THE HANDBOOK OF CANADIAN
PUBLIC ADMINISTRATION

THE HANDBOOK OF CANADIAN PUBLIC ADMINISTRATION

SECOND EDITION

Edited by

Christopher Dunn

8 Sampson Mews, Suite 204
Don Mills, Ontario M3C 0H5
www.oupcanada.com

Oxford University Press is a department of the University of Oxford.
It furthers the University's objective of excellence in research, scholarship,
and education by publishing worldwide in

Oxford New York
Auckland Cape Town Dar es Salaam Hong Kong Karachi
Kuala Lumpur Madrid Melbourne Mexico City Nairobi
New Delhi Shanghai Taipei Toronto

With offices in
Argentina Austria Brazil Chile Czech Republic France Greece
Guatemala Hungary Italy Japan Poland Portugal Singapore
South Korea Switzerland Thailand Turkey Ukraine Vietnam

Published in Canada
by Oxford University Press

First published 2010

Library and Archives Canada Cataloguing in Publication

A handbook of Canadian public administration / edited
by Christopher Dunn. — 2nd ed.
Includes bibliographical references and index.
ISBN 978-0-19-542983-1
1. Public administration—Canada—Textbooks.
I. Dunn, Christopher J. C., 1948–
JL108.H34 2010 351.71 C2010-900187-7

1 2 3 4 — 13 12 11 10

Cover image: Ed Snowshoe/Gettyimages

This book is printed on permanent (acid-free) paper ♾.
Printed in Canada

Contents

Preface

This book came about at the request of colleagues who had used the first edition and wanted another. Their feedback helped me build on the strengths of the first edition: informative pieces, written by expert contributors, that reflect new developments in the field; a consistent style throughout; and a certain edginess, namely a willingness to point out where the field is lacking and where it should be going. I am grateful to such colleagues and to their students.

This book was greatly shaped by the enthusiasm of the contributing authors. In the first book, I assembled a dream team that lent the book a sense of authority—with style. The same dynamic has repeated itself here. Copy editor Leslie Saffrey put it well when she wrote that she had not realized that public administration could be so interesting.

Once again I have thoroughly enjoyed working with Oxford University Press. The professionalism and thoroughness of the staff has lent the same seamlessness and style to this edition as to the first. Eric Sinkins, assistant managing editor in Oxford's Higher Education Division, coached the project along. Jennifer Mueller saw to the slimming of the manuscript in a masterful way. Leslie Saffrey provided sensible and sensitive copy-editing. Lisa Ball, the production coordinator from the Creative Services Division of Oxford, and expert indexers smoothed out the wrinkles in the text. To these and others I may have missed, I offer thanks.

Memorial University has provided me with a wonderful environment for teaching and research. Its Political Science Department has provided collegiality and inspiration, as well as leadership in the discipline. Its students are among the finest and most talented people I have met. Thanks to Megan Sylvester for very fine research assistance.

And lastly, to the people I do this all for. To Hilda, the love of my life; to Christopher, whose passion for life and learning is an inspiration; and to James, the beautiful one born the year of the first book, who gives me a new way of seeing the world.

Contributors

Caroline Andrew is the director of the Centre on Governance in the School of Political Studies at the University of Ottawa. She is also chair of the Board of Echo—the Ontario Women's Health Council.

Carl Baar is a former professor of political science at Brock University, and an adjunct professor of political science at York University.

Jacques Bourgault is a former professeur du science politique à l'Université du Québec à Montréal, adjunct professor at ENAP, and research fellow at the Canada School for Public Service (CSPS).

Kathy Brock is an associate professor in the School of Policy Studies and Department of Political Studies at Queen's University; she is also past director of the Public Policy and Third Sector at Queen's School of Policy Studies.

David C.G. Brown is a senior associate of the Public Policy Forum in Ottawa; a former federal public servant in several central agencies, departments, and in the Office of the Commissioner of Official Languages; and an instructor in the Department of Political Science at Carleton University.

Matthew Burbidge, at the time of his article, was an MPA student at Queen's University.

Christopher Dunn is a professor of political science at Memorial University.

Bryan Mitchell Evans is an associate professor in the Department of Politics and Public Administration at Ryerson University.

Alan Gilmore is a former senior principal in the Office of the Auditor General of Canada and associate of the Ottawa-based Sussex Circle consulting group, which advises senior government clients on policy and finance.

David A. Good is a professor and director of strategic research in the School of Public Administration at the University of Victoria. He has over 30 years of experience as a federal public servant, with 15 as an assistant deputy minister in central agencies (PCO, TBS) and departments.

Andrew Graham is a professor in the School of Policy Studies at Queen's University and teaches at the Queen's University Industrial Relations Centre and at the Canadian Police College. He is a senior research associate of the Conference Board of Canada.

Ian Greene is a professor in the Department of Political Science and the master of McLaughlin College at York University.

Morley Gunderson is a CIBC professor of youth employment with the Centre for Industrial Relations and Department of Economics at the University of Toronto.

Robert Hebdon is a professor in the Faculty of Management at McGill University.

Michael Howlett is the Burnaby Mountain chair in the Department of Political Science at Simon Fraser University and visiting professor at the Lee Kuan Yew School of Public Policy at the National University of Singapore.

Kenneth Kernaghan is a professor emeritus in the Political Science Department at Brock University; he was named to the Order of Canada on 30 December 2008.

Evert Lindquist is a professor and director of the School of Public Administration, University of Victoria.

Henry L. Molot was, until his retirement, senior general counsel, Constitutional and Administrative Law Section, Department of Justice Canada, and the Department's leading authority on administrative law, as well as aspects of constitutional law, parliamentary law, statutory interpretation, and Crown liability.

John Nator, at the time of his article, was an MPA student at Queen's University.

Alasdair Roberts is the Jerome L. Rappaport professor of law and public policy at Suffolk University Law School. Previously, he was a professor of public administration in the Maxwell School of Citizenship and Public Affairs at Syracuse University and an associate professor of public administration at Queen's University.

Scott Sams is a graduate student in the Department of Political Science at the University of Western Ontario.

Andrew Sancton is a professor and director of the Local Government Program in the Department of Political Science at the University of Western Ontario.

Robert Shepherd teaches in the School of Public Policy and Administration at Carleton University.

John Shields is a professor in the Department of Politics and School of Public Administration at Ryerson University.

Richard Simeon is a professor of political science and law at the University of Toronto.

Lorne Sossin is a professor and former associate dean (2004–2007) in the Faculty of Law at the University of Toronto.

Gregory Tardi, BA (Hons), BCL, LLB, is senior legal counsel in the Office of the Law Clerk and Senior Parliamentary Counsel at the House of Commons in Ottawa. He also teaches at the Faculty of Law, McGill University.

Paul Thomas is a Duff Roblin professor of government in the Department of Political Studies at the University of Manitoba.

Annis May Timpson is a professor and director of Canadian studies at the University of Edinburgh.

Nan Weiner is the president of N.J. Weiner Consulting, Inc. in Toronto and an instructor at the Centre for Industrial Relations and Human Resources at the University of Toronto.

David Zussman is the Jarislowsky chair in public sector management at the University of Ottawa, where he also teaches teaching public management. He also serves as a part-time commissioner of the federal Public Service Commission.

Introduction

Shortly after the first edition of *The Handbook of Canadian Public Administration* was published, the country was embroiled in the 'sponsorship scandal'. In 2002, the *Globe and Mail* discovered that the advertising firm Groupaction Marketing Inc. had been paid over half a million dollars for a report that could not be found; Auditor General Sheila Fraser's 2004 report showed that senior officials in government departments involved with advertising and sponsorship contracts in Quebec had broken rules and had essentially wasted more than $100 million in fees to communications agencies, with little to show in return. The Gomery Commission investigated the scandal and reported in two stages, first in November 2005 and then in February 2006; in the latter report, it recommended a comprehensive accountability regime. However, the newly elected Conservative government's Federal Accountability Act (FAA) paid little heed to the report and instead instituted a different, control-oriented regime that supported creating and strengthening financial watchdogs.

Then Ottawa became preoccupied with what many observers, including the secretary to cabinet and the chair of the Prime Minister's Advisory Committee on the Public Service, called 'the web of rules'. Somewhat ironically, the FAA had contributed to this web, but a complex system of rules had formed over time to regulate internal operation of the federal bureaucracy and its relations with external agencies. These rules covered a sweeping range of matters such as official languages, performance management, auditing, confidentiality, financial management, disclosure of interest, staffing, classification, compensation, and privacy. This system prompted such responses as the Independent Blue Ribbon Panel on Grants and Contributions, the Dye Review of Procurement Policy, the Wouters Review of the Financial Management Framework, and the third report of the Prime Minister's Advisory Committee on the Public Service. While most new governments try to gain public support by appearing harsh on overregulation, the efforts made by the federal government late in the decade seemed more consistent than most.

The Advisory Committee's recommendation to mitigate the 'web of rules' by turning to a principles-based risk-management approach in the public sector, balancing risk with managers' knowledge and experience, seemed out of touch with the tenor of the times. Dominance from the centre had become a pervasive theme of federal governance. It affected Parliament, which experienced two early prorogations and shackled committee operations. It affected cabinet, which experienced such a return to centralization that it was dubbed the 'prime minister-centred cabinet', or 'court government'. It affected the public service, and informal talks with federal officials often revolved around the theme of control and its negative effects on innovation and policy entrepreneurship. It is telling that one of the themes of the first edition of this book, the 'Canadian model' of public administration premised on valuing government and the policy role of public officials, is no longer discussed in Ottawa.

After a decade of surpluses, the federal government's budgetary deficit for 2008/9 was $5.8 billion. The projection for 2009/10 was roughly 10 times greater—about $55.9 billion—the result of dramatic stimulus spending, tax cuts, and a war economy. In a 2010 report, the parliamentary budget officer forecast structural deficits between $12.5 billion and $18.9 billion for each of the following five fiscal years, a far more pessimistic outlook than that of the federal government. These developments were also important for the public service, and there were hints that deficit reduction efforts would focus on the federal bureaucracy rather than intergovernmental transfers or taxes.

Some of the causes of the nineties became *causes célèbres* in the next decade. Conservative authors questioned the self-government management of First Nations reserves, and Aboriginal leaders lashed back with accusations of their own. The latter noted that the proposed Indian Act reform suite of 2001–3 was a return to the direct management approach of the past and strengthened the minister's hand instead of recognizing the inherent right of self-government. The legislation died, but the stalemate that had developed lasted into a new government and a new decade. In political theory, the New Public Management became a contested notion rather than conventional wisdom. Robert B. Denhardt offered a comprehensive critique of NPM, calling for it to be overtaken by an approach called 'New Public Service'. Evert Lindquist called the new replacement 'integrated governance'. In technology development, government became less concerned with the nineties' aim to position Canada at the head of the pack in wired nations, and the vision became more diffuse. Intergovernmental affairs went from a vision of a collaborative partnership, as in the Social Union Framework Agreement (SUFA), to a firewall in the Open Federalism vision of Steven Harper, at least initially.

Overview

This new *Handbook* reviews the enduring issues of public administration and analyzes ways of meeting the challenges posed by new issues. It includes a groundbreaking approach to mapping the public administration landscape, and several authors drill down to draw taxonomies of the federal public service itself. Unlike other texts, it challenges Canadian public administration to be more serious about theory and to integrate new theoretical approaches into ongoing research. In response to looming fiscal stringency in the public sector, it offers a new emphasis on budgeting. To counter the lack of mission that some observed in the federal public sector at the end of the last century, it offers a visioning exercise for the next one. Further, it presents some of the first critical observations of new developments, including the Federal Accountability Act, accounting officers, and new agents of parliament. It counterbalances the 'web of rules' by discussing new notions of public servant independence and accountability. And it offers a new assessment of where information technology is going in the new century.

Part I provides an introduction to the new landscape of Canadian public administration. Part II, 'The Organizational Dimension', reviews stability and change in the major institutions of government—the legislative, the central executive, the departments, and the para-public agencies—and their capacity to learn from each other. It also considers what Canadians are getting with the new accounting officers innovation. In Part III, 'The Human Resources Dimension', the articles discuss the need for renewal on both the theoretical and organizational planes in relation to new fiscal realities (such as collective bargaining and compensation in the public sector), workplace equity, pay equity, and human rights in the workplace. Part IV, 'Changing Visions of Public Administration', contrasts the twentieth- and twenty-first-century visions of public administration in Canada; it also considers two different outlooks on the near future—bureaucratic engagement in democratic administration and constant innovation in alternative service delivery. Part V, 'Changing Expectations of Government', deals with societal pressures on the public service to deliver values-based government, equality-based public administration, justice for the third sector, increased freedom to First Nations self-governance, and representative public administration in the North. In Part VI, 'The Policy Dimension', the focus turns to intergovernmental relations. The different eras of Canadian federalism provide a backdrop to the more specialized concerns of the federal spending power, with particular attention to the role of municipal governments in our era of multi-level governance. The section also includes an essay on public policy processes written by Michael Howlett, one of Canada's leading public policy theorists. The final section—Part VII, 'The Management Dimension'—suggests mechanisms that Canadians, particularly members of government, can use to deliver on their visions, expectations, and policies into the future. We'll need to rely on budgeting and examine recent changes in fiscal paradigms and processes. We'll need to use new information technologies. And we'll need quality in deputy minister management and leadership.

All this amounts to a large order. The *Handbook* does not have all the answers. But we believe it asks most of the right questions.

To the memory of my mother, Patricia Mary Gracia Dunn, a former federal public servant who saw the potential in all people and helped it flourish. I love you.

PART I Introduction

Evert Lindquist grapples with the challenge of describing the reach of public administration as a field in the opening chapter to our collection. The paradox is that even in an era of smaller government, the expectations and complexity of public sector governance has increased dramatically.

His chapter attempts to address this problem, by addressing general, then more specific notions. First, it introduces an overarching framework for public administration and a model of public service as an institution. It then reviews evolving conceptions of public administration, followed by a focus on competing interests and perspectives on public sector reform. It provides an agenda for systematic, collaborative, and comparative study of public administration practice, and concludes with speculation about future directions for public sector governance and administration as well as distributed governance. Lindquist's chapter notes that 'integrated governance' has begun to replace a now stale debate between traditional model and the New Public Management (NPM), combining former movements, and emphasizing horizontal, collaborative, and multilevel governance arrangements. He promotes a more comparative research agenda to guide future reform in Canada.

1 Surveying the Public Administration Landscape: *Frameworks, Narratives, and Contours*

Evert Lindquist

Overview

The reach of public administration is stunning; even in an era of ostensibly smaller and 'hollowed out' government, the expectations and complexity of public sector governance have increased dramatically. Even at a high level, it is difficult enough to monitor all the trends, pressures, and opportunities affecting public administration, let alone to trace their real and imagined impacts on the quality of public policy; public service institutions; service delivery to, and engagement of, diverse stakeholders (citizens, business, non-profit organizations, and other levels of government); and democratic accountability. The pace of change, variability of access to information (sometimes too much, and often too little!), scope of the public sector, and complexity of all these factors outstrip our ability to assess definitively developments and impacts; even the first and this second edition of *The Handbook of Canadian Public Administration* provide only selective sketches of impacts and implications.

This chapter attempts to address this problem and is organized as follows. First, it introduces an overarching framework for public administration and a model of public service as an institution, as starting points for embracing and interpreting the contributions to this volume. Second, it reviews evolving conceptions (or *narratives*) of public administration. It examines the differences between the traditional conceptions of public administration and the **New Public Management** and the efforts to rationalize them, and speculates about the contours of the next wave of public sector reform. Third, it focuses on the competing interests in, and narratives on, public sector reform, suggesting that many of our debates are about defining the priorities for reform consistent with these motivations and interpretations. Fourth, the chapter calls for systematic, collaborative, and comparative study of public administration practice in order to get 'underneath' swirling and **competing narratives** for reform. Fifth and finally, it speculates about future directions for public sector governance, and public administration and distributed governance.

A Framework for Comprehending Public Administration

This section outlines a framework to capture the essential features and environment of Canadian public administration, and within that framework presents a model of the Canadian public service as an institution.

A few words about frameworks and models are in order. First, a framework is required in order to situate a model. A framework encompasses the surface features of the system, as well as the conditions, premises, and values that animate it, and identifies the forces affecting key variables. The framework should facilitate monitoring the evolution of key practices and principles of the subject (here, the public service institution); comparisons with other jurisdictions; and explanations and assessments of future challenges and risks. A framework also provides a basis for future research. It should help organize and parse out how we think about the dependent variables, show how different influences, factors, and elements relate to each other, and allow for debate on which historical, current, or future trends might be most relevant to certain issues, capabilities, or functions.

Figure 1.1 shows the general concepts underpinning the public administration framework. The following sections provide details on each component of the framework. There are four.

1. Public Service Institutions: Critical Processes and Values

The work of Philip Selznick, although focused on leadership, contains several starting points to inform a model of a **well-performing institution**. From him we learn that recruitment is crucial for maintaining and developing organizational competence, particularly in maintaining credibility with important stakeholders. Leaders also need to coordinate and align the efforts of the institution's component parts. The institution should hold fast to core values, but it also needs to adapt and learn from experience, and thus requires adroit leadership. Such leadership should be pivotal to developing the organization's norms, cultivating a sense of mission, representing the institution to internal and external audiences, and defending its integrity to key stakeholders.

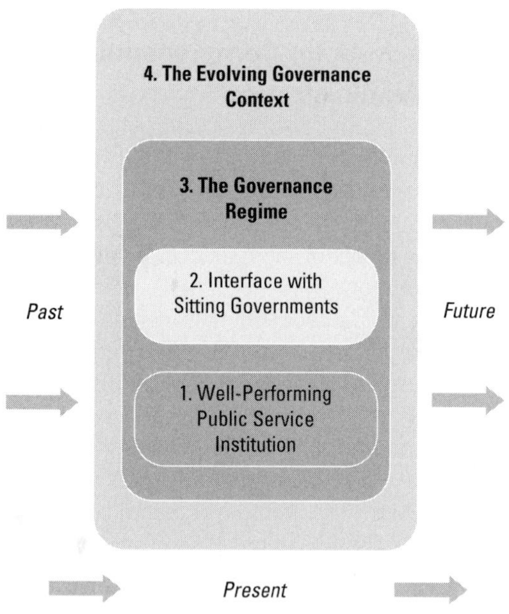

Figure 1.1 General Conceptual Framework

These ideas take on special meaning in the context of public service institutions, which are large, complex organizations serving elected governments by providing policy advice and delivering programs to citizens. By joining these ideas with themes from the literature on the 'Canadian model', which we later examine, we can create a model embracing nine processes and functions critical for sustaining and improving a well-performing public service (see Figure 1.2). These are grouped into three clusters, partly for aesthetic reasons, but mainly because the processes and functions in each cluster relate more to each other than to those in other clusters (although success or failure in a process or function might be attributable to developments in another cluster). This model does not capture all facets of the public service, since models are meant to focus on critical features. Here the focus is on the processes and functions essential for maintaining the capability, credibility, integrity, and adaptability of the public service as an institution.

The first cluster—*managing people, aligning effort*—encompasses three processes. The first process embraces the recruitment and staffing functions: attracting, monitoring, screening, and grooming talent for leadership roles. The second process, particularly important in a complex institution, concerns the macro-management of human resources across the public service, which provides the framework for recruitment and staffing. The final process involves the ways in which the leaders coordinate diverse departments and agencies, including central agency leadership and executive development.

The second cluster—*designing policy and delivering services*—focuses on the central roles that the public service performs for government and citizens. This includes not only the processes and functions of advising government and delivering services (directly and indirectly) to citizens, but also those of working with the government to consult with citizens to inform policy design and service delivery.

The third cluster—*promoting learning, scrutiny, and reform*—captures different ways that

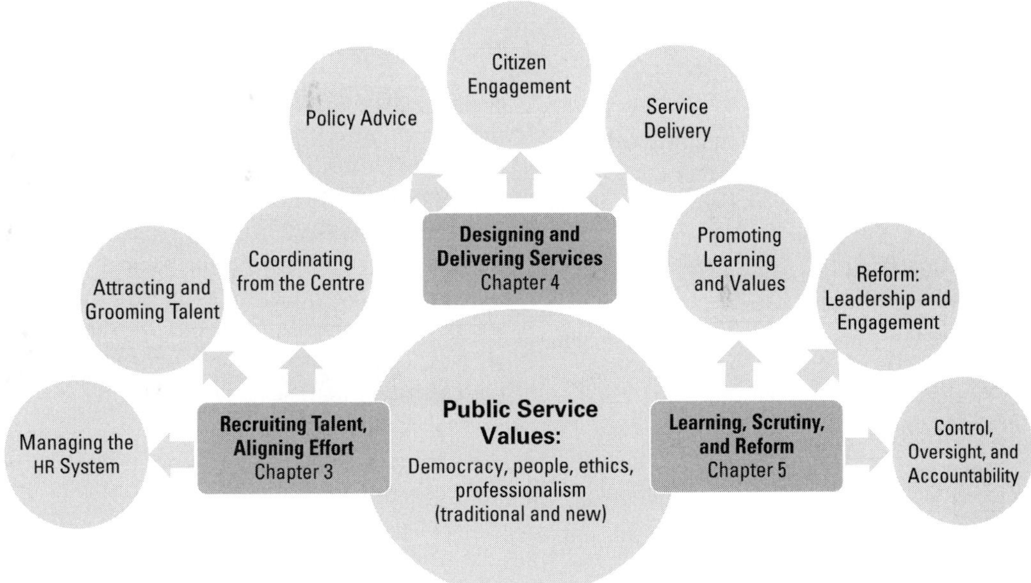

Figure 1.2 Critical Processes and Values in a Well-Performing Public Service Institution

public service institutions learn and adapt. This includes supporting learning and professional development, and promoting essential public service values and ethics. It also includes scrutinizing programs through internal control and challenge systems, and external accountability mechanisms. Finally, it includes continuous efforts by the public service to reform its practices, either reactively or proactively (Aucoin and Heintzman, 2000). But change and innovation may also occur informally, without official programs of reform.

Finally, Figure 1.2 depicts the core values identified by the Task Force on Values and Ethics as animating all clusters. It presumes specific values are invoked or expressed in varying degrees in coordinating and managing staff; designing policy and delivering services; and fostering learning, scrutiny, and reform. For any given activity, some values may be more relevant than others, may conflict with other values, or may require balancing unique to that activity.

This model describes several essential processes for ensuring that a public service institution is competent, responsive, and adaptable, and has integrity. However, the model is only the focal point of a larger framework, and we now turn to reviewing that framework's remaining three elements.

2. The Governance Regime

The public service is deeply affected by Canada's form of Westminster-style government and its federal system (Aucoin, Smith, and Dinsdale, 2004). For our purposes, the **governance regime** has the following features:

- Prime Ministers have extensive power as long as they maintain the confidence of the House of Commons. They are not constrained by a strong party system, as in Australia, nor by an elected Senate or one with provincial representation, nor by proportional representation in the House of Commons. Moreover, Canadian Prime Ministers cannot be removed by caucus, as can happen in Australia and the UK;[1]
- Ministers act under the rule of law and are accountable to the House of Commons, but they are supported by strong central institutions, such as the Prime Minister's

Office and the cabinet system. Canadians have also elected several majority governments in the last few decades, occasionally flirting with other parties or minority governments. Combined with high turnover in the House and a tightly controlled and poorly funded Parliament, this leads to a weak Opposition;[2]
- Provincial and territorial governments have considerable powers, since Canada is one of the world's most decentralized federations and allows for asymmetry in relationships.[3] There is ongoing debate about which level of government takes primacy in different domains of responsibility, and about the fiscal imbalance due to the stronger taxation power of the federal government. Governments compete to demonstrate relevance directly to citizens, communities, and sectors, despite efforts to coordinate services;
- Business, labour, and voluntary organizations are not strongly integrated vertically in Canada, and governments generally do not share power with societal interests, even if they consult and seek advice from those interests.[4] Some interest groups have strong influence in certain sectors, but this influence is affected by the federal division of powers. Interest groups do not have strong influence on the shape of government or on the public service.

In short, the governance regime typically concentrates power in the hands of a majority government led by a strong Prime Minister, whose principal sources of criticism are other levels of government, the Opposition, and the media. A government does not face strong external forces in shaping and controlling the public service as an institution, and, if inclined, can wield enormous influence over the trajectory of the public service, depending on political, policy, and management priorities.

3. The Interactions of Government and the Public Service

A sitting government has an intricate relationship with, and considerable power over, the public service as an institution. Much of this power is exercised by the Prime Minister through the Prime Minister's Office and the Privy Council Office. But the expectations from the cabinet, its committees, and individual ministers and their staffs also influence these interactions with the public service. The framework identifies eight areas of **government power and influence**:

- the mandate and policy priorities of government;
- the design of decision-making processes and machinery of government;
- the appointments of deputy ministers by the Prime Minister;
- the seeking of policy advice from the public service;
- the oversight of departments', agencies', and deputy ministers' performance;
- the government's ideas about public service structure and processes;
- the interest and capabilities of ministerial offices;
- the degree of autonomy of Parliament from the government.

The ways in which the Prime Minister, cabinet ministers, and other Members of Parliament exercise their authority and responsibilities have important implications for, and effects on, the public service as an institution. Interactions between elected representatives and the public service require strategic and sensitive handling by both political and bureaucratic leaders. Good relationships are essential for strong performance of both the government and the public service.

There is not the space to explore the possibilities in detail, but the areas noted above can be interpreted as *variables*. A change in any of them will affect the relationships between government, elected representatives, and the public service.

4. Governance Context: Streams of Influence and Pressure

The governance context continuously presents challenges, trends, uncertainties, and opportunities to policy-makers and public service institutions. The framework identifies four streams of interrelated pressures that constantly vary in importance and vie for the attention of government. These streams are:

- *challenges* such as economic globalization, environmental issues, the information and communications technology revolution, international security and terrorism, the geographical size of the country, regional diversity, income disparity, and identity politics.
- *expectations* of other levels of government—provinces, territories, municipalities, and other countries, including international organizations, as well as those of the private sector, the non-profit sector, and citizens and their communities;
- *ideas* about improving governance from intellectual movements, examples from other jurisdictions, and the country's culture and traditions;
- *precipitating events* such as elections, new government, new ministers, scandals, disasters, and developments in other jurisdictions.

These pressures are best understood as evolving streams of influence that constantly challenge successive governments and the public service, with some streams far more predictable than others (Kingdon, 1995). Our purpose is not to delve into the intricacies of each stream but to show that the public service should anticipate and monitor external developments, advise and assist government in dealing with the challenges, and adapt and renew its capabilities in order to undertake new roles and responsibilities.

Towards a General Framework for Canadian Public Administration

Figure 1.3 presents the entire four-part **general framework**, centred on a model of the Canadian public service as an institution. A more comprehensive version of the framework would include other levels of government and public service, and explicitly acknowledge intergovernmental processes and entities. Such a version, showcasing the entire system of Canadian public administration, would be similar to the Canadian model envisioned by Gow (2004).[5]

The framework allows us to describe the Canadian administrative style and determine whether any elements of that style are unique. Then we can further determine whether the unique elements add up to an overall distinctive administrative approach or style, which might provide an example for other countries to follow. The framework functions as a map, on the one hand showing the different elements or variables that different authors take up in their studies, and on the other showing that even ostensibly disparate elements of managing the public service as an institution—as well as trends and actors in the broader governance system and the federation—are integrally related to others.

Some readers will see in the framework the potential for explanations of current practices and gaps; for others, 'design' challenges will surface. However, this chapter provides a general framework that allows readers to choose the variables to focus on or ignore. Certain intellectual traditions, theories, and professional orientations will emphasize certain variables, issues, forces, and linkages, but that is not for this chapter to judge. Hypothesizing about the driving forces behind public service performance, or how these forces differ in other jurisdictions, moves into the realm of explanation and theory.

Evolving Conceptions of Public Administration: What's Next?

This section focuses on the predominant models of public administration (what Gilles Paquet and I have termed *cosmologies,* and which are referred to later in this chapter as *narratives*). Each of

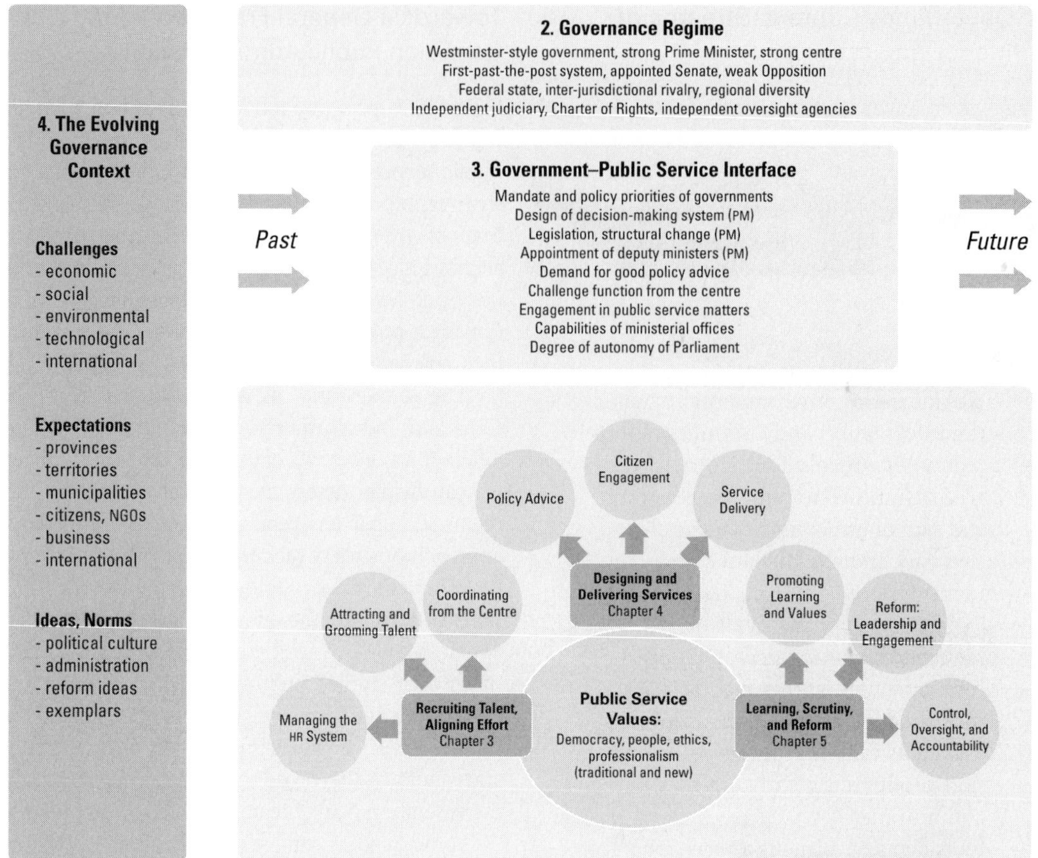

Figure 1.3 Detailed Framework and Model

these models has been contested at one time or another, and each has many elements which persist. It reviews the traditional conceptions of public service and their modernization in the 1960s and 1970s, the challenge emanating from the New Public Management, efforts to reconcile these views, and an overview of current thinking inside and outside Canada on the shape of the 'new' model of public administration.

The Traditional Model and Its Elaboration

The **traditional model** of Canadian public service has been described in the writings of J.E. Hodgetts, Kenneth Kernaghan, John Langford, Iain Gow, and O.P. Dwivedi. These works identified the key public service values and their relationship to the Westminster system of parliamentary government.[6] As Donald Savoie reminds us, many of these principles and practices animating the conduct of government and public servants were developed in simpler times, some almost a hundred years ago (Savoie, 2003). The responsibilities of government were smaller then, and the environment in which government and civil servants worked was considerably less complicated, more personalized, and not mediated by huge institutions.

Beginning in 1918, with the adoption of the merit principle, the Canadian public service has been described as a merit-based, non-partisan, and professional institution, which requires competence, discipline, skills, and knowledge appropriate for specific positions.[7] It is loyal to the duly elected government, which is accountable to the House of Commons and to the public for its decisions and programs. Advice provided by public servants to ministers is confidential; and, in return for this service and loyalty to the government of the day, public servants receive the protection of anonymity. It is also understood that public servants should act with probity.

The merit and recruitment systems mean that public servants begin their careers with entry-level, position-based appointments. Combined with job protections strengthened over the years, this implies that employees can have full careers in the public service. Training focuses on improving skills and knowledge for current positions; career or professional development is either personally financed by the employee or supported by a mentor grooming a promising civil servant for a future position.

Important elaborations to this traditional model emerged during the 1960s and early 1970s as new expectations emerged. They included:

- *Representation.* Bilingualism, and later, minority group representation, both became important new ideas in the public service. They embodied the new desire to make the public service reflect the diversity of the citizens and to give all Canadians equal access to public service employment. Moreover, with such diversity, the public service could provide better advice to ministers and better service to citizens (Benhamadi, 2003).
- *Employee protection.* The Public Service Employment Act and the Public Service Staff Relations Act adopted in the late 1960s formally recognized bargaining agents for different groups of public servants and introduced collective bargaining. This led to more job protection for public servants, regularized procedures for hiring, promoting, and disciplining staff, and created opportunities to challenge the decisions of managers and their departments (Thompson and Fryer, 1999).
- *Planning and coordination.* Since the 1960s, the number of government programs grew dramatically, as did the number of employees, departments, and agencies. Beginning with the Pearson government, prime ministers instituted more complex cabinet structures and decision-making systems. Along with new statutory obligations, this increased the number and scope of central agencies (French with Van Loon, 1984).
- *Control and accountability.* The rapid increase in the scope and size of government led to new approaches to budgeting, such as the Program, Planning, and Budgeting System (PPBS). Concern about the government's ability to monitor and control financial affairs led to the appointment of the Glassco Commission on Government Organization in 1960 and the Lambert Commission on Financial Management and Accountability in 1976. The Auditor General's role was expanded, and the Office of the Comptroller General was created to improve the government's financial management capabilities. The government also reformed the budgetary Estimates procedure and introduced the Policy and Expenditure Management System in the late 1970s.[8]

Many of these developments were mirrored or anticipated by provincial governments. Through these statutory and organizational reforms, the Canadian governments and their public services acquired an international reputation as forward-looking, innovative institutions.

By the early 1980s, the core values of Canadian public administration—merit, professionalism, non-partisanship, loyalty, and anonymity—remained highly valued and relevant, along with the rule of law. But while the traditional understandings of the public service persisted, the complexity of its environment had changed dramatically. The public service had increased in scale and complexity, and more goals, values, and rules guided and constrained departments and public servants.

The Challenge from the New Public Management

A broader challenge to traditional formulations came from a diverse group of ideas and initiatives in the late 1980s and early 1990s that were eventually labelled the New Public Management (NPM). Inspired by private sector values, NPM perspectives rapidly gained currency as governments sought to lower costs, provide better service, contain deficits, and incorporate new technologies. These ideas emerged from efforts to improve specific programs or smaller organizations, often at the local, provincial, or state levels. Sandford Borins identified elements of the new paradigm as:

> providing high quality services that citizens value; demanding, measuring, and rewarding improved organizational and individual performance; advocating managerial autonomy, particularly by reducing central controls; recognizing the importance of providing the human and technological resources managers need to meet their performance targets; and maintaining receptiveness to competition and open-mindedness about which public purposes should be performed by public service as opposed to private sector or non-governmental organizations. (Borins, 2002: 4)

Borins noted that NPM, 'while recognizing the value of a professional public service, puts more emphasis on improving the quality and reducing the cost of public services. It is silent on life-time employment' (Borins, 2002: 4).

Canadian governments and the public service never explicitly invoked NPM as they introduced initiatives in the late 1980s and the 1990s; the concept was then an academic invention that had only recently seeped into the discourse of public service executives in Canada. And, as Dwivedi and Gow observed, many of NPM's ideas have long animated public administration discourse and can be found in the Glassco Commission, the Lambert Commission, the Public Service 2000 exercise, and many reports from the Treasury Board and the Office of the Auditor General (Dwivedi and Gow, 1999).

Views differ as to whether NPM entails significant structural change in addition to new ways of managing and rewarding work. Peter Aucoin, among others, chronicled how the structure of an entire public service may profoundly change as the logical result of these changes in public management: if the focus was to be on improving service, measuring results, and increasing accountability, then an argument could be made for separating policy development from service delivery. Such logic informed the dramatic restructuring of government in both New Zealand and the United Kingdom (Aucoin, 1995).

Borins observes that Canadian governments, unlike these other countries, did not embrace this agenda as a result of political conviction, but rather over many years, pragmatically and from the bottom up, often in response to growing economic pressures. In short, NPM values and initiatives do not require wholesale restructuring of government machinery and can be adopted in a variety of less dramatic but, over time, equally profound ways.

Reconciling Traditional and NPM Values and Practices

In 1996, the Canadian Centre for Management Development Task Force on Values and Ethics tried to reconcile traditional and new public sector management values with the downsizing and upheaval in the federal public service resulting from the June 1993 restructuring and Program Review decisions. The task force identified four overlapping clusters of values (Tait, 1997), which can be summarized as:

- *democratic values* embracing responsible government, respect for the rule of law, support for democracy, respect for the authority of elected office-holders, neutrality and non-partisanship, due process, and the public interest and common good;

- *professional values*, which were grouped into two categories:
  - *traditional values,* such as neutrality, non-partisanship, merit, excellence, effectiveness, economy, frankness, objectivity or impartiality, speaking truth to power, balancing complexity, and fidelity to the public trust;
  - *new values,* such as quality, innovation, initiative, creativity, resourcefulness, horizontality, service orientation, and teamwork.
- *ethical values* promoting integrity, honesty, probity, prudence, impartiality, equity, disinterestedness, discretion, and the public trust;
- *people values,* including respect, concern, caring, civility, courtesy, tolerance, openness, collegiality, participation, fairness, moderation, decency, reasonableness, humanity, and courage (Tait, 1997).

The Task Force recognized that these values, though all laudable, were often difficult to uphold in the face of downsizing, restructuring, time pressures, and budget constraints, and that this was a major reason for the loss of credibility of Public Service 2000 in the eyes of public servants. Interestingly, the Task Force disputed the notion of a guarantee of employment security.

It is important to recognize, too, that the New Public Management has in practical terms meant different things in different jurisdictions, with reforms introduced in varying mixes and degrees, and at varying speeds. For example, in contrast to the dramatic restructuring of New Zealand's core public service and Crown sector announced in the late 1980s, Australia introduced NPM principles in a less episodic, more sustained approach across governments. Halligan (2007 and other writings) describes how Commonwealth governments steadily drove reform through successive financial management and budget reforms, and by devolving human resource management and other corporate responsibilities to departments, thus putting initiative and innovation in the hands of departments. In the United Kingdom, following downsizing and financial management reforms under Prime Minister Thatcher, and the subsequent move towards executive agencies, Prime Minister Blair drove public sector reform towards the end of his first term in office by promoting 'joined-up government' and instituting a performance oversight and challenge regime for departments and other service providers. In Canada, after the 1993 restructuring of cabinet and the public service, and the downsizing and alternative service delivery (ASD) initiatives flowing from the subsequent Program Review, successive governments proceeded with a pragmatic approach on different fronts, such as adopting the service agency model in areas such as food inspection and revenue collection (Lindquist, 2006). More recent analysis of continental European models in the English literature (e.g., Christensen and Lægreid, 2007; Pollitt and Bouckaert, 2004) shows that many countries have long operated on a decentralized basis, and, though not early adopters, have embraced some NPM ideas.

This diversity leads observers to acknowledge different degrees of interest, trajectories, and mixes of initiatives for public sector reform around the world. This diversity is driven by two things. First, it is now well understood that countries proceed with reform from fundamentally different circumstances and with political leaders showing varying degrees of support for, and engagement with, public sector reform. Not surprisingly, this affects the mix, pacing, and overall coherence of reform initiatives. These differences arise from factors such as different government or state traditions, the priority and interest that a government attached to what Barzelay (2001) refers to as 'public management policy', the substantive policy challenges and goals confronting a government, the government's capabilities, and the actions of other countries functioning as exemplars or points of reference. Second, NPM is best understood not as a coherent, integrated program of reform (Aucoin, 1995), but rather, as a family of ideas or a collection of aspirations, instruments, and approaches, sometimes working in contradiction to each other (e.g., responsiveness might come at the expense of efficiency, special-purpose entities at the expense of client-oriented service, and so on).[9] These include, but are not limited to, focusing on achieving desired results, separating policy-making from operations, focusing on service (a 'customer' orientation), providing budgetary and financial management tools such as accrual accounting systems, increasing flexibility for managers, fostering innovation, encouraging political direction and oversight, using contracts and performance agreements, instituting more competitive appointment regimes, and adopting performance regimes.

Barzelay (2001) provides a trenchant critique of how precisely public administration scholars have delineated assumptions and the strands of NPM they are working with, but it is this very diversity of NPM-inspired thinking that allows governments to choose, combine, and pace management reform initiatives in unique combinations.[10] Indeed, a set of sensibilities and prescriptions were variously built up under a succession of labels—managerialism, re-inventing government, ASD, NPM, and so on—and were debated and acknowledged as the best contending ideas for moving away from the status quo. The fiscal stress on governments of the late 1970s and the 1980s led to declining credibility and satisfaction with traditional governance models (due to across-the-board cutbacks), and competence. The quality of governance and public administration became a political issue and needed to be dealt with. NPM ideas were leading contenders to underpin change, and in political and economic environments where business practices and institutions were acceptable in public management, many Western governments and international institutions like the Organisation for Economic Co-Operation and Development (OECD) were anxious to be at least seen to be embracing these ideas—what Meyer and Rowan (1977) would call 'normative alignment'.

Beyond the New Public Management: Integrated Governance?

At least a decade has transpired since the widespread restructuring of the late 1980s and early 1990s. Many governments were able to rein in or conquer deficits. Without large deficits, these governments are in a better position to invest in new policies, placing a greater premium on the performance of government funding and on improving service to citizens; there is simply less room for these governments to cut back services and more incentive to improving service quality. Ensuring value for tax dollars spent remains important in an era of fiscal rationalization, and, in this context, so also does political and bureaucratic accountability, particularly for governments to make good on election commitments. It is in this context that many governments and academic observers have argued that NPM-inspired reforms are less relevant: the next wave of reform will consist of integrated, horizontal, joined-up, and collaborative government along with stronger central government (UK, 2000; Canada, 2001, 2002; Australia, 2004; Christensen and Lægreid, 2007; Halligan, 2007; Shergold, 2007). Despite the many different NPM trajectories of different countries, almost all seem to echo these concerns.

Most of the recent calls for **integrated governance**, joined-up government, and horizontal or collaborative government, however, are aspirations and do *not* describe how public service institutions currently work, even if a government can point to noteworthy instances or initiatives. I meet many public servants from different jurisdictions who, while well aware of these calls and ambitions, describe a world where silos prevail due to incentives, vertical lines of accountability, and scant resources and time for boundary-spanning activity. They would argue that, even if they see the need for horizontal approaches, in their workaday worlds they remain firmly in the realm of the New Public Management, working hard to implement and maintain a subset of those instruments, and continuing to balance them with traditional Westminster expectations of government (responsiveness to ministers, Question Period, low tolerance for error according to older precepts of accountability, and so on). They would see the latest reform ideas as compelling and worthy at one level, but as little more than veneer at another (unless they get to lead a central coordinating secretariat) and hardly likely to form a wave that rolls through and reshapes their workplaces. Indeed, given that NPM styles of reporting persist in annual reports and estimate documents of many governments, it is difficult to ascertain how integrative reform has been realized in the work of public servants, service delivery agents, and those whom they serve.

Finally, it is worth observing that many ideas that are now the centrepieces of the integrative governance perspective were elements of NPM and earlier thinking. Shared services were part of the NPM family of concepts, either through internal single-window delivery or by outsourcing to firms specializing in corporate services. Certainly the idea of multi-level governance co-provision of services was part of Canada's alternative service delivery thinking in the early 1990s. Can we forget the earlier notions of 'co-production' and 'co-participation' in the design and delivery of public services? The focus on accountability and performance reaches back to the 1970s as part of the policy and public sector reform movements in many jurisdictions.

Moreover, it is worth wondering whether the drivers for reform will really come from policy and other imperatives, and *not* across-the-board public management regimes (can we really have complete horizontal or integrated governance on all issues?). Some issues already driving reform over the last few years include the new security environment flowing from the terrorist attacks on the United States of 11 September 2001 and the war on terrorism, economic and weather-related upheavals, public health crises (such as preventing a flu epidemic), and the steady stream of possibilities afforded by new information and communications technologies (most recently energized by the brave Government 2.0 marketing). In Canada, significant shapers of reform include demographic change (for example, in British Columbia the government assumes the provincial public service will decrease by one-third over its planning horizon; across the country First Nations are the fastest-growing communities), the adoption of transportation gateways to move minerals and other resources, and a series of scandals during the early 2000s which led to an onerous federal accountability regime, already itself in need of reform.

There may be a coalescing of interest in integrated governance, but it is not clear if the touted next wave of imagined reform is significant in scope or essentially different from a checklist of ideas long circulating in public sector management. It is clear, however, that many important and often competing ideas and values shape and inform public management reform initiatives: ideas from Westminster precepts, classical administrative and organization theory, the public sector reform movements of the 1960s and 1970s, and NPM. It is no wonder that many of the stakeholders of public sector reform might be a bit confused or even cynical.

Competing Narratives and Public Sector Reform

Public administration practitioners and academics are not alone in having a sense of déjà vu about the values and ideas underpinning the latest waves of reform. Consider three very different perspectives.

- In *Harkoun and the Sea of Stories*, Rushdie (1990) imagines a sea filled with snippets and elements of stories that can be picked up by the skilled storyteller to weave and build a new story or narrative for the purposes at hand.
- Most human resource competency frameworks and leadership programs address strikingly similar issues. Once, when designing a professional development program, a colleague observed that 'the client will always emphasize three or four competencies, but they are all connected to each other as part of a web—you are focusing on a subset for the purposes of design and pulling the others along as if on a string'.
- Roe (1994) argued that, in domains with high uncertainty and complexity, policy analysts need to ascertain the narratives and antinarratives

> swirling around, as well as their logical foundations and degree of completeness, and must then try to construct a metanarrative.

There are parallels here with the various themes of public sector reform: integration and horizontality may be emphasized, but this does not make irrelevant other elements of NPM and traditional ideas and values. There is a common element in the perspectives; each implies a designer or weaver of a narrative or story for a purpose at hand.

Many of us would argue that it is a responsibility, and sometimes an impulse of political and organizational leadership to provide new narratives to engage followers. Indeed, despite cynicism about the 'next' acronym or corporate initiative (we will later discuss what it takes for new narratives to burst through this cynicism), humans nevertheless powerfully yearn for coherence and a compass to guide strategy and work. I am interested not so much in identifying all the narratives and values underpinning public sector reform and their associated critiques, as in suggesting that our academic literature and official pronouncements on public sector reform can be seen as competing narratives about what should be or has been done. This leads one to explore the different motives and vantage points for developing narratives. By doing so, we can explain in some measure the multiplicity and dynamics of narratives found in debates over directions for public sector reform.

- A government seeks to establish credibility in public management, as one part of the overall image it wishes to project, by ensuring that the public service is competent in providing advice and implementation, that it appears to be under control and accountable, and that it is innovative by international standards.
- Top public service leaders seek to build coherence by providing a picture to the government, public servants, and citizens about the capabilities and repertoires it requires to advise governments and manage its own renewal, as well as outlining its history and status quo.
- Reform advocates (both inside and outside the government) and the public service seek to move the organization in new directions by pointing to failures, drawing lessons, and identifying new models from other jurisdictions, as well as promoting new frames of reference for understanding issues and possibilities.
- Opposition parties, watchdog organizations, and journalists monitor performance, pointing out errors, inefficiencies, unresponsiveness, unrealistic promises, gaps between auditors' recommendations and public service performance, and lack of direction from the government, as well as sometimes identifying best practices.
- Academics, former public servants, and think-tanks seek to make sense of reforms (or of inability to initiate reforms in response to discernable problems), their internal contradictions, and the ongoing activities and dynamics of public service institutions through description, comparative analysis, explanation, theory-building, critique, and advocacy.

Across and within each of these categories there will be contending perspectives on which issues are worthy of debate and which have potential solutions—a multiplicity of narratives about the quality and priorities of public service institutions, and the directions that they should take. Given that public sector institutions are huge and complex, examining them in aggregate can send mixed messages and create confusion. Relying only on the narratives of governments and public service leaders can leave out a large part of the story.

As we step back, there is a broader narrative we should have in mind, a longer pendulum that is swinging. In the face of growing deficits and seemingly unresponsive public services, there was general concern and disappointment about the performance of government across the OECD nations by the 1980s. This laid the groundwork for a more decisive approach by many governments, often leading to significant budget rationalization and restructuring of programs. This was a fertile environment for New Public Management ideas, which were partially informed by the perceived superiority of business in grappling with change, and which were acted on in varying degrees. Given that it took about 20 years for the deficit and performance problems to reach a peak, Lindquist (1997) suggested that restoring trust or a sense of proportion about the appropriate role and competence of government might be a similar 20-year proposition. The pendulum will not swing back to precisely where it started, of course, but new notions of public sector roles, new approaches to service delivery (Heintzman and Marson 2005), and stronger engagement with citizens and communities could combine to raise the credibility of government and public sector careers among citizens, particularly younger people. The higher-level discourse, which so easily and often celebrates business practice, may begin to even out.

Finally, there are other lenses for making sense of the narratives on public sector reform emanating from sitting governments and public service leadership. These lenses come from one stream of the organization theory literature, which has emphasized how organizations symbolically and ritually use information, and how organizations will alter their formal structures and nomenclature in order to 'align' with larger organizational fields in which they compete, collaborate, or seek to maintain status and reputation (Meyer and Rowan, 1977; Feldman and March, 1981; DiMaggio and Powell, 1983; Greenwood and Hinings, 1996; and Christensen et al., 2007). In this sense, the significance of the next public sector reform initiative may be less about effecting concrete change inside public service institutions and for those whom they serve, and more about being *seen* to be introducing reform, and being part of larger national and international discussions. With this in mind, we can see debates and efforts to formulate new strategies as means for:

- showing government and other political leaders that the public service *is* modern and interested in change;
- indicating to political leaders that the public service can reform itself, and securing broad political support for reform initiatives (without detailed political engagement);
- demonstrating cohesion across a complex, often disaggregated and loosely coupled multi-organizational public service;
- shaping values and providing a sense of proportion, making sense of recent history and complexities, and demonstrating continuity while embracing change;
- promoting employee pride and recognition in public service institutions, retaining top talent, and attracting new talent;
- developing new narratives and initiatives for engaging counterparts in other jurisdictions bilaterally or multilaterally, for both prestige and drawing lessons at high levels;
- engaging with, mimicking, adapting, and aligning with the most promising ideas and practices of exemplar and selected referent organizations.

These are not cynical observations—I am merely suggesting that government and public service leaders not only have an incentive to promulgate new reforms but that they also have special meaning and purpose in complex public service systems, with many organizations collectively serving elected governments. Indeed, it is critically important for institutional leaders to engage in such activities as those listed for these very reasons.

The flip side of this literature, however, is often ignored; a key point is that institutional alignment—in top structures, announcements, or nomenclature—is often *decoupled* from the 'technical core' or program of an organization. In other words, the organization projects an image aligned with or rationalized by external needs but this image becomes myth if it does not match the real operations of the organization. At worst, such strategies can be seen as 'buffering' technical cores from criticism or view while maintaining a good external reputation. This raises the possibility, then, that narratives and the latest candidates and themes for reform initiatives can be out of sync with organizational realities. The next section considers how we capture those realities.

How Is Government Working? What Are Its Contours and Reach?

The writing on institutional isomorphism and formal structure as rationalized myth is only one strand of an incredibly diverse literature on organizations. Indeed, it arose to counter ecological perspectives that depicted developments in the environment of an organization as 'selecting' certain structures and approaches—in other words, the view that external factors determine the structure of an organization, such that the organization forms a structure to suit its external environment (Hannan and Freeman, 1977). It also arose to counter other perspectives that saw the formal structure of an organization as a solution to coordinating the tasks and relationships among its work units (e.g., Thompson, 1967). Subsequent work suggested that these top-down and bottom-up processes could be working simultaneously (Meyer et al., 1983). But the conclusion that the technical core could be decoupled, at least partially, from the formal and symbolic undertakings of the leadership of the organization remains an important insight. We know that unwieldy hierarchy, faulty communications, strained capacity, and other problems can create similar gaps. This suggests that one way to determine the effectiveness of previous reform initiatives, and to better understand where the organization stands before taking on another round of reform, is to appreciate how the organization is structured and has evolved.

At first, this would seem an easy undertaking—after all, programs and tasks are what organizations do! But one of the by-products of NPM's focus on performance, which influenced the way in which many governments now report on programs, is a relatively narrow focus on outputs and outcomes of programs at the expense of more detailed reporting on inputs and activities. Often only high-level figures are provided on inputs. These reports are not only difficult for non-experts to follow year over year, but also, and more importantly, the level of aggregation is usually quite high, making it difficult for readers to get a good sense of how specific programs work, how many people work in them, and precisely what resources were allocated for them. This is complicated by contracting out programs, public-partnership arrangements, and other forms of distributed governance. And, whatever the merits of accrual accounting from a resource allocation perspective, when combined with a focus on outputs and outcomes, it serves to further hide the allocations for specific programs; only experienced officials can fruitfully read between the lines to find this information.

Not surprisingly, it is difficult for observers to get underneath the high-level announcements and rhetoric to determine the effect of public reform initiatives. Guiding questions might include:

- How have the contours of government, departments, and specific programs changed over the years?
- What is the value-for-money of performance against resources?
- How well organized are activities comprising specific program areas?

Auditors General attempt to answer some of these questions, but often they work within a narrow mandate and accounting perspective, and do not acknowledge the broader demands on departments and managers and the emergent quality of public sector work. Rarely do public auditors rely on systematic comparative analysis at this level of detail.

This analysis suggests that we need finer-grained ways and more accurate nomenclature to capture and track the work of government. One could suggest mandating more detailed reporting from government departments, since the needed information has to be in the system somewhere. Another way would be to rely on detailed academic studies on specific functions; there have been some interesting examples (Christensen and Lægreid, 2007; James, 2004; Hood et al., 2004). These studies take a long time, and some of them are selective and idiosyncratic; but they do try to link high-level reform themes across agencies or jurisdictions through on-the-ground comparisons.

A third possibility would be to establish a database and taxonomy for categorizing and tracking the work of public organizations. Lindquist (1992) reviewed the literature on organizational taxonomies (e.g., McKelvey, 1982) with this idea in mind.[11] One cannot understand what has happened in specific programs without appreciating institutional direction, culture, history, and capabilities, but conversely, we need to get far better at understanding capabilities and innovation from a bottom-up perspective. One could begin to respond to assertions about the benefits ascribed to different governance regimes; is it true, for example, that jurisdictions that adopted policy-operation splits under NPM have less policy capability that those jurisdictions that did not? Do programs that appear to be effective still seem so when compared to other jurisdictions?

Such a strategy would not deal with the important matter of assessing the evolving reach of government through specific programs. It would be important to go beyond ascertaining the levels and use of staffing and financial resources, to capture the instruments that government bureaus use to influence other governments, citizens, and organizations. For example, we could imagine that a program might well decline dramatically in staff size and budget, but also that its capability may have devolved to a service delivery network or public–private partnership. Development of indicators would need to be informed by the perspectives of markets, hierarchies, and networks (Powell, 1990). Making such assessments is critically important in the context of multi-level governance and collaborative environments across jurisdictions.

Proceeding with such a proposal would be a significant enterprise, involving public servants and academics alike, focusing on certain broad functions (e.g., social service programs) as a point of departure, and working as a network across different jurisdictions and countries. My purpose here is *not* to propose the development of a taxonomic classification system for public organizations. I am suggesting that we do not have very good information on the contours and reach of programs, which allows for competing narratives about the progress of, and possibilities for, public-sector reform. Institutional themes and narratives will tend to trump program-level perspectives.

A fourth approach would be systematic research into the state of practice in Canadian public administration. The literature, with a few exceptions, has tended to focus on corporate initiatives and the broad directions of public-sector reform in Canada without delving into their impact on the workings of the public service and on key stakeholders. Nor has it explored how the effects of reform in our system compare to those of other public administration systems. Despite the recent resurgence in comparative research on public sector reform, many studies are so broad they cannot produce detailed information about organizational, on-the-ground effects of reform, including service levels and outcomes.

Figure 1.4 offers closer, more detailed 'probes' of the state of Canadian public administration in specific areas; however, other topics could be added, which would reflect the scope of this volume and other worthwhile topics. In some instances useful information may have been collected by central agencies and departments, but it has not been widely shared. This suggests a program of strategic and collaborative research among practitioners and academics brokered by government entities such as the Canada School of Public Service (CSPS). Such an agenda also points towards a new program of collaborative academic research given the extensive

Recruiting Talent, Aligning Effort	Designing Policy and Delivering Services	Learning, Scrutiny, and Reform
Attracting and Grooming Talent Comparative studies are required for the following: • evolving career patterns in the public service • trends and regimes for handling temporary staff • retention strategies, particularly in critical areas • recruitment and succession programs • complexity and time for staffing actions • employment protections for public servants • PSMA delegation	*Renewing Interest in Policy Capabilities* • Conduct a baseline comparative study of policy capabilities, including FTEs and contracts. • To what extent are external networks used? • Explore the differences between capabilities of operating versus core policy departments. • Examine cohesiveness of the functional community. • Analyse the external competition. • Assess forward-looking capabilities and outputs?	*Learning and Values* • What is the amount spent for learning and development per employee, and who pays? • What is the best executive development for deputy ministers and other executives? • What are the different sources of motivation for public servants in different roles? • Examine comparative practice in 'whistle-blowing' • How many public servants are aware of the Code of Conduct?
Managing the Human Resource System • How do HR practices vary across departments and agencies in the Canadian public service? • How will PSMA affect the quality and pace of recruiting in workplaces? • Do executives and staff identify more with departments or the entire public service? • How long has it taken to introduces selective HR reforms in different jurisdictions? • What are the different audit regimes in HR systems? • What is the efficiency of staffing actions in centralized and decentralized systems? • How are terminations, discipline, appeals, etc., to be handled?	*Service Delivery* • How have the contours of departments changed over the last 10 years? • What services are delivered by the Canadian public service in contrast to other jurisdictions? • Has service quality (and efficiency) been improved by retaining or spinning off units? • Which services are handled electronically, and how has the modality mix been changing? • Do programs in departments innovate more quickly than in SOAs and service agencies? • What approaches to regional structures and representation are evolving in departments and agencies?	*Control and Accountability* • What are the impacts of tightening controls on public servants and on clients and contractors? • How do these impacts compare with other countries? • Do MPs and SCs use performance reports? • What is the depth of review of programs by ERC, TBS, and standing committees? How does this compare to other jurisdictions? • How do internal and external audit compare to those of other jurisdictions? • How has the conduct of performance reviews of DMs and their departments evolved?
Coordinating from the Centre • Patterns in managerial and executive careers, proportion from other sector and governments • Role of PMs versus central agency autonomy • Study of how different Clerks managed the Privy Council Office, COSO, and the public service reform agenda • Patterns in DM meetings, involvement in task forces, and the role of APEX compared • Administrative styles of central agency units in different functional domains	*Citizen Engagement* • What is the role of department-based consultations versus those of standing committees or commissions? • What is the quality of consultation materials? Do they convey sufficiently complex information for the consultations at hand? • Evaluate the informational content and efficiency of different consultation instruments. • Take an inventory of annual consultations across the public service, perhaps by type.	*Public Service Reform* • How can we convey the diversity of reforms and institutional changes to MPs and citizens? • How are the effects of successive reforms felt in different departments? What is the cumulative impact in terms of structure, service, FTEs, etc.? • How well do governments and PS leaders monitor the implementation of reforms? • When do central reforms get to the front line? • How do governments convey the extent of change, as well as reforms, to constituencies?

Figure 1.4 An Agenda for Comparative Research

list of topics in Figure 1.4. Detailed collaborative research is well beyond the resources of individual researchers in Canada. This suggests assembling international teams of researchers and practitioners. The program of research could build on and complement the previous work of the International Governance Network and the CSPS action-research roundtables. Depending on the research topics, funding could come from central agencies, operating departments, the Social Sciences and Humanities Research Council, and from counterparts in other jurisdictions.

Public service institutions in Westminster-style, Anglo-American parliamentary systems, such as Australia, Canada, New Zealand, and the United Kingdom form a natural cluster for systematic comparative research. These countries have parliamentary systems, strong executives, and centralized institutions. However, depending on which issue or practice is being investigated, other jurisdictions could be explored, including sub-national systems. A critical issue concerns where the responsibilities for policy direction, coordination, and service delivery rest; therefore it will also be essential to discover the distribution of responsibilities *within* and *across* levels of government. In other words, the work would have to account for the differing contexts of federal and multi-level governance systems, which this volume explores.

The proposed strategy would delve into the fine details of government and public service institutions and their practices. However, also important are studies that try to make sense of and anticipate higher-level public administration trends and directions both inside and outside Canada. Indeed, the scrutiny of more narrowly defined topics would not supplant, but could illuminate higher-level frameworks and debates.

Some Public Administration Scenarios to Consider

In addition to taking stock of the effectiveness of previous reforms, observers and leaders in public administration systems always look for *emerging* pressures and uncertainties in their organizations, sectors, and networks. Scenario-building exercises are useful for anticipating uncertainty. These exercises encourage participants to identify and embrace diverse views and possibilities, and require that the many issues, variables, trends, organizations, sectors, and different levels of analysis identified are *integrated* into each scenario, regardless of the critical uncertainties, which usually emerge after considerable debate and dialogue. Such exercises can be very extensive, and there is certainly not the space here to fully outline the process. Rather, my goal here is more modest: to stimulate broad thinking on the different directions that the Canadian public administration system could go, and encourage readers of this *Handbook* to carry forward their thinking about the issues and trends from one chapter to the next and throughout the book.

There are many trends, pressures, issues, and opportunities: demographic change, succession in Canadian workplaces, evolving information and communications technology, globalization, economic gyrations caused by changes in the US economy and world resource markets, budget and equalization stresses, climate change, security threats, increased demands for transparency and accountability, and so on. Here I suggest that underlying these larger problems and policy challenges are genuine uncertainties about the extent to which government will reform key elements of the governance regime by modernizing national representative institutions and further experimenting with ASD across governments and with partners in the non-profit and private sectors. Note that any of these problems or challenges could precipitate changes in governance.

Figure 1.5 summarizes four possible scenarios suggested by these critical contingencies.[12] At one end of the horizontal dimension, we see that reform of representative institutions could be quite modest: strengthening standing committees, increasing research budgets, and engaging elected representatives more systematically in the consultation and legislative process. But reform could be more substantial, perhaps implementing some form of proportional representation in the

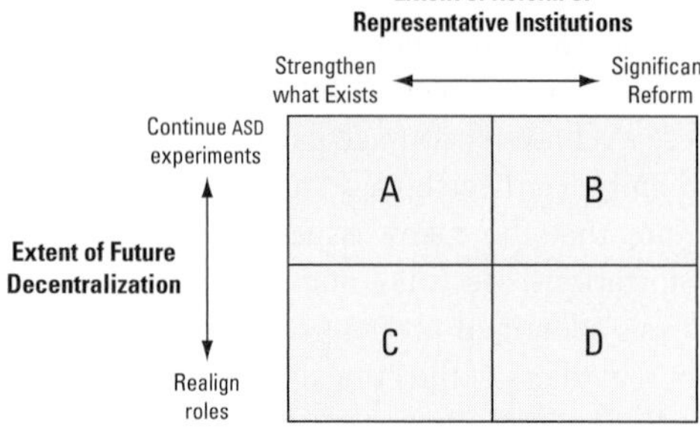

Figure 1.5 Different Institutional Environments for the Canadian Public Service

House of Commons and an elected Senate (as in the Australian electoral system), and perhaps in other legislatures. The vertical dimension shows the range of possibilities for public administration: government could proceed modestly, adopting new ways to deliver services, or could commit to a more radical steering model, relying heavily on the for-profit and non-profit sectors to deliver services, and more extensively collaborating with the other levels of government.

What challenges would these four scenarios pose for the Canadian public administration system during the next couple of decades? In any future, ministers and public servants—as well as various service delivery agents—will face greater scrutiny by elected representatives and the public, with increasing pressure for greater transparency in their dealings. This *Handbook* shows how adjustments in one area will have implications, sometimes significant ones, for other actors in Canada's public administration system. Even in the least radical scenario—with strengthened, more engaged representative legislatures monitoring a modest stream of current and new ASD arrangements—there will be great interest in value-for-money, fairness in contracting, and monitoring performance, focusing not only on ministers and public servants, but also on the private sector, non-profit organizations, and other levels of government, including First Nations organizations.

A key risk in any of the scenarios is how ministers and public service executives will balance attending to demands for external accountability and internal scrutiny with closely monitoring policy advising, considering new service delivery models, and fostering positive learning and work environments. Failure to achieve a good balance leads to the further risk that accountability and scrutiny will significantly reduce public service time spent on policy advising, service delivery, and learning. As the public service moves away from Scenario A in Figure 1.5 towards any of the other scenarios, these tensions will only increase. Proactive institutions should invest in identifying appropriately skilled staff, developing more widely shared and understood rules of engagement, and identifying efficient ways to gather and convey information to handle accountability demands.

Conclusion

This chapter sets out a high-level framework to map out topics, institutions, levels of analysis, and variables associated with studying the public administration system in Canada. It also reviews the succession and evolution of several guiding cosmologies for public administration, and evaluated the latest candidate for the next overarching cosmology of 'integrated governance', noting that many of its elements are not new. This leads to a discussion of the existence of competing narratives of public administration reform, often deriving from the distinct vantage points of different actors in the public administration system. Debates over the most appropriate and persuasive narratives, as well as the dominant narratives that hold sway for some time, take place in the realm of ideas, articles, and press releases. At the same time, there are real and continuous changes in the contours and workings of public administration institutions and front-line service delivery agents delivering programs dictated and guided by policy and management regimes. We know little about these changes, and this chapter calls for a more systematic and comparative approach to shed light on several important topics. Readers of this volume could undoubtedly add to this list of topics.

Important Terms and Concepts

competing narratives
general framework
governance regime
government power and influence
integrated governance
New Public Management
traditional model
well-performing institution

Study Questions

1. What are some strategies for determining what government is actually 'doing'? Which are the most realistic?
2. Working from the extensive nature of this general framework of public administration, can you think of areas that are not covered in this *Handbook* (we had to stop somewhere!), but could be in future?
3. Can one really combine elements of the traditional model and NPM, or are they mutually exclusive?
4. Is the integrated model a satisfactory strategy for governance in the future?
5. Is there a case for an integrated comparative research program in public administration and governance?
6. Can you suggest any areas for international collaborative research that are not covered in the 'Agenda for Comparative Research'?

Useful Websites

Canada. Auditor General of Canada. 1988. 'Well-Performing Institutions'. Report of the Auditor General for 1988.

www.oag-bvg.gc.ca/internet/English/parl_oag_198811_04_e_4231.html

Blythe, D. Marie, and D. Brian Marson. 1999. 'Good Practices in Citizen-Centred Governance'. Citizen-Centred Service Network, Canadian Centre for Management Development.

www.csps-efpc.gc.ca/pbp/pub/pdfs/P88_e.pdf

McDavid, James C., and D. Brian Marson, eds. 1990. *The Well Performing Government Organization*. Publications of IPAC.

www.iapc.ca/PublicationsdelIAPCpartheme

James, Oliver. 2002. 'New Public Management: Enduring Legacy or Fatal Remedy?', *International Review of Public Administration*, 6:2.

www.kapa21.or.kr/down/2001/IRPA/02-Oliver_James.pdf

Notes

1. This stands in considerable contrast to the United States, Australia, and many European countries that provide important checks and complications on prime ministerial or presidential leadership. With few qualifications, a Canadian Prime Minister's principal focus is to secure and maintain power in the House of Commons, although managing cabinet, the government caucus, and public opinion are critical challenges. See, for example, Weller (1989) and Savoie (1999).
2. A reviewer noted that in the last 11 elections, Canadians have elected six majority governments. Still, a high proportion of 'governing time' over the last few decades has proceeded under majority governments.
3. See 'Federalism in Canada' in Manning and Parison (2004: 88).
4. In Sweden and Germany labour and business are coherently represented, which also obtains with the UK for the voluntary sector. See Atkinson and Coleman (1989) and Phillips (2003: 17–71).
5. Gow (2004) argued that the 'contours' of a Canadian model of public administration should embrace public

service reform, managerial reform, and different modes of operation; relationships with the government, Parliament, provincial and territorial governments, the judiciary, Aboriginal governments; and relationships with political parties, interest groups, the media, and citizens. He creatively identifies studies and indicators of patterns in the Canadian model and signs of Canadian distinctiveness. He endorses Bourgon's formulation, agreeing that Canada's approach to public service reform has been 'pragmatic and moderate'. He also suggests the following characteristics of the Canadian model are the most striking: (1) strong political control; (2) strong legal framework, through the Charter, courts, and independent agencies; (3) an autonomous, professional public service; (4) political and public service leaders guided by pragmatism and moderation; and (5) fairly strong tolerance for ambiguity in a federal system with citizens who have multiple loyalties. Gow suggests that the most 'original' features of the Canadian model include the power of the Prime Minister and central agencies, de-politicization of public service appointments, the accent on becoming learning organizations, recognition of minority rights, and moderation on the part of leaders and the public.

6. Hodgetts (1973), Kernaghan and Langford (1990), Dwivedi and Gow (1999), Gow (2004), and Lindquist (2000: 7).

7. All of these ideas were supported by then-current Weberian precepts for managing large-scale bureaucratic organizations, such as chain of command, unity of command, hierarchy, rules and procedures, authority, spheres of responsibility, and specialist expertise.

8. PEMS was an approach to setting priorities and financial discipline in a complex institutional environment that changed the cabinet committee system, budgeting and created additional central agencies. See Richard Van Loon (1984), 'Planning in the Eighties' in French with Van Loon, *How Ottawa Decides*, 157–90.

9. Christensen et al. (2007: 128) write that NPM is 'not a consistent and integrated theory for modernizing the public sector, but is better characterized as a wave of reforms composed of some principle reform ideas together with a loose cluster of reform initiatives pointing in various directions'.

10. Greenwood and Hinings (1996) argue that institutional inertia, culture, structure, and imperfect understanding of strategies adopted by other organizations elsewhere shape the ability and interest of an organization to take on radical, as opposed to incremental, change. In this case, then, the pre-existing diversity in structure, repertoires, and culture of government institutions—along with specific political and policy needs—leads to great diversity in the adoption of reforms. Indeed, Greenwood and Hinings argue that radical change is more likely when there is pent-up demand for reform and relatively impermeable environmental fields—radical change is necessary to overcome such inertia. However, radical change does not simply happen; there must be internal re-alignment of power to foster commitment and designers with the vision and capacity to imagine an alternative state and manage the transition in a concerted way (pp. 1039–40). This analysis describes very well the 1980s New Zealand experience with public sector reform, as well as the experiences in other jurisdictions where, in varying degrees, governments adopted more selective reforms, in part because the environments were more permeable and limited reforms could proceed, and in part because there was an insufficient confluence of interest in radical change at the political and bureaucratic levels.

11. There was little take-up of earlier efforts to establish taxonomies nor McKelvey's (1982) seminal *Organizational Systematics*, owing to the early focus of the literature on informing empirical analyses of assorted organizational variables and a later focus that saw developing taxonomies as part of the population ecology movement. No one saw the potential role of organizational taxonomy in the sense discussed here: to categorize and monitor the evolution of specific programs and their 'comp pools' over time and, by implication, which areas were embraced by specific portfolios.

12. For background on scenario building, see Rosell (1995), van der Heijden (1996), and Ringland (1998).

References

Atkinson, Michael, and William D. Coleman. 1989. *The State, Business and Industrial Policy.* Toronto: University of Toronto Press.

Aucoin, Peter. 1995. *The New Public Management: Canada in Comparative Perspective.* Montreal: Institute for Research on Public Policy.

———, and Ralph Heintzman. 2000. 'The Dialectics of Accountability for Performance in Public Management Reform', *International Review of Administrative Sciences* 66: 43–53.

———, Jennifer Smith, and Geoff Dinsdale. 2004. *Responsible Government: Clarifying Essentials, Dispelling Myths and*

Exploring Change. Ottawa: Canadian Centre for Management Development.

Australia, Management Advisory Committee. 2004. *Connecting Government: Whole of Government Responses to Australia's Priority Challenges*. Canberra: Commonwealth of Australia.

Bakvis, Herman, and Luc Juillet. 2004. *The Horizontal Challenge: Line Departments, Central Agencies and Leadership*. Ottawa: Canada School of Public Service.

Barzelay, Michael. 2001. *The New Public Management: Improving Research and Policy Dialogue*. Berkeley and Los Angeles: University of California Press and Russell Sage Foundation.

Benhamadi, Bey. 2003. 'Governance and Diversity within the Public Service in Canada: Toward a Viable and Sustainable Representation of Designated Groups (Employment Equity)', *International Review of Administrative Sciences* 69: 505–19.

Borins, Sandford. 2002. 'Transformation of the Public Sector: Canada in Comparative Perspective' in Christopher Dunn, ed., *The Handbook of Canadian Public Administration*, 1st edn. Toronto: Oxford University Press, 3–17.

———, Kenneth Kernaghan, David Brown, Nick Bontis, Perri 6, and Fred Thompson. 2007. *Digital State at the Leading Edge*. Toronto: University of Toronto Press.

Boston, Jonathan, John Martin, June Pallot, and Pat Walsh. 1996. *Public Management: The New Zealand Model*. Oxford: Oxford University Press.

Canada, CCMD Roundtable on the Management of Horizontal Initiatives. 2001. *Moving From the Heroic to the Everyday: Lessons Learned From Leading Horizontal Projects*. Ottawa: Canadian Centre for Management Development.

Canada, CCMD Roundtable on Horizontal Mechanisms. 2002. *Using Horizontal Tools To Work Across Boundaries: Lessons Learned and Signposts for Success*. Ottawa: Canadian Centre for Management Development.

Charih, Mohammed, and Art Daniels, eds. 1997. *The New Public Management and Public Administration in Canada*. Toronto: Institute of Public Administration in Canada.

Christensen, Tom, and Per Lægreid, eds. 2007. *Transcending New Public Management: The Transformation of Public Sector Reforms*. Aldershot, Hampshire: Ashgate.

———, ———, Paul G. Roness, and Kjell Arne Rovik. 2007. *Organization Theory and the Public Sector: Instrument, Culture and Myth*. London: Routledge.

DiMaggio, P.J., and W.W. Powell. 1983. 'The Iron Cage Revisited: Institutional Isomorphism and Collective Rationality in Organizational Fields', *American Sociological Review* 48, 2: 147–60.

Dwivedi, O.P., and James Iain Gow. 1999. 'The New Public Management Movement Comes to Canada' in O.P. Dwivedi and James Iain Gow, eds, *From Bureaucracy to Public Management*, 125–59.

———. 1999. *From Bureaucracy to Public Management*. Peterborough, Ont.: Broadview Press.

Edwards, Meredith, and John Langford, eds. 2002. *New Players, Partners and Processes: A Public Sector Without Boundaries?* Canberra and Victoria: National Institute of Governance, University of Canberra, and Centre for Public Sector Studies, University of Victoria.

Feldman, Martha S., and James G. March. 1981. 'Information in Organizations as Signal and Symbol', *Administrative Science Quarterly* 26, 2 (June): 171–86.

Flanagan, Tom. 1995. *Waiting For the Wave: The Reform Party and Preston Manning*. Toronto: Stoddart.

French, Richard D., with Richard Van Loon. 1984. *How Ottawa Decides: Planning and Industrial Policy-Making 1968–1984*, 2nd edn. Toronto: Lorimer.

Gow, James Iain. 2004. *A Canadian Model of Public Administration?* Ottawa: Canada School of Public Service.

Greenwood, Royston, and C.R. Hinings. 1996. 'Understanding Radical Organizational Change: Bringing Together the Old and the New Institutionalism', *The Academy of Management Review* 21, 4 (October): 1022–54.

Halligan, John. 2001. 'Comparing Public Sector Reform in the OECD', in Brendan C. Nolan, ed., *Public Sector Reform: An International Perspective*. New York: Palgrave, 3–18.

———, ed. 2003. *Civil Service Systems in Anglo-American Countries*. Cheltenham, UK: Edward Elgar.

———. 2007. 'Reform Design and Performance in Australia and New Zealand', in Christensen and Lægreid (2007, ch.3).

Hannan, M.T., and J.H. Freeman. 1977. 'The Population Ecology of Organizations', *American Journal of Sociology* 82: 929–64.

Heijden, Kees van der. 1996. *Scenarios: The Art of Strategic Conversation*. New York: Wiley.

Heintzman, Ralph, and Brian Marson. 2005. 'People, Service and Trust: Is There a Public Sector Service Value Chain?', *International Review of Administrative Sciences* 71, 4: 549–75.

Hodgetts, J.E. 1973. *The Canadian Public Service: A Physiology of Government 1867–1970*. Toronto: University of Toronto Press.

Hood, Christopher, Oliver James, B. Guy Peters, and Colin Scott. 2004. *Controlling Modern Government: Variety, Commonality and Change*. Cheltenham, UK: Elgar.

James, Oliver. 2004. *The Executive Agency Revolution in Whitehall: Public Interest Versus Bureau-Shaping Perspectives*. Houndsmills, Basingstoke, Hampshire: Palgrave.

Kernaghan, Kenneth, and John Langford. 1990. *The Responsible Public Servant*. Toronto and Halifax: Institute of Public Administration of Canada and Institute for Research on Public Policy.

Kingdon, John W. 1995. *Agendas, Alternatives, and Public Policies*, 2nd edn. New York: Harper Collins.

Lindquist, Evert. 1992. 'Classification and Relevance: A Strategy for Developing a Data-base and Taxonomy of Public Organizations in Canada', a paper presented to the 1992 Annual Meetings of the Institute of Public Administration of Canada.

———. 1997. 'The Bewildering Pace of Public Sector Reform in Canada', in Jan-Erik Lane, ed., *Public Sector Reform*. London: Sage.

———. 2000. 'Government Restructuring and Career Public Service in Canada: Introduction and Overview', in Evert Lindquist, ed., *Government Restructuring and Career Public Service in Canada*. Toronto: Institute of Public Administration of Canada.

———. 2006. *A Critical Moment: Capturing and Conveying the Evolution of the Canadian Public Service*. Ottawa: Canada School of Public Service.

———. 2007. 'Public Administration and Organization Theory: Recovering Alternative Perspectives on Public Service Institutions', a paper prepared for a symposium on the 90th Birthday of T.E. Hodgetts, University of Guelph, September.

McKelvey, B. 1982. *Organizational Systematics: Taxonomy, Evolution, Classification.* Berkeley, CA: University of California Press.

Manning, Nick, and Neil Parison. 2004. *International Public Administration Reform: Implications for the Russian Federation.* New York: The World Bank.

Meyer, John W., and Brian Rowan. 1977. 'Institutionalized Organizations: Formal Structure as Myth and Ceremony', *American Journal of Sociology* 83, 2 (September): 340–63.

———. Richard W. Scott, and Terrence Deal. 1983. 'Institutional and Technical Sources of Organizational Structure', in H.D. Stein, ed., *Organization and the Human Services.* Philadelphia: Temple University Press, 151–78.

Phillips, Susan D. 2003. 'Voluntary Sector–Government Relationships in Transition: Learning from International Experience' in Kathy Brock and Keith G. Banting, eds, *The Non-Profit Sector in Interesting Times: Case Studies in a Changing Sector.* Montreal and Kingston: McGill-Queen's University Press.

Pollitt, Christopher, and Geert Bouckaert. 2004. *Public Management Reform: A Comparative Analysis*, 2nd edn. Oxford: Oxford University Press.

Powell, Walter W. 1990. 'Neither Market nor Hierarchy: Network Forms of Organization', *Research in Organizational Behavior* 12: 295–336.

Ringland, Gill. 1998. *Scenario Planning: Managing for the Future.* New York: Wiley.

Roe, Emery.1994. *Narrative Policy Analysis: Theory and Practice.* Durham, NC: Duke University Press.

Rosell, Steven A. 1995. *Changing Maps: Governing in a World of Change.* Ottawa: Carleton University Press.

Rushdie, Salman. 1990. *Haroun and the Sea of Stories.* New York: Viking Books.

Savoie, Donald. 1999. *Governing From the Centre.* Toronto: University of Toronto Press.

———. 2003. *Breaking the Bargain: Public Servants, Ministers, and Parliament.* Toronto: University of Toronto Press.

Scott, Graham. 2001. *Public Management in New Zealand: Lessons and Challenges.* Wellington: New Zealand Business Roundtable.

Shergold, Peter. 2007. Keynote address to the Australia–New Zealand School of Government Conference on Collaborative Government, Canberra, June.

Tait, J. 1997. 'A Strong Foundation: Report of the Task Force on Public Service Values and Ethics', *Canadian Public Administration* 40, 1 (Spring): 1–22.

Thompson, James D. 1967. *Organizations in Action.* New York: McGraw-Hill Ryerson.

Thompson, Mark, and John Fryer. 1999. 'Changing Roles for Employers and Unions in the Public Service' in Lindquist (2000: 41–67).

Tufte, Edward. 1990. *Envisioning Information.* Cheshire, Conn.: Graphics Press.

United Kingdom, Cabinet Office. 2000. *Wiring It Up: Whitehall's Management of Cross-Cutting Policies and Services.* London: Performance and Innovation Unit.

Weller, Patrick. 1989. *Malcolm Fraser PM: A Study in Prime Ministerial Power in Australia.* Ringwood, Victoria: Penguin.

2 Departments and Other Institutions of Government

Gregory Tardi

Fundamentals of Democratic Institutional Design

The purpose of this chapter is to define and circumscribe the framework of the institutions that conduct public administration. Departments and other administrative institutions must be explained in their proper democratic context.

At the time of the establishment of British colonies in North America, the rules regarding reception of common law held that the provision of the original institutions of government was a matter of royal prerogative. Among the institutions so originated was the council, the body of executive councillors (only later to be known as ministers) forming the executive (see Hogg, 1997: ss. 2.2[c], 2.6, 93). With the advent of responsible government during the early nineteenth century, the formation of a council of ministers remained a prerogative power but the prerogative devolved from the monarch to the Prime Minister. To this day, the design of a government, that is, the determination of ministerial portfolios, as well as the selection of ministers, is one of the PM's prerogatives. Consequently, the principal departments of government are the administrative institutions necessary to enable ministers invited into the government by the Prime Minister to carry out the mandates he or she assigns to them. The development of the principal departments was based on the major portfolio areas of political responsibility traditionally inherent to government. It has come to include the administrative and regulatory domains that evolved during the twentieth century in regard to concepts of governance. The creation of departments also reflects the particular priorities of the head of government of the day.

While the determination of portfolios remains a prime ministerial prerogative, the establishment of departments and the conduct of their life cycle had become a matter of law in Canadian practice between the Union Act of 1840 and the time of Confederation. A significant reason for this seems to be that, as of 1840, executive councillors were assigned specific portfolios and were paid amounts specified in the schedule to the Union Act itself; Parliament used the power of the purse to assert its control over the creation of the departmental institutions underlying these portfolios. The Constitution Act, 1867 confirmed that the powers, authorities, and functions relating to government previously exercised under legislation should continue to be so exercised. It also provided that all laws then in force, including those that had established departments, continue to have effect, subject to amendment by the appropriate legislative body.[1] Notwithstanding the nineteenth-century constitutional language, which now seems arcane, it is clear that in the perception of the Fathers of Confederation, government departments need to be grounded in legislation. The modern authors also express the unanimous opinion that departments are required to be established by statute.

> Federal and Quebec Departments are established by an Act.... Generally speaking,

> therefore, Parliament alone is responsible for establishing those preferred instruments for the application of laws. This method of establishing Departments, which may at first glance appear rather inflexible, provides the indisputable advantage of conferring upon a particular sector of administrative activity the importance which is normally suggested by setting the legislative process in motion. As well, it contributes to guaranteeing publicity for the functions and attributes of these centralized structures and to allowing representatives of the people to pronounce upon the formation of the administrative structures which are essential to the exercise of parliamentary control over the Administration. (Dussault and Borgeat, 1985, vol. 1: 83–4)

The principal conclusion of this historical evolution is that the domain of state administration relating to public institutions is based on law; its democratic essence is that it is dependent on the will of Parliament.[2] Public institutions are departments only when statutes declare them to be so. Moreover, departments are what the legislation says they are and have authority to perform those functions for the public interest and benefit that the law attributes to them. Departmental legislation must, naturally, respect the bounds of federalism set out in ss. 91 and 92 of the Constitution Act, 1867 as well as abide by the guides on governmental action provided in the Canadian Charter of Rights and Freedoms.

Principal Departments of Government

While it is now well established that departments and other institutions of government in Canada are grounded primarily in law, to achieve a comprehensive understanding of their status it is necessary to discern not only the legal but also the policy and the political characteristics that inform them, and, indeed, to observe how the different types of instruments interact in guiding their functioning. No single code for governmental institutions exists. However, the laws and other instruments of governance that establish and direct departments reveal a pattern of consistent and cohesive practice in which the similarities far exceed the distinctions.

Statutory Foundations

Government departments are established primarily through a number of **self-standing statutes**; as well, some departments have been created through provisions in **substantive statutes**. There is no correlation between the apparent importance or significance of a department within the government and the legislative technique by which it was brought into existence.

Most departments are founded by a particular statute in which the key phrase is, for example, 'There is hereby established a department of the Government of Canada called the Department of Justice over which the Minister of Justice appointed by commission under the Great Seal shall preside.' Such wording may render it difficult to distinguish between the ministerial office that is political in nature and that which is an institution of public administration; the two are distinct, however, in law and in practice. Also, there is no necessary correlation between departments and ministers, as a number of portfolios and ministerial tasks are not supported by departments. Some deviations from this form are worth mentioning. In the case of the Department of Finance, the provision creating the institution and the ministerial portfolio are included in the Financial Administration Act. The Treasury Board Secretariat, which for all intents and purposes functions as any other department, is also a creature of the Financial Administration Act. The political figure at its helm has ministerial rank but is formally known as the President of the Treasury Board. This department is unique in that the Treasury Board itself is a committee of the cabinet. In a manner parallel to the Department of Finance, the Department of National Defence arises out of the National Defence Act.

Another particularity of departments is the location of their headquarters. Most departments are located in Ottawa. For political reasons, however, the Department of Veterans Affairs was moved to Charlottetown. Several of the departments that conduct economic development activity have also been decentralized; in these instances, the reasons were based on policy and practicality.

On the basis of early custom, which has become enshrined in legislation, a few institutions of a departmental nature and rank owe their existence to another mode of establishment. Cabinet portfolios can also be created by the provision of funds pursuant to the Salaries Act. Thus, for example, is the ministerial position of the President of the Queen's Privy Council for Canada staffed. Through consistent practice, which is not legislated, ministers so created can have offices that are, in essence, very small departments. By contrast, the Leader of the Government in the Senate, who also derives his tenure from the Salaries Act, has no office.

Another way of creating departments is through the Ministers and Ministries of State Act, legislation that dates only from 1968. Offices of secretaries of state can in most respects be treated as comparable to the principal departments. Throughout the Pierre Trudeau and Brian Mulroney administrations, the mechanism of this statute was used to set up a number of *ministries* of state. In Jean Chrétien's time as Prime Minister, the Act was used only to create positions of *ministers* of state, who now function essentially as ministers of state to assist ministers. In popular parlance, they are called junior ministers. Prime Minister Stephen Harper has continued this practice of having *ministers* of state but there are no more *ministries* of state.

What is the effect of the creation of departments by this range of means? Some scholars argue that departments have no legal personality, being synonymous with the Crown or the government. However, in 1973, the Supreme Court of Canada decided that the statutory declaration of the corporate existence of an entity created by governmental power for the performance of public functions endowed that entity with legal personality.[3] This ruling has since been followed. Practically, given their status in law and their political legitimacy, departments have the competence and ability to carry out their public mandates and to make decisions that are both legally binding and politically valid.

Powers, Duties, and Functions

To fulfill the constitutional responsibilities of the state to govern, departments are mandated to administer and achieve the political and policy purposes in their respective domains of public affairs. How they carry out their responsibilities determines the quality of democracy and whether or not the governance of the country is accomplished effectively and efficiently. Here also, as in the establishment of departments, there is a pervasive blending of law, politics, and public administration in regard to both goals and means.

The most fundamental and permanent tasks of departments are laid out in the statutes that establish them. Such tasks are allocated through the minister responsible for the portfolio. Thus, each such statute provides that 'The Minister holds office during pleasure and has the management and direction of the Department.' The statutes go on to state, for example, in the case of the Department of Agriculture, that 'The powers, duties and functions of the Minister extend to and include all matters over which Parliament has jurisdiction, not by law assigned to any other department, . . . relating to . . . agriculture.' Some departmental statutes include additional and more specific mandates. These sections, read together, provide the basic skeleton onto which the work of the executive branch of government is grafted. They both secure the necessary legal mandate for each department to undertake work, and divide the overall work of government into distinct portfolios, which have evolved through the last two centuries of governmental practice, in conformity with the inner logic of public administration. The consequence of assigning mandates to governmental institutions by law is that departments may exercise only those powers with which they are endowed. In instances where they seek to extend their mandates without the authority of Parliament, the courts will not hesitate to strike down their resulting actions.[4]

Within the parameters of federalism required by ss. 91 and 92 of the Constitution Act, 1867, the panoply of Canadian departments is mirrored within the provinces. It is worth noting that the division of governments into departments of public administration is also comparable across a wide variety of modern democracies, with the local variations necessitated by the particular circumstances of each country.

In Canadian practice, the powers, duties, and functions attributed to specific departments are not immutable, however. They reflect the rise and demise of public policy issues that government needs to address. Many departments thus have defined life cycles. In this country's political history since Confederation, a number of departments in due course were deemed to be no longer required. In this category are included the Departments of the Interior, of Overseas Military Forces, of Soldiers' Civil Re-establishment, and of Reconstruction. In one relatively recent case, that of the Ministry of State for Urban Affairs, a department was wound up as a result of political problems based on federalism. The federal authorities realized that the overlap in powers relating to municipal affairs favoured the provinces and, in the context of the run-up to the 1980 referendum, decided to pull back. Some departments, such as the Ministries of State for Economic Development and for Social Development, have been phased out for reasons of political convenience, with their responsibilities being taken over by other institutions of government. Other departments serving long-term public policy goals have undergone metamorphoses involving changes in the powers, duties, and functions assigned to their ministers. Such, for example, is the case with the tasks presently assigned to the Department of Industry; in earlier incarnations, each time with a different emphasis on the set of tasks assigned to it, this has been the Department of Trade; of Trade and Commerce; of Industry, Trade and Commerce; of Regional Industrial Expansion; of Regional Economic Expansion; and finally of Industry, Science and Technology. Today it is once again the Department of Industry.

As public policy needs arise, new departments can also be established. Thus, under the impact of the terrorist attacks on the United States of 11 September 2001, the administration of Prime Minister Chrétien contemplated setting up a department to deal with matters of security. Such a body would not only mirror the newly created American Office of Homeland Security and the ministries of interior that have long existed in European countries. It would also revive a plan formulated but not carried out by Prime Minister Campbell to set up a Ministry of Public Security. The portfolio is presently entitled Public Safety and it is meant to encompass all the national security, policing, prison and parole, border protection, and emergency preparedness functions of the federal government.

The legal framework derived from the statutes is, alternatively, neither explicit nor comprehensive enough by itself to provide guidance for departmental operation. The statutes are therefore complemented by texts of a political nature and by others required in the course of public administration. Government-wide, the collective work of departments is affected by the platform of the party coming into office. This can be particularly true when the governing party has made specific written electoral promises in its party platform, as the Liberal Party did in its 1993 and 1997 campaigns. Such promises invariably are reflected in the departmental briefing books for incoming ministers. Upon the assumption of office by a government, as well as on every occasion a new minister is appointed to head a department, the Prime Minister sends the minister a letter called a 'mandate letter', presumably setting out the PM's expectations with respect to the portfolio involved and his notion of the minister's contribution to the overall work of the government. It is difficult to comment on this conventional form of instrument of advice passing from the hands of the Prime Minister to those of an incoming minister, however, as its use is known but the text of each instrument is highly confidential.

Since the late 1980s, yet another form of instrument stating departmental mandates has come into vogue—the statement of mission, mandate, or values. This is a declaration adopted by a department on the basis of internal consultation. Such a mission statement sets out the department's own view of its role in line with the overall goals of the government and in the 1990s context of increased workloads and fewer resources. These statements in some respects can be seen as emulating the internal motivational practices of private sector corporations. While not binding, they are useful indicators of departments' public administration strategies. In the Department of Justice, for example, the effect of the statement was described as follows:

> The statement of mission and values is obviously a key component in Justice in the 1990s, as it is intended to guide us all in our decision-making. The statement is a guiding factor in setting our priorities and strategic directions which, in turn, will lead to the setting of clearer and more relevant objectives and workplans at all levels of the Department, including the corporate, sectoral, branch, unit and individual levels. (Department of Justice, 1990: 4)

Still other clarifications of the tasks assigned to departments and undertaken by them can be gleaned from various documents, such as the annual Estimates Part III, which are required to be submitted to Parliament; from the testimony of ministers and deputy ministers before parliamentary committees; from departments' annual reports; and on occasion from the recommendations of Royal Commissions looking into their management. All these documents of a general nature are, at least in theory, translated into work programs and job descriptions of individual public servants or groups of them.

Departmental Structures

The traditional organizational model of departments is also enshrined in law. Most statutes, in addition to establishing the position of minister with responsibility for presiding over the department and having management and direction of it, provide for the appointment of a deputy minister. The only statutory description of the deputy minister's function is that he or she is to be the 'deputy head' of the department. The unwritten but universally understood meaning of these assignments is that the minister is the political head of the department while the deputy minister is its public service head, implying the notion of permanence and political neutrality. In reality, these two officials must work in close conjunction for the department to be able to administer and develop part of the public interest.

The one minister/one deputy minister form of departmental administration, long in use, can no longer be said to be the unique norm, however. Departments are structured, rather, to suit specific public policy goals and the current requirements of governance. For example, in the 1980s the Department of National Revenue was nominally an integrated department dealing with the collection of funds due to the government under different legislative schemes. In reality, the integration applied at the ministerial level only. Below the minister were two deputy ministers, one responsible for taxation and another for customs and excise. Each deputy headed what effectively were parallel departments. In more recent times, this department was fully integrated with a single minister and a single deputy minister at its head, but that structure was changed more recently to yet another model, as we shall see below.

Another singular case is that of the portfolio tasks performed today in part by the Department of Citizenship and Immigration and in part by the Department of Human Resources Development. In 1976, Parliament adopted the Employment and Immigration Department and Commission Act.[5] This legislation made one minister responsible for the development and use of labour market resources, employment services, unemployment insurance, and immigration. Pursuant to the same Act, the deputy minister was also made chairman of the Canada Employment Insurance Commission, while the associate deputy minister was made the Commission's vice-chair. Of the overall tasks assigned to the minister, the duties and functions relating to labour market resources and immigration were assigned to the Commission, and other matters also may be referred to it by the Governor-in-Council (i.e., cabinet). As a result of the restructuring of the government begun during the tenure of Kim Campbell as Prime Minister and completed by her successor, Jean Chrétien, this arrangement of responsibilities was done away with. As a result, the successor institutions were the Department of Citizenship and Immigration and the Department of Human Resources Development, both of them based on the more traditional pattern. Following further rearrangements during the tenure of office of Prime Minister Paul Martin and subsequently adopted by Prime Minister Stephen Harper, the human resources portfolio activities of the federal government are divided between the Department of Human Resources and Skills Development and the Department of Social Development. One minister is in charge of both departments. He or she wears the blended title of Minister of Human Resources and Social Development, indicating that at some time in the future, these departments may become unified in law and public administration practice. Moreover, pursuant to the Department of Human Resources and Skills Development Act, there is also a Minister of Labour.

The development of new activities within government, in particular the advances in public sector management, has led to significant increases in the number of officials within departments who have deputy ministerial rank. Thus, while there is still only one titular deputy minister in each department, many departments have associate deputy ministers who, for all intents and purposes, report to their minister as deputies and manage specified sectors of departmental activity. The most prominent of these deputy ministerial clusters is in the Prime Minister's entourage, where in addition to his or her political deputy equivalent, the principal secretary, the Privy Council Office has six deputy-ranked officers. Foreign Affairs also has six, Justice, four, and Finance, three. In the Department of National Defence, in addition to the four civilian officials who rank at the deputy level, the Chief of Defence Staff, who is charged with control and administration of the Canadian Forces, is also effectively of that rank.

Below the level of leadership, the units within departments generally tend to be similar. One hallmark of public sector organization is its hierarchical nature, that is, the structure of departments tends to be pyramidal, operating through upward-reporting relationships. While it is most difficult to do away with this, the interesting innovations in public sector management have been the efforts to combine this type of structure with increasingly localized and therefore divergent decision-making authorities. This trend gives rise within the public service to intense discussion about the relative merits and advantages of using legal or other types of instruments to effect reform. Such debates often focus on the binding nature and permanence of legal instruments, as opposed to the flexibility of policy instruments. Another constant tendency in the public service is its practice of internal restructuring. Departmental structures are often modified to serve evolving legal mandates, the political goals of governing parties and ministers, and the requirements of managerial objectives and renewal. In recent years the primary such requirement has been economy.

Rearrangement and Transfer of Duties

In the same manner that individual departments restructure themselves in order to execute their mandates, the government as a whole must have a legal device to give itself the capacity to arrange the duties carried out by its various departments in accordance with its political program and its policy goals. This was recognized as soon after Confederation as the administration of Sir Robert Borden. In the House of Commons debate of March 1918, Prime Minister Borden introduced the first version of the **Public Service Rearrangement and Transfer of Duties Act** and justified it by stating that:

> This Bill authorizes the Governor in Council to change any department or any branch of a department from the direction of one minister to the direction of another. It has become evident that some re-arrangement of certain departments is necessary. . . . This is a general power; it does not permit an increase in the number of departments, but it does permit the transfer of a department or a branch thereof from one minister to another. It permits also an amalgamation of two departments under one minister.[6]

With relatively minor modifications, this statute has been a feature of the Canadian system of government organization since that time. In practice, it provides the mechanism to hold together the components of the executive branch of government. It enables the government to transfer powers, duties, and functions, along with the branches of departments that execute them and the public servants who carry out those functions, from one minister to another. The advantage of this Act is that by authorizing the cabinet to proceed by Order-in-Council, it obviates the need for legislative amendment every time ministerial or departmental responsibilities are shifted, thus saving time on the parliamentary agenda and increasing the flexibility so vital to good government.

Given the nature of this power as encompassing the entire government, it falls into the domain reserved for the Prime Minister, who uses it extensively. The practice successive prime ministers have adopted includes using the Act to shift powers, duties, and functions from one portfolio to another or to transfer them to ministers designated by name, reflecting political arrangements within cabinet. With respect to the structure of the government and the timely reorganization of portfolios and departments, the Prime Minister is advised by a group within the Privy Council Office entitled the Machinery of Government Secretariat. This is in effect the PCO's political science department, ever watchful of the Prime Minister's interests, his need for institutional flexibility, and his primacy among his cabinet colleagues. In some instances, the mechanism of this Act has been used to override a departmental statute that specifically assigns a subject task to the department. Orders under the Public Service Rearrangement and Transfer of Duties Act can thus effectively supersede statutes enacted earlier, creating a deviation from the strict construction of the rules of statutory interpretation. The use of this Act poses two problems. The first is the lack of a centralized registry of orders made under it. Over the lifespan of a government, it can become difficult, without constant reference to the *Canada Gazette*, to keep an up-to-date and cohesive picture of what public sector task is where. More significantly, in relation to the reforms conducted under Prime Minister Jean Chrétien, this Act is not useful for transferring powers to the provinces or to joint federal–provincial agencies.

Responsibility and Accountability

Beyond providing for the establishment of government departments and assigning mandates to them, the Canadian constitutional system has also developed conventions for harnessing the powers that ministers exercise through their departments. Given the necessarily permanent requirement for the institutions of government, these control mechanisms of responsibility and accountability are greatly personalized in regard to ministers and deputy ministers. With variations in degree, however, all professional members of the public service can be said to be accountable.

The concepts of 'responsibility' and 'accountability' were characterized in a recent government Task Force report as being 'related but distinct' (Public Service of Canada, 1997). In many practical respects the two concepts are so similar that it is difficult to draw useful distinctions between them. While 'responsibility' is far more extensively referred to by constitutional and legal scholars, preoccupation with 'accountability' is more prevalent among experts in public administration and has indeed attained the status of a universal buzzword. Both concepts can be viewed as positive incentives to perform according to the rule of law, constitutionally, and with professional conscience and ability. Despite definition problems, it is clear that the two concepts combined constitute the most appropriate modus operandi of government institutions in parliamentary democratic regimes and the best description of professional incentive in governance, in contrast to the profit motive in the private sector. Under either definition, ministers are answerable before Parliament for the administration of their particular department, portfolio, or both. In Hogg's view, **responsibility** entails representing the department before Parliament, piloting legislation relating to the work of the department through the legislative process, ensuring acceptance of departmental estimates of proposed expenditures, and explaining and defending the policies and practices of the department. According to Osbaldeston, the **accountability** process consists of setting expectations, pursuing expected goals, and holding public sector officials to account for their performance. The two descriptions seem to merge conveniently (Hogg, 1997; Osbaldeston, 1989).

The counterpart of ministerial accountability is that of the deputy minister. In the practice developed since the Trudeau administration, deputies are appointed by the Prime Minister, often after consultation with the relevant minister. The deputy ministerial function is grounded within the non-partisan public service, but deputies must have finely tuned political senses to understand their minister's outlook and to aim departmental management towards the desired goals.

Responsibility and accountability relate principally to the general direction of a department, that is, to its policies and programs. In this respect ministers must practise the art of the possible, by assuring Parliament that the goals they have selected can be achieved politically and administratively. The less political and more administrative aspects of accountability are those involving management and the soundness of departmental finances. A further aspect of this control mechanism is the allocation of public responsibility for maladministration, misconduct, or unexpected results of governance. The doctrines of responsibility and accountability are primarily political. In Canadian practice, the ultimate sanctions on ministers—resignation or immediate dismissal from the cabinet—are rare. In the longer term, however, ministers who run into problems of accountability tend to lose power in cabinet, influence within the party, and ultimately their position. For deputies, the most common resolution of accountability problems is transfer to another function.

Only a limited part of the doctrines of responsibility and accountability has been defined through litigation. Traditionally, ministerial responsibility has included liability for the actions of public servants in a minister's department. In a case where the issue at stake was whether a minister could be subject to contempt proceedings because one of her public servants did not deliver documents to the court within a prescribed time period, the Supreme Court of Canada rejected the notion of the minister's personal liability:

> In the case of Ministers of the Crown who administer large departments and are involved in a multiplicity of proceedings, it would be extraordinary if orders were brought, routinely, to their attention. In order to infer knowledge in such a case, there must be circumstances which reveal reason for bringing the order to the attention of the Minister.[7]

It must be acknowledged that dealing with issues of political responsibility and accountability in such manner, by law, is rare. In contrast to the political ability flowing from these doctrines, departments are subject to far more extensively applied legal liability for their operations.

No discussion of accountability as a doctrine of democratic governing would be complete without mentioning the new **Federal Accountability Act**.[8] The perceived need for this Act, one of the most broad-scoped items of federal legislation since Confederation, and certainly the most extensive statute in Canadian history to deal with machinery of government, arose from the *Report of the Commission of Inquiry into the Sponsorship Program and Advertising Activities*, commonly known as the Gomery Report.[9] That report was itself the direct consequence of the so-called 'sponsorship scandal' of 2003–4. Following the strong showing by the 'Yes' side in the 1995 Quebec secession referendum, the Chrétien government used existing public service programs and mechanisms to promote federalism in Quebec through advertising and sponsoring public events. It allowed these activities to become politicized and to be conducted without adequate internal or external controls. Amounts of money that were rather significant in themselves, but small in relation to the government's overall budget, were misspent. The institutional response, set out in the Federal Accountability Act, was to impose various new layers of expenditure control and review and to establish several new offices, all aimed at keeping the system accountable and improving deputy ministerial responsibility and accountability. The Federal Accountability Act is extremely complex legislation; its full effects on democratic governing have not yet been experienced and are perhaps not yet understood.

Particularities of Major Centres of Power

The political landscape, to be sure, is not uniform among all governmental bodies or even among all the principal departments. Some present specific characteristics worth noting because they are based on the unique traits of Canadian political society among like-functioning democracies and they thus contribute to the particularly Canadian variety of governance. They are called **clusters of power in the executive**.

The Prime Ministerial Cluster

Even a brief outline of the institutions of federal government in Canada must delineate the cluster of departments and ministerial offices constituting the apex of public power in this country. The **prime ministerial cluster** is the group of institutions serving the Prime Minister in his or her capacities as political head of the government, of the executive branch for each of the two Houses of Parliament. This group of institutions is of interest in regard to both governmental structure and the processes of governance that it organizes and manages. In Canadian practice, this cluster is the institutional underpinning of what used to be designated in Gaullist terms as *le domaine réservé* of the head of government. Here, the vital interests of the state are combined with the legitimate exercise of political power at its highest levels.

Nominally, the pinnacle of public power in this country is occupied by the monarch in her capacity as (the non-resident) Queen of Canada and by her local representative, the Governor-General. While each of these has a constitutional role in support of the legitimacy of Canadian government, in reality their functions today are largely ceremonial, their genuine powers having been taken over by elected officials.

The genuine focus of power is the Prime Minister and the institutions that serve him or her directly. Arguably, the PM has been the linchpin of governance ever since Confederation (and perhaps even earlier). It is difficult to dispute, however, that in the last few decades, especially since Pierre Elliott Trudeau organized and modernized the departmental structure serving the prime ministerial function, the PM's overall control of governmental operations has become more effective. Donald Savoie (1999) argues that this centralization of the levers of power may even have gone too far, although it is not at all unusual to find such centralization of authority in the executive office in modern democracies, either among the long-standing Western ones or among those that have democratized more recently.

The most central of government departments, that which is in effect the department of the Prime Minister in public service terms, is the Privy Council Office (PCO). This institution originally served primarily as the cabinet secretariat. In more recent times, it has also become the mechanism for substantive policy advice to the PM and the mechanism to enable him or her to coordinate and focus the various policies of the government he or she leads. A key role in the PCO is that of its Clerk, the PM's deputy minister. He or she is the principal adviser to the Prime Minister on the latter's entire range of responsibilities as head of the government. The Clerk of the Privy Council provides the support required for the PM to lead the cabinet, and is also the head of the public service. Despite its proximity to political power, the PCO is exclusively a public service institution. Thus, while it needs to be politically sensitive—aware of, and attuned to, the bonds between the political program and preferences of the governing party and national policy—it remains non-partisan in the sense of serving the state rather than the party and knowing how to keep the two distinct. Within the PCO, under various designations over the years, the two pivotal components with fundamental roles in the substantive fields of government have been the secretariats that deal with economic and social affairs. Today they are called the Economic Union Secretariat, which looks after the Cabinet Committee on the Economic Union, and the Social Union Secretariat, which looks after the Cabinet Committee on the Social Union. In terms of process and the management of governmental processes, the PCO also comprises the Legislation and House Planning and Counsel Secretariat, which coordinates the preparation and scheduling of legislation before its introduction into Parliament. This Secretariat, as its name suggests, also provides legal and parliamentary advice to the Prime Minister.

The Prime Minister's Office (PMO) is the political department of the PM. This institution has grown out of custom and practice rather than statute or constitutional convention. It is in fact a hybrid, in that it is staffed by officials drawn from the party and advises the PM on political matters rather than governmental issues. Yet, it is implicitly recognized as a part of the state apparatus. The PMO concentrates the governing party's influence on the administration of the state. It is headed by the PM's Chief of Staff and its most influential members are the PM's senior policy advisers and his legislative adviser. It also counsels the Prime Minister on his relations with the caucus of the governing party.

The Finance Cluster

The importance of the Department of Finance reflects the intimate link between the management of public policy and the state of the economy. While the appropriate provisions in the Financial Administration Act only establish this department and attribute specific functions to it, the actual power, influence, and prestige of the institution are largely based on the conventions and the public administration practices that surround and complement the Act. The institution itself is no less fundamental to Canadian public administration than the position of its minister. Within the governmental system, Finance is structured principally for the following purposes:

- to analyze the economic and fiscal situation of the country;
- to recommend measures in taxation, borrowing, and government expenditure;
- to manage the Consolidated Revenue Fund and the government's financial holdings;
- to advise on balance of payments, exchange reserves, international monetary and fiscal arrangements, and coinage;
- to deal with all other matters relating to the national, federal–provincial, and international financial affairs and economic issues of Canada.

With this astonishing breadth of tasks, the department has the ability to keep its hand on the macroeconomic pulse of Canada.

Through the combination of the knowledge so acquired and its participation at the pinnacles of policy-making, the department exercises its greatest function—the power of the purse. The Minister of Finance has the determining hand in shaping the federal (and, through the mechanisms of federalism, to a large extent the national) budget. He or she forecasts levels of government revenues, determines the levels of expenditure, and makes aggregate spending decisions for the government as a whole, including the choices involving taxation, tax credits, outright expenditures, and intergovernmental transfers. Consequently, other departments depend on Finance to secure their portfolio budgets for their own mandates. A 1999 decision of the Federal Court, Trial Division, which has not been appealed, upheld the discretion of the Minister of Finance to use the principle of the 'effectiveness of government' in deciding whether or not the disclosure of government documents could cause damage to his or her public policy role. Not only did the Court thus strengthen the minister's hand, but it went even further by admitting explicitly that there was little role for it in overseeing this discretion.[10] Even though this decision was on a specific issue of access to information, the recognition of ministerial discretion as to the issue of effectiveness, together with the Finance Minister's other powers, give the minister and the department a preponderant role not only within the government but, in effect, on the economy of the country as a whole.

Several points highlight the pivotal role of the Department of Finance in public administration. Apart from the Speech from the Throne, the Budget Speech of the Minister of Finance is the only expression of government policy that necessarily engages the confidence of the House of Commons in the government. Moreover, as a result not only of the budget but of Finance's other work as well, this department is the initiator of more legislation, and its issues therefore occupy more parliamentary attention, than any other institution of government. To support this work, the Department of Finance is staffed with a complement of a Secretary of State for International Financial Institutions and three officials at the level of deputy minister. In addition, however, it is the home of the most unusual public servant in Canada below the deputy minister level, the only assistant deputy minister simultaneously accredited to the Finance and Justice departments, who wears the title of 'Senior Assistant Deputy Minister, Public Law and Central Agency Portfolio' in Justice and that of 'Counsel to the Department' in Finance. His or her function is to ensure the linkage between these two department systems and to ensure thereby that financial matters are handled in accordance with law and democratic principles.

The role of the Finance Department in both federal–provincial and international economic relations is also significant. Domestically, there is much consultation and coordination among the finance departments of various jurisdictions, a process in which the federal department is the most senior. On the world stage, the department assumes much of Canada's participation in the OECD, the G-8 and G-20, the World Bank, and the regional banks, such as the European Bank for Reconstruction and Development.

The Department of Finance is at the head of the **Finance cluster**—the cluster of institutions performing related financial functions, throughout which the minister exercises not so much influence as co-operative networking. In particular, the Finance Minister maintains an arm's length, but nevertheless close working relationship with the Governor of the Bank of Canada, and also oversees the Office of the Superintendent of Financial Institutions. The Treasury Board Secretariat, which, among other matters, deals with the allocation to departments of funds appropriated by Parliament and with labour relations in the public sector, can also be considered part of the Finance cluster.

The Justice Cluster

The characteristic of the Justice portfolio that attracts observers' particular interest is its unique independence from politics within government. The entire evolution of Canadian political history, as summarized in the preamble to the Constitution Act, 1982, is that this country's democratic system is based on the rule of law. The practical application of this principle is that in the conduct of public affairs, whether at the political level or in public administration, law is fundamental, a *sine qua non*; the rule of law is pervasive, binding, and unavoidable. The corollary to this principle is that law is independent of politics.

The cardinal guide to legality in public administration derived from the rule of law is the definition of the role of the Minister of Justice and Attorney General. The most often used expression to describe this political figure is that he or she is the 'chief law officer of the Crown'. What does this really mean? The person heading the Department of Justice has a double function. In that individual's capacity as Minister of Justice, he or she is the specific *legal* member of the cabinet and must, as expressed in the Department of Justice Act, ensure that the administration of public affairs is in accordance with law. The Justice Minister also oversees all matters connected with the administration of justice at the federal level and is charged with advising the Crown on legislation. As Attorney General, the minister conducts litigation, with the office representing the government before the courts, and advises the heads of the other government departments on all matters of law.

The most noteworthy element of this set of tasks is the position of the Minister of Justice within cabinet as legal adviser to the Crown. The Prime Minister and all other ministers must, given the tenets of democracy and the rule of law, act in a legal fashion; their principal motivation, though, is political success. Their loyalty is to the party whose colours they carry—its electoral platform, program, and policies. The conventional constitutional obligation and the political motivation of the Minister of Justice are different. Within the context of loyalty to party and the desire to convert its policy preferences into politics, the minister's greater function is to ensure that law prevails, that ministers' legal duties are observed, and that legal considerations are appropriately and adequately addressed in all facets of public administration. In regard to the organization of government and the conduct of departmental business, where there is a distinction between institutional loyalty and wilful adherence to, and application of, law, the function of the Minister of Justice is to ensure that the latter prevails. This is a variation of the principle of accountability, namely, the doctrine of accountability to law.

In tendering advice to the Crown and in acting as legal adviser to the government within cabinet, this doctrine endows the Minister of Justice with a quality of independence. In the language of responsibility and accountability discussed above, this minister's first professional duty is to the Constitution and to the law; only thereafter does the Justice Minister owe allegiance to the government. This is true, as well, of the Department of Justice officials and staff. Law is inextricably linked to politics but independent of it. The relationship of influence between them necessarily runs in both directions. However, it is in the interest of democracy that law bear a greater weight on the conduct of politics and public administration than vice versa. To preserve and develop the rule of law, it is imperative that law be subservient neither to politics nor to public administration.

The **Justice cluster** has been profoundly affected by the 2006 Federal Accountability Act. As the examples amply illustrate, in Canada there had always been an understanding that the Minister of Justice, in his or her capacity as Attorney General, would always exercise prosecutorial decisions purely on the basis of legal considerations. This is the accepted dogma, even despite the two institutional dilemmas. To recapitulate, first, this minister is charged with making justice policy and with carrying out criminal prosecutions, which can on occasion involve him or her in contradictory considerations. The second challenge is that from a constitutional perspective he or she is the legal advisor to the government, while in an institutional perspective he or she is but one of a number of ministers around the Cabinet table where political and party considerations complement considerations of State policy.

The government of Prime Minister Stephen Harper has taken a different view than that of its predecessors of the manner in which the prosecutorial function needs to be carried out. This view is expressed in Part 3 of the Federal Accountability Act, which, upon enactment and proclamation became the self-standing Director of Public Prosecutions Act.[11] This statute essentially withdrew the exercise of prosecutorial discretion from the Minister of Justice and Attorney General and vested the authority in the Director of Public Prosecutions (DPP). Let us note for the sake of precision that the jurisdiction of the DPP is focused on prosecutorial discretion. This means that it extends to initial or first-level prosecutions. Given that appeals, even in criminal cases, are matters of law, and that from the perspective of the State they are matters relating to the development of the law, rather than to prosecutorial decision-making, criminal appeals are still the purview of the Department of Justice. Further, there are some special cases generally thought of as delving into criminal law, such as extradition, which are also still handled within the Department of Justice.

The DPP has the rank and status of a deputy minister; his or her Office and staff consist of that branch of the federal Department of Justice which previously conducted criminal prosecutions. Interestingly, he or she is assigned duties and functions 'under and on behalf of the Attorney General'.[12] At the time of writing, the experience of the new public prosecution service is too recent to enable observers to draw conclusions.

The Foreign Affairs Cluster

Until not long ago, a single minister and one department of government, the Department of External Affairs, dealt with international relations. A separate Trade Commissioner Service, situated within the Department of Industry, Trade and Commerce, provided sectoral work in that field. Since the early 1950s, the Canadian International

Development Agency was active in the field of foreign aid. Over the 1980s and 1990s, institutions of the federal government dealing with international matters were fundamentally restructured. In one respect, this reform has been necessary to achieve greater efficiency, effectiveness, and especially focus within Canadian governmental circles on the outside world. Even more to the point, the changes of the previous two decades were designed to enable this country to confront the trend of global integration and interdependence. Today, the Department of Foreign Affairs is the focal point for all international activities of the Canadian government. Having absorbed or subsumed other parts of the public service dealing with trade and development, this cluster is remarkable for the fact that it is politically led by three ministers, among whom the Minister of Foreign Affairs is the most senior. In addition to this portfolio, there are two positions of statutorily established ministers to assist, one for international trade and one for international co-operation. We must also remember that until recently, there were also three regional secretaries of state, for Latin America and Africa, Asia-Pacific, and the Francophonie.

The principal roles of the Department of Foreign Affairs include development and coordination of the government's international policies, advocacy of Canadian interests and values, and the provision of assistance to Canadians overseas, including in the areas of trade and investment. The priorities adopted by the department to fulfill these roles particularly include contributing to democracy, human rights, and good governance by such means as advancing democratic transitions and electoral observation.[13]

One of the major objectives of the **Foreign Affairs cluster** is to speak for Canada in the world with one voice. This involves issues of not only governmental organization but also political coordination and conflict. Many federal line departments (defined below) conduct technical international relations within their own sectors. Foreign Affairs has succeeded in structuring these units into a network, resulting in the meshing of political and sectoral technical considerations in the conduct of the international relations of the other departments. There is some broader overlap between Foreign Affairs and Finance on international economic and trade issues, which are handled jointly. There is also a jurisdictional balance to be maintained between Foreign Affairs and Justice on matters of international law. Both departments have units dealing with this topic; it seems that Foreign Affairs takes the lead but is advised by Justice on the progressive development of international law, and a Justice unit within Foreign Affairs deals specifically with the domestic implementation of Canada's international legal obligations.

The federal government's desire to have Canada speak abroad with one voice certainly creates political difficulties in the domestic intergovernmental arena. Several provinces, such as Ontario and Alberta, have representation offices in foreign cities significant to their trade patterns. These offices are not fully diplomatic or consular and are, in general, politically docile. Quebec, however, has been developing a system of offices abroad that it perceives to be an embryonic diplomatic service dealing not only with trade but also with political and cultural relations. The activities of this network and the conflicts that sometimes arise between Department of Foreign Affairs representatives and those of Quebec reflect Canada's vibrant internal discussion as to the nature of its identity.

Whatever its institutional benefit may be, the single-voice issue can occasionally become politicized. For example, during the 39th federal general election campaign in 2005–6, the platform of the Conservative Party of Canada included a plank supporting the autonomous representation of Quebec in some international agencies, particularly UNESCO. The constitutional underpinning of this proposal was that Canadian governmental activities in foreign affairs could follow the domestic federal–provincial division of powers. In this logic, given that culture was acknowledged to be under provincial legislative jurisdiction, Quebec would be justified in adding its voice to that of Canada in the world community in this sphere.

From an institutional perspective, the foreign affairs cluster also contains a most interesting example of the interaction of law, public administration, and politics. This example is also recent enough to be of immediate instructive merit.

When Prime Minister Paul Martin assumed office in December 2003, he believed that the Department of Foreign Affairs and International Trade would operate more effectively, and would better serve the interests of Canadian citizens and businesses, if it were severed into two separate departments, one for the political, and one for the trade aspects of our international relations. Therefore, starting on 12 December 2003, he used the legal means available to carry out the intended reforms. By Order-in-Council made pursuant to the Public Service Rearrangement and Transfer of Duties Act, the Governor-in-Council transferred from the Minister of Foreign Affairs and International Trade to a newly minted Minister of International Trade the supervision and control of that portion of the public service known as the Department of International Trade.[14] Other Orders-in-Council, in sequence:

- designated the Minister of International Trade to head the Department of International Trade;[15]
- transferred from the previous Department of Foreign Affairs and International Trade to the new Department of International Trade supervision and control of specifically listed portions of the public service;[16]
- transferred from the Department of Industry to the new Department of International Trade control and supervision of other specifically listed portions of the public service;[17]
- designated the Department of International Trade as a department for public service purposes.[18]

These measures, taken together, were sufficient to establish the Department of International Trade in law. The public service administrative reorganizations, which were meant to give effect to this change in the legal position, were begun.

Following the 38th federal general election, held on 28 June 2004, the government moved to consolidate the splitting of the foreign affairs portfolio by enshrining it in statute. Therefore, on 7 December 2004, the House of Commons gave first reading to Bill C-31, The Department of International Trade Act, and Bill C-32, An Act to amend the Department of Foreign Affairs and International Trade Act and to make consequential amendments to other Acts. These legislative proposals were intended to supersede the Orders-in-Council listed above.

In these initial phases, there was no divergence from the practice of earlier governments of various political stripes. The 2004 general election had, however, produced a minority government, and on 15 February 2005 the government's motions that bills C-31 and C-32 be read a second time and referred to committee were both defeated.

Notwithstanding the defeat of these items on its legislative agenda, the Martin government determined that it would move ahead with the plan to divide the portfolio activities between the two departments. The argument in favour of this position was that even though the legislation could not be adopted because it had been voted down, the Orders-in-Council had been validly adopted and in the absence of the new statutes, the government would merely revert to the subordinate legislation, which stood on its own, without the need for the new and amended statutes.

To counter this, on 17 February 2005, the Opposition House Leader, Jay Hill, MP for Prince George–Peace River (BC) raised a question of privilege in the House. He objected to the comments made by the Minister for International Trade on the day following the defeat at second reading of the bills. In the words of the Speaker,

> The hon. Opposition House leader... pointed to articles in the *Globe and Mail* and the *Ottawa Citizen* which quoted the minister as saying that the two departments would continue to work independently even though Parliament had voted against the bills that proposed to split the two entities, the former Department of Foreign Affairs and International Trade.
>
> The hon. Opposition House leader alleges that the minister's words suggest that the passage or defeat of legislation

> was inconsequential to the separation of the departments and, in so doing, showed disregard for the role of the House of Commons. He argues that this shows such disrespect as to constitute, in his opinion, a contempt of the House.[19]

The underlying machinery-of-government issue at stake was whether self-standing legislation was necessary to set institutional reform in motion, or whether the government's intended changes could be brought about merely under the legislation empowering Orders-in-Council, together with the Orders-in-Council themselves. With the involvement of the Speaker, the parliamentary issues were overlaid on the basic matter. The first of these was whether a government could continue to effect institutional reform in a manner not specifically mandated by Parliament. Also of concern was whether a government defeated in the House in trying to achieve an institutional reform by one legal means could seemingly ignore the will of the House and proceed by another method legally available. The difference here is of course that bills C-31 and C-32 would have had to be adopted by Parliament, the legislative branch, whereas the Orders-in-Council were the instruments of, and made within, the executive branch.

The Speaker, Peter Milliken, ruled on the question of privilege on 23 March 2005. First, he noted that the intent of the Public Service Rearrangement and Transfer of Duties Act was to reorganize existing functions of government for which Parliament had voted funds. He also recollected that existing statutes gave the government leeway in proceeding with any reorganization. In this, he recognized that the Canadian custom was to complete or confirm such rearrangements by way of legislation. The Speaker thus ruled that the comments made by the Minister of International Trade had not amounted to a breach of parliamentary privilege.

> In the opinion of the Chair, the authority to begin the process of separating the departments rests on the series of orders in council adopted December 12, 2003 pursuant to existing statutory authorities granted to the government by Parliament. That authority is set out in the law and it is not for me to judge whether it is sufficient in this case.
>
> Following a search of our precedents, I am unable to find a case where any Speaker has ruled that the government, in the exercise of regulatory power conferred upon it by statute, has been found to have breached the privileges of the House. Indeed, the hon. Member is not arguing that. He seems to be suggesting that the minister's comments amounted to a breach of privilege, but if the minister was stating the legal position, it could hardly constitute a breach.[20]

The Speaker's further and more general comments are significant to the life cycle of departments as the principal institutions of government. While making it clear that he was ruling on the procedural (parliamentary) issue, his comments nevertheless have a strong indicative bearing on the legal institutional practice.

> The procedural consequence is clear. Bill C-31 and Bill C-32 will not proceed further in this session.
>
> The legal consequence is not for me to address. The Chair is unable to determine what future legislative measures the government may bring forward to complete or confirm the division of the two departments. This is for the government to determine.
>
> I can only assume that the minister, in stating his intention to continue with the establishment of the Department of International Trade, is planning to proceed for the moment under existing authorities.
>
> It seems to me that in making the statement outside the House, which gave rise to the point of privilege of the hon. Opposition House leader, the minister might only have meant to indicate that the reorganization by orders in council

> continue to have legal effect. If that was the intent of the minister's remark and the actions taken are legally valid, which I must assume is the case, it is difficult to find this comment offensive to the dignity of the House and therefore a prima facie breach of privileges.
>
> That is not to say that the comments, if reported accurately, do not concern me. I can fully appreciate the frustration of the House and the confusion of hon. Members, let alone those who follow parliamentary affairs from outside this chamber. The scrutiny of legislation is arguably the central role of Parliament.
>
> The decision of the House at each stage of government bill determines whether or not the proposal can go forward. How can the decisions of the House on these bills be without practical consequence?
>
> We appear to have come upon a paradox in Canadian practice. Bill C-31 and Bill C-32 aimed to confirm executive action, action already taken pursuant to statutes by non-legislative means, and the House of Commons has refused to give that confirmation. It leaves the government and the House in a most unfortunate conflict on the matter but, on the information I have, I cannot find that this constitutes a prima facie breach of the privileges of the House.[21]

For quite some time thereafter, the Martin government held to its view and to its plan, despite diverging opinions even within the governing party. The legislative proposals for splitting the Department of Foreign Affairs and International Trade were not reintroduced in Parliament. Since the subsequent 39th federal general election made Stephen Harper Prime Minister, neither has such legislation been introduced. Today, the statutory structure is still entitled the Department of Foreign Affairs and International Trade. In practice, however, Canada's international activities are headed by the Minister of Foreign Affairs and the Minister of International Trade, distinctly.

Functional Categorizations

For several generations, writers about Canadian public affairs have been able to distinguish ways in which power is focused in different locations throughout the public sector. As John Porter (1965) describes it, starting in the 1930s a network of senior officials, many of them graduates of Queen's University and centred particularly in the Department of Finance, exercised a powerful collegial influence on the development of public policy and administration. In the 1960s, especially during the first tenure of office of Prime Minister Trudeau, this era of powerful mandarins evolved into a system of powerful institutions. In analyzing the principal departments of government as components of the overall federal public service since then, the most patent observation is that all departments are nominally equal but some departments are in fact more equal than others. As is true in all conglomerate organizations, the functions that specific departments perform determine their centrality to the government and the bureaucracy, their power, their influence, and, not least, their access to public funds, resources, and staff.

Central Agencies

There is no acknowledged definition of what constitutes a **central agency**. The best way to characterize such bodies is therefore to list their particular functions as being the coordination of the interdepartmental development of substantive policy, the development of government-wide managerial and administrative policies that other departments are bound to follow, and the monitoring of the performance of other departments. Central agencies are some of the bodies that Sutherland and Doern classified as the new 'control' bureaucracy:

> Our Canadian political culture at the federal level encourages a proliferation of central supervisory control agencies that exist to back up the peculiarly Canadian notion of the positive collective responsibility of cabinet for the overall quality of management. This is reinforced by a love for reorganization and, as noted earlier, a strong attachment

to the pre-eminent American principles of efficiency and pluralism. Central executive control agencies are set above the normal heads of the permanent executive. They play a watchdog role over the bureaucracy on behalf of the government for the efficiency and effectiveness of bureaucratic process as opposed to the substance of policy. (Sutherland and Doern, 1985: 45)

The two most obvious examples of central agencies are the Prime Minister's Office (the PM's political department) and the Privy Council Office (the public service department of the Prime Minister that also serves as the secretariat to the cabinet). Given its pivotal role as the determinant of financial, fiscal, and trade policy, as well as its reputation for gathering the best thinkers and long-term planners in the government, the Department of Finance also has a secure position as a central agency.

Line Departments and Common Service Departments

Departments that administer substantive sectors of public affairs rather than managing the process of governance itself are commonly known as **line departments**. This category includes the greatest number of departments; among them, the most senior and highly regarded ones are Justice, Foreign Affairs, National Defence, Health, and Industry.

Common service departments, on the other hand, are those that provide goods and services to other branches of the public sector. Today, the most prominent one among these is the Department of Public Works and Government Services, an amalgamation of the former Department of Public Works with that of Supply and Services.

Officers of Parliament

The majority of tasks in government are accomplished by departments. Ministers who are the political heads of these bodies are members of the government as well as Members of Parliament, or in some cases Senators. The staffs of departments are members of the Public Service of Canada. Generally, these departments can be said to be exclusively within the executive branch of government.

Some functions of democratic governing, however, ought to be more appropriately carried out by institutions which function as if they were government departments but which are in fact independent of the government in the sense of not being in the executive branch. Institutions in this category are ones which do not provide services to citizens or regulate social, economic, legal, or international activity. Rather, these institutions create, administer, and enforce rules of public policy and administration which are meant to determine how the State, the government, public servants, and in some cases parliamentarians carry out their respective mandates and functions. The appropriateness of carving these areas of responsibility out of the structure of departments and assigning them to institutions independent of government derives from the need to avoid self-direction, self-regulation, self-assessment, and accountability to oneself by government departments. Collectively, such bodies are called the offices of Officers of Parliament.

Over the past several decades, there have been five generally recognized Officers of Parliament, despite the fact that there is no formal definition of the concept either in law, public administration, or political science. These are the Chief Electoral Officer,[22] the Auditor General,[23] the Information Commissioner,[24] the Privacy Commissioner,[25] and the Commissioner of Official Languages.[26]

The recent preoccupation of the Canadian body politic with public sector ethics and the related enactment of the Federal Accountability Act in 2006 have resulted in the establishment of more such officials. These are the Conflict of Interest and Ethics Commissioner,[27] the Senate Ethics Officer,[28] the Public Sector Integrity Commissioner,[29] and the Registrar of Lobbyists.[30] Given that the concept of Officer of Parliament allows some fluidity, it may also be possible to include the Parliamentary Budget Officer[31] and eventually, when it is formed, the Public Appointments Commission[32] in this category.

These offices differ from departments in a number of ways. Officers of Parliament who head them have the rank and status of deputy ministers.

But the method of their appointment, more significantly their fixed term of tenure in office, and even the method of their divestiture distinguish them from ordinary deputies. Moreover, although they are deputy ministers, they do not report to ministers of the Crown. Rather, they report through a minister or the Speaker to the House of Commons. In terms of both public law and public administration, the core particularity of Officers of Parliament is that they have independent decision-making authority based on the criteria set out in the statutes that govern them. Commensurate with this power, their independence from the government, in the sense of independence from both the executive branch and from the government of the day, is assured by their financial autonomy. Their funding is assured outside the ordinary paths of appropriations and is more secure than that of government departments.

Indispensable Components of Canadian State Administration

While scholarly observation is always more focused on the principal institutions of government, the departments headed by ministers by no means constitute the full extent of the bodies that, in one sense or another, make up the entire public sector. In order to carry out all the governmental functions inherent to it, the Canadian state comprises a great number of other, generally smaller organizations, all of which are nonetheless vital to its functioning. One of the most interesting problems in the analysis of Canadian government is to determine how extensively to cast the institutional net. In other words, what activity is government per se and what is more properly classified as being activity within the parapublic sector? In more recent times, the corollary to this line of thinking has been the question of what is ripe for devolution or privatization.

Institutions of the Legislative Branch

In classical political science, the legislative branch is Parliament alone. In modern public administration, the institution of Parliament cannot function without the support of organized staff, called **institutions of the legislative branch**, to provide necessary services so that elected representatives can perform their duties. On the basis of the provisions set out in sections 17 through 57 of the Constitution Act, 1867, which establish the House of Commons and the Senate as distinct parliamentary institutions, each house of Parliament is supported by what in effect is its own department-like service. These services are primarily geared to the legislative work of the members and the senators. The important streams within them are thus those of legal advisers and committee staffs. In the last two decades, management experts, in particular financial managers, and protective forces have taken on added significance. In fact, it was only in 1986 that litigation brought the existence of this parliamentary public service into focus.[33] The Library of Parliament, which serves both houses and can be considered part of this public service, has no institutional independence but is functionally separate from both the Commons and the Senate.

The legislative branch consists of a number of bodies other than Parliament itself. For constitutional reasons relating to the division of functions between the government and Parliament, these are not part of the departmental structure but report directly to Parliament. These include the Public Service Commission and the various other bodies that, from time to time, regulate the Public Service of Canada. At present, the Public Service Agency of Canada, previously encumbered with the awkward designation of Public Service Human Resources Management Agency of Canada, is the most significant such institution. The offices of the Officers of Parliament, discussed above, can also be considered part of this category. The most significant feature of these bodies is their independence from the government of the day. This independence manifests itself in a number of ways. The heads of these parliamentary agencies are at the deputy minister level, that is, at the top rank of the public service, but they do not report to ministers. They are appointed by Parliament itself and are protected from removal except through complex parliamentary procedures. The government cannot interfere with their decision-making and, significantly, they have wide degrees of financial autonomy. Most important of all, the independent status of these institutions is safeguarded by the convention of non-interference and self-restraint on the part of the government. Indeed, their characteristic as self-standing centres of diffused power is one of the fundamental elements of Canadian democracy.

Institutions of the Judicial Branch

The independence of the judiciary from the government in the Canadian system is even more sacrosanct than that of parliamentary institutions. Centuries of constitutional evolution, at first inherited from the United Kingdom, but amply developed within this country and all of its component jurisdictions, have reinforced the independence of the courts. This independence is highlighted by the incorporation of the Charter of Rights and Freedoms into Canadian law and politics and the consequential erosion of the boundary between the legal and political elements of public life. **Institutions of the judicial branch** exist to support the judiciary administratively while protecting judicial independence, or to supplement the work of the judiciary.

To assist the judges in their adjudicative work, each of the courts at the federal level—the Supreme Court of Canada, the Federal Court, and the Tax Court—had its own structures. These small court secretariats also functioned as if they were separate departments. In July 2003, with the coming into force of the Courts Administration Service Act, the two latter courts came to be served by the Courts Administration Service (CAS), leaving the Supreme Court with its own administration. The mandate of the CAS is to provide administrative support to the Federal Court of Appeal, the Federal Court, the Court Martial Appeal Court of Canada and the Tax Court of Canada.

Canadian governance has spawned a group of quasi-judicial administrative tribunals, which may also be mentioned in this category. Bodies such as the Canadian Radio-television and Telecommunications Commission and the Immigration and Refugee Board are included here, singled out in sections 18 and 28 of the Federal Court Act as 'federal boards, commissions and other tribunals'. Each of these also functions in department-like fashion, but with a degree of independence based in each case on its constitutive statute and in all cases very much more limited than the courts.

Independent Advisors

The government formed following the 39th federal general election of 29 January 2006 has woven new elements into Canadian practice in institutional design. Prime Minister Stephen Harper's political philosophy differs considerably from that of several of his predecessors. He intended to conduct a government that would be, and that would also appear to be, new and different from earlier ones. As a long-time critic of earlier methods and styles of governing, he also publicly expressed distrust of certain established mechanisms of power. For these reasons, the current government has made greater use than its predecessors of a new, non-institutional vehicle of governing. This is the '**independent advisor**'.

The first time the government appointed an individual outside the public service to offer it independent advice was during the summer of 2006. On 6 August, the Prime Minister announced that Wajid Khan, MP would henceforth be a Special Advisor to the Prime Minister on South Asia and the Middle East. He was to travel to the Middle East on a fact-finding mission and present his findings in a report, which could then form the basis of State policy. The inherent difficulty was that until his appointment, Mr Khan had been a Liberal—a member of the Opposition. This made the appointment of the Advisor appear to be motivated as a means to have Mr Khan cross the floor of the House of Commons. In fact, this is what eventually happened. This experiment with going outside traditional channels was not successful. Its combination of policy and party politics generated negative commentary. The fact that the Advisor's Report was not made public, despite the initial expectation that it would be, also reduced the effectiveness of the model.

In the next two years, on several other occasions the Prime Minister used better-defined and more elaborately framed versions of the independent advisor vehicle. The first was the appointment on 14 November 2007 of Professor David Johnston, President of the University of Waterloo, as Independent Advisor into the Allegations Respecting Financial Dealings between Mr Karlheinz Schreiber and the Right Honourable Brian Mulroney. Professor Johnston's mandate was to define the terms of reference for an inquiry. He reported first on 9 January 2008 and again, after a renewed mandate, on 4 April 2008.

The most serious and significant use of the independent advisor mechanism was the establishment on 12 October 2007 of the Independent Panel on Canada's Future Role in Afghanistan, headed by former Deputy Prime Minister, the Hon. John Manley. This Panel comprised notable citizens, all knowledgeable about public affairs and with considerable experience in government. It reported on 22 January 2008 in a book made available not only to the government but also to the public. It elicited much useful public commentary and analysis.

While the time in office of the Conservatives is still relatively short, we can set out some initial observations of the use of the independent advisor mechanism. What is most plain is that independent advisors are temporary mechanisms, not permanent institutions. Their work does not naturally fall into the jurisdiction of an established department of government, although it could be made to fit into that mould. It must therefore be asked why such a mechanism is used. Each independent advisor addresses a single issue. More to the point, these are important policy issues, are politically difficult and controversial, and are real or potential problems for the government and perhaps indeed for the State itself.

Certain elements are both common to independent advisors and pivotal to their role. Their mandate is determined by, or on behalf of, the Prime Minister, the highest instance of executive power. They deal with matters that are similarly of the highest order, matters of national interest, involving a mixture of national politics, governing party interest, policy in its broadest sense, and legality. Such advisors draw on the public service for support and assistance, but they offer advice personally to the head of government. They report directly to the Prime Minister, bypassing not only the public service but also Parliament and even the cabinet. Thus, in institutional terms, they are accountable only to the Prime Minister. However, in a broader perspective, they can also be said to be accountable to the nation. In all these respects, independent advisors are a unique form of conducting governmental matters or resolving State and governmental issues.

The Evolution of Government Institutions

Departments and other institutions of government are never rigid and immobile over time. In response to the vagaries of political life, they are permanently subject to the ebb and flow of reform. In the context of Canadian federalism, institutions and their managerial practices are also affected by the patterns of accommodation and conflict arising out of federal–provincial relations.

Diversification: Parallel Institutions

The fundamental reality of the federal nature of governance in Canada is reflected in the distribution of institutions among the levels of government. Many of the areas of legislative and executive authority outlined under sections 91 and 92 of the Constitution Act, 1867 necessitate either only federal or only provincial institutions to support them. Several of these powers, however, are split and therefore need parallel federal and provincial departments to administer the entire public realm involved. Nowhere is this more true than in the field of justice. The founders of Confederation mandated the federal authorities to legislate on criminal law and procedure but placed property and civil rights, as well as the organization of the court system and the administration of justice, within the jurisdiction of the provinces. Consequently, departments of Justice, Attorney General, or both, are required at both levels. In other fields, such as the environment, the silence of the original constitutional scheme has necessitated the development of parallel institutions. From an institutional perspective, the challenge presented by parallel and sometimes competing bodies regulating the same topic and governing a single population has been to devise effective methods of co-operation.

In addition to being based on the constitutional division of powers, the syndrome of parallel institutions also arises in the realm of administrative arrangements based on political deals. This is the case in some instances with government communications. Normally, each government handles its own communications, but in 1986 the federal and Quebec authorities concluded an accord whereby in that province, officials of Communications-Quebec would dispense information about federal policies and programs as well. Given the sharply divergent ideological stance of these two governments, this arrangement was highly politicized. 'How long could it last?' was the key question. In fact, during the late summer of 1999, the federal minister responsible announced the termination of this deal. Thenceforth, parallel structures would again replace the single-window concept for citizens in regard to this activity of their governments. The only explanation for either the deal or its unravelling is to be found in the characters of the protagonists and the political circumstances at hand. Canadian public life is full of such politically motivated duplications.

Unification: National Institutions

The fluctuating nature of public administration in federal states induces not only inherent inefficiencies but also centripetal forces based in part on political trends and in part on rationalization. In the past, the most noticeable example of this tendency has been the Royal Canadian Mounted Police (RCMP). This federally established agency conducts all federal policing throughout Canada. In addition, on an ad hoc basis that has become quasi-permanent, the RCMP has been providing policing to most of the provinces in lieu of the establishment of parallel police forces (and it has used this arrangement with a number of municipalities).

The convergence of political necessity and public administration rationalization has made adoption of a modern variation of the 'national' model of service delivery highly desirable. In the last few years, two organizations, the Canadian Food Inspection Agency and the Parks Canada Agency, have been set up along the model of **unity of service**, building on the RCMP experience and going much further. The most ambitious such venture, however, is the Canada Revenue Agency, which was brought into existence on 1 November 1999[34] and the institutional designation of which was changed from Canada Customs and Revenue Agency to Canada Revenue Agency, effective 12 December 2005.[35]

The first element to note about this institution is the form of its existence. The legislation that brought the Agency into force ended the existence of the Department of National Revenue. The ministerial portfolio, however, is maintained. The Minister of National Revenue is said in the Act establishing the Agency to be responsible for it; this is different from the standard formula of a minister having management and direction of a department. It should be taken to mean that the Minister of National Revenue, at the least, reports to Parliament for the Agency and is responsible and accountable for it to Parliament. In addition, the minister has powers, duties, and functions enumerated in a manner similar to that set out in traditional departmental legislation. Management and direction of the Agency are the responsibility of the Commissioner, who is its chief executive officer. There is no deputy minister. By contrast, oversight of the organization is the responsibility of a Board of Management. In the composition of this Board we can detect the first element of the legislators' desire to render the Agency a national—as opposed to an exclusively federal—institution. The Board, comprising 15 members, includes one nominated by each of the provinces and one by the territories, as well as four members who ostensibly speak for the federal interest.

The national or centripetal tendency in the creation of this institution is even more marked in the statutory attribution of duties to the Agency. It is responsible for supporting the administration and enforcement of program legislation, that is, all federal legislation dealing with the revenues of Canada; this includes in particular the Income Tax Act. The new Act goes on, however, to empower the Agency to enter into and implement agreements with other federal departments and agencies to carry out an activity or administer a program, with provinces or public bodies performing a governmental function to carry out an activity or administer a tax or program, as well as with Aboriginal governments to administer a tax.

In short, the Canada Customs and Revenue Agency is authorized to create a web of relationships with all governmental entities in Canada to collect internal taxes. As a first step, it is collecting federal personal and corporate income taxes, the Goods and Services Tax, the Harmonized Sales Tax. In a kind of grid pattern across the country, it is also collecting provincial income taxes in some provinces and provincial sales taxes at the Canadian border for some provinces. To expand its domain of responsibility, the Agency will attempt to sell its collection service capacity and ability to other jurisdictions. With these current and prospective lines of public administration work, the Agency is a hybrid of a federal and a national entity. At the time of its formation, it was also entirely *sui generis* and a distinct innovation on the Canadian institutional scene.

There is more to the Canada Revenue Agency than the mere desire on the part of government to avoid duplication and overlap, although that by itself would be sufficient reason for rationalization of services. As with so many other developments, this one has been influenced by the cost-benefit/population ratio. With a total population of only 30 million people in Canada and the strong will to retain the gains of deficit fighting, all governments have felt the need to maximize use of public resources and to minimize the costs involved with delivering public services.

The constitutional aspect is a further and even more fundamental point at stake in initiating such national schemes as this Agency. In the wake of the 1995 Quebec referendum on sovereignty, the federal government defined its arguments and favoured methods for keeping the country united. The so-called 'Plan A', the more progressive, pragmatic, and less confrontational approach, included the formation of national (jointly federal and provincial) institutions in areas where this could be made to work. These, it was believed, would demonstrate the ability of different layers of government to co-operate in the interests of the single citizenry and show would-be skeptics that federalism can be both workable and economic. The constitutional view underlying this pragmatism is asymmetrical federalism. This is reinforced in the present case by the consensual basis of the Agency's expansion of its mandate. Some may see in this an erosion of provincial autonomy, but no province is forced to join the Agency's activity, except through the desire of its own population and in particular its electorate for economies in public expenditures. Moreover, to date, there seems to have been no court challenge to the constitutional validity of the Agency on grounds of federalism.

It is as possible that the experience of the Canada Revenue Agency will engender the creation of other similar agencies as it is that other original and different forms of national institutions may arise.

By enacting the Canada Border Services Agency Act in 2005, Parliament decided to transfer responsibility for customs, excise and other trans-boundary forms of revenue to an agency different from the Canada Revenue Agency. The organizational logic of this was most likely so as to unify all aspects of border control, as the United States had done, as a result of pressures arising from the events of 9/11.

Current Trends and Prospects

While resort to the expression '*plus ça change, plus c'est la même chose*' would be an exaggeration, it is true that relative permanence is more characteristic of public institutions in Canadian governance than is rapid change. Governments and the bureaucracies that administer in the public interest on their behalf are, by reason of their nature and in tune with the trends of Canadian political history, organizations that evolve gradually. Fundamental change in such institutions occurs rarely; rather, incrementalism and harmonization enable government departments to progress and to reform permanently even if, to outside observers, the speed of such reforms is painstakingly slow. Similarly, despite grand pronouncements, only infrequently do governments set out to conduct comprehensive institutional reforms. Political circumstances dictate the necessary reforms, and there seems to be little use of comprehensive, systematic master plans.

The most marked trend in Canadian governmental institutional behaviour and reform is the constant striving for constitutional democracy, legality, and, in the wording of the Constitution itself, 'good government'. Thus, for example, in the medium to long term, the changes initiated by the advent of the Charter are still rippling through the public sector.

Two inherent traits of institutional organization ought specifically to be observed. In the design of public organizations, the attribution of tasks to them, and their management, the machinery of government tends to follow the adoption of public policies and purposes. The aim in setting up departmental or other structures is always to accomplish a set of public policy goals, rather than vice versa. Whatever structure is devised, the Canadian practice has also been to build flexibility into the system. These pragmatic, non-ideological tendencies are so ingrained into our collective consciousness that the prospects for their continuity are great.

The most solid prospect of all for Canada's public institutions is that they will continue to evolve pragmatically and that the directions of this evolution will contribute to the creation of federal/national 'winning conditions', contributing to the achievement by Canadians of their collective social and political aspirations.

Appendix Evolution of Major Federal Departments and Portfolio Functions

Portfolio/Department	Original Departmental Statute	Current Departmental Statute
Agriculture	An Act for the Organization of the Department of Agriculture 31 Vict., c. 53; 22 May 1868	Department of Agriculture and Agri-Food Act R.S.C. 1985, c. A-9
Canadian Heritage	An Act providing for the organization of the Department of the Secretary of State of Canada and for the management of Indian and Ordinance Lands 31 Vict., c. 42; 22 May 1868	Department of Canadian Heritage Act S.C. 1995, c. 11
Citizenship and Immigration	An Act respecting the Department of Immigration and Colonization 8–9 Geo. V, c. 3; 12 April 1918	Department of Citizenship and Immigration Act S.C. 1995, c. 31
Environment	Government Organization Act, 1970 19–20 Eliz. II, c. 42, Part II; 10 June 1971 Department of the Environment Act	Department of the Environment Act R.S.C. 1985, c. E-10
Finance	An Act respecting the Department of Finance 32–3 Vict., c. 53; 22 June 1869	Financial Administration Act R.S.C. 1985, c. F-11
Fisheries and Oceans	An Act for the organization of the Department of Marine and Fisheries of Canada 31 Vict., c. 57; 22 May 1868	Department of Fisheries and Oceans Act R.S.C. 1985, c. F-15
Foreign Affairs	An Act respecting the Department of External Affairs 2 Geo. V, c. 22; 1 April 1912	Department of Foreign Affairs and International Trade Act S.C. 1995, c. 5
Health	An Act respecting the Department of Pensions and National Health 18–19 Geo. V, c. 39; 11 June 1928	Department of Health Act S.C. 1996, c. 8
Human Resources Development	Conciliation Act 63–4 Vict., c. 24; 28 July 1900	Department of Human Resources and Social Development Act S.C. 2005, c. 34 Department of Social Development Act S.C. 2005, c. 35

(*continued*)

(Continued)

Portfolio/Department	Original Departmental Statute	Current Departmental Statute
Indian Affairs and Northern Development	An Act providing for the organization of the Department of the Secretary of State of Canada and for the management of Indian and Ordinance Lands 31 Vict., c. 42; 22 May 1868	Department of Indian Affairs and Northern Development Act R.S.C. 1985, c. I-6
Industry	An Act respecting the Department of Trade and Commerce 50–1 Vict., c. 10; 23 June 1887	Department of Industry Act S.C. 1995, c. 1
Justice	An Act respecting the Department of Justice 31 Vict., c. 39; 22 May 1868	Department of Justice Act R.S.C. 1985, c. J-2
Labour	Conciliation Act 63–4 Vict., c. 24; 18 July 1900	Department of Labour Act R.S.C. 1985, c. L-3, as amended
National Defence	An Act respecting the militia and Defence of the Dominion of Canada 31 Vict., c. 40; 22 May 1868	National Defence Act R.S.C. 1985,c. N-5
National Revenue	An Act constituting the Department of Customs 31 Vict., c. 43; 22 May 1868	Canada Revenue Agency Act S.C. 1999, c. 17
Natural Resources	Department of Mines and Technical Surveys Act 13 Geo. VI (2nd Sess.), c. 17; 10 December 1949 Department of Resources and Development Act 13 Geo. VI (2nd Sess.), c. 18; 10 December 1949	Department of Natural Resources Act S.C. 1994, c. 41
President of the Privy Council	An Act respecting the Governor-General, the Civil List and the Salaries of certain Public Functionaries 31 Vict., c. 33; 22 May 1868	Salaries Act R.S.C. 1985, c. S-3
Public Safety	Government Organization Act, 1966 14–15 Eliz. II, c. 25, ss. 2–5; 16 June 1966	Department of Public Safety and Emergency Preparedness Act S.C. 2005, c. 10
Public Works and Government Services	An Act respecting the Public Works of Canada 31 Vict., c. 12; 21 December 1876	Department of Public Works and Government Services Act S.C. 1996, c. 16
Transport	An Act respecting the offices of Receiver General and Minister of Public Works 42 Vict., c. 7; 15 May 1879	Department of Transport Act R.S.C. 1985, c. T-18
Treasury Board	Government Organization Act, 1966 14–15 Eliz. II, c. 25, s. 32; 16 June 1966	Financial Administration Act R.S.C. 1985, c. F-11
Veterans Affairs	Department of Veterans Affairs Act 8 Geo. VI, c. 19; 30 June 1944	Department of Veterans Affairs Act R.S.C. 1985, c. V-1
Western Economic Diversification	Western Economic Diversification Act R.S.C. 1985, c. 11 (4th Supp.)	Western Economic Diversification Act R.S.C. 1985, c. 11 (4th Supp.)

Important Terms and Concepts

accountability
central agency
clusters of power in the executive
common service departments
departments
Federal Accountability Act
Finance cluster
Foreign Affairs cluster
independent advisor
institutions of the judicial branch
institutions of the legislative branch
Justice cluster
line departments
prime ministerial cluster
Public Service Rearrangement and Transfer of Duties Act
responsibility
self-standing statutes
substantive statutes
unity of service model

Study Questions

1. What is the purpose of the following statutes, which departments do they create, and how do they create them? (a) Self-standing statutes; (b) Substantive statutes.
2. Statutes are not the only way that ministers receive mandates for departments. List some other measures that instill mandates, and explain how each supplements the statutory mandates of ministers.
3. The Rearrangement and Transfer of Duties Act dates back to 1918 and has been a mainstay of flexibility for federal administrators. It allows the Governor-in-Council (effectively, the cabinet) to transfer departments, or branches of departments, from one minister to another; to amalgamate two departments under one minister; to shift powers, duties, and functions from one minister to another; and to shift public servants between ministers. Despite the flexibility inherent in this instrument, it poses some problems. What are the problems?
4. What are the differences between responsibility and accountability, as perceived by the author? What sanctions can be used to enforce responsibility and accountability?
5. What are the characteristics of each 'cluster of power in the executive government'? Give short, capsule descriptions of the elements within each cluster as of the time of writing (e.g., the PCO), and describe what binds the elements into each cluster. List the agencies and departments in each cluster at the time of writing, and those in each cluster today, if they have changed.

Useful Websites

Government of Canada—the primary internet access point for finding information about the federal (and provincial governments):

http://canada.gc.ca/main_e.html

Links to the home pages of each ministry and agency of the Government of Canada:

http://canada.gc.ca/depts/major/depind-eng.html

Home page of the Prime Minister of Canada:

http://pm.gc.ca/

Canada. Privy Council Office. 2008. *The Role and Structure of the Privy Council Office*. November.

www.pco-bcp.gc.ca/docs/information/publications/Role/docs/2008/role2008-eng.pdf

Department of Finance:

www.fin.gc.ca

Treasury Board and the Treasury Board Secretariat:

www.tbs-sct.gc.ca

Public Service Commission of Canada (PSC):

www.psc-cfp.gc.ca

Inside Canada's Parliament: the Institutions:

www2.parl.gc.ca/Sites/LOP/AboutParliament/InsideParliament/institutions-e.asp

Thomas S. Axworthy. 2008. 'Everything Old Is New Again: Observations on Parliamentary Reform'. Centre for the Study of Democracy, Queen's University. April. (Contains some information on the administration of Parliament.)

www.queensu.ca/csd/documents/2008_EverythingOldIsNewAgain_CSDreport_ExpertiseInParliament-3.pdf

Information on, and decisions of, the Supreme Court of Canada:

www.lexum.umontreal.ca/csc-scc/en/index.html

Canada's Court System—a publication containing some information on judicial administration:

www.justice.gc.ca/eng/dept-min/pub/ccs-ajc/

Parks Canada Agency:

www.parcscanada.gc.ca/

The Canada Food Inspection Agency:

www.cfia-acia.agr.ca/

The Canada Revenue Agency:

www.cra-arc.gc.ca/gncy/menu-eng.html

Notes

1. For the federal government, the applicable provisions are ss. 12 and 129 of the Constitution Act, 1867; for the provinces, they are ss. 65 and 129.
2. The writings of Paul Lordon (1991), who approaches the issue from the government practitioner's point of view, and of Professor Patrice Garant (1987), who looks at it from the academic perspective, also accord with this view.
3. *Westlake v. Ontario* (1973), 33 D.L.R. (3d) 256.
4. *Ontario (Chicken Producers' Marketing Board) v. Canada (Chicken Marketing Agency)* (1993), 1 F.C. 116.
5. S.C. 1976–7, c. 54.
6. Hansard, 20 March 1918, 50; 21 March 1918, 83.
7. *Bhatnager v. Canada (Minister of Employment and Immigration)* (1990), 2 S.C.R. 217.
8. S.C. 2006, c. 9.
9. The Fact Finding Report, entitled *Who Is Responsible?* was issued on 1 November 2005. The Final Report, entitled *Restoring Accountability*, was completed on 1 February 2006.
10. *Canadian Council of Christian Charities v. Canada (Minister of Finance)*, Federal Court, Trial Division, 19 May 1999; not yet reported.
11. S.C. 2006, c. 9, s. 121.
12. Director of Public Prosecutions Act, S.C. 2006, c. 9, s. 121, at s. 3(3).
13. See the 1999–2000 Estimates of the Department of Foreign Affairs.
14. P.C. 2003–20047, made pursuant to the Public Service Rearrangement and Transfer of Duties Act.
15. P.C. 2003–2048, made pursuant to the Financial Administration Act.
16. P.C. 2003–2049, made pursuant to the Public Service Rearrangement and Transfer of Duties Act.
17. P.C. 2003–2050, made pursuant to the Public Service Rearrangement and Transfer of Duties Act.
18. P.C. 2003–2052, made pursuant to the Public Service Employment Act.
19. Hansard, 23 March 2005, page 4498.
20. Hansard, 23 March 2005, page 4499.
21. Hansard, 23 March 2005, page 4500.
22. Canada Elections Act, S.C. 2000, c. 9.
23. Auditor General's Act, R.S.C., c. A-17.
24. Access to Information Act, R.S.C. 1985, c. A-1.
25. Privacy Act, R.S.C., c. P-21.
26. Official Languages Act, R.S.C. 1985, c. 34 (4th Supp.).
27. Parliament of Canada Act, R.S.C. 1985, c. P-1.
28. Parliament of Canada Act, R.S.C. 1985, c. P-1.

29. Public Sector Disclosure Protection Act (commonly called the 'Whistleblowing Act'), S.C. 2005, c. 46.
30. Lobbying Registration Act, R.S.C. 1985, c. 44 (4th Supp.).
31. Parliament of Canada Act, R.S.C. 1985, c. P-1.
32. Salaries Act, R.S.C. 1985, c. S-3.
33. *House of Commons v. Canada* (1986), 27 D.L.R. (4th) 481.
34. S.C. 1999, c. 17.
35. S.C. 2005, c. 38.

References

Department of Justice Canada. 1990. *Mission and Values*. Ottawa, 22 May.

Dussault, R., and Louis Borgeat. 1985. *Administrative Law: A Treatise*. 2nd edn. Toronto: Carswell.

Garant, P. 1987. *Précis de droit des administrations publiques*. Cowansville, Que.: Les Éditions Yvon Blais.

Hogg, P. 1997. *Constitutional Law of Canada*. 4th edn (loose-leaf). Toronto: Carswell.

Lordon, P. 1991. *Crown Law*. Toronto: Butterworths.

Osbaldeston, G. 1989. *Keeping Deputy Ministers Accountable*. Toronto: McGraw-Hill Ryerson.

Porter, John. 1965. *The Vertical Mosaic*. Toronto: University of Toronto Press.

Public Service of Canada. 1997. *A Strong Federation, Report of the Task Force on Public Service Values and Ethics*. Ottawa, Feb.

Savoie, D.J. 1999. *Governing from the Centre: The Concentration of Power in Canadian Politics*. Toronto: University of Toronto Press.

Sutherland, S., and G. Bruce Doern. 1985. *Bureaucracy in Canada: Control and Reform*. Toronto: University of Toronto Press.

Tardi, Gregory. 2004. *The Law of Democratic Governing*. 2 vols. Toronto: Thomson Carswell.

PART II
The Organizational Dimension

An important part of public administration is describing the organizational dimension. Often it is a matter of describing both the forest *and* the trees. One must be able to offer a significant amount of detail on the machinery of government, but also grasp 'big picture' views of new developments in governance. The *Handbook's* contributors manage to do this nicely.

The organization of government is central to public administration, for how government is structured determines in large part what the public service can do and how it is to be done. Gregory Tardi, in Chapter 2, outlines the structure of the Canadian government, including the legislative, executive, and judicial branches. One of Canada's leading interpreters of the statutory structure of Canadian government, Tardi describes the Canadian constitutional context for government by the executive, the statutory foundations of such government, the major 'clusters' of power in government, and the three types of functions used to categorize executive departments. This chapter also provides an overview of the administrative elements of the legislative and judicial branches of government. In addition, Tardi examines the forces behind the evolution, current state, and probable future of the public service in Canada. The recent evolution of public administration in Canada has resulted from two major forces: drives for political reform and federal–provincial relations. Future changes to the structure of government, Tardi anticipates, will result from incrementalism, continued efforts at intergovernmental harmonization, and form following function.

What Lindquist does for governance, Henry L. Molot, QC, for years one of the Department of Justice's most respected constitutional experts, does for Canada's public service. He assumes the task of providing a definitional and constitutional overview of Canada's public service. This involves first outlining the constitutional underpinnings of the public service and its organizational definitions. Then he leads the reader in understanding how the five ways by which various organizational components of the public service are established, before undertaking the challenging task of understanding the half-dozen or so classes of governmental organization. Having done this, he concentrates on three of the most important—ministerial departments, crown agencies, and crown corporations—all the while describing the internal controls and accountability regimes that apply to them. He also makes sense of the new complications added to the Federal Accountability Act of 2006. These complications, he notes, have tended to multiply in recent years, adding to a difficult balancing act between additional bureaucracy and rules on the one hand and efficiency and effectiveness on the other.

Alan Gilmore in Chapter 4 notes that Canadians may not be getting what they thought they were, with the new position of 'accounting officer' in the Government of Canada. Introduced in the Federal Accountability Act of 2006, the position seemed at first glance to be the same in nature as the British Accounting Officer. Gilmore, however, discovers several differences. The Canadian accounting officer has narrower responsibility compared with the UK: no personal responsibility, and no responsibility for overall management or for seeing that standards of financial management are high. The deterrence value of the Canadian position is less; Canadian officers are not required to report ministerial overrulings of their advice to the Public Accounts Committee, which hears about disagreements only after disputes are referred to the Board. Lastly, it dilutes ministerial responsibility by transferring responsibility from the minister to a body of ministers, the Treasury Board. He is puzzled why Canadians had to accept a scaled-down version of the position. Perhaps this article will force discussion on the topic.

Christopher Dunn, in Chapter 5, poses a question about where change in the federal central executive is headed. His chapter asks whether or not cabinet has evolved to a new stage. It is by now fairly standard to argue that there were two stages of cabinet development in the latter part of the twentieth century: (1) the unaided (or departmental or unstructured) cabinet, and (2) the institutionalized (or structured) cabinet. Many scholars are now saying that a new stage has been entered, some even suggesting the restructuring process redounds to the benefit of the Prime Minister. This new Prime Minister-centred cabinet would then be the third stage in cabinet development. Dunn hesitates to accept this conclusion, suggesting instead that the move away from the institutionalized cabinet may have been overstated, at least in regard to provincial cabinets, and that qualifications can be made to the deinstitutionalization of the federal cabinet. He also examines the conflicting lessons that emerge from decades of experimentation with the central executive.

In Chapter 6, Paul G. Thomas provides a comprehensive look at Parliament and the Canadian public service(s) and considers the often problematical relationships between them. Although Thomas examines at length the problems inherent in trying to steer the modern ship of state with an institution that dates back about 800 years, he concludes on an optimistic note.

Public service reform and parliamentary accountability should logically reinforce each other, but in contemporary Canada they have not. Such reform, Thomas notes, historically has been somewhat contrary to long-standing parliamentary traditions, and this has been in evidence in three recent sets of reforms: the 'steering not rowing' slogan, the adoption of special operating agencies (SOAs), and the various related elements of the recent orientation towards the private sector, including privatization, contracting out of service delivery, and public–private partnerships. Thomas notes that Parliament has given very little attention to debates or issues regarding public sector reform. Annual reports of the head of the public service and the chair of the Public Service Commission, even reports of prestigious Royal Commissions, such as the Lambert Report (1979) and Public Service 2000 (1990), engender little interest in parliamentary circles. This is obviously a bad portent for parliamentary supervision of the public bureaucracy. A reversal of this situation, Thomas believes, is paramount for reformers.

Although many texts ignore this area, public administration extends even to the judicial system. As Carl Baar and Ian Greene explain in Chapter 7, the study of judicial administration did not really exist in Canada until 30 years ago. Baar and Greene outline the history of judicial administration in the US and Canada, examines the different parameters that bound it, and reviews some outstanding issues in judicial administration. Paradoxically, despite being the youngest in the public administration family, in some ways judicial administration has become a model for it.

Some of the interesting work being done in judicial administration involves caseflow management, the relationship between courts and the public, alternative dispute resolution, and integrated justice. *Caseflow management* posits the primary responsibility of the courts and judges for determining how cases proceed, as opposed to the traditional assumption of common-law procedure, that of party (in effect, lawyer) control of the process. Such a management approach thus requires an integrated series of processes and resources necessary to move a case from filing to disposition. Just as it focuses attention on new types of procedural reforms, the concept of judicial administration offers new perspectives on the relationships of *courts and the citizenry*. It highlights the importance of concepts like broadened access to justice, the differential effects of law on different segments of the population, and heightening public trust and confidence. *Alternative dispute resolution* (ADR) is one sign of a new commitment to increasing access to justice. ADR means finding alternatives to the court itself or else moving to alternatives *within* the court. *Integrated justice*, which involves the use of computer technology to facilitate court procedures, is the most innovative and ambitious concept in modern judicial administration. It means, as Baar and Greene say, 'seamless automated processes with a single point of entry'.

3 The Public Service of Canada

Henry L. Molot, QC

According to **separation-of-powers theory**,[1] the legislative arm of government makes the laws, the executive arm implements and administers those laws, and the judicial arm adjudicates cases based on those laws. The theory is to some extent acknowledged in Canada's Constitution[2] which calls Part III 'Executive Power', Part IV 'Legislative Power', and Part VII 'Judicature'.

Section 9 of the Constitution Act, 1867 vests the 'Executive Government and authority of and over Canada' in the Queen's representative, the Governor-General. However, neither that official nor his or her Canadian ministers could personally hope to administer the many statutes, regulations, and laws of Canada. How then is this essential function of government to be carried out? In the case of Canada's federal government, it is the Public Service of Canada, variously described by individual legislative enactments,[3] which acts as the principal vehicle for the exercise of the executive power of Canada's government.

But what exactly is Canada's **public service**? And what is its underlying purpose and role? These questions have both definitional and constitutional significance and are addressed below in 'Constitutional Underpinnings'.

The public service, as we shall see, is organizational in nature. The many bodies it contains vary enormously in composition, purposes served, manner of operation, and method of establishment.[4] Often form takes its shape from the purpose meant to be served by the organization. How public service organizations are created is discussed below in 'Formation of Public Service Organizations'.

The next three sections consider the principal types of public service organizations. In particular, what are their forms or structures? Why are such organizations established; what roles and purposes are they intended to serve? How are they established to achieve their purposes?

Are there oversight or accountability regimes to which such bodies are subject and, if so, to what extent is the application of such regimes a function of an organization's purpose and form? This vital issue is discussed in the section 'Ministerial Departments'. The new enhanced oversight mechanisms are briefly considered in 'The Federal Accountability Act'.[5]

Constitutional Underpinnings

To better appreciate the role and purpose that the public service is intended to play within the Government of Canada, let us begin with a little constitutional history.

The executive arm of Canada's federal government has its formal constitutional origins in section 9 of the Constitution Act, 1867, where 'The Executive Government and authority of and over Canada is declared . . . to continue and be vested in the Queen'.

The Sovereign does not of course personally exercise all of this executive authority. As was noted by Mr Justice Dickson of the Supreme Court of Canada, 'Like a corporation, the Crown must act through agents or servants'.[6] The Queen's principal agents are the various ministers appointed to act for and assist her, for example, in the administration of laws and formulation of policy within each minister's authority and mandate. Because ministers too cannot possibly undertake all of this personally, officers, clerks, and others are employed to help them carry out their responsibilities.

In Canada, the executive role of the Queen is generally exercised by the Governor-General, whose authority is conferred principally by his or her instrument of appointment,[7] the Constitution Acts of 1867 and 1982, and Canadian legislation. However, the Governor-General, like the Queen, does not exercise his or her authority alone. Based on constitutional convention, s. 11 of the 1867 Act, and individual enactments, the Governor-General acts through and with the advice of the Queen's Privy Council for Canada, a body composed of ministers of the Crown.[8] It is these ministers, acting both collectively as the Privy Council and individually in carrying out their respective mandates, who are principally responsible for the performance of the executive authority of Canada's government.

While, as noted above, it is Crown employees who support ministers and other government organizations in carrying out their responsibilities, the public service itself is by nature organizational and is not to be equated with its employees. It is true that the Public Service Commission is concerned with government employment and hence with staffing and personnel, but that does not signify that employees and employment lie at the heart of what is meant by 'public service'. So, for example, the definitions of 'public service' in the various statutory components of the new Modernization Act[9] are organizational in nature. Moreover, the context in which ss. 2 and 3 of the Public Service Rearrangement and Transfer of Duties Act[10] use the phrase 'portion of the public service of Canada' makes clear that 'public service of Canada', as it formerly appeared in that statute, is intended to have a purely organizational meaning. This is confirmed by the French version's use of '*secteur de l'adminstration publique*' which s. 224 of the Modernization Act retained, even while the English version of the term was replaced in the Rearrangement Act and in more than 100 other statutes by 'federal public administration'.[11]

This construction is confirmed by s. 102 of the Constitution Act, 1867,[12] which established Canada's Consolidated Revenue Fund 'to be appropriated for the Public Service of Canada'. Section 106 echoes this by providing that the payments there referred to 'shall be appropriated by the Parliament of Canada for the Public Service'. Neither provision limits the purpose of such appropriations to persons employed within the public service.

Formation of Public Service Organizations

How are the various organizational components of Canada's public service established or formed?

Statute

Statute is probably the most common technique for creating a new government entity. Such a statute may provide in great detail for the new body's structure, composition, mandate, internal management, powers, and procedures; or it may simply legislate a skeleton statute supplemented by the authority to make regulations and rules that flesh out less essential matters in greater detail. The current preference is for more rather than less statutory detail. For example, comparing the Atomic Energy Control Act[13] establishing the Atomic Energy Control Board, and the Nuclear Safety and Control Act[14] establishing the Board's replacement, the Canadian Nuclear Safety Commission, shows that the newer Act is much more detailed than the one it supplanted.

Statute is the most public, and hence most transparent, manner in which to proceed. The public nature of the legislative process itself has the added virtue of enabling legislators, as well as interested members of the public, to participate in the formation of the new body. Not only should this lead to more considered legislation and a better organization, but also it is likely to give the new entity greater public acceptance, credibility, and authority.

Statutes are published, which makes the primary legislation governing the organization more accessible and universally known. This also makes it easier for the public to learn about and participate in the activities of the organization.

Except when an emergency or some other factor induces an expedited parliamentary process, enacting a statute can, however, be slow and uncertain. Consequently, not only may proceeding by statute take a long time, but also it may make it more difficult to reform and update the statute by way of amendment. But to some extent, the statute can provide for making regulations outside the legislative process and administrative authority to deal with details.

Subordinate Legislation

A second source of authority is **subordinate legislation**. For example, commissions of inquiry (or, as they are sometimes labelled, 'royal commissions') are established by Order-in-Council made pursuant to the Inquiries Act.[15] Other examples include legislation authorizing the Governor-in-Council to establish a Public Appointments Commission,[16] a minister to establish advisory committees,[17] and the Governor-in-Council to make regulations establishing review panels.[18] Nevertheless, great care must be taken to ensure that there is adequate statutory authority to establish an organization in this manner[19] and to flesh out its mandate and ability to operate effectively.

While the use of subordinate legislation may be less transparent, regulations and Orders-in-Council are now more likely than in the past to be published in Part II of the *Canada Gazette*. Admittedly, an order or regulation published in the *Gazette* may be less easy to find than a statute, but these instruments are now available, and may be searched, electronically.[20]

However, public accessibility is no answer to a more basic constitutional issue if an organization is given authority to adversely affect individual or property rights. That is why it is unusual for an entity with this sort of power to be established by subordinate legislation. If it does have that authority, as in the case of commissions of inquiry, it is probably because the matter is considered so urgent or necessary that the public interest favours this technique.

But public accessibility after enactment does not address the issue of prior public participation in the enactment process. This concern is to some extent met by legislative provisions and internal government policies, which require in certain circumstances pre-publication of a proposed regulation so that the public can review and comment on it before it is enacted.

Traditionally, one important reason for preferring to proceed by way of subordinate legislation is to avoid the slow and uncertain parliamentary process. Subordinate legislation is usually within the exclusive purview of the executive branch and therefore can be given expedited treatment. However, statutory pre-publication requirements as well as the Treasury Board Policy on the Regulatory Process[21] may have diluted this advantage.

Royal Prerogative

Thirdly, government organizations may be established pursuant to the **royal or Crown prerogative** which:

> . . . according to Professor Dicey, . . . is 'the residue of discretionary or arbitrary authority, which at any given time is left in the hands of the Crown'. Dicey, *Introduction to the Study of the Law of the Constitution* 10th ed. (London: Macmillan, 1959) at p. 424. Dicey's broad definition has been explicitly adopted by the Supreme Court of Canada and the House of Lords. See *Re The Effect of the Exercise of the Royal Prerogative of Mercy upon Deportation Proceedings*, [1933] S.C.R. 269 at 272–73 and *A.G. v. DeKeyser's Royal Hotel*, [1920] A.C. 508 at 526 . . . [22]

It is rare in Canada for the prerogative to be the legal basis for establishing components of the public service. By contrast, in the United Kingdom, the royal prerogative has been used to establish, for example, the Criminal Injuries Compensation Board[23] and non-statutory royal commissions of inquiry. Even in the case of ministerial departments, which in the UK and Australia appear to be based on prerogative authority, Canada's constitutional history signals a preference for such organizations being established by statute. Nevertheless, the prerogative has been used as the basis for creating the Canadian Heraldic Authority.[24] This source of legal authority may also explain the origins of Canada's Privy Council Office.

The purely executive nature of an exercise of the prerogative clothes it with a degree of secrecy that is the very antithesis of transparency and openness expected of modern democratic government. Moreover, a major limitation of the prerogative is that it does not provide the authority to compel an individual or to adversely affect his or her rights, for example, by empowering a royal commission to compel evidence. One reason for the UK enacting the 1921 Tribunals of Inquiry (Evidence) Act,[25] which conferred such powers on a prerogative-based commission of inquiry, was to overcome this limitation. These factors may help explain why traditionally Canada has rarely relied on the royal prerogative to create new organizations.

Contract

Fourthly, a governmental organization may be formed through a **contract or agreement**. For example, a minister may, by contract, engage the services of several people to act as a committee to conduct a study, inquiry, or hearing. It is true that such an organization may be nothing more than an unincorporated association that has no legal personality of its own and that cannot be clothed with compulsory powers under the contract.[26] Although such a body may lack legal powers and have to operate on a consensual basis, it can be created expeditiously and with a minimum of formality.

Administrative/Limited-Purpose Body

A fifth type of government organization is one that is not so much legally constituted or established as an **administratively formed organization**, being perhaps little more than a section, branch, or portion of a legally established ministerial department or Crown agency, which is then clothed with limited legal status for specific internal governmental purposes. For example, certain 'divisions or branches of the federal public administration' appearing in Schedule I.1 of the Financial Administration Act[27] were not created by statute or any of the other legal techniques discussed above. They were simply added to the schedule, pursuant to section 3 of the Act, by Order-in-Council. As a result, they found themselves included in that Act's definition of 'department' but only for the limited purposes of that Act. Within those limits, such an organization receives a measure of autonomy, particularly in relation to the department or agency of which it formerly was no more than an administrative unit.

For example, the Labour Branch of the Department of Human Resources Development was plucked from that Department and added to Schedule I.1 pursuant to the Financial Administration Act, its administrative name newly re-styled as the Department of Human Resources and Skills Development.[28] In this manner, the Department of Human Resources and Skills Development, though not a legally constituted organization for general purposes,[29] became a 'department' for the limited purposes of that Act. Subsequent Orders-in-Council adding that Department to schedules under the Public Service Staff Relations Act,[30] the Privacy Act,[31] and the Access to Information Act[32] expanded the law applicable to this newly formed 'department'.

Public Service Rearrangement and Transfer of Duties Act

A sixth method does not so much form the basis for a wholly new organization as it provides the necessary authority for clothing it with legal powers and duties. The source of this unusual authority is the very brief, three-section **Public Service Rearrangement and Transfer of Duties Act**.[33]

Without entering into detail about how this statute operates, it is important to recognize its immense usefulness as a vehicle for reorganizing the Government of Canada quickly. Except in the case of clear contrary parliamentary intent,[34] the Act authorizes the Governor-in-Council, among other things, to:

> transfer any powers, duties or functions or the control or supervision of any portion of the federal public administration from one minister to another, or from one department in, or portion of, the federal public administration to another.[35]

The Act has been used to effect both large and small government reorganizations. Even those reorganizations that are subsequently ratified by statute can begin operating immediately upon the making of the orders. Useful examples illustrating the scope of this authority can be found in the orders passed pursuant to this and related statutes (and published in Part II of the *Canada Gazette*) in order to implement the two major reorganizations of 25 June 1993 and 12 December 2003.

Since the first major non-statutory government reorganization in June 1993, this technique has become more commonly used. While it has the virtue of quick implementation, it lacks the transparency of a statute and the parliamentary process. On the other hand, except for such issues as ensuring that the public is fully aware of which minister or organization has the lawful authority to act, and who is the minister responsible for a given area, it can be argued that any such initiatives are merely matters of internal organizational changes, which have no effect on the existence and exercise of statutory and other legal powers and duties, and the delivery of government programs. In any event, major administrative reorganizations of this sort have invariably been confirmed and ratified by subsequent statutory legislation.

This technique is often used in conjunction with the administrative/limited purpose method discussed above. For example, prior to the enactment of the Canada Border Services Agency Act in 2005,[36] the Canada Border Services Agency was formed in 2003 by means of the following process:

- An Order-in-Council[37] made under section 3(1)(a) of the Financial Administration Act plucked out a purely administrative unit of the Department of Citizenship and Immigration, the Intelligence and Enforcement Operations Branch, and added it as a 'department' for purposes of that Act to Schedule I.1 of that Act under the new name, Canada Border Services Agency, with the Minister of Citizenship and Immigration as the Agency's 'appropriate minister'.
- An Order-in-Council[38] made pursuant to the Public Service Rearrangement and Transfer of Duties Act transferred from the Minister of Citizenship and Immigration to the Solicitor General of Canada the control and supervision of the new Agency.
- The next Order-in-Council[39] amended Schedule I.1 of the Financial Administration Act by replacing the Minister of Citizenship and Immigration with the Solicitor General of Canada as the Agency's 'appropriate minister'.
- A two-pronged Order-in-Council[40] was then made pursuant to the Public Service Rearrangement and Transfer of Duties Act (1) transferring supervision and control of a number of administrative units of the Department of Citizenship and Immigration from the Minister of Citizenship and Immigration to the Solicitor General of Canada, and (2) transferring the powers of the Minister of Citizenship and Immigration under section 77(1) of the Immigration and Refugee Protection Act to the Solicitor General of Canada.
- Two Orders-in-Council made pursuant to the Rearrangement and Transfer of Duties Act then transferred to the Canada Border Services Agency supervision and control of (1) a number of administrative units in the Canada Customs and Revenue Agency;[41] and (2) that portion of the Operations Branch of

> the Canadian Food Inspection Agency described in the order.[42]

While the 2005 statute formally 'established' the Canada Border Services Agency,[43] its transitional provisions made sure to expressly confirm and ratify all of the acts and activities carried out by the 2003 Agency.[44]

Classes of Government Organizations: General

It only takes an examination of schedules of certain statutes such as the Financial Administration Act and of the Government of Canada's website[45] to reveal that Canada's public service is composed of a wide variety of types of organizations.

By way of illustration, the definition of 'department' in section 2 of the Financial Administration Act includes 'departments' named in Schedule I; departmental corporations in Schedule II; and 'divisions or branches of the federal public administration set out in column I of Schedule I.1'. In addition, section 2 refers to 'Crown corporations' as another class of organization.

A **department** listed in Schedule I can appear there only by virtue of statute. It is therefore more difficult for such a department to be added to or removed from the Schedule. A statutory amendment is required. This is in marked contrast with the other schedules, where organizations may be added or deleted by executive act in the form of an order made by the Governor-in-Council.

In the case of the '**departmental corporation**', that type of organization is defined in section 2 of the Financial Administration Act as a corporation listed in Schedule II. By virtue of section 3(1)(a.1) of the Act, such a corporation is required to be 'established by an Act of Parliament', and to perform administrative, research, supervisory, advisory or regulatory functions of a governmental nature.[46]

Schedule III of the Act contains the names of 'parent Crown corporations',[47] a class of organization principally governed by Part X of the Act. Most of these are listed in Part I of the Schedule. To be in Part II requires 'the Governor-in-Council (to be) satisfied that . . . the corporation . . . operates in a competitive environment, is not ordinarily dependent on appropriations for operating purposes, . . . ordinarily earns a return on equity; and . . . there is a reasonable expectation that the corporation will pay dividends'.[48] The recent decline in importance of commercial corporations as a vehicle for carrying out government policy is evident from the fact that, at present, only three corporations are listed in Part II.

Schedule I.1 has the luxury of being subject to none of the definitional limitations governing Schedules II and III. All that is required is that the organization be a 'division or branch of the federal public administration'. The discussion of administrative/limited purpose bodies above illustrates the degree of flexibility the government has in amending this Schedule and thus reshaping and modifying Canada's machinery of government.

The Financial Administration Act contains three other schedules of organizations. Schedules IV and V relate to human resource management and the operation of sections 11 to 13 of the Act. For those purposes, in the definitional provisions of section 11(1), the term 'core public administration' is defined by reference to 'the departments named in Schedule I and the other portions of the federal public administration named in Schedule IV'; the definition of 'separate agency' is based on the portions of the federal public administration named in Schedule V; and '**public service**' is defined to mean departments named in Schedule I, other portions of the federal public administration named in Schedule IV, separate agencies listed in Schedule V, and any other part of the federal public administration designated by the Governor-in-Council.

Schedule VI relates to the new departmental responsibility for internal audit committees and for accounting officers—persons responsible for reporting to Parliament on administrative matters within a department. For a department listed in Part I of Schedule VI, the deputy minister is the department's accounting officer. For a department listed in Part II or III of Schedule VI, the accounting officer is identified by position in the Schedule.

The Financial Administration Act is not, of course, the only statute that identifies and classifies federal machinery of government. It is, however, that statute's definitions that are most often relied on by other legislation applicable to government organizations and employees. For example, the staffing or employment provisions of the Public Service Employment Act[49] use definitions that refer directly to Schedules I, IV, and V of the Financial Administration Act. In this way, the mandate of the Public Service Commission is defined by reference to 'core public administration' and 'separate agencies' as defined in section 11(1) of the Financial Administration Act. This is also the manner in which the Public Servants Disclosure Protection Act[50] defines 'public sector', and in which the Access to Information Act[51] and the Privacy Act[52] define 'government institution'. On the other hand, a statute such as the Official Languages Act uses its own definition of 'federal institution', which relies neither on a schedule of organizations nor on the schedules of the Financial Administration Act.

The three most important types of government organizations will now be considered in greater detail.

Ministerial Departments

No matter the legal basis upon which a minister's authority rests, most ministers simply have too much to do to be able to carry out all of their responsibilities personally. In addition, few ministers possess the knowledge and expertise to deal with the enormous number and the huge variety of matters falling within their mandate, which usually includes the exercise of legal authorities, the administration of particular programs, and the development of policy initiatives. It is principally for these reasons that a minister requires the support of staff who have the necessary authority and qualifications to perform the myriad powers, duties, and functions of their minister.

This can be illustrated by picturing a minister sitting atop a pyramid of officers and employees who have no other purpose than to support their minister. The pyramid itself does not include the minister,[53] who is not usually appointed pursuant to the statute establishing his or her department but rather on the basis of the royal prerogative.[54] Moreover, a minister is not appointed to a department. Most departmental statutes recognize this distinction by providing that the minister 'presides over' the department. The pyramid therefore represents the departmental organization in which those officers and staff are employed, whereas the minister stands outside the departmental pyramid.

In the case of a federal government minister, the department's only role is to support its minister.[55] As was noted by the Lambert Report:

> Departments are the principal delivery arm of government: through them, the Government manages its programs and delivers its services. They are instruments under the direction and management of ministers and through which ministers discharge mandates conferred on them by Parliament in departmental acts. Each departmental statute sets out a minister's area of jurisdiction and prescribes his responsibility for direction and management.[56]

The very close and dependent relationship that a department is intended to have with its minister is emphasized in several ways.

First, such departments are the only ones contained in Schedule I of the Financial Administration Act, which, unlike the other schedules, can be amended only by statute. Second, the language of most departmental statutes authorizes ministers to manage and direct their departments. This power to manage would, for example, ordinarily be broad enough to grant a minister authority in personnel management and staffing in his or her department. Only because of sections 11 and 12 of the Financial Administration Act and section 29 of the Public Service Employment Act is that authority conferred on others to the exclusion of the minister.[57] Exceptions such as these underscore the minister's degree of control and direction over the department for matters that fall within his or her mandate. Even when a departmental employee has independent discretion on a given matter, a ministerial guideline or policy, although not binding in this situation, will influence the employee's decisions and actions.[58]

Third, ministerial departments provide an exception to the general legal principle that discretionary authority can be exercised only by the person upon whom that power is conferred, unless statute expressly authorizes its delegation to some third person. Discretionary authority conferred on a minister may, without benefit of delegation authority or any formal act by the minister, be exercised by an appropriate departmental employee on behalf of the minister.[59] As will be later more fully explained,[60] generally speaking, a ministerial department and its employees have no other role or purpose than to support their minister in the performance of the powers, duties, and functions assigned to him or her.

Internal Controls and Accountability

History and experience, however, have demonstrated the inadvisability of allowing a minister to manage departmental employees and financial resources. In the case of personnel, general legislation such as sections 11 to 13 of the Financial Administration Act and the Public Service Employment Act ensure that a minister does not have personal authority regarding the department's human resources. First, section 29 of the latter Act clothes the Public Service Commission with exclusive power to make appointments to the department; and secondly, the broad delegation provisions of that Act[61] do not authorize any part of the Commission's staffing monopoly to be handed over to the minister. This precaution is echoed in the provisions of the Financial Administration Act, under which the non-staffing aspects of human resources management of a Schedule I department are allocated to the Treasury Board and that department's deputy minister.[62] Again, ministers are purposely excluded from that role.

To the same effect are provisions of the Financial Administration Act regulating the public moneys of individual departments. Not only does the Treasury Board have a significant role in the financial administration of public moneys, but controls on departmental disbursements are assigned by the Act, not to ministers but to deputy ministers[63] and to persons authorized by the minister.[64]

It is worth noting here that although a minister may not have any personal authority in managing personnel and the financial and other resources of his or her department, the basic constitutional principle of ministerial responsibility still applies. A minister therefore remains responsible to the House of Commons for his or her department's human resources as well as for how public moneys appropriated for departmental purposes are administered by the department. At a more practical level, it is the department's deputy minister who has the day-to-day task of ensuring the department acts properly and complies with legal and policy requirements concerning such matters.[65] This practical responsibility of deputy ministers is acknowledged in recent amendments to the Financial Administration Act that formally recognize deputy ministers as 'accounting officers' and make them accountable to parliamentary committees for such matters.[66]

How then is a minister to exercise the innumerable legal powers and duties that typically are his or her responsibility? Strictly speaking, of course, it is not the department, but its employees, that act for the minister. Moreover, unlike a corporation, a department is not a juridical entity and therefore does not have the necessary legal personality at common law to act as an agent in the exercise of legal authority. While, occasionally, legislation may expressly delegate ministerial authority to employees of the department, more usually, reliance is placed on paragraphs (c) and (d) of section 24(2) of the Interpretation Act[67] as well as the common law principle that it reflects.[68] That principle was developed based on these factors: (1) the practical impossibility that a minister could physically exercise all of the powers, duties, and functions for which he or she is responsible; (2) departments and departmental employees have no raison d'être other than to support their minister in carrying out his or her mandate; and (3) while such employees may act in support of the minister, it is the latter who remains constitutionally responsible to the House of Commons for what departmental employees may do on the minister's behalf.

Crown Agencies

It may be recalled that the ministerial department has no legal powers and duties of its own to carry out. Powers and duties are rather assigned to its minister. The role of the minister's department is to support its minister through appropriate departmental employees exercising the minister's legal authority for, and on behalf of, the minister. In contrast, a **Crown agency** may be assigned powers and duties of its own to be exercised by and in the name of the agency. In reality, however, to paraphrase Mr Justice Dickson, the agency '. . . must act through agents or servants'.

In other words, while, strictly speaking, legislation may confer authority directly on an agency, the latter is an inanimate body that can only operate and exercise that authority by means of human actors, that is, its officers and employees.

As far back as fifteenth-century England, when legislation first provided for sewer commissions,[69] it was recognized that there were activities that neither the central government (principally ministers and the Privy Council) nor local officials (such as justices of the peace and local courts) were equipped to manage and administer.

One early Canadian example of a Crown agency is the Heir and Devisee Commission[70] established by Upper Canada in 1797 and described as 'the forerunner of the quasi-judicial tribunals that are familiar to Canadians today'.[71] The Board of Railway Commissioners established in 1903 is taken to be the first administrative tribunal of the federal government.[72] Crown agencies having corporate status, commonly referred to as Crown corporations, are said to have originated in Canada in 1852 when it was enacted that the Montreal Harbour commissioners, 'shall be a Body Corporate and Politic'.[73] Comparable legislation was later enacted for other Canadian harbours, the Ottawa Improvement Commission in 1899[74] and the National Battlefields Commission in 1908.[75]

Crown agencies within Canada's public service are now so numerous and so varied in composition, powers and duties, procedures, accountability mechanisms, and relationships that it would not be easy to accommodate all of them in a single comprehensive analysis. As the Lambert Commission reported:

> The number and variety of functions as well as organizational models that characterize Crown agencies pose two major issues. The first is the identification and classification of Crown agencies. The second is the clarification and rationalization of the arm's length relationships of Crown agencies with Government and Parliament.[76]

The extensive discussion of these issues in the Lambert Report[77] underscores the definitional and classification difficulties that abound here. For purposes of recommending 'appropriate accountability for management and for the implementation of public policy in accordance with mandates',[78] the Report ultimately broke down Crown agencies into three groups: independent deciding and advisory bodies; Crown corporations; and shared enterprises and quasi-public corporations.[79]

Sixteen years later, the Law Reform Commission of Canada issued a Report dealing only with 'independent administrative agencies'.[80] Even though such agencies were restricted to those making decisions, the Commission was still unsure whether its list of agencies was exhaustive.[81]

Nevertheless, even a cursory perusal of the current schedules (other than Schedule 1) of the Financial Administration Act makes clear that the Lambert Report's classification of Crown agencies is now quite inadequate. Many non-corporate bodies do not qualify as either independent deciding or advisory bodies. There are those, such as the Atlantic Canada Opportunities Agency, the Economic Development Agency of Canada for the Regions of Quebec, Infrastructure of Canada, and the Canadian International Development Agency, whose principal mandate is one of subsidy, that is, to make grants and contributions. Then there are the

Courts Administration Service, the Office of the Governor-General's Secretary, and the Library and Archives of Canada, all of which are responsible for managing certain government properties and services.

In some cases, specific policy issues or programs are extracted from a ministerial department and placed with Crown agencies in order to give them some degree of organizational independence (e.g., the Office of the Superintendent of Financial Institutions, the Office of the Commissioner for Federal Judicial Affairs, the Public Health Agency of Canada, the Indian Residential Schools Truth and Reconciliation Commission Secretariat, and the Office of the Communications Security Establishment). Then too, it may be considered essential that the Crown agency established to administer a program have an arm's-length relationship with the minister and department having policy responsibility for that program (e.g., the Canadian Food Inspection Agency, the Parks Canada Agency, and the Canada Revenue Agency).

In the recent past, concerns about the manner in which government itself operates, and the potentially adverse impact that its activities might have on certain constitutional and other important legal rights of citizens, have led to the creation of Crown agencies such as the Information Commissioner, the Privacy Commissioner, and the Official Languages Commissioner.[82] Needless to say, there is even greater concern about the independence of such appointees, inasmuch as it is the government (formally through the Governor-in-Council but in reality through cabinet ministers) that both appoints them and has direct jurisdiction over their activities. In order, therefore, to enhance the independence of these appointees, legislation requires that their appointment be approved by the House of Commons and the Senate, that both houses concur in their removal by the Governor-in-Council,[83] and that they report directly to Parliament rather than through a minister.

As varied as the organizations in this category may be, it excludes those that, regardless of their relationship to the government, are not strictly speaking part of the 'federal public administration'. Among those excluded are parliamentary institutions and officers (even though appointed by the Governor-in-Council),[84] superior court judges, and organizations that do not satisfy the criteria referred to above.[85] However, Schedules I.1 and IV of the Financial Administration Act show that parliamentary staff, the Registrar and staff of the Supreme Court of Canada, and the Court Administration Service supporting the other four federal superior courts[86] are included.

In sum, the reason why such bodies were thought to be necessary, and were considered in certain circumstances to be a superior form of administration than the traditional ministerial department, was the subject of the following comment in the Lambert Report that introduced its treatment of 'non-departmental bodies':

> The extensive resort to Crown agencies is a legitimate response by government to the problem of developing alternative instrumentalities to cope with demands imposed by the assumption of new roles that require independent sources of policy advice, regulation of important sectors of the economy, objective determination of rights, and outright government ownership and operation of numerous business-like undertakings. Crown agencies serve a necessary and useful purpose in lightening the burdens on ministers caused by the growth of programs and added responsibilities within conventional departments.[87]

Crown Corporations

As mentioned in the previous section, a special sub-category of the Crown agency is the **Crown corporation**. Why should a Crown agency be established in the form of a corporation? There are, first, the strictly legal reasons for clothing such an agency with corporate status. A statutory non-corporate Crown agency has only the capacity and powers conferred on it by legislation. However, in addition to whatever powers constitutive legislation confers on a corporation, that body, by its very nature, has the capacity to sue and be sued, to make contracts, and to acquire and dispose of personal property.[88] Where the purposes of a Crown agency require it to own and manage property or to rely on commercial agreements and contractual transactions, it would be a reasonable expectation on the part of those dealing with the agency that it would act much like a normal commercial enterprise, that is, like a business corporation.

In addition,

> . . . Crown corporations have often been established to give a measure of independence to the management of certain types of activities. That independence takes two forms: independence from the close financial and personnel controls that accompany departmental administration and independence from interference by Parliament and the government in the day-to-day management of the activities of the Crown corporations'.[89]

It may be useful to give examples in order to illustrate why successive governments have chosen Crown agencies as the preferred organizational vehicle for carrying out certain governmental activities.

The historical corporations cited above were established in order to manage and regulate government property for a particular public purpose. This could be accomplished more simply and effectively by an organization that could acquire and dispose of property and enter into contracts, and that was not burdened with the financial and personnel strictures and limitations of ordinary government departments. In the past, these and other factors applied to the public harbour commissions, which were reformed by the Canada Marine Act,[90] and to government-owned airports prior to the enactment of the Airport Transfer (Miscellaneous Matters) Act.[91] Current corporations of this sort include the Canada Lands Company Limited, the Queens Quay West Land Corporation, and not-for-profit organizations such the National Gallery of Canada and the various Canadian government museums.

Subsidies form one of the many activities of government no matter which party is in power. For example, the government may provide financial support for Canadian business ventures and enterprises here and abroad;[92] for important social purposes such as housing;[93] and for credit and investment protection.[94] A Crown corporation may be established to administer a grants or subsidy program (e.g., Social Sciences and Humanities Research Council, Natural Sciences and Engineering Research Council, Canadian Institutes of Health Research, and Enterprise Cape Breton Corporation). It is hoped that keeping these programs at arm's length from the responsible minister and the minister's department will depoliticize the process of deciding who qualifies for a grant or subsidy. On the other hand, it is also true that most, if not all, ministerial departments administer grants and contributions programs. And yet, there are departments,[95] as well as Crown agencies,[96] which have no role other than to administer what are in effect subsidy programs that do not have an arm's-length relationship with their minister.

Crown corporations may also be established to operate what is, in effect, a public utility[97] or to implement marketing agency programs such as the Canadian Dairy Commission and the Freshwater Fish Marketing Corporation. All of these examples contemplate an agency that in effect carries on a business enterprise, including commercial transactions and the need for contracts and agreements. History has demonstrated that a corporation is better able than a department to carry out these activities. Not only is a government department ill-equipped to undertake such activities, but the degree of detail that would have to be contained in legislation in order to establish such an agency and to ensure it had comprehensive authority to operate the business in all its facets would make this an unnecessarily cumbersome, and therefore inefficient and ineffectual, vehicle for meeting policy objectives. Independence from political considerations is another reason for insulating the implementation of such programs from possible ministerial pressure.

On the other hand, where the role of the Crown agency is to regulate, not operate, a public utility or some other important sector of the Canadian economy, the agency would not be expected to engage in commercial and property transactions in order to accomplish its policy mission. And so, Crown agencies such as the Canada Industrial Relations Board, the Canadian International Trade Tribunal, the Canadian Radio-television and Telecommunications Commission, the Canadian Transportation Agency, and the Copyright Board of Canada have not been given corporate status. Such an agency accomplishes its objectives through regulations that apply general norms and conditions within its field, and through licensing, which gives economic actors the right to conduct activities in that field.

Recently, the corporate model was adopted for administering regulatory programs that in the past had been the subject of ordinary departmental administration. These include the Canadian Food Inspection Agency, the Canada Revenue Agency, and the Parks Canada Agency. The preamble of the Canadian Food Inspection Agency Act offers some explanation why the administration of food safety programs, which in the past had been administered by three different departments, was turned over to a single corporate body. In addition to enhanced 'effectiveness and efficiency' and better and more uniform 'consumer protection' which would result from the consolidation of food inspection and related activities, a corporation could more easily 'pursue a greater degree of collaboration and consultation between federal departments and with other orders of government in this area'.[98] It is true that the Act expressly authorizes such agreements. However, rigidities under the Act had limited co-operation and joint programs between two or more ministerial departments.[99]

The corporation model provides an additional vehicle for promoting federal–provincial co-operation. Boards of directors or of management normally regulate a corporation's internal affairs, which by appropriate legislation can require provincial representation. For example, the Canada Revenue Agency's Board of Management include a director 'nominated by each province and one director nominated by the territories'.[100]

Internal Controls and Accountability

What sort of management and administrative controls have been placed upon Crown agencies and the manner in which they operate? In particular, is the management of their human and financial resources subject to external controls?

The Financial Administration Act, which regulates financial administration and the management of human resources, draws a distinction between a Crown agency that is a Crown corporation[101] and other Crown agencies including 'departmental corporations'.[102] Crown corporations include 'parent Crown corporations'[103] and their 'wholly-owned subsidiaries'. Much of the supervisory and regulatory responsibility for managing this sort of corporation is specially provided for in Part X of the Act. It seeks to place some limits on how Crown corporations operate while preserving relative 'independence from the close financial and personnel controls that accompany departmental administration'.[104] Examples of Part X controls include the authority conferred on the Governor-in-Council to appoint the officers and directors of parent Crown corporations,[105] to fix the remuneration payable to their directors, chief executive officers and chairpersons,[106] to 'make, amend or repeal' their bylaws,[107] and to approve their annual corporate plans.

As for non-corporate Crown agencies, supervision and control of how they use and manage their financial resources are also governed by the Financial Administration Act. At one end of the spectrum may be a provision such as section 41(3) of the National Defence Act,[108] which expressly stipulates that the Financial Administration Act 'does not apply to non-public property'. Not surprisingly, no reference to non-public property is to be found in any of the schedules of the Act. At the other end of the spectrum are ministerial departments listed in Schedule I and those Crown agencies included in the Act's definition of 'department', which are not otherwise exempted from the full panoply of financial controls imposed under that Act.

For the human resources of Crown agencies that are not Crown corporations, sections 11 to 12.4 of the Financial Administration Act[109] establish regimes for dealing with this matter. Which regime applies will depend on whether the Crown agency in question qualifies as part of the 'public service';[110] as a 'separate agency';[111] as part of the 'core public administration';[112] or only as part of the undefined 'federal public administration'.[113] The Act does not provide for staffing or the employment of particular individuals. It focuses rather on establishing the employment framework, including terms and conditions of employment, within which staffing can then take place. To that end, Treasury Board is thereby authorized, among other things, to determine human resources requirements, to provide for the classification of positions and persons, to determine and regulate pay, hours of work and leave, and to provide for other terms and conditions of employment.[114]

Generally speaking, under the Public Service Employment Act it is the Public Service Commission that has the staffing jurisdiction, particularly the exclusive jurisdiction to appoint or employ persons. However, that exclusive jurisdiction[115] is limited to positions in 'the public service' where no other authority to employ has been conferred by an Act of Parliament. Two limitations are here imposed. First, the Crown agency to which appointments are made must be part of the 'public service', a term having the same definition in section 2(1) of the Public Service Employment Act as it has in section 11(1) of the Financial Administration Act. The Commission therefore has no authority to appoint persons to an agency that is not listed in Schedules I, IV, or V of the Financial Administration Act. But second, even if an agency is so listed, the Commission has no authority to appoint if an Act of Parliament provides otherwise. For example, while the Office of the Auditor General appears in Schedule V, section 15 of the Auditor General Act[116] authorizes the Auditor General to staff that organization.

The acts and activities of Crown agencies are, generally speaking, subject to jurisdictional limits. Such agencies are more usually established or formed by or under legislation which directly or indirectly defines the mandate or jurisdiction of the agency, and provides for its powers and procedures. Where the Crown agency is a statutory corporation, it is the legislative provisions setting forth the corporation's objects or purposes, any prohibited activities, and the powers the corporation may exercise in carrying out the mandate of the corporation, which define its jurisdiction. To stray beyond those jurisdictional limits is to commit an invalid act. As the matter was described by the Supreme Court of Canada:

> The presumption at common law is that corporations created by or under a statute have only those powers which are expressly or impliedly granted to them. To the extent that a corporation acts beyond its powers, its actions are *ultra vires* [beyond its authority] and invalid.[117]

While Mr Justice Iacobucci considered that in the case of modern corporations 'the general abolition of the doctrine of *ultra vires* is in accordance with sound policy and common sense', there are other policy reasons that support retention of the doctrine in the case of 'corporations created by special act for public purposes'.

The doctrine of *ultra vires* also applies to non-corporate Crown agencies created by or under statute to fulfill a specific policy objective or purpose and to do so in the manner provided for in the legislation. As was noted recently by the majority judgment of the Supreme Court of Canada:

> By virtue of the rule of law principle, all exercises of public authority must find their source in law. All decision-making powers have legal limits, derived from the enabling statute itself, the common or civil law or the Constitution. Judicial review is the means by which the courts supervise those who exercise statutory powers, to ensure that they do not overstep their legal authority . . .
>
> Administrative powers are exercised by decision makers according to statutory regimes that are themselves confined. A decision maker may not exercise authority

not specifically assigned to him or her. By acting in the absence of legal authority, the decision maker transgresses the principle of the rule of law. Thus, when a reviewing court considers the scope of a decision-making power or the jurisdiction conferred by a statute, the standard of review analysis strives to determine what authority was intended to be given to the body in relation to the subject matter . . .[118]

Federal Accountability Act[119]

On 1 February 2006, the Commission of Inquiry into the Sponsorship Program and Advertising Activities (more commonly known as the Gomery Commission) issued its final report[120] concerning the serious mismanagement of the government's Sponsorship Program by ministers, senior political officials, and public servants. The new Conservative government acted swiftly; little more than two months after the report was published, they introduced into the House of Commons the Federal Accountability Act,[121] which proposed sweeping legislative changes 'to make government more accountable'.[122] The Act was not, of course, drafted in a vacuum but was built on accountability mechanisms and procedures[123] already operating within the Canadian government. To this end, this long compendious Bill of 314 sections accomplished its goal by enacting two new statutes and amending dozens of existing ones.

The following is a thumbnail sketch of the principal accountability measures in the **Federal Accountability Act** which apply to ministers and the public service. What follows therefore omits reference to those provisions relating, for example, to candidates for election to the House of Commons, to members of the House and of the Senate, and to lobbyists.

Part 1 of the Act enacts a new Conflict of Interest Act[124] dealing with the accountability of ministers, their staff, and their advisers, and of office-holders appointed by ministers and the Governor-in-Council. It establishes conflict-of-interest prohibitions as a condition of a person's appointment or employment. A new Conflict of Interest and Ethics Commissioner, appointed by the Governor-in-Council with the approval of the Senate and House of Commons, has investigative powers and authority to order compliance, including the imposition of administrative monetary penalties.

This is not the first oversight scheme relating to this class of office-holder. However, the scheme set up by Prime Minister Mulroney more than 20 years earlier was not only more limited in scope but was only in the form of administrative guidelines. This informal scheme was replaced in 2004 by amendments to the Parliament of Canada Act,[125] establishing an Ethics Commissioner who, Janus-like, was given the mandate to apply one conflict-of-interest scheme to public office-holders and another to members of Parliament.

Part 2 of the Act augments the financial accountability of the Executive to Parliament. At the time of enactment, the principal source of financial accountability lay with the Auditor General. The Act establishes a new Parliamentary Budget Officer to provide both Houses of Parliament with objective analyses of the estimates and of the state of the nation's finances and economic trends, and to undertake research for Parliamentary committees and provide estimates of the cost of proposals contained in private member bills.

Part 3 enacts a new statute[126] creating the office of Director of Public Prosecutions in order to better ensure the political independence of the prosecutorial role of the Attorney General. The nub of the problem lies in the conflicting responsibilities of the Minister of Justice and the Attorney General of Canada and the fact that one individual holds both offices. For example, as Minister of Justice, he or she is responsible for recommending judicial appointments (of superior court judges, both federal and provincial) to the Governor-in-Council and is responsible for the Judges Act governing judicial administration, but, as Attorney General, this same person is responsible for prosecutions and for representing the federal Crown in litigation before these judicial appointees. While the offices of Minister of Justice and Attorney General continue to exist and to be held by the same person, it is now the responsibility of the Director of Public Prosecutions to initiate and conduct prosecutions under the jurisdiction of the Attorney General of

Canada. The independence of this new officer is enhanced by a seven-year non-renewable term and good-behaviour tenure.

Part 3 also strengthens the 'whistle-blower' provisions of the Public Servants Disclosure Protection Act[127] by augmenting the jurisdiction of the Public Sector Integrity Commissioner to deal with complaints of wrongdoing and of reprisals[128] in relation to the public sector, and by creating a judicially manned Public Servants Disclosure Protection Tribunal, having as its principal role the authority to adjudicate reprisal claims and to make remedial orders in favour of reprisal victims. Part 3 also addresses concerns about what often appear to be partisan and unqualified Governor-in-Council appointments, by authorizing the Governor-in-Council to establish a Public Appointments Commission, to establish a code of practice for such appointments and to oversee, review, audit, and publicly report on the operation of, and compliance with, the code.[129]

A centrepiece of the Gomery Report was the apparent failure of departments to properly account for appropriated moneys and spending on their programs. To that end, Part 4 amends the Financial Administration Act to import the British reform of 'accounting officers'. Designated as such, deputy ministers of departments and chief executive officers of other government organizations are thereby made 'accountable' to parliamentary committees for such matters as the organization of resources to deliver programs, systems of internal control, and the signing of accounts.

Part 5 reforms the contract bidding process by establishing a Procurement Auditor who is responsible for reviewing current procurement practices and making recommendations for their improvement, and for dealing with complaints of non-compliance with procurements laws and the administration of particular procurement contracts by departments.

Conclusion

Canada's public service is an extraordinarily multifaceted, flexible, and versatile universe of organizations that can be formed for purposes of accomplishing almost any purpose or objective the government wishes to achieve, subject always to the limitations imposed by the Constitution Act, 1867 and the Charter of Rights and Freedoms. It is true that the number of organizations within the public service is quite large, but it is interesting to note how many more, over the years, have been dissolved and therefore no longer exist.[130]

Because these are government organizations, their accountability to ministers, to Parliament and, in effect, to the people of Canada imposes upon them a superadded duty that is perhaps more confining than for organizations in the private sector. The additional supervisory and monitoring mechanisms that have been put into place in recent years underscore the high degree of accountability expected of public service organizations. The irony is that additional accountability mechanisms usually translate into additional organizations, levels of bureaucracy, and rules, which must be balanced against the public interest in public service efficiency and effectiveness. Can that balance be achieved? Time will tell!

Important Terms and Concepts

administratively formed organization
contract or agreement
Crown agency
Crown corporation
department
departmental corporation
Federal Accountability Act
public service
Public Service Rearrangement and Transfer of Duties Act
royal or Crown prerogative
separation-of-powers theory
statute
subordinate legislation

Study Questions

1. What is Canada's 'public service'?
2. How are its various organizational components established?
3. What are the advantages and disadvantages of these various methods of establishing parts of the public service?
4. Explain the complexities inherent in the 'crown agencies' sector.
5. To what extent is the Federal Accountability Act a continuation of past reforms?

Useful Websites

The Canada Gazette:

www.gazette.gc.ca

Canada Public Service Agency's Population Affiliation Report:

www.tbs-sct.gc.ca/pas-srp/overview-apercu_e.asp

Halliday, W.E.D. 1959. 'The Executive of the Government in Canada', *Canadian Public Administration* 2 (December), 229–41.

www3.interscience.wiley.com/cgi-bin/fulltext/119883136/PDFSTART

Letters Patent Constituting the Office of Governor General of Canada:

www.efc.ca/pages/law/cons/Constitutions/Canada/English/LettersPatent.html

Public Service Rearrangement and Transfer of Duties Act, R.S.C. 1985, c. P-34:

www.canlii.org/en/ca/laws/stat/rsc-1985-c-p-34/latest/rsc-1985-c-p-34.html

Treasury Board's Guide to the Regulatory Process:

www.tbs-sct.gc.ca/ri-qr/processguideprocessus-eng.asp

Treasury Board's Common Services Policy:

www.tbs-sct.gc.ca/pubs_pol/dcgpubs/TB_93/csp-psc01_e.asp#_Toc147652578

Gomery Commission *Report*, Phase Two:

http://epe.lac-bac.gc.ca/100/206/301/pco-bcp/commissions/sponsorship-ef/06–03–06/www.gomery.ca/en/phase2report/index.asp

Federal Accountability Act:

www2.parl.gc.ca/HousePublications/Publication.aspx?Docid=3294507&file=4

Notes

1. Montesquieu, *The Spirit of the Laws* (1748).
2. Constitution Act, 1867, 30 & 31 Vict. c. 3 (UK), as amended by s. 50 of Sch. B of Canada Act 1982, 1982, c. 11 (UK).
3. The variety of terminology is illustrated by the current statutory definitions and use of 'public service', 'core public administration', and 'federal public administration' in the amended Financial Administration Act (s. 8 of Public Service Modernization Act, S.C. 2003, c. 22), the new Public Service Labour Relations Act (s. 2 of the Public Service Modernization Act), and the new Public Service Employment Act (ss. 12 and 13 of the Public Service Modernization Act), in place of the former 'Public Service' and 'public service of Canada' in the older, now repealed legislation. Other comparable terminology used and defined in legislation include 'public sector' (e.g., Conflict of Interest Act, S.C. 2006, c. 9, s. 2; Public Sector Compensation Act, S.C. 1991, c. 30; Public Servants Disclosure Protection Act, S.C. 2005, c. 46) and 'federal institution' (Official Languages Act, R.S.C. 1985, c. 31 [4th Supp.]).

4. A better appreciation of these matters may be gleaned from the Canada Public Service Agency's Population Affiliation Report, www.psagency-agencefp.gc.ca/pas-srp/overview-apercu_e.asp, which lists more than 300 'departments, agencies, Crown Corporations and other Government of Canada entities'.
5. S.C. 2006, c. 9.
6. *R. v. Eldorado Nuclear Ltd.*, [1983] 2 S.C.R. 551 at 562.
7. Letters Patent 1947. See R.S.C. 1985. Appendices, No 31. See www.efc.ca/pages/law/cons/Constitutions/Canada/English/LettersPatent.html.
8. Based on constitutional convention, the role of the Queen's Privy Council for Canada is performed by current Ministers of the Government of Canada who sit as a committee of Council, more familiarly known as the cabinet: see Halliday (1959: 229); Mallory (1971: 67–8).
9. See note 3.
10. R.S.C. 1985, c. P-34.
11. It is worthy of note that neither the current term 'federal public administration' nor its predecessor 'public service of Canada' has ever been defined by federal legislation. Nevertheless, included among the factors that have been applied to help assess whether an organization is part of the 'public service of Canada'/'federal public administration' are: (1) Is it an agent of the Crown? This test signifies a close association or nexus between the organization and the Government of Canada and a significant degree of control over the organization by the Crown; (2) Is it listed in any of the schedules of the Financial Administration Act? Inclusion in such a schedule reflects a parliamentary intention to subject the listed organizations to central agency control in financial administration, human resources, and public property; (3) Does it depend for its operations on public moneys appropriated by Parliament? (4) Does legislation expressly deem an office-holder or employee of a particular organization 'to be employed in the federal public administration for the purposes of the Government Employees Compensation Act and any regulations made under section 9 of the Aeronautics Act? That express statutory language of inclusion gives rise to an inference that in the absence of such a provision the organization in question would not be part of the 'federal public administration'.
12. Supra note 1.
13. R.S.C. 1985, c. A-16.
14. S.C. 1997, c. 9.
15. R.S.C. 1985, c. I-11.
16. Sec. 227 of Federal Accountability Act, adding s. 1.1 to Salaries Act, R.S.C. 1985, c. S-3.
17. E.g., see s. 15 of the Department of Industry Act, S.C. 1995, c. 1.
18. S. 67(j) of the Pest Control Products Act, S.C. 2002, c. 28.
19. E.g., *Steve Dart Co. and D.J.Duer & Co.*, (1974) 46 D.L.R. (3d) 745 (F.C.T.D).
20. See http://canadagazette.gc.ca/partII/2007/20071231-c/html/index-e.html.
21. See www.tbs-sct.gc.ca/ri-qr/processguideprocessus_e.asp.
22. *Black v. Chrétien* (2001), 199 D.L.R. (4th) 228 at para. 25 (Ont.C.A.). In contrast with 'Dicey's broad definition', Blackstone limits true prerogative powers to those which are peculiar to the Crown, a definition that in principle excludes those rights and authority of the Crown which the Queen, who is both a natural person and a corporation sole, may exercise as such. That authority would include making contracts, acquiring and disposing of property, and making gifts.
23. *R. v. Criminal Injuries Compensation Board ex p. Lain*, [1967] 2 Q.B. 864.
24. See *Canada Gazette*, Part 1, 11 June 1988, pages 2226–7.
25. 11 & 12 Geo. 5, c. 7 (UK).
26. Generally speaking, this type of body is illustrated by the traditional unincorporated trade union that as a result of a certain degree of statutory recognition is elevated to the status of 'a legal entity'. See *Berry v. Pulley*, [2002] 2 S.C.R. 493 at paras. 46 and following.
27. E.g., Canadian Intergovernmental Conference Secretariat, Canadian International Development Agency, and Office of Infrastructure of Canada.
28. SOR/2003–419.
29. It was not until S.C. 2005, c. 34, was enacted that legislation formally 'established' this Department.
30. SOR/2003–421.

31. SOR/2003–422.
32. SOR/2003–423.
33. R.S.C. 1985, c. P-34.
34. E.g., conferring 'exclusive' authority on a Minister or Crown agency: sec. 29(1) of Public Service Employment Act; sec. 10(2) of Defence Production Act, R.S.C. 1985, c. D-1.
35. Sec. 2(a).
36. S.C. 2005, c. 38.
37. SOR/2003–431; P.C. 2003–2059.
38. SI/2003–214; P.C. 2003–2061.
39. SOR/2003–433; P.C. 2003–2062.
40. SI/2003–215; P.C. 2003–2063.
41. SI/2003–216; P.C. 2003–2064.
42. SI/2003–217; P.C. 2003–2065.
43. Sec. 3(1).
44. Secs. 16 to 28.
45. As well as the Population Affiliation Report (see note 3 above) and the Public Accounts of Canada.
46. Only for purposes of section 29.1 and 42 and Parts VIII and X of the Act are departmental corporations apparently singled out.
47. Section 3(1) (b).
48. Section 3(5). Insofar as the Financial Administration Act is concerned, the distinction between the two Parts appears to be recognized only by sections 123 and 130.1 of the Act.
49. S.C. 2003, c. 22, ss. 12, 13.
50. 2005, c. 46.
51. R.S.C. 1985. c. A-1.
52. R.S.C. 1985, c. P-21.
53. See *Canada (Information Commissioner) v. Canada (National Defence)* 2008 FC 766, 19 June 2008.
54. See para. IV of 1947 Letters Patent of Governor-General, supra note 15.
55. In the case of so-called junior ministers whose statutory role is usually to 'assist' another, more senior, minister, legislation may be quite explicit that he or she 'shall make use of the services and facilities of the department . . . concerned' (Ministries and Ministers of State Act (R.S.C. 1985, c. M-8, sec. 12; Department of Foreign Affairs and International Trade Act, R.S.C., 1985, c. E-22, sec. 5; Department of Human Resources and Skills Development Act, S.C. 2005, c. 34, sec. 18(4).
56. Royal Commission on Financial Management and Accountability (Lambert Report, 1979) at 175.
57. *Brown v. PSC*, [1975] F.C. 345 at 348–9 (C.A.).
58. *Wimpey Western Ltd. v. Director of Standards and Approvals of the Department of the Environment* (1983), 2 D.L.R. (4th) 309 (Alta. C.A.).
59. Sec. 24(2) of the Interpretation Act, R.S.C. 1985, c. I-21, s. 24, as amended by S.C. 1992, c. 1, s. 89; *Carltona, Ltd. v. Commissioners of Works*, [1943] 2 All E.R. 560 (C.A.).
60. See below at page 12.
61. Ss. 15(1) and 24.
62. Ss. 7(1) (e), 11, 11.1 and 12 of the Financial Administration Act. See para. (a) of the definition of 'deputy head' in s. 11(1) of the FAA.
63. Ss. 31 and 34(1).
64. Ss. 33(1) and 34(1).
65. See generally, Osbaldeston (1989).
66. See new Part I.1 of the Act, enacted as s. 259 of the Federal Accountability Act, S.C. 2006, c. 9.
67. Supra note 22.
68. Reflecting the seminal English Court of Appeal decision on the issue: *Carltona, Ltd. v. Commissioners of Works*, supra note 22.
69. See Henderson, (1963: 28–35).
70. 37 Geo. III, c. 3 (UC).
71. Romney, Mr. Attorney: The Attorney General for Ontario in Court, Cabinet, and Legislature, 1791–1899 (1986 Osgoode Society).
72. Ircc, Report on Independent Administrative Agencies (1985, No. 26). See also Ircc, Working Paper on Independent Administrative Agencies (1980, No. 25). See Benidickson (1991).

73. S.C. 1852, c. 24, s. 3. See generally Privy Council Office, Submissions to the Royal Commission on Financial Management and Accountability (1979).

74. S.C. 1899, c. 10, s. 4.

75. S.C. 1908, c. 57, s. 1.

76. At 269.

77. Chap. 16.

78. At 269.

79. Chaps. 18 to 20.

80. Ircc, Report on Independent Administrative Agencies (1985, No. 26). See also Ircc, Working Paper on Independent Administrative Agencies (1980, No. 25).

81. See Appendix A of Report at page 81.

82. Long antedating these officers, the Auditor General of Canada serves as a precedent for the manner in which they have been established.

83. See sec. 54 of Access to Information Act (R.S.C. 1985, c. A-1); sec. 53 of Privacy Act (R.S.C. 1985, c. P-21); sec. 49 of Official Languages Act (R.S.C. 1985, c. 31 (4th Supp.); sec. 81 of the Parliament of Canada Act (R.S.C. 1985, c. P-1, as am. S.C. 2006, c. 9, s. 28).

84. E.g, Speaker of the Senate.

85. Supra note 9.

86. Federal Court of Appeal, Federal Court, Court Martial Appeal Court and Tax Court.

87. At 269.

88. Sec. 21(1) of Interpretation Act, R.S.C. 1985, c. I-21.

89. See Canada (1977: 15).

90. S.C. 1998, c. 10.

91. S.C. 1992, c. 5

92. E.g., Business Development Bank of Canada, S.C., 1995, c. 28; Export Development Act, R.S.C. 1985, c. E-20; Canadian Commercial Corporation Act, R.S.C. 1985, c. C-14.

93. Canada Mortgage and Housing Corporation Act, R.S.C. 1985, c. C-7.

94. Canada Deposit Insurance Corporation Act, R.S.C. 1985, c. C-3, Farm Credit Canada Act, S.C. 1993, c.14.

95. E.g., Economic Development Agency of Canada for the Regions of Quebec Act, S.C. 2005, c. 26; Western Economic Diversification Act, R.S.C.1985, c. 11 (4th Supp.).

96. Canadian International Development Agency and the Office of Infrastructure of Canada.

97. E.g., Canada Post Corporation, Federal Bridge Corporation Limited, Blue Water Bridge Authority, Atomic Energy of Canada Limited, and the Royal Canadian Mint.

98. Canadian Food Inspection Agency Act, S.C. 1997, c. 6.

99. In certain areas of government activity, legislation and Treasury Board policies have tried to enhance 'effectiveness and efficiency' as between ministerial departments, by recognizing that the expertise that field of government activity. So, for example, the Department of Justice is considered to have the exclusive mandate to conduct the Crown's litigation (sec. 5(d) of the Department of Justice Act, R.S.C. 1985, c. J-2); and the Minister of Public Works and Government Services has exclusive jurisdiction to procure goods for other departments, as well as the Armed Forces (sec. 9 of the Department of Public Works and Government Services Act, S.C. 1996, c. 16; sec. 10(2) of Defence Production Act, R.S.C. 1985, c. D-1). Treasury Board's Common Services Policy (www.tbs-sct.gc.ca/pubs_pol/dcgpubs/TB_93/csppsc01_e.asp#_Toc147652578) recognizes certain Common Services Organizations which other departments may be required (Appendix E), or have the option (Appendix F), as the case may be, to use or obtain a specific service.

100. Canada Revenue Agency Act, S.C. 1999, c. 17, s. 14.

101. As defined in section 83(1) of the Financial Administration Act.

102. Which are all listed in Schedules I.1, II, IV and V of the Financial Administration Act.

103. Listed in Schedule III.

104. See note 88.

105. Sec. 105.

106. Sec. 108.

107. Sec. 114.

108. R.S.C. 1985, c. N-5.

109. Sec. 8 of the Modernization Act, S.C. 2003, c. 22.

110. Defined in section 11(1) by reference to organizations in Schedules I, IV, and V, including others designated by the Governor-in-Council.

111. Defined as an organization in Schedule V.

112. Defined as organizations in Schedules I and IV.

113. See note 9 supra.

114. See section 11.1(1) of the FAA.

115. Section 29(1) of the Employment Act (S.C. 2003, c. 22, sec. 12).

116. R.S.C. 1985, c. A-17.

117. *Communities Economic Development Fund v. Canadian Pickles Corp.*, [1991] 3 S.C.R. 388 at 402.

118. *Dunsmuir v. New Brunswick*, 2008 SCC 9, paras. 28–30.

119. S.C. 2006, c. 9.

120. http://epe.lac-bac.gc.ca/100/206/301/pco-bcp/commissions/sponsorship-ef/06–03–06/www.gomery.ca/en/phase2report/index.asp.

121. Bill C-2, 1st Session, 39th Parliament: www2.parl.gc.ca/HousePublications/Publication.aspx?DocId=2334012&Language=e&Mode=1.

122. President of the Treasury Board introducing the Bill on 2nd reading (H.C. Debates 25 April 2006).

123. See, for example, Tait (1996).

124. S.C. 2006, c. 8, s. 2.

125. S.C. 2004, c. 7, s. 4.

126. S.C. 2006, c. 9, s. 121.

127. S.C. 2005, c. 46.

128. 'Reprisal' under the Act is basically any adverse action taken against a public servant because he or she has initiated or participated in an act of whistle-blowing.

129. Now s. 1.1 of Salaries Act.

130. Population Affiliation Report: www.psagency-agencefp.gc.ca/pas-srp/report-rapport_e.asp?cat=k.

References

Benidickson, Jamie. 1991. 'The Canadian Board of Railway Commissioners: Regulation, Policy and Legal Process at the Turn-of-the-Century', *McGill Law Journal* 36, 4: 1222–81.

Canada, Privy Council Office. 1977. *Crown Corporations: Direction, Control, Accountability.* Ottawa: Privy Council Office.

Halliday, W.E.D. 1959. 'The Executive of the Government of Canada', *Canadian Public Administration* 2 (December): 229–41.

Henderson, Edith. 1963. *Foundations of English Administrative Law.* Cambridge, Mass.: Harvard University Press.

Mallory, J.R. 1971. *The Structure of Canadian Government.* Toronto: Macmillan.

Osbaldeston, Gordon. 1989. *Keeping Deputy Ministers Accountable.* Toronto: McGraw-Hill.

Romney, Paul. 1986. *Mr. Attorney: The Attorney General for Ontario in Court, Cabinet, and Legislature, 1791–1899.* Toronto: University of Toronto Press.

Tait, John. 1996. *A Strong Foundation: Report of the Deputy Minister Task Force on Public Service Values and Ethics.*

The Canadian Accounting Officer: *Has It Strengthened Parliament's Ability to Hold the Government to Account?*

Alan Gilmore

Since 1866, the British have regarded the permanent secretaries (the equivalent of deputy ministers) of UK government agencies as accounting officers. British government documents state that **accounting officers** have 'personal responsibility for the overall organization, management, and staffing of the department and for department-wide procedures'.[1] They must ensure that 'standards of financial management are high, and they have a particular responsibility to see that appropriate advice is tendered to **ministers** on all matters of financial propriety and regularity and more broadly as to all considerations of prudent and economical administration, efficiency and effectiveness and value for money'.[2] Accounting officers 'answer personally to the Committee of Public Accounts on these matters, within the framework of Ministerial accountability to Parliament for the policies, actions and conduct of their departments'.[3]

After a long confusing debate Canadians have their own Accounting Officers. The **Federal Accountability Act** received Royal Assent on 12 December 2006. The Act is touted by the government as strengthening accountability.[4] One of its chief means of achieving this objective is to designate **deputy ministers** and deputy heads of agencies as 'accounting officers' for their organizations.[5] But what did Canadians really get? While the title is the same, just how similar is the Canadian accounting officer to his or her British namesake? To draw any conclusions, it is necessary to review the history of the debate in Canada and to critically examine the Canadian version of the accounting officer.

The British accounting officer came into being after a long battle for parliamentary control over the public purse in the United Kingdom. The first major steps towards establishing government financial accountability to Parliament were taken in the 1860s. William Gladstone, Chancellor of the Exchequer from 1859 to 1866, led the reform movement. His 1866 Exchequer and Audit Departments Act established a 'circle of financial control' for public funds: the House of Commons would authorize expenditure, accounts would be produced by departments and audited by the UK Comptroller and Auditor General and the results of the audits would be reviewed by a dedicated parliamentary committee, the Committee of Public Accounts (PAC), which Gladstone also established in 1861.[6] Starting in the 1870s, senior officials, usually permanent departmental secretaries, testified at PAC meetings. In 1920, the Treasury Department recommended, and the PAC adopted, the procedure of designating permanent secretaries as accounting officers.[7]

Why Did this Evolution Not Occur in Canada?

The Consolidated Revenue and Audit Act, 1878 was one of the earliest Canadian attempts to control the public purse. The Act required deputy heads and others charged with the expenditure of public money to audit the accounts accurately.

In practice, each department developed its own bookkeeping system, many of which were unreliable. This led to increasing calls for reform.

Not surprisingly, one recommendation was to adopt the British accounting officer concept, which placed greater responsibility and accountability on the shoulders of deputy ministers and vested review authority with the PAC. Instead, the government chose, through the Consolidated Revenue and Audit Act, 1931 to centralize responsibility in a Comptroller of the Treasury, responsible to the Minister of Finance. In his classic work, *The Public Purse*, Professor Norman Ward concluded that this occurred because the Canadian Public Accounts Committee was inactive and maintained a total silence during the debate (Ward, 1951: 166).

The steep rise in spending during and after World War II led to calls for a new framework for financial control. The government's response was the **Financial Administration Act**, 1951. It replaced the Consolidated Revenue and Audit Act, 1931 but continued the centralized approach to accounting and auditing.

In 1962, the Report of the Royal Commission on Government Organization (Glassco Commission) said it was time 'to let the managers manage'.[8] Seven years later, in 1969, the Government amended the Financial Administration Act, creating a decentralized system of accounting and auditing, similar to the system created in 1878. The position of Comptroller of the Treasury was abolished, and deputy ministers were given some of the same administrative responsibilities as the UK accounting officer. However, they remained accountable to ministers without the protections afforded to permanent heads in the UK should they disagree with ministers.

Eight years later, in 1975, the issue was raised again as a result of the Auditor General's report. The report concluded that Parliament—and indeed the government—had lost, or was close 'to losing, effective control of the public purse'. In part, this was the result of deputy heads neglecting their financial control statutory responsibilities given them in 1969. To address this issue the report proposed adopting the British accounting officer concept.[9]

The importance of the issues raised by the Auditor General led to yet another Royal Commission, the Royal Commission on Financial Management and Accountability (Lambert Commission.) Its 1979 report recommended that the deputy ministers be held accountable for departmental management before the PAC.[10] But the government pre-empted the Lambert Commission report in 1978 and re-created the position of **Comptroller General** within the Treasury Board. The Comptroller General was to act as chief financial officer. While the title sounded similar to those of the past, the authority was very different. The office focused on developing financial and management policies; it had no control over expenditures. (In 1993, the office was combined with the position of Secretary to the Treasury Board. It has recently been re-established as a separate entity for the third time.)

The Privy Council Office Position[11]

Since at least 1977 the **Privy Council Office** (PCO), with the support of most deputy ministers, has successfully argued against adopting the accounting officer concept. In its 1977 submission to the Lambert Commission, *Responsibility in the Constitution*, the PCO argued that adopting the accounting officer concept would undermine Canada's 'classical' style of Westminster democracy. However, the PCO has never clearly explained how a practice followed in the UK since 1866 was not part of classical Westminster democracy, and how it would undermine Canada's parliamentary system, which the British North America Act, 1867 states was established 'with a Constitution similar in Principle to that of the United Kingdom'.

The PCO did recognize that the accounting officer function enabled the UK Parliament 'to scrutinize and to some extent to control the exercise of administrative authority' and to hold officials rather than ministers accountable for administration, but it concluded that this was only made possible by the non-partisan practices of the UK PAC.

The PCO appeared to have mistakenly concluded that UK accounting officers were accountable to the PAC. While accounting officers appear before the PAC on matters of administration, they do so within the framework of ministerial accountability to Parliament. The PAC has no authority to punish accounting officers. Thus, when questions infringe on policy and politics, accounting officers refer them to ministers.

This error has led to much confusion and concern in Canada about dividing deputy minister and ministerial responsibility. The PCO argued that *direct* accountability of officials to Parliament for 'administrative matters would divide the responsibility of ministers and politicize deputy ministers; result in 'unsound management' and 'artificial' distinctions between questions ministers and officials would answer'; and offend Parliament's preference for holding ministers accountable.

Recognizing the contradiction between its position and parliamentary practice, the PCO conceded that as matter of 'observation' officials were 'in a sense accountable *before* Parliament for matters of administration'. However, it argued that this situation was acceptable because if questions were related to policy or politics, officials could refer the questions to ministers, which as indicated has been the practice in the UK for over a century.

Still concerned, the PCO sought to ensure that there would be no question of deputy ministers being held accountable by Parliament, and introduced into the already obtuse debate the distinction between '**accountability**' and '**answerability**'. Accountability was defined as accounting to Parliament for how ministerial responsibilities have been carried out and problems corrected, and accepting personal consequences for any problems caused. In contrast, the duty of deputy ministers was only answerability—to inform and provide explanations to Parliament.

Continuing Concern

The accounting officer concept refused to go away. In 1985, it was raised again by the Special Committee on Reform of the House of Commons (McGrath Committee). As part of its package of reforms to strengthen the role of the House of Commons, the Committee proposed that deputy ministers be called before committees using an approach similar to the accounting officer concept (House of Commons, 1985: 20–21). While the government accepted this proposal, it did not clarify the responsibility and accountability of officials vis-à-vis ministers. This left officials in an increasingly awkward position before committees, which at times held them accountable for major problems. Alternatively, it created a situation of 'mutual plausible deniability' of accountability between ministers and deputy ministers, with each party referring the matter under review to the other.

Things became more complicated in 1989, when the Canadian Council of Public Accounts Committees developed *Guidelines for Public Accounts Committees in Canada,* which called for PACs to 'hold public servants accountable for their performance of the administrative duties and implementation activities which have been delegated to them'; and that it was 'unacceptable for them to be able to use the principle of ministerial responsibility when they are asked to account for their decisions and actions'.[12] In 1991 the Council reported that the federal PAC had implemented its recommendation.[13]

The issue of ministerial accountability continued to surface, in part because of the expanding practice of the PAC and other parliamentary committees to call senior officials to testify. The confusion caused by the half-way adoption of the UK practice led the 1996 report of the deputy minister Task Force on Public Service Values and Ethics (Tait Report) to observe that many public servants find the concept of ministerial responsibility unclear, outdated, 'just unreal', or 'meaningless'. The report concluded that because of the evolving nature of parliamentary government and the continuing confusion, it would be useful to develop a clear statement of ministerial responsibility for ministers, public servants, and the public (Task Force on Public Service Values and Ethics, 1996: 18). The 2000 **Auditor General** report on 'Values and Ethics in the Public Sector' found the government had made little progress in addressing the recommendations of the Tait report; and it endorsed the call for clarifying the accountability of ministers and officials as a prerequisite for maintaining sound values and ethics in government (Office of the Auditor General, 2000: 12, 68).

Two years later, in 2002, in response to the controversy over the management of grants and contributions in Human Resource Development Canada, the government announced an eight-point plan of action on government ethics. The plan included strengthening public service management and accountability for public funds, and mechanisms for more explicit accounting of departmental affairs by deputy ministers, possibly using the UK accounting officer as a model (Office of the Prime Minister, 2002: 12). In response to objections from current and former deputy ministers, the government rejected its own proposal and maintained the status quo in its 2002 *Guide for Ministers and Secretaries of State* (Privy Council Office, 2002: 13–14).

However, the government's June 2003 *Guidance for Deputy Ministers* appeared to take some hesitant steps towards adopting the accounting officer concept by stating that deputy ministers when requested 'should personally appear before parliamentary committees to give an account of their stewardship of the department' (Privy Council Office, 2003: s. II, p. 15). The November 2003 Auditor General Report *Accountability and Ethics in Government* highlighted the statement and discussed its implications for improving government accountability to Parliament (Office of the Auditor General, 2003: para. 2.37). Subsequently, the PCO in its December 2003 publication, *Governing Responsibly: Guide for Ministers and Ministers of State,* withdrew this possible concession and restated the PCO's 1977 position that deputies only provide information to parliamentary committees.[14]

Sponsorship Inquiry

The matter may have rested at the PCO's 1977 position if not for the accountability failures of the sponsorship program and the subsequent reports of the PAC to the House of Commons and of the **Commission of Inquiry into the Sponsorship Program and Advertising Activities** (Gomery Commission). In its 2005 *10th Report to the House of Commons*, the PAC expressed frustration with a situation where 'those with responsibility are able to avoid accountability'.[15] It recommended that to clarify responsibility and accountability 'Deputy Ministers be held to account for the performance of their duties and for the exercise of their statutory authorities before the House of Commons **Standing Committee on Public Accounts**'.[16] The House of Commons agreed with the PAC report. However, the government restated the 1977 PCO argument that ministerial and deputy ministerial responsibility and accountability was already clear.[17]

Despite the government's position, the 2006 Gomery Commission's report *Restoring Accountability: Recommendations* urged clearing up the long-standing problem of fuzzy accountability for mismanagement. The worst manifestations of this problem, according to the Commission, were displayed during its inquiry. The Commission recommended 'the Government should modify its policies and publications to explicitly acknowledge and declare that Deputy Ministers and senior public servants who have statutory responsibility are accountable in their own right for their statutory and delegated responsibilities before the Public Accounts Committee'.[18]

So, What Are Canadians Getting?

The Federal Accountability Act designates deputy ministers and heads of agencies as accounting officers. How close is the Canadian accounting officer to its British precedent?

Given past practice, the Canadian accounting officer is a step towards clarifying responsibility and accountability in the federal government. However, Canadians are clearly not getting the equivalent of the British accounting officer. It is unclear why they should have to settle for a markedly weaker model and particularly one that weakens the bedrock principle of individual ministerial accountability to Parliament. The Canadian accounting officer's responsibility and accountability is much narrower, the function's deterrence value to mismanagement is weaker, and it dilutes the principle of ministerial responsibility it was supposed to reinforce. Table 4.1 compares the responsibility and accountability of UK and Canadian accounting officers.

Unlike their UK counterparts, Canadian accounting officers don't have a 'personal

Table 4.1 Comparison of the Responsibility and Accountability of the UK and Canadian Accounting Officer

	UK Accounting Officer	**Canadian Accounting Officer**
Responsibilities	As principal accounting officers, permanent secretaries in the United Kingdom have personal responsibility for the overall organization, management, and staffing of the department and for department-wide procedures. They must ensure that standards of financial management are high, that financial systems promote the efficient and economical conduct of business and safeguard financial propriety and regularity, and that decisions on policy proposals fully take into account financial considerations. They have a particular responsibility to see that appropriate advice is tendered to ministers on all matters of financial propriety and regularity, and more broadly as to all considerations of prudent and economical administration, efficiency, effectiveness, and value for money.	The Act designates the deputy minister or head of an agency as its 'accounting officer [who] is accountable before the appropriate committees of the Senate and the House of Commons for a) the measures taken to organize the resources of the department to deliver departmental programs in compliance with government policies and procedures; b) the measures taken to maintain effective systems of internal control in the department; c) the signing of the accounts that are required to be kept for the preparation of the Public Accounts pursuant to section 64 [of the Financial Administration Act]; and d) the performance of other specific duties assigned to him or her by or under this or any other Act in relation to the administration of the department.'
Relation to Minister	If a minister contemplates a course of action that would infringe on the above matters, the accounting officer is required to object in writing and indicate that it is his or her duty to notify the Treasury and the Comptroller and Auditor General without undue delay should the advice be overruled. If ministers do proceed, accounting officers must obtain a written instruction to take the action and then inform the Treasury and the Comptroller and Auditor General. A similar course of action is expected when the issues relate to the accounting officer's wider responsibilities for administrative economy, efficiency, and effectiveness.	Where the minister and the accounting officer for a department or agency 'are unable to agree on the' interpretation or application of a policy, directive or standard issued by the Treasury Board, the accounting officer shall seek guidance in writing on the matter from the Secretary of the Treasury Board. And, where guidance is provided and 'the matter remains unresolved, the appropriate minister shall refer the matter to the Treasury Board for a decision'. The Board is required to put its decision in writing and provide the **Auditor General of Canada** with a copy.
Accounting Officer's Personal Responsibility	If the above procedure has been followed, the Public Accounts Committee holds that the accounting officer bears no personal responsibility.	[Not addressed]

(continued)

Table 4.1 (Continued)

	UK Accounting Officer	Canadian Accounting Officer
Relation to Public Accounts Committee	Accounting Officers answer personally to the Committee of Public Accounts on these matters, within the framework of ministerial accountability to Parliament for the policies, actions, and conduct of their departments.	Accounting officers are obliged to 'appear before the appropriate committee of the Senate or the House of Commons and answer questions related to carrying out of the responsibilities and the performance of the duties' described above.
	Accounting officers are required to disclose to the Public Accounts Committee instances involving propriety and regularity where they have been overruled by ministers. The Comptroller and Auditor General must report cases where ministers have overridden the accounting officers' advice on administrative efficiency, economy, and effectiveness.	[Not addressed]

Sources: United Kingdom. HM Treasury. *The Responsibilities of an Accounting Officer.* London: HMSO, 1991. Annex # 4.1. (s.5) p 2; The UK Code of Conduct and Guidance on Procedures for Ministers; Canadian Federal Accountability Act.

responsibility' and their responsibilities do not include the overall management, including staffing and department-wide procedures. Nor are they responsible for ensuring that 'standards of financial management are high' and that financial systems promote the efficient and economical conduct of business and safeguard financial propriety and regularity. In addition, they do not have a responsibility to ensure that decisions on policy proposals fully take into account financial considerations and that ministers are given advice on financial propriety and regularity and 'prudent and economical administration, efficiency and effectiveness and value for money'.

In addition, unlike their UK counterparts, Canadian accounting officers are not required and probably cannot disclose to the PAC or the Auditor General instances where their advice has been overruled by ministers. The Auditor General will only receive the decision of the **Treasury Board** (a cabinet confidence) when a minister refers a dispute to the Board. This procedure weakens the deterrence value of the accounting officer regime to prevent imprudent and improper behaviour. The number of times a UK accounting officer has actually reported disputed issues to the Treasury department, the Comptroller and Auditor General, and the PAC can be counted on one hand. However, the fact that this could happen makes for a strong deterrent. Without this deterrence the effectiveness of the proposed Canadian accounting officer function will be significantly reduced.

As noted, the role of the UK accounting officer was intended to reinforce Parliament's control over the public purse by clarifying the principle of **ministerial responsibility** through the identification of the responsibilities of the permanent secretary. The objective is to reinforce individual ministerial responsibility. In contrast, the Canadian version actually dilutes the principle of ministerial responsibility by transferring final accountability for departmental administration from the responsible minister to a group of ministers called the Treasury Board. Some may argue that because the Treasury Board makes administrative policy, referring matters for decision to the Board increases its accountability. However, the Board is not responsible for running a department; that is the statutory responsibility of the minister. Surprisingly, there has been little objection to substituting the collective accountability of Treasury Board ministers to Parliament for the direct individual accountability of the responsible minister.

The government indicated that it was adopting the accounting officer concept because 'it is vital to government accountability that, within the framework of the minister's overall responsibilities and his or her accountability to Parliament, the roles and responsibilities of deputy ministers are clear'. Given this principle, it is unclear why Canadians should have to accept a scaled down version of the UK accounting officer.

Did Canadians Get Even a Scaled-Down Version?

Subsequent to the passage of the Federal Accountability Act, the House of Commons and the government have disagreed over the meaning of the designation 'accounting officer'. Even the limited mandate given Canadian accounting officers is being contested.

In March 2007, the PCO published *Accounting Officers: Guidance on Roles, Responsibilities and Appearances Before Parliamentary Committees* which essentially stated that the Federal Accountability Act has changed nothing. The objective of the document is to 'help accounting officers understand the nature of their responsibilities' under the Act and to provide 'practical guidance for their appearances before committees of Parliament'. The document states that the accounting officer provisions only 'codify long-standing practices whereby deputy ministers appear before parliamentary committees'.[19] The 2008 *Guide for Ministers and Ministers of State* restates this position (Privy Council Office, 2008: 12–13). Taken aback by the government's approach, the PAC in the same month issued its own *Protocol For The Appearance of Accounting Officers as Witnesses Before the Standing Committee on the Public Accounts*. (Prior to issuing the protocol, the PAC had tried without success to discuss drafts of its document with the Treasury Board Secretariat.) According to the PAC protocol, accounting officers 'should ensure that financial administration in their department or agency meets the standards of compliance and prudence and probity'. The protocol asserts that accounting officers 'answer as the holders of responsibilities in their own right before the Public Accounts Committee', and that while ministers 'may provide general direction in areas where the accounting officers possess statutory responsibility, [they] cannot provide direction on specific activities in these areas'.[20]

The Chair of the **Public Accounts Committee**, Shawn Murphy, noted that the PCO was maintaining its traditional position. In an article in the *Canadian Parliamentary Review* he observed that if the PCO 'interpretation is correct, then the question that begs a response is what is the purpose of enacting [the accounting officer provisions] of the Federal Accountability Act?' (Murphy, 2007: 6). He further stated that:

> the Protocol was equally clear that accounting officers hold certain statutory and delegated authorities in their own right and that they—not their ministers—could expect the Committee to hold them—not their ministers—accountable before it for the use of these authorities (which are largely set forth in the Financial Administration Act, but are also found in the Public Service Employment Act and the Official Languages Act). Furthermore, the Protocol makes it plain that the Committee expects that even if an accounting officer is transferred to another department or agency of government, or retires, he or she can still be held for account before the Committee for decisions taken under his or her watch. (Murphy, 2007: 6)

The meaning of the 'accounting officer' designation is being worked out by parliamentary committees and the deputy ministers that appear before them. Ultimately, it will be day-to-day practice in hearings of parliamentary committees that defines the role of the Canadian 'accounting officer', and the working definition of the day will be subject to which party holds a majority on the committees, and to the partisan political interests at work. By not adopting the UK accounting officer model, the PCO may have wrought what it so fervently wanted to avoid—the politicization of deputy ministers and officials. It would have been much easier and more effective for all concerned if the UK accounting officer model and its conventions had been adopted, rather than creating a new untested and disputed position that has the potential to create further controversy in an already severely frayed system of accountability.

Important Terms and Concepts

accountability
accounting officer
answerability
Auditor General of Canada
Commission of Inquiry into the Sponsorship Program and Advertising Activities
Comptroller General of Canada
deputy minister
Federal Accountability Act
Financial Administration Act
minister
ministerial responsibility
Privy Council Office
Public Accounts Committee
Standing Committee on Public Accounts
Treasury Board of Canada

Study Questions

1. What is the purpose of creating an Accounting Officer?
2. What is the mandate of the Standing Committee on Public Accounts?
3. To whom are ministers and deputy ministers accountable?
4. Why is there a debate over deputy minister accountability?
5. What accountability failures did the Commission of Inquiry into the Sponsorship Program of Advertising Activities (Gomery Commission) find?
6. To what extent is the Federal Accountability Act addressing the recommendations of the Gomery Commission regarding deputy minister accountability?
7. Given the differences in the perspectives of the Public Accounts Committee and the Privy Council Office, how do you think the deputy ministers will act before the Committee?
8. Do you think deputy ministers should be accountable to the House of Commons for their legislative responsibilities?

Useful Websites

Privy Council Office, Reports and Publications:

www.pco.gc.ca/index.asp?lang=eng&page=information&sub=publications

Gomery Commission Report:

http://epe.lac-bac.gc.ca/100/206/301/pco-bcp/commissions/sponsorship-ef/06–03–06/www.gomery.ca/en/phase1report/index.asp

Treasury Board of Canada on Accountability Act:

www.faa-lfi.gc.ca/index-eng.asp

Reports of the Treasury Board Secretariat:

www.tbs-sct.gc.ca/reports-rapports/index-eng.asp

Auditor General of Canada:

www.oag-bvg.gc.ca/internet/English/admin_e_41.html

Canada School of the Public Service, Publications:

www.csps-efpc.gc.ca/pbp/pub/lte-eng.asp

Canadian Council of Public Accounts Committees

www.ccpac.ca/

Notes

1. United Kingdom. HM Treasury. *The Responsibilities of an Accounting Officer.* London: HMSO, 1991. Annex # 4.1. (s.5), 2.
2. Ibid.
3. Ibid.
4. Government of Canada, Federal Accountability Act, Federal Accountability Action Plan, www.faa-lfi.gc.ca/docs/ap-pa/ap-pa00-eng.asp.
5. Ibid., See section titled 'Strengthening auditing and accountability within departments', www.faa-lfi.gc.ca/docs/ap-pa/ap-pa13-eng.asp.
6. Franks (1997: 629). Also see history of the United Kingdom Audit Office, www.nao.org.uk/about_us/history_of_the_nao.aspx. For further reading on ministerial responsibility and the accounting officer see Aucoin et al. (2004); Kernaghan (2001, 2003); Good (2003); Savoie (2003); Mitchell (1997).
7. Ibid.
8. The Royal Commission on Government Organization, The Canadian Encyclopedia, http://thecanadianencyclopedia.com/index.cfm?PgNm=TCE&Params=A1ARTA0003349.
9. *Report of the Auditor General of Canada to the House of Commons (for the Fiscal Year Ended March 31, 1975).* See the *Supplement to the Annual Report of the Auditor General to the House of Commons (for the Fiscal Year Ended March 31, 1975).* Ottawa: Information Canada, 1975, para. 10.5.
10. Royal Commission on Financial Management and Accountability, *Lambert Commission, Final Report* (Ottawa: Supply and Services, 1979), Chapter 9, Recommendations 9.1 and 9.2.
11. The full position of the Privy Council Office can be found in its publication *Responsibility in the Constitution*, see Chapter VII, Constitutional Responsibility and Accountability, sections titled 'Accountability in Parliamentary Government—the Minister', and 'Accountability in Parliamentary Government—the Deputy Minister', www.pco-bcp.gc.ca/index.asp?lang=eng&page=information&sub=publications&doc=constitution/ch07-eng.htm.
12. Canadian Council of Public Accounts Committee, *Guidelines for Public Accounts Committees in Canada* (Ottawa: Canadian Council of Public Accounts Committees, 1989), s.2.6(i).
13. Canadian Council of Public Accounts Committee, *Comparative Jurisdictional Implementation Survey* (Ottawa: The Canadian Council of Public Accounts Committee, 1991), Heading No. 7.
14. See Section III.3, 'Parliamentary Committees and the Role of Departmental Officials', in *Governing Responsibly: Guide For Ministers and Ministers of State* (Ottawa: Privy Council Office, 2003), www.pco-bcp.gc.ca/index.asp?lang=eng&page=information&sub=publications&doc=ag-gr/2003/table-eng.htm.
15. See 'Conclusion' in Standing Committee on the Public Accounts Report 10, *Governance in the Public Service of Canada: Ministerial and Deputy-Ministerial Accountability*, House of Commons, Ottawa. Adopted by the Committee on 3 May 2005; presented to the House on 10 May 2005; concurred in by the House on 22 November 2005.
16. Ibid., Recommendation 2.
17. See 'Government Response to Tenth Report of the Standing Committee on Public Accounts, *Governance in the Public Service of Canada: Ministerial and Deputy Ministerial Accountability*'. Presented to the House on 17 August 2005.
18. Commission of Inquiry into the Sponsorship Program and Advertising Activities, Restoring Accountability, Ottawa, 2006, Recommendations, p. 100, Recommendation 4.
19. See 'Introduction' in Privy Council Office of Canada, *Accounting Officers: Guidance on Roles, Responsibilities and Appearances Before Parliamentary Committees*, 2007, www.pco-bcp.gc.ca/docs/information/publications/ao-adc/2007/ao-adc-eng.pdf.
20. See 'Summary of What the Protocol Means' in Standing Committee on Public Accounts, Report 13, *Protocol for the Appearance of Accounting Officers as Witnesses before the Standing Committee on Public Accounts.* Adopted by the Committee on 26 March 2007; presented to the House on 27 March 2007; concurred in by the House of Commons on 15 May 2007, www2.parl.gc.ca/content/hoc/Committee/391/PACP/Reports/RP2798921/391_PACP_Rpt13/391_PACP_Rpt13-e.pdf.

References

Aucoin, Peter, Jennifer Smith, and Geoff Dinsdale. 2004. 'Ministerial Responsibility', Part 2 in *Responsible Government: Clarifying Essentials, Dispelling Myths and Exploring Change.* Ottawa: Canadian Centre for Management Development, 25–47. Available at: www.csps-efpc.gc.ca/pbp/pub/pdfs/P120_e.pdf.

D'Aquino, Thomas, Bruce G. Doern, and Cassandra Blair. 1983. *Parliamentary Democracy in Canada: Issues for Reform.* Toronto: Methuen.

Dobell, Peter. 2000. 'Reforming Parliamentary Practice: The views of MPs', *Policy Matters* 1, no. 9.

Doern, G.B. 1977. *The Relevance and Transferability of Selected British Institutions of Financial Accountability to Canada: A Report and Briefing Document Prepared for the Royal Commission on Financial Management and Accountability.* Ottawa: Supply and Services Canada.

Finer, S.F. 1989. 'Individual Responsibility of Ministers', in Geoffrey Marshall, ed., *Ministerial Responsibility.* Oxford: Oxford University Press.

Franks, C.E.S. 1997. 'Not Anonymous: Ministerial Responsibility and the British Accounting Officers', *Canadian Public Administration* 40, 4 (Winter): 626–52.

Good, David A. 2003. *The Politics of Public Management.* Toronto: University of Toronto Press.

House of Commons. 1985. *Report of the Special Committee on Reform of the House of Commons.* Ottawa: Queen's Printer for Canada.

Huntington, Ron, MP, and Claude-Andre Lachance, MP. 1982. *Accountability: Closing the Loop.* Submission to the Special Committee on Standing Order and Procedure. November 8.

Kernaghan, Kenneth. 2001. *Ministerial Responsibility: Interpretations, Implications and Actions.* Report 4 of the Access to Information Review Task Force. Ottawa: Government of Canada.

———. 2003. *The Future Role of a Professional Non-Partisan Public Service in Ontario.* Report to the Panel on the Role of Government. Toronto: Ontario Law Reform Commission.

Manion, J.L. 1993. 'The Challenge of the New Administrative Order: Post-Modern Accountability', in *Values in the Public Service,* No. 1 in the Dewar Series, Perspectives on Public Management. Ottawa: Canadian Centre for Management Development.

Marshall, Geoffrey, ed. 1989. *Ministerial Responsibility.* Toronto: Oxford University Press.

Mitchell, J.R. 1997. 'Reply to C.E.S. Franks', *Canadian Public Administration* 40, 4 (Winter): 653–7.

———. 2006. *Authority and Accountability: Reflections on the Gomery Report.* Available at: www.SussexCircle.com/ideas.

Murphy, the Hon. Shawn, MP. 2007. 'The Appearance of Accounting Officers before the Public Accounts Committee', *Canadian Parliamentary Review* 30, 2 (Summer): 4–9.

Office of the Auditor General. 2000. 'Values and Ethics in the Public Sector', Chapter 12 in *2000 October Report of the Auditor General of Canada.* Ottawa: Office of the Auditor General of Canada.

———. 2003. 'Accountability and Ethics in Government', Chapter 2 in *2003 November Report of the Auditor General of Canada.* Ottawa: Office of the Auditor General of Canada.

Office of the Prime Minister. 2002. 'Prime Minister announces New Ethics Guidelines for The Ministry and New Appointment Procedure for Ethics Counsellor'. Ottawa: Office of the Prime Minister, June 11.

Oreskes, Michael. 2004. 'Where Does the Buck Stop? Not Here', *New York Times Weekend Review* (New York edition), March 28, section 4, p. 1.

Osbaldeston, Gordon. 1989. 'Executive Summary' in *Keeping Deputy Ministers Accountable.* London: National Center for Management Research and Development.

Pitfield, Michael. 1983. 'Bureaucracy and Parliament', speech delivered to Ottawa Kiwanis Club, 25 February.

Plumptre, Timothy. 1988. *Beyond the Bottom Line: Management in Government.* Halifax, Nova Scotia: The Institute for Research on Public Policy.

Privy Council Office. 2002. *A Guide for Ministers and Secretaries of State.* Ottawa: Privy Council Office. Available at: http://dsp-psd.pwgsc.gc.ca/Collection/CP22–65–2002E.pdf.

———. 2003. *Guidance for Deputy Ministers.* Ottawa: Privy Council Office.

———. 2008. *Accountable Government: A Guide for Ministers and Ministers of State.* Ottawa: Privy Council Office. Available at: www.pco.gc.ca/docs/information/publications/ag-gr/2008/docs/ag-gr-eng.pdf.

Savoie, Donald. 2003. *Breaking the Bargain: Public Servants, Ministers and Parliament.* Toronto: University of Toronto Press.

Schaefer, Arthur. 1999. 'A Wink and a Nod: A Conceptual Map of Responsibility and Accountability in Bureaucratic Organizations', *Canadian Public Administration* 42, 1: 5–25.

Sutherland, S.L. 1991. 'Responsible Government and Ministerial Responsibility: Every Reform is its own Problem', *Canadian Journal of Political Science* 24, 1: 91–120.

Task Force on Public Service Values and Ethics. 1996. *A Strong Foundation: Report of the Task Force on Public Service Values and Ethics.* Ottawa: Canadian Center for Management Development.

Tasse, Roger OC, QC, and Malcolm Rowe, QC. 1996. 'Ministerial Accountability', Part 1 in *Examining Key Questions,* Vol 4 of Deputy Minister Task Force on Service Delivery. Ottawa: Government of Canada.

Ward, Norman. 1951. *The Public Purse.* Toronto: University of Toronto Press.

5 The Central Executive in Canadian Government: *Searching for the Holy Grail*

Christopher Dunn

The central executive is the fulcrum of governance in the cabinet-parliamentary system. It provides leadership, coordination, and facilitation. As such, it is an appropriate focus for public administration.

First things first, however. Of what earthly good is it to study a relative handful of people so earnestly and in such depth? One answer is simple, if deceptive. First, it is part of the search for the Holy Grail. Much of this chapter is an attempt to render lessons of good governance from the massive experimentation of 11 jurisdictions and a complex world of reform of governance. Second, it also attempts to render lessons from what many, but not all, consider to be bad governance, the over-domination of the executive in Canada. It therefore examines executive dominance and alternatives to it. By necessity some of these two topics overlap in the following text.

The focus here is not on the whole of executive government, but the central executive. The **central executive** refers to the collective political and non-political elements of the executive who are engaged in generating and coordinating central policy. It can be said to include the cabinet, its committees, the Prime Minister's Office (the Premier's Office, or similar entity, at the provincial level), the Privy Council Office (Executive Council Office at the provincial level), the Department of Finance, Treasury Board Secretariat, and other relevant central agencies and central departments.

This chapter starts with an introduction to the basic machinery of cabinet governance. It investigates the constitutional position and organizational design of the federal and provincial executives, describes the various paradigmatic frameworks of the central executive, reviews what generations of observers have held to be the lesson of design of the machinery of government, and ends with a prognosis for the future.

The Constitution and the Executive

It is one of the great paradoxes of the Westminster or parliamentary system that the Prime Minister (or Premier) and cabinet exercise enormous power while they do not exist in a constitutional sense. Their roles have evolved through convention over centuries due to the exigencies of leadership and parliamentary performance in Britain and its former colonies.

The Constitution Act, 1867 does not refer to cabinets by name at either the federal or provincial levels, consistent with constitutional convention. The Act does, however, provide for their legal foundations. 'The Queen's Privy Council for Canada' is established by virtue of section 11 'to aid and advise in the Government of Canada'. Executive councils in Ontario and Quebec are created by section 63. Since these provinces were being created *de novo*, section 63 specified the composition of the initial cabinets of each: Attorney General, Provincial Secretary, Provincial Treasurer, Commissioner of Crown Lands, Commissioner of Agriculture and Public Works, with the addition of two more for Quebec, the Speaker of the Legislative Council and the Solicitor

General. The executive authorities in Nova Scotia and New Brunswick were to continue as they had existed at the Union (section 64), an arrangement duplicated in later instruments admitting British Columbia, Prince Edward Island, and Newfoundland.

Statutes creating Manitoba, Saskatchewan, and Alberta similarly established executive authorities in those provinces. Of course, section 92(1) of the 1867 Constitution dealing with amendment of provincial constitutions implied that the composition of the executive councils and indeed the structure of the executive government (save for the office of Lieutenant-Governor) was a matter of purely provincial jurisdiction. Section 45 of the Constitution Act, 1982 replaces section 92(1).

To understand cabinet government it is useful to think in terms of dichotomies: first, power and authority, and second, the dignified and efficient executive. It is also helpful to remember that the dichotomies themselves did not always exist. In the era of the autocratic monarch they were unnecessary, since the king exemplified the unity of formal and informal power structures. Over time, as the king's power became constrained by Parliament, it became necessary to distinguish between authority, the formal designation of who was enabled to perform public acts, and power, the informal political influence that made sure they got performed in the first place. A crude differentiation is to say that authority was possessed by the dignified executive and power was possessed by the efficient executive. This dichotomy between 'dignified' and 'efficient' is the simplest way to understand the structure of the federal and provincial executives. As well, each of the two executives has further subdivisions, as the Table 5.1 shows.

There is, in the dominion and provincial constitutions, a distinction between 'cabinet' and the Privy Council (or 'executive council' for the provincial executives). The **Privy Council**/Executive Council is the 'formal' or 'dignified' executive. The Lieutenant-Governor-in-Council 'shall be construed as referring to the Lieutenant-Governor of the Province by and with the Advice of the Executive Council thereof' (section 66, Constitution Act, 1867). The cabinet is the 'effective' executive in that it is the main policy-initiating and administering body and operates according to constitutional conventions that are more or less similar in all Commonwealth countries.

Table 5.1 The Executive

The Dignified Executive	The Efficient Executive
Queen	Prime Minister (Premier)
Governor-General (Lieutenant-Governor)	Cabinet
Privy Council (Executive Council)	Public Service

The executive council can be considered the provincial analogue of the Privy Council. The main difference between federal and provincial executives is that federal ministers do not relinquish membership in the Queen's Privy Council for Canada upon resignation from cabinet, although for reasons of convention ex-ministers do not participate in actual executive power. In provinces, membership in cabinet and membership in the executive council are synonymous.

First Ministers and Cabinets: Federal and Provincial Comparisons

The provincial executives are not miniature versions of their federal counterparts. They have separate and unique traditions and histories. A study of the federal and provincial cabinets is essentially a comparative search for the Holy Grail of the machinery of government. First, let us deal with some similarities between the two levels of government.

Federal and Provincial Similarities

The first similarity is that the federal and provincial governments adopted the **institutionalized cabinet** model (a highly structured cabinet, discussed later) at about the same time in the 1960s and 1970s. The instigators of the institutionalized cabinets were Pierre Trudeau (government of Canada), W.R. (Bill) Bennett (British Columbia),

Peter Lougheed (Alberta), T.C. Douglas (Saskatchewan), Duff Roblin (Manitoba), William G. (Bill) Davis (Ontario), the first government of Robert Bourassa (Quebec), Richard Hatfield (New Brunswick), G.I. Smith (Nova Scotia), Alexander (Alex) Campbell (Prince Edward Island), and Frank Moores (Newfoundland). (To make sense of the term 'institutionalization', the reader may feel compelled to skip ahead in this chapter to 'Stages of Cabinet Development'.)

A second area of similarity is the virtually identical conventional and political powers enjoyed by prime ministers and premiers. The Prime Minister (or Premier) is the sole interlocutor between cabinet and the Governor-General (or Lieutenant-Governor). Only he or she can choose cabinet ministers and hence has the power to make or break careers (Mallory, 1984: 89). The First Minister is the sole architect of the general machinery of government (cabinet size, **cabinet committees**, central agency support and procedures, and the number and roles of departments). The First Minister can advise the Governor to dissolve or prorogue the legislature. The party depends disproportionately for its electoral fortunes on the popularity of the First Minister, giving him or her a privileged bargaining chip—or alternately, a tenuous hold on power. The Prime Minister is also the prime dispenser of patronage. The First Minister enjoys the instant attention of the press and, with it, the possibility of shaping the public policy agenda. Thus, both Premier and Prime Minister have at hand the five 'P's of power: prerogative, Parliament, party, patronage, and press.

A third area of federal and provincial similarity relates to the conventions of cabinet government, most notably those involving cabinet formation, individual responsibility, and collective responsibility. Conventions dictate the process of **cabinet formation**. The Governor first appoints a Prime Minister or Premier. Whom to choose is usually obvious: in the case of a majority government, it is the parliamentary leader of the majority party. In a minority situation, the Governor has the right to consult with parliamentary leaders to ascertain which leader is likely to command a durable majority in the House. The Prime Minister or Premier then, by convention, has the sole right to advise the Governor on who shall be selected as ministers in the new government. The general practice, both federally and provincially, is to choose ministers from among those who have been elected to the House, but there are exceptions. It is possible for senators to enter the cabinet. Generally, there will only be one senator in cabinet, but in governments in which some regions have not elected enough (or any) government-side members, the number may go as high as three or four, as was the case in the Clark (1979–80) and Trudeau (1980–4) governments. As well, there are several precedents for appointing non-elected ministers—but these individuals are expected to seek election soon thereafter.[1] There are several provincial cases of non-elected officials 'temporarily' entering cabinet as well.[2]

The convention of sectional or regional representation in the federal cabinet is so basic that it has been called the fundamental characteristic of government in Canada (Mallory, 1984: 89). There is not much formal literature on the matter of regional provincial cabinet balance. However, research has determined that a similar convention indeed holds in each province (see Dunn, 2006).

Textbooks on Canadian cabinets may one day refer to a convention of gender equality in provincial cabinets. Rules regarding gender representation are still in the formative stage, and the party recruitment environments that affect this differ between regions. However, given the availability of qualified female government caucus members, the premiers of the 1990s began to make efforts to achieve increased gender balance in the cabinet.[3] The situation was about the same at the federal and provincial levels in the year 2000, as indicated in Table 5.2. By 2008, there had been marginal improvement in the proportional representation of women in five provincial cabinets from 2000 (in percentage terms from 30 to 47 in Quebec, 19 to 29 in Alberta, 23 to 28 in Ontario, 8 to 16 in Nova Scotia, and 10 to 18 in PEI); and two provinces had maintained respectable percentages (Manitoba 33 per cent both years, Newfoundland and Labrador 31 per cent in 2000, 29 per cent in 2008). Three had actually slipped

Table 5.2 Women in Canadian Cabinets, 2000 and 2008

Premier in 2008	Number of Women in Cabinet (2000 figure in brackets)	Total Number in Cabinet (2000 figure in brackets)
Stephen Harper, Canada	(8) 5	(27) 27*
Gordon Campbell, British Columbia	(8) 5	(20) 23
Ed Stelmach, Alberta	(4) 7	(21) 24
Brad Wall, Saskatchewan	(5) 4	(19) 18
Gary Doer, Manitoba	(5) 6	(15) 18
Dalton McGuinty, Ontario	(6) 8	(26) 28
Jean Charest, Quebec	(8) 9	(26) 19
Rodney MacDonald, Nova Scotia	(1) 3	(12) 18
Shawn Graham, New Brunswick	(3) 2	(15) 19, 1 MoS**
Robert Ghiz, Prince Edward Island	(1) 2	(10) 11
Danny Williams, Newfoundland and Labrador	(5) 5	(16) 17

*Does not include four Secretaries of State, two of which were men and two are women.
**Minister of State.

(BC had slipped substantially from 40 per cent in 2000 to 21 per cent in 2008; Saskatchewan from 26 per cent to 22 per cent; and New Brunswick from 20 per cent to 10 per cent). (The table does not show the 'pool' of elected government caucus members from which to choose, but in most jurisdictions it is substantial.)

Individual **ministerial responsibility** holds at the provincial cabinet level as well as the federal. The concept involves the duty of the minister to lead, to defend, and, if deemed necessary, to resign. The minister is responsible or accountable to the House for the proper leadership of a governmental department. The minister must defend his or her actions and those of his or her departmental officials; the minister bears full political and legal responsibility for officials' actions regardless of any lack of foreknowledge of them. The minister must resign for a serious breach of ethics or a serious mistake in policy, with the Premier, effectively, being the final judge. A special case of individual responsibility involves the culpability of the Finance Minister for any release of a budget prior to the official budget day; but this convention is as hard to enforce at the provincial level as it is at the federal.

Similar to the federal case, the doctrine of ministerial responsibility has proven to be hard to define in practice. Some situations are more likely to generate successful calls for the resignation of the minister, as Andrew Heard has revealed. Wrongdoing by departmental officials and administrative ineptitude appear not to constitute convincing thresholds for ministerial resignation. However, the allegation of conflict of interest and violations of the personal code of ethics of the minister appear to be more formidable reasons (Heard, 1991: ch. 3).

Collective responsibility, as Heard reminds us, has three aspects: first, the responsibility of the cabinet to the monarch, second, to itself (through cabinet solidarity and cabinet secrecy), and third, to the elected House (Heard, 1991: 62). The first is marked when the Governor loses confidence in the cabinet and asks it to resign. This, for example, occurred in reaction to political corruption in Quebec in 1891 with the Mercier government and in British Columbia in 1903 with the Prior government; and the Lieutenant-Governor threatened to do so in Manitoba with the Roblin government in 1915 unless it appointed a Royal Commission to investigate the legislative building scandal. It did.

In the second sense, provincial cabinets have made significant, if inadvertent, contributions to establishing the parameters of the venerable, once thought absolute, convention of cabinet secrecy. In *Smallwood v. Sparling* (1982) the court refused former Premier Joseph Smallwood a general injunction based on cabinet secrecy as a form of Crown immunity (or public interest immunity). The decision stated that Crown immunity is not absolute but relative, involving the balancing of injury to the public interest and injury to the administration of justice. In *Carey v. The Queen* (1986) a court ordered that Ontario cabinet documents relating to Minaki Lodge be revealed; cabinet documents, as *Sparling* had established, did not enjoy immunity as a class and must be revealed unless disclosure of them would interfere with the public interest. Cabinet secrecy is supposed to aid proper functioning of government, not improper conduct by the government. In 1988, the Nova Scotia Supreme Court, Appeal Division, maintained in favour of the Donald Marshall Inquiry that cabinet ministers could be compelled to testify about the general nature of discussions in cabinet. Provinces have even begun to follow the example of British commissions, as well as the McDonald Commission, which was the first Canadian inquiry to get access to federal cabinet papers. In 2002 Ontario's Walkerton Commission Report asserted that its mandate 'constituted a waiver of Cabinet privilege by the province' (Ontario, Walkerton Commission, 2002: 486–7). D'Ombrain shows that Walkerton 'had the effect of gaining the commission access to whatever documents it wanted subject to procedures for putting them into evidence' (D'Ombrain, 2004: 357, fn. 48). Nevertheless, disclosure of cabinet papers is the exception rather than the rule.

Collective responsibility is as much a provincial convention as a federal one. Federal governments have been forced to resign due to losing votes of confidence in 1873 (Macdonald, in the Pacific Scandal), 1926 (King, after a customs scandal), again in 1926 (Meighen, in legislative realignments after a short four days in power), 1963 (Diefenbaker, in a vote of confidence), 1974 (Trudeau, after losing a budget vote), 1979 (Clark, after losing a budget vote), and 2005 (Martin, in a vote of confidence). There have been fewer cases of governments losing the confidence of provincial assemblies, and hence fewer cases about which to theorize and to compare. A notable, somewhat bizarre case was the fall of the Howard Pawley government in Manitoba in 1988 occasioned by NDP MLA Jim Walding voting against his own government in a closely balanced budget vote.

Federal–Provincial Differences

Many of the dissimilarities between federal and provincial cabinets involve political dynamics arising from the pursuit of politics on a smaller scale. One difference is the degree to which the size of the cabinet can be and is used as a control mechanism in the provincial context. Federal cabinets regularly comprise around 10 per cent or less of the size of the Commons, whereas a much larger percentage of the provincial assembly is covered by cabinet membership. The percentage of the governing caucus covered by cabinet membership is even greater, often with more people in cabinet than there are backbenchers. These two sets of factors give a significant degree of power to the cabinet, and the Premier who appoints them, as against the backbenchers on both sides.

A second difference is that provincial cabinets are more likely than a federal one to *integrate the caucus* into a meaningful policy development role. Federal caucuses have traditionally served as the *ex post facto* sounding posts for decisions or directions made by the federal cabinet. This is also true in some provinces, but others, including British Columbia, Alberta, Saskatchewan, Manitoba, Prince Edward Island and, recently, Ontario, have made significant attempts to involve all the elected governing party members. The government of Gordon Campbell (2001–) in British Columbia has made the practice of caucus integration even more integral with the initiation of government caucus committees.

Third, there are different types of ministers at the federal and provincial levels. At the federal level, one found a distinction in the Martin government (2003–6) between the cabinet and the ministry; in the former were the traditional cabinet ministers, and in the latter were the secretaries of state as well, who are members of the Privy Council but not of the cabinet, and who, like cabinet ministers, are bound by the convention of collective responsibility. They earned three-quarters of the salary of a cabinet minister, their job being to assist ministers in specific areas of their portfolios. Stephen Harper has retained this 'in the ministry but not the cabinet' distinction but has further provided that each of the secretaries of state attend the cabinet committee meetings pertaining to their area of responsibility. They represent ministers at events, stakeholder meetings, parliamentary committees, and question periods and demonstrate policy leadership in areas specified by the PM or minister but do not preside over any area of the public service.

Provinces have varying arrays of ministers to augment the standard form of departmental minister. Quebec has had a long history of using ministers of state (Lévesque and Bourassa), delegated ministers (Bourassa), two-tiered ministers (one set of ministers for good government, another to plan for Quebec independence, under Parizeau), and 'superministers' (Lucien Bouchard). The Charest Liberal government had both traditional and new aspects. There were three types of ministers in Quebec's *conseil executif*: 'minister of' (regular line minister), 'minister for' (minister of state), and 'minister responsible for' (autonomous policy ministers). New Brunswick under Frank McKenna introduced junior ministers called ministers of state in order to develop ministerial talent. Alberta had associate ministers at various times over the last quarter century. They became less common in the new millennium. Ralph Klein had three of them in 2000, eliminated one in a 2000 reorganization, and then the other two in a 2001 reorganization. Ed Stelmach had three briefly from June 2007 to February 2008.

In Ontario, there has also been some experimentation. Premier Rae expanded upon Peterson's modest use of ministers without portfolio. Since 2000, there has been a new type of minister introduced to the Ontario cabinet system. The Harris and Eves cabinets included 'associate ministers' assigned to support a portfolio minister. These individuals were first appointed by the Lieutenant-Governor as ministers without portfolio and then named by Order-in-Council as Associate Ministers. The responsibilities could be assigned by the Premier and portfolio minister or else by an Order-in-Council, which assigned specific duties, statutory responsibilities, or both. There was one associate minister assigned at the end of the last Harris government, in 2001, and four in the Eves governments. Both Harris and Eves established the chief government whip as a minister without portfolio. Dalton McGuinty halted this pattern for five years, but finally on 20 June 2008 appointed Gerry Phillips as minister without portfolio, with responsibility as Chair of Cabinet.

Visibility is also a difference between federal and provincial cabinets. With a few exceptions, provincial cabinet ministers tend to be higher profile than their federal counterparts. This is not due to any personal failings on the federal side, but rather to reasons of scale, policy, and perception. Provincial ministers are more involved in operational matters, and are seen more often in their communities. Provincial ministers for the most part defend their departmental estimates on the floor of the legislature, whereas the federal estimates are parcelled out to committees.

Territorial Executives

While one is on the subject of inter-jurisdictional differences, one should also take a look at the territorial executives and in what ways they are similar to and different than their federal and provincial counterparts. Yukon, the Northwest Territories (NWT), and Nunavut all share certain characteristics of southern/Westminster executive forms and norms. All operate according to the principles of collective and individual responsibility. All adhere to the norms of cabinet secrecy, cabinet solidarity, and cabinet confidentiality. Some, like Yukon, also include government caucus members on cabinet committees, as some provinces do. All had premiers (in 2008 Paul Okalik, Nunavut; Floyd Roland, NWT; Dennis Fentie, Yukon) with important policy and coordination roles. As elsewhere in Canada it is possible for governments to fall.

There is even an analogue of the provincial Lieutenant-Governor in each territory, called the Commissioner. The Commissioner historically served in a more direct administrative role as the representative of the federal government, who not only chose but chaired the executive council, but the introduction of responsible government in the late twentieth century ended these practices. The Commissioner is now a symbolic figure who is chosen by the federal Governor-in-Council and who performs many of the roles of Lieutenant-Governor, with the notable exception of representative of the monarch.

There are committees. In Yukon, there is Management Board, established by statute, and Legislation; advisory committees to cabinet on social, economic, and environmental matters have been established by past governments, but not by the Fentie government. The NWT cabinet has 'ministerial committees' but not cabinet committees. All have institutionalization of their cabinets—there are principal secretaries/chiefs of staff, cabinet secretaries, deputy cabinet secretaries, cabinet secretariats, secretariat analysis of ministerial proposals, records of decisions, and so forth. Several central officials attend cabinet, as necessary.

There are central agencies as well. Central agencies support the Premier and Executive Council in making decisions and shaping policy. In Yukon, central agencies are the Executive Council Office (ECO) and a Management Board Secretariat. All cabinet submissions are in fact reviewed by a hybrid body named the Policy Review Committee (PRC), which is chaired by the Director of Policy in the ECO, but composed of policy directors from all the departments. It is actually a subcommittee of the Deputy Ministers' Review Committee (DMRC). In the NWT, several bodies are considered central agencies: Department of Executive, Financial Management Board Secretariat, and the departments of Human Resources, Finance, Justice, and Aboriginal Affairs and Intergovernmental Relations. In Nunavut the central agencies are the Department of Executive and Intergovernmental Affairs, which provides support to cabinet and policy coordination, and the Department of Finance and Administration, which provides advice on fiscal and economic management. The Department of Human Resources also has some central agency functions.

Yet there are significant differences, even between the territories themselves. The cabinet and legislature of Yukon operate on the basis of party politics, whereas NWT and Nunavut both operate as 'consensus governments'. In Yukon, each of the Progressive Conservatives (now Yukon Party), New Democrats, and Liberals have formed the government since 1979. In each of NWT and Nunavut, there is no party system and no official opposition; each candidate for office runs as an independent. The legislative assembly, acting under the authority of the Legislative Assembly and the Executive Council Act in each territory, chooses the Premier and members of the executive council by secret ballot, but ministerial assignments are made by the Commissioner in Executive Council, who acts upon the advice of the Premier. It is thus possible to be a member of executive council, in effect cabinet, but not a minister. Executive domination does not figure to the same extent as in the south, since the legislature is an active elective chamber, and the cabinet is in a minority, necessitating constant compromise with members of the Assembly and its committees. The dynamics are somewhat like those in coalition governments, but with aboriginal consensus traditions added.

Stages of Cabinet Development

Cabinets, like many other social creations, have not remained static. They have evolved from relatively small bodies with modest purposes to large institutions with a multiplicity of roles. This is the case at both the federal and provincial levels. The one characteristic, however, that unites the cabinets of all eras is that they were collective organisms, bodies that tended to make decisions in plenary form. There is now a tendency among some observers to see a pathology in modern cabinet governance: the notion that cabinet, rather than being the driver of government decision-making, is becoming (or has become) irrelevant. The First Minister now steers the ship of state, or so the theory goes.

The modes of cabinet operation have been succinctly summed up by J. Stefan Dupré. In 1985 Dupré noted that the federal and provincial cabinets had gone through three historical modes of operation, which he called the traditional cabinet, the departmentalized cabinet, and the institutionalized cabinet. The latter two were associated with greater and lesser 'workability' of executive federalism (that is, relative conduciveness to negotiation, consultation, and exchange of information among intergovernmental actors in Canada) (Dupré, 1985: 1–32). The **traditional cabinet** predominated in Canada before the rise of the administrative state, that is, at a time when the role of government was modest and executive federalism was not yet the practice, the federal cabinet being the primary mechanism of federal–provincial adjustment. The main business of cabinet ministers was to aggregate and articulate regional and local concerns, and to dispense patronage. It lasted from about 1867 to the 1920s.

The next stage was that of the **departmentalized cabinet** (1920s to 1960s). In this era, government departments and ministers were the engines of public sectoe expansion. Ministers were accorded a significant degree of decision-making autonomy and demonstrated 'portfolio loyalty'—or primary commitment to their departments—because they were judged primarily by departmentally oriented client groups and relied on departmental experts for policy formulation and implementation (Dupré, 1985: 1–5).

Some have termed the departmentalized cabinet the 'unaided cabinet', and added some characteristics. The unaided cabinet is simple in structure, with few standing committees, and features restricted collegiality (that is, limited collective decision-making and power-sharing as regards departmental policy). The Prime Minister or Premier is the architect of personnel choice and is usually, but not always, the dominant politician. There are 'central departments': departments that perform a service-wide facilitative and coordinative role but are headed by a minister other than the Premier. There are few cabinet-level staff. Budgeting has narrow aims—usually fiscal control predominates—and employs narrow means. Planning is seen as an optional rather than essential function of government. The unaided cabinet promotes a decision-making style featuring few sources of alternative advice to cabinet other than deputy ministers. Restricted collegiality is the order of the day (Dunn, 1995: ch. 1).

Beginning around the 1960s (or, in the case of Saskatchewan, the 1940s) and lasting into the 1990s, the institutionalized cabinet came to replace the unaided cabinet. This cabinet, Dupré notes, has 'various combinations of formal committee structures, established central agencies and budgeting and management techniques [combined] . . . to emphasize shared knowledge, collegial decision making, and the formulation of government-wide priorities and objectives' (Dupré, 1985). There were now 'central agency ministers' who reflected the collective concerns of cabinet and 'special interest ministers' who continued the older pattern of special interest politics.

The institutionalized cabinet, as has been noted elsewhere, has a complex cabinet structure with many standing committees and expanded collegiality (that is, greater collective decision-making and power-sharing as regards departmental policy). The Prime Minister or Premier's role is expanded to include the responsibilities of organizational architect as well as architect of personnel choice. There are now both central departments and central agencies, the latter being those service-wide facilitative and coordinative bodies directly responsible to the Prime Minister or Premier. Cabinet receives both partisan ('PMO-type') and policy/technocratic ('PCO-type') input. Cabinet-level staff are relatively numerous. Budgeting features wider aims and wider means than the control-oriented budget process of the traditional cabinet. Planning is still considered optional by cabinet, but there is generally more recourse to it. A 'planning-budgeting nexus', or explicit link between the two functions, is common. There are alternative sources of information to cabinet other than the responsible minister and his or her deputy. Decision-making is more centralized in the structured cabinet. Cabinet makes a wider range of decisions and central bureaucrats monitor departments to a greater extent. Not surprisingly, there is almost constant tension between the centre and the departments (Dunn, 1995).

Several writers have contended, implicitly or explicitly, that the days of the institutionalized cabinet have ended. Rand Dyck says that the Chrétien government had 'reverted to the St Laurent model of a departmental cabinet in which individual ministers and departments were allowed to look after their own affairs. The maze of cabinet committees was reduced, as was the scope of many other coordinating central agencies. Departments were allowed more leeway in moving funds from one program to another as long as they did not exceed their overall allotment' (Dyck, 1996: 493–4). Similarly, Peter Aucoin saw elements of the earlier phases of cabinet development in the Chrétien government—collegial, conglomerate, command, and corporate—but says that the Prime Minister, judging from the cabinet/ministry model he introduced, clearly leaned towards the conglomerate model (Aucoin, 1995: 189). The conglomerate model was essentially the same as the departmentalized cabinet that Dupré describes. 'The modern equivalent of this mode of cabinet government finds expression in efforts since the mid-1980s to decentralize decision making from cabinet and cabinet committees (and thus the central policy and management agencies of government) to individual ministers and their operational departments' (Aucoin, 1995: 183). Cabinet was restricted to performing strategic planning and resolving interministerial conflicts.

Donald Savoie's *Governing from the Centre* (1999) was the most extensive critique of the institutionalized model then mounted. Savoie argued that the cabinet decision-making process (i.e., institutionalized cabinet process), which was designed to be a collective one, and specifically managed as such by central agencies, now 'belonged' to the Prime Minister and was emphatically not a collective one. It was not even a case of a *retour en arrière*: 'the days of the departmental Cabinet, when individual ministers "were very much in charge of government decision making" as it applied to their own departments are clearly over, and have been since the 1970s' (Savoie, 1999: 325).

In the current phase of cabinet history, Savoie says, power shifted away from the ministers and their departments towards the centre, and at the centre, away from cabinet and cabinet committees to the Prime Minister and his senior advisers. Cabinet committee decisions are rarely challenged in the plenary cabinet, but this does not imply cabinet minister power, the chairs of these committees being hand-picked, process-oriented choices of the Prime Minister. Central agencies, rather than being neutral facilitators of collective decision-making, are now engaged as actors in the process itself, as extensions of the Prime Minister. Comprehensive policy agendas gives way to the Prime Minister governing by 'bolts of electricity'—a handful of key objectives he pursues and pushes through the system. In pursuing these priorities, the First Minister, Finance Minister, and central agencies essentially make the decision-making system a bifurcated one: there is one set of rules for the (nominal) 'guardians' like the Prime Minister, Finance Minister, and President of the Treasury Board (whose major job traditionally was to protect the public purse) and the 'spenders' (who traditionally tried to evade them). The priority programs of the guardians sail through with little difficulty, whereas those of regular line ministers are subject to the regular cabinet committee decision-making process, where they are subject to the contending wishes of other ministers and the control of the central agencies (that is, the Prime Minister) and seldom emerge as their drafters originally intended. What is involved, Savoie says, is widespread institutional failure. The relevance of Parliament is even further cast in doubt; the power and influence of cabinet are threatened; the media have become actors, not narrators; and the public service has become an instrument for protecting the interests of the Prime Minister.

Nearly a decade later, Savoie was making a somewhat similar argument about 'court government' (or prime minister-centred government) the difference being in degree of centralization (Savoie, 2008). The cabinet had become marginalized in a context that could only be characterized as resembling a (presumably medieval) court government. Cabinet government in both Canada and the UK has been moved away from by stealth and 'all but destroyed' (Savoie, 2008: 229). 'Individuals now rule, starting with the Prime Minister and his most trusted courtiers, carefully selected ministers, and senior civil servants, and they have more power in a court-style government than they do when formal policy and decision making processes tied to cabinet decision making are respected' (Savoie, 2008: 230). Instead of a collective ethos ruling, there is differentiation of status within cabinet. 'Ministers now have to learn to work with the prime minister's court more than they have to learn to work with cabinet and cabinet colleagues' (Savoie, 2008: 238).

The contrast between the unaided (departmental), institutionalized, and court government or a Prime Minister-centred cabinet is presented in Table 5.3.

The blanket characterization of cabinet governance as Prime Minister-centred needs to be tempered. The design of government is remarkably personalistic. First ministers come and go. Chrétien perceived himself hindered by the offshoots of the Trudeau institutional cabinet—excessive use of ministerial time, excessive paperwork, weakening of strong ministers (Chrétien, 1994: 84)—but a future Prime Minister unencumbered by such personal experiences, and taking a team approach, may revert to the institutional approach. Paul Martin, successor to the centralist Chrétien, had a more inclusive mode of governing. Martin, with nine, had more cabinet committees than Chrétien ever had, and garbed them with important policy and financial management roles; included parliamentary secretaries as privy councillors; created new secretariats and roles in the PCO; and juxtaposed these arrangements with a new democratic action plan for Parliament which was nominally aimed at lessening executive domination. This was institutionalization redux. Even the same first minister might reverse him- or herself. Glenn (2001) says the Harris government in Ontario first decreased, then increased, cabinet institutionalization. Of course, Martin was followed by the hyper-centralist Harper, but this probably speaks to a notion of a rhythm of centralization giving way periodically to a more collective cabinet.

Ian Loveland reminds us that such a rhythm has been the case in the UK. There has been some support for Crossman's thesis (Crossman, 1975: 77) that most of cabinet had to go along with decisions taken by the 'inner cabinet'. Cases include Clement Attlee concealing his atomic weapons policy from cabinet, James Callaghan directing economic policy by his 'Economic Seminar', Margaret Thatcher bypassing her first cabinet and its 'wet' ministers, and Tony Blair governing in a 'command and control' style. Yet there were cases of collective governance: Harold Wilson made significant use of cabinet committees in decision-making, and John Major also shifted to a collective cabinet (Loveland, 2006: 321–6). By 2008, even Gordon Brown, having been one half of the Blair–Brown 'duopoly' that dominated cabinet government, found himself as a Prime Minister beset by bad polls, tolerating an end to ministerial submissiveness (Richards, 2008). Could there be lessons for Canada in all this?

At the federal level, a more nuanced perception is warranted. David A. Good in this volume and elsewhere analyzes budget behaviour from the perspective of stylized roles rather than from institutionalized organizations. Good notes that the so-called 'spender–guardian dichotomy' is outmoded, and that public spending in the federal government is actually affected by four sets of actors. 'Spenders' are generally spending ministers (and occasionally the Prime Minister and Finance); 'guardians' are Finance and Treasury Board; priority setters are the Prime Minister, PMO and PCO; and the principal watchdog is the Office of the Auditor General (OAG), to which has been added the new Harper-created watchdogs—the Parliamentary Budget Officer, the chief audit executive in each department, accounting

Table 5.3 The Unaided, Institutionalized, and Prime Minister-Centred Cabinet

Unaided or Departmental Cabinet	Institutionalized Cabinet	Court Government (Prime Minister-Centred Cabinet)
Prime Minister and Cabinet		
Personnel choice by First Minister Dominant First Minister Restricted collegiality Simple cabinet structure	First Minister now has two jobs in the institutionalized cabinet (IC): personnel choice plus design of the machinery of government Greater collegiality Complex cabinet structure	Same two jobs as in the IC; but PM now has policy-making role in any dossier as well Dominant First Minister who holds court Cabinet is a discussion forum and not a decision forum Cabinet structure streamlined, less complex It is not clear what types of decisions require collective Cabinet deliberation; PM and his 'courtiers' (carefully selected ministers and senior civil servants) pick and choose their issues at will
Central Agencies		
Central departments Few cabinet staff Little cabinet-level analysis	Central agencies as well as central departments More cabinet staff Extensive cabinet-level analysis	Same central bodies Large numbers of staff in Prime Minister's Office and central agencies develop ideas and provide extensive central agency analysis for PM's pet projects and purposes Proposals they are not interested in are subject to extensive, slow, porous, and consultative (often intergovernmental) decision-making process The civil service, beset with conflicting demands, has 'lost its way'
Budgeting and Planning		
Budgeting centralized Major role played by First Minister Budgeting aim: mostly control Budgeting means: traditional (annual budget cycle)	Budgeting collegial Budgeting aim: broader than control Budgeting means: both traditional and political/off-budget controls Planning: still optional, but where practised is collective, comprehensive	Not much mention is made by Savoie of internal governmental budget decision-making, but there are hints that practices revealed in the 1999 book still hold: Budgeting centralized under the PM and Finance Minister Most priorities made by PM and court, with cabinet deciding matters of lesser importance Planning not a noticeable feature

(continued)

Table 5.3 (Continued)

Unaided or Departmental Cabinet	Institutionalized Cabinet	Court Government (Prime Minister-Centred Cabinet)
Planning: optional, but either project-oriented or indicative Short-term coordination by First Minister or Finance Minister	Planning-budgeting nexus (balance, complementarity of the two functions)	There is little attention to the traditional 'challenge' function of the bureaucracy and presentations of options is no longer standard practice No mention of the 1999 book's guardian/spender dichotomy and its two sets of rules: one for 'guardians' (no collective constraints) and one for 'spenders' (collective constraints)
Decision-Making Modes		
Hierarchical channels of policy advice, from senior officials to the cabinet with no competing sources Decentralized decision-making: departmental autonomy favoured over power of the central executive	Alternative channels of policy advice for cabinet and committees Centralized decision-making: power of the central executive favoured over departmental autonomy	Nothing happens in Canadian (and UK) governments without a 'strong central push'. Centralized decision-making, meaning the PM's power, is favoured over that by full cabinet, line ministers, and the federal bureaucracy. 'Horizontal government' makes it difficult for ministers to influence policy. Policy advice and briefing are primarily for the PM and his delegates; media play an inordinately influential role. The centre, instead of line ministers, announces new policies and initiatives, because the latter lack profile and the policies would go unnoticed. The majority of cabinet documents are now prepared by consultants rather than by the bureaucracy.

Source: Abstracted and modified from Dunn (1995, 1998) and Savoie (1999, 2008).

officers in each department, an independent procurement officer, and a Public Sector Integrity Commissioner. The watchdogs exercise a kind of cautionary control of public spending. All have different interests, but guardians and priority setters have, despite their differences, arranged to combine to control the effects of spenders and watchdogs (Good, 2007: 294).

The nuances involve discerning where observers coincide in their views and where they do not. Both Savoie and Good, for example, agree that cabinet and its committees have ceased to have an effect on budget priorities and spending decisions. Both agree that there are a limited set of priorities annually and that these are centrally determined. Both would agree with Good that 'priority setters who can stand apart and above the day-to-day scrimmages between the spenders and guardians can have considerable influence not only in shaping shifts in fiscal directions but also in determining the priorities to be included within the budget' (Good, 2007: 116).

However, the Ottawa that Good describes seems to be a different place than Savoie's Ottawa. In Good's view, departments are not as dominated by the centre as Savoie indicates; if they do their homework, develop a clientele, 'think like guardians', and develop ties to key sectoral and regional ministers, they may convince the Prime Minister to adopt their concerns as priorities—witness Kyoto-related activity in the Liberal era. One of the major differences is that Savoie, having been one of the major popularizers of Schick's spender–guardian dichotomy in earlier writings, now does not even mention it in his 2008 book on court government. Good, on the other hand, uses the dichotomy skilfully, seeing the 'old village' where it applied superseded by the 'new town' of complex four-way multilateral relationships. This allows Good to highlight where the centre is weak—for example that one of the guardians, Treasury Board, is now virtually a non-actor because of its lack of control over the departmental A-bases and decades of decentralization of management prerogatives to departments. It also allows him to emphasize the 'challenge function' of the PCO, which sees itself as a 'counter-balance' willing to challenge the spending proposals of both Finance and the departments, and occasionally even of the PM, to weed out risky proposals and to make sure that the policy is needed, costed, workable, and likely to be effective (Good, 2007: 109–10). There is not much mention of challenges to the centre in Savoie.

The Provinces and the Institutionalized Cabinet

Whether or not the provinces have passed beyond institutionalization to a new phase of cabinet evolution is a natural question, given the ferment in academic coverage of the federal scene. Any response will have to be tentative because of the lack of new research on provincial cabinets.

One the one hand, there are some indications that the degree of provincial institutionalization has decreased. Diminished numbers of cabinet committees were characteristic from the 1970s to the 1990s. In British Columbia, Premier Bill Vander Zalm had 12 committees. At the beginning of the Harcourt administration there were eight; in September 1993, the number was further reduced to five. In Alberta, Ralph Klein reduced the total number of committees to five, including Treasury Board. In 1990, New Brunswick and Nova Scotia each had five cabinet committees; by 1995 they and PEI got by with only two committees, Policy Board (Policy and Priorities in New Brunswick) and Board of Management (Treasury Board in PEI). The later Bourassa government of Quebec, like the Lévesque government before it, had several standing (or permanent) committees; the latter covered legislation, regional development, economic development, social development, and greater Montreal (Lachapelle et al., 1993: 241–4). The Parizeau government reduced the number of committees to four: a (reactivated) Priorities Committee, the Treasury Board (retained), the Legislation Committee (retained), and a special committee for greater Montreal.

On the other hand, there are some clues that many provinces have remained in the institutionalized phase, with meaningful recognition given to the collective nature of executive decision-making:

- *Academic reviews of provincial cabinets.* Some academics see Savoie's picture replicated at the provincial level,[4] but several do not. Graham White, for example, does not believe in the myth of the autocratic First Minister in Canada, especially at the provincial level, and quotes several Premiers to that effect (White, 2001). The concept of collegiality can exist within the administration of an influential Premier. What some outside observers may see as autocratic behaviour by a First Minister may be misleading. Even Ontario, which some authors gave as an example of a Premier-centred executive in the 1990s, in fact oscillated between institutionalized and Premier-centred patterns. The determining factor in the Mike Harris years, between June 1995 and March 2002, contends Ted Glenn, was the Premier's assessment of the state of the economy and the deficit (Glenn, 2005). The last Progressive Conservative cabinet, under Eves, had a plethora of cabinet committees. Of Quebec, Bernier says, the power of the Premier has been seriously attenuated since the 1960s because of the tendency for the governing parties to turn against Premiers who are electoral liabilities and for PQ governments to be riven by intra-party and intra-caucus challenges (Bernier, 2005). Dunn says the strong Premier tradition of Newfoundland was mitigated by the tendency of Premiers to lose influence the longer they stayed in office (Dunn, 2005), although the Williams government has not been yet studied. In Saskatchewan, maintain Rasmussen and Marchildon, the legacy of the institutionalized cabinet continues to be a powerful presence and that there endured for over half a century an 'institutionalized legacy'—three poles of influence. 'These three cabinet committees—the Planning Board, the Government Finance Office and the Treasury Board—and their central agency support structures, formed a planning troika that has remained an enduring feature of the Saskatchewan system' (Rasmussen and Marchildon, 2005: 191).

- *Static or growing numbers of cabinet committees*. When surveyed in 1995, 1998, 2004, and 2008, the provincial cabinets revealed a tendency towards even more structure. There were static or growing numbers of cabinet committees between 1995 and 2008. Four provinces had increased the numbers of committees, three had retained the same number of committees, and only three (Saskatchewan, Manitoba, and Newfoundland and Labrador) had reduced the numbers. Of these three, Manitoba and Newfoundland and Labrador still had numerous cabinet committees, at six and five respectively. Table 5.4 shows the evidence.
- *Internal cabinet hierarchy*. One of the historical tendencies of federal and provincial institutionalized cabinets was towards a hierarchy in the committee structure. Whereas this may not in and of itself reveal collegiality, it demonstrates that the Premier has to share authority with at least a handful of fellow ministers, and is therefore

Table 5.4 Numbers of Provincial Cabinet Committees, 1995–2008

	Number of Cabinet Committees			
Province	**1995**	**1998**	**2004**	**2008**
British Columbia	4 (and 4 'working groups')	5 (and 3 'working groups')	5	8
Alberta	8	10	10	10
Saskatchewan	6	9	5	3
Manitoba	12	7	6	6
Ontario	8 (and 2 subcommittees)	4 (and 4 subcommittees)	8	8
Quebec	4	7	5	6
New Brunswick	2	2	6	6
Nova Scotia	5	1	1	5
Prince Edward Island	2	3	5	3
Newfoundland and Labrador	6	6	5	5

Sources: Dunn (1998, 2006); Privy Council Office (1998); Correspondence with Clerks of the Executive Councils, February–June, 2008; Provincial Executive Council Websites, accessed June 2008.

not the only power in cabinet. All provinces in both 1995 and 1998, except Manitoba, had some version of the planning and priorities type of cabinet committee. These committees characteristically regroup all the most powerful ministers in cabinet and include the chairs of the standing committees of cabinet. To some extent the existence of cabinet committees implies power dispersion as well as functional necessity. In 2008, there were still priorities committees in Quebec, Alberta, Saskatchewan, and Newfoundland and Labrador.

- *The use of deputy premiers.* While not perhaps a hallmark of institutionalization per se, the practice of having deputy premiers became a fixture of most provincial cabinets in the 1990s, after having earlier started in central Canadian provinces. Deputy premiers are not merely administrative conveniences; progressively, they have become more institutionalized actors whose presence denotes another power centre in cabinet. They can therefore further the power-distribution effects of cabinet institutionalization.

What Have We Learned from Experiments with the Central Executive?

Students of Canadian public administration and political scientists have poured an inordinate amount of time into the study of the central executive. Not all have explained why. This chapter suggests that the metaphor of the Holy Grail is useful when trying to explain the fascination with the subject. The notion of attaining a satisfactory decision-making structure is irrepressibly attractive, but always seems beyond discovery by ordinary mortals. Even though they may not enunciate this goal most people study the central executive to search for this particular grail.

This literature leaves one impression above all: the contradictions. At one point cabinet committees were not very acceptable, and later they were quite acceptable for dealing with the complexities of public policy. At first committees were not supposed to be garbed with decision-making powers, ostensibly to safeguard collective responsibility, then they were, even to the extent that collective cabinet came to make few real decisions. Individual ministerial autonomy was once highly prized, then it was an inconvenience to be offset by the collective authority of cabinet committees. The control culture of central agencies, especially that of Treasury Board, was stifling initiative and entrepreneurialism, then when Treasury Board gave too much control to departments, this was bemoaned. Some suggested that there be an uncommitted majority in cabinet, by keeping numbers in cabinet committees small; others called for an involvement by most in cabinet on committees, to the extent that there were sometimes a dozen committees. Some First Ministers felt compelled, often by regionalism, to have large cabinets; others were compelled by the dictates of austerity to have smaller ones. For every Savoie who says that dominant First Ministers are the problem, there is a Bakvis or a White saying that the problem is overrated, as are the needs for exaggerated reforms. Even Savoie feels at the beginning of the decade that cabinet government can be salvaged, only to despair of the notion at the end of it, and calling for the PM's role to be fixed instead. What is one to make of all this?

In some ways such contradictions are to be expected. The design of the central executive is largely (although not entirely) a prerogative of the First Minister. And consistency, as Ralph Waldo Emerson said, is the hobgoblin of little minds: first ministers often bring a great deal of creativity, hence variation, to the design of government and it would be a surprise if they all thought alike.

Another reason it might be expected is that over time, the stages of evolution of cabinet have occurred in tandem with those of stages of the party system (Table 5.5). This is because a cabinet system is not only about managing policy, but also about managing parties, within parliament and without. Some cabinet forms and practices are more useful in certain times than they are in others.

The traditional cabinet has always been described as little more than a forum for log-rolling and other political deals, and this makes it a good fit for the patronage-oriented first party system. The strong regional ministers who are the backbone of the second party system find it convenient not to be disturbed in their departmental bailiwicks so important in the departmental cabinet era, and if there is interchange in cabinet, it is in the context of regional brokerage politics prevalent in this era. The leader-directed, pan-Canadian, regional development policies of the third party system take central planning and coordination, and this is what the institutionalized cabinet promises to deliver. To make it clear that the regions have not been forgotten, the makeup of the cabinet and central agencies takes on a moderately regional hue.

In the fourth stage, the multiparty system ushered in by the election of 1993, it becomes apparent that the traditional parties, the New Democratic Party included, have been unable to accommodate the new regional power centres. It becomes important to be more strategic and to have focused policies and programs to offset and destabilize multiple political enemies. This is exactly what Chrétien did, and Harper does, in the central executive. This is what Martin did not do, and lost. Eddie Goldenberg says of Chrétien, 'He saw his own policy role as focusing on a few priorities that he viewed as crucial to the government agenda' (Goldenberg, 2006: 72). The Prime Minister designs a small set of priorities with a view to establishing or re-establishing regional and demographic coalitions. To the extent they insist on these, they are branded as running 'prime ministerial' cabinets. And so it is that one can expect differences in lessons over the eras, since the world the Prime Ministers and cabinets are facing are themselves different.

Table 5.5 Canadian Party and Cabinet Systems

Party Systems	Cabinet Systems
1. Two-party system: cadre parties, patronage and corruption 1867–1917	Traditional 1867–1920s
2. Two-party-plus system: cadre parties, brokerage politics, strong regional ministers 1917–1958	Departmental 1920s–1960s
3. Three-party system: rise of pan-Canadian appeals, primacy of leader, leader directs regional economic development 1958–1993	Institutionalized 1960s–early 1990s
4. Multiparty system: some regional strongholds for parties 1993–present	More Prime Minister-centred 1993–present

The lessons that are put forward in each era can be seen as reflections of the values of that particular era. Most eras sought to regain a balance that had been lost. The departmental cabinet prized ministerial initiative and departmental expertise, and ignored the importance of cabinet-level coordination. The institutionalized cabinet, on the other hand, prized coordination and saw the need for a system of central-departmental counterweights. However, as the system matured, it was perceived to be increasingly dysfunctional: too many ministers, departments, and cabinet committees; too much interest-group influence; but too little policy coherence, regionally sensitive input, and attention to cost control. The apparent concern in the Prime Minister-centred era is that the pendulum has swung too far towards the power of the First Minister and that, if counterweights are to be constructed, they should in fact be put in place against him or her as formal, institutionalized roles for the PM, Parliament, parties, and departments. Provincial reviews see this as less of a problem and tend to see maintaining the collective aspect of decision-making as the main challenge.

To the extent that prime-ministerial government is deemed problematic, there are cures provided. Three major categories of literature speak to the subject. First there are those who perceive the problem as Parliament's role being overshadowed by the executive, and propose measures to bolster the former's status. Others suggest that the problem is the Prime Minister's domination within the executive, and propose balancing reforms within government restructuring of the public sector bargain. Others also see the problem as being executive centred, but propose measures that balance power between government and society.

Federal and provincial jurisdictions can learn from the experiences of each other. For the federal government, the lessons from the provincial governments are that the demise of the institutionalized cabinet may be premature; that Ottawa is notoriously inward-looking and it is useful to learn from provincial experience with central decision-making processes; that pragmatism and personalities must be taken into consideration in cabinet decision-making processes; and that there is room for caucus involvement in the work of cabinet. For the provincial governments, the lessons from the federal government have to do with enhancing the policy capacity of the central executive and encouraging policy communities that transcend the boundaries of government.

For all the contradictions and inconsistencies however, there are enduring principles, as our review of the lessons of federal and provincial government have taught us. They amount to a distillation of the wisdom of the Westminster system.

- The engagement of the First Minister is a necessary part of the success of government's policy initiatives.
- Cabinet functions best when it functions collectively, dominated by neither the First Minister nor departmental visions, but rather by a collective vision, collectively generated.
- The job of cabinets and central agencies is to maintain the integrity of the decision-making process, namely, to facilitate the disinterested, open-minded consideration of available public policy options.
- Policy coherence entails both horizontal coordination (not being constricted by departmental boundaries) and vertical coordination (involving provincial and regional officials in the policy-making process).
- The departments are normally the repository of policy and implementation expertise and should be allowed leeway by central agencies, but pragmatically, in proportion to their relative expertise.

The points above are not therefore radical propositions, but reiterations of decades of experience of cabinet-parliamentary systems. In another sense however they are a wakeup call to those promoting prime-ministerial government. To the extent that this form of government is a problem—and the jury is still out on that one—these principles offer a rebuke to the centralization that such government implies. Prime-ministerial government violates the principles of procedural fairness and threatens to undermine the legitimacy of the political system. This is the message of the chief of staff of a US domestic policy council, as well as research by Tyler: 'Individuals who felt that they played a role in the decision-making process were more accepting of the outcome, regardless of its nature…Those who felt that the process was biased, or that their views were not being considered by those responsible for policy development, were more apt to exit from the formal decision-making process and evade its decisions' (Tyler, 1990: 163; Shambaugh and Weinstein, 2003: 8–9).

In a sense, we have come full circle in the examination of the central executive. Seeking new lessons in governance from experimenting in the machinery of government, governments and their attentive publics have discovered the canons of cabinet government that were there all along. The job of First Ministers is to lead; the job of cabinets is to deliberate; and the job of officials is to help both to do their jobs. It is not the grail, but it is advice that will have to do until we find it.

Acknowledgement

Information for a small portion of this chapter came from Dunn (1996). Permission to use this was received from Broadview Press/University of Toronto Press and is gratefully acknowledged.

Important Terms and Concepts

cabinet committees
cabinet formation
central executive
collective responsibility
departmentalized cabinet
institutionalized cabinet
ministerial responsibility
Privy Council
traditional cabinet

Study Questions

1. What is the difference between the 'dignified executive' and the 'efficient executive'?
2. Are federal and provincial cabinets more alike than they are different?
3. Considering the various models of cabinet development, which one best describes the current state of the federal central executive? What proof can you offer?
4. Assess the model of cabinet development currently in operation in your province.
5. Review some guidelines that have been offered for successful cabinet operations, and assess if they are realistic or not.
6. Are there in fact grounds for drawing connections between the party systems and cabinet evolution?

Useful Websites

Canada. Privy Council Office. 2007. *Accountable Government: A Guide for Ministers and Secretaries of State.*

http://pm.gc.ca/grfx/docs/guidemin_e.pdf

The Prime Minister of Canada:

www.pm.gc.ca

The Privy Council Office:

www.bcp-pco.gc.ca/index.asp?lang=eng

The Treasury Board and its Secretariat:

www.tbs-sct.gc.ca/home_e.html

Blondel, Jean. 1990. 'Types of Party System', in Peter Mair, ed., *The West European Party System* (Oxford: Oxford University Press): 302–10.

http://janda.org/c24/Readings/Blondel/blondel.html

Christian, William. 'Party System', in The Canadian Encyclopedia online:

www.thecanadianencyclopedia.com/index.cfm?PgNm=TCE&Params=A1ARTA0006128#SUBReadings

Notes

1. Between 1867 and 1984, 76 people entered the federal cabinet who were neither MPs nor senators (Heard, 1991: 49). The most recent examples have been Michel Fortier, appointed Minister of Public Works and Government Services in February of 2006; Brian Tobin, Minister of Industry in October 2000; Stéphane Dion, Minister of Intergovernmental Affairs, January 1996; and Pierre Pettigrew, Minister for International Co-Operation, January 1996. A few weeks after entering the cabinet, Fortier was made a 'temporary' appointment to the Senate on the condition that he step down and run in the next general election. Tobin was subsequently elected in the general election of 2000 and the latter two in March 1996 by-elections. For a complete list of outsiders entering the federal cabinet, see the Parliamentary Information site (PARLINFO) found at www2.parl.gc.ca/parlinfo/Compilations/FederalGovernment/OutOfParliamentMinisters.aspx?Language=E.

2. Newfoundland, British Columbia, and Quebec can be used to demonstrate provincial cases. Joseph R. Smallwood of Newfoundland chose the then-unelected Clyde Wells, John Crosbie, and Alex T. Hickman for his cabinet in 1966 and all three successfully won seats in the general election of September of that year. In 1971 the mayors of St John's and Corner Brook, William Adams and Noel Murphy, were elevated to cabinet directly from the mayoralty. Ed Roberts entered the Wells cabinet in February 1992 and was subsequently elected in a by-election in June of that year. Since 1882 there have been 15 unelected people appointed to BC cabinets. An 'outsider' had not been appointed since 1952 when Bill Vander Zalm was appointed Premier and Finance Minister in August 1986. He went on to win seat in a general election two months later. In October 2000 Premier Ujjal Dosanjh appointed Grand Chief Edward John, a former Carrier-Sekani Tribal Council chief, to his cabinet (Canadian Press Newswire, 2000). The list of people made cabinet ministers before being elected in Quebec is long: Premier Jean Lesage chose Eric Kierans for Labour Minister; Jean-Jacques Bertrand picked Jean-Guy Cardinal as Education Minister; Robert Bourassa selected Claude Castonguay to Health and Jean Cournoyer to Labour; and René Lévesque made Francine Lalonde the Status of Women Minister. Pierre-Marc Johnson chose four civilians (Louise Beaudoin, Jean-Guy Parent, Lise Denis, and Rolande Cloutier) for his cabinet in 1985 (Lachapelle et al., 1993: 240).
3. In October 1990, Premier Bob Rae of Ontario chose 11 women for his 26-member cabinet; in a February 1993 shuffle the number of women remained the same while the size of cabinet was reduced to 20. The first Harcourt cabinet in BC in November 1991 included seven women in an 18-member cabinet and featured a woman deputy premier, Anita Hagen. Premier Roy Romanow of Saskatchewan chose four women for his slimmed-down 'war cabinet' in November 1991, and in 1993 chose the first woman Finance Minister in Canadian history. In Quebec, the Jacques Parizeau cabinet of September 1994 had only five women out of 19 ministers but there was male–female equality on the Government Priorities Committee. (Later there was approximate equality. The Government Priorities Committee at the time of the referendum in 1995 had seven members: Jacques Parizeau, Bernard Landry, Guy Chevrette, Jean Campeau, Louise Harel, Louise Beaudoin, and Pauline Marois.) The May 1995 election in Manitoba saw five women elected on the government side; Premier Filmon appointed three to cabinet and one to the Speaker's chair.
4. A minority of contributors to the Bernier et al. book *Executive Styles in Canada* (2005) adopt what might be called the 'Savoie perspective'. The evidence on the other side is mixed. Norman Ruff says that BC's Liberal government under Gordon Campbell has a different administrative style than its Premier's Office-dominated predecessors. 'If there is a newly emergent BC administrative style', he says, 'it is that of a "corporate collegiality" facilitated by the shared political mandate which must be referenced by every cabinet member and that in turn informs the sweeping Core Services Review and the rolling three year Strategic Plans begun in 2002'. He also notes that there has been a growth of somewhat fragmented central departments and central agencies. Despite this collegial aspect, Ruff saw a counter tendency: 'Beneath its organizational jigsaw, British Columbia had many of the characteristics of what Dunn has described as a post-institutionalized cabinet with an increase in the already considerable concentration of power within the Office of Premier at the expense of Cabinet'. In a similar vein, Keith Brownsey maintains that the institutional cabinet once dominated in Alberta, but its reign was restricted to the eras of Peter Lougheed (1971–85) and Don Getty (1985–92).

References

Aucoin, Peter. 1986. 'Organizational Change in the Machinery of Canadian Government: From Rational Management to Brokerage to Brokerage Politics', *Canadian Journal of Political Science* 19, 1: 3–27.

———. 1994. 'Prime Minister and Cabinet', in James P. Bickerton and Alain-G. Gagnon, eds, *Canadian Politics*, 2nd edn. Peterborough, Ont.: Broadview Press, 267–87.

———. 1995. 'The Prime Minister and Cabinet', in Robert M. Krause and R.H. Wagenberg, eds, *Introductory Readings in Canadian Government and Politics*. Toronto: Copp Clark, 169–92.

———, and Herman Bakvis. 1988. *The Centralization–Decentralization Conundrum: Organization and Management in the Canadian Government*. Halifax: Institute for Research on Public Policy.

———, and ———. 1993. 'Consolidating Cabinet Portfolios: Australian Lessons for Canada', *Canadian Public Administration* 36, 3: 392–420.

Bagehot, Walter. 1867. The English Constitution. 1963 Edition. London: Fontana.

Bernier, Luc. 2005. 'Who Governs in Quebec? Revolving Premiers and Reforms', in Bernier et al. (2005).

———, Keith Brownsey, and Michael Howlett, eds. 2005. *Executive Styles in Canada: Cabinet Structures and Leadership Practices in Canadian Government.* Toronto: University of Toronto Press.

Blakeney, Allan, and Sandford Borins. 1992. *Political Management in Canada.* Toronto: McGraw-Hill Ryerson.

Campbell, Colin, and George J. Szablowski. 1979. *The Superbureaucrats: Structure and Behaviour in Central Agencies.* Toronto: Macmillan.

Canada. 1990. *Public Service 2000: The Renewal of the Public Service of Canada.* Ottawa: Government of Canada.

Canada. Privy Council Office. 2007. *Accountable Government: A Guide for Ministers and Secretaries of State.* Available at: http://pm.gc.ca/grfx/docs/guidemin_e.pdf.

Canadian Press Newswire. 2000. 'Chief Edward John brings aboriginal experience to BC Cabinet', 1 Nov.

Chrétien, Jean. 1994. *Straight from the Heart.* Toronto: Key Porter Books.

Crossman, Richard Howard Stafford. 1975–7. *The Diaries of a Cabinet Minister.* Three volumes (*v1. Minister of Housing, 1964–66; v2. Lord President of the Council and Leader of the House of Commons, 1966–68; v3. Secretary of State for Social Services, 1968–70).* London: Jonathan Cape.

D'Ombrain, Nicholas. 2004. 'Cabinet Secrecy', *Canadian Public Administration* 47, 3: 332–59.

Dunn, Christopher. 1995. *The Institutionalized Cabinet: Governing the Western Provinces.* Montreal and Kingston: McGill-Queen's University Press.

———. 1996. 'Premiers and Cabinets', in Dunn, ed., *Provinces: Canadian Provincial Politics.* Peterborough, Ont.: Broadview Press, 165–204.

———. 1998. 'The Utility of the Institutionalized Cabinet', in Paul Barker and Mark Charlton, eds, *Crosscurrents: Contemporary Political Problems.* Toronto: ITP Nelson, 244–63.

———. 2005. 'The Persistence of the Institutionalized Cabinet: The Central Executive in Newfoundland and Labrador', in Bernier et al. (2005).

———. 2006. 'Premiers and Cabinets', in Dunn, ed., *Provinces: Canadian Provincial Politics*, 2nd edn. Peterborough, Ont.: Broadview Press, 215–54.

Dupré, J. Stefan. 1985. 'Reflections on the Workability of Executive Federalism', in Richard Simeon, ed., *Intergovernmental Relations*, vol. 63 of the Research Studies for the Royal Commission on the Economic Union and Development Prospects for Canada. Toronto: University of Toronto Press, 1–32.

Dyck, Rand. 1996. *Canadian Politics: Critical Approaches*, 2nd edn. Toronto: Nelson Canada.

Glenn, Ted. 2001. 'Politics, Leadership, and Experience in Designing Ontario's Cabinet', *Canadian Public Administration* 44, 2: 188–203.

———. 2005. 'Politics, Personality and History in Ontario's Administrative Style', in Bernier et al. (2005: 155–70).

Goldenberg, Eddie. 2006. *The Way it Works: Inside Ottawa.* Toronto: McClelland and Stewart.

Good, David A. 2007. *The Politics of Public Money: Spenders, Guardians, Priority Setters, and Financial Watchdogs in the Canadian Government.* Toronto: University of Toronto Press.

Heard, Andrew. 1991. *Canadian Constitutional Conventions: The Marriage of Law and Politics.* Toronto: Oxford University Press.

Heeney, Arnold. 1972. *The Things That Are Caesar's: Memoirs of a Canadian Public Servant.* Toronto: University of Toronto Press.

Lachapelle, Guy, Gérald Bernier, Daniel Salée, and Luc Bernier. 1993. *The Quebec Democracy: Structures, Processes and Policies.* Toronto: McGraw-Hill Ryerson.

Loreto, Richard, and Graham White. 1990. 'The Premier and the Cabinet', in Graham White, ed., *The Politics and Government of Ontario.* Toronto: Nelson Canada.

Loveland, Ian. 2006. *Constitutional Law, Administrative Law, and Human Rights.* Oxford: Oxford University Press.

McIlroy, Anne. 2000. 'Rock's grand plan was news to the PM: Health Minister's home-care program shared with the media before the PMO staff read it', *Globe and Mail*, 4 March, A3.

Mallory, J.R. 1984. *The Structure of Canadian Government*, rev. edn. Toronto: Gage Publishing.

Matheson, W.A. 1976. *The Prime Minister and the Cabinet.* Toronto: Methuen.

Ontario. Walkerton Commission of Inquiry. 2002. *Report: Part One: The Events of May 2000 and Related Issues.* Toronto: Queen's Printer.

Osbaldeston, Gordon. 1989. *Keeping Deputy Ministers Accountable.* Toronto: McGraw-Hill Ryerson.

———. 1992. *Organizing to Govern.* Toronto: McGraw-Hill Ryerson.

Parliament of Canada 2008. 'Ministers Named from Outside Parliament'. Available at: www2.parl.gc.ca/parlinfo/Compilations/FederalGovernment/OutOfParliamentMinisters.aspx?Language = E.

Privy Council Office. 1998. *Decision-Making Processes and Central Agencies in Canada: Federal, Provincial and Territorial Practices.* Ottawa: Privy Council Office.

Rasmussen, Ken, and Gregory P. Marchildon. 2005. 'Saskatchewan's Executive Decision-Making Style: The Centrality of Planning', in Luc Bernier, Keith Brownsey, and Michael Howlett, *Executive Styles in Canada: Cabinet Structures and Leadership Practices in Canadian Government.* Toronto: University of Toronto Press.

Richards, Steve. 2008. 'Gordon Brown Cannot Stand Alone in the Storm—He Needs His Cabinet', *The Independent.* 29 April.

Roberts, Alasdair. 1997. 'Worrying About Misconduct: The Control Lobby and the PS 2000 Reforms', *Canadian Public Administration* 39, 4: 489–523.

Robertson, Gordon. 1971. 'The Changing Role of the Privy Council Office', *Canadian Public Administration* 14: 487–508.

Royal Commission on Financial Management and Accountability (Lambert Commission). 1979. *Final Report.* Ottawa: Supply and Services Canada.

Royal Commission on Government Organization (Glassco Commission). 1962. *Report.* Ottawa: Queen's Printer.

Royal Commission on the Economic Union and Development Prospects for Canada (Macdonald Commission). 1985. *Report*, 3 vols. Ottawa.

Savoie, Donald. 1999. *Governing from the Centre: The Concentration of Power in Canadian Politics.* Toronto: University of Toronto Press.

———. 2008. *Court Government and the Collapse of Accountability in Canada and the United Kingdom.* Toronto: University of Toronto Press.

Schacter, Mark, with Phillip Haid. 1999. *Cabinet Decision-Making in Canada: Lessons and Practices.* Ottawa: Institute on Governance.

Shambaugh, George E., and Paul J. Weinstein. 2003. *The Art of Policy Making: Tools, Techniques and Processes in the Modern Executive Branch.* New York: Longman.

Stewart, Edward E. 1989. *Cabinet Government in Ontario: A View from Inside.* Halifax: Institute for Research on Public Policy.

Trudeau, P.E. 1968. *Federalism and the French Canadians.* Toronto: Macmillan.

Tyler, Tom. 1990. *Why People Obey the Law.* New Haven, Conn.: Yale University Press.

White, Graham. 2001. *Cabinets and First Ministers.* Vancouver: University of British Columbia Press.

Young, Walter D., and J. Terence Morley. 1983. 'The Premier and the Cabinet', in Morley et al., *The Reins of Power: Governing British Columbia.* Vancouver: Douglas & McIntyre, 45–81.

Parliament and the Public Service

Paul Thomas

Introduction

Parliament's relationship to the public service is not a widely examined aspect of Canada's political system. In general, relations between **Parliament** and the **public service** are informal, indirect, changeable, and often characterized by mutual wariness. The nature of the relationship derives from three main sources: a set of constitutional principles which are largely unwritten; a limited number of statutory provisions; and the dynamic context of the wider political system, particularly the nature of the issues before government and the state of party competition during a particular time period.

With limited recognition for the role of the public service in constitutional and statutory law, its relations with Parliament have been mainly based on the changing interpretation of a series of unwritten constitutional conventions. These conventions were derived from the parliamentary experience of the United Kingdom and were adopted in Canada in the latter part of the nineteenth century when the activities of government were limited and the public service was a small, largely unprofessional entity. As the public sector expanded and became more complicated during the twentieth century, Parliament found it difficult to cope with the rise of a sprawling administrative apparatus wielding growing power. There were from time to time expressions of concern about potential conflicts between bureaucracy and democracy, but for many decades Parliament changed little in terms of its structures and procedures to cope with the increased volume and complexity of public policy and public administration.

In the 1960s Parliament took some steps to strengthen its scrutiny of the public service, mainly by creating a more extensive and active committee system. While progress has been made during the four decades, the task of providing comprehensive and in-depth review of the use of bureaucratic power has at the same time become more difficult as governments have experimented with new approaches to the design and delivery of public programs.

This chapter examines the two issues of how public bureaucracies can be held accountable through the parliamentary process, and how this task has been complicated by a series of public service reforms over the past two decades. The discussion proceeds as follows. First, the historical and constitutional context in which Parliament developed its relations with the bureaucracy is discussed. Second, a number of interrelated functions of Parliament are identified. The review of existing policies and the surveillance of administrative performance are tasks that compete with other, more politically rewarding activities. Third, five roles played by Parliament in relation to the public service are identified. Fourth, the aims and impediments to the conduct of a more thorough parliamentary review of the activities of the public service are discussed. Finally, the chapter speculates on Parliament's future relations with the public service in light of recent reforms within government and possible future developments.

The chapter focuses on the Parliament of Canada. In popular usage, Parliament refers to the 308 members of the House of Commons, but the institution also consists of the 105 members of the Senate and the Governor-General as the representative of the Crown. In terms of legislative authority, the Senate is almost coequal to the House of Commons in the sense that all bills must be approved by the upper chamber. However, the fact that senators are appointed by the Governor-General on the recommendation of the Prime Minister and serve until the age of 75 means that the Senate lacks democratic legitimacy. As patronage appointees, senators from the governing party seldom challenge government positions. Senate critics, of whom there are many, insist that partisanship has seriously compromised the original role of the Senate as a voice for regional concerns. From the beginning of the country the Senate has been the target of reform efforts but it remains unchanged in its fundamental features.

Still the Senate is not, as its harshest critics suggest, a completely useless institution. In terms of the focus of this chapter, the Senate, mainly though its committee system, has conducted valuable reviews of the ongoing policies, programs, and operations of departments and non-departmental bodies. While the remainder of the chapter focuses mainly on the House of Commons, it also includes a brief discussion of the Senate's oversight role.

Any discussion of Parliament as if it were a unified institution is misleading. Several divisions exist within Parliament. The most important dividing lines are between political parties. All important aspects of Parliament's organization and procedures are dominated by the fact of competition among disciplined political parties. Under the fused cabinet-parliamentary model, the cabinet is a part of Parliament. It represents the leadership of the governing party, which usually holds a majority of the seats in the Commons. Most of the initiative in terms of bills, spending proposals, and other business comes from the government and it seeks to exert tight control over the agenda and proceedings of Parliament. Opposition parties are expected to debate government proposals and to expose flaws in the government's performance. Most of the ideas, energy, and intensity of parliamentary life come from the adversarial process of parties competing for public support. Nearly all issues tend to be viewed and acted upon on the basis of partisanship, not an objective or neutral search for the truth.

While the clash between the government and the opposition represents the main division within Parliament, there are also disagreements within parties on matters of substance and process. Such disagreements are expressed mainly in the privacy of party caucuses, which meet on a weekly basis when Parliament is in session. Intra-party divisions can be along ideological, policy, and regional lines, as well as between the parliamentary leadership of each party and its backbench followers. In summary, notwithstanding constitutional rhetoric to the contrary, Parliament seldom acts on a collective basis, all members of Parliament are not equal, and not all of them wish to see the institution strengthened, if this means a loss of cabinet control or a reduction of the prominence of the party leadership in its proceedings. How Parliament approaches its dealings with the bureaucracy and its success in providing oversight of bureaucratic performance are significantly affected by these inter- and intra-party dynamics.

Provincial governments operate on the same principles of cabinet-parliamentary government as the government of Canada and these principles play a major part in shaping the role of provincial bureaucracies. However, it would be wrong to generalize from the national level to the provincial level about relations between legislatures and public services. Each province represents a distinctive history, set of political traditions and cultures, patterns of party competition, and contemporary political dynamics. Most provincial political systems are much smaller than the national political system, including the size of the bureaucracies involved. Other important differences between the national and the provincial political systems include: some provinces have experienced long periods of one-party rule;

cabinets often represent a more domineering presence in **provincial legislatures**; control over nearly all aspects of legislative life is considered a prize for winning power; procedural, organizational, and staff resources to ordinary legislators tend to be limited; legislative sessions are typically shorter; committee systems are less extensive and active in the smaller provincial legislatures; there are no upper houses at the provincial level; and, in terms of the themes of this chapter, there is more political control by the cabinet at the provincial level over the public service (White, 2006). We cannot conclude from these characteristics that provincial legislatures never exert control or influence on governments and public services. Generally, however, provincial legislatures face even greater political and procedural obstacles than does the House of Commons in holding ministers and public servants accountable on an ongoing basis. The remainder of the chapter focuses on the relations between Parliament and the public service at the national level.

The Constitutional Context

The level of bureaucratic accountability achieved within any political system is a function of numerous factors. **Accountability** refers to an obligation to explain and to justify how an individual or an institution discharges its responsibilities, the origins of which may be constitutional, political, hierarchical, or contractual (Thomas, 2008). There is not the space here to analyze the different types and mechanisms of accountability that have emerged within the Canadian political system. Suffice it to say that accountability has become a dynamic, multi-faceted process and that public servants, in a given set of circumstances, may face a number of competing accountability requirements.

The starting point for an understanding of accountability is the Constitution. The Canadian Constitution consists of both legal rules and political conventions (Heard, 1991). Both sets of provisions are meant to be binding upon politicians and public servants. Constitutions promote the rule of law by setting forth the parameters of public power, describing the relationships that ought to exist among the various institutions of government, and defining the relationships between individuals and the state. By doing this, constitutions are meant to protect and to promote the rule of law, which means, in simple terms, that no one, no matter how important or powerful, is above the law, and this includes the government and the bureaucracy.

Important parts of the Canadian Constitution consist of unwritten conventions that have emerged from long-standing political practices. These constitutional conventions vary in the extent to which they are seen as morally binding on ministers, parliamentarians, public servants, and others in public life. Although recognized by the courts, conventions must be enforced through political rather than legal processes. Given the unwritten and non-legal nature of conventions and the fact that we live in a cynical age, many Canadians believe that politicians and public servants cannot be trusted to accept responsibility for breaches of the written and unwritten rules of government.

Under Canadian constitutional arrangements public servants are not directly and personally accountable to Parliament. Instead, the preservation of the rule of law and the promotion of bureaucratic accountability are sought through the principles of **collective responsibility** and individual **ministerial responsibility**. These principles represent a statement of the relationships that ought to exist between cabinets and parliaments, between cabinet ministers and the public service, between the public service and parliaments, and between all office-holders and the citizens they serve. Collective and individual ministerial responsibility is based mainly on political conventions rather than on statutory provisions.

Centralization of power and secrecy are inherent in the cabinet-parliamentary system. Collective ministerial responsibility concentrates authority for policy formulation and for the provision of leadership to the public service in the hands of the Prime Minister and the cabinet. The cabinet-parliamentary system then seeks to hold this small group of partisan politicians accountable to the elected representatives of the public on a continuing basis through a number of mechanisms, most notably through the so-called confidence rule. This rule requires that at all times a government must maintain the support of the majority of MPs in the House of Commons or it can be forced to resign and/or to request dissolution of Parliament leading to a general election. In the case of straight votes of no confidence presented by the opposition parties in response to the Throne Speech (outlining the government's legislative program), the Budget Speech (which presents its taxing and spending decisions), and certain Opposition Supply Motions (in which government policy as reflected in spending is criticized), there is no question that the government must resign. Apart from such explicit votes of no confidence, uncertainty and controversy surround the defeat of particular bills or items of spending. The consensus among authorities is that governments are left to decide the seriousness of such political setbacks and resignations seldom occur. In fact, with a majority government and party discipline, defeats of any kind are rare.

In short, in practice today the Prime Minister and cabinet largely control Parliament, the opposite of what the pure theory of cabinet-parliamentary government implies. However, governments are still obliged to explain and to defend their actions and inactions before the public's elected representatives through events like the daily Question Period. The constitutional principle of collective ministerial responsibility has been weakened by the rise of disciplined parties and by increased prime ministerial power. While collective ministerial responsibility represents a less than perfect accountability system, there is still value in focusing responsibility on a readily identifiable group of political office-holders, in combination with the requirement that they 'boast and confess' in public on a regular basis.

Individual cabinet ministers are made legally responsible for the departments they lead under the statutes passed by Parliament that create those departments (see Chapter 2). This legal arrangement provides a basis for holding ministers politically answerable before Parliament for the performance of those departments. Orthodox constitutional theory insists that all actions of public servants within a department are done in the name of the minister and that she or he can be forced to resign from cabinet for serious policy mistakes or major administrative errors. There has been a gradual retreat from this strict theory of individual ministerial responsibility as a result of a number of trends and developments:

- The policies that ministers and their departments carry out often reflect the wishes of the Prime Minister and the cabinet, and if these policies become controversial the conventions of cabinet solidarity and partisan competition lead the governing party to protect the minister under attack.
- Departments have become large and complicated undertakings in which ministers are involved with only a small percentage of the decisions made daily in their name.
- In addition to their departments most ministers answer to Parliament for the activities of several semi-independent, non-departmental bodies, such as Crown corporations and regulatory agencies, which make up part of the minister's portfolio.

The result of these trends is that individual ministers seldom resign in the face of parliamentary criticism of the policies or administrative actions of their departments. From these facts, critics conclude that individual ministerial responsibility has become a myth and no longer provides a reliable basis for holding ministers (directly) and public servants (indirectly) accountable for their joint efforts in policy formulation and implementation.

Defenders of the existing practices insist that the flexibility of the convention of ministerial responsibility has enabled Parliament to assign it a different meaning under changing circumstances. They insist that individual ministerial responsibility never operated the way that the 'pure' theory implied. Sharon Sutherland (1991a) examined the historical record and could find only two examples of ministers leaving office for reasons of maladministration in their departments. Most ministers resigned for career changes, policy problems, or personal transgressions. In other words, individual ministerial responsibility has not died—it never lived, at least not in the way that orthodox theory implied. Today, it is seen as no longer realistic to assign absolute responsibility to ministers for all administrative actions and to insist that they resign when mistakes, or simply unforeseen and unwanted developments, take place. Loss of political reputation, not loss of office, has become the real sanction behind ministerial responsibility. In the tough league of the House of Commons, the risk of damaging one's career causes most ministers to keep in touch with the activities of their departments and the other components of their ministerial portfolios.

Defenders of the status quo insist that ministers continue to be answerable before Parliament, they are expected to take corrective actions when problems within their departments are identified, they can still be forced to resign for purely personal transgressions, and it is not unheard of for prime ministers to remove ministers from cabinet who have become a liability to the government. Clearly there is life left in the doctrines of collective and individual ministerial responsibility, but the widespread public perception today is that the Canadian political system lacks real accountability because neither ministers nor public servants appear to pay a serious price when mistakes occur.

The Constitutional Role of the Public Service

This brings us to the constitutional conventions respecting the role of the public service within the cabinet-parliamentary system. Although developed separately, the conventions respecting the public service reinforce the principles of ministerial responsibility. These conventions stress the value of an anonymous, neutral, professional, and relatively permanent public service appointed and operated on the basis of merit and competence so that it can provide intelligent and objective policy advice to ministers and deliver programs in an efficient and impartial manner. In traditional constitutional terms the public service is said to serve the Crown, which in practical terms is taken to mean the government of the day. Recently, it has been argued that the public service should be recognized in public law as a separate entity with a measure of independence from the government of the day and an obligation to defend 'the public interest' when it is threatened by short-term, opportunistic political decision-making or undue political interference in the administrative process which might impair the rule of law (Sossin, 2005). This controversial reform notion is discussed near the conclusion of the chapter.

Historically, public servants have shunned publicity and practised a discreet reticence in sharing their knowledge with those outside of government. There is an implicit bargain between public servants and the ministers they serve. In return for the best policy advice the public service can provide and the professional implementation of programs, ministers are expected to avoid blaming in public individual public servants for mistakes. Such matters are to be dealt with privately within the department. Unfortunately, the internal and often confidential nature of such disciplinary action creates the false impression for parliamentarians, the media, and the public that there are no negative consequences for public servants when errors are made or abuses of authority occur.

Just as wider trends within the political system have altered the practices of ministerial responsibility, a number of developments are modifying the conventions of an anonymous, neutral, and permanent public service:

- the difficulty of providing objective policy advice during a period of ideological disagreement over the future role of government;
- changing concepts of political and bureaucratic representation reflected in

programs to ensure the public service is more representative of the various publics it serves and is more open and responsive to outside influences through various consultative mechanisms;
- greater fragmentation of the public sector through the creation of new-style organizations (such as special operating agencies) and the growing reliance on the private sector (through contracting out and public/private partnerships) to deliver public programs;
- increased parliamentary surveillance of the public service through the estimates process, performance reporting, and wider auditing processes;
- greater transparency respecting bureaucratic performance produced by access to information laws and the rise of a more adversarial media;
- a growing role for the courts under the Charter of Rights and Freedoms and other statutes to review the actions of administrative agencies to ensure that they act on the basis of public law, respect Charter principles, and dispense natural justice;
- the promotion of a new entrepreneurial public service culture in which such values as leadership from public servants, innovation, risk-taking, rewards for results, revenue generation, and service contracts supplement or displace traditional values such as loyalty to the minister, reticence in sharing their views publicly, prudence, process compliance, and trusteeship of the public interest (Mitchell and Sutherland, 1999; Thomas, 2008).

Under these conditions, what it means to be a professional, responsible, and accountable public servant has become more complicated, problematic, and controversial. Public servants must balance respect for the law, loyalty to the minister, compliance with internal rules and procedures, the enforcement and respect for contracts with outside parties, responsiveness to various groups, and adherence to their own internalized norms and standards of professionalism. Increasingly, how well this balancing act is performed by senior public servants has become the subject of publicity and controversy. The recent application of the New Public Management approach within the public service is adding to the strain on both ministerial responsibility and the conventional understandings of the relationship between public servants and Parliament.

Parliament's Functions in the Political System

The constitutional framework described above creates both opportunities and constraints for Parliament in dealing with the public service. Under the doctrine of ministerial responsibility, the organization of government is an executive prerogative. In fact, it has become a recognized right of the Prime Minister to determine the size of cabinet, the composition of ministerial portfolios, and the makeup of various departments in terms of combinations of organizational components and programs. Primary responsibility for leadership, direction, and control over departments resides with ministers, both collectively and individually. While Parliament cannot be ignored, it normally has limited influence on the organization and management of the public service. Concentration of authority in the hands of the Prime Minister and cabinet means that in theory the public service is subject to unified political direction and does not face competing demands. In contrast, the system of divided powers and checks and balances contained in the US Constitution means that the public service looks to both the President and Congress for mandates and money and consequently exhibits divided loyalties.

In analyzing Parliament's relations with the public service we must start, therefore, with the fundamental fact that Parliament is limited to scrutiny and influence, not direct control and real power. We must also recognize that scrutiny of the performance of the public service is only one of a number of functions performed by Parliament within the Canadian political system.

Table 6.1 sets forth a list of functions commonly attributed to legislatures. Simply put, **functions of the legislature** represent the contribution to and the effect upon the political system made by Parliament. A list of particular activities that contribute to the performance of these functions is also shown in Table 6.1. Some functions are formally recognized or explicit, whereas others are implicit or latent in the activities of Parliament. The functions overlap in practice—particular activities can contribute to more than one function and inclusion of any function or activity in the table suggests nothing about how successfully or unsuccessfully Parliament performs in this dimension.

The point of this discussion of legislative functions is that scrutiny of the performance of the public service has traditionally not been a high priority for Parliament. Overseeing the administration has not developed as a well-defined function. As a consequence Parliament's efforts have been sporadic, unsystematic, issue-oriented, short-term, ad hoc, shallow, and marginal in terms of impacts. There appear to be several reasons why Parliament has not taken its scrutiny function seriously. First, the Constitution may have represented an obstacle since the conventions of public service anonymity and confidentiality represent a protective shield against parliamentary inquiry. Second, governments were not likely to welcome Parliament poking and prying around in administrative matters, not least because most such scrutiny activity would be led by opposition MPs who could be counted on to seek maximum political advantage from any embarrassing discoveries. Not surprisingly, governments have been reluctant to provide Parliament with the procedural opportunities, the relevant information, and the staff resources needed to conduct more extensive and thorough investigations into how programs and departments are performing. There was also the fact that governments often ignored reports from parliamentary committees dealing with deficiencies in departments and programs, and this pattern produced a sense of futility among MPs. Despite this, it would be naive to assume that, were there no constitutional inhibitions or restrictions imposed by governments, the majority of MPs would jump into the scrutiny function with both feet. As is explained below, the job of reviewing bureaucratic performance is usually difficult, often tedious, frustrating, low-profile, and therefore politically unrewarding work. Not surprisingly, only a minority of MPs exhibit a sustained interest in this function.

Table 6.1 Functions of Legislatures

I Policy-Making Functions

- law-making
- control over taxing and spending
- scrutiny of the government and of the bureaucracy

II Representational Functions

- recruiting and identifying leaders
- dealing with the bureaucracy on behalf of constituents
- an educational function of clarifying policy choices for the electorate

III Systems/Maintenance Functions

- creating governments
- making the actions of governments legitimate
- mobilizing public support for the outcomes of the policy process
- managing conflict within the political system
- contributing to integration within the political system

Numerous factors, both inside and outside of the political system, can potentially affect the effectiveness of Parliament in performing all of its functions. There is not the space here to discuss these factors in detail. Again at the risk of oversimplification, four broad sets of factors potentially affect the strength of Parliament within the Canadian political system:

- the constitutional arrangements, the incentives they create for parliamentarians to engage in certain kinds of behaviour, and the opportunities available

within the political system to change these written and unwritten rules of 'the political game';
- the types of issues that arise within society and make it onto various institutional agendas of government in any given period and over time;
- the social backgrounds, personal qualities, motivations, and aspirations of parliamentarians;
- the internal organization, procedures, and resources of Parliament, particularly staff and informational resources.

The problem for would-be reformers who want to strengthen Parliament within the policy process is that only the fourth broad set of factors can be 'easily' changed in a deliberate and planned fashion. Strengthening Parliament is difficult because it is dominated by competitive political parties who see procedural and organizational arrangements as tactical devices to be used in the *permanent* election campaign, which is the essence of much, though not all, Commons activity. Obviously, most governments do not wish to upset the existing political equilibrium in ways that might work to their disadvantage.

During the three decades from the 1960s to the 1990s, the House of Commons underwent more study and reform than any previous time in its history, but the payoffs in terms of enhanced parliamentary influence were marginal at best. C.E.S. Franks (1987) and others have described the long list of reforms. Without examining them in detail, it can be argued plausibly that the reforms all amounted to tinkering; they did not change the basic power relationships of the cabinet-parliamentary system, which clearly gives the Prime Minister and the cabinet the upper hand. Many reformers naively assumed that they could increase Parliament's influence without detracting from the government's control. Dissatisfaction with political process, declining respect for all public officials (especially politicians and to a much lesser extent public servants), and concern about the undue concentration of power within government led during the 1990s to a shift in focus away from 'parliamentary' reform in favour of 'democratic' reform involving more public input into policy-making and more direct accountability of public servants to citizens.

Parliament's Roles in Relation to the Public Service

Based on the functions/activities identified above, five broad **roles of Parliament in relation to the public service** can be identified (Slatter, 1982): legitimization, policy-maker, creator, financier, and scrutineer. Parliament's involvement in the first four of these roles is more formal than real; it consists mainly of ratifying and sometimes refining decisions taken within government. Accordingly, these four roles will be considered only briefly and the following discussion will focus mainly on the purposes, impediments, and techniques of parliamentary surveillance of the bureaucracy.

Parliament plays an important but not easily measured role in *legitimizing* the actions of government. Legitimacy refers to the satisfaction and support of citizens for the processes, decisions, and outcomes of government. There are both procedural and substantive dimensions to legitimacy. Not only must decisions be made according to recognized and well-accepted rules and procedures; they also must reflect and be consistent with widely held values in society. In other words, legitimacy goes much deeper than the latest public opinion polls showing levels of public support for a particular government. It entails the principles and values upon which we agree to be governed. It appears from sophisticated opinion research that governments in Canada began losing legitimacy with their citizens over the three decades from the 1960s to the 1990s. The causes of this erosion are numerous and controversial (Nevitte, 1996). Increased public cynicism and declining trust and confidence are targeted mainly at political institutions, but they also affect the esteem of the public service.

Public bodies wield considerable power over the operations of private organizations and over the lives of individual citizens. They dispense benefits and impose burdens. They set standards of behaviour and coerce compliance through sanctions. They make judgments about the competing claims of various interests within society, often on the basis of private negotiations and complicated factual and ethical calculations about what is in the public interest. Public servants can only do these things, or do them effectively, if they are perceived to be acting in a legitimate manner on the basis of public law that has been approved by Parliament. Parliament is not the only, or even the most important, source of legitimacy, but administrative agencies will not be successful over time if Parliament finds their policies and practices unacceptable.

A second role of Parliament is *policy-making*. To understand this role requires a brief description of the wider context in which it occurs. The conditions under which governments operate today mean that policy-making at the national level in Canada has become complicated, extended, specialized, fragmented, interdependent, and uncertain. In institutional terms, power is concentrated in the hands of the Prime Minister, central agencies, and, to a lesser extent, cabinet and the bureaucracy. In broader process terms, however, power is increasingly shared and exercised collaboratively with outside pressure groups, provincial governments, and supra-national and international institutions. Governments also face the challenge of combining elite-based decision-making with the public's demands for more consultative and participatory approaches. In short, governments are to some extent tied down by multiple linkages to the economy, society, and other parts of the political system.

More and more leadership and power are exercised collaboratively rather than unilaterally. So even though the appearance of prime-ministerial rule remains and the Prime Minister potentially has firm control over issues once they reach the institutional agenda of government, the image of one-person rule tends to neglect the wider situational constraints that face all governments today. As more issues move upward to international bodies, or downward to provincial, local, and non-governmental bodies, there is a loss of policy-making capacity for both cabinet and Parliament at the national level. Achieving coherence in national policy-making has also been complicated by recent experimentation with alternative service delivery mechanisms (discussed below), which make direction and control from the centre of government more problematic.

All of this being said, it is still the case that the cabinet-parliamentary model concentrates decision-making on issues before government in the hands of a relatively small number of political and bureaucratic insiders. The growing power of the Prime Minister, the fact of party discipline, the cabinet's access to the expertise of the public service, the limited access to information and staff resources by parliamentarians, and the government's use of procedural devices to ensure the completion of its business all reduce Parliament to a marginal, albeit still important, role in the policy process.

During most of the twentieth century, long periods of rule by the Liberal Party, combined with close relationships between the party and the senior ranks of the public service, led some commentators to suggest that power had shifted first from Parliament to cabinet and subsequently from the cabinet to the bureaucracy. Table 6.2 lists some of the other factors usually cited to explain the growing influence of senior public servants within the policy process. The list reflects the fact that policy-making is usually an extended process, involving several different stages and decision-making on a number of different levels. In terms of stages in the policy cycle, the initial formulation of policy tends to be undertaken by public servants in various departmental and interdepartmental bodies. Policy formulation often reflects pressures and advice from individuals and institutions outside of government. The actual selection or adoption of policy to be presented to Parliament in the form of bills, budgetary measures, and other actions is the prerogative of ministers and cabinets, although those choices are clearly influenced by the advice flowing from the public service.

Another level of policy-making in government involves the medium- and lower-level policy-making that takes place daily within departments,

Table 6.2 Sources of Bureaucratic Influence

- the professional backgrounds and relative permanence of senior public servants compared to ministers and other parliamentarians
- the possession of expert knowledge and specialized information
- the ongoing relationships between the public service and pressure groups, which represent a source of ideas and legitimacy for their policy advice to ministers
- the role of public servants in the important field of intergovernmental negotiations, which obliges governments to grant them autonomy to bargain over policy and its implementation
- the weakness of Canadian political parties as vehicles for the development of public policy, which means whether in government or opposition, parliamentarians have a restricted range of alternatives to the policies being presented by the bureaucracy
- the limits of Parliament's own policy-making capabilities due to the partisan theatrics that govern its proceedings and its reliance on vague policy in legislation, with the details to be provided by the bureaucracy through delegated legislative authority

Crown corporations, regulatory commissions, and other administrative agencies. In these instances, Parliament has passed laws in very general language and it is left to the bureaucracy to refine and to carry out the statutory purposes. On the basis of such delegated legislative authority enormous discretion is granted to public servants (acting presumably under the supervision of responsible ministers) to formulate and to apply rules of various kinds. In quantitative terms, based upon the hundreds of thousands of 'small rules' which they formulate and apply, public servants have become the 'real lawmakers'. Parliament has a committee to supervise the exercise of this discretionary power but, as is discussed later, there are limits to its effectiveness.

Only under very fortuitous circumstances can Parliament play a role in delaying or modifying the policy proposals of ministers. If this takes place, it happens in the private meetings of the government caucus, which consists of all the MPs and senators on the government side of Parliament or, less frequently, in the standing committee of the House of Commons where bills are sent for review after second reading (Thomas, 2008). It is necessary to be realistic, but not completely dismissive, concerning Parliament's policy-making role. For constitutional and practical reasons Parliament must be content with discussing, approving, and perhaps refining policies that are formulated elsewhere, usually within the bureaucracy, often in collaboration with outside interest groups. There is less excuse, however, for Parliament's weak performance in terms of the review of existing policies, which is a theme of the later discussion of Parliament's role as a scrutineer of the bureaucracy.

A third and related role of Parliament is that of *creator* of administrative bodies. Since departments and non-departmental bodies such as Crown corporations, regulatory agencies, and special operating agencies have a statutory basis, Parliament plays a role in creating these. However, as already mentioned, there is a recognized right for the Prime Minister to initiate organizational changes and a number of statutes enable the cabinet to set up new administrative agencies. The general practice has been to create such new entities by statute, and therefore there is the opportunity for Parliament to debate the organizational format (departmental or non-departmental), the mandate, and the powers of new undertakings. In practice such debates may occur well after the fact, as was the case with the major 1993 reorganization of the federal bureaucracy. This reorganization saw the number of departments reduced from 32 to 23. Parliament did not approve all the legislation confirming the consolidations for three or four years, long after the new 'mega-departments' were operational. In the interim the cabinet was free to act under the Public Service Rearrangement and Transfer of Duties Act, which allows for the transfer of duties between ministers and departments.

This Act does not apply to such independent administrative agencies as regulatory bodies. Prior to 1984 the cabinet was free to create Crown corporations by Order-in-Council, but amendments to the Financial Administration Act passed in that year require that Parliament approve the creation of all new Crown corporations and the privatization of existing corporations.

In summary, it is an exaggeration to state that Parliament creates the administrative machinery; it is more accurate to say that it reviews ministerial decisions respecting the mandate, organizational format, and powers of the different types of organizations used by government. During the 1980s governments began to experiment with alternative organizational designs such as large consolidated departments, special operating agencies, mixed enterprises, and public–private partnerships. These developments are discussed in the later section of this chapter on future trends. The implications for parliamentary control of the move away from the traditional, integrated department have received little attention, including within Parliament itself.

A fourth role for Parliament in relation to the bureaucracy is that of *financier*. Parliament has three main functions in the field of public expenditure. The first involves authorizing sufficient spending to allow the government to carry on its activities. This is done through the debate and passage of appropriation bills. All new spending must originate with the government (or more formally, the Crown). Motions to reject or to reduce expenditures have been viewed by governments as matters of confidence and party discipline applies. The result is that while constitutional theory places Parliament at the centre of the expenditure process, in practice its direct control and even its indirect influence have been minimal.

Second, it is part of Parliament's financial role to submit expenditure proposals to scrutiny as part of a more general questioning of government policy and management of the public service. Under the rules of the House of Commons, 25 days are allowed in each parliamentary session when the opposition parties can introduce motions criticizing the government, and on six of these—so-called supply or opposition days—the debate ends with a vote of no confidence. Such debates tend to be wide-ranging and rarely focus exclusively on fiscal matters. The supply process represents an opportunity for Parliament to convey its views to the government and the various administrative agencies. Detailed examination of the estimates of the various departments is supposed to take place in the 17 standing committees of the Commons. Although they are theoretically free to recommend changes to the government's financial plans, the committees rarely do this, mainly because they are under tight government control. Government control is lost or reduced in minority government situations, such as has existed from January 2006.

Several reforms have been introduced since the late 1960s to streamline and revitalize the supply process. In 1968 the detailed examination of the Estimates was transferred to the standing committees of the House of Commons with the hope that a more constructive approach involving an actual examination of spending would occur. Instead, the partisan policy debates of the past were simply carried over from the full House of Commons into the committees. In 1982 a new three-part format for the Estimates was introduced with the promise of allowing MPs to examine the substance of departmental performance and future plans by reporting on accomplishments against planned results. Under the new system the committees faced a juggernaut of several hundred documents annually; few MPs became comfortable working with the new documents, departments were frustrated that there was little or no informed interest in their work, and the whole exercise resembled a largely futile make-work project since government maintained tight control on both the committees and spending.

A new Expenditure Management System announced by the Liberal government in February 1995 dealt mainly with reforms to the process within the executive, but it also promised Parliament and other interested parties 'improved information on program performance to aid in decision-making and to facilitate accountability' (Canada, Treasury Board Secretariat, 1995). For the purposes of enhanced accountability to Parliament and to allow it influence over future spending, departments began to publish 'outlook' documents, which are condensed and expurgated versions of internal business plans. These documents, subsequently renamed Reports on Plans and Priorities, are referred to the relevant standing committees of the Commons during the spring when the government's estimates are before Parliament. For the fall sitting of Parliament, departments present the committees with performance reports, which ideally track the progress of departments and programs. Well over 100 performance reports now flow into the Commons committee system each September, and theoretically the review of these documents allows the committees to offer advice to the government about expenditure priorities for a budget to be presented in February or March of the following year.

The last attempt to reform the supply process arose from a 1997 report by a subcommittee of the House of Commons Procedure and House Affairs Committee (Canada, House of Commons, Subcommittee on the Business of Supply, 1997). The subcommittee made 52 recommendations. The most important were to set up a separate Estimates committee, made up of MPs who are experts and interested in the financial side of government, and a change to the rules that would allow MPs to reallocate funds among expenditure items within the total amount recommended by the government. These proposals recognized both that only a small minority of MPs had a real interest in the difficult and unrewarding work of mastering financial matters, and the feeling among most MPs that their input into budgets was largely ignored. While agreeing that the supply process had to be improved, the Liberal government largely dismissed the subcommittee's report. A super Estimates committee, with adequate staffing, was rejected and the power to reallocate money was denied, supposedly because the Constitution allowed only the government to initiate spending. The government also refused to budge on the question of non-confidence on the budget and allow MPs to vote against certain items without fear of party discipline. Protecting their dominance over the budgetary process is a long-standing habit of Canadian governments. It is only a slight exaggeration to conclude that recent steps to improve the supply process represent in many ways an attempt to revive a corpse that never really lived.

Parliament's Financial Watchdog: The Office of the Auditor General

The third financial duty of Parliament is the retrospective scrutiny of the Annual Public Accounts. It performs this task with the support of the Office of the Auditor General of Canada (OAG), which has existed almost since the country was founded. As a parliamentary 'watchdog' on spending, the OAG has become an important actor in the parliamentary system. Traditionally, the role of the OAG consisted of financial and compliance auditing, which meant that the office assisted Parliament in ensuring the legality and accuracy of expenditures. As the auditor of the Public Accounts of Canada, the OAG examines annually the financial records of departments and agencies and files reports to Parliament that are automatically referred to the House of Commons Standing Committee on Public Accounts, chaired by an opposition MP. The Public Accounts Committee considers the OAG's report and presents its own conclusions and recommendations to the House of Commons.

Since 1977 the OAG has also been authorized to practise comprehensive or value-for-money auditing (VFM). VFM examines the legality and efficiency of expenditure transactions, but more importantly it evaluates the adequacy of the management and information systems used to ensure economy, efficiency, and effectiveness in government decision-making.

The OAG insists that it does not conduct actual program evaluations because to do so would potentially entangle it in partisan controversy. It claims to limit itself to the issue of whether information is available or could be made available to answer questions about program effectiveness. However, in refining the VFM approach the OAG has moved well beyond strictly financial matters and outside the parameters of its lead discipline of accountancy. Fully one-third of the OAG's staff now have backgrounds in fields other than accountancy. In addition to widening the scope of its audits, the OAG has added a number of other activities to its repertoire: the review of the sustainable development strategies of departments; special examinations of the performances of Crown corporations, and progress reports on the various public service reform initiatives introduced in recent years. By broadening the scope of its activities, the OAG has contributed to the functioning of Parliament beyond supporting its financial duties. Originally the work of the OAG was mainly used in the Standing Committee on Public Accounts because the annual report focused on issues of financial management. Today the OAG's staff work with many parliamentary committees and its various reports are cited in Question Period, debates on legislation, the supply process, committee inquiries, and media reports.

In providing support to Parliament the OAG is required to perform a balancing act. To ensure parliamentary, media, and public attention for its findings, it must present reports that are controversial enough to be noticed. At the same time it must avoid drifting into policy controversies and focusing only on negative developments because such approaches will produce a backlash and lack of co-operation from ministers and departments. There is also a balance to be maintained between identifying waste and error, and emphasizing constructive criticism and organizational learning.

The expanded scope of the legislative audit has taken the OAG into politically sensitive areas and, not surprisingly, made it the target of criticism. A list of the challenges to the Office would include the following points:

- By using the term 'audit' loosely the OAG creates a false aura of objectivity and validity for its findings.
- The OAG presumes clear and measurable objectives for departments and programs and on this basis promotes a shallow, managerialist conception of accountability.
- The OAG fails to recognize that 'policy' is made on several levels within government and ends up violating its own rule of not commenting on policy.
- The OAG does not recognize sufficiently the political and bureaucratic constraints faced by public servants and ends up distorting the principle of ministerial responsibility by placing blame where it does not belong, i.e., with public servants rather than ministers.
- By its emphasis on mistakes, the assignment of blame, and the promotion of a mentality of error-free administration, the OAG is a part of a 'control lobby' within government that has stifled the emergence of a less rule-bound, less risk-averse, and more entrepreneurial public service.
- With its $83 million budget for 2007–8, large professional staff (approximately 600 employees), and capacity to generate publicity for its findings, the OAG ends up setting the agenda of Parliament, especially of the Public Accounts Committee, rather than taking direction from and responding to the concerns of parliamentarians.
- By promoting the notion that all its reports reflect scientific auditing principles and practices applied in a completely objective manner, the OAG claims to speak 'the truth' and by doing so elevates certain kinds of information and knowledge over other modes of inquiry and analysis.

Of course, the OAG denies many of the concerns of its critics. In terms of its relationship to Parliament, the OAG represents a potentially valuable resource to parliamentarians (Aucoin, 1998; Holmes, 1996; Power, 1997; Roberts, 1996; Sutherland, 1980; Thomas, 1999). If Parliament, especially through its committees, fails to provide direction to the OAG and if its reports disappear into a parliamentary 'black hole', the OAG probably has no choice but to act unilaterally to bring matters to the attention of parliamentarians, only a small minority of whom has exhibited sustained interest in financial and managerial issues.

Parliamentary Scrutiny of the Public Service

The fifth role of Parliament is that of *scrutineer* of the public service. This role is implicit in the previous four. Until the last three decades this role received little definition and separate attention from Parliament. As the consensus grew that ministerial responsibility was inadequate as an accountability mechanism and that ministers were unable to manage the public service, Parliament began to develop the scrutiny function. In general, Parliament saw that it had a duty to probe the operations of the bureaucracy, to make its operations more transparent, to deter the misuse of power, and to galvanize the norms of responsible behaviour on the part of public servants. Table 6.3 presents a list of more specific purposes behind the various mechanisms used by Parliament to provide surveillance of the bureaucracy.

Since the mid- to late 1960s Parliament has adopted a variety of procedural and organizational measures to strengthen its surveillance function. An implicit bargain has often been at the heart of these reforms. In return for speedier passage of its business, the government was prepared to allow Parliament, mainly through its committees, to inquire into the performance of the bureaucracy, but only if this was done in a politically non-threatening fashion. To some extent governments also wanted to use Parliament as an ally in the struggle by ministers to force the bureaucracy to be efficient and accountable. On these grounds governments agreed to Commons rules obliging them to furnish Parliament with certain kinds of information on a regular basis and to respond to parliamentary opinion, such as the requirement that governments respond to committee reports within 150 days.

Table 6.3 The Purposes of Parliamentary Surveillance of the Bureaucracy

- to ensure that laws are implemented as intended
- to review whether laws, policies, programs, or activities of government need to be changed
- to promote accountability among permanent public officials
- to discover waste and mismanagement, and to promote economy, efficiency, and effectiveness in public programs
- to discover and to prevent abuses of discretionary authority
- to allow parliamentarians to act as liaison agents with the bureaucracy on behalf of their constituents

Parliament has also been allowed to create a number of auxiliary agencies (usually called **Officers of Parliament**) to assist it with the task of holding ministers and public servants accountable (Thomas, 2003). Examples of such agencies are the Office of the **Auditor General**, the **Office of the Information Commissioner**, the **Office of the Privacy Commissioner**, and the **Canadian Human Rights Commission**. In response to the so-called 'sponsorship scandal', in December 2006 Parliament passed the **Federal Accountability Act** (FAA). The FAA introduced a consistent appointments process for Officers of Parliament with a more meaningful role for parliamentarians in reviewing the qualifications of nominees; added a Public Sector Integrity Commissioner to oversee a whistle-blower protection law; created a **Parliamentary Budget Officer** to assist Parliament with its financial duties; established a Public Appointments Commission to review cabinet appointments to agencies, boards, and commissions; expanded the Access to Information Act to cover all Crown corporations and their subsidiaries; ended the practice of giving priority treatment to political staff of ministers when they apply to join the public service; created a new, independent Commissioner of Lobbying with stronger powers to oversee lobbying rules; and introduced a new conflict of interest code to be enforced by a new Conflict of Interest and Ethics Commissioner. It also strengthened the internal auditing regime within departments and gave the Auditor General serving Parliament more authority to audit public foundations and to follow money for grants and contributions to third parties outside of government. Finally, the FAA introduced the **accounting officer** model for deputy ministers, a reform which is discussed more fully below.

Table 6.4 presents a summary listing of the main surveillance mechanisms now available to Parliament. Impressive in number, it must be remembered that all the mechanisms operate in a political context of partisan competition where the government is usually in charge. On the other hand, these surveillance mechanisms do force governments to explain themselves on a regular basis before the elected representatives of the public—which is not an insignificant requirement in a democracy.

Question Period, members' statements, and debates of various kinds can be used as spot checks to bring administrative issues before Parliament, but they do not allow for systematic, in-depth coverage. The best opportunities for such scrutiny come through the work of parliamentary committees. The Commons currently has 26 standing committees, each of which covers a broad policy sector. (See Appendix A for a listing.) The committees perform three broad functions: the examination of bills after second reading, the review of the Estimates, and the conduct of general inquiries. Reference is made elsewhere in this chapter to how the committees undertake these functions. In all cases there is a tension between the government's insistence on tight control over committee proceedings and the aspiration of parliamentary reformers to create independent and influential committees. Since a more active committee system was created in the late 1960s, successive governments have used their majorities on the committees, the appointment of government MPs as chairpersons, and the insistence on party discipline to restrain committees in the use of their newly acquired powers (Franks, 1987; Docherty, 2003).

Table 6.4 Parliamentary Techniques for Surveillance of the Public Service

- Question Period
- members' statements
- debates of bills and periodic reviews of legislation
- review and approval of spending
- creation of standing committees that cover broad policy sectors and are somewhat independent of the executive
- the conduct of general inquiries by parliamentary committees and the requirement that ministers reply to reports
- requirements that ministers present Parliament with information on a regular basis, e.g., the annual report on the public service and the annual report on the Crown corporation sector
- the provision of professional staff to committees and to individual parliamentarians
- the creation of the Joint Committee on the Scrutiny of Regulations to review the exercise of delegated law-making authority
- the adoption of an Access to Information Act to promote openness in government
- the appointment of a number of Officers of Parliament to assist Parliament with its scrutiny function for various purposes, such as the Auditor General, the Office of the Information Commissioner, the Privacy Commissioner, the Commissioner of Official Languages, the Public Sector Integrity Commissioner, and the Commissioner of Lobbying

On paper the Commons committees have significant powers to review departmental performance. The rules of the House of Commons allow committees to initiate inquiries and to report on all matters related to the mandate, management, and operations of departments. They have the authority to summon witnesses, compel testimony, and order documents to be provided. On several occasions in recent years public service witnesses have been asked to swear an oath before a committee that they will tell the truth. In the past, it was presumed such witnesses would always be truthful within the limits of the rules respecting public service confidentiality.

Committees can require a government response to their reports and recommendation within 150 days, but, of course, they cannot force governments to take their views seriously. A 2008 report from the Public Accounts Committee documented the lack of meaningful responses by government to its reports and made a number of recommendations to improve the situation. Committee influence depends on a fortuitous combination of circumstances, such as the willingness of ministers and senior public servants to receive advice, the quality of that advice, the degree of cross-party support for reports, the existence of outside pressures for the recommended changes, and so on.

Over the years since 1968, when the standing committees were made the main working units of the Commons, there have been occasional examples of committees demonstrating independence from the government. This has occurred mainly when committees were conducting inquiries into departments and evaluations of programs deemed to be in trouble. In these instances the responsible ministers may have allowed the inquiries in order to shake up their departments. There have also been cases where government MPs, who had perhaps forsaken the possibility of a cabinet posting, provided aggressive leadership as chairpersons of committees. For example, during the 35th Parliament (1993–7), George Baker, a Newfoundland Liberal MP, led a study by the Commons Committee on Fisheries and Oceans. The Committee compelled departmental representatives to appear and produced a stinging report blaming the Department of Fisheries and Oceans for the collapse of the east coast cod fishery. In a similar fashion, the Commons Committee on the Environment issued several reports critical of the Chrétien government's environmental policies and the Justice and Human Rights Committee conducted a useful study of the operations of the controversial Young Offenders Act. These cases are the exception, however.

A fundamental limitation on Parliament's capacity to enforce bureaucratic accountability is the sheer size of the surveillance task. No matter what procedures it adopts, no matter what organizational arrangements it creates, and no matter how many professional staff it employs, Parliament can never come close to providing continuous scrutiny over the wide range of administrative decision-making taking place on a daily basis. Also, beyond some not easily identified point, parliamentary involvement with administrative matters becomes counterproductive if it robs the public service of the flexibility to apply its professional expertise in the most efficient manner possible. Close relations between departments and parliamentary committees with real power to dispense rewards and punishments would potentially leave senior public servants serving two masters—the minister and the designated parliamentary committee. We need look no further than the Congress in the United States to see the danger of micromanagement of the public service and the divided loyalties this produces when powerful legislative committees exist. There is little danger of such relationships developing in Canada; if anything, the greater risk is too little rather than too much parliamentary scrutiny of the bureaucracy, especially scrutiny that is systematic and constructive.

Obstacles to Parliamentary Surveillance of the Bureaucracy

In addition to the vast scope and technical complexity of the public sector, which complicate the surveillance task, Parliament faces other obstacles, some of which have been alluded to earlier. The constitutional framework concentrates authority over the public service in the hands of ministers and the governing party exercises tight control over the standing committees of the House of Commons, which represent the main forums where systematic examination of bureaucratic performance might take place. Elected as part of a 'team', having participated in caucus deliberations and conscious of the potential damage to their prospects of entering cabinet, government MPs are naturally reluctant to embarrass the minister and the government by exposing mismanagement or the abuse of power. This means that most of the serious challenges on bureaucratic performance come from opposition MPs, who can usually be counted on to interpret any revelation of a problem in the worst possible light. This focus on error identification and blaming causes ministers, government MPs, and public servants to adopt a protective stance. Frustrated by the shallowness and distortion of parliamentary performance reviews conducted mainly on a partisan basis, public servants tend to be less than candid and forthcoming in providing information to committees for fear that it might embarrass the minister and damage the department's or their own reputation.

It is often suggested that parliamentarians suffer from a lack of information, but this is not really accurate. The real problem is that they are often faced with voluminous and complicated information, which does not relate to the issues of public policy and public management making headlines at the time. There is, in fact, more information around today than most MPs and senators have time to consume. However, not all of it is relevant, reliable, or easily understood. Packaging information to serve the needs of 308 MPs and 105 senators is a huge challenge because of the diverse and shifting interests of parliamentarians. There is also the complication that parliamentarians do not approach the gathering and use of information on the performance of the bureaucracy in a completely objective manner; they are often more interested in 'vindicators' that reinforce their partisan positions than they are in 'indicators' that accurately report on performance.

Whereas parliamentary committees were once forced to get along with only the services of a clerk who provided advice on procedural matters, they can now seek research support from a number of sources: the Research Branch of the Library of Parliament, the Parliamentary Budget Officer (which was established in March 2008), lawyers from the Legislative Counsel Office, outside consultants (hired from budgets provided to committees), research staffs provided to the party caucuses, and the assistants who work in the offices of individual MPs and senators. As part of its overall budgetary restraint policy, the Liberal government had after 1993 cut the budget of Parliament, and one impact was to curtail committee activity involving paid consultants and travel. Even though Parliament remains better off in terms of information and analytical capability than it was during earlier decades, it still remains no match for the government, which has access to the vast storehouse of accumulated public service knowledge.

To gain greater access to that storehouse of knowledge, Parliament has adopted a number of procedures to oblige the public service to share information. One such approach is to bring public servants before parliamentary committees. This has been done with increasing frequency over the past three decades in conjunction with the examination of bills after second reading, the review of the Estimates, and the conduct of general inquiries into matters of public policy. Normally, public servants voluntarily appear before committees, but there have been several instances where they have been summoned. The rules of engagement for such encounters between neutral public servants and partisan politicians are not entirely clear. In constitutional terms, public servants appear on behalf of their minister and not on their own behalf. They are expected to be honest and forthcoming with information (thus respecting the role of Parliament) and at the same time respecting their obligations to the minister not to disclose confidential policy advice or sensitive information regarding administrative matters (thus respecting ministerial responsibility). To help public servants balance these considerations a number of guidelines have been published and courses are offered to senior public servants on how to prepare for appearances before committees. While helpful, such devices are inevitably general and are no substitute for the situational judgment that public servants develop through actual experience before parliamentary committees.

Since parliamentary committees are primarily political forums there are risks for public servants in appearing there. There are few clear rules governing the behaviour of parliamentarians in their encounters with public servants. To avoid entanglement in partisan controversy or embarrassment to the minister, public servants may refuse to answer certain questions. In most cases, parliamentarians accept the reasons given by public servants for refusing to answer. Such reasons include commenting on government policy, providing information about matters outside of a public servant's responsibility, providing a legal opinion, and providing an answer that could affect a commercial transaction (McInnes, 1999). Ministers (when they are present in committees), parliamentary secretaries (who are government MPs serving as assistants to ministers), and chairpersons of committees (who are normally government MPs or senators) will normally protect public servants against political attacks. The usual assumption might be that public servants need protection exclusively from opposition MPs who are determined to embarrass the government, but this is not true. Both Liberal and Conservative MPs when their party was in office have accused public servants of withholding information and misleading committees.

Under rules of the House of Commons adopted in 1985, Commons committees have the authority to summon all nominees for non-judicial Order-in-Council appointments (such as deputy ministers, presidents of Crown corporations, and chairpersons of regulatory commissions) to review their qualifications. Unlike congressional committees in the US, the Commons committees cannot veto such appointments; they can only report their views on candidates. Back in 1985 the new procedure took Parliament into uncharted constitutional waters and during the first few years of its operation both the government and the opposition sought partisan advantage from the process (Colwell and Thomas, 1987). As a result the procedure was used less and less often.

On a limited but growing number of occasions ministers have failed to uphold their obligation to protect public servants against political attacks and have even blamed individual public servants. The most notorious example was the so-called Al-Mashat affair, involving the fast-tracking of the entry of a former ambassador from Iraq into Canada. In this case Conservative ministers used their majority on a parliamentary committee to shift the blame to a career public servant. According to Sharon Sutherland (1991b) this case was unprecedented and damaging because a parliamentary committee driven by the government majority bypassed ministerial responsibility and criticized the behaviour of a career public servant, sending a chill throughout the public service.

More recently the investigation by the Public Accounts Committee into the so-called 'billion-dollar boondoggle' of the Human Resources and Development Canada's (HRDC) grants and contributions programs saw a parliamentary committee attack the actions and reputations of public servants for flaws in programs which were highly political in their origins, content, and operations (Good, 2003). The most drastic potential action in relation to public servants is to hold them in contempt for misleading Parliament, which is a rarely used sanction. From 1913 to 2008 it was never used, although in 2003 it was threatened in relation to Canada's Privacy Commissioner who was found by a parliamentary committee to have misused his staffing and budgetary authority. It was actually used on 10 April 2008 when a vote in the House of Commons found the deputy commissioner of the RCMP in contempt for testimony she gave during an inquiry by the Public Accounts Committee into the misuse of the Mounties' pension and insurance funds. After the earlier HRDC, privacy, and sponsorship scandals, MPs were determined to send a strong message that they would not tolerate being misled or being given less than the full story.

The Senate

As an appointed body whose members are selected mainly on the basis of political patronage, the Senate lacks democratic legitimacy and credibility with the public. The list of complaints against the present Senate is long and of long standing. Basically, the Senate is seen to have been a failure in terms of performing the three roles officially ascribed to it: it has failed to provide an effective voice for regional concerns because party loyalty has to take precedence; it has failed to serve as a body of 'sober' second thought and a check on government because the patronage appointees of the Prime Minister have shown their gratitude, and the government could usually take Senate approval for granted; and finally, it has failed to protect the rights of minorities. Over the past century and a quarter, numerous schemes to reform the Senate have been proposed, but all failed the tests of constitutional and political feasibility. After taking office as a minority government in January, 2006, Prime Minister Stephen Harper proposed a gradual, incremental plan for the creation of an elected Senate. The plan dealt neither with the powers of an elected Senate nor with the distribution of Senate seats among the provinces and territories, two highly contentious aspects of the overall topic of reform of Senate.

The complaints about the present Senate are somewhat overdrawn. Many of its deficiencies can be blamed more on successive governments than on senators themselves. Also, in recent years a new generation of senators has taken steps to improve the operations of the institution. There is not the space here to detail those reforms. However, one largely unrecognized and unsung contribution of the Senate has been its reviews of the operations of government policies and programs. Most of this work has been done in the Senate's standing and special committees (see Appendix B for a listing).

There are a number of reasons for the success of Senate committee investigations. Many senators have experience and knowledge of public policy issues from their previous careers. Senators approach investigations in a more non-partisan manner than occurs in Commons committees. The Senate has the time and can take a longer-range view of issues than the Commons, which faces re-election pressures. Lastly, Senate investigations do not suffer from excessive media attention, which would promote political grandstanding (Franks, 1987: 188–90; Thomas, 2003: 189–228). It should also be noted that unlike Royal Commissions of inquiry, senators often exhibit a greater sense of political feasibility in their recommendations and remain in office to lobby for their implementation.

Measuring the influence of Senate committees on government and bureaucratic thinking is difficult, but they do add to a climate of opinion in the country (Pattee and Thomas, 1985).

Public Service Reform and Parliamentary Accountability

Even before the ideas of 'reinventing government' and 'New Public Management' began in the late 1980s to be applied within government, there were strains on the conventions of ministerial responsibility, public service anonymity, and parliamentary accountability. Whether the managerial reforms adopted during the 1990s have increased and strengthened accountability on several levels or whether, by multiplying the types of responsibility being promoted, they have further blurred the accountability picture is debatable. In the remainder of this chapter it is possible to provide only a brief, rather general discussion of the potential implications of the public service reform (PSR) movement for the future of parliamentary democracy.

An initial, brief point is that the PSR movement involves many different ideas, not all of which are consistent with one another. Only a few of the leading ideas can be mentioned here. Second, most informed observers agree that the primary purpose behind PSR was to deal with the fiscal crisis of government and to improve the efficiency of the public sector. Other aims, such as improving service quality, promoting citizen engagement, and restoring the professional pride and commitment of public servants were initially secondary considerations. Third, implications of managerial reforms for parliamentary accountability were not central to the discussions over PSR. A plausible argument can be made that the new managerial approaches being applied within government were not consistent with parliamentary traditions and with the political culture of Parliament. To illustrate this point, three sets of reforms will be discussed briefly.

First, on the basis of the slogan calling for a separation of 'steering from rowing', governments have moved gradually and subtly to narrow further the scope of ministerial responsibility and to identify a growing zone of managerial activity where senior public servants will be held directly and personally answerable before Parliament for the performance of the organizations they administer. The culmination of this line of thinking is the adoption of the accounting officer model in the Federal Accountability Act passed by Parliament in December 2006. Put simply, this concept makes deputy ministers directly and personally accountable before

Parliament for the prudent financial management of their departments. However, working out the operational meaning of the concept has proven to be contentious.

In opposition during the sponsorship scandal, the Conservative Party of Canada had endorsed a pure version of the concept in which deputy ministers would be personally answerable before parliamentary committees. In office, however, Conservative Prime Minister Harper (based, it appears, on the advice of the Privy Council Office) eventually took the view that when deputy ministers appear before the Public Accounts Committee to answer questions related to financial management, they were appearing on behalf of their ministers. The opposing view, which is represented by the Public Accounts Committee, is that deputy ministers should answer on their own behalf for the exercise of managerial prerogatives delegated to them under the Financial Administration Act. The committee is not demanding the authority to reward or punish deputy ministers for their performance as financial managers; this would remain the prerogative of the Clerk of the Privy Council (the most senior public servant, the deputy minister to the Prime Minister, and the secretary to cabinet). At the time of writing (2008), when a minority government is in office, it is unclear which philosophy regarding the accounting officer will prevail. Likely controversy will persist over how far Parliament can and should go in insisting on a modification to the principle of ministerial responsibility to enforce direct bureaucratic accountability.

Second, the adoption of **Special Operating Agencies** to deliver programs in a more business-like manner, the privatization of Crown corporations, the contracting out of service delivery to third parties, and the development of public-private partnerships are all prominent features of the PSR process. All of these approaches involve the splitting of policy and operations, faith in competition, efforts to create market-type conditions in the public sector, and greater reliance on private sector management techniques. They also involve transferring or sharing of public power with private parties. By definition they involve a reduction in the scope of political accountability operating through Parliament. How ministerial responsibility applies within the shifting contours of the public sector is not at all clear. Unless governments are clear in their aims, invest seriously in the capability to monitor performances of the third parties, and are able to take action to protect the public interest, ministers will not be in a position to render a satisfactory accounting to Parliament. To date, Parliament has paid little systematic attention to these types of developments. There is a Standing Committee on Government Operations and Estimates in the House of Commons which might investigate how these new arrangements are working but there has been neither encouragement from government nor interest among MPs to do so. In contrast, a parliamentary committee on public administration in the UK has produced some useful reports on the consequences of the new governance approaches for parliamentary accountability.

Performance measurement and reporting is a third prominent feature of PSR. Since 1995 the government of Canada has required departments and agencies to produce business plans, to develop performance measures, and to present performance reports to Parliament. In the spring of each year as part of the supply process, departments make available to the relevant standing committees of the House of Commons an 'outlook' document—a condensed and sometimes expurgated version of its business plan, which is used for internal purposes only. The outlooks are meant to explain significant resource shifts and initiatives over a three-year horizon. In contrast to the future orientation of the outlook document, the performance reports made available in the fall, when consultations on the next year's budget are underway, are meant to focus on measures of performance in relation to results of commitments. Today there are hundreds of reports on plans and performance tabled in Parliament annually. The hope was that such documents would shift parliamentary debates and investigations away from the sensational and often trivial aspects of spending and program operations and lead to more focus on substantive outcomes.

To state that Parliament has found it difficult to practice 'results-based accountability' would be a gigantic understatement. The documents produced at considerable cost in terms of both staff time and money are seldom referred to in debates and committee proceedings. There are several explanations for this non-use of performance data. First, there is such a vast amount of information in printed and electronic form and it is so overwhelming, complex, or irrelevant, parliamentarians have found it difficult to work with the material. Second, most of the data deal with inputs and outputs (such as the levels of services provided) rather than the 'real world' outcomes or impacts that most interest MPs. Third, performance data are open to conflicting interpretations and parliamentarians do not approach information with completely open minds. As partisan politicians operating in a competitive arena, MPs tend to be more interested in 'vindicators' that justify their party's positions than they are in valid, reliable, and relevant 'indicators' of performance. Finally, as was already mentioned, Parliament is problem-oriented, short-range, and shifting in its approach; the new information system presumes that it can become systematic, priority-conscious, and more objective in its approach to the review of government performance. If the goal of achieving a more result-based approach to accountability is to be achieved, parliamentarians will have to take the program review function more seriously, governments will have to allow their own backbenchers more freedom to investigate, and ministers and their officials will have to take more seriously parliamentary committee reports, especially if those reports are more meaningful and constructive in tone.

Conclusion

Historically the relationships between Parliament and the public service have been shaped by unwritten, vague constitutional conventions, most notably the principles of ministerial responsibility and the related concepts of a neutral, anonymous public service, and by the changing parliamentary practices which reflect the shifting issues of the day. Always characterized by a certain amount of mutual wariness, those relationships have become over the past two decades more suspicious, negative, and blame oriented, as evidenced by the examples of parliamentarian attacks on senior public servants noted earlier in this chapter. Both long-term trends and short-term developments, outside and inside of government, have caused this deterioration: a series of scandals; a strong anti-politics public mood; political attacks on the public service; an increased likelihood that ministers will name public servants when something goes wrong rather than assume ministerial responsibility; access-to-information laws and a greater insistence on transparency; more oversight bodies whose sole job is to publicize mistakes and wrongdoing; more aggressive media; and new management doctrines which treat government as a business and seek to put operational matters beyond political influence, leading to a generally blurred accountability picture.

In response to these trends there is an emerging acceptance of the idea that the public service is a separate constitutional entity with its own identity and ethos. Lorne Sossin refers to a similar idea in his chapter '**Bureaucratic Independence**'. It is no longer seen as a neutral instrument which owes unconditional loyalty to the government of the day. It is expected to be responsive to the government in office, but it is also expected to show independence in providing policy advice and in delivering programs in a professional, impartial manner without undue political interference. This line of thinking implies that the public service is a fourth branch of government—joining the legislature, the political executive and the courts—and that it is expected to contribute to defining the public interest and upholding the rule of law. Logically this leads to recommendations to codify the constitutional role of the public service and to develop domains and mechanisms of parliamentary accountability for it outside the boundaries of ministerial responsibility. The adoption of the accounting officer role for deputy ministers is the leading practical example of this trend. Reducing the scope of ministerial responsibility to acknowledge separate accountability for public servants entails the risk that ministers will not ask about operational matters and deny knowledge of problems when they arise. Whatever the weakness of ministerial responsibility, it does pinpoint responsibility and thereby contributes to democratic accountability by requiring an identifiable individual to answer before the public's elected representatives in Parliament.

When it comes to the public service, discussion, publicity, and influence are the extent of Parliament's involvement except when it is asked to approve legislative and budgetary initiatives of the government. If we think of Parliament as mainly a discussion forum rather than a decision-making body, we can identify several possible contributions it might make to the future of public service reform. These contributions derive from what is often seen as a weakness of the institution, namely, its non-technical approach to issues of public management. As part of their ongoing efforts to demonstrate political responsiveness, parliamentarians are particularly attuned to the problems, concerns, and opinions of their constituents. On this basis they can bring to the discussion of public organizations and their programs, insights and sensitivities that are beyond the perception and direct knowledge of experts, even those in the public service who manage programs on the basis of pressure group representations and client surveys.

In my view the discussions of government performance that take place in Parliament represent a potentially valuable source of education for ministers, public servants, the media, interest groups, and the public at large. However, the central importance of the concepts of opposition and adversarial politics within the parliamentary systems puts a premium on error avoidance and defensiveness within the cabinet and the senior public service. Generally parliamentarians assign a low priority to the systematic scrutiny of bureaucratic performance. This is mainly an opposition function, because members of the governing party are not encouraged to probe into possible weakness of policies and programs. Even for the opposition parties the incentives to assign time, resources, and energy to scrutiny are weak, unless there is a case which will draw media and public attention and detract from the reputation of the government. So long as Parliament most resembles a permanent election campaign, where the focus is mainly on error identification and blaming, governments will remain reluctant to grant the public service the degree of autonomy implied by the rhetoric of the contemporary public management literature. Reconciling modern public management approaches with the traditions and practices of parliamentary accountability represents a serious challenge. For Parliament to engage in a constructive dialogue with the public service will depend less on institutional innovation and more on a shift in attitudes among parliamentarians in the direction of a less partisan and less adversarial approach.

Appendix A

Standing Committees of the House of Commons (22), April 2008

Aboriginal Affairs and Northern Development
Access to Information, Privacy and Ethics
Agriculture and Agri-Food
Canadian Heritage
Citizenship and Immigration
Environment and Sustainable Development
Finance
Fisheries and Oceans

(continued)

(Continued)

Foreign Affairs and International Trade
Government Operations and Estimates
Health
Human Resources, Skills and Social Development and the Status of Persons with Disabilities
Industry, Science and Technology
International Trade
Justice and Human Rights
Liaison
National Defence
Natural Resources
Procedure and House Affairs
Public Accounts
Status of Women
Transport, Infrastructure and Communications
Veteran Affairs

Appendix B

Standing Committees of the Senate (15), April 2008

Aboriginal Peoples
Agriculture and Forestry
Banking, Trade and Commerce
Conflict of Interest for Senators
Energy, the Environment and Natural Resources
Fisheries and Oceans
Foreign Affairs and International Trade
Human Rights
Internal Economy, Budgets and Administration
Legal and Constitutional Affairs
National Finance
National Security and Defence
Privileges, Standing Rules and Orders
Social Affairs, Science and Technology
Transport and Communications

Appendix C

Standing Joint Committees (3), April 2008

Library of Parliament
Official Languages
Scrutiny of Regulations

Important Terms and Concepts

accountability
Accounting Officer
Auditor General
bureaucratic independence
Canadian Human Rights Commission
collective responsibility
Federal Accountability Act
functions of the legislature
ministerial responsibility
Office of the Information Commissioner
Office of the Privacy Commissioner
Officers of Parliament
Parliament
Parliamentary Budget Officer
performance measurement and reporting
provincial legislatures
public service
roles of Parliament in relation to the public service
Special Operating Agencies

Study Questions

1. Provincial legislatures should not be simply amalgamated with Parliament in discussions of public service reform. What distinguishes them?
2. What leads Thomas to conclude that 'clearly there is life left in the doctrines of collective and individual ministerial responsibility, but the widespread public perception today is that the Canadian political system lacks real accountability'?
3. What is the nature of the 'implicit bargain between public servants and the ministers they serve' and what developments have made this bargain hard to maintain as a central organizing concept?
4. Outline, in the author's view, the meaning of each of the parliamentary roles in relation to the public service—legitimizer, policy-maker, creator, financier, scrutineer—and the relative *effectiveness* of each role.
5. Considering the evidence presented, as well as additional evidence you may be able to muster, what answer would you give to the question 'Does Parliament play a meaningful role in controlling the public service?'
6. Are there arguments for strengthening the first four parliamentary roles that are usually dismissed as 'formal' (legitimizer, policy-maker, creator, financier)? Offer some arguments both for and against this notion.

Useful Websites

Parliament of Canada:

www.parl.gc.ca/

The Public Service Commission of Canada:

www.psc-cfp.gc.ca/index-eng.htm

The Auditor General of Canada:

www.oag-bvg.gc.ca/internet/index.htm

Canada, Parliament of Canada, 'At Work in Committees':

www.parl.gc.ca/information/about/process/house/RTC2008/rtc2008_06-e.html

House of Commons Procedure and Practice:

www2.parl.gc.ca/MarleauMontpetit/Document Viewer.aspx?DocId=1001&Sec=Ch001&Seq=1&Lang=E

Canada, House of Commons, *Compendium: House of Commons Procedure Online:*

www.parl.gc.ca/compendium/web-content/c_g_typicalsittingday-e.htm#11

References

Aucoin, Peter. 1995. *The New Public Management: Canada in a Comparative Perspective.* Montreal: IRPP.

______. 1998. *Auditing for Accountability: The Role of the Auditor General.* Ottawa: Institute on Governance.

Canada, House of Commons, Subcommittee on the Business of Supply. 1997. *Completing the Circle of Control.* Ottawa.

Canada, Office of the Information Commissioner. 1999. *Annual Report, 1998–1999.* Ottawa.

Canada, Treasury Board Secretariat. 1995. *The Expenditure Management System of the Government of Canada.* Ottawa: TBS.

Colwell, R., and Paul G. Thomas. 1987. 'Parliament and Patronage', *Journal of Canadian Studies* 22, 2 (Summer): 163–76.

Docherty, David C. 1998. *Mr Smith Goes To Ottawa: Life in the House of Commons.* Vancouver: University of British Columbia Press.

______. 2003. 'Canada: Political Careers between Executive Hopes and Constituency Work', in Jens Borchert and Juergen Zeiss, eds, *Politics as a Profession*, rev. English edn. Oxford: Oxford University Press.

Franks, C.E.S. 1987. *The Parliament of Canada.* Toronto: University of Toronto Press.

______. 1997. 'Not Anonymous: Ministerial Responsibility and the British Accounting Officers', *Canadian Public Administration* 40, 4 (Winter): 626–52.

Good, David. 2003. *The Politics of Public Management: The HRDC Audit of Grants and Contributions.* Toronto: University of Toronto Press.

______. 2007. *The Politics of Public Money: Spenders, Guardians, Priority Setters and Financial Watchdogs inside the Canadian Government.* Toronto: University of Toronto Press.

Heard, Andrew. 1991. *Canadian Constitutional Conventions: The Marriage of Law and Politics*. Toronto: Oxford University Press.

Holmes, J.W. 1996. 'The Office of the Auditor General and Public Service Reform: An Insider's Perspective', *Canadian Public Administration* 39, 4 (Winter): 524–34.

McInnes, David. 1999. *Taking It to the Hill: The Complete Guide to Appearing Before (and Surviving) Parliamentary Committees*. Ottawa: University of Ottawa Press.

Mitchell, J.R. 1997. 'Reply to C.E.S. Franks', *Canadian Public Administration* 40, 4 (Winter): 653–7.

______, and S.L. Sutherland. 1999. 'Ministerial Responsibility: The Submission of Politics and Administration to the Electorate', in Martin W. Westmacott and Hugh P. Mellon, eds, *Public Administration and Policy: Governing in Challenging Times*. Scarborough, Ont.: Prentice-Hall Allyn and Bacon Canada, 21–38.

Nevitte, Neil. 1996. *Decline of Deference: Canadian Value Change in a Cross-National Perspective*. Peterborough, Ont.: Broadview Press.

Pattee, R.P., and Paul G. Thomas. 1985. 'The Senate and Defence Policy: Subcommittee Report on Maritime Defence', in David Taras, ed., *Parliament and Canadian Foreign Policy*. Toronto: CIIA, 101–20.

Power, Michael. 1997. *The Audit Society: Rituals of Verification*. Oxford: Oxford University Press.

President of the Treasury Board. 1998. *Managing For Results, 1998*. Ottawa.

Roberts, Alisdair. 1996. 'Worrying About Misconduct: The Control Lobby and Bureaucratic Reform', *Canadian Public Administration* 39, 4 (Winter): 489–523.

Royal Commission on Financial Management and Accountability. 1979. *Final Report*. Ottawa: Supply and Services.

Savoie, Donald J. 1999. *Governing from the Centre: The Concentration of Power in Canadian Politics*. Toronto: University of Toronto Press.

Slatter, Frans F. 1982. *Parliament and Administrative Agencies*. Ottawa: Law Reform Commission of Canada.

Sossin, Lorne. 2000. 'Speaking Truth to Power? The Search for Bureaucratic Independence in Canada'. *University of Toronto Law Journal* 55, 1: 1–59.

______. 2005. 'Speaking Truth to Power? The Search for Bureaucratic Independence in Canada', *University of Toronto Law Journal* 55, 1, (Winter): 1–59.

Sutherland, S.L. 1980. 'On the Audit Trail of the Auditor General: Parliament's Servant, 1973–1980', *Canadian Public Administration* 23, 4 (Winter): 616–44.

______. 1991a. 'Responsible Government and Ministerial Responsibility: Every Reform Is Its Own Problem', *Canadian Journal of Political Science* 24, 1 (March): 91–120.

______. 1991b. 'The Al-Mashat Affair: Administrative Responsibility in Parliamentary Institutions', *Canadian Public Administration* 34, 4 (Winter): 573–603.

Thomas, Paul G. 1979. 'Theories of Parliament and Parliamentary Reform', *Journal of Canadian Studies* 14, 2 (Summer): 57–67.

______. 1991. 'Profile of the Private Member', *Canadian Parliamentary Review* 14, 2 (Summer): 12–15.

______. 1993. 'Effectiveness of Parliamentary Committees', *Parliamentary Government* 44 (Aug.): 10–12.

______. 1994. 'Parties and Parliament: The Role of Party Caucuses', in Alain G. Gagnon and A. Brian Tanguay, eds, *Canadian Parties in Transition*, 2nd edn. Toronto: Nelson.

______. 1996. 'Evaluation of Information Disclosure Standards for the Improved Reporting to Parliament Project', paper prepared for the Treasury Board Secretariat, Ottawa.

______. 1997. 'Ministerial Responsibility and Administrative Accountability', in Mohamed Charih and Arthur Daniels, eds, *New Public Management and Public Administration in Canada*. Toronto: IPAC.

______. 1998. 'Contracting Out: Policy and Management Issues', in Peter Aucoin and Donald J. Savoie, eds, *Managing Strategic Change: Learning From Program Review*. Ottawa: CCMD, 169–222.

______. 1999. 'Change, Parliament and the Future of the Legislative Audit', paper prepared for the Office of the Auditor General of Canada.

______. 2003. 'The Past, Present and Future of Officers of Parliament', *Canadian Public Administration* 46, 3 (Fall): 287–314.

______. 2008. 'The Swirling Meanings and Practices of Accountability in Canadian Government', in David Siegel and Ken Rasmussen, eds, *Power, Professionalism and Public Service: Essays in Honour of Kenneth Kernaghan*. Toronto: University of Toronto Press, 43–75.

United Kingdom, House of Commons, Public Service Committee. 1996. *Ministerial Accountability and Responsibility*. London: HMSO.

White, Graham. 1996. 'Comparing Provincial Legislatures', in Christopher Dunn, ed., *Provinces: Canadian Provincial Politics*. Peterborough, Ont.: Broadview Press, 205–28.

______. 2006. 'Evaluating Provincial and Territorial Legislatures', in Christopher Dunn, ed., *Provinces: Canadian Provincial Politics*. Peterborough: Broadview Press.

7 Judicial Administration

Carl Baar and Ian Greene

Judicial administration refers to the organization, management, and operation of courts and court systems. Judicial administration as a field of study is quite recent in Canada. Perhaps the first comprehensive examination of the area was the three-volume *Report on the Administration of Ontario Courts* published in 1973 by the Ontario Law Reform Commission, and the first scholarly book in the field was *Judicial Administration in Canada* by Judge Perry Millar and Professor Carl Baar, published in 1981 as part of the Canadian Public Administration Series.

Judicial administration was already established as a field of study in the United States, but even there its origins have usually been traced only as far back as 1906, when Roscoe Pound, later to become Dean of Harvard Law School and the most prolific writer in sociological jurisprudence, gave his famous and controversial address to an American Bar Association meeting in St Paul, Minnesota: 'The Causes of Popular Dissatisfaction with the Administration of Justice'. By mid-century, a text (W.P. Willoughby's *Judicial Administration*) and a law school casebook (Maynard Pirsig's *Judicial Administration*) had been published, along with major reports by the American Bar Association (e.g., Vanderbilt, 1949) and articles by Pound and other law reformers. The American Judicature Society had been founded in 1913, and its journal, originally the *Journal of the American Judicature Society* and for many years simply *Judicature*, had provided a forum for scholarly and professional writing on the reform of judicial selection, bar governance and discipline, and court organization and procedure. New Jersey Chief Justice (and former ABA president) Arthur Vanderbilt had just completed constitutional reform of his state's court system, and in 1951 would found the Institute of Judicial Administration at New York University Law School.

A new surge of interest in the field would begin in the mid-1960s with the growing American concern about crime, marked by the 1967 publication of the report of the presidential crime commission, *The Challenge of Crime in a Free Society*. By 1973, when the Ontario Law Reform Commission's report was completed, the flagship American text in the field, *Managing the Courts*, by Ernest C. Friesen, Jr, Edward C. Gallas, and Nesta M. Gallas, was in widespread use. New centres of research and education—the National Judicial College, founded in 1960; the Institute for Court Management (ICM), founded in 1969; and the National Center for State Courts, founded in 1971—had been established. Three specialized master's degree programs in judicial administration were in operation, at the University of Denver Law School, the School of Public Administration at the University of Southern California, and American University in Washington, DC. And a new refereed journal, the *Justice System Journal*, sponsored by ICM, was about to begin its first volume.

In fact, the practice and problems of judicial administration could be traced back well before the twentieth century. While references to the eternal verity of the law's delay are often sprinkled through the orations of judges and lawyers, efforts to address these and other central concerns of the administration of justice go back thousands of years. Chapter 18 of the Book of Exodus describes how Jethro, concerned that his son-in-law Moses has kept the people of Israel waiting 'from the morning unto the evening' to ask him how to resolve their disputes in accordance with God's law, advises Moses to appoint a number of 'able men' to decide the large number of routine cases, leaving only the most difficult matters for Moses himself (Exodus 18: 13–27).

Furthermore, while court administration as a profession has only begun to emerge over the past 30 to 40 years, administrative officials have always played key roles in the support of judicial power. When Michel Foucault introduces his classic *Discipline and Punish* with an account of a public execution in 1759 in France, he describes how the clerk of court is called when the executioner is unable to carry out the sentence; the clerk returns to the courthouse and confers with the judges about how to draw and quarter the man before he is hanged (Foucault, 1979: 3–5). When former Ontario Premier E.C. Drury is rewarded at the close of his political career with a patronage post as Local Registrar of the Supreme Court, Sheriff of Simcoe County, and Clerk of the Simcoe County Court in Barrie, he still must arrange in the late 1940s for construction of a gallows to execute a person convicted of a capital offence in the county (Drury, 1970).

While these local court officials played important roles, they were not part of a larger coherent administrative system. Thus when two neophyte senior court administrators in Manitoba decided to assemble their provincial counterparts at a small conference in September 1975, the two did not even know whom to contact in the other provinces. There were clearly identified senior officials (though varying in title, rank, and legal qualifications) in British Columbia, Saskatchewan, Ontario, Quebec, New Brunswick, and Nova Scotia, but Alberta, Newfoundland, and Prince Edward Island still divided responsibility for court support services among diverse officials (as BC, Ontario, and Nova Scotia had done until only a few years earlier). Following some early stops and restarts, these officials have become the core of a growing national organization that meets annually in locations across Canada.

As late as 1980, when Brock University initiated Canada's first graduate-level course of study in court administration, there wasn't even general agreement on an appropriate label for the field. The Brock program was referred to as an MA degree specializing in Judicial Administration, while the national organization's members settled on court administration, naming their group the Association of Canadian Court Administrators. One ACCA leader felt that the term 'judicial administration' was confined to those matters within the responsibility of the judges themselves, and excluded a variety of court support services in the hands of court administrators. Judge Perry Millar, who had attended the inaugural meeting in Winnipeg of what was to become ACCA, felt that the term 'court administration' was too close to the earlier term 'court services', and that many officials who held the title 'Director of Court Services' needed to bring a broader managerial perspective to their work. He felt the term 'judicial administration' did in fact encompass both the traditional court support functions and the new managerial requirements (Millar and Baar, 1981: 17–18). Today, in fact, both terms—'judicial administration' and 'court administration'—are used widely and interchangeably, reflecting the emergence of a coherent field of study and practice. In 2000, when York University created its Graduate Diploma in Justice System Administration, it was thought that the name of the new program would signal both 'judicial administration' and 'court administration', and would also empower the program to examine administrative issues in parts of the justice system beyond courts.

The purpose of this chapter is to introduce some of the major terms, topics, and preoccupations of the field of judicial administration. At the same time, the chapter will also argue that the field, although non-existent less than 40 years ago in Canada, and seen as backward and marginal in the United States, has emerged today as a model for other areas of public administration in an era when the ability to manage professionals, to manage flexibly, to manage contextually, and to deliver specific programs effectively is critical to success in managing a wide range of public sector initiatives.

Provincial Responsibility

In Canada, authority over judicial administration lies largely with the provinces and is therefore affected by the managerial and fiscal environment of provincial and territorial governments. This differentiates judicial administration from many of the larger, older, and more established areas of public administration, and reinforces its distinctive character.

Provincial authority is easily understood and explained, because the administration of justice has been a provincial responsibility since Confederation in 1867, as specified in section 92(14) of the British North America Act (today known as the Constitution Act, 1867). Prior to that time, courts had been organized within each province from the time of the earliest permanent civilian settlements. Upper Canada (now Ontario) gets its own special footnote in North American history, for in 1795, within a few years of the establishment of its first courts, a group of lawyers met in Niagara-on-the-Lake, the province's first capital, and set up the Law Society of Upper Canada as the governing body of the legal profession; the Law Society is now the oldest group of self-governing lawyers on the continent, and was the model for integrated bar reforms in the United States in the first half of the twentieth century (McKean, 1963: 33).

Four caveats are necessary to modify the general statement that court administration is a provincial responsibility. First, the judges of the superior courts of each province (the judicial hierarchy is discussed below) are appointed, and their salaries and expenses paid, by the federal government. Thus, an important aspect of the responsibility for and administration of the courts is divided between federal and provincial authorities. No similar system would be conceivable in either the American or Australian federations. In fact, the Canadian approach would be unique had not the Indian Constitution of 1949 borrowed and entrenched it in their fundamental law. No principled reason for this division can be gleaned from Canadian Confederation debates of the 1860s, and the general view is that federal appointment power reflected the patronage preferences of key political allies Macdonald and Cartier. In retrospect, federal appointment may re-enforce the separation of the judges from a key source of potential dependence on governments responsible for day-to-day administration of the courts, but there is no sign that the Constitution's framers had Locke or Montesquieu in mind when the judicature provisions (sections 96–101 of the Constitution Act, 1867) were drafted.

Second, criminal law and procedure are federal responsibilities under section 91(27), so that provincial efforts to address issues of court delay, for example, must either stay away from changes in the federal Criminal Code or await support and co-operation from Ottawa, speaking through the Department of Justice Canada, before being able to act. For example, grand juries have long been seen as antiquated; once provinces had replaced citizen-initiated prosecution with professional prosecutors, the citizen grand jury no longer provided real protection for persons accused of crime or meaningful participation of the public in the law enforcement process. But provinces that sought to eliminate the grand jury often had to wait many years for federal parliamentary concurrence (Nova Scotia was the last, in 1992). Today, provincial attorneys general often call for an end to preliminary inquiries that take up many hours of Provincial Court time, arguing that the Supreme Court of Canada's post-Charter decision requiring pretrial disclosure of evidence by Crown prosecutors (*R. v. Stinchcombe*, 1991) makes the preliminary hearing redundant. Criminal defence lawyers, however, disagree, and Justice Canada has refused to act on recommendations that go back over 25 years.

Third, the federal government is responsible for the administration of certain specialized courts set up by federal statute under the authority of section 101: 'for the better Administration of the Laws of Canada'. Earliest among these were the Supreme Court of Canada and the Exchequer Court of Canada. (It is interesting to realize that the Supreme Court itself was not created until 1875, a full eight years after Confederation. Presumably there was no rush, since a final appeal could still go to five members of the House of Lords in England, sitting as the Judicial Committee of the Privy Council.) While the Supreme Court has become the jurisprudential leader in reality as well as formality, the Exchequer Court, with its specialized jurisdiction over federal tax matters, was abolished and replaced in 1971 by the Federal Court of Canada, with broader authority to handle appeals from federal administrative agencies and other matters under federal law (see, generally, Russell, 1987). Later in the 1970s, the existing Tax Review Board was transformed into the Tax Court of Canada. Each of these three courts has had its own administrative apparatus, including professional administrators charged with overall responsibility for managing the records, the staff, and the courthouse space; and registrars and trial coordinators who deal with the day-to-day movement of cases and courtroom proceedings. In 2002, federal legislation created the Courts Administration Service (CAS) by merging the administrative staffs of the Federal Court, Tax Court, and Court Martial Appeals Court, and placing the CAS at arm's length from the Ministry of Justice; the innovation has been noticed and praised as far away as Australia (Alford et al., 2004: Ch. 7). The Supreme Court remains a separately administered body.

Finally, federal institutions have developed in recent decades to support the common efforts of provincial judiciaries. Thus the Canadian Judicial Council, founded in 1971, includes all federally appointed chief justices and associate chief justices, even though the vast majority of them sit on provincially administered superior courts. The Council has statutory responsibility for discipline of section 96 judges, and has also supervised important research on issues and policies of direct concern to the administration of justice. The Canadian Centre for Justice Statistics was established in 1981 as a satellite of (or section within) Statistics Canada and operates today under the guidance of liaison committees of provincial justice officials. And the National Judicial Institute was established in 1988 to provide judicial education programs for all judges, regardless of whether they are appointed by the federal or provincial government.

The Judicial Hierarchy

Courts throughout the world are organized in hierarchies that reflect the process of litigating cases and making authoritative decisions. Cases proceed from trial to appeal; since appellate courts have the last word in a case, they are referred to as 'higher courts'. Trial courts are typically categorized into **superior and inferior courts**; the former are often given the statutory name of Superior Court (*cour superieure* in Quebec). The two types of courts, properly identified by more neutral terminology as courts of general jurisdiction and courts of limited jurisdiction, are often distinguished by the seriousness of the cases they handle, but there are numerous and growing exceptions.

The hierarchical distinction remains important in legal terms, especially in common-law countries where past decisions establish precedents binding in future cases. Thus, whether a judgment constitutes a binding precedent depends first on the hierarchical relationship of the court that set the precedent and the court that is asked to follow the precedent. A decision of a provincial court of appeal is binding on all the trial courts of that province. A decision of the Supreme Court of Canada is binding on all other Canadian trial and appellate courts. In turn, the decision of a provincial superior court is binding on all other trial courts within that province. (For the names of the various provincial trial courts, see Dunn, 2006: 287.)

The decisions of common-law courts that are not legally superior to one another are not binding, but may be persuasive. Thus, the judgment of a court of appeal in one province is often cited in the courts of appeal of other provinces as a rule that ought to be followed, but it does not govern. Similarly, a superior court judge need not follow the precedent set by another judge on the same superior court.

Constitutionally, superior courts also have what is legally termed 'inherent jurisdiction', which is derived from their link to superior courts in England and their constitutional entrenchment in section 96 of the Constitution Act of 1867. Thus superior courts, unlike trial courts whose jurisdiction is limited to powers conferred by statute, have inherent authority to enforce their own orders (e.g., through use of the contempt power).

Historically, appeals in Canadian provinces were not handled by a separate court, but by superior court judges assembled to review the original judgment of one of their fellow judges. As provinces grew in size, courts of appeal became differentiated entities with judges appointed specifically to those tribunals. Newfoundland's superior court had only three judges from its inception in 1825 until 1963; as a result it was not unusual for a trial judge to sit on a three-judge panel reviewing one of his own decisions (Goodridge, 1991). In Alberta, the historic link between its current Court of Appeal and Court of Queen's Bench is such that trial judges often sit by special appointment to hear appeals (but never from their own judgments).

The superior courts were supplemented by a set of county courts and district courts in the nine English-Canadian provinces. These courts, also staffed by federally appointed judges, did the bulk of the civil and criminal trials in county towns throughout the country. Over time, the work of the county and district courts came to overlap the work of the superior trial courts, and beginning in 1973, the two courts were merged to form a single section 96 trial court in each of the provinces.

At the lowest level of the judicial hierarchy stood the **Magistrate's Courts**. In the first half of the twentieth century, it would have been appropriate to apply the term 'inferior courts' to them in more than a formal legal fashion. Magistrates themselves were sometimes called police magistrates, reflecting their role in criminal cases—and typically their location in local police stations (where their successors were found until much later in the century). Magistrates were usually non-lawyers (the first women judges in Canada were non-lawyer magistrates, including Emily Murphy of the 'Persons Case', whose criminal sentences could be notoriously harsh), serving on a part-time basis, often paid on a piecework basis (the more warrants signed, the higher the pay), and serving at the pleasure of the government. In pioneer Alberta, the local magistrate could be the commander of the local RCMP detachment. Until 1939 in British Columbia, magistrates were paid only when they entered a conviction; the practice continued for some matters until 1960 (Watts, 1986: 79–81).

Beginning in Quebec and Ontario in the 1960s, these courts were transformed over two decades in every province into modern, professional **Provincial Courts**. Their work today is primarily in criminal matters, but some have been given expanded jurisdiction in civil matters (originally small claims, but now extending to claims currently as high as $25,000 in British Columbia, Alberta, and Nova Scotia, and $25,000 in Ontario as of 1 January 2010) and in family law. All of these courts have exclusive jurisdiction over young offenders under the federal Young Offenders Act. The criminal jurisdiction of Provincial Courts has expanded to the point where a large majority of serious offences (termed 'indictable offences' in Canada, generally parallel to 'felonies' in the United States) are tried in these courts. Thus, in practice, superior courts have tended to specialize in civil litigation, and Provincial Courts in criminal matters, limiting the salience of the superior–inferior legal relationship between the two levels of trial courts.

These changes, coupled with the desire of Provincial Court judges to erase the difference in status between the two levels, have led to proposals for a **unified criminal court** at the superior court level. The unified criminal court would replace the current division, whereby only superior courts can hold jury trials and

Provincial Court judges cannot preside at murder trials. In the 1980s, the proposal received the unanimous support of provincial attorneys general, but opposition by superior court judges and the Canadian Bar Association stopped the proposals. (For a detailed analysis of the issues, see Baar, 1991.) Renewed interest surfaced again early in this century, and a major national conference was held on the topic in 2002 (see Russell, 2007).

A more successful innovation has been the **unified family court**, designed so that litigation on family issues (divorce, separation, custody and access, division of property) would no longer be divided between superior courts and Provincial Courts. Specialized family courts with unified jurisdiction now operate in seven provinces.

The existence of a legal hierarchy has had important administrative consequences. In a sense, judicial administration is inherently non-hierarchical in character. The most difficult administrative work is often at the front end of the system. Visualize the paperwork (or computer capacity) necessary to support the activities in a criminal intake court that hears first appearances, deals with applications for pretrial release, takes guilty pleas, metes out sentences, and schedules dates for trials and preliminary hearings. Or picture the support work at the counter in a civil court, where many claims are filed and judgments issued without a case ever going before a judge. The pressure and complexity of this work reflect the fact that court administrators must manage processes and smooth the flow of incoming work. Yet the existence of a judicial hierarchy, in which the courts with the greatest legal authority handle fewer cases than courts in a legally subordinate position, could distort administrative priorities.

In the United States, critics have noted that because judicial salaries increase as judges move up the legal hierarchy, so do the salaries of court administrators, meaning that courts with the largest volume of cases, as well as the largest amount of fee and fine collection, are managed by administrators with the lowest salaries and status (Stott, 1982). The chief justices of state supreme courts can often dictate administrative policy in high-volume courts of limited jurisdiction. As court administration has evolved as a distinct field and the professional requirements for court managers are increasingly recognized, processes for court governance are likely to evolve that separate the requirements for a hierarchy of legal judgments from the requirements for effectively administering justice.

Judicial Independence

Judicial independence is the central concept in understanding how courts are administered. This independence reflects the fundamental values of the judiciary as a distinct public institution. It is seen as a necessary condition for any court system to perform its functions (in current terminology, achieve its mission). It is also a constraint on the management of courts and a challenge to court administrators everywhere.

Judicial independence refers to the ability of the individual judge to perform his or her adjudicative function, whether sitting in court hearing cases or sitting in chambers writing judgments and hearing motions, free from external interference. Historically, that interference took the form of pressure from government on the judiciary to hand down decisions consistent with governmental preferences, and that pressure is still visible today in many countries throughout the world (including Canada and the United States). Judicial independence can also be undermined by interference from outside pressure groups, or even from 'inside' interference, for example, if the chief judge of a court criticizes the work of one of that court's judges and perhaps threatens to take that work away (see *Chandler v. Judicial Council of the Tenth Circuit*, 1970, in the US, and *Reilly v. Wachowich*, 2000, in Canada; for related commentary, see Bouck [2006]).

This is not to say that judges do or should operate free from external influences when they hear and decide cases. Governments are the most frequent litigators (parties) in court. Every criminal case is prosecuted by a Crown attorney (a full-time government official) or a person that the Crown attorney designates. Federal and provincial governments are parties or intervenors in every case arising under the Canadian Charter of Rights and Freedoms. Numerous interest groups participate in litigation as well. But these roles are clearly defined and public. Parties argue for their positions, both orally and in writing, through formal processes that are either public, or conducted with all contending parties present (e.g., proceedings under the Young Offenders Act), or subject to review and appeal (e.g., *ex parte* proceedings brought by one party alone on an emergency basis). Thus, if a government lawyer meets privately with a judge to discuss a pending case, as occurred during a war crimes proceeding in the Federal Court of Canada, that meeting is seen as a violation of judicial independence (*Canada [Minister of Citizenship and Immigration] v. Tobiass*, 1997; and see Baar, 1998).

Judicial independence is closely linked to the concept of **judicial impartiality**: that a judge is bound to decide only on the relevant law and facts presented in court. Interference by any individual or official not playing a formal role in the proceeding (that is, someone who is not a witness, advocate, or adjudicator in that case) could prevent the judge from coming to an impartial judgment. Thus judicial independence is seen as a necessary condition for an impartial tribunal. However, it is not a sufficient condition, since an independent adjudicator might still not act impartially. If that occurs, judicial independence requires that it be remedied through appropriate formal procedures (e.g., an appeal to a higher court, or a motion by a party that the judge recuse him- or herself from the case, or a complaint to a judicial disciplinary body), not by a personal attack from a government official or members of the public.

Similarly, judicial independence and impartiality do not prevent politicians, academics, or citizens from criticizing the judgments of a court on the grounds that the court misread the law or misconstrued facts, or made policy best left to others (or declined to make policy when a legitimate opportunity arose to do so). Judges are not accountable in the sense that employees in a government department are; they are not required to follow orders that restrict their exercise of judicial discretion. But judges are accountable in the sense that their discretion is subject to review, whether by a higher court or by those who follow their work and question its quality.

In a liberal democratic theory of society and politics, judicial independence is critical to the ability of courts to do justice by the impartial application of the law to parties in individual cases. It is also a legitimate and important constraint on governments that is often missing in non-democratic regimes, where judges sit and apply the law but may be sanctioned when their judgments are seen to undermine the government in power.

In the Charter era, the constitutional guarantees surrounding judicial independence have been given additional meaning, particularly in the context of disputes over the salaries of provincial court judges in the 1990s. As a result of disputes in four provinces, the Supreme Court of Canada imposed constitutionally required salary commissions in each province, to limit negotiation between elected officials and judges. (See McCormick's excellent article [2004] on these developments.) Following criticism of the breadth of the holding in the Remuneration Reference, the Court subsequently modified its judgment (*Provincial Court Judges' Assn. of New Brunswick v. New Brunswick*, 2005).

But how does the fundamental concept of judicial independence fit into the study and practice of judicial administration? First, the preservation and enhancement of judicial independence becomes one of the purposes of court administration (see Friedland, 1995). At an operating level, clerical employees must know what documents need to go in a case file for the judge to review before going into court, and court administrative staff often become a buffer between the judiciary and the public. Those who design courthouses have to ensure that jury rooms are private and that judges can move in and out of court without passing through public hallways where parties to a case could make statements not properly in evidence. Those who prepare the court's budget must ensure that officials with fiscal authority do not act to undermine judicial independence.

Second, the management of an organization whose core activities are performed by autonomous professionals becomes a challenge for court administration. Unlike most parts of the public sector, in which civil servants deliver services to the organization's clients in the community, the justice services of the court are not provided by public servants but by independent judges not subject to direct supervision by any manager. In many provinces, court administration defines its clients as the judges themselves rather than the public, only to find that many judges react unkindly to that label.

Third, court administration is made even more challenging in Canada because administrators in every province are part of executive branch ministries responsible to the government of the day. Thus, court administrators must serve two masters—judiciary and government—and two potentially conflicting principles: judicial independence and responsible government. This conflict has been addressed differently in various judicial systems. Courts in the United States are conceived as a third branch of government, so that court administrators are responsible to the judges of their courts—either to a Chief Justice, the court as a whole, or a judicial council. Courts in England and Wales have been administered by an executive department, the Lord Chancellor's Department, but the Lord Chancellor is both a judge and a cabinet minister. (Recent legislation replacing the Lord Chancellor's Department with a Department of Constitutional Affairs was very controversial and created difficulties for court administration; see Lord Justice Phillips [2008].) In Australia, a number of courts have evolved arm's-length relationships to the government of the day, so that their administration resembles that of independent agencies in Canada. In Ireland, an innovative Irish Courts Service has shifted responsibility for court administration from the government to an independent board of judges, lawyers, court administrators, and public representatives. Elsewhere in Europe, and in Asia and Latin America, where government has traditionally played a central role in court administration, a diverse array of countries—including Sweden, Singapore, India, and Cuba—have developed administrative forms separate from the executive.

Canada has traditionally separated adjudication from court administration, so that judges and administrators can define distinct spheres of activity. Judges expect government to provide them with the necessary staff and material resources to conduct legal proceedings, but they have no authority to hire or fire administrative staff or to supervise the purchase of necessary equipment. However, procedural and technological changes urged by judges to reduce delay and increase efficiency are often delayed or denied by government ministries responsible for court administration—usually provincial ministries of the attorney general that are also responsible for prosecuting criminal cases in those courts.

Beginning in 1981, when the late Chief Justice Jules Deschenes of the Quebec Superior Court wrote a 198-recommendation report, *Masters in Their Own House*, many students of the courts have called for some form of **judicial administrative independence** that reflects the unique role of the courts within a traditional cabinet system. But no major change has been accomplished. British Columbia began in 1976 to shift parts of the court administrative staff to a separate judicial administration budget controlled by the judges, but no further shifting of responsibility has taken place in over two decades. In the late 1980s, the Quebec government offered to adopt the principles in the Deschenes Report. The province's three chief justices (from the Court of Appeal, the Superior Court, and the *Cour du Québec*) were supportive, but the rest of the judiciary resisted, fearing that administrative autonomy would be accompanied by substantial budget cuts that the government would leave the judiciary to implement. More recently, Ontario judges and ministry officials attempted to negotiate a 'court services agency' model similar to that in Ireland, but no consensus was ever reached, and current section 96 chief justices prefer the status quo.

While a new set of practical issues has led to increased collaboration between judiciary and government in a number of provinces, the issue of administrative autonomy remains a lightning rod for executive-judicial conflict. A major report of the Canadian Judicial Council, *Alternative Models of Court Administration*, was released in Fall 2006. It tried to reopen the issue by showcasing a wider variety of alternative approaches, but any breakthrough is still pending.

Caseflow Management

Court administration has often been associated with court reform, the periodic efforts of legal and political elites to change the way court cases proceed from initiation to resolution. Roscoe Pound's 1906 address to the American Bar Association, recognized as the beginning of the study of judicial administration, was primarily a comprehensive agenda for procedural and organizational reform of common-law courts.

In the 1990s, court reform has moved from a focus on changes in the jurisdiction and organization of courts to the revamping of court processes to reduce cost and delay and to increase access to justice, particularly in civil cases brought by private parties. At the heart of court administrative reforms is the concept of '**caseflow management**', which refers to 'the continuum of processes and resources necessary to move a case from filing to disposition, whether that disposition is by settlement, guilty plea, dismissal, trial or other method' (Solomon and Somerlot, 1987; see also Church et al., 1978; Mahoney, 1988; Steelman, 1997, 2006). The term was coined in the United States 40 years ago to convey a new conception of the court's role in the monitoring and supervision of all matters before it.

Caseflow management rests on a set of principles that derive from the notion that courts and judges are responsible for how cases proceed. This may sound trite to those unfamiliar with the internal workings of the judicial system, but it represents a challenge to one of the underlying assumptions of common-law procedure and the **adversary system**: party—and hence lawyer—control of the process (Jacob, 1987). In the traditional common-law proceeding, cases are initiated when one party (the plaintiff in a civil proceeding, the Crown in a criminal proceeding) files an appropriate document with the court. This may be a statement of claim or an application (in civil proceedings), or an information or indictment (in criminal proceedings). Once the defendant has responded (by filing a statement of defence in a civil proceeding or appearing in court to enter a plea in a criminal proceeding), the case then proceeds through preliminary steps taken by the parties (e.g., exchange of documents in civil cases or Crown disclosure in criminal cases). Only when the parties are ready to proceed to a trial, or perhaps earlier to a pretrial conference or a preliminary hearing, do they approach court staff and ask for a trial date (or have the matter placed on a list for trial). Only when a case moves to this stage is the court responsible for expediting its disposition. Thus a case may have been filed in court months or even years earlier, as, for example, the parties await medical evaluations in a personal injury case, additional investigation in a criminal case, or the availability of busy counsel. In this paradigm, lawyer delay is separate from court delay (the number of weeks or months the parties must wait for a trial once they have requested a trial date from the court).

The theory of caseflow management is that the court is responsible for the case from the time it is initiated. Caseflow management rules and procedures typically include a set of time standards for all stages of litigation and a procedure for monitoring those cases that exceed the time standards (Civil Justice Review, 1995). In criminal cases, the Supreme Court of Canada has constitutionalized some of these time standards through use of section 11(b) of the Charter of Rights (*R. v. Askov*, 1990; *R. v. Morin*, 1992). As a result, courts may dismiss cases if the parties do not proceed, or they may force parties on when they believe the litigants are unnecessarily delaying the litigation. By monitoring the flow of cases, courts hope to speed up the pace of litigation, avoid having parties use delay for strategic purposes, and increase the predictability of trial or last-minute settlement in cases that are set down for trial.

Caseflow management may encompass a variety of different techniques and elements. Some courts set general guidelines and standards, for example, by using a 'fast track' for cases that need to proceed more expeditiously. Other courts may establish 'directions hearings' or 'case conferences' at the early stage of a larger or more complex case, so that a customized set of time standards may be established by a judicial officer in consultation with the parties and their lawyers; these procedures are often labelled '**case management**' or 'individual case management'. Some courts encourage the use of settlement processes as part of a caseflow management program (e.g., settlement conferences conducted by a judge, or **mediation** conducted by a professional mediator).

While caseflow management projects and procedures have been used in a number of jurisdictions in the United States, and more recently in Canada, parties themselves still typically control the civil litigation process, at least in its preliminary stages. In Canada, criminal case processing is now typically controlled by the courts, although the Crown—and even the police—still play major and perhaps determining roles in setting trial dates.

The concept of caseflow management came later to England, but after a wide-ranging inquiry by Lord Woolf (1995), who later became the Master of the Rolls and then Lord Chief Justice, a comprehensive system of civil caseflow management was initiated in April 1999 throughout England and Wales. The Woolf reforms, as they are known, make up the most important changes in English civil procedure in over a century, and suggest that the changes begun in the United States 40 years ago are likely to continue there and in Canada.

Caseflow management reforms have also shifted the field of judicial administration from its traditional concern with jurisdictional divisions and judicial independence to a focus on operational processes and effective teamwork (both among teams of judges and between judges and lawyers and court staff). In fact, concepts of case management are increasingly used in other fields (e.g., medicine and social services). The field of court administration has thus been in the forefront of widespread public administration efforts to redirect attention away from formal structures and functions over to core processes and purposes.

Courts and the Public

Judicial administration has not only embraced the analysis of operational processes, but has also given increased attention to the relationship of courts and their clientele. A pioneering set of Trial Court Performance Standards developed over a decade ago by the National Center for State Courts in the United States focused not only on delay reduction and judicial independence, but also on access to justice and on maintaining public trust and confidence in the courts. Court administration has always been premised on efforts to improve the quality of justice (on court effectiveness rather than more narrowly defined issues of court efficiency). What has emerged in the 1990s is a change in the issues courts define as central to achieving and maintaining the quality of justice. Court reform has shifted its orientation from internal professional issues to external public service issues, and from a focus on adjudication in courtrooms and chambers to litigation within and outside the courthouse itself.

One important manifestation has been the recognition that diversity has never been adequately understood or its effects on justice acknowledged. The rule of law is based on principles of universality—rejecting in theory the favouritism and bias that arose when individuals could use their power and influence to exempt themselves from laws that applied to others. But those general laws could have different effects on the population, reflecting historical differences in the treatment of men and women, Aboriginal people and settlers, and people of different races and social conditions. The judiciary, made up primarily of men from dominant ethnic groups and economic classes, would be particularly vulnerable to critics of the gap between the theory and practices of legal institutions.

In the United States, a number of state court systems responded to these concerns by creating internal judicial task forces, to consider, first, gender bias and then racial bias (Baar, 1994). The Canadian judiciary lacked the administrative authority to initiate similar inquiries, but provincial law societies initially filled the gap (Law Society of British Columbia, 1992), and the Canadian Bar Association set up a gender bias task force, chaired by retired Supreme Court Justice Bertha Wilson, that produced an important and controversial report that spurred the development of judicial education programs on this and related topics (Canadian Bar Association Task Force, 1993: ch. 10). A broader commitment to ensuring access to justice is still new to the field of court administration, but this is increasingly defining the reform agenda (see Hughes, 1988; Zuber, 1987).

Near the beginning of the new century, Ian Greene was invited to join the team of the Canadian Democratic Audit to write a book about the strengths and weaknesses of Canadian courts. His book, *Courts*, reviews the successes and failures of various reforms in the justice system, and concludes that 'Canadian courts are doing very well in some areas, such as their contribution to independence and impartiality. But there is a great deal of room for improvement in other areas, such as public participation in court administration and judicial selection, responsiveness to problems of unnecessary delay, support for self-represented litigants, and the respectful treatment of juries, witnesses and litigants' (Greene, 2006: 163). There are signs, however, that the civil justice system in Canada is addressing the need to respond to public criticism of its inefficiencies. For example, since 2003 the Canadian Forum on Civil Justice, a non-profit independent agency located at the University of Alberta, established to promote improvements to Canada's civil justice system, has spearheaded a collaborative research program entitled 'The Civil Justice System and the Public'. Among other things, the project supports research that provides the civil justice system with more complete and accurate information about public concerns, so that the system can respond appropriately.

Alternative Dispute Resolution (ADR)

The earliest, most visible evidence of this reorientation of court administration was the development of **alternative dispute resolution (ADR)** mechanisms. These were already well known in other fields: arbitration had been a staple of labour relations for decades, and mediation had roots as diverse as religious communities, family counselling processes, and commercial and workplace committees.ADR received added visibility among court reformers in the 1976 Pound Conference in St Paul, Minnesota, convened on the seventieth anniversary of Roscoe Pound's pioneering ABA address. Pilot projects followed under the impetus of the Carter administration's Justice Department, both as free-standing alternatives to the court itself, and as alternatives to adjudication within the court (the beginning of the concept of the multi-door courthouse).

Mediation and settlement conferences have become an option—and occasionally a requirement—in Canadian and American trial courts, in civil cases, and in family law matters. What began as a movement proposing a new paradigm for dispute resolution, energized by a culture of peace and a theory of a facilitative interest-based transformative process, has been seen by some as an increasingly professionalized and mainstream option, often rights-based in character and sometimes even staffed by retired judges.

The role of ADR is still evolving. But as the concept of alternative dispute resolution has threatened to go mainstream, it has also been supplemented by a more radical conception of **restorative justice**. Australian criminologist John Braithwaite, its best-known theoretician, went far enough to identify it as a replacement for a system of criminal justice that he considers one of the worst institutional failures since the Industrial Revolution. For Braithwaite, all disputes require a restoration of the balance of relationships within a community, and thus the participation of members of the larger community in individual cases.

In Canada, the most visible moves towards restorative justice have come in recommendations for separate Aboriginal justice systems (Law Reform Commission of Canada, 1991) and the adaptation of traditional sentencing circles for use in Provincial Courts to advise judges on the length and terms of criminal sentences. Other examples are less well known. Victim–offender rehabilitation programs have been undertaken by Mennonites and Quakers, and courts handling cases under the Young Offenders Act have used panels of young people to advise the judge on terms of sentences.

Court Technology and Integrated Justice

Judicial administration, like other elements of the public sector, has also responded to the technological changes associated with computerization. Beginning with the advent of automated management information systems in the 1970s (Millar and Baar, 1981: ch. 10), judges and court administrators have worked to adapt a wide range of electronic technology to the justice environment.

Quebec was the early leader in court technology. By the 1970s, the province had replaced traditional court reporters with recording technology—so centralized in the massive *Palais de Justice* in Montreal that 90 courtrooms were served by a single recording centre. Since then, court reporters in English Canada have upgraded their transcript preparation technology through CAT (computer-assisted transcription) systems, staving off elimination in several provinces and creating the anomalous situation that a province with recording technology may not be able to prepare a transcript necessary for an appeal as effectively as a province with a traditional court reporter.

Today, advocates of technology talk of a paperless courthouse, with parties and their lawyers filing documents electronically, and judges reviewing court records on a computer screen instead of a paper file. E-filing and similar developments are still in the pilot stage, and have taken longer to develop than experienced systems engineers expected. But even now, one can walk into an appellate court in British Columbia or Ontario and observe judges listening to oral argument while taking notes on their laptop computers. And the monitoring and scheduling of cases are automated in every trial centre of any size throughout the country.

The most ambitious concept in the field today is labelled '**integrated justice**'. It is based on the notion of seamless automated processes with a single point of entry. For criminal cases, integrated justice means that data on criminal charges would move electronically from police to prosecution to courts to corrections, without personnel at each stage having to re-enter the names, charges, and other information about every person accused of an offence. Electronic filing by private parties in civil and family cases is the counterpart of integrated justice in criminal proceedings.

So far, provincial aspirations for integrated justice have run ahead of achievements, as pioneering efforts in British Columbia and New Brunswick were scaled down and large-scale private partnerships were abandoned. Ontario tried to build on these experiences, but its integrated justice project faced added costs necessary to bring courts up to the level needed to begin to move information electronically into and out of the adjudicative process (Baar, 1999), and was finally abandoned.

New Professionalism

As this account is written, courts face resource constraints common throughout the public sector. And in some respects, the pressures and constraints on court administration are even greater. While other government departments can downsize by reducing their complement of senior staff, judges cannot be laid off, and they serve until retirement ages generally well beyond any others (age 75 for superior court judges, Federal

Court judges, justices of the Supreme Court of Canada, and some Provincial Court judges). And judges are continually replaced, usually by cabinets and governments with no direct interest in or understanding of the courts' financial needs or of the reality that justice in individual cases cannot easily be repackaged in bulk or turned over to the private sector for delivery.

Yet court administrators in recent years have approached their work with renewed engagement and a level of professional skill unknown in the past. Previously, experienced clerks, familiar with arcane rules of procedure but limited in professional training, supervised court services at the local level, while civil servants drawn from other government departments or other fields (with little or no operational experience in the courts or understanding of how management principles must be modified to be effective in a court environment) directed court services provincially. Today, court administrators have developed distinctive skills increasingly important throughout the public sector: how to manage work processes rather than simply directing people (when key people cannot be subject to formal lines of bureaucratic accountability); how to deal with clientele under stress and often in conflict with the system (in the words of a senior management scholar who had studied the US space agency, courts are more complex because on any given day, half the participants don't want them to work); and how to maintain a commitment to broader institutional purposes (to see that justice is done, and is seen to be done).

In 2000, the ACCA (the Association of Canadian Court Administrators) held its 25th anniversary conference, as it reached a larger membership and expanded its educational and communication activities. As a further sign of the field's professional development, York University's Business School and Arts Faculty established a Graduate Diploma in Justice System Administration, building on the original Brock University program in judicial administration. The core course for the diploma is now built into the Administrative Law stream of York's part-time LLM program. The reform agenda for court administration is as challenging as ever, but enhanced skills and a renewed commitment to advance the agenda provide cause for optimism.

Important Terms and Concepts

adversary system
alternative dispute resolution (ADR)
case management
caseflow management
integrated justice
judicial administration
judicial administrative independence
judicial impartiality
judicial independence
Magistrate's Court
mediation
Provincial Courts
restorative justice
superior and inferior courts
unified criminal court
unified family court

Study Questions

1. Outline what each of these sections of the Constitution Act, 1867 say, and what the implications are for judicial administration in Canada: s. 96, s. 91(27), and s. 101.
2. Why does Baar think that the superior/inferior characterization sometimes used to characterize higher and lower trial courts in the provinces is misleading? How have reformers sought to erase, or lessen, the difference in status between the two levels? What are the *administrative* consequences of the legal hierarchy?
3. What is the relationship of judicial independence and judicial administration?

4. Spell out in detail the differences in processes under the traditional and caseflow management supervision of court administration.
5. What has been the effect of the Charter on the administration of justice?
6. What seem to be some skills, orientations, approaches, and reforms that the larger public administration community could import, to its advantage, from the judicial administration field?

Useful Websites

Alford, John, Royston Gustavson, and Philip Williams. 2004. 'The Governance of Australia's Courts: A Managerial Perspective' (the concluding chapter mentions Canadian federal judicial administration):

www.aija.org.au/online/GACCh7.pdf

Baar, Carl, et al. 2006. *Alternative Models of Court Administration.* Ottawa: Canadian Judicial Council.

http://papers.ssrn.com/sol3/papers.cfm?abstract_id=1352223

Speech by Lord Phillips of Worth Matravers, Lord Chief Justice of England and Wales, 15th Australian Institute of Judicial Administration Oration 'Courts Governance', 2 June 2008.

www.judiciary.gov.uk/docs/speeches/lcj_melbourne_0508.pdf

Supreme Court of Canada (SCC) decisions:

www.lexum.umontreal.ca/csc-SCC/en/index.html

SCC cases referenced in the chapter:

R. v. Askov, 1990:

http://scc.lexum.umontreal.ca/en/1990/1990rcs2–1199/1990rcs2–1199.html

R. v. Morin, 1992:

http://scc.lexum.umontreal.ca/en/1992/1992rcs1–771/1992rcs1–771.html

Regina v. Stinchcombe, [1991] 3 S.C.R. 326:

http://scc.lexum.umontreal.ca/en/1991/1991rcs3–326/1991rcs3–326.html

Provincial Court Judges' Assn. of New Brunswick v. New Brunswick (Minister of Justice); Ontario Judges' Assn. v. Ontario (Management Board); Bodner v. Alberta; Conférence des juges du Québec v. Quebec (Attorney General); Minc v. Quebec (Attorney General), [2005] 2 S.C.R. 286:

http://scc.lexum.umontreal.ca/en/2005/2005scc44/2005scc44.html

References

Alford, John, Royston Gustavson, and Philip Williams. 2004. *The Governance of Australia's Courts: A Managerial Perspective.* Melbourne: Institute of Judicial Administration of Australia.

Baar, Carl. 1991. *One Trial Court: Possibilities and Limitations.* Ottawa: Canadian Judicial Council.

———. 1994. 'Independence, Impartiality and Gender Fairness in the Courts', paper prepared for annual meeting of the Canadian Political Science Association.

———. 1998. 'Judicial Independence and Judicial Administration in the *Tobiass* Case', *Constitutional Forum* 9, 2: 48–54.

———. 1999. 'Integrated Justice: Privatizing the Fundamentals', *Canadian Public Administration* 42: 42–68.

Bouck, John C. 2006. *Exploding the Myths: An Insider's Look at Canada's Justice Systems.* Edmonton: Juriliber.

Canada (Minister of Citizenship and Immigration) v. Tobiass, [1997] 3 S.C.R. 391.

Canadian Bar Association Task Force on Gender Equality in the Legal Profession. 1993. *Touchstones for Change: Equality, Diversity and Accountability.* Ottawa: Canadian Bar Association.

Canadian Judicial Council. 2006. *Alternative Models of Court Administration.* Ottawa: Canadian Judicial Council.

Chandler v. Judicial Council of the Tenth Circuit (1970), 398 U.S. 74, 90 S.Ct. 1648, 26 L.Ed. 2d 100.

Church, Thomas, Jr, et al. 1978. *Justice Delayed: The Pace of Litigation in Urban Trial Courts.* Williamsburg, Va: National Center for State Courts.

Civil Justice Review. 1995. *First Report.* Toronto: Ontario Court of Justice and Ministry of the Attorney General.

Deschenes, Jules. 1981. *Masters in Their Own House.* Montreal: Canadian Judicial Council.

Drury, E.C. 1970. *Farmer Premier.* Toronto: McClelland & Stewart.

Dunn, Christopher, ed. 2006. *Provinces,* 2nd edn. Peterborough, Ont.: Broadview Press.

Foucault, Michel. 1979. *Discipline and Punish.* New York: Vintage Books.

Friedland, Martin L. 1995. A Place Apart: Judicial Independence and Accountability in Canada. Ottawa: Canadian Judicial Council.

Friesen, Ernest C., Jr, Edward C. Gallas, and Nesta M. Gallas. 1971. *Managing the Courts.* Indianapolis: Bobbs-Merrill.

Goodridge, Chief Justice Noel. 1991. 'Remarks to Provincial Judges Association', St John's, Nfld, photocopy.

Greene, Ian. 2006. *Courts.* Canadian Democratic Audit. Vancouver: University of British Columbia Press.

———, Carl Baar, Peter McCormick, Geroge Szablowski, and Martin Thomas. 1998. *Final Appeal: Decision-Making in Canadian Courts of Appeal.* Toronto: Lorimer.

Hughes, The Hon. E.N. 1988. *Access to Justice: Report of the Justice Reform Committee,* report presented to the Attorney General of British Columbia.

Jacob, Sir Jack. 1987. 'Fundamental Features of English Civil Procedure', in W.E. Butler, ed., *Justice and Comparative Law: Anglo-Soviet Perspectives on Criminal Law, Evidence, Procedure, and Sentencing Policy.* Dordrecht: Martinus Nijhoff, 155–69.

Law Reform Commission of Canada. 1991. *Aboriginal Peoples and Criminal Justice.* Ottawa.

Law Society of British Columbia. 1992. *Gender Equality in the Justice System: A Report of the Law Society of British Columbia Gender Bias Committee.* Vancouver.

McCormick, Peter James. 1994. *Canada's Courts.* Toronto: Lorimer.

———. 2004. 'New Questions about an Old Concept:The Supreme Court of Canada's Judicial Independence Decisions'. *Canadian Journal of Political Science* 37:4 (December): 839–62.

McKean, Dayton David. 1963. *The Integrated Bar.* Boston: Houghton Mifflin.

Mahoney, Barry. 1988. *Changing Times in Trial Courts.* Williamsburg, Va: National Center for State Courts.

Millar, Perry S., and Carl Baar. 1981. *Judicial Administration in Canada.* Montreal and Kingston: McGill-Queen's University Press.

Ontario Law Reform Commission. 1973. *Report on the Administration of Ontario Courts,* 3 vols. Toronto.

Phillips, Lord Justice of Worth Matravers. 2008. '15th Australian Institute of Judicial Administration Oration:"Courts Governance"'. 2 June. Available at: www.judiciary.gov.uk/docs/speeches/lcj_melbourne_0508.pdf.

Pirsig, Maynard. 1942. *Judicial Administration.* St Paul, Minn.: West Publishing Company.

Pound, Roscoe. 1906. 'The Causes of Popular Dissatisfaction with the Administration of Justice', address to the American Bar Association, St Paul, Minn.

President's Commission on Law Enforcement and the Administration of Justice. 1967. *The Challenge of Crime in a Free Society: A Report by the President's Commission on Law Enforcement and Administration of Justice.* Washington: US Government Printing Office.

Provincial Court Judges' Assn. of New Brunswick v. New Brunswick (Minister of Justice); Ontario Judges' Assn. v. Ontario (Management Board); Bodner v. Alberta; Conférence des juges du Québec v. Quebec (Attorney General); Minc v. Quebec (Attorney General), [2005] 2 S.C.R. 286.

Regina v. Askov, [1990] 2 S.C.R. 1199.

Regina v. Morin, [1992] 1 S.C.R. 771.

Regina v. Stinchcombe, [1991] 3 S.C.R. 326.

Reilly, P.C.J. v. Wachowich, C.J.P.C. (2000), 266 A.R. 296–320 (Alberta Court of Appeal).

Russell, Peter. 1987. *The Judiciary in Canada: The Third Branch of Government.* Toronto: McGraw-Hill Ryerson.

———. 2007. *Canada's Trial Courts: Two Tiers or One.* Toronto: University of Toronto Press.

Solomon, Maureen, and Douglas K. Somerlot. 1987. *Caseflow Management in the Trial Courts: Now and for the Future.* Chicago: American Bar Association.

Steelman, David C. 1997.' 'What Have We Learned About Court Delay, "Local Legal Culture", and Caseflow Management Since the Late 1970s?' *The Justice System Journal* 19: 145.

———. 2006. *Caseflow Management: A Brief Guide for Family Court Judges.* New York: New York State Judicial Institute.

Stott, E. Keith, Jr. 1982. 'The Judicial Executive: Toward Greater Congruence in an Emerging Profession', *Justice System Journal* 7: 152–79.

Vanderbilt, Arthur T., ed. 1949. *Minimum Standards of Judicial Administration: A Survey of the Extent to Which the Standards of the American Bar Association for Improving the Administration of Justice Have Been Accepted Throughout the Country.* New York: New York University Law Center.

Watts, Alfred, QC. 1986. *Magistrate–Judge: The Story of the Provincial Court of British Columbia.* Victoria: Provincial Court of British Columbia.

Willoughby, W.P. 1927. *Judicial Administration.* Washington: Brookings Institution.

Woolf, The Rt. Hon., Lord. 1995. *Access to Justice.* London: Interim Report to the Lord Chancellor on the civil justice system in England and Wales.

Zuber, The Hon. T.G. 1987. *Report of the Ontario Courts Inquiry.* Toronto.

PART III The Human Resources Dimension

Human resource management (HRM) refers to the wide range of policies relating to the organization of people in the workplace. It involves job design, staffing, training, communications, scheduling, compensation, union–management relations, and forecasting and adjusting to future needs.

Evert Lindquist, though he does not deal with HRM in particular, provides a critical overview of public administration/organization theory that gives context for Chapter 8. His avenue for this is an analysis of the work of the 'dean of public administration' in this country, Ted Hodgetts. Hodgetts, in work covering the Canadian public service, managed to set out a research plan for the immediate generations following him, from the 1970s forward. They were, he argued, to avoid the more esoteric elements of organizational theory, because the basics of theory-informed research—decision-making, internal processes, dealing with external stakeholders, and accountability—had not yet been satisfactorily researched in Canada. One had to walk, he argued, before one could fly into more esoteric realms. Things did not go according to plan, however, argues Lindquist. The immediate generation did what they were asked, but the ensuing generations did not. All modern Canadian single-authored public administration textbooks offer what he calls 'fossilized insight', with scant reference to true organizational theory past the 1960s. There is no reference to contemporary literature on organizational analysis from the 1970s onward; no literature on organizations, tasks and environments, and no research into these areas by the authors themselves. Lindquist offers a menu of research directions to correct these gaps, and suggests a variety of research directions beyond the confines of organizational theory. Some, the reader will discover, involve HR questions.

The last century witnessed remarkable growth in rights consciousness, and the workplace was one of the primary places where reformers sought to extend rights. Nan Weiner, in Chapter 9, discusses workplace equity in terms of the rights and rights-related regimes that have transformed the Canadian public sector workplace to make it more diverse and inclusive. She suggests that the recent wave of change is not over yet. Workplace equity includes initiatives resulting from the Canadian Charter of Rights and Freedoms, human rights legislation, employment equity measures, and pay equity initiatives. The Charter, especially section 15, provides for equality rights and effectively constitutionalizes affirmative action (or employment equity) programs. Human rights legislation in Canada evolved from a focus on fair employment practices, to anti-discrimination measures, and finally to human-rights commissions. Over time there was an expansion of protected groups, recognition of the quasi-constitutional nature of human rights legislation, and a growing awareness of systemic discrimination. Employment equity, which seeks to expand the representativeness of public sector employment in reference to designated groups, began in the mid-1980s and expanded in scope and effect thereafter. Pay equity is 'equal pay for work of equal value' (a step up from the previous iteration, which was 'equal pay for equal work'); it began in Quebec in 1976 and in the federal government in 1978.

Human resources policy is concerned with public sector labour relations, but as Morley Gunderson and Robert Hebdon emphasize in Chapter 10, collective bargaining is only one aspect of labour relations. Determining the future of public sector labour relations requires an understanding of where it has been.

Labour relations in the Canadian public sector have a mixed history of market determination, collective bargaining, and legislative and regulatory action. Perhaps, as Gunderson and Hebdon suggest, its development can be considered an evolution from 'collective begging' to 'collective bargaining', and in the 1990s, as a result of legislated initiatives, a partial return to the begging mode. Initially, small portions of the public sector—for example, in municipal governments—were covered by the same legislation that applied to the private sector. There followed a period of informal bargaining between governments and employee associations, which represented large parts of the public sector workforce, setting the precedent for modern collective bargaining between governments and large employee unions.

Formal collective bargaining in the public sector began in 1944 in Saskatchewan and evolved gradually in other Canadian jurisdictions. Societal impulses combined with increasing power of public sector employees has resulted in higher unionization rates here (30 per cent) than in the US (15 per cent). Various legislative options have been used to mediate relations between governments and their employees, including reliance on legislation drafted for private sector labour relations, modifications of this legislation to accommodate the public sector, and hybrids of the above. Dispute resolution mechanisms have included the right to strike, a limited right to strike, binding arbitration, arbitration requested by either party, and choice of procedure in advance of negotiation. The unfettered right to strike is most common, but no uniform pattern prevails for all of the public service even within one jurisdiction or across all jurisdictions. The differences reflect varying effects of parties, interest groups, special events, and sometimes merely inertia.

Despite the existence of formal strike rights on paper, strikes and collective bargaining can be circumscribed by various means. Designated (or 'essential') employees may be prohibited from striking, arbitration chosen by one party may neutralize the strike weapon, and the public service employer may not have an incentive to settle if it retains its revenue-garnering potential during strikes. In the case of broad collective bargaining, there are also structural impediments: a multiplicity of fragmented bargaining units; legalistic, adversarial government attitudes; and a patchwork of narrow job classifications that inhibit teamwork. Even pay-equity legislation can be considered a legislated method of wage determination, removing the issue from the sphere of conventional collective bargaining. Without these constraining factors, strike activity in the public sector would be much wider than it has been. At issue is whether the public sector bargaining model, especially the traditional system of collective bargaining present in Canada today, can deal with the new issues emerging in the public sphere.

The future of the public sector depends partly on its attractiveness to new recruits, and this revolves to some extent around the comparative compensation that the public and private sectors can provide. In Chapter 11, Gunderson untangles the issue of public and private sector compensation. The current interest in public/private pay differences stems from various sources: concern about deficits and debts; constraints placed on public sector expenditures by globalization; changes in private sector labour markets; fear of spillovers of excessive wage settlements from one sector to the other; and morale/brain-drain problems that periodically beset the public sector. Wage differentials between the two sectors can be attributed largely to three theoretical determinants: the use of higher wages to compensate for other job characteristics; short-run demand changes; and non-competitive factors, which, according to Gunderson, appear to have the most explanatory power. Some interesting differences can be found between the private and public sectors, not the least of which is a pure government pay premium of approximately 5 to 10 per cent.

Public Administration Research and Organization Theory: *Recovering Alternative Perspectives on Public Service Institutions*

Evert Lindquist

Introduction

Ted Hodgetts' *The Canadian Public Service: A Physiology of Government 1867–1970*, published in 1972, is rightly regarded as a classic study in the field of Canadian public administration. It provides an assessment of an important national institution, exploring its historical evolution, and the mandates and interests of line and central agencies, and coins the term 'structural heretics'. It also identifies emerging issues and tensions during a time when the public service was growing quickly in a rapidly changing governance environment, many of which three generations of scholars have wrestled with to this day. Aside from its elegant and often wry rendering of the state of public administration at the national level, *The Canadian Public Service* is intriguing to this reader because Hodgetts draws on concepts and models from organization theory (among other sources) to analyze a complex, evolving institution, and anticipates approaches later elucidated in that literature.

Much has changed in the world of public administration and governance in the last 35 years, but this chapter argues that the field of Canadian public administration has not kept up with and taken advantage of the organization theory literature, while recognizing there are many other rapidly expanding fields to monitor, including our own. Indeed, our collective understanding of organization theory seems to have virtually frozen since *The Canadian Public Service* was published. With some exceptions, we have not kept abreast of the literature on organizations, a diverse interdisciplinary field (often grouped into the broad and overlapping areas of organization theory, organizational behaviour, and organizational change and development) that exploded beginning in the early 1970s, and therefore public sector organizations have not received the attention in organizational studies that they should. This paper argues that the existence of such gaps is worthy of note, deserves some explanation, and has implications for how research and faculty renewal in public administration, along with 'network' strategies, might evolve in the years to come.

This chapter has five parts. It begins with a closer look at *The Canadian Public Service*, particularly drawing attention to Hodgetts' references to the organization theory and the metaphors he invokes to describe and analyze the institution. The second part attempts to gauge contemporary use of organization theory by surveying some well-known texts on Canadian public administration and identifying what strands of the literature they emphasize, and by considering examples of selected use in articles and books. The paper then identifies strands of the more recent organization theories that have not been recognized or utilized in studying Canadian public administration, and the kind of research agendas these strands imply. The fourth part attempts to explain why the gap emerged after the 1960s and possible implications for the field of Canadian public administration, including the narrowing of our relevance over a broader set of issues that confront governments. The paper concludes by considering where and how our field of public administration might address this gap, particularly since there are many other fields that could equally inform our analyses. I suggest that we need to recover the posture of Hodgetts in the 1960s with respect to organization theory and other fields pertinent to public sector governance, but that to do so requires adopting network strategies.

Hodgetts' 'Physiology' of Government: Working at Many Levels

For most readers *The Canadian Public Service* is a seminal and comprehensive account of the state of Canadian public administration at the national level in the early 1970s, exploring the internal dynamics and the state of the institution as a whole. For readers with some background in organization theory, turning the pages of *The Canadian Public Service* is a revelation because of the work it taps into and the later theoretical currents it anticipates. Though the book does not revolve around organization theory nor use it for scaffolding, Hodgetts is clearly aware of both early and more recent contributions to the literature. In what follows we consider Hodgetts' intentions, the authors he cites, and the metaphors and perspectives he invokes or anticipates.

The book is best understood as offering, in part, a dialogue with emerging approaches from organization theory, as well as with others from systems analysis and behavioural traditions. In the preface to the volume, John Meisel wrote:

> Professor Hodgetts, while fully cognizant of—and ever ready to draw on—the insights and benefits provided by organization theory, systems analysis, functionalism–structuralism, and most of the other props which have enriched our studies of society, remains closely attached to the historical and environmental parameters within which the public service performs its tasks. (p.vii)

The book accomplishes what the author set out to do: primarily to convey the state of the Canadian public service and issues and tensions emerging during an era of great growth and new forms of political oversight. Hodgetts sought perspectives to assist in this project, rather than using the opportunity to showcase certain streams of theory.

Hodgetts, however, does see *The Canadian Public Service* as providing an opportunity to broaden horizons and open up new theoretical horizons. He writes:

> The major part of this book, relying on relatively straightforward techniques of analysis, is directed to an attempt to open up the subject, to dissect and describe the anatomy and physiology of the federal public service. If it provides the incentive for others to launch studies to fill the many obvious gaps, using more sophisticated research techniques, this volume will have attained the limited objectives imposed by the prevailing state of our studies. (p. xiii)

In this regard Hodgetts anticipates criticism about whether he relies too heavily on early insights from the organization and administrative literature, and on a historical–legal perspective as his primary empirical approach:

> The public service, both in the tasks it is required to perform and in the ways it is organized to accomplish these tasks, is a reflection of the community it exists to serve. The verification of this hypothesis is attempted in the first four chapters. While this so-called 'ecological approach' to public organizations is in keeping with contemporary academic fashions, other portions of this book may be viewed by

> many students as wedded too closely to the classical school of public administration theorists who enjoyed their heyday in the 1930s. (p. xii)
>
> The failure to adopt these exciting contemporary tools of analysis is not a mark of disapproval or disagreement: the preference for more pedestrian modes of inquiry is simply based on an old-fashioned notion that we must first learn to walk before we can fly. In this respect, such weaknesses as this study exposes are reflections of the comparative neglect of the subject by students of Canadian public administration and the retarded stage of development in which it languished. (p. xii)

With this frank assessment of the state of the field, Hodgetts identifies priority areas where colleagues should invest their energies. He recommends that they focus on deepening their understanding of decision-making, exchange and transactions with the public and inside the bureaucracy, internal adaptive processes, and bureaucratic accountability. Anticipating some push-back from colleagues, he writes:

> There is a simple, straightforward defence that can be mustered in favour of the procedures used for analyzing the allocation of programmes to departments and agencies and for exploring the internal division of labour: it has not been done yet it should be done before we fly off to the esoteric realms inhabited by modern-day organizational theorists and administrative behaviouralists. (p. xii)

It was interesting ground to choose given that Hodgetts monitors and invokes many of the early and emerging precepts of organization theory in analyzing public administration developments in Canada. Some might argue that this remains a compelling argument to this day—one this author has been mindful of when crafting this paper.

While Hodgetts does not see theory-building as a priority for the field of Canadian public administration, he is aware of currents in the organization theory literature. In addition to the classical theorists—Weber, Fayol, Taylor, Gulick, Urwick, and White—he notes Simon's *Administrative Behavior* and Selznick's *Leadership in Administration* and is undoubtedly aware of the salvos against the 'proverbs' of administration (Simon, 1945; Dahl, 1947); really a debate about different notions and standards for 'sciences' of administration. Through his reading, but also through secondary sources (Pfiffner and Presthus, 1967; March, 1965), Hodgetts would be aware of emerging concepts of power, goals, decision-making, leadership, survival, and external environment in the study of organizations from economics, politics, sociology, psychology, management, and informatics; theoretical and experimental approaches to understanding individual and group behaviour, including personality, motivation, strain (what we now call stress), and socialization in workplaces and organizations; ideas about the importance of size and complexity of organizations, and their implications for structure; and the effects of new technology such as computers.

That he does not choose to produce a huge bibliography and adopt a more conceptual approach in *The Canadian Public Service* reflects nothing more than a proper focus on the specific task at hand, providing perspective on the evolution, and rapidly increasing complexity, of a large-scale organization. However, Hodgetts repeatedly invokes metaphors that point towards new analytic and methodological approaches, as well as towards ones that emerge later in organization theory. His master metaphor, of course, is that of 'physiology' (pp. 1, 87), but a closer look—in part with the benefit of hindsight and more supple terminology that has since emerged in the field of organization theory—shows that Hodgetts points to many different aspects of organization in a public sector context. These included the following perspectives:

- *Natural organism*. Hodgetts characterizes the public service as an organism that would experience 'birth, growth, adaptation, and decay' (p. 5). Elsewhere in the book, he depicts the Canadian public service as interested in survival and thus in adapting goals, structure, or position to perceived threats and competition (p. 1). This perspective is consistent with the framework outlined by Selznick (1948) in the **structural-functional tradition** with a focus on co-optation.

- ***Cybernetics***. Elements of the excerpts from the *Encyclopaedia Britannica* on 'physiology' supplied by Hodgetts point to the notion that an organization—like an organism—monitors, anticipates, and adapts to change in its environment. Leaving the strict biological analogy, however, allows one to variously label such perspectives as cybernetics, information-processing, and learning perspectives.
- *Organizational repertoires*. Hodgetts does not cite Cyert and March's (1963) *A Behavioral Theory of the Firm*, but takes considerable space to describe the public service as a complex organization with a variety of programs and routines, as well as efforts to introduce new routines and procedures for coordination and control. Later this becomes a central feature of Allison's *Essence of Decision* (1971).
- *Transactions and exchange*. Hodgetts wonders how the Canadian public service engages in 'mutual exchange' with citizens and other elements in its environment (p. 17), and presumably among constituent programs, departments, and agencies. This interest not only reflects the work of exchange theorists such as Homans (1958), Levine and White (1961), and Blau (1968), but later is taken up in a very different way by Williamson (1981) to explain how organizations structure themselves to minimize the costs of transactions.
- *Tasks and technology*. If there is a foundational concept in organization theory, it is not goals, but tasks (Dill, 1958), which often defines not only the immediate task environment but also the culture of those conducting the tasks as well as the individuals and organizations they deal with. Hodgetts is aware of, but does not delve into tasks, although tasks are closely related to exchange. Tasks are also closely linked to technology, and while he is interested in and understands the importance of technological change (pp. 26–30), the approach in the book is more historical, and does not utilize emerging ideas from the literature. The nature of tasks and technology later becomes a pivotal dimension for analysis in the hands of Thompson (1967) and later Tushman and Anderson (1986).
- ***Morphology***. Hodgetts' notion of physiology is also invoked to consider how the structure of an institution might evolve like an organism (biologists would call this morphology), not only going through natural stages of growth and maturity, but also intentionally aligning workings and structure with new environments or even *altering* their external environments. There is a distinction and a tension between these two drivers of morphological change.
- ***Ecological perspectives*** *and natural selection*. Hodgetts identifies competitive processes both inside and outside the public service arising from its concern for survival—in this sense, survival strategy or reflex arises from a threat from either the internal or the external environment. Hodgetts, like the literature at the time, does not have a well-developed notion of evolving environments, which would come later, but he puts his finger on another core issue: whether institutions have the

ability to alter strategy and structures, as opposed to being compromised or 'selected' by their environments, such as new governments or different economic circumstances (Child, 1972; Chandler, 1962; Hannan and Freeman, 1989).

- ***Punctuated equilibrium***. This is certainly not a concept that was circulating in social science circles in the 1960s, since it is coined by Eldredge and Gould (1972) as a perspective from paleontology on evolutionary dynamics (see also Gould, 2002). But it is worth noting that Hodgetts' historical–institutional–legal perspective relies heavily on having sufficient time to discern and make sense of change. Hodgetts is very aware that he is observing an institution in an era of rapid growth and significant and complex internal and external change, with profound implications for the shape and survival of its structures.
- *Organization design and change*. Hodgetts, of course, is interested in the design of organizational structures, even if this is largely derived from the classical tradition of allocating formal responsibility to central, departmental, regional, and non-core public service forms (pp. 129–37). He is aware of growing interest in the sources of motivation for individuals and groups (Argyris, 1957; Herzberg 1966), and the need for new structures and approaches to coordination, many of which are cascading from the political level. From his ecological and physiological vantage point, though, he sees this as a process of adaptation and repositioning.

Hodgetts' *The Canadian Public Service* is remembered for its synoptic view of a key institution, using deft historical brushstrokes to depict and explain the institution's trajectory and challenges as it entered a period of great change. But in rendering and analyzing this picture, he brings to bear considerable diversity and nuance in conceptual perspectives, even if social science terminology takes a few years to catch up. This observation, in my view, is possible only if one understands a range of theoretical concepts and traditions from the contemporary organization theory. Hodgetts, of course, does not run all of these concepts and forms of analysis through the book—it is not his intention. Many of these concepts are squarely juxtaposed with those of systems theorists like David Easton and Gabriel Almond, so popular at the time.

Based on his evaluation of the 'retarded state of development' of Canadian public administration, Hodgetts identifies the research priorities of decision-making, internal processes, dealing with external stakeholders, and accountability. The next two generations of enormously productive scholars (Aucoin, Borins, Bourgault, Doern, Dwivedi, Good, Gow, Kernaghan, Langford, Phidd, Prince, Pross, Savoie, Schultz, Sutherland, Tupper, Van Loon, Wilson, and Zussman, as well as their students) effectively took this seriously, rapidly exploring the processes, instruments, actors, and values animating the Canadian public service. With these priorities largely addressed, did the field since 'fly off to the esoteric realms inhabited by modern-day organizational theorists and administrative behaviouralists'?

Canadian Public Administration and Organization Theory: Fossilized Insight?

Where might we go to gauge the extent of understanding and use of organization theory precepts in Canadian public administration? One place to begin is with the best-known textbooks in the field. Several nicely crafted textbooks include Kernaghan and Siegel (1999), Inwood (2004), Johnson (2006), and Barker (2008). Each contains one or more dedicated chapters on organization theory.[1] In varying degrees they contain references to the following authors and themes:

- ***Formal organization***. Typically there is reference to the works of Weber, Fayol, Gulick, and Urwick on the bureaucratic form and its underpinnings such as goals, hierarchy, offices, and legal authority. All of these books describe Simon's attack on the 'proverbs of administration' on the early efforts to identify principles for design.
- ***Informal organization*** *and motivation*. Each book reviews the contributions of Barnard, Follett, the Hawthorne experiments (Mayo, Roethlisberger, and Dickson), Maslow, Herzberg, Argyris, and McGregor. The focus here is on the informal and human dimensions of organizations, and different leadership styles. Some books, in highly selective, idiosyncratic ways, delve into certain models of decision-making and participatory management.
- ***Scientific management***, *Total Quality Management, and change*. The books spend considerable time on Taylor and scientific management, which is equally critical and demanding of workers and managers alike. They all consider TQM and, in varying degrees, the principles and approaches to organizational development.
- *Systems and environmental perspectives*. Some texts, in less thorough and accurate fashion, describe the arrival of **systems theory** and cybernetic perspectives and its linkages to Thompson's seminal *Organizations in Action* (1967), as well as contingency perspectives. One book mentions, in passing, population ecology perspectives.

The reviews are concise and generally dispassionate. Little effort is made to integrate across these approaches, except to make room for the critics. The cited literature on true organizational theory rarely extends beyond the 1960s, except in reference to popular writers or, as we discuss shortly, the New Public Management. There is virtually no reference to contemporary literature on organizational analysis from the 1970s and beyond in any of the categories used (i.e., no effort to provide the latest thinking and empirical studies in each tradition). None in any way meaningfully reviews the literature on organizations, tasks, and environments. There is no evidence that any of the authors have conducted research in any of these areas or are familiar with recent relevant research published in journals.[2]

Another way to assess the research is to identify scholars who invoke or rely on concepts from organization theory to focus or illuminate their work. Some examples include:

- Peter Aucoin and Herman Bakvis's *The Centralization–Decentralization Conundrum* (1988) relies on the concepts of **organization differentiation and integration**, among others, from Lawrence and Lorsch's seminal (1967) article.
- Doug Stevens' *Corporate Autonomy and Institutional Control: The Crown Corporation as a Problem in Organization Design* (1993) taps into the strategy-structure literature, as well as contingency and **transaction–cost economics** perspectives, to inform his analytic framework on how to balance autonomy and control of Crown corporations by governments.
- Jim Desveaux in *Designing Bureaucracies: Institutional Capacity and Large-Scale Problem Solving* (1995) provides a detailed examination of how the Department of Energy, Mines and Resources mobilized the capacity to design and announce the National Energy Program, and then out-negotiate Alberta counterparts.
- Lindquist marries concepts from the organizational literature on tasks and task environments with policy network concepts in 'New Agendas for Research

on **Policy Communities**' (1996) to develop the beginnings of a more elegant theory of central agency internal interactions.

- Barbara Wake Carroll and David Siegel's *Service in the Field* (1999) taps into the literature on organizational culture, differentiation and integration, front-line and street-level bureaucrat perspectives, self-correcting organizations, dimensions of bureaucracy, public choice and behavioural perspectives on organizations, and matrix organization.
- Jonathan Malloy's dissertation and book *Between Colliding Worlds* (2003) uses concepts from organization theory, such as boundary-spanning, institutional isomorphism, role conflict, and self-designing organizations, to explore the tensions and dynamics of central secretariats in government designed to respond to social movements advocating for women and Aboriginals.

Undoubtedly there are more examples of the use of organization theory concepts by Canadian public administration scholars, but I suspect we would quickly conclude that, even with additional examples, it still constitutes selective use and is certainly not the focus of empirical investigations of public administration scholars. And, it would also serve to underscore a key point: the use of such concepts and perspectives from contemporary organization theory is not recognized in the textbooks that define the field in Canada. Moreover, these approaches are not likely taught in any traditional PhD-level core course on public administration in departments of political science unless someone has a strong interest in the area.[3] We have come a long way from the early days of public administration when there was a substantial overlap in scholarship and lesson-drawing from the field of organization theory, and vice versa. Arguably, the peak period for such lesson-drawing and influence lasted from the 1930s to the 1970s.

This stands in considerable contrast with US public administration scholarship. My sense is that a higher proportion of public administration scholars south of the border have strong grounding in organizational analysis—it may not be a majority of scholars, but is a sufficient number to keep ideas in circulation, canvass newer insights from organization theory, and share them with colleagues. This is attributable to a far stronger presence of quantitative, behavioural, and rational choice traditions in US departments of political science, and, relatedly, more interdisciplinary public policy and public administration schools and programs of scale. Scale means not only that it will be more likely that one or more colleagues in a program will take an interest in organization theory (and such a person could be from business, political science, sociology, economics, law, or even public administration), but also that the sheer number of specialists in any sub-discipline or sub-field greatly increases the chance that there will be scholars who cross over to or mine other disciplines. Examples of cross-over scholars include Moe (1984; 1990), La Porte (e.g., 1970, 1996; with Frederickson 2002), Chisholm (1989), Kelman (2005), and O'Toole and Meir (2004). Such interest has been fostered by journals that welcome articles using organization theory concepts among other contributions—such as *Administrative Science Quarterly*, *Public Administration Review*, and *Administration and Society*—as well as journals that specialize in making such connections, such as the *Journal of Public Administration Research and Theory* and, more recently, *International Journal of Public Management*.

These positive perceptions, however, might be overstated. Steven Kelman, as the new editor of *International Journal of Public Management*, has aggressively committed himself to fostering a dialogue between scholars from the worlds of organization theory and public administration. This has been reflected in appointments to the editorial board of scholars with strong credentials in organization theory. So, even if the knowledge and linkages in the US look richer from the vantage point of Canada, the connections may be tenuous. This view is buttressed by a recent review by Pfeffer (2006) of the *Oxford Handbook of Public Management* entitled 'Like Ships Passing in the Night: The Separate Literatures of Organization Theory and Public Management'.

He sees a disjuncture between the literatures and missed opportunities: on the one hand, a lack of theory illuminating public management issues and practice, and, on the other, a lack of learning from public organizations for the purposes of theory-building.

Recovering Perspectives from Contemporary Organization Theory

One can imagine that a challenge would soon emerge from public administration scholars: if organization theory is so wonderful, why doesn't it spill over onto our radar scopes and meet us more than halfway? Perhaps, as Hodgetts suggested many years ago, however intriguing, the literature is simply too esoteric, theoretical, and even normatively unaligned with the field of public administration!

With these reasonable caveats in mind, what horizons might a fuller appreciation of the organization theory literature lead to? Here are some snapshots of the possibilities:

- *Institutionalized environments*. In contrast to the political science institutional literature, this body of work considers an organization's need for symbolism and positioning, and examines ways in which an organization decouples central administration from its 'technical core', thereby providing a 'buffer' from the broader environment (Meyer and Rowan, 1977; Meyer et al., 1981; DiMaggio and Powell, 1983, 1991; Weick, 1976). Interestingly, this is inherently a comparative perspective, exploring how classes of organizations align (or appear to align) with broader regimes in their environments.
- *Ecological perspectives*. Borrowing concepts from biology and ecology used to examine the rise and fall of natural species, this literature studies narrow classes of organization (Hannan and Freeman, 1977, 1989). It aggressively relies on the concept of natural selection, has interesting models of the nature of environmental change, and presumes organizations find it difficult to adapt their structures and strategies to environmental change. More recent contributions consider how specific organizational forms evolve with other forms (Astley, 1985; DiMaggio, 1994; Rao, 2002). When these concepts are combined with organizational systematics (below), there is potential to ascertain how public service institutions have been evolving, and what is getting 'selected' in and out.
- *Organizational systematics*. This approach (McKelvey, 1982) borrows heavily from the fields of systematics and phylogenetics in biology, which seek to identify different species according to key features reflecting reproductive integrity, and to inform assessments and debates about ontogeny (the evolving structure and development over a typical life of a species member) as well as the evolutionary trajectory of a species as a whole. Organizational systematics attempts to adapt this logic and methodology to study organizations, and would appear to be fraught with all kinds of difficulties (e.g., what should be the unit of analysis: organizational structure, technology, compools?). However, we have precious little data and indicators about how the contours of public service institutions and their constituent elements have been changing, and this could be a comparative approach within and across institutions.
- *Organizational fields and networks*. In political science and policy studies, there has been tremendous progress in recognizing and characterizing **policy**

networks and communities (see Pross, 1986; Atkinson and Coleman, 1989; Coleman and Skogstad, 1990), and even in how to manipulate and nurture them (Kickert et al., 1997; Lindquist 1992a). But, arguably, there has been less progress and realization of the original promise (Atkinson and Coleman, 1989) with respect to systematic assessments of the dynamics and learning in these networks (Lindquist, 1992b) and to carefully understanding how individuals, information, and other resources move through these networks, and if and how they can adapt to deal with the broad challenges confronting the sector. To build and work in more robust and flexible networks, particularly from public service institutions, there may be benefits in returning to the original organizational field perspectives (Levine and White, 1961; Evan, 1966; Warren, 1967) and joining these up with the societal sector approach (Scott and Meyer, 1991) and with finer-grained network theory from sociology and related disciplines, anticipated by Kickert et al. (1997) who tap into organization theory perspectives.

- *Transaction costs economics and institutional design*. One key reason for delving into networks and systematics from a public administration perspective is that the core responsibilities in public service institutions have evolved, ostensibly from 'rowing' to 'steering' roles such as policy design, network facilitation, and monitoring and evaluating programs and performance. But this is the rhetoric, and there is little analysis of how alternative service delivery arrangements such as public–private partnerships actually work with respect to risk, costs, decisions, error, oversight, and so on. One analytic approach for exploring such matters is the transaction–cost economics set out by Williamson (1981, 1990) which relies on careful examination of task structure, exchange, and institutional arrangements. The key research question here is: when services are spun 'outside' the public service, is this really the case? Such analysis would inform how we typically think about the more formal contours of public service institutions.
- *Real-time decision-making*. For many public administration scholars, the notion of 'loose-coupling' applied to their field (Weick, 1976; Orton and Weick, 1990) may seem beyond the pale, but Perrow (1984), Frederickson and La Porte (2002), Roe et al. (2005)—to name but a few examples—have used this concept to analyze how high-reliability organizations (Lerner, 1986) work under stress when monitoring and guiding critical public infrastructure, and how better to design the system and co-ordinating capabilities. Reminiscent, in part, of the Mintzberg (1973) empirical study of executive work, this style of research involved close observation and mastery of the technical, cognitive, and decision-making strategies of 'operators'. It is hard to overstate its importance and relevance, focusing on specific constellations of tasks and responsibilities.
- *Organizational engagement and culture*. Public sector leaders have indicated that they want to change organizational cultures, instilling leadership and improving the feedback loops to executive teams and institutional leaders. Although there has been much ink spilled in academic and applied journals about organizational development and change strategies, there appears to be relatively little analysis of the extent to which organizational cultures change, which in turn requires capability to measure, characterize, and monitor different organizational cultures. There are many examples of frameworks for doing so (e.g., Cameron and Quinn, 2006), and

> tremendous potential for joining these frameworks, theories of motivation, and assessments to analyze employee engagement surveys. Some work has been done on workplace dynamics (e.g., Lowe, 2000; Verma and Lonti, 2001; Lonti and Verma, 2003; Lonti et al., 2002), but more should be done on this important theme associated with the early days of public administration and organization research.

Similar suggestions for research agendas based on conceptual groundwork could be made with respect to radical organizational change and development (i.e., Tushman and O'Reilly, 1996; Greenwood and Hinings, 1996; Freeman and Cameron, 1993; Gersick, 2003); learning and information utilization incentives (Feldman and March, 1981; March 1988, 1991); and the adoption of new technologies by organizations, especially that involving discontinuities (Barley, 1990; Benner and Tushman, 2003; Tushman and Nelson, 1990; Tushman and Smith, 2002; Tushman and Anderson, 1986), but there is not the space to delve into these areas here.

Contemporary organization theory can be seen as incredibly intriguing and diverse: it has a bewildering array of different guiding metaphors, levels of analysis, conceptual frameworks, and methodological approaches (Morgan, 1980; March, 1965; Scott, 2003; Baum, 2002). But it is also a field where colleagues working in all of its myriad traditions seem to delight and celebrate in this diverse and evolving mix, and spend episodic moments trying to make sense of it (March, 1965; Nystrom and Starbuck, 1981; Perrow, 1986; Williamson, 1990; Powell and DiMaggio, 1991; Clegg et al., 1996; Tsouksas and Knudsen, 2003). None of this curiosity and ferment makes its way into Canadian public administration textbooks and very little into our research literature. Indeed, for a fan of the literature it is hard not to be disappointed by its limited use in Canadian public administration.

In making these points and heaving audible sighs of regret, I should clarify my position in several important ways. First, I do not want my words to be construed as saying that the field of Canadian public administration research and teaching should become heavily skewed towards organization theory; there are other disciplinary and professional directions in which it could also grow. Nor am I suggesting that delving into each strand of the literature will necessarily yield a sea-change in how we perceive public organizations. Nor do I want to argue that the strands or currents in the classic organization theory literature long identified by Canadian scholars as part of the canon be ignored or rejected. That said, Canadian textbooks claiming to impart the state of organization theory to students and colleagues need to re-evaluate their claims, and they should make every effort to showcase more recent empirical studies.

As Kelman and Pfeffer argue in the US context, an ostensibly multidisciplinary field of Canadian public administration needs to move beyond its reliance on two dominant disciplines. One direction should entail reconnecting to the rich literature on organizational theory, behaviour, and change. Contributions to this literature provide concepts and ideas that may clarify or raise the level of discussion in the probing of complex phenomenon such as the public sector. Taking this literature seriously may lead to new research agendas requiring different levels of analysis, new methodologies, and different collaborations. But immersion into these research directions does not mean devaluing public organization and Canadian perspectives, and would probably strengthen them. And, given the ubiquity, scale, and economic and democratic importance of public organizations, we should have far more influence on the research on organizations more generally, and this simply is not happening.

Explanations and Implications of the Public Administration–Organization Theory Gap: Are We Falling Behind?

Before considering what directions Canadian public administration might take to recover its trade in ideas with organization theory, it will be useful to consider how we have arrived at the current state of affairs.

First, all disciplines have fanned out since the 1960s; it is difficult to keep up with ones own discipline and its sub-disciplines, let alone with others expanding equally quickly, if not considerably more. In the case of organization theory, the 1960s and the 1970s witnessed a remarkable proliferation of analytic and methodological perspectives, and eventually an increase in the number of journals in the area. Even scholars fully committed to organizational theory find it hard to keep abreast of all the field's currents.

Second, Canadian political science has been remarkably impervious to American and other literatures, particularly when it comes to rational and public choice perspectives, and, aside from election and public opinion studies, the application of empirical methods to other areas of the discipline has not been as aggressive. To the extent that organization theory, in many quarters, relies on sophisticated quantitative methodologies, this may have created barriers to the monitoring and exchange of approaches, insights, and findings.

Third, most programs and schools of public administration in Canada are not genuinely interdisciplinary in the way that departments of geography, agriculture, and business have been for a long while. These programs tend to be dominated by political scientists and, to a lesser extent, economists. There are few sociologists or business-school graduates who have been hired sporting comprehensives in organizational analysis. Our programs and schools tend to be 'bi-disciplinary' at best, and each of those disciplines has experienced considerable proliferation in perspectives. Complementing this is that fact that the field of public administration, at least until recently, has been moved forward by a relatively small group of productive scholars, mainly trained in political science. Moreover, there was little hiring during the 1980s, when the gaps between Canadian public administration and organization theory were not as large and could have been more easily bridged.

Fourth, one can shift vantage points and ask: to what extent has the organization theory literature reached out to public administration? The answer here has to be 'very little', even though most contributors to the literature would claim that they are indifferent about the kinds of organizations that get studied. Indeed, public organizations would be treated no differently than for-profit and third-sector organizations, but public administration scholars would be less likely to see common cause as a result. Contributors to this literature would be less likely to use as their points of departure the notions of democratic legitimacy and responsible government—they would be more likely to focus on tasks, interactions, environments, structures, and culture.

Leaving aside the question of which organizations tend to be the focus of attention, it is certainly true that with its amazing conceptual, theoretical, and methodological diversity, the literature on organizations does not seem very coherent and can look like a hodgepodge to outsiders. This is well understood by core contributors, as any review of the major volumes dedicated to reviewing the state of the field will demonstrate: March (1965); the two-volume Nystrom and Starbuck (1981); the two editions of Clegg et al. (1996); Baum (2002), and other integrating volumes, such as five editions of Scott (2003), Perrow (1986), Williamson (1990), and Aldrich and Ruff (2006).

Conversely, it is important to recognize that there is much more to public administration than organization theory! One has only to review the many compelling topics captured by the *Handbook of Public Administration* edited by Peters and Pierre (2003) to see this is true, even if the handbook is dominated by scholars with political science backgrounds. But there are many *other* perspectives and substantive areas that have received insufficient attention, particularly in the eyes of practitioners. These include information technology adoption and its impacts, supply chain management, motivation and engagement of public servants, marketing and conveying of public service work to outside audiences, better use of information, studies on the nature and organization of work in different program areas (as opposed to the politics and managing networks in those areas), making public organizations environmentally sustainable, creating and managing diversity in public administration, the day-to-day governance and management of departments and agencies (as opposed to outlining the principles of accountability, which several Canadian scholars have done very well). It should be easy to identify other equally compelling lines of investigation. All of this serves to reinforce the point that although organizations may be ubiquitous, there are many themes to mine from different disciplinary and professional perspectives, and organization theory perspectives constitute only one part of this mix.

This line of argument, even if deemed persuasive, needs to be put in perspective: the disinterest in modern organization theory by public administration scholars in Canada (because this has not been the case in the United States and in some European quarters), and the juxtaposition of other equally important topics noted above, are certainly not unique problems for our field. Indeed, perhaps it is best to see them as part of a larger challenge confronting our public administration scholarly community. Here is our condition: we are a small band of academics (mostly with backgrounds in political science), with an interest in democratic public organizations, and who collectively attempt to keep abreast of international, national, provincial, territorial, municipal, and Aboriginal developments at the intersection of political and administrative realms. Our revealed preferences are that we believe it important to keep our eye on the high-level governance ball, because that is where authority and reform often (though not always!) flow from. Individually, but sometimes in pods, we make forays into more selective areas (voluntary sector, diversity, specific policy domains, public–private partnerships, service delivery, ethics, etc.). Governments have steadily reached beyond public administration scholar-experts to move goalposts forward in areas such as service quality, technology, alternative service delivery, engagement, leadership, and so on, and as a group, we typically play catch-up in these areas, no matter how good the scholarship. Governments are reaching out, as they should, to experts and scholars in many other disciplines (and do this far better than we do as an interdisciplinary enterprise). Sometimes we get pulled into these initiatives, but it is clear where the insight, demands, and energy come from.

The implication is that even as our best scholars continue to play and exercise influence in important ways (think of accountability, federalism, voluntary sector initiatives, etc.), and we continue to remind practitioners and the next generation of public servants at all levels of important values and organizing principles in government, we could fall behind in important ways as a scholarly field.

Conclusion: Emulating Hodgetts in the Early Twenty-First Century

I have entered into these larger questions from the vantage point of organization theory, but really, the argument could have come from any one of many other directions and would have wound up in more or less the same place. These sorts of issues have been broached at meetings of the Canadian Association of Programs in Public Administration and at the Canada School of Public Service, so some of these points are not new. I am not suggesting that all public administration scholars should be trained in organization theory, but I worry that too few of our PhD students are aware of the existence of that field, and that, because of the smallness of the public administration field in Canada, the chances are low that some scholars might mine certain veins of organization theory literature and marry them to public administration topics. (Or, those interested in organization theory may have to move to other fields or countries to get such grounding.) To me, it implies a multi-part question:

- if scholars (and practitioners) need to keep abreast of the insights produced by other disciplines and professions, and, more dramatically, to work with colleagues from those disciplines and professions, to be on the leading ('bleeding') edge; and
- if we agree that traditional public administration and political science perspectives are *essential linchpins* for filtering information and ensuring its evaluation in the appropriate context, and that therefore these perspectives must retain a robust role for reminding all concerned about the distinctiveness of public organizations and how to apply alternative perspectives in a public sector context; and
- if, even though our community of scholars in public policy and administration schools is growing, the number of public administration scholars remains relatively small and possibly shrinking compared to the governance challenges, knowledge demands, and requisite methodological and disciplinary perspectives;
- then, how do we organize ourselves to operate in this environment?

While one partial solution is to write a compelling book that more fully makes the case outlined in this chapter (but that requires less devotion to administrative duties!), my view is that making significant progress is beyond the scope of any one scholar, or even of any one school or program. It requires cultivating a posture among a community of scholars and schools, where our networks of colleagues and programs across Canada can together find ways to scan, partner, coordinate, and exercise leverage in a more systematic and intelligent manner.

The foundations arguably are in place: the Canadian Association of Programs in Public Administration has grown steadily more robust over the years and, as noted above, these sorts of issues have been tabled (but no real action has been taken). I believe that most of our colleagues would have a genuine interest in fostering, tapping into, and working in an interdisciplinary environment (though this would not be everyone's cup of tea, nor should it be). This requires assiduously cultivating or tapping into networks of expertise outside the usual public administration beats. Indeed, developing such networks and repertoires would be an excellent way to engage government. The goal, however, would *not* be to align all of this activity with the needs of governments and other sponsors, precisely because individual understandings of needs and directions are important sources of innovation, and the need for certain kinds of insight cannot be anticipated. This model would entail encouraging individuals or groups to monitor and report on different areas of literature in various fields, including organization theory, behaviour, and change.

As I consider these possibilities and juxtapose them against the capabilities we have in our field, and the amount of change in public sector governance, there are interesting parallels to the decisions Ted Hodgetts had to make when writing *The Canadian Public Service: A Physiology of Government*. There were so many institutional and theoretical developments that he decided on a synoptic and suggestive study, rather than a comprehensive one, which meant that he did not delve into various domains as deeply as he could have. Only a master of the field of public administration and political science, with one eye firmly on emerging trends and issues in public sector institutions, and the other eye scanning other fields such as organization and systems theory, could strike such an intriguing and productive balance. This paper is suggesting that we consider collectively adopting a similar strategy at the network level to move our field forward by levering and anchoring insights from other fields with our own.

Important Terms and Concepts

cybernetics
ecological perspectives
formal organization
informal organization
institutionalized environments
morphology
organization differentiation and integration
organizational systematics
policy communities
policy networks
punctuated equilibrium
scientific management
structural-functional tradition
systems theory
transaction–cost economics

Study Questions

1. What made J.E. Hodgetts a good example of how to use organizational theory?
2. At what stage of organizational theory are most textbooks in Canada, and does this matter?
3. Of what fields of organization theory should Canadian public administrationists be more aware?
4. What explains the delay of Canadian public administrationists in catching up to what is happening in organization theory elsewhere?
5. Reseach and explain what is meant by each entry in 'Important Terms and Concepts'.

Useful Websites

Dowding, Keith. 1995. 'Model or Metaphor? A Critical Review of the Policy Network Approach', *Political Studies* 43: 136–58.

www3.interscience.wiley.com/cgi-bin/fulltext/121436327/PDFSTART

Evans, Mark. 2001. 'Understanding Dialectics in Policy Network Analysis', *Political Studies* 49, 3: 542–50.

www3.interscience.wiley.com/cgi-bin/fulltext/119015610/PDFSTART

Marsh, David, and Martin Smith. 2000. 'Understanding Policy Networks: Towards a Dialectical Approach', *Political Studies* 48, 1: 4–21.

www3.interscience.wiley.com/cgi-bin/fulltext/119037593/PDFSTART

Notes

1. Inwood's (2004) Chapters 2 and 3 are respectively on 'Theories of Organization' and 'Organization Theory and Canadian Public Administration'; Johnson's (2006) Chapter 5 is 'Theory of Organizational Design and Management Decision-Making'; and Kernaghan and Siegel (1999) and Barker (2008) have Chapters 2, 3, and 4 respectively titled: 'Public Administration and Organization Theory: The Structural Foundation'; 'Public Administration and Organization Theory: The Humanistic Response'; and 'Public Administration and Organization Theory: The New Public Management'.

2. The only modern work that gets explored is the more popular management-guru literature like In Search of Excellence and Reinventing Government and so on. One volume casts the New Public Management (NPM) as a theory of organization as opposed to a management and political philosophy. Any reference to NPM as having been inspired by organization theory, of course, is a misrepresentation of the literature. NPM proponents were inspired by the public choice literature, and while this does constitute a theory of organization, it emanated from practitioners who sought out economics and political science

perspectives, and only later was identified as tradition by academics. While a public administration PhD course should require students to read such literature (the popular and more academic renderings), such reading would not materialize in a standard organization theory course. NPM had no influence on the organization theory literature—indeed, many of the limitations and appropriate expectations for the NPM approach could have been anticipated by utilizing well-understood ideas in the modern literature if anyone had bothered to do so.

3. Many years ago I taught 'Organization Theory and Public Organizations' at the University of Toronto's Department of Political Science. A similar course now constitutes one of the three core fields of the PhD Program in Public Administration at the University of Victoria.

References

Aldrich, Howard E., and Martin Ruff. 2006. *Organizations Evolving*, 2nd ed. Thousand Oaks, Calif.: Sage.

———, and J. Pfeffer. 1976. 'Environments of Organizations', *Annual Review of Sociology* 2, 79–105.

———, and D.A. Whetton. 1981. 'Organization-Sets, Action-Sets, and Networks: Making the Most of Simplicity', in P.C. Nystrom and W.H. Starbuck, eds, *Handbook of Organizational Design*, Vol. 1. New York: Oxford University Press, 385–408.

Allison, Graham T. 1971. *Essence of Decision: Explaining the Cuban Missile Crisis*. New York: Little, Brown.

Argyris, Chris. 1957. *Personality and Organization*. New York: Harper.

Astley, W.G. 1985. 'The Two Ecologies: Population and Community Perspectives on Organizational Evolution', *Administrative Science Quarterly* 30, 224–41.

Atkinson, Michael, and William Coleman. 1989. *The State, Business, and Industrial Change in Canada*. Toronto: University of Toronto Press.

Aucoin, Peter, and Herman Bakvis. 1988. *The Centralization–Decentralization Conundrum: Organization and Management in the Canadian Government*. Ottawa: Institute for Research on Public Policy.

Barker, Paul. 2008. *Public Administration in Canada*, brief edn. Toronto: Thomson Nelson, chs 2–4.

Barley, Stephen. 1990. 'The Alignment of Technology and Structure through Roles and Networks', *Administrative Science Quarterly* 35, 1 (Mar.): 61–103.

Baum, Joel A.C., ed. 2002. *Blackwell Companion to Organizations*. Malden, Mass.: Blackwell.

———, and Tim Rowley. 2002. 'Companion to Organizations: An Introduction', in J.A.C. Baum, ed., *The Blackwell Companion to Organizations*. Malden, Mass.: Blackwell, 1–34.

Benner, Mary J., and Michael L. Tushman. 2003. 'Exploitation, Exploration, and Process Management: The Productivity Dilemma Revisited'. *Academy of Management Review* 28, 2: 238–56.

Blau, Peter M. 1968. 'The Hierarchy of Authority in Organizations', *American Journal of Sociology* 73: 453–67.

———. 1974. 'Social Exchange', Chapter 12 in *On the Nature of Organizations*. New York: John Wiley, 204–14.

Cameron, K.S., and Robert E. Quinn. 2006. *Diagnosing and Changing Organizational Culture*, rev. edn. San Francisco: John Wiley & Sons.

Carroll, Barbara Wake, and David Siegel. 1999. *Service in the Field: The World of Front-Line Public Servants*. Montreal and Kingston: McGill-Queen's University Press.

Chandler, Alfred D. Jr. 1962. *Strategy and Structure: Chapters in the History of the American Industrial Enterprise*. Cambridge, Mass: MIT Press.

Child, J. 1972. 'Organizational Structure, Environment and Performance: The Role of Strategic Choice', *Sociology* 6 (June): 1–22.

Chisholm, Donald W. 1989. *Coordination without Hierarchy: Information Structures in Multiorganizational Systems*. Berkeley: University of California Press.

Clegg, S.R., C. Hardy, and W.R. Nord, eds. 1996. *Handbook of Organization Studies*. Thousand Oaks, Calif.: Sage.

Coleman, William D., and Grace Skogstad, eds. 1990. *Policy Communities and Public Policy in Canada: A Structuralist Approach*. Toronto: Copp Clark Pitman.

Cyert, Richard, and James G. March. 1963. *A Behavioral Theory of the Firm*. Englewood Cliffs, NJ: Prentice-Hall.

Dahl, R.A. 1947. 'The Science of Public Administration: Three Problems', *Public Administration Review* 7, 1 (Winter).

Desveaux, James A. 1995. *Designing Bureaucracies: Institutional Capacity and Large-Scale Problem Solving*. Stanford: Stanford University Press.

Dill, W.R. 1958. 'Environment as an Influence on Managerial Activity', *Administrative Science Quarterly* 2: 409–43.

DiMaggio, Paul. 1994. 'The Challenge of Community Evolution', commentary in Joel Baum and Jitendra Singh, eds, *Evolutionary Dynamics of Organizations*. New York: Oxford University Press, 444–50.

———, and Walter W. Powell. 1983. 'The Iron Cage Revisited: Institutional Isomorphism and Collective Rationality in Organizational Fields', *American Sociological Review* 48, 2 (April): 147–60.

———, and ———. 1991. 'Introduction', in Walter W. Powell and Paul J. DiMaggio, eds, *The New Institutionalism in Organizational Analysis*. Chicago: University of Chicago Press.

Duncan, Robert B. 1972. 'Characteristics of Organizational Environments and Perceived Environmental Uncertainty', *Administrative Science Quarterly* 17, 3 (September): 313–27.

Dunn, Christopher, ed. 2002. *The Handbook of Canadian Public Administration*. Toronto: Oxford University Press.

Eldredge, N., and S.J. Gould. 1972. 'Punctuated Equilibria: An Alternative to Phyletic Gradualism', in T.J.M. Schopf, ed.,

Models in Paleobiology. San Francisco: Freeman, Cooper, 82–115.

Emery, F.E., and E.L. Trist. 1965. 'The Causal Texture of Environments', *Human Relations* 18 (February): 21–32.

Evan, W. 1966. 'The Organization-Set: Toward a Theory of Interorganizational Relations', in J.D. Thompson, ed., *Approaches to Organizational Design.* Pittsburgh: University of Pittsburgh, 173–91.

Feldman, Martha, and James March. 1981. 'Information in Organizations as Signal and Symbol', *Administrative Science Quarterly* 26, 2 (June): 171–86.

Frederickson, H.G., and Todd R. La Porte. 2002. 'Airport Security, High Reliability, and the Problem of Rationality', *Public Administration Review* 62 (September), Special Issue on Homeland Security: 34–44.

Freeman, S., and Kim Cameron. 1993. 'Organizational Downsizing: A Convergence and Reorientation Framework', *Organizational Science* 4: 1 (February): 10–29.

Gersick, Connie J.G. 2003. 'Revolutionary Change Theories: A Multilevel Exploration of the Punctuated Equilibrium Paradigm', *Academy of Management Review* 16, 1: 10–36.

Gould, Stephen Jay. 2002. *The Structure of Evolutionary Theory.* Cambridge, Mass.: Belknap of Harvard University Press.

Greenwood, Royston, and C.R. Hinings. 1996. 'Understanding Radical Organizational Change: Bringing Together the Old and the New Institutionalism', *The Academy of Management Review* 21, 4: 1022–54.

Gulick, Luther. 1937. 'Notes on the Theory of Organization', in Luther Gulick and L. Urwick, eds, *Papers on the Science of Administration.* New York: Institute of Public Administration.

Hannan, Michael T., and John Freeman. 1977. 'The Population Ecology of Organizations', *American Journal of Sociology* 82, 5 (March): 929–64.

———, and ———. 1989. *Organizational Ecology.* Cambridge: Harvard University Press.

Herzberg, Frederick. 1966. *Work and the Nature of Man.* Cleveland: World Publishing.

Hodgetts, J.E.H. 1972. *The Canadian Public Service: A Physiology of Government, 1867–1970.* Toronto: University of Toronto Press.

Homans, George C. 1958. 'Social Behavior as Exchange', *American Journal of Sociology* 63, 6 (May): 597–606.

Inwood, Gregory. 2004. *Understanding Canadian Public Administration: An Introduction to Theory and Practice*, 2nd edn. Toronto: Pearson Prentice Hall.

Johnson, David. 2006. *Thinking Government: Public Sector Management in Canada*, 2nd edn. Peterborough, Ont.: Broadview.

Kelman, Steven. 2005. *Unleashing Change: A Study of Organizational Renewal in Government.* Washington, DC: Brookings Institution.

Kernaghan, Kenneth, and David Siegel. 1999. *Public Administration in Canada: A Text*, 4th edn. Toronto: Nelson.

Kickert, W.J.M, E.H. Klijn, and J.F.M. Koppenjan, eds. 1997. *Managing Complex Networks.* London: Sage.

La Porte, Todd R. 1970. 'The Recovery of Relevance in the Study of Public Organizations', in F. Marini, ed., *Toward a New Public Administration.* San Francisco: Chandler Press, Chapter 2.

———. 1996. 'Shifting Vantage and Conceptual Puzzles in Understanding Public Organization Networks', *Journal of Public Administration Research and Theory* 6, 1 (January): 49–74.

Landau, Martin. 1969. 'Redundancy, Rationality, and the Problem of Duplication and Overlap', *Public Administration Review* 29, 4: 346–58.

———. 1999. 'On Multiorganizational Systems in Public Administration', *Journal of Public Administration Research and Theory* 1, 1: 5–18.

Lawrence, Paul R., and Jay W. Lorsch. 1967. 'Differentiation and Integration in Complex Organizations', *Administrative Science Quarterly* 12, 1 (June): 1–47.

Lerner, A.W. 1986. 'There is More than One Way to be Redundant: A Comparison of Alternatives for the Design and Use of Redundancy in Organizations', *Administration and Society* 18, 3 (November): 334–59.

Levine, S., and P.E. White. 1961. 'Exchange as a Conceptual Framework for the Study of Interorganizational Relations', *Administrative Science Quarterly* 5, 4: 583–601.

Lindquist, Evert. 1992a. 'Classification and Relevance: A Strategy for Developing a Data-Base and Taxonomy of Public Organizations in Canada', paper presented to the Annual Meetings of the Institute of Public Administration.

———. 1992b. 'Public Managers and Policy Communities: Learning to Meet New Challenges', *Canadian Public Administration* 5, 2: 127–59.

———. 1996. 'New Agendas for Research on Policy Communities: Policy Analysis, Administration, and Governance', in L. Dobuzinkskis, M. Howlett, and D. Laycock, eds, *Policy Studies in Canada: The State of the Art.* Toronto: University of Toronto Press, 219–41.

Lonti, Zsuzsanna, and A. Verma. 2003. 'The Determinants of Flexibility and Innovation in the Government Workplace: Recent Evidence from Canada', *Journal of Public Administration Research and Theory* 13, 3: 283–309.

———, Sara Slinn, and Anil Verma. 2002. 'Can Government Workplaces be Made World-Class? Policy Challenges for Labour and Management', *Canadian Labour & Employment Law Journal* 9, 3: 335–60.

Lowe, Graham S. 2000. *The Quality of Work: A People-Centred Agenda.* Toronto: Oxford University Press.

McKelvey, Bill. 1982. *Organizational Systematics.* Berkeley: University of California Press.

Malloy, Jonathan. 2003. *Between Colliding Worlds: The Ambiguous Existence of Government Agencies for Aboriginal and Women's Policy.* Institute of Public Administration of Canada Series in Public Management and Governance. Toronto: University of Toronto Press.

March, James G., ed. 1965. *Handbook of Organizations.* Chicago: Rand McNally.

———. 1988. *Decisions and Organizations.* Oxford: Basil Blackwell.

———. 1991. 'Exploration and Exploitation in Organizational Learning', *Organization Science* 2, 1: 71–87.

———. 1999. *The Pursuit of Organizational Intelligence.* Oxford: Basil Blackwell.

Meyer, J.W., and B. Rowan. 1977. 'Institutionalized Organizations: Formal Structure as Myth and Ceremony', *American Journal of Sociology* 83, 2 (September): 340–63.

———, W.R. Scott, and T. Deal. 1981. 'Institutional and Technical Sources of Organizational Structure: Explaining the Structure of Educational Organizations', in H.D. Stein, ed., *Organization and the Human Services.* Philadelphia: Temple University Press, 151–79.

Mintzberg, Henry. 1973. *The Nature of Managerial Work.* Harper & Row.

Moe, Terry M. 1984. 'The New Economics of Organization', *American Journal of Political Science* 28, 4 (November): 739–77.

———. 1990. 'The Politics of Structural Choice', in O.E. Williamson, ed., *Organization Theory: From Chester Barnard and Beyond.* New York: Oxford University Press.

Morgan, Gareth. 1980. 'Paradigms, Metaphors, and Puzzle Solving in Organization Theory', *Administrative Science Quarterly* 25, 4: 605–22.

———. 1986. *Images of Organization.* Newbury Park, California: Sage.

Nohria, Nitin, and Robert Eccles, eds. 1992. *Networks and Organizations: Structure, Form and Action.* Boston: Harvard Business School.

Nystrom, Paul C., and William H. Starbuck, eds. 1981. *Handbook of Organizational Design*, vols. 1 and 2. New York: Oxford University Press.

Orton, Douglas, and Karl Weick. 1990. 'Loosely Coupled Systems: A Reconceptualization', *Academy of Management Review* 15, 2 (April): 203–23.

O'Toole, Jr., Laurence, and Kenneth J. Meier. 2004. 'Desperately Seeking Selznick: Cooptation and the Dark Side of Public Management in Networks', *Public Administration Review* 64, 6 (November–December): 681–93.

Perrow, Charles. 1984. *Normal Accidents: Living with High-Risk Technologies.* New York: Basic Books.

———. 1986. *Complex Organizations: A Critical Essay*, 3rd ed. New York: Random House.

Peters, Guy, and Jon Pierre, eds. 2003. *Handbook of Public Administration.* London: Sage.

Pfeffer, Jeffrey. 2006. 'Like Ships Passing in the Night: The Separate Literatures of Organization Theory and Public Management', *International Journal of Public Management* 9, 4: 457–65.

Pfiffner, John M., and Robert Presthus. 1967. *Public Administration*, 5th edn. New York: Ronald Press, Chapters 11–13.

Powell, Walter. 1990. 'Neither Market nor Hierarchy: Network Forms of Organization', *Research in Organizational Behaviour* 12: 295–336.

———, and Paul J. DiMaggio, eds. 1991. *The New Institutionalism in Organizational Analysis.* Chicago: Chicago University Press.

Pross, Paul. 1986. *Group Politics and Public Policy.* Toronto: Oxford University Press.

Rao, Hayagreeva. 2002. 'Interorganizational Ecology', Chapter 23 in Joel A.C. Baum, ed., *The Blackwell Companion to Organizations.* London: Blackwell, 541–56.

Roe, Emery, Paul Schulman, Michel van Eeten, and Mark de Bruijne. 2005. 'High-Reliability Bandwidth Management in Large Technical Systems: Findings and Implications of Two Case Studies', *Journal of Public Administration Theory and Research* 15, 2: 263–80.

Scott, W. Richard. 1995. *Institutions and Organizations.* Thousand Oaks: Sage.

———. 2003. *Organizations: Rational, Natural, and Open Systems*, 5th ed. Newark, NJ: Prentice-Hall.

———, and J.W. Meyer. 1991. 'The Organization of Societal Sectors: Propositions and Early Evidence', in W.W. Powell and P.J. DiMaggio, eds, *The New Institutionalism on Organizational Analysis.* Chicago: University of Chicago Press, 108–17.

Selznick, Philip. 1948. 'Foundations of the Theory of Organization', *American Sociological Review* 13, 1: 25–35.

———. 1957. *Leadership in Administration: A Sociological Perspective.* New York: Harper & Row.

Simon, Herbert A. 1945. *Administrative Behavior: A Study of Decision-Making Processes in Administrative Organizations.* New York: Free Press.

———, Donald W. Smithburg, and Victor A. Thompson.1962. *Public Administration.* New York: Alfred Knopf.

Stevens, Douglas F. 1993. *Corporate Autonomy and Institutional Control: The Crown Corporation as a Problem in Organization Design.* Montreal and Kingston: McGill-Queen's University Press.

Stinchcombe, A. 1965. 'Social Structure and Organizations', in J.G. March, ed., *Handbook of Organizations.* Chicago: Rand McNally, 142–93.

Terreberry, S. 1968. 'The Evolution of Organizational Environments', *Administrative Science Quarterly* 12, 4 (March): 590–613.

Thompson, James D. 1967. *Organizations in Action.* New York: McGraw-Hill.

Tsouksas, Haridimos, and Christian Knudsen, eds. 2003. *The Oxford Handbook of Organization Theory.* Oxford: Oxford University Press.

Tushman, Michael L., and Philip Anderson. 1986. 'Technological Discontinuities and Organizational Environments' *Administrative Science Quarterly* 31, 3: 439–65.

———, and Richard Nelson. 1990. 'Introduction: Technology, Organizations, and Innovation', *Administrative Science Quarterly* 35, 1 (March): 1–8.

———, and C. O'Reilly. 1996. 'Ambidextrous Organizations: Managing Evolutionary and Revolutionary Change', *California Management Review* 36, 4: 8–30.

———, and Wendy Smith. 2002. 'Organizational Technology', Chapter 17 in Joel A.C Baum, ed., *The Blackwell Companion to Organizations*. London: Blackwell, 386–414.

Verma, Anil, and Zsuzsanna Lonti. 2001. *Changing Government Workplaces*. CPRN Discussion Paper No. W11. Ottawa: Canadian Policy Research Networks.

Warren, R. 1967. 'The Interorganizational Field as a Focus for Investigation', *Administrative Science Quarterly* 12, 3 (December): 396–419.

Weick, Karl. 1976. 'Educational Organizations as Loosely Coupled Systems', *Administrative Science Quarterly* 21, 1 (March):1–19.

———. 1995. *Sensemaking in Organizations*. Thousand Oaks, Calif.: Sage.

Williamson, Oliver E. 1981. 'The Economics of Organization: The Transaction Cost Approach', *American Journal of Sociology* 87, 3 (November): 548–77.

———, ed. 1990. *Organization Theory: From Chester Barnard to the Present and Beyond*. New York: Oxford University Press.

Wilson, James Q. 1989. *Bureaucracy: What Government Agencies Do and Why They Do It*. New York: Basic Books.

9 Workplace Equity: *Human Rights, Employment, and Pay Equity*

Nan Weiner

Introduction

Governments make laws. In addition, government organizations are employers governed by some of these laws. With respect to workplace equity laws, significant changes occurred from the 1960s through the 1990s on a national level. '**Workplace equity**' is increasingly used to refer to a number of laws, programs, and concerns related to the fair treatment of employees and the elimination of discrimination in the workplace. Human rights, the equality section of the **Canadian Charter of Rights and Freedoms**, pay equity, employment equity, anti-harassment efforts, and, increasingly, diversity all come under the rubric of workplace equity. This chapter focuses on human rights, employment equity, and pay equity in the public sector, with brief consideration of how these issues relate to the Charter.

While each of these aspects of workplace equity will be discussed in detail, it will be helpful to provide a brief definition at this point. **Human rights** provides protection to individuals or groups based on a characteristic (e.g., age, gender, race, religion) to ensure they are not adversely affected by discrimination. Human rights legislation provides protection in the areas of employment, services (e.g., accessibility to restaurants), and accommodation (i.e., place to live). Since this chapter focuses on workplace concerns, only human rights related to employment will be discussed. Human rights legislation provides protection to everyone; for instance, men and women are covered under the protected group 'gender'. **Employment equity** (EE) addresses four **designated** (or target) groups: Aboriginal people, persons with disabilities, visible (racial) minorities, and women. EE requires that employers determine if their workforce reflects the proportion of each of these groups in the occupations they employ compared to the external labour supply from which they recruit. If an under-representation exists (internal workforce has a lower proportion than the labour supply), employers are required to identify and remove barriers believed to be preventing representation. **Pay equity** (PE) or comparable worth[1] requires equal pay for predominately female jobs of equal value to predominately male jobs. PE differs from other workplace equity concerns in that it focuses on jobs, not people. Both men and women working in predominately female jobs (e.g., child-care workers, librarians, secretaries) benefit from pay equity protection. Women and men working in predominately male jobs do not.

The history of workplace equity is provided in the next section. This includes a discussion of the evolution of our understanding of discrimination (direct and systemic). Historical development provides the background for current workplace equity legislation and an understanding of recent Supreme Court decisions. The current situation is delineated in terms of significant human rights cases and the impact employment equity and pay equity legislation has had. Speculation regarding the future of workplace equity is provided in the last section of this chapter.

Historical Development

The actual chronology of the passage of various types of workplace equity legislation is not consistent with the evolution of thought in the area. The focus here is on the evolution of workplace equity thinking, with particular consideration of the Charter of Rights and Freedoms, human rights, employment equity, and pay equity.

Canadian Charter of Rights and Freedoms

The Canadian Constitution was patriated in 1982. One part of the Constitution, the Canadian Charter of Rights and Freedoms, became effective in 1985. It is the foundation of workplace equity legislation affecting government. The Charter regulates only governmental organizations so as not to infringe on the rights of individuals. Governments include the federal government, provincial and territorial governments (excluding Quebec, which replaced the Canadian Charter with its own), municipal governments, and bodies that receive their powers from statutes, such as police commissions. The Charter covers a wide range of issues, such as right to assembly and association, democratic rights, mobility rights, and minority-language rights. Of most relevance to workplace equity is the Equality Rights section. Section 15(1) reads:

> Every individual is equal before and under the law and has the right to the equal protection and equal benefit of the law without discrimination and, in particular, without discrimination based on race, national or ethnic origin, colour, religion, sex, age, or mental or physical disability.

The Charter, like human rights legislation, lists protected groups. However, under the Charter, the listing of protected classes is illustrative, not exhaustive. This means the courts can decide that groups not listed are covered by Charter protection. Under human rights legislation, only those groups listed have protection.

The references in Section 15(1) to protection 'before the law' and 'under the law' and to 'equal protection and equal benefit of the law' ensure that equality means more than just the same application of a law to everyone. Rather, it requires a determination of whether the same application of a law creates inequities for protected groups. For example, there used to be a law that if an Aboriginal woman married a non-Aboriginal man she lost her 'Indian' status. An Aboriginal man who married a non-Aboriginal woman retained his status. Before the Charter this was not seen as discriminatory since the law was applied equally to all Aboriginal women and equally to all Aboriginal men. The requirements of the Charter recognize the discriminatory aspect of treating Aboriginal women differently from Aboriginal men. This is one way that the Charter incorporates broader thinking about equity and rights than had human rights legislation. Thus the Charter is conceptually the foundation for workplace equity even though it is more recent than human rights legislation.

Section 15(2) of the Charter allows employers to enact special programs that may appear to favour some groups over others, e.g., an Aboriginal Internship Program. These programs are allowed where:

- they are directed at disadvantaged individuals or groups;
- their purpose is the amelioration of such disadvantage.

Employment equity and pay equity efforts fulfill this definition since they are directed at redressing historical disadvantages and are designed to ameliorate (eliminate) past disadvantage. This is also true of recent legislation in Ontario to make organizations in the province more accessible to persons with disabilities, which is discussed later.

The Charter does set a limit on equality in section 1, which notes that rights and freedom are subject to 'reasonable limits . . . as can be demonstrably justified in a free and democratic society'. An example of this limit was a decision by the Supreme Court in 1990 on mandatory retirement. The Court said that mandatory retirement at 65 *is* discrimination on the basis of age but that this is nonetheless reasonable in a free and democratic society (*McKinney v. University of Guelph*, 1990).

Human Rights

Legislation to address discrimination has been in place for a long time. Ontario had a Religious Freedom Act as early as 1897. However, modern human rights began after World War II as a reaction to the Nazis' attempt to eliminate whole peoples (e.g., Jews, gypsies, and homosexuals). Early post-war human rights legislation focused on fair employment practices and put the full responsibility for resolution on those who felt discriminated against. The courts at this time were not sympathetic to human rights issues. Beginning in the 1960s and through the 1970s all Canadian jurisdictions passed human rights legislation designed to recognize the dignity and worth of every person by redressing discrimination. Human rights commissions were established to investigate complaints and provide educational assistance. Remedies moved from apologies to financial remuneration. Over time, human rights protection has increased in three important ways:

- expansion of protected groups;
- recognition by the Supreme Court that human rights legislation is quasi-constitutional;
- greater understanding of how discrimination actually works.

Expansion of protected groups. Protected groups are those specifically mentioned as being covered by human rights legislation. Certain protected groups have always been found in all human rights legislation, for example, age groups and racially defined groups. Other protected groups have been added to legislation in various jurisdictions over time. 'Disability', for example, was first added to the New Brunswick Act in 1974 and has since become part of all human rights legislation. While various Canadian jurisdictions differ somewhat in the groups they protect, the vast majority provide protection on the basis of the following:

- age
- ethnicity (including ancestry, citizenship, nationality, and place of origin)
- disability
- family status and/or marital status
- gender (sex)
- religion (creed)
- race and colour
- sexual orientation

In addition, most jurisdictions include other, more unique categories, such as criminal charge or record (Ontario, Yukon), political conviction (Quebec), and language (Quebec). Further, human rights legislation prohibits harassment of the members of the protected groups.

Expansion of a protected group occurred in 1989 when the Supreme Court of Canada ruled that discrimination on the basis of pregnancy was included under the prohibition of discrimination on the basis of gender (*Brooks v. Canada Safeway Ltd*). In 1998 the Supreme Court decided that certain groups are so discriminated against that they must be 'read into' (assumed to be covered by) human rights legislation even if they are not specifically mentioned (*Vriend v. Alberta*). *Vriend* was a Charter case brought because discrimination on the basis of sexual orientation was not protected under Alberta's human rights legislation. The Supreme Court said that clearly there is discrimination against gays and lesbians and so they must have protection in human rights legislation.

Quasi-constitutional. The highest court in Canada has declared that human rights legislation is quasi-constitutional. The Constitution, including the Charter of Rights and Freedoms, is the highest law in the land. By interpreting[2] human rights legislation to be quasi-constitutional, the Court effectively stated that human rights statutes have precedence over all legislation other than the Constitution. For instance, human rights legislation takes precedence over health and safety legislation and other workplace equity legislation. This does not mean, however, that health and safety concerns are unimportant, but that they do not override human rights considerations. For example, a mining company concerned about the potential effect of some of its processes on fetuses had a policy prohibiting all women of child-bearing age from working in certain jobs. The Ontario Board of Inquiry in this case,

Wiens v. Inco Metals Co. (1988), declared this policy too broad—all women of child-bearing age are not pregnant or about to become pregnant. The company needed a policy that did not violate human rights *and* that took into account realistic health and safety considerations. Looking at effect rather than intent is a major breakthrough in human rights thinking and facilitated an understanding of systemic discrimination.

Systemic discrimination. In the early 1980s, human rights theorists began to realize that discrimination did not operate solely in the manner assumed by human rights legislation. Human rights legislation is premised on the assumption that discrimination, whether malicious or not, is the result of intentional behaviour of one person towards another. Such behaviour can be due to negative prejudice or presumed to be for 'someone's own good' (e.g., the concern that someone using a wheelchair could not get out of the building in case of fire). It was assumed that discriminatory behaviour is not desired by the organization and that stopping it was simply a matter of getting particular individuals not to discriminate.

While this kind of direct or interpersonal discrimination continues to exist, it is now clear that another kind—'systemic discrimination'—also operates. **Systemic discrimination** results from the unintended negative consequences of established employment systems and practices that disadvantage members of certain groups. Barriers that have an adverse impact on some groups (e.g., people of colour) and not on others (e.g., whites) can unwittingly be built into employment systems. An example of systemic discrimination found in many organizations is the typical educational assistance program. The program allows employees to be reimbursed upon successful completion of a course. However, many of those in lower-paying jobs cannot manage the cash flow required in paying for a course ahead of time and being reimbursed months later. Because visible minorities, Aboriginal people, persons with disabilities, and women are found disproportionately in lower-paying jobs, traditional educational assistance programs affect these groups more negatively than others.

In 1984, the Report of the Commission on Equality in Employment (the Abella Report) highlighted the presence of systemic discrimination and the need to address such discrimination with systemic remedies. In 1985, the Supreme Court ruled in two human rights cases—*Ontario (Human Rights Comm.) and O'Malley v. Simpson Sears* and *Canadian National Railway Co. v. Canada (Human Rights Comm.) and Bhinder*—that the effect, not the intent, must be assessed to determine if discrimination has occurred. Thus, policies and practices that employers did not intend to be discriminatory could be in violation of human rights legislation because of their adverse impact on the members of certain groups protected under human rights legislation.

Systemic discrimination is often subtle and difficult to detect unless one is looking for it because such discrimination operates through employment systems that:

- clearly have an acceptable purpose;
- are assumed to be non-discriminatory since no one intended them to discriminate;
- have often been in place so long that the system is not really 'noticed' (it is assumed this is the way 'things' must be done).

Differences between direct and systemic discrimination are provided in Table 9.1.

While there has been increased recognition of systemic discrimination and attempts to address it through human rights legislation, for the most part the complaint nature of the legislation is not conducive to redressing systemic discrimination. Problems of a systemic nature have been best addressed by separate legislation designed with an understanding of the employment systems to be examined; employment equity and pay equity legislation are examples of this.

Employment Equity

The Abella Report (1984) called for systemic remedies to redress systemic discrimination. Enactment of the federal Employment Equity Act in 1986 was the response. The original legislation was weaker than that called for by the Abella

Table 9.1 Comparison between Direct and Systemic Discrimination

Characteristic	Direct Discrimination	Systemic Discrimination
Occurrence of discrimination	Exception or aberrant incident due to behaviour of one or more individuals.	A policy, procedure, or system that has a valid purpose also has an unintended adverse impact on one or more groups protected by human rights legislation.
Detection of discrimination	Discrimination is known or suspected and a complaint is filed and investigated.	Proactive examination of systems is necessary to identify the operation of such discrimination. Statistical analysis is often used to detect the adverse impact of specific policies and practices.
Appropriate remedies	'Make the person whole' as if the discrimination had never occurred. This holds whether the discrimination is intentional or not, and whether it is malicious or not. Such a remedy requires looking back in time to determine what would have happened if the discrimination had never occurred.	Typically, there is more than one way to change the system to remove the adverse impact while ensuring the intended purpose of the system continues.
Appropriate timing of the remedy	Liability begins at the time of the complaint. Because the orientation is to the past, retroactivity is often required.	A systemic remedy is required. The remedy may need to be phased in, since a reasonable period of time to correct the system is required, while the non-discriminatory purpose of the system needs to continue. There is usually a future orientation, since the emphasis is to ensure discrimination does not continue.

Report, but in 1995 amendments were added to strengthen the Act. The initial Employment Equity Act covered federally regulated industries (e.g., banking, communication, and transportation) and federal Crown corporations. The federal public service was excluded from the 1986 Act but included in the 1995 amendment. In addition, a Federal Contractors Program has been operating since 1986. It involves businesses that are not covered by federal legislation but that must agree to implement employment equity if they want to do business with the federal government. However, it applies only to businesses that provide at least $200,000 of goods or services in a single contract to the federal government.[3] In this way the federal government has extended the concept of employment equity to its suppliers. Quebec legislation covers provincial departments and agencies and public sector organizations that have a $100,000 contract, subcontract, or grant under its contract compliance program.

Based on an understanding of systemic discrimination, employment equity legislation is premised on the presumption that systemic discrimination could exist within workplaces and is likely to affect the four designated groups (Aboriginal people, persons with disabilities, visible minorities, and women) adversely. Because it is understood that systemic discrimination is difficult to detect, the Act requires proactive efforts to look for barriers affecting the four designated groups. These four groups have been identified as being disadvantaged in Canadian workplaces.

While human rights legislation covers everyone within each protected group (e.g., able-bodied persons and persons with a disability), human rights experience shows that certain subgroups (e.g., persons with a disability) are discriminated against more than others—specifically, women more than men; racial minorities, including Aboriginal people, more than whites; and persons with a disability more than able-bodied persons. Consistent with human rights complaints, statistical data show these same groups to be disadvantaged in the workplace: they have higher levels of unemployment, a lower proportion in positions of authority, and lower pay for their level of skill. Because of this, the four designated groups require more than human rights protection—they need proactive measures to ameliorate the effects of discrimination built into employment systems. This is substantive equality. Table 9.2 describes the steps required to achieve employment equity.

Every aspect of employment equity is derived from the goal of 'representation'. **Representation** means that an organization's workforce reflects the available labour supply for each of the four designated groups for each occupational grouping (see Table 9.3) in the geographic area from which the organization recruits. For example, let us assume that in Winnipeg, 10 per cent of the 'economist' occupational group are members of a visible minority (VM) and that one of the federal departments has an office in Winnipeg and currently employees 6 per cent visible minorities in this occupational group. This is under-representation. A measure of representation relative to labour market availability is the **Index of Representativeness** (IR), which is calculated as follows:

$$\text{IR} = \frac{\text{Current representation}}{\text{Availability in labour market}} \times 100$$

If this index is 100 (or more) then representation exists. Where there is a high under-representation (IR $<$ 80) then employment equity efforts are a priority. So in the Winnipeg example, the 6 per cent representation with a 10 per cent availability (IR = 6/10 = 60) is considerably below the acceptable level. On the other hand, if 18 per cent of the economists in this department are women, where the availability of women is 20, the IR would be 90 (= 18/20). In this situation more effort should be put into hiring more VM economists. The index (IR) is useful for making comparisons. An employer can compare the IR for each designated group to determine priorities (lowest IR), or comparison can be made between employers for the same designated group, or an employer's progress can be assessed by comparing a designated group's IR over time.

Workforce survey and analysis. Two pieces of information are needed to determine whether representation exists: (1) the proportion, by occupational groupings, of each of the designated groups within the organization's current workforce; and (2) the proportion of these same demographic groups available in the external labour force for each occupational group. (If the organization promotes from within, then the internal labour supply is relevant.) Gaining information on the organization's current workforce requires a survey asking employees to self-identify regarding their disability status, gender, and race. Since such information must be given voluntarily, it is vital for employees to understand why it is needed and how it will (and will not) be used. That is, employment equity needs to be well explained. External availability data are provided by Human Resources Development Canada based on census data. These data are based on the broad occupational groupings in the National Occupational Classification (NOC) codes. For example, financial auditors and accountants are in the same broad NOC code. When comparing to the external (NOC) data, an employer need only compare to those occupations actually employed in the organization. For example, an engineering firm would look at the availability of women in engineering jobs but not those in nursing (both of which are in the broad NOC of 'Professionals'). Table 9.3 lists the 14 occupational groups into which over 500 more narrow NOC codes are grouped for employment equity purposes (the federal public service uses its own unique occupational groupings).

Table 9.2 Steps Required to Achieve Employment Equity

1. Identify any equity problems	A workforce survey is used to determine how representative an employer's workplace is; that is, how well does it reflect the proportion of the four designated groups in the broader labour market?	Employees are asked to self-identify in terms of their characteristics relative to the four designated groups and this information is compared to the availability of members of each group in the external labour market.
	Where an under-representation is found (fewer members of a designated group in the organization than in the labour market) the organization must examine its employment systems (e.g., hiring, training, promotion) via an employment systems review (ESR) to identify the barriers which are likely causing the under-representation.	
2. Set goals and timetables	Based on the under-representation found, the barriers identified in the ESR, and the organization's expected hiring and promotion over the next year, goals are set, which are designed to move the organization towards full representation.	Numerical goals are required (e.g., attempt to hire persons with disabilities for 20 per cent of accounting positions).
		System goals are required; these can be focused on eliminating barriers, changing employment systems (e.g., review all qualifications required for entry level jobs to ensure they reflect what is actually needed), and establishing special programs (e.g., provide special training for designated group members).
3. Write and monitor a three-year Employment Equity Plan	Based on steps 1 and 2 above, an EE plan is written and communicated to employees.	
	The EE plan is monitored and revised to ensure that goals are being achieved and that it is having the desired effect on representation and is creating employment systems which benefit everyone.	

For the purposes of this discussion the workforce survey and analysis (see calculation of Index of Representativeness) have been presented in a straightforward manner. Reality is more complex. However, the basic outcome of the analysis is that for any given location a single number exists for *each* of the designated groups for *each* of the relevant occupational groups. For an organization operating in a single geographic location, this could be at the most 56 (four designated groups × 14 occupational groups) indices indicating if representation exists or not.

If an under-representation exists for any of the designated groups in any occupational group, then the following steps are required by the EE Act (see Table 9.2):

Table 9.3 List of 14 Occupational Groupings used for Employment Equity Purposes among Federally Regulated Industries and Crown Corporations

Senior managers
Middle and other managers
Professionals
Semi-professionals and technicians
Supervisors
Supervisors—crafts and trades
Administrative and senior clerical
Skilled sales and service personnel
Skilled crafts and trades workers
Clerical personnel
Intermediate sales and service personnel
Semi-skilled manual workers
Other sales and service personnel
Other manual workers

- An employment systems review is to be undertaken.
- An employment equity plan is to be developed.
- The EE plan is to be monitored and revised.

Employment systems review. Where an under-representation exists, the employer (and union) must look for possible causes (barriers) in the following employment systems, policies, and practices: recruitment, selection, and hiring; development and training; promotion; retention and termination; and accommodation of special needs of members of designated groups. It is not enough just to look at written policies; an employment systems review is required of the actual practices and organizational culture operating in different organizational units. The purpose of this review is to identify the underlying causes for the under-representation so that they can be redressed.

Employment equity plans. EE plans are based on the findings of the workforce analysis and employment systems review. Both numerical targets and qualitative goals must be included in the plan. Numerical goals indicate how many of each designated group for each occupation the organization will make a 'reasonable effort' to hire over the three-year life of the EE plan. Such numerical targets are based on the degree of under-representation and the amount of hiring expected. Such goals are truly targets, not quotas. Quotas mean that if a member of a designated group cannot be found the position goes unfilled. Targets require that the organization make a reasonable effort to hire members of the under-represented designated group. If it is unable to, the organization can fill the position with another. Qualitative goals set out the special efforts or measures that will be made to eliminate the barriers identified in the employment systems review. Some of these measures will benefit all employees (e.g., introduction of flexible work hours) while others will only benefit designated group members. These latter are only temporary until representation is achieved.

Monitoring and revising EE *plan.* There is no time limit as to when representation must be achieved. Rather, organizations continue to monitor the progress they are making in fulfilling their goals and, every three years, must revise their EE plan. Over time, the 'solution' of some problems will create other problems that need to be addressed. For example, organizations that have increased their representation of persons with disabilities by allowing them to work from home may find that such individuals may not be appropriately considered for promotions because of being 'out of sight'.

It is necessary to monitor an EE plan while it is being implemented to ensure it is having the desired results, to learn from experiences, and to prepare for revisions in the next plan. External audits of EE plans can be made by the Canadian Human Rights Commission, which, since the 1995 amendments, is responsible for overseeing compliance with the federal Employment Equity Act.

Pay Equity

Pay equity (PE) is discussed last because it is narrower in scope than other workplace equity legislation. Specifically, it looks at only one employment system—compensation—and is concerned about providing fairness for men and women working in 'female' jobs. There is a presumption that systemic discrimination exists within the compensation system of employers such that female jobs are underpaid relative to their value to the employer. The Act requires employers to examine their wage-determination process and, if underpayment of women's jobs is found, to correct it over time. Pay equity is defined as 'equal pay for work of equal value'. The female and male jobs may be totally different in content (e.g., secretary, carpenter), but if they are equal in their value to the employer, they must be paid the same.

Before pay equity there was a requirement to ensure 'equal pay for equal work' between female and male jobs. This required that men and women performing substantially the same jobs (e.g., nurse's aides and orderlies; airline stewardesses and stewards) be paid the same. Ontario passed the first equal pay for equal work law in 1951 (Female Employees Remuneration Act). Since then equal pay for equal work has become part of employment standards or human rights legislation in all the provinces and territories, and under the federal jurisdiction. However, this approach had a limited effect because men and women have historically worked (and continue to work) in different jobs. Even as women have gone into what have traditionally been male occupations they tend to work in different areas. For example, within the human resources field there are more women in staffing and training than in labour relations. In 1976 Quebec became the first province to legislate pay equity; the federal government followed in 1978. Both Quebec and the federal government included pay equity in human rights legislation, which had a complaint-based approach (rather than a proactive approach) to redressing discrimination; this did not recognize the systemic nature of the problem and thus did not apply a **systemic remedy**. In 1985 the modern period of pay equity legislation began when Manitoba, recognizing the systemic nature of the discrimination, passed the first proactive pay equity legislation. Proactive legislation required employers to examine their compensation systems to determine if pay inequities existed, and if so, to correct them—a systemic approach. Between 1985 and 1996 proactive pay equity measures were introduced in every province except Alberta.[4] Not all the provinces have PE legislation; many entered into voluntary agreements with their unions. While Quebec has changed from a complaint-based to a proactive pay equity process, the federal government has not, even though a 2004 task force on PE strongly recommended a proactive approach.

Pay equity is primarily a public and broader public sector initiative. Only under the federal jurisdiction, where legislation covers certain private sector industries (e.g., banking, communications, and transportation), and in Ontario are private sector organizations covered. Pay equity requires the following three steps. (1) Predominantly female and male jobs need to be identified. (2) All jobs must be evaluated using the same gender-neutral job evaluation process. (3) Female jobs must be compensated the same as male jobs of equal value.

Identify female and male jobs. Even today, jobs tend to be performed by members of one gender or the other. Women are found in clerical, child-care, elementary school teaching, library, and nursing work while men predominate in trades, management, and university teaching. A few jobs, such as residential real estate agent, are gender-neutral (not associated with one gender or the other). Ontario's legislation has the most complete way to identify the gender of jobs based on the following three criteria:

- percentage cut-off (if 60 per cent of the incumbents are female, it is likely a female job; if 70 per cent are male, it is likely a male job);
- historical incumbency (which gender has traditionally performed the job within the organization);
- gender stereotype (the gender that typically performs the job in society).

Evaluate all jobs using the same gender-neutral job evaluation process. Job evaluation (JE) is a standard compensation tool for assessing the relative worth of jobs within an organization. The aspects of work that an employer values (i.e., wants to pay for) are identified—these are criteria or subfactors on which jobs will be evaluated. Under the most popular job evaluation system—a point factor system—a scale is derived for each sub-factor indicating differing levels of each criterion (e.g., different levels of decision-making;

exposure to disagreeable working conditions). Jobs are assessed on each of these sub-factors and given points for the level that best describes the job content. The points for all sub-factors are summed for each job—jobs with more points are deemed to be of higher value to the organization, thus warranting higher pay. Job evaluation is not so precise that a difference of a few points indicates differences in value, so typically points are banded together (e.g., jobs with 100 to 199 points) to indicate jobs of comparable value. However, JE has been found to historically be gender-biased because they have tended to exclude aspects of work that are relevant to female jobs (e.g., proof-reading and editing, multi-tasking, and providing emotional support); minimize aspects of work relevant to female jobs; or measure inadequately aspects of female jobs (e.g., not recognizing the 'dirt' found in nursing work).

Pay equity legislation specifies that female and male jobs must be assessed in terms of skill, effort, responsibility, and working conditions. Exactly how each of these is defined is left to the employer (and the union, in some cases) as long as the way they are defined is free of gender bias. In addition, how information about jobs is collected and how jobs are evaluated (i.e., typically by committee) must also be free of gender bias.

Compensate female jobs the same as male jobs of equal value. Where an organization finds that female jobs are of comparable value to male jobs, the female jobs must have the same salary maximum as the male jobs. In no case can the salary for the male jobs be lowered. Where pay equity is being completed under a proactive model, employers are required to allocate up to 1 per cent of their payroll each year towards the goal of achieving pay equity. In two jurisdictions (federal and Yukon) pay equity is pursued under a complaint-based model, and any adjustments must be made restorative to the date of the complaint. The pay equity process does allow individual employees doing jobs of comparable value to be paid different amounts based on individuals' seniority or performance. However, all individuals in jobs of comparable value must be able ultimately to earn the same salary given the same level of seniority or performance.

Pay and Employment Equity

Many people confuse pay equity and employment equity; others see them as incompatible. Both are needed to address different aspects of the same concern—occupational segregation. The fact that men and women tend to be employed in different kinds of jobs underlies the need for both pay and employment equity. However, each addresses a different aspect of occupational segregation. Employment equity challenges such segregation by removing barriers that have kept women out of traditionally male-dominated jobs. On the other hand, pay equity 'accepts' that men and women do different kinds of work and strives to get fair pay for those doing traditionally women's jobs. Both are needed to redress different kinds of systemic discrimination. Not all women (nor all men) want to work in traditional male jobs, and yet they deserve fair pay. It is not enough, however, to pay women's work fairly; there also must be ways for all individuals to be considered for work for which they are interested and qualified. Table 9.4 summarizes the differing but complementary approaches of human rights legislation, employment equity, and pay equity.

Current State of Workplace Equity

Assessment of the current status of human rights, employment equity, and pay equity indicates how these approaches to a more equitable society differ. Human rights legislation is given skin and bones by court decisions, particularly those of the Supreme Court. Employment equity and pay equity can be assessed in terms of the accomplishments each has achieved. In addition, there is new proactive legislation in Ontario to help persons with disabilities, which is discussed at the end of this section.

Human Rights

Unlike criminal cases, which use 'reasonable doubt' as a basis for determining if a defendant is guilty or not guilty, human rights decisions are based on a

Table 9.4 Comparison of Human Rights, Employment Equity, and Pay Equity

	Human Rights	Employment Equity	Pay Equity
Objective	Freedom from discrimination based on certain characteristics, e.g., age, disability, gender, race, religion, sexual orientation	Removal of systemic barriers to ensure a workforce representative of the labour market from which an organization recruits	Equal pay for work of equal value
Concern	All aspects of employment	All aspects of employment	Compensation
Focus	All aspects of employment Individuals	All human resource systems Individuals	Compensation system Jobs
Who is covered	Protected groups listed in the legislation	Aboriginal people Persons with disabilities Visible minorities Women	Men and women working in female-dominated jobs
Orientation	Complaint-based	Proactive process to determine if systemic discrimination exists and, if so, to correct it	Proactive except for federal and Yukon, where it is complaint-based
Implementation	Complaints are investigated and where discrimination is found the goal is to 'make the person whole'	Identification and removal of barriers via workforce surveys and analysis; employment systems review; setting of goals, timetables; and special programs in an EE plan	Gender-neutral evaluation of female and male jobs; equal compensation for jobs of comparable value

'balance of probabilities'. That is, of the two versions of events presented, which is most likely or probable to have occurred? While human rights legislation differs in different jurisdictions, a decision of the Supreme Court under one piece of legislation can affect the legislation of other jurisdictions. For example, the decision in *Canada (Treasury Board) v. Robichaud* found that the employer, the federal Department of National Defence, was liable for sexual harassment of one of its employees, and this decision impacted on all employers, public and private, regardless of the specific human rights legislation that covered them. Some areas where the courts have given very clear signals regarding the interpretation of human rights are religion, the duty to accommodate, and harassment.

Religion. Canada is a Christian country—78 per cent of the population is either Catholic (44 per cent), Protestant (29 per cent), or another Christian denomination (5 per cent) (Statistics Canada, 2001).[5] The courts have been very clear: freedom to practise one's religion is sacrosanct in Canada. Key Supreme Court decisions in this area include *O'Malley v. Simpsons-Sears* (1985), *Central Alberta Dairy Pool v. Alberta* (1990), *Central Okanagan School Dist. No. 23 v. Renaud* (1992), *Shapiro v. Peel* (1997), *Multani v. Commission scolaire Marguerite-Bourgeoys* (2006), and *Bruker v. Marcovitz* (2007). For instance, in the *Central Alberta Dairy Pool* case, the plaintiff's choice to observe the preference of his church, the World Wide Church of God, that its members not work on Easter Monday was upheld by the Court even though Mondays are the busiest day of the week at the Dairy Pool.

The Court's decisions require the employer and/or the union to accommodate religious practices. In *Renaud*, for example, a school janitor, a Seventh Day Adventist whose religion forbade him to work from sundown Friday to sundown Saturday night, sought an exception to the regular hours he was expected to work. The Supreme Court ruled that Mr Renaud must be allowed to work a Sunday night to Thursday night shift rather than a Monday to Friday shift despite the collective agreement. The Court discussed the union's duty to accommodate, which arises when the union is involved in formulation of the work rule that has the discriminatory effect, and whether it impedes the reasonable efforts of an employer to accommodate.

Duty to accommodate. The **duty to accommodate** goes beyond religious observance. It can also affect persons with a disability who may have special needs requiring accommodation, such as having an attendant at work with them, arriving before or after most workers arrive to avoid the crowd, working from home, working shorter hours, and so on. Further, there may be other protected groups with accommodation needs. The Court in *O'Malley* said that when systemic discrimination is found, it is 'incumbent upon the employer to make a reasonable effort to accommodate the . . . needs of the employee, short of undue hardship to the employer'. What is undue hardship has not been clearly defined by any Court decision but it is clear that 'undue' hardship means that 'some' hardship may be required. While health and safety, along with financial considerations, should be taken into account there must be actual evidence of hardship rather than just an assumption that hardship will occur. What has been clear is that each situation is unique and must be judged on its own merits. For example, a major department store's ability to accommodate an employee who cannot work on Saturday (as happened in the *O'Malley* case) is different from that of a small dress shop. In the landmark Merion case (*Public Service Employees Relations Commission v. B.C.G.S.E.U*, 1999) the Supreme Court made it very clear that accommodation is required on an individualized basis. That is, it is not enough to say that all women need a given accommodation, but rather it must be ascertained what accommodation a particular woman requires.

Accommodation could be required by:

- applicants during the selection process;
- employees regarding the terms and conditions of employment;
- employees regarding how a job is performed.

It is clear that employees also have obligations with respect to accommodation. They must communicate in a timely fashion their need for an accommodation and become involved in identifying the appropriate accommodation (Keene, 1992: 14).

Harassment. Harassment is a course of vexatious conduct that is unwelcome or should be known to be unwelcome. Generally, harassment is understood to involve a victim who is a member of a protected group under human rights legislation. Sexual harassment is probably the first kind of harassment people think of, though it is not the only kind. It does differ from all other types of harassment in that it can involve quid pro quo harassment. This occurs when an employee is promised a 'reward' for engaging in sexual behaviour (or threatened with being unfavourably treated if the employee does not engage in sexual behaviour). The first major harassment case, *Robichaud*, involved quid pro quo harassment where a supervisor threatened a female employee that she would not pass her probationary period unless she engaged in sex with him. The other form of harassment, which can be sexual in nature or based on any of the other protected categories, is 'poisoned environment' harassment. Human rights complaints have been brought on the basis of race, disability, and gender (rather than sex, this has to do with the status of being a man or a woman, e.g., being told women should not be in the workforce). A poisoned work environment is intimidating, hostile, or offensive, and thus interferes with an employee's work performance or causes the employee to become ill or to leave her or his job.

The decision in *Robichaud* made it clear that employers are liable for the behaviour of their employees. An employer can mitigate its liability by having an anti-harassment policy, doing timely and complete investigations when there is a complaint, and fulfilling its obligations for a harassment-free work environment.

While few harassment cases have gone to the Supreme Court (*Robichaud* being an exception) there has clearly been an increase in understanding that this is a serious problem, as well as increases in financial remuneration when courts and tribunals have found harassment to exist. Recently, in *Lippe v. Quebec Public Security Department* (1998), a $143,000 award was given to a woman because her work environment, a prison where she was a guard, was poisoned with pornographic posters, sexist remarks, reference to the complainant being a lesbian, and threats of assault and rape. The employer had an anti-harassment policy but had not adequately communicated or applied it.

Until recently employers have sometimes felt themselves in a Catch-22 with regard to dealing with harassment, when an employee fired for harassment has then won a wrongful dismissal case. In 1998 two decisions (*Bannister v. General Motors of Canada Ltd.* and *Gonsalves v. Catholic Church Extension Society of Canada*) by the Ontario Court of Appeal clearly said that employers who conduct a thorough investigation can fire employees who harass others.

Employment Equity

Experience in the federal public service. Federal employment equity legislation passed in 1986 required employers to file reports on their progress in achieving representation. In addition, the federal public service (FPS) also has published reports on its progress. This allows two interesting comparisons: the FPS's achievement of representativeness and a comparison between the FPS and those in federally regulated industries covered by the Employment Equity Act. In 2005, the FPS (in total; various departments could have quite different results) achieved overall representation for Aboriginal people, women, and persons with disabilities (based on 2001 census) but had under-representation for visible minorities (IR = 78).[6] This shows significant progress from 1993, when the FPS had just about reached representation only for women. Table 9.5 provides the Index of Representativeness for the federal public service for 1993 and 2006, which shows the progress that has been made.

Table 9.5 Comparison of Index of Representativeness for Federal Public Service, 1993 and 2000

Designated Group	March 1993 IR	March 2000 IR
Aboriginal people	77	168
Persons with disabilities	60	161
Visible minorities	42	78
Women	99	102

Note: Revenue Canada not included.
Sources: Treasury Board of Canada (1995) and Employment Equity Act: Annual Report 2006 (Canada, 2007).

The IRs for the federal public service and the private sector are quite different (Canada, 2007). Among private sector organizations covered by the Employment Equity Act, representation has been achieved for visible minorities (IR = 110) and is close for women (IR = 92), but is quite poor for Aboriginal people (IR = 69) and persons with disabilities (IR = 51). Comparing these IRs to the year 2000, private sector organizations have remained virtually the same for women (decreased from 95 to 92) and increased moderately for Aboriginal people (63 to 69). The most progress has been made for persons with disabilities (35 to 51).

It must be remembered that overall representation is only one of many pieces of data important to understanding if employment equity has been achieved. One needs to also consider the representation of designated groups in various occupations. For instance, the IR for each of the four groups in senior and middle management for private sector organizations is shown in Table 9.6.

With respect to middle management, all groups except Aboriginal people are doing well, while for senior managers, only persons with disabilities are.

The Canadian Human Rights Commission (CHRC) oversees the compliance with the Employment Equity Act, while Human Resources and

Table 9.6 Index of Representativeness for Managerial Occupations in Private Sector Organizations Covered by the Federal Employment Equity Act

Designated Group	Senior Management	Middle Management
Aboriginal people	28	67
Persons with disabilities	129	104
Visible minorities	67	100
Women	88	118

Social Development Canada (HRSDC) provides support for employers. In addition, the CHRC has issued guidelines to help employers and has a schedule to audit all employers covered by the Act.

A common misunderstanding about employment equity is that it imposes quotas; that is, it requires employers to hire members of designated groups to the exclusion of non-designated group members. No employment equity legislation requires quotas. Rather, the law calls for 'reasonable effort' to achieve numerical goals based on the degree of under-representation. Interestingly, however, quotas have been required very occasionally under human rights legislation where discrimination has been found. In the *Action Travail des Femmes* case (1987) the Supreme Court upheld a quota system to redress the under-representation of women in trades jobs at CN Rail. Again in 1997, a Canadian Human Rights Tribunal imposed promotion goals on Health Canada to bring more visible minorities into its managerial and executive positions when it was shown that a glass ceiling existed.[7]

Again, this points to the difference between employment equity and human rights. The former requires employers to look for potential systemic discrimination and, if it is found, to eliminate it over time through reasonable efforts. On the other hand, where discrimination has been found to exist through a complaint process, the requirements to redress it can be more stringent.

Pay Equity

One of the long-range impacts pay equity legislation has had is to change job evaluation systems to make them better able to assess fairly the work found in both female and male jobs. Ontario's 1998 pay equity legislation has been the most extensive, covering the province, all municipalities, and broader public sector organizations such as universities and hospitals (in addition to private sector organizations). A study for the Pay Equity Commission (SPR Associates, 1991) found that pay equity adjustments tended to be larger in the public sector. It was noted that it was not possible to determine whether many female jobs were underpaid or not, a situation that was corrected in the 1993 amendments to the Act. Larger public sector organizations were better able to identify comparative male jobs (male jobs of equal value to female jobs), which jobs were found for about 74 per cent of female jobs within municipalities. Fifty-eight per cent of female job classes within municipalities received adjustments; 25 per cent were found to be fairly paid already, and comparative male jobs could not be found for 16 per cent of female jobs. Municipalities spent 2 per cent of payroll on pay equity adjustments, the province 2.5 per cent. The types of female jobs most likely to receive adjustments in the public sector were clerical jobs. Table 9.7 provides some comparisons of pay equity results in some Canadian provinces and the state of Minnesota.

All the jurisdictions in Table 9.7 were operating under proactive pay equity legislation and required only two years to identify adjustments needed. The payout schedule for proactive pay equity is 1 per cent of payroll per year, so PEI, for example, could have taken up to five years to pay out all of its adjustments. The federal government, on the other hand, is required to achieve pay equity under its complaint-based Human Rights Act. Treasury Board and two of its unions, the Professional Institute of the Public Service of Canada (PIPS) and the Public Service Alliance of Canada (PSAC), worked on pay equity (evaluating female and male jobs fairly) for many years. The employer and unions agreed jointly on everything until it came time to determine the adjustments, which Treasury Board, as the employer, made and presented to the unions. However, the

Table 9.7 Comparison of Pay Equity Results for Some Canadian Provinces and One US State

Jurisdiction	Per Cent Female Employees in Jurisdiction	Average Adjustment (per year)	Range of (non-zero) Adjustment (per hour)	Number of Employees in Female Jobs Receiving Adjustment	Cost as a Percentage of Total Payroll
Manitoba	42	$3,600	up to $3.27	4,900	3.3
Nova Scotia	51	$2,800	$.22–5.10	5,537	3.7
Ontario	39	$3,000	$.02–7.76	N/A	2.5
PEI	58	$3,100	$.19–3.07	1,934	4.9
Minnesota	41	$1,600	N/A	8,225	3.7

Sources: Minnesota: Commission on the Economic Status of Women, 'Pay Equity: The Minnesota Experience', June 1985; Manitoba: talks by John Cumberford, Manitoba Compensation Department, Thunder Bay, 22 Jan. 1988, and Bob Pruden, Manitoba Labour Relations Department, Ottawa, 3 Feb. 1989; Ontario: Ontario Human Resources Secretariat, Pay Equity Background Information and Pay Equity Plans for Bargaining Unit and Management and Excluded Provided by Pay Equity Section (Pay and Classification Branch), Mar. 1990; Nova Scotia: memo to All Departments, Agencies and Institutions from Joint Union/Management Pay Equity Committee regarding Pay Equity Adjustments for Classes Covered by Phase I of the Pay Equity Act. Missing information received from Nova Scotia Pay Equity Commission; PEI: data from staff of Pay Equity Commission.

methodology used was questioned by the unions and they filed a case with the Canadian Human Rights Tribunal in 1991. Over time PIPS settled, but in 1998 the Human Rights Tribunal decided the case in favour of PSAC. This provides an illustration of the length of time it can take with a complaint-based process. In addition, publicity around the case referred to a $5 billion cost. This vast sum is owed because the case is under a complaint-based process, which means that even while the parties were working together towards a settlement, financial remedies were owed to the complainants. In proactive pay equity such retroactivity does not exist. Retroactivity under a proactive scheme is needed only when an organization does not identify pay equity adjustments in the time allotted for such assessment.

The initial 1988 Ontario Pay Equity Act used a methodology which made it impossible to determine whether many female jobs were underpaid or not (i.e., a job-to-job comparison method). This was corrected in the 1993 amendments to the Act, which allowed for a different methodology (referred to as Proportional Value or wage line method). Many people assume that pay equity is 'done'. The law is still in place and recent efforts by the Review Services of the PE Office are reminding employers of this and increasing compliance with the Act.

Accessibility for Persons with Disabilities

The only significant legislative push since 2000 was in Ontario, with the passage of two bills related to persons with disabilities: the Ontarians with Disabilities Act (ODA), 2001 and the Accessibility for Ontarians with Disabilities Act (AODA), 2005. It is the second of these that will have more effect. It requires all businesses and organizations (e.g., provincial and municipal governments) providing goods and services in the province to comply with accessibility standards in five areas: customer service, transportation, information and communications, the built environment, and employment. The standards cover people with all disabilities (physical, sensory, mental, developmental, and learning). Accessibility standards are being developed by members of the disabled community and other stakeholders (e.g., the provincial government). Standards are introduced gradually; new standards are published every four to five years, with different implementation periods based on the type and size of the organization. Private sector organizations of fewer than 20 people have more time to meet the standards. Public sector organizations, regardless of size, and larger private sector organizations are to meet the standards sooner, as well as to fulfill several requirements that do not apply to the smaller private sector organizations. All standards are to be in place by 2025.

Training and other assistance is available to help employers fulfill their obligations; a major source of assistance is online. The ODA remains in effect and requires Ontario ministries and broader public sector organizations to develop annual accessibility plans which include the identification, removal, and prevention of barriers to access. However, the AODA is much broader in that it covers the private sector, both in the development of specific standards and in enforcement. The ODA provides no enforcement mechanisms; however, the AODA requires organizations to file accessibility reports on compliance with standards, and charges penalties for non-compliance; further, the reports must be publicly available. The creation of standards, which are obviously not unique to Ontario, could have a major impact nationally and even internationally.

The Future

Concern for workplace equity has increased in Canada between the 1960s through the 1990s. However, since then there has been less innovation in workplace equity, with the exception of the Accessibility for Ontarians with Disabilities Act. And, of course, there have been changes in social values, such as related to gay and lesbian rights. Human rights legislation, of course, will continue to be needed, as it is unlikely that individual acts of discrimination will ever totally cease. It is likely that age discrimination cases may become more prevalent as the baby-boomer generation moves into their later fifties and sixties. Clearly, the Accessibility for Ontarians with Disabilities will aid the boomers, as they are likely to become more disabled as they age. While employment equity success is a long way off, it is possible to envision a time when employment policies and practices no longer contain systemic discrimination. At some point in the future, equity in employment may well have been achieved for the current designated groups but may be needed for other groups. At present only the federal government and Quebec have employment equity legislation. This is similar to the situation that existed in the pay equity area between 1976 and 1985—when pay equity was required only by the federal government and Quebec. Then, beginning in 1985, every other province except Alberta either passed legislation or voluntarily agreed to establish pay equity criteria.

One of the biggest forces supporting employment equity goals is the shortage of labour for many kinds of skilled and unskilled work. When employers are unable to find the workers they need, they are more likely to look to those who have not traditionally been considered for such work (e.g., women for trades jobs). Canada relies on immigration for any growth in its labour force, since Canadians are not having enough children to replace themselves. However, immigrants face a number of barriers to being fully utilized in the workplace. First, many overseas credentials (educational degrees, licences, and certificates) and skills are not recognized in Canada. The Ontario government has recently passed the Fair Access to Regulated Professions Act, 2006, which requires the organizations which regulate professions (e.g., medicine, architecture, nursing, engineering, teaching) to find ways to more effectively and efficiently assess foreign credentials so that the proverbial doctor is not driving a taxicab. Other barriers include language, requirement for Canadian experience, and discrimination (in addition to facing discrimination for being immigrants, most immigrants are visible minorities). Efforts to teach 'technical' English or French are increasing, since to work in various professions one needs to know the jargon of the field, not just everyday conversational language. The requirement for 'Canadian experience' often masks unspecified concerns that immigrants do not understand Canadian workplace norms. Such norms need to be made explicit and taught to newcomers. Labour shortages propel the efforts to address these problems, so that Canada continues to be a desirable place for immigrants. Canada must compete globally for immigrants; if it takes too long for one's immigration to be processed or there are unnecessary barriers to working in one's field, immigrants will go elsewhere.

Pay equity provides both encouragement and a cautionary tale about the elimination of systemic discrimination. In the short period of six years, pay equity requirements were found in virtually every jurisdiction except one—beginning in 1985 when Manitoba passed its legislation until 1991 when Saskatchewan required pay equity for provincial government and a number of Crown corporations. While pay equity legislation and programs require that pay equity be maintained, there is the danger that even after systems have been corrected, bias will be reintroduced. One lesson learned is that as discrimination is addressed, it becomes more and more subtle.

Another concern is that equity be achieved in an appropriate manner. Alan Borovoy of the Canadian Civil Liberties Association has raised the concern that equity seekers have lost sight of liberal values—freedom of expression, equality of treatment and concern, and procedural fairness. Equality of treatment is of most concern to workplace equity. Borovoy (1999: xiii) notes that equality does not necessarily mean the same treatment for everyone, but rather that in all cases human dignity and the right to be judged on one's individual merit rather than group membership are preserved. This is why it is important to ensure that EE is implemented in a manner that removes barriers to allow, among other results, the recognition of merit among the designated group members who have traditionally been seen as unacceptable for certain kinds of work. The acceptance and understanding of religious and ethnic minorities is being studied by the Bouchard-Taylor Commission on reasonable accommodation.

A future development is the focus on diversity. Diversity is concerned with all relevant differences within an organization and how to capitalize on them (Weiner, 1997). It includes all the kinds of differences found in human rights legislation plus other differences that are relevant to organization. Like human rights legislation, it is concerned with all aspects of these differences—both female and male under gender, for example. Yet, diversity is an expansion of the principle of employment equity—that it is good to have differences within work organizations. But diversity is not legislated. It developed in the US after organizations had been involved in **affirmative action** (employment equity) for over 30 years. Diversity does not replace EE: if people who are different in terms of disability status, gender, and race are not in an organization, then the organization cannot capitalize on these important differences. In addition, diversity is concerned with differences in thinking styles, socio-economic status, professional orientation, rural–urban orientation, and so on.

Some proponents of EE distrust diversity efforts because they fear they will dilute the work needed to achieve representation. But experts in the US make it clear that diversity needs to build on and support EE (Thomas, 1991). The goal of diversity is inclusivity, which requires that people are not just in the organization but that their differences are valued. This concept is totally consistent with other aspects of workplace equity.

Important Terms and Concepts

affirmative action
Canadian Charter of Rights and Freedoms
designated groups
duty to accommodate
employment equity
human rights
Index of Representativeness
pay equity
representation
systemic discrimination
systemic remedy
workplace equity

Study Questions

1. What is the purpose of workplace equity legislation?
2. What are the key similarities and key differences between human rights and employment equity legislation, and between employment equity and pay equity legislation?
3. Is it possible that other groups will be added to the four designated groups currently addressed by employment equity legislation? Could any of the four current groups be dropped?
4. Should pay equity be extended beyond the public sector as it was in Ontario? If so, what would the impact be on the public sector?
5. Why will human rights legislation always be needed but employment equity and pay equity legislation could at some point in the future not be needed?
6. The public sector is presumed to lead on workplace equity issues; for example, it is expected to promote equity even without legislation. Why do you think this is?

Useful Websites

Statistics Canada:

www.statcan.ca/start.html

Human Resources and Social Development Canada: Equity in the Workplace:

www.hrsdc.gc.ca/en/labour/equality/index.shtml

Employment equity guidelines provided by Labour Programs of Human Resources and Social Development Canada:

www.hrsdc.gc.ca/en/lp/lo/lswe/we/legislation/guidelines/index-we.shtml

Employment Equity Annual Report, 2006:

www.hrsdc.gc.ca/en/lp/lo/lswe/we/ee_tools/reports/annual/2006/index-we.shtml

Human Resources and Social Development Canada: Pay Equity:

www.hrsdc.gc.ca/en/labour/equality/pay_equity/index.shtml

Report of federal Task Force on Pay Equity:

www.justice.gc.ca/eng/payeq-eqsal/6000.html

Ontario Pay Equity Commission:

www.payequity.gov.on.ca/index_pec.html

Canadian Human Rights Commission:

www.chrc-ccdp.ca/default-en.asp

Notes

1. 'Comparable worth' is the term commonly used in the US while 'pay equity' is commonly used in Canada, though the phrases 'equal value' and 'equal wages' are sometimes used in the Canadian federal jurisdiction.
2. The quasi-constitutional nature of human rights legislation was discussed in the *O'Malley v. Simpsons-Sears* case in 1985, which involved religious freedom and the duty to accommodate it, and *Action Travail des Femmes v.* CN *Railroad* (1987), which involved discrimination against women wanting to work in trades jobs. In this case the Supreme Court upheld using a quota system as part of the remedy.
3. In the US, a much larger country, businesses with contracts of $25,000 are covered by a contractors' program.
4. Nunavut has not done anything about pay equity. For a summary of pay equity legislation see www.hrsdc.gc.ca/en/lp/spila/clli/eslc/table_pay_equity.pdf (dated July 2006; retrieved 7 April 2008).

5. Non-Christians include: Muslims 2 per cent; Jews, Buddhists, Hindus, and Sikhs 1 per cent each; and 17 per cent of the population have no religious affiliation.

6. Representation, availability, and IR for each of the four designated groups in the FPS is given below for 2006 (Canada, 2007). An index of 100 means that adequate representation has been achieved; an index of more than 100 overall does not indicate if all the members of designated groups are evenly distributed across organizational levels, or if the designated group members are more concentrated into lower level jobs which is problematic even if the overall representation is high.

	Representation	Availability	IR
Aboriginal people	4.2%	2.5%	168
Persons with disabilities	5.8%	3.6%	161
Visible minorities	8.1%	10.4%	78
Women	53.5%	52.2%	102

7. *National Capital Alliance on Race Relations v. The Queen*, Canadian Human Rights Tribunal, 19 March 1997.

References

Abella, Rosalie Silberman. 1984. *Equality in Employment: A Royal Commission Report*. Ottawa: Minister of Supply and Services.

Borovoy, A. Alan. 1999. *The New Anti-Liberals*. Toronto: Canadian Scholars' Press.

Canada. 2007. *Employment Equity Act: Annual Report 2006*. Ottawa. Available at: www.hrsdc.gc.ca/en/lp/lo/lswe/we/ee_tools/reports/annual/2006/EEA_AR06_e.pdf.

Keene, Judith. 1992. *Human Rights in Ontario*. Toronto: Carswell.

SPR Associates. 1991. *An Evaluation of Pay Equity in Ontario: The First Year*. Report prepared for the Ontario Pay Equity Commission. Toronto, 29 April.

Statistics Canada. 2001. *Census of Canada*. Ottawa: Statistics Canada. Available at: www40.statcan.ca/l01/cst01/demo30a.htm?sdi = religion. Retrieved 7 April 2008.

Thomas, R. Roosevelt, Jr. 1991. *Beyond Race and Gender*. New York: AMACOM.

Treasury Board of Canada. 1995. *Employment Equity in the Public Service, Annual Report, 1993–94*. Ottawa.

———. 2001. *Employment Equity in the Public Service, 1999–2000*. Ottawa: Minister of Public Works and Government Services.

Weiner, Nan. 1997. *Making Cultural Diversity Work*. Toronto: Carswell.

Cases

Action Travail des Femmes v. CN Railroad.

Bannister v. General Motors of Canada Ltd. (1998), 112 O.A.C. 188, 98, C.L.L.C. 210–031, 164 D.L.R. (4th) 325 (Ont. C.A.).

Brooks v. Canada Safeway Ltd., [1989] 1 S.C.R. 1219, 10 C.H.R.R. D/6183, 26 C.C.E.L. 1:78.

Bruker v. Marcovitz, 2007 S.C.C. 54.

Canada (Treasury Board) v. Robichaud, [1967] 2 S.C.R. 84, 8 C.H.R.R. D/4326; D/76, D/215, D/244, D/368, D/390.

Canadian National Railway Co. v. Canada (Human Rights Comm.) and Bhinder, [1985] 2 S.C.R. 561, 7 C.H.R.R.

Central Alberta Dairy Pool v. Alberta (Human Rights Comm.), [1990] 2 S.C.R. 561, 7 C.H.R.R. D/3093; D/173, D/259, D/435.

Central Okanagan School Dist. No. 23 v. Renaud, [1992] 2 S.C.R. 970, 16 C.H.R.R. D/425.

Gonsalves v. Catholic Church Extension Society of Canada (1998), 112 O.A.C. 164, 98 C.L.L.C. 210–032, 164 D.L.R. (4th) 339, (Ont. C.A.).

Lippe v. Quebec Public Security Department, Quebec Human Rights Tribunal, 2 Nov. 1998.

McKinney v. University of Guelph, [1990] 3 S.C.R. 229.

Multani v. Commission scolaire Marguerite-Bourgeoys, [2006] 1 S.C.R. 256, 2006 S.C.C. 6.

National Capital Alliance on Race Relations v. The Queen, Canadian Human Rights Tribunal, 19 Mar. 1997.

Ontario (Human Rights Comm.) and O'Malley v. Simpson-Sears Ltd., [1985] 2.S.C.R. 536, 7 C.H.R.R. D/3102.

Public Service Employee Relations Commission v. B.C.G.S.E.U., [1999] 3 S.C.R. 3 (known as the Merion decision).

Shapiro v. Peel (Regional Municipality) (No. 2) (1997), 30 C.H.R.R. D/172.

Vriend v. Alberta, [1998] 31 C.H.R.R. D/1.

Wiens v. Inco Metals Co., Ontario Division (1988), 9 C.H.R.R. D/4795 (Ontario Board of Inquiry).

10 Collective Bargaining and Dispute Resolution in the Public Sector

Morley Gunderson and Robert Hebdon

There are three main mechanisms for regulating the employment relationship: (1) the market mechanism (often termed 'private ordering' in legal parlance); (2) collective bargaining; and (3) laws and regulations. All three mechanisms are at work to various degrees in the different elements of the Canadian public sector. As discussed subsequently, their relative importance has also changed substantially over time so that the Canadian public sector thereby serves as an interesting laboratory for analyzing the pros and cons of the different mechanisms.

Issues pertaining to collective bargaining and dispute resolution in the public sector have taken on increased importance for a variety of reasons, many of which are analyzed in more detail subsequently. The vast majority of the Canadian public sector is covered by collective agreements and the two largest unions in Canada are now in the public sector;[1] hence, it is crucial to understand how collective bargaining operates in that sector. In contrast to collective bargaining in the *private* sector, where Canada has largely followed the US model, Canada's public sector has broken new ground and has a longer and more extensive history of bargaining (Goldenberg, 1988). This longer history and extensive provincial variation (with labour matters falling under provincial jurisdiction) provide a laboratory of 'natural experiments' for analyzing collective bargaining and dispute resolution.

With increased emphasis being placed on 'reinventing government' to be more responsive to the needs of the public and to be complementary to private sector competitiveness, increased attention is being paid to whether the traditional models of collective bargaining are a hindrance or a help in meeting those objectives. This is especially the case given the increased emphasis on downsizing, **privatization**, and deregulation in various elements of the public sector, as well as the increased use of user charges and private sector partnerships and delivery systems.[2]

Demands on the public sector will also be changing in the future as a result of the aging population, with longer life expectancy supported by a smaller (and increasingly mobile) taxpaying base. This will likely lead to increased emphasis on deinstitutionalization, community-based care, and volunteer activity, all of which will likely place new strains on the collective bargaining system.

Volunteer activity, for example, appears to be taking on increased importance for persons at both ends of the age spectrum—youths and persons who are retiring earlier. The hope is that such activity will help to fill a vacuum both in their own time availability and in the need for public services created by a retrenching role of the state. Yet potential conflicts could develop if, for example, volunteers displace public employees or are the subject of a grievance or are involved in legislative violations.

There is often a perception that the public sector should not be immune to the competitive pressures that have inundated the private sector under globalization, free trade, and increased economic integration. At times, this appears to take on a 'mean-spirited' tone—'if it happened to us, it should happen to them.' At other times it is a more reasoned response—that the public sector should be restructured to ensure that it provides the crucial public infrastructure essential for competitiveness of the private sector.

In that vein, governments are under strong pressure to compete with other governments for business investment and the jobs associated with that investment (Gunderson, 1998). With globalization and freer trade, capital is increasingly mobile and able to locate in countries and particular jurisdictions within countries that provide an investment climate conducive to their competitive needs. Governments 'getting their own house in order' with respect to their own public sector can be an important ingredient of that process, especially since governments wear two hats in this area: they set the rules and regulations under which the parties operate; and they are themselves a major employer. This spotlight on the public sector is important not only because of its size (especially in the collective bargaining arena) but also because public sector activities can have important spillover effects on the private sector. The public sector is under strong political pressure to be a **model employer**. At times this can mean progressive practices; at other times it can mean a model of restraint.

Issues of dispute resolution take on heightened importance in the public sector since the decline in strike activity that has been prominent in recent years has been much smaller in the public sector than in the private sector. With the increased emphasis on **alternative dispute resolution** (ADR) procedures to reduce conflict, the public sector is a natural target for such actions.

In essence, the public sector has taken 'centre stage' in recent years. This is highlighted by the opening sentence in Swimmer's *Public Sector Labour Relations in an Era of Restraint and Restructuring*: 'The 1990s will probably go down as the most stressful decade for public sector industrial relations since the inception, 25 years earlier, of collective bargaining for public sector workers' (Swimmer, 2001: 1). In that setting, it is crucial to understand the process of collective bargaining and dispute resolution in the public sector.

In this restructuring environment, another key question is the role of the private sector in the provision of services and the consequences of privatization for workers, unions, and collective bargaining.

The purpose of this chapter is to provide such an understanding. The evolution of collective bargaining and dispute resolution is first discussed, followed by a description of the current legal framework governing collective bargaining and the alternative dispute resolution procedures. Special attention is paid to arbitration and the increasing role of legislation in circumscribing—indeed, supplanting—collective bargaining. The means for settling disputes in public sector strikes are then analyzed, followed by a discussion of the growing importance of legislative interventions through pay and employment equity. The chapter concludes with a summary and discussion of the key policy issues.

Evolution of Collective Bargaining

The history of bargaining in the Canadian public sector has been described as an evolution from 'collective *begging* to collective *bargaining*'. Prior to the mid-1960s, the terms and conditions of employment in the public sector were generally dictated by the state both as employer and as the entity that establishes laws and regulations. This is epitomized in the statement of one public official that 'The Queen does not negotiate with her subjects' (cited in Goldenberg, 1973). Nevertheless, during that earlier period, the foundations were being laid for subsequent collective bargaining through three main elements.[3]

First, municipal workers in Canada (except for police and firefighters) were generally covered under the private sector labour relations laws and regulations in each jurisdiction. Hence, they had the same bargaining rights, including the right to strike, as did workers in the private sector. Since they often provided '**essential services**' for which there was not a viable private sector alternative (public transportation, road maintenance, garbage collection, sewage, and water), collective bargaining and even strikes in such areas were not unknown. The precedence had already been set for extending such rights to other elements of the public sector.

Second, a precedent for collective bargaining and the right to strike even for the *civil service* had been established in 1944 when a left-wing government in Saskatchewan granted such rights to its own civil service at the same time as its original private sector labour relations legislation was enacted.

Third, even though formal collective bargaining rights were seldom granted in the public sector, there was the precedent of informal bargaining through consultation between governments and employee associations that represented much of the public sector workforce. Such associations were generally dominated by white-collar and professional workers who rejected the notion of being members of a conventional union, especially one that would exercise the right to strike. Nevertheless, the employee associations and consultation process did provide the foundations for subsequent bargaining by providing leadership, institutional structure, and bargaining experience that could serve as a springboard for subsequent collective bargaining.

While the foundations and precedents for collective bargaining were present, they required a catalyst to be transformed into genuine collective bargaining. That catalyst was provided by the socio-political-economic environment of the 1960s, characterized by such factors as the civil rights movement, anti-Vietnam War protests, campus militancy, and the Quiet Revolution in Quebec (Ponak and Thompson, 1995: 422). All of these forces questioned the unfettered sanctity of the state and led to a mistrust of government. In such circumstances it was easy to extend that mistrust to the unilateral determination of the wages and working conditions for its employees. If 'people power' was expanding to question governance in general, it was a logical extension to expand it to question governance of the workplace. As well, the public sector was expanding rapidly, hiring younger workers with more radical ideas and experiences that were conducive to questioning the idea of being a civil *servant*. The expansion also shifted bargaining power into the hands of public sector employees who were needed to fill the jobs of the expanding state sector at that time.

The fortuitous combination of the basic foundations for public sector collective bargaining (established by the precedents of bargaining on the part of municipal workers in all jurisdictions and civil servants in Saskatchewan, as well as the experience of consultation with employee associations) with the catalyst of the socio-political-economic environment precipitated the legislative initiatives of the 1960s that established broad-based collective bargaining in the public sector throughout Canada. The watershed legislation in this area was the federal Public Service Staff Relations Act (PSSRA) of 1967, which fulfilled a promise made in 1963 by Prime Minister Lester Pearson to grant federal employees broad collective bargaining rights, including the right to strike. This had been preceded by similar legislation in Quebec in 1965. All provincial jurisdictions almost immediately followed suit, although not always granting all employees the right to strike.

By the mid-1970s, the basic structure was in place. Collective bargaining rights had come to the public sector. In fact, collective bargaining dominated the public sector and it was to be the mechanism for determining the terms of employment in the public sector more so than in the private sector.

Interestingly, the divergence of unionization rates in Canada and the United States also began during the mid-1960s (Riddell, 1993). Until then, both countries had similar rates of unionization, at around 35 per cent of the non-agricultural paid workforce. Thereafter, unionization rates dropped steadily in the US, so that today less than 15 per cent of the American workforce is unionized. In contrast, in Canada, the unionized workforce has been maintained at about 30 per cent, over twice the US rate. It would be interesting to know if the higher unionization rates in Canada could have been sustained without the legislative boost given to public sector unionization in the late 1960s and early 1970s.

The Structure of Collective Bargaining

The current structure of collective bargaining in Canada's public sector can best be described by a number of its components: collective agreement coverage; collective bargaining legislation; dispute resolution procedures; arbitration requirements; the restitution of the dominant role of the state; and increased attention to market forces. These components also illustrate the interplay among the three main mechanisms for regulating the employment relationship: the market; collective bargaining; and government legislation and regulation.

Collective Agreement Coverage

As indicated in Table 10.1, over three-quarters of workers in the public sector are covered by a collective agreement, much higher than the 20 per cent coverage rate in the private sector. The coverage rate in each of the four main components of the public sector is higher than in any other industry, with the highest rate in the private sector being 45 per cent in transportation and warehousing (Akyeampong, 1999: 48). When one considers that a large component of the public sector (i.e., managerial personnel) is not eligible for unionization or covered by a collective agreement, the 75 per cent coverage figure suggests that the vast majority of workers in the public sector who could be covered by a collective agreement are covered.

As a result of this high coverage rate, the public sector now also makes up the majority of persons covered by collective agreements in Canada.[4] Clearly, unionization and collective bargaining are important phenomena in the public sector.

Collective Bargaining Legislation[5]

Labour relations in Canada are under provincial jurisdiction, with only about 10 per cent of the workforce under federal jurisdiction (e.g., federal civil service, transportation, communication, banking, and the postal service). Yukon, the Northwest Territories, and Nunavut also tend to follow the federal jurisdiction. The 11 different jurisdictions (federal plus the 10 provinces) have often followed quite different legislative regimes to govern the conduct of collective bargaining in the various elements of the public sector (e.g., public administration at the federal, provincial, and local levels; education; health; police;

Table 10.1 Unionization Rates and Collective Agreement Coverage, Private and Public Sectors, 2006

Sector	Employees (000s)	Union Density (%)	Collective Agreement Coverage (%)
Private	10,575	17.0	18.9
Public*	3,229	71.4	75.1
Education	1,145	68.3	72.7
Utilities	119	68.5	72.5
Public administration	833	67.3	72.5
Health & social assistance	1,546	54.2	56.5

*The public sector refers to employees in government departments or agencies, Crown corporations, or publicly funded schools, hospitals, or other institutions. The subcomponents of the public sector (education, utilities, public administration, health and social services) are ones where the employer usually but not always is a government. Similarly, government employees occasionally are found outside of these industries. For this reason, the sum of employees in those sectors (3,643,000) does not equal the sum in the public sector (3,229,000). Furthermore, the overall collective agreement coverage rate in the public sector, at 75.1 per cent, is higher than the rate in each of those components, since the coverage rate will be much lower for private sector employers in those components.

Source: Akyeampong (2006) based on data from the Labour Force Survey.

and firefighters). The main legislative options include:

- private sector labour relations legislation;
- private sector legislation, but with specific modifications for particular elements of the public sector, usually pertaining to the right to strike and the scope of bargaining;
- separate collective bargaining statutes for different elements of the public sector;
- hybrids of the above.

Although there is almost always an exception, the different elements of the public sector tend to be covered as follows:

- Civil servants tend to be covered by separate civil servant legislation, although in Saskatchewan they are covered by the general private sector labour relations legislation.
- Teachers tend to be covered by separate statutes, but in some jurisdictions they are covered under the general private sector labour relations legislation.
- Hospital workers tend to be covered by the general private sector labour relations legislation, but sometimes by separate legislation and even by the civil service statutes.
- Police and firefighters are sometimes covered by separate statutes, sometimes by separate sections within the private sector labour relations legislation, and sometimes by a hybrid of the two, with the private sector statute covering some aspects of bargaining and special legislation covering other aspects of bargaining.
- Employees of government-owned corporations are usually covered by the relevant private sector labour relations legislation, but sometimes by separate statutes.

Clearly, there is no uniform pattern across all jurisdictions and with respect to the different elements of the public sector. As such, public sector collective bargaining legislation in Canada has been described as exhibiting a 'crazy quilt' pattern. The pattern likely reflects the peculiarities of political pressures, interest groups, special events, and inertia more than it reflects the different needs and circumstances in each jurisdiction. As well, the different legislative regimes can likely deliver similar outcomes even though the process is 'packaged' differently.

Dispute Resolution Procedures, Arbitration, and the Right to Strike

The dispute resolution procedures that prevail across the different elements of the public sector and across the different jurisdictions also exhibit a crazy quilt pattern. The main **dispute resolution** procedures are:[6]

- the right to strike, with the same procedures that prevail in the private sector;
- the limited right to strike, where certain designated employees who are regarded as essential are not allowed to strike;
- **binding arbitration** when strikes are not allowed;
- arbitration at the request of either party, and sometimes at the request of the Minister of Labour;
- **choice of procedure** where the union is allowed to choose in advance of negotiation either the strike or arbitration route.

As indicated in Table 10.2, the most common dispute resolution procedure (52 per cent of the cases) is the unfettered right to strike, as that right also exists in the private sector. This right exists for municipal workers in all jurisdictions and it is common for workers in government enterprises and teachers. Arbitration, with no right to strike, is the next most common procedure, required in 20 per cent of the cases. It is never required across all jurisdictions for any one element of the public sector, although it is required in Alberta for all but municipal workers and teachers. The other procedures are spread out across the different jurisdictions and elements of the public sector.

Based on a more detailed tabulation of the alternative dispute resolution procedures for the different elements of the public sector workforce across the different jurisdictions, Gunderson and Hyatt (1996) provide the following generalizations.

1. There is no uniform pattern with any one jurisdiction requiring a single procedure for all elements of the public sector (except for British Columbia, which formally[7] allows the right to strike for all elements) or with any one element of the public sector having the same procedure across all jurisdictions (except for the right to strike for municipal workers).
2. There is a slight tendency to restrict the right to strike in the 'most essential' services, such as police services and firefighting, and to allow it in what are considered less essential services, such as municipal services, government enterprises, and teaching, albeit the patterns are certainly not uniform.
3. There is also a slight tendency for some jurisdictions to be more restrictive than others. Alberta, for example, appears to be the most restrictive, allowing the right to strike only for municipal workers and teachers while requiring arbitration in all other sectors. British Columbia, in contrast, allows the right to strike across all elements of the public sector, although general legislation may restrict designated employees from striking. Saskatchewan and Nova Scotia also allow the right to strike across all elements of the public sector, but arbitration at the request of either party is required for firefighters in Saskatchewan and for the civil service in Nova Scotia. Newfoundland and Quebec also allow the right to strike in many elements of the public sector, with the other provinces generally having a variety of procedures across the different elements of the public sector.
4. While there are these 'slight tendencies' for some jurisdictions to be more restrictive and for the right to strike to be more limited the more essential the service, there certainly is no strong, uniform pattern.
5. In fact, discrepancies appear to exist even within a jurisdiction in that the right to strike is allowed in what generally would be regarded as an essential service (e.g., police) while it is prohibited and arbitration required in what would be regarded as a less essential service (e.g., civil service).

As with the different legislative regimes that prevail, the pattern of dispute resolution procedures likely reflects the peculiarities of political pressures, interest groups, special events, and inertia more than it reflects the different needs and circumstances in each jurisdiction. It is hard to believe, for example, that police would be more essential than civil servants in one jurisdiction but less essential in another jurisdiction.

The choice of procedure regime, which is an unusual and innovative procedure, is only used in the federal jurisdiction.[8] Under this procedure the union gets to choose, in advance of the negotiation, whether it wants the ultimate dispute resolution procedure to be arbitration or a strike. This is different from arbitration being chosen by either party (or sometimes required by the Minister of Labour), which effectively also allows the employer to choose arbitration and hence to be insulated from a strike. Under the federal regime, the weaker bargaining units initially chose the arbitration route, hoping that they would be granted the same wage increases established by the pattern in the more powerful units that chose the strike route. Over time, however, the unions increasingly opted for the strike route, feeling that they could gain more through the ultimate strike threat.

Factors Circumscribing the Strike Weapon in the Public Sector

The data in Table 10.2 could certainly indicate that the right to strike is the dominant dispute

Table 10.2 Dispute Resolution Procedures in Seven Elements of the Public Sector Across 11 Canadian Jurisdictions

Dispute Resolution Procedure	Number	%
Right to strike	40	51.9
Limited right to strike, non-designated employees	8	10.4
Binding arbitration with no strike	9	11.7
Arbitration at request of either party	15	19.5
Choice of procedure	5	6.5
Total (11 jurisdictions, seven elements* of public sector)	77	100.0

*The seven elements of the public sector are: civil service, municipal, government enterprises, police, firefighters, teachers, and hospitals.
Source: Gunderson and Hyatt (1996), compiled from information in Swimmer and Thompson (1995) and Thompson and Ponak (1992).

resolution procedure in the various elements of the public sector in Canada. This is so not only because the right to strike is the single-most important procedure, existing in 52 per cent of the cases, but also because it can be invoked under the limited right-to-strike procedure, as well as under the choice of procedure and when arbitration can be requested by either party. In fact, only the arbitration procedure, which exists in 12 per cent of the cases, explicitly prohibits strikes.

While the right to strike is an important dispute resolution procedure in many elements of the public sector, its ultimate threat is extremely circumscribed in a variety of ways. As indicated previously, even when the strike is allowed, general legislation often specifies that designated employees may be required to continue to work. When the limited right to strike exists and permanently designated employees are prohibited from striking, the power of the union is emasculated by the fact that the organization can generally carry out its essential tasks with the designated employees.[9] The costs that the union can impose are largely ones of 'inconvenience'. These are not the same as the inconvenience costs imposed in the private sector when customers are forced to shift to a producer not on strike. Here, the producer whose workers are on strike runs the risk of permanently losing customers. In the public sector, there are usually no other producers to shift to, with the non-essential services having to be postponed rather than not provided.

In situations where a strike is possible but arbitration can be requested by either party, the option of arbitration effectively means that the parties are insulated from the threat of the strike when it is most likely to be an effective weapon for one of the parties. In such circumstances, the strike weapon is effectively emaciated by the fact it can be neutralized by one party choosing arbitration.

Even under the choice of procedure, where the union can opt for arbitration or the strike, designated employees are not allowed to strike if the strike option is chosen. This is an especially important constraint because the proportion of employees who have been designated as essential has increased substantially over time, amounting to over half of the employees in the bargaining units that have opted for the strike route.[10] If over half of the employees are required to continue working, and these are the workers most essential to the operation, the threat of the strike is clearly circumscribed, especially in the public sector where a permanent loss of customers is not generally involved. This would be analogous in the private sector to bringing in replacement workers (who could immediately do the most important tasks) to fill over half of the jobs, and to restricting customers from going to alternative providers.

Clearly, these subtle institutional features change the picture from one where strikes appear to be the dominant dispute resolution procedure in the public sector to one where the threat from the strike is severely circumscribed. The threat from strikes is further circumscribed by the more general proposition that when strikes occur in the public sector, those on strike lose income but employers generally do not lose revenues even though the services are not provided. This is very different from the private sector where employers lose revenues, perhaps even on a permanent basis if customers shift to other providers. In such circumstances, public sector employers may not have a financial incentive to settle. In fact, they may have a perverse incentive not to settle so as to reduce their deficits if revenues keep coming in but costs are not incurred during the strike. The threat from strikes may be further reduced by the fact that the public perception, generally, is that the union 'causes' the strike, for the public does not always recognize that it takes two parties to create a dispute. Employers can be just as much the cause of such strikes by refusing to bargain in a meaningful way.

Arbitration

When the right to strike is prohibited or not opted for when the parties can choose to strike, or when the parties are ordered back to work via legislative enactments, binding arbitration is the method of dispute resolution in the public sector. In determining awards arbitrators tend to use the following criteria:

- comparability, especially with private sector settlements if similar ones exist, but often with other public sector settlements if private sector ones do not exist;
- the employers' ability to pay;
- cost of living, especially to keep up with inflation;
- productivity increases in the economy as a whole;
- minimum living standards, especially for low-wage groups (Gunderson, 1983; O'Grady, 1992).

By far the dominant criterion, however, is comparability. This can create a form of de facto **pattern bargaining** since key settlements get emulated across similar groups. Just as in the private sector, however, such pattern bargaining is becoming less prominent, with more attention being paid to local conditions and the employers' **ability to pay**. In fact, governments have increasingly enacted legislation requiring arbitrators to pay attention to the ability to pay without having to engender tax increases.

Arbitration in Canada tends to be of the conventional type rather than one of the forms of final-offer arbitration more common in the United States (O'Grady, 1992; Ponak and Falkenberg, 1989). Reasons for this are not obvious, since the pros and cons of **final-offer arbitration** would appear to apply equally in both countries. Requiring the arbitrator to choose *either* the employer's *or* the union's offer, final-offer encourages the parties themselves to compromise and to settle in advance of the arbitration to avoid the risk of an all-or-nothing settlement. They are under strong pressure to sort out their own internal trade-offs so as to craft a reasonable offer that is likely to be accepted. On the other hand, final-offer imposes a degree of risk, it may lead to unworkable settlements, and it can foster an adversarial 'win-lose' environment. This win-lose aspect of final offer arbitration may account for the significantly higher number of job actions of police unions in New Jersey under final offer versus conventional arbitration (Hebdon, 2005). These negative consequences can be mitigated, however, by the fact that arbitrators in subsequent arbitrations (or even the parties themselves in subsequent bargaining) are likely to take into account any one-sided nature of earlier awards (Swimmer, 1975).

The Pendulum Swings: Legislative Enactments

The previous discussion focused on how the strike threat has been increasingly circumscribed by features such as restricting the strike to non-designated employees and giving employers the option of arbitration. Furthermore, arbitrators are increasingly called on to pay attention to the employer's ability to pay. These, however, are marginal 'tinkerings' with the fundamental mechanism of collective bargaining as it is used to determine employment conditions in the public sector. They are marginal relative to the mechanism of legislation and regulation that has effectively replaced collective bargaining in many elements of the public sector in recent years. While the earlier transformation may be characterized as being from collective begging to collective bargaining, the pendulum may have swung back. Although it may no longer be appropriate to characterize the current situation as one where 'the Queen does not negotiate', it is not a far cry to depict it as one where 'the government does not negotiate'. This is illustrated in a wide range of legislative enactments with respect to bargaining in the public sector.

Legislative **wage controls** were a common feature of the 1970s and early 1980s.[11] The 1975 wage control program that applied across the country was applicable to both the private and public sectors, but it had features that made its application more binding in the public sector. As well, public sector employers are less likely to try to evade legislative initiatives given the scrutiny they are under. The wage control programs of the early 1980s were restricted to the public sector. They were set off by the federal '6-and-5' program limiting public sector wage increases to 6 per cent in 1982 and 5 per cent in 1983. Five provinces followed suit with their own programs and the other five provinces limited their spending explicitly to constrain public sector wages, with Quebec going so far as to institute a 20 per cent rollback.

The public sector wage control programs of the early 1980s were followed by a series of other legislative and regulatory initiatives in the early 1990s that effectively controlled public sector wages. In 1991, the federal government froze wages and suspended collective bargaining for a period that lasted until 1997. The Atlantic provinces, Quebec, Ontario, and Manitoba followed with public sector wage freezes and sometimes even mid-contract wage rollbacks. In some circumstances these were accompanied by so-called **social contracts** where employees were given mandatory unpaid leave days as part of the freezes.

In Saskatchewan, Alberta, and British Columbia public sector wage restraint was negotiated with the unions, albeit under the obvious shadow of what was happening in the other provinces. The BC negotiations were closest to true negotiations (likely reflecting the NDP government) since they involved extensive consultation and bargaining over a wide range of issues including job security, restructuring, and human resource and workplace practices (Fryer, 1995).

Back-to-work legislation has also increasingly been invoked to 'settle' disputes in the public sector in both Canada (Gunderson et al., 2001) and the US (Lund and Maranto, 1996). Such legislation, which is invariably preceded by a strike, establishes arbitration to set the terms and conditions of the new contract. The importance of legislative enactments (wage controls, the suspension of collective bargaining, social contracts, back-to-work legislation) as a dispute resolution procedure in the public sector is amply illustrated in Table 10.3. During the 1990s, 22.4 per cent of contracts were settled through such legislative enactments. This dwarfed the direct use of arbitration (4.2 per cent) or strikes (3 per cent). After 1999, however, legislated settlements dropped to a three-decade low of 2.4 per cent.

The state was clearly instrumental in establishing collective bargaining in the public sector in Canada in the mid-1960s, especially through the commitments made in 1963 culminating in the Public Service Staff Relations Act of 1967, as well as legislation in Quebec in 1965. In the 1980s and 1990s, however, the state was equally instrumental in putting the genie back in the bottle through various legislative enactments including wage controls, the suspension of collective bargaining, social contracts, and back-to-work legislation. What the state gives, the state can clearly take away.

As pointed out by Swimmer (2001), some have interpreted this as the end of collective bargaining in the public sector of Canada, although others, such as Thompson (1998), argue that the basic structure is still in place and can be modified to deal with the new issues. In contrast, Panitch and Swartz (1984, 1993) argue that the government legislative interventions represent the nail

Table 10.3 Proportion of Contracts Settled by Different Means, Public and Private Sectors, 1980–2007

Means of Settlement	Public Sector			Private Sector		
	1980–9 (%)	1990–8 (%)	1999–2007 (%)	1980–9 (%)	1990–8 (%)	1999–2007 (%)
Bargaining*	74.5	70.4	71.5	83.8	88.0	69.1
Arbitration	8.6	4.2	6.4	0.9	1.6	4.2
Strike	4.2	3.0	4.8	15.1	9.5	8.8
Legislation	12.7	22.4	2.4	0.2	0.9	0.0
Conciliation	N/A	N/A	13.2	N/A	N/A	16.8
Other	N/A	N/A	1.5	N/A	N/A	1.0
Total, all means	100.0	100.0	100.0	100.0	100.0	100.0

*Includes settling at the stage of direct bargaining with no third-party assistance, as well as settling at the stages where there was some third-party assistance—conciliation, post-conciliation, mediation, or post-mediation.

Source: Compiled from data in Gunderson et al. (2001: Table 4). The original data source is the Bureau of Labour Information's Major Wage Settlements database, for major collective agreements of 500 or more employees.

in the coffin from a series of government assaults on trade union freedoms.

Despite the documented record of massive intervention, the institution of collective bargaining was recently bolstered by the Supreme Court of Canada (2007). In limiting the ability of the BC government to invalidate existing agreements with health care workers, the Court found that the constitutional guarantee of freedom of association in the Charter of Rights includes the right to collective bargaining. The decision will undoubtedly restrict the ability of governments to restructure by means of legislation that bypasses the collective bargaining process.

Nonetheless, conventional collective bargaining in the public sector has permanently changed. Warrian (1995, 1996) claims that the end of conventional bargaining in the public sector is a result of the inability of the Wagner model of collective bargaining to adapt to the new needs of public sector bargaining. The Wagner model was designed for the private sector and largely transplanted into the public sector. The characteristics of the conventional private sector **Wagner model** that make it ill-suited for the changing needs of the public sector include:

- a multiplicity of fragmented bargaining units that inhibits unions from bargaining 'with one voice';
- a legalistic, adversarial orientation that emphasizes the distributive separate nature of employee and employer interests and that therefore inhibits them from joint co-operative 'win-win' initiatives;
- a multiplicity of narrow job classifications and seniority-based work rules that inhibit teamwork and employee involvement in service delivery.

These characteristics may not have had serious negative consequences when the public sector was expanding and not under pressure to restructure. However, they are ill-suited to deal with the new issues of restructuring, downsizing, job security, and flexibility in both wage structures and wage levels.

These are the crucial new issues given the transformation of the public sector and hence of the internal labour markets and workplace practices in that sector. Elements of this transformation include:

- slower employment growth and downsizing;
- a reorientation from government being a service provider to a service coordinator, with a core of public employees providing policy advice and coordinating service delivery often through the private sector;

- increased emphasis on service delivery and customer orientation in activities where governments are involved;
- increased non-standard employment in such forms as contractually limited appointments and subcontracting;
- privatization of a wide range of conventional public sector activities and deregulation in others;
- increased performance-based budgeting being applied to public sector organizations, with that pressure filtering down to performance evaluations of employees;
- pressures to merge units and to restructure for cost-effective delivery.

These and other pressures in turn have important implications for a wide range of industrial relations and human resource practices in the public sector. These include successor rights, transfer rights, merging of seniority lists in newly integrated units, retraining, job classifications, relocation, and work-sharing as an alternative to layoffs. At issue is whether the public sector bargaining model, with its fragmented bargaining units, narrow job classifications, and adversarial emphasis, can deal with these new issues. What is not at issue, however, is that conventional collective bargaining has been circumscribed by legislative requirements pertaining to such factors as designated employees and impositions on arbitrators to pay attention to ability to pay, as well as more direct interventions in such forms as wage controls, wage freezes, suspension of bargaining, social contracts, and back-to-work legislation.

Strikes and Other Settlement Stages in Public and Private Sectors

Table 10.3 provides additional information on the stages at which collective agreements are settled in the public and private sectors. During the decade of the 2000s, 69.1 per cent of the agreements in the private sector tended to be settled by the parties themselves. The comparable figure in the public sector is about the same, at 70 per cent. In the private sector, when contracts were not settled by the parties themselves, they were usually settled at conciliation (16.8 per cent), with arbitration and back-to-work legislation being rare. The strike rate in the private sector also dropped considerably over the period, from 15.1 per cent in the 1980s to 8.8 per cent in the 2000s.

In contrast, in the public sector, strikes occurred in only 4.8 per cent of the cases in the 2000s, up slightly from 4.2 per cent in the 1980s and 3 per cent in the 1990s. Table 10.4 gives the strike rate for the different elements of the public sector separately for the 1980s, 1990s, and 2000s. Over the full period, the public sector rate was highest in Crown corporations, followed by provincial administration and local administration, all of which were above the average strike rate of 4.0 per cent of contracts in the public sector. As indicated in the public and private totals for these decades, the strike rate in the public sector rose steadily over the period from 28 per cent (i.e., 4.2 ÷ 15.1) of the rate of the private sector in the 1980s, to 32 per cent (i.e., 3.0 ÷ 9.5) in the 1990s, to 55 per cent in the 2000s (i.e., 4.8 ÷ 8.8).

In general all strikes declined steadily from an annual average of 794 in the 1980s to 394 in the 1990s, and time lost from 541 workdays per 1,000 employees in the 1980s to 233 in the 1990s (Akyeampong, 2006). But there has been a modest reversal of this trend in the 2000s with the public sector accounting for a significant share of the increase. The increase in strikes and time lost occurred in 2005, with strikes jumping to 261 and time lost increasing to 301 workdays.

An examination of these increases by industry over the three-year period 2003–5, as shown in Table 10.5, reveals that the public sector education, health, and social services and public administration together accounted for 27.3 per cent of strikes (second only to manufacturing at 28.5 per cent) and the largest share of time lost at 33.3 per cent. This reversal perhaps reflects the adversarial relationship fostered by the years of

Table 10.4 Strike Rates for Various Elements of the Public Sector, 1980–2007

Element of Public Sector	1980–9	1990–8	1999–2007	1980–2007
Parliamentary employees	0.0	0.0	0.0	0.0
Federal administration	1.5	0.0	0.0	0.5
Provincial administration	7.6	3.9	5.7	5.7
Local administration	6.3	3.1	5.9	5.1
Education/health/welfare	3.3	3.1	5.7	4.0
Utilities	2.4	4.7	5.6	4.2
Crown corporations	5.7	2.3	25.7	11.2
Total public sector	4.2	3.0	4.8	4.0
Total private sector	15.1	9.5	8.8	11.1
Ratio public/private	0.28	0.32	0.55	0.36

Source: Calculations based on special data request from Labour Canada's Major Wage Settlements database, for major collective agreements, usually of 500 or more employees. 'Strikes' refers to both strikes and lockouts.

Table 10.5 Strikes and Lockouts and Person-Days not Worked by Major Industry, 2003 to 2005

	Strikes and Lockouts		Days not Worked	
		(%)	(000s)	(%)
All industries	743	100.0	9,068	100.0
Primary	19	2.6	454	5.0
Utilities	6	0.8	81	0.9
Construction	13	1.7	102	1.1
Manufacturing	212	28.5	1,572	17.3
Wholesale and retail trade	76	10.2	706	7.8
Transportation and warehousing	51	6.9	275	3.0
Information and cultural industries	12	1.6	2,202	24.3
Finance	48	6.5	82	0.9
Education, health and social services	159	21.4	1,454	16.0
Entertainment and hospitality	103	13.9	567	6.3
Public administration	44	5.9	1,573	17.3

Note: Data may not add to total due to rounding.
Source: Statistics Canada, *Perspectives on Labour and Income* 7, 8 (2006): 8 (from data provided by: Human Resources and Social Development Canada, Workplace Information Directorate; Statistics Canada, Labour Force Survey).

persistent government intervention in the collective bargaining process.

Pay and Employment Equity Legislation

Legislative interventions have also been important in the areas of pay and employment equity, since these are largely public sector phenomena. Employment equity legislation requires that employers have the designated groups (women, visible minorities, Aboriginal persons, disabled persons) represented throughout the occupational structure of their organization in the same proportion as they are represented in the external labour pool. Such legislation exists only in the federal jurisdiction, the federal public service, and for firms that bid on federal contracts.[12]

Pay equity legislation requires that female-dominated jobs be paid the same as male-dominated jobs of the same 'value', where value is determined by a gender-neutral job evaluation scheme. It exists in all Canadian jurisdictions except Alberta and Saskatchewan but is confined to the public sector in all jurisdictions except Ontario, Quebec, and the federal jurisdiction, where it can also apply to the private sector. In those jurisdictions, however, it is still largely a public sector phenomenon. In the federal jurisdiction and in Quebec until 1998, pay equity required a complaint to be initiated and almost all complaints were from the public sector. In Ontario, where employers were required to have a pay equity plan whether or not a complaint had been placed, the wage adjustments were considerably higher in the public sector than in the private sector (Gunderson, 1995).

Pay equity can be an especially important legislative factor influencing wages in the public sector because its applications have been mainly in the public sector and because the wage adjustments have been fairly substantial where they have occurred.[13] Clearly, legislative initiatives have again become an important ingredient of wage determination in the public sector, making them one more step removed from being determined by conventional collective bargaining. It is true that unions are often instrumental in the pay equity adjustment process and pay equity has become an important instrument in the arsenal of weapons used by unions to garner wage gains. Nevertheless, such gains occur through the legislative route rather than through conventional collective bargaining.

Conclusion

Collective bargaining in the public sector in Canada has been described as evolving from collective begging to collective bargaining. The foundations for the transformation to collective bargaining were established by earlier precedents including the rights of municipal workers in all jurisdictions to bargain and strike and similar rights granted to civil servants in Saskatchewan, as well as by a structure and history of consultation through employee associations. These combined with the socio-economic environment of the 1960s—student protests, the Quiet Revolution in Quebec, and an expanding public service of young persons prepared to question the idea of being civil *servants*. Thus, legislation from the mid-1960s to the mid-1970s essentially established collective bargaining as the dominant mechanism for determining the terms and conditions of employment in the public sector.

The legislation was very diverse across the different jurisdictions and across the different elements of the public sector. The legislative options included the private sector labour relations legislation, the private sector legislation with specific modifications usually pertaining to the right to strike and the scope of bargaining, separate statutes for different elements of the public sector, and hybrids of the above. Diverse dispute resolution procedures also prevailed. These included the right to strike, the limited right to strike, binding arbitration, arbitration at the request of either party, and the choice of procedure.

While legislation and regulations were instrumental in establishing collective bargaining in the public sector, they were also instrumental in severely curtailing that right throughout the 1980s and 1990s. This was done through various mechanisms, such as expanding the number of designated workers, requiring arbitrators to pay attention to ability to pay, and instituting wage controls, wage freezes, suspensions of collective bargaining, social contracts, and back-to-work legislation. It will be interesting to see whether the constitutionalization of collective bargaining will curtail future government intervention.

Over the 1980s and 1990s, strike activity declined in the public sector but not by as much as it declined in the private sector, so that by the mid-1990s the public sector contributed more to overall strike activity than did the private sector. Perhaps as a reaction to the intervention in the 1980s and

1990s, the decline reversed in 2005, with the public sector accounting for much of the increase.

If contracts settled by back-to-work legislation were added to strike activity on the grounds that the legislation was instituted after a strike, and if social contracts were included as strikes on the grounds that unpaid leave was required (analogous to unpaid strike days), then strikes would be the dominant form of dispute resolution in the public sector when the parties did not settle themselves.

Legislation in the form of **employment equity** and pay equity has also played a prominent role in the public sector, again highlighting the role of legislation in determining the terms and conditions of employment in that sector.

There is considerable debate over the motivations for the increasing role of governments in using legislation and regulation to circumscribe—indeed supplant—collective bargaining in the public sector. There is also considerable debate over the ability of the traditional system of collective bargaining, which was imported largely from the private sector, to deal with the new challenges facing the public sector. There is little debate, however, over the fact that the twenty-first century will still face challenges in striking a balance over how the public sector will be affected by the three main mechanisms for governing labour relations: the market, collective bargaining, and legislation and regulations.

Important Terms and Concepts

ability to pay
alternative dispute resolution
binding arbitration
choice of procedure
dispute regulation
employment equity
essential services
final-offer arbitration
model employer
pattern bargaining
privatization
social contracts
wage controls
Wagner model

Study Questions

1. What are the historical antecedents to modern collective bargaining?
2. What are the effects of modern collective bargaining legislation?
3. There is a 'crazy quilt' approach in Canada regarding collective bargaining legislative regime options, different types of coverage for different elements of the public sector, and dispute resolution procedures. Discuss what this means. How did this state of affairs come to be? Should there be more standardization?
4. Examine the 2007 Supreme Court of Canada decision *Health Services and Support–Facilities Subsector Bargaining Assn. v. British Columbia*, [2007] 2 S.C.R. 391, 2007 SCC 27 (see 'Useful Websites'). What reasoning did the Supreme Court use in its decision? What is the significance of the decision?
5. Has the traditional collective bargaining model been circumscribed? If so, by what and to what extent? If not, what remains of it?
6. Do you think that government intervention in the collective bargaining process has repercussions on strike and dispute settlement rates?

Useful Websites

Health Services and Support–Facilities Subsector Bargaining Assn. v. British Columbia, [2007] 2 S.C.R. 391, 2007 SCC 27.

http://scc.lexum.umontreal.ca/en/2007/2007scc27/2007scc27.html

Reference Re Public Service Employee Relations Act (Alta.), [1987] 1 S.C.R. 313.

http://scc.lexum.umontreal.ca/en/1987/1987rcs1–313/1987rcs1–313.html

C.A.T.C.A. v. The Queen, [1982] 1 S.C.R. 696.

http://scc.lexum.umontreal.ca/en/1982/1982rcs1–696/1982rcs1–696.html

Industrial relations legislation in Canada, public and private sectors:

www.hrsdc.gc.ca/eng/labour/labour_law/ind_rel/index.shtml

Collective bargaining dispute resolution process in the public and parapublic sectors in Canada, as of the end of 2008:

www.hrsdc.gc.ca/eng/labour/labour_law/ind_rel/pub.shtml

Federal Public Service Staff Relations Act (R.S., 1985, c. P-35) (Act current to 17 September 2009):

http://laws.justice.gc.ca/en/P-35/index.html

Public Service Employment Act (R.S., 1985, c. P-33) (Act current to 11 November 2009; see relevant regulations):

http://laws.justice.gc.ca/eng/P-33.01/index.html

Canada Labour Code (R.S., 1985, c. L-2) (Act current to 17 September 2009):

http://lois.justice.gc.ca/en/showtdm/cs/L-2

Employment Equity Act (1995, c. 44). (Act current to 17 September 2009; see relevant regulations):

http://laws.justice.gc.ca/en/E-5.401/index.html

Canadian Human Rights Act:

http://laws.justice.gc.ca/eng/H-6/index.html

Equal Wages Guidelines, 1986 (SOR/86–1082):

http://laws.justice.gc.ca/en/ShowTdm/cr/SOR-86–1082//20091015/en

Statistics Canada. 2006. *Perspectives on Labour and Income*, current issue:

www.fedpubs.com/subject/labour/persp.htm#current

Notes

1. The two largest unions in Canada are the Canadian Union of Public Employees (CUPE) with about 10 per cent of total union membership, and the National Union of Public and General Employees (NUPGE) with about 7.8 per cent of total union membership. They are followed by two mainly private sector unions: the Canadian Autoworkers (CAW) with about 5.7 per cent of total union membership, and the United Food and Commercial Workers (UFCW) with about 5.1 per cent. These figures are from the author's calculations based on data from Human Resources Development Canada (1998).
2. For recent discussions of these issues, see, for example, Auditor General of Canada (1998), Gunderson and Hyatt (1996), Swimmer (1996, 2001), Thompson (1998), Thompson and Ponak (1992), and Warrian (1995, 1996).
3. Details of the earlier history and evolution of collective bargaining in the public sector, from which this section draws, are given in Finkelman and Goldenberg (1983), Goldenberg (1973, 1988), Gunderson and Hyatt (1996), Ponak and Thompson (1995), Rose (1995), Swimmer (1995, 1996), and Thompson and Ponak (1992). Those studies also contain references to earlier material on the subject.
4. Applying the 75.1 per cent coverage rate to the 2,604,000 employees in the public sector yields 1,955,000 persons covered, while applying the 20.2 per cent coverage rate of the private sector to the 9,009,000 employees yields 1,820,000 employees covered.
5. Discussions of the statutes governing collective bargaining in the public sector in Canada are given, for example, in Gunderson and Hyatt (1996), Ponak and Thompson (1995), Swan (1985), and Swimmer and Thompson (1995).

6. Dispute resolution procedures are discussed in the studies indicated in note 5, as well as in Currie and McConnell (1991) and Gunderson et al. (1996).

7. Although British Columbia allows the right to strike, general legislation in that province stipulates that employees providing essential services may be forbidden from striking.

8. Detailed discussions of the choice of procedure regime in the federal jurisdiction are given in Ponak and Thompson (1995), Subbarao (1985), Swimmer (1978, 1989, 1995), and Swimmer and Winer (1993). Ponak and Thompson (1995) indicate that the choice of procedure has occasionally been used in some of the provinces on an experimental basis, but in such cases it has subsequently been abandoned.

9. Recent court decisions have further enhanced the power of employers with respect to the designation of employees who do not have the right to strike. In *C.A.T.C.A. v. The Queen*, the Supreme Court of Canada held that the employer had the right to determine the level of service regarded as essential—a determination that effectively gives government the power to determine the employees who are designated as providing essential services and hence who will not have the right to strike. Furthermore, that decision indicated that designated employees were to perform *all* of their functions, not just those considered essential.

10. Calculations given in Gunderson and Hyatt (1996: 254) based on data from Swimmer (1995: 379).

11. Discussions of the earlier wage control programs with their relevance to the public sector are given in Fryer (1995), Gunderson and Hyatt (1996), Panitch and Swartz (1984), Ponak and Thompson (1995), Thompson (1988), and Thompson and Ponak (1991).

12. Employment equity legislation was introduced by the Rae NDP government in Ontario in 1993, but was subsequently rescinded by the Harris Conservative government in 1995. In that period it was never actually implemented in a formal sense.

13. Gunderson (1995) indicates that the adjustments have been in the neighbourhood of $4,000 per recipient or a 20 per cent wage increase, averaging 4 to 8 per cent of payroll. The 1999 Bell Canada settlement of $59 million for 20,000 current and former employees averaged about $3,000 per employee. The federal pay equity settlement with the Public Service Alliance of Canada in October 1999, for a case that started in 1983, was for approximately $3.5 billion and affected 230,000 current and retired federal employees, such as clerks, secretaries, and librarians, in female-dominated positions. That averages to a little over $15,000 per recipient including back pay.

References

Akyeampong, Ernst. 1999. 'Unionisation: An Update', *Perspectives on Labour and Income* 11, 3: 45–65. Statistics Canada Cat. no. 75–001–XPE.

———. 2006. 'Unionization', *Perspectives on Labour and Income* 18, 3. Statistics Canada Cat. no. 75–001-XIE.

Auditor General of Canada. 1998. 'Expenditures and Work Force Reductions in the Public Service', *Report of the Auditor General of Canada*. Ottawa: Public Works and Government Services, 1.1 B 1.33.

Currie, Janet, and Sheena McConnell. 1991. 'Collective Bargaining in the Public Sector: The Effect of Legal Structure on Dispute Costs and Wages', *American Economic Review* 81: 693–718.

Finkelman, Jacob, and Shirley Goldenberg. 1983. *Collective Bargaining in the Public Service: The Federal Experience in Canada*. Montreal: Institute for Research on Public Policy.

Fryer, John L. 1995. 'Provincial Public Sector Labour Relations', in Swimmer and Thompson (1995a: 341–67).

Goldenberg, Shirley B. 1973. 'Collective Bargaining in the Provincial Public Services', in J.F. O'Sullivan, ed., *Collective Bargaining in the Public Service*. Toronto: Institute of Public Administration of Canada, 11–44.

———. 1988. 'Public Sector Labor Relations in Canada', in B. Aaron, J. Najita, and J. Stern, eds, *Public Sector Bargaining*, 2nd edn. Washington: Bureau of National Affairs, 266–313.

Gunderson, Morley. 1983. *Economics Aspects of Interest Arbitration*. Toronto: Ontario Economic Council.

———. 1995. 'Gender Discrimination and Pay Equity Legislation', in L. Christofides, K. Grant, and R. Swidinsky, eds, *Aspects of Labour Market Behaviour: Essays in Honour of John Vanderkamp*. Toronto: University of Toronto Press, 225–47.

———. 1998. 'Harmonization of Labour Policies Under Free Trade', *Relations Industrielles/Industrial Relations* 53: 11–41.

———, Robert Hebdon, and Douglas Hyatt. 1996. 'Collective Bargaining in the Public Sector: Comment', *American Economic Review* 86: 315–26.

———, and Douglas Hyatt. 1996. 'Canadian Public Sector Employment Relations in Transition', in D. Belman, Gunderson, and Hyatt, eds, *Public Sector Employment Relations in a Time of Transition*. Madison, Wis.: Industrial Relations Research Association, 243–81.

———, ———, and Allan Ponak. 2001. 'Strikes and Dispute Resolution', in Gunderson, Ponak, and D. Taras, eds,

Union-Management Relations in Canada, 4th edn. Toronto: Addison-Wesley.

———, and Frank Reid. 1995. 'Public Sector Strikes in Canada', in Swimmer and Thompson (1995a: 135–63).

Hebdon, Robert. 1991. 'Ontario's No Strike Laws: A Test of the Safety-Valve Hypothesis', in D. Carter, ed., *Proceedings* of the 28th conference of the Canadian Industrial Relations Association, 347–57.

———. 2005. 'Toward a Theory of Workplace Conflict: The Case of US Municipal Collective Bargaining', *Advances in Industrial and Labor Relations*, Vol. 14: 35–67.

———, and Robert Stern. 1998. 'Tradeoffs among Expressions of Industrial Conflict: Public Sector Strike Bans and Grievance Arbitrations', *Industrial and Labour Relations Review* 51: 204–21.

Human Resources Development Canada. 1998. *Directory of Labour Organizations in Canada.* Ottawa: Canadian Government Publishing.

Lund, John, and Cheryl Maranto. 1996. 'Public Sector Law: An Update', in D. Belman, M. Gunderson, and D. Hyatt, eds, *Public Sector Employment Relations in a Time of Transition.* Madison, Wis.: Industrial Relations Research Association, 21–58.

O'Grady, John. 1992. 'Arbitration and Its Ills', paper prepared for Governments and Competitiveness Research Program, Institute of Policy Studies, Queen's University.

Panitch, Leo, and Don Swartz. 1984. 'Free From Collective Bargaining to Permanent Exceptionalism: The Economic Crisis and the Transformation of Industrial Relations in Canada', in M. Thompson and G. Swimmer, eds, *Conflict or Compromise: The Future of Public Sector Industrial Relations.* Montreal: Institute for Research on Public Policy, 403–35.

———, and ———. 1993. *The Assault on Trade Union Freedoms: From Wage Controls to Social Contracts.* Toronto: Garamond Press.

Ponak, Allan, and Loren Falkenberg. 1989. 'Resolution of Interest Disputes', in A. Sethi, ed., *Collective Bargaining in Canada.* Scarborough, Ont.: Nelson Canada, 260–97.

———, and Mark Thompson. 1995. 'Public Sector Collective Bargaining', in M. Gunderson and A. Ponak, eds, *Union-Management Relations in Canada.* Toronto: Addison-Wesley, 415–54.

Riddell, Craig. 1993. 'Unionization in Canada and the United States: A Tale of Two Countries', in D. Card and R. Freeman, eds, *Small Differences That Matter: Labor Markets and Income Maintenance in Canada and the United States.* Chicago: University of Chicago Press, 109–48.

Rose, Joseph B. 1995. 'The Evolution of Public Sector Unionism', in Swimmer and Thompson (1995a: 20–51).

Statistics Canada. 2006. *Perspectives on Labour and Income* 7, 8.

Subbarao, A. 1985. 'Impasse Choice in the Canadian Federal Service: An Innovation and an Intrigue', *Relations Industrielles* 40: 567–90.

Supreme Court of Canada. 2007. *Health Services and Support–Facilities Subsector Bargaining Assn. v. British Columbia*, [2007] 2 S.C.R. 391, 2007 SCC 27. Available at: http://scc.lexum.umontreal.ca/en/2007/2007scc27/2007scc27.html.

Swan, Ken. 1985. 'Differences among Provinces in Public Sector Dispute Resolution', in D. Conklin, T. Courchene, and W. Jones, eds, *Public Sector Compensation.* Toronto: Ontario Economic Council, 49–75.

Swimmer, Gene. 1975. 'Final Position Arbitration and Intertemporal Compromise: The University of Alberta Compromise', *Relations Industrielles* 30, 3: 533–6.

———. 1978. 'The Impact of the Dispute Resolution Process on Canadian Federal Public Service Wage Setttlements', *Journal of Collective Negotiations in the Public Sector* 16, 1: 53–61.

———. 1989. 'Critical Issues in Public Sector Industrial Relations', in A. Sethi, ed., *Collective Bargaining in Canada.* Scarborough, Ont.: Nelson Canada, 400–21.

———. 1995. 'Collective Bargaining in the Federal Public Service of Canada: The Last Twenty Years', in Swimmer and Thompson (1995a: 368–406).

———. 1996. 'Provincial Policies Governing Collective Bargaining', in C. Dunn, ed., *Provinces: Canadian Provincial Politics.* Peterborough, Ont.: Broadview Press, 351–78.

———, ed. 1996. *How Ottawa Spends 1996–97: Life Under the Knife.* Ottawa: Carleton University Press.

———. 2001. 'Public Sector Labour Relations in an Era of Restraint and Restructuring: An Overview', in Swimmer, ed., *Public Sector Labour Relations in an Era of Restraint and Restructuring.* Toronto: Oxford University Press, 1–35.

———, and Mark Thompson. 1995a. *Public Sector Collective Bargaining in Canada.* Kingston: IRC Press.

———, and ———. 1995b. 'Collective Bargaining in the Public Sector: An Introduction', in Swimmer and Thompson (1995a: 1–19).

———, and Stanley Winer. 1993. 'Dispute Resolution and Self-Selection: An Empirical Examination of the Federal Public Sector, 1971–1982', *Relations Industrielles/Industrial Relations* 48, 1: 146–62.

Thompson, Mark. 1988. 'Public Sector Industrial Relations in Canada: The Impact of Restraint', in *Proceedings of the Annual Spring Meeting of the Industrial Relations Research Association.* Madison, Wis.: IRRA.

———. 1995. 'The Industrial Relations Effects of Privatization: Evidence from Canada', in Swimmer and Thompson (1995a: 164–79).

———. 1998. 'Public Sector Industrial Relations in Canada: Adaptation to Change', paper presented at the 11th Congress of Industrial Relations, Bologna, Italy, Sept.

———, and Allan Ponak. 1991. 'Canadian Public Sector Industrial Relations: Theory and Practice', in D. Sockell, D. Lewin, and D.B. Lipsky, eds, *Advances in Industrial and Labor Relations*, vol. 5. Greenwich, Conn.: JAI Press, 59–93.

———, and ———. 1992. 'Restraint, Privatization and Industrial Relations in the 1980s', in R. Chaykowski and A. Verma, eds, *Industrial Relations in Canadian Industry.* Toronto: Dryden Press, 284–322.

Warrian, Peter. 1995. 'The End of Public Sector "Industrial" Relations in Canada?' KPMG Centre for Government Foundation.

———. 1996. *Hard Bargain: Transforming Public Sector Labour-Management Relations.* Toronto: McGilligan Books.

11 Compensation in the Public Sector

Morley Gunderson

Issues of compensation in the public sector have given rise to a variety of interrelated questions. What in the current environment makes this issue one of importance for practical and policy purposes? What are the main issues? Are there theoretical reasons to believe that compensation may differ between the public and private sectors? Do these reasons shed light on the direction of the difference and how it may vary by such factors as time, element of the public sector, level of government, gender, and pay level? What do these reasons for public–private pay differences imply about future predictions of such differences? How is the compensation picture affected by differences in non-wage benefits such as pensions, job security, and stock options? What are the impacts of particular institutional features that characterize the public sector, such as unionization, pay and employment equity, different dispute resolution procedures, and arbitration? How are such pay differences commonly measured? And—most importantly—what does the empirical evidence say about the public–private pay differences? Do they exist? Do they spill over from the public to the private sector? How have they changed over time? Where are they greatest? What are the policy implications?

The purpose of this chapter is to deal with these questions, highlighting what we know and what we also do not know in this important area. The chapter first considers why the issue is of increased importance for policy and practical purposes. It then deals with the theoretical reasons for expecting public–private pay differences and the factors that will give rise to such differences. Empirical procedures for estimating the differences are briefly outlined, followed by a discussion of the evidence. The chapter concludes with a discussion of the policy issues.

Why the Current Interest in Public–Private Pay Differences?

Over the past decade much concern was expressed over government deficits and the accumulated debt. Such deficits can be reduced only by increasing taxes or reducing expenditures. Tax increases are often regarded as political suicide, with tax reductions being regarded as the politically appealing option in an era of taxpayer revolt. This leaves reduced expenditures as the main political option. Given the significance of labour costs in public expenditures, public sector wages certainly attract the political spotlight.

The pressure to constrain public sector expenditures is enhanced by increased globalization. In a world of footloose capital and reduced tariff and non-tariff barriers to trade, corporations can more easily locate their plants or outsource to countries with lower taxes and regulations, and export back into the countries with higher taxes and regulations. This reduction in business investment also means a reduction in jobs associated with that investment. In such circumstances, governments increasingly find themselves constrained in their taxation and expenditure decisions. They are more under the '**hard' budget constraint** of the international capital markets and bond ratings, and less under the '**soft' budget constraint** of the political processes. For some, this is a desirable discipline of market pressures simply compelling governments to deliver their services in a cost-effective fashion. To others it represents the sovereignty of the state being subservient to the sovereignty of the market. In either case, public sector wages are under more scrutiny.

The forces of globalization and international competition have led to dramatic changes in private sector labour markets in such forms as downsizing, restructuring, layoffs and plant closings, deregulation, mergers and acquisitions, and outsourcing. There is often the perception that the public sector should not be immune from such pressures. Hence, the pressure for such initiatives as 'reinventing government', privatization, performance-based management, and infusing private sector workplace practices into the public sector. Pressures that were brought to bear on private sector labour markets in the 1970s and 1980s are now being felt in the public sector—some would say, with a vengeance.

There is also concern that 'excessive' wage settlements in the public sector may spill over into the private sector, jeopardizing competitiveness and fuelling inflation. Such settlements could also be a burden on future generations of taxpayers, especially if the compensation occurs in forms of deferred compensation such as seniority-based wage increases, liberal retirement and pension plans, and job security into the future. This **intergenerational burden** could come on top of those associated with pay-as-you-go schemes such as the Canada/Quebec Pension Plan and workers' compensation, as well as the burden associated with health-care expenditures for an aging population with increased life expectancy.

These various policy concerns, which are of practical importance, generally focus on public sector pay being 'excessive' and out of line with pay in the private sector. Yet there are potential concerns also in the other direction. Pay restraint can lead to morale problems, especially if it is accompanied by downsizing that leaves the remaining workforce feeling 'overworked and underpaid'. Underpaying can lead to a 'brain drain' of public sector workers, as has occurred in nursing, just as it can lead to a loss of executives or information technology personnel. Public sector infrastructure can be an important ingredient of private sector competitiveness. Education is crucial for productivity improvements, for adapting to technological change, and for the **high-performance workforce** of the new information economy. A viable health-care system can save on the expense of private health expenditures or insurance and thereby enhance competitiveness. Both roads and the information highway can be crucial in a world of just-in-time delivery. The key is cost-effectiveness, not cost-minimization, and this applies to public sector wages as well as to other public expenditures.

Clearly, a wide array of issues of practical and policy importance apply to public sector wage determination. While most of these issues focus on ensuring that public sector wages are not excessively high, there are potential concerns in the opposite direction—that they not become excessively low. In a world where the law of one price increasingly applies, it is crucial to 'get prices right' in this important area as well.

Theoretical Reasons for Public–Private Pay Differences

As a benchmark, basic labour market theory posits that wage differentials across industries for the same type of worker should not prevail in the long run since 'underpaid' workers would, at the margin, leave the low-wage sector for the high-wage sector. The supply exodus from the low-wage sector would increase wages in that sector, and the supply influx into the high-wage sector would reduce wages in that sector until the same wage was paid for the same type of labour in each sector. This does not require all workers to leave one sector for the other—only that there be sufficient adjustment in the long run at the margin through such forces as attrition, turnover, mobility, recruitment, and retention. Such competitive forces would dissipate pure inter-industry wage differentials, ensuring that the law of one price would apply for similar workers across industries, including between the various elements of the public and private sectors. The public sector is an industry, with sub-sectors of government (federal, provincial, and local) as well as the broader public sector, which includes health, education, and social services.

According to this perspective, inter-industry wage differentials, including public–private differentials, could persist only if they reflected the following characteristics: **compensating wages** paid for other aspects of employment; **short-run demand changes**; and non-competitive forces. This provides a convenient framework for categorizing the theoretical determinants of public–private wage differences and how they may relate to other characteristics.

Compensating Wages for Other Job Characteristics

The characteristics of public sector jobs are generally regarded as desirable: safety; job security; good pensions and retirement plans; and reasonable fringe benefits. As such, public sector jobs would generally be expected to pay lower wages, given the higher non-wage benefits. Some characteristics, however, can work in the other direction. Stock options are not available for higher-level personnel as they often are in the private sector. Opportunities to receive the prize of a 'superstar' salary are also not available. As well, in recent years, job security is no longer guaranteed, and stress may be high for the smaller core of remaining personnel who often have the same amount of work after downsizing.

Nevertheless, public sector jobs are generally regarded as having better non-wage conditions of employment compared to private sector jobs. Certainly, it is reasonably safe to say that any public sector wage premium that prevailed would not be a premium for compensating for the less desirable non-wage aspects of employment in the public sector.

Short-Run Demand Changes

Inter-industry wage premiums can also reflect premiums necessary to attract new workers to a growing sector. In general, the public sector has been contracting in recent years (Peters, 1999; Swimmer, 2001) and hence any public sector wage premium that prevails would not be a premium necessary to attract new workers.

Since many public services are associated with the provision of services to various specific demographic groups, however, there may be demand changes for public sector workers emanating from the changing demographics of the population. In the near future, for example, as the baby-boom population ages and lives longer because of increased life expectancy, there should be an increased demand for public services associated with elder care and the general health care of older persons.[1]

Non-Competitive Factors

Wage differentials can prevail across industries (i.e., between the public and private sectors) if **non-competitive factors** prevent mobility from arbitraging such differentials. If competitive forces are not in operation, public sector wage premiums can prevail and be sustained even in the long run.

The public sector generally does not operate under the profit constraint (albeit many of the new pressures of privatization, reinventing government, subcontracting, school choice, vouchers, user charges, and performance-based budgeting are often designed to introduce elements of competition). Businesses in the public sector generally do not go out of business if they do not show a profit. In fact, the concept of profit is often not applicable since products and services are often not sold and revenues come from budgetary allocations.

The public sector operates more under a political constraint than a profit constraint, and the political constraint is generally regarded as less binding than the profit constraint. There is a large disconnect between revenues from tax payments and public services provided. There is often political pressure to be a model employer and not to pay 'what the market will bear', especially for low-wage and other disadvantaged workers. Issues of fairness and a **fair wage** are much more prominent. Public sector workers are voters and can be very influential in that process. Initiatives like pay equity and employment equity are largely a public sector phenomenon, and even when they apply in the private sector (as is the case with pay equity in Ontario) adjustments are much more prominent in the public sector (Gunderson, 1995b). Public sector pay practices can prohibit executives in the civil service from earning more than elected politicians earn. Unionization is much more prominent in the public sector than the private sector, with about 75 per cent of workers in public administration being covered by a collective agreement, a rate that is almost four times the rate of 20 per cent in the private sector (Gunderson and Hyatt, 1996: 247).

Arbitration is a common method for determining wages in the public sector, and arbitrators seldom pay attention to competitive pressures as reflected in such factors as **queues or shortages** of applicants in setting wages. Ability to pay has been increasingly emphasized as a criterion for arbitrators to follow, but that is at best an elusive concept given the 'deep pockets' of governments and taxpayers. Certainly, public sector unions or arbitrators would not be constrained extensively by the possibility that they may put their employer into bankruptcy, as is the case in the private sector. Nor are they constrained by the possibility that the employer (a government, school board, or hospital) may move to the non-union South in the United States, to the Maquiladoras in Mexico, or to a low-cost country in Asia.

While most of the political constraints suggest that higher wages would be paid in the public sector compared to the private sector, where the profit constraint is more operative, other forces can work in the opposite direction. Political capital can now often be made by appearing to be a guardian of the public purse and paying low wages in the public sector, even if that leads to problems of recruiting, morale, and turnover. Governments can influence the balance of power in favour of public sector employers through a wide range of mechanisms, including back-to-work legislation and restricting the right to strike for large numbers of designated workers (see Chapter 10).

While the non-competitive forces, in theory, can work in either direction, in practice they likely work in the direction of facilitating public sector pay premiums or rents above the pay of comparable workers in the private sector. This, in part, occurs because of the asymmetry of market forces or mobility to arbitrage public–private pay differences. If the public sector 'underpays' it will have problems recruiting and retaining its workforce and hence will be under pressure to increase pay in order to provide public services. However, if it 'overpays' it will not be under the same competitive pressure to reduce wages simply because there is a large queue of applicants. Market forces dictate a floor but not a ceiling to public sector wages, and consequently create the potential for compensation to be higher in the public sector.

This is further exacerbated by the possibility that public sector employers may have an incentive to pay **deferred compensation**, the obligation of which falls on a future generation of taxpayers and politicians who are not 'at the table' in the current rounds of bargaining. This can be especially appealing to political parties, knowing that opposition parties are likely to be in power at some time in the future. The process is not likely to be overt, with current governments saying 'let's pass this bill to future taxpayers.' It can be subtle. If a cash-strapped government faces two options—a 5 per cent wage increase with no pension obligation, or a 1 per cent wage increase with a generous pension plan that will be paid by future taxpayers—there certainly may be political pressure to opt for the latter option. The same can apply to agreeing to seniority-based wage increases and job security, both of which, effectively, are forms of deferred compensation.

Some 'market' checks can constrain the use of such deferred compensation, but they are not as strong in the public sector as in the private sector. (In the private sector, a firm that pays in the form of deferred or '**back-loaded' compensation** eventually has to pay that compensation, while in the public sector it is paid by future taxpayers.) The 'market' checks in the public sector come in the form of the downgrading of government bond ratings if governments have large future debt obligations, or in reductions in property values if deferred compensation obligations are capitalized into lower property values because owners of property expect large future tax obligations to pay for the deferred compensation. While these pressures can exist, they are not likely to be as prominent as the pressures private sector employers face if they incur such future compensation obligations.

In summary, there are theoretical reasons to believe that public sector compensation premiums will prevail and that such premiums will be larger for low-wage and other more disadvantaged workers. Furthermore, deferred compensation in such forms as seniority-based wage increases, liberal pension and retirement benefits, and job security will be more prominent in the public sector. Public sector compensation premiums may have dissipated in recent years, given the pressures to downsize and to introduce competitive elements, but this may be offset by other pressures, such as those associated with pay equity.

Empirical Procedures

Before we examine the empirical evidence in public–private compensation differences, it is instructive to outline briefly the procedures used to estimate these differences. Three main methods have typically been used to determine if compensation differences exist between workers in the public and private sectors.[2]

Job-to-Job Comparisons

The simplest and most readily understood procedure is to compare public and private sector wages in the same jobs in the public and private sectors (for Canada, see, e.g., Daniel and Robinson, 1980; Gunderson, 1978, 1980). The same job generally involves the same narrowly defined occupation, and preferably within the same labour market (e.g., region, city). This is what is commonly done when employers use wage surveys to benchmark their own wages, and it is commonly used by arbitrators to establish 'comparability' with the private sector. It is also sometimes done by researchers through the use of published data sets.

The job-to-job comparison procedure compares jobs in the public sector with comparable jobs in the private sector, irrespective of the characteristics of the individuals who do the jobs. Additional experience, for example, could compensate for a lack of formal education. What matters is that the individual can do the job. Difficulties arise in determining the relevant comparison groups. Advocates of higher public sector pay, for example, generally argue that the comparisons should only be with large employers and the unionized sector. As well, difficulties exist in situations where there are no comparable private sector jobs or only a few similar jobs in the private sector.

People-to-People Comparisons and Wage Equation Decompositions

The most common procedure for making public–private wage comparisons is regression analysis to estimate **wage equations** for workers in the public sector and in the private sector (for Canadian examples, see Gunderson, 1979; Gunderson and Riddell, 1995; Gunderson et al., 1999; Robinson and Tomes, 1984; Shapiro and Stelcner, 1989; Stager, 1988). The determinants of wages (explanatory variables) typically include **human capital variables** such as education and experience, as well as such other factors as gender, marital status, occupation, region, firm size, union status, and whether the individual is a visible minority, an Aboriginal, or an immigrant. The estimates are usually based on extensive micro-data files such as the census or the labour force survey.

Public sector wage premiums can be estimated by including public sector dummy variables for the different components of the public sector, with the omitted reference category being the private sector. Alternatively, separate wage equations can be estimated for each of the elements of the public sector as well as the private sector. The average public–private wage differential can then be decomposed into two component parts: one is attributable to differences in the average endowments of wage-determining characteristics (explanatory variables) between workers in the public sector and in the private sector; the other component is attributed to differences in the pay (regression coefficients) that workers receive for the same characteristics. The former component is a measure of differences in the human capital and other wage-determining characteristics of workers in the two sectors; the latter is a measure of the rent or pure public sector wage differential (if positive) paid to workers in the public sector. Refinements are also often made to account for the possible selection bias that may occur because workers may sort themselves or be sorted into the public sector or private sector on the basis of unobserved characteristics that are not controlled for in the regression analysis.

In contrast to the job-to-job comparisons, this procedure essentially involves a comparison of the pay that individuals with the same human capital and other wage-determining characteristics would get if they were in the private sector compared to the public sector. It involves comparing persons with the same observable characteristics.

Queues or Shortages

An indirect measure of whether the public sector pays 'too much' or 'too little' relative to the private sector is based, respectively, on queues or shortages of applicants. To my knowledge, no Canadian empirical studies have examined supply and demand factors to determine wage differentials between the public and private sectors. The potential use of the procedure for determining appropriate wage awards under interest arbitration in the public sector is discussed in Gunderson (1983), and O'Grady (1992) provides a critique of such procedures. US studies that have used measures of queues and shortages to infer compensation differences between the public and private sectors include Borjas (1982), Krueger (1988a, 1988b), Long (1982), Moore and Newman (1991), and Utgoff (1983). Ippolito (1987) points out, however, that lower quits in the public sector could reflect the greater use of deferred compensation (especially through pensions) and not necessarily rents.

These indirect measures allow individual workers to evaluate the '**total compensation**' of the job (i.e., wages, fringe benefits) relative to the working conditions, and then to 'vote with their feet' by applying for the job or by leaving one sector for the other. Queues of qualified applicants that are greater in the public sector than in the private sector would be a sign that the pay in the public sector is excessive relative to the pay in the private sector, albeit the exact magnitude of the rent would not be determined.

Evidence of Public–Private Pay Differences

Based on the studies cited previously in the empirical procedures, the following generalizations emerge with respect to public–private pay differences in Canada:

- There is a pure government pay premium of approximately 5 to 10 per cent.
- It is larger for females than for males and larger for low-wage workers than for high-wage workers, likely reflecting political pressures not to discriminate or to pay simply 'what the market will bear' for less-skilled workers.
- The 'premium' is likely negative at the higher pay level for executives, and certainly there are no 'super salaries' with stock options in the public sector.
- The public sector wage premium is likely a conservative estimate of the

total compensation premium since fringe benefits, pensions, and job security are generally also greater in the public sector.

- This also highlights that the public sector likely tends to pay more deferred or 'back-loaded' compensation in such forms as seniority-based pay increases, job security, and liberal pension and retirement schemes.
- It is difficult, if not impossible, to disentangle the pure public sector pay premium from the union pay premium since most public sector workers are covered by a collective agreement. The limited evidence, however, suggests the following: there is a union impact in the public sector over and above the pure public sector wage impact; the earlier evidence indicated that the union impact is smaller in the public sector than in the private sector; this is more than offset by the fact that unionization is much more prominent in the public sector than in the private sector so that unions do contribute slightly to the public sector wage premium. More recent US evidence, however, suggests that the union impact has increased in the public sector and decreased in the private sector so that they are now similar in the two sectors (Bellman, Haywood, and Lund, 1997; Blanchflower and Bryson, 2007: 88; Gunderson, 2007).
- There is not much difference in the public sector pay premium across the three levels of government; if anything, it may be slightly lower in the federal sector than in the provincial or local government sectors.
- The pay premiums are now negligible in both the health and, especially, the education sectors.
- Somewhat surprisingly, the overall government pay premium has not declined since the 1970s, in spite of the retrenchment and political pressures for restraint that have been placed on the public sector. This is a result of offsetting forces, however, with the government pay premium rising for females (likely as a result of pay and employment equity initiatives) and falling for males.
- There is no evidence of wage spillovers from the public sector to the private sector; that is, high public sector settlements in any given year do not affect private sector settlements in the long run.
- Public sector settlements are often volatile in the short run, with high settlements often occurring in a particular year; however, this frequently reflects a need to catch up from having lagged behind private sector wages in previous years, and the unusually high settlements are often dissipated over time.
- There appears to be a slight upward bias to arbitrated settlements that are set under **binding wage arbitration**, compared to when public sector workers have the right to strike.[3]
- Privatization and deregulation tend to reduce costs, in part through reductions in wages.[4]
- These results for Canada are generally in line with those for the United States and other developed countries. (See Gunderson, 1980, 1995a, 1998; Gunderson et al., 1999.)

Illustrations of the Evidence

A 'flavour' of the empirical evidence upon which many of these generalizations for Canada are based can be illustrated through two sets of empirical tabulations: aggregate wage changes for the public and private sectors; and public sector wage premiums estimated from regression equations.

Aggregate Wage Changes Over Time

Table 11.1 gives the average annual changes in **base wages** in major collective agreements in

Table 11.1 Effective Base Wage Increases, Major Collective Agreements, 1978–2007

	Private	Public	Federal	Provincial	Local	Educ. Health	Federal Crown	Utilities
	(1)	(2)	(3)	(4)	(5)	(6)	(7)	(8)
1978	8.7	7.1	7.2	7.7	7.3	6.8	6.4	7.2
1979	11.1	9.5	8.4	9.0	9.4	8.2	14.4	9.8
1980	11.7	10.9	11.3	11.1	10.8	10.8	11.1	10.6
1981	12.6	13.1	12.7	13.3	12.7	13.5	12.7	13.1
1982	9.5	10.4	8.2	11.8	12.1	11.4	9.9	12.5
1983	5.5	4.6	5.4	4.9	5.7	3.6	5.6	6.4
1984	3.2	3.9	5.0	4.7	3.3	3.1	4.6	2.8
1985	3.3	3.8	3.2	4.4	4.7	3.4	4.0	3.3
1986	3.0	3.6	3.6	3.8	3.2	3.6	3.7	3.3
1987	3.8	4.1	3.4	4.4	4.3	4.1	3.0	2.4
1988	5.0	4.0	3.5	4.3	4.6	3.9	3.2	2.9
1989	5.2	5.2	4.2	5.7	6.2	5.7	3.9	4.7
1990	5.7	5.6	5.3	6.6	4.9	5.5	4.6	4.8
1991	4.4	3.4	1.7	3.6	4.9	3.7	4.2	2.2
1992	2.5	2.0	0.0	2.1	3.3	1.7	3.2	2.9
1993	0.8	0.6	0.0	0.4	0.7	0.8	2.3	1.5
1994	1.2	0.0	0.0	0.1	0.6	−0.3	2.1	0.3
1995	1.4	0.6	0.0	0.9	0.5	0.5	1.0	0.0
1996	1.7	0.5	0.0	0.2	1.1	0.5	0.4	0.9
1997	1.8	1.1	2.3	1.1	1.2	1.0	1.4	1.3
1998	1.8	1.6	2.2	1.7	1.5	1.4	2.3	1.4
1999	2.7	1.9	2.9	1.6	2.3	1.8	2.1	2.5
2000	2.4	2.5	2.1	2.6	2.5	2.6	2.2	3.6
2001	3.0	3.4	3.1	3.4	2.6	3.6	3.7	2.8
2002	2.6	2.6	2.9	2.3	3.0	3.0	2.8	3.0
2003	1.2	2.9	3.1	1.6	2.7	3.3	3.0	2.3
2004	2.3	1.4	2.4	1.9	2.5	0.9	3.0	3.2
2005	2.5	2.2	2.6	2.0	3.1	2.1	2.6	2.6
2006	2.2	2.6	2.7	2.7	3.2	2.6	2.5	2.5
2007	3.1	3.4	3.1	3.8	3.3	3.5	2.7	2.7

Note: Base wages are typically the lowest wage rate in the collective agreement. Major collective agreements involve 500 or more employees. The effective wage includes the imputation for any cost-of-living adjustment (COLA) that may be part of the collective agreement. For the more recent years, predicted inflation rates are used for imputing the COLA. These are then revised subsequently when actual inflation rates become available. For this reason, the figures are constantly adjusted and hence can differ slightly from those in published sources. Published sources include Labour Canada, Bureau of Labour Information, Major Wage Settlements until 1995, and Human Resources Development Canada, Workplace Gazette for years after 1995.

Source: Special tabulations provided by Human Resources Development Canada, through the assistance of Angele Charbonneau.

Canada over the period 1978–99. A comparison of the private sector settlements (col. 1) with the overall public sector settlements (col. 2) highlights that periods of unusually high settlements in the public sector (e.g., 1981–2; 1984–7) are usually preceded by periods when they are below those of the private sector and are followed by periods when they dissipate relative to the private sector. Of particular note, over the full decade of the 1990s settlements in both sectors were low, and they were lower in the public sector in every year.

The separate results for the different components of the public sector highlight that the pattern of unusually high settlements reflecting **catch-up**, and subsequently being dissipated, prevails across most sectors. Settlements in the federal sector exceeded those in the private sector in 11 of the 30 years. A similar pattern prevailed in the education, health, and welfare sector. Furthermore, in neither of those two sectors did settlements exceed those in the private sector during the 1990s. In fact, in the 60 'cells' reflecting the six components of the public sector over the 10 years of the 1990s, settlements in the public sector exceeded those in the private sector only 10 times. Clearly, the 1990s were a time of overall public sector wage restraint, at least with respect to base wages.

The cumulative effect of these patterns is illustrated in Table 11.2. Wages in 1978 were set equal to a common index of 100 and then the cumulative wage increases were calculated from the annual percentage changes of Table 11.1.

Table 11.2 Cumulative Effective Base Wage Increases, Major Collective Agreements, 1978–2007

	Private	Public	Federal	Provincial	Local	Education/ Health/ Welfare	Federal Crown	Utilities
	(1)	(2)	(3)	(4)	(5)	(6)	(7)	(8)
1978	100.0	100.0	100.0	100.0	100.0	100.0	100.0	100.0
1979	108.7	107.1	107.2	107.7	107.3	106.8	106.4	107.2
1980	120.8	117.3	116.2	117.4	117.4	115.6	121.7	117.7
1981	134.9	130.1	129.3	130.4	130.1	128.0	135.2	130.2
1982	151.9	147.1	145.8	147.8	146.6	145.3	152.4	147.2
1983	166.3	162.4	157.7	165.2	164.3	161.9	167.5	165.6
1984	175.5	169.9	166.2	173.3	173.7	167.7	176.9	176.2
1985	181.1	176.5	174.5	181.4	179.4	172.9	185.0	181.2
1986	187.1	183.2	180.1	189.4	187.8	178.8	192.4	187.2
1987	192.7	189.8	186.6	196.6	193.9	185.2	199.5	193.3
1988	200.0	197.6	193.0	205.3	202.2	192.8	205.5	198.0
1989	210.0	205.5	199.7	214.1	211.5	200.3	212.1	203.7
1990	220.9	216.2	208.1	226.3	224.6	211.8	220.4	213.3
1991	233.5	228.3	219.1	241.2	235.6	223.4	230.5	223.5
1992	243.8	236.0	222.9	249.9	247.2	231.7	240.2	228.4
1993	249.9	240.7	222.9	255.2	255.3	235.6	247.9	235.1
1994	251.9	242.2	222.9	256.2	257.1	237.5	253.6	238.6
1995	254.9	242.2	222.9	256.5	258.6	236.8	258.6	239.3
1996	258.5	243.6	222.9	258.8	259.9	238.0	261.2	239.3
1997	262.9	244.9	222.9	259.3	262.8	239.2	262.3	241.5
1998	267.6	247.6	228.0	262.1	266.0	241.6	265.9	244.6
1999	272.4	251.5	233.0	266.6	269.9	244.9	272.1	248.0
2000	279.8	256.3	239.8	270.9	276.2	249.3	277.8	254.2
2001	286.5	262.7	244.8	277.9	283.1	255.8	283.9	263.4
2002	295.1	271.6	252.4	287.3	290.4	265.0	294.4	270.8
2003	302.7	278.7	259.7	294.0	299.1	273.0	302.6	278.9
2004	306.4	286.8	267.7	298.7	307.2	282.0	311.7	285.3
2005	313.4	290.8	274.2	304.3	314.9	284.5	321.1	294.4
2006	321.3	297.2	281.3	310.4	324.6	290.5	329.4	302.1
2007	328.3	304.9	288.9	318.8	335.0	298.1	337.6	309.6

Source: Calculated by setting 1978 to an index of 100 and then cumulating the annual increases from Table 11.1.

Over the full period, the cumulative effect of the wage changes was fairly similar between the private and public sectors. Between 1978 and 2007, wages had increased by 3.3 times in the private sector and by 3.04 times in the public sector. A base wage of $10 per hour in 1978 would have been $32.83 per hour by 2007 in the private sector and $30.49 in the public sector—not a large difference over a 30-year period.

The cumulative differences are more substantial, however, when compared across the different elements of the public sector. Specifically, the cumulative increases are lowest in the federal jurisdiction (index of 289 by 2007), followed by education/health/welfare (298) and utilities (310). The cumulative increases in the provincial governments (319), local governments (335), and Crown corporations (338) are similar to those in the private sector (328). In essence, over the full 30-year period, base wages in collective agreements increased slightly less in the overall public sector compared to the private sector, almost completely as a result of lower cumulative increases in the federal sector, in health/education/welfare, and in utilities.

The changes were most pronounced over the 1990s. As of 1989, the cumulative indexes were remarkably similar across all sectors (210 in the private sector and 205 in the public, with the lowest of 200 in the federal jurisdiction and the highest of 214 in the provincial jurisdiction). Over the first half of the 1990s, the cumulative increases were smallest in the federal jurisdiction and in health/education/welfare so that by the end of the 1990s these two sectors had the lowest cumulative wage index. This is especially apparent in the wage freezes in the federal jurisdiction from 1992 to 1996 and the very low increases in the health/education/welfare sector over that period (indicated in Table 11.1). Interestingly, these two sectors with the lowest wage increases also had the lowest index by the beginning of the 1990s.

Overall, the following generalizations emerge from wage settlements in major collective agreements over the period 1978–2007:

- Public sector settlements exhibited more volatility, with large settlements often reflecting catch-up and being dissipated over time.
- Cumulatively, there was little difference, although public sector settlements were slightly lower, especially during the 1990s.
- The lower public sector settlements were almost exclusively a result of lower settlements in the federal jurisdiction, in health/education/welfare, and in utilities.

Public sector Premiums from Regression Estimates

Table 11.3 illustrates recent public–private wage differentials estimated from human capital regression equations—essentially the 'people-to-people' procedure discussed previously.[5] The overall public sector wage premium is 7.6 per cent. For both sexes, a public sector premium exists in each of the elements of the public sector. For the three levels of government it is lowest in the federal sector and highest in provincial and local governments. It is a 'normal' premium in the education sector, and effectively zero in the health sector. For all elements of the public sector except provincial governments, the public sector premium is larger for females than males. This provides a specific illustration of many of the generalizations from the empirical evidence discussed previously.

Table 11.3 Public Sector Wage Premiums, Regression Estimates from the November 1997 Labour Force Survey

Public Sector	Both Sexes	Males	Females
Federal	7.0	5.5	8.8
Provincial	11.4	12.8	11.2
Local	10.3	12.2	5.9
Education	6.9	4.9	7.8
Health	0.8	–14.2	4.9
Transport/ Communication/ Utilities	9.2	7.6	14.9
Religion/Other	6.8	3.0	11.8

Source: Gunderson et al. (1999).

Policy Implications

The previously discussed theoretical considerations and empirical evidence highlight a number of important policy implications. First and foremost, a difficult policy trade-off is involved since a policy of restraint on public sector pay (which may be warranted, given the pay premium) would disproportionately fall on females and low-wage workers—groups generally considered disadvantaged in their labour market status. As well, reducing public sector payrolls by restraining salaries at the high end will likely lead to severe problems of recruiting and retaining executive talent because, as it is, such persons generally receive lower pay in the public sector compared to the private sector, and there are no 'super salary prizes'.

Certainly, a policy of continued vigilance is in order since both theory and empirical evidence suggest that public sector pay will be higher than private sector pay. Yet, extreme actions seem unwarranted because the premium is not large, much of it is a normal union wage premium, and the effect would likely disproportionately fall on females and low-wage workers.

The area where most vigilance is merited is with respect to the tendency to pay deferred compensation in the form of seniority-based wage increases, job security, and liberal pension and retirement schemes. While there may be good reasons for such compensation arrangements in the public sector, they are also consistent with the possibility that governments are simply trying to save on current wage costs (when they are in power) and to shift the costs to future generations of taxpayers (when another government may be in power). Unfortunately, it is difficult to be vigilant in this area since future generations of taxpayers are not at the bargaining table when such arrangements are made.

Predicting the future is extremely difficult in the area of public sector wage determination, in part because it involves predicting political pressures. The pressures for restraint will likely continue into the near future, albeit they may be tempered by government budget surpluses that are replacing deficits and by the fact that the political pressures are not all in the direction of using the surpluses for tax cuts.

Nevertheless, the political pressures are now much more likely to be circumscribed by the forces of global competition, free trade, and capital mobility, including human capital mobility through the brain drain. In such a world, companies are able to locate in political jurisdictions that have lower taxes (including taxes used for public sector payrolls) for a given level of public services and to export back into the higher-tax jurisdictions. Political jurisdictions are under more pressure to compete for that business investment and the associated jobs. One way to compete is to provide public services in the most cost-effective fashion, with the removal of public sector rents (pay premiums above the competitive wage paid in private sector firms) being one mechanism.

In such circumstances, it is questionable whether governments will be able to continue their more egalitarian pay practices with respect to women and low-wage workers in general. Similarly, the threat of a brain drain to the private sector or to other jurisdictions means that they may not be able to continue the practice of 'underpaying' high-level personnel. This is especially the case if such personnel are regarded as important in leading the public sector through the dynamic restructuring that will be required because of the inter-jurisdictional competition for business investment and the associated jobs. To the extent that this inter-jurisdictional competition becomes a more powerful force, it suggests an overall dissipation of the public sector rents, with that dissipation being largest for women and low-wage workers and with a concomitant rise in the pay of higher-level personnel in the public sector.

To the extent that they occur, these changes in compensation will likely occur in subtle forms. Pay and employment equity initiatives may be put more 'on hold', not so much through the repeal of laws as through the de facto emaciation of administration and enforcement resources. Low-wage workers in the public sector will not have their wages directly cut to 'what the market will bear', although this can occur indirectly through privatization, subcontracting, and the injection of competitive pressures as part of reinventing government. Higher-level personnel in the public sector will also not likely have their pay rise dramatically, as did the pay of CEOs in recent years. Nevertheless, this can occur indirectly, again through privatization and subcontracting for the delivery of public services through the private sector.

Whatever the future holds—and the crystal ball is cloudy—it will likely be an interesting period for public sector compensation. This is as true for the compensation dimension of public administration as it is for other dimensions in this important area. What is clear is that public administration will be under increased pressure to deliver its services in a cost-effective fashion—with compensation being an important component of that delivery.

Important Terms and Concepts

base wages
binding wage arbitration
catch-up
compensating wages
deferred (or back-loaded) compensation
fair wage
hard and soft budget constraints
high-performance workforce
human capital variables
intergenerational burden
non-competitive forces/factors
queues or shortages
short-run demand changes
soft budget constraints
total compensation
wage equations

Study Questions

1. How does one determine whether there are public–private compensation differentials?
2. What are the difficulties inherent in determining public–private compensation differentials?
3. According to labour market theory, what characteristics may explain public–private wage differentials?
4. What are some theoretical reasons for believing that public sector compensation premiums will prevail and that such premiums will be larger for low-wage and other, more disadvantaged, workers?
5. What evidence for public–private pay differences exists? According to what studies? For which sectors and levels?
6. What are the policy implications and trade-offs following upon existing compensation theory and empirical evidence presented by Gunderson and Hebdon?

Useful Websites

Canadian Federation of Independent Business. 2008. 'Wage Watch: A Comparison of Public Sector and Private Sector Wages'. 2 December.

www.cfib-fcei.ca/cfib-documents/rr3077.pdf

Canadian Labour Congress. 2008. 'Summary and Analysis of CFIB's Research Report: Wage Watch: A Comparison of Public Sector and Private Sector Wages'. 11 December.

www.canadianlabour.ca/sites/default/files/pdfs/12–11-CFIB_Study.pdf

Gunderson, Morley, Douglas Hyatt, Craig Riddell. 2000. 'Pay Differences between the Government and Private Sectors: Labour Force Survey and Census Estimates'. Canadian Policy Research Networks (CPRN), 20 June.

www.cprn.org/doc.cfm?doc=22&l=en

Notes

1. For a contrary view, see Gee and Gutman (2000).
2. The empirical procedures discussed here refer to those used to compare the *level* of compensation between public- and private sector workers at a point in time. They do not refer to aggregate annual wage *changes* between the public and private sectors (although such figures are reported later in the chapter). Nor do they refer to the estimation of aggregate wage equations (augmented Phillips curves) based on such aggregate wage changes. The latter equations do not illustrate whether wages are higher or lower in the public sector compared to the private sector. Rather, they illustrate the sensitivity of public and private wage changes to economic conditions such as the business cycle, and they can be used to determine whether there is a spillover effect across the sectors. Such studies in Canada include Auld et al. (1980), Auld and Wilton (1985), Cousineau and Lacroix (1977), Riddell and Smith (1982), and Wilton (1986). The generalizations based on these studies are incorporated into the summary of evidence discussed here.
3. Canadian studies in this area include Anderson (1981), Curie and McConnell (1991), Downie (1979), Gunderson et al. (1996), Ponak and Falkenberg (1989), and Saunders (1986).
4. Gunderson and Riddell (1991) discuss some of the empirical evidence in this area. They also indicate, however, that 'Unfortunately, much of the empirical evidence is anecdotal; more research is needed to provide a clear picture.'
5. Control variables include age, marital status, education, full-time/part-time work, tenure, type of work (permanent, seasonal, contract, casual), collective agreement coverage, establishment size, province, city, and occupation. Estimates were based on the micro-data files of the November 1997 Labour Force Survey, with a usable sample of 48,385.

References

Anderson, J. 1981. 'The Impact of Arbitration: A Methodological Assessment', *Industrial Relations* 20: 129–48.

Auld, D., L. Christofides, R. Swidinsky, and D. Wilton. 1980. 'A Microeconomic Analysis of Wage Determination in the Canadian Public Sector', *Journal of Public Economics* 13: 369–88.

———, and D. Wilton. 1985. 'Wage Settlements in the Ontario Public Sector and the Ontario Controls Program', in D. Conklin, T. Courchene, and W. Jones, eds, *Public Sector Compensation*. Toronto: Ontario Economic Council, 80–108.

Belman, D., J. Haywood, and J. Lund. 1997. 'Public Sector Earnings and the Extent of Unionization', *Industrial and Labor Relations Review* 50: 610–28.

Blanchflower, D., and A. Bryson. 2007. 'What Effect Do Unions Have on Wages Now?', in J. Bennett and B. Kaufman, eds, *What Do Unions Do?: A Twenty-Year Perspective*. London: Transaction Publishers, 79–113.

Borjas, G. 1982. 'Labor Turnover in the US. Federal Bureaucracy', *Journal of Public Economics* 19: 187–202.

Cousineau, J.M., and R. Lacroix. 1977. *Wage Determination in Major Collective Agreements in the Private and Public Sectors*. Ottawa: Economic Council of Canada.

Currie, J., and S. McConnell. 1991. 'Collective Bargaining in the Public Sector: The Effect of Legal Structure on Dispute Costs and Wages', *American Economic Review* 81: 693–718.

Daniel, M., and W. Robinson. 1980. *Compensation in Canada: A Study of the Public and Private Sectors*. Ottawa: Conference Board of Canada.

Downie, B. 1979. *The Behavioral, Economic and Institutional Effects of Compulsory Interest Arbitration*. Ottawa: Economic Council of Canada.

Gee, E.M., and G.M. Gutman, eds. 2000. *The Overselling of Population Aging: Apocalyptic Demography, Intergenerational Challenges, and Social Policy*. Toronto: Oxford University Press.

Gunderson, M. 1978. 'Public–private Wage and Non-Wage Differentials in Canada: Some Calculations from Published Tabulations', in D.K. Foot, ed., *Public Employment and Compensation in Canada: Myths and Realities*. Toronto: Butterworths for Institute for Research on Public Policy, 127–66.

———. 1979. 'Earnings Differentials between the Public and Private Sectors', *Canadian Journal of Economics* 12: 228–41.

———. 1980. 'Public Sector Compensation in Canada and the US.', *Industrial Relations* 19: 257–71.

———. 1983. *Economic Aspects of Interest Arbitration*. Toronto: Economic Council.

———. 1995a. 'Public Sector Compensation', in G. Swimmer and M. Thompson, eds, *Public Sector Collective Bargaining in Canada*. Kingston: IRC Press, 103–34.

———. 1995b. 'Gender Discrimination and Pay Equity Legislation', in L. Christofides et al., eds, *Aspects of Labour Market Behaviour: Essays in Honour of John Vanderkamp*. Toronto: University of Toronto Press, 225–47.

———. 1998. *Government Compensation: Issues and Options*. Ottawa: Canadian Policy Research Network.

———. 2007. 'Two Faces of Union Voice in the Public Sector', in J. Bennett and B. Kaufman, eds, *What Do Unions Do?: A Twenty-Year Perspective*. London: Transaction Publishers, 401–22.

———, R. Hebdon, and D. Hyatt. 1996. 'Collective Bargaining in the Public Sector: Comment', *American Economic Review* 86: 315–26.

———. and D. Hyatt. 1996. 'Canadian Public Sector Employment Relations in Transition', in D. Belman et al., eds, *Public Sector Employment in a Time of Transition*. Madison: Industrial Relations Research Association, 1–20.

———, ———, and C. Riddell. 1999. *Pay Differences between the Government and Private Sectors: Labour Force Survey and Census Estimates*. Ottawa: Canadian Policy Research Network.

———. and C. Riddell. 1991. 'Provincial Public Sector Payrolls', in M. McMillan, ed., *Provincial Government Finances*, vol. 2. Toronto: Canadian Tax Foundation, 164–92.

———. and ———. 1995. *Public and Private Sector Wages: A Comparison*. Kingston: Government and Competitiveness Series, School of Policy Studies, Queen's University.

Ippolito, R. 1987. 'Why Federal Workers Don't Quit', *Journal of Human Resources* 22: 281–99.

Krueger, A. 1988a. 'The Determinants of Queues for Federal Jobs', *Industrial and Labor Relations Review* 41: 567–81.

———. 1988b. 'Are Public Sector Workers Paid More Than Their Alternative Wage? Evidence from Longitudinal Data and Job Queues', in R. Freeman and C. Ichnioski, eds, *When Public Sector Workers Unionize*. Chicago: University of Chicago Press, 217–40.

Long, J.E. 1982. 'Are Government Workers Overpaid? Alternative Evidence', *Journal of Human Resources* 17: 123–31.

Moore, W., and R. Newman. 1991. 'Government Wage Differentials in a Municipal Labor Market', *Industrial and Labor Relations Review* 45: 145–53.

O'Grady, J. 1992. *Arbitration and Its Ills*. Kingston: Institute for Policy Analysis Program on Government and Competitiveness.

Peters, J. 1999. *Statistical Profile of Employment in Government*. Ottawa: Canadian Policy Research Network.

Ponak, A., and L. Falkenberg. 1989. 'Resolution of Interest Disputes', in A. Sethi, ed., *Collective Bargaining in Canada*. Scarborough, Ont.: Nelson Canada, 260–90.

Riddell, W.C., and P. Smith. 1982. 'Expected Inflation and Wage Changes in Canada', *Canadian Journal of Economics* 15: 377–94.

Robinson, C., and N. Tomes. 1984. 'Union Wage Differentials in the Public and Private Sectors: A Simultaneous Equations Specification', *Journal of Labor Economics* 2: 106–27.

Saunders, G. 1986. 'The Impact of Interest Arbitration on Canadian Federal Employees' Wages', *Industrial Relations* 25: 320–7.

Shapiro, D., and M. Stelcner. 1989. 'Canadian Public–private Sector Earnings Differences, 1970–1980', *Industrial Relations* 28: 72–81.

Stager, D. 1988. 'Lawyers' Earnings in the Canadian Private and Public Sectors', *Relations Industrielles/Industrial Relations* 43: 571–89.

Swimmer, G. 2001. 'Public sector Labour Relations in an Era of Restraint and Restructuring: An Overview', in Swimmer, ed., *Public sector Labour Relations in an Era of Restraint and Restructuring*. Toronto: Oxford University Press, 1–35.

Utgoff, K.C. 1983. 'Compensation Levels and Quit Rates in the Public Sector', *Journal of Human Resources* 18: 394–406.

Wilton, D. 1986. 'Public Sector Wage Compensation', in W.C. Riddell, ed., *Canadian Labour Relations*. Toronto: University of Toronto Press, 257–84.

PART IV Changing Visions of Public Administration

Most observers would agree that government has changed substantially in the last few decades. Charting the exact nature of the changes, however, is less likely to elicit agreement. In Part 3, the contributors discuss these changes in public administration and the practical reasons for, and visions behind, the changes that have occurred in recent years.

In Chapter 12, Alasdair Roberts takes a very complex subject—the evolution of the Canadian government—and simplifies it for the reader by considering the history of government in Canada in identifiable periods. Roberts reminds us that a sense of 'mission' marked a number of periods during the evolution of the Canadian public service in the twentieth century. Paradoxically, with a new era of budget surpluses starting as early as the mid-1990s, there was no overarching conception, after so many years of deficits, as to how to spend these surplus government funds. Policy-makers were wary about preaching big government as a panacea for every problem. Promotion of the 'knowledge-based economy' is a likely candidate for the new mission. However, he says, the same problems that bedevilled the last century would likely continue, particularly policy area disputes between the federal and provincial governments and various international areas of contention, especially between Canada and the US. Roberts provides both a useful summary of where we have been and a challenge to determine where we should be going.

Kathy L. Brock, Matthew P.J. Burbidge, and John L. Nator take up the challenge established by Roberts. They acknowledge that the old century ended with the federal public service lacking a clear guiding vision or purpose. They respond in Chapter 13, however, by attempting to lay the groundwork for a vision for the public service in the new century. The record of the Canadian public service over the long haul, from 1867 on, shows a public service with important adaptive qualities. The legacies of the past must be linked with the realities of the present day. The legacies of the past are impressive. The country, despite challenges of geography and jurisdiction, managed to develop a competent, fiscally responsible public service based on merit, promotions, and political neutrality in the era of the expansive vision, 1867–1928; managed a 'grand vision' of public service, despite its earlier 'faltering vision', in the period 1929–1945; and then transformed this into government as 'benevolent Leviathan' in the era of the welfare state, 1946–1973. However, in the 1974–1998 period, one of fiscal crisis and the 'hollowed-out state', there was a lack of confidence and sense of vision, and this continued even when balanced budgets and surpluses returned in the fifth period, 1999–2008. The old emphasis on aligning political masters and public servants in a common mission of service to the public must once again prevail in the face of present-day realities. Significant external challenges to the public sector now exist (globalization, digital governance), as well as internal ones (internal and external demographics, new accountability models which undermine collaboration and horizontality, and the need for new leadership styles to replace the narrow transactional style of the [old] New Public Management popular in the 1990s). Optimism prevails in this pithy mission statement.

David Zussman, in Chapter 14, has completely rewritten his important chapter on Alternative Service Delivery (ASD), since much has changed since the first edition in 2002. He provides a current definition of ASD in Canada, outlines its current context, reviews its various models and classifications and its current status, and assesses its legacy. ASD is a 'creative and dynamic process of public sector restructuring that improves the delivery of services to clients by sharing governance functions with individuals, community groups and other entities'. It aims at three objectives: a more cost-effective delivery, improved effectiveness and delivery, and promoting managerial decision-making closer to the point of delivery. Most of the pressures promoting ASD covered in the first edition—IT, deficit-fighting, demography, and so on—are still operative, but one new one stands out: the need for 'governing by network', not by hierarchy: not managing people, but coordinating resources for producing public value. A model in Zussman's chapter (Figure 14.1) gives a review of the significant number of options that are available to ASD reformers; and the Ontario government continuum of ASD options provides a comprehensive guide to the range of ASD options. However, classification techniques should be used to arrange the various options. He eschews the standard ones—structure, financing, degree of government involvement—in favour of a more useful functional classification system capturing the intended goals and objectives of ASD initiatives: service efficiency, management flexibility, and collaborative arrangements.

Zussman foresees a day when alternative service delivery will be the 'standard' rather than an 'alternative' in public sector management. However, at present, it is plainly a very modest part of the federal government's strategy for transformation of the public sector when compared to leaders such as the UK, NZ, and Australia. Despite the relatively modest commitment to ASD, there were indications, with Service Canada, federal foundations and special operating agencies, that the Canadian government was continuing its commitment to service transformation early in the decade. Most recently, however, the federal government has taken a sharp turn away from ASD and has focused instead on management reform. As a result, ASD has become one strategy among many in the pursuit of better management practices. Yet the promise it holds is significant for public administration writ large.

NPM is only one view of the future for Canadian public administration.

It is instructive to consider what Lorne Sossin, in Chapter 15, says about another, contending paradigm, that of 'democratic administration'. This view of public administration sees the public services in a broad social context—through a deliberative model of bureaucrat–citizen interaction or, even better bureaucratic engagement—and is preoccupied with ensuring citizen empowerment. Public officials in this approach are committed to facilitating public deliberation about policy, consulting with citizens before reaching decisions, establishing frameworks for engaging with vulnerable citizens, fostering mutuality and trust relationships with citizens, and providing direct accountability to citizens who are dependent on their decisions.

Democratic administration is not a simple extension of New Left thinking of the last century. Its strength is in integrating the powerful participation and accountability themes from both the New Left and the New Right, while recognizing that the implementation techniques of both had serious deficiencies. Democratic administration, in this sense, would appear to transcend both ideologies. It positions public officials as mediators who give equal weight to interactions with their political masters and interactions with citizens. It aims to give substance to what previously have been only slogans of public sector reform. Sossin suggests that democratic administration will come into effect 'when the recipients of public goods and services demand it, and administrative bodies can no longer avoid it'.

12

A Fragile State: *Federal Public Administration in the Twentieth Century*

Alasdair Roberts

Introduction

Government as we know it today—so-called '**big government**', with its extensive array of mechanisms for redistribution of wealth and other modes of social and economic regulation—is a relatively new invention. In fact, it may be the most important invention of the twentieth century, surpassing in significance any of the scientific and technical advances of that period and often serving as a prerequisite for these other advances.

The invention of 'big government' was partly a cultural project and partly an exercise in organizational engineering. The cultural project involved a transformation in popular understandings about the role that the state should play in the regulation of society. The foundation for this transformation was laid in the nineteenth century, when ideas about the 'sacred' nature or '**sacrality**' **of the state** became ensconced in popular thought, and the symbols and rituals designed to promote 'patriotic love' of the state—such as flags and anthems—became familiar parts of everyday life.[1] By the latter third of the twentieth century, the state had become something more than an object of devotion: it had acquired responsibility for regulating broad swaths of social and economic affairs. Furthermore, it had acquired the extensive administrative apparatus needed to fulfill these broad new obligations.

The development of the Canadian federal government followed a path that was similar in many respects to those followed by the central governments of many other capitalist democracies. On the whole, it was characterized by growing confidence among policy-makers about the capacity of government to remedy the defects of an unregulated capitalist economy and the elaboration of programs to manage economic activity and redistribute wealth. However, the story was not a simple one of steady expansion. Instead, it was a story punctuated by crisis and experimentation. Two world wars provided governments with unexpected lessons about the potential of large-scale economic and social planning.

In Canada, the evolution of central government was also shaped by distinctive local conditions. The exercise of consolidating control over territory—the most basic requirement for nationhood—continued in Canada long after it had been completed in other nations. Even after territorial control was established, fears about political and economic sovereignty persisted, driven by the threat of domination by the United States. Urbanization and industrialization, and the pressures that they imposed on government, also occurred later than in other nations. The growth of the national government was moulded as well by the realities of federalism. Except in wartime, the federal government was hobbled by constitutional limits on its powers and by the need to manage conflicts with provincial governments. The result was an administrative apparatus that featured weakly developed tools for economic regulation, a heavy reliance on state-owned enterprises, highly decentralized arrangements for delivery of social benefits, and a distinctive capacity for intergovernmental negotiation and collaboration with economic elites.

A combination of crises struck the Canadian government in the last quarter of the twentieth century, compelling significant changes in its administrative arrangements. Some of these developments—such as increasing popular distrust of political authority, doubts about the competence of government in economic planning, and rapid growth in government indebtedness—were experienced in many nations. In addition, the Canadian government struggled with growing regional alienation and support for secession within the province of Quebec. At the end of the century, the problems of indebtedness and secessionism seemed to have been held in check. However, the federal government's influence in social and economic affairs had declined significantly. There was a sense of uncertainty about its role that had not been experienced since the early years of the Great Depression.

The Railway State, 1900–1928

A history of the development of the administrative apparatus of the federal government in the twentieth century can be divided into four parts, each comprising roughly one-quarter of the century and marked by distinctive preoccupations. In the first quarter of the century, the evolution of government was driven by one basic imperative: the drive for **territorial consolidation**. Most of the capitalist democracies with which Canada is now compared had, by 1900, established effective control of the land over which they claimed sovereignty. Even the United States—the nation whose experience most closely paralleled that of Canada—had divided its western territories into states and linked substantial settlements on both coasts through a system of transcontinental railways.

The Canadian situation was more tenuous. Maps that showed the Dominion consuming a broad swath of North America were highly misleading. Its population of 5.3 million was still largely settled on the southern shores of the Atlantic Ocean, the St Lawrence River, and the lower Great Lakes. Only 600,000 lived west of the Ontario–Manitoba border.[2] Most of the land over which Canada asserted sovereignty remained under direct federal administration as part of its Northwest Territories. This included all the land that now constitutes the upper halves of Manitoba, Ontario, and Quebec, as well as the land that would later form the provinces of Saskatchewan and Alberta, the Yukon Territory, and Nunavut. Most of the Atlantic coast was claimed by Newfoundland, still a separately administered colony of Great Britain. Canadian ownership of the Pacific coast was contested by the United States.

One way of transforming 'Canada' from an assertion to a fact was to settle the vast western territories. Immigration into Canada exploded, from 42,000 persons in 1900 to 401,000 in 1913. The influx was motivated by a growing market for the wheat that could be grown on new western farms. Seventy-three million acres of new farm holdings were established between 1901 and 1921. The steady flow of people into the West—and of grain out of the West—demanded an expansion in transportation facilities. Part of the challenge was an improvement in canals on the St Lawrence River and Great Lakes to accommodate larger grain carriers. But the larger task was an expansion of national railroads. The railway system was not a legacy of the nineteenth century, as is commonly thought. At its peak in the mid-twentieth century, Canada's rail system comprised about 60,000 miles of track. Only 18,000 miles of track had been built by 1900. Almost all of the remaining track would be laid between 1900 and 1926, as a result of expansion into western and northern lands.

The administrative structure of the federal government in this period was primitive and heavily geared towards the task of territorial consolidation. In 1912, the government employed 15,000 people, excluding the 5,100 who worked for the Post Office (Table 12.1). Over 3,000 employees worked in Customs houses, largely because of the government's support for protectionist trade policies and its dependence on tariffs as its principal source of revenue. Otherwise, most federal employment could be related directly to the expansion of rail and water transportation capacity; the promotion of immigration, and processing of immigrants; the sale of federal lands to immigrants; and support to these new farmers.

Table 12.1 Largest Departments in the Federal Public Service, 1912–1999

1912		**1935**	
Total employment	20,016	Total employment	40,709
Post Office	5,082	Post Office	10,780
Transport	4,235	National Revenue	5,374
Customs	3,214	Transport	4,678
Public Works	1,400	Public Works	3,620
Interior	1,270	Agriculture	2,280
1945		**1970**	
Total employment	115,908	Total employment	244,197
National Defence	28,137	Post Office	45,482
Post Office	13,770	National Defence	39,027
Finance	12,772	National Revenue	18,967
National Revenue	10,706	Transport	17,556
Veterans Affairs	7,364	RCMP	12,253
1985		**1999**	
Total person-years	260,049	Total employment	186,314
National Defence	37,018	Revenue Canada	43,216
Solicitor General (RCMP)	32,462	Human Resources Development	21,848
National Revenue	29,594	National Defence	18,644
Employment and Immigration	24,823	Correctional Service	12,232
Transport	22,976	Public Works and Government Services	11,418

The Post Office became a Crown corporation in 1981 and was excluded from the public service count after that date. Before 1970 and after 1985, only RCMP administrative staff were included in the public service count.
Sources: Data for 1912 to 1970: (Leacy, 1983). Data for 1985 from Estimates. Data for 1999: (Treasury Board Secretariat, 1999).

Employment figures may understate the federal government's preoccupation with the expansion of transportation systems in the years preceding World War I. Between 1901 and 1913, half of the government's total expenditures were dedicated to transportation and communication functions. The bulk of this was comprised of subsidies to support rail line expansion by private firms, such as the Canadian Pacific Railway and Grand Trunk Railway. Other inducements—such as federal guarantees for private borrowing and gifts of federal land to private firms—were at least as important but never appeared in the tabulation of federal expenditures. Where inducements failed, the federal government would resort to direct ownership. At the time of Confederation, it had built and operated the Intercolonial Railway; later, it built and leased the National Transcontinental Railway; and, in 1917–19, the federal government took over the bankrupt Canadian Northern and Grand Trunk railways. In 1920, the government consolidated its own operations into the Canadian National Railways, which controlled 40 per cent of all Canadian rail lines.

The evolution of the Canadian government in this period differed significantly from that of the American federal government. Within the United States, the task of territorial consolidation had been completed by the turn of the century; its new challenge was to manage pressures associated with rapid industrialization and urbanization. The American government was pushed by Progressive reformers to expand its regulatory functions to protect the new industrial working class and the growing mass of urban consumers against new concentrations of corporate power. The Progressive era was marked by the assertion of a federal role in assuring safe foods and medicines, regulating labour relations, and breaking up or regulating trusts and monopolies (Eisner, 1994: 161–7).

For a combination of reasons, there was no comparable expansion of federal responsibilities in Canada. One was the slower pace of industrialization and urbanization in Canada. In 1920, most Canadians still lived in unincorporated rural areas or worked in agricultural enterprises. The degree of urbanization already achieved in the United States would not be matched in Canada until 1950. The Canadian government was also hobbled by constitutional restrictions that gave much authority for social regulation to provincial governments. As a senior public servant within the Laurier government, William Lyon Mackenzie King attempted to expand the federal government's role in managing industrial relations and succeeded in persuading Parliament to adopt an Industrial Disputes Investigation Act in 1907 (Robertson, 1991: 112). But the law was struck down as an infringement of provincial jurisdiction.

Nor was the Canadian political climate as favourable to regulatory actions intended to check corporate power. Americans, unworried about the problems of territorial consolidation or foreign economic domination, saw only the abuses that might flow from the emergence of monopolies in key sectors such as oil, steel, or banking. The Canadian government, on the other hand, had concluded from its experience in the development of the railway system that the cultivation of more powerful corporate interests might often be in the national interest. There was no enthusiasm for 'trust-busting'. Although a Combines Investigation Act had been adopted by Parliament in 1910, it was poorly drafted and weakly enforced (Brecher, 1960). In one case, western farmers were told that a cartel of grain elevator companies served the public interest by ensuring the 'orderly marketing' of grain (Rea, 1999).

Crisis and Drift, 1929–1945

Popular opinion about the virtues of King's 'prosperity budgets' was badly shaken after the onset of the **Great Depression** in late 1929. The Depression is often regarded as a catalyst that led to a quick and dramatic expansion of governmental responsibilities. In fact, the transformation of government was slow and tentative. The severity of the economic decline—often described, even in its early years, as a 'crisis' or 'emergency'—was widely understood. There was less agreement on how government should respond. The idea that government might take an active role in economic management did not gain influence for more than a decade, and only after another war provided another public demonstration of the power of central economic planning.

Many factors contributed to the onset of the Great Depression. A glut on the wheat market cut western incomes; this was followed by several years of drought and pestilence. After the crash of the American stock market in October 1929, foreign demand for Canadian natural resources and manufactured goods also plummeted. The economic collapse was unparalleled in its severity. Unemployment increased from 3 per cent in 1929 to 23 per cent in 1933, and almost two million Canadians had no source of earned income at all (McNaught, 1986: 246).

At first, many governments floundered. The King government, like the Hoover administration in the United States, was too firmly committed to the doctrine of budgetary balance to contemplate increased spending for economic relief. Both governments—like many others—had tried to improve conditions by increasing tariffs, but this early experiment at intervention actually exacerbated the economic decline. Each government intended to preserve domestic markets for domestic manufacturers, but the cumulative effect was to close off export markets worldwide.

Only after both leaders were defeated—King in the general election of 1930, Hoover in 1932—did governments become more willing to take steps to ameliorate economic distress.[3] But there was still uncertainty about the best course of action, and significant differences existed in the paths taken in the United States and Canada. The Roosevelt administration dramatically expanded spending on federally run public works projects, such as construction of transportation facilities and improvement of federal lands. The Canadian government, by contrast, put little emphasis on direct spending, choosing instead to emphasize larger grants in support of provincially administered relief projects. Transfer payments to the provinces increased from roughly 5 per cent of federal expenditures in 1929 to a Depression-era peak of 25 per cent in 1937 (US Bureau of the Census, 1976: 1123–34; Statistics Canada, 1988: Table 44; Strick, 1999: 204).

There were other differences as well. As part of its 'New Deal' program, the Roosevelt administration expanded the government's role in regulating economic conditions, introducing new mechanisms to control securities markets, a new law on collective bargaining and conditions of work, and new programs to regulate agricultural production and encourage planning within the manufacturing sector. A system of unemployment insurance and a contributory pension plan were introduced in 1937.

In some of these areas, such as securities market regulation and collective bargaining, there were clear constitutional limitations on the Canadian government's ability to act. In other areas, however, the government's authority was more ambiguous. Shortly before the 1935 election, the Conservative government of R.B. Bennett proposed its own version of the New Deal, including new laws to regulate conditions of work, control the marketing of agricultural products, proscribe unfair trade practices, permit joint planning in the manufacturing sector, and introduce unemployment insurance. King, still reluctant to usurp provincial authority, opposed the proposals, and after his electoral success asked the Supreme Court of Canada for a judgment about their constitutionality. The Court's answer was decisively negative.[4] King then appointed a Royal Commission to consider Bennett's proposals further. The Rowell–Sirois Commission did not issue its report—which included a strong endorsement of constitutional amendments to permit a more active federal role—until after the start of World War II. Provinces fiercely opposed most of the Commission's recommendations. However, a modest constitutional amendment to permit the introduction of unemployment insurance was adopted in 1940. Parliament adopted its Unemployment Insurance Act a few months later—11 years after the onset of the economic crisis (McConnell, 1968, 1971; McNaught, 1986: 257).

There were other, more modest ways in which the authority of the federal government was expanded in the Depression years. A new central bank—the Bank of Canada—was established in 1935 to improve regulation of private banks and control over the nation's money supply.[5] A federally owned airline—Trans-Canada Airlines—was added in 1937, as was a federally owned radio service, the Canadian Broadcasting Corporation. These were not radical innovations. The Canadian National Railways had set the precedent for government ownership of modes of communication that were thought to be vital to the project of nation-building. TCA and the CBC merely applied the precedent to new technologies.

Building the 'New Social Order', 1946–1973

This second post-war transition was distinctive in other ways as well. The aim at the end of World War I had been a return to pre-war conditions, remembered as a time of expansion and social peace. In 1945, no one wanted a return to the circumstances of the Depression years, which had come to be regarded as proof of the inability of a capitalist economy to regulate itself properly. The success of the wartime effort to manage economic affairs seemed to strengthen the case for an expanded government role in social and economic planning. Furthermore, the federal government now had the administrative capacity to undertake a larger role: over the course of the previous three decades it had built a professional civil service, an ability to collect ample tax revenues, the required statistical services, and improved structures for central decision-making.

The case for a larger federal role could also be rationalized by appeal to a new economic doctrine first proposed by the British economist, John Maynard Keynes. Keynes argued that national governments could have avoided the worst effects of the Depression by taking steps to promote public demand for goods and services. Such steps might have included direct government expenditures like the American public works projects; alternatively, governments could introduce social programs that assured citizens of a minimum income. Keynes's influence was evident in Britain's 1942 Beveridge Report, which advocated a range of new unemployment, welfare, health-care, and pension programs. Canadian bureaucrats and academics, conscious of developments in Britain, argued for similar policies in a succession of wartime reports.[6]

By 1945, Prime Minister King could see that the Beveridge proposals might be good politics as well as sound policy. British voters had already replaced the wartime Conservative government with a Labour government committed to the Beveridge plan. Canada's new social democratic party, the Co-operative Commonwealth Federation (CCF), almost won the 1943 Ontario election and formed a government in Saskatchewan in 1944. Before the general election of June 1945, King's Liberal Party promised a more active role for the federal government in the post-war years. The Liberals, King said, would build a '**New Social Order**' in Canada (Newman, 1995: 348; Morton, 1997: 231).

However, pre-war realities reasserted themselves at a conference of provincial premiers two months later. In many areas the federal government could not act without the co-operation of the provinces, which balked at the assertion of federal power. Construction of Canada's New Social Order would consequently follow a different path from that in Britain: it would proceed more slowly and unevenly, relying less on direct administration of services by federal departments, and more on financial inducements to encourage action by provincial governments. Nevertheless, the project of building the New Social Order did proceed, encouraged by the high rates of economic growth that typified the next quarter-century. The amount of money the federal government paid directly to citizens increased steadily (see Table 12.2). A Family Allowance program providing federal assistance directly to families with children was begun in 1945. The Unemployment Insurance program begun in 1940 was also expanded, by eliminating rules that restricted eligibility to low-income earners.

Table 12.2 Federal Government Transfers, per Capita, in 1995 dollars, 1940–1995

Year	Payments to Persons	Payments to Governments
1940	$62	$71
1945	$296	$122
1950	$310	$127
1955	$457	$167
1960	$581	$293
1965	$561	$423
1970	$748	$658
1975	$1,267	$912
1980	$1,324	$925
1985	$1,859	$1,163
1990	$2,027	$1,098
1995	$2,388	$1,140

Note: Transfer payments to persons include CPP payments.
Sources: For data on transfer trends, see Statistics Canada (1988) and CANSIM data.

Programs to aid elderly Canadians grew as well, although the federal role was checked by constitutional difficulties. A 1951 constitutional amendment permitted the federal government to extend pension programs, but with an important qualification: no federal law could override any existing or future provincial pension law. The Old Age Assistance (OAS) program, established in 1952, provided a basic level of direct financial assistance to any Canadian resident over 70 years of age. A second program—the Guaranteed Income Supplement (GIS)—was added later to provide aid to low-income OAS recipients. In 1966, OAS and GIS were supplemented with a third scheme, the Canada Pension Plan (CPP), providing payments to senior citizens that were tied to contributions made during income-earning years. However, the province of Quebec exercised its prerogative under the 1951 constitutional amendment to establish an independent program, the Quebec Pension Plan. The remaining provinces acquiesced to the federal scheme only when the federal government promised that it would be jointly controlled.[7] In 1970, all three programs were expanded by lowering the threshold for eligibility from 70 to 65 years of age.

The growth of governmental responsibilities entailed an expansion in the federal bureaucracy—and in particular, a burgeoning of the central agencies that formulated policy and coordinated departmental activities. In 1966, the Treasury Board Secretariat—responsible for oversight of departmental spending—was separated from the Department of Finance. In the next decade, its staff increased fourfold. In the same period, the Finance Department's own staff doubled from 3,000 to 6,000, the Privy Council Office staff grew from 400 to 900, and the Justice Department staff increased from 300 to 1,800. Several 'ministries of state', whose principal responsibility consisted only of coordinating policy among other departments, were established throughout the 1970s (Savoie, 1990: 63). Within departments, the number of staff solely responsible for formulation and evaluation of policy increased as well, partly in response to the new demands emanating from central agencies.

The post-war boom was brought to a jarring halt in 1973, when a cartel of oil-exporting nations raised the price of fuel. An economy that had been built on the availability of cheap energy was hobbled, and began to experience rapid inflation in wages and prices. The 1973 oil shock—and a smaller 1979 oil shock—initially encouraged the federal government to strengthen its capacity for direct management of the economy. The Supreme Court of Canada was persuaded that the government had constitutional authority to impose peacetime wage and price controls, administered by a new Anti-Inflation Board between 1975 and 1978. (A second and less restrictive wage and price control scheme operated from 1982 to 1984.) The government also tightened its hold on the energy sector. A new government-owned corporation, Petro-Canada, was intended to 'Canadianize' the industry through acquisition of its foreign-owned competitors (Strick, 1999: 241). The 1980 National Energy Program included a range of subsidies and regulatory reforms aimed at hastening this Canadianization through preferential treatment of domestically owned firms (Foster, 1982: 149–50).

Instability and Retrenchment, 1974–1999

In the last quarter of the century, the federal government was challenged in three ways: by popular discontent about the concentration of governmental authority and doubts about its competence in managing the economy; by pressure to restrain the growth of government debt; and by regional disaffection and secessionist pressures. This led, in the last decade of the century, to substantial **retrenchment** within the federal government and uncertainty about the role it would play in national life in the next century.

During the two world wars, the extension of economic controls and government ownership had been widely accepted as a necessary—and effective—method of responding to emergency conditions. But the experiments of the 1970s were not received so well. On the contrary, they often provoked deep resentment. Some Canadians complained about the emergence of a class of 'superbureaucrats' (Campbell and Szablowski, 1979) whose influence over everyday life seemed contrary to democratic principles. Fears about the expansion of governmental authority were fuelled by the 1976 Lambert Royal Commission, which described 'a grave weakening, and in some cases an almost total breakdown, in the chain of accountability' within the federal government.

The Westminster system of government had always been criticized for the degree to which it concentrated political authority in the hands of cabinet ministers and bureaucrats, but now these criticisms seemed to gather new force. This was not simply a result of economic dislocation. Throughout the post-war period, there had been a growing emphasis on the importance of protecting basic human rights against arbitrary government action. Even in Canada, fears about abuse of power were encouraged by the Watergate scandal and the resignation in 1974 of President Richard Nixon.

The result of all these trends was a tightening of legislative and constitutional checks on executive power. In 1977, Parliament amended the Auditor General Act to give the Office of the

Auditor General broader authority to determine whether government expenditures were producing 'value for money'. The Canadian Human Rights Act, adopted in the same year, established an independent Commission to provide remedies for discrimination by federal organizations. In 1982, Parliament established two more oversight organizations. The Privacy Act gave the Office of the Privacy Commissioner a mandate to regulate the collection of personal information from citizens by the federal government. The companion Access to Information Act established a limited right of access to federal government records, which is enforced by the Office of the Information Commissioner. Later in the decade, new legislation and administrative codes were adopted to regulate relationships between public officials and lobbyists.

The most important of these new checks on executive power was probably the Charter of Rights and Freedoms, one of several reforms to the Canadian Constitution completed in 1982. The Charter, which proscribes government action that interferes unjustifiably with specified civil liberties, had a profound effect on the formulation of policy within the federal bureaucracy. It also strengthened the role of the federal Justice Department, which provides opinions on the constitutionality of proposed policies and was said to have acquired 'a range of power and influence rivalling only that of the Finance Department' (Monahan and Finkelstein, 1993: 7; Hiebert, 1999).

Declining faith in the capacity of the federal government to manage the economy eventually led to a dismantling of much of the administrative apparatus that had been built up in preceding years. The Progressive Conservative government elected in 1984 began to sell off many government-owned enterprises in an attempt to 'reduce the size of government in the economy . . . [and] improve market efficiency' (Strick, 1999: 77) (see Table 12.3). The **privatization** program was slowed because of the government's preoccupation with national unity issues and its worry that privatization could lead to job losses and increased regional alienation (Savoie, 1990: 265). However, the Liberal government elected in 1993 continued the effort. The oldest and most venerable enterprise, Canadian National Railways, was privatized in 1995 (Bruce, 1997).

Other mechanisms for economic regulation also were weakened by the Conservative government. Rules restricting foreign acquisition of Canadian businesses were loosened. The Foreign Investment Review Agency was transformed into a new entity, Investment Canada, with a mandate to encourage foreign investment in Canada. The 1980 National Energy Program was abandoned and the regulatory role of the National Energy Board Limited. The federal government surrendered the role traditionally played by the Canadian Transport Commission in regulating competition in the railway and airline industries. However, there was less enthusiasm for deregulation of the broadcasting and telecommunications sectors, given the important role these industries continued to play in maintaining Canada's 'identity and sovereignty' (Doern and Wilks, 1998: 124). Cabinet also limited its role in providing direction to the Bank of Canada regarding the development of Canadian monetary policy (Thiessen, 1998).

Since 1945, governments had been negotiating trade agreements aimed at reducing barriers to international trade. In the 1980s, trade liberalization efforts intensified, resulting in a series of agreements—such as the 1989 US–Canada Free Trade Agreement, the 1994 North American Free Trade Agreement, and the 1994 Uruguay Round trade agreements. The immediate effect of these agreements was to limit the capacity of the federal government to protect Canadian industries against foreign competitors through the imposition of high import tariffs. However, the agreements also imposed increasingly tight restrictions on non-tariff barriers, such as government subsidies or regulations that unfairly favoured domestic producers. In 1999, for example, the World Trade Organization directed the Canadian government to dismantle programs run by the Canadian Dairy Commission and the Department of Industry, which it said constituted unfair practices under the Uruguay Round agreements.

These efforts at **economic liberalization** did not solve another growing problem: the imbalance of federal expenditures and revenues following

Table 12.3 Privatization of Federally Owned Enterprises, 1985–1999

Enterprise	Activity	Year
Northern Transportation	trucking	1985
de Havilland Aircraft of Canada	aircraft manufacture	1986
Canadair	aircraft manufacture	1986
Canadian Arsenals	munitions	1986
Nanisivik Mines	mining	1986
Pêcheries Canada	fish processing	1986
Route Canada	trucking	1986
Teleglobe Canada	telecommunications	1987
Canada Development Corporation	venture capital	1987
Fishery Products International	fish processing	1987
CN Hotels	hotels	1988
CNCP Telecommunications	telecommunications	1988
Northern Canada Power Commission	electricity generation and distribution	1988
Terra Nova Telecommunications	telecommunications	1988
Air Canada	air transportation	1989
Eldorado Nuclear	uranium mining and processing	1991
Co-Enerco Resources	oil and gas production	1992
Nordion International	nuclear-based industrial and medical products	1992
Telesat Canada	satellite telecommunications	1992
Canadian National Railways	rail transportation	1995
Petro-Canada	petroleum production and retailing	1991–5
Nav Canada	air navigation systems	1996
Canada Communications Group	printing and publishing	1996–7
National Sea Products	fish processing	1997
Theratronics International	radiation therapy equipment	1998

the 1973 oil shock. By the 1980s, the federal government regularly relied on borrowing to finance over 20 per cent of its annual spending. As federal indebtedness grew, so did the proportion of federal spending that was absorbed on interest charges. The federal government, said Finance Minister Michael Wilson, was on a 'treadmill of borrowing money to pay interest on the past debt' (Strick, 1999: 191) (see Table 12.4).

The drive to restrain expenditures was prolonged and painful. By necessity, key targets for restraint included transfer programs, which accounted for the largest proportion of government spending. Eligibility for the Family Allowance program was restricted in 1989; in 1993, the program was replaced with a new, limited-eligibility Child Tax Benefit. Benefits under the Unemployment Insurance program were reduced throughout the 1990s. (Its name was changed to Employment Insurance in 1996.) Eligibility for the Old Age Security program was also restricted in 1989. In 1996, the federal government attempted to replace this program and the Guaranteed Income Security program with a new, more limited 'seniors' benefit', but withdrew the proposal in 1998. Net benefits under the Canada Pension Plan were reduced and a new body, the CPP Investment Board, was established to oversee the investment of CPP funds in the stock market.

Federal payments to provinces were also controlled. In 1977, the federal government adopted a new model for grants, known as Established Programs Financing (EPF), which limited its liability for provincial health and education costs. In 1986 and again in 1990, EPF was amended to

Table 12.4 Federal Deficit and Interest Payments as per cent of Total Expenditures, 1974–1998

Year	Deficit (%)	Interest on Debt (%)
1974	−6.4	10.3
1975	8.5	10.4
1976	6.7	11.5
1977	14.6	11.6
1978	19.7	13.1
1979	16.3	15.1
1980	15.9	16.0
1981	8.0	18.8
1982	18.3	19.6
1983	22.0	18.8
1984	24.2	20.2
1985	24.7	21.6
1986	18.6	22.5
1987	15.3	22.6
1988	13.3	24.1
1989	13.7	26.5
1990	15.9	27.1
1991	17.2	24.9
1992	16.1	23.5
1993	18.1	22.9
1994	15.3	23.6
1995	13.2	26.1
1996	5.6	26.5
1997	−5.2	26.3
1998	−5.9	26.1

Source: Statistics Canada, National Economic and Financial Accounts, Catalogue no. 13–001.

control the rate of increase in assistance to provinces. New restrictions on the other major transfer program, the Canada Assistance Plan (CAP), were also imposed in 1990. In 1996, EPF and the CAP were consolidated into a single program, the Canada Health and Social Transfer (CHST). At the same time the federal government announced its intention to reduce CHST payments by 40 per cent over the next three years (Maslove, 1996; Strick, 1999: 213–16).

These efforts at retrenchment caused deep concern, and not only because of the harm that might be done to vulnerable citizens or valued public services. Over 30 years, these social programs had become powerful instruments for promoting a shared identity among the citizens of a weak federal state. The federal government, and other proponents of a stronger federation, used these programs as reifications of a 'common Canadian identity' that was said to trump regional and linguistic differences. As a 1991 Ontario government report observed:

> A national system of health care, an array of income support programs, free public and secondary education, and affordable post-secondary education are claims that all Canadians make on their governments. Taken together, these programs represent and symbolize Canadians' sense of themselves as members of a community where solidarity and mutual responsibility are fundamental social norms. (Newman, 1995: 343)

The erosion of federal spending on universal social programs led some observers to worry about a concomitant growth in constitutional instability.

Other institutions that had served as instruments for national integration also suffered setbacks. The Canadian Broadcasting Corporation experienced sharp reductions in appropriations, compelling it to reduce services and provoking worries about the threat that might be posed to national culture (Manera, 1996: 21, 187). The Department of National Defence was obliged to abandon an ambitious modernization plan that had been laid out in a 1987 White Paper. It attempted to reduce the impact of budget cuts by deferring acquisitions, contracting-out functions, and reducing personnel, but by the end of the 1990s the department still suffered from the twin problems of inadequate equipment and slumping morale.

The last but most serious crisis confronted by the federal government over the last decades of the century arose as a result of the intensification of separatist sentiments in the province of Quebec. The Royal Commission on Bilingualism and Biculturalism (1963–71) described one language-based cause of alienation: the exclusion of francophones from key posts in the federal civil service and the use of English as the language of business within government. (This was one of the unanticipated consequences of the civil service reforms undertaken at the turn of the century [Granatstein, 1998; Roberts, 1999].) The government took steps to improve recruitment and promotion of francophones through the 1969 Official Languages Act, which established French and English as the languages of work in federal institutions and created an Official Languages Commissioner to see that the policy was enforced (Hodgetts et al., 1972: 473 et seq.). 'Official bilingualism' was a contentious policy. In 1976, for example, many pilots went on strike in response to federal attempts to apply the principle to air traffic control within the province of Quebec (Borins, 1983).

The separatist movement shaped the federal bureaucracy in other ways. Following the FLQ crisis of October–December 1970, the federal internal security service—then part of the Royal Canadian Mounted Police—began clandestine operations against political and cultural groups within Quebec that it considered to be potentially dangerous (French and Béliveau, 1979). Public revelations about these operations provoked an independent inquiry and ultimately an overhaul of the RCMP. In 1984, a separate Canadian Security Intelligence Service was set up to be monitored by an independent review agency, the Security Intelligence Review Committee.

The federal government also began to expand its capacity to undertake extensive communications programs. Federal expenditures on advertising increased by 70 per cent in real terms between 1978 and 1992 (Rose, 2000), and the amount spent on polling and market research and other modes of communication probably increased similarly. This period of expansion began with the government's attempt to use mass communications to win over voters in Quebec's May 1980 referendum on sovereignty-association. By 1990, however, it was using similar techniques for other purposes, as in its 1989–90 campaign to quell popular opposition to the new Goods and Services Tax (Rose and Roberts, 1995).

Intergovernmental discussions about constitutional reforms that would respond to the separatist threat intensified in the early 1970s. This contributed to the expansion of staffs specializing in federal–provincial relations. In 1975, the federal government created a new central agency, the Federal–Provincial Relations Office, comprised of staff formerly located in the Privy Council Office (Savoie, 1999: 148–53). Traditionally, negotiations on constitutional reform were undertaken by the Prime Minister and the premiers in closed-door meetings—a mode of decision-making characterized as 'executive federalism' (Smiley, 1987). However, citizens and non-governmental organizations grew increasingly impatient with these processes, calling them undemocratic. The defeat in 1990 of the Meech Lake Accord constitutional reforms was partly attributable to such complaints. In 1992, the federal government used a different approach, emphasizing widespread consultations and employing a referendum for final ratification of yet another set of constitutional proposals. These proposals—the Charlottetown Accord—were also defeated, but it seemed that the federal government had entered a new era in which public consultations on proposed policy changes would become the norm rather than the exception (Boyer, 1992: 223–58; Sterne and Zagon, 1997).

Since 1992, no serious attempts at constitutional reform have been attempted. After Quebec separatists were narrowly defeated in a second referendum in 1995, the federal government sought to devolve powers in other ways. It began to give provinces responsibility for the design and delivery of federally funded labour-market training and social housing programs. New and more independent bodies, such as the Canadian Tourism Commission and the Canadian Food Inspection Agency, were created to encourage closer federal–provincial collaboration in those areas. The government promised that it would only use its spending power to encourage the establishment of new provincial social programs with the consent of a majority of provinces, and with a provision for provinces to opt out by designing distinct, but still federally supported, programs. In contrast to the methods used during the constitutional tumult of the early 1990s, these reforms were made through the traditional method of closed-door negotiations between federal and provincial officials.

The Next Transformation

As the century ended, so, too, did the period of retrenchment within the federal government. The federal budget produced a surplus for the first time in 23 years, with more surpluses expected in following years. The advent of this new era of surpluses produced new calls for a re-expansion of federal programs. The government responded with modest initiatives, including steps to address the 'quiet crisis' within the federal public service (Clerk of the Privy Council, 1997). However, policy-makers remained chary of 'grand gestures' that might upset the government's books (Chrétien, 1999). 'Never again,' Finance Minister Paul Martin told Parliament, 'will we allow the spectre of overspending to haunt this land. Never again will we let old habits return—of defining bigger government as better government, of believing that every problem requires another program' (Martin, 1998).

The federal government was not simply bound by fiscal pressures. It also seemed to confront a crisis of mission. In the early years of the century, the central purpose of the federal government—the consolidation of its claim to a vast territory—had been clear enough. By mid-century, the task of territorial consolidation had been largely completed and the federal government had moved on to a second project: the construction of a web of regulatory and redistribution programs designed to remedy the excesses of an unrestrained capitalist economy. But this project now seemed to have exhausted itself—because of disenchantment with the effects of intervention, new proscriptions within international agreements on interventionist policies, and public unwillingness to bear the costs of redistribution. A sense of malaise now seemed to settle on federal policy-makers. Even if surpluses were available, there was no grand conception of government that helped to explain how they might be spent. Observers complained about a 'policy vacuum' within federal institutions (DeMont and Lang, 1999). Even the Finance Minister seemed to agree that the government was in the midst of another transformation:

> Central governments such as Canada's have become too small to deal with the big, global issues, yet they remain too large and distant to deal with problems of local concern. So the challenge is to redefine the role of central government as an institution that can do a limited number of things well, instead of continuing to pretend it can do everything for everybody. (Newman, 1995: 357)

The unresolved question was how to choose the 'limited number of things' that government would do.

The most promising candidate for a new national project was built upon the concept of '**competitiveness**' within the international trading system (Porter, 1990, 1991). This new paradigm put a premium on lowering trade barriers, overseas trade promotion, and improvement of the capacity of workers and firms to innovate and adapt to the demands of the global marketplace. The Liberal government explained in its 1999 Throne Speech: 'In the global, knowledge-based economy, the advantage goes to countries that are innovative, have high levels of productivity, quickly adopt the latest technology, invest in skills development for their citizens, and seek out new opportunities around the world' (Privy Council Office, 1999).

Many other governments had begun to frame debates about the role of government in similar terms. Many of the traditional functions of government—such as education, health care, and welfare expenditures—were now recast as 'investments' designed to create a globally competitive workforce. Social programs that were once defended on humanitarian grounds became 'economic assets' instead (DeMont and

Lang, 1999: 195). In Canada, however, the project of promoting 'competitiveness' ran afoul of a familiar problem. Jurisdiction over many of the relevant policies remained with provincial governments. For example, the new paradigm emphasized the development of a 'highly qualified, well-educated' workforce (DFAIT, 1999), but education was an area of provincial jurisdiction. As a consequence, the federal government proceeded cautiously, going to extraordinary lengths to assuage provincial concerns about incursions on their authority. To run a new national scholarship program, the federal government established a quasi-private institution run by a board appointed in part by provincial governments (Martin, 1998). Even with these precautions, however, the program was attacked as a violation of provincial prerogatives.

Whether 'competitiveness' will prove to be a transient or enduring preoccupation remains an open question. In the twenty-first century, Canada will be confronted with a range of internal and external challenges. The proportion of elderly Canadians will double, and overall population growth will slow significantly. Canada's place in the world, measured either by share of population or by economic activity, will be reduced. Its environment may be dramatically altered as a consequence of global warming. Any of these trends—or events that cannot yet be foreseen—may cause a dramatic transformation in popular opinion about the proper role of the federal government.

Important Terms and Concepts

'big government'
competitiveness
economic liberalization
Great Depression
'New Social Order'
privatization
retrenchment
'sacrality' of the state (or 'sacralized state')
territorial consolidation

Study Questions

1. What was the nature of the territorial challenges Canada faced in its first quarter-century? What were the effects on the federal government's administrative structure, employment figures, and expenditures? Why was the expansion of federal responsibilities in Canada in this period so modest compared with the United States?
2. Over and above the general factors affecting Canada's fortunes in the first part of the twentieth century, there was, of course, World War I (1914–18). What specific effects did it have on federal public administration?
3. How did the Great Depression of the 1930s and then World War II affect federal public administration in Canada?
4. What was the effect of the growth of 'big government' (1946–73) on the federal public administration? Summarize the purposes of the social and economic programs introduced in this era. How many are still with us?
5. In the last quarter of the twentieth century, public administration saw a series of checks on the executive government, dismantling of the state apparatus, deregulation, restraint, cutbacks, and public service management reforms. What programs, policies and administrative moves were examples of initiatives in each of each of these categories?
6. Summarize the missions apparent in each of the last four quarter-centuries in Canada. Is Roberts accurate when he says that the modern public sector tends to lack a 'mission'? Describe what you think what a tenable mission for the next quarter-century could be, based on present trends.
7. Review tables 12.3 and 12.4. Put into words the significance of these figures and facts. Analyze the trends in the data, and give some probable explanations for them.

Useful Websites

Canada, Library and Archives Canada, LAC Forum on Canadian Democracy, Centenary of the Public Service Commission of Canada, 1908–2008:

www.collectionscanada.gc.ca/democracy/023023–3100.1-e.html

Canada, Treasury Board of Canada Secretariat, Office of the Chief Human Resources Officer:

www.tbs-sct.gc.ca/chro-dprh/default.asp

Clark, D. 2002. 'Neoliberalism and Public Service Reform: Canada in Comparative Perspective', in *Canadian Journal of Political Science* 35, 4 (December) : 771–3.

www.jstor.org/stable/pdfplus/3233289.pdf

Dwivedi, O.P., and James Iain Gow. 1999. *From Bureaucracy to Public Management: The Administrative Culture of the Government of Canada.* Peterborough, Ontario: Broadview Press. Available in ebook form through various university libraries, such as:

http://site.ebrary.com/lib/memorial/Doc?id=10173345

Organisation for Economic Co-Operation and Development (OECD). 1999. 'The State of the Higher Civil Service after Reform: Britain, Canada and the United States'.

www.olis.oecd.org/olis/1999doc.nsf/LinkTo/PUMA-HRM(99)1

Notes

1. The emergence of the 'sacralized state' in the American context is described by Delbanco (1999). A **sacralized state** is one that has become established as a font of important values and as an object of quasi-religious devotion among citizens. Such a state becomes an instrument through which individuals imbue their own lives with meaning. The phrase 'true patriots' love' is taken from the 1908 version of 'O Canada', written by Alexander Stanley Weir. The last stanza of Weir's lyrics conflated patriotism and religious devotion.

   Ruler Supreme, who hearest humble prayer
   Hold our dominion within thy loving care;
   Help us to find, O God, in thee
   A lasting, rich reward,
   As waiting for the Better Day
   We ever stand on guard.

   The original French lyrics by Sir Adolphe-Basile Routhier achieved a similar conflation. In translation:

   Canada! Land of our forefathers
   Thy brow is wreathed with a glorious garland of flowers
   As in thy arm ready to wield the sword,
   So also is it ready to carry the cross.
   Thy history is an epic of the most brilliant exploits.
   Thy valour steeped in faith
   Will protect our homes and our rights
   Will protect our homes and our rights.

2. The statistics in this section are taken from Urquhart (1965). For good surveys of Canadian history in this period, see McNaught (1986) and Morton (1997).
3. The Roosevelt administration, which began in March 1933, was also elected on a commitment to budgetary balance, although it quickly recanted.
4. The Supreme Court's decision was referred to the final judicial authority for Canada at the time, the Judicial Committee of the Privy Council in London. The Judicial Committee affirmed the Supreme Court's decision.
5. The Bank was first established as a privately run entity in 1935, and then nationalized in 1938 (Granatstein, 1998: 49–56).
6. The two most influential were the report of the Advisory Committee on Reconstruction, published in February 1943, widely known as the Marsh Report, and the White Paper on Employment and Income, published in 1945.
7. Changes to the federal plan require the consent of two-thirds of the remaining provinces representing two-thirds of the population.

References

Borins, S.F. 1983. *The Language of the Skies: The Bilingual Air Traffic Control Conflict in Canada.* Montreal and Kingston: McGill-Queen's University Press and Institute of Public Administration of Canada.

Bothwell, R., I. Drummond, and J. English. 1989. *Canada Since 1945.* Toronto: University of Toronto Press.

Boyer, P. 1992. *Direct Democracy in Canada: The History and Future of Referendums.* Toronto: Dundurn Press.

Brecher, I. 1960. 'Combines and Competition: A Re-Appraisal of Canadian Public Policy', *Canadian Bar Review* 38: 522–93.

Bruce, H. 1997. *The Pig That Flew: The Battle To Privatize Canadian National.* Toronto: Douglas & Macintyre.

Campbell, C., and G.J. Szablowski. 1979. *The Superbureaucrats: Structure and Behaviour in Central Agencies.* Toronto: Macmillan of Canada.

Chrétien, J. 1999. Notes for an address on the occasion of the 69th Annual General Meeting of the Canadian Chamber of Commerce, Saint John, NB. Office of the Prime Minister, 13 Sept. 1998.

Clerk of the Privy Council. 1997. *Fourth Annual Report on the Public Service of Canada.* Ottawa: Privy Council Office, 3 Feb.

Delbanco, A. 1999. *The Real American Dream.* Cambridge, Mass.: Harvard University Press.

DeMont, P., and J.E. Lang. 1999. *Turning Point.* Toronto: Stoddart.

Department of Foreign Affairs and International Trade (DFAIT). 1999. *Human Resources in Canada: Our People Make the Difference.* Ottawa: DFAIT, Aug.

Doern, G.B., and S. Wilks. 1998. 'No Longer "Governments in Miniature": Canadian Sectoral Regulatory Institutions', in Doern and Wilks, eds, *Changing Regulatory Institutions in Britain and North America.* Toronto: University of Toronto Press, 108–32.

Duxbury, L., L. Dyke, and N. Lam. 1999. *Building a World-Class Workforce.* Ottawa: Treasury Board Secretariat, Jan.

Eisner, M.A. 1994. 'Discovering Patterns in Regulatory History: Continuity, Change, and Regulatory Regimes', *Journal of Policy History* 6, 2: 157–87.

Foster, P. 1982. *The Sorcerer's Apprentices.* Toronto: Collins.

French, R., and A. Béliveau. 1979. *The RCMP and the Management of National Security.* Montreal: Institute for Research on Public Policy.

Granatstein, J.L. 1998. *The Ottawa Men: The Civil Service Mandarins, 1935–1957.* Toronto: University of Toronto Press.

Greenspon, E., and A. Wilson-Smith. 1996. *Double Vision: The Inside Story of the Liberals in Power.* Toronto: Doubleday Canada.

Hiebert, J. 1999. 'Wrestling with Rights: Judges, Parliament, and the Making of Social Policy', *Choices* 5, 3: 3–31.

Hilliker, J. 1990. *Canada's Department of External Affairs.* Montreal and Kingston: McGill-Queen's University Press.

Hodgetts, J.E., W. McCloskey, R. Whitaker, and V.S. Wilson, eds. 1972. *The Biography of an Institution.* Montreal and Kingston: McGill-Queen's University Press.

Howlett, M., A. Netherton, and M. Ramesh. 1999. *The Political Economy of Canada.* Toronto: Oxford University Press.

Leacy, F.H., ed. 1983. *Historical Statistics of Canada*, 2nd edn. Ottawa: Supply and Services Canada.

Lindquist, E. 1996. 'On the Cutting Edge: Program Review, Government Restructuring, and the Treasury Board of Canada', in G. Swimmer, ed., *How Ottawa Spends, 1996–97.* Ottawa: Carleton University Press, 205–52.

McConnell, W.H. 1968. 'The Judicial Review of Prime Minister Bennett's "New Deal"', *Osgoode Hall Law Journal* 6, 1: 39–91.

———. 1971. 'Some Comparisons of the Roosevelt and Bennett "New Deals"', *Osgoode Hall Law Journal* 9, 2: 221–60.

McNaught, K. 1986. *The Pelican History of Canada.* Harmondsworth, UK: Penguin Books.

Manera, T. 1996. *A Dream Betrayed.* Toronto: Stoddart.

Martin, P. 1998. *Budget Speech 1998.* Ottawa: Department of Finance, 24 Feb.

Maslove, A. 1996. 'The Canada Health and Social Transfer: Forcing Issues', in G. Swimmer, ed., *How Ottawa Spends, 1996–97.* Ottawa: Carleton University Press, 283–301.

Monahan, P.J., and M. Finkelstein. 1993. 'The Charter of Rights and Public Policy', in Monahan and Finkelstein, *The Impact of the Charter on the Public Policy Process.* Toronto: York University Centre for Public Law and Public Policy, 1–48.

Morton, D. 1997. *A Short History of Canada.* Toronto: McClelland & Stewart.

Newman, P. 1995. *The Canadian Revolution: From Deference to Defiance.* Toronto: Penguin Books.

Organisation for Economic Co-Operation and Development (OECD). 1997. *Trends in Public Sector Pay in OECD Countries.* Paris: OECD.

Porter, M.E. 1990. *The Competitive Advantage of Nations.* New York: Free Press.

———. 1991. *Canada at the Crossroads: The Reality of a New Competitive Environment.* Ottawa: Business Council on National Issues and Minister of Supply and Services.

Privy Council Office. 1999. *Speech from the Throne.* Ottawa: Privy Council Office, 12 Oct.

Rea, K.J. 1999. Canadian Economic Development: The Prairie Wheat Economy. 30 Aug. Available at: www.chass.utoronto.ca/~echist/lecnotes/lec7_p.htm.

Roberts, A. 1996. *So-Called Experts: How American Consultants Remade the Canadian Civil Service, 1918–1921.* Toronto: Institute of Public Administration of Canada.

———. 1997. 'Worrying about Misconduct: The Control Lobby and Bureaucratic Reform', *Canadian Public Administration* 39, 4: 489–523.

———. 1999. 'The Duelling Commissioners: Linguistic Politics in the Early Public Service', unpublished manuscript.

Roberts, L. 1957. *C.D.: The Life and Times of Clarence Decatur Howe.* Toronto: Clarke, Irwin and Company.

Robertson, B. 1991. *Sir Wilfrid Laurier: The Great Conciliator.* Kingston: Quarry Press.

Rose, J. 2000. *Making 'Pictures in Our Heads': Government Advertising in Canada.* Greenwood, Conn.: Praeger Publishing.

———, and A. Roberts. 1995. 'Selling the Goods and Services Tax', *Canadian Journal of Political Science* 28, 2: 311–30.

Savoie, D. 1990. *The Politics of Public Spending in Canada.* Toronto: University of Toronto Press.

———. 1992. *Regional Economic Development: Canada's Search for Solutions.* Toronto: University of Toronto Press.

———. 1999. *Governing from the Centre.* Toronto: University of Toronto Press.

Shortt, A., and D.O. Malcolm. 1911. Memorandum on improvements required in the Dominion Public Service, Queen's University Archives, Adam Shortt Papers.

Smiley, D. 1987. *The Federal Condition in Canada.* Toronto: McGraw-Hill Ryerson.

Spence, E.J. 1947. *Wartime Price Control Policy in Canada.* Ottawa: Wartime Prices and Trade Board, Apr.

Statistics Canada. 1988. *National Income and Expenditure Accounts.* Ottawa: Supply and Services Canada.

Sterne, P., and S. Zagon. 1997. *Public Consultation Guide: Changing the Relationship between Government and Canadians.* Ottawa: Canadian Centre for Management Development, May.

Strick, J. 1999. *The Public Sector in Canada.* Toronto: Thompson Educational Publishing.

Taylor, G. 1997. *Canada 2005: Implications for the Public Service Commission.* Ottawa: Public Service Commission, Feb.

Thiessen, G.G. 1998. 'The Canadian Experience with Targets for Inflation Control', 1998 Gibson Lecture. Kingston: School of Policy Studies, Queen's University.

Treasury Board Secretariat. 1999. *Employment Statistics for the Government of Canada.* Ottawa: Treasury Board Secretariat.

Urquhart, M.C., ed. 1965. *Historical Statistics of Canada.* Toronto: Macmillan Company of Canada.

US Bureau of the Census. 1976. *The Statistical History of the United States.* New York: Basic Books.

Ward, N. 1962. *The Public Purse: A Study in Canadian Democracy.* Toronto: University of Toronto Press.

Worton, D. 1998. *The Dominion Bureau of Statistics.* Montreal and Kingston: McGill-Queen's University Press.

13 A Resilient State: *The Federal Public Service, Challenges, Paradoxes and a New Vision for the Twenty-First Century*

Kathy Brock, Matthew Burbidge, and John Nator[1]

Introduction

A variety of visions have animated the Canadian state since its inception in 1867. In a previous chapter Alasdair Roberts refers to them as 'missions'. From its origins at Confederation as a small, patronage-filled body to the 255,000 professional public servants of the twenty-first century (Clerk of the Privy Council, 2008), the public service has evolved to meet the needs and aspirations of an increasingly diverse citizenry and to address the challenges posed by social and economic events. Not always successful and its role often contested, the state has been critical in the formation of Canada's identity both internationally and in the eyes of its citizens. Today, a public service designed for small, representative government faces the new challenges of an expansive state governing an increasingly technologically sophisticated and diverse society demanding a more responsive, participatory style of government.

Indeed, as the twentieth century drew to a close, the legitimacy of the Canadian state was being challenged by significant social, economic, and political events. The public service, beleaguered both by the rapid changes in Canadian economic and social life and by cuts within its ranks, wandered in the wilderness, lacking a clear guiding vision or purpose.

This chapter takes up the challenge established by Roberts. We acknowledge his statement about a lack of 'mission'—or vision—in the federal public service in the latter part of twentieth century. Here, therefore, we attempt to lay out a new vision. Past attempts to assert political dominance over the bureaucracy had limited effect as the public service grew. Current political masters have also had limited success in harnessing the full potential and power of their administrative servants or in crafting an effective guiding vision for the public sector. Consequently, it remains uncertain whether the political executive and its administrative arm can transform the challenges of the first decade of the twenty-first century into opportunities and advantages for a stronger Canadian state. The fate of responsible, representative, responsive government depends on this uncertain outcome. Whether the state is resilient enough to meet these new challenges is being tested.

An Overview of the Animating Visions of the Public Sector: Lasting Legacies

Five phases capture the distinct visions animating the Canadian state over the past 150 years. In each phase, the idea of responsible, representative government at the core of the Westminster model evolved to meet the changing demands of society and the economy. Even as its political masters shaped and reshaped the public sector to respond to new conditions, the public service gained authority and autonomy. Under the Westminster model of government, the public service should exist in a tight, symbiotic relationship with the elected governing officials; in recent decades, however, tensions have entered this relationship. For its part, the political executive should provide leadership and policy direction to the public service, but has been remiss in its duties. Similarly, the public service should offer the political executive policy advice and execute the government's plans faithfully, but has been fitful in the performance of its duties. As both the political and permanent executives have evolved, sometimes working together and at other times seemingly working at odds with one another, the roles of the two bodies and their responsibilities to each other and to Canadians have become blurred. As a consequence, the legitimacy of the state has suffered, leaving an ambiguous legacy for the future. To understand how the Canadian state arrived at this point, we must return to 1867 and briefly travel the path from there.

An Expansive Vision: Territorialism and Professionalism, Pre-1867–1928

Prior to Confederation and into the 1920s, three key principles guided the public service. First, geography was the key determinant of the structure and priorities of Canada's public service. Civil servants in the colonies were faced with the challenges of settling the West, consolidating the vision of Canada, and delivering services over a vast geographic expanse (Savoie, 2003: 25–6; Hodgetts, 2005: 9). Second, public officials realized the economic development, transportation, and settlement needs of Canadians could not be met by government action alone, but required joint action with the private sector. The public service therefore adopted a 'businessman's approach' to service delivery, a form of partnering with private industries that surged back into vogue at the end of the twentieth century (Hodgetts, 2005: 15). Third, the spirit of federalism infused the public sector due to the constitutional division of powers, the deliberate strengthening of the federal principle by the Judicial Committee of the Privy Council (serving as the final court of appeal for Canada), and federal payments to the provinces to supplement their revenues and build their public sectors (Hogg, 1992: 110–11, 411; Vipond, 1991; Strick, 1999: 202–3).

In response to increasing demands for standards and non-partisanship in the public service, the Canadian government enacted the Civil Service Act, 1908, which created a Civil Service Commission to set entrance examinations and oversee appointments. By 1918, spurred on by World War I and the perceived need for a competent, fiscally responsible public service, the entire civil service (with a few minor exceptions) was subject to the independent Commission. Thus, by the end of this period, the foundations of the modern professional public service were established and embraced the principles of merit, promotions, competence, accountability, and political neutrality characterizing the public service today (Dawson, 1966: 272–3, 279; Hodgetts, 1972: 26).

Faltering Visions: Depression and War, 1929–1945

Despite the creation of a professional public service, the Canadian government was unable to produce a grand vision to solve the economic crisis of the Great Depression in the 1930s. The proposed Canadian version of the American 'New Deal' would have transformed the federal public service into a more interventionist and expansive body equipped to handle economic and social demands, but was sharply curtailed by the Judicial Committee of the Privy Council, ever vigilant of provincial jurisdiction (Hogg, 1992: 454–5). However, a grand vision of the federal public service re-emerged during World War II when prevailing circumstances allowed the federal government to escape from the judicial strictures.

Four key features characterized this vision. First, in response to the financial pressures brought on by the war, the provinces co-operated with the federal government in instituting fiscal agreements that regularized the negotiation of federal–provincial financial arrangements in subsequent periods (Strick, 1999). Second, as the government assumed control of businesses essential to the war effort and brought business leaders into government to operate these enterprises (Roberts, 2002: 24), the principle of public ownership of private enterprise was firmly entrenched. Third, the number of appointments to the public service rose from 6,406 in 1938 to 56,342 in 1943 (Privy Council Office [PCO], 2008),[2] increasing the influence of central agencies like the Department of Finance and Privy Council Office. The principle of central planning within the federal public sector was established and closed Cabinet-run government was no more (Savoie, 1999: 28). Fourth, the seeds for citizen suspicion of government were sown by the vast delegation of powers to the federal government to govern for the 'security, defence, peace, order and welfare of Canada', during the war. These powers enabled public officials to abrogate the rights of citizens on the basis of race or mere suspicion of actions prejudicial to public safety (Dawson, 1966: 291–2). Combined with a new universal awareness of rights, the exercise of these powers provided a key impetus to the loss of faith in Parliament and government as the protector of citizens and led to the demand for more secure human, social, and economic rights for individuals. Paradoxically, big government inspired public confidence but also generated calls for more control both within the public service and on government.

Benevolent Leviathan: The Rise of the Welfare State Vision, 1946–1973

At the end of World War II, the vision guiding the Canadian government shifted from one of big government designed to fight a war abroad to one of a benevolent leviathan at home. Canada was a leader among Western nations in embracing the principles of Keynesian economics, which promote a large public service empowered to stimulate economic growth at will (Savoie, 1999: 33). With this rise of the welfare state came the 'superbureaucrats' (Campbell and Szablowski, 1979): public servants wielding significant powers over their compatriots in the bureaucracy, as well as over Canadian social and economic development, in order to counter the ill effects of capitalism witnessed in the Depression, and ensure a fairer and more just social order. This growing role of government in society and the economy was reflected in the actual growth of the public sector. In 1946, the number of federal public servants was 120,557. By 1977—the peak year—this number had more than doubled to 282,788 (Dwivedi and Gow, 1999: 90).

Even as Canadians turned to their government to provide a better life for them, suspicion of the big state born in the war years gave rise to a federal Bill of Rights and calls for a constitutionally entrenched Charter of Rights and Freedoms. While the superbureaucrats viewed the trend towards recognition and legislative enactment of rights as part of their benevolent care of Canadians, the trend was also a reaction against the often unfettered discretion of these same mandarins engaging in profound economic and social reforms, economic regulation, and the creation of quasi-judicial tribunals to adjudicate rights and entitlements of citizens (Dawson, 1966: 294–5), and in the process, imposing their will on the private sector and citizens. As high inflation and unemployment cast doubt on the effectiveness of Keynesian economics in the late 1960s and early 1970s, support for big government began to wane and distrust in public servants grew (Savoie, 2003: 69–70). The 1973 oil crisis heightened these economic concerns, while fears of separatism, heightened by the 1970 Quebec crisis and the 1976 election of the separatist party in Quebec, validated deep-seated worries that the federal government could no longer manage society. Benevolence became impotence at best, authoritarianism at worst.

A Loss of Vision with Confidence, 1974–1998

Despite attempts at instituting political control over the bureaucracy from the 1960s onward, the fundamental problems of lack of policy coordination and political responsiveness remained (Aucoin, 1986; Savoie, 2003). In the 1980s, following the lead of Britain, New Zealand, Australia, and the United States, the Canadian government embraced the New Public Management theory of government as its guiding vision. Focusing on alternative service delivery, privatization, and taking policy-making out of the hands of the career public servant led to the 'de-Sir Humphreyfying' of government, in which many 'superbureaucrats' were toppled and left Ottawa for provincial public sectors (Hood, 1990; Savoie, 1999: 276–7). Under New Public Management, a smaller bureaucracy intends to provide citizens high-quality services with greater efficiency, public responsiveness, and accountability (Borins, 2002a: 4; cf. Lister, 2007: 5).

The continuing decline in public confidence in the administrative state as an economic manager resulted in a revisiting of the principles of public ownership, government control of industrial enterprises, and nation-building. In the 1990s, financial necessity arising out of the mounting deficit and national debt, and criticism of Canada within the G-7 countries, led the Canadian government to make large cuts to both the budgets and the size of the public service. Primarily through attrition, privatization, and layoffs, the size of the public service decreased by about 25 per cent or 50,000 positions (from 234,000 in 1988 to 184,000 in 1998) while extensive program review exacted a 10 per cent cut in program spending (Roberts, 2002: 30; Courchene, 2005). In the mid-1990s, the federal government unilaterally cut transfer payments to provinces, generating a vociferous protest and tension in intergovernmental relations.

This retreat from its traditional jurisdiction meant that for many Canadians the Canadian government lost its identity and rationale. Efforts at achieving public service reform and a more efficient policy process coordinated by effective central agencies largely failed (Lindquist, 2006: 61). Hollowed out, the state failed to define a new vision to carry the public sector into the twenty-first century or to project a convincing and inspiring image to citizens (cf. Linquist, 2006: 61). Instead, both morale within the public service and public confidence in the Canadian state reached new lows (Shields and Evans, 1998: 14–15). Further doubts about the ability of the public service were raised by the increasing public scrutiny and criticism of government operations through the newly empowered offices of the Auditor General and Privacy Commissioner, through the media under changes to freedom-of-information rules, and through the courts in the era of the Charter of Rights and Freedoms. Continuing fiscal challenges to the national well-being deepened this skepticism.

Money Can't Buy Vision: The Era of Balanced Budgets and Surplus, 1999–2008

The ambivalence and lack of vision for the public service that prevailed when the government was running deficits and downsizing continued in the era of balanced budgets and surpluses. Canada's journey from the verge of losing its top credit rating to being the 'fiscal virtuoso' of the G-7 caused some political commentators to call balanced budgets a 'Canadian fiscal value' (Courchene, 2005); but the Canadian government lacked a clear vision of where it was leading Canadians and the public service. The short-lived Paul Martin Liberal government (November 2003 to January 2006) attempted to sculpt a vision with its return to big government, national programs, and social justice. The election of the Conservatives to federal office in early 2006 under Prime Minister Stephen Harper ended these plans, introducing an era of fiscal prudence and respect for the division of federal and provincial powers (House of Commons, 2007; Brock, 2008). Re-election of the minority Conservative government in 2008 has generated calls for interparty co-operation in Ottawa, but without a coherent vision for the future policy announcement in 2010.

Facing Challenges and Finding Opportunities

Canada is a recognized world leader in public administration, consistently receiving high grades on international measures of governance and public institutions (World Bank, 2007). Widely admired are the resiliency of the state in the face of serious social and economic challenges and its ability to adapt the core values and traditions of the public service under the Westminster model of government to changing times and circumstances. However, while public trust in the public sector has rebounded from its lows in the 1990s, it remains disturbingly low (Lister, 2007: 3, 5). As Ian Greene warns, 'In a public service world of increased networking and partnering, management of complex, and often contested, issues and navigating in ambiguous circumstances—trust is an essential commodity' (2007: 18). The shift from a hierarchical bureaucratic style to a more participatory **post-bureaucratic organizational model** introduces a new tension between citizens and the public sector, discussed in the next section. Despite considerable efforts by the political executive to improve the quality of the public service and reinforce the public's trust in national institutions, serious challenges remain.

There exist both internal and external challenges to the public sector. These will become even more pressing in the coming years.

The External Challenges: Globalization and Digital Governance

Globalization

Globalization poses a challenge for the Canadian government just as it does for other nations. Definitions of globalization are hotly contested but most commentators agree that **globalization** is about interconnectedness, interdependence, and a perception that the world is 'smaller' than it used to be.[3] Globalization is not a unidirectional process, but one that links the local and the global. As Friedman argues, 'It is the inexorable integration of markets, nation-states and technologies to a degree never witnessed before—in a way that is enabling individuals, corporations and nation-states to reach around the world farther, faster, deeper and cheaper than ever before, and in a way that is enabling the world to reach into individuals, corporations and nation-states farther, faster, deeper and cheaper than ever before' (2000: 9). The process of globalization is not reduceable to a neo-liberal, corporate experience but must be understood in its fullest sense as an economic, political, social, cultural, and psychological phenomenon. Held and McGrew (2000) suggest that globalization affects social time and geographic space by embedding the local in the regional, interregional, and global. Local occurrences can have global effects and vice versa, much faster and to a greater degree than ever before. Distance 'shrinks', borders 'disappear', and connections multiply and strengthen, signifying a cognitive shift away from the nation-state. As a result, government powers are transferred upward to transnational and supranational organizations that challenge domestic policy; outward to regimes that constrain the economic and regulatory scope of government through international and domestic actors; and downward to private and non-profit sector actors and empowered citizen groups who vie with the government for power, and to local governments as city-states rise to challenge national authority (Courchene, 2001: 17–25). The state is thus transformed.

These changes mean that the Canadian public service needs to learn to build relationships with actors beyond the provincial governments, including city regions like Toronto, Montreal, Vancouver, and Calgary, and non-profit and private sector organizations, if it is to continue to be effective in this new global order. Approaching the question of globalization from a different perspective, Louise Frechette reaches a similar conclusion: 'In the coming decades, new global issues are likely to rise to the surface as the need for energy and raw materials continues to grow and water shortages threaten the well-being of millions. These problems cannot be solved by any country working in isolation within national borders' (Frechette, 2007). Government is increasingly having to share the 'public policy dance floor with a growing array of other actors, including non-governmental organizations, think tanks, advocacy groups, lobbyists, ministerial staff, political consultants, and the media' (Lister, 2007: 6; Savoie, 2006: 53). The Canadian government will need to learn not to lead only but also to follow its partners; this entails sharing powers and information, two highly coveted goods in the public service.

Digital Governance

Globalization works in tandem with the digital revolution. The public sector 'state of mind' is being transformed as information flow and technology challenge the way government does business (Courchene, 2001). **Digital governance** is the result. As Tony Dean, the former Secretary of Cabinet and Head of the Public Service in Ontario has summed it up, information technology 'creates the possibility of enterprise approaches to the design and delivery of services in large and complex organizations, including payroll, accounts receivable, purchasing, customer relationship information, sharing data between enforcement agencies and the delivery of multiple service offerings through common counters' (2007: 9). This change 'provides for standardization, cost transparency and the development of common service standards' (Dean, 2007: 9). The impact of information technologies (IT) on the public service is evident in the increase in knowledge workers over 10 years, from approximately 40 per cent in 1997 to 58 per cent in 2007 (Jauvin, 2007). The importance of new technologies in the operation of the federal government is reflected in its expenditures; in 2000 the government spent $4 billion or 10 per cent of its operations budget on IT (Borins, 2002b: 459). As Brown observes in this volume (Chapter 29), the commitment to and use of new technologies is only increasing. In short, it provides government with a new way to do business that is more efficient and responsive, and has a greater reach among citizens and around the world.

Despite the obvious advantages that IT brings to large public sector organizations, IT also creates new and complex challenges. With new technologies come higher levels of scrutiny and public access to information, and also a greater need for privacy and control of information (Borins, 2002b: 460). Even as accountability is being emphasized in government, both citizens and organizations 'have less control over who knows what and when' (Lister, 2007: 6; cf. Savoie, 2006: 53). The new technologies enable greater and more immediate public scrutiny of government actions; the result is more frequent crisis management by government. This approach to governing holds politicians to the centre, where they can exert more control, and disrupts strategic planning by forcing political leaders to expend resources on relieving immediate or short-term problems (MacKinnon, 2003: 274–5). And the introduction of new technologies and sophisticated goods in the private sector and for consumers has resulted in escalating demands on government for corresponding public goods (Strick, 1999: 59–60). Information technology requires an information highway largely supported by government.

The information highway poses an even more profound challenge for the Canadian government and governments everywhere. First, the inability of the state to control and police the flow of information and some of its potentially harmful associated activities, such as the promotion of pornography and terrorism, reinforces citizens' perception of the state as weak and ineffectual, or worse, arbitrary and autocratic. Second, the homogenizing impact of information and cultural content received through new technologies may diminish local culture. Canadian policies aimed at developing the information highway have been directed towards technologies rather than content. Darrin Barney, however, suggests that successful implementation of technology lies in effective collaboration with other governments, both provincial and international (2000: 239–500), while the key to regulating content lies in Grant's admonitions about the need to protect Canadian culture and mediate the effects of liberalism and capitalism offered in the 1960s (2000: 251–61).

The information revolution is two-sided. On the one hand, it offers the Canadian state new tools to reach citizens more effectively and deepen the democratic tradition; the legacy of public lack of trust and confidence in the state can be reversed. On the other hand, increased public scrutiny of state actions and questions about its efficacy in a digital era may deepen public disillusionment with the state, particularly as challenges to any attempts by the state to mediate the effects of the information flow and associated activities are mounted in the courts under the Canadian Charter of Rights and Freedoms. Public sector officials will need to advise their political masters wisely and cautiously if these perils are to be avoided while the benefits of the new technology are realized by the public sector and citizens alike.

The Internal Challenges: Demographics, Accountability, and Leadership

Demographics and a Shifting Political Culture

Internal and external demographics pose a serious challenge to the public sector in four ways. First, a shrinking Canadian labour pool combined with an increasing demand for highly qualified and highly educated professionals means a more competitive environment for attracting new talent. Second, the increasing complexity of policy and the policy process necessitates continuity and mentoring in the public service at a time when retaining staff is more difficult (Savoie, 2003: 279). Third, the increasingly racial and ethnic diversity of the Canadian public calls for similar diversity within the public sector; an expectation encouraged by the values embedded in the Canadian Charter of Rights and Freedoms as well as human rights codes (Al-Waqfi and Jain, 2008). Fourth, the new generation of public servants are part of the 'X' and 'Y' generations—less willing than previous generations to accept long working days or traditional authority structures or to bide their time learning new skills and acquiring routine knowledge before promotions, and more likely to challenge past practices and desire more meaningful work earlier in their careers (Coupland, 1991; Dagnino 2009). These generations of new workers expect a respectful, employee-oriented working environment that supports family and personal time more than in past generations. The sense of entitlement is strong.

The shifting age profile of the public sector reveals how critical recruitment and retention of public servants are in this increasingly competitive and challenging world of labour. The federal public sector has responded with an increasingly aggressive recruitment strategy. In 2008, the Clerk of the Privy Council, Kevin Lynch, noted the need for a five-year recruitment strategy and began by setting a target of hiring 3,000 new post-secondary graduates into the public service (Clerk of the Privy Council, 2008: 12). In fact, by 31 March 2008, over 4,000 new graduates had been recruited into the public service (including two of the authors of this chapter) (Clerk of the Privy Council, 2008: 12). In a significant shift from the centralized hiring practices established under the Public Service Commission by 1916 and the Treasury Board by 1961 as discussed above, the Clerk recommended that 'departments and their leadership...[should] have the primary responsibility for recruitment' (Lynch, 2008). A more personal, timely, and targeted strategy that leverages the advantages of working in the public service as well as particular departments 'can trump more lucrative financial offers from the private sector' (Lynch, 2008). To ensure higher retention rates, Lynch proposed providing 'employees with the challenging variety of work experiences which we have, with targeted development training and leadership skills, and with more supportive and flexible work–life balance that meets the operational and professional needs of the public service and the personal needs of highly qualified public servants' (Lynch, 2008). In sum, Lynch developed a strategy targeting **generations X and Y**.

This hiring strategy is part of a larger shift from a bureaucratic to a post-bureaucratic organizational model. Kernaghan, Marson, and Borins explain that this signifies a shift from a policy culture based on organizational needs, control and command, rules and procedures, unit autonomy, status quo, and procedural accountability to one based on citizen needs, participatory decision-making, empowering employees, collective action, innovation, and results-based accountability. In this shift, centralization, departmental operation of programs, budgeting, and government delivery of services give way to decentralization, multiple program-delivery mechanisms, revenue recovery, and competition with private and non-profit service delivery (2000: 3). The result is a diffusion of responsibility for policy advice, decisions, and implementation; empowered employees with a strong sense of entitlement and independence; weaker leadership at the centre; an emphasis on public sector-defined innovation; and increased efficiency. While these values are consonant with the new and changing generation of public employees, they may be less attuned to citizens' needs than first thought.

Indeed, newly embedded public sector expectations might need to be balanced with citizen expectations in at least three important ways.[4] First, decentralization within government, collective decision-making, and partnering with other governmental and non-governmental organizations diffuse both authority and responsibility. Citizens may have more trouble navigating the bureaucracy to locate the individuals who are responsible for policy and those who actually deliver the services. Despite the renewed emphasis on accountability and transparency discussed in the next section, government appears to be a black box where decisions are not traceable to particular points or people. And with the growth in government, ministerial accountability is similarly diluted. As Good notes about the shift to the new culture, the change embraced in the new slogans may obscure 'the hidden dichotomy of competing values that at some point will need to be reconciled through rebalancing' (2003: 178). The gains to the citizen may be diluted until this rebalancing is achieved.

Second, empowered employees may raise public service morale and improve workplace culture at the expense of citizens. Empowered, well-educated employees reinforced by collective decision-making and diffused authority are less likely to be receptive to constructive criticism; even if they are sympathetic they may not have sufficient individual power to reverse decisions. For example, in the case of Maher Arar, the federal government took over five years to admit its errors and offer him a (reduced) compensation package for his unjust and appalling treatment as an accused terrorist despite clear evidence in his favour. Had the case not had such a high public profile, Mr Arar might not have been released from prison in Syria and the Canadian redress might have taken longer, if achieved at all.

Further, empowerment can cause employee interests to clash with the public interest during periods of financial restraint. Generation X and Y staff are likely to expect higher salary and fuller compensation packages than did previous generations, but without the willingness of older and previous employees to work longer hours. Salary cuts are more difficult to negotiate than previously, given both a competitive labour pool and stronger unions. To borrow a recent example from the US: as California in December 2008 faced bankruptcy, Governor Arnold Schwarzenegger announced a 10 per cent reduction in the public sector payroll and two unpaid days off per month for the state's 235,000 employees. The outcry was immediate and the Governor was immediately labelled 'Grinch'. As Canada grapples with a dire economic situation in 2009, similar measures may elicit similar protests or an out-migration, as happened in the 1990s when able civil servants left Ottawa for the provinces. Quality of service declines, morale suffers, and citizens lose.

Third, as the public sector strives to become more diverse through its aggressive hiring policies, it continues to struggle with the challenges posed by a more ethnically and racially diverse citizenry. In a recent study, Al-Waqfi and Jain conclude that while 'access' discrimination has been more effectively eliminated in both the public and private sectors, 'treatment' discrimination has been harder to combat (2008: 448–9). Further, they document the rise in racial discrimination complaints in public administration organizations from 16.7 per cent of cases filed in the 1980s to 42.9 per cent in the 1990s. Based on the number of cases, and their duration and complexity, they conclude that 'the problem of discrimination might be more complicated and more difficult in the public services sector' (2008: 449). Similarly, Barbara Arneil argues that aiding community and citizen empowerment by partnering with the non-profit and private sectors for delivering programs and services may harm the interests of certain populations, unless the state addresses the configuration and nature of civic services provided by non-profit and private organizations to ensure that all populations are served (2006: 219–20). She points out that partnering and program devolution do not entail a diminished role for the state in breaking down barriers to citizen participation; developing policies to foster inclusion of diverse communities (e.g., educational policies for First Nations); and attacking economic marginalization and inequality, 'political duplicity' in treatment of different groups, and the continuing misrecognition of women and cultural minorities (Arneil, 2006: 221). If the public service is not vigilant, partnering and conformity within the collective approach of the post-bureaucratic model may suppress the ability of the public service to be responsive and meet its implicit goals of equity. In the era of the Charter, such lapses might only further embed legacies of citizen distrust and suspicion of government.

Accountability and Transparency

The decline in trust of public servants by both their political masters and the Canadian public has spawned a new emphasis on accountability and transparency in the policy process. The principles of accountability and open government are embedded in the doctrine of responsible, representative government so central to the Westminster model (Green, 2007: 21). However, the Westminster model was designed for small government, and the traditional lines of accountability involving the Minister answering for his or her department in the House of Commons have been attenuated as the public sector has grown. In a departure from the tradition of respecting the political anonymity of the civil service, cabinet ministers began to publicly criticize their officials for their part in embarrassing political decisions by the 1990s (Sutherland, 1991). More recently, sensational media stories about the sponsorship scandal under the Chrétien government and about the Auditor General's findings of bureaucratic wrongdoing and misspending have spurred renewed interest in strengthening accountability measures (Good, 2003). This interest has only been heightened by the increased prominence of the office of Prime Minister and the questioning of the loyalty and neutrality of public servants who are more activist in the policy process, personally active in politics (including elections), and less deferential than in the past (Savoie, 1999: 350–2, 276–7; 2003: 7). Breaking the traditional bargain of political neutrality and anonymity for public servants (Savoie, 2003: 5–7), new accountability measures are increasingly drawing public servants into public scrutiny.

Recent actions to enforce accountability are threefold. First, the **Federal Accountability Act**, 2006 is a focused attempt to improve accountability and transparency in the decision-making process across government, and to increase public trust in government. The Act 'makes substantive changes to 45 statutes and amends over 100 others, delivers on the Government's promise to put in place a five year lobbying ban, to eliminate corporate and union donations, and to protect whistle-blowers, among other reforms' (Government of Canada, 2006). Most notably, it extends the powers of the Auditor General across departments to include departmental action plans and progress reports on department responses to the Auditor General's reports, and to include federal agencies, Crown corporations, and individuals and organizations receiving federal monies (Government of Canada, 2006). In the case of Crown corporations, a paradox is created: an organization created at arm's length from government to run more efficiently, free from government interference, is being brought back into the bureaucratic world through increased audits and access-to-information requests.

Second, under a companion piece of legislation, the **Financial Administration Act**, deputy ministers and deputy heads of designated entities are designated 'accounting officers' of their organizations, and are required to appear before parliamentary committees to answer questions on their management responsibilities. They may be questioned about complying with administrative policies and procedures, maintaining effective systems of internal control, financial accounting, and the legal aspects of their units, including human resources practices. There is much confusion on the role and significance of the accounting officer, even to knowledgeable observers of Parliament (Savoie, 2006: 265). It is clear, however, that the creation of this role represents an evolution in the principle of responsible government and strengthening of the relationship of departments to Parliament.

Third, two additional areas of scrutiny have been strengthened. The rules on freedom of information have been strengthened, requiring greater disclosure. Most notably, the Accountability Act extends access-of-information requirements to the seven officers of Parliament, all Crown corporations, the Canadian Wheat Board, and five foundations under federal jurisdiction. Also, the role of the Ethics Commissioner has been strengthened with the passage of a new conflict-of-interest act (Government of Canada, 2006). The appointment of a highly respected former Associate Deputy Minister of Justice, Mary Dawson, to this office has only strengthened its credibility.

To date, the emphasis on accountability has yielded mixed results. In particular, the 'rising bar' of accountability has provided opposition parties with a lash to whip government, and has introduced another layer of bureaucratic process while not necessarily yielding improved quality and representativeness in government (Green, 2007: 21). Instead, 'accountability models that reinforce centralized, hierarchical, and defensive structures at best neglect, and at worst undermine, the collaboration, horizontality, risk-taking and learning that need to underpin future public service efforts' (Green, 2007: 23). Or as David Good explains, there is a tension between accountability for control (the old model) and accountability for assurance and for learning (post-bureaucratic model). Just as the balance struck following the Human Resources Development Canada (HRDC) scandal was not right (Good, 2003: 177), the current measures may reflect a swing towards a degree of control that is not consistent with the new values in the public sector. Further, if accountability measures are too stringent, a perceived chill goes through government, dampening enthusiasm for innovation and lowering morale. Or, as comedian Rick Mercer has observed, the Auditor General appears to have the 'power and authority of the Pope, the Queen, and the Dalai Lama all wrapped up in one' (Mercer, 2007), with the final lash lying in the media and public reactions to his or her reports. Public servants, fearing the scrutiny of the Auditor General, become averse to risk-taking and innovation. The balance between accountability and the needed discretion to innovate and serve Canadians most effectively is lost in the process.

Leadership

A renewed public service capable of meeting the challenges of the twenty-first century requires a new style of **collaborative leadership**. According to Tony Dean, 'If public service leaders want to truly transform large and complex public sector organizations they must step out of the shadows and be seen and heard. They need to embrace some part of the huge accountability currently absorbed by ministers. Public sector leaders have a responsibility to determine at any given point what is worth protecting as well as what must necessarily change' (Dean, 2007: 6). They must defend the core values of the public service as laid down in its creation without becoming defensive. Open to change, they must be able to discern the key features of the policy process and public service that should remain constant. While exercising discretion and tact, they must offer the best advice possible, particularly when it concerns the future of their organization. 'The nature of this type of working environment will require that leaders rely more than ever on personal and corporate values, an awareness of their personal preferences, and their inclusive communication and relationship building skills' (Coté, 2007: 22). All the while, they cannot lose sight of the public good.

Effective collaboration necessitates a new style of leadership. Gone are the days of transactional leadership popularized under New Public Management, when leaders in the public sector, like their private and non-profit sector counterparts, concentrated on positioning their organizations, obtaining maximum benefits from relationships, and terminating partnerships of little immediate value: in sum, they practised rational self-maximization. This form of leadership is myopic (Reich, 2001: 207–12). It prevents organizations from engaging in alliances that may incur costs in the short term but that will yield benefits in the longer term, or causes narrowly defined organizational interests to preclude awareness of the broader good of the organization in pursuing relationships. In both cases, the public good is not served.

To transcend these dangers, leaders must conceive of the interests of their organizations more broadly within the context of the public well-being; that is, articulate a vision that serves the organization as an actor in civil society (Reich, 2001: 208–13; Scott, 2002: 6–7). As a corollary, it is necessary to learn to blend these visions with those of the other sectors. As Brock concluded regarding NGO-military relations in sudden disasters:

> Leaders who are able to work co-operatively with others, compromise, understand the limitations and strengths that their side brings to the situation are more likely to appreciate the need for forging a good working relationship with the other sector. Leaders who are jealous of their territory, insecure in their position or unable to heed advice will be less capable of building the trust and understanding so critical to these alliances. A certain dexterity is required to bridge the divide in values, method of operation and objectives of the two types of organization. (Brock, 2005)

Clarity of vision and purpose effectively communicated within the public sector to the actual individuals working in relationships with the other sectors will help ensure a successful relationship that benefits the public as well as the organizations.

This new style of leadership requires managing not only the complexities of the new policy world but also the paradoxes. André Coté remarks that 'the enduring challenges of increasing complexity and speed within the system, the growing need to work with other levels of government and with non-governmental actors, the continuing need to build and maintain relationships, the ever-present paucity of resources, the continued maintenance of public service neutrality and professionalism, and the requirement that they actively advance institutional values, seem to paint a disquieting picture' (Coté, 2007: 22). Needs conflict; transparency and openness are offset by privacy, accountability by innovation, partnering by control, public service renewal by the loss of institutional memory, stability in policy by changing citizen needs, and more political control by administrative neutrality. Tolerance for ambiguity, for managing through paradox, and for serving multiple authorities is a prerequisite for leaders in the public sector and a valuable, albeit largely unacknowledged, quality of successful public servants.

Building a Vision for the Future: Values and Operational Principles

The Public Service of Canada has travelled a long way from Sir John A. Macdonald's railroad to Stephen Harper's e-government. But the public service is in flux, lacking a guiding vision akin to the one that illuminated policy choices in Canada's early history. If the government and public service are to develop a guiding vision, market themselves effectively to Canadians, and regain lost lustre then they must link the legacies of the past with the realities of the present day. Only then will they restore the image of the federal government (of whatever political stripe) and the public service as able to manage and guide society and the economy effectively in the twenty-first century. This is an important task, as Kevin Lynch has recently reminded Canadians, since 'a well-functioning and values-based public service is critical to the success of every country in today's complex and interconnected world. As a national institution, a high quality merit-based Public Service is part of Canada's comparative advantage and a key to competitiveness in the global economy' (2008). What can be done?

Revitalization of the public service will be critical in guiding the Canadian state in the future. Permanent and political officials will need to harness the potential of one of the most highly regarded public administrations in the world. As the accountability chill seeps through the public sector, policy creativity and innovation are threatened and suppressed. To escape the legacy of past experiences with accountability measures and to ensure that the values of a post-bureaucratic public service are entrenched and operative, political masters and public officials will need to find the right balance between accountability for control, for assurance, and for learning. As a new sense of pride and empowerment enters the public service with the new ideas and people, leaders will need to ensure that the arrogance of past superbureaucrats is not re-created in a workforce protected and emboldened by collective decision-making. This requires ensuring that the value of serving citizens and the public good is primary and that any policies and programs can be, and are, defended publicly. While this is risky in an ever-vigilant world populated by a cynical and distrustful citizenry, it is essential to rebuilding trust. Mistakes must be admitted but explained, and corrective actions taken in a timely manner. And policy triumphs should be extolled. Only then will the public again begin to see the public service as a worthy manager of society and the economy.

In the Westminster model of parliamentary government, political masters and public servants must work together if the system is to function in the best interests of the citizenry. This entails elected officials respecting the public service and using the full potential of a professional, merit-based administrative body by encouraging creative thought and innovative ideas. It involves the public service accepting the political direction of the government of the day and offering its best advice using the new tools within those parameters. If they can work together to develop a vision of the future for Canadians and then construct an effective plan for executing that vision, they may rebuild trust among citizens as proper managers of the economy and society in a challenging time and reverse some of the negative legacies of the past. Wisdom and strong leadership are critical in this task but so are an active, confident public service and an engaged public. The public servant of today—unlike the bureaucrat of yesterday—must not only serve the public, but also engage the public in imagination and action.

Important Terms and Concepts

collaborative leadership
digital governance
Federal Accountability Act
Financial Administration Act
generations X and Y
globalization
post-bureaucratic organization model

Study Questions

1. What are the key features of each of the five phases of the life of the public service in Canada?
2. Describe the key principles governing the public service that were entrenched in the first phase of its existence.
3. In your view, given the history of the Canadian public service recounted here, has it been an effective institution?
4. Why has the government of Canada been less effective in developing a guiding vision for the public service in recent years?
5. What are the key challenges facing the Canadian public service in the twenty-first century?

6. Which challenge is most important in your view? Is the public service likely to meet that challenge, in your opinion?
7. What is a responsible public servant? How has this definition changed in recent years?

Useful Websites

Office of the Chief Human Relations Officer:

www.tbs-sct.gc.ca/chro-dprh/index-eng.asp

Public Service Commission of Canada. 2008. 'A Timeline of the Public Service Commission of Canada'. Ottawa: Public Service Commission of Canada, 10 March.

www.psc-cfp.gc.ca/abt-aps/tpsc-hcfp/index-eng.htm

Government of Canada Privy Council Office:

www.pco-bcp.gc.ca/premier.asp

Federal Accountability Act:

www2.parl.gc.ca/HousePublications/Publication.aspx?Docid=3294507&file=4

Federal Accountability Act background information:

www.tbs-sct.gc.ca/media/nr-cp/2006/1212_e.asp

Jauvin, Nicole. 2007. 'Demographic Challenges Facing the Federal Public Sector', speech to the Standing Committee on Government Operations and Estimates, 17 April.

www.tbs-sct.gc.ca/nou/n20070417-eng.asp

World Bank: Governance Matters 2009: Worldwide Governance Indicators 1996–2008:

http://info.worldbank.org/governance/wgi/index.asp

Notes

1. Kathy L. Brock is associate professor, School of Policy Studies, Queen's University, Kingston, Ontario. At the time of writing, Matthew P.J. Burbidge and John L. Nator were MPA candidates, School of Policy Studies, Queen's University.
2. Most of these appointments were temporary (PCO, 2008) with women bearing the brunt of public service shrinkage since they were expected to resign their positions upon the return of war veterans, as well as when they married, well into the late 1950s. This set the legacy of viewing female public servants as unequal to men into the 1970s (Dwivedi and Gow, 1999: 109) and leaving a cold shadow into the 2000s.
3. For an overview of the various definitions offered by technological enthusiasts, *marxisant* pessimists, pluralist pragmatists, and skeptic internationalists, see Vic George and Paul Wilding (2002: 1–24).
4. Kernaghan, Marson, and Borins consider the positive cases of post-bureaucratic culture in their study without examining the costs to citizens (2000: 15–43). For example, the study of Canada Post discusses the benefits of franchising postal outlets but neglects the reduction in rural delivery and the elimination of certain routes that recent employees have deemed more dangerous.

References

Al-Waqfi, M., and H.C. Jain. 2008. 'Racial Inequality in Employment in Canada: Empirical Analysis and Emerging Trends'. *Canadian Public Administration* 51, 3 (September): 429–454.

Arneil, B. 2006. *Diverse Communities: The Problem with Social Capital.* Cambridge: Cambridge University Press.

Aucoin, P. 1986. 'Organizational Change in the Machinery of Canadian Government: From Rational Management to Brokerage Politics'. *Canadian Journal of Political Science* 19,1 (March): 3–27.

Barney, D. 2000. *Prometheus Wired: The Hope for Democracy within the Age of Technology.* Vancouver: University of British Columbia Press.

Borins, S. 2002a. 'Transformation of the Public Sector: Canada in Comparative Perspective', in C. Dunn, ed., *The Handbook of Canadian Public Administration*, 1st edn. Don Mills: Oxford University Press.

———. 2002b. ''Information Technology in the Public Sector', in C. Dunn, ed., *The Handbook of Canadian Public Administration*, 1st edn. Don Mills: Oxford University Press.

Brock, K.L. 2005. 'Weak States and Sudden Disasters and Conflicts: The Challenge for Military-NGO Relations—Final Reflections', Ottawa: IRPP, 7 June. Available at: www.irpp.org/events/archive/0605NGOpap.htm.

———. 2008. 'The Politics of Asymmetrical Federalism: Reconsidering the Roles and Responsibilities of Ottawa', *Canadian Public Policy* 34, 2 (June): 143–61.

———, and K. Webb. 2006. 'Creating Sustainable Relations among the Public, Private and Nonprofit Sectors to Prevent Human Tragedy: The Global Road Safety Initiative', paper presented to the Seventh International Conference of The International Society for Third Sector Research, Bangkok, Thailand, 9–12 July.

Campbell, C., and G.J. Szablowski. 1979. *The Superbureaucrats: Structure and Behaviour in Central Agencies*. Toronto: Macmillan.

Clerk of the Privy Council. 2008. *Fifteenth Annual Report to the Prime Minister on the Public Service of Canada*. Ottawa: Privy Council Office, 31 March. Available at: www.pco-bcp.gc.ca/docs/information/publications/ar-ra/15-2008/pdf/rpt-eng.pdf.

Coté, A. 2007. 'Leadership in the Public Service: Leaders, the Leadership Environment, and Canada's Public Service in the 21st Century'. Ottawa: Public Policy Forum.

Coupland, D. 1991. *Generation X: Tales for an Accelerated Culture*. New York: St Martin's Press.

Courchene, T. 2001. *A State of Minds: Toward a Human Capital Future for Canadians*. Montreal: IRPP.

———. 2005. 'Balanced Budgets: A Canadian Fiscal Value', paper prepared for *The Long-Term Budget Challenge: Public Finance and Fiscal Sustainability in the G7*. Washington, DC: IRPP, 2–4 June. Available at: www.irpp.org/events/archive/jun05/courchene.pdf.

Dagnino, M. 2009. *The Changing Face of the Workplace* (forthcoming). Description available at: www.michelledagnino.com/newsletter/0408.html.

Dawson, R.M. 1966. *The Government of Canada*, ed. N. Ward. Toronto: University of Toronto Press.

Dean, T. 2007. 'Modernizing Public Sector Organizations', in *Five Trends that Are Transforming Government*. Ottawa: Public Policy Forum.

Dwivedi, O.P., and J.I. Gow. 1999. *From Bureaucracy to Public Management: The Administrative Culture of the Government of Canada*. Toronto: Broadview Press.

Frechette, L. 2007. 'The Public Service and Global Governance', in *Five Trends that Are Transforming Government*. Ottawa: Public Policy Forum.

Friedman, T.L. 2000. *The Lexus and the Olive Tree: Understanding Globalization*, rev. edn. New York: Anchor Books.

George, V., and P. Wilding. 2002. *Globalization and Human Welfare*. New York: Palgrave.

Good, D. A. 2003. *The Politics of Public Management: The* HRDC *Audit of Grants and Contributions*. Toronto: University of Toronto Press.

Government of Canada. 2006. 'The Federal Accountability Act Becomes Law', news release. Ottawa: Treasury Board Secretariat, 12 December. Available at: www.tbs-sct.gc.ca/media/nr-cp/2006/1212_e.asp.

Greene, I. 2007. 'The Public Service and Trust', in *Five Trends that Are Transforming Government*. Ottawa: Public Policy Forum.

Held, D., and A. McGrew, eds. 2000. *The Global Transformations Reader*. Cambridge: Polity Press.

Hirst, P., and G. Thompson, eds. 1999. *Globalization in Question*, 2nd edn. Cambridge: Polity Press.

Hodgetts, J.E. 1972. *The Biography of an Institution: The Civil Service Commission of Canada 1908–1967*. Montreal and Kingston: McGill-Queen's University Press.

———. 2005. 'Challenge and Response: A Retrospective View of the Public Service of Canada', in Barbara Carroll, David Siegel, and Mark Sproule-Jones, eds., *Classic Readings in Canadian Public Administration*. Toronto: Oxford University Press.

Hogg, P.W. 1992. *Constitutional Law of Canada*, 3rd edn, student edn. Scarborough: Carswell.

Hood, C. 1990. 'De-Sir Humphreyfying the Westminster Model of Bureaucracy: A New Style of Governance', in *Governance* 3, 2 (April): 205–14.

House of Commons of Canada. 2007. 'Speech from the Throne; Strong Leadership. A Better Canada'. Hansard Journals. 39th Parliament, 2nd session, no. 1, 16 October.

Jauvin, Nicole. 2007. 'Demographic Challenges Facing the Federal Public Sector', speech to the Standing Committee on Government Operations and Estimates, 17 April. Available at: www.tbs-sct.gc.ca/nou/n20070417-eng.asp.

Kernaghan, K. 2000. 'The Post-Bureaucratic Organization and Public Service Values', in *International Review of Administrative Sciences* 66, 1: 91–104.

———, B. Marson, and S. Borins. 2000. *The New Public Organization*. Toronto: L'Institute D'Administration Publique du Canada/The Institute of Public Administration of Canada.

Klein, P. 2008. 'How Web 2.0 Can Reinvent Government', *Expert Voice*, 1 April. Available at: www.cioinsight.com.

Lindquist, E. 2006. *A Critical Moment: Capturing and Conveying the Evolution of the Canadian Public Service*. Ottawa: Canada School of Public Service. Available at: www.csps-efpc.gc.ca/pbp/pub/pdfs/P134_e.pdf.

Lister, M. 2007. 'Government and Globalization: What Kind of Public Service Does Canada Need in Order to Survive in the Knowledge Economy?' Ottawa: Public Policy Forum.

Lynch, K.G. 2008. 'The Public Service of Canada: Too Many Misperceptions', remarks by Clerk of the Privy Council, Secretary to the Cabinet, and Head of the Public Service to Federal Public Servants. Vancouver, 18 February.

MacKinnon, J. 2003. *Minding the Public Purse: The Fiscal Crisis, Political Trade-Offs, and Canada's Future*. Montreal and Kingston: McGill-Queen's University Press.

Mercer, R. 2007. 'Rick's Rant' on *The Rick Mercer Report*. Toronto: CBC Television, 20 February.

Privy Council Office. 2008. 'Accounting Officers: Guidance on Roles, Responsibilities and Appearance before Parliamentary Committees 2007'. Ottawa: Privy Council Office, 13 February.

Reich, R. 2001. *The Future of Success*. New York: Alfred A. Knopf.

Roberts, A. 2002. 'A Fragile State: Federal Public Administration in the Twentieth Century', in C. Dunn, ed., *The Handbook of Canadian Public Administration*. Toronto: Oxford University Press.

Savoie, D. 1999. *Governing from the Centre: The Concentration of Power in Canadian Politics*. Toronto: University of Toronto Press.

———. 2003. *Breaking the Bargain: Public Servants, Ministers, and Parliament*. Toronto: University of Toronto Press.

———. 2006. 'The Canadian Public Service Has a Personality', *Canadian Public Administration* 49, 3 (September): 261–81.

Schirle, T. 2008. *Greener Pastures: Understanding the Impact of Retirement Incentives in Defined-Benefit Pension Plans*. Toronto: C.D. Howe Institute.

Scott, R. 2002. *Working Better Together: How Government, Business, and Nonprofit Organizations Can Achieve Public Purposes through Cross Sector Collaboration, Alliances, and Partnerships*. Washington, DC: Independent Sector. Available at: www.independentsector.org/PDFs/working_together.pdf.

Shields, J., and B.M. Evans. 1998. *Shrinking the State: Globalization and Public Administration 'Reform'*. Halifax, Nova Scotia: Fernwood.

Strick, J.C. 1999. *The Public Sector in Canada: Programs, Finance and Policy*. Toronto: Thompson Education.

Sutherland, S. 1991. 'The Al-Mashat Affair: Administrative Accountability in Parliamentary Institutions', *Canadian Public Administration* 34, 4 (Winter): 573–603.

Thurow, L.C. 1996. *The Future of Capitalism*. New York: Morrow.

Vipond, R. 1991. *Liberty and Community: Canadian Federalism and the Failure of the Constitution*. Albany: State University of New York Press.

Webb, K. 2005. 'Sustainable Governance in the Twenty-First Century: Moving Beyond Instrument Choice', in Pearl Eliadis, Margaret Hill, and Michael Howlett, *Designing Government: From Instruments to Governance*. Montreal and Kingston: McGill-Queen's University Press.

World Bank. 2007. 'Governance Matters 2009: Worldwide Governance Indicators 1996–2008'. Washington, DC: World Bank. Available at: http://info.worldbank.org/governance/wgi/index.asp.

14 Alternative Service Delivery in Canada

David Zussman

Introduction

Public sector governance has continued to evolve and adapt over the past decade as leaders in the public sector strive to look for creative and innovative methods of serving citizens. A significant contributor to this evolution has been the rise of **alternative service delivery** (ASD), resulting in a fundamental shift in the traditional role of government. Hierarchical, vertically integrated departments have proven to be too rigid and unresponsive to an environment that is increasingly complex, turbulent, and demanding. Gordon Osbaldeston, a former Clerk of the Privy Council and Secretary to Cabinet in Canada's federal Public Service once said that 'governing is an untidy business'—a bold but true statement that reflects the complexity and interdependence of federalism in Canada, the country's geographic size, its cultural diversity, and the need to govern both horizontally and globally (Wilkins, 2003: 173).

As governments at all levels rethink the way they do business, they look to ASD as a means to provide the public service with creative solutions to complex challenges. ASD can contribute to the modernization and restructuring of government to improve service delivery, increase efficiency and effectiveness, enhance inter-jurisdictional co-operation, and take advantage of the strengths and capacities of other sectors. No longer is ASD merely an experiment in new forms of governance. It is now an integral part of the administrative structures and practices of governments around the world.

Much has happened in the world of ASD since a chapter on ASD was included in the first edition of this book, published in 2002 (Zussman, 2002)—so much so that this chapter has been completely re-written to provide the reader with a new perspective on how ASD has advanced within Canada over the past five years. The purpose of this chapter is not to provide a summary of the myriad ASD arrangements currently in operation in Canada. Rather, it analyzes what has happened in recent years and provides insight into the current evolution of ASD in Canada.[1] The chapter has been divided into five sections: (1) our current definition of ASD in Canada; (2) the current context surrounding ASD; (3) classification, models, and practice; (4) insight into the current status of ASD in Canada; and (5) the legacy of ASD.

What Is ASD?

ASD has developed widespread appeal throughout governments around the world, and each has developed its own definition of ASD. Within Canada, the Treasury Board Secretariat defines it as 'the pursuit of new and appropriate organizational forms and arrangements, including partnerships with other levels of government and other sectors, in order to improve the delivery of programs and services' (TBS, 2002b: 1). In the broadest sense, ASD is any new or altered approach in the institutional arrangements for the delivery of government programs and services. A more succinct working definition of ASD is a 'creative and dynamic process of public sector restructuring that improves the delivery of services to clients by sharing governance functions with individuals, community groups and other entities' (Ford and Zussman, 1997: 6).

These definitions have stood the test of time and continue to capture the breadth of activity within the ASD arena in Canada. ASD is seen as a strategy for innovation and for managing change, and therefore encourages new ways of thinking in public sector management that transcend traditional boundaries. No longer is there one best way to deliver a service. ASD approaches provide a toolbox from which governments can tailor various options to meet their own needs and demands. It allows public servants the flexibility to adapt to their future environment and to consider the best mechanism to respond to a particular set of circumstances.

More specifically, ASD works towards three main objectives. First, it aims to establish a more cost-effective, responsive delivery of government services to Canadian citizens. Second, it aims to change organizational structure and management practices within the various departments, in order to improve effectiveness and performance. Third, it seeks to give more authority to managers in order to move decision-making closer to the point of delivery, that is, to the Canadian communities and citizens served (TBS, 2002b: 2).

Supporters of ASD come from different places on the ideological spectrum. Those on the right appreciate that it reduces the size and scope of government. Those on the left approve of moving the delivery of services to a more local, responsive level and away from the bureaucracy. For pragmatists, it is a way to get people to consider a variety of delivery options. But despite the fact that ASD began as a uniquely Canadian term (Wilkins, 2000), when compared to other countries such the United Kingdom, Australia, and New Zealand, Canada has been modest in its approach to ASD. Implementation of alternatives has been incremental, small-scale, experimental, and on a case-by-case basis.

The Context Influencing ASD

The previous edition of this chapter cited six pressures for change that were top of mind in the early years of the first decade of the twenty-first century. They include:

- the rapid rise of information technology developments, which have created service delivery opportunities and have led to globalization and intensified international competition;
- public concern over deficit financing, the accumulated debt burden, and finding the right balance between taxation levels and provision of public services;
- a dramatic shift in how workers relate to their jobs and to their employers;
- changing public perceptions regarding the role and performance of public institutions and the services they deliver;
- business groups' demands to provide cost-efficient public services and an investment-friendly climate;
- changes in the demographic profile, such as an aging population, high unemployment, higher levels of education, and increased racial heterogeneity (Zussman, 2002).

These pressures are still relevant to today's public service leaders; however, new developments nationally and globally over the past five years influence public sector reform and governance.

Information technology not only has proven to be a platform for new service delivery opportunities, but also it has led to a more limited role for government. Citizens are increasingly bypassing traditional political channels and using the Internet as a means of socializing, seeking advice, networking, and finding information. Government in this new era is merely one voice among many and must now compete for the attention of its citizens.

Public service renewal has also evolved from PS 2000 in the early 1990s to La Relève later in that decade, to the development and passage of the Public Service Modernization Act in 2003, bringing about the potential for significant reforms in staffing and labour relations within the federal public service. However, recent recruitment and staffing efforts within the ranks of the public service have not entirely compensated for several reorganizations over the past 15 years. Renewal efforts will need to address two key challenges in order to preserve and strengthen the government's ability to deliver excellent services and policy advice: first, an aging workforce nearing retirement in substantial numbers, especially at the senior levels; and second, the increasing complexity of the issues affecting Canada and its place in the world (Lynch, 2007, 2008).

Recent trends and experiences also indicate that the traditional hierarchical model of governance is being eclipsed by 'governing by network', in which public service leaders redefine their core responsibilities from managing people to coordinating resources for producing public value. Most major public policy issues require activating, nurturing, and managing networks of federal, provincial, and local governments, private businesses, contractors, and non-profit organizations. Technological advances have enabled coordination with internal and external stakeholders to a degree simply not possible just 15 years ago. Citizens' expectations of integrated, seamless service have increased accordingly (Eggers, 2005).

Perhaps one of the most influential changes to the Canadian governance context over the past few years has been heightened sensitivity to accountability and the need to demonstrate responsible government to citizens who have become increasingly distrustful of government. The federal sponsorship program in Quebec and the resulting inquiry led by Judge Gomery in 2004 placed accountability front and centre in Canadian politics for over a year. Consequently, new accountability measures have been adopted and the transactional costs of responding to the myriad accountability requirements have escalated.

Classification, Models, and Practice

A Framework for ASD

The origins of ASD can be traced to the early 1990s when David Osborne and Ted Gaebler convinced the world that government should focus more on developing policy and allow its implementation to be taken over by external organizations. Now known commonly as the 'steering versus rowing' debate, this argument provided the initial intellectual framework within which ASD mechanisms were legitimized. Three years later, the Treasury Board Secretariat released its first *Framework on Alternative Program Delivery* that is still in use today.

Figure 14.1 captures the breadth of options available for consideration when analyzing various service delivery alternatives. Governments can choose the extent of control they want to exert over the delivery of the service; whether a private, public, or hybrid delivery mechanism is appropriate; and the level of commercialization that the service should embody.

At the provincial level, Ontario has taken a systematic approach to alternative service delivery and has established the following continuum of ASD options:

- ***Direct delivery***. Government delivers the services directly through its ministries, through business planning, focusing on results, cost recovery, getting the best value for the tax dollar, and customer service.
- ***Agencies***. Government delegates service delivery to a scheduled agency operating at arm's length from the ongoing operations of government, but maintains control over the agency.
- ***Devolution***. Government transfers the responsibility for delivering service to: a) other levels of government, b) profit or non-profit organizations that receive transfer payments to deliver the service.
- ***Purchase of service***. Government purchases the services under

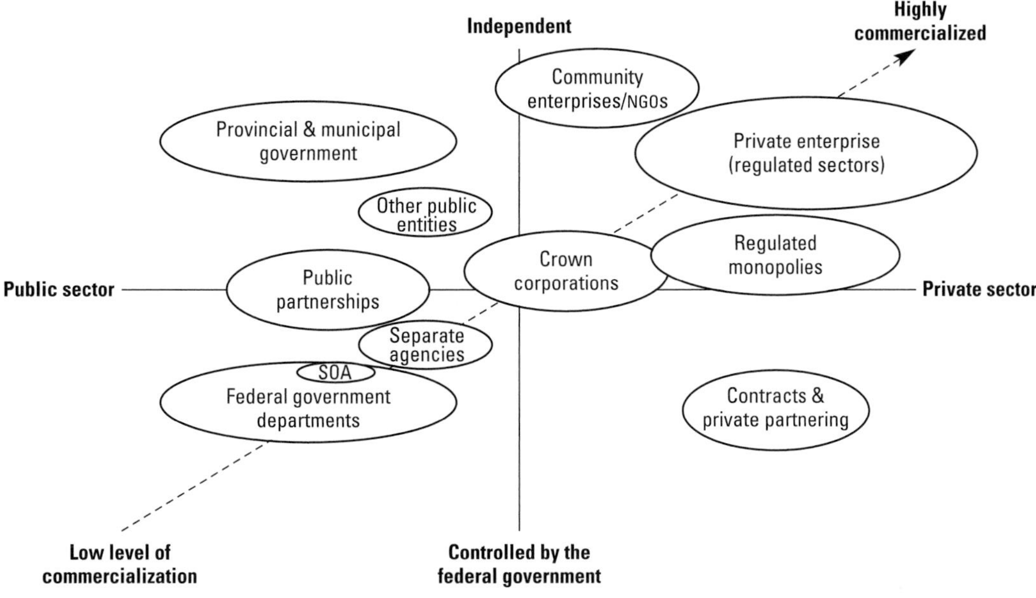

Figure 14.1 Opportunities for Program Delivery Alternatives

contract from a private firm, but retains accountability for the service. This includes contracting out and outsourcing of services.

- ***Partnerships***. Government enters into a formal agreement to provide services in partnership with other parties where each contributes resources and shares risks and rewards.
- ***Franchising/Licensing***. For franchising, the government confers to a private firm the right or privilege to sell a product or service in accordance with prescribed terms and conditions. For licensing, the government grants a license to a private firm to sell a product or service that unlicensed firms are not allowed to sell.
- ***Privatization***. Government sells its assets or its controlling interest in a service to a private sector company, but may protect the public interest through legislation and regulation (Good and Carin, 2003: 7).

Classifying ASD

Given the broad range of approaches to ASD, it is often difficult to define the boundaries of ASD and to classify different ASD initiatives. Some analysts classify ASD options according to governance structure; others focus on financing arrangements, and still others look at the extent of change or the degree of government responsibility.

While each of these classification systems provides special insights into the breadth of ASD approaches, they do not capture the intended goals and objectives of ASD—seeking ways and means to deliver programs and services more efficiently, with greater flexibility, and with the active engagement of other levels of government, the private and voluntary sectors, and citizens.

Using a functional classification system captures the intended goals and objectives of ASD initiatives: service efficiency, management flexibility, and collaborative arrangements. As with other classification systems, however, grouping

ASD initiatives by function should not be viewed as a rigid compartmentalization but as an organizational instrument with a heuristic value. Often, ASD initiatives will contain elements that allow them to be classified under all of the functional categories. In such circumstances, we must choose the function that seems the most important.

Service Efficiency

Rapid developments in the application and availability of information technologies have created opportunities to rethink how traditional public services are delivered. This, combined with growing public demand for improved standards of service delivery, has focused attention on the efficiency of government service delivery—quicker, more convenient, and accessible services delivered at the lowest possible cost to taxpayers. Seeking ways and means to deliver programs and services more efficiently is a fundamental goal of ASD. Service efficiency initiatives include the following as stand-alone mechanisms or in combination with each other:

- electronic service delivery;
- single-window delivery;
- co-location.

Management Flexibility

Management flexibility, in the context of ASD, refers to the increased autonomy from central agency regulations in areas such as staffing, procurement, and financing, so that managers are faced with fewer restrictions in attempting to meet performance targets (see Table 14.1). As a means of improving service delivery, this flexibility has long been a preoccupation within public management reform. In Canada, management flexibility options include:

- Crown corporations;
- Special operating agencies;
- Service agencies;
- Departmental corporations;
- Shared governance entities.

Collaborative Arrangements

Under a range of legal, financial, and administrative arrangements, and within the context of alternative service delivery, governments are increasingly collaborating or 'partnering' with other levels of government and the private and third sectors in the design and delivery of public goods and services. While a number of different terms exist to describe **collaborative arrangements**, the most common is 'partnership'. However, with so many meanings and applications, partnerships have become a moving target for public policy analysis and evaluation. Collaboration in general, however, suggests mutual contribution—financial, institutional, and intellectual—as well as shared objectives, decision-making, and benefits. Some examples of collaborative ASD arrangements include:

- contracting out and franchising;
- partnerships–between different levels of government and across sectors;
- devolution;
- privatization.

ASD in Practice

ASD, however, needs to be more than a choice of one among many mechanisms for a quick-fix solution. A threshold test is required to determine which specific ASD option, under what particular circumstances, might be a useful way to proceed. Leaders and analysts require a critical thinking process to assess the consequences of ASD alternatives, to account for policy imperatives and political variables, and to anticipate managerial challenges arising from the chosen delivery option (Good and Carin, 2003: 8). In Canada, the critical thinking process is aided by the framework for program review used widely by departments and agencies in the federal government (see Table 14.2).

Having moved through the six test questions and decided that ASD is an appropriate option, leaders then develop a rigorous case analysis of

Table 14.1 Degrees of Management Flexibility Inherent in Various ASD Options

Organizational Model	Method of Establishment	Independent Decision-Making	Financial Flexibility	Human Resources	Accountability	Management
Department	Established by legislation	No	Annual appropriations through budget process	Under PSEA	Minister	Minister and deputy minister
Special Operating Agency (SOA)	Established by Treasury Board approval Legislation is not required Operates as a unit of a department	Uses department's legislative framework and authorities May have some flexibility over financial and human resources	Annual appropriations through budget process May be given authority to operate under revolving funds	Under PSEA or separate-employer status	Framework document and business plan establish accountability; approved by deputy minister, minister, Treasury Board Accountable to department for results	Deputy head
Separate Agency	Established by legislation or Order-in-Council Is administrative entity Is considered department for purpose of complying with Financial Administration Act (FAA)	Policy framework established by minister More independent than SOA	Annual appropriations through budget process Statutory funding possible	Under PSEA or separate-employer status	Deputy head reports to minister	Deputy head

(continued)

Table 14.1 (Continued)

Organizational Model	Method of Establishment	Independent Decision-Making	Financial Flexibility	Human Resources	Accountability	Management
Departmental Corporation	Established by legislation as corporate body with legal liability implications of being a corporation Performs administrative, research, supervisory, or regulatory functions	More independent than SOA or separate agency	Annual appropriations through budget process May be given authority to re-spend revenues through net vote revolving funds Statutory funding possible	PSEA or separate-employer status Most have separate-employer status with direct control over personnel management and collective bargaining	Governed by corporate business plan CEO reports to minister	Chief Executive Officer, with authority of deputy head Board of Directors or Commission
Crown Corporation	Established by legislation, by letters patent, or by articles of incorporation under CBCA Governance, control, and accountability provisions for most parent Crown corporations set out in FAA Part X Created to achieve specific public policy goals within commercial environment	Yes Operates under broad policy framework established by government Day-to-day operations managed at arm's length from government	Financial self-sufficiency desirable but not necessary Corporations under FAA Schedule III, Part I receive parliamentary appropriations Corporations under FAA Schedule III, Part II operate in competitive environment and are expected to be profitable Can borrow money	Most have separate-employer status with direct control over personnel management and collective bargaining	Accountable to government through minister	CEO and Board of Directors

(*continued*)

Table 14.1 (Continued)

Shared Corporate Governance	Is corporate entity without share capital Federal government has right to appoint/nominate one or more members of governing body	Yes	Yes	Employees are not public servants	Varies	CEO and Board of Directors
Partnership	Established by formal agreement that specifies terms of relationship between federal government and partners for delivery of program or service Partners may include other levels of government, international governments, private sector and non-profit organizations	Yes	Joint investment of financial resources by partners May be financially independent, depending on extent of funding provided by levels of government and other funding partners	Employees are not public servants	Formal agreement specifies delineation of authority and responsibility among partners	CEO and Board of Directors

Source: Adapted from Sutcliffe and Tilson (2005).

Table 14.2 ASD Framework Test Questions

Strategic Focus	Question
Public Interest Test	Does the program or service continue to serve a public interest?
Role of Government Test	Is there a legitimate and necessary role for government in this program or service?
Jurisdictional Alignment Test	Is the lead responsibility for this program or service assigned to the right government jurisdiction?
External Partnership Test	Could or should this program or service be provided in whole or in part by the private or voluntary sector?
Business Principles Test	If the program or service continues within the existing government context, how could its efficiency and effectiveness be improved?
Affordability Test	Is the program or service affordable within fiscal realities?

the specific services being considered. The case analysis often includes:

- a more detailed investigation into the issue of the public interest;
- client satisfaction and service improvement priorities;
- results commitments;
- accountability framework;
- cost-benefit analysis;
- risk-management strategy;
- measurement and reporting framework for assessing the results and reporting publicly;
- the mechanisms and authorities available to proponents, departmental ministers, and central management board ministers to take corrective action once the initiative is implemented.

Where Are We Now In Canada?

Canada has continued to place service excellence at the forefront of public sector improvement initiatives. Survey data confirm that Canadians' level of service satisfaction appears to have a strong influence on their trust and confidence in government (ICCS: 2004). With trust in government on the decline for the past two decades, the service relationship provides governments with an avenue to citizens that can help to rebuild trust and confidence in public institutions.

The Government of Canada's service transformation agenda in recent years has become a pillar within the broader reform agenda of the federal public service. In the 2005 Budget, the government announced initiatives designed to 'work smart', pay attention to the needs of Canadians, and react more quickly to change. Under the banner of modernizing government, a commitment was made to improved, integrated, and efficient service for Canadians. The next year, the Clerk of the Privy Council and Secretary to Cabinet underscored the need to service Canadians more efficiently and effectively, recognizing that excessive rules and regulations can create obstacles to achieving those goals.

While service transformation projects are continuing to move ahead across departments and agencies, recent years have also marked the conclusion of two high-profile service initiatives: Government On-Line and the Service Improvement Initiative. Both of these initiatives have made significant contributions to Canada's rank in the top tier of global e-government leaders, and Canada continues to look at ways to use technology to improve service to Canadians.

In February 2006, the Service Transformation Office was established to provide oversight on the progress and impact of service transformation initiatives across the government. The current wave of service initiatives focuses on the transformation of services that are internal to government, including corporate and administrative shared services, pay and pension modernization, procurement transformation, real property reform, and IT shared services. These service modernization initiatives are highly complex, transformative, and intended to have government-wide departmental impact. They are intended to enhance service to Canadians through faster and more reliable delivery of financial transactions and enhanced back office operations for external service delivery.

Service Canada

The most tangible manifestation of the government's commitment to continued service transformation was the creation of **Service Canada** in 2005 as a new model for the delivery of government services. Its primary purpose was *integrated* service delivery—bringing and fitting together a wide range of government programs and services from across federal departments and other levels of government to provide citizens with integrated, easy-to-access, personalized service.

In effect, Service Canada is a modern manifestation of ASD arrangements described as 'one-stop-shops' or 'single windows'. These types of arrangements have multiplied worldwide and the development of Service Canada has been informed by service improvement initiatives in other governments, including Canadian provinces and Australia's Centrelink.

Service Canada employs over 22,000 people to serve the country's 32 million citizens. It operates more than 490 points of service across the country and has taken over responsibility for the Government of Canada's one-stop telephone call centre (1-800-O CANADA) and the Government of Canada's Internet Portal (www.canada.gc.ca). Each year, Service Canada answers more than 56 million telephone calls (over 80 per cent of all calls to the federal government, excluding those to the Canada Revenue Agency) and handles 14 million unique visits to its website (Flumian, Coe, and Kernaghan, 2008: 4).

Canada, like its international counterparts, had traditionally approached service delivery via several departments, each with its own responsibilities for programs and services. As a result, Canadians could experience different levels of service across a complex and fragmented array of choices. Consequently, Service Canada was created to collaborate across agencies and jurisdictions to bring public service offerings together in a single service-delivery network.

In keeping with the philosophy behind ASD innovations, it is envisaged that policy departments will no longer need to build and maintain separate delivery networks. These departments will be able to concentrate on the development of outcomes-focused policies and programs, while Service Canada concentrates on improving the delivery of programs and services. A strengthened focus on service will help improve the achievement of policy outcomes by better connecting citizens and communities to the services and benefits they need. The information gathered through citizen-centred service delivery is also expected to inform the policy and program development process and to foster a whole-of-government approach to socio-economic outcomes. The creation of Service Canada provides a clear point of accountability for service in the federal government. Departments will remain accountable for the policies and programs under their mandates. Service Canada will be accountable for how programs and services are delivered. Service Canada and its partner departments will share responsibility for aligning policy and service outcomes and will work together to report on and ensure the achievement of these outcomes (Flumian, Coe, and Kernaghan, 2008: 7).

From a governance perspective, Service Canada is a horizontal service-delivery organization that currently operates within the legislative framework of its host department. The current organizational form of Service Canada is intended to be an interim arrangement as an initial phase of its implementation. Its future organizational form is undecided but will need to incorporate vertical and horizontal dimensions of accountability, robust performance management strategies based on integrative results, secure and stable funding for horizontal service delivery, and mechanisms and authorities for ensuring effective partnerships.

Special Operating Agencies

In the mid-1980s, pressures for governments to be more businesslike focused reform attention on improving service delivery by addressing impediments in government *structures*, notably the inflexibilities in staffing, purchasing, and decision-making. The federal government began identifying departmental service functions that could be separated from core policy and regulatory functions and managed by more autonomous units of public enterprise.

In 1989, the Treasury Board Secretariat introduced a unique method of creating autonomous service units within traditional departments. These autonomous service units, known as **special operating agencies (SOAs)**, were created through negotiated agreements between the sponsoring departments and the Treasury Board Secretariat, pursuant to the Financial Administration Act. Canada currently has 16 SOAs, almost all of which were created in the 1990s.

Despite an initial flurry of SOA activity in the 1990s, only two SOAs have been created within the federal government over the past five years. The Industrial Technologies Office was created in 2007 by Industry Canada as an evolution of a previously existing SOA called Technology Partnerships Canada. Interestingly, Industry Canada is home to the most SOA structures under one government department (four) and it has very tactically used this type of ASD mechanism as a strategic response to improve service to its clients.

The Canadian Coast Guard (CCG) was established as an SOA in 2005 and brings with it a much more turbulent story. In the mid-1990s the CCG was moved from Transport Canada to Fisheries and Oceans Canada with the intent of realizing cost savings through merging the two fleets. With funding for programs cut and difficulties integrating organizations with different structures and cultures, the merger proved to be a failure. After 10 years of trying to fit the CCG into the departmental structure of Fisheries and Oceans, the decision was made to separate it from the departmental structure through the use of an SOA mechanism.

The SOA status allows the CCG to operate in a more business-like manner, facilitates enhanced service delivery to its clients, and provides greater control of its financial resources. The change also positions the CCG to respond to its enhanced role under Canada's national security agenda. In an associated action, the government also transferred all policy and regulatory responsibilities associated with maritime safety to Transport Canada. It is anticipated that the transfer of responsibilities will result in a better service to Canadians by providing a single point of contact for all maritime safety policies and regulations.

Federal Foundations

In 1997, the federal government created a new instrument of public policy—the foundation. **Federal foundations**, of which there were 14 in 2009 (listed in Table 14.3), are designed to promote science, education, technology, and research. Each foundation is established as an independent, not-for-profit corporation with its board of directors populated by experts in the foundation's mandate.

Operating at arm's length from the government, the foundations function independently of the partisanship and bureaucracy that are

Table 14.3 Federal Foundations

Aboriginal Healing Foundation
Asia Pacific Foundation
Canada Foundation for Innovation
Canada Health Infoway
Canada Health Services Research Foundation
Canadian Foundation for Climate and Atmospheric Sciences
Canadian Institute for Research on Linguistic Minorities
Clayoquot Biosphere Trust
Frontier College
Genome Canada
Green Municipal Fund
Pacific Salmon Endowment Fund Society
Pierre Elliott Trudeau Foundation
Sustainable Development Technology Canada

believed to impede the focused and flexible response necessary to address the specific challenges facing knowledge growth.

Foundations share six defining characteristics that are used as tools to deliver public policies:

- They are independent, autonomous organizations established by legislation or as not-for-profit corporations under the Canada Corporations Act or similar legislation.
- They are created with the express purpose of delivering a focused service or range of services to satisfy needs that are not currently addressed by existing government programs or services.
- They are funded by up-front payments of conditional grants that provide multi-year funding over a fixed time period or in the form of a perpetual endowment.
- Mandates and governance structures are established in their legislation or articles of association. Funding agreements between the Government of Canada and individual foundations establish the objectives, governance, and accountability requirements, and terms and conditions for the use of the transferred funds.
- They operate, for the most part, by providing funding for third-party projects and activities selected on the basis of merit. Selection processes typically involve assessments against comprehensive selection criteria and the use of peer review processes. Most foundations also require beneficiaries to obtain matching funding for their projects.
- Governance is provided by boards composed of members with relevant expertise and experience, and who for the most part come from outside the federal government (although some foundations have government officials sitting as ex-officio members of their boards). A minority of board members are appointed by the government (TBS, 2007: 2).

The Legacy of ASD

We are now in an era where ASD has become ingrained in the very roots of public sector governance and administration. What may have started out as just another public sector reform initiative in the late 1980s has truly changed the way governments operate.

Twenty years later we can appreciate the transformative effects it has had on the role of governments and their ability to deliver services to citizens. The wide-reaching effects of ASD can be seen in governments around the world, despite different political systems, administrative cultures, and electoral choices. Large and small, at the national, regional, and municipal levels, ASD has been used in varying shapes and forms to help governments operate in a more efficient and effective manner.

So what does this mean for leaders and practitioners of public sector administration? Have we crossed the finish line and won the race?

More Efficient and Effective Government

Alternative service delivery evolved within the broader framework of New Public Management—an approach to public administration that defined itself against traditional hierarchical bureaucracy. With governments growing larger each year and struggling with layers of management and red tape, New Public Management introduced a bottom-line mentality with an overriding focus on efficiency. It was an effort to incorporate private sector principles to the fiscal and governance challenges of the 1980s and 1990s.

As an element of the reform agenda, ASD emerged as a new and effective instrument of public policy. In Canada, ASD mechanisms have become too numerous to count and service efficiency has improved accordingly. The use of ASD mechanisms has produced more flexible and focused service delivery arms for the public service. And perhaps more importantly, it has provided the *mechanisms* to support a citizen-centred *approach* to service delivery. Innovative structures for service delivery are meaningless without a corresponding commitment to manage government in a way that places the citizen at the heart of service. In this respect, Canada has proven to be a world leader in marrying the commitment to improved service with the ability to execute on its promises.

Complexity and Fragmentation

ASD, however, is not without its challenges. This new and flexible approach to service delivery brings with it the threat of fragmentation. If we were to look down on the federal government from a bird's eye view, we would see a complex network of governance structures, accountability frameworks, financial mechanisms, and relationships. The proliferation of semi-autonomous public, private, and hybrid entities has become almost dizzying in its scale. In one sense, ASD evolved as a strategy to reduce the size and scope of government. And in some respects this has happened. In cases where it made little sense for government to deliver a service that could be better operated by others, ASD has simplified public sector operations. For example, Ontario chose to partner with private sector specialists to develop and manage an electronic land registry system called Teranet. The government has benefited from lowering its costs, installing the land registry system more quickly, and creating more jobs and job skills. The private sector partners bring to Teranet business skills, a marketing network, and equity, and they get an immediate financial return, long-term contracts, access to government expertise, and access to international markets.

But regardless of whether the size and scope of government has decreased, on a broad scale, ASD has deepened the complexity of government. And with complexity comes the danger of fragmentation and disjointed government. As governments continue to innovate and look for new methods of delivering service to Canadians, a careful watch will need to be kept on how all of the pieces strategically fit together as a cohesive whole.

The Accountability Dilemma

Perhaps more than any other aspect of alternative service delivery, Canada has adopted a particular focus on accountability in recent years. As discussed earlier in the chapter, the accountability environment in Canada is a result of many different circumstances, often unrelated to ASD. Nevertheless, ASD brings with it unique challenges, and the accountability frameworks that have been developed to support ASD mechanisms have gone under the microscope.

In many cases, accountability mechanisms have proven to be more than adequate in protecting the public interest and providing an optimal balance of independence and oversight. But the sign of a healthy public sector is a willingness to continually evaluate efforts, learn from mistakes, and take corrective action.

Canada's Office of the Auditor General has played an important role in shining the light on accountability frameworks within the federal government that lack rigour or appropriate safeguards. As an example, the Auditor General voiced a number of concerns regarding the functioning of the accountability mechanisms of federal foundations in the 1999 and 2002 reports. In response to these assessments and in light of the experiences gained through the establishment and administration of foundations, adjustments have been made. These adjustments include, as TBS reported in its Evaluation of Foundations:

- introducing consistent expectations regarding the preparation of annual corporate plans and performance reports;
- conducting independent audit and evaluation studies;
- submitting these reports to the responsible ministers and disclosing them publicly;
- allowing discretion for responsible ministers to commission their own independent evaluation and performance audit studies;
- creating consistent conditions under which the Crown may intervene in

> the event of non-compliance with the requirements of funding agreements (TBS, 2007: 8).

Canadian leaders have learned that careful analysis is needed in order to choose the types of services that are to be given the arm's-length treatment often characterized in ASD arrangements, and accountability continues to be a live issue that deserves to stay at the forefront of ASD evaluations.

High Performance Leadership

No longer is the decision to deliver a service a simple one. Departments and agencies must rigorously analyze options, costs, and benefits, with the sometimes difficult choice of what instruments of public policy are best suited to the circumstances at hand.

As ASD mechanisms proliferate throughout government, the complexity of leadership has also intensified. Leaders, especially deputy ministers, must be able to manage multi-faceted relationships with other government departments, other levels of government, private industry, and third-sector organizations. Leaders at all levels are now expected to be able to build support for government initiatives through engagement, influence, negotiation, and the creation of strategic alliances while balancing national and regional interests.

Strategic thinking has also become an imperative to high-performance leadership. In the Government of Canada, this competency is defined as 'innovating through analysis and ideas' (PSHRMAC/PSC, 2005). Leaders are expected to frame issues with a thorough understanding of enabling legislation and governance parameters. They must also be able to identify links between global, societal, and economic trends; stakeholder concerns; the policy agenda; public service values; and departmental, regional, and horizontal issues. And from all this, they must be able to extract key issues from complex, ambiguous, rapidly changing contexts.

High-performance leadership is demanding and sometime elusive. One of the most important and enduring competitive advantages that a country can have today is a lean, efficient, honest civil service (Friedman, 1999). As the service delivery environment continues to evolve, public sector leadership will play a key role in keeping Canada at the leading edge of service innovation.

The Learning Organization

Alternative service delivery is able to increase the effectiveness and efficiency of government operations, but within a structure that often separates policy development from service delivery. From an efficiency perspective, the separation is necessary and admirable. But the difficulty occurs when there is too much distance between the designers of policy and those tasked with delivering it on the ground.

This is not a new challenge in government, but is one that can be exacerbated by ASD mechanisms. Policy can be insufficiently informed by front-line experience and knowledge. To offset this difficulty, public sector organizations need to do a better job of *becoming* learning organizations—talking is not enough. Linkages between policy and service delivery need to be explicitly created and knowledge management strategies should be prioritized (Lodge, 2007: 17). Learning practitioners will agree that this is easier said than done. Nevertheless, organizational learning will be a critical aspect of public sector excellence in the years to come.

The Ability to Innovate

Canada has proven itself to be a leader in creating and implementing ASD mechanisms. However, experience over the past decade indicates that we may be becoming complacent. The fact that ASD has become ingrained in the everyday operations of government is a success story. But ASD within the federal public service has now become merely transactional and more often than not, service delivery choices lean towards tried and true options.

In order to stay at the leading edge of service delivery innovation, Canada needs to continue to experiment with new ideas and strategies for service excellence. In the private sector, innovation often falls into two categories: (1) incremental innovations that result in small but important improvements, and (2) disruptive innovations that fundamentally change the nature of a business. ASD was the public sector equivalent of a disruptive innovation in the 1990s and it still holds the potential to create fundamental improvements to service delivery.

While service continues to be at the top of Canada's public sector priorities, it has been subsumed within the broader renewal agenda. As a result, there is no leadership imperative or public sector champion to encourage the public service to continue be innovative in the use of ASD mechanisms. Service Canada is a case in point. The vision for the organization is innovative and its potential to fundamentally change service delivery across Canada is far-reaching. Sadly, what started out as an exciting initiative seems to have reached a plateau in its evolution. Despite the fact that it has demonstratively moved the bar on improving service to Canadians, there seems to be little appetite to move it to the next phase of implementation. As a result, it remains within a departmental governance structure with questions as to its future independence and scope of operations.

Conclusion

Canada was once a major player in the development of modest initiatives in the reform of service to citizens. On the world stage, Canada has differed in its approach to ASD in that it did not move towards a full-scale overhaul of the service delivery function as can be seen in other countries, such as the United Kingdom and Australia. Rather, we strategically adopted the best of New Public Management principles where circumstances allowed. In this respect, Canada has been a leader in the evolution of service standards, metrics, accountability, improved governance, business planning, and reporting on performance.

The past decade has witnessed the creation of a small number of new agencies and some tinkering with the machinery of government. Most recently, the federal government has taken a sharp turn away from ASD and has focused instead on management reform. As a result, ASD has become one strategy among many in the pursuit of better management practices.

In the early years of the decade, leaders began to realize that the public service would soon face severe human resources challenges as a result of demographics, the need for new talent, and a recognition that the human resources system was not functioning effectively. This shifted the focus away from service innovation towards management reform and modernization.

In 2003, the **Public Service Modernization Act** became law and ushered a new management structure into the federal government with the deputy minister at the centre of the accountability 'tree' and the central agencies as service providers, planners, and oversight organizations. Public service reform and renewal initiatives have continued under the Clerk of the Privy Council's leadership, and the work of the Prime Minister's Advisory Committee on the Public Service under the chairmanship of Paul Tellier and Don Mazankowski. The work currently underway in Canada on public service renewal is of utmost importance and will set the necessary conditions for the next generation of public service leadership in Canada.

That said, ASD is no longer an articulated government priority. It is certainly not dead, but it has morphed into an emphasis on better management. Indeed, the Treasury Board Secretariat no longer has a dedicated team working on ASD, and without committed central agency oversight it has become difficult to track ASD movements in Canada.

The future continues to hold great promise for new variations of ASD. Technological improvements will continue to provide solutions to address the problems and challenges associated with an increasingly complex government. Canada will continue to lead in the area of metrics. From 'Reporting to Canadians' to the Management Accountability Framework, there is an expanded awareness of the importance of measuring outcomes and outputs and relating them back to both financial and human inputs.

Canada's modest experiment with ASD has certainly resulted in a significant emphasis on governance of all kinds of public institutions. This has and will continue to serve Canada well as leaders and students of public sector innovation continue to look for new ideas and approaches to governance and service delivery excellence.

Acknowledgements

I am especially indebted to Susan Snider, a former student and research assistant, and now a friend, for her help in completing this chapter. Her organizational skills and knowledge of ASD developments in Canada were especially helpful. I would also like to thank Dr Barry Stemshorn and Ouassim Meguellati of the Graduate School of Public and International Affairs at the University of Ottawa for their insights into recent trends in ASD.

Important Terms and Concepts

agencies
alternative service delivery
collaborative arrangements
devolution
direct delivery
federal foundations
franchising/licensing
partnerships
privatization
Public Service Modernization Act
purchase of service
Service Canada
Special Operating Agencies (SOAs)

Study Questions

1. The reasons to turn to ASD have evolved as much as the concept of ASD itself. Comment.
2. What are the goals and objectives of ASD?
3. How does one go about determining which ASD option is the one to adopt?
4. Is the ASD concept a mixed blessing?
5. Where does one stop in the drive to move away from the standard departmental form?
6. What are the benefits of the standard departmental form?

Useful Websites

Accenture. 2007. *Leadership in Customer Service: Delivering on the Promise.* Report at:

http://nstore.accenture.com/acn_com/PDF/2007LCSReport_DeliveringPromiseFinal.pdf

Annual Report to the Prime Minister on the Public Service of Canada: Sixteenth Report, for the year ending 31 March 2009. And links to previous, and related, reports:

www.pco-bcp.gc.ca/index.asp?lang=eng&page=information&sub=publications&doc=publications-eng.htm

Auditor General of Canada. 2007. *Assessing Alternative Service Delivery Arrangements.*

www.oag-bvg.gc.ca/internet/English/meth_gde_e_10195.html

Canadian Council on Public–Private Partnerships. *About PPP: Definitions and Models:*

www.pppcouncil.ca/aboutPPP_definition.asp

Fyfe, Toby. 2004. 'Alternative Service Delivery—Responding to Global Pressures', *International Review of Administrative Sciences* 70, 4, 637–44.

http://ras.sagepub.com/cgi/content/abstract/70/4/637

Public Service Human Resources Management Agency of Canada [now called Canada Public Service Agency]/Public Service Commission of 2005. *Key Leadership Competencies.* Ottawa: Government of Canada.

www.psagency-agencefp.gc.ca/leadership/klc-ccl/intro_e.asp

Treasury Board Secretariat. 2002. 'Policy on Alternative Service Delivery' (Archived).

www.tbs-sct.gc.ca/pubs_pol/opepubs/TB_B4/asd-dmps-eng.asp

The World Bank. Updated 2005. 'Alternative Service Delivery Mechanisms'.

www1.worldbank.org/publicsector/civilservice/alternative.htm

The World Bank. 2008. 'Administrative and Civil Reform':

http://web.worldbank.org/WBSITE/EXTERNAL/TOPICS/EXTPUBLICSECTORANDGOVERNANCE/EXTADMINISTRATIVEANDCIVILSERVICEREFORM/0,,menuPK:286372~pagePK:149018~piPK:149093~theSitePK:286367,00.html

Note

1. An overview of ASD activity in Canada has been written by Paul Barker in a book titled *Public Administration in Canada.* Thompson Nelson, 2008: 128–39.

References

Accenture. 2007. *Leadership in Customer Service: Delivering on the Promise.* Accenture.

Auditor General of Canada. 2007. *Assessing Alternative Service Delivery Arrangements.* Ottawa: Ottawa: Her Majesty the Queen in Right of Canada.

Barker, Paul. 2008. *Public Administration in Canada,* brief edn. Toronto: Thomson Nelson.

Boase, Joan. 2000. 'Beyond Government? The Appeal of Public–Private Partnerships', *Canadian Public Administration* 43, 1: 75–92.

Borins, Sandford, et al. 2007. *Digital State at the Leading Edge.* Toronto: IPAC-University of Toronto Press.

Boston, Jonathan. 2000. 'Organizing for Service Delivery: Criteria and Opportunities', in Guy Peters and Donald Savoie, eds., *Governance in the Twenty-First Century.* Montreal: McGill University Press.

Canada, Clerk of the Privy Council.2006. *Annual Report to the Prime Minister on the Public Service of Canada: Thirteenth Report.* Ottawa: Ottawa: Her Majesty the Queen in Right of Canada.

———. 2007. *Annual Report to the Prime Minister on the Public Service of Canada: Fourteenth Report.* Ottawa: Ottawa: Her Majesty the Queen in Right of Canada.

Canadian Council on Public–Private Partnerships. nd. *About PPP: Definitions and Models.* Available at: www.pppcouncil.ca/aboutPPP_definition.asp

Carroll, Barbara Wake. 2008. Editor's introduction to the special issues on public–private partnerships, *Canadian Public Administration* 51, 1: 1–4.

Desautels, Denis. 1999. 'Accountability for Alternative Service Delivery Arrangements in the Federal Government: Some Consequences of Sharing the Business of Government', in Susan Delacourt and Donald Lenihan, eds., *Collaborative Government: Is There a Canadian Way?* Toronto: Institute of Public Administration of Canada.

D'Ombrain, Nicholas. 2000. 'Alternative Service Delivery: Governance, Management and Practice', in *Change, Governance, and Public Management: Alternative Service Delivery and Information Technology.* Ottawa: Public Policy Forum.

Dunn, Christopher, ed. *The Handbook of Canadian Public Administration,* 1st edn. Toronto: Oxford University Press, 2002.

Dyck, Rand. 2004. *Canadian Politics: Critical Approaches,* 4th edn. Scarborough: Thomson Nelson.

Eggers, Bill. 2005. *Government 2.0: Using Technology to Improve Education, Cut Red Tape, Reduce Gridlock, and Enhance Democracy.* Lanham, Md.: Rowman and Littlefield.

Flumian, Maryantonett, Amanda Coe, and Kenneth Kernaghan. 2008. '*Transforming Service to Canadians: The Service Canada Model*'. Unpublished paper.

Ford, Robin, and David Zussman.1997. 'Alternative Service Delivery: Transcending Boundaries', in *Alternative Delivery: Sharing Governance in Canada.* Toronto: IPAC-KPMG.

Friedman, Thomas L. 1999. *The Lexus and the Olive Tree.* Washington: Harper Collins.

Fyfe, Toby. 2004. 'Alternative Service Delivery—Responding to Global Pressures', *International Review of Administrative Sciences* 70, 4: 637–44.

———, Michael McConkey, and Patrice Dutil. 2004. *Reinventing Service: Processes and Prospects for Municipal Alternative Service Delivery*. New Directions series (no. 14). Toronto: IPAC.

Good, David, and Barry Carin. 2003. 'Alternative Service Delivery'. Unpublished paper.

Heron, Anne Louise, and Douglas Lychak. 2008. 'Government Performance: Alternative Service Delivery Approaches', EcDevJournal.com. 21 March.

Human Resources and Social Development Canada. 2003. *Government On-Line 2003 Public Report*. Available at: www.hrsdc.gc.ca/eng/cs/comm/gol/2003.shtml.

Institute for Citizen Centred Service. 2004. *Alternative Service Delivery*. Available at: www.iccs-isac.org/en/clearinghouse/asd.htm.

Inwood, Gregory. 2007.*Understanding Canadian Public Administration: An Introduction to Theory and Practice*, 3rd edn. Toronto: Pearson Prentice-Hall.

Kernaghan, Kenneth, and David Siegel. 1999. *Public Administration in Canada*, 4th edn. Toronto: Nelson.

Lodge, Guy. 2007. *Lost in Translation? International Perspectives on Civil Service Reform*. London: Institute for Public Policy Research.

Lynch, Kevin G. 2007. *Fourteenth Annual Report to the Prime Minister on the Public Service of Canada*, for the year ending 31 March 2007. Available at: www.pco-bcp.gc.ca/index.asp?lang=eng&page=information&sub=publications&doc=ar-ra/14report2007/14threport-eng.html.

———. 2008. *Fifteenth Annual Report to the Prime Minister on the Public Service of Canada*, for the year ending 31 March 2008. Available at: www.pco-bcp.gc.ca/index.asp?lang=eng&page=information&sub=publications&doc=ar-ra/15-2008/table-eng.htm.

Ontario Public Sector Restructuring Secretariat. 1999. *Alternative Service Delivery in the Ontario Public Sector*. Toronto: The Secretariat.

Osbaldeston, Gordon. 1992. *Organizing to Govern*. Toronto: McGraw-Hill Ryerson.

Osborne, David, and Ted Gaebler. 1992. *Reinventing Government*, Reading, Mass.: Addison-Wesley.

Pal, Leslie. 2001. *Beyond Policy Analysis: Public Issue Management in Turbulent Times*, 2nd edn. Toronto: ITP Nelson.

PSHRMAC [Public Service Human Resources Management Agency of Canada, now called Canada Public Service Agency] Public Service Commission of Canada. 2005. *Key Leadership Competencies*. Ottawa: Government of Canada. Available at: www.psagency-agencefp.gc.ca/leadership/klc-ccl/intro_e.asp.

Public Service Alliance of Canada. 2006. *Policy: Defending Quality Public Services*. Available at: www.psac.com/issues/dqps-dspq/index-e.shtml.

Sutcliffe, Judy, and Melodie Tilson. 2005. 'Sport and Physical Activity in Canada: National Leadership Models'. Unpublished paper.

Tapscott, Don, and Anthony Williams. 2006. *Wikinomics: How Mass Collaboration Changes Everything*. Toronto: Portfolio.

Treasury Board Secretariat. 2002a. *New Policy Strengthens Oversight of Alternative Service Delivery Arrangements and Respects Official Language Principles*. Available at: www.tbs-sct.gc.ca/media/nr-cp/2002/0220-eng.asp.

———. 2002b. 'Policy on Alternative Service Delivery'. Available at: www.tbs-sct.gc.ca/pubs_pol/opepubs/TB_B4/asd-dmps-eng.asp.

———. 2007. *Final Report: Evaluation of Foundations*. Prepared by KPMG on behalf of the Government of Canada between September 2006 and January 2007. Available at: www.tbs-sct.gc.ca/report/orp/2007/ef-fe/ef-fe-eng.asp.

West, Darrell. 'E-Government and the Transformation of Service Delivery and Citizens Attitudes', *Public Administration Review* 64, 1: 15–27.

Wilkins, John K. 2000 (updated 2005). 'Alternative Service Delivery Mechanisms', *Administrative & Civil Service Reform*. Washington, DC: The World Bank. Available at: www1.worldbank.org/publicsector/civilservice/alternative.htm.

———. 2003. 'Conceptual and Practical Considerations in Alternative Service Delivery', *International Review of Administrative Sciences* 69, 2: 173–89.

The World Bank. Updated 2005. 'Alternative Service Delivery Mechanisms'. Available at: www1.worldbank.org/publicsector/civilservice/alternative.htmThe World Bank. 2008. 'Administrative and Civil Reform'. Available at: http://web.worldbank.org/WBSITE/EXTERNAL/TOPICS/EXTPUBLICSECTORANDGOVERNANCE/EXTADMINISTRATIVEANDCIVILSERVICEREFORM/0,,menuPK:286372~pagePK:149018~piPK:149093~theSitePK:286367,00.htm.

Zussman, David. 2002 . 'Alternative Service Delivery', in Dunn (2002).

15 Democratic Administration

Lorne Sossin

> The taste for participation is whetted by participation: democracy breeds democracy.
>
> (Barber, 1984: 265)

Introduction

Both inside and outside of government, from the left and the right of the ideological spectrum, democratic administration, it seems, had come of age in the 1990s. In 1991, a conference held at York University in Toronto heralded the arrival of a new and different kind of state. Leo Panitch, one of the conference organizers, referred to the rise of **democratic administration** as 'a remarkable development taking place in the political culture of the liberal democracies, one that in the future may come to be seen as marking a historic turning point, a moment of departure in political time' (Panitch, 1993: 2). That same year, a 'Citizen's Charter' was adopted by a Conservative government in the United Kingdom, which affirmed the obligations of the government and entitlements of citizens with respect to the administration of public services and programs.[1] The following year, the national non-fiction best-seller list in the US was dominated by *Reinventing Government* (Osborne and Gaebler, 1993), a book about how to enable public organizations to better serve citizens. This approach shortly thereafter was adopted as a blueprint for the reform of the American federal public service,[2] with significant repercussions for administrative reform in Canada as well (Peters and Savoie, 1993; Trebilcock, 1994).

The emergence of democratic administration, however, coincided with a massive restructuring of government and its bureaucracy. By the close of the 1990s, after a decade of downsizing, outsourcing, off-loading, privatization, and trying to do more with less, the promise of a new era of revitalized and democratized public administration remained unfulfilled. In the early years of the twenty-first century, the focus of the democratic administration movement appears to have shifted away from participatory government towards greater accountability and transparency in governance.

The purpose of this chapter is to explore the past, present, and future of democratic administration and its diverse practices. This analysis will be divided into three sections. The first section will examine the idea of democratic administration as a response to the Weberian ideal of rational administration. The second section will look at the dynamics of democratic administration in the 1990s, and specifically the appeal of democratic administration within both the New Left and the New Right. Finally, the third section will consider the future of democratic administration in the twenty-first century, first, by exploring the possible roles bureaucrats might play in deliberative and communicative politics; and second, by examining the implications of new social and economic dynamics, such as the rise of the Internet, the deepening influence of globalization, and the continuing evolution of the state itself.

What Is Democratic Administration?

Before commencing this examination, it is important first to explore what is meant by 'democratic administration'.[3] This term, unsurprisingly, means different things to different people; however, in virtually every case, citizen 'empowerment' lies at its core. **Citizen empowerment**, in turn, leads to two central critiques of conventional forms of bureaucracy: the first critique relates to the issue of accountability; the second emphasizes the issue of participation.

In the first critique bureaucrats are viewed as insufficiently accountable to citizens for their actions and decision-making. When we speak of empowering citizens in a liberal democracy, we usually are referring to the ballot box. A political party provides citizens with a slate of policy initiatives and claims to good government, on the basis of which the party is elected or defeated; and, if that party does not fulfill its promises once elected, voters can turn them out at the next election.[4] With respect to the actions of bureaucrats, accountability usually refers to the doctrine of ministerial responsibility, under which a cabinet minister is accountable to Parliament for everything that occurs in her or his ministry (Sutherland, 1991; Smith, 2006). While ministerial responsibility may compel a government to explain policies and actions that otherwise would not be subject to public scrutiny, it is unrealistic to expect ministers to be aware of all the actions taken by public officials in their ministries, much less to assume any direct role in them. Ministers resign infrequently, and governments own up to errors and publicly try to rectify them even less often. The nature, extent, and implications of ministerial responsibility are subject to the whim of the government of the day, the persistence and interest of the media, and the dynamics of party and caucus discipline. Other governmental figures, such as the Auditor General, have responsibility for reviewing bureaucratic conduct, but their role is merely to publicize when that conduct is questionable. The courts provide perhaps the significant supervision of administrative action. Courts have the authority not just to publicize bureaucratic wrongdoing, incompetence, or malfeasance, but to impose remedies as well. Judicial review, however, depends on a person's willingness and resources to challenge an adverse decision. This may occasionally lead to individual accountability but rarely to institutional accountability. Advocates of democratic administration generally favour institutional reforms that would render the decision-making process transparent and subject to meaningful citizen review. This may involve more administrative officials being elected directly, more officials coming under the direct supervision of democratic institutions (e.g., citizen boards, community groups), and/or more informal administrative settings where citizens can have decisions reviewed more easily.

One of the most active areas of democratic administration is policing. Here the recognition that those subject to police authority are often among the most vulnerable in society has led to multiple forms of accountability. For example, the activities of the Toronto Police Service are subject to an internal accountability structure (i.e., police discipline); an independent Toronto Police Services Board, which comprises both provincial and city appointees; the Special Investigations Unit, which is a provincial investigations body created to examine cases where anyone dies or is seriously injured as a result of a police officer's actions; and a province-wide Civilian Commission on Police Services (Sossin, 2006). Such overlapping forms of accountability may mean a particular police activity is subject to several different investigations (and the investigating bodies listed above do not include civil and criminal legal action, which also may result from perceived police misconduct). The goal is to enhance both the transparency of policing and community confidence in the police. Accountability, in other words, is a mechanism for infusing democracy into administration.

The second critique of **conventional bureaucracy** asserts that there is too little scope for public participation in the administrative process and that citizens experience a pervasive sense of powerlessness when adversely affected by bureaucratic decision-making. This critique views democracy as more than merely holding decision-makers to account for their decisions or requiring transparency in public decision-making; rather, citizens should have access to, and involvement in, decisions that affect their interests or the public interest more broadly.

Democracy, in this context, is a spectrum rather than a threshold that is or is not crossed (Cunningham, 1987: 25–31). The issue is not whether to introduce democratic features into administrative practices, but rather what degree and dimension of democratic features are appropriate for various administrative settings. Democratic administration is concerned with exploring administrative structures that would 'deepen the experience of democracy' (Shields and Evans, 1998: 118). Town-hall meetings, public hearings, interest group and stakeholder consultations, and referenda all have been raised as possible avenues of infusing public participation into public administration. However, citizens may convey their input in less-visible ways outside of state structures as well. They may move from an area poorly served by public services (e.g., hospitals, schools) to an area well served by them; they may evade taxes or pay them; they may co-operate with the police or withhold information.

Democratic administration, whether seen as a reform project for increased accountability or for increased participation, raises the same fundamental question, namely, how to transform people from the object into the subject of government. But where does this question come from? How did citizens become the object of government in the first place? Why have bureaucracy and democracy evolved as opposing forms of decision-making? In order to address these questions, it is first necessary to review the origins of democratic administration.

The Origins of Democratic Administration

The departure point for an understanding of democratic administration is Weber's ideal type of rational–legal public administration. This is the dominant ideology of bureaucratic organization and authority in most liberal democracies, including Canada. As Fred Dallmayr observes, 'We are today the heirs—the reluctant heirs—of Max Weber. . . . It was Max Weber who, in the opening decades of this century, captured the path of Western society as a process of relentless rationalization geared towards greater efficiency—a process of which we are both the beneficiaries and the . . . victims' (Dallmayr, 1994: 49).

Weber identifies a variety of criteria that, in his observation of various administrative systems, render bureaucracies efficient and effective. These include: impartiality; neutrality; tenure of office; the provision of fixed salaries to officials; the organization of bureaucratic units along hierarchical lines; the regulation of entry and promotion according to merit; the regulation of operations according to general, consistent, and abstract rules; and, most importantly, the separation of administration from politics (Weber, 1947: 328–40). Bureaucrats, under this ideal, are independent and beholden only to the duties of their office, not to any master, political or otherwise.

This model of bureaucratic organization made possible the dramatic expansion of public administration into social and economic life, but posed normative problems for liberal democracy. As Eva Etzioni-Halevy concludes, 'It follows that the very same superiority that has made bureaucracy so essential to modern society also poses a threat to modern democracy' (Etzioni-Halevy, 1985: 33). Investing appointed officials with vast discretionary authority threatens the premise of liberal democracy, under which those with power are said to be accountable to the electorate.[5] Moreover, the people subject to this authority often experience it as an 'iron cage', constructed, in Weber's words, by 'specialists without spirit, sensualists without heart' (Weber, 1958: 182). For Weber, bureaucracy was domination through knowledge.

Critics emphasize that Weber did not celebrate the triumph of bureaucracy, but rather was haunted by the spectre of bureaucrats assuming mastery of the state over both citizens and their political representatives, as experts manipulating dilettantes (Etzioni-Halevy, 1985: 32–5). The prospect of the politicians exercising any substantive supervision over the conduct of public officials is remote. To address these democratic anxieties over the extent of bureaucratic authority, advocates of Weberian bureaucracy stress the functional distinctions between politics and administration. According to this **politics–administration dichotomy**, politics is devoted to the development of laws, policies, and public values, while administration is devoted to the technical process or implementing those laws, policies, and values.[6] By improving technical methods through scientific refinement, administration can be rendered efficient, anonymous, and mechanistic (Taylor, 1947). In this way, bureaucracy is construed as a tool to be used by politicians for whatever ends they view as worthwhile; it poses no more of a threat to democracy than a typewriter poses to a writer. The flaw in this understanding of bureaucratic power is that people are not machines and administration cannot be cleansed of politics.

The attempt to disentangle politics and administration originally had a democratically beneficial intent. The scourge of the nineteenth century had been the system of patronage appointments to public service by which large portions of bureaucracy were beholden to the partisan interests of the party in power (Simpson, 1988; Skowronek, 1982). Patronage led to corrupt, wasteful, and arbitrary public administration. Exchanging jobs for votes undermined public confidence in both democracy and bureaucracy. Therefore, emphasizing the technical nature of public service and the need for hiring and promotion according to merit, the development of training and education programs in administrative management was designed to foster professionalism and thereby to distinguish between the political and administrative spheres of government.

This politics–administration dichotomy, however, rested on a myth. In practice, it is not possible to remove all political considerations from public administration. The nature of the choices that public officials make in their day-to-day activities has a direct impact on the distribution of resources, influence, and power in society. The dissonance between the premise and the practice of public administration became more pronounced as the state's role in social and economic life deepened and its political aspects became more apparent. State intervention in health, welfare, education, social services, and economic development led bureaucratic authority into virtually every corner of daily life. As more and more scrutiny focused on public officials, the myth became more and more untenable.

The growth of the welfare state gave rise to new ideas about bureaucratic organization and put new strains on the politics–administration dichotomy. Canada's version of the **Keynesian welfare state** emerged more gradually and less coherently than in the United Kingdom and Northern Europe (partially as a result of Canada's complex relationship between federalism and social policy); nevertheless, by the 1960s and 1970s, Canadian public policy embraced the goal of full employment and a comprehensive social safety net for those unable to achieve self-sufficiency in the market economy (Guest, 1985; Banting, 1987). The success of the welfare state, however, was tied to the prosperity generated by the market. A decline in profits and productivity in the 1970s, the rise of multinational corporations and capital flight in the 1980s, the shifting of manufacturing to newly industrializing centres in the developing world, and a process of deindustrialization in many developed countries all contributed to the diminished economic viability of the welfare state by the 1990s (McBride and Shields, 1997: 46–52). Rising state deficits, cycles of inflation and stagflation, and economic instability undermined public confidence in the apparatuses of government and their ability to sustain the prosperity that the post-war generation had attained and come to assume. As Peter Aucoin concludes, 'The coalitions that had brought about the interventionist-welfare state everywhere began to collapse into various states of disarray' (Aucoin, 1995: 119).

The rise of the 'administrative state' in the post-war era led to an analogous breakdown of its institutional logic (Waldo, 1940; Cairns, 1990). The volume, complexity, and unanticipated consequences of administrative decision-making made the notion of a 'science' of public administration implausible. This welfare state led to a more pragmatic understanding of administrative decision-making as 'disjointed incrementalism' (Lindblom, 1959). The hierarchical divisions of bureaucratic organizations, which were designed to convey directions from the political masters at the top to the rank-and-file officials through to the bottom were shown to be dysfunctional. A 'human relations' school of bureaucratic management emerged by which ideas were supposed to flow from the bottom to the top as well as from the top to the bottom (McGregor, 1960: 33–4; Kernaghan and Seigel, 1991: 63–78). Eventually, a flood of new managerial theories, many imported from the private sector, began to erode the Weberian approach to administrative organization. These attacks on the orthodoxy of rational administration sowed the seeds for democratic administration.

Recognizing the political content of administrative action, being open to bottom-up communication, and valuing pragmatism all helped to create the conditions for the critique of public administration on democratic grounds to emerge. The infiltration of the state into new areas of society and the economy provided the fertile soil for this idea to grow. As public officials came more into contact with the everyday lives of citizens (deciding who should receive social welfare, affordable housing, tax benefits, scholarships, economic subsidies, etc.), the bureaucracy's isolation from the way citizens thought and reasoned was highlighted. Bureaucracy became synonymous with remoteness. The distance between citizens and public officials, which once had been seen as a prerequisite for good government, now appeared as a symptom of bureaucratic malaise.

Bureaucracy became an easy target for the failures of the welfare state in the 1970s and 1980s. Whereas civil servants had once been seen as the human face of the welfare state, attracting many of the finest educated, civic-minded professionals of the 1930s and 1940s, the expansion of the welfare state led to more reliance on centralization, new technologies, and volume efficiencies. Clerical staff replaced social workers; inscrutable forms and regulations left little room for compassion, and targets for moving recipients off the welfare rolls became the only performance measure that mattered; citizens, as a result, experienced bureaucracy more as numbers than as people (Simon, 1983: 1199), and bureaucrats more as entrepreneurs than as agents of public support (Diller, 2000). In Ontario, the government contracted out welfare intake to regional call centres, where staff read a script in order to fill out entries in a database to determine eligibility. In such a setting, applying for benefits becomes both disembodied and disconnected from the reality of the applicants' lives (Sossin, 2004).

The alienation of citizens from public life (and from public administration in particular) led to the distinct but related movements for more accountability and greater participation in administrative action. The accountability movement, which originated mostly from the right of the ideological spectrum, sought to make public officials answerable for the waste and inefficiencies of public enterprises (Savoie, 1994: 87–115). The stereotype of the self-aggrandizing, bungling, indolent bureaucrat became a more frequent fixture in the election campaigns and academic invectives of those on the political right (Goodsell, 1994: 49–76). The participatory administration movement, which originated mostly from the left of the ideological spectrum, sought more intervention from public officials to redress social and economic inequalities, to protect the environment and vulnerable communities, and to spearhead political empowerment.[7] What these disparate points on the ideological spectrum had in common was the rhetoric of taking government away from 'the bureaucrats' and returning it to 'the people'. This became a powerful symbol of public administration reform in the 1990s. However, as I discuss in the following section, such symbols have thus far failed to alter the substance of public administration in Canada.

The State of Democratic Administration

The idea of democratic administration has been frequently applauded but rarely implemented (Munroe, 1990). Indeed, it may well be that this idea was universally praised precisely because it so rarely altered the facts of administrative life. In this section, I investigate why the popularity of the symbol of democratic administration has not been matched by its substance. The two most significant and coherent programs to reform (or transform) conventional bureaucracy on democratic grounds broadly may be characterized as the New Left and the New Right. The **New Left** has pursued the empowerment of citizens through advocating the increased participation of users, particularly disadvantaged users, in the development and implementation of government policies and programs. The purpose of restructuring public administration in this fashion is to redress the social and economic inequalities produced by the market. The **New Right** has pursued the empowerment of citizens through advocating increased competition, choice, and freedom of contract between the users of public goods and services and the government. The purpose of this restructuring is to have the state mirror the market. While each of these streams may share certain prescriptions for administrative reform (e.g., increased decentralization, responsiveness to community needs), they do so with a dramatically different ideal of state action in mind.

The New Left

For the Old Left, democracy and bureaucracy were simply incompatible. Socialist transformation of economic life was intended to pave the way for self-government and the apparatus of the state was seen simply as an extension (i.e., the executive committee) of the ruling class and the bureaucracy its administrative arm. For Marxists, in short, 'bureaucracy is a circle from which no one can escape' (Marx, 1978: 24; Lenin, 1926: 155). In the 1960s and 1970s, however, the New Left emerged, which accepted that the bureaucracy could in fact act contrary to the interests of the ruling class, at least if it was necessary to shore up the legitimacy of the welfare state, though this autonomy was bounded and contingent (Miliband, 1969; Poulantzas, 1973; Nordlinger, 1981). The welfare state thus could function as a vehicle for progressive, albeit limited, social change. Democratic administration was seen, especially by the social movements spawned by the New Left (e.g., feminism, environmentalism), as a means of empowering citizens through collective action in order to attain those progressive ends.

The New Left not only views bureaucratic relationships as a venue for class conflict and as a threat to the ideal of citizenship, but also as a 'violent form of abstraction' (Habermas, 1987: 361–3; Habermas, 1990a: 51). This abstraction is the result of bureaucracies denying personal relationships with citizens and treating them instead as data to be entered or files to be closed. To counter this reification of public life (i.e., the treatment of people as though they were things), a number of New Left theorists have adopted and adapted what Jürgen Habermas has termed a 'communicative action' approach (Sossin, 1993). Communicative action involves the justification of public decision-making by recourse to consensually agreed-to 'good reasons' (Habermas, 1990b). Good reasons are distinguished from bureaucratic reasons because good reasons presuppose universal moral claims about fairness and justice, whereas bureaucratic reasons rely solely on instrumental rationality and technical expertise. According to Habermas, since all people possess the intuitive capacity to reason practically—to deliberate, dialogue, debate, and ultimately be persuaded by the best argument—all people are capable of commanding influence in public decision-making through the search for good reasons. However, as Habermas's critics have observed, assuring that 'good reasons' emerge from a dialogue in which persuasive ability is often a product of wealth and education, as well as ethnic, regional, racial, gender, and linguistic background, is always daunting and sometimes impossible (Fraser, 1985; Alexander, 1991).

Critical theorists of the New Left, whether supportive or critical of this venture, rarely dealt in significant detail with the administrative complexities of putting their participatory ideas into practice.[8] As Orion White and Cynthia McSwain note:

> advocates of participation never theorized the details of an effective participatory

> process and the role that relevant expertise needs to play in it. The result was that actual experiments in participation frequently devolved into interminable meetings, according to Robert's Rules of Order or incoherent 'rap sessions' of intolerable length. (McSwite, 1997: 213–14)

For many activists, therefore, theorizing about participatory structures was not enough. Communities had to be organized, public officials had to be pressured, and established interests had to be undermined. The first large-scale experiment in this form of participatory administration took place in the United States as part of President Johnson's War on Poverty in the 1960s (Levitan, 1969). The first prong focused on empowering the poor through legal challenges intended to entrench a right to obtain and keep welfare benefits and to prevent employment-related discrimination. The second prong involved community organizing. The Economic Opportunity Act, which created new community action agencies to receive and administer federal anti-poverty funds, mandated that those agencies be 'developed, conducted, and administered with maximum feasible participation of the residents.' The federal government bypassed local municipal bureaucracies and directly funded an advocacy body, Community and Legal Services. Money was provided to grassroots organizations specifically to fund advocates who represented the poor before city agencies. However, this left local political networks with a vested interest in the demise of Community Action Projects. In most urban areas they set to accomplishing with far more vigour then they had ever displayed at combatting poverty. Community Action Projects were also undermined by the advocacy and activism of their own administrators, who tended not to recognize any line between politics and administration in the context of social welfare and civil rights. This led both to unprecedented activism in harnessing public benefits for the poor and to a serious erosion of public support for those benefits programs. Widespread administrative irregularities led to the end of the Office of Economic Opportunity funding for Community Action Projects.

Despite advances in the areas of community involvement and civil rights, the War on Poverty intentionally steered clear of undermining the welfare state. The singular priority of these programs was to provide access to existing jobs in an expanding economy and existing benefits in the expanding state. Rather than focusing on the structural defects in the post-war economy, the Great Society attacked instead the limitations that poverty placed on personal advancement in the economy—directing funds to education, training, and skills development in poor districts (Katz, 1989: 101).

A similar development was taking place in Canada as part of Prime Minister Pierre Elliott Trudeau's 'Just Society' initiatives in the late 1960s and early 1970s. Legal clinics, mental health clinics, crisis centres, battered women's shelters, neighbourhood associations, peer self-help groups, and outreach centres, among many other institutional forms, demonstrated the benefits of community activism in public administration (Handler, 1996: 93–6). These organizations not only advocated more participation in public decision-making on matters that affected them, but they were often themselves administered along more democratic lines than conventional government agencies.

Two significant social movements, feminism and environmentalism, have also embraced democratic administration, but on slightly different terms. The feminist movement within the New Left has attempted both to challenge and to reconceptualize the meaning of the state (Fraser, 1997; Phillips, 1991; Young, 1990; Nedelsky, 1989; MacKinnon, 1989; Gould, 1988). Feminists encompass diverse and shifting approaches to the state and administrative life. Liberal feminists may view the state in terms of whether it enhances or obstructs the goal of gender equality; other feminists are more concerned with the relationship between the state and the structures of patriarchy. For most feminists, however, the state is seen as a 'multifaceted ensemble of power relations' that creates subjects who are 'bureaucratized, dependent, disciplined and gendered' (Brown, 1992).

The feminist literature on public administration has been particularly interested in public agencies and offices that interact with vulnerable citizens. In such settings, women tend to constitute a majority of both the providers and recipients of state benefits. The feminist critique of this interaction generally revolves around the treatment of individuals in need as cases to be resolved, rather than as members of social groups, made not agents, but the passive recipients of predefined services (Fraser, 1990: 212). The welfare bureaucracy is a salient example.

The **feminist analysis of the state** embraces contradictory tendencies. While one stream of feminist analysis conceives of ways to transform the nature of the state, another conceives of new strategies for feminist representation in state institutions (Findlay, 1993).

A similar tension has animated environmental approaches to the state. The first wave of environmentalism in the 1960s focused on persuading the government of the day to adopt environmentally friendly laws and regulations, and relied on the expertise of administrators as guardians of the public interest. The second wave, which began in the 1970s and 1980s with the rise of Greenpeace in North America and the Green Party in Europe and continues to this day, seeks more environmentally sound public policies, but in addition seeks to transform the development and implementation of policies (Paehlke, 1989; Dryzek, 1994; Seccombe, 1993). This second wave has specifically challenged the assumption that environmental decisions are technical in nature and instead views such determinations as political, contested, and value-laden (Paehlke, 1990: 39). Environmentalists continue to lobby for a more open environmental assessment process, and occasionally have been successful in pressuring governments to provide more input into environmental decision-making (Mazmanian and Nienaber, 1994; Babe, 1994) or to launch public inquiries or Royal Commissions into environmental matters (Berger, 1977). However, while incremental policy change remains a goal of environmental activism, that activism also, increasingly, has been directed towards attaining a greater role in the policy process. As Robert Paehlke observes, 'environmentalism cannot be successful in the long run without a continuous enhancement of opportunities for democratic participation' (Paehlke, 1990: 51). Thus far, attempts at participatory environmental governance appear mixed, as the sponsoring agencies of the participatory forums often steer the resulting public involvement to pre-determined outcomes (Dorcey and McDaniels, 2001).

Despite the different approaches to democratic administration evident in social movements such as environmentalism and feminism, both advocate the use of the state to regulate, control, and in some cases restrain the effects of the market economy. The New Right, by contrast, has adopted the opposite premise, namely, that to attain citizen empowerment the state must facilitate (and imitate) the market.

The New Right

The New Right posits that the state's role in social and economic life should be as minimal as possible and that the state should facilitate rather than regulate the market (Kristol, 1995; Pierre, 1995). The New Right looks to economic liberalism, entrepreneurialism, and individualism as counterpoints to the Keynesian welfare state and its collectivist premise (Hoover and Plant, 1989). While many of these tenets were also embraced by the old right (which reached its apex of influence during Barry Goldwater's 1964 bid for the US presidency), that movement was also seen as elitist, marginal, and aloof. The New Right, by contrast, has had remarkable success in tapping into popular discontent with government. This has resulted in an ambivalent position with respect to democratic administration. For the New Right, bureaucratic restructuring entails not only the familiar marketization strategy (e.g., deregulation, privatization, and contracting out), but also empowering citizens to assert their rights in bureaucratic settings. Citizens as consumers, in this view, should be entitled to shop for goods and services from the state as they do from the local mall. New Right prescriptions for reforming public administration include simplifying forms and procedures, reducing 'red tape', delayering bureaucracy, and decentralizing authority to 'let managers manage'. Clients of state services are now routinely asked to fill out 'customer satisfaction' cards. Put simply, the New Right seeks to treat government like a business.[9]

This ideology has had a number of ripple effects in administrative reform in Canada. One such ripple is the rise of the '**New Public Management**'. Like Total Quality Management and other related management trends, the New Right's prescription for reforming public administration emphasizes bottom-up lines of communication and responsiveness to the needs and concerns of users. Public managers, under this approach, are expected to mimic their counterparts in the private sector (and, indeed, many reform proposals made recruiting private sector managers a priority) and foster inter-bureaucratic competition, entrepreneurial ventures (preferably in partnership with the private sector), and income generation (profits) through user fees and competing for vouchers (Howse, 1993; Howse et al., 1990; Daniels and Trebilcock, 2005).

In addition to altering *how* governments operate, the New Right has also advocated altering *what* governments operate. This has led to calls not only for privatizing large (and profitable) public enterprises and Crown corporations, but also for delegating (or downloading) many government functions to voluntary associations in the mushrooming 'third sector'. Unlike the New Left, which justifies its support for certain voluntary associations on the grounds they provide a voice for vulnerable citizens and can help access public goods and services, the New Right supports voluntary associations because they reduce the size and the budget of public agencies and return public administration, especially in the fields of social welfare, to communities (Kramer, 1994; Hall and Reed, 1996).

As Osborne and Gaebler (1993: 180–6) argue, the creation of a public market—including competitive government agencies and non-profit, commercial, and voluntary institutions all providing public goods and services—is intended to allow consumers of those goods and services to convey their concerns directly to service providers, who, in turn, have greater capacity and incentive to respond directly to those concerns. However, as with the prescriptions for democratic administration from the New Left, the operation of public markets runs into difficulties when put into practice. Jon Pierre explains this dilemma in the following terms:

> Clearly, this is a model that, in theory at least, empowers citizens vis-à-vis the government. That said, it is equally clear that the model causes tremendous problems for public sector managers. How are public organizations supposed to be able to conduct any type of planning in this new system, given the uncertainty introduced by the customer-choice-based model? How are these organizations going to be able to get some return from facilities set up in socially problematic neighbourhoods? How are they going to be able to cope with increasing demand, for instance, in schools in attractive neighbourhoods? (Pierre, 1995: 73–4)

More disconcerting, this model appears to conflate market empowerment with political empowerment, and market accountability with democratic accountability (Aucoin, 1995: 188–97). Choice, competition, and consumer-based entitlements may increase the efficiency and effectiveness of public administration. The Citizen's Charter in the United Kingdom, for example, gave users of public services a tangible advantage in terms of courtesy, access to information, and responsiveness. The complaints mechanism established under the Charter to deal with 'dissatisfied customers' represented an important form of direct accountability from public officials to citizens. Such mechanisms, however, cannot question the underlying justness or fairness of administrative action. That one is provided with a choice between a green sweater or a red sweater, a sweater on sale or one with a premium-brand label, does not afford that person any meaningful control over the decision-making structures of the local mall or the retail industry. The same might be said of the value of choice and competition in public goods and services. It may tend to improve the quality and lower the price of the goods and services in question (at least at first), but it does not lead to substantive citizen influence over the decision-making process. Indeed, the very fact that the same values are invoked to distribute sweaters as to distribute social benefits denies the 'public' ethos of public administration altogether (Woodhouse, 1997: 221–32). The result is an administrative process emptied not only of political participation but of all public content.

Democratic Administration's Future: Reflecting on the Twenty-First—Century Bureaucrat

Both the New Right and the New Left arguably are in decline.[10] Neither massive state intervention in, nor massive state withdrawal from, social and economic life enjoys widespread support (Graves, 1999: 56–65).

Canadians' traditional deference to those in authority has been replaced with skepticism, cynicism, and suspicion (Nevitte, 1996). This is partially due to the heightened public scrutiny of administrative action, to which the media, interest groups, and political parties running 'against government' have all contributed. It may also be attributed, in part, to the traditionally closed nature of the administrative state, which has prevented trust from being fostered between bureaucrats and citizens. As Panitch predicted, Canadians are clamouring more than ever for a 'different kind of state'. Frank Graves of Ekos Research Associates explains this phenomenon in the following terms:

> If a key engine of discontent with government is a perception that it has lost its focus on public interest, that citizens are excluded from real power and decision-making, and that public values are inadequately reflected in government, the **'citizen engagement' model** becomes a theoretically attractive remedy for these problems. Our recent work on citizen engagement shows that only about one in four Canadians think that average citizens have a lot of power, but three in four think that they should. (Graves, 1999: 50)

While substantive citizen participation in administrative life and administrative accountability to citizens for bureaucratic decision-making remain largely unfulfilled goals, they continue gradually to redefine the ideal of public administration. Because citizens have bought into the symbols of democratic administration, they are becoming attuned to its substance. Further, substantive citizen involvement in public decision-making is increasingly a significant measuring stick for evaluating the success of administrative action. While many of the ideological tenets of the New Left and the New Right seem of diminishing relevance at the cusp of the twenty-first century, the ideal of democratic administration resonates more than ever.

Democracy is ultimately not about outcomes but about the process of reaching outcomes. The classic depictions of small nineteenth-century New England towns, with citizens taking part in every event and decision, cannot be easily replicated in modern, urban settings, where people are more often strangers to one another their entire lives. However, few people are strangers to public administration. No matter how isolated we may be from one another, virtually all of us are in constant (though perhaps not always welcome) contact with state officials: the tax collector, the welfare case worker, the police officer, the court registrar, or one of scores of licensing and permit offices, agencies, boards, tribunals, and commissions that regulate and mediate our social and economic lives.

How should public officials in these diverse settings engage with citizens to bring isolated individuals, groups, and perspectives together in a public forum? How would these relationships change if we took the substance of democratic administration seriously? One approach would be to view public officials as promoters of what has been termed '**deliberative democracy**' (Cohen, 1997). This approach is often associated with the 'civic republican' movement that rose to prominence in the United States in the 1980s (Fallon, 1989). Citizenship in this model means equal partnership in public affairs and is contrasted to the pluralist model in which individuals seek to maximize their self-interest through capture of political institutions. Deliberation is both a means and an end—a means to determining what is in the public interest and an end to creating a truly public sphere of political decision-making. In his article, 'A Civic Republican Justification for the Bureaucratic State', Mark Seidenfeld articulates the mission of public officials in this scheme in the following terms: 'government's primary responsibility is to enable the citizenry to deliberate about altering preferences to reach consensus on the common good' (Seidenfeld, 1992: 1514).

The problem with the deliberative model of bureaucrat–citizen interaction is that it assumes that the people brought together to 'deliberate' have equal (or, for that matter, any) desire or capacity to do so. As noted above, grafting increased deliberation onto a society of stark social and economic inequalities is likely to exaggerate those inequalities, as those people with greater resources, better education, and more stature would tend to dominate the discussion and disproportionately influence the resulting consensus (Young, 1990). It is difficult for the best argument in a public debate to succeed if some people can purchase advertising space on television and others cannot. A second approach seeks to address this imbalance in communicative skills and participatory opportunities through more direct bureaucratic intervention. In both cases, the initiative towards citizen empowerment cannot succeed without bureaucratic support and, in some cases, bureaucratic initiative (see Table 15.1).

Table 15.1 Substantive Citizen Empowerment: the Bureaucratic Commitment

Bureaucrats should facilitate public deliberation about public policy.
Bureaucrats should consult with citizens before reaching decisions.
Bureaucrats should adopt frameworks of engagement with vulnerable citizens.
Bureaucrats should foster relationships of mutuality and trust with citizens.
Bureaucrats should be accountable directly to those citizens who depend on their decisions.

In this **bureaucratic engagement model**, public officials do not serve only as neutral moderators and arbiters of public deliberation but instead are encouraged to form personal and meaningful relationships with citizens (especially vulnerable or disadvantaged citizens) to ensure their interests are adequately represented in the public domain. The goal of engagement is not to undermine existing bureaucratic channels but rather to transform them. Joel Handler has emphasized that the task of public officials should be to break down hierarchies and 'explicitly introduce values, commitments, and intuitions . . . to create the conditions whereby people talk to each other' (Handler, 1988). Jennifer Nedelsky (1993: 7–8) sees this process as replacing a rights-based discourse with one premised on relationships. This requires giving public officials increased discretion to form such relationships and reconceiving the basic normative foundations of public administration to accommodate attachment rather than detachment. On this view, values such as trust, engagement, and self-disclosure would come to characterize bureaucratic behaviour.

Substantive citizen involvement in the administrative process would require a fundamental restructuring of bureaucratic norms that would transcend the labels of the New Left and New Right. Such a restructuring would have as its goal a form of public administration in which public officials would view their interaction with citizens on a similar footing to their interaction with political officials—as a source of authority, legitimacy, and policy direction. To achieve this goal, public officials would have to mediate (and perhaps even facilitate) a vast and potentially unwieldy public deliberative process, as well as remain responsive to their political masters.[11] By the same token, citizens would have to demand a far more active role in everyday governance (Stivers, 1990). Facilitating such demands will require a substantial economic and social investment by the state.

Notwithstanding some sporadically successful experiments in democratic administration, it may not be realistic to expect governments to change their thinking in such a fundamental fashion unless compelled to do so. For example, for as long as there has been a Canadian state, Aboriginal groups have been demanding a greater say in state decisions which affect their lands, customs, and interests. With key Supreme Court of Canada decisions as a catalyst, Canadian and provincial governments have entered into arrangements with Aboriginal peoples giving Aboriginal communities unprecedented new roles in their own government. One such arrangement, the territory of Nunavut, came into existence in April, 1999 with a pledge to conduct public administration in a fashion consistent with Inuit tradition and culture. Another such arrangement, the Nisga'a Lisims Government established through a treaty in 2000, between the Nisga'a people and the governments of Canada and British Columbia, recognizes the Nisga'a nation's right to self-government. A third arrangement, created by the Supreme Court in the 2004 *Haida Nation* decision, imposes a duty on all government officials to consult with Aboriginal people whose claimed land may be affected by a government decision (such as allowing a mining company to exploit mineral resources in disputed land). This 'duty to consult' includes not only a requirement that affected Aboriginal communities have an opportunity to express their concerns, but also the requirement that those concerns be accommodated by government.

Changes in the relationship between government and those affected by their decisions, whether resulting from confrontation, litigation, negotiation, co-optation, or infiltration, could well have far-reaching and unanticipated consequences for bureaucratic life. Realizing a substantive democratic form of public administration will increase the importance of those the state recruits into the bureaucracy; of how those recruits are trained, evaluated, and promoted; of how bureaucratic offices are organized; of the professional and ethical rules of conduct that govern administrative action; and, perhaps most importantly, of the legislation by which public officials are empowered to act, which sets out the criteria to guide their decision-making. To take one example, what will the bureaucracy of Aboriginal self-government look like? Will it operate on principles of hierarchy or consensus? Will it feature different relations with elected branches of government than those in the Westminster system which operates in the rest of Canada?

According to advocates of democratic administration, the result of transformations such as Aboriginal self-government may well be a more representative and responsive public service. It raises questions about how the public service might change as a result of multiculturalism in Canada and the desire to have a bureaucracy that reflects the society it serves (Sossin, 2006b).

In short, democratic administration posits a new ideal-type of public administration, one that aims at attachment rather than detachment, relationships rather than isolation, transparency rather than secrecy, flexibility rather than rigidity. Thus, democratic administration sees the means *as an end* rather than only the means *to an end.*

The nature of this democratic ideal, however, precludes generalizing about its applications. Some kinds of bureaucratic settings have been democratized, at least to a point, with little upheaval (e.g., local environmental planning). Other settings require more imagination to envisage them as participatory venues (e.g., national budgetary planning). Democratic administration will have different implications for policy development than for service delivery. What may work in the context of a benefits program may not work in a regulatory context. The premise of democratic administration is simply that every bureaucratic setting can and should be evaluated according to how fully the goals of participation and accountability have been achieved.

Democratic administration is concerned not only with inward change, but also with external constraints. The state influences, and is influenced by, social and economic trends. Two related trends—the rise of new technologies and the increasing globalization of economic production—promise new possibilities and present new dangers for democratizing public administration in the twenty-first century (Diebert, 1997).

The first development is the rise of new technologies, most saliently the Internet, which has made possible (though not necessarily accessible) the widespread and effective dissemination of information as well as interactivity among citizens, officials, and politicians. A burgeoning literature on 'digital democracy' has begun exploring how citizen participation in government may be transformed by these new technologies. The Internet has opened up the possibility of citizens receiving information from and providing information to the government without the traditional intermediaries (e.g., the media, political parties, interest groups) (Grossman, 1995). According to Leslie Pal's study of political mobilization on the Internet, interconnectivity is 'intrinsic' to this medium, enhancing broader coalition-building and wider mobilization than would have been possible through conventional communications media (Pal, 1998: 113). The democratic participation that new technologies may usher in, however, also has a darker side. The lack of uniform access to computers and of the knowledge to use them may exacerbate existing social and economic inequalities (May, 1998), and the establishment of competing, overlapping, and unbounded 'virtual communities' may further fragment and atomize the democratic process (Cross, 1998).

The second development likely to shape the future of democratic administration is premised on a different kind of knowledge, one elusive to democratic input. Globalization threatens to remove citizens entirely from the realm of meaningful political decision-making. '**Globalization**' is the umbrella term for a number of interrelated movements culminating in the emergence of an international economic system beyond the control of any single state (Savoie, 1995). As Harry Arthurs has argued, this dynamic has special resonance in Canada:

> we are not only vulnerable to pressure from both foreign governments and foreign investors, we are acutely sensitive about our own vulnerability. Fluctuations in the Canadian dollar and in the market for Canadian bonds and securities, complaints (often spurious) about our 'unfair' trade practices, threats by multinationals to close Canadian plants or offers to expand them: such concerns cast their long shadow over virtually all aspects of public policy formation.... Thus, we make policy timidly, not merely because of possible domestic economic or political repercussions, not merely to avoid violating our treaty obligations, but because we do not wish to offend foreign investors or disquiet global markets. (Arthurs, 1997: 37)

This 'cult of impotence' in the face of global markets and foreign investors presents a real and tangible threat to democracy in Canada (McQuaig, 1998), as does the reality of globalization and its impact on the state (Clarkson and Lewis, 1999; Panitch, 1994; Boyer and Drache, 1996). In this scenario, the state, held hostage by global markets over which they have little or no influence, has no choice but to capitulate to corporate demands for less regulation and more access to resources, in order to avoid the pulling out of investment and jobs. The future of democratic administration is premised on the fallacy of this belief.

For advocates of democratic administration, globalization is a choice, not a fact, and one made by the state, not beyond it. Therefore, it should not be seen as obviating the possibility of participation and accountability; rather, it has created a new and critical arena in which to explore those possibilities. Flows of capital, jobs, and timber are all subject to state regulation and, therefore, permeable to more democratic forms of regulation. While the fear of scaring off foreign investment is a palpable risk, it is a palatable one if a substantial proportion of the population has indicated, through participation in the process, its willingness to shoulder the consequences in exchange for tighter environmental standards, better working conditions, or other socially desirable policy outcomes.

One reason why democratic administration is poised to become the dominant approach to public administration in the twenty-first century is the fear that new technologies and the 'new world order' are conspiring to render people powerless and democracy irrelevant. At the same time, faith in bureaucratic experts and political elites has steadily deteriorated. The very terms 'backroom' and 'closed-door' have come to connote a shadowy and suspect species of anti-democratic deal-making. These policies are now attacked, not because they are unsound or undesirable, but rather because they are developed without sufficient public involvement. The once far-fetched notion that the public is entitled to know about and influence the development and implementation of all major government policies now seems not just plausible but inevitable.

The roles of political parties, political staff, and partisan interests in bureaucratic settings have come under scrutiny as never before in the wake of the Gomery Inquiry. The view that the bureaucracy serves the Crown has been supplanted with the view that public officials serve the public interest. The question should no longer be whether politics and administration can be kept apart, but rather how bureaucracy might be transformed to legitimate its central role in political decision-making.[12] This question begs a larger one: what should be the purpose of the state in the twenty-first century? The study of democratic administration is directed towards addressing this question.

Important Terms and Concepts

bureaucratic engagement model
citizen engagement model
conventional bureaucracy
deliberative democracy
democratic administration
feminist analysis of the state
globalization
Keynesian welfare state
New Left
New Public Management
New Right
politics–administration dichotomy

Study Questions

1. What is 'conventional bureaucracy' and what indictments can be made against it?
2. Explain the rise and fall of Weberian bureaucracy.
3. What similarities and differences exist between the Old Left and the New Left?
4. What is 'New Right administrative thought' and what critiques of it does Sossin advance?
5. What difference could democratic administration make?
6. What are some external constraints that democratic administration faces? Are they insurmountable?
7. Assess the claim that democratic administration is poised to become the dominant approach in the twenty-first century.

Useful Websites

Collection of writings by and about Max Weber by Sociosite, Social Science Information System based at the University of Amsterdam:

www.sociosite.net/topics/weber.php

Habermas links (collected by Antti Kauppinen):

www.helsinki.fi/~amkauppi/hablinks.html

'Contemporary Philosophy', 'Critical Theory', and 'Postmodern Thought' links (collected by Martin Ryder, School of Education, University of Colorado at Denver):

http://carbon.ucdenver.edu/~mryder/itc_data/postmodern.html

'Critical Theory on the Web—Selected Links, (compiled by Dr Malinda S. Smith, University of Alberta):

www.arts.ualberta.ca/~courses/PoliticalScience/661B1/resources.htm

MASS LBP official website:

www.masslbp.com/journal.php

The Deliberative Democracy Consortium:

www.deliberative-democracy.net/

Involve:

www.involve.org.uk/

Supreme Court of Canada Aboriginal consult and accommodate decision—*Haida Nation v. British Columbia (Minister of Forests)* 2004 SCC 73:

http://csc.lexum.umontreal.ca/en/2004/2004scc73/2004scc73.html

Demos:

www.demos.co.uk/

PBS. *Commanding Heights: The Battle for the World Economy*. An interactive site dealing with issues of globalization:

www.pbs.org/wgbh/commandingheights/

PBS. *Commanding Heights* storyline:

www.pbs.org/wgbh/commandingheights/shared/minitext/tr_show01.html#1

BBC. 'On This Day'. Review of Prime Minister John Major's Citizens' Charter.

http://news.bbc.co.uk/onthisday/hi/dates/stories/july/22/newsid_2516000/2516139.stm

National Performance Review. *From Red Tape to Results: Creating a Government that Works Better and Costs Less: Report of the National Performance Review.*

http://govinfo.library.unt.edu/npr/library/nprrpt/annrpt/redtpe93/index.html

Notes

I would like to thank Geoffrey Kennedy for his excellent research assistance in the preparation of this chapter.

1. The Charter established six principles of public service: standards, information and openness, choice and consultation, courtesy and helpfulness, putting things right, and value for money. Public services are required under the Charter to set, monitor, and publicize the standards that citizens can expect, and a complaints mechanism has been established for citizens who believe these standards have not been met. See Woodhouse (1997: 49–51); Lovell (1992: 395–404).
2. Vice-President Al Gore's National Performance Review (NPR) set out in 1993 to transform the basic culture of federal organizations to make them more performance-based and customer-oriented (see Gore, 1993). For a review of the consequences of this initiative, see *Public Administration Review* (1996).
3. 'Democratic administration' should at the outset be distinguished from 'administrative democracy', which refers to the transformation of the administrative workplace along democratic lines. For discussion of democratizing bureaucracy from both within and without, see Frug (1990); Tuohy (1990). For other ways of distinguishing these concepts, see Pollitt (1986).
4. In Canada, the democratic process is entrenched by virtue of sections 3–5 of the Charter of Rights and Freedoms, under which a government must call an election within five years and must conduct the electoral process in a fair and lawful fashion.
5. It is worth noting that it is not just bureaucratic authority that has come under this criticism, but judicial authority as well, especially after the expansion of the scope of judicial review of government action with the enactment of the Constitution Act, 1982. See, for example, Monahan (1987); Mandel (1994).
6. See Wilson (1887), in which Woodrow Wilson distinguishes between political questions (about the ends of government action) and administrative

questions (about the means of government action). See also Goodnow (1900). It is worth recalling that Wilson's justification for the isolation of administration from politics was the strengthening of democracy by providing a 'counterweight' to the vagaries of the popular will. For a discussion of this position, see Waldo (1952).

7. While some early public administration theorists devoted attention to the value of public participation (see, notably, Metcalfe and Urwick, 1940), this idea first received widespread scholarly attention with the publication of Carole Pateman's *Participation and Democratic Theory* (1970). For a discussion of the development of public administration theory, see McSwite (1997: 198–237).

8. For a notable exception, see Forester (1985).

9. As John Shields and Brian Evans (1998: 56) explain, 'Marketization of the state and the broader public sector is viewed, from a neo-liberal perspective, as the proper means of reintroducing effectiveness and efficiency into the public sector. The fundamental principles of the state marketization thesis are the conversion of citizens into consumers and the commodification of public goods. The restructuring of the public sector through privatization, commercialization and contracting out provides the means for imposing market discipline upon public sector organizations by demanding competitive delivery of public services and establishing trends towards user pay systems, economic incentives for improved efficiency and more stringent financial accountability. . . . This concept is often captured in the term 'entrepreneurial government' which refers to the kinds of governments and administrations that can anticipate problems, are free to react in the most appropriate manner and can encourage competition, especially with respect to enhancing consumer choice.'

10. On the New Right, see Campbell (1999); on the New Left, see Panitch and Leys (1997).

11. Calls for such widespread public deliberation have until now been associated with major policy initiatives, such as constitutional amendments or new social contracts. See, for example, Simeon (1994).

12. The politics–administration dichotomy has proven curiously resilient. As Donald Savoie (1994: 23) asserts, 'Although there are now precious few students of public administration who still adhere to the politics–administration dichotomy to explain how the real world of government actually works, the principle still haunts many public services and individual government officials. Government bureaus everywhere cling to the difference between policy decisions and policy execution in describing their work: decisions flow from politics and execution from administration, they insist.'

References

Adams, Guy B., Priscilla V. Bowerman, Kenneth M. Dolbeare, and Camilla Stivers. 1990. 'Joining Purpose to Practice: A Democratic Identity for the Public Service', in H. Kass and B. Catron, eds, *Images and Identities in Public Administration*. London: Sage, 219–40.

Albo, Greg. 1993. 'Democratic Citizenship and the Future of Public Management', in Albo et al. (1993; 17–33).

———, Leo Panitch, and David Langille, eds. 1993. *A Different Kind of State? Popular Power and Democratic Administration*. Toronto: Oxford University Press.

Alden, Edward. 1999. 'US. Companies Go on Spree in Canada's Bargain Basement', *Financial Times*, 7 July, 5.

Alexander, Cynthia J., and Leslie A. Pal, eds. 1998a. *Digital Democracy: Policy and Politics in the Wired World*. Toronto: Oxford University Press.

———, and ———. 1998b. 'Introduction: New Currents in Politics and Policy', in Alexander and Pal (1998a: 1–22).

Alexander, Jeffrey. 1991. 'Habermas and Critical Theory: Beyond the Marxian Dilemma?', in Axel Honneth and Hans Joas, eds, *Communicative Action*. Cambridge, Mass.: MIT Press, 49–73.

Arthurs, Harry. 1997. 'Mechanical Arts and Merchandise: Canadian Public Administration and the New Economy', *McGill Law Journal* 42: 29–61.

Aucoin, Peter. 1995. 'Politicians, Public Servants and Public Management: Getting Government Right', in Peters and Savoie (1995: 113–37).

Babe, Barry. 1994. 'Beyond NIMBY: Participatory Approaches to Hazardous Waste Management in Canada and the United States', in Fischer and Sirianni (1994: 622–43).

Banting, Keith. 1987. *The Welfare State and Canadian Federalism*, 2nd edn. Montreal and Kingston: McGill-Queen's University Press.

Barber, Benjamin. 1984. *Strong Democracy: Participatory Politics for a New Age*. Berkeley: University of California Press.

———, et al. 1997. *The State of 'Electronically Enhanced Democracy': A Survey of the Internet*. Rutgers, New Jersey: Walt Whitman Center for the Culture and Politics of Democracy, Department of Political Science, Rutgers University.

Benhabib, Seyla. 1992. *Situating the Self.* New York: Routledge.

Berger, Thomas. 1977. *Northern Frontier/Northern Homeland,* 2 vols. Ottawa: Supply and Services Canada.

Boyer, R., and D. Drache. 1996. *States Against Markets: The Limits of Globalization.* London: Routledge.

Brown, Wendy. 1992. 'Finding the Man in the State', *Feminist Studies* 18, 1: 7–34.

Cairns, Alan. 1990. 'The Past and Future of the Canadian Administrative State', *University of Toronto Law Journal* 40: 320–61.

Campbell, R. 1999. 'The Fourth Fiscal Era: Can There Be a "Post-Neo-Conservative" Fiscal Policy?', in Pal (1999: 113–50).

Carroll, William K., ed. 1992. *Organizing Dissent: Contemporary Social Movements in Theory and Practice.* Toronto: Garamond Press.

Cartier, Genevieve. 2005. 'Willis and the Contemporary Administrative State: Administrative Discretion as Dialogue', *University of Toronto Law Journal:* 629–656.

Clarkson, S., and T. Lewis. 1999. 'The Contested State: Canada in the Post-Cold War, Post-Keynesian, Post-Fordist, Post-National Era', in Pal (1999: 293–340).

Cohen, Joshua. 1997. 'Deliberation and Democratic Legitimacy', in James Bohman and William Rehg, eds, *Deliberative Democracy: Essays on Reason and Politics.* Cambridge, Mass.: MIT Press, 67–92.

Cross, Bill. 1998. 'Teledemocracy: Canadian Political Parties Listening to their Constituents', in Alexander and Pal (1998a: 132–48).

Cunningham, Frank. 1987. *Democratic Theory and Socialism.* Cambridge: Cambridge University Press.

Dallmayr, Fred. 1994. 'Max Weber and the Modern State', in Asher Horowitz and Terry Maley, eds, *The Barbarism of Reason: Max Weber and the Twilight of Enlightenment.* Toronto: University of Toronto Press, 49–67.

Daniels, Robert, and Michael Trebilcock. 2005. *Rethinking the Welfare State: Government by Voucher.* London: Routledge.

Diebert, Ronald J. 1997. *Parchment, Printing and Hypermedia: Communication in World Order Transformation.* New York: Columbia University Press.

Diller, Matthew. 2000. 'The Revolution in Welfare Administration: Rules, Discretion, and Entrepreneurial Government', *New York University Law Review* 75: 1121–220.

Dorcey, A.H.J., and T. McDaniels, 2001. 'Great Expectations, Mixed Results: Trends in Citizen Involvement in Canadian Environmental Governance', in E.A. Parson, ed., *Governing the Environment: Persistent Challenges, Uncertain Innovations.* Toronto: University of Toronto Press.

Dryzek, J.S. 1994. 'Ecology and Discursive Democracy: Beyond Liberal Capitalism and the Administrative State', in M. O'Connor, ed., *Is Capitalism Sustainable?* New York: Guilford, 176–97.

Etzioni-Halevy, Eva. 1985. *Bureaucracy and Democracy: A Political Dilemma.* London: Routledge & Kegan Paul.

Fallon, Richard H., Jr. 1989. 'What Is Republicanism and Is It Worth Reviving?', *Harvard Law Review* 102: 1695–735.

Ferguson, Kathy. 1984. *The Feminist Case Against Bureaucracy,* 2nd edn. Philadelphia: Temple University Press.

Findlay, S. 1993. 'Democratizing the Local State: Issues for Feminist Practice and the Representation of Women', in Albo et al. (1993: 155–64).

Fischer, Frank, and Carmen Sirianni, eds. 1994. *Critical Studies in Organization and Democracy.* Philadelphia: Temple University Press.

Forester, John, ed. 1985. *Critical Theory and Public Life.* Cambridge, Mass.: MIT Press.

Fox, C., and H. Miller. 1995. *Postmodern Public Administration: Toward Discourse.* Thousand Oaks, Calif.: Sage.

Fraser, Nancy. 1985. 'What's Critical about Critical Theory: The Case of Habermas and Gender', *New German Critique* 35: 97–131.

———. 1990. 'Struggle Over Needs: Outline of a Socialist–Feminist Critical Theory of Late-Capitalist Political Culture', in Linda Gordon, ed., *Women, the State, and Welfare.* Madison: University of Wisconsin Press.

———. 1997. 'Rethinking the Public Sphere', in Fraser, ed., *Justice Interruptus.* New York: Routledge.

Frug, Gerald. 1984. 'The Ideology of Bureaucracy in American Law', *Harvard Law Review* 97: 1276–1388.

———. 1990. 'Administrative Democracy', *University of Toronto Law Journal* 40: 559–86.

Goodnow, Frank. 1900. *Politics and Administration.* New York: Macmillan.

Goodsell, Charles. 1994. *The Case for Bureaucracy,* 3rd edn. Chatham, NJ: Chatham House.

Gore, Albert. 1993. *From Red Tape to Results: Creating a Government that Works Better and Costs Less: Report of the National Performance Review.* New York: Plume Books.

Gould, Carol. 1988. *Rethinking Democracy.* Cambridge: Cambridge University Press.

Graves, Frank. 1999. 'Rethinking Government as if People Mattered: From "Reaganomics" to "Humanomics"', in Pal (1999: 37–74).

Grossman, Lawrence K. 1995. *The Electronic Republic: Reshaping Democracy in the Information Age.* New York: Viking.

Guest, D. 1985. *The Emergence of Social Security in Canada,* 2nd edn. Vancouver: University of British Columbia Press.

Habermas, Jürgen. 1987. *Theory of Communicative Action: Lifeworld and System.* Boston: Beacon Press.

———. 1990a. 'The New Obscurity: The Crisis of the Welfare State and the Exhaustion of Utopian Energies', in Habermas, ed., *The New Conservatism: Cultural Criticism and the Historian's Debate,* trans. S. Nicholson. Cambridge, Mass.: MIT Press, 48–70.

———. 1990b. 'Discourse Ethics: Notes on a Program of Philosophical Justification', in Seyla Benhabib and Fred Dallmayr, eds, *The Communicative Ethics Controversy.* Cambridge, Mass.: MIT Press, 60–110.

Hague, Barry, and Brian London. 1999. *Digital Democracy: Discourse and Decision-Making in the Age of Information.* London: Routledge.

Hall, Michael, and Paul B. Reed. 1996. 'Shifting the Burden: How Much Can Government Download to the Non-profit Sector?', *Canadian Public Administration* 41: 1–20.

Handler, Joel F. 1986. *The Conditions of Discretion: Autonomy, Community, Bureaucracy.* New York: Russell Sage.

———. 1988. 'Dependent People, the State, and the Modern/Postmodern Search for the Dialogic Community', *UCLA Law Review* 35: 999–1113.

———. 1992. 'Discretion: Power, Quiescence, and Trust', in Keith Hawkins, ed., *The Uses of Discretion*. Oxford: Clarendon Press, 331–60.

———. 1996. *Down From Bureaucracy: The Ambiguity of Privatization and Empowerment*. Princeton, NJ: Princeton University Press.

Hoover, K., and R. Plant. 1989. *Conservative Capitalism in Britain and the United States*. London: Routledge.

Howse, Robert. 1993. 'Retrenchment, Reform or Revolution? The Shift to Incentives and the Future of the Regulatory State', *Alberta Law Review* 31: 455–92.

———, Robert Pritchard, and Michael Trebilcock. 1990. 'Smaller or Smarter Government?', *University of Toronto Law Journal* 40: 498–558.

Hummel, Ralph P. 1982. *The Bureaucratic Experience*. New York: Free Press.

Katz, Michael. 1989. *The Undeserving Poor: From the War on Poverty to the War on Welfare*. New York: Pantheon.

Kernaghan, Kenneth, and David Seigel. 1991. *Public Administration in Canada*, 2nd edn. Toronto: Nelson.

Kettl, D. 1995. 'Building Lasting Reform: Enduring Questions, Missing Reforms', in Kettl and J. Dilulio Jr, eds, *Inside the Reinvention Machine: Appraising Government Reform*. Washington: Brookings Institution, 14–83.

Kramer, Ralph. 1994. 'Voluntary Agencies and the Contract Culture: Dream or Nightmare?', *Social Service Review* 68: 33–60.

Kristol, Irving. 1995. *Neoconservatism: Autobiography of an Idea*. New York: Free Press.

Lenin, V.I. 1926. *The State and Revolution*. New York: Vanguard Press.

Levitan, Sar A. 1969. *The Great Society's Poor Law: A New Approach to Poverty*. Baltimore: Johns Hopkins University Press.

Lindblom, Charles. 1959. 'The Science of Muddling Through', *Public Administration Review* 19: 79–88.

Lovell, Roger. 1992. 'Citizen's Charter: The Cultural Challenge', *Public Administration* 70: 395–404.

Loxley, John. 1993. 'Democratizing Economic Policy Formulation: The Manitoba Experience', in Albo et al. (1993: 186–94).

McBride, Steven, and John Shields. 1997. *Dismantling a Nation: The Transition to Corporate Rule in Canada*, 2nd edn. Halifax: Fernwood.

McGregor, Douglas. 1960. *The Human Side of Enterprise*. New York: McGraw-Hill.

MacKinnon, Catherine. 1989. *Toward a Feminist Theory of the State*. Cambridge, Mass.: Harvard University Press.

McQuaig, Linda. 1998. *The Cult of Impotence*. Toronto: Penguin.

McSwite, O.C. [pseudonym for Orion F. White and Cynthia J. McSwain]. 1997. *Legitimacy in Public Administration: A Discourse Analysis*. Thousand Oaks, Calif.: Sage.

Magnusson, Warren. 1993. 'Social Movements and the State: Presentation and Representation', in Albo et al. (1993: 122–30).

Mandel, Michael. 1994. *The Charter of Rights and Freedoms and the Legalization of Politics in Canada*, rev edn. Toronto: Thompson.

Marx, Karl. 1978. 'Contribution to the Critique of Hegel's Philosophy of Right', in Robert C. Tucker, ed., *The Marx–Engels Reader*. New York: Norton, 16–25.

May, James H. 1998. 'Information Technology for Indigenous Peoples: The North American Experience', in Alexander and Pal (1998a: 219–37).

Mazmanian, Daniel, and Jeanne Nienaber. 1994. 'Fishbowl Planning: Environmental Regulation, Economic Development and Democratic Technique', in Fischer and Sirianni (1994: 601–21).

Metcalfe, H.C., and L. Urwick, eds. 1940. *Dynamic Administration: The Collected Papers of Mary Parker Follett*. New York: Harper.

Miliband, Ralph. 1969. *The State in Capitalist Society*. London: Weidenfeld & Nicholson.

Monahan, Patrick. 1987. *Politics and the Constitution*. Toronto: Carswell.

Munroe, James A. 1990. *The Democratic Wish: Popular Participation and the Limits of American Government*. New York: Basic Books.

Nedelsky, Jennifer. 1989. 'Reconceiving Autonomy: Sources, Thoughts and Possibilities', *Yale Journal of Law & Feminism* 1: 7–33.

———. 1993. 'Reconceiving Rights as Relationship', *Review of Constitutional Studies* 1: 1–26.

Nevitte, Neil. 1996. *The Decline of Deference*. Peterborough, Ont.: Broadview Press.

Nordlinger, Eric. 1981. *On the Autonomy of the Democratic State*. Cambridge, Mass.: Harvard University Press.

Osborne, D., and T. Gaebler. 1993. *Reinventing Government: How the Entrepreneurial Spirit Is Transforming the Public Sector*. New York: Penguin.

Paehlke, Robert. 1989. *Environmentalism and the Future of Progressive Politics*. New Haven: Yale University Press.

———. 1990. 'Democracy and Environmentalism: Opening a Door to the Administrative State', in Paehlke and Douglas Torgerson, eds, *Managing Leviathan: Environmental Politics and the Administrative State*. Peterborough, Ont.: Broadview Press, 35–55.

Pal, Leslie. 1998. 'A Thousand Points of Darkness: Electronic Mobilization and the Case of the Communications Decency Act', in Alexander and Pal (1998a: 105–31).

———, ed. 1999. *How Ottawa Spends 1999–2000. Shape Shifting: Canadian Governance Toward the 21st Century*. Toronto: Oxford University Press.

Panitch, Leo. 1993. 'A Different Kind of State?', in Albo et al. (1993: 2–16).

———. 1994. 'Globalization and the State', *Socialist Register, 1994*. London: Merlin.

———, and Colin Leys. 1997. *The End of Parliamentary Socialism: From New Left to New Labour*. London: Verso.

Pateman, Carole. 1970. *Participation and Democratic Theory*. Cambridge: Cambridge University Press.

Peters, B. Guy, and Donald Savoie. 1993. *Reinventing Osborne and Gaebler: Lessons from the Gore Commission*. Ottawa: Canadian Centre for Management Development.

———, and ———, eds. 1995. *Governance in a Changing Environment*. Montreal and Kingston: McGill-Queen's University Press.

Phillips, A. 1991. *Engendering Democracy*. University Park: Pennsylvania State University Press.

Pierre, Jon. 1995. 'The Marketization of the State: Citizens, Consumers and the Emergence of the Public Market', in Peters and Savoie (1995: 55–81).

Piven, Frances Fox, and Robert Cloward. 1993. *Regulating the Poor: The Functions of Welfare*. New York: Vintage.

Pollitt, Christopher. 1986. 'Democracy and Bureaucracy', in David Held and Christopher Pollitt, eds, *New Forms of Democracy*. London: Sage, 158–91.

Poulantzas, Nicos. 1973. *Political Power and Social Classes*, trans. Timothy O'Hagen. London: New Left Books.

Public Administration Review. 1996. Symposium on 'Reinventing Public Administration', 56: 245–304.

Reid, Grant. 1993. 'Public Participation in Welfare: The Winnipeg Child and Family Services System', in Albo et al. (1993: 195–207).

Savoie, Donald J. 1990. *The Politics of Public Spending in Canada*. Toronto: University of Toronto Press.

———. 1994. *Thatcher, Reagan, Mulroney: In Search of a New Bureaucracy*. Pittsburgh: University of Pittsburgh Press.

———. 1995. 'Globalization, Nation States and the Civil Service', in Peters and Savoie (1995: 82–112).

Seccombe, Wally. 1993. 'Democracy and Ecology: Envisioning the Transition to a Green Economy', in Albo et al. (1993: 101–9).

Seidenfeld, Mark. 1992. 'A Civic Republican Justification for the Bureaucratic State', *Harvard Law Review* 105: 1511–76.

Shields, John, and B. Mitchell Evans. 1998. *Shrinking the State: Globalization and Public Administration 'Reform'*. Halifax: Fernwood.

Simeon, Richard. 1994. *In Search of a Social Contract: Can We Make Hard Decisions as if Democracy Matters?* Toronto: C.D. Howe Institute.

Simon, William. 1983. 'Legality, Bureaucracy and Class in the Welfare System', *Yale Law Journal* 92: 1198–269.

Simpson, Jeffrey. 1988. *Spoils of Power: The Politics of Patronage*. Toronto: W. Collins & Sons.

Skowronek, Steven. 1982. *Building a New American State*. New York: Cambridge University Press.

Smith, David E. 2006. 'Clarifying the Doctrine of Ministerial Responsibility as it Applies to the Government and Parliament of Canada', in *Commission of Inquiry into the Sponsorship Program and Advertising Activities; Restoring Accountability*, Research Studies, Volume 3 (*Linkages: Responsibilities and Accountabilities*). Ottawa: PWGSC.

Sossin, Lorne. 1993. 'The Politics of Discretion: Towards a Critical Theory of Public Administration', *Canadian Public Administration* 36: 364–91.

———. 1994. 'Redistributing Democracy: Authority, Discretion and the Possibility of Engagement in the Welfare State', *Ottawa Law Review* 26: 1–46.

———. 2002. 'Law and Intimacy in the Bureaucrat–Citizen Relationship', in N. des Rosiers, ed., *No Person is an Island: Personal Relationships of Dependence and Independence*. Vancouver: University of British Columbia Press, 120–54.

———. 2004. 'Boldly Going Where No Law Has Gone Before: Call Centres, Intake Scripts, Database Fields and Discretionary Justice in Social Welfare', *Osgoode Hall Law Journal* 42: 363–414.

———. 2006a. 'Oversight of Executive-Police Relations in Canada: The Constitution, The Courts, Administrative Processes and Democratic Governance', in M. Beare and T. Murray, *Police and Government Relations: Who's Calling the Shots?* Toronto: University of Toronto Press, 96–127.

———. 2006b. 'Discretion and the Culture of Justice', *Singapore Journal of Legal Studies* (December): 356–84.

Stivers, Camilla. 1990. 'Active Citizenship and Public Administration', in G.L. Wamsley et al., eds, *Refounding Public Administration*. Thousand Oaks, Calif.: Sage, 246–73.

———. 1993. *Gender Images in Public Administration: Legitimacy and the Administrative State*. Newbury Park, Calif.: Sage.

Sutherland, S. 1991. 'Responsible Government and Ministerial Responsibility: Every Reform Is Its Own Problem', *Canadian Journal of Political Science* 24: 91–120.

Taylor, F.W. 1947. *Scientific Management*. New York: Harper.

Trebilcock, Michael. 1994. *The Prospects for Reinventing Government*. Toronto: C.D. Howe Institute.

Tsagarousianou, R., et al., eds. 1998. *Cyberdemocracy: Technology, Cities, and Civic Networks*. New York: Routledge.

Tuohy, Carolyn. 1990. 'Bureaucracy and Democracy', *University of Toronto Law Journal* 40: 598–605.

Unger, Roberto. 1975. *Knowledge & Politics*. New York: Free Press.

Wainwright, Hilary. 1987. *A Taste of Power: The Politics of Local Economics*. London: Verso.

———. 1993. 'A New Kind of Knowledge for a New Kind of State', in Albo et al. (1993: 112–21).

Waldo, Dwight. 1940. *The Administrative State*. New York: Ronald Press.

———. 1952. 'Development of a Theory of Democratic Administration', *American Political Science Review* 47: 81–103.

Weber, Max. 1947. *The Theory of Social and Economic Organization*, trans. A.M. Henderson. New York: Free Press.

———. 1958. *The Protestant Ethic and the Spirit of Capitalism*, trans. T. Parsons. New York: Charles Scribner & Sons.

Wilson, Woodrow. 1887. 'The Study of Administration', *Political Science Quarterly* 2, 1: 197–222.

Woodhouse, Diana. 1997. *In Pursuit of Good Administration: Ministers, Civil Servants and Judges*. Oxford: Clarendon Press.

Young, Iris Marion. 1990. *Justice and the Politics of Difference*. Princeton, NJ.: Princeton University Press.

PART V

Changing Expectations of Government

As Kenneth Kernaghan reminds us in Chapter 16, different eras in public sector reform are distinguished by different sets of values. Recently *traditional values* in the public sector (accountability, efficiency, integrity, neutrality, responsiveness, and representativeness) have been challenged by *new values* (service, innovation, quality, teamwork). Yet values are not the only core ideas in Canadian public service: constitutional conventions are intimately linked with public service values. The three conventions integral to the Canadian system (the 'East Block conventions') are (1) ministerial responsibility, (2) public service anonymity, and (3) political neutrality. Kernaghan traces the action of all three in constructing Canada's values and ethics regime since 2003.

A shift in government expectations may not yield the changes expected, as B. Mitchell Evans and John Shields explain in Chapter 17, examining the role of the 'third sector' in Canadian politics and society. In an era of neo-liberal restructuring, the state has encouraged a new expectation of the third sector—partnership. Partnership implies—in its broadest definition—sharing power, a common forum for dialogue, and multi-actor input into policy development. This has not happened. The new arrangements—adoption of NPM, a changing conception of governance, and reconceptualization of state, market, and societal boundaries—engendered new expectations of the role of third-sector agencies. Rather than being agents of community, solidarity, and collective responsibility, they are however increasingly agents of the state, or 'shadow state'. As quasi-governmental agents, they often must forgo important research and advocacy to focus on producing the results required by government. Evans and Shields regret that neo-liberal restructuring contributes to deteriorating social cohesion and hampers the development of social capital. Notions of community, solidarity, and collective responsibility are being displaced by an atomized society where the ethic of what C.B. Macpherson critiqued as 'possessive individualism' prevails.

In Chapter 18, Caroline Andrew cautions against simplistic forecasts about women in the public sector. She wants scholarship to abandon ideas of 'linear progress' with an ineluctable improvement in women's status; to focus on resistance to women's entry; and to abandon a view of women as homogeneous. The 1970 report of the Royal Commission on the Status of Women sparked optimism that public sector structures could achieve equality for women. By the late 1980s resistance to women's greater involvement had developed, necessitating a Task Force on Barriers to Women in the Public Service. Since then, there have been innovations aimed at promoting women's participation, but their effects are problematic. New macroeconomic, political, and administrative movements can prevail over specific machinery. Women in the public sector must be analyzed in terms of public–private sector relations, and the differential impacts of public policy on women and men better understood.

Robert Shepherd covers First Nations' and governments' contrasting expectations of Aboriginal governance today. For government officials, community mismanagement stems from the lack of financial aid and policy control. For First Nations, it occurs as a result of systemic problems associated with financial dependency and 'outside' control over their affairs, which breeds lackadaisical attitudes towards financial and organizational performance. Lack of agreement about the nature of the problem of accountability has led both sides to pose incompatible solutions. For government, it is more stringent bureaucratic controls; for First Nations it is a separation of First Nations and Canadian governance. One important challenge, moreover, derives from the governance models in play. Shepherd examines the complications of promising the 'inherent right' of self-government, only to deliver the weaker 'delegated' self-government model. The latter goes hand in hand with the restrictive New Public Management practised by federal authorities.

Annis May Timpson explores in Chapter 20 how Inuit values, culture, and language are being embedded in the design, operation, and policy of Nunavut's territorial government, which serves all its citizens, regardless of ethnicity. Its Inuit orientation ensures both the full employment and full representation of Aboriginal citizens in the territory, and the embedding of Inuit culture and language in government operations. Article 23 of the Nunavut Land Claims Agreement specifies that staffing of both territorial and federal public services in Nunavut should reflect the territory's ethnic composition. As roughly 85 per cent of Nunavut's population is Inuit, it will likely become the first North American jurisdiction with a public service predominantly staffed by Aboriginal people. The challenges lie in achieving this objective while delivering services to residents of 28 small communities spread over one-fifth of Canada's land mass, and ensuring that the elected territorial government responds to the needs of its Aboriginal population.

One of the most striking examples of changing expectations—the possibility of a distinct identity for the public service of Canada—comes in Chapter 21, where Lorne Sossin argues that there are two versions of the role of the public service. One version grants the public service little independence. A key constitutional principle says that no public servant can make a decision not authorized by a statute or government. The alternative view, taken by Sossin, is that the public service is an organ of government. While public servants owe loyalty to the government of the day, they also must be able to exercise independence to protect the neutrality of the public service and the rule of law. Even though Canada's constitutional texts are silent on the role and responsibilities of the public service, the courts have recognized a range of unwritten constitutional conventions and principles which give rise to obligations, responsibilities, and constraints on the public service. Together, argues Sossin, these confer constitutional status on the public service as an organ of government. However, if bureaucratic independence is to be a reality, the public service must distinguish between loyalty to the government and its higher duty to the Crown.

16 East Block and Westminster: *Conventions, Values, and Public Service*

Kenneth Kernaghan

Introduction

'Westminster conventions', that is, non-legal rules of the British constitution, are central to the operation of Canada's parliamentary democracy. Indeed, the preamble to Canada's founding constitutional document—the British North America Act, 1867—states that Canada is to have 'a constitution similar in principle to that of the United Kingdom'. **Constitutional conventions** are 'rules that define major non-legal rights, powers and obligations of office-holders in the three branches of government, or the relations between governments or organs of government' (Marshall, 1984: 210). These conventions are frequently described as principles or, less commonly, as doctrines, traditions, or customs. While they are crucial components of the constitution, they are not set out in written form. They are of enduring importance but they are subject over time to gradual change in their interpretation and application.

Three constitutional conventions—ministerial responsibility, public service anonymity, and political neutrality—have extremely important implications for the public service in Canada's federal and provincial governments. These governments, unlike municipal governments, are modelled on the Westminster system of cabinet-parliamentary government. To distinguish the Canadian version of these three conventions from usage in Britain and in other Westminster-style democracies, the conventions are described here, symbolically, as the *East Block* conventions. The East Block 'is the oldest essentially unaltered structure on Parliament Hill.... in the course of more than a century most government departments at some time were centred there.... In the year of Confederation, it was even possible to have thirteen branches of government housed within it' (Pearson, 1967).

The East Block conventions provide a framework for determining the nature and propriety of relationships among politicians, public servants, and the public. These conventions are closely related to **public service values**, which are enduring beliefs that influence the choices public servants make from among available means and ends. The conventions are especially tightly linked to such *democratic* values as accountability, loyalty, and impartiality. In fact, the conventions themselves are sometimes treated as values in that they constitute enduring beliefs that influence public servants' attitudes, actions, and choices. Political neutrality, in particular, is often referred to as a public service value as well as a constitutional convention.

In general, three features of the East Block conventions distinguish them from public service values. First, the conventions have constitutional status. Second, they are interdependent parts of a coherent system: a change in one usually results in a change in one or both of the others. While some public service values (e.g., representativeness and responsiveness) can be interdependent, values are often in a state of tension or conflict (e.g., accountability versus efficiency). Like the East Block conventions, public service values have considerable staying power, but changes in their meaning and application occur over time—and new values emerge. Third, public servants do not commonly perceive the East Block conventions as values; none of them appeared among the top 20 values in a 1994 study of public organizations in Canada (Kernaghan, 1994a: 620). However, accountability, which is closely tied to the convention of ministerial responsibility, ranked near the top of the list.

The interpretation and application of public service conventions and values are influenced by a wide variety of political, economic, and social factors. For example, the decision by political executives to restructure and downsize the public service led to the adoption of new forms of organization and new approaches to management that, as explained later, have significant consequences for conventions and values. This chapter examines these conventions and values, both separately and in relation to one another, with particular reference to recent and anticipated public service reforms. The chapter begins by explaining the meaning and evolution of the conventions of ministerial responsibility, political neutrality, and public service anonymity. The second section outlines the meaning and evolution of the concept of public service values. The third section examines the implications of public sector reforms for conventions and values, and the final section outlines predictions and prescriptions for the future.

The East Block Conventions

The East Block Conventions Defined

The essence of each convention is set out below. It will be evident that in practice both cabinet ministers and public servants have departed, sometimes significantly, from the requirements of these conventions.

Ministerial responsibility has both a collective dimension and an individual dimension. ***Collective* ministerial responsibility** (often described as cabinet responsibility) requires that ministers, in their capacity as members of the cabinet, are responsible for the policies and management of the government as a whole. If the government loses a vote of confidence in the legislature, it is required to resign. In addition, ministers are obliged to resign if they cannot support government decisions in public (or at least refrain from publicly criticizing them), regardless of their personal views about the decisions. ***Individual* ministerial responsibility** has two closely related components. First, ministers must resign in the event of a major error that they have personally committed or that has been committed by public servants in their department. Second, ministers must answer to the legislature, in the form of explanation or defence, for their own actions and for all of the actions of their departmental public servants.

Public service anonymity is a corollary of individual ministerial responsibility. It requires that public servants provide advice to ministers in confidence and refrain from activities that bring them into the public spotlight or involve them in public controversy. *Political neutrality* requires that public servants not engage in activities that impair or seem to impair their impartiality or the impartiality of the public service as a whole.

East Block Conventions and the Political Neutrality Model

As noted above, the East Block conventions are interdependent. For example, if a minister does not answer publicly for the actions of public servants, he or she may be drawn into the political arena to explain or defend those actions, in part perhaps by criticizing the minister. The result would be a diminution in their political neutrality and their anonymity—and, in all likelihood, their career prospects.

The intertwining of the conventions can be demonstrated by reference to an ideal model of **political neutrality** (Kernaghan, 1976). This model is composed of the East Block conventions. It provides an analytical framework for examining relationships between public servants and politicians, especially cabinet ministers, in a parliamentary democracy of the Westminster variety. The model is not ideal in the sense of most desirable; rather, it is an *ideal-type* construct depicting the characteristics of a public service that is neutral in an absolute or pristine sense. The components of the model are these:

1. Politics and policy are separated from administration; thus, politicians make policy decisions and public servants execute these decisions.
2. Public servants are appointed and promoted on the basis of **merit** rather than of party affiliation or contributions.
3. Public servants do not engage in partisan political activities.
4. Public servants do not express publicly their personal views on government policies or administration.
5. Public servants provide forthright and objective advice to their political masters in private and in confidence; in return, political executives protect the anonymity of public servants by publicly accepting responsibility for departmental decisions.
6. Public servants execute policy decisions loyally, irrespective of the philosophy and programs of the party in power and regardless of their personal opinions; as a result, public servants enjoy security of tenure during good behaviour and satisfactory performance.

As a public service or a particular public organization departs in practice from each of these characteristics, it becomes more politicized. The term 'politicization' refers here to the involvement of public servants not only in partisan political activities but also in politics in the broad sense of the authoritative allocation of social values through policy advice and policy implementation.

Evolution of the East Block Conventions

The evolution of the East Block conventions since Confederation is explained below by reference to each of the six components of the model of political neutrality.

Separation of Politics, Policy, and Administration

One of the most famous statements in the history of public administration is the 1887 assertion by Woodrow Wilson (later President of the United States) that 'the field of administration is a field of business. It is removed from the hurry and strife of politics...administrative questions are not political questions.... "Policy does nothing without the aid of administration", but administration is not therefore politics' (Wilson, 1966 [1887]). This statement of what is widely described as the **politics–administration dichotomy** was preceded by a more narrow but similar statement of a House of Commons Select Committee, which emphasized in 1877 the importance of separating politics from administration so as to promote the values of political neutrality and efficiency:

> As a general principle appointments, promotions and the whole management of the [public] service should be separated as far as possible from political considerations. The service should be looked upon merely as an organization for conducting the public business and not as a means of rewarding personal political friends. (Canada, House of Commons, 1877: 5)

There was recognition at this time also of the inevitability of public servants exercising power in the policy process and the likelihood of this power being used on occasion to obstruct the will of elected officials. George Casey, the head of the Select Committee, noted that:

> We all speak with horror of government by 'bureaucracy', but we forget that we can never wholly get rid of its influence. Every official must have some freedom of action in the interpretation and performance of his duties, some power to obstruct, facilitate, or prevent the operation of those laws with whose execution he is charged. (Casey, 1877: 83)

Thus, it was clear more than a century ago that politics and policy cannot in practice be easily separated. It soon became clear also that while elected officials have final authority over policy decisions, public servants have considerable influence on these decisions and exercise substantial power through their dominance of the policy implementation process. The balance of power between politicians and public servants was a constant issue during the twentieth century. As governments grew larger and more complicated, ministers became increasingly dependent for policy advice on the knowledge and experience of public servants. Over the period 1935–57, a small number of federal senior public servants, known as 'the mandarins', played an especially influential policy role in Canadian government (Granatstein, 1982; Kernaghan and McLeod, 1982). They were at the same time, however, strong proponents and practitioners of the East Block conventions.

By the early 1960s, the policy role had begun to be shared by a larger group of public servants. By this time also, the power of the public service had been more openly acknowledged. The Glassco Royal Commission on Government Organization concluded in 1962 that 'permanent officials are also participants in the exercise of power, rather than mere instruments through which it is wielded by ministers' (Canada, Royal Commission on Government Organization, 1962, vol. 5: 74). And Professor J.E. Hodgetts noted in 1964 that 'the shift from laissez-faire to collectivism has been accompanied by an unprecedented shift in the balance of real power, discretion and initiative—away from courts, legislatures and even cabinets to public servants' (Hodgetts, 1964: 421). The power of public servants in relation to other political actors has ebbed and flowed since the 1960s, depending to a large extent on the determination of the governing party to exercise political control over the public service. This story has been told elsewhere (Aucoin, 1995; Savoie, 1994; Mitchell and Sutherland, 1997). It is a story that demonstrates the difficulty, in practice, of separating politics and policy from administration.

Merit, Not Patronage

The pre-Confederation practice of appointing and promoting public servants on the basis of partisan political considerations rather than of merit continued unabated after Confederation. Vigorous efforts by reformers over a 50-year period led to the formal abolition of **patronage** appointments in the federal sphere by the Civil Service Act of 1918 (Canada, 1918). These efforts served the twin objectives of promoting the political neutrality and the efficiency of the public service.

A substantial number of patronage appointments continued to be made after 1918, but they were gradually reduced to the point where by the early 1960s such appointments had been largely eliminated from the regular departments of the federal government (Canada, Royal Commission on Government Organization, 1962: 371). However, in the provinces, most governments by this time still presented 'only the facade of a **merit system**, while combatting charges of patronage and personal favouritism in their public services' (Hodgetts and Dwivedi, 1976: 347). The provincial performance gradually improved after the mid-1960s, but some provinces have continued to make patronage appointments to the lower levels of the public service, and, on occasion, with a change in the governing party a substantial number of senior public servants have been replaced by political appointees.

In both the federal and provincial spheres, patronage appointments are still made to semi-independent agencies, boards, and commissions. While the hope is that governments will not risk embarrassment by appointing incompetent partisans to these bodies, there is less concern about these appointments than about the practice of appointing partisans to senior positions in regular government departments. Among the arguments against this practice is that political appointees block the career path of permanent public servants and they bring into government persons who may not share or understand the conventions and values of the public service.

No Political Partisanship

As a basis for assessing the propriety of public servants' participation in partisan politics, it is helpful to specify what kind of participation is at issue. For public servants, involvement in partisan politics can take the form of such modest activities as casting a vote or being a silent spectator at political meetings; but it can also take the form of such highly visible and potentially controversial activities as door-to-door fundraising and seeking elected office.

To combat patronage, public servants were prohibited from participation in virtually all forms of **partisan political activity** for a very large portion of Canadian history. The 1918 Civil Service Act provided, on pain of dismissal, that no deputy minister or other public servant 'shall engage in partisan work in connection with any election or contribute, receive or in any way deal with any money for party funds.' Despite the gradual decrease in patronage appointments after that time, these restraints were maintained until they were loosened somewhat by the Public Service Employment Act of 1967 (Canada, 1966–7). Under this Act, all public servants, with the exception of deputy ministers, were allowed to stand for election so long as the Public Service Commission was satisfied that the person's usefulness as a public servant would not be impaired. In addition, public servants were allowed to donate money to a political candidate or party and to attend political meetings. All other forms of political activity were prohibited until 1991, when the Supreme Court of Canada decided that most of the remaining constraints on the political rights of public servants were unduly restrictive (*Osborne v. Canada*, 1991).

The challenge has always been to achieve the greatest possible measure of **political rights for public servants** while maintaining the political neutrality and efficiency of the public service. The traditional arguments for *restricting* the political rights of public servants are these:

1. To preserve public trust in government, public servants must be—and must appear to be—politically impartial in the development and implementation of public policy. Members of the public must be assured that political affiliation is not a consideration in any dealings they may have with public servants.
2. Public servants must be—and must appear to be—politically impartial so as to retain the trust of political superiors who are dependent on them for objective policy advice and for effective policy implementation.
3. Opposition parties must have trust in the political impartiality of public servants so that there will not be a politically motivated turnover of public servants with a change of government.
4. The expansion of political partisanship may result in the re-emergence of the patronage system of hiring and promotion with a consequent decline in merit and in public service efficiency and effectiveness. Both the public and public servants must be assured that appointment and advancement in the service are based on merit rather than on party affiliation.
5. Public servants must be protected against financial or other forms of exploitation by political or administrative superiors who are affiliated with a specific political party or candidate.

The traditional arguments for *expanding* the political rights of public servants are these:

1. Public servants should be permitted to exercise the fundamental rights of freedom of expression and of association guaranteed to all citizens; they should not be treated as second-class citizens.
2. Limits on the political activities of public servants deprive both the general public and political parties of valuable information and insights on public affairs.
3. Limits on the political activities of public servants restrict the involvement in partisan politics of a large percentage of the labour force.
4. The application of the merit principle protects the public service against political or bureaucratic patronage based on the partisan affiliation of public servants.
5. Knowledgeable and skilled persons whose talents are needed in government will be

unwilling to accept employment in the public service if their political rights are unduly restricted (Kernaghan, 1991: 220–31).

Over the past decade, in the provinces as well as in the federal sphere, the current has been running strongly in the direction of increased political rights for public servants. As a result, the substantial variation in political rights regimes that used to exist from one government to another has been considerably reduced.

No Public Comment

The term 'political rights' refers not only to partisan political activity but to **public comment** as well. Traditionally, public servants have been prohibited from criticizing or praising government policies or personalities in public. Clearly, it is tougher for public servants to follow this admonition if they are actively engaged in partisan politics. Several of the arguments for and against political activity outlined above also apply to public comment. On the one hand, there is concern that public servants be seen as politically neutral by politicians and the public; on the other hand, there is a danger of restricting unduly the political rights of a large body of well-educated and well-informed citizens.

It has proved difficult for governments to develop specific rules regarding the permissible limits of public comment, in part because there are so many types of public comment and in part because there is considerable debate as to what types should be permitted and what types should be prohibited. There is general agreement that public servants should be allowed to comment publicly by providing information and analysis of a technical or scientific nature, describing the machinery of government, and explaining the content of policies. There is general agreement also on the risky or prohibited nature of such activities as providing even constructive criticism of government policies, denouncing these policies, or making overtly partisan statements.

There is, however, a grey and controversial area that includes such activities as discussing, within the framework of settled policy, the solution of problems through new or modified programs, commenting on issues on which policy has not yet been decided, explaining the political and policy process in government, and proposing reforms in the machinery of government (Kernaghan, 1991: 252). Nevertheless, as with partisan political activity, the trend is in the direction of extending the permissible rights of public servants to engage in public comment.

Ministerial Responsibility and Public Service Anonymity

As early as a decade after Confederation, the extent to which ministers could effectively monitor the details of departmental administration was a subject of parliamentary debate (Canada, 1878: 1588, 1610, 1614–15). The growth in the scale and complexity of government during the twentieth century, especially after 1945, meant that ministers could not reasonably be required to resign to atone for public servants' errors about which they had no personal knowledge. Indeed, in Canadian political history, no minister has ever resigned in response to mistakes made by his or her public servants.

However, ministers have, with a few exceptions (Kernaghan, 1979; Sutherland, 1991), adhered to the second component of individual responsibility: they have usually answered to the legislature for all of the acts of their department. They have thereby protected public service anonymity—the anonymity of individual public servants. Nonetheless, public service anonymity has been eroded somewhat by other developments, including expanded media coverage of public servants' activities and their frequent appearances before legislative committees, sometimes to testify about politically controversial issues.

When the issue of individual ministerial responsibility is raised in a partisan context, it quickly becomes evident that where one stands on this issue often depends literally on where one sits. Legislators sitting on the Opposition benches interpret the convention in a way that will support their calls for a minister's resignation while government members insist that the opposition has misunderstood or misapplied the requirements of the convention of ministerial responsibility. In addition, some commentators argue that ministerial responsibility is a myth. This argument is based largely on the 'corrosive and unhelpful' nature of 'the proposition that a minister of a department is responsible for everything that happens in the department' (Segal, 1998: 232). The argument is also based in part on the belief that the convention protects both ministers and public servants from being held adequately accountable for their decisions. Critics of the convention often suggest that public servants should be held directly accountable to the legislature for their decisions (Segal, 1998: 238), but they fail to draw out the full political and public service implications of this suggestion and to provide a realistically viable option to the convention of ministerial responsibility.

Those who support the preservation of the convention usually present the following arguments regarding its meaning and importance:

- The convention is intended to protect the authority and accountability of ministers for government decisions.
- It is a positive and pervasive force for accountability in the myriad day-to-day operations of government.
- The meaning and application of the convention are often distorted by undue emphasis on ministerial blame and calls for resignation. While ministers are responsible for answering to the legislature for the errors of administrative subordinates, they do not thereby accept personal blame for these errors.
- It is unreasonable to hold a minister personally responsible, to the extent that she or he must resign, for the errors of administrative subordinates.
- Ministers usually resign in the event of serious personal misconduct or in cases where they have directed public servants to take a specific action that turns out to be a serious mistake.
- Public servants answer to legislative committees for administrative matters, but not for policy or politically controversial matters; this answerability takes the form of explanation, not defence, of departmental actions.
- Ministers have a commitment to protect the conventions of political neutrality and public service anonymity (Kernaghan, 1998: 229–30).

Tenure in Office

The issue of security of tenure for public servants demonstrates well the interdependent nature of the East Block conventions. Traditionally, public servants have enjoyed permanence in office 'during good behaviour and satisfactory performance'. Their security can be tenuous, however, if they become too closely associated with certain policy decisions, if they were appointed on partisan grounds and there is a change in the governing party, or if they engage too actively in partisan political activity or make controversial public comments on government policies.

In general, public servants have served the government of the day with loyalty and impartiality regardless of their personal opinions about the government's policies and decisions. In response, public servants have usually been secure in their positions despite a change of government. In some provincial governments, however, a change in the governing party has led to the removal of a considerable number of senior public servants and their replacement by patronage appointees, as occurred in Ontario in 1990 with a newly elected NDP government. The danger here, for advocates of a professional, non-partisan public service, is that the next government will be tempted to replace these appointees with its own supporters.

Since the mid-1980s in particular it has become clear that public servants can be dismissed for reasons unrelated to acceptable performance and appropriate behaviour. A large number of public servants have lost their jobs as a result of the staff reductions accompanying the downsizing of government. Moreover, the notion of lifelong employment that has historically been associated with the concept of a career public service is now widely questioned, and the expectation is that employees will move frequently during their careers between the public and private sectors. We shall see below that there is a close connection between these East Block conventions and certain public service values.

David Good (2008) has affirmed that the behaviour of politicians and public servants does depart substantially from the ideal model of the doctrine of political neutrality outlined above. Indeed, since the model was first formulated in the mid-1970s, pressure to depart in practice from its requirements has increased substantially. Good concludes that:

> the widening gap between the ideal model and actual practice is more than stretching the limits of those who are responsible for interpreting the doctrine. It also appears to be giving licence to some for the way in which they practice the doctrine and subsequently report on their practice. As the interpreters or enforcers of the doctrine struggle to provide meaningful guidance to public servants and politicians in a world that is changing in fundamental ways, their interpretations are finding less resonance. (Good, 2008: 81)

Public Service Values

Values are an enduring and pervasive element of intellectual enterprise and daily experience (see Kernaghan, 2000). Several academic disciplines are centrally concerned with the concept of values. Political science is concerned with the practice of politics as the authoritative *allocation of social values*. Psychology studies how *individuals* develop, understand, and use human values. Sociology adds a *group*-based dimension by examining the impact of social experience on human values. And philosophy brings a *normative* dimension by asking what values people should hold (Gortner, 1994: 375ff.). The study of public administration draws ideas and insights on values from each of these disciplines.

D.B. Dewar, a former federal deputy minister, has explained the practical use of values:

- They help us to visualize ideal outcomes and thus to establish goals.
- They motivate and energize us to work towards these goals.
- They serve as standards to help us measure progress, decide perplexing questions, and choose between alternative courses of action.
- By doing all this, they help us to define who we are and how we should relate to the world.

Dewar has explained also that values tend to be long-lasting and resistant to easy change but should be 'open to change for compelling reasons.... The toughest questions about values arise when we are confronted by circumstances that force a choice between two values in our framework—between loyalty and integrity, for example' (Dewar, 1994: 2–3). And Ralph Heintzman has observed that 'public servants who do not realize they function in a world in which, say, democratic values may be in tension with, say, professional values are stumbling in the dark' (Heintzman, 2007).

Types of Public Service Values

For analytical purposes, this essay classifies public service values into four categories: ***ethical* values** (e.g., integrity), ***democratic* values** (e.g., rule of law), ***professional* values** (e.g., innovation), and ***people* values** (e.g., caring). Some values can be found in more than one category. For example, accountability is usually considered to be both an ethical value and a democratic value—and some commentators include it in the professional category as well. Each of these categories can in turn be divided into traditional values and new values. Among the major **traditional values** are accountability, efficiency, effectiveness, integrity, neutrality, responsiveness, and representativeness

(Kernaghan, 1978). Among the most important **new values** are service, innovation, quality, and teamwork. Most of the new values fall into the category of professional values.

Evolution of Public Service Values

Values have long been an important concept in scholarly writings on public administration, especially in the United States (Kaufman, 1956; Gilbert, 1959).

Since the mid-1980s the concept of values has become increasingly central to the study and practice of public administration in many countries around the world, including Canada. This heightened interest in values has resulted from five main developments.

First, the public sector experienced the spillover effect of the private sector's emphasis on the concept of corporate culture, and statements of values. Second, some public organizations have been successfully transformed by focusing on a change in their values rather than in their structures (Denhardt, 1993). Third, the increased emphasis on *results* than on *process* favoured values over the more intrusive alternative instruments of rules, directives, and guidelines. Fourth is the concern about the perceived undermining of traditional public service values by some public-sector reformers.

A fifth and final explanatory factor has been the steadily rising interest since the late 1960s in **public service ethics**—a concept so tightly intertwined with that of public service values that many commentators use the terms 'values' and 'ethics' interchangeably. However, not all values are ethical values, that is, not all values relate to questions of right and wrong, good or bad. It is helpful, therefore, to distinguish ethical values from democratic, professional, and people values.

While the relative significance of the traditional values noted above has changed over time, their overall significance has endured. Reference to these traditional values provides a framework for explaining and assessing past, present, and anticipated public service reforms. For example, several reforms between Confederation and 1918 were designed to promote the values of neutrality and efficiency; the 1960 Glassco Royal Commission was concerned with promoting efficiency, economy, and improved service; and the 1978 Lambert Commission focused on accountability (Kernaghan, 1997).

During the past two decades, new values (e.g., innovation, quality) have risen to prominence and certain traditional values (e.g., accountability) have become relatively more important. The Public Service 2000 White Paper published by the federal government in 1990 noted the continuing importance of traditional values such as accountability, integrity, and fairness, but recommended reforms reflecting the growing emphasis on such professional values as innovation and empowerment. Similar mixtures of values are found in other reports and statements.

Reforms, Values, and Conventions

Private Sector Influence on Public Sector Reform

Since the mid-1980s, a strong wind of public sector reform has swept through many countries. The major means by which this reform has been accomplished include partnerships, empowerment, restructuring, re-engineering, information technology, citizen-centred service, and continuous learning (Kernaghan et al., 2000). Most of the scholarly literature on this reform movement has focused on its organizational, managerial, and political implications. Much less attention has been paid to its implications for public service values and ethics.

Several of the new public service values (e.g., service, innovation) are identical to prominent private sector values. This reflects the fact that many of the recent public sector reforms have been inspired by private sector experience. Concern has arisen about the impact of this private sector influence on the ethical values and constitutional conventions of the public service. The public sector has been affected not only by certain business values (e.g., risk-taking) but also by increased business involvement in the conduct of government activities (e.g., contracting out, partnerships). Several scholars have argued that this business influence will undermine the ethical performance of the public sector (Frederickson, 1993; Doig, 1995). The British parliamentary Committee on Standards in Public Life warned in 1994 that public sector functions are increasingly being performed by those, notably business persons, who have not been socialized to core public service values: 'it cannot be assumed that everyone in the public service will assimilate a public service culture unless they are told what is expected of them and the message is systematically reinforced' (United Kingdom, 1994: 16).

There is particular concern about the extent to which it is possible to infuse program delivery agencies (e.g., service agencies in Canada) with core public service values, especially if the organizations are headed by persons brought in from the private sector to manage them on a more 'businesslike' basis. The creation of agencies at arm's length from ministerial control raises concern as to ministers' responsibility for the agencies' decisions. Moreover, the appointment of business people to head public agencies and the increased mobility of employees between the public and private sectors threaten political neutrality by increasing the likelihood of partisanship and patronage (Canada, Deputy Ministers' Task Force, 1996).

Old and New Values

Value conflict is a pervasive reality for public administrators. There are frequent tensions and clashes among democratic, ethical, professional and people values, and between old and new values. In assessing the value implications of public service reforms, administrators have to consider both the relative merits and the compatibility of a wide range of pertinent values. As explained below, it is helpful to identify core public service values and to establish priorities among them so as to narrow the range of values that decision-makers are obliged to consider. The 1994 study mentioned above found that the value statements of 93 public organizations contained a total of 164 different values (Kernaghan, 1994a: 630). There was substantial agreement among the organizations on the top dozen values but most organizations also espoused values related to their particular responsibilities (e.g., safety for a transportation agency).

From among the several means mentioned earlier whereby public organizations can carry out reform, we shall focus here, by way of illustration, on partnerships. Partnerships involving public organizations and various non-governmental entities (especially business organizations) are widely viewed as an effective means of promoting citizen-centred service, collaboration, decentralization, non-departmental forms of organization, and cost recovery. Partnerships are also promoted as an effective means of pursuing such traditional professional values as efficiency and effectiveness and such new professional values as service and innovation. A major impetus for the widespread creation of partnerships since the mid-1980s has been the need to respond to the public's demand for more or better service with fewer resources. Many of these partnerships have been remarkably innovative in meeting this need (Rodal and Mulder, 1993; Kernaghan, 1993).

There is tension between the use of partnerships to pursue these professional values and the need to respect several traditional democratic and ethical values, especially accountability, which may be the dominant value in contemporary public administration. All those individuals and organizations in society who exercise power over us have a duty to account for the proper exercise of that power—and this duty is centrally important for public officials in a democratic system of government. While accountability has long been a central public service value, it has taken on new life and new importance in the context of recent reforms, including the use of partnerships.

Some partnerships—especially truly collaborative ones in which public organizations share power and risk with their partners—have provoked concern about the accountability of the partners to ministers, legislators, and taxpaying citizens. Partnerships in general and innovative ones in particular can be risky, especially for politicians. The political risk is especially problematic in Westminster-style governments like Canada's where, as explained in the earlier discussion of the East Block conventions, cabinet ministers are required to answer to the legislature for the errors of their departmental subordinates. Consider, for example, the political consequences of partnerships in which substantial public money is lost and the business partners cannot, or are not obligated to, bear a reasonable share of the loss.

Partnerships also have significant implications for traditional ethical values like integrity and fairness. The creation of partnerships often involves public servants exercising discretionary authority during protracted negotiations with business firms, thereby increasing the opportunity for conflict-of-interest situations. Fairness is also an issue in partnership arrangements. Thus, if a business firm brings a good partnership idea to government, is it fair to give other firms an opportunity to compete for involvement in the partnership so as to ensure the best possible deal for the taxpayer?

This brief examination of the implications for accountability of using partnerships illustrates the kind of analysis that can be performed for other instruments of reform (e.g., restructuring, technological innovation, empowerment). Reformers need to conduct such analysis so as to take adequate account of both the growing importance of professional values and the enduring importance of democratic and ethical ones.

Predictions and Prescriptions

Predictions

The evolution of the East Block conventions and public service values will depend on a complex mix of political, economic, and social changes that are difficult to foresee. In the absence of a clear statement as to the appropriate meaning and application of the conventions, they may be eroded by certain public service reforms. Paul Thomas (1997: 151–2) has warned against producing the worst of both worlds, that is:

> a serious undermining of the traditional constitutional framework based on misunderstandings and distortions as to how it was meant to operate and how it actually operates, together with a failure to offer an alternative approach to the democratic control of political and bureaucratic power that matched the old framework in terms of its theoretical consistency, practical value and inherent flexibility.

Historical experience in Canada suggests that the relative importance of public service values is likely to shift. The direction and extent of the shift will be determined by the particular features of the environment for governance.

The use of three governance scenarios developed by the federal government (Canada, Deputy Ministers' Task Force on the Future Public Service, 1997: 4) as an analytical tool for strategic thinking and planning provides some insight into possible shifts in the importance of public service values. These scenarios are presented here in a brief and oversimplified fashion. Among the future challenges to government and the public service associated with the *Evolution* scenario are providing basic programs and services with fewer resources, making new management reforms (including new delivery mechanisms and new accountability regimes), and fostering creativity in a risk-averse milieu. The emphasis in this scenario is on the professional values of service and innovation and the democratic/ethical value of accountability. The challenges that arise in the *Market* scenario include fostering private sector innovation and competitiveness, operating in a more businesslike fashion, and encouraging mobility between the public and private sectors. This scenario brings to the fore the professional value of efficiency, the democratic value of political neutrality, and the ethical value of integrity (e.g., avoiding the use of public office for private gain). In the final scenario—*Renaissance*—the challenges to government and the public service include promoting collaboration among a wide variety of policy actors; balancing party politics, organizational hierarchy, and ministerial responsibility with partnerships and co-operative working relationships; and recruiting high-calibre employees devoted to the public good. The emphasis in this scenario is on the professional values of collaboration and innovation, the democratic values of accountability and the public interest and the people values of participation and openness.

Each of the scenarios has different implications for the East Block conventions. For example, the emphasis on risk-taking in the Evolution scenario must be balanced by sensitivity to the answerability of ministers for departmental errors; the Market scenario's emphasis on mobility between the public and private sectors raises the question of whether short-term employees moving in and out of government will be sufficiently attuned to the requirements of the East Block conventions; and the Renaissance scenario's emphasis on collaboration (across departments) must be accompanied by agreement as to which minister(s) will be accountable for results.

Prescriptions

The preceding discussion suggests the need for all policy actors to have as clear an understanding as possible of what the core values and conventions of the public service are and how they should be interpreted. A formal statement of these conventions and values, both for the public service as a whole and for individual public organizations, could provide a foundation for assessing the value consequences of public servants' decisions, including the likely consequences of proposed reforms (Kernaghan, 2003). Montgomery Van Wart (1998: xvii) contends that 'being clear about and managing values is an organizational priority of the highest order.... Lack of clarity about the values to be endorsed, their priority, their application in different situations, their support, and their enforcement leads to ineffectiveness as employees work at cross-purposes.' And Steven Cohen and William Eimicke (1999: 72) argue that public servants are not:

> fully equipped to determine the degree of risk in a particular innovation and accurately assess the ethical questions it may encompass. Nor are they clear about the proper process to follow when seeking to make decisions regarding risk, innovation and ethics. The solution is not to discourage public entrepreneurship but rather to establish practical principles to ensure that it is exercised in an effective and ethical manner.

Several Westminster-style democracies have responded to actual or anticipated problems arising from reforms by drafting or strengthening a **code of conduct**, sometimes called a statement of values or a statement of principles (New Zealand, 2007; United Kingdom, 2006). The experience of these countries suggests that governments need to take careful account of the value implications of reforms before they implement them. There is significant congruence in the core public service values adopted by the Westminster-style democracies of Australia, New Zealand, and the United Kingdom, where ministerial responsibility is a central constitutional convention. The value statements of these three countries contain a mix of democratic, ethical, professional, and, to a lesser extent, people values. Foremost among the democratic values are accountability and impartiality, while integrity, honesty, and fairness are the most prominent ethical values.

In 2003, Canada adopted a Values and Ethics Code that applies to all federal employees. The Code's purposes are:

- to articulate the values and ethics of public service to guide and support public servants in all their professional activities;
- to maintain and enhance public confidence in the integrity of the public service;
- to strengthen respect for, and appreciation of, the role played by the public service within Canadian democracy.

The Code's four chapters contain a statement of public service values and ethics, conflict of interest measures, post-employment measures, and avenues of resolution. The Code recognizes that public servants' decisions are inevitably influenced by a substantial number of values. The several values in the Code are divided into four categories or 'families' of public service values: the democratic, ethical, professional, and people values discussed above. For example, the section 'People Values' refers to 'demonstrating respect, fairness and courtesy in . . . dealings with both citizens and fellow public servants' (Canada, Treasury Board Secretariat, 2003).

Since 2003, there has been further thinking and action regarding Canada's values and ethics regime. The Public Servants Disclosure Protection Act, which was enacted in late 2005 and came into force in 2007, protects public servants who disclose wrongdoing in government—often described as 'blowing the whistle'. In addition, the Act's preamble commits the federal government to adopting a Charter of Values of Public Service 'to guide public servants in their work and professional conduct' (see Kernaghan, 2006). Moreover, section 4 of the Act requires the Treasury Board to establish a Code of Conduct applicable to the public sector. The heads of departments and agencies are required to establish codes for their organizations that are consistent with the Code.

The emphasis in most current codes is on *traditional* democratic, ethical, and professional values. Few statements reflect the increased importance of new professional values such as innovation and creativity and little effort is made to reconcile traditional and new values. Part of the explanation for these apparent deficiencies is the view of some government officials that the so-called 'new' values are a passing fancy or are at best second-order values that are less central to successful governance than the traditional ones. A review of the scenarios discussed above, however, suggests that the importance of certain professional values, especially innovation, is likely to endure. This means that public servants must be mindful of these values when developing codes of conduct and sensitive to the tension between professional values and other categories of values (e.g., innovation versus accountability and integrity). Ontario's 2007 statement, *OPS Organizational Values*, highlights eight values: trust, fairness, diversity, excellence, creativity, collaboration, efficiency, and responsiveness. Elaboration on the value of creativity refers to the importance of public servants being innovative.

A major theme in recent public service reforms is reducing the number of rules so that empowered public servants, who will be held more accountable for results and less accountable for process, can be more creative, and even entrepreneurial. However, some reforms create pressure for more, not fewer, rules (e.g., conflict of interest, non-partisanship). Fostering shared values across the public service and in individual organizations can help to reduce the overall need for rules and to increase the use of guidelines—a less intrusive management instrument. Public servants are then more likely to comply with the rules that remain and to respect the guidelines if they see the connection between the intent of these rules and guidelines and fundamental public service values. For example, one approach to managing conflict of interest is to provide lengthy and detailed rules against it. Another approach is to explain that the need to avoid conflict of interest is grounded in basic and enduring democratic and ethical values such as impartiality and fairness; to develop broad conflict-of-interest guidelines based on these values; and then to draw from these guidelines a limited number of rules. 'The best accountability systems recognize . . . that control is normative . . . rooted in values and beliefs' (Mintzberg, 1996: 81).

Ralph Heintzman, in discussing the relationship between values and rules, notes that 'there can never be enough rules to cover every decision a public servant would ever need to make. Which means there will always be lots of discretionary space between the rules, space that can only be filled in by judgment and values.' Thus, 'even when a due reverence for rules is present, an understanding of their spirit, of the values of public service that underlie the rules, is needed to explain them, and to guide their interpretation and application' (2008: 578).

It is unrealistic to expect that a code of conduct alone will be sufficient to foster shared values and high ethical standards in the public service. A code should be viewed as an essential component of a broad regime for preserving and promoting values-based behaviour (Kernaghan 2003; OECD 1997: 4). This framework could include not only a code of conduct but also such measures as ethics rules and guidelines, ethics training and education, ethics counsellors or ombudspersons, and the evaluation of ethical performance as a basis for appointments and promotions, especially at the senior leadership level. While codes of conduct can serve important purposes, they can be severely undermined by leaders who do not model the organization's values. Public servants are more effectively motivated by concrete examples of values-based leadership than by written declarations of values. Nevertheless, a code of conduct can provide a powerful incentive and complement to exemplary leadership.

Important Terms and Concepts

code of conduct (statement of values)
collective ministerial responsibility
constitutional conventions
individual ministerial responsibility
merit
merit system
partisan political activity
patronage
political neutrality
political rights for public servants
politics–administration dichotomy
public comment
public service anonymity
public service ethics
public service values
- democratic values
- ethical values
- new values
- people values
- professional values
- traditional values

Study Questions

1. Explain the meaning of the three 'EastBlock' conventions, how they are related to one another, and their connection to public service values.
2. Explain the six components of the model of political neutrality. To what extent does the contemporary behaviour of politicians and public servants depart from this 'ideal-type' model?
3. What are the arguments for and against permitting public servants to exercise full political rights?
4. Assess the importance of the constitutional convention of ministerial responsibility.
5. Explain the meaning and importance of public service values and describe, with examples, the various types of values.
6. Assess the importance of values statements and codes of conduct, with particular reference to Canada's *Values and Ethics Code for the Public Service.*

Useful Websites

Canada, Deputy Ministers' Task Force on Public Service Values and Ethics. 1996. *A Strong Foundation: Discussion Paper on Values and Ethics in the Public Service.* Ottawa: Privy Council Office.

www.ccmd-ccg.gc.ca/publications.html

Canada. Office of the Prime Minister. 2007. *Accountable Government: A Guide for Ministers.*

www.pcobcp.gc.ca/docs/information/Publications/guidemin/ag-gr/2007/accountable-guide2007_e.pdf

Canada Public Service Agency. Office of Public Service Values and Ethics. 2005. '*Duty of Loyalty*'.

www.tbs-sct.gc.ca/rp/icg-eng.asp

Canada Public Service Agency, Office of Public Service Values and Ethics:

www.tbs-sct.gc.ca/chro-dprh/ve-eng.asp

Canada, Public Service Agency, *Values and Ethics Code for the Public Service*:

www.tbs-sct.gc.ca/pubs_pol/hrpubs/tb_851/vec-cve-eng.asp

Canada. Public Service Commission. 2004. 'Personal Favouritism in Staffing and Recruitment within the Federal Public Service'.

www.psc-cfp.gc.ca/adt-vrf/rprt/2004/ptrn-fvrt/index-eng.htm

References

Aucoin, P. 1995. *The New Public Management: Canada in Comparative Perspective.* Ottawa: Institute for Research on Public Policy.

Canada. 1878. *House of Commons Debates.*

———. 1918. *Statutes.* 8–9 George V, c. 12.

———. 1966–7. *Statutes.* c. 71.

———. Civil Service Commission. 1958. *Personnel Administration in the Public Service: A Review of Civil Service Legislation by the Civil Service Commission of Canada.* Ottawa: Queen's Printer.

———. Deputy Ministers' Task Force on the Future Public Service. 1997. *Report.* Ottawa: Privy Council Office. Available at: www.ccmd-ccg.gc.ca/documents/dmtf/intromtf.html.

———. Deputy Ministers' Task Force on Public Service Values and Ethics. 1996. *A Strong Foundation: Discussion Paper on Values and Ethics in the Public Service.* Ottawa: Privy Council Office. Available at: www.ccmd-ccg.gc.ca/publications.html.

———. House of Commons. 1877. *Journals*, Appendix no. 7.

———. Royal Commission on Government Organization. 1962. *Report.* Ottawa: Queen's Printer.

———. Treasury Board Secretariat. 2003. *Values and Ethics Code for the Public Service.* Minister of Public Works and Government Services.

Casey, G.E. 1877. 'Civil Service Reform', *Canadian Monthly* 11 (Jan.): 83–91.

Charih, M., and A. Daniels, eds. 1997. *New Public Administration and New Public Management in Canada.* Toronto: Institute of Public Administration of Canada.

Cohen, S., and W. Eimicke. 1999. 'Is Public Entrepreneurship Ethical? A Second Look at Theory and Practice', *Public Integrity* 1 (Winter): 54–74.

Denhardt, R. 1993. *The Pursuit of Significance: Strategies for Managerial Success in Public Organizations.* Belmont, Calif.: Wadsworth.

Dewar, D.B. 1994. 'Public Service Values: How to Navigate in Rough Waters', in *Values in the Public Service.* Ottawa: Canadian Centre for Management Development, 1–13.

Doig, A. 1995. 'Mixed Signals? Public Sector Change and the Proper Conduct of Public Business', *Public Administration* 73 (Summer): 191–212.

Frederickson, H.G. 1993. 'Ethics and Public Administration: Some Assertions', in Frederickson, ed., *Ethics and Public Administration.* New York: M.E. Sharpe.

Gilbert, C.E. 1959. 'The Framework of Administrative Responsibility', *Journal of Politics* 21 (1959): 373–407.

Good, David. 2008. 'An Ideal Model in a Practical World: The Continuous Revisiting of Political Neutrality and Ministerial Responsibility', in David Siegel and Ken Rasmussen, eds, *Professionalism and Public Service: Essays in Honour of Kenneth Kernaghan.* Toronto: University of Toronto Press, 63–83.

Gortner, H.F. 1994. 'Ethics and Values', in T. L. Cooper, ed., *Handbook of Administrative Ethics.* New York: Marcel Dekker, 373–90.

Granatstein, J.L. 1982. *The Ottawa Men: The Civil Service Mandarins, 1935–1957.* Toronto: University of Toronto Press.

Heintzman, Ralph. 2007. 'Public-Service Values and Ethics: Dead End or Strong Foundation?', *Canadian Public Administration* 50: 4 (Winter): 573–602.

Hodgetts, J.E. 1955. *Pioneer Public Service: An Administrative History of the United Canadas.* Toronto: University of Toronto Press.

———. 1964. 'Challenge and Response: A Retrospective View of the Public Service', *Canadian Public Administration* 7 (Dec.): 409–21.

———, and O.P. Dwivedi. 1976. 'Administration and Personnel', in D.J. Bellamy, J.H. Pammett, and D.C. Rowat, eds, *The Provincial Political Systems: Comparative Essays.* Toronto: Methuen, 341–56.

Hondeghem, A., ed. 1998. *Ethics and Accountability in a Context of Governance and New Public Management.* Amsterdam: IOS Press.

Kaufman, H. 1956. 'Emerging Conflicts in the Doctrines of Public Administration', *American Political Science Review* 50, 1 (Dec.): 1059–73.

Kernaghan, K. 1976. 'Politics, Policy and Public Servants: Political Neutrality Revisited', *Canadian Public Administration* 19 (Fall): 432–56.

———. 1978. 'Changing Concepts of Power and Responsibility in the Canadian Public Service', *Canadian Public Administration* 21 (Fall): 389–406.

———. 1979. 'Power, Politics and Public Servants: Ministerial Responsibility Revisited', *Canadian Public Policy* 3 (Summer): 383–96.

———. 1991. 'The Political Rights of Canada's Federal Public Servants', in M. Cassidy, ed., *Democratic Rights and Electoral Reform*, Royal Commission on Electoral Reform and Party Financing, vol. 10. Toronto: Dundurn Press, 213–67.

———. 1993. 'Partnership and Public Administration: Conceptual and Practical Considerations', *Canadian Public Administration* 36 (Spring): 57–76.

———. 1994a. 'The Emerging Public Service Culture: Values, Ethics and Reforms', *Canadian Public Administration* 37 (Winter): 614–30.

———. 1994b. 'Rules Are Not Enough: Ethics, Politics and Public Service in Ontario', in J. Langford and A. Tupper, eds, *Corruption, Character and Conduct: Essays on Canadian Government Ethics*. Toronto: Oxford University Press, 174–96.

———. 1997. 'Shaking the Foundations: Traditional Versus New Public Service Values', in Charih and Daniels (1997: 47–65).

———. 1998. 'Is the Doctrine of Ministerial Responsibility Workable?', in M. Charlton and P. Barker, eds, *Crosscurrents: Contemporary Political Issues*. Toronto: Nelson, 222–31.

———. 2000. 'The Post-Bureaucratic Organization and Public Service Values', *International Review of Administrative Sciences* 66, 1 (Mar.): 91–104.

———. 2003. 'Integrating Values into Public Service: The Values Statement as Centerpiece', *Public Administration Review* 63 (November–December): 711–19.

———. 2006. 'Encouraging "Rightdoing" and Discouraging Wrongdoing: The Case for a Public Service Charter and Disclosure Legislation'. Study for Gomery Commission of Inquiry into the Sponsorship Program and Advertising Activities, *Restoring Accountability*. Research Studies, vol. 2: 71–114.

———, and T.H. McLeod. 1982. 'Ministers and Mandarins in the Canadian Administrative State', in O.P Dwivedi, ed., *The Administrative State*. Toronto: University of Toronto Press, 17–30.

———, B. Marson, and S. Borins. 2000. *The New Public Organization*. Toronto: Institute of Public Administration of Canada.

Marshall, G. 1984. *Constitutional Conventions*. Oxford: Oxford University Press.

———, and G. C. Moodie. 1967. *Some Problems of the Constitution*, 4th edn. London: Hutchinson.

Mintzberg, H. 1996. 'Managing Government: Governing Management', *Harvard Business Review* (May–June): 75–83.

Mitchell, J.R., and S.L. Sutherland. 1997. 'Relations between Politicians and Public Servants', in Charih and Daniels (1997: 181–97).

New Zealand, State Services Commission. 2007. *Standards of Integrity and Conduct: A Code of Conduct Issued by the State Services Commissioner*. Wellington: State Services Commission. Available at: www.ssc.govt.nz/upload/downloadable_files/Code-of-conduct-StateServices.pdf.

OECD. 1997. 'Ethics Infrastructure', *Public Management Focus* 4 (Mar.).

Osborne v. Canada (Treasury Board) (1991), 82 D.L.R. (4th) 321 (S.C.C.).

Pearson, L.B. 1967. 'Foreword', in R.A.J. Phillips, *The East Block of the Parliament Buildings of Canada*. Ottawa: Department of Public Printing and Stationery.

Rodal, A., and N. Mulder. 1993. 'Partnerships, Devolution and Power-Sharing: Issues and Implications for Management', *Optimum*: 27–48.

Savoie, D.J. 1994. *Thatcher, Reagan, Mulroney: In Search of a New Bureaucracy*. Toronto: University of Toronto Press.

Segal, H. 1998. 'Ministerial Responsibility: Confronting the Myth', in M. Charlton and P. Barker, eds, *Crosscurrents: Contemporary Political Issues*. Toronto: Nelson, 232–9.

Sutherland, S.L. 1991. 'Responsible Government and Ministerial Responsibility: Every Reform Is Its Own Problem', *Canadian Journal of Political Science* 24 (1991): 91–120.

Thomas, P. 1997. 'Ministerial Responsibility and Administrative Accountability', in Charih and Daniels (1997: 141–63).

United Kingdom. Committee on Standards in Public Life (Nolan Committee). 1994. *First Report*. London: HMSO. Cmd. 2850–1.

———. 2006. *The Civil Service Code*. London: Cabinet Office. Available at: www.civilservice.gov.uk/documents/pdf/cscode/cs_code.pdf.

Van Wart, M. 1998. *Changing Public Sector Values*. New York: Garland.

Wilson, W. 1966 [1887]. 'The Study of Administration', reprinted in Jay M. Shafritz and Albert C. Hyde, eds, *Classics of Public Administration*. Chicago: Dorsey, 10–25.

17 The Third Sector and the Provision of Public Good: *Partnerships, Contracting, and the Neo-Liberal State*

B. Mitchell Evans and John Shields

Introduction

The **third sector**—that space between the state and market realms where not-for-profit organizations operate—has only recently been identified as an active and vital component of society. Academics and policy-makers have largely neglected the contributions that non-profit organizations make to the provision and public administration of the 'public good'. In fact, the role of third-sector organizations has largely been hidden from history, so much so that the third sector has even been labelled the 'invisible sector' (Hall, 1997: 74). Yet third-sector organizations are doing more of the work for which governments once took full responsibility and the sector is expected to play an increasingly central role in the future health and well-being of society (Amin et al., 2002: vii).

The central point to be made in this chapter is that restructuring, guided by neo-liberal and third-way thinking, has assigned a key role to the third sector as an agent of the state in the production and delivery of 'public goods'. The contract relationship that has developed between the state and non-profit organizations, however, has worked to transform the third sector, moving it away from its core mission, commercializing the sector's operations, and compromising its autonomy. These developments have had profound implications for governance, encompassing inclusive citizenship, the health of civil society, the development of social capital, the enhancement of social cohesion, and the well-being of public service provision.

The Canadian Third Sector in Perspective

Various terms have been used in the attempt to capture the essence of this newly visible sector including 'non-profit sector', 'social economy', and 'third sector'. The Organisation for Economic Co-Operation and Development (OECD) Ahas usefully described the sector in the following way:

> A sector between the state and market, filling both economic and social missions, which pursues a general interest, and whose final objective is not the redistribution of profit. Each of these terms underlines only one aspect of the sector. So, while the term 'non-profit sector', born in the USA, refers mainly to the absence of the redistribution of profits, the term 'social economy'... underlines the socio-economic dimension of the sector, and the term 'third sector' highlights its position between the state and the market (OECD, 2003: 10).

Key concepts that express the distinctive values that set the third sector off from the market and government sectors are philanthropy, altruism, charity, reciprocity, mutuality (Shields and Evans, 1998: 89), and the ethic of giving and caring. Four basic categories of third-sector organizations can be identified. *Funding agencies or fundraising intermediaries* (e.g., the United Way) generally do not provide services themselves but 'channel resources to those who do'. *Member-serving organizations* (e.g., business and professional associations and trade unions) serve their immediate members rather than the public at large. *Public benefit organizations* (e.g., nursing homes, daycares and other social service organizations, cultural institutions) 'exist primarily to service others, to provide goods or services (including information or advocacy) to those in need or otherwise to contribute to the general welfare.' *Religious organizations* (e.g., churches and religious societies) are involved in the pursuit of 'essentially sacramental and religious functions' (Salamon, 1995: 54). The sector embraces a considerable diversity of organizations with varying aims and perspectives. Our focus will primarily be public benefit/service-providing organizations.

The size, scope, and economic contribution of the third sector are considerable although difficult to fully measure (Hall and Banting, 2000). In 2003 there were some 161,000 formally constituted non-profit bodies in Canada, of which 80,000 were registered charities (Statistics Canada, 2004: 4, 12). Canada's third sector, measured 'as a share of the economically active population' is the second largest in the world, standing at 11.1 per cent of the workforce in 2000, behind only the Netherlands and well ahead of the US, at a more modest 9.8 per cent (Hall et al., 2005: 9–10).

On the whole, third-sector organizations are small, with two-thirds of them processing annual revenues of less than $100,000 (Panel on Accountability and Governance in the Voluntary Sector, 1998: 4). There are, of course, some large organizations in the sector and the general trend is that these bigger non-profits are growing larger (Statistics Canada, 2004: 10) in order to take advantage of economies of scale to better compete for government funding for program delivery. In sources of funding, non-profit organizing received some 51 per cent of their revenues from government, 39 per cent from fees and sales, and only 9 per cent from private philanthropy. Service-providing non-profits are more dependent on government sources of revenue than are other types of non-profit organizations.

The Third Sector in Historical Context

The early role of voluntary organizations in Canada was paternalistic; charity was directed towards the social and moral regulation of society (Valverde, 1995). Charitable organizations in this period were often financially assisted by the state in carrying out their 'charitable functions'. However, the state deliberately resisted directly providing health and social welfare to forestall a public perception that it would always be obliged to provide such support (Maurutto, 2005).

Non-profit organizations assumed a very different role during the period of welfare-state construction and consolidation. Keynesian-inspired public policy and public management approaches legitimated an extensive expansion of the state's role in society and economy. The state took the lead in providing for the health and welfare of Canadians, thus displacing paternalistic charity. Non-profit involvement in social service provision, however, did not disappear but rather was reconfigured, as third-sector organizations transformed into community-based partners with the state for welfare provision. Rather than being a state monopoly, the Canadian welfare state was based on a **mixed social-economy model** where services were delivered through a combination of state and privately run and administered programs (Valverde, 1995). Non-profit service providers were joined up with the state through public financing of many of the programs they offered.

In this arrangement the non-profit sector assumed a secondary place in the Keynesian welfare state structure, but even as a junior partner to the state the third sector played a very important role in a greatly expanded array of service provision. Contrary to popular belief, as the welfare state grew, third-sector organizations also rapidly expanded. A symbiotic and dynamic relationship between the state and non-profits emerged, with each building up and enhancing the other (Salamon, 1995). Non-profit service delivery was seen as less bureaucratic, and more innovative and flexible (Deakin, 2003: 196) and geographically and culturally close to the communities being served. The third sector was, however, seen as structurally limited in its capacity to deliver comprehensive 'collective goods' to all (Salamon, 1995: 16). Hence, non-profits were limited to supporting the state, which was able to provide comprehensive and uniform welfare state supports.

The relationship between the Keynesian state and non-profit service providers is distinguished from the neo-liberal period in a number of important respects: (1) state financing of non-profit service providers was centred on base funding, allowing organizations a good deal of latitude in spending; (2) funding was stable and long-term, allowing non-profits to build capacity and to become deeply rooted in the communities they served; (3) relationship between the state and the third sector were primarily based on trust and mutual respect rather than regulated by the narrow bonds of business contracts; (4) non-profit service providers were not meant to replace the state but were to enhance and complement the state's welfare-building role; and (5) relationships between the state and non-profits were not based on a coherent forward-planning vision but were ad hoc and uneven (Evans, Richmond, and Shields, 2005: 76). The relationship that evolved between third-sector organizations and the state, while far from ideal, did represent meaningful **partnerships** where non-profit organizations were respected by the state and allowed scope for autonomous operation.

In the welfare-state era, a number of distinctive roles for the third sector can be identified. First, the mandate of non-profits is 'to do good works', to provide **services** to the community (Cappe, 1999: 2). The third sector delivered a wide variety of services that are both tangible (clothing, shelter, food, training, health) and more intangible (counselling, support, collective worship). Some of these service activities were in partnership with the state, while others were independent actions.

Advocacy is a second area of non-profit activity. In its broadest sense advocacy can take a number of forms, including public education about an issue or societal problem and more direct advocacy/lobbying directed at improving the conditions of a particular client group or aimed at what are considered to be laws or policies that are unjust or against the public good. Third-sector organizations contribute to an ongoing 'public policy dialogue' (Cappe, 1999: 2). The advocacy role of third-sector organizations has been critical for broadening the democratic experience in the post-war period (Edwards, 2004: 78–81). Non-profit community groups facilitated involvement and voice within the political process. During the welfare-state era, governments guided by a reform agenda provided funding for the advocacy role to allow 'organizations of women, Natives, disabled, official language minorities and poor people to be heard among the voice of the economically powerful' (Phillips, 1991: 197). The political role of many non-profit organizations in this regard has been viewed as a 'critical counterweight to states and corporate power' (Edwards, 2004: 14). A publicly supported advocacy role for non-profit organizations helped to facilitate enhanced societal inclusion.

Also, third-sector organizations can often play a '**mediation**' role within society; that is, they can bring together people across a spectrum, such as a geographic area involving various neighbourhoods, where they are able to work out issues and help develop a common understanding, a consensus, or compromise (Scott, 1997: 46–7). This mediation role is very much an aspect of third-sector organizations' part in building '**social capital**' and maintaining **social cohesion** within society. Social capital 'refers to features of social organization such as networks, norms, and social trust that facilitate coordination and co-operation for mutual benefit' (Putnam, 1995: 67). Non-profit organizations foster the kinds of relationships that enable groups of people to work together efficiently in the pursuit of their shared goals (Halpern, 2005).

'Social cohesion' may be defined as involving building shared values and communities of interpretation, reducing disparities in wealth and income, and generally enabling people to sense that they are engaged in a common enterprise, facing shared challenges, and that they are members of the same community' (Judith Maxwell, as quoted in Policy Research Committee, 1996: 44). A cohesive society is one where public, private, and non-profit institutions are able to manage conflict; where institutional supports exist to foster inclusiveness; and where disparities within society are prevented from growing too wide.

A fourth role for third-sector organizations is helping to build citizenship (Phillips, 2001: 145). **Citizenship** is ultimately about participation and membership in a community (Barbalet, 1988: 2). In the second half of the twentieth century, citizenship came to be defined as social citizenship, i.e., the entitlement to basic social and economic rights associated with the welfare state as well as civil and political rights (O'Connor, 1998: 184–5). Moreover, citizenship was seen to encompass a more active dimension involving deep participation within the community/society. As Cappe (1999: 2) notes, third-sector organizations offer 'a unique way of social organizing' constructed on the values of 'independence (freedom of association), altruism (concern for others), [and] community (collective action)'. In addition, what makes community-based organizations different 'is that they are as much about participation as provision; as much about citizenship as service' (Nowland-Foreman, 1996: 4).

Third-sector organizations are a central part of civil society. Civil society can be conceived as occupying that space in society where 'uncoerced human association' and 'relational networks—formed for the sake of family, faith, interests and ideology' occur (Walzer, 1991: 293). Civil societies act 'as a reservoir of caring, cultural life and intellectual innovation' schooling people in the 'skills of citizenship' (Edwards, 2004: 14). As Michael Walzer notes, 'poor people with strong families, churches, unions, political parties, and ethnic alliances are not likely to be dominated or deprived for long' (Walzer, 1991: 299–300). To date, the contribution of an independent third sector to citizenship and civil society has been little acknowledged, yet clearly this sector has added a fuller, deeper, and more meaningful dimension to the idea of citizenship and has contributed to the creation of vibrant civil societies.

The Turn to Neo-Liberalism

The switch towards a neo-liberal public philosophy of the Canadian state over a welfare-state orientation began to take hold in the mid-1970s in the wake of a severe economic crisis that called into question the established Keynesian order. By the 1990s a neo-liberal governance paradigm had become firmly established. **Neo-liberalism** represents a fundamental assault on the Keynesian welfare state.

The neo-liberal project is widely accepted as comprising the following elements: the need to reduce the state's intervention in economic and social domains; deregulation of and allowing flexibility in labour and financial markets; and the elimination of barriers to the movement of capital, goods, and services (Navarro, 2007: 9). Neo-liberalism associates these changes with the so-called 'problem of *government failure*'. Their solution is to downsize the state and allow the market and individual initiative to be given freer rein and the creation of a new 'lean state' (Shields and Evans, 1998).

Harvey suggests, in addition to this, a much more profound process is at work wherein 'neoliberalism values market exchanges as . . . it emphasizes the significance of contractual relations in the marketplace. It holds that the social good will be maximized by maximizing the reach and frequency of market transactions, and it seeks to bring all human action into the domain of the market' (2005: 3). It is with respect to this meta-process within neo-liberalism that new relationships and roles for non-profit organizations vis-à-vis the state begin to emerge. This process is closely associated with the central place that neo-liberalism assigns to marketization and privatization in its restructuring agenda.

Marketization is the application of 'market criteria for allocating public resources and also to measure the efficiency of public service producers and suppliers according to market criteria' (Pierre, 1995: 56). In terms of productivity, the assumption is that competition between potential producers will 'reduce cost and increase quality of social services' production and delivery (Fabricant and Burghardt, 1992: 71–2).

Privatization is a complex concept that defies a singular definition (Hartley, 1990: 180). The standard definition of privatization is typically 'the withdrawal of the state from the production of goods and services' (Veljanovski, 1987: 1). Increasingly privatization is associated with the alignment of public sector employment and management practices with those in the private sector (Bach, 2004). Consequently, privatization may proceed through several different methods: (1) eliminating or reducing public services with the expectation that the private sector will pick up the slack left by the receding state; (2) restraining or cutting the financing of public programs with the possibility of finding compensatory private financing; (3) increasing consumer contributions; (4) transferring responsibilities for service delivery directly to private firms—including non-profit agencies; (5) contracting out service delivery while retaining responsibility for policy development; and (6) selling publicly owned assets such as land and housing (Drakeford, 2000: 28).

With respect to social services, 'privatization more often takes the form of a partial inroad into the public sector' (Walker, 1984: 25). The implication is that there will necessarily be 'greater reliance on the voluntary, informal and commercial sectors in financing and delivering social services' where market criteria, such as ability to pay, serve to ration the delivery of services (Rekart, 1993: 29–30). The key point is that the provider is not the state but rather non-governmental organizations, whether for-profit or non-profit. Privatization in this sense refers 'to the transfer of responsibility . . . from the collectivity to the individual and from the state to the home' (Armstrong, 1997: 53) and to non-profits.

It is possible to discern four distinct 'episodes' in the history of neo-liberalism. The early 1970s can be characterized as the period of 'proto neo-liberalism' where the central concern was to establish intellectual legitimacy. The second period, in the 1980s, is the one most readily associated with aggressive neo-liberal restructuring. Referred to as 'roll-back neo-liberalism', it was primarily in this decade that Thatcher and Reagan, and, in Canada, Mulroney and Bennett, among others, directed the power of the state against the policy regimes and structures, both within the state sector as well as civil society, most closely identified with the post-war Keynesian welfare state and the political foundations upon which it had been constructed. Through much of the 1990s and into the first decade of the twenty-first century we observe the advent of a roll-back neo-liberalism. This expression of neo-liberalism emerged as a response to the political limitations and extreme economic consequences flowing from the prior policies of austerity, privatization, and shrinking of the actual size and role of the state sector in the production of goods and services. This may be understood as the displacement of Thatcherism by the politics of the 'third way'.

The **third way** can be conceived as a 'soft' form of neo-liberalism which seeks to re-employ the state, but this time to contain the damage and dysfunction wrought by the policies of roll-back neo-liberalism (Peck and Tickell, 2002: 388–9). Jessop described 'third wayism' as a 'flanking strategy' in support of neo-liberalism, as the problems and contradictions of the roll-back phase surfaced and threatened to undermine the viability of the project (2002: 458). This is a critical aspect of the adaptation of neo-liberal strategies to address the political and economic tensions of its own making (Graefe, 2006: 71). Third-way advocates assert that new times require a new politics based on a new pragmatism, but one that fundamentally accepts the new order brought in by neo-liberal 'reform' (Powell, 2003: 102).

In brief, the politics of the third way are distinguished by a number of features. The third way accepts the neo-liberal idea of the problem of government failure, and hence the need to rely more on market mechanisms to increase society's wealth and provide services. But the third way also acknowledges *market failure* and suggests that there is consequently a need (greater than is allowed by hardline neo-liberals) for the state and civil society to correct resulting deficiencies. The third way seeks to harness the market to increase efficiency but it also seeks to use the state and civil society, including non-profit organizations, to provide the measure of equity necessary to support a more socially cohesive society (Powell, 2003: 103). In this context, third-way advocates are more open to investing in services than are hardline neo-liberals. However, such services will still be constructed and delivered using market-based models and contracted third-party delivery agents.

In Canada, freed by fiscal surplus, both the Liberal Chrétien government in its latter years and Martin's subsequent minority Liberal government engaged in cautious third-way–inspired reforms. The election of Stephen Harper's minority Conservative government represented a definite shift away from third-way approaches back towards the orthodoxy of the neo-liberal paradigm. The weakness of this minority government in terms of both seats and public support (Simpson, 2006), however, made this administration more tentative in implementing neo-liberal policy. At the provincial level, the Ontario Liberal government of Premier Dalton McGuinty is the clearest and most consistent expression of third-way politics and policy. What is inescapable, however, is the extent to which this government has worked within the constraints established by the Harris neo-liberal 'Common Sense Revolution' of the late 1990s (Evans and Albo, 2007; Peters, 2007).

Neo-Liberalism and Public Administration

Neo-liberalism and its third way offshoot required a new model of public administration based on reconstructing the state and its activities to resemble and mimic market economics and so to increase public sector productivity (Stewart and Walsh, 1992). The transition from the Keynesian welfare state to the neo-liberal state is a project in building a different kind of state where the 'purposes and operating values are considerably different from that which was characteristic' of the Keynesian period as 'the goal is no longer to protect society from the market's demands but to protect the market from society's demands' (Cohn, 1997: 586). Henceforth, it would not be so much a matter of market regulation but rather regulating the state.

At its most fundamental level the problem of public administration in the Keynesian era was seen to be rooted in its Weberian and Taylorist foundations. The ineffectiveness of government was seen to be a function of such innate characteristics such as size, complexity, and the absence of a pricing mechanism for public services. Such 'structural difficulties are accentuated by the emphasis on formal rules and authority as the guides for action within traditional public organizations, rather than depending upon either market signals or the entrepreneurial spirit of individuals to guide decisions' (Peters, 1993: 10). The OECD criticized this model, contending that organizational effectiveness was impeded by 'highly centralised, rule-bound, and inflexible organisations that emphasize process rather than results' (OECD, 1995: 7). Consequently, the restructuring of these characteristics became one of the central objectives of neo-liberalism; although, ironically, new contracting arrangements would impose a government-based 'web of rules' onto non-state actors.

In public administration neo-liberalism was imposed through **New Public Management** (NPM) which consists of two basic streams: managerialism and modes of control. Managerialism is defined as involving: (1) continuous increases in efficiency; (2) the use of ever more sophisticated technologies; (3) a labour force disciplined to productivity; (4) clear implementation of the professional management role; and (5) managers being given the right to manage (Pollitt, 1990: 2–3). Modes of control deals with the emergence of indirect control or 'centralized decentralization' as a means of managing from a distance and which operates through such means as: (1) continuous quality improvement; (2) an emphasis upon devolution; (3) information systems; (4) an emphasis upon contracts and markets; (5) performance measurement; and (6) an increased emphasis on audit and inspection (Walsh, 1995: xiv).

The prominent place that NPM has come to play within the third sector has led to a 'cultural take-over by stealth' of non-profit service provision by business values and practices (Taylor, 2002: 98–9). The introduction of a new funding regime and accountability measures as central control mechanisms through which the state has restructured its relationships with non-profits is clearly visible and suggests intent on the part of neo-liberal policy-makers. The use of funding contracts and strict administrative accountability systems was designed to solidify funder control of program costs and structure (Handy, 1990: 94). Non-profits would be compelled to bend to neo-liberal accountability schemes and human resource strategies: 'the use of contracts to regulate state finance of services provided by private organisations indicates more, not less, government regulation' (Ascoli and Ranci, 2002: 5).

Neo-Liberalizing the Third Sector

In the international context, Harvey has observed that 'NGOs have in many instances stepped into the vacuum in social provision left by the withdrawal of the state from such activities. This amounts to privatization by NGO. In some instances this has helped accelerate further state withdrawal from social provision. NGOs thereby function as "Trojan horses for global neoliberalism"' (Harvey, 2005: 177). The same process of transforming non-profits is well underway in Canada. And here the 'business model' is being imported into the third sector and is expressed by the adoption of practices previously unknown in that sector, drawn from the world of for-profit business enterprise. Whereas the same phenomenon entered the public sector in the 1980s and 1990s under the aegis of NPM, it has now proceeded into the third sector where the 'increasing use of these tools and approaches, adopted to ensure funding flows, plus the increasing professionalization of the NGO sector, pushes many NGOs into becoming carriers of these concepts, values and practices' (Wallace, 2004: 203).

The increasingly central place of non-profit agencies in the delivery of a diverse range of social services, not in a support role but as primary agent in a new 'partnering relationship' with the state, stands out under neo-liberalism. This is a form of privatization of social service provision where the responsibility for financing of social services remains a public responsibility but provision is contracted out to third parties, including non-profit agencies. It is in this context that the third sector was reconstituted in the 1980s and 1990s (Borzaga and Santuari, 2003: 38–9).

The neo-liberal demand that government be *reinvented* has drawn attention to the role and place of non-profit organizations in society. This has occurred because of the moves by neo-liberal governments to download former public responsibilities onto the market, non-profit organizations, and individuals; the neo-liberal desire to forge new 'partnership' relationships with such non-state actors as voluntary bodies in order to develop alternative service delivery options; and the neo-liberal *false* assertion that intrusive government has worked to undermine voluntary citizen participation, charitable giving, and self-help. There is little empirical evidence that neo-liberal policies have resulted in greater civic activism in voluntary organizations. The neo-liberal rhetoric about a revival of voluntarism and a more 'participatory' civic culture is, in fact, about the process of transferring many social support functions to the third sector. This speaks to the neo-liberal desire to *disinvest* government responsibilities for various citizenship rights in the social and economic spheres and, in the process, to transform the state's caring role in society. Moreover, in the government's shift to develop a more contractually based relationship with non-profit organizations (to set the government–non-profit relationship on a more commercial footing), the non-profit sector is being significantly and negatively altered (Evans, Richmond, and Shields, 2005). In short, neo-liberalism is about downsizing the state, slashing state support for programs (including those shifted to non-profit organizations), and placing most other human activities on a more market-based footing.

The Contracting Regime and Accountability: Controlling the Third Sector

The former grants-based regime, characterized by third-sector organizations acting as clients to the state, has been displaced by a new 'contracting regime' in the neo-liberal era. Program-based funding of non-profit service providers, regulated through strict contracts, has come to dominate the state–non-profit relationship. The market-oriented logic of the system, as described above, has been the main way in which the neo-liberal state has pushed the restructuring of the third sector. These contracts are: (1) competitive (non-profit providers bidding against one another); (2) short-term (usually one-year contracts to maximize funder control and oversight); (3) rigid in terms of how contracted dollars must be spent; and (4) generally inadequately funded (financing fails to fully cover the real costs of program delivery). The model assumes that non-profit volunteers and charitable donations will make up any funding shortfalls (Eakin, 2001: 2). One study calculated the underfunding of real program costs to be 7–15 per cent of the value of the actual contract (Eakin, 2002: 8). This approach to non-profit financing has been called 'hollow core funding' where the third sector subsidizes government programming (Eakin, 2004, 2005).

This **contract funding** regime has had a number of negative effects on non-profits, including (1) increasing levels of income instability and vulnerability among non-profit service providers; (2) reducing organizational effectiveness and flexibility as organizations struggle to compete for contracts and meet the narrow rules governing program funding; (3) creating wage depression and insecure employment in the sector because of underfunding and short-term financing; (4) greatly increasing the administrative burden on organizations due to onerous reporting requirements; (5) taking away the ability of many non-profits to engage in rational long-term planning because of the short-term nature of funding; (6) cultivating a climate of 'advocacy chill' where non-profits become afraid to voice criticism of government that they depend on financially; (7) commercializing operations by pushing non-profits to impose fee structures and sell other products to make up for funding shortfalls; and, (8) creating 'mission drift' as organizations juggle missions and mandates to fit government funding priorities (Reed and Howe, 2000: 17–18; Scott, 2003: 36; O'Sullivan and Salamon, 2004).

The presence of such a 'funding regime' points to the existence of 'a unified set of values and regulations governing the relationship between the non-profit and voluntary sector and their stakeholders, including funders' (Scott, 2003: 35). Market/business principles, fiscal restraint, and government control through the contract all clearly rest at the centre of this 'funding regime'. Moreover, third-sector organizations are being positioned to police their contracts with the state. Non-profits mediate between citizens and the state to ensure the contract terms are fulfilled. However, where they depend on the state for funding service delivery, they are not autonomous to negotiate on behalf of their client groups. In this process non-profits are being transformed into one-dimensional alternative service delivery agents and stripped of their multi-purposed origins.

An important dimension of this contract-funding regime is the new accountability system imposed on non-profit providers. **Accountability** is the 'obligation to explain how a responsibility has been discharged' and this requirement is particularly important where public trust is involved (Panel on Accountability and Governance in the Voluntary Sector, 1998: 8). Since third-sector organizations exist to be of public and mutual benefit there is 'a clear ethical obligation to perform according to promise and, as with all contracts, to be subject to evaluation and ready to answer for a failure to perform' (Jeavons, 1994: 197). Hence, non-profits have long operated under rules of accountability. The current challenge is the extent to which contract funding has worked to shift non-profit accountability away from its community roots towards the domination of accountability to the state. McCambridge notes that the use of service contracts to regulate non-profits does not in itself equal full accountability. It may work in fact to deflect attention away from a more fundamental accountability that non-profits owe to the cause they were established to benefit (2005: 3).

Unlike private for-profit enterprise driven by bottom-line logic, non-profits have multiple lines of accountability. Non-profits are accountable to clients, members, volunteers, staff, partners, donors, funders, and the public at large. These accountabilities often coexist uneasily (Panel on Accountability and Governance in the Voluntary Sector, 1998: 8). For instance, clients may be most concerned with improving the quality and human dimension of the service offered, while government funders may be most concerned with enhancing the 'efficiency' of service delivery and improving the bottom line. Under the new funding regime, accountability to government funders is coming to trump all other kinds of accountability.

Accountability under the neo-liberal funding regime has come to be defined as a 'value neutral' demand linked tightly with efficiency. The values of market-based notions of efficiency are, of course, embedded in this association. This approach also promotes the artificial separation between 'administrative accountability' and 'public accountability'. Administrative accountability is essentially reporting that funds have been spent in accordance with the conditions laid out in the funding contract. Public accountability is the responsibility of state authorities to fully and publicly account for their support for the provision of public goods and services. This responsibility should ensure that adequate financial support, infrastructure, and long-term vision sustain the public support of desired services.

Under NPM administrative accountability has been defined narrowly and has come to overshadow public accountability. Driven by 'audit chill', administrative accountability imposed on contracted services has also become extremely burdensome to administer. It is designed both to control actions from the centre and to shift risk downward. In this way the state is able to evade responsibility for underfunding services and transfer blame for deteriorating service quality onto third-party non-profit service deliverers (Taylor, 2002: 106).

Conclusion

Over the last few decades there has been an ideological shift from a Keynesian public-policy and public-administration orientation to the adoption of neo-liberal prescriptions and a corresponding assault on the post-war welfare state. The third sector, located between state and market, has been strategically positioned to facilitate the long-term neo-liberal strategy of marketization of public goods and services. Advancing the marketization of the public sector is an essential step on the road to the market society. The enhanced role awarded to non-profits in the production and delivery of public goods has been a key instrument of such a neo-liberal structural adjustment strategy. This new role of the third sector has had profound implications for the sector itself in terms of lost autonomy vis-à-vis the state and in regard to risks being transferred to third-sector agents of the state. Moreover, the capacity of this sector to take a greatly expanded position of supplier of social provision is highly problematic. The third sector is simply too small and vulnerable to adequately fill the vacuum left by a hollowed-out welfare state (Hall and Reed, 1998: 18). This in turn has negative implications for the development of social capital, enhancement of social cohesion, and the health of civil society in general.

The array of public goods and services that came to define the post-war social contract, most importantly the state provision of social programs as a citizenship entitlement, served to broaden and deepen the meaning of citizenship well beyond the narrow definition of civil and political rights to encompass social and economic needs.

In this sense the **Keynesian welfare state** was a developmental state in which the expansion of social provision contributed to social cohesion. The cohesive society was built within the context of a growth paradigm predicated on political commitments to high levels of good employment, macroeconomic management, a strong social safety net, and the provision of political voice—often facilitated by non-profit advocacy (Burke, Mooers, and Shields, 2000).

Neo-liberal restructuring is contributing to the deterioration of social cohesion and is hampering the development of social capital. In terms of civil society, notions of community, solidarity, and collective responsibility are being displaced by an atomized society where the ethic of 'possessive individualism' (Macpherson, 1962) prevails. Social citizenship is under challenge and the narrower idea of the citizen as consumer and client is coming to predominate (Mooers, 1999). The diminishing of the advocacy role of the third sector is deterring access to the policy-making process, especially for the most marginal and underrepresented in society. In this sense the idea of the third sector as a voice for society is under threat. As Paul Leduc Browne notes, non-profits' 'autonomy and identity will be eclipsed as they are forced into the straightjacket of [the] commercialized public sector's managerial norms and procedures' (Browne, 1996: 69). In the neo-liberal era, unlike the Keynesian, there has been the tendency to *use* the third sector rather than *support* it (Hudson, 1999: 221).

Hence, neo-liberal restructuring is changing the character and ethos of many non-profit organizations, thereby threatening the roles that they have traditionally performed in society. The changing nature of government funding to non-profit bodies has thrown the third sector into fiscal stress. Downloading many welfare-state services to the third sector has taxed the capacity of the sector to the breaking point. The drive of policy-makers to 'facilitate' the creation of new partnerships between non-profit organizations, the state, and for-profit organizations is forcing the non-profit sector to act in a more entrepreneurial fashion, diminishing its community orientation. This is an environment where markets prevail over the interests of the larger community.

Important Terms and Concepts

accountability
advocacy
citizenship
contract funding
Keynesian welfare state
marketization
mediation
mixed social economy model
neo-liberalism
New Public Management
privatization
services
social capital
social cohesion
third sector (non-profit sector)
third way

Study Questions

1. According to Evans and Shields, how does the role of the third sector change over the evolution from early stages, to the Keynesian welfare state, to the neo-liberal era?
2. What are the differences in characteristics from era to era?
3. How has neo-liberalism evolved over time, and what significance does this hold for the third sector?

4. What is the nature of public administration in the neo-liberal state?

5. What are the characteristics, size, and extent of the third sector?

Useful Websites

Eakin, Lynn. 2001. 'An Overview of the Funding of Canada's Voluntary Sector', prepared for the Voluntary Sector Initiative Working Group on Financing, September.

www.vsi-isbc.org/eng/funding/overview_of_funding.cfm

The Voluntary Sector Initiative Reports: Around 100 specialized reports sponsored by this unique venture, jointly led and managed by the federal government and voluntary sector:

www.vsi-isbc.org/eng/products/reports.cfm#policy

The Voluntary Sector Roundtable:

www.voluntary-sector.ca/

Eakin, Lynn. 2005. *The Policy and Practice Gap: Federal Government Practices Regarding Administrative Costs When Funding Voluntary Sector Organizations*, prepared for Voluntary Sector Forum.

http://lynneakin.com/wp-content/uploads/2006/11/policy_practice_gap.pdf

McMullen, Kathryn, and Grant Schellenberg. 2002. 'Mapping the Non-Profit Sector—Human Resources in the Non-Profit Sector' (with links to related reports). Canadian Policy Research Networks.

www.cprn.org/doc.cfm?doc=60&l=en

The Third Sector in the UK: Third Sector: Charities/Voluntary Organizations/Social Enterprise:

www.thirdsector.co.uk/

International Society for Third Sector Research:

www.istr.org/

The Public Policy and Third Sector Initiative at the School of Policy Studies, Queen's University, Kingston:

www.queensu.ca/sps/third_sector/

The Center for Civil Society Studies of the Johns Hopkins Institute for Policy Studies:

www.ccss.jhu.edu/index.php?section=content&view=20

References

Amin, Ash, Angus Cameron, and Ray Hudson. 2002. *Placing the Social Economy.* London: Routledge.

Armstrong, Pat. 1997. 'The Welfare State as History', in Raymond B. Blake, Penny E. Bryden and J. Frank Strain, eds, *The Welfare State in Canada: Past, Present and Future.* Concord, Ont.: Irwin.

Ascoli, Ugo, and Constanzo Ranci. 2002. 'The Context of New Social Policies in Europe', in Ugo Ascoli and Constanzo Ranci, eds, *Dilemmas of the Welfare Mix: The New Structure of Welfare in an Era of Privatization.* New York: Kluwer Academic/Plenum Publishers, 1–24.

Bach, Stephen. 2004. *Labour and Social Dimensions of Privatization and Restructuring: Health Care Services.* Geneva: International Labour Office Action Programme on Privatization, Restructuring and Economic Democracy.

Baines, Donna. 2004. 'Caring for Nothing: Work Organization and Unwaged Labour in Social Services', *Work, Employment and Society* 8, 2: 267–95.

Banting, Keith G. 2000. *The Non-Profit Sector in Canada: Roles and Relationships.* Kingston: School of Policy Studies, Queen's University.

Barbalet, J.M. 1988. *Citizenship: Rights, Struggle and Class Inequality.* Minneapolis: University of Minnesota Press.

Borzaga, Carlo, and Alceste Santuari. 2003. 'New Trends in the Non-Profit Sector in Europe: The Emergence of Social Entrepreneurship', in OECD, *The Non-Profit Sector in a Changing Economy.* Paris: Organisation for Economic Co-Operation and Development, 31–77.

Browne, Paul LeDuc. 1996. *Love in a Cold World? The Voluntary Sector in an Age of Cuts.* Ottawa: Canadian Centre for Policy Studies.

———. 1999. 'Post Social Democracy, or the Dialectic of the Social Economy', in Dave Broad and Wayne Antony, eds, *Citizens or Consumers? Social Policy in a Market Society.* Halifax: Fernwood, 206–11.

Burke, Mike, Colin Mooers, and John Shields. 2000. *Restructuring and Resistance: Public Policy in an Age of Global Capitalism.* Halifax: Fernwood.

Byrne, David. 2005. *Social Exclusion.* Maidenhead, UK: Open University Press.

Cappe, Mel. 1999. 'Building a New Relationship with the Voluntary Sector', speech to the Third Canadian Leaders' Forum on the

Voluntary Sector, Association of Professional Executives, Ottawa, 31 May. Available at: www.pco-bcp.gc.ca/ClerkSP-MC/voluntary_e.htm.

Cohn, Daniel. 1997. 'Creating Crises and Avoiding Blame: The Politics of Public Service Reform in the New Public Management in Great Britain and the United States', *Administration and Society* 29, 5: 584–616.

Daly, Tamara J. 2003. 'Responding to State Retrenchment: An Historical Perspective on Non-Profit Home Health and Social Care in Ontario', in Paul LeDuc Brown, *The Commodity of Care: Home Care Reform in Ontario*. Ottawa: Canadian Centre for Policy Alternatives.

Deakin, Nicholas. 2003. 'The Voluntary Sector', in Pete Alcock, Angus Erskine, and Margaret May, eds, *The Student's Companion to Social Policy*. Oxford: Blackwell, 191–9.

Drakeford, Mark. 2000. *Privatisation and Social Policy*. Essex: Pearson Educational.

Eakin, Lynn. 2001. *An Overview of the Funding of Canada's Voluntary Sector*. Ottawa: Voluntary Sector Initiative Working Group on Financing, September.

———. 2002. *Supporting Organizational Infrastructure in the Voluntary Sector*. Ottawa: Voluntary Sector Initiative Secretariat, May.

———. 2004. *Capacity Draining: The Impact of Current Funding Practices on Non-Profit Community Organizations*. Toronto: Community Social Planning Council of Toronto.

———. 2005. *The Policy and Practice Gap: Federal Government Practices Regarding Administrative Costs When Funding Voluntary Sector Organizations*. Ottawa: Voluntary Sector Forum, March.

Edwards, Michael. 2004. *Civil Society*. Cambridge, UK: Polity.

Elson, Peter R. 2007. 'A Short History of Voluntary Sector-Government Relations in Canada', *The Philanthropist* 21, 1: 36–74.

Evans, Bryan, and Greg Albo. 2007. 'Limited Horizons: Assessing Ontario's Election', *Relay* 20 (November/December): 4–7.

———, Ted Richmond, and John Shields. 2005. 'Structuring Neoliberal Governance: The Non-Profit Sector, Emerging New Modes of Control and the Marketisation of Service Delivery', *Policy and Society* 24, 1: 73–97.

Fabricant, Michael, and Steve Burghardt. 1992. *The Welfare State in Crisis and the Transformation of Social Service Work*. Armonk, New York: M.E. Sharpe.

Ford, Robin. 1998. 'Trends and Issues in Governance and Accountability', unpublished manuscript.

———, and David Zussman, eds. 1997. *Alternative Service Delivery: Sharing Governance in Canada*. Toronto: KPMG and the Institute of Public Administration of Canada.

Graefe, Peter. 2006. 'Social Economy Policies as Flanking for Neoliberalism: Transnational Policy Solutions, Emergent Contradictions, Local Alternatives', *Policy and Society* 25, 3: 69–86.

Graves, Frank L. 1999. 'Rethinking Government As If People Mattered: From "Reaganomics" to "Humanomics"', in Leslie A. Pal, ed., *How Ottawa Spends 1999–2000. Shape Shifting: Canadian Governance Toward the 21st Century*. Toronto: Oxford University Press, 37–73.

Hall, Michael. 1997. 'Comments', in Ronald Hirshhorn, ed., *The Emerging Sector: In Search of a Framework*. Ottawa: Canadian Policy Research Networks, 72–4.

———, and Keith G. Banting. 2000. 'The Non-Profit Sector in Canada: An Introduction', in Keith G. Banting, ed., *The Non-Profit Sector in Canada: Roles and Relationships*. Kingston: School of Policy Studies, Queen's University, 1–28.

———, Cathy W. Barr, M. Easwaramoorthy, S. Wojciech Sokolowski, and Lester M. Salamon. 2005. *The Canadian Non-Profit and Voluntary Sector in Comparative Perspective*. Toronto: Imagine Canada.

———, and Paul B. Reed. 1998. 'Shifting the Burden: How Much Can Government Download to the Non-Profit Sector?', *Canadian Public Administration* 41, 1 (Spring): 1–20.

Halpern, David. 2005. *Social Capital*. Cambridge, UK: Polity.

Handy, Charles. 1990. *The Age of Unreason*. Boston: Harvard Business School Press.

Hartley, K. 1990. 'Contracting Out in Britain: Achievements and Problems', in J.J. Richardson, ed., *Privatization and Deregulation in Canada and Britain*. Dartmouth: Institute for Research on Public Policy.

Harvey, David. 2005. *A Brief History of Neoliberalism*. Oxford: Oxford University Press.

Hirshhorn, Ronald, ed. 1997. *The Emerging Sector: In Search of a Framework*. Ottawa: Canadian Policy Research Networks.

Hoggett, Pail. 1991. 'A New Management in the Public Sector', *Policy and Politics* 19, 4: 243–56.

Hudson, Pete. 1999. 'The Voluntary Sector, the State and Citizenship in the UK', in Dave Broad and Wayne Antony, eds, *Citizens or Consumers? Social Policy in a Market Society*. Halifax: Fernwood, 212–24.

Independent Sector. 1998. 'Overview and Executive Summary: The State of the Independent Sector', Washington, Independent Sector. Available at: www.indepsec.org/programs/research/almanac_overview.html.

Jeavons, Thomas H. 1994. 'Ethics in Non-Profit Management: Creating a Culture of Integrity', in Robert D. Herman & Associates, eds, *The Jossey-Bass Handbook of Non-Profit Leadership and Management*. San Francisco: Jossey-Bass, 182–207.

Jenson, Jane, and Susan D. Phillips. 1996. 'Regime Shift: New Citizenship Practices in Canada', *International Journal of Canadian Studies* 14 (Fall): 111–35.

Jessop, Bob. 2002. *The Future of the Capitalist State*. Cambridge: Polity Press.

Kay, Fiona M., and Paul Bernard. 2007. 'The Dynamics of Social Capital: Who Wants to Stay in if Nobody Is Out?', in Fiona M. Kay and Richard Johnston, eds, *Social Capital, Diversity, and the Welfare State*. Vancouver: University of British Columbia Press, 41–66.

Kernaghan, Ken. 1992. 'Choose your Partners—It's Innovation Time!', *Public Sector Management* 3, 2 (Fall): 16–17.

———. 1993. 'Partnership and Public Administration: Conceptual and Practical Considerations', *Canadian Public Administration* 36, 1 (Spring): 57–76.

Langford, John. 1997. 'Power Sharing in the Alternative Service Delivery World', in Robin Ford and David Zussman, eds, *Alternative Service Delivery: Sharing Governance in Canada*.

Toronto: KPMG and the Institute of Public Administration of Canada, 59–70.

McCambridge, Ruth. 2005. 'Is Accountability the Same as Regulation? Not Exactly', *The Non-Profit Quarterly* 12 (Special Issue): 3–5.

Macpherson, C.B. 1962. *The Political Theory of Possessive Individualism*. Oxford: Oxford University Press.

Maurutto, Paula. 2005. 'Charity and Public Welfare in History: A Look at Ontario, 1830–1950', *The Philanthropist* 19, 3: 159–67.

Means, Robin, Hazel Moreby, and Randall Smith. 2002. *From Community Care to Market Care: The Development of Welfare Services for Older People*. Bristol: The Polity Press.

Mooers, Colin. 1999. 'Can We Still Resist? Globalization, Citizenship Rights and Class Formation', in Dave Broad and Wayne Antony, eds, *Citizens or Consumers? Social Policy in a Market Society*. Halifax: Fernwood, 285–98.

Murray, The Honourable Lowell. 1999. *Final Report on Social Cohesion*. Ottawa: Standing Committee on Social Affairs, Science and Technology, June. Available at: www.parl.gc.ca/36/1/parlbus/commbus/senate/com-e/SOCI-E/rep-e/repfinaljun99-e.htm.

The Muttart Foundation. 2006. *Talking About Charities 2006: Tracking Canadian's Opinions About Charities and the Issues Affecting Them*. Edmonton: The Muttart Foundation.

Navarro, Vicente. 2007. 'Neoliberalism as a Class Ideology: Or, The Political Causes of the Growth of Inequalities', in Vicente Navarro, ed., *Neoliberalism, Globalization and Inequalities: Consequences for Health and Quality of Life*. Amityville, NY: Baywood.

Nowland-Foreman, Garth. 1996. 'Governments, Community Organisations and Civil Society—A Beginner's Guide to Dissection of a Golden Goose', *The Jobs Letter*, New Zealand. Available at: www.jobsletter.org.nz/art/artn0001.htm.

O'Connor, Julia S. 1998. 'Social Justice, Social Citizenship, and the Welfare State, 1965–1995: Canada in Comparative Context', in Rick Helmes-Hayes and James Curtis, eds, *The Vertical Mosaic Revisited*. Toronto: University of Toronto Press, 180–231.

OECD (Organisation for Economic Co-Operation and Development). 1995. *Governance in Transition*. Paris: OECD.

———. 2003. *The Non-Profit Sector in a Changing Economy*. Paris: OECD.

———. 2005. *Modernizing Government: The Way Forward*. Paris: OECD.

O'Sullivan, Richard, and Lester M. Salamon. 2004. 'Stressed but Coping: Nonprofit Organizations and the Current Fiscal Crisis'. Johns Hopkins University, Center for Civil Society Studies, Institute for Policy Studies. 19 January. Available at: www.jhu.edu/listeningpost/news/pdf/comm02.pdf.

Panel on Accountability and Governance in the Voluntary Sector. 1998. *Helping Canadians Help Canadians: Improving Governance and Accountability in the Voluntary Sector*. Discussion Paper, May. Available at: http://www.pagvs.com/helping.html.

Peck, Jamie, and Adam Tickell. 2002. 'Neoliberal Space', *Antipode* 34, 3: 380–404.

Peters, B. Guy. 1993. *The Public Service, The Changing State and Governance*. Ottawa: Canadian Centre for Management Development.

———, and Donald J. Savoie, eds. 2000. *Governance in the Twenty-First Century: Revitalizing the Public Service*. Montreal and Kingston: Canadian Centre for Management Development and McGill-Queen's University Press.

Peters, John. 2007. 'Liars, Twits, and the Ennui of Democracy: The McGuinty Victory and the Problems of Third Way Politics in Ontario', *Relay* 20 (November/December): 8–12.

Phillips, Susan D. 1991. 'How Ottawa Blends: Shifting Government Relationships with Interest Groups', in Frances Abele, ed., *How Ottawa Spends 1991–1992: The Politics of Fragmentation*. Ottawa: Carleton University Press, 183–227.

———. 2001. 'From Charity to Clarity: Reinventing Federal Government–Voluntary Sector Relationships', in Leslie A. Pal, ed., *How Ottawa Spends 2001–2002: Power in Transition*. Don Mills: Oxford University Press.

Pierre, Jon. 1995. 'The Marketization of the State: Citizens, Customers, and the Emergence of the Public Market', in B. Guy Peters and Donald Savoie, eds, *Governance in a Changing Environment*. Montreal and Kingston: McGill-Queen's University Press.

Policy Research Committee. 1996. *Growth, Human Development, Social Cohesion*, Draft Interim Report. Ottawa: Policy Research Secretariat, Government of Canada, 4 Oct.

Pollitt, Christopher. 1990. *Managerialism and the Public Services*. Oxford: Blackwell.

Powell, Martin. 2003. 'The Third Way', in Pete Alcock, Angus Erskine, and Margaret May, eds, *The Student's Companion to Social Policy*. Oxford: Blackwell, 100–6.

Putnam, Robert. 1995. 'Bowling Alone: America's Declining Social Capital', *Journal of Democracy* 6, 1 (Jan.): 65–78.

Reed, Paul B, and Valerie J. Howe. 2000. *Voluntary Organizations in Ontario in the 1990s: Non-Profit Knowledge Base Project Reports*. Ottawa: Statistics Canada.

Rekart, Josephine. 1993. *Public Funds, Private Provision: The Role of the Voluntary Sector*. Vancouver: University of British Columbia Press.

Salamon, Lester M. 1995. *Partners in Public Service: Government–Non-Profit Relations in the Modern Welfare State*. Baltimore: Johns Hopkins University Press.

Sava, E.S. 1987. *Privatization: The Key to Better Government*. Chatham, NJ: Chatham House.

Schwartz, Herman. 1994. 'Small States in Big Trouble: State Reorganization in Australia, Denmark, New Zealand and Sweden in the 1980s', *World Politics* 46, 4: 527–55.

Scott, Jacquelyn Thayer. 1997. 'Defining the Non-Profit Sector', in Ronald Hirshhorn, ed, *The Emerging Sector: In Search of a Framework*. Ottawa: Canadian Policy Research Networks, 43–51.

Scott, Katherine. 2003. *Funding Matters: The Impact of Canada's New Funding Regime on Non-Profit and Voluntary Organizations*. Ottawa: Canadian Council on Social Development.

Seidle, Leslie. 1995. *Rethinking the Delivery of Public Services to Citizens*. Montreal: Institute for Research on Public Policy.

———. 1997. 'Responsiveness and Accountability: The Drivers of Alternative Service Delivery', in Ford and Zussman (1997: 88–103).

Shields, John, and B. Mitchell Evans. 1998. *Shrinking the State: Globalization and Public Administration 'Reform'*. Halifax: Fernwood.

Simpson, Jeffrey. 2006. 'Why the Conservatives are Doing So Poorly', *Globe and Mail*, 6 September, A17.

Social Planning Council of Metropolitan Toronto (SPC). 1997. *Merchants of Care? The Non-Profit Sector in a Competitive Social Services Marketplace.* Toronto: SPC, April.

Statistics Canada. 2004. *Cornerstones of Community: Highlights of the National Survey of Non-Profit and Voluntary Organizations.* Ottawa: Statistics Canada.

Stein, Janice. 2001. *The Cult of Efficiency.* Toronto: Anansi Press.

Stewart, J., and K. Walsh. 1992. 'Change in the Management of Public Services', *Public Administration* 70: 499–518.

Taylor, Marilyn. 2002. 'Government, the Third Sector and the Contract Culture: The UK Experience So Far', in Ugo Ascoli and Constanzo Ranci, eds, *Dilemmas of the Welfare Mix: The New Structure of Welfare in an Era of Privatization.* New York: Kluwer Academic/Plenum Publishers, 77–108.

Tuohy, Carolyn. 1999. *Accidental Logics: The Dynamics of Change in the Health Care Arena in the United States and Canada.* New York: Oxford University Press.

United Kingdom, Department of Health. 1989. *Caring for People: Community Care in the Next Decade and Beyond,* White Paper. London: HMSO.

Valverde, Mariana. 1995. 'The Mixed Social Economy as a Canadian Tradition', *Studies in Political Economy* 47 (Summer): 33–60.

Veljanovski, Cento. 1987. *Selling the State: Privatisation in Britain.* London: Weidenfield and Nicolson.

Voluntary Sector Task Force. 1999. *Working Together: A Government of Canada/Voluntary Sector Joint Initiative.* Ottawa: Privy Council Office, August.

Walker, Alan, 1984. 'The Political Economy of Privatisation', in Julian LeGrand and Ray Robinson, eds, *Privatisation and the Welfare State.* London: George Allen and Unwin.

Wallace, Tina. 2004. 'NGO Dilemmas: Trojan Horses for Global Neoliberalism?', in Leo Panitch and Colin Leys, eds, *The Socialist Register 2004: The New Imperial Challenge.* London: Merlin Press, 202–19.

Walsh, Kieron. 1995. *Public Service and Market Mechanisms: Competition, Contracting and the New Public Management.* New York: St Martin's Press.

Walzer, Michael. 1991. 'The Idea of Civil Society', *Dissent* (Spring): 293–304.

Ware, Robert. 1999. 'Public Moral Values, the Fabrication of Communities and Disempowerment', in Dave Broad and Wayne Antony, eds, *Citizens or Consumers? Social Policy in a Market Society.* Halifax: Fernwood, 299–312.

Wright, J. David, and Alti B. Rodal. 1997. 'Partnerships and Alliances', in Mohamed Charih and Arthur Daniels, eds, *New Public Management and Public Administration in Canada.* Toronto: Institute of Public Administration of Canada, 263–91.

18 Women and the Public Sector

Caroline Andrew

Introduction

The relationship of women to the public sector is a huge, complex, and fascinating story riddled with contradictions, ambiguities, and uncertainties. It is, at one and the same time, one of the fundamental themes of feminist analysis, a detailed account of **government machinery**, and a lens of analysis for public policy and public policy-making.

Looking at the public sector in relation to women raises the whole set of issues of how women have been associated with the private realm and men with the public realm. One of the major themes of the modern **feminist movement** has been to contest the definitions and boundaries of public and private and to argue both for the presence of women in the public realm and for the reconceptualization of the public–private dichotomy. In one sense, our use of 'public sector' in this chapter is more modest in that it largely refers to the government bureaucracies of the Canadian state: federal, provincial, and municipal. However, the larger debates about public/private and male/female cannot be dismissed as they emerge constantly—in discussions about work–family reconciliation and women's careers, about municipal policy on women's security, about the policy areas where there are more women senior officials. All of these questions come back to basic arguments about how women relate, and are seen to relate, to public and private spheres.

A second major theme—in some ways contradictory to the first—is the comparison between the place of women in the organizations of the public sector and in those of the market sector. The public sector has certain characteristics—greater reliance on formal rules and formal procedures, more weight given to formal education as a criterion for positions—that suggest it might be easier for women to enter and to be promoted within the public bureaucracies than within the market sector. Women and the public sector can thus be seen as one of the areas where there was at least some transformation during the second half of the twentieth century.

Linked to this is the fact that the modern Canadian feminist movement has given considerable importance to the issue of work in the public sector. As we shall see, since the *Report of the Royal Commission on the Status of Women* (1970), the conditions of work for women in the public sector have been of ongoing interest to the women's movement. It is therefore interesting to examine this question over 35 years after the *Report* to see to what extent women have succeeded in realizing their goals for public sector employment. To explore this question we must also be sensitive to the major shifts that have taken place in the role of the public sector in Canada. To simplify greatly, we can think of three periods: the pre-expansion period; the period of the expanding public sector or the development of the Canadian welfare state; and, finally, the period of the questioning of the public sector with the moves to decentralization, privatization, and reconfigurations of public sector organizations. At present, we seem either to be still in this third period or to be in transition from the period of the cutbacks to a new period as yet unclearly defined. These shifts have major consequences for the relations between women and the public sector; indeed, these consequences are far greater than any explicit policies or programs that exist. Our attempts, therefore, to think in terms of future trends must be based on a reading of the overall role of the public sector in Canadian society.

This chapter is organized according to a logic that combines chronology and issues, inspired in part by Martha Hynna's overview (Hynna, 1997) of women in the federal public service. Hynna examines how the issue has evolved over the previous 30 years. At the beginning it was dominated by questions of numbers, but more recently administrative culture and styles of decision-making have become more important. This discussion brings us back to a recognition of the importance of the formal structures or governmental machinery (increasingly in a comparative framework) and, finally, to policy, as well as structure, as a way of thinking about the impact of women on the public sector. Looking at policy-making and policy allows us to evaluate how women fare in, and from, the public sector.

The Early Years

Women have been employed in the federal public service since the 1870s. John Taylor (1990: 3) dates the first full-time permanent female appointment in the inside service as that of Miss Annie Samuels, as of 1 May 1876, in the Post Office Department. By the time of the Royal Commission on the Civil Service in 1907, of an estimated 3,000 employees in Ottawa, 700 were women (ibid., 4). Women had entered the public sector in part because the salaries were so low that men were not attracted to the civil service.

The defining moment of the early development of the civil service in relation to women came in 1908 when, following the Royal Commission of 1907, the Civil Service Amendment Act was passed. This instigated a double-entry system, with an officer class at the top and a 'routine' class, largely clerical and destined to be highly female, at the bottom. The civil service list of 1910 indicates only one woman in the top class (ibid., 19). Taylor links this with the professionalization of the civil service and the desire of middle-class men to create good jobs for themselves. This corresponds as well to Graham Lowe's analysis of the feminization of clerical work. Lowe (1987: 71) states that 'the treatment of women in the Canadian federal civil service is one of the more blatant examples available of how some major employers used sophisticated bureaucratic measures to corral women into the lowest occupational grades.' In addition to the 1908 introduction of a double-entry system, in 1918 legislation allowed the Civil Service Committee to limit job competitions on the basis of sex and, in 1921, to bar married women from permanent posts (ibid., 73).

What is important to underline is not so much the specific detail of these policies but the general trend that links the modernization and professionalization of the public sector with the creation of a female clerical ghetto and the virtual exclusion of women from the officer rank. Merit and women were seen as contradictory; women were seen 'as having limited abilities; as needing to be managed; as needing to be protected; and as willing to work for less' (Taylor, 1990: 11). The merit system prevailed and the modern federal civil service was developed on a highly gendered basis. These patterns are important for understanding the present and future place of women in the public sector. As Nicole Morgan argued in her study of women in the federal public service from 1908 to 1987, an adequate research perspective requires abandoning certain traditional ideas; instead of focusing on women's lack of qualifications one should look at men's resistance to women's entry, abandon linear views of progress whereby slowly and steadily women's position improves, and, finally, set aside the idea that women form a homogeneous unit (Morgan, 1988: 1). These early years of the Canadian civil service are instructive in reinforcing Morgan's argument, for the position of women certainly did not follow a pattern of linear progression. The early patronage civil service was more open to women than was the merit-based, professionalized bureaucracy that followed it.

State Expansion and the Role of Women: The Royal Commission on the Status of Women

World War II was a crucial period both for the expansion of the public sector in Canada and for the increase in the participation of women in the paid labour force. These two phenomena interconnect and the development of the Canadian welfare state in the post-war period, through the expansion of government involvement in education, health, and social services, is clearly linked to female employment.

In 1967, when the federal government decided to create a Royal Commission on the Status of Women, one of the specific areas for investigation was the 'laws, practices and policies concerning the employment and promotion of women in the Federal Civil Service, by Federal Crown Corporations and by Federal Agencies' (Royal Commission, 1970: viii). The federal government was the largest employer of women in Canada, with more than 81,000 women employed. The concern of the Commission was with numbers, but with numbers linked to levels. Large numbers of women were employed by the federal government but almost all were concentrated at the bottom. One striking statistic was that in the most senior level of the federal public service at the time, the Senior Officer class, there were 349 officers of which only three were women (ibid., 109). At the other end of the scale, 83 per cent of the office support and administrative support category were female, and 41 per cent of female employees received less than $4,000 per year (as compared to 7 per cent of male employees) (ibid., 106). The Commission's *Report* is full of numbers indicating that 'women do not have equal opportunity to enter and advance in Government Service' (ibid., 138). This was a central question to the Commission and its vision was that the federal government should not only be a good employer but should be a model to demonstrate 'Canada's commitments to working women' (ibid., 139). The Commission recommended that the federal government, in addition to issuing a policy declaration, should set up a Women's Program Secretariat in the Privy Council Office, with coordinators named in each department, and that this agency be responsible for a 'program for equality of opportunity for women in the Federal Government Service and the greater use of their skills and abilities' (ibid., 140).

The *Report* of the Commission is important in regard to women and the public sector for a number of reasons. First of all, it underlined the dramatic imbalance of power and of good jobs and, in terms of a concern for increasing **gender equality**, this clearly called for strong collective action and the creation of specific government machinery. Second, it articulated a justification for federal action—the federal government was to be a model of commitment to working women. Third, by its recommendations relating to the need for support for voluntary associations it articulates the basis for alliances and coalitions between people working within the government and women active in women's groups. This is a theme to which we will return, but certainly the Commission helped to lay out a clear basis for support by government of the activities of civil society that were furthering public policy goals. Also of note is that the recommendations of the Royal Commission illustrate the optimism of the period, when the public sector was expanding and a sense of confidence existed in its capacity to realize the goals given to it by Canadian society. The logic of the recommendations is that with specific policy machinery and the elimination of systemic barriers, women's employment conditions in the federal public service would improve so substantially that equality could be reached.

And there was progress. As Hynna reports, the percentage of women in the highest category of the civil service went from less than 1 per cent in 1967 to 12 per cent by 1988 and to 23 per cent by 1997 (Hynna, 1997: 620). Indeed, by 2005–6 the percentage of women in the EX category was 38.8 per cent (Canada Public Service Agency, 2006). However, the optimism of the Royal Commission was not borne out as progress has been slower and more difficult to achieve than had been envisaged, particularly concerning the representation of female diversity. But implementation of its recommendations led to the creation of some specific procedures and structures aimed at increasing female employment in senior positions and sensitizing the bureaucracy to the importance of gender equality. Progress within the federal government on these issues also came from the adoption in 1985 by the federal government of the principle of **employment equity** following Rosalie Abella's 1984 report, *Equality in Employment*. This involved the development of plans by each federal department and agency for the fairer representation of women, disabled persons, Aboriginal people, and members of visible minority groups. The plans included numerical objectives and special initiatives (Status of Women, 1989: 26). In addition, the federal government accepted a plan of action for applying equal pay for work of equal value throughout the federal public service. This last issue has had a particularly long history—it took over 15 years, and several court decisions, for the federal government to agree to implement decisions on pay equity. In fact, only in the late fall of 1999 did the federal government agree to make retroactive payments.

By the late 1980s concern about the slowness of progress led to the creation of a Task Force on Barriers to Women in the Public Service. By this time, the civil service was facing important downsizing. Pat Carney, the minister responsible for launching the idea of the task force, stated in her Foreword to the *Report* presented by this Task Force that 'at first, the bureaucracy was cool to this particular ministerial initiative. In a period of downsizing, reduced promotion opportunities and possible male backlash to employment equity initiatives by the Government, few people wanted to tackle the issue of women in the public service' (Task Force on Barriers, 1990, vol. 1: Foreword). Once more, we come back to the themes elaborated by Nicole Morgan—progress is not linear and resistance to women's entry must be taken into account. The heterogeneity of women also emerges in the Task Force *Report*.

This *Report* is of particular interest because of the evolution in the analysis of the reasons for women's position in the federal civil service. The Task Force mandate was to analyze the barriers to women's equality and the *Report* accords the greatest importance to attitudes, certainly a major shift from the structural vision of the earlier Royal Commission. The three major barriers are described as attitudes, corporate culture, and balancing work and family responsibilities (ibid., 60). The principal recommendations were to make 'visible, clearly-articulated persistent commitment from the top', to treat gender balance as a management problem, to take action on system improvements that had been recommended in the past, and, finally, to tackle the questions of attitudes and corporate culture (ibid., 125, 124).

This view of the problem has been important in recent times and has brought to the fore the differences in management styles between men and women, the whole range of issues relating to work–family balance, and the issue of gender-based harassment. This shift in understanding can and has been interpreted in various ways. For some, it reflects a fuller understanding of how women's current position in the public sector is constructed. For example, Martha Hynna (1997: 623) argues that the issue has moved to one of **managing diversity**: 'an approach that emphasizes valuing and managing diversity is probably more difficult to implement than employment equity because of the need to change the culture of the organization.' Others have argued that a move from structures and systems to culture and attitude is a watering-down of the federal commitment to equality in that the government appears to take less responsibility by emphasizing questions of broad socialization patterns for which it cannot be held directly accountable. If the problem is attitude, then everyone, and perhaps no one, is responsible for solutions. It is an interesting, and important, question to think about whether or not this emphasis on culture and attitude facilitates or constrains the possibilities of focusing on the intersections of gender and other markers of equity, such as visible minority status, Aboriginal status, or disability (Hankivsky, 2005), as it is these questions of **intersectionality** that have become increasingly salient to the examination of women and the public sector.

Government Machinery

It should not be suggested, however, that the interest in structures and systems has entirely disappeared. Ever since the Royal Commission on the Status of Women, there has been a clear interest in issues of government machinery at both the federal and provincial levels. Our description of government machinery requires a jump back in time to situate the creation of the first government agency interested in women's issues, the establishment in 1954 of the Women's Bureau of the Department of Labour, although the major innovations in machinery emerge subsequent to the 1970 Royal Commission.

Starting first with the federal government, in 1971 a position of Minister Responsible for the Status of Women was created, as was an Office of the Coordinator of the Status of Women reporting to the minister. In 1973 the Women's Program was established within the Department of the Secretary of State and the Canadian Advisory Council on the Status of Women was established. In 1976 the Office of the Coordinator became a self-standing organization, Status of Women Canada, and in 1981 the first meeting was held of the federal, provincial, and territorial ministers responsible for the status of women. Finally, in 1994 the Advisory Council was abolished and its research and information functions absorbed by Status of Women Canada, along with the Women's Program (originally with the Secretary of State). The policy research program within Status of Women Canada was eliminated in 2007.

There have been five major components to the government machinery for women in Canada: advisory bodies; government agencies concerned with policy advocacy, coordination, and development; programs and agencies to fund women's groups and activities aimed at gender equality; policy-specific agencies such as those related to health and employment (the Women's Bureau at the federal level was originally in the Department of Labour and now is housed in Human Resources Canada) and government-funded research and knowledge translation centres working on areas relevant to women. In addition to looking at these components, we must consider recent trends in governments' commitments to specific machinery for women.

Advisory councils have been created in a number of jurisdictions. At the present time, the most important example is the Conseil du Statut de la femme du Québec. Others, including the federal Advisory Council on the Status of Women and the Alberta Council, have been eliminated. At the municipal level, Whitzman (2002: 10) reports that 'women's committees were the exception rather than the norm in Canadian cities of the 1980s and 1990s. There has therefore been a move away from using advisory councils—either to eliminate them entirely or to integrate the responsibility for women's issues to agencies fully within government. This integration can be seen as a move either to strengthen the position of women in making their concerns a more integral part of the public sector or to control more directly these concerns by reducing the kind of advocacy role that advisory bodies can play. An exception to these trends was the creation in 2004 of the Conseil des montréalaises.

Marie Lavigne's analysis (1997) of the Conseil du Statut de la femme du Québec situates clearly the delicate balance such bodies must maintain—linked to the women's movement and to government but distinct from both. The attempt to maintain a sympathetic understanding and a critical distance vis-à-vis both government and the women's movement has led some of these advisory bodies to focus on research in order to develop a base for policy recommendations independent of government and the women's movement. Research was certainly the major activity for the federal Advisory Council during its existence and research is an important component of the work of the Quebec council.

The example most often given for the potential of a research agenda to advance debate is the early study on violence against women produced for the federal Advisory Council by Linda MacLeod (1980). MacLeod's study defined violence against women as a public issue that Canadian society must respond to. In addition, it emphasized a role for the federal government. MacLeod's research played a significant role in articulating this issue as a public policy question. Given the huge amount of legal, social service delivery, and public education policy that has taken place at federal, provincial, and municipal levels in relation to violence against women (Kérisit and Andrew, 1995; Andrew, 1995, 1997), the whole question of how public consciousness of this as an issue requiring collective action has been constructed in Canada is central to the task of understanding the relationship between women and the public sector. That the earliest articulation of the issue began as research done for an advisory body to government is instructive.

The second type of government agency is that concerned with policy advocacy, coordination, and development. At the federal level, Status of Women Canada plays this role, in Ontario, the Ontario Women's Directorate, and in Quebec, the Secrétariat à la condition féminine. One example of the kind of policy development role filled by these bodies is the work of Status of Women Canada in promoting gender-based analysis (GBA) within the federal government (Dwyer-Renaud, 1998; Siltanen, 1999) or 'l'analyse differenciée selon les sexes', the approach used by the Quebec government's agency.

As with advisory bodies, the analysis of women's policy agencies also involves understanding the delicate balance to be achieved between links to the community and to the women's movement and links to the government. Naomi Alboim, in discussing the evolution of the Ontario Women's Directorate (OWD) from 1983 to 1990, makes this point with reference to the staffing policies of the OWD. In the first years OWD staff were seconded from other ministries for relatively short periods. One positive result is that women with OWD experience are now in important positions throughout the Ontario government. On the negative side have been 'constant turnover' and a 'lack of continuity' (Alboim, 1997: 226). In the following period, the OWD hired permanent staff, often from the community, with experience in women's issues. Positive results have included a 'broader range of women's interests' and more work on diversity. On the negative side, staff have 'less knowledge of government process and of the ability to influence government from the inside' (ibid.). Thus, these agencies must be analyzed in terms of their strategies for creating beneficial contacts both inside government and outside in their efforts to influence policy.

Agencies and programs that fund women's groups and activities in the community aimed at gender equality are a third component of government machinery. The fundamental justification for such activities relates to our analysis of the Royal Commission on the Status of Women and the argument about the need for support for voluntary associations. Government funding has been variously analyzed as indicating that the activities being supported are part of public policy goals that the state wants to achieve, as a sign of the electoral and/or political strength of the women's movement and/or women, and as an indication of the state's desire to control, neutralize, and/or buy off the women's movement (Masson, 1998, 1999; Ng, 1988; Lamoureux, 1997).

Within the federal government, Status of Women Canada funds activities that promote gender equality. Until recently, the government provided core funding to about 20 national women's groups but this funding is now all on a project basis. Indeed, in the past few years many of these groups, such as the Canadian Research Institute on the Advancement of Women (CRIAW), have seen their funding dramatically reduced or completely eliminated. Funding is available to community-based organizations, and indeed now to private sector for-profit groups, for activities aimed at achieving the full participation of women in the economic, social, and democratic life of Canada. The Women's Program in Status of Women Canada is responsible for this funding.

Funding for community-based activities is generally targeted by the state, although the project focus for this funding can be relatively broad. For example, the Ontario Women's Directorate funds the following programs:

- Employment Training Pilot Program
- Training Programs (Innovations Fund)
- Investing in Women's Futures
- Promoting Healthy Equal Relationships
- Information Technology Training for Women
- Women in Skilled Trades (Ontario Women's Directorate, 2008)

In some cases, the link to government policy directions is particularly clear. For instance, in Quebec the Secrétariat à la condition féminine set up a program in 1999, 'À égalité pour décider', to fund activities designed to increase the representation of women within local and regional structures (Secrétariat à la condition féminine, 1999). The context is clearly the Quebec government's policy on regionalization, with an aim to increase the responsibilities of regional and local levels of the state and a realization, by the government, that this policy will not be successful, and politically will be vulnerable to criticism by the women's movement, if it is not accompanied by an increased role for women at these levels. Funding is available for projects aimed at one or more of the following objectives: facilitating and promoting women's access to local and regional decision-making positions; increasing the pool of candidates for these positions; preparing women for these positions; helping women remain in these positions; and sensitizing local and regional institutions to the importance of gender equity among decision makers. This program has produced a wide variety of tools, training programs, and resource kits aimed at encouraging greater participation by women in municipal and regional decision-making.

Governments, particularly provincial and municipal ones, fund a vast number of local services to women through grants to groups and agencies. Transition houses for battered women, women's health centres, rape crisis centres, employment programs, information centres, and many other services receive funds that either fully or partially cover the services offered. In many cases, government funding is supplemented by a variety of methods of community fundraising, including United Way campaigns, individual campaigns, and specialized activities (walks, auctions, dinners, art sales, raffles, and the like). These programs can be compared in terms of both overall budgets and the focus, or breadth, of the activities to be funded.

The fourth type of government agency specializes in one particular policy area in relation to gender equity. Some of the first of these existed in relation to women's employment issues and, more recently, in relation to health. For instance, Health Canada has a Women's Health Bureau, established formally in 1993. The Bureau works to integrate questions of gender within all the operations of Health Canada and it is also responsible for the funding of the five centres of excellence in the area of women's health (discussed below). This Bureau and similar agencies often have this kind of double mandate that includes responsibility for specific women-centred activities and for **mainstreaming** gender issues in the more general program activity. As the Director of the Women's Health Bureau stated: 'This demonstrated how it is important to undertake not only a women-centred research program, but to integrate gender into the better endowed mainstream programs where most of the money and the thrust are located' (Ponée, 1998). The existence of these agencies raises classical questions of public administration—how best to coordinate both horizontally (gender) and vertically (health, employment, anti-violence). These questions exist within each level of government and, of course, across levels of government. There are, for instance, meetings of federal, provincial, and territorial ministers to look at existing programs aimed at the elimination of violence against women.

Our last type of government agency is perhaps more of a 'quango' (quasi non-governmental organization); the research and knowledge translation centres funded by governments but set up outside formal government structures. These research centres have been set up in the areas of violence against women (five centres, by regions) and women's health (four regional centres, a centre on Aboriginal Women's Health and Healing Research, and the Canadian Women's Health Network). The Metropolis Research Centres can also be at least partially included in this list, as the five Metropolis centres have produced a good deal of intersectional research looking at the relationships between gender and immigrant settlement and integration. Another model, this time provincial, is Echo, the Ontario women's health agency. An earlier version, the Ontario Women's Health Council, was part of the Ontario Ministry of Health but the new agency, created in 2007, has a more independent status.

This discussion of government machinery involved in gender equality in Canada is not intended to describe all that now exists or what has existed over the past 35 years. The intention is rather to indicate the kinds of structures and machinery that do exist and also to suggest the complexity of the evolution of these structures. There have been some dismantling of women's machinery within some of the provincial governments (as well as the federal cuts that we have described above) but the wholesale dismantling that many predicted in the 1990s has not taken place. To give a brief profile of provincial and territorial government machinery: seven jurisdictions have both a government body and an external advisory committee—Manitoba, Quebec, New Brunswick, Prince Edward Island, Newfoundland and Labrador, Yukon, and the Northwest Territories; Saskatchewan has a government body and an internal advisory committee; Ontario has a government body; and Nova Scotia has an external advisory committee. In British Columbia, Alberta, and Nunavut the focus on women appears to have been subsumed into departments renamed around children, youth, and families. We might conclude that considerable activity and machinery continue to exist, but that the levels of impact and of funding are extremely variable. At the same time, women's machinery has become more **institutionalized**, and is increasingly viewed as part of 'legitimate state structures' (Haussman and Sauer, 2007: 3).

Public Policy and Women

A discussion of government machinery leads fairly naturally into a consideration of public policy and the impact this machinery has had on changes in and the results of government policy. Our discussion of GBA indicates that most, if not all, areas of public policy have gender implications. One dimension of particular importance to our focus on women and the public sector is the relationship between women working within the public sector and policy outputs of interest to women. In other words, are women more interested in gender equality and policies promoting gender equality? Is there a relationship between the presence of women in important political and administrative decision-making positions and the gender emphasis of the policy outputs?

The answers to these questions are both simple and complex. Most studies indicate that women are more interested than men in gender equality, but this is certainly not universally true. In addition, such factors as party policies, party discipline, and administrative structures also are important in the overall policy-making framework. Ministers responsible for women's equality have tended, more often than not, to be women, but studies have often made the point that a senior male minister, combining this responsibility with others, might be far more powerful and effective than a junior female charged uniquely with women's equality (Alboim, 1997; Bégin, 1997; O'Neil and Sutherland, 1997). At the same time there are numerous examples of women, at both the political and administrative levels, being instrumental in advancing policy for women. For example, at the municipal level evidence from surveys on uses of women's safety audits—where areas of the city are examined with an eye to improving urban security for women—suggests that the existence of female elected officials is related to the successful implementation of such audits (Andrew, 2000). There is some basis, therefore, for suggesting a link between the substantial presence of women in decision-making positions and the likelihood of policy that takes gender into account.

On the other hand, debate about the impact of globalization and state restructuring on policies of interest to women suggests that macroeconomic and political trends are of even greater importance than the existence of female decision-makers. Books, such as those by Brodie (1996) and Bakker (1996), argue that neo-liberalism and subsequent state restructuring have had a negative effect on women despite an increasing presence of women within the policy-making structures. Brodie and Bakker both argue that budget cuts and program changes have reduced services to women, increased social control on women, increased victimization, and, in general, increased the marginalization and vulnerability of women. Jenson and Phillips (1996) argue that these changes stem in part from ideological changes on the part of governments and that the federal government attack on special interests indicates a major change in the government's view of its relationship to civil society. Rather than seeing women's and other interest groups as part of the federal government's strategy for achieving its own policy goals, the groups are seen as pushing for increased government spending to further their own particular goals rather than the broad goals of the society. Still other studies (e.g., Masson, 1998) have focused on the political dynamics of the relations between the women's movement and the state. In the case of Quebec, Masson argues that the result of this relationship cannot be interpreted as the co-optation of the women's movement but rather as a more equal struggle between the articulations of policy demands by the women's groups and policy directions by the state.

Some policy areas have been more influenced by gender considerations than others, and some have not been influenced at all (Recherches féministes, 1999; Clark, 1997; Bégin, 1997). Recently, the emphasis on children and child poverty has been seen by some as bypassing and marginalizing gender. On the other hand, as described above, the funding of centres for policy research and knowledge translation indicates support for gender-sensitive health research, research on violence against women, and research to better understand the conditions for the integration of immigrant women.

Conclusion

We can look at our overall question of how women have been treated in, and by, the public sector in a number of ways. We can, for instance, examine the evolution of concern for this question within the public sector and the government machinery, as well as in terms of public policy results. Doing this should reinforce our position that a concern for gender equality does not evolve in a linear fashion; it is influenced by macroeconomic, political, and administrative trends. Periods of affluence have led to more generous public policy and greater willingness to include gender considerations. Political shifts, clearly related to but distinct from economic trends, also influence gender equality both directly and indirectly. Neo-liberal and/or neo-conservative trends emphasized traditional family values, a diminished role for the state, and a lessened importance for equality. All of these attitudinal shifts have had an impact on policies for women, although they may not address the question specifically. Trends in administration also influence gender considerations, as the introduction of the merit principle in the federal civil service illustrates. And, more recently, some people have argued that a drastically reduced civil service will disproportionately eliminate women because they tend to be more recently hired and more junior.

Our examination of government machinery indicates a considerable increase in organizations, services, and programs that specifically relate to women's equality. The effectiveness of this machinery is much more difficult to establish. Ultimately one can look at policy outcomes, but, here again, we come back to the questions of the weight of overall economic, political, and administrative trends that outweigh the impact of specific machinery.

We can also return to our initial formulation of the importance of the analysis of women and the public sector in terms of the relationship between public and private sector, male and female, and the difficulty, for women, of clearly establishing their claims to be actors in the public sector on an equal footing with men. To what extent does the variable success of specific pieces of government machinery relate to this fundamental difficulty for society to accept the presence of women in the public sector? Does this acceptance require the prior transformation of the private realm so as to eliminate the greater responsibilities of women within this sector? These questions go far beyond the scope of this chapter but they are useful, and necessary, as a frame to our discussion, which focused on the importance of understanding the machinery of government as it relates to gender equality, the need for analyzing public policy in terms of its impacts on women and men, and the significance of doing this within the context of the broader economic, political, and administrative trends that play themselves out in our society. The relationship of women to the public sector is indeed complex.

Important Terms and Concepts

employment equity
feminist movement
gender equality
government machinery
institutionalization of the women's movement
intersectionality
mainstreaming (of gender)
managing diversity

Study Questions

1. To what extent is it important to have women as decision-makers? If it is important, is it more important to have women as elected representatives or as bureaucrats?
2. Has government policy around the issue of violence against women been influenced by the feminist movement in the past 15 years? If so, what has been the influence?
3. Has the world-wide trend towards decentralization made the question of the role of women in municipal government increasingly important? If so, is the traditional definition of municipal responsibilities as related to hard infrastructure services a constraint to increasing the place of women in municipal decision-making?
4. The priority around the representation of women has now become that of the representation of the full diversity of women. To what extent had this led to new strategies either on the part of grassroots women's organizations or on the part of governments?
5. What are the benefits and costs of the institutionalization of the women's movement?

Useful Websites

Canadian Women's Health Network:

www.cwhn.ca/

Centre for Research and Education on Violence against Women and Children:

www.crvawc.ca/

Centres of excellence for women's health, with links to the organizations supported by the Women's Health Centre Program:

www.cewh-cesf.ca/en/index.shtml

Conseil du Statut de la femme, Gouvernement du Québec:

www.csf.gouv.qc.ca/fr/leconseil

Le centre de recherche interdisciplinaire sur la violence familiale et la violence faite aux femmes(CRI-VIFF):

www.criviff.ca

Muriel McQueen Ferguson Centre for Family Violence Research:

www.unbf.ca/arts/CFVR/

Ontario Women's Directorate:

www.citizenship.gov.on.ca/owd/

Provincial Advisory Council on the Status of Women—Newfoundland and Labrador:

www.pacsw.ca/

Research and Education for Solutions to Violence and Abuse (RESOLVE):

www.umanitoba.ca/resolve/

Secrétariat à la condition féminine, Gouvernement du Québec:

www.scf.gouv.qc.ca

Status of Women Canada:

www.swc-cfc.gc.ca

The FREDA Center for Research on Violence against Women and Children:

www.harbour.sfu.ca/freda/reports/rapidindex.htm

References

Abella, R. 1984. *Equality in Employment: A Royal Commission Report.* Ottawa: Queen's Printer.

Alboim, N. 1997. 'Institutional Structure as Change Agent: An Analysis of the Ontario Women's Directorate', in Andrew and Rodgers (1997: 220–7).

Andrew, C. 1995. 'Getting Women's Issues on the Municipal Agenda: Violence against Women', in J. Garber and R. Turner, eds, *Gender in Urban Research.* Thousand Oaks, Calif.: Sage Publications, 99–118.

———. 1997. 'Les femmes et le local: les enjeux municipaux à l'ère de la mondialisation', in M. Tremblay and Andrew, eds, *Femmes et représentation politique au Québec et au Canada.* Montréal: Remue-ménage, 179–96.

———. 1998. 'Les Femmes et l'État-providence: Question revue et corrigée', *Politiques et Sociétés* 17, 1–2: 171–82.

———. 2000. 'Les enquêtes de sécurité: stratégie de pouvoir pour les femmes ou outil de contrôle étatique?', in Actes de séminaire, *Genre et gestion urbaine et environnementale.* Montréal: Institut d'urbanisme.

———, and S. Rodgers. 1997. *Women and the Canadian State.* Montreal and Kingston: McGill-Queen's University Press.

Bakker, I. 1996. *Rethinking Restructuring.* Toronto: University of Toronto Press.

Bégin, M. 1997. 'The Canadian Government and the Commission's Report', in Andrew and Rodgers (1997: 12–26).

Brodie, J. 1996. *Women and Canadian Public Policy.* Toronto: Harcourt Brace.

Canada Public Service Agency. 2006. 'Employment Equity in the Public Service of Canada 2005–2006—Annual Report to Parliament'.

Clark, L. 1997. 'Reminiscences and Reflections on the Twentieth Anniversary of the Commission Report', in Andrew and Rodgers (1997: 3–11).

Dwyer-Renaud, H. 1998. 'Reforming Public Policies for Gender Equality', paper presented at the Fifth Women's Policy Research Conference, Washington, DC.

Hankivsky, O. 2005. 'Gender vs Diversity Mainstreaming: A Preliminary Examination of the Role and Transformative Potential of Feminist Theory', *Canadian Journal of Political Science* 38, 4: 997–1001.

Haussman, M., and B. Sauer. 2007. *Gendering the State in the Age of Globalization.* Lanham, Md.: Rowman and Littlefield.

Hynna, M. 1997. 'Women in the Public Service—A Thirty-Year Perspective', *Canadian Public Administration* 40, 4: 618–25.

Jenson, J., and S. Phillips. 1996. 'Regime Shift: New Citizenship Practices in Canada', *International Journal of Canadian Studies* 14: 111–36.

Kérisit, M., and C. Andrew. 1995. 'La violence affichée', *Revue: femmes et droit* 8, 2: 337–70.

Lamoureux, D. 1997. 'Les services féministes—de l'antiétatisme à l'intégration subsidiaire', in Andrew and Rodgers (1997: 145–54).

Lavigne, M. 1997. 'Structures institutionnelles en condition féminine—le cas du Conseil du Statut de la femme du Québec', in Andrew and Rodgers (1997: 228–40).

Lowe, G. 1987. *Women in the Administrative Revolution.* Toronto: University of Toronto Press.

MacLeod, L. 1980. *Wife Battering in Canada: The Vicious Circle.* Ottawa: Minister of Supply and Service Canada.

Masson, D. 1998. 'With and Despite the State: Doing Women's Movement Politics in Local Service Groups in the 1980s in Quebec', PhD thesis, Carleton University.

———. 1999. 'Repenser l'État: Nouvelles perspectives féministes', *Recherches féministes* 12, 1: 5–24.

Morgan, N. 1988. *Jouer à l'égalité : les femmes et la fonction publique fédérale.* Ottawa: Canadian Advisory Council on the Status of Women.

Ng, R. 1988. *The Politics of Community Service.* Toronto: Garamond Press.

O'Neil, M., and S. Sutherland. 1997. 'The Machinery of Women's Policy: Implementing the RCSW', in Andrew and Rodgers (1997: 197–219).

Ontario Women's Directorate. 2008. OWD Grant Programs. Available at: www.citizenship.gov.on.ca/owd/english/organizations/.

Ponée, D. 1998. 'Treating Women Differently', paper presented at the Fifth Women's Policy Research Conference, Washington, DC.

Recherches féministes. 1999. Special issue: 'Femmes, État, Société', 12, 1.

Royal Commission on the Status of Women in Canada. 1970. *Report.* Ottawa: Information Canada.

Secrétariat à la condition féminine. 1999. *À égalité pour décider: Guide d'information.* Québec: Secrétariat à la condition féminine.

Siltanen, J. 1999. 'Connecting Theory, Research and Policy—Issues with "Gender" in Gender-Based Analysis', paper presented at the annual meeting of the Canadian Sociology and Anthropology Association, Sherbrooke, Que.

Status of Women Canada. 1989. *Dimensions of Equality: An Update of the Federal Government Work Plan for Women.* Ottawa: Status of Women Canada.

Task Force on Barriers to Women in the Public Service. 1990. *Report of the Task Force on Barriers to Women in the Public Service: Beneath the Veneer,* 4 vols. Ottawa: Minister of Supply and Service Canada.

Taylor, J. 1990. 'The Rights of Men and the Privilege of Their Own Sex As Well: Image and Place of Women in the Canadian Civil Service, 1867–1921', paper presented at the annual meeting of the Canadian Historical Association, Victoria.

Whitzman, C. 2002. *The Voice of Women in Canadian Local Government.* Montreal and Kingston: McGill-Queen's University Press.

19 First Nations and the Public Sector: *Understanding Accountability and Its Impacts on Governance Relationships*

Robert Shepherd

> I'm too old for meetings . . . I'm tired of meetings, I'm tired of promises. I want this assembly to produce an action plan so our people don't have to wait anymore for those promises that are made many years ago and made with great faith, made with a mutual respect.
>
> Chief Lawrence Joseph (Bernhardt, 2008)

Introduction

It is widely accepted that the state of relations between Canada's First Nations and its federal, provincial, and territorial governments has been adversarial, antagonistic, and distrustful. These relations have been under a great deal of strain at the best of times for many reasons, particularly due to the aftermath of the federal government's assimilationist policies of the past century. All governments face increasing pressure to resolve ongoing and long-standing disputes: land claims, specific claims, and grievances against the Crown. In addition, there have been notable shortfalls (relative to the Canadian population) in overall First Nations community health and programming, including gaps in education, social security, and other basic services that have gone unresolved.[1]

Although Canadian and First Nations governments have had poor relations for several decades, limited progress has been made in improving them. Time and again Canadian governments have attempted on several fronts to repair the damage of past intrusions. For example, some progress has been made in reducing the number of outstanding land claims.[2] Aboriginal leaders, however, have called for more fundamental change premised on the fact that Canada's **Aboriginal** peoples are founding nations with the right of self-determination, as expressed in such important documents as the Royal Proclamation, 1763 (Johnson, 1996: 182–5).

One of the key challenges has been to build more effective accountability relationships with on-reserve, status First Nations. Accounting for funding used on reserves is rigorous; a recent Auditor General of Canada report that found status First Nations governments are required to complete no fewer than 168 federal reports annually, depending upon the type of funding arrangement (Auditor General of Canada, 2002: 9). There have been several attempts to repair and improve the accountability relationships, but, not surprisingly, First Nations leaders have reacted negatively when the federal government attempted to set its own terms in accountability initiatives that hold communities to account for the use of public funds.

Both the federal and provincial/territorial governments and First Nations acknowledge that funding for basic programs and services will continue to be provided by government departments, even under self-government. This raises questions about how to ensure an appropriate balance between the accountability requirements of the state, especially for public money, and the particular accountability needs and requirements framing the relationships between First Nations governments and their citizens. Indeed, an important point of contention in almost all self-government negotiations to date has been ensuring that the content and degree of status First Nations' accountability to federal and provincial/territorial governments does not dilute the primacy of First Nations governments' accountability to their citizens.

Given the complexity of policy relationships and cultural, spatial, and other differences among Aboriginal peoples, defined as First Nations, Inuit, and Metis, this chapter focuses exclusively on status, or registered,[3] First Nations people living on reserves as defined in the Indian Act, 1876. The first section of this chapter provides a profile of First Nations in the overall context of Aboriginal peoples in Canada. The second section describes the accountability relationship between First Nations and Canadian governments, premised in large part on the principal–agent version of accountability informed increasingly by the **New Public Management** (NPM). This section highlights the different funding agreements that frame this contractual relationship between the federal government and status Indian bands. The third section describes the persistent dominant discourse in defining how the federal government has 'managed' the relationship using mainly administrative mechanisms, mostly over First Nations' objections. Finally, the chapter concludes with some thoughts on the current accountability relationship and the impact of the New Public Management. It posits that NPM has done little to resolve the many challenges inherent in the relationship. The federal government's Weberian command and control structure remains firmly intact and there does not appear to be any letting up in governmental control of the accountability relationship any time soon.

Profile of Status Indians in Canada

Defining 'Status Indian' and 'First Nation'

Defining the term 'status Indian' is not a straightforward task. However, it is important to clarify the terms 'status', 'legal', and 'registered' because all of these refer generally to 'Indians' that come under the explicit jurisdiction of the Indian Act. **Status Indians** are defined in legal terms as opposed to other 'Aboriginal people' who lack legal recognition under the Act. The original Indian Act, 1876 has been amended on several occasions since Confederation, as has the legal definition of 'Indian', thereby causing complex understandings of the term. In brief, an '**Indian**' is a person registered, or entitled to be registered, as an Indian, pursuant to the Indian Act.[4] Being **registered** means that the person is attached, or is a member of, a band recognized by the Department of Indian and Northern Affairs Canada (INAC). It also means that the person is on the **Indian Register** and legally entitled to access federal programming and funding for status Indian people.

This definition is exceedingly important because it constitutes the federal government's conception of its jurisdiction under section 91(24) of the British North America Act, 1867, which states that the federal government has exclusive jurisdiction over 'Indians, and lands reserved for the Indians'. For several decades, a number of different criteria have been used by the department to determine who is and who is not an Indian. For example, since the Indian Act was instituted in 1876, and even earlier in some cases, the following groups of people have been defined as Indians, and at other periods have been disqualified or denied access to the benefits of the Act:

- 'half-breeds' outside of Manitoba who accepted scrip (addressed in 1951 version of the Act);
- Indians with a university degree (addressed in 1951 version of the Act);
- Indians residing outside Canada for more than five years (addressed in 1951 version of the Act);
- Indian women married to non-Indian men (1876 version of the Act, addressed with Bill C-31 in 1985);
- children of non-Indian mothers and whose father had a non-Indian mother (1876 version, also addressed with Bill C-31 in 1985).

A key change instituted by the federal government was the introduction and passing of **Bill C-31** in its amendments to the Indian Act in 1985. Three key changes were introduced:

- the reinstatement of Registered Indian status to those individuals, mainly women, who had lost their registration through marriage, as stipulated in earlier versions of the Indian Act, and the first-time registration of their children;
- new rules governing entitlement to Indian registration for all children born after 16 April 1985 (section 6);
- the opportunity for individual bands to develop and apply their own rules governing First Nations membership (section 10).[5]

Under these changes to the Act, more than 114,000 persons were added to the Indian Register and are entitled to access federal programming for First Nations communities (INAC, 2005: Introduction). Many First Nations communities voiced their concerns about these changes to the Act, because for many communities, having several individuals or families return to their reserves would place significant pressure on already overstretched resources. Many communities lobbied the department to ensure that additional funds would be forthcoming for new homes and to bolster education and other programs. Today, many communities across the country are still reeling from not only the economic effects of this bill but also the added strain of creating yet another distinction between individuals. Now, there are not only status versus **non-status** distinctions, but also status versus 'C-31' status. In fact, in some communities there is a view that '**C-31 Indians**' are merely 'Indian Act Indians'—ironic, given that 'status Indian' is also a manifestation of the Act. This reflects in part the unfortunate state of relations between Indian peoples and the federal government.

The term 'First Nation' refers to an organic political and cultural entity or 'band' as defined under section 2 of the Indian Act: '(a) for whose use and benefit in common, lands, the legal title to which is vested in Her Majesty, have been set apart before, on or after September 4, 1951; (b) for whose use and benefit in common, moneys are held by Her Majesty, or (c) declared by the Governor in Council to be a band for the purposes of this Act'. First Nations include both on-reserve and off-reserve members who are listed on the Indian Register maintained, in part, by the Department of Indian and Northern Affairs. Some bands maintain their own registry and provide this information to the department, especially those which manage their own membership codes under Bill C-31.

The Nature of the Accountability Relationship

The Dominant Model of Accountability with Respect to First Nations

At its most basic level, **accountability** 'refers to an authoritative relationship in which one person is formally entitled to demand that another... provide an account of his/her actions; rewards or punishments may be meted out to the latter depending on whether those actions conform to the former's wishes' (Harmon, 1995: 25). To say that a person is accountable means that he or she is held responsible for sanctions, either positive or negative, according to an authoritative rule, decision, policy, or criterion enforceable by someone else, usually in a superior position of hierarchical authority. In this sense, accountability tends to be individualized or targeted because authoritative rewards and punishments are difficult, although not impossible, to dispense to collectives of individuals.

This form of accountability is called in management practice the 'principal–agent version'. An authoritative 'principal' assigns, or delegates, responsibilities to individuals in the hierarchy who carry out these responsibilities according to established expectations. These individuals are then required to provide an accounting of how these responsibilities were carried out. Differences between traditional public administration premised on command and control and NPM conceptions of accountability based on the achievement and performance of results are related to the scope of relationships and the selection of measurement and accounting processes. NPM expressions of accountability tend towards reporting and other mechanisms that place priority on value-for-money, whereas traditional forms ensure that process and procedure are enforced. As such, the variations between traditional and NPM conceptions relate more to differences in priorities of what agents are to be held accountable for, rather than the method under which they will be held to account. Romzek and Dubnick refer to this shift in priority as a movement away from 'bureaucratic' forms of accountability to forms based on 'performance'.[6] The accountability relationships between First Nations under the Indian Act and government have undergone various changes, as has the overall relationship with Aboriginal peoples, given new land and self-government agreements. Likewise, the procedural requirements of accountability which apply to status First Nations are constantly changing under NPM, but the rigour associated with these requirements remains firmly intact.

Bureaucratic accountability (sometimes referred to as 'hierarchical' accountability) is rooted in the classical Weberian model based on close supervision of individuals who have low work autonomy and are subject to strict internal command and control, established in rules and regulations. This type of accountability model ensures that decisions are technically and legally correct. Although straightforward in theory, such hierarchical forms operate best in stable environments but do not support dynamic environments with changing client demands, as in the relationships between First Nations and federal and provincial/territorial governments (Bovens, 1998: 155).

Historically (before the 1970s), the federal bureaucracy was governed by the principles of traditional public administration, including the values of hierarchy, command and control, objectivity and impartiality, and rationality (i.e., specialization and legality), and focused mainly on managing resource inputs (Gow, 2004: 19–22). It was driven by utilitarian concern for the distribution of resources and bureaucratic requirements that ensured that those resources were used according to rules established by Parliament and central agencies. The relationship between donor governments and First Nations was that of a guardian to ward, with routine relations buried deep within the department and with various regional program and financial units. (In 1950, the Indian Affairs Branch became part of the Department of Citizenship and Immigration, where it remained until 1965. Between 1936 and 1950, it had been part of Mines and Resources. Before this the Superintendent General of Indian Affairs had responsibility for Indians.) When, the department devolved its program responsibilities to First Nations governments beginning in the 1950s, contractual financial agreements known as **Contribution Agreements** became the conduit linking the federal government with local First Nations bureaucracies, thereby replacing the Indian Agents. Elected First Nations leaders became responsible for band affairs and for overseeing the activities of the bureaucracy without compromising departmental policy. These agreements for the most part remain to this day, although the priorities for which bands are held to account are slowly changing to a results-based, or NPM, orientation.

Under performance accountability arrangements, externally imposed performance criteria are applied, which specify output and/or outcome objectives spelled out in various instruments, including new funding agreements. In Canada, performance measures have been more commonly applied to ensure programs meet specified cabinet objectives and expectations. In accordance with NPM 'culture', performance-based accountability includes minimal bureaucratic constraints on how services are delivered, thereby maximizing the administrative autonomy and flexibility of service delivery agencies including First Nations governments. However, autonomy over program policy remains low, meaning that local program policy and budgeting is subject to federal preferences and requirements.

Applying Accountability: The Funding Agreements

Funding agreements between INAC and band governments are the main tools used to transfer funds for the provision of basic services. These characterize a contractual relationship which provides for a detailed set of obligations on the part of the federal government and of band governments spelled out in terms and conditions for the delivery of treaty-based responsibilities. The difficulty for many First Nations leaders with these agreements is that the definition of these responsibilities has been dictated almost exclusively by the federal government. Phil Fontaine, Grand Chief of the Assembly of First Nations, explains:

> Treaties are not simply contracts to us. They're not merely a real estate transaction. They are sacred agreements that are intended to guide our relationship as long as the sun shines and the rivers flow. The treaties weren't designed and negotiated to have one party impose its will on the other party... to have one party deprive the other of its rights and interests... or to have one party impoverish the other party. Unfortunately, that has been our history. (Bernhardt, 2008)

Since the creation of newer funding instruments in the mid-1980s, a key objective has been to ensure an appropriate balance between ministerial and First Nations responsibility. Therefore, these new fiscal arrangements tend to ensure that donors are able to monitor program and services delivery through audit and reporting requirements while promising First Nations the highest degree of program flexibility and the ability to develop accountability systems with community members.

The basis for receipt of funding determines the manner in which funding is allocated. That is, fiscal arrangements could grant funding as a matter of entitlement such as a treaty right, through an unconditional grant program such as provincial equalization, through a regular program conditional transfer, or through a one-time spending and program conditional transfer such as a contribution agreement for a basic service. From the first to the last of these possibilities, the degree of recipient autonomy diminishes and accountability requirements to the donor government increase. The last two possibilities imply an accountability relationship where the donor decides on programs and provides funding while the agent merely delivers the services. Typically, Canadian government departments rely on one-time conditional transfer mechanisms. Although some funding is provided through grants, this type of funding tends to be minimal relative to the overall budget of the band government.

INAC uses three main funding arrangements for Indian Act First Nations governments and tribal councils, now referred to as the Contribution Agreement (CA), Comprehensive Funding Arrangement (CFA), and the DIAND[7]/Canada–First Nations Funding Arrangement (DFNFA/CFNFA). These arrangements have undergone several iterations and name changes since they were introduced. INAC also uses grants to fund self-governing First Nations communities using an agreement generically called the Self-Government Financial Transfer Agreement (SGFTA).[8] Although the SGFTA is negotiated individually for each treaty, the core elements of the instrument, including the definition of programs and services to be delivered, are premised on the same principles as those of the CFNFA. Oddly, conditions still apply under this agreement for the provision of mandated programs and services although the extent of these conditions varies with each self-government arrangement.

Table 19.1 shows the menu of funding arrangements available and the funding authorities for each. A 'funding authority' is defined as the set of specific conditions and rules to spend public money as allowed by Parliament.

Contribution Agreement and Contributions Funding Authority

The Contribution Agreement (CA) is a single-year, single purpose or program contractual funding instrument that involves the greatest degree of accountability and control for government. As stand-alone agreements, CAs are used mainly for funding major capital projects on strict time schedules or for time-limited special program offerings by donor departments. This form of agreement was used as the main contractual agreement between First Nations and donor departments from 1950 to about 1980. Bands typically signed several of these agreements to access

Table 19.1 INAC Funding Arrangements and Funding Authorities

Funding Arrangement	Funding Authorities
Contribution Arrangement (CA) Single year	• Contributions
Comprehensive Funding Arrangement (CFA) (Specifies services funded according to a particular authority) Single year	• Contributions • Flexible Transfer Payment (FTP) • Grant
DIAND/Canada–First Nations Funding Arrangement (CFNFA) Multi-Year	• Block Funding—Alternative Funding Arrangement (AFA) • Targeted Funding[9]—Contributions • FTP
Self-Government Financial Transfer Agreement (SGFTA)	• Grant (Negotiated terms in legislation)

funds for specific programs. The CA was widely criticized as affording bands little opportunity to set their own program management priorities, given its extensive accountability requirements and limited term. This form of agreement was the focus of attention in a special parliamentary committee study led by Liberal MP Keith Penner in 1983 (further discussed below).

Not to be confused with the CA, the 'Contributions authority' is one of a combination of authorities that encompasses spending rules in other funding agreements developed as a result of the Penner parliamentary study.[10] It is used widely to fund several types of programs including capital initiatives and social assistance. The Contributions authority sets out rigid terms and conditions that stipulate matters such as what service is to be provided and to whom, and what expenses are eligible for reimbursement. In this sense, it is a 'bottom-up' form of funding in which expenses incurred by the recipient are submitted to the responsible donor for reimbursement up to a specified maximum amount.[11] Any unexpended balance or unallowable expenditure is an amount due to the Crown. Likewise, any deficit supported by claims eligible for reimbursement is an amount receivable by the First Nations government. Programs and services must be administered in accordance with the donor's relevant program policies and/or procedure manual.

From a government perspective, this type of authority provides high control over local spending but significantly reduces management flexibility over that spending. For local bands that are growing in population, this type of authority provides some degree of security. For example, if the number of social assistance recipients is increasing annually, this authority provides full repayment to the band government for all expenses incurred as a result of the increase in program usage. Clearly, there is a trade-off: high security versus low management autonomy and flexibility. In an era of increasing emphasis on accountability at all levels of public management, there is evidence to suggest that the Treasury Board is demanding greater use of this authority despite progress in the 1980s and 1990s towards affording local band governments greater ability to set their own program and spending priorities and to allocate funds accordingly.

Comprehensive Funding Agreement (CFA)

The Comprehensive Funding Arrangement is the current default arrangement used by INAC to consolidate funding to First Nations governments and tribal councils.[12] The CFA is program-budgeted: programs are budgeted in their entirety rather than by individual program items as in the CA approach. This funding arrangement comprises three funding authorities: Contributions (described above),

Flexible Transfer Payment (FTP), and Grants. The Contributions portion continues to be used where extensive interaction is required with the government funding authority, especially in capital projects and social development.

The FTP funding authority was approved by the Treasury Board on 26 July 1989 to 'be used where agreements are established on a formula basis or where total expenditures are based on a fixed cost approach' (Treasury Board Secretariat, 1989). FTPs have simplified terms and conditions relative to Contributions. Like Contributions, FTP funding is a conditional transfer in accordance with specific program terms and conditions but these are fixed amounts of funds being disbursed, rather than expenses being reimbursed. In this sense, it is a top-down funding authority. For INAC, the FTP focuses on 'program performance', thereby freeing up local administrators to monitor the effectiveness of their programs and services rather than to record how each dollar is spent (as required under the Contributions authority). For First Nations governments, the FTP portion of funded services consolidates several budgets, thereby reducing reporting requirements. Other federal departments such as Health Canada are also using this type of authority in some of their local program agreements. In all cases, a final audit is required.

The Grants portion of the INAC agreement, albeit a minor element, eliminates all reporting and other accountability requirements and is used primarily to fund pilot and other programs where government intervention is not required.

DIAND/Canada First Nations Funding Agreement (CFNFA)

On 7 November 1985, cabinet authorized the development of the *optional* block five-year funding agreement, then called Alternative Funding Arrangements (AFA), and on 26 June 1986 the Treasury Board approved the implementation of the AFA funding authority 'to create a relationship between Indian bands and the Minister of Indian Affairs and Northern Development which increases accountability of Indian leaders to their own community and in which Bands have greatly expanded scope to establish program policies and to apply funds in accordance with community priorities'.[13] This agreement was developed to assist those bands with aspirations for self-government. DIAND used this agreement to facilitate progress in this direction but under a clearly federal perspective of self-government.

A notable criticism of the CFNFA is that its minimum accountability standards for the recipients are high.[14] The principal advantage for First Nations governments utilizing the CFNFA is that it facilitates long-range budgeting, as long as they do not anticipate drastic increases in demand for services that could make program costs exceed fixed budget amounts.

The Self-Government Financial Transfer Agreement (SGFTA)

The Government of Canada announced in 1995 that it was recognizing the inherent right of self-government. The Self-Government Negotiations Funding Support (SGNFS) program within INAC was created based on the 1998 paper ***Gathering Strength**: Canada's Aboriginal Action Plan*. The main objective of SGNFS is to provide funding to assist First Nations in negotiations to 'reach practical agreements on self-government and to achieve harmonious and clear relationships among Aboriginal, federal and provincial jurisdictions'. Self-government negotiations are expected to result in 'increased self-sufficiency of Aboriginal people and a corresponding lessening dependency on the Crown' (Treasury Board Secretariat, 1996). Generally, self-government agreements require recipients to submit an annual report on the delivery of programs and services and an audited financial statement to Parliament. Funding is provided by government departments, implying that funding is at their discretion and is subject to change. As of 2007, 15 of these agreements have been signed with the federal government.

Key Initiatives in the Administrative Relationship

Legislative and policy reform is nothing new in Canada's long-standing relationship with First

Nations. Reform of the Indian Act especially has been an ongoing priority for many ministers of Indian Affairs, efforts that have been generally misdirected and have done little to build a government-to-government relationship. The discourse of 'administrative reform' is long-standing. Whereas the federal government understands First Nations governance authority as delegated from the Crown, First Nations believe they have an **inherent right of self-government**. This difference in understanding underpins the fiscal and administrative framework outlined in the previous section, which persists despite the government's eventual recognition of the inherent right of self-government.

Penner Report (1983)

In response to the failure of the 1969 White Paper and various reforms of the Indian Act in the 1970s, the federal government created a Special Parliamentary Committee on Indian Self-Government in 1982, chaired by MP Keith Penner 'to examine the Government of Canada's total financial and other relationships' with Indian people. Its mandate was twofold: to study the provisions of the Indian Act dealing with band membership and Indian status; and to make recommendations to Parliament on possible new legislation and improved administrative arrangements to apply to some or all band governments on reserves (House of Commons, 1983: 3).

A key aim of the committee, which reported in 1983, was to propose alternatives to the 1950s–style direct program delivery by the federal government. The high degree of federal departmental control was 'rationalized by a conviction that Indian people lack the capacity to administer their own affairs and are the natural response of a bureaucracy anxious to retain control of its programs. They are also rationalized on the basis of criticisms from the Auditor-General about the inadequacies of financial controls' (House of Commons, 1983: 82). Specifically, First Nations voiced their criticisms of the administrative process arguing that, 'Just as control of the purse was fundamental to the evolution of our own parliamentary system of government, it is also fundamental to the survival and growth of government bureaucracies. Thus, Indian self-government comes into conflict with bureaucratic processes, and it is not surprising that real decision-making power, which depends on having unrestricted funding, has not been transferred to Indian bands and councils' (Coopers & Lybrand, 1983: 18). Arguably, this view among federal officials has changed little since the Penner findings were released.

The **Penner Report** recommended 'that Indian self-government must be supported by new funding arrangements that would enable Indian First Nations governments to decide how best to meet their peoples' needs' (House of Commons, 1983: 94). In particular, it recommended the use of direct grants based on a modified per-capita formula, five-year global funding of operational programs, and corrections for infrastructure deficiencies that would place fewer conditions on recipients. The Committee argued that contractual agreements such as Contributions Agreements were appropriate for departmental agents delivering programs on behalf of INAC but that the department should adopt a funding approach for First Nations whereby bands could identify their program requirements as part of their own budgetary processes. Federal funding would be based on a single agreement which would state the amount of the grant and community responsibilities. Accountability would consist of an audited annual financial statement confirming that funds had been expended for the agreed purposes. In addition, each First Nation would be free to allocate funds according to their own priorities and policies (House of Commons, 1983: 96) and grants would be made only to Indian governments that had an appropriate accountability system (House of Commons, 1983: 57). Although bands would be responsible for setting out their own priorities, programs would have to meet certain program and policy criteria. While praised at the time, the report has been criticized by later standards because First Nations authority would continue to be subject to departmental scrutiny (Graham et al., 1996). However, the

Penner Report remains an important benchmark for financial relations, because even its most modest recommendations regarding simplified block transfers have yet to be realized.

The Committee also promoted an enhanced municipal-type government within a revised federal legislative framework which would constitute a 'distinct order of government' with **delegated powers**. For example, First Nations authority would be recognized in specific areas including education, child care, and membership. In some areas there would be no need to negotiate self-government authority, but in more controversial areas such as fisheries and other resources, federal approval through negotiation would be required. This fundamentally defines the current approach to contemporary treaties in Canada: selected administrative responsibilities and powers are delegated to First Nations with financial accountability to the Crown for the use of public funds.

Legal Rights and Legislative Reform (1984–1988)

Following the tabling of the Penner Report, INAC drafted the Indian Nations Recognition and Validating Act (Bill C-52) in December 1983. In some respects, the Act went further than Penner's recommendations especially in reducing the discretion of government officials in recognizing a First Nation. The Act validated the traditional laws of each nation to the extent that they did not conflict with the laws of Parliament. Each nation would have all powers under section 91(24) except those withdrawn by Parliament.

The Assembly of First Nations attempted to convince chiefs and councils that Bill C-52 would fulfill the promises made in the Penner recommendations. However, chiefs and councils rejected the bill on the grounds that it failed to reflect the diversity of regional and local First Nations circumstances, aspirations, and interests surrounding self-government. As such, when the legislation was presented to cabinet in 1984, it was promptly dismissed because the Minister of Indian Affairs, John Munro, 'declined to endorse self-government as an aboriginal right and rejected the notion of pushing section 91(24) to its limits' because First Nations were unwilling to support the bill (Tennant, 1985: 330).

At the same time that Bill C-52 was being reviewed by cabinet, Prime Minister Mulroney created the **Nielsen Task Force on Program Review** in late 1984 with a mandate to cut federal spending and address inefficiencies, and to reduce government programs and services including Aboriginal and First Nations programs. In 1985, the Aboriginal programs study team reported on the status of federal programs and services and recommended the transfer of these responsibilities to the provinces and communities, and that federal funding be contained and targeted towards youth and education (Abele, Graham, and Maslove, 1999: 267–8). A report to the Task Force concluded that 'the continuing dilemma of high government expenditures and socioeconomic inertia demands significant adjustments to government policy' (DIAND, 1986: 21). It argued that services being provided exceeded the federal government's constitutional and legislative responsibility, maintaining that 25 per cent of expenditures were connected to treaty or Indian Act obligations, 38 per cent were attributable to statutory provincial responsibilities, and 37 per cent were considered 'discretionary' spending (DIAND, 1986: 21–2). The Task Force believed that three-quarters of First Nations funding could be either transferred to other jurisdictions or eliminated altogether. Accordingly, the Task Force made several recommendations that would address the issues of universality and government standards for service delivery, including deconcentrating programs within INAC, eliminating programs that duplicated provincial programs, reducing expenditures in high-cost areas such as health care and post-secondary education, capping program expenditures on-reserve through greater use of other funding authorities, introducing user fees for capital, and operations and maintenance, and removing incentives for housing assistance and health-care benefits (DIAND, 1986: 32–8).

The recommendations spoke directly to the first wave of NPM measures designed to devolve responsibilities both within the federal government and to outside institutions, privatizing programs and services that did not fit with government responsibilities, and building partnership arrangements with other institutions and jurisdictions with a stake in First Nations programs. The Task Force acknowledged that First Nations might not agree with the recommendations but opined that in due course they would accept the 'new way of doing business'.

For their part, the Neilson Task Force recommendations on First Nations programming were received poorly by First Nations, who referred to the report as 'The Buffalo Jump of the 1980s' because it called for a return to the rejected 1969 White Paper. First Nations suspected that the White Paper would become the government's unofficial policy guide for devolving First Nations provincial-type programs and services to bands and the provinces, and their suspicions were realized (Wilson, 1988: 37–8). This meant that any accountability arrangements would have to adhere to provincial program guidelines.

As it turned out, almost all of the Task Force recommendations were submitted to cabinet for approval. The most controversial recommendations such as privatizing Indian trusts and negotiating federal–provincial arrangements were slated for implementation over the long term. In November of 1986, one of the most fundamental recommendations was implemented. Indian Affairs was granted formal authority from Treasury Board to 'devolve, over time, to the greatest extent possible within existing legislation and current administrative arrangements, its programs and services to Indian people' (Treasury Board Secretariat, 1986b). The Treasury Board was assured by the department that devolution of government programs would not result in an increase in existing program and service expenditures and that these activities would facilitate further reductions and departmental downsizing.[15]

Community-Based Self-Government Program (1986–1988)

Consistent with the Neilson Task Force review, the federal government announced the Community-Based Self-Government Program (CBSG) in 1986. The program proposed transferring specific departmental programs such as policing and fisheries management to other departments, and creating new funding arrangements including the Alternative Funding Agreement that would allow communities more flexibility in using federal transfers. The federal government promised that First Nations would have greater flexibility, more certainty with respect to funding levels, and increased accountability to their own communities. However, only bands that met strict eligibility criteria would be able to take advantage of this new agreement.

The CBSG program was not well received by First Nations. They objected to the lack of community consultation, to the control imposed by the department over the eligibility criteria, and to the limits placed on the program responsibility areas that could be negotiated. The department expected proposals to be submitted, not only to develop community distinctiveness, 'but also to focus on subject areas targeted for negotiation. Community proposals that failed to identify specific concerns, or simply duplicated the proposals of other communities, were rejected' (McDonnell and Depew, 1999: 355). The program essentially 'offered' self-government on the department's terms, in that the accountability for program funding resided ultimately with the minister. As per NPM, the program was concerned mainly with economic development rather than self-identified 'community' concerns.

By May of 1988, fifteen developmental and seventeen framework proposals were on file with the Self-Government Negotiations Branch at INAC. These proposals involved 135 bands (of 604 at the time) from across the country, including several tribal councils (INAC, 1988: iii). Despite these optimistic results, the program was hardly a departure from the federal government's devolution strategy. Rather, it had First Nations bands assuming the federal role of managing programs and services, without any real power over policy and legislative decision-making. The Sechelt Agreement was the first one reached under CBSG; it was also the last. The remaining files were transferred under the new Inherent Right of Self-Government Policy introduced in 1995.

Liberal Party Red Book, Program Review, and the Inherent Right Policy (1993–1995)

When the Liberal government under Jean Chrétien came to office in 1993, it inherited a massive national debt and deficit, Québec separatism was on the rise, and foreign creditors and bond-rating agencies were demanding tighter control over the deficit. Canadians were growing impatient with ballooning costs, giving rise to the Reform Party under Preston Manning, and an increasing profile to cost-cutting provincial governments under Mike Harris of Ontario and Ralph Klein of Alberta. Within this hostile environment, First Nations issues were pushed off the agenda.

For First Nations, hopes were raised when the Liberal Party established the Aboriginal Peoples' Commission in 1990 which was co-chaired by David Nahwegahbow and Marilyn Buffalo. Its purpose was to advise the Policy Platform Committee of the Liberal Party on a new Aboriginal policy direction for the country for the next federal election. The Liberal Party promised that 'the role of a Liberal government will be to provide Aboriginal people with the necessary tools to become self-sufficient and self-governing. Our priority will be to assist Aboriginal communities in their efforts to address the obstacles to their development and to help them marshal the human and physical resources necessary to build and sustain vibrant communities'.[16] Given that First Nations and the Liberal Party worked together to construct the platform statement, and that it was presumed Chrétien had learned from the 1969 White Paper debacle, expectations of progress were high. These expectations would soon be dashed with the announcement of the Liberal government's Program Review exercise in 1994 and the Inherent Right Policy in 1995.

Within INAC, the Program Review was carried out internally in 1994 without consulting with First Nations regarding the programs being considered for review. Few cuts were made to housing, post-secondary education, specific and comprehensive claims, and social development programs, given that these were considered significant 'Red Book pressures' (INAC, 1995: Annex C). Several programs, however, underwent dramatic cuts to their operating and program budgets, including the self-government program.

Two important changes occurred during the Program Review exercise that affected administrative policies related to First Nations. First, the department's mandate underwent significant reform. Second, the definition attached to 'Indian monies' was amended. Interestingly, both changes went virtually unnoticed by the public and even within the federal government itself.

In 1995, the federal government announced the **Inherent Right of Self-Government Policy**, which was intended to address the Liberal Party's Red Book obligations for streamlining the self-government negotiations process. Political pressure from First Nations had been mounting steadily throughout the 1990s following the Oka Crisis, and bands in British Columbia pressed to increase the pace of negotiations.[17] The Red Book promised increased First Nations participation in policy development. However, this did not happen with respect to the Inherent Right Policy. The federal government delivered a policy that facilitated the aggregation of programs and services management at the tribal council and regional representative organizational levels. It was not surprising, therefore, that between 1995 and 1998 the number of tribal councils increased by 26 per cent, totalling 96 in December 1997. By the end of 1998, 80 per cent of bands were affiliated with a tribal council (INAC, 1998b). Once again, the federal government rejected the 'inherent' authority for self-government and embraced a delegated model which, in lockstep with NPM, aggregated services with tribal councils in order to improve program efficiency (MacDonnell and Depew, 1999: 356). Such a divergence from the Liberal Party Red Book signalled a souring of relations between First Nations and the Chrétien government. For some prominent First Nations leaders, 'it seems obvious that Chrétien never intended to drop [the **White Paper of 1969**], not in 1969 and not even in 1993 when he was running for the leadership of the country... Having observed Mr. Chrétien's conduct on Indian policy over the years, I believe that he refuses to believe the White Paper was wrong!' (Nahwegahbow, 2003: 5).

RCAP and Gathering Strength (1996–1998)

The release of the ***Report of the Royal Commission on Aboriginal Peoples*** in 1996 compelled the federal government once again to consider the Crown's obligations to First Nations with respect to self-government. RCAP advocated the regeneration of the approximately 60 to 80 Aboriginal 'nations' as the basis for self-determination (Canada, 1996a: 25). It also identified four principles upon which to base this new relationship: recognition, respect, sharing, and responsibility. Underlying these principles was the assumption that Aboriginal peoples have distinct rights and responsibilities as the original occupants of 'Turtle Island' (North America) and that financial accountability for First Nations government is principally at the community level (Canada, 1996c: 675–96). Most First Nations supported the work of the Royal Commission and hoped that its report 'has helped to establish both a language and benchmarks for productive dialogue' (Castellano, 1999: 109).

From 1995 to 1996, the federal government again considered amending the Indian Act and began consultations with several First Nations representative organizations. First Nations were assured that only changes with their support would proceed.[18] In December 1996, the Minister of Indian Affairs tabled Bill C-79, the Indian Act Optional Modification Act, after several revisions from First Nations. As the bill's title implies, First Nations would be able to opt into, but not out of, its package of changes to the Indian Act. The 'new' bill put forward changes to the legal capacity of bands, ownership of reserve lands, band council elections and law-making authority and rules of succession. In addition, it contained a non-derogation clause under which neither the Act nor its amendments were to be construed as abrogating or derogating from existing Aboriginal treaty rights, including the inherent right of self-government. These were not new ideas: these have surfaced in various forms since the 1969 White Paper. The bill was ultimately rejected by First Nations because the government did not take into consideration differing First Nations priorities and capacity, the Minister's powers were still intact, and they saw the bill as having a deleterious effect on their treaty rights.[19] Bill C-79 died on the Order Paper in the spring of 1997 when Parliament was dissolved. Despite the failure of the bill to pass, the government would return to its provisions as the basis for further attempts at reform.

In response to the RCAP report, INAC released *Gathering Strength: Canada's Aboriginal Action Plan* in 1998, which outlined departmental commitments for the future including recognition of the government-to-government, treaty-based approach advocated by the RCAP. It also committed to address social and economic problems in First Nations communities and develop a training strategy that would more fully allow them to improve their collective health (INAC, 1998a: 13). It promised to strengthen First Nations governance, to design a new fiscal relationship, and to sustain the growth of strong, healthy communities. However, the statement was silent as to how it would go about implementing this new relationship. The clearest clue was the Action Plan's statement on instituting self-government: 'certain provisions in self-government agreements with First Nations, Inuit, Métis and off-reserve Aboriginal peoples could be constitutionally protected as treaty rights under section 35 of the Constitution Act, 1982' (INAC, 1998a). This suggested a continued reliance on the Inherent Right Policy. Once again, the federal government had returned to a delegated model of self-government and an accountability relationship that placed governmental requirements ahead of local priorities.

The Indian Act Reform 'Suite' of Legislation (2001–2005)

The encore to Bill C-79 and *Gathering Strength* came in 2001 when the federal government committed to 'strengthening its relationship with Aboriginal People' in its Speech from the Throne.[20] It took a multi-pronged approach to legislative reform by introducing four controversial, independent but related pieces of legislation: The Specific Claims Legislation Act (Bill C-6),[21] the Land Management Act (Bill C-49), the First Nations Governance Act (Bill C-61, later to be reintroduced as Bill C-7), and the First Nations Fiscal and Statistical Management Act (Bill C-19). Instead of reforming the entire Indian Act, the federal government attempted to replace parts of it through these stand-alone pieces of legislation. The strategy was clever in that it would presumably divide First Nations' time and resources for participation. It would become clear that the most controversial of these bills was the First Nations Governance Act.

Cabinet approved extensive consultations on the entire **Indian Act reform suite** in April 2001, called the 'Communities First: First Nations Governance Initiative'. Between April and November of that year, more than 10,000 individuals participated in the consultations. From the start, First Nations were critical of the process because they believed the consultations were flawed. Nonetheless, the federal government's objective was 'to provide the tools many First Nations leaders and individuals have called for to run their communities efficiently and fairly' (INAC, 2001). INAC set out to ascertain the views of all Aboriginal peoples on the priority areas identified in the former Bill C-79, except for issues related to status and band membership, First Nations women's concerns related to land ownership (this would come later in a separate bill), and the delivery of programs and services. INAC excluded the delivery of programs and services specifically because it did not intend to reform that relationship between INAC and First Nations. To do so would have meant restructuring its accountability arrangements. Instead, it chose to concentrate on that part of federal accountability emphasizing the accountability between band governments and its citizens by incorporating into legislation the principles of transparency, disclosure, and redress.

Following the consultations, Indian Affairs Minister Robert Nault tabled the **First Nations Governance Act** (Bill C-61, later re-titled Bill C-7) on 14 June 2002. The bill outlined three principal objectives: '(a) to provide bands with more effective tools of governance on an interim basis pending the negotiation and implementation of the inherent right of self-government; (b) to enable bands to respond more effectively to their particular needs and aspirations; and (c) to enable bands to design and implement their own regimes in respect of leadership selection, administration of government, and financial management and accountability, while providing rules for those bands that do not choose to do so' (Canada, 2002).

The new Act would require band governments to create several regulatory codes in the three areas noted in (c). If bands did not create these codes, the Act stipulated that the Minister of Indian Affairs may 'make regulations applicable to bands during any period when a band code is not in force and on all other matters related to First Nations governance covered in the Act'. Essentially, it was the federal government's intent to ensure the minister's obligations for open and accountable First Nations government was realized.

For First Nations, such codes were seen to increase the powers of the Minister over band affairs, not diminish them. More importantly, the fact that a default regime was in place suggested a minimum threshold within which band governments were to operate and be held to account. First Nations argued that they alone should be responsible for setting out the rules managing their administration, governance, and programs (Assembly of First Nations, 2002: 11).

Overall, First Nations regarded the First Nations Governance Act as a reinforcement of the 1995 Inherent Right Policy and a return to pre-1980s **direct management approach** by the Department of Indian Affairs. Although First Nations validated that improved accountability and transparency in their local communities was desirable and that, indeed, band governments were striving towards this goal, Bill C-7 and its distinctly federal approach to control was not regarded as the way forward. In fact, several protests erupted across the country in 2002 and 2003. However, the bill also had its supporters and it was this fact that prompted Minister Nault to argue in 2003 that 'The AFN leadership is clearly out of sync with... the people for whom they claim to speak. Many First Nations people are too frightened to speak of their support of the bill, for fear of reprisals' (*The Gazette*, 2008). Ultimately the bill died on the Order Paper with the prorogation of Parliament on 12 November 2003 and was not reintroduced. There is some evidence to suggest, however, that the bill continues to enjoy some support of senior officials in Ottawa.

Federal Accountability Act (2006)

Responding to widespread claims from citizens that its governments are unresponsive to their concerns and perceived failings in the management of public services resulting from various scandals, including Justice Gomery's inquiry into the Sponsorship Program and Advertising Activities, Prime Minister Stephen Harper introduced Bill C-2, the **Federal Accountability Act**, on 11 April 2006 with the promise that, 'With the Federal Accountability Act, we are creating a new culture of accountability that will change forever the way business is done in Ottawa' (Treasury Board Secretariat, 2006). Improving the accountability of government was a major element of the Conservative government's election platform in 2005. The Act was, and remains, a significant rules-based reform of federal government operations with widespread implications for almost every aspect of its responsibilities, including those related to the management of First Nations communities.

The Federal Accountability Act received Royal Assent on 12 December 2006, only eight months since it was introduced. It created two new Acts of Parliament: the Conflict of Interest Act intended to clarify situations where real conflicts of interests can occur with respect to public office-holders; and the Director of Public Prosecutions Act which separates functions relating to criminal prosecutions from the Justice department. The Federal Accountability Act also made substantive changes to 45 federal Statutes and amended over 100 other Acts of Parliament. These amendments are being implemented over time through the Federal Action Plan in the form of thirteen broad commitments comprising forty specific actions. In essence, the Act seeks three broad areas of reform: improving the accountability of Parliament (e.g., strengthening the role of the Auditor General, improving government budgeting, improving access to information); improving the accountability of departments and agencies (e.g., improving government procurement provisions, instituting accounting officers, permitting 'whistle-blowing'); and attempting to improve the overall culture of accountability across the federal government (e.g., through an Ethics Commissioner and a Lobbyist Commissioner).

The Act arguably affects the management and governance activities of First Nations. For example, First Nations responded to the increased powers of the Auditor General in sections 304–307 of the Act. Band funding agreements were captured under early versions of section 304 which made these open to audit by the Auditor General. Equally relevant, band governments were considered 'recipients' and again, considered open to audit. However, after considerable lobbying by the Assembly of First Nations and other Aboriginal organizations, a section was added to the list of exempted institutions in the Financial Administration Act.[22]

Although First Nations are not captured directly under the revised section 304, the idea that the federal government may inquire into the use of funds still holds. Under the Act, the Auditor General is authorized to 'follow the money' (Canada, 2007) and inquire into the use of public money under any funding agreement to determine whether appropriate reporting mechanisms are in place and that recipients maintain records that speak to the effective performance of programs and services (Canada, 2008: s. 307). Because the Act aims to improve transparency and accountability in government, the Minister of Indian Affairs still reserves the authority to prepare funding agreements in line with these provisions of the Federal Accountability Act. In fact, Indian Affairs Minister Chuck Strahl announced in March 2008 that his department 'notified funding recipients that it intends to amend 2008–2009 funding agreements to include an audit clause. The addition of this clause will ensure INAC's right to conduct audits of funding agreements to make certain that contributions are used for intended programs and services'. The announcement was linked directly to the federal government's Accountability Act commitments. He also explained that, 'What we're saying is if we're going to give money, we want to be able to do an audit on it to make sure that it's serving its purpose, that it's being spent on the programs that it was intended. We just want to make sure that—especially first nations—but all taxpayers know the money is being well spent' (INAC, 2008). In other words, First Nations remain accountable and subject to federal legislation.

Not surprisingly, First Nations responded negatively to the announcement by the Minister. According to the Assembly of First Nations, the announcement 'plays on the false impression that has been spread about first nations and accountability. Those who believe the myths might like the idea that "something is finally being done", but they would be wrong again' (Curry, 2008a). The AFN linked the announcement directly to the federal government's attempts to strengthen accountability and control to the failed First Nations Governance Act, 2006.

Conclusion

This chapter has illustrated the painstaking and stubborn single-policy directedness on the part of the federal government with respect to First Nations governance and administrative policy preferences. The federal government believed that its administrative reform efforts under NPM regarding the improvement of bureaucratic efficiency and First Nations accountability would be universally accepted by First Nations. It assumed that in order to rectify the deficiencies and failures of the Indian Act and presumably poor management on reserves, First Nations would naturally embrace any measures that assigned greater responsibilities for programs and services management and increased authority over monitoring, accountability, and achieving results. Although NPM provided greater management authority over program and service delivery for First Nations, they were still subject to rigorous accountability requirements by the federal government, which placed government preferences for results and accountability ahead of local First Nations preferences. First Nations insisted that the dominance of such accountability arrangements meant that their inherent right to self-government was subordinate to the federal government. It is striking that First Nations arguments to this effect have remained consistent throughout the many federal governmental reform efforts from the 1980s to the present. One of the clearest examples was the consultations on the First Nations Governance Act. The policy had as one of its objectives to further 'municipalize' First Nations governments—the same tried and true trajectory of administrative reform the federal government has followed from the introduction of public administration in the nineteenth century to the White Paper of 1969 to the present day. It does so by continuing to strengthen federal accountability arrangements through such instruments as funding agreements, legislation, and even self-government agreements. Ultimately, the First Nations Governance Act would have created federal municipalities with delegated authority for program management and delivery. Likewise, the Federal Accountability Act further reinforces these efforts.

In this respect, at least three themes are visible and even remain consistent in this ongoing narrative. First, NPM as an administrative framework continues to be unresponsive to First Nations policy and program concerns. Programs and services are being imposed on First Nations that have little to do with their actual needs.

Second, NPM continues to impose a strict accountability regime premised on performance accountability, which reinforces a delegated and principal–agent relationship, again disrespectful of the relationship envisaged in the treaties. Not only are First Nations required to respect programs and services funding rules, they are also required to meet the results-based management objectives set out in new program policies. Such governmental preferences for results are not negotiable, implying that First Nations cannot stray from defined results.

Finally, NPM continues to be regarded by First Nations as overly rules-bound, not unlike traditional public administration, thereby stifling any possibility for greater autonomy. Whereas NPM recognizes that local systems for managing accountability relationships are important, the federal government imposed an additional layer of accountability to its already stringent accountability requirements—ensuring that First Nations incorporate the principles of transparency, disclosure, and redress into their regular program operations. In other words, First Nations are required to impose a set of accountability rules on their band government operations that may or may not be consistent with their inherent systems. The effect of such rules is to further entrench and municipalize band governments consistent with the First Nations Governance Act vision of First Nations government. What is missing from NPM is confidence that First Nations want to manage their affairs in ways that maximize financial and program effectiveness and efficiency. The Minister's recent announcement about auditing First Nations despite the lack of evidence that management on reserves is weak or corrupt, speaks to this overwhelming lack of confidence in First Nations.

The effect of NPM so far has been increased control over First Nations governance and program management regimes. Almost every initiative launched by the federal government to date has been aimed at improving financial accountability or the management of reserves according to federal preferences for efficiency. If real and sustained progress towards a respectful relationship is to be achieved, First Nations governments must be thought of less as extensions of federal departments and more as equals in the effort to resolve the many challenges faced by this community.

Important Terms and Concepts

Aboriginal
accountability
Bill C-31
C-31 Indians
Contribution Agreements
delegated powers
direct management approach
Federal Accountability Act
First Nations Governance Act
Gathering Strength
Indian
Indian Act reform
Indian Register
inherent right of self-government
Inherent Right of Self-Government Policy
New Public Management (NPM)
non-status Indians
Penner Report
registered Indian
Report of the Royal Commission on Aboriginal Peoples
status Indians
White Paper of 1969

Study Questions

1. What is accountability, and what are the different variants of accountability that can apply in the case of a First Nation?
2. How are First Nations financed?
3. What effects do various finance agreements have?

4. What is the difference between delegated governance and the inherent right of self-government?
5. Which of these two theories of governance is most in evidence in the administrative relationships between First Nations and the federal government?

Useful Websites

Office of the Auditor General of Canada. 'Streamlining First Nations Reporting to Federal Organizations', Chapter 1 of *2002 Report*.

www.oag-bvg.gc.ca/internet/English/parl_oag_ 200212_01_e_12395.html

Clatworthy, Stewart. 2005. 'Indian Registration, Membership and Population Change in First Nations Communities'. Ottawa: INAC.

www.ainc-inac.gc.ca/pr/ra/rmp/int_e.html

AFN-INAC Joint Technical Working Group. 2008. *First Nations Registration (Status) and Membership Research Report*.

www.afn.ca/misc/mrp.pdf

Federal Accountability Act:

www2.parl.gc.ca/HousePublications/Publication.aspx?Parl=39&Ses=1&Mode=1&Pub=BW&Doc=C-2_4&Language=E

Library of Parliament. 2003. Legislative Summary: 'Bill C-7: The First Nations Governance Act'. Ottawa: Library of Parliament (see, especially, Appendix: Selective Overview of Indian Act History).

www2.parl.gc.ca/Sites/LOP/LegislativeSummaries/Bills_ls.asp?lang=E&ls=C7&source=library_prb&Parl=37&Ses=2

Minister of Indian Affairs and Northern Development, and Federal Interlocutor for Métis and Non-Status Indians. 2009. *Discussion Paper on Needed Changes to the Indian Act Affecting Indian Registration and Band Membership McIvor v. Canada*. Ottawa.

www.ainc-inac.gc.ca/br/is/mci-eng.asp

Turtle Island Native Network News:

www.turtleisland.org/news/news-landclaims-governance.htm

Notes

1. Several stories have been reported in the media in this respect over several decades. For example, in an episode of CBC Radio 'Ontario Today' (17 March 2008), NDP MP Charlie Angus called on the Government of Canada to take action to remedy the critical situation of youths in the native community of Attawapiskat. He criticizes federal departments for the lack of action on the high rates of suicide and violence.
2. Indian Affairs Minister, Chuck Strahl, confirmed that 54 land claims had been resolved as of 31 March 2008, of which 37 involved financial settlements. This is opposed to the usual 14 claims settled each year. This marked a 34-year high in such settlements (Curry 2008b).
3. According to the 2001 Census, 976,305 people reported 'Aboriginal identity'. This represents the total number of people identifying themselves as either a status or non-status Indian, Inuit, or Métis. This population increased to 1,172,785 persons as of the 2006 Census. As a percentage of the total population, the proportion of Aboriginal peoples increased from 3.3 per cent in 2001 to 3.7 per cent in 2006. Approximately 62 per cent of Aboriginal respondents in the census reported that they were Indian, 30 per cent who said they were Métis, and almost 5 per cent who said they were Inuit. (See: Statistics Canada, 2001 and 2006 *Census of Canada*; INAC, Indian Register; INAC, *Registered Indian Population Projection Series 2004–2029* [Ottawa: INAC, 2004]; Statistics Canada, *2005–2056 Population Projection Series* [Ottawa: Statistics Canada, 2004].) The total Aboriginal population is growing at a rate of approximately 1.8 per cent per year which is more than twice the overall Canadian growth rate. The median age of all Aboriginal peoples is 27 years of age in 2006 compared with 40 years for all Canadians. In addition, approximately 48 per cent of all Aboriginal peoples is under the age of 25 years. (Statistics Canada, 2001 and 2006 *Census of Canada* [Ottawa: Supply and Services, 2001 and 2006].)

   With respect to the status Indian population specifically, there were 558,175 who self-identified in 2001 compared with 623,780 on 2006, an increase of 11.75 per cent. The status Indian population is even younger than the overall Aboriginal identity population at 20 years of age. Approximately 40 per cent of Indians are under the age of 20 compared with 24 per cent for the overall Canadian population. As of 2007, approximately 57 per cent of status Indians live on a reserve or 460,300 people. The remainder, approximately 345,000 status Indians, reside off-reserve and live in larger urban centres. The on-reserve status Indian population is expected to increase by about 50 per cent between 2007 and 2029, compared with about 18 per cent for the Canadian population as a whole over the same time period. (INAC, *Registered Indian Population Projection Series 2004–2029* [Ottawa: INAC, 2004]; Statistics Canada, *2005–2056 Population Projection Series* [Ottawa: Statistics Canada, 2004].)

There are 615 First Nations communities in Canada comprising more than 50 nations or cultural groups, and speaking more than 50 Aboriginal languages. Approximately 59 per cent of First Nations communities have fewer than 500 residents and about 8 per cent have more than 2,000. Approximately 35 per cent of on-reserve status Indians live in urban areas, 45 per-cent in rural areas, and 20 per cent in remote or special access areas.

To assist with on-reserve programs, two-thirds of all federal programs directed to First Nations are funded by Indian and Northern Affairs Canada amounting to $6.85 billion in fiscal years 2007/8. INAC has primary but not exclusive responsibility for meeting the federal government's constitutional, treaty, political, and legal responsibilities to First Nations, Inuit, and Northerners. Thirteen other federal departments are responsible for on- and off-reserve programming and contribute approximately $3.5 billion combined for such programs as health care, fisheries management, residential schools, emergency preparedness, justice, and natural resources. The greatest expenditures occur in elementary/secondary education, schools infrastructure, specific and comprehensive claims, and social assistance. Interestingly, self-government and economic development programs constituted less than 14 per cent of INAC's total budget.

4. For a fuller definition of 'Indian', see sections 11, 12, and 13 of the Indian Act, 1876.

5. See INAC, 'Indian Registration, Membership and Population Change in First Nations Communities', (Ottawa: INAC, 2005) at: www.ainc-inac.gc.ca/pr/ra/rmp/int_e.html. Note that because not all bands provide their membership information to the department, an accurate account of population is not possible.

6. Romzek and Dubnick (1987) describe four types of accountability in their model: hierarchical (or bureaucratic), legal, professional, and political. I have added 'performance-based' as a specific form of bureaucratic accountability.

7. DIAND stands for Department of Indian Affairs and Northern Development, the former name of the Department of Indian and Northern Affairs Canada (INAC).

8. The exception to this is that the British Columbia INAC regional office uses the CFNFA as the base document to initiate discussions regarding federal funding under the federal self-government negotiations process. However, this is a regional approach that has been accepted by the Province of British Columbia and participating First Nations in the BC Treaty Negotiations process.

9. Targeted programs are those that are developed to address a specific problem or project on the part of the department or government as a whole. First Nations complain that instead of such 'one-off' programs being funded under their funding arrangement, they are funded separately under a mechanism that relies on high control and extensive accountability and reporting requirements (INAC, 1996: 19–21).

10. The funding authority used to support the 'Contributions funding authority regime' of the 1960s and 1970s remains intact. However, it now constitutes one authority among others in the new arrangements. See House of Commons (1983: 81–104) and Canada (1996b: 280–7).

11. A reimbursement of actuals regime requires significant staff resources because it requires the recording of how each dollar is spent. It should be noted that a traditional Contribution Agreement would not be capped. One of the principal reasons INAC has relied less on the traditional format is because costs were increasing at the local level at a rate that could not be sustained over the long term.

12. The agreement type was developed jointly with Health Canada and Justice Canada (Treasury Board, 1989: 13).

13. In this case, the block arrangement and the funding authority were given the same title. This created a great deal of confusion at the time but was rectified with a name change to the arrangement in 1994 (Treasury Board, 1986a: 3).

14. During the term of the CFNFA, recipients must adhere to 'minimum accountability requirements' including (1) INAC will ensure that the Council demonstrates the capacity to implement an accountability framework

that reflects accountability of Council to its members that provides for (a) transparency and openness in the Council's decision-making processes including a written conflict-of-interest code, (b) disclosure of the Council's administrative procedures and policies by making various documents including audited financial statements, fiscal plans, program evaluations, annual reports, and other documents available to members, and (c) redress for members by ensuring that policies and procedures are in place to address disputes related to block-funded services and targeted programs; (2) INAC will ensure that the Council has in place an accountability framework to recipients which provides for (a) transparency and openness in the Council's decision-making processes as these relate to block-funded services and targeted programs, (b) disclosure of the Council's written standards or procedures with respect to the delivery of programs, and (c) redress for recipients affected by decisions of Council that relate to the delivery of block-funded and targeted programs; (3) INAC will ensure that the Council has the listed policies in place which will be provided to the Department upon request; (4) INAC will obtain a copy of the Council's annual report on its program activities that it provides to its members. Note the similarity to First Nations Governance Act legislative requirements (discussed in the next section).

15. 'The departmental downsizing plan provided for a net reduction of 1,230 person years and approximately $36 million in annual expenditures (excluding reductions in the Northern Affairs Program). While part of these reductions was independent of program transfers, other parts were either directly or indirectly contingent on program transfers' (Treasury Board Secretariat, 1986b).

16. Specifically, the plan calls for a renewal of the relationship and to 'act on the premise that the inherent right of self-government is an existing Aboriginal and treaty right . . . . A Liberal government will be committed to gradually winding down the Department of Indian Affairs at a pace agreed upon by First Nations, while maintaining the federal fiduciary responsibility' (Liberal Party of Canada, 1993: 97–8).

17. The Inherent Right Policy included the *Framework for Implementation of the Inherent Right and the Negotiation of Self-Government* (Canada, 1995), the *British Columbia Treaties Mandate for Negotiations* (November 1995), the *Federal Policy for the Settlement of Native Claims* (Canada, 1993), and the *Comprehensive Claims Policy* (Canada, 1986).

18. Potential amendments to the Indian Act were circulated to First Nations governments in September of 1995 related to reserve lands, natural resources, estates, Indian monies, elections, by-laws, and education. Many of the recommendations came out of the LRT Review in 1993.

19. For greater detail, see Library of Parliament (2003: Appendix: 'Selected Overview of Indian Act History', iv).

20. See Canada (2001: 'Sharing Opportunity'). Despite these assurances, it would not be the first time such a promise was made. For example, in its October 1999 Speech from the Throne the federal government committed it would 'develop relationships with Aboriginal people based on the principles of partnership, transparency, predictability and accountability'.

21. It was announced by Robert Eyaphaise, Senior Advisor of Department of Indian Affairs, on 28 September 2005 at a meeting of the National Research Directors in Winnipeg that Bill C-6 will be withdrawn by the federal government in its entirety (Telephone discussion with a senior INAC official, 28 September 2005).

22. Canada, Federal Accountability Act (Ottawa: Supply and Services, 2006), s. 307. The following was added: '(c.1) a band, as defined in subsection 2(1) of the Indian Act, any member of the council or any agency of the band or an aboriginal body that is party to a self-government agreement given effect by an Act of Parliament or any of their agencies.'

References

Abele, Frances, Katherine Graham, and Allan Maslove. 1999. 'Negotiating Canada: Changes in Aboriginal Policy over the Last Thirty Years', in Leslie A. Pal, ed., *How Ottawa Spends 1999–2000: Shape Shifting: Canadian Governance Toward the 21st Century.* Don Mills: Oxford University Press.

Assembly of First Nations. 2002. 'Preliminary Analysis: First Nations Governance Act'. Ottawa: AFN, 14 June. Available at: www.afn.ca/Legislation%20Info/FNGA%20ANALYSIS.pdf.

Auditor General of Canada. 2002. 'Streamlining First Nations Reporting to Federal Organizations', *Report of the Auditor General of Canada.* Ottawa: Supply and Services.

Bernhardt, Darren. 2008. 'First Nation leaders speak out as treaty conference begins', Saskatoon: *Star Phoenix*, 26 March.

Bovens, Mark. 1998. *The Quest for Responsibility: Accountability and Citizenship in Complex Organizations.* New York: Cambridge University Press.

Canada. 1986. *Comprehensive Claims Policy*. Ottawa: INAC.
———. 1993. *Federal Policy for the Settlement of Native Claims*. Ottawa: INAC.
———. 1995. *Framework for Implementation of the Inherent Right and the Negotiation of Self-Government*. Ottawa: INAC, August.
———. 1996a. *People to People, Nation to Nation: Highlights from the Report of the Royal Commission on Aboriginal Peoples*. Ottawa: Royal Commission on Aboriginal Peoples.
———. 1996b. *Restructuring the Relationship*, vol. 2 of *Report of the Royal Commission on Aboriginal Peoples*. Ottawa: Royal Commission on Aboriginal Peoples.
———. 1996c. 'The Principles of a Renewed Relationship', ch. 16 of *Looking Forward, Looking Back*, vol. 1 of *Report of the Royal Commission on Aboriginal Peoples*. Ottawa: Royal Commission on Aboriginal Peoples.
———. 2001. 'Speech from the Throne to Open the First Session of the 37th Parliament of Canada'. Ottawa: Privy Council Office, 30 January. Available at: www.pco-bcp.gc.ca/default.asp?Language=E&Page=InformationResources&sub=sftddt&doc=sftddt2001_e.htm.
———. 2002. 'Bill C-7: First Nations Governance Act'. Ottawa: Supply and Services.
———. 2006. Federal Accountability Act. Ottawa: Supply and Services.
———. 2007. 'Federal Accountability Act and Action Plan: Strengthening the Powers of the Auditor General'. Available at: www.faa-lfi.gc.ca/fs-fi/16/fs-fi-eng.pdf.
———. 2008. Federal Accountability Act, ss. 306, 307. Ottawa: Supply and Services.
Castellano, Marlene Brant. 1999. 'Renewing the Relationship—A Perspective on the Impact of the Royal Commission on Aboriginal Peoples', in John H. Hylton, ed., *Aboriginal Self-Government in Canada*, 2nd edn. Saskatoon: Purich, 92–111.
Coopers, and Lybrand. 1983. 'Special Committee on Indian Self-Government Research Project on Federal Expenditures and Mechanisms for their Transfer to Indians'. Ottawa: House of Commons, 13 May.
Curry, Bill. 2008a. 'New Tory policy to audit reserves prompts outcry'. *The Globe and Mail*, 3 April.
———. 2008b. 'Tories hit mark on land claims: Fifty-four settlements resolved after public servants given target last year', *The Globe and Mail*, 28 March.
DIAND. 1986. *Indian and Native Programs: A Study Team Report to the Task Force on Program Review*. Ottawa: Supply and Services.
The Gazette. 2008. 'Paul Martin still wrong about Aboriginal issues' (editorial). *The Gazette* [Montreal], 11 April.
Gow, Iain. 2004. *Basic Research: A Canadian Model of Public Administration?* (Ottawa: Canada School of Public Service).
Graham, Katherine A., Carolyn Dittburner, and Frances Abele. 1996. *Soliloquy and Dialogue: Overview of Major Trends in Public Policy Relating to Aboriginal Peoples*. Ottawa: Royal Commission on Aboriginal Peoples.
Harmon, Michael. 1995. Responsibility as Paradox: A Critique of Rational Discourse on Government. Thousand Oaks, Calif.: Sage Publications.
House of Commons. 1983. *Indian Self-Government in Canada*. Report of the Special Committee on Indian Self-Government. Ottawa: Queen's Printer.
INAC. 1988. Forms of Self-Government: Community-Based Self-Government Negotiations. Ottawa: INAC Self-Government Branch.
———.1995. Program Review: Programs and Activities Requiring Full Reviews and Strategic Action Plans. Ottawa: INAC.
———.1996. 'Overview of DAEB Evaluation Studies of INAC Funding Arrangements'. Ottawa: INAC, October.
———. 1998a. *Gathering Strength: Canada's Aboriginal Action Plan*. Ottawa: INAC.
———. 1998b. *Indian Register*. Ottawa: INAC, Indian Registration Branch.
———. 2001. 'Communities First: First Nations Governance'. Consultation package. Published at: www.fng-gpn.gc.ca/samp_mat_e.asp (Link now inactive).
———. 2005. 'Indian Registration, Membership and Population Change in First Nations Communities', (Ottawa: INAC). Available at: www.ainc-inac.gc.ca/pr/ra/rmp/int_e.html.
———. 2008. 'Indian and Northern Affairs Canada (INAC) Continues to Strengthen Its Fiscal Management and Accountability' (press release). Ottawa: INAC, 31 March.
Johnson, Darlene. 1996. 'Native Rights as Collective Rights: A Question of Group Self-Preservation', in Will Kymlicka, ed., *The Rights of Minority Cultures*. New York: Oxford University Press.
Liberal Party of Canada. 1993. *Creating Opportunity: The Liberal Plan for Canada*. Ottawa: Liberal Party of Canada.
Library of Parliament. 2003. Legislative Summary: 'Bill C-7: The First Nations Governance Act'. Ottawa: Library of Parliament, December.
McDonnell, R.F., and R.C. Depew. 1999. 'Aboriginal Self-Government and Self-Determination in Canada: A Critical Commentary', in John H. Hylton, ed., *Aboriginal Self-Government in Canada*, 2nd edn. Saskatoon: Purich, 352–76.
Nahwegahbow, David. 2003. 'Statement by David Nahwegahbow, Former Co-Chair of the Aboriginal Peoples' Commission of the Liberal Party of Canada' (press release). 1 June.
Romzek, Barbara, and Melvin Dubnick. 1987. 'Accountability in the Public Sector: Lessons from the Challenger Tragedy', *Public Administration Review* 47, 3: 227–38.
Tennant, Paul. 1985. 'Aboriginal Rights and the Penner Report on Indian Self-Government', in Menno Boldt, J. Anthony Long, and Leroy Little Bear, eds, *The Quest for Justice*. Toronto: University of Toronto Press: 321–32.
Treasury Board Secretariat. 1986a. 'Decision of the Treasury Board—Meeting June 26, 1986'. Ottawa: TBS, 26 June.
———. 1986b. 'Decision of the Treasury Board Meeting of November 27, 1986 [Minutes of Meeting]'. Ottawa: TBS, 27 November.
———. 1989. 'Decision of the Treasury Board: Meeting of July 26, 1989'. Ottawa: TBS, 26 July.
———. 1996. 'Treasury Board Submission for Funding to Support Inherent Right Negotiations'. Ottawa: TBS, 2 January.
———. 2006. 'Accountability Restored with Landmark Legislation—Federal Accountability Act introduced to rebuild confidence and trust of Canadians' (press release). Ottawa: TBS, 11 April.
Wilson, V. Seymour. 1988. 'What Legacy? The Nielson Task Force Program Review', in Katherine A. Graham, ed., *How Ottawa Spends 1988–89: The Conservatives Heading into the Stretch*. Ottawa: Carleton University Press.

20 Inuit Approaches to Public Governance, Public Administration, and Public Policy in Nunavut

Annis May Timpson

A new era of Inuit-oriented governance is developing in northern Canada, reflected in the creation of the territorial government of Nunavut and regional governments in Nunatsiavut, Nunavik, and the Inuvialuit Settlement Region in the Northwest Territories. These long-negotiated initiatives, which are part of a broader process of decolonization in Canada, have encouraged new thinking about **indigenous approaches to public administration**. This chapter contributes to those reflections by exploring how Inuit values, culture, and language are being embedded in the design, operation, and policy initiatives of the territorial government of Nunavut.

The idea of creating a jurisdiction in the eastern Arctic where the Inuit language and culture would be fully recognized was a dream that galvanized a generation of Inuit activists in the late 1960s as, listening together at their residential school in Churchill, they absorbed broadcasts relaying news of civil rights campaigns in the United States. It was an aspiration that inspired Tagak Curley—now a member of the Nunavut Legislative Assembly—to call the first meeting of the Inuit Tapirisat of Canada in a church basement in Ottawa in 1971. Moreover, it was an objective that motivated a generation of Inuit negotiators who toughed it out—pragmatically—in protracted trialogues with federal and territorial government representatives.

These negotiations led eventually to the signing of the most comprehensive land claims agreement in Canadian history and the creation of Canada's first Aboriginal-focused public government. The dream of creating an Inuit-oriented territory was fulfilled, in part, with the signing of the Nunavut Land Claims Agreement (NLCA) in 1993, and the creation of the new territorial government of Nunavut in 1999. Nonetheless, the process of establishing a new public government centred on Inuit values is complex, not least because the Canadian federation has long prioritized settler approaches to governance. Only in recent years have adjustments been contemplated that can begin to address Aboriginal ideas about how approaches to governance might evolve in Canada. By exploring some of the complexities that have arisen in the process of developing an Aboriginally sensitive jurisdiction in Nunavut, we can begin to understand the potential for developing more inclusive approaches to public administration in Canada that take fuller account of Aboriginal perspectives.

Inuit-Oriented Public Government

The territorial government of Nunavut is a public government that serves all citizens in the jurisdiction, regardless of their ethnicity. Nonetheless, from the outset, it has always been developed with a specific Inuit orientation to ensure both the full employment and full representation of Aboriginal citizens in the territory and also the embedding of Inuit culture and the Inuit language in government operations. In Nunavut, the **Aboriginal** orientation arises not only because the territorial government's very existence is embedded in Article 4 of the constitutionally protected Nunavut Land Claims Agreement (NLCA) but also because Article 23 of this agreement specified that the public services in Nunavut (be they territorial or federal) should, in the long run, be staffed so as to reflect the ethnic composition of the territorial population. Indeed, Nunavut is significant because around 85 per cent of its 31,000-strong population is Inuit, and as a result it is likely to become the first jurisdiction in North America with a **public service** that is predominantly staffed by Aboriginal people. The challenges for Nunavut lie in achieving this objective, while delivering services to residents of 28 small communities spread over one-fifth of Canada's land mass, and ensuring that the elected territorial government responds to the needs and interests of a population that is predominantly Aboriginal.

This chapter addresses three core issues that have characterized the Government of Nunavut's approach to developing North America's first Aboriginal-oriented public government. It looks first at the institutional design of the new government, then at the creation of an ethnically reflective public service, and, finally, at the way key policies developed by the new government have reflected cultural priorities of the territory's mainly Inuit population.

Institutional Design and Public Government

How has the challenge of developing an **Inuit-oriented public government** been addressed in the design and operation of the institutions of governance in Nunavut?

The Legislative Assembly of Nunavut—known as 'the leg'—was designed to reflect the non-partisan, consensual approach to governance that became the hallmark of the Legislative Assembly of the Northwest Territories (Henderson, 2007: 111–12). Interestingly, however, when the Nunavut Implementation Commission (NIC) was overseeing plans for the new Legislative Assembly of Nunavut, it hoped that the design and composition of the assembly would ensure that legislative processes in Nunavut reflected traditional Inuit values. First, in contrast to the Legislative Assembly of the Northwest Territories, where the public gallery overlooks the debating chamber, the Legislative Assembly of Nunavut was designed to draw legislators, Elders, and community members into an intimate circular space, suggesting the interior of an igloo. The debating chamber in the Legislative Assembly of Nunavut was arranged with three concentric circles: the inner circle for legislators, the middle one for Elders, and the outer circle for members of the public and visitors to the Assembly. Second, to reflect the interdependence of men and women essential to survival in Inuit outpost camps, the NIC called for an innovative electoral system that would ensure that each riding would be represented by both a male and female member of the assembly.

These significant innovations, designed to bring Elders and women more directly into the operation of the Nunavut Legislative Assembly have had limited effect. The sealskin-covered seats reserved for Elders routinely remain unoccupied, reflecting perhaps the disconnection between contemporary governance and traditional decision-making in Inuit communities. Moreover, the NIC's proposal to create a gender-equal legislative assembly was not ratified in the 1997 gender parity referendum, held prior to the creation of Nunavut: only 37 per cent of the eligible electorate turned out to vote with 57 per cent voting against the objective (Henderson, 2007: 146). Very few women have been elected to office in Nunavut and, at the time of writing, Premier Eva Aariak is the only woman to hold office in the Legislative Assembly of Nunavut.

As in the Northwest Territories, legislative procedures reflect a hybrid approach that, on the one hand are grounded in established parliamentary routines found in legislative assemblies throughout the Commonwealth, and on the other reflect a consensual style of governance and cabinet selection that became the hallmark of procedures in the Legislative Assembly of the Northwest Territories (Legislative Assembly of Nunavut, 2007; Cameron and White, 1995, 53–7). Nonetheless, despite the theoretical commitment to **consensus government**, legislators in this new 'Westminster of the Arctic' do not systematically operate in consensus mode (White, 1991). Indeed, at a relatively early stage in Nunavut's first Legislative Assembly, when regular members began to hold the cabinet to account over the slow growth of Inuit employment in the public service and the government's limited commitment to embedding Inuit values in its operation, an oppositional atmosphere was often in evidence between the ten regular members, sitting on one side of the legislative circle, and the eight members of cabinet sitting on the other (*Nunatsiaq News*, 2001a).

Moreover, as legislative debates, in contrast to traditional decision-making procedures, involve the production of written text—in the form of 'The Blues' and then of Hansard—problems occasionally emerge in their translation from Inuinnaqtun, the Inuit dialect in the west of the territory, to Inuktitut, the Inuit dialect in the Baffin region. This highlights the complexities of shifting from traditional community governance, where one indigenous dialect would have been spoken, to contemporary forms of representation in a multilingual assembly, where translation of debates is the norm.

In designing the departments of the new territorial government, the Nunavut Implementation Commission emphasized 'the need to respect the unique culture, language and history of the aboriginal residents of Nunavut' (Nunavut Implementation Commission, 1995: 28). Its proposal that the Department of Executive and Intergovernmental Affairs 'coordinate relations with aboriginal organizations' brought a new dimension to thinking about the way governments in Canada should conduct external relations (ibid.). Similarly, its recommendation that the Department of Justice 'provide a justice system relevant to the life style, customs and culture of Nunavut' marked a key stage in a much longer process of reconciling contemporary Canadian jurisprudence with traditional Inuit law (ibid.). This process, incidentally, was encouraged by the Government of Nunavut's decision to fund Akitsiraq, a program run by the University of Victoria and Arctic College to train Nunavut's first cohort of Inuit lawyers. In 2005 a group of 11 Inuit students graduated with LLB degrees: their legal education had included training in both conventional Western law and traditional Inuit law (University of Victoria, 2005).

In designing the infrastructure of the new government, the NIC also recommended the creation of program departments that would sustain Inuit values in policy development. Particularly noteworthy is its design of the Department of Sustainable Development, and of the Department of Culture, Language, Elders and Youth.

The Department of Sustainable Development—or simply 'Sustainable', as it became known—was established to bring issues of the environment, economy, and human development together to preserve Inuit knowledge of the land and encourage the use of traditional knowledge alongside scientific approaches to resource management (Nunavut, Department of Sustainable Development, 2000: 1). This was an innovative departmental structure that had the potential to reframe policy approaches in the North by linking questions about the land and environmental management, economic development, and welfare resources together. It was hoped that by linking core aspects of the Inuit economy in the eastern Arctic, this integrated department would facilitate new forms of economic planning for the development of the healthy, sustainable communities that lay at the heart of the first government's strategic plan.

The importance of connecting elders and youth to preserve Inuit culture in a period of modernization led also to the creation of the Department of Culture, Language, Elders and Youth (CLEY). The first department of its kind in Canada, CLEY was created to 'bring Inuit language and culture into the everyday lives and work of the residents of Nunavut,' preserve and promote Inuit culture and language, and ensure that the youngest citizens of Nunavut acquire cultural wisdom from Elders in the territory (Nunavut Implementation Commission, 1995: 28).

Although both departments were central to creating Inuit-oriented institutions of government, only CLEY (the department with the lowest budget within the Nunavut government) has survived. The demands on officers in Sustainable Development, both from within and outside the Government of Nunavut (GN) became extensive and, as a result, Sustainable proved to be unsustainable as a department. In 2004 it was split into the departments of Environment and of Economic Development and Transportation (Nunavut, 2004a).

The experience of designing an Aboriginally sensitive infrastructure for the GN carries important messages for future initiatives. On the one hand the GN's institutional base reinforces the centrality of Aboriginal concerns in the new government. On the other hand, it demonstrates how internal and intergovernmental pressures can overwhelm Aboriginal-oriented departments as senior officials in these units find themselves working on multiple intergovernmental files that in most other jurisdictions are serviced by separate departments (Timpson, 2005: 216). While department restructuring becomes inevitable, it is only if Aboriginal cultural perspectives are kept front and centre that the objective of maintaining an Aboriginally oriented government infrastructure will be met.

While this chapter focuses on the territorial government, it is important to note that public government in Nunavut has both territorial and federal dimensions, with a significant number of federal government departments represented in Nunavut through regional offices and the Nunavut Federal Council. These public dimensions of governance contrast with the services delivered through Nunavut Tunngavik Incorporated (NTI), the Inuit organization established in 1993 to manage the benefits that flow to Inuit as a result of the NLCA. NTI acts in the interests of Inuit beneficiaries of the NLCA and is accountable to them through its elected officers. Its relations with the territorial government of Nunavut are guided by the 1999 *Clyde River Protocol* and its 2004 update *Iqqanaijaqatigiit* ('working together') (Nunavut and Nunavut Tunngavik Incorporated, 1999; Nunavut Tunngavik Incorporated and the Government of Nunavut, 2004). These documents set out the intention of sharing issues of mutual interest and embedding a series of meetings between senior officials from both the GN and NTI. Relations between the two organizations vary—at times NTI becomes a kind of official opposition to the GN and at other times they work in collaboration, particularly in lobbying the federal government for financial resources for Nunavut.

These different dimensions of public and ethnically focused governance in Nunavut are drawn together by a series of land claims boards known as Institutions of Public Government (IPGs). These boards address key issues of land-use planning and wildlife management, providing an important and effective example of contemporary 'treaty federalism' (White, 2002). Moreover, these IPGs have played a critical role in ensuring that Inuit knowledge is integrated into the development of public policy in Nunavut.

Representative Public Service

One of the core objectives of Inuit land claim negotiators was to ensure that the staff of the new territorial government's public service would reflect the ethnic composition of the population. This was particularly important given that the Government of Nunavut would become the major employer in the new territory. It was also important to avoid a repetition of the Inuit experience of governance in the Northwest Territories that, as Peter Jull has noted, was one in which 'well-meaning whites turned Aboriginal lives upside down' (Jull, 2000: 14). Inuit negotiators realized this objective and as a result Article 23 of the NLCA obliges federal and territorial governments and the designated Inuit organization—NTI—to 'co-operate in the development and implementation of employment and training' in order to 'increase Inuit participation in government employment in the Nunavut Settlement Area to a representative level' (Canada, Indian and Northern Affairs, 1993: 191). In a territory with a population that is close to 85 per cent Inuit, this article gives constitutional backing (under section 35 of the Charter) to the creation of the first public service in North America to be staffed predominantly by Inuit at all occupational groupings and grade levels. For this reason alone, the development of the public sector in Nunavut deserves our attention.

From the federal government's perspective, the development of a **representative public service**—a public service that reflects the population in Nunavut—made sense. It fit with the broader ethos of federal employment equity programs and the longer history of building representative bureaucracies in Canada (Kernaghan, 1978; Timpson, 2006). It also made demographic sense to ensure that a rapidly expanding Inuit population would be effectively employed. As Thomas Berger noted, in his 2006 report on Nunavut: 'The need for educational and career opportunities for Inuit is pressing. . . . Nunavut's population has doubled in a single generation, from 15,000 in 1981 to almost 30,000 today. . . . It is the youngest population in Canada, with approximately 60 per cent of residents under 25 years of age, 92 per cent of whom are Inuit' (Berger, 2006: 40).

Training programs to facilitate the creation of a representative public service were essential. Initial funding of $39.8 million for this purpose was channelled into the Nunavut Unified Human Resources Development Strategy, designed both to expand the pool of trained Inuit in Nunavut by developing training opportunities for unemployed Inuit who wanted to enter public service employment and to provide in-service training for Inuit public servants who wished to increase their responsibilities and remuneration (Fortier and Jones, 1998). A variety of training programs have continued since the territory's inception and the government has developed a broader commitment to culturally sensitive hiring interviews which aim to focus on applicants' transferable skills, in order to facilitate the shift between subsistence and wage-based economies. Nonetheless, both the GN and NTI consider that the federal government has not sustained its financial contribution to this project. Indeed, 10 years into its existence, the Government of Nunavut still relies heavily on a southern Canadian workforce.

Inuit employment statistics, published by the GN, demonstrate uneven progress towards the creation of a population-reflective public service. In the years following the creation of Nunavut, as the territorial public service developed, Inuit representation declined marginally, appearing to reach a low point of 42 per cent in June 2003 (Nunavut, Human Resources, 2003). The representation of Inuit in the public service has since improved, reaching an overall level of 52 per cent in June 2008 (Nunavut, Human Resources, 2008). However, the greatest increase in Inuit employment has been concentrated in the paraprofessional and administrative support categories. Indeed, by 2006 almost all posts in the lowest rung of the territorial government's six employment categories were filled by Inuit and, although data on the gender breakdown is not published, these posts appear to be primarily filled by women (Timpson, 2009). Moreover, while there has been a gradual improvement in the representation of Inuit in professional and managerial categories, *Qallunaat* (non-Inuit) still account for three-quarters of the people employed in these posts.

Why have initiatives to build a population-reflective public sector in Nunavut not taken root more rapidly or on more gender-neutral lines? Perhaps training programs were not developed soon enough to ensure the creation of a more Inuit-representative workforce. More emphasis may need to be placed on in-service mentoring and support systems to encourage progress through the ranks of the public service. Indeed the idea of working in a bureaucratic post within government is not likely to appeal to all *Nunavummiut* (residents of Nunavut) and is probably least likely to appeal to those Inuit men who are still directly engaged in harvesting country food that remains intrinsic to household economies.

The entry of Inuit into government employment is also affected by competition for skilled Inuit in Nunavut. The GN has to compete with the private sector and with the range of Inuit organizations that are affiliated with NTI and that, in many respects, provide a more Inuit-oriented working environment (*Nunatsiaq News*, 2001b: 20). Moreover, as the government is currently operating at about three-quarters of its planned staffing capacity, the demands of working for the

GN can be stressful (Nunavut, Human Resources, 2008).

Frustration with the slow rate of growth in Inuit employment in Nunavut was aired by Inuit leaders in the GN and NTI during lengthy negotiations with the federal government to ensure that the initial ten-year Planning Period Funding that underwrote the Land Claim Implementation Contract was renewed for a further period in 2003 (Bell, 2003). Negotiators from Nunavut argued that the federal government needed to invest more heavily in Inuit employment training to meet its commitments under the NLCA. The federal government, by contrast, took the position that while it had provided start-up funds to support the territory's unified human resource strategy, it was for the territorial government to support long-term training from its block-grant territorial transfer funds.

The difficulty in negotiating additional federal investment in training led NTI and the GN to appoint the international accountants, PricewaterhouseCoopers, to assess the costs of not implementing Article 23. Their report reinforced the argument that 'full implementation of Article 23 would ensure that Inuit have the power to develop and administer government policies in a manner consistent with Inuit values and culture, in direct proportion to the percentage of the population they represent' (PricewaterhouseCoopers, 2003: 15). It also identified persistent barriers to Inuit employment in the territorial government, including Inuit perceptions of limited work available, low educational attainment among Inuit, the absence of sufficient mentoring of Inuit within the public sector workplace, and the prevalence of English as the language of work in the GN (ibid., 7).

Interestingly, the report emphasized the direct and indirect costs of not achieving an ethnically representative public service in Nunavut. It estimated that 'Inuit would have earned $258 million in compensation if Article 23 had been fully implemented' (ibid., 9). It also argued that 'Inuit under-representation in Government, particularly in the high paying positions [meant that] $123 million of this compensation was expected to go to non-Inuit in 2003 [and that] the total value of lost wages [for Inuit], if representation rates remain[ed] at [that] level, [was] estimated to be $2.5 billion over the next 18 years' (ibid.). The problem therefore, from the perspective of NTI (which exists to protect the interests of Inuit beneficiaries), is that, in core financial terms, the employment opportunities emerging through federal transfer funds to the territorial government are benefiting *Qallunaat* (non-Inuit) disproportionately to their representation in the population.

Although the report reinforced perceptions in Nunavut about the importance of additional federal government resources being poured into Nunavut to further the training needed to achieve the objectives of Article 23, the federal government's reluctance to do so led to NTI initiating legal action in 2006 against the Government of Canada for being in breach of the contract that underscored Article 23 (Nunavut Tunngavik Incorporated, 2006). At the time of writing the outcome of that court challenge is not yet known.

Culturally Relevant Public Administration

How has the Government of Nunavut begun to address the challenge of embedding Inuit culture in the public administration of the territory? All the territorial government's strategic plans for the long-term development of Nunavut have emphasized how ***Inuit Qaujimajatuqangit*** (IQ) ('that which is long known by Inuit') should 'provide the context [for developing] an open, responsive and accountable government' (Nunavut, 1999a: 4). Nonetheless, it has taken some time for officials in government to work out how traditional Inuit values might best be translated into government policy and operations.

The process has been emotionally intense, in part because the concept of Inuit knowledge is not easily understood by many *Qallunaat* public servants in the senior ranks of the territorial public service. Moreover, interpretations of traditional Inuit knowledge vary across communities, genders, and generations. In addition, it has been difficult to achieve consensus within the GN about the most effective way to integrate Inuit knowledge into bureaucratic practice.

Nora Sanders, formerly deputy minister of Justice in the GN, reflected how 'there isn't a day that goes by within the Nunavut Government [without] a discussion somewhere, (or several) [discussions], about what Inuit Qaujimajatuqangit means, and how it is to be understood and incorporated into the Government's practices' (Sanders, 2005: 8). This process began when CLEY (the department with overall responsibility for the development of IQ policies within the GN) led a major IQ workshop in Apex in September 1999 (Nunavut, 1999b). It continued in November 2000 when the minister of CLEY appointed an Inuit-only Task Force (made up of two Nunavut government employees, two members of the Nunavut Social Development Council, and two elders) to consider the development of a government-wide strategy on IQ.

When the Task Force reported in August 2002, it urged the government to rethink its approach to IQ and develop strategies that would encourage the GN to 'incorporate itself into Inuit culture' rather than only seeking to 'incorporate Inuit culture into itself' (Nunavut, Culture, Language, Elders and Youth, 2002: 1). In response, the government developed core principles around which *Inuit Qaujimajatuqangit* could be developed and required government departments to begin IQ audits—evaluating departmental policy objectives in their annual business plans in terms of IQ.

When the second Legislative Assembly of Nunavut took office in 2004 it codified the principles of IQ in its new strategic plan. Although many of these principles, when translated into government practice, reflect best-practice objectives that would ideally be found in the public service of any government in Canada, others are less familiar. For example, the 2004 strategic plan specified that core Inuit values of silence being integral to communication; consensus-building as a prerequisite for decision-making; innovation as necessary for survival and progress; and respect and care of the land, animals, and the environment should be embedded as fundamental objectives of the GN and its public service (Nunavut, 2004b: 3–4).

While there was significant debate in the early days of Nunavut about the disconnection between traditional Inuit decision-making and contemporary forms of public government, IQ initiatives have provided opportunities for Elders to advise officers in the GN about ways in which working practices and policies could reflect fundamental aspects of traditional Inuit culture. Elders were directly involved in the 1999 IQ workshop. They were key members of the GN's IQ Task Force. In 2001 the Department of Justice created the post of Elder-in-Residence, to advise public servants about how the department could take account of traditional Inuit law and to be directly involved in teaching traditional law to students registered in the Akitsiraq Law School program (Sanders, 2005: 19).

The Nunavut experience highlights the complexities of transposing traditional Aboriginal knowledge into the contemporary bureaucratic framework of public governance. It also reveals the significance of such an exercise in empowering Aboriginal public servants to connect the project of a new government with the body of traditional knowledge developed through intergenerational survival on the land. This highlights the importance not just of connecting Elders and youth through intergenerational cultural projects but also of connecting Elders and professional public servants in designing and developing culturally relevant procedures of governance. Moreover, the process of developing IQ not only has provided Inuit public servants with the opportunity to work on a significant cultural project with Inuit colleagues, but also has provided them with the critical experience of working in policy committees within the GN that function entirely in their own language.

Public Policy on the Inuit Language

The process of ensuring that Inuit culture is embedded in the processes of territorial governance not only concerns questions about IQ but also, more broadly, questions about the recognition and use of the Inuit language in the public service. In a community that still has direct understanding of the oppressive experience of having its indigenous language suppressed in residential schools, the idea of being able to reclaim this language in a public space and use it in managing the operation of government is a powerful objective to keep in mind.

Inuit politicians have long considered the development of the Inuit language as central to their vision of Nunavut. As the Nunavut Constitutional Forum noted in 1983, 'perhaps there is no more fundamental goal of a Nunavut government, nor one more essential to guarantee the survival and unique contribution of Inuit in Canada. . . . Official status for Inuktitut will hasten the full participation by Inuit in employment opportunities in Nunavut . . . testify to the unique cultural nature of Nunavut and . . . encourage other residents of Nunavut to learn the language of the majority' (Nunavut Constitutional Forum, 1983: 18).

When the first elected government of Nunavut took office it stated that the territory should become 'a fully functional bilingual society, in Inuktitut and English, respectful and committed to the needs and rights of French speakers, with a growing ability to participate in French' (Nunavut, 1999a: 7). It also emphasized that efforts would be made to ensure that 'Inuktitut, in all its forms, is the working language of the Government of Nunavut' (ibid., 4). That objective moved a step closer to being realized in 2008, when the Legislative Assembly of Nunavut passed legislation to recognize and protect the Inuit language.

Making the Inuit language an official language of Nunavut and protecting its erosion are central not only to the full realization of Article 23 of the NLCA but also to the integration of *Inuit Qaujimajatuqangit* into government operations. As Thomas Berger noted in 2006, 'No other province or territory has a majority of Aboriginal people speaking a single language . . . Nunavut remains, in terms of the reality on the ground, a jurisdiction where the first language of the vast majority of the population is Inuktitut' (Berger, 2006: 16, viii).

Nonetheless, indigenous language use in Nunavut is complex. Inuit in Nunavut speak seven different dialects. Six of these are collectively referred to as Inuktitut, which uses a syllabic script and is spoken throughout the Baffin and Keewatin regions. The seventh dialect—Inuinnaqtun—uses Roman orthography and, though severely endangered, is still spoken in the western Kitikmeot region of Nunavut (Hicks and White, 2000: 100, note 48). In recent public documents the term 'the Inuit language' has been used to embrace both Inuktitut and Inuinnaqtun (Nunavut, Culture, Languages, Elders and Youth, 2006: 4).

Developing the Inuit language as an official language of work in the GN is important as most Inuit speak primarily Inuktitut or Inuinnaqtun at home but find themselves shifting between their indigenous language and English in the workplace (Nunavut, Nunavummit Kiglisiniartiit/Nunavut Bureau of Statistics, 2003). Moreover, in the western Kitikmeot, where Inuinnaqtun is most endangered, indigenous language skills are even more limited than in the Inuktitut-speaking regions of the territory, increasing the probability that Inuit employees in this region will speak and use English more easily than their indigenous language (ibid.). Moreover, Inuit children in Nunavut will most likely be educated in the Inuit language for part or all of their elementary school education, but then educated almost entirely in English once they move on to high school. It is not surprising, therefore, as Berger noted, that not only do 'Inuit of Nunavut have the lowest rate of literacy in English in the country' but the '"early exit immersion" model [of language training in the territorial school system] . . . provides students with an insufficient foundation in their first language and too sudden an immersion in the second' (Berger, 2006: iv, 28–9).

Not all Inuit working for the GN have complete communication skills in the Inuit language or in English. Furthermore, most *Qallunaat* working for the GN have nothing more than rudimentary skills in the Inuit language. Nonetheless, except at the most senior level, language training initiatives within the GN have focused almost exclusively on equipping *Qallunaat* employees with rudimentary Inuit language skills, requiring all new *Qallunaat* employees to take a basic ten-week course in Inuktitut on appointment to the GN, with the option to move beyond this with further language training (Nunavut, Human Resources, 2001: 15). Only since 2006 have senior level employees been expected to develop their Inuit language skills beyond this preliminary level (CBC North, 2006). Interestingly, the decision to require senior officials in the GN to develop their Inuit language skills then had key Inuit and *Qallunaat* public servants working together in thrice-weekly language training sessions, an initiative that has started to address a much broader problem of Inuit and *Qallunaat* employees acquiring the linguistic capacity to communicate in each other's primary language.

Interpretation services are critical to the development of an effective public service in Nunavut. These services, however, involve not only interpretation of Inuktitut for those speaking Inuinnaqtun, and vice versa, but also interpretation between indigenous and settler languages. They also require extensive development of new terminology. While the GN does not yet have the facilities to ensure simultaneous electronic translation, *Asuilaak* (an online living dictionary) has been created to develop a central data bank of terminology in Inuktitut, Inuinnaqtun, English, and French. Although interpreters are present for the Legislative Assembly and at key meetings of the GN, greater consideration needs to be given to making such services available for routine use within the public service. After all, this would create an environment in which unilingual public servants could feel at ease discussing policy matters. In addition, it would ensure that all GN offices could deliver services directly to unilingual *Nunavummiut* (residents of Nunavut).

The development of the Inuit language as an official language of government requires legislative development, particularly as the official language legislation that the GN inherited from the Government of the Northwest Territories reflected language use in that territory. The first Legislative Assembly of Nunavut consulted extensively about the most appropriate way to revise this legislation for Nunavut (Nunavut Legislative Assembly, 2002). But it was only when the second Legislative Assembly of Nunavut assumed office in 2004 that the GN committed itself to developing 'made-in-Nunavut language legislation to foster the use of Inuktitut in the workplace and in the public and private sectors' (Nunavut, 2004b: 12). Even then it was only in the final two sittings of the second Legislative Assembly that language legislation was passed. Moreover, at the time of writing, the 2008 Official Languages Act of Nunavut has not been ratified by the federal government as formally required under section 28 of the 1993 Nunavut Act (the federal legislation that created the new territory of Nunavut).

The policy instruments passed by the Legislative Assembly of Nunavut are double-edged. The Official Languages Act is designed to ensure that the Inuit language is placed on par with English and French as one of three official languages in Nunavut. By contrast, the Inuit Language Protection Act is designed to protect the Inuit language from further erosion. This legislative division ensured that the promotion of the Inuit language as an official language of Nunavut would not diminish the status of English or French in the territory.

The Preamble to the 2008 Official Languages Act asserts that the Inuit language is 'the indigenous language of Nunavut, the spoken and preferred language of a majority of Nunavummiut, [and] a defining characteristic of the history and people of Nunavut' (Nunavut, 2008a: Preamble, b, c). It also considers the Inuit language to be 'a necessary element in the improvement of Inuit social, economic and cultural well-being... and the development of the public service, and of government policies, programs and services, as contemplated by the Nunavut Land Claims Agreement' (ibid.: Preamble, d.i, ii).

In order to ensure that the Inuit language is used in government communications and services in Nunavut, the legislation requires that every territorial institution in Nunavut shall 'display its public signs...make and issue its instruments...in the Official Languages' (ibid., s. 11.1a). Resonating with language legislation elsewhere in Canada, it also requires that signs or notices in official languages ensure that each official language has 'an equal prominence, impact or effect with all the other Official Languages used' (ibid., s. 11.1c). It also requires the administrative head of the relevant unit to ensure that a member of the public can exercise their 'right to communicate with and receive the services of a territorial institution in an Official Language' (ibid., s. 12.1).

The Official Languages Act specifies the appointment of two key officials to oversee the implementation of the legislation. First, a Minister of Languages (a post currently held by the minister with responsibility for Culture, Language, Elders, and Youth) is responsible for overseeing the implementation of official languages legislation in the territory, including developing and implementing an official languages plan that involves Inuit and members of both the English and French official language communities (ibid., s. 13.3c, d). In addition, the act formalizes the powers of the Languages Commissioner of Nunavut to ensure compliance with the legislation. Interestingly, the act specifies that in investigating compliance the Languages Commissioner can proceed by 'developing mediation and other methods consistent with Inuit Qaujimajatuqangit, and using these methods when appropriate to resolve concerns about the performance of legislative, policy or procedural language obligations' (ibid., s. 22.2b). In addition, the Act specifies that the Languages Commissioner may, in the course of exercising the powers and duties of the post, 'consult with or engage Elders for assistance with dispute resolution, or... Inuit Qaujimajatuqangit' (ibid., s. 21.2).

While the Official Languages Act attempts to set the indigenous and settler languages on par in Nunavut, the new Inuit Language Protection Act links this objective with broader commitments to embed the Inuit language in the community and grant *Nunavummiut* territorially based rights to receive their education and to work in the Inuit language.

The Inuit Language Protection Act reinforces the GN's commitment to embedding the Inuit language in signage by requiring that all public sector, municipal, and private sector organizations in Nunavut display their signs in the Inuit language in a way that ensures that 'the Inuit Language text of its public signs, posters and commercial advertising is at least equally prominent with any other language used' (Nunavut, 2008b: s. 3.1c). It also requires such organizations to ensure that their client and reception services are made available in the Inuit language. In addition the act seeks to ensure that essential services to *Nunavummiut* will be provided in the Inuit language.

The Act states that 'every parent whose child is enrolled in the education program in Nunavut...has the right to have his or her child receive instruction in the Inuit Language' (ibid., s. 8.1). It also requires the GN, 'in a manner that is consistent with Inuit Qaujimajatuqangit, [to] design and enable the education program to produce secondary school graduates fully proficient in the Inuit Language, in both its spoken and written forms; [and to] develop and implement appropriate Inuit Language competency targets necessary for the achievement of full proficiency for all stages of learning within the education program' (ibid., s. 8.2a, b). While these proposals are in keeping with the recommendations of Berger's 2006 report they raise serious questions about the availability of teachers who have the linguistic skills to deliver this level of language instruction.

Thirdly, the Inuit Language Protection Act reinforces the GN's commitment to embedding the Inuit language as the language of work in government institutions. It specifies that 'the Inuit Language is a language of work in territorial institutions, and every employee of a territorial institution has the right to use the Inuit Language at work to the extent and in the manner provided in this Act and the regulations' (ibid., s. 12.1). As a result managers in the territorial public service are required to ensure that people can apply for positions in the Inuit language, and that 'applicants' assessed level of competence in the Inuit

Language is a criteria that receives value in the assessment of his or her overall qualifications for the position' (ibid., s. 12.2c, ii). In addition, the act requires managers to 'determine through an active offer made at the commencement of employment, whether the new employee prefers the Inuit Language as his or her language of work,' and, if this is the case, to make provisions for the new public servant to work, receive communications and supervision in the Inuit language, and, if necessary file grievances in the Inuit language (ibid., s. 12.2e, f). In addition, managers are required to ensure that all employees are able to undertake 'Inuit Language training, upgrading and assessment' and, interestingly, they are also required to 'maintain records concerning the individual attainment and overall outcomes from the training and upgrading provided to employees' (ibid., s. 12.2g).

Finally, the Inuit Language Protection Act establishes an Inuit *Uqausinginnik Taiguusiliuqtiit* (Inuit Language Authority) to 'expand the knowledge and expertise available with respect to the Inuit Language, and to consider and make decisions about Inuit Language use, development and standardization' (ibid., s. 16.1). In addition the act reinforces the powers of the Minister of Languages to develop plans to promote the Inuit language and guide the implementation of this Act (ibid., ss. 24–7). It also ensures that the Languages Commissioner of Nunavut, operating within the framework of core IQ principles, has extensive powers for monitoring the Inuit language plans of institutions and ensuring their compliance with the legislation (ibid., ss. 27–42).

The evidence from Nunavut is that the creation of an Aboriginally oriented public service cannot be completed without legislation to ensure that Aboriginal languages have official recognition in the relevant jurisdiction and that, as a result, Aboriginal people can use their own language as employees or service recipients in the public sector. But the process is more complex than the historical examples of recognizing French and English as official languages of Canada in the late 1960s, which took place in the context of each language having already been embedded in educational curricula. Encouraging the use of Aboriginal languages as official languages of work can only prove effective as part of a broader Aboriginal language protection strategy that links education and government employment as critical means of Aboriginal empowerment. The Inuit Language Protection Act is a significant development for Nunavut, because it stands as territorial legislation regardless of the federal government's decision on whether or not to approve Nunavut's new Official Languages Act. Nonetheless, its emphasis on language rights still leaves the fundamental problem of resources for language education and development unresolved.

Conclusion

The development of Nunavut in the first decade of its existence as a territorial jurisdiction raises two very different issues. On the one hand, it highlights the importance of ensuring that questions about institutional design, culture, and language are embedded in broader discussions about creating public institutions, employment opportunities, administrative services, and public policies in Canada that are sensitive to the needs and identities of Aboriginal communities. On the other hand, Nunavut highlights the costs, complexities, time, and negotiation involved in building capacity to develop Aboriginally sensitive approaches to public administration.

Both issues need to remain on the radar screen as new initiatives in Aboriginal governance are developed in Canada. In addition, the experience in Nunavut indicates that the project of building public institutions that fully represent Canada's indigenous citizens numerically, culturally, and linguistically cannot be addressed solely in the sphere of government. These issues have to be addressed over the long term within the education system. Government employment is not a quick-fix solution: full Aboriginal employment and representation within and beyond the public sector will only be realized if it is linked to the longer-term development of educational institutions that embrace more Aboriginally sensitive curricula and are staffed, more fully than at present, by Aboriginal educators (Kovach, 2009). Nonetheless, the first decade of Nunavut is important for understanding the challenges and the potential implicit in developing models of public governance, public administration, and public policy that take account of indigenous perspectives in ways that may benefit the future development of Aboriginal communities in Canada.

Words and Phrases in the Inuit Language

Aqitsirak: To strike out disharmony and wrongdoing and to render justice
Inuinnaqtun: Inuit language spoken in western area of Nunavut
Inuit Qaujimajatuqangit: That which is long known by Inuit
Inuit Uqausinginnik Taiguusiliuqtiit: Inuit Language Authority
Inuktitut: Inuit language spoken in Nunavut
Iqqanaijaqatigiit: Working Together
Nunavummiut: Residents of Nunavut
Qallunaat: Non-Inuit
Tunngavik: Foundation

Important Terms and Concepts

Aboriginal
consensus government
indigenous approaches to public administration
Inuit-oriented public government
Inuit Qaujimajatuqangit
public service
representative public service

Study Questions

1. How has the challenge of developing an Inuit-oriented public government been addressed in the design and operation of the institutions of governance in Nunavut?
2. Does the new Nunavut territorial government reflect the ethnic composition of population?
3. Why have initiatives to build a population-reflective public sector in Nunavut not taken root more rapidly or on more gender-neutral lines?
4. How has the Government of Nunavut begun to address the challenge of embedding Inuit culture in the public administration of the territory?
5. What measures have been taken to reclaim the Inuit language in the public space and use it in managing the operation of government?
6. Does the Nunavut government demonstrate potential for developing more inclusive approaches to public administration in Canada that take fuller account of Aboriginal perspectives?

Useful Websites

Government of Nunavut:

www.gov.nu.ca

Legislative Assembly of Nunavut:

www.assembly.nu.ca

Nunatsiaq News:

www.nunatsiaq.com

Nunavut Tunngavik Incorporated:

www.tunngavik.com

Knowledge and Use of Inuktitut among Inuit in Canada, 1981–2001, Inuit Tapiriit Kanatami and Research and Analysis Directorate Research Project, Strategic Research and Analysis Directorate Indian and Northern Affairs Canada March, 2007.

http://dsp-psd.pwgsc.gc.ca/collection_2009/ainc-inac/R2-468-2007E.pdf

Asuilaak: Inuktitut Living Dictionary/Dictionaire Vivante:

www.livingdictionary.com

Nunavut. 1999a. *Pinasuaqtavut: The Bathurst Mandate, 1999.*

www.austlii.edu.au/au/journals/AILR/2000/11.html

Berger, Thomas R. 2006. *Conciliator's Final Report: 'The Nunavut Project'.* Nunavut Land Claims Agreement Implementation Contract Negotiations for the Second Planning Period 2003–2013. 1 March.

www.ainc-inac.gc.ca/al/ldc/ccl/fagr/nuna/lca/nlc-eng.asp

Nunavut's Official Languages Act. S.Nu. 2008, c. 10:

www.justice.gov.nu.ca/apps/authoring/dspPage.aspx?page=STATUTES+OF+NUNAVUT+(ANNUAL+VOLUMES)+PAGE&year=2008

Nunavut's Inuit Language Protection Act. S.Nu. 2008, c.17:

www.justice.gov.nu.ca/apps/authoring/dspPage.aspx?page=STATUTES+OF+NUNAVUT+(ANNUAL+VOLUMES)+PAGE&year=2008

References

Bell, Jim. 2003. 'Inuit Employment in Government Moving Backward', *Nunatsiaq News.* 2 May. Available at: www.nunatsiaq.com.

Berger, Thomas R. 2006. *Conciliator's Final Report: 'The Nunavut Project'.* Nunavut Land Claims Agreement Implementation Contract Negotiations for the Second Planning Period 2003–2013. 1 March. Available at: www.ainc-inac.gc.ca/al/ldc/ccl/fagr/nuna/lca/nlc-eng.asp.

Cameron, Kirk, and Graham White. 1995. *Northern Governments in Transition: Political and Constitutional Development in the Yukon, Nunavut and the Western Northwest Territories.* Montreal: Institute for Research in Public Policy.

Canada. Indian and Northern Affairs Canada. 1993. *Agreement between the Inuit of the Nunavut Settlement Area and Her Majesty the Queen in Right of Canada.* Ottawa: Minister of Indian Affairs and Northern Development and the Tungavik. Available at: www.canlii.org/en/ca/laws/stat/sc-1993-c-29/latest/sc-1993-c-29.html.

CBC North. 2006. 'Learn Inuktitut or *iqqanaijaaqajjaagunniiqtutit*, Mandarins Told', 7 June. Available at: www.cbc.ca/canada/north/story/2006/06/07/nor-bilignual-senior.html.

Fortier, Marcel, and Francine G. Jones. 1998. 'Engineering Public Service Excellence for Nunavut: The Nunavut Human Resources Development Strategy', *Arctic* 51, 2: 191–94.

Henderson, Ailsa. 2007. *Nunavut: Rethinking Political Culture.* Vancouver: University of British Columbia Press.

Hicks, Jack, and Graham White. 2000. 'Nunavut: Inuit Self-Determination through a Land Claim and Public Government?' in Jens Dahl, Jack Hicks, and Peter Jull, eds, *Nunavut: Inuit Regain Control of Their Lands and Their Lives.* Copenhagen: International Work Group for Indigenous Affairs, 30–115.

Jull, Peter. 2000. 'A Blueprint for Indigenous Self-Government: The Bathurst Mandate', *Indigenous Law Bulletin* 4, 27: 14–18.

Kernaghan, Kenneth. 1978. 'Representative Bureaucracy: The Canadian Perspective', *Canadian Public Administration* 21, 4: 489–512.

Kovach, Margaret. 2009. 'Being Indigenous in the Academy—Creating Space for Indigenous Scholars', in Annis May Timpson, ed, *First Nations, First Thoughts: The Impact of Indigenous Thought in Canada.* Vancouver: University of British Columbia Press.

Legislative Assembly of Nunavut. 2002. Special Committee to Review the Official Languages Act, *Interim Report,* Fifth Session, First Legislative Assembly, March.

———. 2007. *Rules of the Legislative Assembly of Nunavut.* April. Available at: www.assembly.nu.ca/public_docs/rules_english.pdf.

Nunatsiaq News. 2001a. 'Nunavut Legislative Round-Up: MLAs End Review with Warning to Cabinet', 30 Nov. Retrieved at: www.nunatsiaq.com.

———. 2001b. 'Inuk Staffing Still Low', 8 June. Retrieved at: www.nunatsiaq.com.

Nunavut. 1999a. *Pinasuaqtavut: The Bathurst Mandate, 1999.* Available at: www.austlii.edu.au/au/journals/AILR/2000/11.html.

———. 1999b. *Report from the September 1999 Inuit Qaujimajatuqangit Workshop.* Iqaluit: Government of Nunavut.

———. 2004a. 'Civil Service Changes Underline Government's Commitment to Economic Prosperity and Inuit Qaujimajatuqangit', News release, 10 March 2004. Available at: www.gov.nu.ca.

———. 2004b. *Pinasuaqtavut, 2004–2009: Our Commitment to Building Nunavut's Future*. Available at: www.gov.nu.ca/pinasuaqtavut/engcover.pdf.

———. 2008a. Official Languages Act. S.Nu. 2008, c. 10. Available at: www.justice.gov.nu.ca/apps/authoring/dspPage.aspx?page=STATUTES+OF+NUNAVUT+(ANNUAL+VOLUMES)+PAGE&year=2008.

———. 2008b. Inuit Language Protection Act. S.Nu. 2008, c.17. Available at: www.justice.gov.nu.ca/apps/authoring/dspPage.aspx?page=STATUTES+OF+NUNAVUT+(ANNUAL+VOLUMES)+PAGE&year=2008.

Nunavut and Nunavut Tunngavik Incorporated.1999. *Clyde River Protocol*. Available at: www.tunngavik.com/index.php?iDocCat=41.

Nunavut Constitutional Forum. 1983. *Building Nunavut: A Working Document with a Proposal for an Arctic Constitution,* Tabled in the Legislative Assembly of the Northwest Territories, 17 May.

Nunavut, Culture, Language, Elders and Youth. 2002. *The First Annual Report of the Inuit Qaujimajatuqangit (IQ) Task Force*. Iqaluit: Government of Nunavut.

———. 2006. *Language Legislation for Nunavut: A Consultation Paper*. Iqaluit: Government of Nunavut.

Nunavut, Department of Sustainable Development. 2000. *2000/2001 Business Plan,* Honourable Peter Kilabuk, Minister, March. Tabled in the Legislative Assembly of Nunavut on 19 April 2000. Tabled Document No.87.

Nunavut, Human Resources. 2001. *Combined 1999–2000 and 2000–2001 Public Service Annual Report*. Iqaluit: Government of Nunavut. Available at: www.gov.nu.ca/hr/site/psannualreport.htm.

———. 2003. *Towards a Representative Public Service: Statistics as of June 30th, 2003*. Available at: www.gov.nu.ca/hr/site/doc/trpsjune2003eng.pdf.

———. 2008. *Towards a Representative Public Service: Statistics as of June 30th, 2008*. Available at: www.gov.nu.ca/hr/site/doc/TRPS_updates/June%202008/TRPS%20June%202008%20Eng.pdf.

Nunavut Implementation Commission. 1995. *Footprints in New Snow: A Comprehensive Report from the Nunavut Implementation Commission to the Department of Northern Affairs and Northern Development, Government of the Northwest Territories and Nunavut Tunngavik Incorporated Concerning the Establishment of the Nunavut Government, March 31*. Iqaluit: Nunavut Implementation Commission.

Nunavut, Nunavummit Kiglisiniartiit/Nunavut Bureau of Statistics. 2003. 'Language Data from the 2001 Nunavut Household Survey', Powerpoint presentation, Mar. Available at: www.tunngavik.com/english/pub.html.

Nunavut Tunngavik Incorporated. 2006. 'NTI Launches Lawsuit Against Government of Canada for Breach of Contract', *News release 06-24*, 6 December. Available at: www.tunngavik.com/index.php?iDocCat=8.

———, and the Government of Nunavut. 2004. *Iqqanaijaqatigiit—Working Together*. 28 May. Available at: www.tunngavik.com/index.php?iDocCat=41.

PricewaterhouseCoopers. 2003. *The Cost of Not Successfully Implementing Article 23: Representative Employment for Inuit within the Government,* 17 February. Available at: www.tunngavik.com/English.pub.html.

Sanders, Nora. 2005. 'Through Cultural Eyes: Perspectives on Aboriginal Governance and Leadership', Keynote Address, First Nations/First Thoughts, 30th Anniversary Conference, Centre of Canadian Studies, University of Edinburgh, May 2005. Available at: www.cst.ed.ac.uk/Events/Conferences/index.html.

Timpson, Annis May. 2005. 'The Challenges of Intergovernmental Relations for Nunavut', in Michael Murphy, ed, *Reconfiguring Aboriginal–State Relations—Canada: The State of the Federation 2003*. Montreal and Kingston: McGill-Queen's University Press, 207–35.

———. 2006. 'Stretching the Concept of Representative Bureaucracy: The Case of Nunavut', *International Review of Administrative Sciences* 72, 4: 517–30.

———. 2009. 'Rethinking the Administration of Government: Inuit Representation, Culture and Language in the Nunavut Public Service', in Annis May Timpson, ed, *First Nations, First Thoughts: The Impact of Indigenous Thought in Canada*. Vancouver: University of British Columbia Press.

University of Victoria, 2005. Akitisiraq Law School. *Media Releases: Backgrounder*. 21 June.

White, Graham. 1991. 'Westminster in the Arctic: The Adaption of British Parliamentarianism in the Northwest Territories', *Canadian Journal of Political Science* 24, 3: 499–523.

———. 2001. 'And Now for Something Completely Northern: Institutions of Government in the Territorial North.' *Journal of Canadian Studies* 35, 1: 80–99.

———. 2002. 'Treaty Federalism in Northern Canada: Aboriginal–Government Land Claims Boards', *Publius* 32, 3: 89–114.

21 Bureaucratic Independence

Lorne Sossin

Introduction

This chapter explores the concept of **bureaucratic independence** and the legal relationship between the public service and the government of the day.[1] Traditionally, the public service has been seen as the operational arm of the government. In other words, the **public service** takes instruction from elected politicians through either laws passed in the legislature or direction from the cabinet—these are the means by which government achieves its ends. Indeed, one of the most important constitutional principles in Canada is that no public servant can make a decision or take any action not authorized by a statute or government directive. On this view, there is little room for the public service to exhibit 'independence'.

The alternative view, however, elaborated in this chapter, is that the public service is an organ of government. While public servants owe a duty of loyalty to the government of the day, they also must be able, in certain circumstances, to exercise independence from the government of the day, in order to protect the neutrality of the public service and the rule of law.

In Canada, as in most constitutional democracies, there is a separation of powers between the legislative, executive, and judicial branches of government. In brief, the legislative branch makes laws, the executive applies laws, and the judiciary interprets laws. While everyone is clear on who constitutes the legislative branch (i.e., elected members of the legislature, etc.) and who constitutes the judicial branch (i.e., judges appointed by provincial, territorial, and federal governments), there is no such clarity when it comes to the executive branch of government. At its head, the executive consists of the Prime Minister and cabinet. Ministers stand at the head of bureaucratic departments. For example, the Minister of Citizenship and Immigration heads up a ministry of over 3,000 public servants. The Minister is also responsible for independent adjudication of immigration and refugee claims through the Immigration and Refugee Board (IRB). While IRB members are not public servants, they are also part of the executive branch of government. The ministry also funds a range of programs and services delivered through NGOs and community agencies, which are fulfilling policy objectives and are accountable for the public funds they receive, but which are not part of the executive branch of government.

The focus of this analysis is on the relationship between the political executive (that is, the Prime Minister, cabinet, and their political staffs, often concentrated in offices like the Prime Minister's Office (PMO) and the public service (that is, the employees of government).

The point of departure for this relationship is the Canadian Constitution. However, constitutional theory must be applied to political reality and in some cases political expediency (Savoie, 2003). For example, while it may be legally permitted, or even legally required, for public servants in some circumstances to refuse to follow government direction, it is equally true that the government could not function if the policies of the political executive were held hostage to the preferences or personal views of public servants.

The relationship between the public service and the political executive lay at the centre of the 'sponsorship affair'.[2] In his report, Justice Gomery raised the possibility of a separate constitutional identity for the public service and confirmed its separate statutory and legal status.[3] A remarkable letter from 60 or so former politicians and civil servants cautioned the government against accepting this view or accepting some of the concrete recommendations on the nature and role of deputy ministers and the Clerk of the Privy Council.[4] Even more remarkably, the Prime Minister personally penned a response, indicating that he agreed with the critics of the Gomery Report, and that his government would not accept those aspects of the Gomery Report.[5]

This view echoed the position of the public service itself. Treasury Board is the government department responsible for public service management. In the recent Treasury Board 'Review of the Responsibilities and Accountabilities of Ministers and Senior Officials',[6] prepared as a response to the 2003 Auditor General report into the sponsorship program, the lack of constitutional status of the public service is described in the following terms:

> Departments, as apparatuses for the exercise of authority and responsibilities that reside in ministers, are the basic organizational unit of executive administration in the Westminster system, and ministers act principally through the public servants in their department. The role of the Public Service is to advance loyally and efficiently the agenda of the government of the day without compromising the non-partisan status that is needed to provide continuity and service to successive governments with differing priorities and of different political stripes. In order to do this, public servants must provide candid, professional advice that is free of both partisan considerations and fear of political criticism, which in turn requires that they remain outside the political realm. But, while public servants provide advice, the democratically elected ministers have the final say, and public servants must obey the lawful directions of their minister. In short, all government departments, and all public servants who work for them, must be accountable to a minister, who is in turn responsible to Parliament. Were this not so, the result would be government by the unelected. *In keeping with these principles, public servants as such have no constitutional identity independent of their minister.*[7] [Emphasis added]

Canada's constitutional texts are silent on the role and responsibilities of the public service. Courts, however, have recognized a range of unwritten **constitutional conventions** and principles which give rise to obligations, responsibilities, and constraints on the public service. Together, these arguably confer constitutional status on the public service as an organ of government (Sossin, 2005a; Savoie, 2006).

The letter to Prime Minister Harper mentioned above suggested such recognition would 'represent a major departure from how governments function in Canada' and lead to 'confusion as to who was accountable to Parliament for what'.[8] As I discuss below, recognizing the constitutional identity of the public service is a way of enhancing accountability, and represents a return to, rather than a departure from, Canada's core democratic values.

The Constitutional and Legal Terrain

Constitutional Boundaries

At least two constitutional principles directly address the role and responsibility of executive decision-makers: first, the constitutional convention of **bureaucratic (or political) neutrality** ensures that public servants owe a primary obligation to the Crown (and, by extension, to the people of Canada) and not to the party which happens to control the government of the day; and second, the **rule of law** ensures that executive decision-making is animated only by proper purposes, good faith, and relevant criteria set out by law. Together, these principles represent a constitutional norm of bureaucratic independence, because when it comes to ensuring the integrity of bureaucratic neutrality and the rule of law, the public service cannot take direction from the government of the day. Consequently, this norm requires separation between bureaucratic and political decision-making. This separation varies according to the context. In some areas, it will be near absolute, as in the case of criminal justice decision-making, where Crown prosecutors make operational decisions with no room for political interference whatsoever. In other cases, such as policy-making spheres or intergovernmental relations, for example, where political direction may be decisive, the separation may be subtle.

The Constitutional Convention of a Non-Partisan Public Service

The point of departure for any discussion of public service independence as a constitutional norm is the constitutional convention that the public service remains neutral between partisan interests (the 'Convention') (Kernaghan and Langford, 1990; Siegel, 1986; Hodgetts, 1973). Kenneth Kernaghan has outlined the content of the Convention in an oft-cited list of six key principles:

1. Politics and policy are separate from administration; thus, politicians make policy decisions and public servants execute these decisions.
2. Public servants are appointed and promoted on the basis of merit rather than of party affiliation or contributions.
3. Public servants do not engage in partisan political activities.
4. Public servants do not express publicly their personal views on government policies or administration.
5. Public servants provide forthright and objective advice to their political masters in private and in confidence; in return, political executives protect the anonymity of public servants by publicly accepting responsibility for departmental decisions.
6. Public servants execute policy decisions loyally, irrespective of the philosophy and programs of the party in power and regardless of their personal opinions; as a result, public servants enjoy security of tenure during good behaviour and satisfactory performance (Kernaghan, 2003, 2002, 1986).

There is, in my view, an important omission in this list. The Convention also, by necessary implication, includes the duty of public servants to question instructions that are motivated by improper partisan interests and if necessary to decline to follow them. While ministers are responsible for the decisions of the department, officials alone are responsible for their obligation to remain non-partisan. In relation to the Crown, the public service is the guardian of the public trust (and, by extension, of the public purse). In addition to their primary constitutional obligations towards the Crown, public servants also owe a legal obligation of loyalty to the government of the day, which includes a duty to carry out lawful instructions and not publicly criticize government policy or take public sides in partisan debates. The limit on this secondary obligation of loyalty to the government is dictated by the primary obligation of responsibility to the Crown, and by extension to the public. In other words, it is not constitutionally permissible for public servants to discharge their loyalty to the government of the day where to do so would require public servants to take part in partisan activities (or, as discussed below, to contravene the rule of law).

While the Convention could suggest that the public service operates independently of the political executive, in many if not most governmental contexts, government could not function on such a basis. Public servants are deeply enmeshed in supporting the political executive as it forms and finalizes policy preferences. Public servants help in shaping legislation and have a leading role in the drafting of regulatory and policy instruments to further legislative aims. Public servants give life to government programs through the exercise of discretion and control over implementation. Public servants are responsible for oversight through internal audits and accountability measures. In many of these settings, senior public servants work hand in glove with political staff in the employ of ministers (who used to be referred to federally as 'exempt staff' as they are exempted from the terms of the legislation which applies to the public service), who themselves may be deeply enmeshed in decision-making around policy formation and issues management. As a former senior public servant once observed, the idea that you can keep the political and bureaucratic roles distinct at the highest levels of government decision-making is 'naïve and non-productive' (Stewart, 1989; Dunn, 2002). It is because of this integration of the bureaucratic and the political, however, that the constitutional principles which demarcate the appropriate sphere of bureaucratic and political activity become so crucial.

The interdependence of the bureaucratic and political domains of the executive can be threatened in two ways: first, when the political executive seeks to politicize the public service for its own advantage; and second, when public servants act for partisan ends on their own initiative. In the case of the sponsorship affair, as highlighted in the Gomery Report, this Convention was compromised in both senses.

It has been in response to such threats that the courts, elaborating upon the Convention, have played a central role.[9] The importance of courts in elaborating constitutional conventions is noteworthy as conventions themselves are unenforceable. The power of the courts lies not in requiring or prohibiting the government action in question, but rather through moral suasion and political accountability. The classic example of this judicial role in Canadian politics was the *Patriation Reference* in 1981. The court held that it could not prevent the federal government from unilaterally patriating the Constitution from Great Britain, but that a constitutional convention required that a substantial majority of provinces concur in such a change before it could be considered in keeping with Canada's constitutional traditions.

Constitutional conventions are not part of written constitutional texts but arise from historically accepted practices and customs with respect to the machinery of government. In *OPSEU v. Ontario (A.G.)*,[10] the Supreme Court offered the following observation on conventions:

> As was explained in Re: Resolution to amend the Constitution, [1981] 1 S.C.R. 753, at pp. 876–78, with respect to the Constitution of Canada—but the same can generally be said of the constitution of Ontario—'those parts which are composed of statutory rules and common law rules are generically referred to as the law of the constitution'. In addition, the constitution of Ontario comprises rules of a different nature but of great importance called conventions of the constitution. The most fundamental of these is probably the principle of responsible government which is largely unwritten, although it is implicitly referred to in the preamble of the Constitution Act,1867 . . .[11]

To say that the political neutrality of the public service is a constitutional convention, in other words, is to recognize it as a rule of long-standing which has become part of the fabric of Canada's democratic and legal system.

The constitutional convention of a politically neutral public service is part of what is sometimes referred to in the public administration literature as the 'iron triangle' of conventions consisting of political neutrality, ministerial responsibility, and public service anonymity (Marshall, 1984). The fact that these duties are not part of the written constitution does not detract from their centrality to Canada's constitutional system (Heard, 1991). Put differently, a non-partisan public service is as important as ministerial responsibility to Canada's constitutional order. However, as Wade and Forsyth explain, writing in the British context, the convention of neutrality and anonymity for public servants may be seen as interwoven with ministerial responsibility:

> The high degree of detachment and anonymity in which the civil service works is largely a consequence of the principle of ministerial responsibility. Where civil servants carry out the minister's orders, or act

> in accordance with his policy, it is for him and not for them to take any blame. He also takes responsibility for ordinary administrative mistakes or miscarriages. But he has no duty to endorse unauthorised action of which he disapproves, though he has general responsibility for the conduct of his department and for the taking of any necessary disciplinary action (Wade and Forsyth, 2000: 29).

Conventions do not and cannot exist in the abstract. They are constitutional rules whose contours are set by practice over time; they are determined to a considerable extent by a particular view of history. The history of the public service, however, reveals several different stories. At least since the time of Confederation, a principal feature of responsible government in colonial Canada was security of tenure for public servants, but the merit system did not take hold in Canada until the late nineteenth and early twentieth centuries (Savoie, 1994). Patronage was rampant, and remains common in a variety of board and agency appointments and is not precluded even at the highest levels of the public service (Smith, 1995). Public service anonymity is now routinely breached (Kernaghan, 2003). Not only are such breaches of anonymity common, they are, I would suggest, now expected. In an era where 'secret guidelines' and 'behind-closed-door' politics are viewed as inconsistent with transparent accountability, public service anonymity would be viewed favourably in few quarters. Naming public officials, however, should not be interpreted as sanction for the public humiliation of public officials. The value at stake in such settings is not secrecy but respect for the public service as an institution.

The principle of bureaucratic neutrality has been described by courts as 'a right of the public at large to be served by a politically neutral civil service',[12] as an 'essential principle' of responsible government,[13] as a matter of the 'public interest in both the actual, and apparent, impartiality of the public servant',[14] and finally, as an 'organ of government'.[15] Can a non-partisan public service be simultaneously a 'right' of the people, an 'essential principle' of responsible government, and a 'policy' in the public interest? The answer is undoubtedly that constitutional conventions (as well as norms and principles) can and do have multiple rationales and serve multiple ends. This is consistent with what might be accurately characterized as the plural nature of the executive branch in Canada's constitutional system (Sossin, 2006). Another example of a plural requirement in Canada's constitutional order is the requirement to preserve and promote the rule of law, to which my analysis now turns.

The 'Rule of Law'

Public servants are entrusted with public authority in order to implement the policy agenda of the political executive. They have no legitimate alternative set of interests or agendas and the existence of such alternative public servant interests and agendas would pose a threat to democratic accountability and Westminster principles under which all public authority must adhere to the rule of law.[16] Parliament, the political executive, and the public service all must conform to the rule of law and this is a separate and independent duty on each organ of government.

The obligation to comply with the rule of law would be a straightforward constraint on government action but for the fact that the rule of law is a deeply contested notion which also must be balanced against other unwritten constitutional principles such as democracy and Parliamentary sovereignty.[17] While the rule of law has been recognized as the animating principle for the judicial review of administrative action,[18] and is mentioned alongside the supremacy of God in the preamble to the Charter of Rights, the rule of law remains largely unexplored as a constitutional norm by courts in Canada (Hogg and Zwibel, 2005). In the *Secession Reference*, where the Supreme Court affirmed the rule of law as an underlying constitutional principle, it described the importance of the rule of law in terms of subjecting executive authority to legal accountability and protecting citizens from arbitrary state action:

> The principles of constitutionalism and the rule of law lie at the root of our system of government. The rule of law, as observed in *Roncarelli v. Duplessis*, is 'a fundamental postulate of our constitutional structure'. As we noted in the *Patriation Reference*, supra, at pp. 805–6, '[t]he "rule of law" is a highly textured expression, importing many things which are beyond the need of these reasons to explore but conveying, for example, a sense of orderliness, of subjection to known legal rules and of executive accountability to legal authority'. At its most basic level, the rule of law vouchsafes to the citizens and residents of the country a stable, predictable and ordered society in which to conduct their affairs. It provides a shield for individuals from arbitrary state action.[19]

The executive accountability to legal authority referred to in this passage is accomplished by another constitutional postulate—all executive authority is subject to judicial review on the grounds that the rule of law has been contravened.[20]

While the rule of law imposes a special set of duties on government lawyers and the Attorney General as Chief Law Officer (which includes, for example, the obligation on a Deputy Attorney General to resign if an Attorney General rejects advice that a particular course of action is unconstitutional and a correlative duty on Attorneys General to resign if cabinet refuses their advice on similar questions) (Freiman, 2002), its reach is not, and should not be, limited to lawyers or judges. The rule of law doctrine imposes a public trust obligation on public servants to ensure that the rule of law is respected and that government directions which are inconsistent with the rule of law are not followed. To view the administrative state in terms of rule of law means, for example, that it would be unlawful for a public servant to carry out an exercise of public authority which was based purely on political whim, or the desire to curry favour with political authorities or through improper political pressures (Dyzenhaus, 2002). This also suggests that public servants have a constitutional obligation not to carry out directions which are themselves unlawful.[21] But how is the rule of law, in this sense, to be enforced?

If the rule of law is to play a constructive role in boundary drawing between political and public servant spheres, it will have to do so through the inculcation of administrative culture. Courts, tribunals, Auditors General, and public service commissions all provide important venues where these boundaries are identified and developed, but it is what lies below the surface that matters most. Bureaucratic independence, in other words, rises or falls with the day-to-day values of the public service (and of the political executive) rather than with the occasional, ex-post pronouncements of those exercising oversight (Sossin, 2005b). Without a rule of law culture, proliferating rules and procedures are unlikely to produce accountability or compliance with a set of institutional boundaries.

To understand how the rule of law may shape the relationship between the public service and the political executive, consider the example of the 'Magna Budget' affair in Ontario. In the spring of 2003, the then Tory government announced it was going to present its annual budget, not in the Legislature, but rather in a closed-circuit studio hastily erected at a Magna auto parts plant owned by a prominent and generous supporter of the Progressive Conservative Party. A minor constitutional crisis ensued. Critics in the media and opposition decried the arrogance of the decision to 'end-run' legislative debate on the budget, while the Speaker of the Legislature obtained a legal opinion suggesting the decision violated Parliamentary and constitutional convention.[22] The budget was later introduced in the Legislature in the usual manner.

The Magna Budget implicated bureaucratic independence in at least two ways. First, it fell to the constitutional lawyers of the Attorney General's office to ensure that the government was not embarking on an unconstitutional course of action, and second, it fell to Cabinet Office to ensure that public servants and public resources were not deployed in support of partisan activities. The Attorney General, when pressed, would neither confirm nor deny that an opinion on the budget delivery had been sought from government lawyers, but reiterated that he would be compelled to resign if an opinion had been sought and if it had indicated that the proposed course of action was unconstitutional. Therefore, by negative implication presumably the AG was signalling either that no opinion had been sought or that the opinion sought was not unfavourable (Baillie, 2003). The Secretary of Cabinet was asked by the Liberals, then in opposition, to prevent the public service from being dragged into a partisan exercise by providing their services to facilitate the delivery of the budget at the auto parts plant.[23] The Secretary later issued a press release indicating 'no civil servant was involved in any inappropriate activity'.

The Magna Budget reflects both the possibilities and limits of bureaucratic independence. On the one hand, it remained within the power of the Attorney General and Cabinet Office effectively to prevent the budget from being delivered outside the legislature. Each of the AG and Secretary of Cabinet were called upon to give, in effect, their imprimatur to the action contemplated by the government. On the other hand, the political realities made that approval almost a foregone conclusion. This is so for at least three reasons. First, determining whether a proposed course of action violates the constitution is more often an exercise in risk analysis than in raising red flags. Even if a Charter breach is apparent, it is much more difficult to say with certainty how a court will respond to section 1 evidence. At most, government lawyers could identify a high risk with respect to one course of action over another. Whether a government has infringed a convention is a still less certain determination.[24]

Thus, occasions when an Attorney General must advise a government not to pursue its desired course will be rare (especially if the AG wishes to remain in cabinet). Second, it is unclear whether the Secretary of Cabinet may seek legal advice independent of the Attorney General's office. Therefore, although the government of the day and the public service might not always have identically convergent interests, they remain bound by the same ambiguities in relation to government legal opinions. Third, there are few if any means to resolve disputes between the head of government and the head of the public service who is herself or himself a political appointee (other than the head of the public service resigning or being fired, neither of which impose any accountability on the political executive). When push comes to shove, it is the public service that more often than not ends up back on its heels.

Constitutional crises like the Magna Budget affair are rare.[25] They reflect only the visible tip of a largely submerged iceberg of political and bureaucratic entanglements. Most forms of political pressure on public service decision-making arise and are resolved quietly, without the anxiety of a constitutional crisis, through a phone call or email between the Clerk of the Privy Council's office and a Minister's office, or between Attorney General lawyers and line ministries, on a weekly and sometimes daily basis. Occasionally, once a month or so, one or two might bubble to the surface and become issues, briefly, between a minister and a deputy minister, or between Cabinet Office and the Premier's Office. In rare instances, a leaked memo or document leads to some news coverage and perhaps the attention of opposition parties. In the overwhelming majority of cases, few records will attest to the tensions such friction might produce and more rare still will be records of how such friction will be resolved (e.g., did one side blink or lack backbone, or was a compromise fashioned?). It is far from clear that the status quo provides the public service with the capacity (and legitimacy) to fulfill its obligations to ensure respect for the rule of law. In the current climate, we are left to question whether a culture of intimidation is more likely than a culture of rule of law to prevail when political pressure is brought to bear on public servants. Can a rule of law culture, however, flourish in contexts where public servants owe duties of loyalty to carry out governmental direction? It is to this aspect of the relationship between the political executive and the public service that I now turn.

The Duty of Loyalty

I would contend that neither the Convention of a non-partisan public service nor adherence to the rule of law is incompatible with the public service's **duty of loyalty** to the government of the day. The ability of that political executive to carry out its policy mandate depends entirely on the loyalty and professionalism of the public service. As the Ontario Law Reform Commission noted, however, one cannot understand the relationship between political neutrality and independence without also factoring in the common law duties of loyalty, good faith, and confidentiality:

> The common law duties of loyalty, good faith and confidentiality should be seen, then, as having two essential roles, both of which are manifestations of the 'public interest': to secure the sound administration of the various branches of government, and to foster and maintain the traditional independent role of the public service. However, it is essential to emphasize that the 'public interest' so served is not monolithic; rather, it is the result of the delicate balancing of frequently competing interests, that of the employee wishing to exercise individual rights of expression and to engage in political activity, and that of the government, wishing to maintain the existence and the appearance of independence and impartiality in the public service and to ensure effective administration in the Province.[26]

At least in theory, the duties of loyalty and neutrality are complementary attributes. The relationship between the two was aptly summarized by Sir C.K. Allen in the following terms:

> . . . the civil servant is expected to give, and with very few exceptions does give in full measure, the qualities of loyalty and discretion. He is not to obtrude his opinion unless it is invited, but when it is needed he must give it with complete honesty and candour. If it is not accepted, and a policy is adopted contrary to his advice, he must and invariably does, do his best to carry it into effect, however much he may privately dislike it. If it miscarries, he must resist the human temptation to say 'I told you so'; it is still his duty, which again he invariably performs, to save his Minister from disaster, even if he thinks disaster is deserved. (Allen, 1965: 281–2)

In *Fraser* (1985), Dickson CJ states that the characteristics of impartiality, neutrality, fairness, and integrity are associated with the public service and a person entering the public service is deemed to understand that these values require caution when it comes to criticizing the government.[27] Knowledge, fairness, integrity, and loyalty all are core characteristics which characterize the public service's aspirations.[28] Dickson CJ recognized a qualified rather than absolute duty of loyalty owed by public servants.[29]

It has fallen to subsequent courts interpreting the qualified nature of this duty to resolve the dilemma raised by *Fraser*—how disputes should be resolved in which the ideals of neutrality and loyalty come into conflict. Importantly for the present purposes, these cases have concerned breaches of loyalty where public servants have criticized the governments.

A number of labour law cases involving disputes between public servants and the government followed the release of *Fraser* and explored the boundaries of the duty of loyalty owed by public servants to the government of the day. One such case, *Haydon v. Canada*,[30] demonstrates how rarely loyalty and neutrality are in fact complementary values. The case concerned two Health Canada scientists who spoke on national television about their concerns regarding the drug review process in Canada. They raised serious allegations, including the claim that the scientific integrity of Health Canada was undermined by the undue influence of partisan political considerations. In the government's submissions, the two scientists were said to have breached their duty of loyalty to the government. The Director of the Bureau where the two scientists worked issued a written reprimand to the scientists, emphasizing, 'Your decision to pursue your outstanding complaints in a public forum is in my view in conflict with your obligations as a public servant. . . . Public denunciation of management is incompatible with a public servant's employment relationship'.[31]

The issue for the Federal Court in *Haydon* was both whether the duty of loyalty itself violated the expressive freedom of public servants and whether the Associate Deputy Minister of Health Canada acted reasonably in denying the scientists' grievance over the reprimand. Tremblay-Lamer J. held that the common law duty of loyalty, as articulated in *Fraser*, did not in and of itself violate the freedom of expression found in the Charter because the exceptions set out in Fraser embraced matters of public concern. She concluded that, 'the common law duty of loyalty does not impose unquestioning silence'.[32]

While the framework in *Fraser* provides a helpful point of departure for this balancing exercise, too often the tendency of lower courts faced with adversarial disputes between public servants and government has been to treat that framework as a 'test'. Rather than thoughtful reflection on, and flexible application of the principles underlying *Fraser*, the courts have contented themselves with a narrow analysis of whether the impugned activity in a given case fits within any of the exceptional categories recognized in *Fraser*. This approach leaves open how a Court might respond to a public servant who fails to raise red flags where rule of law or neutrality issues arise—in other words, does *Fraser* permit public servants to criticize the government publicly (or refuse to carry out government direction) where it is justified to do so, or does it require such action if there is no other reasonable means for the improper activity to come to light?

The issue of when whistle-blowers will receive legal protection has been clarified by statute. In 2006, as its first legislative priority, and as its response to the Gomery Inquiry, the federal government introduced the Federal Accountability Act. Among other initiatives, such as the creation of a Director of Public Prosecutions and new audit measures for government departments, the Act creates the office of the Public Sector Integrity Commissioner with the power to enforce the **Public Servants Disclosure Protection Act**. The Act also creates a new Public Servants Disclosure Protection Tribunal with the power to order remedies and discipline.

The Public Servants Disclosure Protection Act defines wrongdoing in the public sector as:

1. Violating any Act of Parliament or any Act of the legislatures of Canada's provinces and territories. This includes violating any regulations made under these Acts.
2. Misusing public funds or a public asset.
3. Gross mismanagement.
4. Doing something—or failing to do something—that creates a substantial and specific danger to the health, safety, or life of persons or to the environment.
5. Seriously breaching the public sector Code of Conduct or the organization's Code of Conduct.
6. Knowingly directing or counselling a person to commit wrongdoing as defined above.[33]

While whistle-blowing protections reflect an important recognition of public servants as agents of accountability, the content of bureaucratic independence must address, at a minimum, what conditions, structures, guarantees or protections are required to ensure the political neutrality of the public service, adherence to the rule of law and respect for the duty of loyalty. A primary bulwark against politicization remains the merit principle for public service hiring and promotion.[34] The integrity of the public service, however, cannot end with labour relations but must also extend to the day-to-day interaction between the political executive and the public service. In these settings, there must be an equivalent 'merit' principle at stake.

Ultimately, however, the greatest guarantee against political interference is not objective in character; rather, it emanates from political will and leadership. Judicial intervention in high profile disputes is unlikely to change a culture which sees appointments of friends and partisan associates to senior public service management as a vehicle for implementing policy. Constitutional principles cannot be left entirely in the hands of the political executive or the public service to work out as they please. The courts have a role to play in resolving disputes and elaborating boundaries. The fact that the relationship between organs of executive government involves constitutional principles, however, does not imply that it must be left entirely for lawyers to define either. Bureaucratic independence engages norms of constitutional and administrative law, the political process, and public administration. Only measures which resonate in all of those spheres will be effective.

The Institutions of Bureaucratic Independence

In the sections above, I have emphasized the role of the courts and judicial review in recognizing and elaborating the concept of bureaucratic independence. Judicial review, however, is an awkward, expensive, and ultimately ineffective means of governing relations between public servants and the government. In the wake of the Gomery Inquiry and the rise of what may been termed a 'culture of accountability' in Canada, there has been growing attention focused on how best to institutionalize public service accountability.

There are several institutions of importance in understanding the public service, discussed below. While I will refer to the federal public service for the purposes of this analysis, most of the offices below, with sometimes modified names, also exist at the provincial and territorial levels of government as well.

Public Service Commissions

While the courts clearly perform a critical role in establishing and elaborating the boundaries between political and public service spheres, as discussed in the first part of this chapter, they are not ideal institutions to deal with monitoring or refining those boundaries. This may well fit better the flexibility and specialized expertise of a commission or tribunal. Most Canadian jurisdictions in fact have public service commissions of one kind or another, but their mandate does not extend to governing the relationship between cabinet ministers and public servants.

As part of the federal government's modernization of the public service governance, the Canadian Public Service Commission became in December of 2005 an independent institution which reports to Parliament. This same legislation provides that the Commission's reports, like the reports of the Auditor General, are to be tabled in Parliament. Further reinforcing the independence of the public service commission is the fact that Parliament approves the appointment of the President of the Commission and that the President will serve for fixed seven-year terms. Protecting the political impartiality of the public service is one of the core missions of the Commission under its new empowering legislation. The Public Service Commission has multiple mandates, which include the development of policy, investigation, auditing, adjudicating, and remedial measures (including ordering the termination of a public servant's employment).[35]

However, the scope of the Commission's power in relation to the non-partiality of the public service is limited in at least two key areas. First, the Commission is concerned with narrowly party-related political activity. This would catch activities by public servants—for example, to advance the interests of the Liberal Party of Canada, as occurred in relation to the sponsorship program—but not activities designed to advance a particular political cause but unrelated to a particular party—for example, to promote Quebec separatism. Second, the Commission's role in relation to political activities relates primarily to oversight over public servants who wish to run for office or become involved in political campaigns. The Commission is not designed to monitor and enforce protections against political interference on a day-to-day basis (the one exception to this is in the field of staffing where the Commission plays a key role in ensuring that staffing decisions are made without partisan manipulation). There is also some question as to the sufficiency of the Commission's resources and its capacity to obtain the resources it would need should it seek to fulfill a broader mandate. In this regard, it may be advisable to clarify one of the Commission's most important powers, which is to act as a Commission of Inquiry with all the necessary powers under the Inquiry Act where necessary.

Another potential limitation to the independence of the Commission is its reliance on Department of Justice lawyers for legal advice. This raises a crucial dilemma—who has the last word when it comes to the nature and scope of public service duties under the constitution? The Attorney General must have the last word for the government on matters of constitutional propriety (and must resign if the cabinet rejects her or his advice). If it is not for the Attorney General to speak for the Public Service Commission (or the Clerk of the Privy Council) then whose view prevails where there is a conflict between the constitutional position of the political executive and the position of the public service? And further, what if there is a conflict between the Clerk and the President of the Commission in this regard? Resolving this dilemma in part relates to reforms to the Clerk of the Privy Council's mandate and the protections against politicized appointments to this position.[36] Since the role of the Clerk is to represent the public service to government, I would suggest it cannot also be to represent the government to the public service. This potential conflict between voices articulating constitutional and legal boundaries between political and public service spheres will be complicated still further if and when new whistleblower legislation is enacted, which would create yet another body with authority over the interface between political and public service spheres.

Clerk of the Privy Council

While the Public Service Commission governs the merit process that lies at the heart of the independence of the public service, the Clerk of the Privy Council is the senior public servant in the federal bureaucracy, and since 1993 has been formally recognized as the 'head of the public service'.[37] The Clerk heads the Privy Council Office (PCO) which is the bureaucratic arm of the federal cabinet and the nerve centre for the policy process. The Clerk's position has been described as 'the executive of the Canadian State' (Sutherland, 2006: 23).

The Clerk also functions as the deputy minister to the Prime Minister, and in this sense works hand in glove both with cabinet and with the Prime Minister's political arm, the Prime Minister's Office (PMO). The Clerk is the most important non-political adviser to the Prime Minister and cabinet and in this sense serves as a bridge between public servants and political advisers on matters of public policy.

The Clerk thus has two constituencies—the public service as a whole which she or he leads, and the government of the day which she or he serves. On occasion, these obligations may conflict. The only tool at the Clerk's disposal to deal with such a conflict is resignation, which is hardly satisfactory. Because the Clerk serves at the pleasure of the Prime Minister, however, there are few other options. The strength of the Clerk is the credibility that this individual enjoys with senior public servants (the Clerk in fact plays a key role in the appointment of deputy ministers and other senior executives) and with government. If this credibility is lost, the effectiveness of the Clerk will be significantly diminished. In this sense, the Clerk's ability to 'speak truth to power' depends on the willingness of those in power to hear and heed such advice.

Treasury Board

While the Clerk provides leadership and direction to the public service, Treasury Board, a committee of the Privy Council, provides ministerial accountability for the performance of the public service. Treasury Board represents the only cabinet committee created by law in the federal government, and wields more power than most other cabinet committees, which are less formal and subject to change. The President of the Treasury Board serves as a cabinet minister. The Treasury Board President provides a voice respecting the public service in cabinet, and also initiates reforms aimed at the public service. Treasury Board is also the manager of the federal civil service, in the sense that it negotiates labour agreements with the public service unions, serves as Comptroller General, and issues the policies governing the working conditions and accountability measures for federal public servants.

Public Sector Integrity Commissioner

If there is one federal office particularly concerned with the nature and scope of bureaucratic independence, it is the public service integrity commissioner. The mandate of the Public Sector Integrity Commissioner is set out in the Public Servants Disclosure Protection Act, which entered into force on 15 April 2007, and is mentioned above. The Commissioner is appointed as an Agent of Parliament by an Order-in-Council and approved by resolution of both Houses of Parliament.

The Commissioner and her or his office provide for a means and mechanism for public servants to disclose potential wrongdoing in their workplace, and to be protected from reprisal for making such disclosures. This mandate has five main responsibilities:

1. to accept disclosures of wrongdoing in or relating to the public sector made by public servants and other Canadians;
2. to investigate these disclosures and report findings to the concerned chief executive, which may also include recommendations for the chief executive on corrective measures to be taken;
3. to enforce the prohibition against reprisal by receiving all reprisal complaints from public servants;
4. to investigate complaints of reprisal, which may include conciliation attempts to remedy a complaint or, if unresolved, application to the Public Servants Disclosure Protection Tribunal to determine whether reprisal took place and to order appropriate remedial action;
5. to report to Parliament.

In order to gain the protection of the legislation, whistle-blowers must make their disclosure to the Commissioner (who is also authorized to assist with the legal expenses associated with a complaint). The Public Servants Disclosure Protection Act, in other words, requires public servants to follow established procedures to secure the handling of information that the public sector is taking measures to protect. The Act also stipulates that public servants making disclosures of wrongdoing provide no more information than is reasonably necessary to make the disclosure. Further, this Act places important limitations on disclosure, including not violating confidences of cabinet.

While the Commissioner does not exercise a leadership role in the public service, by clarifying the nature and scope of conflicts of interest in political and bureaucratic relations, this office may provide moral leadership in the articulation of bureaucratic independence.

Conclusions

In this chapter, I have attempted to demonstrate that constitutional and legal boundaries do exist between the public service and the political executive, and that the independence of the public service forms part of the foundation of the Westminster model of Parliamentary democracy. Further, I have emphasized that these boundaries are dynamic, contextually determined 'lines in the sand'. While they may be constitutional in origin, I have emphasized that these boundaries must develop, through the institutions of the public service, not simply by judges interpreting constitutional conventions and common-law principles. Finally, if bureaucratic independence is to be a reality, it will involve an integrated and concerted effort to orient public service culture to distinguishing between the duty of loyalty to the government of the day and a higher duty to the Crown and the public interest to ensure the integrity of democratic government. Such an initiative cannot, furthermore, be limited to the public service. It is the relationship between the political executive and the public service which must embrace this framework, and do so on the basis of mutual respect and a shared commitment to the rule of law, the Convention of a non-partisan public service, and accountability for the exercise of public authority. Ultimately, therefore, bureaucratic independence must start with political will.

Important Terms and Concepts

bureaucratic independence
bureaucratic (or political) neutrality
constitutional conventions
duty of loyalty
institutionalization of bureaucratic independence
Public Servants Disclosure Protection Act
public service
rule of law

Study Questions

1. What is the traditional view of the role of the public service and its constitutional identity?
2. What supporting arguments can be mustered for this traditional view of the public service?
3. What is the new view of the role of the public service described by Sossin?
4. What supporting arguments can be mustered for this new view of the public service?
5. If you were to devise an agenda for reforms related to bureaucratic independence, which would you include?
6. Is it a 'good thing' to have a Public Service Integrity Commissioner (PSIC)?

Useful Websites

Public Servants Disclosure Protection Act (2005, c. 46):

http://laws.justice.gc.ca/en/showtdm/cs/P-31.9

Public Service Integrity Commissioner (PSIC):

www.psic-ispc.gc.ca/index.php

Public Service Commission:

www.psc-cfp.gc.ca/index-eng.htm

Public Service Impartiality: Taking Stock. Public Service Commission paper (see in particular Chapter 7 on the constitutional identity of the Public Service):

www.psc-cfp.gc.ca/plcy-pltq/rprt/impart/index-eng.htm

Clerk of the Privy Council:

www.pco-bcp.gc.ca/index.asp?lang=eng&page=clerk-greffier

Treasury Board Secretariat:

www.tbs-sct.gc.ca/tbs-sct/index-eng.asp

Savoie, Donald. 2006. 'The Canadian Public Service has a Personality', *Canadian Public Administration* 49, 3: 261–81.

www3.interscience.wiley.com/journal/119819726/issue

Gomery Report, Phase 2:

http://epe.lac-bac.gc.ca/100/206/301/pco-bcp/commissions/sponsorship-ef/06-02-10/www.gomery.ca/en/phase2report/default.htm

Letter from the critics of the Gomery Report dated 3 March 2006:

www.pm.gc.ca/grfx/docs/gomery_toaupm_e.pdf

Letter from PM Stephen Harper to the critics of the Gomery Report, dated 14 December 2006:

www.pm.gc.ca/grfx/docs/gomery_fromdupm_e.pdf

Roncarelli v. Duplessis, [1959] S.C.R. 121:

http://csc.lexum.umontreal.ca/en/1959/1959scr0-121/1959scr0-121.html

Fraser v. P.S.S.R.B., [1985] 2 S.C.R. 455:

http://csc.lexum.umontreal.ca/en/1985/1985scr2-455/1985scr2-455.html

Osborne v. Canada (Treasury Board), [1991] 2 S.C.R. 69:

http://csc.lexum.umontreal.ca/en/1991/1991scr2-69/1991scr2-69.html

Notes

1. This chapter includes material originally published as 'Defining Boundaries: The Constitutional Argument for Bureaucratic Independence and Its Implication for the Accountability of the Public Service', a paper commissioned by the Inquiry into the Sponsorship Affair (Gomery Inquiry) (February 2006); see www.gomery.ca/en/phase2report/volume2/CISPAA_Vol2_2.pdf. I am grateful to Jamie Liew and Erica Zarkovich, for their superb research assistance.

2. The culture of 'fear and intimidation' which led to egregious political interference in the operation of the sponsorship program is now documented in detail in the first report of this Commission. See *Who Is Responsible: Phase 1 Report* at www.gomery.ca/en/phase1report/ (hereinafter 'Phase I Report').

3. See *Restoring Accountability*, Phase 2 Report at pp. 62–3.

4. Letter dated March 3, 2006, at www.pm.gc.ca/grfx/docs/gomery_toaupm_e.pdf (accessed 7 May 2008).

5. Letter dated December 14, 2006 at www.pm.gc.ca/grfx/docs/gomery_fromdupm_e.pdf (accessed 7 May 2008).

6. www.tbs-sct.gc.ca/report/rev-exa/ar-er_e.rtf

7. Ibid., at p.13.

8. Supra note.

9. While the jurisprudence on bureaucratic neutrality is significant, it is worth highlighting that this issue is typically secondary to the actual dispute at hand. The actual dispute is more likely to be a labour issue involving either an individual sanction being grieved or a dispute between a public sector union and the government. This is even more apparent in cases elucidating the duty of civil service loyalty to the government of the day, as discussed below.

10. [1987] 2 S.C.R. 2.

11. Ibid., at para. 85.

12. See Federal Court of Appeal's reasons in *Osborne v. Canada.*

13. *Osborne v. Canada* [1991] 2 S.C.R. 69 at 88. Sopinka J. rejected the government's argument that s. 33 of the Public Service Act was immune from Charter scrutiny because it codified a constitutional convention, but did observe that the fact a provision reflects this convention 'is an important consideration in determining whether in s. 33, Parliament was seeking to achieve an important political objective'.

14. *Fraser*, supra.

15. *OPSEU*, supra, at para. 93.

16. *Roncarelli v. Duplessis*, [1959] S.C.R. 121 at 142. In that case, Rand J. stated that 'there is always a perspective within which a statute is intended to operate' (at 140). In other words, every grant of statutory authority has an implied limitation which restricts its exercise to proper and not improper purposes, in good faith and not in bad faith, and based on reasoned and not arbitrary or discriminatory factors.

17. See *British Columbia v. Imperial Tobacco Canada Ltd.* 2005 SCC 49 at paras. 57–68.

18. See *Baker v. Canada (Minister of Citizenship and Immigration*, [1999] 2 S.C.R. 815, at paras. 53, 56.

19. *Secession Reference*, supra, at para. 70.

20. See *Crevier v. Quebec*, [1981] 2 S.C.R. 220.

21. In New Zealand, for example, public servants are informed that ministers' directions should be rejected if 'it is reasonably held that instructions are unlawful because it would be unlawful for the minister to issue them . . . where it would be unlawful for the officials to accept them . . . where officials would have to break the law in order to carry out the directive.' New Zealand, State Services Commission, *The Senior Public Servant*, p. 28, quoted in Kernaghan (2003: 22).

22. Two other opinions sought by the Government House leader contradicted this conclusion and found that no convention requiring the announcement of a budget in the House existed.

23. From Mallan (2003): 'Also yesterday, Liberal Leader Dalton McGuinty's chief of staff sent a letter to the province's top bureaucrat, Secretary of Cabinet Tony Dean, questioning the Conservative government's use of non-partisan public servants in the release of what he termed a plan that is "clearly partisan in nature". Philip Dewan asked Dean to prevent civil servants from being drawn into a political exercise. "I believe the leadership of the OPS (Ontario Public Service) has an obligation to ensure that . . . Ontario's dedicated

and professional public servants are not placed in the compromising circumstance of assisting with preparations for a partisan event."'

24. This is attested to by the conflicting constitutional opinions produced by the Speaker of the Legislature and the Tory Government House Leader, which are on file with the author (the opinion produced by the Attorney General, if there was one, was never released).

25. The last chapter in the Magna Budget affair ended in a courtroom. Following the delivery of the budget, a court application was brought by a citizen seeking a declaration from the court that the delivery of the budget outside the Legislature violated parliamentary conventions. The suit was dismissed on a preliminary motion on justiciability grounds. See *Martin v. Ontario* (decision of Superior Court of Ontario, released 20 January 2004).

26. OLRC Report, supra, at p.34.

27. *Fraser,* supra at 471.

28. Ibid., at 470.

29. This was characterized by the Ontario Law Reform Commission as a functional approach to loyalty, in which 'Loyalty is necessary to the effective operation of the public service, and the effective operation of the public service is a constitutional imperative that legitimizes some limitation on the individual rights of public servants.' Supra note 54, at p.47–8.

30. [2001] 2 F.C. 82 (F.C.T.D.). This litigation continues; for the most recent decision confirming that the standard of review of grievance adjudicators is reasonableness and that the adjudicator's finding against Ms Haydon was reasonable, see [2005] FCA 249.

31. Ibid., at para. 32.

32. Ibid.

33. For the exact language used in the Act, visit http://laws.justice.gc.ca/en/showtdm/cs/P-31.9.

34. For an example of how the merit principles works, consider Australia's Public Service Act which provides that employment decisions be made on the basis of merit and that a decision relating to hiring and promoting is based on merit if: '(a) an assessment is made of the relative suitability of the candidates for the duties, using a competitive selection process; (b) the assessment is based on the relationship between the candidate's work-related qualities and the work-related qualities genuinely required for the duties; (c) the assessment focuses on the relative capacity of the candidates to achieve outcomes related to the duties; and (d) the assessment is the primary consideration in making the decision', cited in Kernaghan (2003: 15).

35. See Public Service Commission's submission to this Inquiry. See also its last annual report at www.psc-cfp.gc.ca/centres/annual-annuel/index_e.htm.

36. While it is beyond the scope of this paper, I have argued elsewhere that the Clerk should not be a political appointment. I would go further and also question the propriety of deputy ministers being appointed by the Prime Minister. The system in the UK, whereby the head of the Civil Service Commission chairs selection committees for deputy ministers to ensure they are non-partisan appointments has much to commend it as a practice in keeping with the constitutional values advanced in this analysis.

37. See Public Service Employment Act, 1993.

References

Allen, C.K. 1965. *Law and Orders*, 3rd edn. London: Stevens.

Baillie A. 2003. 'Contempt ruling shocks PCS; Government lawyers told Tories moving budget venue was illegal'. *Toronto Star*, 9 May, A1.

Dunn, C. 2002. 'The Central Executive in Canadian Government: Searching for the Holy Grail', in C. Dunn, ed., *The Oxford Handbook of Canadian Public Administration*, 1st edn. Toronto: Oxford University Press.

Dyzenhaus, D. 2002. 'Constituting the Rule of Law: Fundamental Values in Administrative Law', *Queen's University Law Journal* 27: 445.

Freiman, M. 2002. 'Convergence of Law and Policy and the Role of the Attorney General', *Supreme Court Law Review* 16 (2nd): 335.

Ganz, G. 1987. *Quasi-Legislation: Recent Developments in Secondary Legislation.* London: Sweet & Maxwell.

Heard, A. 1991. *Canadian Constitutional Conventions: The Marriage of Law and Politics.* Toronto: Oxford University Press.

Hodgetts, J.E. 1973. *The Canadian Public Service: A Physiology of Government.* Toronto: University of Toronto Press.

Hogg, P., and C. Zwibel. 2005. 'The Rule of Law in the Supreme Court of Canada', *University of Toronto Law Journal* 55: 715.

Kernaghan, K. 1986. 'Political Rights and Political Neutrality: Finding the Balance Point', *Canadian Public Administration* 29: 639.

———. 2002. 'East Block and Westminster: Conventions, Values, and Public Service', in C. Dunn, ed., *The Handbook of Canadian Public Administration*, 1st edn. Toronto: Oxford University Press.

———. 2003. 'The Future Role of a Professional, Non-Partisan Public Service in Ontario', paper prepared for the Panel on the Role of Government in Ontario. Toronto. June. Available at: www.law-lib.utoronto.ca/investing/reports/rp13.pdf.

Kernaghan, K., and J. Langford. 1990. *The Responsible Public Servant*. Halifax and Toronto: IRPP and IPAC.

Mallan, C. 2003. 'Tory backers to provide setting for budget day', *Toronto Star*, 22 March, A6.

Marshall, G. 1984. *Constitutional Conventions*. Oxford: Oxford University Press.

Savoie, D. 1994. *Thatcher, Reagan, Mulroney: In Search of a New Bureaucracy*. Toronto: University of Toronto Press.

———. 2003. *Breaking the Bargain: Public Servants, Ministers and Parliament*. Toronto: University of Toronto Press.

———. 2006. 'The Canadian Public Service Has a Personality', *Canadian Public Administration* 49, 3: 261–81.

Scott, Sir Richard. 1996. 'Ministerial Responsibility', *Public Law*: 410.

Siegel, D. 1986. 'Politics, Politicians, and Public Servants in Non-Partisan Local Governments', *Canadian Public Administration* 37, 1 (Spring 1994): 7–30.

Smith, C., and L. Sossin. 2003. 'Hard Choices and Soft Law: Ethical Codes, Policy Guidelines and the Role of the Courts in Regulating Government', *Alberta Law Review* 40: 867–93.

Smith, D. 1995. *The Invisible Crown: The First Principle of Canadian Government*. Toronto: University of Toronto Press.

Sossin, L. 1999. *Boundaries of Judicial Review: The Law of Justiciability in Canada*. Toronto: Carswell.

———. 2005a. 'Speaking Truth to Power? The Search for Bureaucratic Independence', *University of Toronto Law Journal* 55: 1–60.

———. 2005b. 'From Neutrality to Compassion: The Place of Civil Service Values and Legal Norms in the Exercise of Administrative Discretion', *University of Toronto Law Journal* 55: 427.

———. 2006. 'The Ambivalence of Executive Power in Canada', in Adam Tomkins and Paul Craig eds., *The Executive and Public Law: Power and Accountability in Comparative Perspective*. Oxford: Oxford University Press.

Stewart, E. 1989. *Cabinet Government in Ontario: A View from the Inside*. Halifax: IRPP.

Sutherland, S. 1991. 'Responsible Government and Ministerial Responsibility: Every Reform Is Its Own Problem', *Canadian Journal of Political Science* 24, 1 (March): 91–120.

———. 2006. 'The Role of the Clerk of the Privy Council', in *Linkages: Responsibilities and Accountabilities*, vol. 3 of the Research Papers for the Commission of Inquiry into the Sponsorship Affair. Ottawa: PWGSC.

Wade, H.W.R., and C.F. Forsyth. 2000. *Administrative Law*. Oxford: Oxford University Press.

PART VI The Policy Dimension

Policy development can be reflected through many prisms. Michael Howlett, in Chapter 22, suggests that the literature on policy development is best organized through the perspective of policy stages, which constitute a recurring cycle. One can, as did Harold Lasswell originally, call the stages intelligence-gathering, promotion of options, prescribing a course of action, implementation by the courts and the bureaucracy, and evaluation vis-à-vis original policy aims and goals. Or one can, as in more recent approaches, call the stages agenda-setting, policy formulation, decision-making, policy implementation, and policy evaluation.

This simplified model provides a general framework for understanding the policy development process and points to several of the temporal activities and relationships that should be examined. However, it does not answer key questions about the actual substance of policy, the number and type of relevant actors involved, the manner and sequence in which policy development processes occur, and whether basic patterns of development exist for different issue areas and jurisdictions. Empirical studies aimed at answering these questions and generating more detailed models of the policy-making process were conducted in the 1960s and 1970s, producing several competing approaches to the subject, which Howlett covers in his useful overview chapter.

Richard Simeon, in Chapter 23, examines federalism and intergovernmental relations. This broad area demands close attention to such issues as coordination, competition, collaboration, accountability, transparency, and a host of related matters. If intergovernmental relations is a Canadian success story, it must be told, and Simeon traces it from Canada's beginnings to the present. Canada initially manifested the model of colonial federalism before turning to classical federalism as provinces established new power bases in response to the centralized, Ottawa-based control over policy. As the ravages of war and the Great Depression lingered after World War II, the country turned to a new co-operative federalism, with Ottawa pursuing social reconstruction on behalf of the provinces; however, this paternalism, as some saw it, fostered the growth of competitive federalism, led by the Quebec government, from the early 1960s on. An overlapping period of constitutional federalism aimed at broad constitutional reform in an effort to placate Quebec's nationalistic desires and the increasing demands of other provincial governments for greater powers. The most recent era of Canadian federalism has been called collaborative federalism, a response to perceived excesses of the previous period.

Designing and administering intergovernmental relations is vitally important, Simeon explains, given the less than successful integrative roles played by legislatures and the party system. The plethora of intergovernmental mechanisms that have developed in Canada suggest that the collaborative model is establishing deep roots, but even this model is subject to substantial strains. The Social Union Framework Agreement (SUFA) of 1999, and the new Open Federalism arrangements enunciated in the 2007 budget, were based on collaborative principles but depend for their success on trust relationships that are not always apparent. In addition, questions remain about the policy and administrative aspects of intergovernmental relations, such as the degree to which they should be made contractual, what role there should be for citizen participation, to what extent reforms should attack the democratic deficit in Canadian federalism, what the balance should be between strengthening provinces and strengthening the representative and integrative capacity of Ottawa, and to what extent Ottawa should be the lead government in defining the social and economic union. To put it briefly, how can we exploit the virtues of intergovernmentalism while avoiding its vices?

In Chapter 24, Christopher Dunn reviews the history of the federal spending power, as well as the evolution and details of an agreement that addressed the very problems Simeon has characterized as endemic to Canadian federalism. For years the spending power had been uncontroversial, due largely to its conformance to the nation-building urge that restrained governments and society from emphasizing jurisdictional considerations. There followed a period of the 'constitutional industry'—the period Simeon characterizes as constitutional federalism—that featured attempts to limit federal spending power by constitutional means, the latest example being provisions found in the Charlottetown Accord, 1992. After this, Canada entered a third period of spending power—constitutional minimalism or non-constitutional reform. Now the constitutional industry—dissident provincial governments, members of constitutional task forces, and academic commentators—sought to achieve by other means those reforms they had previously sought by constitutional measures. The SUFA, born in 1999, but more importantly the Harper government's 'Open Federalism', were the results.

Those seeking greater provincial autonomy in the SUFA were disappointed, as the *status quo ante* prevailed. The federal government retained the ability to penalize provinces that do not meet the principles of medicare. Direct federal spending to individuals and organizations faced no significant new impediments other than certain minimal conditions. However, in the 2007 budget, the Harper government outlined measures more philosophically aligned with the constitutional reform industry. It would focus new spending primarily in areas of federal responsibility and limit the use of the 'federal spending power' by ensuring (1) that new cost-shared programs in areas of provincial responsibility have the consent of the majority of provinces to proceed and that provinces; and (2) territories have the right to opt out of cost-shared federal programs with compensation if they offer similar programs with comparable accountability structures. Despite these advances, the Quebec government has outlined a significant number of unmet promises in Open Federalism.

In Chapter 25, Andrew Sancton and Scott Sams examine the intergovernmental theme as it relates to the policy dimension of public administration. They depart from the traditional analytical approach to consider the two levels—provincial and local—as one functional unit for the purposes of analysis. Many provincial functions provided in modern Canada have such intertwined links between provincial and municipal administrations that it does not make sense to separate them.

Sancton and Sams's piece is a reminder not to obsess on federal public administration. It is important to know how the federal government is organized, how its financial management system works, and how its public service is being renewed. But the story of federal government accounts for less than half the story of Canadian public administration, less still if one realizes that much of the federal government's role is to extract money from taxpayers and redistribute it to provinces and people with relatively low incomes. Most of the actual public services on which Canadians depend—health, education, social services, roads, sewers—are provided by provincial and local governments, which were renewing and experimenting with varied institutional arrangements long before the federal authorities entered the field. Unless students of Canadian public administration make the effort to learn more about these, they will know very little about their chosen subject.

22 The Policy Process

Michael Howlett

Introduction: Policy Development as Decision-Making Process

The idea that policy development can be thought of as a series of decision-making processes was first broached systematically in the work of Harold Lasswell (Lasswell, 1956, 1971). For Lasswell, the policy development process began with intelligence gathering, that is, the collection, processing, and dissemination of information for those who participate in the decision process. It then moved on to the promotion of particular options by those involved in the actual decision. In the third stage the decision-makers actually prescribed a course of action. In the fourth stage this course of action was invoked, that is, sanctions were developed to penalize those who failed to comply with the prescriptions of decision-makers. The policy was then applied by the courts and the bureaucracy and ran its course until it was terminated or cancelled. Finally, the results of the policy were appraised or evaluated against the aims and goals of the original decision-makers.

This model was highly influential in the development of the policy sciences. Although not entirely accurate, it helped to advance the policy sciences by expanding the idea of the policy process beyond its traditional confines in the actions of governments and their agencies. It also introduced the notion of the policy process as an ongoing cycle, recognizing that most policies do not have a definite life cycle—moving from birth to death—but rather endlessly reoccur, in slightly different guises, as one policy succeeds its predecessor.

In most recent work, a five-stage model of the **policy process** has been posited. In this model, '**agenda-setting**' is the first stage in the process. This is the earliest stage in a sequence of policy development when a problem is initially sensed by policy actors and a variety of solutions are put forward. During '**policy formulation**', the second stage in the process, specific policy options are developed within government. In this stage the range of plausible choices is narrowed by excluding the infeasible ones, and efforts made by various actors to have their favoured solution ranked highly among the remaining few. '**Decision-making**' is the third stage, when governments adopt a particular course of action or non-action. This can involve the adoption of one, none, or some combination of the solutions remaining at the end of the formulation stage. In the fourth stage, '**policy implementation**', governments put their decisions into effect. This involves the use of some combination of the tools of public administration to alter the distribution of goods and services in society in a way that is broadly compatible with the sentiments and values of affected parties. Finally, the fifth stage in the policy process, '**policy evaluation**', involves both state and societal actors monitoring the results of policies, often leading to the reconceptualization of policy problems and solutions in the light of experiences encountered with the policy in question (Howlett and Ramesh, 2003). This sequence of stages in the policy process, as well as other formulations of it, is often referred to as the '**policy cycle**'.

This simplified model provides a general framework for understanding the policy development process and points to several of the key temporal activities and relationships that should be examined in furthering study of the issue. However, it does not answer several key questions such as the actual substance of policy, the number and type of relevant actors involved in the process, the exact manner and sequence in which actual policy development processes occur, and whether basic patterns of development exist in different issue areas, sectors, or jurisdictions (Sabatier, 1992). Empirical studies aimed at answering these questions and generating more detailed models of the policy-making process were conducted in the 1960s and 1970s and generated several competing 'schools' or approaches to the subject.

Historical Overview: The (Ir)Rationality of Policy Development

Early studies of the policy development process differed considerably in terms of their findings and assumptions about the 'rationality' of the process. While a number of studies indicated that policy-makers went about their business in a calm, methodical, and precise fashion aimed at optimizing or maximizing policy outcomes, others found the process to be much more Byzantine, haphazard, and unpredictable. Several examples of these early works are presented below.

Pure Rational Models

Some early studies of individual policy-making in companies, governments, and organizations, conducted largely by students of public and business administration, found policy-makers attempting to follow a systematic method for arriving at logical, efficient policies. To various extents, they argued that policy-makers established a goal; explored alternative strategies for achieving it; attempted to predict its consequences and the likelihood of each occurring, and then chose the option which maximized potential benefits at least cost or risk (Ward, 1954; Gawthrop, 1971; Weiss, 1977; Carley, 1980).

This model was 'rational' in the sense that it prescribed a standard set of procedures for policy-making that were expected to lead in all circumstances to the choice of the most efficient means of achieving policy goals (Jennings, 1987; Torgerson, 1986). Policy-makers were thought of as neutral 'technicians' or 'managers', who identify a problem and then find the most effective or efficient way of solving it (Elster, 1991).

Limited Rationality Models

Further empirical research into policy-making processes, however, soon led to a re-thinking of many elements of the **rational model**. Policy-makers were often found to be neither neutral nor competent and a second wave of models of the policy-making process tended to argue that this was not accidental, or due to avoidable errors made by policy-makers, but an inherent and unavoidable characteristic of the policy-making exercise. The well-known **incremental model** of policy-making developed by Yale University political scientist Charles Lindblom, for example, attempted to capture the elements of a policy process characterized by only limited rationality (Dahl and Lindblom, 1953; Lindblom, 1951, 1958, and 1959). Lindblom summarized the elements of his model as consisting of the following 'mutually supporting set of simplifying and focusing stratagems':

a) limitation of analysis to a few somewhat familiar policy alternatives . . . differing only marginally from the status quo;
b) an intertwining of analysis of policy goals and other values with the empirical aspects of the problem (that is, no requirement that values be specified first with means subsequently found to promote them);
c) a greater analytical preoccupation with ills to be remedied than positive goals to be sought;
d) a sequence of trials, errors, and revised trials;
e) analysis that explores only some, not all, of the important possible consequences of a considered alternative;

f) fragmentation of analytical work to many (partisan) participants in policy-making, (each attending to their piece of the overall problem domain)'. (Lindblom, 1979: 521)

Lindblom argued that policies were invariably developed through a process of 'successive limited comparisons' with earlier policies with which decision-makers were most familiar. As he put it in his oft-cited 1959 article 'The Science of "Muddling Through"', policy-makers worked through a process of 'continually building out from the current situation, step-by-step and by small degrees' (Lindblom, 1959: 83). For Lindblom, this was due to two related aspects of the policy-making situation. First, since policy-making requires distribution of limited resources among various participants, it is easier to continue an existing pattern of distribution rather than to adopt radically new proposals that alter the established pattern of costs and benefits enjoyed, or borne, by specific actors. Second, the standard operating procedures that are the hallmark of bureaucracy also tend to promote the continuation of existing practices. The methods by which bureaucrats identify options and the methods and criteria for choice are often laid out in advance, which inhibits innovation and perpetuates existing arrangements (Gortner et al., 1987).

The incremental model hence viewed policy-making as a practical exercise concerned with solving problems through trial-and-error processes rather than through the comprehensive evaluation of all possible means of achieving policy goals (Manzer, 1984). Decision-makers, it was argued, did not maximize policy outcomes in the traditional, rational sense, because they considered only a few familiar alternatives for their appropriateness and stopped their search whenever an alternative acceptable to established policy actors was found.

Irrational Models

Perhaps the most noted critic of the rational model was the American behavioural scientist Herbert Simon. In a series of books and articles beginning in the early 1950s, he argued that several hurdles prevented decision-makers from attaining 'pure' comprehensive rationality in their decisions (Simon, 1955, 1957). First, Simon noted definite cognitive limits to the decision-makers' ability to consider all possible options, which forces them to selectively consider alternatives. Second, he argued that the model assumed that it is possible for decision-makers to know the consequences of each decision in advance, while, in reality, no one can predict the future with any degree of certainty. Third, he also noted specific policy options usually entail a bundle of favourable and adverse consequences in different areas of social life, which makes comparisons among them difficult. Moreover, since the same option can often be efficient or inefficient depending on the circumstances, it is not possible for decision-makers to arrive at unambiguous conclusions about which alternative is superior.

Simon concluded that public decisions in practice did not maximize benefits over costs, but merely tended to satisfy whatever criteria decision-makers set for themselves. This '**satisfycing**' criterion, as he put it, was realistic given the '**bounded rationality**' with which human beings are endowed.

A very different model was put forward by one of Simon's co-authors, James March, and his Norwegian colleague Johan Olsen. March and Olsen (1979) asserted that public policy-making was an inherently irrational process. The two authors proposed a so-called **garbage-can model** of decision-making that denied even the limited notion of rationality accepted by incrementalists. They started from the assumption that both the rational and incremental models presumed a level of intentionality, comprehension of problems, and predictability of relations among actors that simply did not obtain in reality. Based on studies they conducted into policy-making exercises carried out in universities and similar large institutions, they argued that policy-making is a highly ambiguous and unpredictable process only distantly related to searching for means to achieve goals. Rejecting the instrumentalism that characterized most other models, March, Olsen, and Michael Cohen argued that decision opportunities were:

> a garbage can into which various problems and solutions are dumped by participants. The mix of garbage in a single can depends partly on the labels attached to the alternative cans; but it also depends on what garbage is being produced at the moment, on the mix of cans available, and on the speed with which garbage is collected and removed from the scene. (Cohen, March, and Olsen, 1979: 327)

That is, they saw policy solutions as only very loosely related to policy problems and the process of matching solutions to problems as a largely ad hoc one that depended on various unpredictable elements such as the personalities of the actors involved, their presence or absence in specific decision-making instances, and the temporary alliances and arrangements made between them in specific cases. The garbage-can metaphor was used deliberately to strip away the aura of science and rationality attributed to decision-making by earlier theorists. March and Olsen sought to drive home the point that goals are often unknown to policy-makers, as are causal relationships. In their view, actors simply define goals and choose means as they go along in a process that is necessarily contingent and unpredictable.

Problems with Existing Models: False Dichotomies and Corrective Syntheses

As is apparent from the above brief overview, each of these early models was constructed on the basis of certain findings and expectations with respect to the behaviour of policy-makers, especially in regard to how policy-makers characterized acceptable policy outcomes and acted so as to achieve them (Cahill and Overman, 1990). Each model was constructed on the basis of some empirical findings, but inherent in both the incremental and garbage-can models was criticism of the concepts contained in their predecessors. Hence incremental critics of the rational model argued that it would generate maximal results only if all possible alternatives and the costs of each alternative were assessed before a decision was made, while garbage-can critics of incrementalism argued that it assumed a constant set of decision-makers who could learn from past experiences. In both cases, empirical evidence to the contrary was cited to bolster arguments made about the unreality of such assumptions.

Defenders of rational models, however, were unwilling to accept the superiority of those alternatives based on limited or restricted notions of rationality. Critics found faults with several aspects of incremental policy-making which, as Forester put it, 'would have us cross and recross intersections without knowing where we are going' (Forester, 1984: 23). The model was criticized, for example, for being unable to explain large-scale change and innovation (Berry, 1990; Lustick, 1980; Weiss and Woodhouse, 1992) and for being undemocratic to the extent that it confined policy-making to bargaining within a select group of senior policy-makers (Gawthrop, 1971). By discouraging systematic analysis and planning and by undermining the need to search for promising new alternatives, it was also said to promote short-sighted decisions which can have adverse consequences for society in the long run (Cox, 1992; Hayes, 1992). In addition to criticisms of the desirability of decisions made incrementally, the model was also criticized for its narrow analytic usefulness. Yehezkel Dror, for example, noted that incrementalism could only work when there is a great deal of continuity in the nature of problems that policies are intended to address and in the means available to address them, conditions that do not always exist (Dror, 1964). Incrementalism was also found to be more characteristic of decision-making in a relatively stable environment, rather than in situations that are unusual, such as a crisis (Nice, 1987) and also was seen to be a more likely explanation where large numbers of actors participate in policy development (Bendor, 1995).

The garbage-can model also generated similar criticisms. While it was found by some authors, including John Kingdon (1984) to be a fairly accurate description of how decisions are made at times in some complex organizations, such as legislatures, its application to all instances of policy development was questioned. Guy Mucciaroni, for example, argued that:

> Perhaps the mode of policy-making depicted by the garbage can model is itself embedded in a particular institutional structure. Put another way, the model may be better at depicting decision-making in certain polities than in others. It may be more useful for describing policy-making in the United States, where the institutional structure is fragmented and permeable, participation is pluralistic and fluid, and coalitions are often temporary and ad hoc. By contrast, policy-making in other countries takes place among institutions that are more centralized and integrated, where the number of participants is limited and their participation is highly structured and predictable.... [Where this occurs] the result has been a process described as 'stable', predictable', orderly', 'rationalistic', 'deliberative' and 'planned' quite unlike the garbage can model's image of decision-making that is more open, fluid and ad hoc. (Mucciaroni, 1992: 466–7)

In addition, it was argued that the model did not well explain the existence of fairly long-term patterns in policy-making and exaggerated the gap existing between problems and solutions in most instances (Mucciaroni, 1992).

These limitations led many analysts to continue to look for alternative models of policy-making processes. Some suggested that the shortcomings of existing models could be overcome by combining elements from each in a new, synthetic, model. One such effort, for example, suggested that optimal decision-making would consist of both a cursory search ('scanning') for alternatives as suggested by incrementalism, followed by a detailed probe of the most promising alternative, as suggested by the rational model (Etzioni, 1967). However, most efforts took to heart the idea put forward by Lindblom late in his career, that a spectrum of policy-making styles existed (Smith and May, 1980). These ranged from 'synoptic' or rational–comprehensive decision-making to 'blundering', that is, simply following hunches or guesses without any real effort at systematic analysis of alternative strategies. The spectrum put forward by Lindblom and Cohen in 1979 is illustrated in Figure 22.1.

While Lindblom did not specify under what circumstances a specific option might be used, other authors have since suggested that the manner with which a policy problem or issue would be developed tends to be established on a relatively permanent basis and can usefully be thought of as a policy 'style' (Freeman, 1985; Coleman, 1994). Richardson, Gustafsson, and Jordan (1982), for example, defined a **policy style** as a typical process of policy development characterized by 'the interaction between (a) the government's approach to problem solving and (b) the relationship between government and other actors in the policy process'. Utilizing these two variables, they argued that a limited number of large-scale, typically national, styles could be identified (see Figure 22.2).

synoptic———	strategic———	disjointed——— incremental	simple——— incremental	blundering
[Proactive	———	——— to ———	———	Reactive]

Figure 22.1 A Spectrum of Policy-Making Types
Source: Adapted from Lindblom and Cohen (1979).

	Dominant Approach to Problem-Solving	
Relationship between Government and Society	Anticipatory	Reactive
Consensus	e.g., German 'rationalist consensus' style	e.g., British 'negotiating' style
Imposition	e.g., French 'concertation' style	e.g., Dutch 'negotiation and conflict' style

Figure 22.2 An Early Model of National Policy Styles
Source: Adapted from Richardson et al. (1982).

Several studies applied this concept with great facility to policy-making in various nations and sectors (Tuohy, 1992; Vogel, 1986). However, others found that few governments were consistently active or reactive; nor did any government always work through either consensus or imposition. Rather than think of policy styles as existing at the national level, they argued that a focus on the sectoral level would be more accurate and more productive (Freeman, 1985).

Elements of a Policy Style

In this section, the results of studies undertaken into the types of styles prevalent at each stage of the policy cycle are presented. Combining the style found to exist at each stage of the policy development process, it will be argued, generates a useful picture of the overall policy style found in any sector and provides a comprehensive overview of typical policy development processes in a jurisdiction.

Agenda-Setting Styles

In the formal study of agenda-setting, a distinction is often made between the *systemic* or unofficial public agenda and the *institutional* or formal, official agenda. The systemic agenda 'consists of all issues that are commonly perceived by members of the political community as meriting public attention and as involving matters within the legitimate jurisdiction of existing governmental authority' (Cobb and Elder, 1972). This is essentially a society's agenda for discussion of public problems, such as crime or health care, water quality or wilderness preservation. The formal or institutional agenda, on the other hand, consists of only a limited number of issues or problems to which attention is devoted by policy elites (Baumgartner and Jones, 1991; Kingdon, 1984).

Each society has literally hundreds of issues that some citizens find to be matters of concern and would have the government do something about. However, only a small proportion of the problems on the public or systemic agenda are actually taken up by policy actors actively involved in policy development. In other words, the public agenda is an agenda for discussion while the institutional agenda is an agenda for action, indicating that the formal policy process dealing with the problem in question has begun.

Over 30 years ago the American political scientists Cobb, Ross, and Ross developed a model of typical agenda-setting styles. They argued that three basic patterns of agenda-setting could be discerned, distinguished by the origins of the issue as well as the resources utilized to facilitate their inclusion on the agenda.

In the **outside initiation** pattern 'issues arise in nongovernmental groups and are then expanded sufficiently to reach, first, the public [systemic] agenda and, finally, the formal [institutional] agenda' (Cobb, Ross, and Ross, 1976). In this case issues are first initiated when some part of the public articulates a grievance and demands its resolution by the government. The aggrieved groups attempt to expand support for their demand, a process that may involve submerging the specific complaint within a more general one and forming alliances across groups. Finally, these groups lobby, contest, and join with others in attempting to get the expanded issue onto the formal agenda. If they have the requisite political resources and skills and can outmanoeuvre their opponents or advocates of other issues and actions, they can often succeed in having their issue enter the formal agenda. Thus, as Cobb, Ross, and Ross summarize it:

> The outside initiative model applies to the situation in which a group outside the government structure 1) articulates a grievance, 2) tries to expand interest in the issue to enough other groups in the population to gain a place on the public agenda, in order to 3) create sufficient pressure on decision-makers to force the issue onto the formal agenda for their serious consideration.

The **mobilization** case is quite different and describes 'decision-makers trying to expand an issue from a formal to a public agenda'. In this model, issues are simply placed on the formal agenda by the government with no necessary preliminary expansion from a publicly recognized grievance. There may be considerable debate within government over the issue, but the public may well be kept in the dark about the policy and its development until its formal announcement. The policy may be specified in some detail or it may just establish general principles whose specification will be worked out later.

In the third, **inside initiation**, pattern, influential groups with special access to decision-makers initiate a policy and do not necessarily want it to be expanded and contested in public. This can be due to technical as well as political reasons. In this model, initiation and specification occur simultaneously as a group or government agency enunciates a grievance and specifies some potential solution to the problem. Expansion is restricted to specialized groups or agencies with some knowledge or interest in the subject. Entrance is virtually automatic due to the privileged place of those desiring a decision. According to Cobb, Ross, and Ross:

> Proposals arise within governmental units or in groups close to the government. The issue is then expanded to identification and attention groups in order to create sufficient pressure on decision-makers to place the item on the formal agenda. At no point is the public greatly involved, and the initiators make no effort to get the issue on the public agenda. On the contrary, they try to keep it off.

From the above discussion, it should be apparent that two of the most critical factors in identifying a typical pattern of agenda-setting in any policy area are the level and extent of public involvement and support for government action (May, 1991), and the response or 'pre-response' of the state in directing, mediating and accommodating this activity (Majone, 1989). The resulting agenda-setting styles are set out in Figure 22.3. As this figure shows, a fourth agenda-setting style—'consolidation'—exists in addition to the three identified by Cobb, Ross, and Ross. In this last style, state actors may initiate debate on an issue with high public support and thus simply consolidate this support in moving the issue on for further development.

	Nature of Public Support	
Initiator of Debate	High	Low
Societal Actors	outside initiation	inside initiation
State	consolidation	mobilization

Figure 22.3 Basic Agenda-Setting Styles

Policy Formulation Styles

Studies of policy formulation have also emphasized the importance of the kinds of actors interacting to develop and refine policy options for government (Freeman, 1955; Linder and Peters, 1990). But unlike agenda-setting, where the public is often actively involved, in policy formulation the relevant policy actors are restricted to those who not only have an opinion on a subject, but also have some minimal level of knowledge of the subject area, allowing them to comment, at least hypothetically, on the feasibility of options put forward to resolve policy problems.

Scholars over the years have developed a variety of taxonomies to help identify the key actors in these **policy subsystems**, what brings them together, how they interact, and what effect their interaction has on policy development (Jordan, 1981, 1990a, 1990b; Jordan and Schubert, 1992). Most of these distinguish between a larger set of actors with some knowledge of the policy issue in question, and a smaller set in which actors not only have requisite knowledge, but also have established patterns of more or less routine interactions with each other (Knoke, 1993).

Membership in knowledge-based **policy communities** extends to actors such as state policy-makers (administrative, political, and judicial), members of non-governmental organizations (NGOs) concerned with the subject, members of the media who report on the subject, academics who follow or research the area, and members of the general public who, for whatever reason, have taken an interest in the subject (Sabatier 1987, 1988). In many issue areas, the policy community also involves members of other organizations such as businesses, labour unions, or various formalized interest groups or professional associations concerned with government actions in their sector. In some cases, international actors, such as multinational corporations, international governmental or non-governmental organizations, or the governments of foreign states, can also be members of sectoral policy communities (Haas, 1992).

A subset of these actors who interact within more formalized institutions and procedures of government are defined as members of **policy networks** (Coleman and Skogstad, 1990; Marin and Mayntz, 1991; Pross, 1992). These policy networks include representatives from the community, but are 'inner circles' of actors, who effectively hold the power to veto many policy options as untenable or infeasible.

In this view, the likely results of policy formulation are contingent upon the nature and configuration of the policy community and network in the specific sector concerned. A key variable, which many observers have argued affects the structure and behaviour of policy networks, is the number of members, which affects aspects of networks such as their level of integration and the types of interactions members undertake (Van Waarden, 1992; Atkinson and Coleman, 1989, 1990; Coleman and Skogstad, 1990). What is important for policy communities, on the other hand, is not the number of participants in the community but the number of relatively distinct 'idea sets' which exist within it. This affects the nature of conflict and consensus in the community and, as a result, affects the behaviour of community actors (Schulman, 1988; Haas, 1992; MacRae, 1993; Smith, 1993; Hessing and Howlett, 1997).

The type and nature of options that come forward to governments from the policy formulation phase are affected by the interaction of networks and communities (Howlett and Rayner, 1995; Smith, 1993, 1994; Howlett and Ramesh, 1998; Howlett 2002a). Figure 22.4 presents a model of policy formulation styles based on the manner in which different types of policy networks and communities interact.

In open subsystems where networks have many members and communities sharing many idea sets, it can be expected that a propensity exists for new, radical alternatives to the status quo to be generated in the policy formulation process. In closed subsystems, where networks have few members and communities are dominated by a single idea set, on the other hand, a status quo orientation will emerge in the policy options developed and put before decision-makers. In subsystems where only a few actors make up

	Policy Network Membership	
Policy Community Idea Sets	Few	Many
Few	status quo options	marginal/incremental options
Many	contested alternative options	radical alternative options

Figure 22.4 Basic Policy Formulation Styles

the network but communities are open to new ideas, significant alternatives to the status quo may emerge from the formulation process, but usually over the opposition of network members. In subsystems where many actors deal with few ideas, as Lindblom suggested, marginal or incremental options tend to develop.

Decision-Making Styles

In some of their early writings, Lindblom and his co-authors held out the possibility that incremental decision-making could coexist with efforts to achieve more 'rational' decisions. Thus Braybrooke and Lindblom, for example, argued that four different styles of decision-making could be discerned, depending upon the amount of knowledge at the disposal of decision-makers, and the amount of change the decision involved from earlier decisions (Braybrooke and Lindblom, 1963). This generated the two-by-two matrix shown in Figure 22.5.

In Braybrooke and Lindblom's view, the overwhelming majority of decisions were likely to be taken in an incremental fashion, involving minimal change in situations of low available knowledge. Three other possibilities existed, however, with the rational model emerging as one possibility and two styles—'revolutionary' and 'analytic'—also existing as infrequently employed alternatives. Although it was somewhat tautological to use 'amount of change' as a variable to help explain the degree of change each decision-making style entailed, as a description of commonly occurring decision-making styles, this type of model was quite useful. Other authors, like Graham Allison (1969, 1971), also developed similar models of distinct decision-making styles, but also did not specify in any detail the variables that led to the adoption of a particular style (Bendor and Hammond, 1992).

Attempting to improve upon these models, John Forester (1984, 1989) argued that there were at least five distinct decision-making styles associated with a variety of decision-making conditions and contexts. Forester began from the position that 'what is rational for administrators to do depends on the situations in which they work'. That is, the decision-making style and the type of decisions made by decision-makers varied according to issue and institutional contexts. As he put it:

Depending upon the conditions at hand, a strategy may be practical or ridiculous. With time, expertise, data, and a well-defined problem, technical calculations may be in order; without time,

	Level of Available Knowledge	
Amount of Change Involved	High	Low
Societal Actors	revolutionary	analytic
State	rational	disjointed incremental

Figure 22.5 An Early Model of Decision-Making Styles
Source: Adapted from Braybrooke and Lindblom (1963).

data, definition, and expertise, attempting those calculations could well be a waste of time. In a complex organizational environment, intelligence networks will be as, or more, important than documents when information is needed. In an environment of inter-organizational conflict, bargaining and compromise may be called for. Administrative strategies are sensible only in a political and organizational context (Forester, 1984).

Forester suggested that decision-making was affected by the number of agents involved in a decision, their organizational setting, how well a problem is defined, the information available on the problem, its causes and consequences, and the amount of time available to decision-makers to consider possible contingencies and their present and anticipated consequences. The number of agents can expand and multiply almost to infinity; the setting can include many different organizations and can be more or less open to external influences, the problem can be ambiguous or susceptible to multiple competing interpretations, information can be incomplete, misleading, or purposefully withheld or manipulated; and time can be limited or artificially constrained and manipulated.

Re-casting Forester's variables allows the development of a simple but effective model of decision-making styles present in the policy development process. 'Agent' and 'setting', for example, can be thought of as elements of how decision-makers are situated vis-à-vis policy subsystems, while the notions of the 'definitional', 'information', and 'time' resources can all be seen as relating to the types of constraints which are placed upon decision-makers. Using these dimensions, the model of styles found in Figure 22.6 can be generated.

In this model, decision-makers situated in complex subsystems are expected to undertake adjustment strategies while those dealing with simple configurations of actors and ideas will be more prone to undertake search-type strategies. The nature of the decision criteria, on the other hand, varies with the severity of the informational, time, and other resource constraints under which decision-makers operate. Hence decision-makers faced with high constraints will tend to favour satisfycing over optimization; itself an outcome more likely to occur in situations of low constraint.

Policy Implementation Styles

Generally speaking, comparative implementation studies have also shown that governments tend to develop specific implementation styles in areas which they regulate (Knill, 1998; Hawkins and Thomas, 1989; Kagan, 1991; Howlett 2002b). These styles combine various kinds of instruments into a more or less coherent whole which is consistently applied in particular sectors. More specifically, such styles combine at least one major type of procedural policy instrument with at least one major type of substantive instrument.

Substantive instruments are those directly providing goods and services to members of the public or governments. They include a variety of tools or instruments relying on different types of governing resources for their effectiveness (Tupper and Doern, 1981; Vedung, 1997; Woodside, 1986; Peters and Van Nispen, 1998; Salamon, 1989). A useful way to classify these (see Figure 22.7) is according to the type of governing resource upon which they rely: nodality or information; authority, treasure, or financial resources, or administrative or organizational ones (Hood, 1986).

Procedural instruments are different from substantive ones in that their impact on policy

	Complexity of the Policy Subsystem	
Severity of Constraints	High	Low
High	incremental adjustment	satisfycing search
Low	optimizing adjustment	rational search

Figure 22.6 Basic Decision-Making Styles

	Governing Resource			
Principal Use	Nodality	Authority	Treasure	Organization
Effectors	advice training	licences user charges regulation certification	grants loans tax expenditures	bureaucratic administration public enterprises
Detectors	reporting registration	census-taking consultants	polling policing	record-keeping surveys

Figure 22.7 A Taxonomy of Substantive Policy Instruments
Source: Adapted from Hood (1986).

outcomes is less direct. Rather than to affect the delivery of goods and services, their principle intent is to modify or alter the nature of policy processes at work in the implementation process (Howlett, 1996; in't Veld, 1998). A list of these instruments is provided in Figure 22.8.

Why a particular combination of procedural and substantive instruments is used in particular sectors is a key question. In the case of substantive instruments, Linder and Peters argued that the features of the policy instruments themselves are important for selection purposes, because some instruments are more suited for a task at hand than are others. They noted that instrument choice was not simply a technical exercise, however, and that variables such as political culture and the depth of its social cleavages could have an impact on instrument selection. They also noted that the choice of an instrument is circumscribed by the organizational culture of the concerned agencies. The context of the problem situation, its timing, and the scope of actors it includes were also cited as having significant potential impacts on choices (Linder and Peters, 1989).

This analysis suggested that the choice of policy instruments is shaped by the characteristics of the instruments, the nature of the problem at hand, past experiences of governments in dealing with the same or similar problems, the subjective preference of the decision-makers, and the likely reaction to the choice by affected social groups. However, in attempting to explain a consistent preference for the use of particular instrument over a wide range of contexts, the influence of the first three somewhat idiosyncratic variables can be discounted. More significant for such purposes are the preferences of state decision-makers and the nature of the constraints within which they operate (Bressers and O'Toole, 1998). States must have a high level of administrative capacity in

	Governing Resource			
Principal Use	Nodality	Authority	Treasure	Organization
Positive	education exhortation advertising training	agreements treaties advisory-group creation	interest-group funding research and intervenor funding	hearings evaluations institutional- bureaucratic reform
Negative	misleading information propaganda	banning groups and associations	eliminating funding	administrative delay information suppression

Figure 22.8 A Resource-Based Taxonomy of Procedural Policy Instruments

order to use authority, treasure, and organization-based instruments in situations in which they wish to affect significant numbers of policy targets. When a state has few of these resources, it will tend to use such instruments as incentives or propaganda, or to rely on existing voluntary, community- or family based instruments (Howlett and Ramesh, 1995). Similarly, a key feature of procedural instrument choice is a governments' capacity to manipulate policy subsystems. Often used to retain or reacquire the political trust or legitimacy needed for substantive instruments to be effective (Weber, 1958; Beetham, 1991; Stillman, 1974), procedural policy instrument choice is also affected by the size of the policy target and the nature of the constraints under which a state is operating. Whether a government faces sectoral de-legitimation or widespread systemic de-legitimation, especially, is a significant constraint affecting the types of procedural instruments a government will employ (Mueller, 1973; Habermas, 1973, 1975; Mayntz, 1975).

Hence, like substantive instruments, procedural instrument choice is affected by the nature of the constraints under which policy-makers operate and the type of target it is attempting to influence. Putting these two types of instruments and variables together leads to the model of implementation styles found in Figure 22.9.

Governments facing a variety of resource or legitimation problems and dealing with large policy targets use low cost substantive instruments, such as exhortation, and procedural ones, such as government reorganization (or 'institutionalized voluntarism') as a preferred implementation style. Faced with lower constraints and similarly large-sized targets, they tend to use 'direct subsidization' involving treasure-based tools, such as offering subsidies to producers of goods and services and extending similar recognition to interest groups to help direct their activities. In a situation where governments face small targets under situations of high constraint, they tend to use forms of authoritative instruments—including such substantive tools as regulation—and procedural ones, such as the extension of financial aid to interest group formation and consolidation, in an implementation style of 'representative legalism'. Finally, in situations where they face low constraints and the same smaller targets, they use substantive tools such as public enterprises and procedural ones such as enhancing public access to information, in a style of 'public provision with oversight'.

Policy Evaluation Styles

The last stage of the cycle is policy evaluation. For many early observers, policy evaluation was expected to consist of assessing if a public policy is achieving its stated objectives and, if not, what could be done to eliminate impediments to their attainment. Thus David Nachmias (1979) defined policy evaluation as 'the objective, systematic, empirical examination of the effects ongoing policies and public programs have on their targets in terms of the goals they are meant to achieve'. However, while analysts often resorted to concepts such as 'success' or 'failure' to conclude

	Nature of the Policy Target	
Severity of Constraints	Large	Small
High	institutionalized voluntarism (exhortation and information manipulation)	representative legalism (regulation and financial manipulation)
Low	directed subsidization (financial and recognition manipulation)	institutionalized public provision (organization and information manipulation)

Figure 22.9 Basic Implementation Styles

their evaluation, as Ingram and Mann (1980) cautioned:

> the phenomenon of policy failure is neither so simple nor certain as many contemporary critics of policy and politics would have us believe. Success and failure are slippery concepts, often highly subjective and reflective of an individual's goals, perception of need, and perhaps even psychological disposition toward life.

In other words, public policy goals are usually not stated clearly enough to find out if and to what extent they are being achieved, nor are they shared by all key policy actors. Moreover, the possibilities for objective analysis are also limited because of the difficulties involved in the attempt to develop objective standards by which to evaluate government's level of success in dealing with subjective claims and socially constructed problems. Furthermore, the formal, overt goals stated by government typically gloss an array of 'latent objectives' that policy also serves. Thus, for example, while governments may attempt to reduce industrial effluents through raising regulatory standards, they also have an interest in preserving conditions for employment and for economic activity, objectives that can easily conflict with increased regulation (Kerr, 1976).

What is significant in the evaluative process is not so much ultimate success and failure, but, as Lindblom correctly anticipated, that policy actors and the organizations and institutions they represent can *learn* from the formal and informal evaluation of policies in which they are engaged. This can lead them to modify their positions in the direction of greater substantive or procedural policy change, or it can lead them to resist any alteration to the status quo (Majone, 1989). That is, policy evaluations do not necessarily result in policy change. While the concept of evaluation suggests that an implicit 'feedback loop' is an inherent part of the policy cycle, in many cases this loop may not be operationalized (Pierson, 1993). This implies that understanding the conditions under which **policy learning** occurs or does not occur is critical to understanding and modelling evaluative styles.

A significant variable in this regard is the capacity of an organization to absorb new information. As Cohen and Levinthal (1990) argued in the case of the private firm:

> the ability to evaluate and utilize outside knowledge is largely a function of the level of prior related knowledge. At the most elemental level, this prior knowledge includes basic skills or even a shared language but may also include knowledge of the most recent scientific or technological developments in a given field. Thus, prior related knowledge confers an ability to recognize the value of new information, assimilate it, and apply it to commercial ends. These abilities collectively constitute what we call a firm's 'absorptive capacity'.

Of course, this is not the only significant variable, as the organization must also be receptive to new information and capable of its dissemination. Hence, as Cohen and Levinthal also suggested, a second significant variable affecting the potential for administrative learning can be found in the kind of links between administrators and their environments. Figure 22.10 presents a model of evaluative styles based on these two variables.

Only when state administrative capacity is high would one expect any kind of learning to occur. However, if a relatively closed network dominates the subsystem, whereby few links join administrators to their environment, then this learning is likely to be restricted to some form of '**lesson-drawing**', in which policy-makers draw lessons from past uses of policy instruments (Rose, 1991; Bennett and Howlett, 1992). If the links between the network and the community are more open, one would expect other forms of learning, such as '**social learning**' in which ideas and events in the larger policy community penetrate into policy evaluations. When state capacity is low, one would expect little learning to occur. If the policy subsystem in such circumstances is dominated by existing networks, one would expect to find

	Type of Policy Subsystem	
State Administrative Capacity	Open	Closed
High	social learning	lesson-drawing
Low	informal evaluations	formal evaluations

Figure 22.10 Basic Policy Evaluation Styles

formal types of evaluation with little substantive impact on either policy instruments or goals. If the subsystem is more open to members of the policy community, one would expect a range of informal evaluations to occur, but still find little substantive impact on policy outcomes or processes (Howlett and Ramesh, 1995).

Conclusion: Policy Development as Policy Style

As Lasswell noted in the 1950s, envisioning policy development as a staged, sequential, and iterative process is a useful analytical and methodological device. Methodologically, such an approach reduces the complexity of public policy-making by breaking down that complexity into a small number of stages and substages, each of which can be investigated alone or in terms of its relationship to any or all the other stages of the cycle.

Analytically, as this chapter has argued, adopting such an approach is also useful because it helps to make sense out of the different approaches to understanding patterns of policy development first developed by Lindblom, March and Olson, and others. More importantly, it also allows the insight of Richardson and his colleagues to be built upon; that is, it is possible to observe and model fairly long-term patterns in policy development processes as *policy styles*, and to construct a general model of sectoral policy development styles on this basis.

The basic components of an overall sectoral policy style are set out in Figure 22.11.

Although this implies that there are quite a large number of possible policy styles, the discussion above highlights how these will tend to fall into several common types. That is, certain common variables reappear at different stages of the policy cycle and influence the styles found at these stages. The nature of the policy subsystem,

Styles Present at Each Stage of the Process	Elements that Combine to Create a Policy Style			
agenda-setting	outside initiation	inside initiation	consolidation	mobilization
policy formulation	status quo options	marginal/incremental options	contested alternative options	contested alternative options
decision-making	incremental adjustment	satisfycing adjustment	optimizing search	rational search
policy implementation	voluntary improvement	directed subsidization	representative legalism	institutionalized public provision
policy evaluation	social learning	lesson-drawing	formal evaluations	informal evaluations

Figure 22.11 Components of a Policy Style

for example, is such a significant, recurring, factor. Since the nature of a subsystem tends to constant over an extended period of time (Baumgartner and Jones, 1991; Blom-Hansen, 1997; Mortensen, 2007), this helps not only to restrict the number of common policy styles, but also to help explain their persistence. This is also true of administrative capacity, a second variable that reappears in various forms as a determining element of the styles found to exist at particular stages of the policy development process.

Analyzing policy development in terms of policy cycles and policy styles is useful for several reasons. Not only does it help to make sense out of the different models put forward earlier in the history of policy studies, such as the rational, incremental, and garbage-can models, it also helps to advance studies of these models by specifying the conditions under which such styles could occur. That is, the type of development process specified by each model is shown not to be a universal one, but rather can be seen as a specific combination or set of styles found at each stage of the process; occurring only in the specific circumstances underlying each stage.

As the analysis presented here demonstrates, while determining which overall style is present in a specific sector is not an easy task, understanding the nature of the possibilities that exist and the factors that lead to their existence is a necessary first step to understanding the policy development process.

Important Terms and Concepts

agenda-setting
bounded rationality
decision-making
garbage-can model
incremental model
inside initiation
lesson-drawing
mobilization
outside initiation
policy community
policy cycle
policy evaluation
policy formulation
policy implementation
policy learning
policy network
policy process
policy style
policy subsystem
procedural instrument
rational model
satisfycing
social learning
substantive instrument

Study Questions

1. What is the 'policy cycle', according to various observers?
2. How is the policy cycle concept useful in studying public policy?
3. Who are the most notable policy theorists of various stages of the policy cycle?
4. Are there any drawbacks or caveats one must keep in mind when using the 'policy cycle' concept?
5. What are some important models of decision-making?
6. What are some important elements of a 'policy style'?

Useful Websites

Michael Howlett's website:

www.sfu.ca/~howlett

Journal of Comparative Policy Analysis (address and linking contracts for this and other journals may vary in different university and institutional libraries):

www.springerlink.com/content/102926

Policy and Society:

www.elsevier.com/wps/find/journaldescription.cws_home/714836/description#description

Policy Studies Journal:

www3.interscience.wiley.com/journal/118539967/home?CRETRY=1&SRETRY=0

Canadian Journal of Political Science:

http://journals.cambridge.org/action/display Journal?jid=CJP

Canadian Public Administration:

www.ipac.ca/pubs/cpa_journal/

References

Allison, Graham. 1969. 'Conceptual Models and the Cuban Missile Crisis', *American Political Science Review* 63: 689–718.

———. 1971. *Essence of Decision: Explaining the Cuban Missile Crisis*. Boston: Little Brown.

Atkinson, M., and W. Coleman. 1989. *The State, Business, and Industrial Change in Canada*. Toronto: University of Toronto Press.

———, and ———. 1990. 'Strong States and Weak States: Sectoral Policy Networks in Advanced Capitalist Economies', *British Journal of Political Science* 19, 1: 47–67.

Baumgartner, Frank R., and Bryan D. Jones. 1991. 'Agenda Dynamics and Policy Subsystems', *Journal of Politics* 53, 4: 1044–74.

Beetham, David. 1991. *The Legitimation of Power*. London: Macmillan.

Bendor, Jonathan. 1995. 'A Model of Muddling Through', *American Political Science Review* 89, 4: 819–40.

———, and Thomas H. Hammond. 1992. 'Re-Thinking Allison's Models', *American Political Science Review* 86, 2: 301–22.

Bennett, Colin J., and Michael Howlett. 1992. 'The Lessons of Learning: Reconciling Theories of Policy Learning and Policy Change', *Policy Sciences* 25, 3: 275–94.

Berry, William T. 1990. 'The Confusing Case of Budgetary Incrementalism: Too Many Meanings for a Single Concept', *Journal of Politics* 52: 167–96.

Blom-Hansen, Jens. 1997. 'A "New Institutional" Perspective on Policy Networks', *Public Administration* 75: 669–93.

Braybrooke, David, and Charles Lindblom. 1963. *A Strategy of Decision: Policy Evaluation as a Social Process*. New York: Free Press of Glencoe.

Bressers, Hans Th. A., and Laurence J. O'Toole. 1998. 'The Selection of Policy Instruments: A Network-Based Perspective', *Journal of Public Policy* 18, 3: 213–39.

Cahill, Anthony G., and E. Sam Overman. 1990. 'The Evolution of Rationality in Policy Analysis', in S.S. Nagel, ed., *Policy Theory and Policy Evaluation: Concepts, Knowledge, Causes, and Norms*. New York: Greenwood Press, 11–27.

Carley, Michael. 1980. *Rational Techniques in Policy Analysis*. London: Heinemann.

Cobb, Roger W., and Charles D. Elder. 1972. *Participation in American Politics: The Dynamics of Agenda-Building*. Boston: Allyn and Bacon.

———, J.K. Ross, and M.H. Ross. 1976. 'Agenda Building as a Comparative Political Process', *American Political Science Review* 70.

Cohen, Michael, James March, and Johan Olsen. 1979. 'People, Problems, Solutions, and the Ambiguity of Relevance', in James March and Johan Olsen, eds, *Ambiguity and Choice in Organizations*. Bergen: Universitetsforlaget.

Cohen, Wesley M., and Daniel A. Levinthal. 1990. 'Absorptive Capacity: A New Perspective on Learning and Innovation', *Administrative Science Quarterly* 35: 128–52.

Coleman, William D. 1994. 'Policy Convergence in Banking: A Comparative Study', *Political Studies* 42: 274–92.

———, and Grace Skogstad, eds. 1990. *Policy Communities and Public Policy in Canada: A Structural Approach*. Mississauga, Ont.: Copp Clark Pitman.

Cox, Robert H. 1992. 'Can Welfare States Grow in Leaps and Bounds? Non-Incremental Policymaking in the Netherlands', *Governance* 5, 1: 68–87.

Dahl, Robert A., and Charles E. Lindblom. 1953. *Politics, Economics and Welfare: Planning and Politico-Economic Systems Resolved into Basic Social Processes*. New York: Harper and Row.

Dror, Yehezkel. 1964. 'Muddling Through—"Science" or Inertia', *Public Administration Review* 24: 154–7.

Elster, Jon. 1991. 'The Possibility of Rational Politics', in David Held, ed., *Political Theory Today*. Oxford: Polity.

Etzioni, Amitai. 1967. 'Mixed-Scanning: A "Third" Approach to Decision-Making', *Public Administration Review* 27: 385–92.

Forester, John. 1984. 'Bounded Rationality and the Politics of Muddling Through', *Public Administration Review* 44.

———. 1989. *Planning in the Face of Power.* Berkeley: University of California Press.

Freeman, Gary P. 1985. 'National Styles and Policy Sectors: Explaining Structured Variation', *Journal of Public Policy* 5: 467–96.

Freeman, J. Leiper. 1955. *The Political Process: Executive Bureau–Legislative Committee Relations.* New York: Random House.

Gawthrop, Louis. 1971. *Administrative Politics and Social Change.* New York: St Martin's Press.

Gortner, Harold, Julianne Mahler, and Jeanne Bell Nicholson. 1987. *Organization Theory: A Public Perspective.* Chicago: Dorsey Press.

Haas, Peter M. 1992. 'Introduction: Epistemic Communities and International Policy Co-Ordination', *International Organization* 46, 1: 1–36.

Habermas, Jurgen. 1973. 'What Does a Legitimation Crisis Mean Today? Legitimation Problems in Late Capitalism', *Social Research* 40, 4: 643–67.

———. 1975. *Legitimation Crisis.* Boston: Beacon Press.

Hawkins, Keith, and John M. Thomas. 1989. 'Making Policy in Regulatory Bureaucracies', in Hawkins and Thomas, eds, *Making Regulatory Policy.* Pittsburgh: University of Pittsburgh Press, 3–30.

Hayes, Michael T. 1992. *Incrementalism and Public Policy.* New York: Longmans.

Hessing, Melody, and Michael Howlett. 1997. *Canadian Natural Resource and Environmental Policy: Political Economy and Public Policy.* Vancouver: University of British Columbia Press.

Hood, Christopher. 1986. *The Tools of Government.* Chatham, NJ: Chatham House.

Howlett, M. 1996. 'Legitimacy and Governance: Re-Discovering Procedural Policy Instruments', Paper presented to the Annual Meeting of the British Columbia Political Studies Association, Vancouver.

———. 2002a. 'Do Networks Matter? Linking Policy Network Structure to Policy Outcomes: Evidence from Four Canadian Policy Sectors 1990–2000', *Canadian Journal of Political Science* 35, 2: 235–68.

———. 2002b. 'Policy Instruments and Implementation Styles: The Evolution of Instrument Choice in Canadian Environmental Policy', in D.L. VanNijnatten and R. Boardman, eds, *Canadian Environmental Policy: Context and Cases.* Toronto: Oxford University Press, 25–45.

———, and M. Ramesh. 1995. *Studying Public Policy: Policy Cycles and Policy Subsystems.* Toronto: Oxford University Press.

———, and ———. 1998. 'Policy Subsystem Configurations and Policy Change: Operationalizing the Postpositivist Analysis of the Politics of the Policy Process', *Policy Studies Journal* 26, 3: 466–82.

———, and ———. 2003. *Studying Public Policy: Policy Cycles and Policy Subsystems.* Toronto: Oxford University Press.

———, and Jeremy Rayner. 1995. 'Do Ideas Matter? Policy Subsystem Configurations and the Continuing Conflict Over Canadian Forest Policy', *Canadian Public Administration* 38, 3: 382–410.

Ingram, Helen M., and Dean E. Mann. 1980. 'Policy Failure: An Issue Deserving Analysis', in Helen M. Ingram and Dean E. Mann, eds, *Why Policies Succeed or Fail.* Beverly Hills, Calif.: Sage.

in't Veld, Roeland J. 1998. 'The Dynamics of Instruments', in B.G. Peters and F.K.M. Van Nispen, eds, *Public Policy Instruments: Evaluating the Tools of Public Administration.* New York: Edward Elgar, 153–62.

Jennings, Bruce. 1987. 'Interpretation and the Practice of Policy Analysis', in Frank Fischer and John Forester, eds, *Confronting Values in Policy Analysis: The Politics of Criteria.* Newbury Park, Calif.: Sage, 128–52.

Jordan, Grant. 1981. 'Iron Triangles, Woolly Corporatism and Elastic Nets: Images of the Policy Process', *Journal of Public Policy* 1: 95–123.

———. 1990a. 'Policy Community Realism versus "New" Institutionalist Ambiguity', *Political Studies* 38: 470–84.

———. 1990b. 'Sub-Governments, Policy Communities and Networks: Refilling the Old Bottles?', *Journal of Theoretical Politics* 2: 319–38.

———, and Klaus Schubert. 1992. 'A Preliminary Ordering of Policy Network Labels', *European Journal of Political Research* 21: 7–27.

Kagan, Robert A. 1991. 'Adversarial Legalism and American Government', *Journal of Policy Analysis and Management* 10, 3: 369–406.

Kerr, Donna H. 1976. 'The Logic of "Policy" and Successful Policies', *Policy Sciences* 7: 351–63.

Kingdon, John W. 1984. *Agendas, Alternatives and Public Policies.* Boston: Little, Brown and Company.

Knill, Christopher. 1998. 'European Policies: The Impact of National Administrative Traditions', *Journal of Public Policy* 18, 1: 1–28.

Knoke, David. 1993. 'Networks as Political Glue: Explaining Public Policy-Making', in W.J. Wilson, ed., *Sociology and the Public Agenda.* London: Sage, 164–84.

Lasswell, Harold D. 1956. *The Decision Process: Seven Categories of Functional Analysis.* College Park: University of Maryland Press.

———. 1971. *A Pre-View of Policy Sciences.* New York: Elsevier.

Lindblom, Charles. 1951. *Bargaining.* Los Angeles: Rand Corporation.

———.1958. 'Policy Analysis', *American Economic Review* 48, 3: 298–312.

———. 1959. 'The Science of Muddling Through', *Public Administration Review* 19: 79–88.

———. 1979. 'Still Muddling, Not Yet Through', *Public Administration Review* 39, 6: 517–26.

———, and D.K. Cohen. 1979. *Usable Knowledge: Social Science and Social Problem Solving.* New Haven, Conn.: Yale University Press.

Linder, Stephen H., and B. Guy Peters. 1989. 'Instruments of Government: Perceptions and Contexts', *Journal of Public Policy* 9.

———, and ———. 1990. 'Policy Formulation and the Challenge of Conscious Design', *Evaluation and Program Planning* 13: 303–11.

Lustick, Ian. 1980. 'Explaining the Variable Utility of Disjointed Incrementalism: Four Propositions', *American Political Science Review* 74, 2: 342–53.

MacRae Jr, Duncan. 1993. 'Guidelines for Policy Discourse: Consensual versus Adversarial', in Frank Fischer and John Forester, eds, *The Argumentative Turn in Policy Analysis and Planning*. Durham, NC: Duke University Press, 291–318.

McWilliams, William C. 1971. 'On Political Illegitimacy', *Public Policy* 19, 3: 444–54.

Majone, Giandomenico. 1989. *Evidence, Argument, and Persuasion in the Policy Process*. New Haven, Conn.: Yale University Press.

Manzer, Ronald. 1984. 'Policy Rationality and Policy Analysis: The Problem of the Choice of Criteria for Decision-Making', in O.P. Dwivedi, ed., *Public Policy and Administrative Studies*. Guelph: University of Guelph, 27–40.

March, James, and Johan Olsen. 1979. 'Organization Choice Under Ambiguity', in James March and Johan Olsen, eds, *Ambiguity and Choice in Organizations*, 2nd edn. Bergen: Universitetsforlaget.

Marin, Bernd, and Renate Mayntz, eds. 1991. *Policy Networks: Empirical Evidence and Theoretical Considerations*. Boulder Colo.: Westview Press.

May, Peter J. 1991. 'Reconsidering Policy Design: Policies and Publics', *Journal of Public Policy* 11, 2: 187–206.

Mayntz, Renate. 1975. 'Legitimacy and the Directive Capacity of the Political System', in Leon N. Lindberg et al., eds, *Stress and Contradiction in Modern Capitalism*. Lexington, Mass.: Lexington Books, 261–74.

Mortensen, Peter B. 2007. 'Stability and Change in Public Policy: A Longitudinal Study of Comparative Subsystem Dynamics', *Policy Studies Journal* 35, 3: 373–94.

Mucciaroni, Guy. 1992. 'The Garbage Can Model and the Study of Policy Making: A Critique', *Polity* 24, 3: 460–82.

Mueller, Claus. 1973. *The Politics of Communication: A Study in the Political Sociology of Language, Socialization and Legitimation*. New York: Oxford University Press.

Nachmias, David. 1979. *Public Policy Evaluation*. New York: St Martin's Press.

Nice, D.C. 1987. 'Incremental and Nonincremental Policy Responses: The States and the Railroads', *Polity* 20: 145–56.

Peters, B.G., and F.K.M. Van Nispen, eds. 1998. *Public Policy Instruments: Evaluating the Tools of Public Administration*. New York: Edward Elgar.

Pierson, Paul. 1993. 'When Effect Becomes Cause: Policy Feedback and Political Change', *World Politics* 45: 595–628.

Pross, A. Paul. 1992. *Group Politics and Public Policy*. Toronto: Oxford University Press.

Richardson, Jeremy, Gunnel Gustafsson, and Grant Jordan. 1982. 'The Concept of Policy Style', in Jeremy J. Richardson, ed., *Policy Styles in Western Europe*. London: George Allen and Unwin.

Rose, Richard. 1991. 'What is Lesson-Drawing?', *Journal of Public Policy* 11, 1: 3–30.

Sabatier, Paul A. 1987. 'Knowledge, Policy-Oriented Learning, and Policy Change', *Knowledge: Creation, Diffusion, Utilization* 8, 4: 649–92.

———. 1988. 'An Advocacy Coalition Framework of Policy Change and the Role of Policy-Oriented Learning Therein', *Policy Sciences* 21, 2/3: 129–68.

———. 1992. 'Political Science and Public Policy: An Assessment', in W.N. Dunn and R.M. Kelly, eds, *Advances in Policy Studies Since 1950*. New Brunswick, NJ: Transaction Publishers, 27–58.

Salamon, Lester M., ed. 1989. *Beyond Privatization: The Tools of Government Action*. Washington: Urban Institute.

Schulman, Paul R. 1988. 'The Politics of "Ideational Policy"', *Journal of Politics* 50: 263–91.

Simon, Herbert A. 1955. 'A Behavioral Model of Rational Choice', *Quarterly Journal of Economics* 69: 99–118.

———. 1957. *Models of Man, Social and Rational: Mathematical Essays on Rational Human Behavior in a Social Setting*. New York: Wiley.

Smith, Gilbert, and David May. 1980. 'The Artificial Debate between Rationalist and Incrementalist Models of Decision-Making', *Policy and Politics* 8, 2: 147–61.

Smith, Martin J. 1993. *Pressure, Power and Policy: State Autonomy and Policy Networks in Britain and the United States*. Aldershot: Harvester Wheatsheaf.

———. 1994. 'Policy Networks and State Autonomy', in S. Brooks and A.G. Gagnon, eds, *The Political Influence of Ideas: Policy Communities and the Social Sciences*. New York: Praeger.

Stillman, Peter G. 1974. 'The Concept of Legitimacy', in *Polity* 7, 1: 32–56.

Torgerson, Douglas. 1986. 'Between Knowledge and Politics: Three Faces Of Policy Analysis', *Policy Sciences* 19: 33–59.

Tuohy, Carolyn. 1992. *Policy and Politics in Canada: Institutionalized Ambivalence*. Philadelphia: Temple University Press.

Tupper, A., and G.B. Doern. 1981. 'Public Corporations and Public Policy in Canada', in A. Tupper and G.B. Doern, eds, *Public Corporations and Public Policy in Canada*. Montreal: Institute for Research on Public Policy.

Van Waarden, Frans. 1992. 'Dimensions and Types of Policy Networks', *European Journal of Political Research* 21: 29–52.

Vedung, Evert. 1997. 'Policy Instruments: Typologies and Theories', in Marie Louise Bemelmans-Videc, Ray C. Rist, and Evert Vedung, eds, *Carrots, Sticks and Sermons: Policy Instruments and Their Evaluation*. New Brunswick, NJ: Transaction Publishers.

Vogel, David. 1986. *National Styles of Regulation: Environmental Policy in Great Britain and the United States*. Ithaca: Cornell University Press.

Ward, Edward. 1954. 'The Theory of Decision-Making', *Psychological Bulletin*: 380–417.

Weber, Max. 1958. 'Politics as a Vocation', in Hans Gerth and C. Wright Mills, eds, *From Max Weber: Essays in Sociology*. New York: Oxford University Press.

Weiss, Andrew, and Edward Woodhouse. 1992. 'Reframing Incrementalism: A Constructive Response to Critics', *Policy Sciences* 25, 3: 255–73.

Weiss, Carol H. 1977. 'Research for Policy's Sake: The Enlightenment Function of Social Science Research', *Policy Analysis* 3: 531–45.

Woodside, K. 1986. 'Policy Instruments and the Study of Public Policy', *Canadian Journal of Political Science* 19, 4: 775–93.

23 Federalism and Intergovernmental Relations

Richard Simeon

Introduction

Federalism and intergovernmental relations are central to the lives of Canadians and their public servants. In designing, financing, and delivering public services, they can seldom ignore the federal dimensions of their roles. Managing intergovernmental affairs is a major part of any senior policy manager's job. The reasons are clear. The hallmark of Canadian federalism, and indeed, of all other modern federations, is *interdependence*. Responsibilities for most major policy sectors—from health, education, and welfare to transportation, economic development, and the environment—are shared among two and often three orders of government. On the fiscal side, taxation systems are deeply intertwined, and intergovernmental financial transfers pervade the system. All of this means that policy responsibilities inevitably spill across jurisdictional lines and that, in field after field, successful policy-making and implementation require coordination among the levels, if duplication, contradiction, and frustration are to be avoided and if the aspirations of Canadians are to be met. Federalism, along with parliamentary government and the Charter of Rights and Freedoms, constitutes one of the principal 'pillars' of the institutional framework within which Canadian governance and policy-making takes place. Many labels have been applied to describe the Canadian model of federalism: competitive, co-operative, collaborative, water-tight compartments, and many others, of which 'open federalism' as enunciated by Prime Minister Stephen Harper is only the most recent. Each such term captures an important element of the Canadian reality; none fully describes the complexity of an intricate system constantly in flux. Indeed federalism has been described not as a steady state, but rather as a continuing process as the system responds to changing economic, social, and political circumstances.

The purpose of this chapter is to describe the key elements of the Canadian federal design and the central dynamics of the relationships between federal and provincial governments that arise from it. These are the two orders of government set out in the Constitution. There is, of course, a third level of government in Canada's multi-level system—local or municipal government. Since municipal governments are the constitutional children of the provinces, they have usually been conspicuously absent from the study of federalism in Canada; and this chapter will continue that admittedly narrow tradition. In addition, Canada now has three territorial governments, Yukon, Northwest Territories, and Nunavut. They have gradually taken on more and more province-like powers. Their leaders are described as First Ministers, and are now routinely involved in most intergovernmental forums.[1] Yet another order of government—Aboriginal governments—may well emerge in the near future. And at the same time, international intergovernmental bodies and treaties such as the North American Free Trade Agreement (NAFTA) and the World Trade Organization (WTO), as well as many others, impinge ever more directly on the Canadian policy process. Thus, multi-level governance in Canada extends well beyond the federal–provincial relationship that is the focus of this chapter.

Federalism is also central to any analysis of public administration in Canada because the working out of relationships among the orders of government takes place almost entirely in the arena of '**executive federalism**'—in close relationships among first ministers, ministers, and senior bureaucrats (Smiley, 1974). Political parties and legislatures play only a minor role. This is because Canada combines federalism with Westminster-style cabinet government, which concentrates power in the hands of the executive (White, 2005).

Two perspectives guide much of this chapter. The first is explanatory. What accounts for the Canadian pattern of federalism and intergovernmental relations? What explains varying levels of conflict and competition, harmony and disharmony, across different time periods and different policy areas? A second perspective is more normative. It asks how we can judge, assess, and evaluate institutions and processes, and how we might think about reform.

Many criteria can be applied to the assessment of governing institutions. In the Canadian context, three are especially important with respect to federalism and intergovernmental relations. First, Canada is a country deeply divided along linguistic and regional lines. Do its federal institutions work towards bridging, ameliorating, and managing these divisions, or do they exacerbate and intensify them? Second, Canada is a country deeply committed to democratic values. Does our federalism enhance or undermine the quality of our democracy? Third, Canada, like all other advanced countries, faces a complex and difficult policy agenda. Does federalism contribute to the effective development, administration, and delivery of public policy, or does it frustrate these goals?

The literature of federalism, and indeed our own experience, suggests there are no easy answers. Federalism is Janus-faced. Yes, it facilitates the management of linguistic and regional conflict, by ensuring that linguistic and regional minorities have sufficient autonomy to defend their vital interests without fear of being overpowered by national majorities. But no, federalism institutionalizes and entrenches in its political structures the very conflicts it is designed to manage. At the extreme it provides the institutional base from which a plausible secessionist movement can emerge.

Yes, it facilitates democracy by ensuring that regional majorities, acting through their provincial governments, are able to enact policies and programs that meet their local needs and preferences, and because it provides multiple avenues—federal, provincial, and local—for political participation. Federalism embraces the idea of 'shared rule' (what the whole community wishes to accomplish together) and 'self rule' (what local or provincial communities can do better on their own). But also no, because managing interdependence in the federal system requires closed-door bargaining between governmental elites, leading to what the Europeans call the '**democratic deficit**'.

Yes, federalism facilitates the development and implementation of effective policy in many ways: by allowing policy solutions to be tailored to local needs, by encouraging experiment and innovation, by encouraging competition among governments to supply preferred options, and, at least in principle, by assigning responsibilities to the level of government most appropriate, whether national or provincial. But no: federalism frustrates effective policy-making by requiring extensive co-operation among governments before policy can be effectively developed and implemented, by placing the political and bureaucratic interests of rival governments at the heart of the policy process and freezing out relevant interest groups, and by building in a tendency towards 'lowest common denominator' policy solutions (Simeon, 2006). Federalism is thus a contested set of concepts about which few easy generalizations can be made (Treisman, 2007).

From a more policy-focused perspective, Herman Bakvis and Grace Skogstad bring a slightly different set of criteria to bear. To what extent, they ask, do Canadian federalism and the practice of intergovernmental relations contribute to the *performance* of the system in developing public policy, to the *effectiveness* of governments in responding to public needs, and to the *legitimacy* of governing institutions in the minds of citizens? Again, the results are mixed (Bakvis and Skogstad, 2008). The larger question, then, is not whether or not to have federalism, since it is deeply embedded in our institutions and in our federal society. It is rather to think of ways to improve its capacities to serve Canadians.

The Development of Canadian Federalism

Federalism has been described as not so much a steady state, but as a process (Simeon and Robinson, 1990). The dynamics of federal–provincial relations—the relative balance between centralization and decentralization, the levels of conflict among governments, and the like—vary over time in response to changing citizen attitudes and changing policy agendas. These attitudes and agendas are themselves products of broader social, demographic, and economic changes. This is certainly true in the Canadian case. Moreover, the legacies of the past cast a very long shadow over the present. Thus we begin with a narrative.

The adoption of a federal system in the Constitution Act, 1867 was the result of several important forces. On the one hand, the British North American colonies sought a closer union to strengthen them against the powerful neighbour to the south, to compensate for declining economic support from Britain, and, eventually, to build a nation spanning the continent. On the other hand, Confederation was a response to the political deadlock that had developed between French and English, Canada East and Canada West, in the United Province of Canada, established in 1840. Each community would now have an independent political space in which to pursue its own development. Thus, like other federations, Canadian federalism was both a 'coming together' and a 'coming part', and this dynamic—centrifugal and centripetal—has persisted throughout our history.

Colonial Federalism

The federal model created in 1867 was, on its face, highly centralized. It appeared to set the federal government in much the same relationship to the provinces that the Canadian colonies had previously had to the British colonial regime. Thus, the major public responsibilities of the time—especially the powers necessary to nation-building—were concentrated in federal hands. So were the most important revenue sources. Moreover, the federal government was given a powerful set of levers with which to control the provinces—the power to appoint the provincial lieutenants-governor, with their ability to 'reserve' provincial legislation for the consideration of the Governor-General, the 'declaratory power' that allowed Ottawa to take control of any 'undertaking' in the provinces, and, most important, the 'disallowance' power that permitted Ottawa to kill any provincial legislation of which it disapproved. This was the **colonial model of federalism**. The chief architect of Confederation, Sir John A. Macdonald, was confident that provinces would come to play a role little more important than that of municipalities. In the early decades of Confederation, Ottawa freely used these powers, so much so that one leading student of federalism concluded that Canada could be considered only 'quasi-federal' (Wheare, 1964).

Classical Federalism

This federal dominance was not to last. Gradually Canada moved towards a more **classical model of federalism**, in which the powers of federal and provincial governments were more evenly balanced, and in which provinces were to be fully autonomous within their designated areas of jurisdiction. Eventually, indeed, the broad discretionary powers of reservation, declaration, and disallowance were to fall into disuse, to become constitutional 'dead letters'. They remain in the constitutional text, but their use today is almost unthinkable. The reasons for this development were complex. A long, late nineteenth-century recession weakened Ottawa's claim to political support. Provincial governments became more assertive. Ontario Premier Oliver Mowat and Quebec's Premier Honoré Mercier developed the 'compact theory' of Confederation, which saw the federal government as the creature of the provinces. In 1887 they convened the first interprovincial conference, which mounted a broad attack on federal powers. The courts (in the Canadian case, the Judicial Committee of the Privy Council in Great Britain) also played a critical role. Over time the JCPC whittled away at broad federal powers established in the Constitution Act, 1867, such as the general power to enact laws for the 'peace, order and good government of Canada' (section 91), the trade and commerce power, and the power to sign international treaties. At the same time, provincial powers—such as the power over 'property and civil rights'—were interpreted expansively. Thus the pendulum swung sharply towards a more decentralized model.

Co-Operative Federalism

That model, however, failed to meet the enormous policy challenges posed by the Great Depression of the 1930s. Provinces were simply unable to alleviate poverty and unemployment on their own, and several, especially on the hard-hit Prairies, came close to bankruptcy. Ad hoc federal financial assistance helped relieve the worst of the crisis, but a more substantial attempt to respond, in the 'Bennett New Deal' of 1935, was rejected in 1937 by the JCPC as beyond the jurisdiction of the federal government. Many commentators suggested that the 'dead hand' of the federal Constitution, as interpreted by the courts, was a fundamental block to the development of an effective state. Indeed, Harold Laski, a leading British scholar, argued that federalism as a system of government, in the modern world of industrialism and capitalism, was simply obsolete. Towards the end of this period, a Royal Commission, the Rowell-Sirois Commission, recommended sweeping reforms to the distribution of powers and to federal–provincial fiscal arrangements in order to respond to the changing political economy and new views about the role of the state. Thus the pendulum was swinging back to federal power.

This was strongly reinforced by the emergency federal powers adopted to allow Canada to conduct its role in World War II. Federalism, in a sense, was suspended for the duration. Provinces surrendered their taxation powers to Ottawa, which made compensating grants to them. A constitutional amendment early in the war gave Ottawa the responsibility for developing a national unemployment insurance system. Following World War II, Canada, like most other Western countries, committed itself to a broad set of new roles and responsibilities for government. Government would now be the instrument for managing the economy, maintaining high levels of employment, and developing a welfare state to cushion the population against the vicissitudes of unemployment, poor health, and poverty.

But how was this 'Keynesian welfare state' to be enacted within the federal system, especially when jurisdiction for most of its major elements, such as health care, lay with the provinces? Many believed that only the central government had the financial resources and political clout to bring this about. Some scholars, echoing Sir John A. Macdonald in an earlier period, predicted a fundamental decline in provincial power. The central axis of politics would shift from federalism and regionalism to the 'creative politics' of class (Porter, 1965). One opinion survey shortly after the war found that a majority of respondents would support the abolition of the provinces.

Reflecting these ideas, Ottawa, in what came to be known as the 'Green Book proposals', suggested major reform to the federal system: federal assumption of responsibility for old age pensions and assistance to the unemployed, along with the sharing of costs in health care. Provincial income taxation would be assumed by Ottawa in return for federal subsidies to the provinces.

Prime Minister Mackenzie King asserted that it was not Ottawa's intention to weaken or subordinate the provinces, or to centralize all powers in Ottawa. 'Our aim is to place the Dominion and every province in a position to discharge effectively and independently its appropriate functions' (quoted in Simeon and Robinson, 1990: 111).

Nevertheless, provinces, especially the larger and richer ones led by Ontario and Quebec, which had profound philosophical objections both to the modern idea of the welfare state and to the perceived threat to their autonomy, strongly resisted the federal proposals. The grand scheme was not implemented. But over the next two decades the major building blocks of the welfare state—various health programs culminating in the medicare program in 1968; aid to those in poverty culminating in the Canada Assistance Plan of 1966; security for the elderly with the old age pension system and later the Canada and Quebec Pension Plans; and federal assistance to post-secondary education—were put in place.

Only two important policy responsibilities were constitutionally shifted to Ottawa—Unemployment Insurance and old age pensions. The other elements, such as medicare, welfare, and support for the disabled, were achieved by the provinces and Ottawa acting together. The key policy instrument in the post-war period was the shared-cost or conditional grant program, by which Ottawa provided support in the form of 'fifty-cent dollars' for the provinces to establish and deliver their own programs, subject to federal norms, standards, and conditions. Such programs proliferated in the fifties and sixties, not only in social policy, but also in such endeavours as the Trans-Canada Highway and bilingual education (Smiley, 1963).

This was the era of '**co-operative federalism**'. With abundant fiscal, bureaucratic, and political resources, Ottawa took the lead, though, as with Saskatchewan's pioneering of medicare, provinces could be important innovators as well. Provinces generally, however, reacted to federal proposals. This period of relative intergovernmental harmony was made possible by the fact that the larger project—building the welfare state—was accepted by all governments. With the important exception of Quebec, it did not divide the country along regional lines. Moreover, during this period, close working relationships developed between federal and provincial program officials working in particular policy areas and sharing similar programmatic norms and values—often they were able to combine against their respective treasuries (see, for example, Dyck, 1976).

Competitive Federalism

This dynamic persisted until the 1960s. But in the next two decades a series of developments began to exert strong pressures for decentralization and for a much more adversarial relationship between federal and provincial governments.

The first significant development was the Quiet Revolution in Quebec following the election of the provincial Liberals under Jean Lesage in 1960. Previous Quebec governments had fought a rearguard battle against the expansion of the welfare state (Royal Commission of Inquiry on Constitutional Problems, 1954). Now Quebec embraced a wide-ranging program of reform in education, health, economic development, and other areas. It modernized and expanded its bureaucracy to undertake these new tasks. Quebec thus embraced the expansionist welfare state, but it was determined to do it on its own terms—to be 'maîtres chez nous' (McRoberts, 1988). To do this, Quebec argued, it needed a much greater share of tax revenues, and it needed to free itself of federal controls and conditions. At the same time, Quebec nationalism was growing, and the Parti Québécois, seeking sovereignty, with an association (later a 'partnership') with Canada, was formed. Ottawa found itself responding to calls for increased provincial tax room, for Quebec to have the right to 'opt out' of shared-cost programs in order for it to follow its own priorities, and for Quebec to establish its own Quebec Pension Plan alongside the CPP for the rest of the country. At first, the federal government acceded to many of these demands—for example, in the Established Programs (Interim Arrangements) Act (1965), which permitted Quebec to opt out of a wide range of grant programs in return for 'compensation' in the form of additional tax room. But after 1968, when Prime Minister Pierre Elliott Trudeau came to power,

Ottawa increasingly argued that further concessions would only fuel sovereignist impulses and put Quebec on a slippery slope to eventual secession. Hence, the federal mantra became that all provinces should be treated equally.

This position escalated the conflict another step: now Quebec argued that only fundamental constitutional change recognizing its distinct role as the primary government of Quebecers would suffice; ad hoc administrative and political accommodations were no longer sufficient. Other provinces also increasingly resisted a paternalistic Ottawa. Partially fuelled by federal grants, but also by the massive growth of policy areas like education within provincial jurisdiction, provincial governments had grown larger, more competent, and more self-confident. They were exercising more fiscal autonomy. They were less and less willing to defer to federal leadership or to allow federal conditional grants to shape their priorities. Their share of total government spending and revenues, and of public employment, was steadily increasing relative to Ottawa. Moreover, at both levels of government, new ideas about public management were leading to the concentration of power in central agencies and to an increasing focus on placing the varied activities of many ministries into an overall strategic plan (see Dupré, 1985).

Third, in the 1970s, another issue arose that was to prove almost as divisive as the debate about Quebec, but this time in the West. Unlike the issues surrounding the welfare state, which divided Canadians by income and class, the energy crisis divided them starkly by region. As oil prices escalated, Alberta and Saskatchewan argued strenuously that oil prices should move to world levels, that they should control the industry, and that they should gain the lion's share of the associated public revenues. Ontario and other consuming provinces wanted Ottawa to regulate the domestic price of oil and to capture a large share of the rents so that they could be shared across the country. 'Petro-dollars', argued Ontario, were rewriting the Canadian Constitution. The battles were intense, culminating in the draconian federal National Energy Program of 1980 (Doern and Tomlin, 1985).

Thus Canada entered a new phase of intensely '**competitive federalism**'. The agenda now focused on large, fundamental issues concerning the very nature of the Canadian polity. Provinces increasingly sought the autonomy to pursue their own economic and social development—'province-building'. Ottawa resisted, asserting its responsibility for 'nation-building'. And Quebec, after the election of the PQ in 1976 and its first referendum on sovereignty in 1980, was increasingly preoccupied with 'Quebec nation-building'. These were competing visions, each advanced by strong governments, which were also deeply concerned with maintaining their own turf and political visibility.

In this atmosphere, the trust relationships built in the earlier period began to break down. More intergovernmental conflicts found their way to the Supreme Court. Governments developed ministries or agencies of intergovernmental relations—such as the Federal–Provincial Relations Office in Ottawa and the Ministry of Federal and Intergovernmental Affairs in Alberta—to monitor the actions of line ministries and develop overall strategies in intergovernmental affairs.

In this period, as well, the frequency of intergovernmental conferences—first ministers, ministers, and officials—was rapidly increasing. Many more now became open to the press and public. But they appeared to function, at least at the ministerial level, less as arenas for co-operation and coordination and more as arenas of conflict and discord. As conflicts escalated, the Constitution itself came to dominate the intergovernmental agenda, pushing aside more mundane issues of intergovernmental coordination on public policy. Between 1968 and 1992 Canada undertook five failed rounds of what Peter Russell calls 'mega-constitutional' discussion (Russell, 2004). The primary arena for these discussions was the executive-centred federal–provincial conference.

Constitutional Federalism

The first round, between 1968 and 1971, was primarily an attempt to come to terms with the new Quebec. It failed when the Victoria Charter was rejected by Quebec because it did not go far enough to recognize its pre-eminence in social policy. In the late 1970s a series of federal proposals in response to the election of the PQ made little progress. Much more consequential was the round of discussions following the Quebec referendum of 1980. Federalists had argued that a 'No' to sovereignty would be a 'Yes' to a reformed federalism. Intensive discussions through the summer of 1980 culminated in a First Ministers Conference in September, where the competing visions of Canada were presented more starkly than ever before. Following its failure the federal government sought to break the log-jam by acting unilaterally, proposing patriation of the Constitution and a new amending formula.[2] Most important, Ottawa proposed a fundamental new addition to Canada's constitutional order, the Charter of Rights and Freedoms. Eight provinces combined to fight this federal unilateralism, thus forcing Ottawa to refer the question of the constitutionality of its action to the Supreme Court of Canada. The Court decided that while Ottawa had a technical right to request an amendment without provincial support, a constitutional convention had been established saying that no constitutional amendment was valid without substantial provincial consent (Russell, 1983). This forced the matter back into the intergovernmental bargaining arena, and in November 1991 Ottawa and nine provinces agreed on a set of changes including patriation, a new amending formula, and the Charter. Quebec, seeing the result as a diminution of Quebec's powers rather than the increased recognition it had sought, refused to sign, and later lost a court battle in which it argued that the convention concerning provincial support also required Quebec's consent to any major amendment.

In 1987, a new federal government, led by Brian Mulroney, enjoying a broad national coalition of support, tried to close the glaring gap of Quebec's omission from the Canadian constitutional family by engineering the Meech Lake Accord. The Accord went a long way towards responding to Quebec's image of its role in Confederation, providing recognition of Quebec as a 'distinct society' within Canada, and acknowledging the special role of the Quebec government to promote and protect that society, limits on the federal spending power, and other elements. The Accord was signed by all 11 governments and initially supported by virtually all Canadian elites. Under the recently adopted amending formula governments had three years to ensure ratification of the Accord in their respective legislatures. But in the meantime, a massive uprising of popular sentiment in English-speaking Canada turned opinion strongly against the Accord (suggesting it would undermine the Charter and threaten progressive social policies) and after the failure of a desperate, last-minute conference designed to rescue it in 1990, two provinces failed to ratify it and the Accord died (Romanow et al., 1984).

There were two fundamental consequences. First was a dramatic upsurge in support for independence in Quebec: to the exclusion of 1981 was now added the 'rejection' of 1990. This led many Quebecers to the view that recognition could only come about if English Canada had a 'knife to its throat', the imminent threat of secession. It also paved the way for the re-election of the PQ, and hence for the sovereignty referendum of 1995.

Second, the Meech Lake experience suggested a transformation of the public environment in which intergovernmental relations took place. In large part this was inspired by the development of the Charter in the previous round. The Charter had deeply engaged most Canadians, leading them to think of themselves as bearers of rights. It had strongly encouraged the realization that the Constitution was not just about the abstract relations among governments, but, rather, was fundamentally about the relations between governments and citizens. The Constitution belonged to them, not to 11 'men in suits' negotiating deals behind closed doors. Thus the legitimacy of executive federalism was profoundly challenged.

There was to be one more attempt at constitutional renewal. This time, the mistakes of Meech would be avoided. There would be far more public consultation—in two parliamentary committees and in a round of federally sponsored national conferences. The agenda would be broadened to include not only Quebec's concerns, but also those of the western provinces, women, Aboriginal peoples, and others. And there would be more voices at the intergovernmental table; now it would include representatives of the Aboriginal peoples and of the northern territories. Once again, an agreement was reached, in the Charlottetown Accord. But this time, it was decided that it should be submitted to the popular will in a national referendum. It was roundly defeated in eight of the 10 provinces, including Quebec (McRoberts and Monahan, 1993).

Thus '**constitutional federalism**' had failed. There was simply no consensus on fundamental features of the Canadian polity. Competing ideas of equality—was Canada a partnership of two nations, 10 provinces, 30 million rights-bearing individuals, Aboriginal and non-Aboriginal peoples, or a multicultural nation?—could not be reconciled. Canada was and is, of course, all those things, but it proved impossible to find the words that could put it all into broadly acceptable constitutional language (Cairns, 1991; Taylor, 1991).

Throughout this period, the day-to-day management of the intergovernmental relationship continued, but the preoccupation with the Constitution had far-reaching effects. Issues that might once have been treated in substantive terms through informal discussion tended to escalate quickly to the constitutional level, making them more symbolic and conflictual. Virtually every issue that arose in the intergovernmental arena was filtered through the lenses of governments' strategic visions and parsed to examine their implications for Quebec nationalism and national unity.

Collaborative Federalism

The failures of Meech Lake and Charlottetown produced an enormous constitutional fatigue. It no longer seemed possible to resolve Canada's tensions by means of constitutional renewal. This led to a widespread view that it was time to focus on non-constitutional mechanisms for reform and renewal and to concentrate on demonstrating the 'workability' of the federal system with its existing institutions (Lazar, 1998).

This is one impetus to the most recent iteration of the intergovernmental relationship, which might be labelled '**collaborative federalism**' (Cameron and Simeon, 2000). Unlike the post-war 'co-operative federalism' led by Ottawa, this image sees intergovernmental relations as a partnership between equals. Unlike the competitive model, it focuses on the search for collective solutions to the challenges posed by interdependent, overlapping responsibilities and the contemporary policy agenda.

Several other forces fuelled the movement towards a more collaborative model. First, globalization and North American economic integration were changing the context within which intergovernmental relations in Canada functioned. The impact of global forces now reached deep into the lives of provinces and municipalities, while intergovernmental divisions within Canada extended beyond our own borders. Hence the need for Ottawa and the provinces to get their act together. Globalization, others suggested, was 'hollowing out' national governments everywhere, with power flowing outward to international institutions and transnational corporations and downward towards regions and localities. Some of what had been the most important policy instruments deployed by Ottawa were now significantly constrained by NAFTA and the WTO. Finally, North American integration was fundamentally reorienting the Canadian economy, from the east–west model embodied in Sir John A's 'National Policy' to a north–south model, in which economic linkages within Canada would substantially decline. This in turn would challenge the commitment to interregional equalization and the very logic of a 'national' economic strategy (Courchene, 1991).

Such considerations underpinned negotiation of the first major accomplishment of the collaborative model—the **Agreement on Internal Trade (AIT)** (1995). Having failed to find ways to reduce internal trade barriers and secure the economic union in the constitutional forum, governments negotiated the AIT as an informal code of conduct, including rules concerning mobility, procurement, and other matters, along with a dispute settlement mechanism (Trebilcock and Schwanen, 1995; Schwartz, 1996).

Of more immediate importance was the preoccupation with debts and deficits that came to dominate thinking by all governments in the 1990s. One effect was a kind of competitive downloading, as governments sought to transfer the political and economic costs of deficit-cutting, from Ottawa to the provinces, from the provinces to municipalities, school boards, and other institutions funded by government, and ultimately to the citizen. Intergovernmental competition now shifted from the competition for credit and approval of an expansionary phase to competition to avoid blame in a period of contraction. Thus, starting with the 1995 federal budget, Ottawa radically reduced its transfers to the provinces, rolling transfers with respect to health, welfare, and post-secondary education into the Canada Health and Social Transfer (CHST) with fewer dollars and, to some degree, fewer federal controls, except for those concerning medicare in the Canada Health Act (see Phillips, 1996; Boychuck, 1996). This, in turn, forced radical economies onto provincial budgets, which were also grappling with reining in their own deficits.

The declining federal fiscal presence in the social policy field raised a number of difficult issues. Most immediately, if Ottawa was no longer paying the provincial piper, what right did it have to continue to call the tune? Provinces, therefore, were increasingly impatient with federal restrictions on their ability to experiment with cost-cutting and restructuring in the health-care field, for example. More generally, if Ottawa no longer had the capacity to define, finance, and enforce 'national standards', and thereby to ensure consistency across the Canadian 'social union', then who was able to do it? Thomas Courchene and others came to argue that provinces, acting together, provided the only alternative (Courchene, 1997). In 1995, provincial premiers, meeting at their Annual Premiers Conference, the APC, mandated their ministers responsible for social policy to work on the question. The ministerial council worked through several drafts before engaging with the federal government in February 1999. The result was the **Social Union Framework Agreement** (SUFA), the second major achievement of collaborative federalism.

SUFA was designed to provide the template for intergovernmental relations in the social policy field. Its rationale could easily be applied to other policy areas. The logic underlying SUFA was that governance in Canada is a partnership among equals. It accepted the federal role in areas of provincial jurisdiction by endorsing the validity of the federal spending power. But it subjected this power to some constraints: existing programs would not be changed without due notice and new programs would not be proposed without securing the prior consent of a majority of the provinces. Governments collectively committed themselves to ensuring an 'adequate' level of social support for Canadians and to ensuring that provincial programs would not impede citizens' mobility across the country. A 'dispute settlement' process was proposed, though it has not yet been developed or put into practice.

Two other elements were important. First, the Agreement emphasized many of the values associated with the New Public Management approach, with its emphasis on setting performance standards, monitoring best efforts, and reducing intergovernmental administrative barriers to seamless delivery of services to Canadians. Second, the Agreement—though it was negotiated in the closed intergovernmental arena—recognized the need to increase transparency and accountability in intergovernmental relations. This collaborative model of intergovernmental relations, which was played out in other policy areas such as labour-force training and environmental policy, recognizes some important features of Canadian federalism. These include the sense that the pervasive interdependence of governments faced with common policy problems means that neither level, on its own, can fully address them; that the governments of the federation are political equals, such that neither level is strong enough unilaterally to define the agenda and set the rules; that there should be greater efficiency in the delivery of public services; and that citizens demand more openness and access, as well as a more seamless delivery of public services.

Yet its future remains very much in question. The agreement was largely a provincial initiative, developed in the face of massive cuts in federal transfers. Ottawa was a reluctant participant from the beginning, and when it did enter the discussions, in the final moment, it pressed successfully for a fulsome recognition of the federal spending power. By the time the final agreement was reached, the federal government had overcome its deficit and foresaw growing surpluses. It was anxious to use these to develop new policy initiatives that could strengthen its links to individual citizens and increase its visibility. It had little interest in constraining its own freedom of action through the rules of the social union.

Provinces were more committed to the document, but their interests differed as well. As in the past, larger wealthier provinces like Ontario and Alberta were interested primarily in enhancing their own freedom to act and in limiting the ability of the federal government to impose conditions. Thus, despite the commitments in the SUFA, there remained considerable hostility and distrust, as both levels were to continue to compete for visibility and public support, to enhance their public standing, and to win political credit and avoid blame. Some of the smaller provinces, more fiscally dependent on Ottawa, were less interested in developing a model that would constrain Ottawa than they were in ensuring that Ottawa would continue to have the ability to generate programs that would benefit them.

Quebec, which had participated throughout the interprovincial development of SUFA, did not sign the final agreement because it failed to adopt the right of provinces to opt out of new federal programs. For Quebec, national standards arrived at by intergovernmental agreement were no more acceptable than those enunciated by the federal government alone. Thus, the depth of the often-stated governmental commitments to the values of consensus, co-operation, and collaboration embodied in the agreement is uncertain.

So is public support. For some active in social policy, the Agreement offers the possibility for an intergovernmental relationship more closely linked to interest groups and policy networks in the private sector; for others the Agreement itself was yet another example of 'closed-door' federalism, and the renewed emphasis on consensus among governments was likely in the future to sacrifice many of their policy concerns (see Kennett, 1997).

Design and Practice: The Institutions of Canadian Federalism

The dynamics of federalism and intergovernmental relations are shaped both by the specific design of federal institutions and by the place of federalism in the larger Canadian political system. As we have noted, Canada combines federalism with a parliamentary system, characterized by the dominance of the cabinet and the executive, and, increasingly, by the concentration of power in the hands of first ministers (Savoie, 1999). Unlike the US, where the separation of powers and weak party discipline in Congress make the legislature an important arena for representing and balancing local and national interests, legislators do not play an important role in Canada. 'Executive federalism' is a natural extension of cabinet government. In most federal systems, the second chamber in the central parliament is designed to bring provincial interests to bear on national policy-making, and thus to integrate national and provincial politics. But, because it is appointed by the Prime Minister, the Canadian Senate is unable to play this role (Smiley and Watts, 1985).

Party systems also play an important role in integrating national and provincial politics and policy in federal systems. This does not occur in Canada. Often, different parties are in power at national and provincial levels, and even when they share the same name, provincial and national parties are institutionally distinct. The national party system is also highly regionalized. The recent experience has been that only rarely has the national governing party been able to build coalitions of support across all regions. Influenced by the electoral system, which rewards regionally concentrated parties and penalizes those whose support is spread across the country, Canada's party system is increasingly fragmented, making minority federal governments more and more common. The resulting image is of a Canada made up of two sets of political institutions, federal and provincial, that are politically and institutionally distinct. Again unlike the US, there is remarkably little mobility of politicians or senior bureaucrats between the two levels. Given the weakness of these other potentially integrative institutions, Canadian governments interact with each other rather like individual countries in the international arena—by 'federal–provincial diplomacy' (Simeon, 1971, 2006). Executive federalism is not simply about achieving coordination of policy; it is also about achieving much broader political accommodations between national and regional interests and between Quebec and the rest of Canada, which other institutions are unable to do. This pattern of what might be called 'divided federalism' (Simeon, 1998) continues when we turn to the federal design itself.

The Division of Powers

The logic of the Canadian federal design set out in sections 91 and 92 of the Constitution Act, 1867 is, as interpreted by the courts, one of 'watertight compartments', with each order of government assigned responsibility for legislating and implementing policy in designated policy areas. Only two responsibilities—agriculture and immigration—were designated as concurrent areas of jurisdiction in 1867; pensions were added later (Simeon and Papillon, 2006).

At the same time, the division of powers provides both levels with a broad set of policy instruments that permit them wide discretion to intervene in emerging policy areas. These include few limits on the powers to tax or to use the spending power; the broad federal power (though narrowed by the courts) to make laws for the 'peace, order and good government of Canada' and to regulate trade and commerce; and, at the provincial level, the open-ended powers to regulate 'property and civil rights' and all matters of a local nature.

The contemporary reality, of course, is one of considerable de facto concurrency. Many issues, such as the environment or communications policy, were not contemplated in 1867; others, such as social policy, have attained much greater significance. In these areas, constitutional jurisdiction has been unclear, and governments have been able to use a wide variety of heads of power to intervene, creating the potential for competition and for overlapping, duplication, and contradiction. Numerous attempts to clarify roles and responsibilities—'disentanglement'—have met with only limited success. Indeed, the conventional wisdom has been that 'overlap is essentially an "evil" in the federal context because . . . its presence can lead to conflicting objectives and confused accountabilities, divide the overall resource efforts of governments so that full economies of scale cannot be achieved, and increase coordination costs across governments.' An alternative view, however, is that too much emphasis on clarity and efficiency obscures the value of redundancy—overlap and duplication—in avoiding error (Lindquist, 1999: 38). Evert Lindquist concludes that 'overlap may not be as dysfunctional as the conventional wisdom suggests, and may contribute in positive ways to meeting the needs of citizens and communities' (ibid., 64).

Fiscal Arrangements

The divided model of federalism in Canada continues into fiscal arrangements, the rules governing revenues and spending in the federal system. How do we achieve 'vertical balance', ensuring that each order of government has revenues appropriate to its constitutional responsibilities? How to achieve 'horizontal balance', ensuring that all provinces, rich and poor, have, as s. 36 of the Constitution puts it, the ability to provide comparable levels of public services at comparable levels of taxation? Both dimensions have become increasingly contentious in the recent years of financial turmoil.

Under the Constitution, both orders of governments have wide autonomy in the raising of revenues, though the provinces are barred from indirect taxation. Each is free to borrow on domestic and international markets.

Since the 'tax rental' agreements that centralized powers over income taxation in federal hands in the post-war period, the fiscal system has progressively decentralized. The provincial–local share of revenues and spending has grown relative to the central government. In a series of negotiated five-year plans, tax rentals became 'tax-sharing' and, more recently, 'tax collection agreements'. Provinces are free to set their own levels of taxation, subject to the federal definition of the tax base. Provinces have gained greater discretion to vary their own tax systems, using income tax credits and other devices, with Ottawa continuing to act as the collection agent. Recently, several provinces, including Ontario and Alberta, have shifted their income tax systems from a percentage of the federal tax (which means that changes in federal tax rates have large consequences for provincial tax revenues) to a 'tax on base', which gives provinces more fiscal independence and further disengages federal and provincial tax regimes (Courchene, 1999). Overall, in financial terms, Canada is one of the world's most decentralized federations (Watts, 2008: ch. 6).

Another important dimension of fiscal federalism is the role of intergovernmental fiscal transfers, generally from the central to the provincial governments. Such grants may be conditional (with various strings or conditions attached), or unconditional. They have played an important role in adapting federalism to changing policy concerns. In particular the federal 'spending power' allows it to transfer funds to provinces (or individuals) even in areas of provincial jurisdiction, such as health. The spending power has always been deeply controversial in Quebec, where it is seen as an instrument for federal invasion of provincial jurisdiction. It has also been controversial in the rest of Canada. In the 2007 Throne Speech, newly elected Prime Minister Stephen Harper promised to introduce legislation to limit the introduction of new spending in areas of provincial jurisdiction, and to allow provinces to 'opt out' with 'reasonable compensation' if they introduced compatible programs of their own (Telford, Graefe, and Banting, 2008).

Intergovernmental transfers have also moved in a decentralizing direction, with Ottawa exercising less and less control over provincial priorities through conditional grants. Over time, shared-cost programs were shifted to block-funding arrangements, with few or minimal conditions attached. One major milestone was passage of the Established Programs Financing Arrangements Act (EPF) in 1977, which de-linked federal payments from actual provincial spending and provided federal financing for post-secondary education with no federal involvement in setting policy. A second was the folding of a number of shared programs in health, education, and welfare into the Canada Health and Social Transfer (CHST) in 1995. Again, federal conditions would be weakened (except under the Canada Health Act), and federal contributions would be further de-linked from actual spending. At the same time the overall federal contributions were significantly reduced, from $18 billion to $12.5 billion—an exercise of what might be called the 'dis-spending' power.

Following a dramatic reduction in federal transfers in the late 1990s, as Ottawa fought to reduce its deficit, federal transfers to the provinces have recently been increasing. Total transfers in 2009–10 were projected to amount to just over $50 billion, of which the largest elements were the Canada Health Transfer ($22.6 billion), the unconditional equalization program ($14.2 billion) and the Canada Social Transfer ($10.6 billion). An additional $2.5 billion finances the three territorial governments (Canada, 2009: ch. 3). Nevertheless, transfers from Ottawa to the provinces account for a smaller proportion of their revenues than in other federations. Only 13 per cent of provincial revenue flows from Ottawa, compared to 26 per cent of state revenues in the US, and 44 per cent in Germany (Watts, 2008: 105).

Another key element of fiscal federalism is the Canadian equalization program, designed to overcome disparities among the provinces by ensuring that they would be able to provide 'comparable levels of services at comparable levels of taxation'. This commitment is enshrined in section 36 of the Constitution Act, 1982. It takes the form of unconditional payments from the federal treasury to provinces with fiscal capacities below the national average. Thus, national financial power is used to finance the equality and autonomy of poorer provinces, often seen as an essential element of the Canadian 'federal bargain'.

Each of these elements of fiscal federalism has been contentious in recent years, especially as governments were preoccupied with the battle against debts and deficits. With respect to the tax collection agreements, provinces have sought and achieved greater flexibility to determine their own systems. With respect to conditional transfers, provinces have also gained additional autonomy. Quebec and other provinces have argued that there is a vertical fiscal imbalance, leaving the federal government in surplus in recent years, while provinces struggle with rising costs in their own fields, such as health care. They have called for a basic shift in revenue to the provinces, to which Ottawa has replied that provinces are fully capable of raising taxes on their own (Quebec, 2002; Council of the Federation, 2007; Institute of Intergovernmental Relations, 2007). However, they have strenuously called for restoration of federal cuts, at the same time demanding greater insulation from the effects of federal budgetary decisions and more opportunity to experiment, especially in health care, freed of some of the conditions in the Canada Health Act. As both orders of government seek to address the challenges of recession, this conflict is likely to increase.

Intergovernmental Relations

Given interdependence, and strong autonomous governments deploying broad political, bureaucratic, and financial resources, an extensive network of intergovernmental relations is central to the management of federalism in Canada. It takes place in the arena of executive federalism. This process is a central element of Canadian governance, but it has no constitutional or legislative status. Unlike similar institutions in the European Union, for example, it has no formal voting rules, nor power to make binding decisions. Executive federalism has grown in an ad hoc, informal way, in response to the needs and ambitions of the component governments. It has been gradually taking on a more permanent and institutionalized form. It has shifted from the relatively harmonious but 'paternalistic' co-operative federalism of the post-war period to a more competitive partnership of equals in the recent periods.

There are number of elements in this machinery. The pinnacle is the First Ministers Conference (FMC), bringing together the Prime Minister, the premiers, and the territorial leaders. These meetings are combined with meeting of federal and provincial ministers, and senior officials. They are coordinated by an intergovernmental body, the Canadian Intergovernmental Conference Secretariat (CICS). In 2009, CICS organized 67 such meetings. Myriad other meetings, phone calls, and emails at all levels constitute the day-to-day operation of the federal system.

The frequency of FMCs or their forerunners has varied considerably over time. From the 1920s until World War II, six Dominion–Provincial Conferences were held, mainly dealing with the economic and social consequences of the Great Depression. From 1945 until 1961, 12 were held, focused on post-war reconstruction and the development of the Canadian welfare state. The pace intensified under Prime Minister Lester Pearson, with the rise of Quebec nationalism, completion of the welfare state with medicare and the Canada Pension Plan, and the start of constitutional negotiations. The Constitution, and to a lesser extent energy the economy, dominated the intense round of FMCs under Trudeau (24 FMCs) and Mulroney (14 FMCs), to 1992. In the decade from 1993 to 2004, just eight conferences, now re-labelled First Ministers' Meetings, were held (CICS, 2006). Simeon and Papillon thus conclude that FMCs have become the 'missing link' in Canadian intergovernmental relations (Simeon and Papillon, 2004). Over the years, several proposed constitutional agreements have called for the institutionalization of regular annual First Ministers Conferences, but none have been acted on.

Another form of First Ministers Conference has, however, become a much more regular part of the intergovernmental scene. This began as the **Annual Premiers Conference (APC)**, bringing together the 10 premiers and the leaders of the three northern territories. Once little more than a social gathering, the APC became an increasingly important date on the intergovernmental calendar. In 2003 it was reconstituted as the Council of the Federation (Institute of Intergovernmental Relations, 2003). It is used to coordinate the often differing provincial interests in order to present a united position to federal authorities and to exchange views and best practices about common problems. In recent years, it has also been the launching pad for initiatives aimed at strengthening the collaborative model of intergovernmental relations, most notably in the development of the Social Union Framework Agreement. The position of chair rotates annually among premiers; and the incumbent chair is widely accepted as the general spokesperson for the provinces.

An increasingly important set of intergovernmental institutions is the growing number (now over 20) of ministerial councils (Simmons, 2004). Some of these include only the provincial and territorial governments (PT); others embrace all three levels (FPT). The latter frequently involve joint chairs. Some meet regularly; others on a more ad hoc basis. Some are restricted to governmental officials and ministers, but others have successfully developed extensive linkages with interest groups in their respective fields (Simmons, 2009). Ministerial councils, which go by a number of different titles, now cover most areas of shared or overlapping jurisdiction, including the environment, social policy, education, and finance. They are the forums in which much of the ongoing work of governance in the federation takes place.[3]

Backing up these conferences are a host of meetings of deputies and other officials. Indeed, intergovernmental relations are pervasive throughout the bureaucracy. Antonia Maioni observes that in the health field alone, 'over fifty intergovernmental health advisory committees already operate at the ministerial, deputy ministerial and administrative levels, covering everything from population wellness to physician supply' (Maioni, 1999: 105).

An important development in modern intergovernmental relations is the creation of specialized intergovernmental agencies or ministries at both levels of government, such as the Federal–Provincial Relations Office (FPRO) in Ottawa, the Ministry of Federal and Intergovernmental Affairs (FIGA) in Alberta, and the Ministry of Intergovernmental Affairs (MIA) in Ontario. Typically, these agencies shape the broad strategic directions of each government in the federal–provincial arena, and in monitoring and advising the intergovernmental operations of line ministries. Their 'client' is usually the First Minister. For example, FPRO is part of the Privy Council Office in Ottawa; and Ontario's MIA has recently been integrated into the Cabinet Office. In some respects such cadres of intergovernmental professionals may facilitate co-operation. But in other respects they may heighten tension by moving relations to a more political level, at which turf, status, visibility, credit-seeking, and blame avoidance become more prominent than they are when line officials, sharing many of the same values and responding to similar interest group networks, get together. Given the crucial role of intergovernmental finance in recent years, finance ministries also play a major role in intergovernmental relations.

If intergovernmental agreements are to become a more central part of Canadian federalism, some important issues arise. First, to what extent should they become enforceable, contractual arrangements, legally binding on the parties? To the extent they do so, then the agreements take on the character of legislation. This is difficult to reconcile with the Canadian pattern of parliamentary sovereignty, in which each government is responsible to its own legislature. Second, to what extent will agreements include a role for citizen participation; and, especially, to what extent should citizens, as well as governments, have access to any dispute settlement mechanisms that are established? Third, what is the status of agreements once arrived at? Should they be enshrined in law, or be legally enforceable contracts? When a government changes, can they simply be repudiated?—as the newly elected Conservative government did in 2006 with a major federal–provincial–Aboriginal agreement, the Kelowna Accord, negotiated in 2005 by its predecessor.

Evaluation and Assessment

At the beginning of this chapter, I suggested three sets of criteria that might be used to judge or evaluate the consequences of Canadian federalism and intergovernmental relations: their contribution to democratic politics, to effective governance or policy-making, and to the management of the regional and linguistic divisions central to Canadian politics.

Intergovernmental Relations and Democracy

The democratic critique of the practice of federalism in Canada—the 'democratic deficit'—focuses on the relatively closed nature of intergovernmental relations. Donald Smiley argued as long ago as 1979 that:

> My charges against executive federalism are these:
>
> First it contributes to undue secrecy in the conduct of the public's business.
>
> Second, it contributes to an unduly low level of citizen participation in public affairs.
>
> Third, it weakens and dilutes accountability of governments to their legislatures and the wider public. (Smiley, 1979)

Many of the characteristics of executive federalism that he described persist, despite the popular revolt against intergovernmentalism manifested in opposition to the Meech Lake and Charlottetown Accords. There was little public involvement in the development of the AIT, the Social Union, or other recent agreements. Intergovernmental meetings continue to be held behind closed doors; and dealings between governments are protected from freedom of information laws. Much of the discourse of federal–provincial relations remains arcane and obscure to citizens. Intergovernmental mechanisms provide few channels for citizen groups to become involved. Thus, despite greater commitments to more transparency in the process, there remains a considerable distance to go.

Moreover, accountability is often blurred. It is often difficult for citizens to know who is responsible for what. This is especially true with respect to intergovernmental transfers: how could voters understand that many provincial cuts in welfare and health care, or increases in post-secondary education fees, could be traced to federal budget decisions made earlier? Government competition to win credit and avoid blame often further confuses the issues. Thus there is a 'democratic' reform agenda for intergovernmental relations in Canada. This might include several elements:

- Greater transparency—with prior publication of scheduled meetings, and their agendas, and with fuller reporting of the results of conferences to legislatures.
- Stronger linkages between ministerial councils and related interest groups in their respective policy areas. This could have the added advantage of providing an external check on governmental preoccupations with their own status and turf.
- Citizen access to the dispute settlement mechanisms in intergovernmental agreements.
- A stronger role for legislatures in the intergovernmental process, through such mechanisms as the establishment of standing committees

on intergovernmental relations; holding of debates or committee hearings before and after major intergovernmental meetings; legislative ratification of major intergovernmental accords; the inclusion of opposition members on government negotiating teams; and perhaps the convening of regular meetings that would bring together legislators, rather than ministers and ministry officials, to discuss common problems.
- Further clarification of roles and responsibilities—not necessarily via constitutional amendment—to improve accountability. (Cameron and Simeon, 2000; Simeon and Cameron, 2001)

It should be remembered, however, that the critique of the conduct of intergovernmental relations from this perspective is not so much a critique of federalism itself, but of the excessive centralization of powers in the hands of the executive in the Canadian version of Westminster-style parliamentary government. Nor is this critique unique to Canada: it is common to all systems of multi-level governance, including those at the international level.

Federalism and Public Policy

Canadian federalism has proved to be a wonderfully adaptable system of government. Born in the mid-nineteenth-century era of limited government, it has been able to accommodate, with remarkably little institutional alteration, dramatic changes in the role of the state and the expectations of citizens. It has permitted wide room for provinces to innovate and experiment in developing policies and programs suited to their needs. At the same time, through constitutional change, use of the federal spending power, judicial decisions, and intergovernmental co-operation, it has permitted the completion of the Canadian welfare state and responded to many of the challenges to that model imposed more recently by globalization and the rethinking of governmental roles.

The broad evolution of public policy in Canada has been shaped by forces wider than those associated with federalism, indeed by forces that have been operating in all Western industrial democracies. The impact of federalism has been felt mainly at the margins. Thus, the 'complexities of federalism' did not block development of the welfare state. But they did, relative to other countries, mean that Canada was somewhat later than many other countries to put it into place (Banting, 1983). Federalism has also ensured that territorial concerns would be a major feature of Canadian public policy. It has constrained the policy instruments available to governments. And it has had profound influence on policy discourse and the policy-making process in many areas.[4]

Nevertheless, there are a number of critiques of the impact of federalism on public policy, especially when those policies require coordination in the intergovernmental arena. Analyzing the cases of German federalism and the European Union, both of which place a high premium on intergovernmental consensus in policy-making, Fritz Scharpf (1988) discusses the 'joint decision trap'. It emphasizes the costs of seeking agreement in consensual decision-making systems—delay, the likelihood of common denominator solutions, and the like. In a similar vein, Steven Kennett argues that a collaborative approach to strengthening the Canadian economic union faces an 'impressive set of obstacles', notably 'the incentives for governments to free-ride and cheat, transactions costs, the bargaining dynamic arising from differing vulnerability to externalities, the risks associated with coalition building and issue linkage, and the politics of collective action in Canadian federalism' (Kennett, 1997: 64). Albert Breton (1985) reinforces this view, arguing that an emphasis on intergovernmental collaboration and co-operation risks replacing government by a multiplicity of actors competing to respond to citizen concerns, with a 'cartel of elites' interested primarily in their own security. And, with respect to health care at least, Antonia Maioni argues that, in a situation where 'the incentive to retain jurisdictional sovereignty is high, while the economic costs of non-co-operation are low', movement towards a confederal model of decentralization would likely lead to a 'deepening of asymmetry' and 'a harmonization that little resembles the health-care systems now in place' (Maioni, 1999: 121).

These observations suggest two distinct models for the evolution of Canadian federalism. The first suggests a sharper delineation of who does what—which policy areas should be federal, and which provincial. Within their assigned areas, each level of government would then act independently, exploiting the full range of its fiscal, jurisdictional, and human resources. The second suggests further development of the collaborative model, which recognizes the inevitable interdependence among governments, and hence the need for an effective partnership. Within the collaborative model, there is a further distinction between a version that emphasizes federal and provincial governments working together and one that emphasizes that national norms and standards can develop through interprovincial partnerships.

Judging the overall impact of federal institutions and practices is a difficult task. So many other variables affect policy decisions and their consequences. Herman Bakvis and Grace Skogstad, drawing on a set of detailed case studies, have proposed a scorecard for the effects of federalism, distinguishing between the performance and effectiveness of the intergovernmental system, and the legitimacy of its processes and results. The result is a mixed bag. In social policy, provision of pensions fares well, but health and child care do poorly or only 'fairly'. International trade and economic development seem to work well in the federal system. Regulating the environment works only fairly—and co-operation on policies to address climate change receive a failing grade. Federal and provincial governments have done quite well in addressing the needs of cities, but much less well in integrating local governments into the federal policy-making system more generally. Similarly, intergovernmental co-operation in meeting the needs of Aboriginal peoples, and involving them in the broader intergovernmental process has been only poor to fair (Bakvis and Skogstad, 2008: ch. 18).

Janice Gross Stein makes a more fundamental critique. Canadian federalism, she argues is 'misaligned', 'out of whack'. Our federal system, as it is currently configured and as it now works 'is not equipping Canadians well to thrive in an environment that is global as well as national and regional, and correspondingly more complex and layered than it was 50 years ago' (Stein, 2008: 348). Our federal institutions and practices have simply failed to adapt to the changing society and economy. 'Highly decentralized federal systems, of the kind we have appear to be especially handicapped in managing economic performance in an era of accelerating globalization' (ibid.: 350). Particularly striking is the absence of urban governments from the intergovernmental negotiating table. These concerns seem even more relevant as Canada, and the world, enter a potentially prolonged period of restructuring our economy and society in light of fiscal crisis and global warming. Stein does not argue for a return to the central government leadership of the post-war period. Instead, she argues for a more fluid, inclusive, multi-dimensional 'networked federalism'. 'Federal, provincial, and municipal governments must work to forge new, more flexible structures that are more nimble, less rigid, less cumbersome and more transparent to Canadians' (ibid.: 356). Whether such changes are possible, however, remains in question. Institutional conservatism or resistance to change remains profound. When the author revisited the practice of federal–provincial diplomacy 35 years after its initial discussion, what struck most was not change in intergovernmental relations, but continuity. *Plus ca change*, despite the massive shifts in Canadian social, economic, and political life.

Federalism, Public Services, and Public Servants

This analysis suggests a number of consequences of public policy in Canada, for citizens, and for public servants. For public policy, the clear implication of the Canadian model of federalism is that policy in most important areas—health, welfare, education, the environment, economic development—is an amalgam of federal and provincial decisions and programs, in some cases coordinated and rationalized through intergovernmental agreements, in others by individual governments acting on their own. The cost is often consistency and clarity; the benefit is variability of policy according to provincial priorities. For citizens, the costs are the lack of clear lines of accountability and transparency, and an intergovernmental process that is often opaque and disconnected; the benefits are that intergovernmental competition is often about competing for public support, opening multiple arenas for intervention.

For public servants in the intergovernmental system, two sets of incentives are in play: to collaborate and to compete. The incentive to collaborate builds on the realization that public servants, federal and provincial, serve the same citizens. They often share similar policy goals and similar clienteles. They have often built strong trust relationships across levels. The lower one goes in the governmental hierarchy, the stronger common interests are likely to be. The incentive to compete arises from the fact that public servants serve governments and first ministers, who have a profound interest in sustaining their own turf, visibility, and status. The fundamental challenge for Canadian federalism, therefore, is to find the means to balance national standards against provincial variation, and to exploit the virtues of intergovernmentalism while avoiding its vices. On a more mundane level, public servants with policy responsibilities must keep the intergovernmental dimension of their work constantly in mind. Networking and information exchange with colleagues across jurisdictions are essential. At senior levels, officials will inevitably find themselves at the intergovernmental negotiating table. The arts and skills of negotiation are therefore critical, and should be a central element in training and evaluation.

More generally, at the heart of Canadian federalism is a deep tension between the need for coordination born of interdependence, shared responsibilities, and citizen expectations, and the logic of our parliamentary, divided federalism, which institutionalizes a deeply competitive relationship among governments.

Important Terms and Concepts

Agreement on Internal Trade (AIT)
Annual Premiers Conference (APC)
classical model of federalism
collaborative federalism
colonial model of federalism
competitive federalism
constitutional federalism
co-operative federalism
democratic deficit
executive federalism
federalism
Social Union Framework Agreement (SUFA)

Study Questions

1. What accounts for the Canadian pattern of federalism and intergovernmental relations? What explains varying levels of conflict and competition, and harmony and disharmony, across different time periods and different policy areas?
2. How we can judge, assess, and evaluate institutions and processes, and how we might think about reform?
3. Canada is a country deeply divided along linguistic and regional lines. Do its federal institutions work towards bridging, ameliorating, and managing these divisions, or do they exacerbate and intensify them?

4. Canada is a country deeply committed to democratic values. Does our federalism enhance or undermine the quality of our democracy?
5. Canada, like all other advanced countries, faces a complex and difficult policy agenda. Does federalism contribute to the effective development, administration, and delivery of public policy, or does it frustrate these goals?
6. Of the various eras of intergovernmental relations in Canada, which seems to have been the most productive, and why?

Useful Websites

Forum of Federations:

www.forumfed.org/en/index.php

The Council of the Federation:

www.councilofthefederation.ca

Canadian Intergovernmental Conference Secretariat:

www.scics.gc.ca

Institute of Intergovernmental Relations, Queen's University. 2003. *Special Series on the Council of the Federation.*

www.queensu.ca/iigr/working/CouncilFederation/FedEN.html

Institute of Intergovernmental Relations, Queen's University. 2006. *Special Series on Fiscal Imbalance.*

www.queensu.ca/iigr/working/fiscalImb.html

Institute of Intergovernmental Relations, Queen's University. 2006. *Open Federalism: Interpretations, Significance.* Kingston: IIGR (ordering information).

www.queensu.ca/iigr/pub/Book/OF.html

Canada. Ministry of Finance. 2007 Budget. (Chapter 4 outlines the Harper government's philosophy on the use of the spending power.)

www.budget.gc.ca/2007/plan/bpc4-eng.html

Quebec's Commission on Fiscal Imbalance: Report and supporting documents, 2002:

www.desequilibrefiscal.gouv.qc.ca/index_ang.htm

Canada West Foundation:

www.cwf.ca/V2/main

Links to Canadian intergovernmental affairs secretariats:

www.queensu.ca/iigr/links/linksProv.html

Notes

1. Intergovernmental bodies now are typically designated as FPT (federal, provincial, territorial) or PT (provincial, territorial).
2. The Constitution had remained a statute of the British Parliament, amendable only by it at the request of Canada. Canadians had not been able to agree on the appropriate formula for amending the Constitution in Canada.
3. At the ministerial level, the frequency of meetings increased slowly between 1973 and 1984, from about 40 to 60 meetings per year. Between 1984 and 1993, during the tenure of Prime Minister Brian Mulroney, the number never dropped below 80 meetings per year, with peaks of 130 in 1985–6 and 127 in 1992–3. The arrival of the Liberal government was accompanied by a drop in the number of meetings, but the number has increased in recent years, with 70 held in 1997–8, and 105 in 1999–2000, an increase over the 10-year average of 78. About 60 per cent of the meetings involved all three levels, while the other 40 per cent were meetings of provinces and territories without a formal federal presence. In 1999–2000, five conferences (all provincial–territorial) involved first ministers, 49 involved ministers, and 48 involved deputy ministers. (Data provided by the Canadian Intergovernmental Conference Secretariat.)
4. This section draws heavily on the analysis in Norrie et al. (1986: ch. 11).

References

Bakvis, Herman, and Grace Skogstad, eds. 2008. *Canadian Federalism: Performance, Effectiveness, and Legitimacy,* 2nd edn. Toronto: Oxford University Press.

Banting, Keith. 1983. *The Welfare State and Canadian Federalism,* 2nd edn. Montreal and Kingston: McGill-Queen's University Press.

———. 1998. 'The Past Speaks to the Future: Lessons from the Postwar Social Union', in Harvey Lazar, ed., *Canada: The State of the Federation, 1998.* Kingston: Institute of Intergovernmental Relations, 36–69.

Boychuck, Gerald. 1996. 'Reforming the Canadian Social Assistance Complex: The Provincial Welfare States and Canadian Federalism', in Brown and Rose, eds, *Canada: The State of the Federation,* 1995. Kingston: Institute of Intergovernmental Relations, 115–44.

Breton, Albert. 1985. 'Supplementary Statement', in Royal Commission on the Economic Union and Development Prospects for Canada, *Report,* vol. 3. Ottawa: Supply and Services, 486–553.

Brooks, Stephen. 1999. 'Comments on Alain Noel's Paper', in Young, ed., *Stretching the Federation: The Art of the State in Canada.* Kingston: Institute of Intergovernmental Relations, 219–25.

Brown, Douglas M. 2003. *Getting Things Done In the Federation: Do We Need New Rules for an Old Game?* Kingston and Montreal: Queen's University Institute of Intergovernmental Relations and IRPP.

———, and Jonathan W. Rose, eds. 1996. *Canada: The State of the Federation, 1995.* Kingston: Institute of Intergovernmental Relations.

Cairns, Alan. 1991. 'Constitutional Change and the Three Equalities', in Watts and Brown, eds, *Options for a New Canada.* Toronto: University of Toronto Press.

Cameron, David, and Richard Simeon. 2000. 'Intergovernmental Relations and Democratic Citizenship', in B.G. Peters and D. Savoie, eds, *Governance in the 21st Century: Revitalizing the Public Service.* Montreal and Kingston: McGill-Queen's University Press, 58–118.

Canada, Ministry of Finance. 2007 Budget. *Annex 1.*

———. 2009. *Budget 2009.* Ch. 3.

Canadian Intergovernmental Conference Secretariat (CICS). 2006. Report to Governments, 2005–6. October. Available at: www.scics.gc.ca/pubs/rep_gov_2005_06_e.pdf.

Council of the Federation. 2007. *Reconciling the Irreconcilable: Addressing Canada's Fiscal Imbalance.* Ottawa: The Council.

Courchene, Thomas J. 1991. *Rearrangements.* Oakville, Ont.: Mosaic Press.

———. 1997. 'ACCESS: A Convention on the Canadian Economic and Social Systems', reprinted, with comments, in *Assessing Access.* Kingston: Institute of Intergovernmental Relations.

———. 1999. 'The PIT and the Pendulum: Reflections on Ontario's Proposal to Mount Its Own Personal Income Tax System', in Young, ed., *Stretching the Federation: The Art of the State in Canada.* Kingston: Institute of Intergovernmental Relations, 129–85.

Dion, Stéphane. 1992. 'Explaining Quebec Nationalism', in R.K. Weaver, ed., *The Collapse of Canada?* Washington: Brookings Institution.

Doern, G. Bruce, and Brian Tomlin. 1985. *The Politics of Energy: The Development and Implementation of the NEP.* Toronto: Methuen.

Dupré, J. Stefan. 1985. 'On the Workability of Executive Federalism', in R. Simeon, ed., *Intergovernmental Relations,* vol. 63 of the Research Studies for the Royal Commission on the Economic Union and Development Prospects for Canada. Toronto: University of Toronto Press, 11–32.

Dyck, Rand. 1976. 'The Canada Assistance Plan: The Ultimate in Cooperative Federalism', *Canadian Public Administration* 19: 587–602.

Fafard, Patrick C., and Kathryn Harrison, eds. 2000. *Managing the Environmental Union: Intergovernmental Relations and Environmental Policy in Canada.* Kingston: School of Policy Studies.

Gibbins, Roger. 1997. 'Democratic Reservations about the ACCESS Model', in Institute of Intergovernmental Relations, *Assessing Access: Towards a New Social Union.* Kingston: IIR, 41–4.

———, and Guy Laforest, eds. 1998. *Beyond the Impasse: Toward Reconciliation.* Montreal: Institute for Research on Public Policy.

Institute of Intergovernmental Relations, Queen's University. 2003. *Special Series on the Council of the Federation.* Available at: www.queensu.ca/iigr.

———. 2006. *Open Federalism: Interpretations, Significance.* Kingston: IIGR. Available at: www.queensu.ca/iigr/pub/Book/OF.html.

———. 2007. *Working Papers on Fiscal Imbalance.* Available at: www.queensu.ca/iigr.

Kennett, Steven. 1997. *Securing the Social Union: A Commentary on the Decentralized Approach.* Kingston: Institute of Intergovernmental Relations.

Lazar, Harvey, ed. 1998. *Canada: The State of the Federation 1997. Non-Constitutional Renewal.* Kingston: Institute of Intergovernmental Relations.

Lindquist, Evert. 1999. 'Efficiency, Reliability or Innovation: Managing Overlap and Interdependence in Canada's System of Governance', in Young, ed., *Stretching the Federation: The Art of the State in Canada.* Kingston: Institute of Intergovernmental Relations, 35–68.

McRoberts, Kenneth. 1988. *Quebec: Social Change and Political Crisis,* 3rd edn. Toronto: McClelland & Stewart.

———, and Patrick Monahan, eds. 1993. *The Charlottetown Accord, the Referendum and the Future of Canada.* Toronto: University of Toronto Press.

Maioni, Antonia. 1999. 'Decentralization in Health Policy: Comments on the ACCESS Proposals', in Young, ed., *Stretching the Federation: The Art of the State in Canada.* Kingston: Institute of Intergovernmental Relations, 97–122.

Noel, Alain. 1999. 'Is Decentralization Conservative?', in Young, ed., *Stretching the Federation: The Art of the State in Canada.* Kingston: Institute of Intergovernmental Relations, 195–219.

Norrie, Kenneth, Richard Simeon, and Mark Krasnick. 1986. *Federalism and the Economic Union in Canada*, vol. 59 of the Research Studies for the Royal Commission on the Economic Union and Development Prospects for Canada. Toronto: University of Toronto Press.

Phillips, Susan D. 1996. 'The Canada Health and Social Transfer: Fiscal Federalism in Search of a Vision', in Brown and Rose, eds, *Canada: The State of the Federation, 1995*. Kingston: Institute of Intergovernmental Relations, 65–98.

Porter, John. 1965. *The Vertical Mosaic: An Analysis of Social Class and Power in Canada*. Toronto: University of Toronto Press.

Quebec. 2002. Commission on Fiscal Imbalance, *Report*. Gouvernement du *Québec, 2002*.

Romanow, Roy, John Whyte, and Howard Leeson. 1984. *Canada Notwithstanding . . . The Making of the Constitution, 1976–1982*. Toronto: Carswell/Methuen.

Royal Commission of Inquiry on Constitutional Problems (Tremblay Commission). 1954. *Report*. Quebec City: Editeur Officiel.

Russell, Peter. 1983. 'Bold Statecraft, Questionable Jurisprudence', in K. Banting and R. Simeon, eds, *And No One Cheered: Federalism, Democracy and the Constitution Act*. Toronto: Methuen, 210–38.

———. 2004. *Constitutional Odyssey: Can Canadians Become a Sovereign People?* Toronto and London: University of Toronto Press.

Savoie, Donald. 1999. *Governing from the Centre: The Concentration of Power in Canadian Politics*. Toronto: University of Toronto Press.

Scharpf, Fritz. 1988. 'The Joint Decision Trap: Lessons from German Federalism and European Integration', *Public Administration* 66: 236–78.

Schwartz, Bryan. 1996. 'Assessing the Agreement on Internal Trade: Towards a More "Perfect" Union', in Brown and Rose, eds, *Canada: The State of the Federation, 1995*. Kingston: Institute of Intergovernmental Relations, 189–219.

Simeon, Richard. 1971. *Federal–Provincial Diplomacy: The Making of Recent Policy in Canada*. Toronto: University of Toronto Press. Re-issued with a new Epilogue, 2006.

———. 1998. 'Considerations on the Design of Federations', *SA Public Law* 13: 42–72.

———, and David Cameron. 2000. 'Federalism and Democracy: An Oxymoron if Ever There Was One?', in Herman Bakvis and Grace Skogstad, eds, *Canadian Federalism*. Toronto: Oxford University Press, 278–94.

———, and Martin Papillon. 2004. 'The Weakest Link? First Ministers' Conferences in Canadian Intergovernmental Relation', in Peter Meekison, Hamish Telford, and Harvey Lazar, eds, *Canada: The State of the Federation, 2002: Reconsidering the Institutions of Canadian Federalism*. Montreal and Kingston: McGill-Queen's University Press.

———, and ———. 2006. 'Canada', in Akhtar Majeed, Ronald L. Watts, and Douglas M. Brown, eds, *Distribution of Powers and Responsibilities in Federal Countries*, Montreal and Kingston: McGill-Queen's University Press, 91–122.

———, and Ian Robinson. 1990. *State, Society and the Development of Canadian Federalism*, vol. 71 of the Research Studies for the Royal Commission on the Economic Union and Development Prospects for Canada. Toronto: University of Toronto Press.

Simmons, Julie. 2004. 'Securing the Threads of Cooperation in the Tapestry of Intergovernmental Relations: Does the Institutionalization of Ministerial Conferences Matter?', in Peter Meekison, Hamish Telford, and Harvey Lazar, eds, *Canada: The State of the Federation, 2002: Reconsidering the Institutions of Canadian Federalism*. Montreal and Kingston: McGill-Queen's University Press.

Smiley, D.V. 1963. *Conditional Grants and Canadian Federalism*. Toronto: Canadian Tax Foundation.

———. 1974. *Constitutional Adaptation and Canadian Federalism*. Document 4, Royal Commission on Bilingualism and Biculturalism. Ottawa: Queen's Printer.

———. 1979. 'An Outsider's Observations on Intergovernmental Relations among Consenting Adults', in R. Simeon, ed., *Confrontation or Collaboration: Intergovernmental Relations in Canada Today*. Toronto: Institute of Public Administration of Canada, 105–13.

———, and Ronald L. Watts. 1985. *Intrastate Federalism in Canada*, vol. 39 of the Research Studies for the Royal Commission on the Economic Union and Development Prospects for Canada. Toronto: University of Toronto Press.

Stein, Janice Gross. 2008. 'Networked Federalism', in John R. Allan, Thomas J. Courchene, and Christian Leuprecht, eds., *Transitions: Fiscal and Political Federalism in an Era of Change Canada: The State of the Federation 2006/7*. Kingston: Institute of Intergovernmental Relations and McGill-Queen's University Press, 347–67.

Taylor, Charles. 1991. 'Shared and Divergent Values', in Watts and Brown, eds, *Options for a New Canada*. Toronto: University of Toronto Press.

Telford, Hamish, Peter Graefe, and Keith Banting. 2008. *Defining the Federal Government's Role in Social Policy: The Spending Power and Other Instruments. Policy Matters* 9, 3. Montreal: Institute for Research on Public Policy.

Trebilcock, Michael, and Daniel Schwanen. 1995. *Getting There: An Assessment of the Agreement on Internal Trade*. Toronto: C.D. Howe Institute.

Treisman, Daniel. 2007. *The Architecture of Government: Rethinking Political Decentralization*. Cambridge: Cambridge University Press.

Watts, Ronald L. 2008. *Comparing Federal Systems*, 3rd edn. Montreal: McGill-Queen's University Press.

———, and Douglas Brown, eds. 1991. *Options for a New Canada*. Toronto: University of Toronto Press.

Wheare, K.C. 1964. *Federal Government*, 4th edn. New York: Oxford University Press.

White, Graham. 2005. *Cabinets and First Ministers*. Vancouver: University of British Columbia Press.

Young, Robert, ed. 1999. *Stretching the Federation: The Art of the State in Canada*. Kingston: Institute of Intergovernmental Relations.

24 The Federal Spending Power

Christopher Dunn

The use, expansion, and control of the federal spending power have occupied generations of practitioners and political observers. The detractors of the spending power, who coalesced into 'the constitutional reform industry' and saw one defeat after another in the latter part of the twentieth century, managed to see a measured victory early in the twenty-first. The defenders of the spending power have yet to recover.

Our job here will be to trace the meaning of the spending power; the factors that led to its expanded use, then to its decline, and then to a kind of rebirth; and lastly to the varied attempts to control it. Such attempts culminated in a new approach to Canadian federalism called 'Open Federalism' or 'the federalism of openness'.

The Spending Power of Parliament

The **spending power of Parliament**, as Prime Minister Pierre Elliott Trudeau noted in 1969, has come to have a special constitutional meaning in Canada. It signifies 'the power of Parliament to make payments to people or institutions or governments for purposes on which it (Parliament) does not necessarily have the power to legislate' (Trudeau, 1969: 4). It has justified federal transfer payments in several domains, including conditional or shared-cost programs with the provinces, unconditional equalization payments to provincial governments, payments to institutions (such as universities until 1966) or to industries as incentives for regional development, and, finally, income support payments to individuals. The spending power is also exercised when the federal government enters directly into a field such as resource development or insurance, or establishes commissions for the purpose of exercising direct legislative control over an area (LaForest, 1969: 36).

The spending power served historically as the basis for a wide variety of programs and subsidies to various bodies. Broadly speaking, there have been three kinds of uses of the spending power in the post-war period.

(1) **Payments to individuals and institutions** have been made for purposes that have been or alleged to have been constitutionally assigned to the provinces. Among these initially were payments to individuals in earlier programs such as federal Family Allowances, Youth Allowances, Canada Council grants, Training Allowances to Adults, and National Research Council grants. Also included were those to institutions and industries, including Area Development Agency grants, research and development incentives for business, plus coal subventions and subsidies. More recently, the spending power has been upheld as the basis for federal loans for student housing, for federal job creation programs involving a federal wage subsidy, and for the tax expenditure provisions of the Income Tax Act (Hogg, 1996: 150–1).

(2) **Shared-cost programs** accounted for the largest percentage of total money paid to the provincial governments and constituted the largest number of programs. These were originally based

on the conviction that certain 'national standards' are desirable in areas that relate to the provincial allocation of powers. In other cases decision-makers desired an incentive effect. Federal representatives, by introducing conditions attached to receipt of federal money, hoped either to spur a greater outlay of provincial funds on particular concerns or to encourage the assumption of these or related programs by the provinces. Under this category fell some of Canada's most important and progressive legislation: Hospital Insurance, the Canada Assistance Plan, Medical Care Insurance, the Health Insurance Fund, capital grants to technical schools, and various forms of technical and vocational aid. Shared-cost schemes also gave Canada a comprehensive highway network.

In 1977, federal funding for hospital insurance, medicare, and post-secondary education was grouped into a large block grant called Established Programs Financing (EPF). The funding changed from cash grants to a combination of cash and tax points, and federal funding was divorced from the sharing of provincial operating costs. These moves diminished the level of conditionality over provincial programs in health. In 1984, the Canada Health Act reinforced conditions that a province had to meet to obtain the full federal cash contribution: comprehensiveness, universality, portability, public administration, and accessibility. In pursuance of the last condition, it established a prohibition against user fees and extra-billing by imposing financial sanctions against provinces that permitted them. Thus, conditionality was heightened. In 1996, both CAP and EPF were rolled into one federal transfer called the Canada Health and Social Transfer, which provided a block fund to assist provinces in providing health, post-secondary education, social assistance, and social services programs. The new transfer continued the Canada Health Act criteria as well as the former CAP prohibition against making eligibility for social assistance conditional upon a residency requirement.

(3) **Unconditional grants**, apart from statutory subsidies, came to play an important role in the support of provincial revenues. These 'equalization grants', or 'fiscal capacity revenue transfers' as they are sometimes called, were designed to compensate for the low per-capita tax yield in the less-endowed provinces so that an average Canadian standard of services might be provided that would not otherwise be possible. Canada's commitment to the principle of equalization was finally constitutionalized, and with remarkably little controversy. Section 36(2) of the Constitution Act, 1982 says that 'Parliament and the government of Canada are committed to the principle of making equalization payments to ensure that provincial governments have sufficient revenues to provide reasonably comparable levels of public services at reasonably comparable levels of taxation.'

Not all aspects of the federal spending power have been equally controversial. Equalization payments are generally safe from provincial criticism because of their unconditional nature. Grants to individuals and institutions are generally a modest notch up in controversy, mostly as they relate to Canada–Quebec relations. However, both pale in comparison to federal shared-cost programs in areas of exclusive provincial jurisdiction, which have borne the brunt of most provincial hostility, as we shall see in the 'rationales' for constitutional controls of the federal spending power provided by the **constitutional reform industry**.[1]

The criticisms in general, however, fall into two categories: federal theory and public administration. Some hold the spending power as exemplified by the shared-cost program to be a violation of the federal principle. Others claim that the use of the federal spending power blurs accountability, distorts the provinces' ability to set priorities, hinders planning, and creates extravagant administrative and decision-making costs. Either way, some kind of control and/or reciprocity for both Ottawa and the provinces seems to be unavoidable if federal–provincial peace is to exist.

The Era of Federal Dominance, 1945–1969

After World War II, the federal government enjoyed a long period of dominance of the intergovernmental scene, largely if not exclusively due to its vastly expanded use of the spending power and of conditional grants in particular. Several factors led to this explosion of federal–provincial shared-cost programs. They amounted to a combination of economic theory, asymmetries of power, the lack of alternative instruments, and functional consensus.

The first was the **Keynesian consensus** that dominated post-war economic thinking in Canada and many other Western nations. John Maynard Keynes, a noted British economist, had argued that downturns in the business cycle could be counteracted by increasing aggregate demand in the economy. To accomplish this, thought Canadian interpreters of Keynesianism such as Ottawa mandarins O.D. Skelton and W.A. Mackintosh, required a commitment to two principles originally floated during the reconstruction planning of World War II: 'a strong government that stressed common national interests; and an interventionist role for the state, one that could employ tools such as tax relief, subsidies, and public works to keep employment up when times were hard' (Granatstein, 1982: 166). To a remarkable degree these core beliefs, which also formed the backbone of the Liberal government's influential White Paper on Employment and Income tabled in Parliament in 1945 (Canada, 1945: 808 ff.), persisted throughout much of the next two decades. They also formed an intellectual bedrock for most of the spending programs of this era.

Another factor associated with the rise of the shared-cost instrument was asymmetry in federal and provincial power. Federal actions in this regard were more akin to filling a vacuum than contesting for position or intergovernmental advantage. By 1955, Ottawa collected three-quarters of all tax revenue in Canada, compared to the one-quarter raised by provinces and municipalities (Smiley, 1970: ch. 3). Provincial public services were smaller and preoccupied with basic infrastructure services, whereas Ottawa had a reputation as a bureaucratic powerhouse able to solve problems ranging from the conduct of war and the Cold War to social and economic modernization. Provincial expenditures on matters under their own constitutional jurisdiction had been restricted by a variety of fiscal emergencies, including depression, war, reconstruction, and demographic growth.

Restrictions on the choice of alternative policy instruments were another consideration. Given the opposition of the Premier of Quebec, Maurice Duplessis, to amending the Constitution, not to mention the more recent history of unsuccessful attempts even to agree on an amending formula, federal policy-makers believed that any attempts to amend the Constitution to change the federal and provincial division of powers would be bound to fail. The Judicial Committee of the Privy Council (JCPC) in London, at the time the final arbiter of constitutional matters for Canada, had decided in 1937 that the federal government could not establish a special fund to finance matters that fell under provincial jurisdiction. Critics maintained that it was contrary to the spirit of federalism to use the declaratory power to render provincial works and undertakings matters of general advantage to Canada and therefore matters of federal jurisdiction. Changes in boundaries to capture externalities, or spillovers, were not seriously considered.

A potent factor in the expansion of the spending power was the flexibility inherent in the instrument itself. Richard Simeon and Ian Robinson have argued that most provinces accepted federal incursions into their areas of jurisdiction because the spending power was a malleable and relatively non-threatening mechanism in Canadian federalism. Contrary to the pattern of detailed supervision inherent in American categorical grants, the federal conditions placed only loose conditions on provinces; the conditions themselves were often developed in conjunction with provincial officials who shared professional values with the federal officials; federal shared-cost programs strengthened, rather than weakened, provincial governments by augmenting their revenue base, the size and expertise of their bureaucracies, and their appeal to provincial publics; and, finally, the federal and provincial governments fundamentally agreed on goals, especially in regard to programs the provinces had pioneered themselves, as was the case with hospital and medical insurance (Simeon and Robinson, 1990).

The reciprocal interaction between intergovernmental coordination and 'departmentalized' cabinet organization also facilitated the shared-cost mechanism. Stefan Dupré has commented that cabinet organization at the federal and provincial levels saw three historical modes of operation: the traditional cabinet, the departmentalized cabinet, and the institutionalized cabinet. The **traditional cabinet** predominated in the days before the rise of the modern administrative state; ministers' jobs were to articulate and aggregate matters of local and regional political concern. Between 1920 and 1960 the **departmentalized cabinet** held sway. This, of course, coincided with the rise of the modern administrative state, which saw government departments as the centre of government decision-making, ministers who demonstrated 'portfolio loyalty', and departmental experts who provided the principal input for government decision-making. Discrete client interests thus focused their attention on the ministers and experts. The **institutionalized cabinet**, which, with some variations, tended to predominate after 1960, featured formal cabinet structures, established central agencies, and new budgeting and management techniques that emphasized shared knowledge, collegial decision-making, and the formation of government-wide priorities (Dupré, 1988: 234–5).

The departmentalized cabinets of the federal and provincial governments promoted shared-cost programs. Ensconced in departmental settings where they were largely masters of their own fate, ministers and officials of the federal and provincial governments could interact with each other in long-term 'trust relationships' according to the 'functional relations model'. Federal and provincial officials who performed analogous functions also shared similar professional values they could transmit to their ministers, and this would result in intergovernmental agreements that were unlikely to be second-guessed by the cabinets or first ministers. Conditional grants formed a financial lubricant that aided the reputations of ministers and the careers of senior officials in both donor and recipient governments; federal–provincial programs tended to be locked in as each level defended against budgetary competition by appealing to the needs of the other level of government or the client group affected by the functional program. To itemize the multiplicity of shared-cost programs is to describe the post-war reconstruction era, as Table 24.1 indicates.

The dominant image of federalism at this time emphasized public administration values. To be sure, clear partisan advantage was gained by expanding the welfare state to serve Canadians who had faced decades of privation, and the indisputable winner in this race was the 'government party', the federal Liberals. However, for various reasons, most governments—of varied stripes—couched their defence of shared-cost programs in the language of the social sciences. Advocates regularly made reference to functional values, efficiency, containment of externalities, and other related terms. A weaker echo in this debate came from the defensive federalism of Quebec's Maurice Duplessis, who attacked the spending power in terms of classical federalism.

The Era of the Constitutional Reform Industry: Proposals to Constitutionalize the Spending Power, 1969–1992

The spending power proved to be a contentious topic in the next few decades. It was shaped by factors that were the opposites of those that explained its earlier prominence. Keynesian economic prominence faded; provincial power, especially Quebec's power, accelerated; alternative instruments were considered; and the institutionalized cabinet reshaped the policy-making world for federal and provincial governments. These factors came together to promote a new phenomenon: a formidable constitutional industry advocated a grand 'megaconstitutional reform' effort involving a comprehensive renegotiation of the federal bargain struck a century before. It treated the spending power reform as one element

Table 24.1 Major Shared-Cost Programs and Years Established

Health Programs		**Social Welfare Programs**	
1948	Hospital Construction	1937/51	Blind Persons' Allowances
1948	General Public Health	1952	Old Age Assistance
1948	Tuberculosis Control	1954	Disabled Persons' Allowances
1948	Public Health Research	1956	Unemployment Assistance
1948	Cancer Control	1966	Canada Assistance Plan
1948	Professional Training (Health)		
1948	Mental Health		
1948/53	Medical Rehabilitation and Crippled Children		
1953	Child and Maternal Health		
1957	Hospital Insurance and Diagnostic Services		
1966	Health Resources Fund		
1968	Medical Insurance ('medicare')		
Technical and Vocational Training Programs		**Economic Development and Infrastructure Programs**	
1937	Student Aid	1900	4H Club Activities
1944	Apprenticeship Training	1909	Railway Grade Crossing Fund
1945	Technical and Vocational Training—Capital Costs Assistance	1913	Premiums on Purebred Sires
		1927	Municipal Airports
1946	Training in Co-Operation with Industry	1944	Urban Redevelopment
1948	Training of Unemployed	1950	Trans-Canada Highway
1950	Training of Disabled	1958	Roads to Resources
1950	Vocational High-School Training	1958	Municipal Winter Works
1953	Rehabilitation of Disabled Persons	1961/5	Agricultural Rehabilitation and Development
1960	Teacher Technical Training	1963	Municipal Development and Loan Fund
1960	Technician Training	1964	Centennial Grants and Projects
1960	Trade and Occupational Training	1966	Fund for Rural Economic Development
1964	Student Loans (interest)	1951/67	Federal Grants to/for Universities

Source: Adapted from Carter (1971: ch. 2); Trudeau (1969); Moore, Perry, and Beach (1966: 114–18). Some programs were folded into others over time. Not all shared-cost programs are listed here.

of broad reform. During this period, not one but many images of federalism were proffered.

The allure of the Keynesian managed economy began to fade in the 1960s and 1970s as it began to be associated with rising deficits. As Alasdair Roberts demonstrates in Chapter 12 of this volume, federal deficits as a percentage of total expenditures increased from 8.5 per cent in 1975 to 15.9 per cent in 1980 and 21.6 per cent in 1985. No longer was it a matter of introducing new shared-cost programs; rather, politicians and bureaucrats sought to limit the growth of programs already in place. This in turn provided provincial treasurers with another in a growing list of complaints about the spending-power instrument, in this case the charge of federal unilateralism. The federal government, keen to control its deficits, introduced the Established Programs

Financing (EPF) arrangements in 1977, linking federal contributions to growth in the economy rather than to actual program costs. Later, in both 1986 and 1990, Ottawa changed the formula to reduce the rate of increase in its contributions. In 1990, Ottawa introduced a new 'cap on CAP', which put a ceiling on the rate of increase of federal contributions under the Canada Assistance Plan (CAP) to the so-called 'have' provinces (Ontario, Alberta, and British Columbia), which were, coincidentally, the provinces with the highest welfare rates.

Provincial power was on the increase after 1960, and this had important effects on the will and capacity of the federal government to introduce new shared-cost programs. There were in fact three dynamics now at work: country-building, province-building, and Quebec nation-building, each implying 'a different sense of community, or collectivity across which benefits are to be maximized and to which primary loyalty or identity will be given' (Evenson and Simeon, 1979: 171). Country-building manifested itself in different forms. The first was the integrative economic provisions of the British North America Act. The second was the Keynesian-inspired federal dominance from the end of World War II to the mid-1960s. Province-building, for its part, was based on a strong sense of regional community and implied major changes: the shift away from shared-cost programs, greater autonomy in economic development and regulation, limitations of the federal spending power and the 'peace, order, and good government' clause, and a greater role in the operation of federal institutions and regulatory agencies that affect them (ibid., 176). Quebec nation-building led to a 'bureaucratic revolution' in the province, featuring massive public sector growth. The Quebec state expanded, requiring new resources and policy levers that were and are under federal control.

Federal, provincial, and Quebec governments therefore began to compete for the allegiance of their respective populations. Evenson and Simeon said this was accompanied by 'institutional failure': the inability of central institutions to represent and integrate regional interests, and the failure of federal–provincial mechanisms to make collective policy that would reconcile regional and national aspirations. This led to a felt need to re-establish a new equilibrium, and the spending power was a central symbol of jurisdictional power. In this context, the trust relationships of the earlier era dissipated.

Governments began considering alternative instruments—other ways of achieving their aims than the spending power. Equalization had started tentatively in 1957, and provinces began to lobby, often successfully, for increases in the amounts accorded under the program, and to see equalization, with its unconditional nature, as a functional replacement for conditional shared-cost grants. In cases with a de facto concurrent jurisdiction in the so-called 'grey areas' of the Constitution, some of the larger provinces argued for the federal government to vacate the area and compensate provinces for running the programs themselves (Strick, 1999: 225). Some, such as Strick (ibid., 233), for example, even called for formal changes in the division of powers to give the provinces the constitutional right to govern over certain areas. Others, such as the Beaudoin–Dobbie Report (Canada, 1992b) and the Charlottetown Accord (Canada, 1992a) took the opposite tack and began to consider the notion of federal–provincial partnership in the design and implementation of new 'national' programs that downplayed jurisdictional prerogatives; in some cases the approval of such programs by a reformed national second chamber was seen as a necessary accompaniment (Canadian Bar Association, 1978; Pepin–Robarts Report, 1979).

The institutional cabinet was now in its heyday and it began to shape the way that the federal and provincial governments determined and implemented policy. The involvement of central agencies in the work of federal and provincial functional negotiators laid to rest what had been a series of trust networks dominated by what Dupré described as a 'workable' model of executive federalism. Instead of the 'fiscal relations model' of federal–provincial summitry underpinned by finance ministers and their officials who spoke a common language and focused principally on financial issues, a fundamental reorientation of federal–provincial relations evolved. Summit consultation was circumvented, the role of provincial treasuries was diluted, and different professional norms clashed and prevented fruitful negotiation. Dupré's prescription for a once-again workable executive federalism was to restrict central agencies' participation in federal–provincial relations to occasional appearances to clarify general policy, taking care to keep them away from ongoing participation in the process of consultation or negotiation and to establish routinized, annual federal–provincial summits (Dupré, 1988).

The notion of a constitutionalized spending power included a number of things. First, of course, it implied the need for a clear description of that power. Other issues also had to be determined: whether the focus was to be on spending-power programs that transfer resources to governments, to institutions, or to individuals; whether new and/or old programs were to be covered; what threshold of agreement was appropriate for new programs; whether shared-cost or unconditional programs were the focus; whether national objectives were desirable and, if so, what mechanisms should be used to achieve them; and, lastly, what form of compensation, if any, was appropriate for governments that choose not to participate in national programs.

The spending power recommendations of these various reports are summarized in Appendix A of this chapter.

The Partnership Push: 1992–2006 Developments on the Spending Power

Since 1992, controls over the federal spending power, which the reform industry maintained were achievable only through constitutional reform, have been sought by intergovernmental fiat. Also, many of the **tests** for the use of the spending power and the **frameworks** for its collective exercise—both of which the reform industry generated—served as guidelines for such intergovernmental efforts. The actors redirected their energies towards new horizons, but the post-1992 agenda was remarkably similar to the pre-1992 agenda.

Federal–provincial discussions and decision-making on the spending power have been shaped by various factors. One was the crisis of purpose experienced by the federal government, as it perceived a public reaction against interventionism and redistribution, and found its policy options increasingly circumscribed by a variety of international agreements. Others involved the continuing, and indeed deepening, fiscal gap between the 'have' and 'have-not' provinces, combined with the increasing fiscal health of the federal government. Quebec nation-building also remained as a potent force, although it appeared to have waned somewhat by the end of the century. The net result of all these factors was the **Social Union Framework Agreement (SUFA)** of 4 February 1999.

In the latter part of the twentieth century, the federal government experienced a certain crisis of identity and purpose, as Alasdair Roberts notes in Chapter 12. Ottawa, Roberts says, seemed to have found its way to a new role, tentatively, through the notion of enhancing Canada's international competitiveness and its embracing of the knowledge-based economy. However, another version of a new role seems to have come about with the new emphasis on direct transfers to individuals.

The varying condition of the fiscal health of the federal government had a galvanizing effect on the state of the spending power and federal–provincial relations in general. The federal deficit ballooned to $42 billion in 1993–4; its net debt was $508 billion, which represented about 70 per cent of GDP; and its debt charges were close to 33 per cent of revenues. By a combination of financial constraint and improving economic conditions, Ottawa by 1998–9 had managed to achieve a surplus of $2.8 billion; the growth rate of its national debt had declined to the extent that the debt was now close to $577 billion, or 64.4 per cent of GDP; and debt charges were under 27 per cent (Canada, Department of Finance, 1999). The federal government revealed in 1999 that its cumulative fiscal surplus could climb as high as to $95 billion between 2000–1 and 2004–5. The Royal Bank was more conservative in its projections, but still projected a cumulative five-year surplus of over $86 billion (Royal Bank, 1999).

The rise in the economic fortunes of the federal government led to calls for the end to restraint in the transfer field, but the federal government countered with the view that its financial affairs, comparatively speaking, were not healthy enough to allow it to act as the banker for the provinces. Provinces, in the aggregate, were in a similar fiscal circumstance to that of the federal government. Seven provinces posted balanced budgets or surpluses in 1998–9. The Royal Bank of Canada, noted the federal Finance Department, forecast a cumulative fiscal surplus for all provinces of over $46 billion between 2000–1 and 2004–5, and it pointed out that the federal and provincial–territorial revenue growth rates had been virtually identical from 1978 to 1998 and that the federal government's debt burden was over twice as large as the aggregate provincial–territorial debt burden ($246 billion in 1997–8) (Canada, Department of Finance, 1999).

Another factor motivating the federal government was Quebec secessionism. When the Quebec government called for a provincial referendum on sovereignty-association in 1995 and then came within a percentage point of winning a simple majority, the federal Liberal government saw a need for supplementing its earlier traditional approach of proving the workability of federalism (nicknamed 'Plan A' by some observers) with a harder-edged strategy of various warnings about the negative implications of separation (nicknamed 'Plan B' by the same). The softer approach would be evident in the devolution of federal program responsibilities and the self-imposed restriction on the spending power undertaken in 1996; the harder version included references to the Supreme Court and a resulting new 'Clarity Act'.

A continuing factor in regard to the spending power was the notion of province-building. Provincial calls continued for autonomy in selected areas of public policy, and a general increase in general-purpose transfers to the provinces allowed them sufficient revenues to fulfill their constitutional responsibilities as they interpreted them. The tendency towards autonomy was strongest in the case of the so-called 'have' provinces, who relied comparatively little on federal transfers in the first place, and disputed the moral and political right of the federal authorities to dictate conditions when they contributed so little. Federal specific-purpose cash transfers, for example, amounted to 8 per cent of British Columbia's total revenue, 9 per cent of Alberta's, and just under 11 per cent of Ontario's in 1997–8 (Canadian Tax Foundation, 1997: 8:3). Periodically, these provinces would threaten to opt out of the shared-cost programs and operate the programs themselves. The spending power became the principal object of provincial discontent during this period because it represented everything they disliked about contemporary federalism: federal unilateralism in deciding levels of transfers to the provinces, and the general lack of ability to plan provincial development that this unilateralism implied. In the 1990s the province-building doctrine was expressed in various terms, but with a common element: a vision of equality of the two orders of government, notably in areas where the federal government had previously dominated the agenda.

The road to the Social Union Framework Agreement was strewn with a number of crises and false starts. These included the Canada Health and Social Transfer, the Social Union talks, the 1996 federal spending power commitment, the Calgary Declaration, and events following the 1997 federal general election.

The Canada Health and Social Transfer

In the federal budget of 1995, federal Finance Minister Paul Martin gave notice of the introduction of the **Canada Health and Social Transfer (CHST)**. The budget noted that it would 'continue the evolution away from cost-sharing in areas of provincial responsibility, which has been a source of entanglement and irritation in federal–provincial relations.' It was the financial substance of the CHST, however, that exacerbated historical grievances about the federal spending power.

The CHST amalgamated the two major federal transfer payments, the block funding mechanism for health insurance and post-secondary education known as Established Programs Financing (EPF) and the Canada Assistance Plan (CAP), a social assistance and welfare transfer, into one large transfer, to begin in 1996–7. As was the case with EPF and the CAP, the CHST was to be a combination of cash and tax points. The new transfer was associated with major cuts in the projected entitlement under the former programs. In 1996–7, the funding was set at $26.9 billion, a reduction of $2.5 billion, and in 1997–8 at $25.1 billion, for a total reduction of $4.3 billion in the two-year period. If only cash transfers were considered, the provinces' take would slide dramatically, from $18.3 billion in 1995–6 to $12.5 billion in 1997–8. (During the 1997 election, the Liberals vowed that the cash floor of the CHST would never fall below $12.5 billion, thus ensuring Ottawa a continuing presence in social policy.) The equalization program, which had been renewed for a five-year period beginning in 1994–5, was allowed to rise in line with annual GDP growth. The CHST was still subject to some conditions. Ottawa would continue to enforce the five principles of the Canada Health Act (comprehensiveness, universality, portability, public administration, and accessibility), and the provinces would be required, as they were under CAP, to provide social assistance without any minimum residency requirements. However, the budget invited the provinces to pursue innovation by eliminating restrictions on cost-sharing that the CAP had contained. As to what lay beyond 1997–8, the provinces were invited 'to work together, through mutual consent, a set of shared principles and objectives that could underlie the new transfer'.

The 1996 Federal Spending Power Commitment

The provinces would indeed begin working together, but it would be within the context of changed federal ground rules. In the Throne Speech of 1996, the federal government made a commitment that it would 'not use its spending power to create new shared-cost programs in areas of exclusive provincial jurisdiction without the consent of a majority of the provinces. Any new program will be designed so that non-participating provinces will be compensated, provided they establish equivalent or comparable initiatives.' In one stroke the federal government had (1) met the test of no unilateralism in the initiation of new shared-cost programs; (2) established a simple consent formula; (3) opened the door to a consent mechanism and to a more detailed consent formula; and (4) outlined a principle of conditional compensation.

Of course, it did not meet all the tests of the constitutional reform industry. It did not constrain itself against unilateralism in established shared-cost programs or fully funded federal programs in areas of provincial jurisdiction. Presumably it was not curtailing its ability to terminate spending power programs or to reduce substantially its funding, as it had in regard to health, education, and welfare programs in the past. It did not constrain federal spending power programs relating to individuals and institutions. Needless to say, it did not meet the continuing demand of the then Quebec Liberal leader, Daniel Johnson, to add to the Constitution a limitation of the federal spending power. However, progress had been made, and the nine provincial governments other than Quebec saw the measure as a positive step (Provincial/Territorial Council, 1997: 7).

Federal–Provincial Consent Mechanisms after the CHST

One of the more remarkable things about federal–provincial relations in the late 1990s was the extent to which the decision-making structures—both extant and proposed—began to resemble those suggested by the constitutional reform industry. While they did not have elevated names like the Council of the Federation, Federal Council, or reconstituted Upper House, functional counterparts of these entities came into existence.

The premiers, reacting to the new federal ground rules and diminished financial presence, established the Ministerial Council on Social Policy Reform and Renewal at their annual meeting in 1995. (Social policy was defined to include health, post-secondary education, income support, labour market programs, social services, housing, and other specific supports.) In December 1995, the Ministerial Council, on which all provinces except Quebec had participated, reached consensus in a report to the premiers (Ministerial Council, 1995). This report called for a rebalancing of federal, provincial, and territorial roles in social policy and to that end presented 15 'principles' to guide social policy reform. It also recommended that the report itself serve as a basis for new dialogue with the Prime Minister, and that the provinces and territories develop a 'national framework' to guide the reform process in areas of provincial/territorial responsibility. The framework would include the 15 principles, the reform agenda being developed by the Council and its sectoral ministerial committees, and a monitoring mechanism that would also aid in 'settling differences' (ibid., 20).

At their June 1996 first ministers meeting in Jasper, the Prime Minister and premiers committed themselves to 'put into practice' the Ministerial Council report and established a committee of ministers to study the issues. This would come to be called the Federal/Provincial/Territorial Council on Social Policy Renewal (the 'F/P/T Council'). Human Resources Development Minister Doug Young was the lead federal minister. For their part, the premiers at their August 1996 Annual Premiers' Conference (APC) adopted the *Issues Paper on Social Policy Reform and Renewal* and established a counterpoint body of their own called the Provincial/Territorial (P/T) Council on Social Policy Renewal. The premiers directed their designates to the P/T Council to report in six months with 'options for mechanisms and processes to develop and promote adherence to national programs and standards' at both the federal/provincial/territorial and provincial/territorial levels (Provincial–Territorial Working Group, 1996: 16). Significantly, the Council was also to review new approaches to the use of the federal spending power to ensure that the federal government could not use it to impose conditions unilaterally on social programs. Over time, deadlock would come to characterize the efforts of the joint F/P/T Council, in contrast to the co-operation of the P/T Council.

The result of the August 1996 APC mandate was the April 1997 options paper of the Provincial/Territorial Council, *New Approaches to Canada's Social Union*, which presented a broad gamut of alternatives, including a broad federal/provincial/territorial framework agreement, a framework agreement on a single issue (like the spending power), step-by-step sectoral agreements with no framework, and parallel federal/provincial/territorial and provincial/territorial agreements (Provincial/Territorial Council, 1997). Its most important immediate effect was to popularize the term 'social union'.

The premiers seem to have gone for the full-meal deal. At their 1997 conference at St Andrew's-by-the-Sea, New Brunswick, they instructed their Provincial/Territorial Council on Social Policy Renewal to 'negotiate with the federal government a broad framework agreement on the social union to address cross-sectoral issues such as common principles, the use of the federal spending power, and new ways to manage and resolve disagreements' (Canadian Intergovernmental Conference Secretariat, 1997a). Parallel fiscal frameworks established by finance ministers and parallel provincial/territorial framework agreements were also mandated for discussion.

Two Faces Have I: Chrétien after the 1997 Federal Election

The provincial approach may have been sophisticated. It may have constituted a phenomenal rebound for a provincial agenda that seemed all but spent with the demise of the Charlottetown Accord. It may have succeeded in luring federal authorities into framework discussions that would have been unthinkable decades before. It may have focused public attention on the spending power in an unparalleled fashion. However, it provided few incentives for the federal government, a government that responded to a far different set of political imperatives. Indeed, there actually were incentives for it to continue interventionism in social policy areas.

What made the renewed federal interventionism initially confusing is that during its first term the Chrétien Liberal government had engaged in a conscious effort to 'rebalance' the federation. As a consequence, it had offered to withdraw from certain areas of provincial jurisdiction, namely labour-market training, social housing, mining, forestry, and recreation. Even though it had decreased cash transfers, the CHST had expanded the freedom of provinces to experiment in social policy, especially in areas previously under the constraints of the Canada Assistance Plan. However, observers were soon able to piece together the motivations for renewed government interest in such intervention. The Liberals cherished their welfare state image, and there was news of an impending 'social dividend' (budget surpluses). Importantly, there was an apparent lack of political payoff for the rebalancing effort. In the 1997 election the Liberals had won fewer seats than in 1993 (155 as opposed to 177); went down in the popular vote to 38.4 per cent from 41.8 per cent; and suffered a decline in regional representation in Atlantic Canada, dropping to 11 seats from 31, and in Western Canada, to 15 from 27. In fact, the Liberals in 1997 received the lowest popular vote for a party forming a majority government since 1867, the previous lowest being 40.9 per cent for the Liberals in 1945; won the second lowest seat percentage for a party forming a majority government, the lowest being the 51 per cent for the Liberals in 1945; and attracted the lowest percentage of eligible voters since Confederation—25.5 per cent—for a party forming a majority government: all of this in an election that featured the lowest voter turnout—66.7 per cent—since 1925 (*The Hill Times*, 1997). To add insult to injury, Quebec took the credit for wresting the 'rebalanced' powers from Ottawa. So what now needed rebalancing, apparently, were Liberal fortunes, not federal and provincial roles.

After the June 1997 federal election, a tendency towards federal intervention would begin to resurrect itself. Jean Chrétien declared himself satisfied with the wording of the Calgary Declaration and the motives of the premiers in calling the late 1997 meeting (Galloway, 1997; Greenspon, 1997). The government did not explicitly renege on the Declaration's 'partnership' theme, but it did not completely honour the spirit of the pledge, either. It unilaterally initiated a spending power program in the form of the Canada Millennium Scholarship Fund, a one-time $2.5 billion program aimed at increasing accessibility to post-secondary education. The 1998 budget announced the creation of 19,000 'internship programs' for youth, presumably as a complement to the Millennium Fund. Ottawa continued to discuss with the provinces the idea of initiating the home care programs touted in the 1997 Liberal Party's 'Red Book' election manifesto, even though the provincial consensus appeared to favour a simpler strategy of reinstating the lost $6 billion CHST cash transfers as opposed to acquiescing to what were informally termed federal 'boutique programs'. At the same time, however, at their December 1997 meeting the Prime Minister and premiers agreed to begin negotiations on an F/P/T framework for Canada's social union. The framework would include principles of social policy, collaborative approaches, dispute settlement arrangements, and clarification of roles and responsibilities in social policy.

Parenthetically, some provinces now began to demand that all new major spending power programs, not just the ones involving cost-sharing (as in the 1996 commitment), should be subject to vetting under a social union framework. Ottawa, for its part, dodged the 1996 commitment bullet by following a strategy of *independence* (initiating transfer programs that did not involve cost-sharing, as with the Millennium Fund) and *integration* (combining resources in a specific policy area, with each government co-operating but retaining separate delivery mechanisms according to areas of expertise, as with the National Child Tax Benefit announced in 1998).

When all provinces—Quebec included, surprising those familiar with Premier Lucien Bouchard's repeated suspicion of the social union concept—finally agreed on the principles of a framework agreement, the federal reaction was predictably muted. At the August 1998 Premiers' Conference, there was unanimous agreement (nicknamed the 'Saskatoon Consensus') on rules the premiers wanted to see in place:

- The federal government should be prohibited from spending money to create or change national social programs without majority provincial consent.

- Provinces should be able to opt out of any new or modified national social program with full financial compensation, providing that they provide a program that 'addresses the priority areas' dealt with in the national program.
- There should be a joint role in setting, interpreting, and enforcing national standards for medicare and other national programs.
- A mechanism should be instituted to give provinces a role in resolving disputes over standards and disagreements when opting-out provinces have met the conditions for receiving compensation. (Thompson and Bryden, 1998)

The similarity of some of these suggested rules to those that emerged from the constitutional reform industry phase is striking. However, some of the demands, like that for dispute resolution mechanism involving the provinces, amounted to an advance over what the constitutional reformers had demanded.

Over and above its agreement to sign on to the social union discussions, Quebec made the additional concession of abandoning its traditional insistence that opting-out provinces receive *unconditional* compensation from the federal government. Now Quebec would be obligated to address the same 'priority areas' as did the federal program from which it opted out. Another surprise would lie in store in the course of the fall 1998 Quebec provincial election when Premier Bouchard announced that he wanted a constitutional amendment to the Canadian Constitution entrenching the social union and the right of provinces to opt out of social programs with compensation, even going so far as to call the entrenchment proposal 'good for Quebec' (Daly, 1998).[2]

In September 1998 Chrétien refused to accept the premiers' August consensus. In particular, he did not agree to give up the federal government's right to spend on social programs if the provinces did not consent to them, and especially where only federal cash was involved. He would not abandon the federal power to enforce medicare standards. He would not accept the premiers' idea of a joint federal–provincial dispute settlement tribunal, alleging that informal federal–provincial consultation already achieves the same effect as would such a formal mechanism. He would not go further in constraining the federal spending power than what was done in the 1996 Throne Speech commitment. He made reference to some (unspecified) compromises he was willing to make, but warned of a total federal boycott if pushed too far, saying that 'if they [the premiers] don't want to take what I'm offering, they take nothing. That's an alternative, too' (Bryden, 1998). The reversal of a Quebec-sensitive 'Plan A' strategy appeared evident in an interview the Prime Minister gave in October 1998 to the Montreal daily, *La Presse*, in which he commented that he had already satisfied Quebec's traditional demands for change, and the Constitution was not a 'general store'. Bouchard gleefully seized upon this as evidence that the Calgary Declaration was too high a threshold of reform for the Prime Minister.

At long last the battle lines were once again drawn in their traditional form. The provinces wanted a constrained and co-determined spending power. The federal authorities were unwilling to accept this vision, opting instead for a kind of traditional co-operative federalism approach. It seemed that once again Canadians were to be treated to a protracted debate on the pros and cons of the spending power. Yet it would soon appear that these were only bargaining positions. A final agreement, of sorts, was on the way.

A Framework to Improve the Social Union for Canadians

The Prime Minister and premiers, expressing dissatisfaction with the embarrassingly slow pace of progress achieved on the dossier, took matters into their own hands and emerged from the Prime Minister's residence on 4 February 1999 with an agreement called *A Framework to Improve the Social Union for Canadians*. Quebec did not sign. The social union agreement was supplemented with a vague Federal–Provincial–Territorial Health Care Agreement that protected medicare and promised an unspecified increase in health funding. The Social Union Framework Agreement included seven sections. Table 24.2

Table 24.2 Summary of 'A Framework to Improve the Social Union for Canadians'

Framework Section	Content of the Section
1. Principles	Governments commit to a number of principles within their respective jurisdictions and powers. These, among others, include greater fairness, equality, diversity, and mutual aid. The needs of Canadians are to be met by ensuring access to essential social services of reasonably comparable quality; by respecting the principles of medicare (comprehensiveness, universality, portability, public administration, and accessibility); and by ensuring adequate, affordable, stable, and sustainable funding for social programs.
2. Mobility within Canada	Governments will ensure that no new barriers to mobility are created in new social policy initiatives. Governments will eliminate, over three years, existing residency-based policies and practices that constrain access to post-secondary education, training, health and social services, and social assistance unless such policies/practices are demonstrated to be consistent with the social union framework principles. Accordingly, sector ministers will submit annual reports to the Ministerial Council identifying such barriers and providing action plans for their elimination. Governments will ensure, by 1 July 2001, full compliance with the mobility provisions of the Agreement on Internal Trade by all entities subject to them; such provisions include the mutual recognition of occupational qualifications and the elimination of residency requirements for employment opportunities.
3. Informing Canadians: Public Accountability and Transparency	Governments' accountability to constituents (*public accountability*) is to be enhanced by a variety of mechanisms: among others, regular reporting to constituents on the outcomes of social programs; the development of comparative indicators between jurisdictions to measure progress on agreed objectives; explaining the respective roles of governments to the public; and public involvement in developing social priorities and reviewing outcomes. *Transparency* is to be enhanced by making publicly available both the eligibility criteria and service commitments established for social programs; installing citizen appeal and complaint mechanisms; and reporting publicly on such appeals and complaints.
4. Working in Partnership for Canadians	Building on the demonstrated benefits of the Ministerial Council experience of joint planning and collaboration, governments agree to share information on social trends and identify priorities for collaborative action; and to provide more effective and efficient service to Canadians in areas such action is identified by, where appropriate, joint development of objectives, clarification of roles and responsibilities, and flexible implementation that recognizes diverse needs, complements existing measures, and avoids duplication. Governments also agree to reciprocal notice, that is, giving each other advance notice when implementing a major change in social policy that affects the other government(s); and to advance consultation before implementing such policy, in order to identify potential duplication and alternative approaches to implementation that are flexible and effective. As well, for any new Canada-wide social initiative, arrangements made with one province or territory will be made available to all, consistent with their diverse circumstances. Co-operation with Aboriginal peoples is pledged.
5. The Federal Spending Power	In order to promote funding predictability, the federal government will consult at least one year prior to renewal or significant funding changes in existing social transfers, and will build in 'due notice provisions' to new social transfers to provinces and territories.

(*continued*)

Table 24.2 (Continued)

	For purposes of establishing new constraints, the Agreement makes a distinction between two types of social programs undertaken through the use of the federal spending power: first, new Canada-wide initiatives supported by transfers to the provinces and territories (intergovernmental transfers), and second, new Canada-wide initiatives funded by direct federal spending (federal transfers to individuals and to organizations).
	(1) Regarding the first, the federal government will no longer unilaterally introduce new Canada-wide initiatives in health care, post-secondary education, social assistance, and social services that are funded through intergovernmental transfers, whether block-funded or shared. Instead, it will collaborate with provinces and territories to identify Canada-wide priorities and objectives and will introduce such new initiatives only upon the agreement of a majority of provincial governments. The federal government will no longer impose programs, but allow each province and territory to determine its own program design and mix. The federal government will no longer require that the total transfer be devoted to a given objective; a provincial or territorial government that, because of its existing programming, does not need the total transfer to fulfill the agreed objective, may reinvest the balance in the same or a related priority area. The federal, provincial, and territorial governments will agree on an accountability framework for new social initiatives and investments. Provincial and territorial governments will receive their share of available funding if they meet or commit to meet the agreed Canada-wide objectives, and agree to respect the accountability framework.
	(2) Regarding the second, new Canada-wide initiatives funded through direct federal spending for health care, post-secondary education, social assistance, and social services, the federal government will give, prior to implementation, at least three months' notice and offer to consult other governments. The governments participating in the consultations will have the opportunity to identify potential duplication and to propose alternative approaches to achieve flexible and effective implementation.
6. Dispute Avoidance and Resolution	Governments commit themselves to working collaboratively to avoid and resolve intergovernmental disputes. Dispute avoidance and resolution, while respecting existing legislative provisions, will apply to commitments on mobility, intergovernmental transfers, interpretation of the Canada Health Act principles, and, as appropriate, on any new joint initiative. Sector negotiations to resolve disputes will be based on joint fact-finding, written reports of which will be submitted before completion to the governments involved to provide them opportunity to comment. Governments involved may seek third-party assistance for fact-finding, advice, or mediation. Fact-finding or mediation reports may be made public at the request of either party in a dispute. Governments will report annually and publicly on the nature of intergovernmental disputes and their resolution. The Ministerial Council will support sector ministers by collecting information on effective implementation, dispute avoidance, and jurisdictional progress reports.
7. Review of the Social Union Framework Agreement	Governments will jointly undertake a full review of the Framework Agreement by the end of the third year of its operation in order to make appropriate adjustments. The review will ensure significant public input and feedback.

Source: Abstracted by the author from Canadian Intergovernmental Conference Secretariat (1999).

reviews, in summary form, the content of what some have called the 'Sussex Accord' or, in more abbreviated form, simply 'SUFA'.

The provincial gains were not as great as some of those involved in the negotiations had hoped, but the dossier had indeed moved forward. There was a commitment to stable funding for social programs (which materialized as equal per capita CHST funding in the 1999 federal budget) and a one-year notice provision for changes to existing transfers. In addition, the federal government had made a commitment to joint planning and consultation in social policy. Provinces now had a legitimate right to suggest modifications to federal policy designs. Also, new national shared-cost programs involved greater flexibility in implementation and funding. As long as they honoured the agreed objectives, provinces and territories could arrange the program design and mix of any new national shared-cost program to suit their own needs and circumstances. They could reinvest the extra portion of federal transfers not spent on the program in question in the 'same or a related priority area'. As well, fact-finding and mediation reports could be made public, a useful tool in the perennial struggle of governments for the hearts and minds of Canadians, and a province could demand, and get, within the bounds of practicality, the same arrangement that Ottawa made with another province. And, finally, there was a nod to a kind of 'equality of status' of the provinces with the federal government implicit in the dispute avoidance provisions.

Yet Ottawa had prevailed over the constitutional industry. To a remarkable extent the status quo ante prevailed. The federal authority retained the ability to penalize provinces that did not meet the principles of medicare. The consent formula for the introduction of new Canada-wide, shared-cost programs remained what Chrétien had decreed it to be in 1996; and there was no mention of a consent formula for changing established shared-cost programs. Direct federal spending to individuals and organizations faced no significant new impediments, other than a three-month notice provision accompanied by an offer to consult. There was no mention of federal compensation for early withdrawal from shared-cost programs, and mutual consent was not required for funding changes, only consultation and 'due notice'. The Agreement did not mention the right to opt out with compensation from new national intergovernmental initiatives. There was to be no binding dispute resolution mechanism, merely a non-binding 'dispute avoidance and resolution' mechanism limited to fact-finding and mediation roles. As well, a host of Quebec demands went largely unanswered.

The advent of a new century did not mute the provincial voices calling for reformed federal decision-making. At their Annual Premiers' Conference (APC) of July 2003, the Premiers agreed to the establishment of a 'Council of the Federation' (COF), with as-yet vague powers, other than to provide leadership and to act as an umbrella for provincial/territorial coordinating bodies (CICS, 2003). However, big things were foreseen for the body, at least from the standpoint of its main progenitors, Premier Jean Charest of Quebec, and his intergovernmental affairs Minister, Benoît Pelletier. 'Ultimately it would be a joint decision-making body, which would oversee areas of overlapping jurisdictions such as health, education, social policy, and interprovincial trade. Mr. Pelletier said it would be funded first by the provinces, which would appoint representatives, with the federal government signing on later' (Aubry, 2003). (Federal membership never came to pass, however.) So far its ambit has seemed relatively restrained, its workplan established in 2004 focusing mostly on research on fiscal imbalance, health-care reform, and interprovincial trade. Privately, Pelletier said that it would not take on the spending power yet because the COF would need to build up a record of successful handling of dossiers, in order not to hand the separatists an issue that they could use to rally support to their cause.

During the Chretien–Martin years, new programming under the spending power began to take on a more economic hue. The agenda of the Liberal government once had shared with the provinces a concern with place and community prosperity; it now came to be replaced by what might be called 'the innovation agenda'. This agenda sees the country more in terms of clusters of communities and less in terms of provinces. This was evident in a series of Liberal government policy documents, such as the *Red Book* (Liberal Party, 1993), the 1994 *Jobs and Growth Agenda: Building a More Innovative Economy* (Canada, 1994), the *Innovation Strategy* (Canada, 2002), and a host of throne speeches and budget addresses.

This led to a new economic use of the spending power which can be called '**urban asymmetry**'. This term signified the special relationships of the federal government with larger urban centres and agglomerations across the country, based on what it considers to be their needs and economic potential. The relationships were not only with cities and metropolitan areas, but also with other regional and local actors like universities, community economic development agencies, special purpose bodies (SPBs), industry associations, research institutes, and so forth. An important implication of the term—indeed it is implied in the expression itself—is that the federal government does not have to treat the actors equitably. It may not even choose to deal with any but a handful of them in certain provinces, for special programs. Urban asymmetry had special implications for both smaller provinces and the municipalities of smaller provinces.

The Chretien–Martin governments liked urban asymmetry because it had overtones of the co-operative federalism of the 1950s and 1960s; it could tailor its programs as a response to the size of jurisdiction; building the knowledge economy (the major focus of the concept) was a new form of 'nation-building'; and it made the federal government highly visible. The politics were also important. The federal Liberal cabinet courted votes in densely populated areas; had a way of picking 'winners and losers' in a seemingly technical, non-obvious fashion; and established a process which entailed an immense information cost for critics who wanted to compare its operation on a regional or provincial basis (Dunn, 2004).

Martin as Prime Minister emphasized both the innovation agenda and a personal crusade he called 'the New Deal for Cities and Communities'. His government's Budget 2005 estimated that the goods and services tax (GST) rebate implemented in budget 2004, the gas tax sharing announced in Budget 2005, and the continuing and enhanced Green Municipal Funds program, would provide Canadian communities with over $9 billion between 2005 and 2010. On 1 June 2005, Infrastructure and Communities Minister John Godfrey announced an additional $800 million over two years for public transit at the Canadian Urban Transport Association (CUTA) annual conference.

The Constitutional Reform Industry Cycles into Saigon: Harper's Conservatives and Open Federalism

By the middle of the first decade of the twenty-first century, the spending power had become a political issue, skilfully manipulated by the new Conservative Party, a union of the former Canadian Alliance and Progressive Conservative parties. It was emphasized by the leader himself, Steven Harper, wrapped up in a broader intergovernmental philosophy called '**Open Federalism**', and made a mainstay of the 2006 federal election. Thereafter it appeared in the context of budget announcements and specialized intergovernmental arrangements.

Whereas various factors led to the other stages in the history of the spending power, there was just one at this stage: electoral politics: specifically, coalition-building. University of Calgary political science professor Tom Flanagan, the single-most important factor in Harper's success, explains the thinking. He had helped the future Prime Minister write a speech for the important 1996 'Winds of Change' Conference, inserting into it a concept he nicknamed the 'Three Sisters Theory'. In the speech, says Flanagan, 'Mr Harper marshalled historical evidence to show that all winning Conservative coalitions in 20th-century Canadian history had been built around three main elements: populist reformers, strongest in the West but also present in rural Ontario; traditional Tories, strong in Ontario and Atlantic Canada; and francophone nationalists in Quebec' (Flanagan, 2006). The election of 1993 saw Brian Mulroney's grand coalition shatter along these ancient fault lines to form an opposition composed of the Reform Party, the separatist Parti Québécois, and a small (two elected members) Progressive Conservative element. Conservatives, to regain national power, had to reconstruct the coalition.

As it turned out, the members of the coalition were charter members of the constitutional reform industry. Quebec nationalists had had issues with Ottawa's historical use of the spending power for decades; Reform Party western populists cited the legal prohibitions against the use of the spending power, which were included in the party's *Blue Book: 1996–1997 Principles and Policies* statement, as a weapon against Liberal centralizers; and eastern Tories had in fact generated the Meech Lake and Charlottetown accords.

So there was little surprise when the Conservative National Policy Convention of March 2005 constructed an intergovernmental platform that faithfully reflected the constitutional reform industry tests. There were to be other iterations of intergovernmental policy that further elaborated the tests as well. This policy would become known as 'Open Federalism'.

The Party revealed its new notion of Open Federalism in its founding *Policy Declaration*. Its policies committed a future Conservative Government to restore the 'constitutional balance between the federal and provincial and territorial governments'; to defend 'the notion of strong provinces within Canada' and 'the federal principle'; to advance specific reforms to respond to both Quebec's reluctance to sign the Constitution as well as Western alienation; to support the new interprovincial forum, the Council of the Federation (which Quebec had proposed); and, famously, to fix the 'fiscal imbalance' by various means including increasing the amounts allocated to provincial transfers, by reducing taxes, or by transferring tax points to the provinces (Conservative Party of Canada, 2005).

With respect to the transfers issue, the Policy Declaration promised to ensure that 'the use of the federal spending power in provincial jurisdictions is limited' (ibid.). Specific ideas on how to limit it, however, were lacking. Clarity on the actual framework for spending power limits would only come a few years later. They were to parallel very closely the constitutional reform industry frameworks.

The 2006 Conservative platform promised a 'Charter of Open Federalism' which never materialized, but the 2007 federal budget did in fact add some detail to the concept (Canada, 2007a). It implicitly characterized it as:

- enhancing the accountability of governments through the clarification of their respective roles and responsibilities;
- using excess federal revenues primarily to reduce taxes rather than to launch new federal programs in areas that are primarily of provincial and territorial responsibility;
- focusing new spending on areas of federal responsibility and where new initiatives are introduced in areas of primary provincial and territorial responsibility, doing it at the request of provinces and territories;
- limiting the use of the 'federal spending power' by ensuring (1) that new cost-shared programs in areas of provincial responsibility have the consent of the majority of provinces to proceed and that provinces; and (2) territories have the right to opt out of cost-shared federal programs with compensation if they offer similar programs with comparable accountability structures;
- aiding transparency by reporting in all future budgets on new investments (1) in areas of core federal and shared responsibility and (2) in transfers to support provinces and territories.

For some months the government said that it would be announcing measures to 'strengthen the federation' in an upcoming Speech from the Throne. In the Throne Speech of 16 October 2007 it became evident that the Prime Minister's Office was mindful of history:

> Our Government believes that the constitutional jurisdiction of each order of government should be respected. To this end, guided by our **federalism of openness** [the new name favoured by the Conservatives] our Government will introduce legislation to place formal limits on the use of the federal spending power for new shared-cost programs in areas of exclusive provincial jurisdiction. This legislation will allow provinces and territories to opt out with reasonable compensation if they offer compatible programs. (Canada, 2007b)

There were only nuanced changes from the 2007 budget wording: the limits would be legislated, formal, and they would apply to *new* shared-cost programs. The Meech Lake Accord of 1987 and the Charlottetown Accord of 1992, two failed federal–provincial constitutional amendment agreements, had of course included similar wording and foreseen the same arrangements. It was *déjà vu* all over again. The only thing that was missing was the degree of contention that had surrounded past efforts to rein in the spending power.

The intergovernmental peace may have been eased, ironically enough, by significant increases in transfers under *old* shared-cost programs. The 2007 budget spoke of 'putting transfers on a long-term principles-based footing'. This meant in practice that cash funding to provinces and territories, which had been $43 billion when the Harper government took office in 2006, would rise to at least $18 billion higher in 2013–14. A modified CST (Canada Social Transfer) would see a rise of $16 billion in new funding over seven years, beginning in 2008–9, for post-secondary education, children and social programs; and infrastructure would also get more than $16 billion in new funding over the next seven years. Budget 2008 did not disturb these figures.

Conclusion

The asymmetric nature of the Social Union Framework Agreement had come back to haunt intergovernmental negotiators. Only a few of the historical concerns with transfers had been addressed. Now there was a new approach to the spending power, embedded in a broader, more classical conception of intergovernmental relations, called Open Federalism.

There were several reasons why it was received without the acrimony that had marked other reform industry efforts. The Conservatives had learned the Liberal lesson that dollars—they now called it 'restoring fiscal balance'—brought intergovernmental peace. The provinces were unlikely to remain satisfied for long with an agreement, SUFA, premised upon the federal government as the senior partner in Canadian federalism. The Saskatoon Consensus of 1998 had been just that—a consensus; a rare show of unanimity on the basics of intergovernmental transfers, and Open Federalism delivered most of what Saskatoon had advocated. Quebec, albeit with a federalist government in power, was now onside. The Liberal opposition, which had built its popularity on the basis of the spending power, was now silent on the question of limiting it. One notable difference in the old packages and the new Open Federalism is that the latter did not include the debilitating links to a variety of controversial institutional changes, as had the accords.

One other lesson, however, bears remembering. Provinces seek power. Open Federalism has not delivered all that it said it would. There is no Charter of Open Federalism. There is no mention of tax transfers, so beloved of Quebec nationalists especially. There is no mention of Quebec distinctiveness in a constitutional context. There is no intergovernmental dispute-resolution mechanism. There is no clarity on the status of old shared-cost programs. These may be avenues down which the advocates of provincial power drive. There they may be met once again in battle by the defenders of the use of the spending power and a vigorous federal role. This is not destined to be a quiet area of public policy.

Appendix A The Spending Power and the Constitutional Reform Industry, 1969–1992

Report	Scope of Power	Consent Formula	Consent Mechanism	Opt Out with Compensation	Opting Out Conditional	Opting Out Unconditional	National Objectives?	Financial Guidelines
Trudeau (1969)	nsc	yes	no	yes (to taxpayer)		yes	no	no
Molgat-MacGuigan (1972)	nsc	yes	no	yes (to govt)		yes (implicit)	yes (portable; increase of fed $)	no
CBA (1978)	nsc	yes	yes (RUH)	yes (to govt)	yes		yes (portable)	no
Pepin-Robarts (1979)	nsc ffp (esc?)	yes	yes (RUH)	yes (to govt)		yes	no	no
Beige Paper (1980)	nsc	yes	yes (FC)	yes (to govt)		yes	yes	no
Meech Lake (1987)	nsc	no	no	yes (to govt)	yes		yes	no
Shaping . . . (1991)	nsc	yes	yes (COF)	yes (to govt)	yes		yes	no
Beaudoin-Dobbie (1992)	nsc	no	no	yes (to govt)	yes		yes	yes
Charlottetown (1992)	nsc	no	no	yes (or stay)	yes		yes	yes

Scope: Refers to the scope of the spending power involved. Alternatives are new shared-cost (nsc), established shared-cost (esc), fully federal program (ffp), equalization (e), direct transfers to individuals and corporations (i&c). The latter two categories do not appear on this chart, nor does any mention of provincial spending power.

Consent Formula: Refers to what threshold of approval, expressed in numerical terms, should be necessary for the initiation of a spending power program: for example, the consent (1) of a specified number of provinces or (2) of a certain percentage of the delegates in a reconstituted upper house.

Consent Mechanism: Refers to whether or not the provincial consent is to be registered by a new intergovernmental mechanism, whether a reconstituted Upper House (RUH), Federal Council (FC), or Council of the Federation (COF).

Opt Out with Compensation: Refers to whether or not the plan envisages financial or fiscal compensation being offered to governments who do not participate in federal spending power programs and run their own similar program.

Opting-Out Conditionality: Refers to the degree of compulsion associated with the compensation for opting-out provinces: (1) conditional opting out means that compensation depends on the province establishing its own program with objectives compatible with those of the national program; (2) unconditional opting out means that the province receives compensation for opting out, but is not obliged to mount a program with objectives compatible to those of the national program.

National Objectives: Refers to whether or not the opting-out provinces would have to comply with 'national objectives' and whether these would be set federally or co-operatively.

Financial Guidelines: Refers to protections against federal unilateralism, such as notice of withdrawal, compensation for early withdrawal, multi-year funding commitments, and mutual consent for changes.

Important Terms and Concepts

constitutional reform industry
departmentalized cabinet
institutionalized cabinet
Keynesian consensus
Open Federalism (Federalism of Openness)
payments to individuals and institutions
shared-cost programs
Social Union Framework Agreement (SUFA)
spending power framework
spending power of Parliament
spending power tests
traditional cabinet
unconditional grants (including equalization)
urban asymmetry

Study Questions

1. What are the various kinds of transfers possible under the spending power, and what kinds have various parties promoted while in power?
2. What is meant by the 'constitutional reform industry' and what tests and frameworks did it promote as ways to undertake intergovernmental relations in Canada? (See note 1.)
3. To what extent did the Harper government's 'Open Federalism' policies reflect the tests and frameworks of the constitutional reform industry?
4. Why did reform of the spending power prove so difficult to achieve for so many decades?
5. What are the various limits that are possible to place on the spending power, and which have been advocated by what actors over the decades?

Useful Websites

A Framework to Improve the Social Union for Canadians:

http://socialunion.gc.ca/news/020499_e.html

Conservative Party of Canada. 2005 *Policy Declaration.*

www.conservative.ca/media/20050319-POLICY%20DECLARATION.pdf

Federal/Provincial/Territorial Ministerial Council on Social Policy Renewal. 2003. Three Year Review Social Union Framework Agreement (SUFA). June.

www.unionsociale.gc.ca/sufa/Three_Year_Review/e/tyrsufa.html#1_

Speech from the Throne, October 16, 2007: The announcement of action to come on the Spending Power:

www.parl.gc.ca/39/2/parlbus/chambus/senate/deb-e/001db_2007-10-16-E.htm?#7

Canada. Ministry of Finance. 2007 Budget. (Chapter 4 outlines the Harper government's philosophy on the use of the spending power):

www.budget.gc.ca/2007/plan/bpc4-eng.html

Notes

1. The 'constitutional reform industry' is a catch-all phrase to describe the main lines of consensus among decentralist forces in Canada from 1968 to 1992. Such reports as Molgat-MacGuigan (Canada, 1972), *Towards a New Canada* (CBA, 1978), Pepin-Robarts (Canada, 1979), the Beige Paper (Quebec Liberal Party, 1980), the Meech Lake and Charlottetown accords, *Shaping Canada's Future Together* (Canada, 1991), and Beaudoin-Dobbie (1992b) would be examples of the reform industry.

Over a period of time, this 'industry' managed to describe a series of tests for measuring the success of federal–provincial relations. As well, it generated relative consensus on what frameworks were preferable in controlling the federal spending power. Together, these amounted to a thesis that the federal spending power should be constitutionally controlled. Their respective tests and frameworks for Canadian federalism are as follows.

Constitutional Reform Industry Tests

The tests to be applied to federal–provincial relations, if the reform industry had its way, were remarkably consistent from 1969 to 1992. (1) The future use of the federal spending power would have to avoid federal unilateralism in the initiation and termination of fully funded federal programs or shared-cost programs in areas of provincial jurisdiction. (2) Clearly, they would have to be policy areas of overriding national importance, however difficult it was to clarify this concept. (3) A co-operative approach to determining national objectives was preferable to unilateral federal definition; the co-operation could occur along either a federal–provincial or interprovincial axis. (4) The federal principle could be encapsulated in the principle of non-subordination: one level of government should not be subordinated to another in areas of its own jurisdiction; put another way, this implied the constitutional equality of the two orders of government. (5) Provinces had a right to say 'no' to the introduction of new shared-cost programs, and a right (if we can judge from the near-unanimity of most reports on this issue) to reasonable fiscal compensation if they operate a program consistent with the national objectives. (6) The spending power was a two-edged sword; too great an attack on it would harm the potential for attaining overarching national objectives and meeting emergency situations, and too great a reliance on it would result in a drift to duplication, inefficiency, lack of accountability, too much government, and a disregard for the division of powers, which was a protection for provincial ways of life.

Constitutional Reform Industry Frameworks

The frameworks suggested by the various reports of the constitutional reform industry also seemed to suggest some overlapping approaches, if one attempts a comprehensive overview based on Appendix A. This generation of 'framework' recommendations suggests the following. (1) There appeared to be a consensus that the most contentious area is the initiation of new shared-cost programs in areas of exclusive provincial jurisdiction. (2) There was an early preoccupation with mandating a threshold of interprovincial consent for initiation of programs. (3) The threshold-of-consent criterion, however, seems to have ebbed in importance and been replaced by a preference for opting-out rights. (4) There was divided opinion on the notion of tying the use of the spending power to a federal–provincial or (5) interprovincial institution. (6) There was nearly unanimous agreement that non-participating governments should be compensated. (7) There was division on whether this compensation should be conditional on the provinces establishing programs with compatible objectives, (8) or simply unconditional, but the later initiatives indicated a provincial comfort level with the former. (9) The new shared-cost programs envisaged by the industry tend to feature national objectives, but the gist of the proposals was towards joint federal–provincial agreement on the nature of the objectives. Despite the concern with federal unilateralism in program initiation, modification, and termination, until recently there was no concern with mandating practical solutions such as (10) mandatory notice of termination, (11) multi-year funding commitments, and (12) mutual consent for changes. In more recent years, these latter three seem to have been more generally accepted.

2. Clause 7 of the Calgary Declaration reads: 'Canada is a federal system where federal, provincial and territorial governments work in partnership while respecting each other's jurisdictions. Canadians want their governments to work together co-operatively and with flexibility to ensure the efficiency and effectiveness of the federation. Canadians want their governments to work together particularly in the delivery of their social programs. Provinces and territories renew their commitment to work in partnership with the Government of Canada to best serve the needs of Canadians.'

References

Aubry, Jack. 2003. 'Quebec sends unity envoy', *National Post*, Monday, 28 April, A7.

Bryden, Joan. 1998. '"Back off," PM tells premiers: Chrétien vows to keep social policy powers', *Ottawa Citizen*, 17 Sept.

Canada. 1945. *House of Commons Debates*. 12 Apr.

———. 1972. Parliament of Canada. *Report* of the Special Joint Committee of the Senate and House of Commons on the Constitution of Canada (Molgat-MacGuigan Report). 1972. Ottawa: Parliament of Canada.

———. 1978. *Report of the Pepin-Robarts Task Force on Canadian Unity*. Ottawa: Queen's Printer.

———. 1991. *Shaping Canada's Future Together*. Proposals. Ottawa: Supply and Services.

———. 1992a. *Charlottetown Accord* (draft legal text). Ottawa: Privy Council.

———. 1992b. *Report of the Special Joint Committee on a Renewed Canada*. (Beaudoin-Dobbie Report). Ottawa: Queen's Printer.

———. 1994. *Jobs and Growth Agenda: Building a More Innovative Economy*. Ottawa: Government of Canada.

———, Department of Finance. 1999. *The Fiscal Balance in Canada*. Ottawa, Dec.

———. 2002. *Canada's Innovation Strategy*. Ottawa: Industry Canada. Available at: http://dsp-psd.pwgsc.gc.ca/Collection/Iu4-5-2002E.pdf.

———. 2007a. *Budget 2007*. Available at: www.budget.gc.ca/2007/bp/bpc4e.html.

———. 2007b. Speech from the Throne. 16 October. Available at: www.parl.gc.ca/39/2/parlbus/chambus/senate/deb-e/001db_2007-10-16-E.htm?#7.

Canadian Bar Association (CBA). 1978. *Towards a New Canada*. Montreal: Pierre DesMarais.

Canadian Intergovernmental Conference Secretariat (CICS). 1997a. 'Social Policy Renewal', news release ref. 850–061/009, St Andrew's-by-the-Sea, N.B., 8 Aug.

———. 1997b. 'Premiers Agree to Consult Canadians on Unity', news release ref. 850–065/04, Calgary, 14 Sept.

———. 1999. *A Framework to Improve the Social Union for Canadians*. Available at: www.scics.gc.ca/info99/80003701_e.htm.

———. 2000. 'New Federal Investments to Accompany the Agreements on Health Renewal and Early Childhood Development'. Available at: www.scics.gc.ca/cinfo00/80003807_e.html.

_____. 2003. 'Premiers announce plan to build a new era of constructive and cooperative federalism', Communique 850-092/006 of the 44th Annual Premiers' Conference, Charlottetown, PEI, July 9–11. Available at: www.scics.gc.ca/cinfo03/850092006_e.html.

Canadian Tax Foundation. 1997. *Finances of the Nation, 1997*. Toronto.

Carter, George E. 1971. *Canadian Conditional Grants Since World War Two*. Toronto: Canadian Tax Foundation.

Conservative Party of Canada. 2005. *Policy Declaration*. Available at: www.conservative.ca/media/20050319-POLICY%20DECLARATION.pdf.

Daly, Brian. 1998. 'Charest accuses Bouchard of waffling on referendum', *Ottawa Citizen*, 5 Nov.

Dion, Stéphane. 1998. 'A New Social Union: Improving the Way Governments Work Together to Serve Canadians', notes for an address by the Honourable Stéphane Dion, President of the Privy Council and Minister of Intergovernmental Affairs, at the Sands Hotel, Regina, Sask., 15 Oct.

Dunn, Christopher. 2004. 'Urban Asymmetry: The New Reality in Intergovernmental Relations', *Policy Options*, November.

Dupré, J. Stefan. 1988. 'Reflections on the Workability of Executive Federalism', in R.D. Olling and M.W. Westmacott, eds, *Perspectives on Canadian Federalism*. Scarborough, Ont.: Prentice-Hall Canada.

Evenson, Jeff, and Richard Simeon. 1979. 'The Roots of Discontent in Canada', in *Proceedings of the Workshop on the Political Economy of Confederation*, Institute of Intergovernmental Relations and the Economic Council of Canada, Queen's University, Kingston, 8–10 Nov. Ottawa: Minister of Supply and Services.

Federal/Provincial/Territorial Ministerial Council on Social Policy Renewal. 2003. Three Year Review Social Union Framework Agreement (SUFA). June. Available at: www.unionsociale.gc.ca/sufa/Three_Year_Review/e/tyrsufa.html#1_ .

Flanagan, Tom. 2006. 'Harper's road map to power', *Globe and Mail*, 23 May, A15.

Fraser, Graham, and Rhéal Séguin. 1997. 'Nine provinces to talk social policy', *Globe and Mail*, 12 Dec.

Galloway, Norma. 1997. 'Chrétien praises premiers' plan', *Ottawa Citizen*, 16 Sept.

Gouvernement du Québec, Secrétariat aux Affaires Intergouvernmentales canadiennes. 1998. *Québec's Historical Position on the Federal Spending Power, 1994–1998*. Available at: www.cex.gouv.qc.ca/saic/english.htm.

Granatstein, J.L. 1982. *The Ottawa Men: The Civil Service Mandarins, 1935–1957*. Toronto: University of Toronto Press. Reprinted 1998.

Greenspon, Edward. 1997. 'Premiers use Quebec unity proposal to expand talks with Ottawa', *Globe and Mail*, 15 Sept.

The Hill Times. 1997. 'Election Numbers Lowest Since Confederation', 16 June.

Hogg, P.W. 1996. *Constitutional Law of Canada*, 4th student edn. Toronto: Carswell.

LaForest, G.V. 1969. *The Allocation of Taxing Power under the Canadian Constitution*. Toronto: Canadian Tax Foundation.

Liberal Party of Canada.1993. *Creating Opportunity: The Liberal Plan for Canada* (Red Book). Ottawa: Liberal Party of Canada.

Ministerial Council on Social Policy Reform and Renewal. 1995. *Report to Premiers.* Dec.

Moore, A. Milton, J. Harvey Perry and Donald I. Beach. 1966. *The Financing of Canadian Federation. Canadian Tax Papers,* no. 43. Toronto: Canadian Tax Foundation.

Provincial/Territorial Council on Social Policy Renewal. 1997. *New Approaches to Canada's Social Union: An Options Paper.* 29 Apr.

Provincial-Territorial Working Group on Social Policy Reform and Renewal. 1996. *Issues Paper on Social Policy Reform and Renewal: Next Steps.* Prepared for the 37th Annual Premiers' Conference, Jasper, Alta, Aug.

Quebec Liberal Party. 1980. *A New Canadian Federation* (Beige Paper). Montreal: Quebec Liberal Party.

Royal Bank of Canada. 1999. *Relative Fiscal Power: Ottawa versus the Provinces.* Sept.

Simeon, Richard, and Ian Robinson. 1990. *State, Society and the Development of Canadian Federalism.* Toronto: University of Toronto Press.

Smiley, D.V. 1970. *Constitutional Adaptation and Canadian Federalism Since World War Two.* Ottawa: Information Canada.

Strick, John C. 1999. *The Public Sector in Canada: Programs, Finance and Policy.* Toronto: Thompson Educational Publishing.

Thompson, Elizabeth, and Joan Bryden. 1998. 'Premiers united on demands on Ottawa', *Montreal Gazette*, 7 Aug.

Trudeau, Pierre Elliott. 1969. *Federal–Provincial Grants and the Spending Power of Parliament.* Ottawa: Queen's Printer.

25 Provincial and Local Public Administration

Andrew Sancton and Scott Sams

The Canadian federal government accounts for less than half of all government spending in Canada. By any measure, Canada is a remarkably decentralized federation. This chapter is about the governments—provincial and local—that spend most of our public funds. It is also an essay about intergovernmental relations, but provincial–local rather than federal–provincial relations. American students of public administration are accustomed to lumping together 'state' and 'local' issues; numerous textbooks on the subject constitute the best evidence. Canadians have been reluctant to make the same connection, perhaps because, since the 1960s at least, so much of our political activity has been directed at elevating our provincial governments to a status that is fully equal to that of the government in Ottawa. If federal and provincial are truly equal, it might seem demeaning to link the latter to the humble local governments that collect garbage and repair potholes.

The federal and provincial governments in Canada share common institutional arrangements. All are parliamentary systems of the Westminster model. As much of this *Handbook* demonstrates, a great deal of what is written about the theory and practice of public administration at the federal level also applies provincially. But this is not true for Canadian local government. As W.B. Munro noted in 1929, our arrangements for local governments have been much more influenced by American practice than British. In the United States, state and local institutions are not radically different from each other; in Canada, provincial and local institutions are quite different. Compare the relative power of a provincial premier and a city mayor within their respective political systems and one begins to sense how profound the differences are.

By treating the provincial and local levels together, this essay aims to provide a different perspective on Canadian public administration. The focus is on how provincial governments arrange for services to be provided. Much more than the federal level of government, provincial governments are constitutionally responsible for delivering services that citizens use on an everyday basis. Long before the term 'alternate service delivery' was in vogue, each province had already worked out elaborate arrangements involving delegation, grants, and regulation whereby institutions other than the government itself delivered a wide range of social, health, and educational services.

Provinces must also grapple with difficult issues involving the organization of municipal governments and **special-purpose bodies (SPBs)**, issues entirely foreign to the kinds of organizational problems that confront the federal government. Perhaps because Canadians are so used to thinking of the federal and provincial as distinct entities that can be and should be disentangled from each other, many provincial policy-makers have attempted to disentangle the provincial–municipal relationship. One of the central themes of this chapter is that such an effort is misguided. Despite the obvious differences in their institutional structures, the concerns of provincial and local governments in Canada are inextricably intertwined.

Rather than attempt to distinguish the inherently provincial services from those that are inherently local, we should instead accept that locally elected councils have great unfulfilled potential to act as the mechanism whereby a wide range of provincial policies and services are adjusted to fit the particular needs of various cities, towns, villages, and townships.

The first section of this chapter outlines the main functions and internal organizational arrangements of Canadian provincial governments. The next looks at how provincial governments use Crown corporations and non-profit organizations for delivering services. The third section examines the organization of **local government** in Canada, both municipalities and special-purpose bodies. This is followed by a discussion of the key issues in provincial–local relations.

Functions and Organizational Structures of Provincial Governments

Sections 92 and 93 of the Constitution Act, 1867 formally outline most of the constitutional responsibilities of Canadian provincial governments. Not surprisingly, this outline bears only a limited relationship to what provincial governments actually do at the beginning of the twenty-first century. The best way now to get a snapshot of what they do is to explore their websites. After allowing for the normal puffery of public relations, the sites provide a remarkable glimpse into the politicians, the finances, and the organizational arrangements of Canada's 10 provinces.

It is the organizational arrangements that are of prime concern here. The Constitution provides that, within each province's parliamentary system, the lieutenant-governor, appointed on the advice of the federal prime minister, acts in place of the monarch. This is the one aspect of a provincial government's organization that the provincial legislature cannot change (without first launching the constitutional amending process). Each province has a head of government known as the premier, who is formally appointed by the lieutenant-governor but who in practice is the leader of the party caucus that commands the support of the majority of the members of the legislature. In some provinces the premier is supported by a distinct department of government with its own deputy minister; in others the premier is supported only by a combination of personal political staff and public servants working in direct support of the cabinet as a collectivity. Whatever the exact details might be, the premier is clearly in charge. He or she appoints all cabinet ministers and deputy ministers. The most senior provincial public servant—often known as clerk of the executive council—in fact works for the premier (Dunn, 1996).

Most cabinet ministers appointed by the premier are the political heads of ministries of government. For our purposes here, the term 'ministry' will be used, even though some provinces use 'department' or 'office'. Every province has a ministry concerned with raising sufficient revenue from taxes to cover provincial expenses. It is called the Ministry of Finance or the provincial treasury. The Constitution prohibits provinces from levying 'indirect' taxes. In practice, this means that provincial legislatures may not approve laws purporting to establish customs or excise duties that are included in the cost of the products or services being taxed. Provincial finance ministries are extremely important in establishing the financial regimes under which all provincial and local public services are provided.

All provinces also have a ministry responsible for ensuring that people charged with violating the law are prosecuted by Crown attorneys in the courts (for details see Chapter 7, Judicial Administration). It is called the Ministry of Justice or Ministry of the Attorney General. Crown prosecutors must work closely with the police, including officers who are members of municipal forces. In most Canadian cities, an alleged murderer, for example, will be arrested by a municipal police officer, charged under the provisions of a federal law (the Criminal Code), and prosecuted by a provincial Crown attorney before a federally appointed judge in a court of law established by the province.

Of special relevance to this essay are provincial ministries in charge of municipal affairs. Most provinces have a ministry with 'municipal' in the name, although some use the terms 'communities', 'local government', or 'intergovernmental affairs'. Their main task is to implement the laws concerning the establishment and operation of municipal governments and to monitor their financial management. Ministries of municipal affairs are most assuredly not the source of all provincial rules and regulations concerning municipal operations. Many other ministries regulate aspects of municipal government involving their particular subject areas. Municipal affairs ministries are left to regulate the municipal electoral process, conflict-of-interest rules, record-keeping, and financial procedures.

All provinces have ministries in charge of operating the legal regime that governs the relationship between employers and employees. They are named ministries of labour, human resources or employment. Since most Canadian workplaces relate to subjects under provincial jurisdiction, these provincial ministries are collectively far more important than the federal one. Various provinces also have ministries charged with internal financial and human resource management and with the provision of facilities and services to other ministries.

Virtually all other provincial ministries are in one way or another concerned with providing services to the public, either directly, through Crown corporations and non-governmental organizations, or through local governments. All provinces have ministries concerned with transportation (mostly highways), education, health, income maintenance programs (but not old-age pensions and Employment Insurance, which are under federal jurisdiction), personal social services, natural resources and energy, agriculture, the environment, and various programs relating to economic development and tourism.

Very few, if any, of these ministries directly provide all of their services. Most provincial ministries responsible for transportation directly manage provincial highways, although long before 'contracting out' became a buzzword they were a source of business for local companies engaged in road-building, maintenance, paving, and snow removal. Ontario's Ministry of Transportation went further: it turned to the private sector for the building, financing, and maintenance of Highway 407, a major toll road that skirts the city of Toronto (Mylvaganam and Borins, 2004). Many transportation ministries converted some provincial highways to local roads, one of the most obvious forms of provincial 'downloading'.

Except in Ontario, Nova Scotia, and Manitoba, provinces directly administer income security (welfare) programs themselves. The incomes of adults below age 65 who are unable to work, either permanently or for extended periods of time, are directly dependent on decisions of provincial officials. Even in Ontario, Nova Scotia, and Manitoba—where municipal bureaucrats are involved—provincial funding and policy-making predominate. But the real story about provincial government activity in Canada is that it is usually some other organization—such as a Crown corporation or provincially funded non-profit organization—that has direct contact with ordinary citizens and consumers.

Crown Corporations and Non-Profit Organizations

Starting in the early twentieth century, Canadian provinces became involved in the generation, distribution, and sale of electricity. The standard mechanism was a Crown corporation, an organization structured in many ways like a private corporation except that the provincial government owns all the shares. Provincial involvement in electricity through Crown corporations was a crucial feature of most provinces' economic development throughout the twentieth century (Nelles, 1974). Some provinces—notably Alberta and Ontario—took steps to break up monopolies and introduce forms of competition, but results have been mixed and the sale of provincially owned assets has been limited. In Alberta, electrical prices soared after the province started selling off its energy interests in 1998. Ontario Hydro was split into five corporations in 1999, but none were privatized. Operation of the Bruce Nuclear Generating Station was licensed to a private company. The province also established an open electricity market, but regulates consumer prices to be less than the market average. For the foreseeable future, most Canadians will, at a minimum, be receiving electricity through a provincial grid owned by their provincial government.

In some provinces, provincial Crown corporations also are in the water business, although such corporations tend to sell to municipalities rather than directly to consumers. At one time or another, there have been provincial Crown corporations relating to an incredibly wide variety of products: potash in Saskatchewan, asbestos in Quebec, urban transit vehicles in Ontario.

But perhaps the most ubiquitous provincial Crown corporations in Canada involve liquor. Ever since the rise of the temperance movement in North America early in the twentieth century, provinces have monopolized the retailing of wine and spirits. The original purpose of direct provincial involvement was to make it as difficult and unpleasant as possible for consumers to purchase alcoholic beverages. But the liquor monopoly proved lucrative. As societal values changed, the mission of provincial liquor operations changed from the suppression of demand to the maximization of profit. Now we enter provincial liquor stores expecting to receive attentive service and to use credit cards. In Quebec wine can be purchased in small grocery stores and in Alberta all is privatized, just as it was before the temperance movement began.

Crown corporations have usually produced and/or marketed products for sale, generally in the expectation that, in the long run, there would be at least full recovery of costs and (as in the case of liquor) even some profit for provincial treasuries. Non-profit organizations, on the other hand, are concerned with activities that, for various reasons, are not always suitable for full-cost recovery from the people who apparently benefit from them. Most of these organizations in Canada have their origins in the nineteenth century and were originally sponsored by churches, charitable organizations, or municipalities. Particularly since World War II, they have become increasingly reliant on provincial funding. For Canadian provinces, the most significant of these institutions are universities, hospitals, and social service agencies.

Canadian universities, regardless of what province they are in, are remarkably similar in their organizational structure and financing (Cameron, 1991). Unlike many American state universities, none of their assets are directly owned by, nor is their financial reporting integrated with, their provincial governments; and their employees are not part of their province's civil service. Unlike private American universities (Harvard, for example), all Canadian universities receive ongoing provincial government operating funds, usually according to a formula that also regulates tuition fees. The assets of Canadian universities are controlled by free-standing boards of governors, only some of whose members are appointed by the provincial government. Controversial as university funding issues often are, there have been few serious calls for fundamental changes in these arrangements.

Such is not the case for hospitals and social services, even though their historical origins, funding, and methods of governance have generally been quite similar to those of universities. Perhaps the major difference is that the bigger provinces have only a few universities, while even the smaller ones have dozens, if not hundreds, of hospitals and social service agencies. During times of fiscal stress, provinces have taken dramatic measures, including merger and closure, to control their costs. One commonly adopted device aimed at bringing order to the health and social services sector has been the establishment of regional councils whose mandate involves coordination and, to some extent at least, the allocation of public funds among competing institutions.

Quebec has gone further along these lines than any other province. In the early 1970s it merged its health and social service ministries and established a network of local community service centres throughout the province (*centres locaux des services communautaires*) staffed by an integrated team of physicians (on salary) and social workers (Sancton, 1985: 172–90). Although these centres have not come close to displacing physicians whose fees for service are covered by provincial health insurance, they remain a distinct part of Quebec's public system for the delivery of health and social services. The centres—along with more specialized social service centres, chronic-care facilities, and hospitals—are coordinated by regional councils for health and social services (*Régies régionales de la santé et des services sociaux*). Subsequent to the establishment of this system in Quebec, other provinces, including Ontario and Alberta, created regional coordinating councils of one kind or another, usually only for health services.

Councils of this type have no taxing authority, nor does the entire citizenry directly elect them. Consequently, they can hardly qualify as governments, local or otherwise. Their main task is to insulate central ministries from constant involvement in local squabbles about which institution gets how much provincial money. The usual problem, however, is that large and powerful local institutions, such as university-affiliated teaching hospitals, are always looking for ways to escape the control of such councils and to deal directly with the key decision-makers at the provincial level. In short, regional councils for health and social services lack legitimacy. The institutions they are supposed to be coordinating are reluctant to accept their decisions.

Of all provinces, Quebec has probably gone the furthest towards fully integrating hospitals and social service agencies directly into the provincial public sector. Quebec, for example, has standard provincial rules about the composition of boards of directors, and labour relations have long been centralized. Ontario, by establishing 'local health integration networks' has gone some way towards institutionalizing a mechanism for regional health-care planning, funding, and coordination (Fenn, 2006). But most personal social services in Ontario—especially those aimed at children—remain in a remarkably anomalous perch between public and private. Child protection services, children's mental health centres, and organizations that deliver services to physically and developmentally handicapped children all remain private charitable institutions in theory. In practice they receive almost all their funding directly from the province. Its field managers are crucially important in making local allocations. Municipal governments are irrelevant. There is no alternative form of local decision-making body—or even an advisory body—for the personal social services (Sancton, 1986).

Universities, hospitals, and social service agencies are all crucially important institutions within every Canadian province. They are prodigious consumers of public funds. More than any other institutions in Canada, they are at the boundary between the public sector and what is increasingly known as '**civil society**', i.e., the network of voluntary organizations that stands between the state, on the one hand, and families and individuals, on the other (Schechter, 1999: 66–7). Our treatises on public administration pay them little attention; our schools of business administration and commerce, even less. But, to understand fully how our provinces affect the lives of Canadians, we need to know much more about how these institutions work, how they spend the public funds entrusted to them, and how they might best develop alternative ways of meeting their objectives.

The Organization of Local Government

There are two kinds of local government: municipalities and special-purpose bodies. Municipalities are responsible for a number of government functions or activities; special-purpose bodies, as their name implies, are usually only responsible for one function or a set of closely related ones. In Canada, the governing bodies of municipalities always comprise only people who have been elected to municipal office, while the governing bodies of special-purpose bodies are sometimes appointed. All provincial legislatures have established a system of municipal government. Some of the populated parts of Ontario and Quebec are covered by two tiers of municipal government, the **upper tier** in Quebec being either a municipal regional county (*municipalité régionale de comté*) or a metropolitan community (*communauté métropolitaine*), while in Ontario it is either a county (in rural areas) or a regional **municipality** (in large urban centres and their immediate rural hinterland). **Two-tier systems** came under severe attack in Ontario under the Harris government because of alleged overlap and duplication. Some (the city of Chatham and Kent County, and the regional municipalities of Hamilton–Wentworth, Ottawa–Carleton, and Sudbury) were converted to **single-tier systems**, the most notable being the creation in 1998 of the new city of Toronto (the 'megacity') from the constituent parts of the Municipality of Metropolitan Toronto (Frisken, 2007).

In the late 1960s British Columbia established a network of **regional districts** covering almost the entire province. These districts brought municipal services to areas that previously had no municipal government and provided a mechanism for co-operation among neighbouring municipalities that were already established. Whether regional districts constitute a distinct tier of municipal government is subject to debate. The minister who established them thought not; that is why he insisted that a 'board of directors' rather than a 'council' govern them. There is evidence, however, that regional districts are evolving. The Greater Vancouver Regional District changed its name to 'Metro Vancouver' in 2007 to raise its profile and better describe its responsibilities. In any event, board memberships comprise only people who have been elected to municipal office or who have been directly elected from otherwise unincorporated areas to represent them on the regional boards (Bish, 1999). All other provinces have only a single tier of municipal government.

Local governments in Canada generally possess the functional responsibilities described in Table 25.1. Absent from this list is public education, provided by special-purpose bodies—school boards—that have lost much of their taxing and policy-making authority. Also absent from the list are public health and income security (welfare), functions that remain at the local level in only a few provinces. Whether a municipality or a special-purpose body carries out a function is a decision made by the provincial government. It is intimately related to the overall pattern of provincial–municipal relations, to be discussed in the next section of this chapter. The rest of this section is concerned with the internal organization of municipal government, focusing especially on how it differs from the way parliamentary systems are organized at the federal and provincial levels.

Table 25.1 Functional Responsibilities of Local Governments

Policing
Fire protection
Emergency planning
Roads and traffic control
Parking
Street-lighting
Public transit
Water supply (and sometimes natural gas, electricity, and telephones)
Sewage collection and treatment
Solid-waste collection and disposal
Land-use planning and regulation
Building regulation and inspection
Economic development and promotion
Public libraries
Parks and recreation
Cultural facilities including museums, concerts halls, and art galleries
Business licensing

As in Britain and the United States, Canadian municipalities are, in legal terms, a form of corporation, not unlike limited liability corporations established for business purposes. Indeed, in terms of their legal origins, the two types of corporations are quite similar. What this means in practice has, in the past, been the subject of considerable legal controversy. Are municipal corporations to be thought of as essentially private organizations comprising property-owners and residents, or are they really small-scale governments? The courts have generally decided that they are small-scale governments, with all the obligations of governments to treat citizens fairly and equitably (Frug, 1999). But, in the English-speaking world at least, they remain outside the formal, or narrow, definition of the state. In British parliamentary systems, the state is the monarch. Parliament, the courts, and ministers (of the Crown) act only on behalf of the monarch. Public servants act only on behalf of ministers. Municipalities are most assuredly not part of this definition of the state. Nothing that municipalities do is directly on behalf of the Crown. Unlike cabinets, they can claim no residual royal authority. They can only do what statutes allow. Consequently, municipal councils approve bylaws, not laws; similarly, their employees are not civil servants (of the monarch), perhaps explaining why the term 'municipal staff' is more commonly employed.

Elected municipal councils, acting collectively, possess all the authority of their municipal corporation. Individual councillors, like private members in federal and provincial legislatures, possess no individual authority. Even mayors have no special authority, unless it is explicitly delegated to them by a provincial statute (Sancton, 1994). What is missing at the municipal level is a cabinet. The municipal council is generally both the local legislature and the local executive, although a very few provincial laws—notably Quebec's for municipal government in Montreal—provide for an executive committee of council to act in the municipality's name without council approval. Even in Montreal, however, there is no legal equivalent of a cabinet minister; individual councillors are not politically accountable for particular aspects of municipal government activity. Legally, all councillors are responsible for everything, which means in practice that none of them are personally responsible for anything. Only in major cities in Quebec—Montreal, Laval, and Quebec City—with functioning local political parties is there any sense of a particular municipal 'administration', headed by a mayor and politically opposed by an organized opposition.

This means that staff in Canadian municipalities generally function in a dramatically different political environment from their federal and provincial counterparts, who are civil servants. Civil servants have a single political boss: their minister. They provide advice to him or her in confidence. The minister takes formal responsibility for all that goes right and all that goes wrong, even if the minister was acting directly (and sometimes even unknowingly) on advice from civil servants.

In municipal government all is different. Municipal staff report only to a collective political entity, the council (Siegel, 1994). Their advice is provided in documents that are usually made public at the same time as councillors first see them. Often they are asked for extemporaneous oral policy advice at public meetings, sometimes by particular municipal councillors anxious to use staff to support their own position against their political opponents of the moment. Senior municipal staff operating in such an environment must develop highly tuned political antennae. By some they can be accused of acting inappropriately in support of one political position or group over another; others might claim that they are too timid in providing the professional advice they are paid to give.

A distinguishing feature of municipal staff, as opposed to federal and provincial civil servants, is that they are much more likely to have been recruited to government service because they were professional experts of one kind or another: civil engineers, land-use planners, accountants, lawyers. Municipal governments have generally not recruited many policy analysts, economists, and management trainees. Instead of being perceived as a single entity that requires high-quality general management at all levels in the organization, municipal government has traditionally been perceived more like a confederation of distinct professionally based services, held together only at the very top. One of the practical effects of this is that municipal professional experts are not reluctant to express their views in their professional capacities, often with little heed to the declared positions of mayors, councillors, and even their own administrative superiors. Indeed, some provincial regulatory tribunals routinely call municipal professionals to the stand to ask them the extent to which the council has been following their declared professional advice. No one is shocked (as they generally would be in our federal and provincial systems) when these same professionals sometimes openly declare that the council majority acted against their advice.

Nearly every municipal staff is headed by a single individual in Canada. Titles for the position abound. The most common are: city manager, chief administrative officer, *directeur-général/directrice-générale* (Quebec), city administrator, and clerk-treasurer (for smaller municipalities). The title says very little about the incumbent's power, although the term 'city manager' usually denotes considerable formal authority. The position of **city manager** has its origins in the American-based Progressive movement of a hundred years ago. The belief was that corrupt urban political machines could be cleaned up by removing elected councillors from any managerial functions and convincing or forcing them to hire a professional manager with broad authority over all municipal staff (Plunkett, 1992).

In the United States city management has emerged as a more or less distinct profession, with academic roots firmly planted in university schools of public administration. City managers often begin as assistants in small places and work themselves up through a series of moves, culminating for the most successful ones by taking charge of the staff in a large municipality. American city managers often have complete control over the hiring of department heads and are the only channel of communication between staff and council. The more flamboyant among them sometimes have a higher public profile than their mayors. Their profession is organized and promoted by the International City Management Association based in Washington, DC.

Even in the US the strong city manager model has been unable to penetrate the larger and more politically complex central-city municipalities. No central-city mayor is willing to surrender that much power and authority to an appointed official. Similar concerns have prevented the model from gaining much currency in Canada, even in smaller municipalities. The largest Canadian municipalities whose staffs are headed by a city manager are Toronto, Calgary and Ottawa, but these positions are not nearly as powerful as their American counterparts.

The more typical Canadian designation was **chief administrative officer (CAO)**. An increasing number of municipalities are adopting the 'city manager' title, but the positions typically remain CAOs in function. Canadian CAOs are involved in the hiring of department heads but do not make the final decision; they are the main conduit of information between staff and council, but not the only one; their public presence is muted, certainly in comparison to the mayor. CAOs must have a privileged relationship with their respective mayors but, unlike the Clerks of the Privy Council in Ottawa or clerks of the executive councils in provincial capitals, CAOs do not have a single boss. As with all municipal staff, CAOs report to all councillors collectively, not to any particular individual. Ontario, however, appears poised to streamline accountability in Toronto by empowering its mayor to hire and fire the city manager. The job is exceptionally difficult. Most attain it after having worked their way up through a particular municipal department. Although there is now much more movement from city to city among experienced Canadian CAOs, there is—unlike the United States—no commonly accepted academic credential for entry into general municipal management positions.

In recent years, senior municipal staff in Canada have been caught up in all the various organizational and policy prescriptions associated with the 'New Public Management'. Many have been quick to point out that the most popular American book on the subject, *Reinventing Government* (Osborne and Gaebler, 1992), contains more examples of innovative management from American municipal government than from either of the other two levels. Similar Canadian success stories have been less frequent, in part because of the greater strength here of public sector unions. Another reason is that in many parts of Canada councillors and staff have been so preoccupied with provincial plans for municipal reorganization that they have had little time to consider new ways of managing. Canadian provinces—more so than American states—have a profound and constant impact on the day-to-day activities of Canadian municipalities. It is to provincial–municipal relations in Canada that we now turn.

Provincial–Municipal Relations

At various times since the mid-1960s municipalities in most Canadian provinces have faced major plans for wholesale municipal reorganization. The merits of such plans have been thoroughly assessed elsewhere (Graham et al., 1998: 65–91; Tindal and Tindal, 2000: 97–191). The political justifications for such reorganizations have changed over time. Initially, in the 1960s, the object of restructuring was to enable municipal government to do more, especially in relation to regional planning and the provision of large-scale infrastructure. In the 1990s, the priority was to cut costs and improve economic competitiveness. For the purposes of this discussion, the point is that the fate of these plans tells us a great deal about the underlying pattern of power within provincial–municipal relations. In Ontario, from the mid-1960s to the mid-1970s, the provincial legislature redrew municipal boundaries in most urban areas of the province. Municipalities were consolidated from 13 to six within the two-tier system of Metropolitan Toronto that had first been created (without boundary changes) in 1953. Thunder Bay was formed from Port Arthur and Fort William. In Ottawa–Carleton, Niagara, Waterloo, Sudbury, Hamilton–Wentworth, and the counties around Metropolitan Toronto, the number of municipalities was drastically reduced and new regional governments were created. In Quebec, the province's second most populous municipality was created when all the municipal units on Ile Jésus, just north of Montreal, were merged to form the city of Laval. In Manitoba, 11 suburbs were joined to the city of Winnipeg to create a new 'Unicity'.

Another round of forced municipal mergers began in the early 1990s. New Brunswick created the city of Miramichi by merging Chatham, Newcastle, and adjoining municipalities (Robison, 1998). Similar amalgamations took place in Cape Breton and Halifax in Nova Scotia. We have mentioned the creation of the megacity in Toronto in 1998; in 1999 the Ontario government announced similar mergers for Ottawa, Hamilton, and Sudbury. The Quebec government actively promoted mergers as well. Restructuring tapered off again at the end of the 1990s, and in Quebec some municipalities were de-amalgamated following referendums (Sancton, 2006).

Unlike what happened in the United Kingdom in the 1960s and 1970s—when the local system was fundamentally restructured in each of England, Scotland, Wales, and Northern Ireland—no Canadian province has legislated a complete redrawing of the municipal map for the entire province all at the same time. Serious proposals along these lines have been made in the past in Ontario, Nova Scotia, and Newfoundland, and in all of these cases municipalities successfully resisted. We can perhaps conclude on the basis of this limited experience that provinces are more likely to attain their reorganizational objectives if they act incrementally rather than comprehensively.

Another form of major change in the provincial–local relationship involves an upheaval in the allocation of functions between the two levels and consequent financial rearrangements. Many such changes occurred in the wake of the Great Depression, when municipalities proved incapable of bearing the burden of what was then called 'relief'. In the second half of the twentieth century, major functional rearrangements occurred in New Brunswick as a result of the 'Program for Equal Opportunity' launched in 1967; in Quebec under the first Parti Québécois government in 1979 when municipalities were allocated most of the property tax revenues that previously went to school boards; and in Nova Scotia and Ontario in the 1990s under what are known as 'service exchange' and 'local services realignment', respectively.

In both Nova Scotia and Ontario, provincial and municipal functional and financial responsibilities were dramatically changed. In both cases, municipalities ended up with more responsibility for roads. In Nova Scotia municipalities were relieved of much of their social welfare responsibilities. In Ontario, the municipal share of welfare funding was increased, while local property tax funding for schools was decreased (Graham et al., 1998: 171–85; Graham and Phillips, 1998). More recently Ontario's provincial government has reviewed the funding and delivery of municipal services and uploaded some costs from municipalities.

One of the most important ongoing issues in provincial–municipal relations is the role of local special-purpose bodies. Two main sets of interests are involved here, best labelled 'professional' and 'municipal', rather than 'provincial' and 'municipal'. The professional interests favour special-purpose bodies; municipal interests are opposed. Let us take the example of policing (Martin, 1995). Most municipal police officers—and the organizations that represent them—do not want to be subject to the direct control of municipal councils. Their worst nightmare is that local politicians would try to 'fix' driving offences for their constituents or try to become directly involved in detecting crimes. Their more justified fear is that they would constantly have to compete with other municipal services for scarce resources. Better to be insulated from direct local political control, they reason. Municipal police officers are generally supported in this view by experts (often former police officers) working at the provincial level and by academic criminologists. The apparently ideal world for municipal police would be one in which they would effectively be self-governing, drawing on local financial resources as required and relying on provincial authorities to help keep them up-to-date with the latest technologies and crime-fighting techniques.

Senior corporate staff (city managers) usually lead municipal interests in large municipalities. Since local tax revenues are required to support municipal police forces, municipal management wants, at a minimum, to be able to control local expenditures—on policing and on all other municipal functions. In their ideal world, they would like to be able to treat the police in the same way as they treat other municipal services, perhaps even integrating their activities, to some extent at least, with local fire and ambulance services. Such views are often supported by elected councillors, but not by ones whose political priorities are directed at fully supporting whatever the police desire. These views are also generally supported by civil servants in provincial ministries of municipal affairs whose bureaucratic objectives usually involve strengthening municipal governments, at least in relation to other provincial ministries. It is in this sense that there is no single provincial interest on this type of issue; different parts of the provincial government have different interests. The differences are ultimately dealt with at the cabinet table.

In provinces such as Ontario, where municipal police have traditionally been removed from the direct control of municipal councils, we can conclude that policing interests have generally prevailed over municipal interests (Beare and Murray, 2007). However, in Quebec, for example, where the police chief reports to the municipal council through the *directeur-général/directrice-générale*, we can conclude the opposite. In relation to Ontario it is important to note that in 1998 municipal interests won a significant victory. Municipal councils now appoint a majority of the members of their local police services board and municipal councils can now refuse to accept a budget from the board. If the board objects to this decision, it can appeal to the Ontario Civilian Police Services Commission, a body that, as its name suggests, is more concerned with the overall well-being of policing than with the financial health of municipalities.

Such is the ongoing dynamic of the conflict between professional and municipal interests as it is played out in relation to special-purpose bodies. The same story can be repeated for different professional groups, with different outcomes in different provinces. Librarians, public-health professionals, land-use planners, and parks managers all can point to some evidence of success in perpetuating their own local special-purpose bodies (Richmond and Siegel, 1994). Managers of public transit operations and municipal utilities could also be included in this list, but their claim to special status derives more from the user charges they bring in than from their unique professional status.

Special-purpose bodies are not standing committees of council, whose recommendations can always be overturned by the larger body. Special-purpose bodies have a degree of independence established by provincial statute. The independence remains, even if municipal councils appoint all members. They often come from diverse backgrounds and are not necessarily experts on the subject matter with which their special-purpose body deals. The point is, however, that members of these bodies usually are sympathetic to the basic interests of the professional group they are supposed to be governing. In the event that this is not the case when they are first appointed, outsiders soon see themselves as part of the professional team. This, of course, is precisely why such an arrangement is so desirable from the point of view of the professionals.

The best-known local special-purpose bodies in Canada are school boards. They are a very special case because, to some extent at least, their existence, unlike that of any other institution of local government, is explicitly protected by the Constitution of Canada. Municipalities first provided public education in Canada. Well before Confederation in 1867, municipalities in what are now Ontario and Quebec were required by statute to have their schools governed by directly elected school boards. Religious minorities (Catholic or Protestant) were then allowed to establish their own school boards within the same territories. In Ontario and Quebec, the Constitution Act, 1867 protected these rights. Similar rights were protected for religious minorities when Manitoba, Saskatchewan, Alberta, and Newfoundland joined Confederation. By two different constitutional amendments in 1997, such rights have been removed for religious minorities in Newfoundland and Quebec. Meanwhile, in 1982, section 23 of the Canadian Charter of Rights and Freedoms effectively guaranteed that French or English linguistic minorities within a province have a right to govern their own schools. At a minimum, this means that the existence of Catholic school boards is protected in four Canadian provinces and that official-language minorities in all provinces have constitutional rights relating to school governance.

Directly elected local school boards exist in all Canadian provinces. In New Brunswick they were abolished in 1996 but re-established in 2001 as 'district education councils'. Traditionally, school boards have had the same statutory rights as municipalities to levy a tax on property. Until the 1970s, municipal officials looked on approvingly as provincial governments increased their grants to school boards, leaving more tax room for municipalities. But during that decade the situation was reversed and municipalities then began lobbying desperately to reduce the financial demands of school boards on the local property tax base. In 1979 the Quebec government responded by largely eliminating the taxation authority of its school boards, replacing their property tax funds with provincial grants and reducing its grants to municipalities accordingly. A few provincial governments have taken over the taxation of property for educational purposes. In short, long-standing conflicts between school boards and municipalities about who is responsible for property tax increases have now been reduced or eliminated in most provinces.

Over the past 25 years, Canadian school boards have lost a great deal of autonomy and power. This is mainly because, despite being directly elected, they were seen by many as having been completely captured by the professional interests they were supposed to be governing. In a sense, their fate demonstrates that even the most powerful of special-purpose bodies cannot remain immune indefinitely from broader societal concerns and priorities, such as teaching children to read rather than creating local bureaucratic empires. Now the search is on to develop new ways of enabling local citizens to influence what goes on in their schools. Evidence seems to suggest, however, that most of the lost power of school boards has passed up to the province rather than down to principals, parents, teachers, and neighbourhoods (Barker, 1999).

As has already been indicated, much of provincial–municipal relations is about money (Hobson and St-Hilaire, 1997). Municipalities in Canada generally have three main fiscal complaints about their provincial governments. The first is that provinces have not provided them with a sufficiently broad or secure revenue base. Most municipalities are effectively limited to restricted areas of **direct taxation**: a tax on property and to various forms of user charges. By beating back school boards from unrestricted access to the property tax, they have won a significant victory. But they would like guaranteed shares of various provincial taxes, especially the tax on gasoline. Exactly how any such guarantees, if given, could ever be enforced over time is far from clear. Municipalities in most provinces have already experienced broken provincial fiscal promises. Ontario, however, granted Toronto significant new taxation powers in 2006. The city has approved taxes on land transfer and personal vehicles.

A second concern has been fiscal downloading. This is the oft-heard claim that municipalities have borne the brunt of federal and provincial cutbacks. Their only alternatives, they claim, have been to raise taxes or cut services. Most have done both during the past 15 years or so. But all this must be kept in historical perspective. It is true that from 1984 to 1994 the local share (excluding transfers from other governments) of total government spending in Canada went up from 9.8 per cent to 11.4 per cent. But the local share in 1965 was 18.6 per cent.[1] The percentage went down so dramatically between 1965 and 1984 because we experienced a remarkable period of local fiscal uploading, a period in which provincial governments were pleased to take over what were previously local functions and/or to provide local governments with various kinds of conditional grants to encourage them to spend more on old services or to begin to provide new ones.

This leads to the third kind of municipal fiscal complaint, one not heard so often in recent years. The complaint is that provincial conditional grant programs have distorted local priorities by inducing municipalities to fund programs at levels they might not have chosen on their own. Many such grant programs have been cut or eliminated. For many municipalities, having the conditional grants now seems in retrospect better than not having them.

The debate about conditional grants is closely connected to the issue of **disentanglement**. During the 1990s most provinces and most municipalities seemed to agree that it is desirable to disentangle the provincial–local relationship. This means clearly defining the role of the two levels of government so that each can be responsible for developing policy for its own assigned functions and raising the necessary funds. In theory at least, such an arrangement would mean the end both of conditional grants and of the need for provincial inspectors and regulators to check that municipalities were following provincial policy in areas of shared jurisdiction.

Much intellectual energy has been applied to the attempt to determine what functions should be provincial and what should be local. Although this might appear to be a relatively simple task, experience has shown that it is not. Almost every apparently local program (such as those relating to parks and recreation) can be seen to have provincial dimensions. Similarly, many provincial programs work best when they are adapted to local conditions by local people who know their communities. For instance, in the 1990s, Ontario decided that public transit was a local function that would no longer receive operating or capital subsidies from the province. New provincial policies and funding programs are being developed, however, to deal with urban transportation crises in Ontario's cities. It appears that it is no longer possible for the provincial government to say that public transit is not their concern.

But the political problems with disentanglement are even greater. It is inevitable that significant functional rearrangements will cause some municipalities to be better off financially and some to be worse off. Sometimes a provincial government can live with the results and sometimes it cannot. Efforts to fix such apparent inequities add complications to a system that disentanglement was meant to simplify. More importantly, a provincial government always has higher priorities. For the Harris government in Ontario, the highest priority in provincial–local financial affairs was to remove the right of school boards to levy a property tax. Once this had been decided, the only real imperative for the province was to ensure that municipalities covered enough costs that were formerly provincial to make up for the revenue from the educational property tax that the province chose to forgo. This is how Ontario municipalities ended up paying a larger share of income security costs. Municipalities now deliver these programs under tight provincial regulation, hardly a sterling example of disentanglement.

It appears that one of the factors that drove policies in some provinces to promote or force municipal amalgamations was a desire to simplify the provincial–local relationship. Larger municipalities have more diverse property tax bases and are less likely to be screaming for provincial assistance if a particular local factory closes down or moves away. Fewer municipalities within a province mean fewer inter-municipal squabbles that might require a provincial referee, and fewer demands from aggrieved parties that the only solution to a problem is to change the municipal boundaries. But, even with large municipalities, the provincial–local relationship will be incredibly messy and complex. Like a teenager's bedroom, it might occasionally be cleaned up—but chaos soon returns.

Conclusion

It is natural for students of Canadian public administration to focus on the federal government. It is the one government we all share in common. It is important to know how the federal government is organized, how its financial management system works, and how its public service is being renewed. But the story of federal government accounts for less than half the story of Canadian public administration, less still if we realize that much of what the federal government does is to extract money from taxpayers and send it out again in cheques to provinces and people with relatively low incomes. Most of the actual public services that Canadians need in their daily lives—health, education, social services, roads, sewers—are provided by our provincial and local governments.

Institutional arrangements within each province vary considerably for each functional activity. Different provinces allocate different functions to municipalities and local special-purpose bodies. For any one person to master the intricacies of all the different arrangements is likely impossible. Unless students of Canadian public administration make the effort, however, they will know very little about their chosen subject.

Important Terms and Concepts

chief administrative officer
city manager
civil society
direct taxation
disentanglement
local government
municipality
regional districts (British Columbia)
single-tier systems
special-purpose body
two-tier systems

Study Questions

1. Why is it difficult to 'disentangle' the provincial and local governments?
2. Where and how have regional bodies become integrated into the provincial public sector?

3. What are the so-called differences in context and status between municipal staff, on the one hand, and federal and provincial public servants, on the other?
4. What effect has American local government had on Canadian local government?
5. What are some common issues that arise in provincial–municipal relations, and in what ways are they likely to be addressed?

Useful Websites

For links to provincial and territorial websites, along with democracy, party, and electoral links:

www.elections.ca/content.asp?section=lin&dir=url&document=index&lang=e

Public Policy in Municipalities:

www.ppm-ppm.ca

Federation of Canadian Municipalities/Fédération canadienne des municipalités (FCM):

www.fcm.ca

Canadian Policy Research Networks (CPRN) ceased operations in 2009 but still has an impressive list of research archived. Cities and Communities research area publications:

www.cprn.org/theme.cfm?theme=26&l=en

Canadian Urban Institute:

www.canurb.com/home.php

Creative City Network of Canada:

www.creativecity.ca

The Metropolis Project:

http://canada.metropolis.net

Infrastructure Canada:

www.infc.gc.ca/infc-eng.html

Public Works and Government Services Canada—Payments in Lieu of Taxes:

www.tpsgc-pwgsc.gc.ca/biens-property/peri-pilt/index-eng.html

Canada, Prime Minister's Caucus Task Force on Urban Issues. 2002. *Canada's Urban Strategy: A Vision for the 21st Century. Interim Report* (Sgro report).

www.udiontario.com/reports/pdfs/UrbanTaskForce_0211.pdf

Sancton, Andrew. 2006. 'Municipal Mergers and Demergers in Quebec and Ontario'.

www.cpsa-acsp.ca/papers-2006/Sancton.pdf

Selected Canadian City Websites

Vancouver:

http://vancouver.ca/

Edmonton:

www.edmonton.ca

Calgary:

www.calgary.ca/portal/server.pt?

Saskatoon:

www.saskatoon.ca/Pages/default.aspx

Regina:

www.regina.ca/site3.aspx

Winnipeg:

www.winnipeg.ca/interhom/

Toronto:

www.toronto.ca/

Ottawa:

www.ottawa.ca/

Montreal:

http://ville.montreal.qc.ca/portal/page?_pageid=5798,38539559&_dad=portal&_schema=PORTAL

Quebec:

www.ville.quebec.qc.ca

Saint John:

www.cityofsaintjohn.com

Moncton:

www.moncton.org/SplashPages/MonctonIndex.htm

Halifax:

www.halifax.ca

Charlottetown:

www.city.charlottetown.pe.ca

St John's:

www.stjohns.ca/index.jsp

Note

1. These percentages calculated from Statistics Canada CANSIM data available at: http://datacentre.epas.utoronto.ca, labels D464264, D464244, D464287, D464285, D464803, and D464801.

References

Barker, Paul. 1999. 'Education in Canada: Options for Change', in Martin W. Westmacott and Hugh P. Mellon, eds, *Public Administration and Policy: Governing in Challenging Times*. Scarborough, Ont.: Prentice-Hall Allyn and Bacon Canada, 171–86.

Beare, Margaret E., and Tonita Murray, eds. 2007. *Police and Government Relations: Who's Calling the Shots*. Toronto: University of Toronto Press.

Bish, Robert L. 1999. *Regional District Review—1999: Issues and Interjurisdictional Comparisons*. Victoria: Local Government Institute, School of Public Administration, University of Victoria.

Cameron, D.M. 1991. *More Than an Academic Question: Universities, Government and Public Policy in Canada*. Halifax: Institute for Research on Public Policy.

Dunn, Christopher. 1996. 'Premiers and Cabinets', in Dunn, ed., *Provinces: Canadian Provincial Politics*. Peterborough, Ont.: Broadview Press, 165–204.

Fenn, W. Michael. 2006. 'Reinvigorating Publicly Funded Medicare in Ontario: New Public Policy and Administration Techniques', *Canadian Public Administration* 49, 4: 527–47.

Frisken, Frances. 2007. *The Public Metropolis: The Political Dynamics of Urban Expansion in the Toronto Region, 1924–2003*. Toronto: Canadian Scholars' Press.

Frug, Gerald F. 1999. *City Making: Building Communities without Building Walls*. Princeton, NJ: Princeton University Press.

Graham, Katherine A., and Susan D. Phillips. 1998. 'Who Does What in Ontario: The Process of Provincial–Municipal Disentanglement', *Canadian Public Administration* 41, 2 (Summer): 175–209.

———, ———, with Allan M. Maslove. 1998. *Urban Governance in Canada: Representation, Resources, and Restructuring*. Toronto: Harcourt Brace Canada.

Hobson, Paul A.R., and France St-Hilaire, eds. 1997. *Urban Governance and Finance: A Question of Who Does What*. Montreal: Institute for Research on Public Policy.

Manzer, Ronald. 1994. *Public Schools and Political Ideas: Canadian Educational Policy in Historical Perspective*. Toronto: University of Toronto Press.

Martin, Maurice A. 1995. *Urban Policing in Canada*. Toronto: University of Toronto Press.

Munro, W.B. 1929. *American Influences on Canadian Government* Toronto: Macmillan.

Mylvaganam, Chandran, and Sandford Borins. 2004. *'If You Build It...': Business, Government and Ontario's Electronic Toll Highway*. Toronto: University of Toronto Press.

Nelles, H.V. 1974. *The Politics of Development: Forests, Mines & Hydro-Electric Power in Ontario 1849–1941*. Toronto: University of Toronto Press.

Osborne, David, and Ted Gaebler. 1992. *Reinventing Government: How the Entrepreneurial Spirit is Transforming the Public Sector*. Reading, Mass.: Addison-Wesley.

Plunkett, T.J. 1992. *City Management in Canada: The Role of the Chief Administrative Officer*. Toronto: Institute of Public Administration of Canada.

Richmond, Dale, and David Siegel, eds, *Agencies, Boards and Commissions in Canadian Local Government*. Toronto: Institute of Public Administration of Canada.

Robison, John. 1998. 'Public Participation in Restructuring Local Government to Create the City of Miramichi', in K.A. Graham and S.D. Phillips, eds, *Citizen Engagement: Lessons in Participation from Local Government*. Toronto: Institute of Public Administration of Canada, 188–99.

Sancton, Andrew. 1985. *Governing the Island of Montreal: Language Differences and Metropolitan Politics*. Berkeley: University of California Press.

———. 1986. *Municipal Government and Social Services: A Case Study of London, Ontario*. Local Government Case Studies, No. 2. London, Ont.: Department of Political Science, University of Western Ontario.

———. 1994. 'Mayors as Political Leaders', in Maureen Mancuso, Richard G. Price, and Ronald Wagenberg, eds, *Leaders and Leadership in Canada*. Toronto: Oxford University Press, 174–89.

———. 2006. 'Fusions et défusions municipales au Québec et en Ontario', in François Pétry, Éric Bélanger, and Louis M. Imbeau, eds, *Le Parti Libéral : Enquête sur les réalisations du gouvernement Charest*. Laval: Les Presses de l'Université Laval. Available in English at: http://www.cpsa-acsp.ca/papers-2006/Sancton.pdf.

Schechter, Michael. 1999. 'Globalization and Civil Society', in Schechter, ed., *The Revival of Civil Society: Global and Comparative Perspectives*. Basingstoke, England: Macmillan, 61–101.

Siegel, David. 1994. 'Politics, Politicians, and Public Servants in Non-Partisan Local Governments', *Canadian Public Administration* 37, 1 (Spring): 7–30.

Tindal, C. Richard, and S. Nobes Tindal. 2000. *Local Government in Canada*, 5th edn. Scarborough, Ont.: Nelson.

PART VII The Management Dimension

Management has been defined in a variety of ways, but in the public sector it is essentially the application of administrative skills to implementation of the political will. It includes a variety of subfields. Here we consider some aspects of management that are undergoing substantial change in Canada: financial and budgetary management, the role of the deputy minister, and information technology.

Chapter 5 noted in passing David A. Good's nuanced view of the recent history of federal government budgeting. Observers of the federal budgeting scene long considered it common wisdom that American Aaron Wildavsky's 'spenders–guardians' dichotomy, dating from the 1960s, applied in Canada as well. Good considers this dichotomy, at one time useful, now outmoded, and explains why in Chapter 26. Four sets of actors now affect public spending: spenders, guardians, priority setters, and financial watchdogs. The first of these are the spending ministers of the Crown, and may include the Prime Minister and Finance Minister; the second last would fall under the strict rubric of guardians in the old spender–guardian dichotomy. The guardians, those with institutional responsibility for curbing excessive spender demands, are Finance and the Treasury Board. The Privy Council Office and the Prime Minister's Office, partly engaged in political direction-setting, are the priority setters. The principal financial watchdog is the Auditor General, but this category has grown in recent years by other officials such as the Parliamentary Budget Officer, chief audit officers in each department, an Independent Procurement Officer, and a Public Sector Integrity Commissioner. This new framework, particularly the priority setters and watchdogs part, emerged over the past decade or more due to several forces acting on government that fundamentally influenced the budgeting process. The need for fiscal restraint, particularly the requirement for a balanced budget or better, along with ideas inherent in the New Public Management, brought to the fore two major issues affecting budgeting: priorities and performance. The new framework is useful because it shows that the guardians are not monolithic, helps paint a more complete understanding of competition and co-operation in the budgetary process, and sheds new light on the front end of the budgetary process.

Andrew Graham complements Good's overview. In Chapter 27 he reviews the basis and main characteristics of public sector financial management. He then addresses the key issues on resourcing public policy: getting the funds, controlling their use for their intended purpose, and accounting for their use. The effective execution of public policy hinges on adequate resources. However, getting the funds through the budgetary process is only the beginning. Once the funds are allocated, they must be managed to ensure maximum impact within both the policy intent and government's regulatory framework. Finally, the results are subject to various levels and means of review, both in terms of the program intention and of compliance with the government's financial standards of practice, reporting requirements, use of funds, and external review or audit. Financial management therefore is central to achieving the policy goal. How funds are managed is also a central preoccupation of accountability and integrity as well as the continuity of the policy and its program. Once you read his review, you will understand why Graham is the central figure in published literature on financial management in Canada today.

One of the major change agents in the governance of Canada and the provinces is among the most traditional management figures: the deputy minister. No one knows more about deputy ministers in Canada than Jacques Bourgault. In Chapter 28, he examines the many and varied roles of deputy ministers (DMs), all of them placing the DM at or near the nexus of change in the public sector. Deputies are designated by the Prime Minister and appointed by the Governor-in-Council to signify the appointment is made by the whole cabinet (that is, of the highest significance). With some exceptions, DMs exercise power through the cabinet minister's authority. They incorporate cabinet priorities into departmental priorities and answer to the minister, but are ultimately accountable to the Prime Minister. Recently, evolution in the DMs' role obliges them to answer questions posed by parliamentary committees, within the context of ministerial responsibility. However, the role of the DM has become more complex, and has been changed by myriad factors, in recent decades: new approaches to accountability; changes in state–citizenry relations; a greater emphasis on fiscal responsibility; the public management movement; challenges of new technologies; globalization; and the changing nature of the DM's role, from managing to empowering others. This complexity can only increase in the future. One major change is the added role of 'accounting officer' to the panoply of the DM's responsibilities. This chapter should be read in concert with Alan Gilmore's Chapter 4, on accounting officers.

In Chapter 29, David C.G. Brown explores five elements of the story of information and technology in Canadian public administration. He starts by looking at the promise of information technology and the phenomenon that it has spawned, 'e-government'. Harnessing information and technology is a critical underpinning of New Public Management thinking; a second part of the discussion is to look at the catalytic effects of a central tenet of NPM, a focus on the citizen. The third section briefly considers politics and policy-making in the electronic environment—what is happening at the front end of public administration. The heart of the chapter is the fourth section, which looks at new spheres and methods of public administration created by information technology and information management, and the chapter concludes with a look at the relationship of these to public sector reform.

Brown reminds us that the modern public service builds on a legacy of past reforms, and the challenge is to continue that process. This challenge can be illustrated in six issues arising from the nature of information and technology in the public administration context: (1) the inherent obsolescence of technology; (2) the fragmented situation of information management; (3) the institutional immaturity of information and technology management, especially compared with financial and human resources management; (4) keeping government as a model user of the information highway—maintaining a link between technology strategies and developments for the public sector and those directed at society at large; (5) managing the problem of communications having become part of the currency of contemporary politics, with the paradoxical effect of isolating the communications function as a discipline within public administration; and (6) whether the political masters of the public sector, the ministers, will encourage technology's further development in public administration or to try to control its use and limit its impact.

26 Budgeting in Canada: *Beyond Spenders and Guardians*

David A. Good

The budgeting of public money is changing inside the Canadian federal government.[1] In government, public money talks. It speaks to the great public purposes of society—where governments place their priorities and what they decide to ignore. It affects the standards of living in the nation and it reflects standards by which politicians and public servants undertake the nation's business. Public money speaks to promises and aspirations. It also speaks to deep concerns—both real and sometimes fabricated—of citizens, taxpayers, and members of Parliament about the way public money is spent. Inside and outside government, matters of public money are filled with great promises and fraught with bitter disappointments.

The Canadian federal **budgetary process** has long been influenced by a simple bilateral relationship between departmental **spenders** and central guardians (the Department of Finance and Treasury Board Secretariat) within an 'old village' conditioned by old norms of behaviour. This chapter examines the extent to which a more complex, multilateral relationship is emerging among spenders, guardians, priority setters (the Prime Minister's Office and the Privy Council Office), and **financial watchdogs** (the Office of the Auditor General) within a 'new town' conditioned by new norms of behaviour.

When Canadian officials from the **budget office** meet annually with their counterparts from the 30 member countries of the Organisation for Economic Co-Operation and Development (OECD), they talk about the 'functions of the budget office'. Dressed up in the latest language, the two-day agenda for the twenty-fourth annual meeting in June 2003 reflected the basic budget office functions: 'the role of fiscal rules', 'the political economy of reallocation', and 'budgeting and managing for performance' (OECD, 2006). This emerging perspective goes beyond the traditional notions of budgeting that have largely focused on matters of allocation—who gets what. Now included in the purview of the budget office officials is an extended set of concerns about public money—how much to spend it, where to spend it, and how it should best be managed. Indeed, as Allen Schick explains, 'all budget systems—reformed and traditional—have three basic budget objectives: (1) to maintain aggregate fiscal discipline, (2) to allocate resources in accord with government priorities, and (3) to promote the efficient delivery of services' (Schick, 1997: 4; Allen and Tommasi, 2001). The story about the changing budgetary process is the story about the changing relative importance of these objectives to government and the changing ways in which governments go about pursuing them.

Spenders and Guardians

Much of our understanding of budgeting has come from studies by academics and articles by practitioners (Ward, 1962; Maslove et al., 1986; Doern et al., 1988; Hartle, 1988; Savoie, 1990; Prince, 2002; Johnson, 1971, 1973; Van Loon, 1981, 1983a, 1983b; Clark, 1994). In

1964, Aaron Wildavsky's book *The Politics of the Budgetary Process* set out the spenders and guardian framework, which for that period and for the remainder of the twentieth century defined not only the way in which most academics thought about the budgetary process but also described how most practitioners experienced budgeting.[2] The budgetary process in the Canadian federal government has been described and practised as a bilateral game between two sets of players—spenders and guardians—with their inherent competitive behaviour conditioned by the kinship and culture of 'village life' on the Rideau River. Budgeting in Ottawa, however, is changing and is being reshaped through powerful outside forces and influential newcomers who are penetrating the expenditure community and creating new norms of behaviour in a new town.

Wildavsky (1964: 160) argued that budgetary outcomes could best be described and explained by examining the interaction of budget players performing stylized institutional roles of spenders and guardians. These roles, or 'expectations of behaviour attached to institutional positions', were the division of labour among the key participants in the budgetary process. In this framework, spenders and guardians interact in a complementary way and their interactions create a stable pattern of mutual expectations, thereby reducing the burden of complex budgetary calculations. As he described it:

> Administrative agencies act as advocates of increased expenditure, and central control organs function as guardians of the treasury. Each expects the other to do its job; agencies can advocate knowing that the center will impose limits, and the center can exert control, knowing that agencies will push expenditures as hard as they can. Thus roles serve as calculating mechanisms. The interaction between spending and cutting roles makes up the component elements of budgetary systems. (Wildavsky, 1975: 7)

These mutual expectations between spenders and guardians serve as conventions to guide and condition behaviour. Some of these conventions are explicit and formal, taking the form of codified rules of budget behaviour. But, as Wildavsky found, most are implicit and informal, shaped and nurtured over a long and sustained process of interaction between spenders and guardians.

Wildavsky viewed the inherent conflict resulting from the spender and guardian interaction as necessary for resolving budget decisions. Separating functions and responsibilities and embodying them with institutional form—central control agencies and spending departments—allowed for specialization and reduced the complexity inherent in budget decisions. Spenders could focus their expert knowledge and experience on designing expenditure programs, and guardians could capitalize on information and analysis about the economic, fiscal, and political situation to set limits for overall expenditures and force choices among competing demands. The result? Year after year a multitude of seemingly endless individual and separate budget decisions could be moulded into a single annual budget.

The interaction between spenders and guardians did not mean that budgeting was a 'free-for-all' fight constrained only by the limits of financial resources. Spenders and guardians had to co-operate as well as compete. Conflicts had to be managed and agreements struck in order for a budget to be made. Complexities had to be simplified and, at times, egos had to be massaged. In determining how much funding to request and how much to grant, budget players relied upon various 'aids to calculation' to reduce conflict and complexity. Both spenders and guardians depended upon past experience, focused on knowable expenditure inputs rather than on uncertain program outputs and unknowable policy outcomes, made annual incremental changes to the budget, and avoided changes to the ongoing base of budget expenditures.

The spenders and guardians framework was particularly powerful, and through numerous studies and applications, it accounted for differences in budgetary behaviour across different political systems and for explaining the impact of different budgetary reforms in countries, provinces, or states under different economic circumstances (Caiden and Wildavsky, 1974; Heclo and Wildavsky, 1974; Wildavsky, 1975; Imbeau, 2000). The framework continues to be widely reflected in the academic literature on budgeting (Hartle, 1988; Savoie, 1990; Dewar and Good, 2004). Through his extensive research, Wildavsky discovered that the roles of spenders and guardians were performed at all levels in both the political and bureaucratic spheres. He also found that these roles were played out at each stage in the budgetary process—the setting of fiscal aggregates, the determination of allocations, and the management of programs.[3]

From Old Village to New Town

Different political systems have shaped and conditioned the behaviour of spenders and guardians differently. When it came to parliamentary systems of government, Wildavsky argued that the behaviour of spenders and guardians was conditioned not so much by formal rules but by the kinship and culture within a tightly knit expenditure community that governed the expectations of spenders and guardians and established their behavioural norms. In Britain and in Canada, budgetary conflict between spenders and guardians has traditionally been privately absorbed and often quietly managed. In the United States, it has been publicly exposed and sometimes not managed at all.

As Heclo and Wildavsky (1974) explained, privacy at the centre of government was the defining characteristic of British parliamentary budgeting. This was 'village life' in Whitehall. It was best understood in terms of a combination of four central concepts. None was absolutely unique to Britain; most parliamentary systems contained most if not all of them, perhaps in less powerful combination. These concepts were (1) a community of insiders that was small, private, and closed; (2) mutual confidence as a 'pervasive bond' governing how insiders dealt with each other and, by extension, strangers on the outside; (3) common calculations to help them deal with the complexity of budget decisions; and (4) the assessment of political climate by public servants and ministers before determining expenditure strategy. Together these four concepts explain much of the behaviour of spenders and guardians in parliamentary government. The kinship and culture of the British expenditure community of Whitehall was not exactly the same in the Canadian federal expenditure community on the Rideau. The 'old tie' and the 'grey suit' were not identical. But when it came to matters of expenditure, the combination of these four concepts has conditioned the behaviour of spenders and guardians in the Ottawa expenditure community.

Budget preparation in Ottawa has traditionally been a private and internal affair in government, run by the Minister of Finance and top officials in the department, with limited tasks assigned to the President of the Treasury Board and the Treasury Board Secretariat, and with the Prime Minister looking over both their shoulders and intervening with the Minister of Finance as and when he wished. Only within the last decade have new processes been put in place in an effort to increase outside input and to condition the expectations and reactions of outsiders. Mutual confidence and trust among and between ministers and public servants and between spenders and guardians has been the traditional underlying ingredient that has sustained relationships, ensured coherence, and facilitated difficult choices. Common calculations have helped spenders and guardians to simplify decisions, reduce complexities, and hedge against the inevitable uncertainties of budget making. By chipping away at the margins of the budget, rather than attacking its base, spenders and guardians have mutually agreed to focus their time and energy around budget increments, with the result that each year budget decisions could be made and deeply divisive conflicts avoided. Assessing the political climate and knowing when 'windows of opportunity' open and when they close have been essential intuitive skills for ministers and officials anxious to push through new expenditures or shut down the demands from others. These norms and beliefs about trust, common calculations, and political assessment have been deeply shared by the community of spenders and guardians who work at the centre of government. Indeed, understanding 'village life' has been critical in understanding budgeting in Ottawa.

The spenders and guardians framework is, however, showing signs of wear. Despite the high-profile promises in early 2004 of the first Martin government for 'a politics of achievement' and a 'continuous culture of reallocation', the seeds of change in the budgetary process were sown years before (Savoie, 2003). Over the past decade, there has been an accumulation of forces that are changing the way budgeting is being done. These changes got underway some time ago, and were perhaps most visibly manifested in the 1995 'Program Review' budget in which expenditures were significantly reduced and many programs dramatically restructured (Aucoin and Savoie, 1998). The result was that federal program spending in 1996 fell to 12.6 per cent of the GDP, a level that had not been achieved since 1949–50. These changes have been more recently reflected in the growing importance and prominence of external financial watchdogs as contained in the Federal Accountability Act brought forward by the Harper Conservative minority government in 2006. The old village has given way to a new town, if not a major city.

Beyond Spenders and Guardians

Some budget scholars have concluded that the spenders and guardians framework is still relevant for explaining the budgetary process and its outcomes (Imbeau, 2000; Kelly and Wanna, 2000). Over the past decade or more, however, there have been several forces on government that are having a fundamental influence on the way in which budgeting is carried out. The necessity for fiscal restraint, particularly the requirement for a balanced budget or better, along with ideas inherent in New Public Management have brought to the fore two major issues affecting the practice of. budgeting. The one major issue can be summed up as priorities, and the other as performance.

With the requirements for restraint and a balanced budget, the government has focused more on strategic planning and priority setting. As long as the economy and budgets were expanding significantly each year there was less need for the government to undertake the difficult and painful task of determining and setting out publicly explicit budget priorities. In the 1950s and 1960s and for much of the 1970s there was sufficient overall funding to increase the budgets of all departments and agencies—the 'fair share' allocation—and the government was spared much of the divisive and conflict-ridden debates over what should increase and what should not. Even when its fiscal flexibility was reduced in the 1980s, the government first minimized conflict and simplified its calculations through the use of across-the-board cuts to all departments—the 'equal sacrifice' treatment—rather than the clear enunciation of specific priorities. However, as more and more of the government's expenditures were being used to finance the increasing costs of carrying the ballooning debt and as many years of across-the-board cuts had significantly reduced the capacity of government to deliver its programs, the government in the 1990s found it necessary to be more selective in where it cut and where it spent. This required that the government be explicit about its expenditure priorities rather than rely upon the implicit norms of 'fair share' and 'equal sacrifice'. Even after budgets had been balanced in the late 1990s, the ongoing strong public commitment to 'a balanced budget or better' requires that the government have clear and explicit priorities for the allocation and reallocation of expenditures.

Along with the need for government to set priorities, there were also increasing demands for better performance from government. With more of the expenditure budget being used to pay for the escalating service costs of the increasing debt, less was available for programs and services. With declining public services and a continued tax burden, citizens became concerned about the government's diminishing performance. To many citizens it seemed that they were paying too much and receiving too little. Starting in the mid-1980s, government focused on a series of initiatives to improve performance ranging from the establishment of service standards to innovations in alternative service delivery. More recently, these initiatives have broadened to include results reporting, performance measurement, accountability frameworks, and improved financial management, as well as expanded internal and external audits.

As the issues and ideas concerned with government priorities and government performance have come to the fore, they have had significant and direct influence on the practice of budgeting. The most important has been the emergence of two entirely new institutional roles in the budgetary process—priority setters and financial watchdogs—separate and distinct from the traditional roles of spenders and guardians.

Two New Roles

As budgeting has moved from allocating the increments to all, to cutting all (some more than others), and then to cutting some while benefiting others, priority setting in budgeting has taken on greater importance. Government is finding that priorities need to be established upfront and early, and it is less prepared to let expenditure priorities simply emerge as seeming by-products from the 'argy bargy' of spender and guardian bilateralism. As a consequence, a new and separate institutional role of **priority setters** has emerged in the budgetary process. In the Canadian federal government, it is embodied in the **Prime Minister's Office (PMO)** and the **Privy Council Office (PCO)**. To be sure these important and distinctly different offices have always played an indirect role in the budget,[4] but in the last decade their roles have been more significant, more direct, and more involved. Indeed, as the budget has become more central to the act of governing, these central agencies have become more directly involved in budget-making (Savoie, 1999).

Priority setters in the PMO and the PCO are creating new space and taking over some old space in the budgetary process that has traditionally been occupied by spenders and guardians. For example, as budgets have become important public communications documents for government, PMO and PCO priority setters are focusing on the political and policy messages that are conveyed to voters and citizens. In the face of continuous fiscal restraint and increasing demands for programs and services, the PMO and the PCO are working more actively with, and on, spenders to shape and position expenditure proposals. They are also working with the Department of Finance to turn back unwanted, low-priority expenditure proposals. They are also creating new space within the budgetary process for the consideration and determination of overall government priorities in advance of budget preparation and, in so doing, are changing the traditional interactions between spenders and guardians.

Priority setters, however, are not the only newcomers to the budget game. Financial watchdogs are now firmly and visibly on the scene. At one time, financial watchdogs only lurked around the edges of the budgetary process, dependent on their bark to effect change. Now with the bite of their public reports and commentary, sharpened by a highly attentive and probing media and a less deferential and more skeptical public, they have become more central to the action.

One way of appreciating the emerging influence of financial watchdogs on the budgetary process and understanding how financial watchdogs think about public money is to examine a theory of budgeting that is separate from, but related to, the spenders and guardians framework. This is the theory of 'the budget-maximizing bureaucrat' which became required reading for certain politicians and bureaucrats and, as this happened and the concepts took root, it became associated with a particular ideology in support of 'smaller government'.[5] The central hypothesis of this public choice model is that bureaucrats attempt to maximize their discretionary budgets and 'since neither the bureaucrats nor the political authorities . . . can claim this discretionary budget as personal income, this surplus is spent in ways that serve the interests of the bureaucrats and the political authorities' (Niskanen, 1991: 16).

The conclusions from the model suggest that these underlying bureaucratic and political biases within government can lead to what taxpayers have come to perceive as inherent inefficiency and waste in public expenditure. In parliamentary systems of government, the long-standing antidote to these natural biases has been the creation of strong independent monitoring or watchdog organizations, operating outside the government of the day, not as agents of the government but as agents of Parliament. The creation of a separate Auditor General (neither a public servant of the government nor a politician) can be seen as an independent check on the behaviour of both political authorities as review agents and bureaucrats as spenders. In order for the independent agent to remain independent, he or she must not engage directly with the government in the act of budgeting—that is, in determining aggregate fiscal levels, allocating resources to government priorities, or deciding on the appropriate mix of expenditure and program inputs for the efficient delivery of services. Instead, auditors general report publicly on events after the fact.

The institutions that represent these two new roles of priority setters (PMO and PCO) and financial watchdogs (Office of the Auditor General) are, of course, not new. The PMO and PCO, usually, although not always, have been aligned with the spenders. The Auditor General has traditionally been viewed as aligned with the guardians and is increasingly seen by many taxpayers as a force for smaller government. What is new is that these stylized roles are taking on a larger and more significant part in describing and explaining the budgetary process and its outcomes.

As with spenders and guardians, priority setters and financial watchdogs operate in a complementary way, creating a stable pattern of mutual expectations. However, unlike spenders and guardians, both are concerned with 'all of government' and they rarely interact directly with each other. Priority setters are concerned with the 'what' and 'who' of public expenditure: are the broad visions of government translated into defined priorities, is money going to them, and is the government achieving its political commitments? They operate under the belief that they are defining and ordering the priorities of government and, by extension, meeting the needs of citizens. Financial watchdogs are concerned with the 'how' of public expenditure: is spending done with due regard for economy, efficiency, and the capacity of government to assess effectiveness? They operate under the belief that they are protecting the taxpayer from the inevitable inefficiency of government and the possible misuse of public money. Each expects the other to do its job. Priority setters can push priorities and the need to fulfill political commitments to the limit, knowing that watchdogs will invariably report on deficiencies in how things were done, and watchdogs can report regularly on deficiencies and transgressions in how things are done knowing that priority setters are focused on what is being done.

Guardians and the Changing Role of the Budget Office

Understanding budgeting begins with understanding the changing role of the budget office. Surprisingly, in Ottawa there is no longer a shared view about the budget office, what it is, where it is, and who runs it. For many years the conventional view has been that the budget office was divided between the Department of Finance and the Treasury Board. In a nutshell, the Department of Finance was responsible for management of the macroeconomy and for the overall fiscal policy, and the Treasury Board Secretariat for the operating budgets of programs and the general management of government. On paper (more recently on websites), this is the way it still appears.

Because budgeting is complex, no single guardian can handle all its aspects. Different guardians therefore come to specialize in one or more of the three main functions of budgeting—determining fiscal aggregates, allocating resources, and ensuring efficiency and sound financial management. The Department of Finance has always had near-exclusive responsibility for the determination of fiscal aggregates and for maintaining overall fiscal discipline. It is the Minister of Finance who sets the **fiscal framework** and through the annual budgets carries on his or her shoulders a government-wide responsibility for overall fiscal management. When the Treasury Board Secretariat was created in 1966 as a separate entity from the Department of Finance, it assumed distinct responsibility for promoting efficiency in the delivery of programs and for sound financial management.[6] The responsibility for resource allocation has traditionally been shared between the Department of Finance and the Treasury Board Secretariat, although over the past decade it has increasingly been assumed by the Department of Finance.

Because budgeting is complex, budget office officials break the budget into five components: (1) major transfer payments to individuals; (2) major transfer payments to provincial and territorial governments; (3) operating and other expenditures—the 'small p' programs; (4) public debt charges; and (5) tax expenditures.[7] The Department of Finance has primary responsibility for everything except for operating and other expenditures, which is the general responsibility of the Treasury Board Secretariat and includes operating and capital, payments to Crown corporations, and minor transfer payments and subsidies (Government of Canada, 2005). Over the last 40 years the expenditure components for which Finance is responsible have increased significantly, whereas the relative share of operating and other expenditures, the responsibility of the Treasury Board Secretariat, has declined significantly. In 1964, operating and other expenditures were nearly 60 per cent of the direct expenditure budget. Forty years later, it was less than 40 per cent.[8]

The differences between the guardians in the Department of Finance and the Treasury Board Secretariat reflect an increasing divergence in the culture of the two organizations. This is a consequence of two fundamental and distinct forces over the past 15 years. One force has been the gradual introduction of various forms and mutations of New Public Management throughout the public service. This was predicated on the view that there were too many central rules and controls standing in the way of departmental performance and efficient programming. The other was the preoccupation with the deficit, a concern that emerged slowly and sporadically over the late 1980s and early 1990s to become the overriding public and political preoccupation in the mid-1990s.

The first force had enormous impact on the Treasury Board Secretariat and its evolving culture as it attempted for years to fundamentally, but only partially, transform itself into a 'management board'. An early step taken in 1996 was the dramatic and far-reaching decision to eliminate the Program Branch, which had been the influential 'budget office' and the backbone of the Secretariat since its inception. A further step was the formal announcement in 1997 by Prime Minister Chrétien that the Treasury Board would be constituted as a 'management board'. The second force—the preoccupation with the deficit—played directly into the hands of the Department of Finance. It reinforced the department's traditional function of being the sole and exclusive manager of the fiscal and expenditure framework and sharpened its new-found role as the government's major budget cutter. As the Treasury Board Secretariat continued to grapple with how to deal with the generation-old cry to 'let the managers manage', the Department of Finance focused exclusively and single-mindedly on eliminating the deficit, 'come hell or high water'.[9]

It is not surprising that these forces—increasing managerial authority for departments and significant cuts to expenditures—have affected the long-standing relationship between guardians in the Department of Finance and the Treasury Board Secretariat. It is not so much a question of differences over issues or approaches to specific expenditure matters. Nor is it simply a powerful Department of Finance exploiting a weakened Secretariat. In one sense it is more fundamental. When it comes to budget allocations, Treasury Board is not so much exploited as it is ignored. The relationship of guardians, once based on clearly defined specialized responsibilities, has been considerably weakened through the changing roles of each.

As Treasury Board officials have become significantly less influential in shaping budget allocations they have lost their capacity to secure program and budget information from spending departments. With less information they have done less expenditure analysis and have less advice to offer on matters of program expenditures, all of which has weakened their position with the Department of Finance, with Privy Council Office priority setters, the spending departments, and the financial watchdogs. Although Finance has temporarily taken on some of this detailed expenditure work itself, it knows that the key to longer-term success rests on working with the Treasury Board Secretariat to rebuild its expenditure analysis and advisory capacity. However, as the increasingly separate guardians of Finance and the Secretariat begin to address this internal challenge in search of new and more effective ways to work together, they continue to face the ongoing external challenge of dealing with the continuous demands and increasing aspirations of spending departments and spending ministers.

Here Come the Spenders

Spenders are everywhere in government. In a small 27-person cabinet, there are 25 spenders and only two guardians—the Minister of Finance and the President of the Treasury Board. In a large 39-person cabinet, there are 37 spending ministers and still only two guardians. In 2004, to a constellation of 27 ministers, Prime Minister Martin added 28 parliamentary secretaries each with assigned responsibilities and all with access to cabinet documents and decisions. All but one, the parliamentary secretary to the Minister of Finance, were spenders.

Standing outside the spenders in Ottawa are the spending premiers, mayors, and First Nations chiefs and other Aboriginal leaders. Premiers see the federation in terms of its alleged fiscal imbalance—a federal government with perpetual and automatic surpluses and provincial governments with increasingly costly expenditure obligations. Provincial premiers and territorial leaders see federal expenditures not only as a means for dealing with pressing policy problems but also in terms of what expenditure increases can mean for them politically and for the autonomy of the governments that they lead. They are the spenders, and they view the federal government as the guardians. Mayors and municipal leaders, traditionally dependent on diminished fiscal transfers from deficit-ridden provincial governments, are increasingly and more successfully making their budget requests directly to the federal government. The approximately 600 First Nations bands, their chiefs, and leaders, who face a history of social and economic neglect for their communities and their peoples, make the federal government the target of their expenditure demands.

Most spending ministers and spending public servants are never content with the same level of budget from one year to the next. Indeed, a large part of their jobs is developing and advocating new policies, programs, and projects, all of which require additional budget resources. During periods of budgetary expansion, they want to ensure that they are getting at least their 'fair share' of the available new money. During periods of budgetary restraint and reduction, they want to ensure that they maintain their budgets, or at a minimum, take no more than their 'fair share' of the budget cuts. Their fundamental concerns are how to get money, how to keep it, and how to spend it.

Ask any number of experienced deputy ministers about how spenders get new money and it invariably comes down to three things: link the proposal to the priorities of government, do your homework, and have a constituency. All three are necessary and all are used by spenders in varying degrees, depending on the circumstances. 'For us to get money', instructs a spending deputy minister, 'we have to do the policy work to show that infrastructure supports the priorities of the government. No matter what the program, you need to show how it helps to achieve the government's priorities. We linked infrastructure to Kyoto, to the environment, and to trade' (Good, 2007: 77).

During periods of significant and prolonged expenditure restraint, spenders shift their attention from getting new money to maintaining their existing base of money. During these times, skilful spenders can actually become part guardians, at least when it comes to the question of total government spending. A former deputy minister explains: 'During all my eight years as a deputy minister and indeed before that as a central agency guardian, the pre-eminent public policy issue was not the constitution, daycare, and defence. It was the huge and yawning **deficit and debt** that the government faced and the very real prospects of becoming an impoverished nation. Like most other deputies of the day, I was convinced that, if we didn't get that under control, there was no point in carrying on with ordinary business' (Good, 2007: 81).

Getting money (or even keeping it) is one thing, spending it is quite another. Whether and how a department has spent its money in the past is an important influence on future spending decisions. Spenders, guardians, priority setters, and financial watchdogs all have a different perspective on past spending. For spenders, the key is the confidence and assurance that come from having in place the program delivery systems to ensure that the money is spent within the time constraints of the fiscal year and the requirements of the programs. For guardians, how well a department spent its resources in the past is the clue to how tough to be on them in the future. For priority setters, departments that have done their spending provide evidence that the government has focused on what it says needs to be done and that it has lived up to its publicly expressed spending commitments. For the financial watchdog, spending provides the opportunity to audit departments and agencies on their compliance with the government financial policies and to assess the performance of their programs and their management.

Spenders know that in order 'to get' they have 'to give' and that means providing information to guardians in exchange for expenditure increases or for protection from budget cuts. The reciprocity of information and budget exchanges between spenders and guardians serves their mutual interests. But spenders don't naturally give information to guardians and guardians don't naturally give expenditure increases to spenders. No spender wants a guardian to use the information later to turn down a request or, worse yet, to cut a program. Spenders will, however, provide information to guardians when it is in their interest to do so and when it strengthens their case for their spending proposal. For spenders, this has increasingly become a matter of providing information about how the new spending proposal contributes to and furthers the government's priorities. Less emphasis is placed on providing budget information about how the proposed new program or program expansion will actually perform.

For the guardians, the information provided by spenders about the linkage of the proposal to government priorities is rarely useful for determining whether one proposal should be funded and not another, or whether the department should absorb the costs from within its existing A-base of expenditures. The information that guardians need for expenditure analysis and expenditure management and planning—a detailed and fine-grain costing of the A-base of expenditure programs that can be easily aggregated and disaggregated in relation to proposals for new spending and for reallocations—is not readily available. It must be created; therefore, there must be an incentive to do it. It must also be relevant to the decisions at hand, and it must be up-to-date.

To get this information, guardians face a fundamental problem. They have learned that the information they receive from spenders is often distorted, incomplete, discontinuous, and inaccurate. Central directives and requests from guardians to spending departments for expenditure and program information yield only generalized information and not the information that guardians need to do effective program and budget analyses. As a result, securing reliable and relevant information from spenders requires that guardians be able to give them something in return. The fate of guardians to acquire this critical information rests on their ability to grant expenditure increases, to provide increased certainty through the commitment of multi-year expenditures, and to allow for financial and management flexibility. When guardians are unable to grant these concessions to departments, the budget information they receive from departments dries up. This is the reciprocity of budgets and information. It is implicitly understood by guardians and spenders at all levels and it affects information flows at all levels. An experienced assistant secretary of the Treasury Board Secretariat explains it this way: 'It is much easier to get information from a department if you deal with budgeting and affect their allocations. It is the dollars that matter, that is how you become relevant' (Good, 2007: 88).

Priority Setters at the Centre

Budgeting goes to the heart of any government. The 'centre' of Canadian government—the Prime Minister's Office and the Privy Council Office—is not prepared to leave budget allocations to be determined simply through the bilateral interplay of spenders and guardians.[10] Individual spenders have their own priorities and they are not necessarily those of the government and may not fit with those of the Prime Minister.

Prime ministers know that it is too late to await the annual budget process if they are to shape the contents of the budget. They also know that determining priorities through strategic planning in government is all too often a daunting and unproductive task, usually producing more paper than actual decisions. Over the past 40 years there has been much written on the various and often failed attempts by prime ministers at strategic planning (Doern, 1971; French, 1984; Clark, 1985; Lindquist, 2001). If there is one trend, however, that is now well established, it is that the Prime Minister, his or her office, and the Privy Council Office more tightly link together election campaign platforms, transition planning, the Speech from the Throne, and the budget. The political groundwork begins with the preparation of the campaign platform by political parties, which can take the form of a single overall document or a series of individual announcements strung out over the course of the campaign.[11] The public service groundwork begins with the transition planning in preparation for a new government and a new Prime Minister. This work is undertaken at the centre of government by the Privy Council Office as well as in each department when an incumbent government nears the end of its mandate.

The formal planning and priority process of the government and cabinet provides a general framework for government direction, but has limited impact in the determination of budget priorities. When it comes to setting priorities for the budget, the key players—priority setters, spenders, and guardians—all know that the priorities of government that emerge from the cabinet planning process never provide the clarity and precision that is required for budget allocations. A top aide to a Prime Minister recalls his years of experience in the 1990s:

> Discussions in cabinet on government priorities were never useful in helping to clarify the precise priorities for budget planning. We would simply hear from ministers that health or national defence was a priority, but ministers never came to a joint view on what specifically should be done. (Good, 2007: 103)

It has not been for want of trying that ministers have had difficulty in determining budget priorities. 'We have tried everything with cabinet ministers', explained one senior PMO official, 'overviews, planning sessions, even voting, but it has never worked' (Good, 2007: 103). Certainly, every cabinet finds it difficult if not impossible to set specific priorities for budgets. The collective agreement on any single, specific budget priority means that the spending ambitions of one, or at best, a few ministers are met, but those of most other ministers are precluded. Individual ministers, if forced to choose, soon learn to prefer that budget priorities remain vague and general so that as many of their own priorities can be justified under the broad, overall general heading. In the end, at best, priorities determined by cabinet remain multiple, conflicting, and vague, with the result that major budget allocations are determined by the Prime Minister and the Minister of Finance.[12]

The Financial Watchdog's Bite

Years ago, in a simpler world of budgeting, the Auditor General and his or her office were viewed as an offspring of the guardians, an independent voice that advocated restraint in government and the prudent and economical management of public spending. However, fundamental changes to the **Auditor General Act in 1976** significantly increased the influence of the **Office of the Auditor General (OAG)** with respect to the management of public money (Aucoin, 1998). With this new act, the focus of the OAG shifted dramatically from financial audit to 'value for money' audit (now called **performance audit**), displacing much of the burden of financial audit to internal auditors in departments and agencies.[13] With this major legislative change, the Auditor General acquired significant, new influence in shaping how the expenditure of 'public money' in the form of budgets would be assessed in terms of the 'value' or performance of government programs. In short, the Auditor General and his or her office—the financial watchdog—had become important players, albeit indirect players, in the budgetary process.

The road that transformed the role of the financial watchdog into a budget player was paved by a significant and important guardian—the Treasury Board Secretariat. Up to the 1960s, when budgeting was done by **line item**, there was no need to link expenditures to programs. No one needed what they could not use. Money was allocated to buy things—planes, pencils, and paper clips—and to pay public servants to undertake assigned tasks. Financial audits—to determine if the financial transactions conformed to the laws and regulations—were sufficient for guardians, parliamentarians, and the public to judge probity and compliance in the use of the public money. However, as Sharon Sutherland (2002: 7) notes, when the Treasury Board Secretariat established the government-wide requirement to link expenditures and programs by introducing the **Planning, Programming, and Budgeting System (PPBS)**, it 'opened the door [for] the OAG to become a future program auditor who would undertake validation of departments' reported program results'. If the government was to have a **program budget**, then the government's auditor should 'audit' the spending departments' evaluative and performance work on their programs. Today, the Auditor General is not just 'a' program auditor; he or she is 'the' program auditor, and as such has become an important player, passing independent judgment on the linkage between the expenditures provided by guardians and the results achieved by spenders.

Since the mid-1960s, the program budget has established the essential logic that not only determines how budgeting is to be done—by program expenditures—but also how achievement is to be measured—by program results. Ironically, the introduction of the program budget has created a major and insurmountable problem; that is, the need to establish on a government-wide basis program results that are true and verifiable and can be linked to program expenditures. Decreeing that this will be done is one thing; making it happen has proved to be quite another. Since 1971 none of the expenditure and performance management reforms and procedures have come close to solving this problem of objectively linking budget expenditures with program performance. The reforms and procedures have been continuous and there have been many.[14] In fact, the Auditor General (2001, 2001, 2005) has developed a 'model' for rating departmental performance reports and has consistently reported on 'the painfully slow progress of departments towards managing for results' and the 'disappointing progress'. As long as this problem cannot be solved—and there is much experience and theory to suggest that it will not be—there is every reason to believe that the financial watchdog will continue to exercise important judgments on what governments have and have not achieved through public expenditures.[15]

Despite their independence, financial watchdogs have considerable dealings with other players in the budgetary process. These interactions are important for their credibility, to ensure that their work is accurate and relevant, and, perhaps most importantly, to avoid charges that they have made mistakes. To preserve and maintain their independence, a set of mutual expectations about their role has developed among various public money players. Everyone—spenders, guardians, and priority setters—accept that the job of the financial watchdog is to keep its eyes on things and, when things start to go wrong, to bark loudly. No one expects the financial watchdog to view a glass of water as half full; it is invariably half empty, because the job is to detect what could or has gone wrong and to compel spenders, guardians, and priority setters to take corrective action. Auditors are pessimistic because all others are expected to be optimistic. Auditors are skeptical because others will be credulous. Auditors are watchers and reporters, and spenders, guardians, and priority setters are planners and doers. Auditors look for mistakes, knowing that when they are publicly exposed, spenders, guardians, and priority setters will be forced to correct them. Spenders, guardians, and priority setters look for opportunities, knowing that they must abide by the constraints of prudent, economical, and efficient public management if they are to avoid negative audit reports. In their dealings with one another, each player expects the other to do his or her job.

A Framework Beyond Spenders and Guardians

The framework which has added priority setters and financial watchdogs to the traditional roles of spenders and guardians has provided a more comprehensive basis for describing and explaining budgeting in contemporary twenty-first-century government. It has helped in understanding the uneasy balance among competing budgetary objectives—determining fiscal aggregates, allocating resources, and achieving efficiency in the management of expenditures. In terms of budget outcomes—controlling total expenditures, linking expenditures to priorities, and ensuring efficiency in expenditure and avoiding financial mismanagement—we see that it is rare that the government can achieve simultaneously high scores in all three areas. Instead, as government focuses its limited attention and scarce resources on one, it gives less priority to another, sometimes with significant and undesirable consequences.

The framework has helped us to understand that guardians are not monolithic. Treasury Board Secretariat analysts are not clones of the Department of Finance who just happen to work on the 'small p' programs of the budget. Instead, with an increasing emphasis on management issues, their focus on budgeting has clearly moved from matters of allocation to matters of management and performance. At the same time, the Department of Finance has extended its capacity and grasp to deal with practically all matters of expenditure allocation. Guardians in the Department of Finance are also spenders, and significant ones at that. In terms of **direct expenditures**, Finance develops and designs programs, particularly those involving 'big money', that often involve major transfers to provinces and territories and major transfer payments to individuals. In the hidden area of **tax expenditures**, which in dollar terms nearly equals the entire direct expenditure budget, Finance has exclusive responsibility for designing the initiatives and determining what goes ahead and what stays on the drawing board. Indeed, the Department of Finance exerts great influence not only because it is a guardian but also because it can act as both guardian and spender and usurp some of the responsibilities of the priority setters in determining budget priorities.

The framework has also helped us to have a more complete understanding of the competitive and co-operative roles inherent in the most important of all relationships in the budgetary process—that between the Minister of Finance and the Prime Minister. The priority setter role of a Prime Minister is important in supporting the Finance Minister in making the unpopular expenditure cuts required in a period of deep fiscal restraint, but it may be still more important in determining a limited set of focused priorities when the government returns to a surplus position. The experience of a former Finance Minister cum Prime Minister indicates that being a good guardian when everyone needs to cut does not guarantee being a good priority setter when some spenders will win and others will not (Simpson, 2006).

The framework sheds light on the front end of the budget process and how governments are increasingly articulating government priorities to determine the aggregate fiscal levels and budget allocations and then using these priorities to explain and sell the budget to the public. Governments have learned that if they do not put their own, readily understandable label on their complex budgets, the media will likely do it for them, and it may well be a label they do not like. The Prime Minister's Office and the Privy Council Office, while starting from different vantage points, work in tandem and are major and influential budget players. They are not just 'framers' who work only on the Speech from the Throne; they are also 'deciders' who shape the themes and contents of the budget. Indeed, prime ministers and their closest advisers are not prepared to leave the determination of budget priorities to the Minister of Finance and his or her department. Prime ministers and ministers of finance have different interests and they will go to great ends, pushing the relationship, sometimes beyond the breaking point, to get what they want. But, in the face of legions of spenders and aggressive watchdogs, they need each other as much as they need the tight cover of confidentiality in order to manage, without publicity and fanfare, their inherent differences.

The framework, which includes a major role for priority setters inside government, can help us to better understand how and when major shifts to the normal incremental process of budgeting take place. In the spenders and guardians model, such **shift points**—when expenditures for a particular department or program area increased quickly and significantly beyond the normal incremental and regular adjustment—were treated, as in a regression analysis, like 'error terms', unexplained by the independent variables of the model: **budgetary base**, increment, limited calculations, trust, and conflict avoidance. To be sure, the origins of shift points will be exogenous to any model of budgeting constructed from variables largely internal to government. However, by including the role of priority setters within the new model, we might better understand how changes in broader societal preferences, attitudes, and political ideology can be channelled and focused by participants within government and thereby affect the internal workings of the budget process and its outcomes.

The framework has helped to shed more light on the back end of the budget process (some call it budget implementation), a part that is increasingly important but has traditionally been neglected by most budget theory. Financial watchdogs, through extensive use of their public reports by parliamentarians and the media, have considerable influence on the public perception of the government when it comes to the management (or mismanagement) of public money. Furthermore, the Harper government's Federal Accountability Act, which came into force in December 2006, expanded significantly the role of watchdogs. It established five new parliamentary watchdogs, strengthened five existing parliamentary watchdogs, created three new internal but independent watchdogs, strengthened one existing internal watchdog, and codified in law the watchdog-like functions of yet another.[16]

In terms of the management and accountability of public money, this legislation represents a major strengthening of the scope, powers, and responsibilities of financial and budget watchdogs. The measures and the language used to describe them were decidedly reformist in nature and in tone: 'ensure truth in budgeting', 'strengthen the power of the Auditor General', 'strengthen auditing and accountability in departments', 'clean up the procurement of government contracts', 'provide real protection for whistle-blowers', and 'designating deputy ministers as **accounting officers**' (see Chapter 4). In all there were six major reforms dealing with the management of public money:

1. The creation of a new budget watchdog, the **Parliamentary Budget Officer (PBO),** is an effort to improve the transparency and credibility of the government's fiscal forecasting and budget planning. It is intended to provide parliamentarians and parliamentary committees with independent information and advice on economic, fiscal, and budget issues.
2. New powers and resources have been provided to the Office of the Auditor General to audit any individual and organization that receives public money from the federal government, allowing the Auditor General to 'follow the money' through the growing number of public, private, and voluntary sector partnerships and other multi-party financial arrangements.
3. The independence and influence of internal audit watchdogs were strengthened with the appointment of a chief audit executive within each department and agency, reporting directly to the deputy minister and reporting functionally to the Comptroller General. In addition, the independence of internal departmental audit committees was strengthened by requiring that their membership be drawn largely from outside government.
4. Designating deputy ministers as accounting officers for their departments to make them accountable before Parliament to answer questions related to their assigned responsibilities. In the event a minister and deputy minister are unable to agree on the interpretation or application of a Treasury Board policy, directive, or standard, the deputy minister is to seek guidance from the secretary of the Treasury Board. If the matter remains unresolved, the minister would refer it to the Treasury Board for a decision. A copy of the Treasury Board decision would be provided to the Auditor General as a confidence of the Queen's Privy Council.
5. Procurement has been given extra attention by enshrining in law a commitment to fairness, transparency, and openness in the government procurement process, and appointing an **independent procurement auditor** to provide additional oversight of the procurement process.
6. Finally, every public servant is encouraged to be a watchdog by providing them with whistle-blower protection and incentives.

This dramatic strengthening of all forms of internal and external financial watchdogs has signalled a change in the traditional dynamic that had operated among spenders, guardians, and priority setters. Less emphasis will be placed on internal reciprocity and adjustment within government and more on external scrutiny by, and independent reporting to, Parliament and those outside government. In short, there is a smaller premium on trust within a community of shared interests and competing requirements and a larger one on public reporting, external scrutiny, and independent verification. These changes signal a significant acceleration in the gradual transformation, which had been underway for several decades, from the 'old village' with its closely knit expenditure community to the 'new town' with its independent and increasingly influential financial watchdogs.

When Canada is compared to other countries using the spenders and guardians framework, the analysis suggests that it has much to learn (Wanna et al., 2003). While this undoubtedly is the case, especially with respect to the changing role of the budget office, the broader framework employed here suggests there are some important and enduring features of the Canadian system that can adapt and are adapting to meet the new challenges in the management of public money. By Schick's standards—'a government has the capacity to budget when it can adjust claims and ration to produce desired outcomes'—Canada comes off quite well (Schick, 1990: 12). The Canadian system finds institutional structure in the central agency network of the Privy Council Office, the Department of Finance, and the Treasury Board Secretariat, the labyrinth of departments, agencies, and Crown corporations, and the influential parliamentary watchdog of the Office of the Auditor General. It is deeply embedded in a parliamentary tradition where the government of the day, in all but a rare minority government situation, has the singular capacity and legitimacy, if it can muster the political will, to act decisively in determining a comprehensive and consistent budget plan for the country and in ensuring its timely implementation. The Parliament, for its part, remains responsible for reviewing overall and departmental budget plans and for holding the government to account on behalf of citizens as voters, taxpayers, and recipients of public services. While Parliament's role in the review of spending needs to be strengthened, it has, with information provided by the independent public auditor, been able to hold governments to account. Through a history of innovation in the design and implementation of federal–provincial and territorial fiscal transfer arrangements and through a tradition of tough intergovernmental bargaining with pragmatic political compromise, the system has accommodated a highly decentralized federation.

The Canadian budgetary system is deeply embedded in the budgetary norms that condition and shape the behaviour of the central budget players—guardians, spenders, priority setters, and financial watchdogs. These players have operated with a minimum of formal budget rules and within traditional organizational structures that are sufficiently elastic that they can be readily adapted and bent to suit the required circumstances and their particular personal styles. Over time, the interaction across these four players creates a stable pattern of mutual expectations, which guide and condition their behaviour. As the influence of one player changes—becoming stronger or weaker—the behaviour of the others slowly adjusts. Through long-standing experience in dealing with the seemingly endless controversies and battles over public money, these central players have developed an innate sense of 'how things are playing (or not playing) in the town'. They have an instinctive feel for when to include and when to ignore the others; when to push ever harder and when to ease off; who to attach to on their way up and who to distance from or provide comfort to on their way down; and when to be satisfied with less for fear of getting nothing at all.

Important Terms and Concepts

accounting officer
Auditor General Act, 1976
budget base
budget increments
budget office
budget roles
budget shift point
budgetary process
direct expenditures
financial watchdogs
guardians
independent procurement auditor
line item budgeting
Office of the Auditor General (OAG)
Parliamentary Budget Officer (PBO)
performance audit
Prime Minister's Office (PMO)
priority setters
Privy Council Office (PCO)
program budgeting
spenders
tax expenditures
Treasury Board Secretariat

Study Questions

1. What are the principal roles in the budgetary process? What are their motivations and interests? What institutions perform them?
2. How do these roles interact to produce budgets?
3. Why is budgeting incremental?
4. When, how, and why are major shifts sometimes made in budgeting?
5. What are the strengths and weaknesses of the federal budgetary process?
6. What improvements should be made to the federal budgetary process?

Useful Websites

Department of Finance, Budget Information:

www.fin.gc.ca/access/budinfoe.html

Department of Finance, Fiscal and Economic Information:

www.fin.gc.ca/access/ecfisce.html

Department of Finance, Taxes and Tariffs:

www.fin.gc.ca/access/taxe.html

Office of the Auditor General of Canada:

www.oag-bvg.gc.ca/internet/English/admin_e_41.html

Privy Council Office:

www.pco-bcp.gc.ca/index.asp?lang=eng

Treasury Board of Canada Secretariat, Estimates of the Government of Canada and Other Supporting Documents:

www.tbs-sct.gc.ca/est-pre/estime.asp

Treasury Board of Canada Secretariat, Expenditure Management Sector:

www.tbs-sct.gc.ca/tbs-sct/organization-organisation/ems-sgd-eng.asp

Treasury Board of Canada Secretariat, Office of the Comptroller General:

www.tbs-sct.gc.ca/tbs-sct/organization-organisation/ems-sgd-eng.asp

Notes

1. This article draws from Good (2007).
2. Wildavsky (1964; revised 1974, 1979, 1984). Like some budgets, the early drafts of his manuscript received 'unusually negative response (nine publishers rejected it)' (Wildavsky, 1988 and 1992: xxvii). According to Wildavsky, 'readers found it too critical of government (if they were in it) or too tolerant of bad practices (if they suffered from them). . . . At first the reaction in the old BOB (Bureau of the Budget) was that none of it was true. After about two years the word was that some of it was true. By the time four years had elapsed the line was that most of it was true, but wasn't it a shame' (Wildavsky, 1974: xx–xxi). It seemed that budgeting by spenders and guardians was what it was, not what some might wish it to be.
3. For an appreciation of his writings on budgeting, see Caiden and White, 1995.
4. Good (1980) and Hartle (1988).
5. Niskanen (1971). Once elected, the Thatcher government assigned one of Niskanen's works, *Bureaucracy: Servant or Master? Lessons from America* (London: Institute of Economic Affairs, 1973), to public servants as 'required reading'. See Goodin (1982: 23–42).

6. For a history of the evolution of the Treasury Board and the creation of the Treasury Board Secretariat, see, White and Strick (1970).

7. Tax expenditures are tax measures such as exemptions, deductions, rebates, deferrals, and credits that are used to advance a wide range of economic, social, and other public policy objectives.

8. One reason for the declining relative size of 'small p' programs has been smaller defence expenditures relative to total direct expenditures. In 1964, defence was 18 per cent of total direct expenditure. In 2004 it was only 6.9 per cent.

9. From the time it was first coined by Grant Glassco in his seminal Royal Commission report on government organization in 1963, 'let the managers manage' became the continuous cry of departments and the constant challenge for the Treasury Board Secretariat. In the fall of 1994 when Finance Minister Martin announced to the Standing Committee on Finance that he would reduce the deficit 'come hell or high water', that slogan became the single target for government achievement that trumped all others.

10. For a personal account of the role of the Prime Minister's Office in budget-making, see Goldenberg (2006).

11. Since the 1990s the written campaign documentation prepared by political parties is both extensive and detailed. Notable examples include the 'Red Book' of the Liberal Party in the 1993 election, the 'Common Sense Revolution' used by the provincial Conservative Party in the 1995 Ontario provincial election, and the 'New Era Document' used by the provincial Liberal Party in the 2001 British Columbia provincial election. In the 2004 federal election, all four major parties provided extensive documents, including the identification of specific priorities and the costing of proposed expenditures. The documents, totalling close to 175 pages, carried the following titles: 'Moving Canada Ahead: The Paul Martin Plan for Getting Things Done'; 'Demanding Better: Conservative Party of Canada Platform'; 'Jack Layton, NDP: New Energy, A Positive Choice'; and 'Un Parti Propre au Québec'. In the 2006 general election campaign, Stephen Harper and the Conservative Party put forward a series of many individual announcements each day over the course of the campaign. These were subsequently rolled into a single document, 'Stand Up for Canada', in the latter stages of the campaign.

12. This has been the underlying explanation in the literature for the lack of cabinet-determined specific budget priorities over most of the last century. See Schick (2002).

13. Performance auditing is not a uniquely Canadian phenomenon as most OECD countries do performance auditing of some sort.

14. To name only a few, there was the Operational Performance Measurement System (OPMS) and Management by Objectives (MBO) in the 1970s; the Policy and Expenditure Management System (PEMS) in the early 1980s; the Increased Ministerial Authority and Accountability (IMAA) in the mid-1980s; the Expenditure Management System, Business Planning, and Program Review in the mid-1990s; Reform of the Estimates and Results for Canadians, and Performance Reporting in the early 2000s.

15. One of the earliest articles, if not the most widely cited, on the inability to determine an objective basis on which to link budget allocations to program outcomes is V.O. Key, Jr (1940: 1137–44). A more recent book on program evaluation describes and explains the extensive professional judgment that is inherent in determining causality in the area of program evaluation. See McDavid and Hawthorn (2006: 401–33).

16. The five new parliamentary watchdogs are the conflict of interest and ethics commissioner; the commissioner of lobbying; the parliamentary budget officer; the public sector integrity officer; and the director of public prosecutions. The four parliamentary watchdogs with increased legislature authority are the chief electoral officer; the privy commissioner; the information commissioner; and the public service agency. The three new internal, independent watchdogs are the public appointments commissioner within the prime minister's portfolio (not in place as of 2010); the independent procurement auditor; and the chief audit executives with each department. The role of the existing Comptroller General is strengthened and deputy ministers have been designated as 'accounting officers', accountable before Parliament for certain responsibilities.

References

Allen, Richard R., and Daniel Tommasi, eds. 2001. *Managing Public Expenditure: A Reference Book for Transitional Countries.* Paris: OECD.

Aucoin, Peter. 1998. *Auditing for Accountability: The Role of the Auditor General.* Ottawa: Institute on Governance.

———, and Donald J. Savoie, eds. 1998. *Managing Strategic Change.* Ottawa: Canadian Centre for Management Development.

Auditor General of Canada. 2001. *Report of the Auditor General of Canada: Reflections on a Decade of Serving Parliament.* Ottawa: Public Works and Government Services Canada.

———. 2002. 'A Model for Rating Departmental Performance Reports', in *Report of the Auditor General of Canada.* Ottawa: Public Works and Government Services Canada, chap. 6.

———. 2004. Opening Statement, November 2003 Report, Press Conference, Ottawa, Ont. 10 February 2004.

———. 2005. *Report of the Auditor General of Canada: Rating Selected Departmental Performance Reports.* Ottawa: Public Works and Government Services Canada. chap. 5.

Caiden, Naomi, and Joseph White, eds. 1995. *Budgeting, Policy, Politics: An Appreciation of Aaron Wildavsky.* New Brunswick, NJ: Transaction.

———, and Aaron Wildavsky. 1974. *Planning and Budgeting in Poor Countries.* New York: Wiley and Sons.

Campbell S.J., Colin and George J. Szablowski. 1979. *The Superbureaucrats: Structure and Behaviour in Central Agencies.* Toronto: Macmillan.

Canada, Department of Finance. 2004. *Budget Speech*, 23 March 2004, Ottawa: Public Works and Government Services Canada.

Clark, Ian D. 1985. 'Recent Changes in the Cabinet Decision-Making System in Ottawa', *Canadian Public Administration* 28, 2: 85–201.

———. 1994. 'Restraint, Renewal and the Treasury Board Secretariat', *Canadian Public Administration* 37, 2 (Summer): 209–48.

Dewar, David I., and David A. Good. 2004. 'Great Books Revisited: Wildavsky on "Rescuing Budgeting from American Administration" and Heclo and Wildavsky on "Village Life in British Budgeting"', *Canadian Public Administration* 47, 1 (Spring): 81–96.

Doern, G. Bruce. 1971. 'The Development of Policy Organizations in the Executive Arena', in G. Bruce Doern and Peter Aucoin, eds, *The Structures of Policy-Making in Canada.* Toronto: Macmillan.

———, Allan M. Maslove, and Michael J. Prince. 1988. *Public Budgeting in Canada: Politics, Economics and Management.* Ottawa: Carleton University Press.

French, Richard D. 1980. *How Ottawa Decides.* Toronto: James Lorimer.

———. 1984. *How Ottawa Decides: Planning and Industrial Policy Making 1968–84*, 2nd edn. Toronto: James Lorimer.

Goldenberg, Eddie. 2006. *The Way It Works: Inside Ottawa.* Toronto: McClelland and Stewart.

Good, David A. 1980. *The Politics of Anticipation: Making Canadian Federal Tax Policy.* Ottawa: School of Public Administration, Carleton University.

———. 2007. *The Politics of Public Money: Spenders, Guardians, Priority Setters, and Financial Watchdogs inside the Canadian Government.* Toronto: University of Toronto Press.

———, Evert Lindquist, Jim McDavid, Angus Carnie, Irene Huse, Jessica Ling, John Montgomery, Erin Scraba, and Justin Young. 2006. *A Comparative Study of the Use of Performance Information for Decision-Making in Selected OECD Countries.* Victoria, BC: School of Public Administration, University of Victoria.

Goodin, Robert E. 1982. 'Rational Politicians and Rational Bureaucrats in Washington and Whitehall', *Public Administration* 60, 1 (Spring): 23–42.

Government of Canada. 2005. 'Table 1: Budgetary Main Estimates by Type of Payment', in Government of Canada, 2004–2005 *Estimates, Part 1: The Government Expenditure Plan.* Ottawa: Minister of Public Works and Government Services Canada.

———. (undated). *Population Affiliation Report.* Available at: www.hrma-agrh.gc.ca/hr-rh/hrtr-or/hr_tools/Intro_e.asp.

Hartle, Douglas G. 1988. *The Expenditure Budget Process of the Government of Canada: A Public Choice—Rent-Seeking Perspective.* Toronto: Canadian Tax Foundation.

Heclo, Hugh, and Aaron Wildavsky. 1974. *The Private Government of Public Money: Community and Policy Inside British Politics.* Berkeley: University of California Press.

Imbeau, Louis M. 2000. 'Guardians and Advocates in Deficit Elimination: Government Intervention in the Budgetary Process in Three Canadian Provinces', in Jurgen Kleist and Shawn Huffman, eds, *Canada Observed: Perspectives from Abroad and from Within.* New York: Peter Lang, 45–56.

Johnson, A.W. 1971. 'The Treasury Board of Canada and the Machinery of Government in the 1970s', *Canadian Journal of Political Science* 4, 3: 240–59.

———. 1973. 'Planning, Programming and Budgeting in Canada', *Canadian Public Administration* 33, 24: 23–31.

Kelly, Joanne, and John Wanna. 2000. 'Are Wildavsky's Guardians and Spenders still Relevant? New Public Management and the Politics of Government Budgeting', in Lawrence Jones, James Guthrie, and Peter Steane, eds, *Learning from International Public Management Reform.* London: Elsevier and Oxford University Press, 598–614.

Key, Jr, V.O. 1940. 'The Lack of a Budgetary Theory', *American Political Science Review.* December: 1137–44.

Lindquist, Evert A. 2001. 'How Ottawa Plans: The Evolution of Strategic Planning', in Leslie A. Pal, ed., *How Ottawa Spends, 2001–2002: Power in Transition.* Don Mills, Ont.: Oxford University Press, 61–93.

McDavid, James C., and Laura R.L. Hawthorn. 2006. *Program Evaluation and Performance Measurement: An Introduction to Practice.* Thousand Oaks, Calif.: Sage, chap. 12, 'The Nature and Practice of Professional Judgment in Program Evaluation', 401–33.

Maslove, Allan M., Michael Prince, and G. Bruce Doern. 1986. *Federal and Provincial Budgeting.* Toronto: University of Toronto Press.

Niskanen, William A. 1971. *Bureaucracy and Representative Government.* Chicago: Aldine Atherton.

———. 1973. *Bureaucracy: Servant or Master? Lessons from America.* London: Institute of Economic Affairs.

———. 1991. 'A Reflection on Bureaucracy and Representative Government', in Andre Blais and Stephane Dion, eds, *The Budget Maximizing Bureaucrat: An Appraisal and Evidence.* Pittsburgh: University of Pittsburgh Press, 16–17.

OECD (Organisation for Economic Co-Operation and Development). 2006. '24th Annual Meeting of OECD Session Budget Officials: Annotation Agenda', retrieved 14 December 2006 from: http://oecd.org/dataoecd/61/21/2633689.doc.

Prime Minister of Canada. 2004. Statement by the Prime Minister at a Press Conference on the Auditor's General Report, Ottawa, Ont., 12 February.

Prince, Michael J. 2002. 'Budgetary Trilogies: The Phases of Budget Reform in Canada', in Christopher Dunn, ed., *The Handbook of Canadian Public Administration,* 1st edn. Don Mills, Ont.: Oxford University Press.

Savoie, Donald J. 1990. *The Politics of Public Spending in Canada.* Toronto: University of Toronto Press.

———. 1999. *Governing from the Centre: The Concentration of Power in Canadian Politics.* Toronto: University of Toronto Press.

———. 2003. *Breaking the Bargain: Public Servants, Ministers, and Parliament.* Toronto: University of Toronto Press.

Schick, Allen. 1990. *The Capacity to Budget.* Washington, DC: Urban Institute Press.

———. 1997. *The Changing Role of the Central Budget Office.* Paris: OECD.

———. 2002. 'Does Budgeting Have a Future?' *OECD Journal of Budgeting* 2, 2: 7–47.

Simpson, Jeffrey. 2006. 'Why Mr Red has the Blues', *Globe and Mail,* 21 January 2006, F1, F4–F5.

Sinclair, Sonja. 1979. *Cordial but Not Cosy: A History of the Office of the Auditor General.* Toronto: McClelland and Stewart.

Sutherland, Sharon L. 2002. 'The Office of the Auditor General of Canada: Government in Exile?' School of Public Policy Studies Working Papers Series, no. 31. Kingston: Queen's University, School of Policy Studies.

Van Loon, Richard. 1981. 'Stop the Music: The Current Policy and Expenditure Management System', *Canadian Public Administration* 24, 2: 175–99.

———. 1983a. 'The Policy and Expenditure Management System in the Canadian Federal Government: The First Three Years', *Canadian Public Administration* 26, 2: 255–85.

———. 1983b. 'Ottawa's New Expenditure Process: Four Systems in Search of Co-Ordination', in G.B. Doern, ed., *How Ottawa Spends: The Liberals, the Opposition and Federal Priorities.* Toronto: James Lorimer, 93–120.

Wanna, John, Lotte Jensen Wanna, and Jouke de Vries, eds. 2003. *Controlling Public Expenditure: The Changing Role of Central Budget Agencies—Better Guardians?* Cheltenham, UK: Edward Elgar.

Ward, Norman. 1962. *The Public Purse: A Study of Canadian Democracy.* Toronto: University of Toronto Press.

White, W.L., and J.C. Strick. 1970. *Policy, Politics, and the Treasury Board in Canadian Government.* Don Mills, Ont.: Science Research Associates, Ltd.

Wildavsky, Aaron. 1964 (rev. 1974, 1979, and 1984). *The Politics of the Budgetary Process.* Boston: Little, Brown.

———. 1975. *Budgeting: A Comparative Theory of Budgetary Processes.* Boston: Little, Brown.

———. 1988 and 1992. *The New Politics of the Budgetary Process.* Boston: Scott, Foresman; New York: Harper Collins.

27 Budgets, Budgeting, and Control in the Public Sector Context

Andrew Graham

This chapter reviews the basis and main characteristics of public sector financial management. It then addresses the key questions associated with how to resource public policy: how to get the funds, how to control their use for their intended purpose, and how to account for their use. The execution of good public policy hinges on adequate resources. However, getting the funds through the budgetary process is only the beginning. Once the funds are allocated, they must be managed to ensure their maximum impact within both the policy intent and the regulatory framework of the government. Finally, the results are subject to various levels and means of review, both in terms of the program intention and of compliance with the government's financial standards of practice, reporting requirements, use of funds, and external review or audit. Financial management therefore is central to achieving the policy goal. How funds are managed is also a central preoccupation in terms of accountability and integrity as well as the continuity of the policy and its program.[1]

What Is a Budget?

A budget is a plan that puts resources in place to implement the goals of the organization. In the public sector, it is the link to policy, legislation, and organization intent. For much of the public sector, a budget is a monetized plan that establishes spending limits for programs. Finally, a budget is time limited, usually for one year, but in multi-year budget forecasting and accrual budgeting, time frames may vary.

A budget looks to the future. It projects both revenues and expenditures for a given time period. This period can vary depending on the nature of the organization. Similarly, the more complex the revenue and expenditure situation of the organization, the more likely it will be that mid-course adjustments are needed during the lifespan of the budget. In government, these adjustments translate into **supplementary budgets** or **estimates** that regularly go before legislatures. In smaller organizations, a **rolling budget** can accommodate mid-course adjustments. In this form of budget, expenditures are directly linked to revenues and other available funds. The organization thus can make continual adjustments to its programs depending on its revenues.

A budget is the basis for financial control and accountability within the public sector organization. Because it not only establishes spending limits, but also as a planning and policy statement states expectations about results of the expenditures, it begins the control cycle for the responsibility centre manager (managers who are responsible for controlling a specific operation). As such, it is a useful benchmark to control the operations of departments, agencies, hospitals, or schools.

Cyclical Nature of the Managerial Budget: Present, Future, and Past

There are three budgets in play at all times for public sector managers: present, future, and past.

The manager's immediate concern is the management of funds within the current fiscal year—the present. This is the realm of control of funds, cash management, and program management. However, the manager also must continuously participate in the long-range policy and expenditure planning process to secure funds for coming years—the future. Finally, the manager must account for historical use of funds—the past. Accounting for the past is both technical (financial accounting, reconciliation, and the closing of the books) and political, in that expenditures must be linked to the desired policy results. Some of the questions that the law requires be answered are:

- Were funds properly spent?
- Were there over-expenditures?
- Were there unused funds left at the end of the year?
- Do all transactions reconcile so that year-end financial statements can be signed off?
- Did the funds accomplish the goals set out?
- Were the estimates correct?
- Were the funds spent according to plan?

Past budgets are critically important in the public sector, because so much of the budgeting process is *incremental*. Many organizations make most of their budget decisions based on past performance and allotments. How much funding was actually used is important. Similarly, unless there is a major policy shift, or programs are changed or large budget cuts are made, public sector budgets generally tend to rise by small amounts each year based on past use and general increases permitted by the central finance authorities.

Understanding the three budget phases is also important because of the need to account to legislative authorities, be it a public accounts committee of a legislature or a city council. Increasingly, public organizations provide annual performance reports of some form. These contain financial performance information of great interest to the stakeholders and granting authorities. Performance information is usually presented comparatively: performance against budget, one year against another, and projections against past and present performance.

We see that budget activity for financial managers takes various forms and spans different times. The great challenge for public officials and their stakeholders is to understand all elements of the budgetary process in order to derive the maximum benefit from it.

Budgeting in the Policy and Administrative Context

No examination of public sector budgets would be complete without contributions from Aron Wildavsky, who first opened up discussions of budgets and budgeting to an analysis that combines cultural studies, political science, economics, and street smarts. Wildavsky's definition of budgeting contains as clear an understanding of the logic of budgeting as found anywhere:

> In the most general definition... budgeting is concerned with the translation of financial resources into human purposes. (Wildavsky, 1964: 1–2)

Thus, Wildavsky's understanding is like that of the commentary in Box 27.1 and other contemporary texts. His 'financial resources' are translated into his 'human purposes' by means of his 'plan of work'.

Understanding budgets and budgetary process of the public sector is important to being an effective financial manager. Similarly, understanding the tenets of managing resources once they are allocated, and monitoring, controlling, and accounting for that use is part of the total package.

However, budgeting is entirely within the tableau of the resource allocation processes that the government, department, or agency uses, for it is through these processes that the public sector

Box 27.1 The Budget as an Instrument of Public Policy and Management

Planning Instrument: Sets goals, priorities, and strategies and coordinates the government/agency resources into an expenditure plan identifying what program or activities will take place and at what levels

Political Instrument: Competing interests attempt to influence a government or agency to form policy favourable to them

Social Instrument: Provides a vehicle to grant and deny privileges and disburse burdens and benefits to individuals and businesses.

Economic Instrument: Offers powerful potential for affecting the growth and productive capacity of the community and its citizens.

Legal Instrument: Grants authoritatively the rights, responsibilities, power, and guidelines that regulate the budget format, timing, and process.

Source: McKinney and Howard (1979)

organization accomplishes a number of important objectives:

1. A budget translates *policy intention* into specific activities through allocating resources to support the policy's goal. This defines just how much is actually to be done, how many clients are to be serviced, and what will be the form of entitlements.[2]
2. A budget is a key outcome of the organization's planning processes, again *translating goals and objectives into action.* Often, through these planning processes a manager can affect the outcome of resource allocations for his or her program.
3. A budget sets *limits of expenditure* to guide managers within the organization. In government, it is dangerous (and often illegal) to surpass those limits.
4. A budget is an *economic document* that allocates resources. Government can and does use budgets to announce policy initiatives and set tax rates.
5. Similarly, through the budgetary process, voluntary sector organizations can *define fundraising targets* or *set fees for services.*
6. Budgetary decisions set the stage for *internal financial controls* and *effective cash management.*

One fault in some budgetary systems is their timing: managers may start their fiscal year not knowing exactly what resources they have. More will be said of this later.

The Functions of a Budget

The proper functioning of the **budget** relates to the four functions it performs:

1. *Authorization function.* All money spent from the public treasury is subject to legislative authorization or the governing body of the organization.
2. *Allocative/distributive function.* The budgetary authorities (executive and legislative branches) compare and trade off all changes in expenditures and revenues both within the entity and to recipients of services, entitlements, grants, or funding.
3. *Macroeconomic function.* The budgetary authorities (executive and legislative branches) decide on the impact upon the economy of totals and composition of expenditure, revenues, and the deficit.
4. *Administrative function.* Budgetary authorities (executive and legislative branches) distribute and control resources within the organization according to the structure and assignment of

responsibilities and use that distribution to assess the cost effectiveness and efficiency of service delivery.

Types of Budgets

Budgets are structured to meet the needs of the organization for which they are created. In the public sector, these needs are varied and complex. However, there are only so many forms that a budget can take and still be seen as a budget rather than a policy or planning document. Therefore, a smaller, less complex public organization might well be served with a straightforward cash budget showing only revenues and expenditures and managed on a flexible budget basis. Larger, multi-departmental governments will require a master or expenditure budget with both operating and capital budgets linked to both policy frameworks and organizational planning documents to support the budgetary process.

Often, a complex budget will be an amalgam of different types of budgets. As already noted, budgets in the public sector serve a number of different purposes: policy, planning, resource allocation, and communication. They also operate at different **levels of expenditure** within the entity: strategic, departmental, and unit. To meet the various needs of the public, stakeholders, decision-makers, budget managers, and staff, budgets can be configured differently. But the possible forms are few and the principles that govern them are straightforward. These forms are not mutually exclusive. The examples that follow demonstrate how they can be created in layers that meet multiple needs.

Relationship of Revenue Budget to the Expenditure or Operating Budget

This chapter focuses on the management of the expenditure side of the budget. In the public sector, as in the private sector, there is a very close relationship between revenue and expenditure. For governments, however, this relationship is often detached from the day-to-day activities of responsibility centre managers. While governments seek to balance revenues and expenditures, they are not fully obliged to do so. They can borrow, using their immense credit capacity to raise funds. Similarly, they can raise funds by increasing taxes and fees that are charged for services. In any public sector environment, this is of course limited by how much debt is tolerable or the politically acceptable level of taxation.

In general, governments manage their revenue strategies at a corporate level and then distribute the results of their policies to departments or units through the budgetary and appropriations process. There are, of course, exceptions. For instance, governments can create **revolving funds** within departments or for unique agencies. These are funds that are theoretically self-financing and are generally permitted to retain all or part of their revenue.

However, the revenue budget is often the result of government policy that is quite separate from most lower-level expenditure planning processes, which tend to be driven by demand. While the revenue capacity of governments certainly dictates the level of funds available for expenditures, this process is on a different track than the expenditure planning and management process. In a large complex government, revenue is managed centrally by the Department of Finance while expenditure is managed in a more decentralized fashion, with overall central control by the Treasury Board or Management Board.

The government's revenue budget serves a number of purposes:

- interpreting and projecting current economic behaviour and patterns in the country as a whole to estimate revenue;
- adjusting basic taxes and credits for both revenue and expenditure, and also to redistribute wealth among income groups;
- adjusting other taxes and credits to implement policy changes (e.g., the federal government's child tax credit); this is known as a tax expenditure;
- making changes in fiscal policies (e.g., acceptable borrowing levels).

Budgets by General Purpose

An organization's general or master budget has two main components: the operating budget and the capital budget.

Operating Budgets

The operating budget contains the plan for revenues and expenditures for the period, usually referred to as a fiscal year. In governmental terms, the expenditure plan represents the authorized limit of expenditures for the operating unit or responsibility centre. In general, government expenditures are not as closely connected with revenues, since government revenues are usually put into a consolidated revenue fund and then distributed among the departments or units.

The operating budget is also called the recurrent budget. Most operating budgets provide funds for staff salaries, benefits, supplies, and other operating expenses, as well as regular grants and disbursements. These expenses carry on from year to year with some adjustments for funds available and policy and program changes. The term 'recurrent budget' also reflects the generally incremental nature of operating budgets.

Cash Budgets

'Cash budget' and 'operating budget' are often used interchangeably, depending on the form and amount of program information contained in the operating budget. It is best to think of a cash budget as a stripped-down version of the operating budget. It contains only planned cash receipts, and disbursements or expenditures. It may break the information down according to line items, which refer to the uses of the money (e.g., staff costs), but goes little further in providing information about the use of the funds in terms of programs or geographic distribution.

Some elements of a cash budget that distinguish it from operating and capital budgets are:

- Cash budgets disregard the principles of accrual accounting, often necessitating the conversion of an accrual-based budget to a cash format by removing depreciation charges.
- Instead of matching expenses with revenues in the periods in which they are incurred, they match cash inflows and outflows in the periods in which they are incurred.
- All cash items regardless of their classification (e.g., expense, asset, fixed cost, variable cost) are accounted for in a cash budget.
- Non-cash items (e.g., amortization) never appear.

Capital Budgets

Capital budgets contain the plans and resource allocations for capital acquisitions to support the organization's program. Capital acquisitions cover a variety of goods. These are treated differently than operating funds because they require more complex, often multi-year, accounting. They often involve complex planning processes with considerable financial risk and cash outlay. Capital acquisitions are often governed by laws and regulations.

Capital budgets involve multi-year expenditure projections with approval for current year expenditures. Increasingly, governments are providing multi-year approvals to ease implementation.

Unlike operating budgets, capital budgets focus on non-recurring or permanent goods. For example, an organization finances the construction of a new building on a one-time basis; this plan would not be automatically carried forward to the next capital budget.

Forms of Non-Budgetary or Off-Budget Expenditures

There are a variety of ways that governments can deliver their services and goods. Not all appear on the budget. Here we explore common non-budgetary measures: valid public instruments that may not appear on budget statements. The role these measures play in the overall budgetary picture varies from one government to another.

A tax expenditure is a transfer of public resources to individuals, groups, or corporations through the reduction of tax obligations, rather than by a direct expenditure. Tax expenditures may be:

- *Exemptions*: amounts excluded from the tax base;
- *Allowances*: amounts deducted from the tax base;
- *Credits*: amounts deducted from tax liability;
- *Rate relief*: a reduced rate of tax applied to a class of taxpayers or taxable transactions;
- *Tax deferral*: a relief that takes the form of a delay in paying tax.

Governments increasingly report tax expenditures to the public, as they are using them more frequently as policy instruments. They have the attraction of being easier to administer than individual entitlement programs.

An **entitlement program** is a financial obligation on the government created by legislation. For example, legislated social assistance programs often set levels of assistance to which any and all eligible individuals are entitled. While budgets may estimate the costs of such programs, there is no budget limit; all entitlements must be paid.

Direct loans and loan guarantees are forms of non-budgetary expenditures that may or may not appear on the budget. Certainly, with the movement towards accrual budgeting and accounting, both of these forms of expenditures are increasingly reported as contingent liabilities.

The Budgetary Process

Most governments, departments, and units have formalized processes to create their budgets. Within operational units, arriving at the final distribution of the operating budget will entail some measure of forecasting, analyzing options, long-term planning, and finally assigning resource levels. This is the budget cycle.

Elements of an Effective Budget Cycle

Budget cycles, planning systems, and procedures form key elements of public sector management. You can call them anything (e.g., strategic planning system, planning, budgeting systems), you can flow chart them, PowerPoint them, and build in all the bells and whistles that the organization needs, wants, and likes. However, some basic requirements have to be met, regardless of the size and complexity of the organization:

- a basic framework with common language, meaning, and reference points for all the players in the process to use;
- a sense of the desired outcomes from the political leadership, be it cabinet or council;
- a link to the strategic plans of the organization, especially for increases or reductions in program levels, investments in new programs, and the multi-year implications of the plan;
- a format used by all units of the organization that will ultimately roll into the organization's spending plan for the defined period (usually a year);
- an agreed-upon timetable for preparation and consideration of budgets;
- instructions that set out the objectives of the current process, any pre-determined budgetary or program limits, and instructions on matters that are handled at the corporate level of the organization rather than at the unit level (e.g., salaries and benefits based on organization-wide collective agreements);
- methodologies for costing and forecasting current program levels, the implications of changes in service demands or standards, and the cost of new initiatives;
- directions on reallocating current funding, absorbing known cost increases, or accessing additional funds.

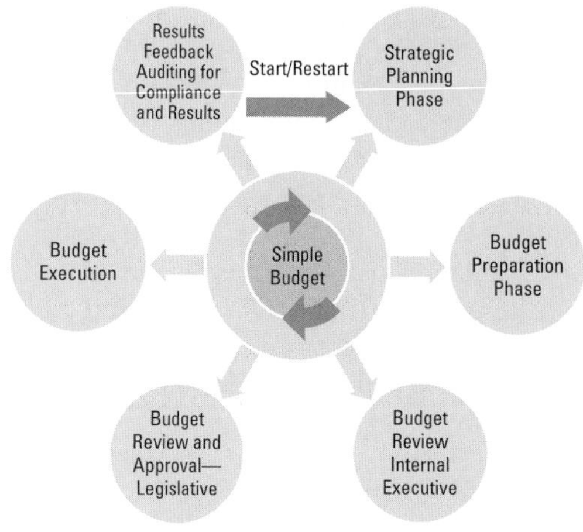

Figure 27.1 A Simple Budget Cycle

Most likely, these requirements would completely be met only in an ideal world. Real-life processes are less clear and often less logical than described above. However, in outlining an effective budgetary process for a public sector organization, it is necessary to establish standard expectations against which the process might be judged. Also, a manager should be looking for these features of the budgetary process, and in their absence attempt to make them happen.

The Simple Budget Cycle shown in Figure 27.1 is a good starting point for understanding the budgetary process. A diagram such as this can be deceiving, as a real-life budget process will not follow the steps of this cycle so clearly. Steps overlap and may not be clearly defined. While one budget is being implemented, the next one is being planned. While one approval phase ends, the review of results of the previous year may begin. The process is non-linear and multi-dimensional.

Strategic Planning Phase

All organizations plan for the future. Making choices about programs and priorities sets a direction, communicates values, distributes resources, and arouses expectations. Some organizations have complex and well-documented planning processes. These can involve many levels of the organization, often working together in the preparation of documents and the provision of information. For others, planning and budgeting is much simpler, as the lines of control and command are shorter and the decision-making is more immediate.

The Expenditure Management System of the Canadian Federal Government as shown in Figure 27.2 is a good example of a complex budget planning system. It is designed to ensure that the final budget of the Minister of Finance, usually announced in April of each year, is the result of a rigorous planning process. Given the breadth of the federal government, this process is necessarily a complex one.

This process takes into account the relationship of the political leadership—cabinet and the Prime Minister, through the Privy Council Office and the Department of Finance, with the bureaucratic leadership through the Treasury Board, which provides the advice and support needed for decision-making. This is both a strategic planning and a budgetary process.

Strategic planning usually takes place outside the context of direct budget planning alone, drawing in the many tools of planning beyond simply resource allocation and distribution. At least, this is the theory: strategic planning is driven by values and outcomes, and the mechanics of financing the vision are left to the next iterative phase of planning. However, the reality is somewhat different. Of course, some aspects of strategic planning should be long-term and visionary. However, organizations cannot plan in a vacuum. So, financial information about the past and present naturally feed the thinking about the future. Similarly, anticipated revenue flows will influence multi-year strategies. Otherwise, the political leadership would be accused of creating false expectations. Thus, the strategic planning process takes into account financial realities.

Some characteristics of strategic planning differ from annual budget preparation. For instance, very few strategic plans are for one year only. For the most part, they go beyond the budgeting horizon of most governments. However, governments today are increasingly

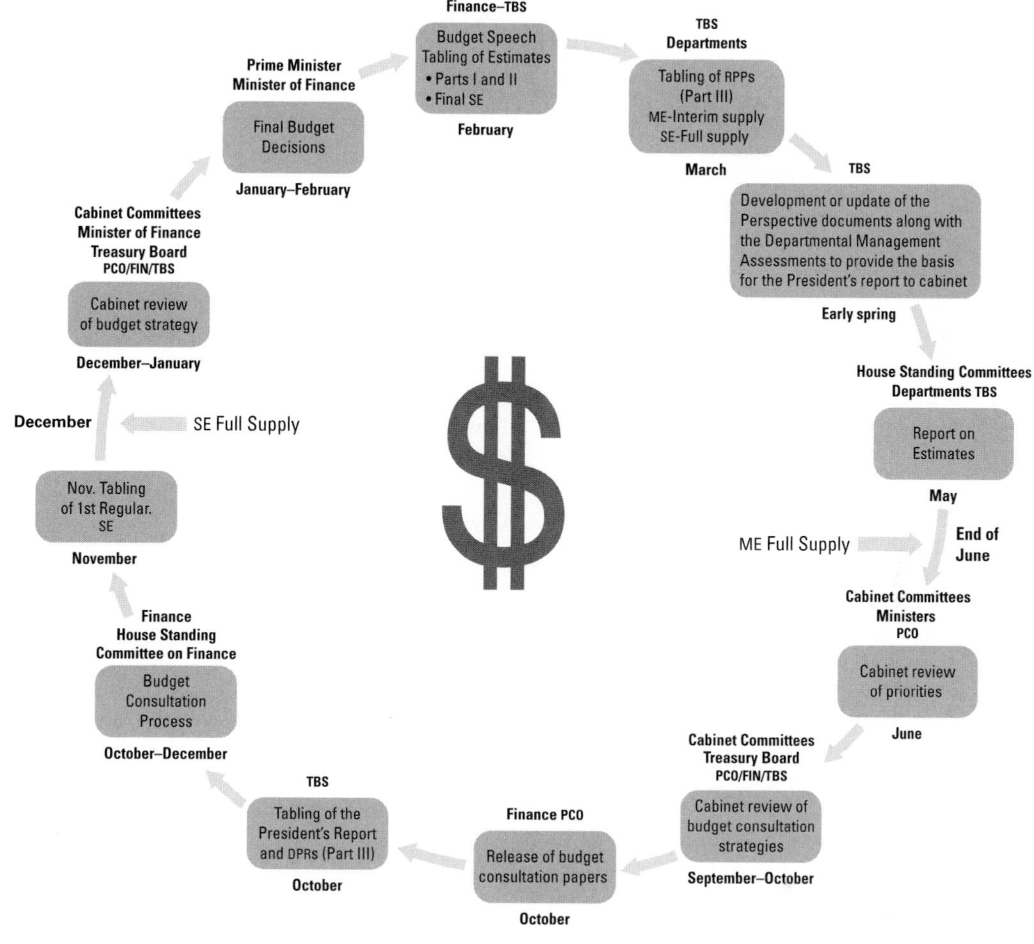

Figure 27.2 The Budget Cycle of the Federal Government of Canada (Expenditure Management System)

projecting their budget costs well into the future to inform public review and decision-making. Similarly, the introduction of accrual budgeting will encourage a multi-year and intergenerational understanding of budget decisions. While this trend provides more information in the budget process, it is still the case that legislatures usually only approve a budget for a single year (although some governments are moving towards the approval of multi-year budgets or the creation of self-managing funds that exist over several years).

Strategic planning is generally program oriented. It involves creating strategic tools that permit the organization ideally to guide decision-making and set priorities for the organization as a whole. It is also important in establishing desired end-states (e.g., a certain level of environmental emissions to reduce pollution) as a means of measuring the outputs desired for the organization.

In sum, most strategic planning is mission- or goal-driven, using long-term and broadly based objectives.

Budget Preparation Phase

Budget preparation is, in most cases, the melding of two processes. The strategic plan provides a set of program objectives, overall goals, and proposals for change. This process involves direction from the central office of the organization on budget limits. These are budget guidelines that a government issues to all responsibility centres to guide the preparation of their budget plans. Many governments formally adopt budget planning guidelines as a cabinet decision to ensure solidarity among departments, which must compete for scarce resources. Such guidelines normally contain direction on the technical aspects of budget calculations, may set spending limits in some or all areas, and give instructions on increasing or decreasing budget items depending on program plans and expectations. The extent of these guidelines varies greatly from one government to another. It also varies according to how authority is delegated and the extent to which senior management wish to provide direction. For instance, where collective bargaining is centrally managed, managers will simply be informed of salary increases based on calculations of their staff complements. In some instances, managers may be instructed to absorb additional costs or negotiate salaries themselves.

Once the budget preparation phase is reached, there is usually very little room for flexibility. With some variation according to the size and style of the organization, a rigorous strategic planning exercise will certainly reduce the scope for budget negotiations. So too will pressures to reduce spending or limit staff size. This first phase is described as 'top-down'; it is usually part of the organization's planning cycle, with a central office overseeing it to ensure that it reflects the direction that the organization's top management wishes to take.

The second element of the budget preparation is the influence of the managers who prepare the budget. As noted, in large organizations that emphasize direction from the top, there is likely little flexibility in negotiating significant budget changes at this phase. However, some variables and flexibility are still in the hands of a manager; for example, the calculation or estimation of workloads and costs. A manager may also be able to propose program changes and improvements, or make a case for increased program funding. In these ways, a manager may be able to exert 'bottom-up' influence on the budget. However, timing is important, and managers must understand how to influence these processes. If they wait too long, boundaries will have been set and the organization will have little appetite for new funding ideas, especially in the near term.

The Appropriation Process: Getting Approval to Spend

It is clear that a budget is a plan. As the process becomes more institutionalized, such as in the Expenditure Management System of the Government of Canada, it engages more players and eventually becomes the formal budget submitted to the authorizing body; for a government, this is the city council, Legislative Assembly, or Parliament. In many cases, the formal budget will also be scrutinized and possibly subject to some form of approval by a senior level of government. Not-for-profit public organizations, such as hospitals, that receive funding from a government usually require some form of provincial government approval of their budgets.

The purpose of submitting the budget to the legislative body is to obtain specific approval to spend money. Such authorization is called an **appropriation**—the approval by a legislative body of an organization's budget, and permission to spend the amounts in the budget. A procedure such as 'voting supply' or 'approval of the estimates' creates the important legal authority for individual managers to spend public funds.

The role of a legislature, however, is not restricted to voting for or against a particular budget plan. There are a number of other functions that it plays that affect the outcome of a particular budget planning cycle, including:

- engaging in budget consultation processes, including setting up public hearings on budget priorities for the government;

- detailed scrutinizing, at committee level, of individual departmental spending plans, including hearing from the Minister and officials as well as interest groups;
- detailed and open decision-making, most notably at the municipal level, of budget plans presented by departments in advance of their approval;
- proposing changes to appropriations for individual departments and submitting these to a committee vote and subsequently to a vote in the legislature (more likely in minority government situations);
- hearing from the legislative auditor, most notably the Auditor General of the jurisdiction, on his or her views of the financial management of the government, which will have an impact on future budget behaviour;
- holding hearings and investigations into specific aspects of the budget that may cross departmental lines, but that are directly relevant to taxpayers (e.g., the impact of various user fees charges by different departments on economic development and small business); thus bringing public attention to such issues and often affecting future government behaviour;
- reviewing past financial and program performance using departmentally-generated performance reports.

Legislatures, then, can participate in the budget cycle. The degree of that participation varies across Canada, but it is clearly increasing as the budgetary process has become increasingly more open over the past 20 years.

Fundamental Tensions in the Budgetary Process

The budgetary process is inherently value-laden and rich in conflict. As we describe planning processes, the need to plan and translate policy into resources, and the various roles of the executive branch and the legislative or oversight branch (e.g., legislature, council, board of directors), it would be naïve not to realize how many tensions play themselves out in the budgeting process. These tensions also have a significant impact on the substantive outcomes of the process itself.

Balancing Revenues and Expenditures

For all public sector organizations, the primary tension in budgeting is between aspiration and capacity. Expenditures should ideally equal revenue. A public sector organization has to make that equation work. Often it does so with a mix of revenue and expenditure adjustments, including changes to taxes and fees to increase revenue, and changes to program levels to reduce expenditures, as well as incurring debt to cover the difference. Extending program expenditure by increasing debt often leaves the country or province with large debt burdens. Similarly, adding fees, secondary taxes, user charges and other sources of revenue (all forms of taxation, voluntary or otherwise) can expand capacity. An example of this is the relatively recent development of many North American governments increasing their dependency on publicly licensed casino revenues (*The Wager*, 2000).

On the other hand, tremendous pressure exists to restrain the growth in taxation in any form and in the size of government as a whole. Some of it is ideological, based on a strong belief that government is too large and does too much, and that the private sector should be used to move so-called public goods into the market. This has manifested itself in much provincial legislation to cap tax increases and government spending.

Complexity versus Clarity

Budgets are made up from a stream of decisions, some that involve spending and some that involve limiting spending. However, seldom is this stream of decisions totally clear. A variety of political, social, and economic factors influence them. For many governments, in order to achieve the objective of public involvement and transparency, the budget process can be long, and involve many different forums, to arrive at a final product. Budget making is complex. Understanding the process itself takes some skill. Managing effectively within it takes another set of skills.

Such complexity can drive out clarity of purpose, unless there is a strong, singular force at play. In budget cutting, it is often the force of a simple objective desired by the leadership that runs up against the complexity of a planning and budgeting process that, left to its own internal dynamic, would have produced quite a different result. In other words, regardless of the process design, it is often necessary to cut through all this if there is an urgent need to make changes, especially to reduce a budget.

The tension in the process becomes the problem of marrying clarity to a necessarily complex process. This often means limiting spending options well in advance of the beginning of the process. It can also mean resorting to across-the-board solutions that have the satisfaction of achieving one result at the cost of vastly distorting program priorities along the way. Regardless, a budgetary process that runs on its own dynamic without direction and leadership will land in a very uncomfortable place. It forces leaders to make decisions contrary to the demands presented to them, which takes strong political will and the potential loss of many allies along the way. It can also take strong bureaucratic will to make such decisions within the organization. Coalitions also have to be made, rebuilt, and occasionally, abandoned to achieve internal budgetary ends.

Managing the Budget: Financial Management, Monitoring, and Control

While the budgetary process, with its power to allocate and reallocate funding, gets much public attention, the process of actually delivering public goods and services starts (or restarts) once the budget is allocated. The purpose of the budget is to efficiently and effectively achieve the objectives of the programs and projects it addresses, while ensuring the proper use of public funds. In any enterprise, this requires a series of controls. The most visible controls are audits and external review; these are but two elements of a full control framework.

Control begins and ends within the management environment. An effective control framework delivers more than accountability for the results of the budget. It provides valuable information to managers about their operations. Similarly, it allows senior managers to evaluate the performance of the managers who report to them. The control framework also informs stakeholders about the organization's performance. Stakeholders might be the client group, interest groups, or even other governments. At a very high level, a stakeholder could be a bond rating agency assessing the credit worthiness of an entire government. Certainly, it provides those governing the organizations—both the executive and the legislature—with the information to assess how the organization is doing financially. Finally, it provides internal and external auditors with information on conformity to the organization's financial practice laws or policies as well as on the use of funds voted.

For both governing and oversight bodies, effective controls mean that rules about financial behaviour and avoidance of misuse of funds, and a common platform for understanding financial statements are in place and are being applied. At one extreme, it means being able to see that no one is absconding with the money. At the other extreme, it means evaluating whether the program is meeting its objectives in a proper manner and with due regard for efficiency.

The Meaning of Control

First, we will define exactly what is meant by 'control'. Then, we will examine the broad range of various forms of control in government, and the challenge of developing the appropriate mix of controls for the organization. Next, we will look at the inherent risks in how controls are set within organizations. Risk is a large topic in itself, and in government, one that receives a great deal of attention. The essential balance in all

Box 27.2 Public Sector Control and What You Never Want to Hear About Your Program

- It ignored your legislative authority
- It overspent its budget and you did not know about it
- It broke your financial rules
- It broke your own contracting rules
- You broke the rules in selecting contractors
- Steps were taken to hide it from public and ordinary scrutiny
- Money disappeared
- It did not do what it was supposed to
- It did other, really bad things instead

organizations is between the agreed-upon risks and the degree of control needed at the program as well as the policy level. Arriving at such determinations is often contentious.

Of particular concern is how to establish sufficient control over funds being spent through third-party arrangements within public organizations. As the voluntary sector increasingly becomes a deliverer of services using public funds, contractual relationships between government and not-for-profit organizations have grown. However, the accountability for the funds remains with the granting agency within government. How this is exercised successfully is an emerging issue for the public sector and often a taxing one for both parties.

An underlying theme of the issue of control is the tension between the level of control exercised over a manager and the degree of freedom or discretion that he or she has in his or her work. This involves a variety of dimensions of management: decision scope, the capacity to reallocate funds, and the ability to respond to emerging situations. On the other hand, the other side involves the amount of delegated authority, reporting requirements, actual discretion and what is seen as the time and money burden of control. The challenge is how to maintain accountability while ensuring that service is being given.

The term 'control' is used in a wide variety of situations to describe many different phenomena (see Box 27.2). Consequently, different disciplines use the term differently. A useful way to describe what is meant by management control in the context of financial management is:

> *Management control systems consist of all organizational structures, processes and subsystems designed to elicit behaviour that achieves the strategic objectives of an organization at the highest level of performance with the least amount of unintended consequences and risk to the organization.*

This definition covers many of the key elements of management control.

- Control cannot occur unless the organization knows what it has to do, has organized that work accordingly and can link it to achieving its strategic objectives.
- Control extends beyond control over transactions and financial reporting, without excluding them.
- The objectives must be achieved at a highest level of performance possible,

i.e., they must seek to be as efficient as possible.

- Risk must be minimized to avoid any chance of unintended consequences either in terms of outcomes or deviations from the rules governing the work.
- Structure refers to the formal task, authority and responsibility assignments in an organization.
- Processes are the activities through which control is accomplished.
- Subsystems support the structures and processes by providing the right incentives to guide behaviour.

The Meaning of a Control Framework

A control framework has certain key features:

- It establishes the organization's goals and objectives.
- It assigns roles and responsibilities.
- It establishes performance standards where possible.
- It promotes an understanding of the risks inherent in the program and the environment in which it is taking place.
- It includes positive mitigation and monitoring tools to continually reassess the risks.
- It includes a series of control procedures and policies to both address the risks identified and to satisfy legislative or policy-based requirements for adequate control.
- It provides monitoring at both the operational and financial level to ensure that the organization fully understands what is happening relative to its goals and the risk environment.
- It provides a system of auditing and evaluation, both internal and external, that provides independent assurance that there is adequate control, that it is put into practice, and that the outcomes, both operational and financial, are as the organization claims.

The Cost of Control

Control comes at a cost. It is a normal part of the administration of a government and its departments and agencies. However, cost can be a major factor in the amount of control that is possible. Even if control costs are transferred to other organizations when government contracts with them to perform services, the level of reporting detail required either increases overall project costs or diverts funds from direct program delivery to supporting control functions.

Risk and politics drive the degree of control that an organization wants. They also determine whether the controls should be *ex ante* (based on forecast results) or *ex post* (based on actual results). In general, *ex ante* controls are applied in high-risk environments. These controls are more costly in that they apply to whole categories of expenditures, all of which must pass through an audit gate to be authorized. Further, they are more costly in the sense that they generally will slow down processes, reduce the efficiency of the operation and, by implication, reduce services to recipients. Means can be found to speed up such processes, such as setting audit gates at a risk level that permits some payments to go through automatically and some to be held because of their risk factors, such as high cost. For example, a dollar threshold may be set; for amounts below the threshold no authorization or pre-audit is needed, while for amounts above the threshold approval or review is needed. This would speed up processes and reduce costs while keeping low the organization's exposure to risk.

Controls can also be costly in that they may limit managerial discretion to respond to unique circumstances. This discretion is usually sought in the name of improved client service or adaptation to special needs in a specific community. Another variant on this is that managers may have to pursue higher cost solutions to problems because policies demand certain processes when there may be advantages to moving more quickly to find low cost solutions. For example, a manager seeking to stretch her funds may see a sale of office furniture at costs significantly below the standing offers that she is required to draw from. Procedures do not permit her to take advantage of such savings.

She could, however, use her local purchase capacity with a government credit card to make lower-cost purchases, meet her office needs, and maximize the budget potential. This would achieve an improved office environment and, hopefully, improve productivity. Is this breaking the rules or using creative applications of them? Managers often have to confront and challenge controls that increase costs and reduce their budgetary potential.

Another cost of controls is that of managerial attention. What is the appropriate balance of focus on the client or program objectives versus focus on the taxpayer rights to sound financial management of their resources? This somewhat rhetorical overstatement of the issue does serve to illustrate the dilemma that many managers and governments face: when is there enough control and to what extent is control reducing organizational effectiveness? While it is cliché to say that a proper balance must be struck, too often government control wins out. This may be followed by accusations of mindless bureaucracy run rampant at the cost of service. Similarly, bureaucrats can become preoccupied with controls as a means to protect themselves from criticism or worse when something goes wrong. This obsession with control, repeated often enough, becomes the actual work of the organization and not the work for which it was created.

Finally, third-party deliverers of public services can suffer when government controls become excessive. In contracting, part of the goal is to transfer many of the administrative burdens to the deliverer. However, governments often demand a level of reporting detail that effectively turns the third party into an arm of government control. Part of what is contracted is the ability to deliver the public good. Often, organizations, especially voluntary organizations, face a reporting burden that distracts from their ability to deliver the goods contracted for.

Whatever the control framework, it must be weighed against its operating costs and the effect it has on the organization itself and its delivery systems. It also has to be weighed against the reasonable expectations of return, that is, good control must be measured against risk and political necessity. Is it worth the money? In the public sector, politics enters very quickly into this calculation; but this is perfectly valid and a valuable part of the democratic process. Hopefully, though, such calculation is informed and considered and not simply rapid knee movements.

Control and the Modernization of Public Management

The various trends of change in public sector management over the past two decades have had an impact on control. While some would characterize these trends as part of the New Public Management movement, it would be more accurate to simply report what elements have changed and made the delivery of government services more complex.[3] The changes in public sector management that are relevant here are:

- privatization and contractualization of services;
- focus on client service and service standards;
- increased reliance on technological solutions;
- abandonment of central controls and uniform standards;
- creation of special agencies, especially in the service delivery;
- alternative service delivery, embracing more partnerships either with other governments or the private sector;
- government being more 'business-like';
- separation of policy and delivery: 'rowing' and 'steering';
- changes in financial accounting systems to be more 'private-sector–like';
- great competition both within government and outside;
- reconceptualization of the citizen to include the notions of customer and consumer;
- introduction of greater and more performance links;
- use of user fees for specific services more common;
- rapid proliferation of new organizational forms, e.g., agencies and quangos,[4] linked to governments around the world.

The Provincial Auditor of Ontario, in a report entitled 'Towards Better Accountability' noted the impact of these changes on control frameworks:

> Public sector controllers have historically focused primarily on establishing basic accounting systems and financial controls to, for example, ensure that government spending is within the levels approved by the Legislature. However, over the last decade there have been a number of initiatives at the federal and provincial government level to expand this traditional role of the controller. (Report of the Provincial Auditor, 2003)

In 1996, the federal government acknowledged that the modernization of the controllership function was key to improving the performance of government. To help achieve this, a federal panel known as the Independent Review Panel on Modernization of Comptrollership in the Government of Canada was established. The Panel issued a report identifying four key elements of modern controllership:

- integrated performance information using both financial and non-financial information and linking the two;
- appropriate control systems;
- a sound approach to risk management;
- a shared set of ethical practices and organizational values.

The Panel also stated that the single most important change needed was a move to a new guiding philosophy for controllership. Essentially, the culture of controllership had to move from a 'command/control' orientation to a 'loose-tight' orientation that would combine a strong commitment to centralized standards and values designed to achieve planned results with a flexible approach to processes and operating results.

The heart of these efforts by several governments to improve their controllership was a recognition that a disconnect had occurred between the goals of the organization and the means to exercise the necessary levels of controls. Part of that disconnect is associated with a failure of the financial community to adequately understand the program goals of many public sector organization and align the control framework to achieve them in a cost effective and legal manner. Generally, the controllers' philosophy was that one size would fit all, regardless of the risk, understanding, and competence of the staff and form of the organization. Modern public sector controllers have had to make a major transition from the public accounting and controllership techniques of the past. The modern controller has to satisfy new organizational demands, including management reporting; being an ethical watchdog, corporate leader, and advisor to other managers; and still getting the monthly closing done on time!

What Is Accountability and How Financial Management Plays a Role

Like control, the concepts of accountability in government have come under equally close scrutiny. There are many definitions and uses of the term 'accountability'. The challenge is to discuss accountability at a sufficiently general level to make it readily understandable, while making the connection to financial management and describing the role it plays in accountability. Let us look at two definitions of accountability that address many important elements of public sector accountability.

Dr Janice Stein of the University of Toronto, in her book *The Cult of Efficiency* defined it in the following way:

> Accountability is about evaluating performance, meeting legitimate standards, fulfilling legitimate commitments, and holding responsible those who fail to meet the standards. The right to judge government performance flows naturally from the role of citizen, as does the right to

> sanction those who fail to meet the standards. (Stein, 2003)

Christine Ryan and Peter Walsh of Queensland University of Technology, in their review of shared accountabilities, note that

> An inherent feature of accountability in the governmental context is that some identifiable individuals or define groups are held responsible for a set of activities that correspond to their actual span of control and capacity to act. (Ryan and Walsh, 2004)

What then, are the principal characteristics of accountability relationships in government? They are:

- *Assignment of authority, power, and resources.* This is the downward delegation of duties to an individual or organization. This can be prescribed by law, by policy, by way of formal delegation matrices, or by the completion of an organizational work plan, budget distribution, or performance contracts. It can also be implicit or indirect, such as using formal position descriptions to describe duties that included delegated authority and, possibly, outcome expectations.
- *Accountability for performance and results.* In accepting the authority, power, and resources described in the previous point, the individual or organization takes on the responsibility to perform the work and account for the results.
- *Assignment of duties.* In assigning duties formally, the granting authority also provides clear direction, legislative or regulatory guidance, and resources consistent with the expectation.
- *Requirement to report.* The necessity to report in a formal way is often prescribed by the granting authority and deals with three elements:
    - results achieved;
    - compliance with legal and procedural requirements;
    - efficiency.
- *Judgement exercised.* At some level, either within the organization and/or in the public at large, public sector accountability involves the right of the granting authority to make judgments about how the accountability has been exercised and act on those judgments. These judgments may range from a clean bill of health on a financial statement by a legislative auditor, to the downfall or re-election of a government—the ultimate test in a democracy such as ours.

The Objectives of Financial and Performance Reporting

At the heart of good reporting is meeting the accountability contract that the individual or organization has with its authorizing body. In government, this relationship is multi-dimensional: accountability relationships start with Parliament and the executive, continue through government as a whole to individual departments, and extend to divisions within those departments as well. Such reporting is based on the capacities, resources, and delegated authority at each level. This relationship conditions all capacity to effectively carry out the work both in the manner demanded and with the efficiency required.

Reports therefore, should, make it possible to:

- assess the discharge of the accountability taken on;
- make decisions about the public good, the means of delivery, the resources allocated to it, and the political consequences of all of these.

To do this, effective public sector financial and performance reporting should meet certain objectives:

- to provide a means to demonstrate the organization's accountability that enables users to asses that accountability in a mutually accepted manner;
- to provide sufficient information to permit users to assess the financial viability of the organization, and to assess whether current revenues and expenses will meet program objectives or impose future liabilities on taxpayers or donors;
- to show that the organization is compliant with its legal financial reporting requirements;
- to show that the organization is compliant with its contractual agreements and requirements;
- to provide information needed to evaluate the organization's operating results for the period under review, including sources and uses of financial resources; objectives, standards, and obligations, and how they were met; and changes in financial condition and viability;
- to provide information about the organization's level of service and capacity.

Annual Reporting: Basic Format Requirements

It would be impossible to display even a representative number of annual reports that governments produce. Format and appearance vary dramatically. In general, all jurisdictions in Canada require their governments to produce annual financial statements. Most governments produce forms of performance reporting, based either on government-wide performance targets or on targets for individual departments.

Most standard-setting accounting organizations for both government and the voluntary sector recommend that annual reports contain information that addresses the following:

- management report: introductory information and management's discussion and analysis;
- financial reports;
- auditor's report;
- notes on the financial statement.

Many governments meet the standards of reporting described above, but increasingly try to link the financial information to performance and risk. As this trend has developed, annual reports have become longer, more linked to the stated objectives of the organization, and often more oriented to public relations (in order, it is argued, to increase readability). In essence, organizations see reports as a way to 'tell their story'. For example, the federal government provides its Reports on Plans and Priorities to Parliament for all departments and agencies.[5] Similarly, most municipalities produce annual reports on expenditures and results to council. Many good examples exist; for instance, the City of Brampton has been noted for the high quality of its financial and performance reporting.[6]

The Role of Audit in the Accountability Process

Effective internal and external audit systems exist to serve the need for public accountability. However, they are not accountability itself; that rests with the individual or organization that has taken on certain responsibilities and powers and that must publicly account for them. **Audits**, in their various forms, are control tools to be used in both assessing performance and assessing compliance with both their own objectives and the means approved to achieve them.

The Canadian Comprehensive Audit Foundation (CCAF) defines audit as follows:

> Audit serves an accountability relationship. It is the independent, objective assessment of the fairness of management's representations on performance or the assessment of management's system and practices, against criteria, reporting to a governing body or others with similar responsibilities. (CCAF, 1991)

The logic behind audits has been with us for a very long time. In fact, the ancient Egyptians used auditors to control transactions for the royal treasury. They also established detailed records of their work and the resulting transactions. Thus the notion of using people and systems to safeguard public funds and provide a check against corruption is deep-seated.

Audits play an important role in the dynamic both within the executive in the Westminster system as well as between Parliament and the executive. As Wayne Cameron, Auditor General of the State of Victoria in Australia points out:

> For minister and departmental officials, the key channel of accountability remains the chain of responsibility, upwards through the departmental hierarchy to the secretary and the minister and, via the minister, to parliament and the public. This central channel is supplemented by a number of other accountability mechanisms, including the accountability of public servants to respond to enquiries by parliamentary committees, to those agencies which through their statutory roles reinforce public accountability such as the Auditor-General, the Ombudsman, tribunals and the courts, as well as freedom of information. (Cameron, 2004)

While this statement is a useful reminder about accountability in general, it also reinforces the need for internal audit capacity in the program departments themselves in addition to using outside bodies when greater transparency is needed. Auditing is an essential part of the control framework. Internal audits must, even within the organization serving senior management, have integrity and independence to investigate and determine the risks in certain programs. The extent and even the degree of internal auditing needed depend on the size of the organization and the degree of risk. Small public organizations function very well with a single auditor who serves both internal roles (e.g., advice on establishing a statement of accounts) and external roles (attesting to the completeness of year-end financial statements). However, the greater the complexity and the greater the risk the more there is need for an internal audit function, in addition to a separate external function.

Large public entities such as governments need to continuously reassess the adequacy of their internal and external audit functions. Most have a history that guides them, as in the office of Auditor General. But there are a range of other external oversight bodies in the federal government that serve audit functions as well. One good example is the Office of Official Languages for the federal government of Canada which regularly audits departmental compliance with the Official Languages Act.

At the heart of the use of audit is the need for public and independent assurances on two fronts:

- *attestation* that management's information is fairly and completely represented, be it financial information (for the most part it is) or any other information that management offers and that it is presented in conformance to practice, standards and rules;
- *assessment* and reporting on management's performance in comparison to the approved purposes of the program, its stated objectives and goals, and the need for economy and efficiency.

Internal Audit Functions

The management system of an organization in government must be able to demonstrate that it can control its resources. An important tool for exercising that control is internal audit capacity. The size of this capacity depends on the organization and the risks that it manages. For government, however, especially for those parts of government that have many financial transactions, either in the area of entitlements (pensions, social assistance, etc.) or grants and contributions, the internal capacity to review, either *ex ante* or *ex post*, is important for internal control.

Some of the functions of an internal audit are:

- to review and provide advice on overall control systems of the organization;
- to assess project control capacity for large, high risk projects;
- to ensure that adequate measures are in place to minimize theft or fraud;
- to ensure that grant and entitlement decision-making reduces errors to a minimum to prevent overpayment and the need for recovery;
- to ensure adherence to regulations covering how funds are spent, recorded, and controlled;
- to attest to the accuracy of the information in the financial and reporting system.

One of the most important roles that internal audit performs is to provide assurances to senior managers that their control systems work.

In ensuring that internal audit can function effectively to meet its objectives, some organizational matters take on importance. Internal audit generally needs a significant degree of independence and needs to be *seen* to exercise that independence. While it clearly serves the needs of the organization and, in particular, the chief executive officer, it must be able to function without interference. Therefore, internal audit should be sufficiently independent of the activities that it audits to enable auditors to make impartial and effective professional judgments and recommendations. The auditors should have no executive responsibilities. This means that they should not be operating or managing any activities that will themselves be a subject to an audit in the future. Further, their involvement in the management structure of the organization should be sufficiently distant from both line and staff functions such that they can readily audit either.

Government: Legislative Auditors

Legislative auditors, now called Auditors General or Provincial Auditors, are appointed by the legislature, based on legislation such as the federal Auditor General Act. They are independent of government and report directly to the legislature.

Originally, many legislative auditors were created as the sole government audit function. Legislation in the late nineteenth century created audit offices in many Canadian jurisdictions. However, their role was dramatically different than it is today. Originally, these auditors serviced government directly by:

- examining all payments before a cheque could be issued;
- reporting to the legislature on an individual basis all payments made within departments;
- preparing a book of accounts for all revenue;
- preparing a uniform system of books for the departments;
- preparing any reports or conducting any investigations desired by the government.

Today, most of these operational functions are either undertaken by internal audit or done by finance staff. For example, very little pre-audit takes place today, except in high-risk areas. The job of creating and maintaining financial statements is generally a matter of general government policy coming from the central agency responsible for financial management (e.g., Treasury Board or Management Board). Thus, generating a book of accounts or preparing financial statements is no longer an audit function.

From the view of legislators, the value of legislative auditors is not simply in their technical expertise—it is also in their ability to conduct audits that may not please those being examined, and to report their findings publicly and independently. They subject the operations of the public sector to regular, independent examinations, acting in the public interest as advocates of transparent government.

Defining the role of legislative auditors in the public accountability process requires examining their independence, their mandate, their reporting obligations, and their expertise in public sector matters.

Comprehensive Legislated Mandate

For most jurisdictions there is an act of the legislature creating the auditor's position and outlining the duties. Some important elements that are usually included in legislation are:

- the scope of audit concern, including all departments and potentially on related organizations such as Crown corporations;
- the authority and duty to report back to the legislature;
- the authority to investigate without encumbrance (a guarantee of independence);
- the identification of the legislative auditor as an officer of the legislature.

Whole-of-Government Mandate

The legislative auditor is generally the only official channel through which legislatures are regularly and consistently kept informed of government's stewardship of public funds and success in achieving value for money. Legislatures have granted their legislative auditors **'whole-of-government' mandates**, covering organizations as diverse as government departments, agencies, commissions, boards, and Crown corporations. The list of organizations covered varies from jurisdiction to jurisdiction.

Public Sector Expertise

Because of the diverse set of organizations they may audit, legislative auditors in Canada meet their objectives by examining a very broad range of issues. It is expected, however, that they conduct audits according to public sector values, taking into account the policy objectives of the programs. To make this possible, legislatures have broadened the scope of the work that legislative auditors may do to obtain the information they need to hold government accountable. They no longer focus strictly on financial information. In fact, they must take public policy, operations, and other matters into consideration.

Furthermore, having a whole-of-government mandate has allowed legislative auditors to speak to legislators about broad government matters and to better identify those accountability and performance issues that have the greatest impact on government.

Reporting to the Legislature

Legislative auditors generally report directly to their authorizing legislatures, at least annually, on anything they think should be brought to the legislators' attention. The auditors' reports become a matter of public record and cover a wide range of issues of interest to legislators and the public, including compliance, propriety, the economy, and the efficiency and effectiveness of government operations. Legislative auditors also have direct access to each legislature's **Public Accounts Committee**. This provides them with a formal means of discussing their reported audit findings with the legislators.

Conclusion

Budgets play an important role in the management of public sector organizations. While they can be organized in a number of different ways, they always serve as important instruments of public policy. Their structure will generally reflect the complexity of the public organization itself. This chapter has revealed some of the complexity. More to say on the subject can be found in the expanding literature on budgeting.

Important Terms and Concepts

appropriation
audits
budget
capital budget
cash budget
entitlement program
legislative auditors
levels of expenditure
Public Accounts Committee
revolving funds
rolling budget
supplementary budgets or estimates
tax expenditure
'whole-of-government' mandates

Study Questions

1. Budgets serve many purposes. What are some of these purposes?
2. What is meant by 'revenue budget' and 'expenditure budget', and what is their relationship?
3. What are the different forms of budget and off-budget expenditures, and why are they used?
4. Explain the nature of the budgetary process.
5. Describe the fundamental tensions inherent in the budget process.
6. What is the meaning and nature of control? Of financial accountability?

Useful Websites

Canadian Tax Foundation (CTF):

www.ctf.ca

CCAF-FCVI Inc. (formerly called the Canadian Comprehensive Auditing Foundation—La fondation Canadienne pour la vérification integrée):

www.ccaf-fcvi.com/english/about/index.html

Treasury Board Secretariat, Estimates Publications and Appropriation Acts (Supply Bills):

www.tbs-sct.gc.ca/est-pre/index-eng.asp

Canadian Federal Budget, 2009:

www.budget.gc.ca/2009/home-accueil-eng.asp

Links to Canadian provincial budgets, 2009:

www.taxtips.ca/provbudgets.htm

Canadian Council of Legislative Auditors (CCOLA):

www.ccola.ca/index_english.cfm

Office of the Auditor General of Canada:

www.oag-bvg.gc.ca/internet/English/admin_e_41.html

Links to legislative auditors across Canada and around the world:

www.auditor.sk.ca/paweb/links.html

Notes

1. A more fulsome presentation of these ideas and a more in-depth review of public sector financial management can be found in Graham (2007).
2. Unless such *entitlements* are established in specific legislation and therefore not a matter of budget decision-making.

3. While reading is extensive in this area, Lester Salamon's *The Tools of Governance* is perhaps the best summarization of these trends.
4. Quasi Autonomous Non-Governmental Organization.
5. The reports for 2005–2006 can be found at www.tbs-sct.gc.ca/est-pre/20052006/p3a_e.asp.
6. See www.city.brampton.on.ca/annual_report/annualreport06.pdf.

References

Bland, Douglas L. 2004. *Canada without Armed Forces?* Kingston: School of Policy Studies, Queen's University.

Cameron, Wayne. 2004. 'Public Accountability; Effectiveness, Equity, Ethics', *Australian Journal of Public Administration* 63, 4 (December): 59–67.

CCAF. 1991. 'Comprehensive Audit Reporting—Concepts, Issues and Practice'. Ottawa: CCAF.

City of Brampton. *Annual Report.* Available at: www.city.brampton.on.ca/annual_report/annualreport06.pdf.

Graham, Andrew. 2007. *Canadian Public Sector Financial Management.* Montreal and Kingston: McGill-Queen's University Press.

Kelly, Joanne, and Dirk-Jan Krann. 2005. *Reallocation: The Role of Budget Institutions.* Paris: OECD.

Lindquist, Evert A. 1994. 'Citizens, Experts and Budgets: Evaluating Ottawa's Emerging Budget Process', in Susan D. Phillips, ed., *How Ottawa Spends 1994–95.* Ottawa: Carleton University Press, 116–22.

McKinney, Jerome B., and Lawrence C. Howard. 1979. *Public Administration: Balancing Power and Accountability.* Oak Park, Ill.: Moore Publishing.

MacKinnon, Janice. 2003. *Minding the Public Purse.* Montreal and Kingston: McGill-Queen's University Press.

Office of the Auditor General of Ontario. 2003. *2003 Annual Report.* Toronto: Office of the Auditor General of Ontario.

Ryan, Christine, and Peter Walsh. 2004. 'Collaboration of Public Sector Agencies: Reporting and Accountability Challenges', *International Journal of Public Sector Management* 17, 7: 612–31.

Salamon, Lester M. 2002. *The Tools of Governance.* New York and Oxford: Oxford University Press.

Stein, Janice Gross. 2003. *The Cult of Efficiency.* Toronto: House of Anansi Press.

Tait, John C., QC, Chair. 1997.' A Strong Foundation: Report of the Task Force on Public Service Values and Ethics' [summary], *Canadian Public Administration* 40: 1.

The Wager. 2000. 'Easy Come, Easy Go. . .Maybe'. *The Wager* [a publication of Harvard Medical School] 5, 43 (November).

Washington, Sally, and Elia Armstrong. 1996. 'Public Management Occasional Paper, No. 14: Ethics in the Public Service: Current Issues and Practice'. Paris: OECD. Available at: www.oecd.org/dataoecd/59/24/1898992.pdf.

Wildavsky, A. 1964. *The Politics of the Budgetary Process.* Boston: Little, Brown.

28 The Role of Deputy Ministers in Canadian Government

Jacques Bourgault

Introduction

The deputy minister's position is essential within the Canadian government based on the Westminster tradition, especially in today's ever-changing context. Being the linchpin between the public administration and the government, the deputy minister (DM) needs to incarnate knowledge and know-how for his or her minister and to represent the political will of the administration. This prestigious central position carries its burden of responsibilities. Now more than ever, the DM's mission is ambitious, with more expectations from the citizenry and more resources, but it encounters far more contingencies. In recent years much has been written about the perils of politicization or of professional submission to the political masters.

This chapter aims to expose the complexity of the federal deputy minister. After a brief description of the profession's context in Canada, its characteristics are depicted in the sections 'Position in the System' and 'Profile of Deputy Ministers'. The challenges faced by the DMs are further described in the sections 'Politicization', 'Managing the Department and Policies', and 'Multiple Accountability'.

Position in the System

A **deputy minister (DM)** is just below the minister in the hierarchy. The deputy minister's role is to assist the minister in his or her functions within the department and advise the minister. All of the legislation establishing departments stipulates simply that a deputy minister *may be appointed,* without specifying the DM's role. The DMs are the civil servants who are closest to the political level; they are outside the merit appointment system of the Public Service of Canada (PSC) but are subject to most provisions of the Public Service Employment Act.

Designation/Selection/Appointment

Being at pleasure. Deputy ministers are a category of what are called discretionary appointments, along with the CEOs of Crown corporations, board members, and ambassadors; however, deputies and ambassadors 'hold office' for an undetermined period, while the others are generally appointed for a determined period. In theory, any Canadian citizen of sound mind and not under any legal prohibition may be appointed to those functions. Out of respect for democratic principles, the architects of the system wanted the government, which is responsible to the elected Parliament, to be able to hire and fire the people it wants to advise ministers, run departments, and implement legislation. They were aware that ministers were kept busy by their duties as parliamentarians, MPs, caucus members, and members of cabinet, as well as by their symbolic functions as representatives of the state or the government at local, national, and foreign events. Moreover, it is fair to say that ministers are not always chosen on the basis of their specialized education or experience in the field for which they are to be responsible. As a result, the deputy minister has an important role to play in advising the minister and keeping the department on an even keel.

Designation. Though the Prime Minister has full discretion in choosing deputy ministers, today a DM is seldom designated by the Prime Minister or the minister alone, and never by the governing party per se. Most often, they are civil servants who have been tagged as up-and-comers, groomed over the long term by senior officials and sometimes ministers, and promoted to positions closer and closer to the circle of power. Our research indicates that in recent decades only a tiny number of federal deputy minister appointments have been arranged primarily through political channels, which in fact usually means personal networks with a political tinge.

Selection. Up-and-comers are promoted to assistant deputy minister and associate deputy minister before they move up to DM. The Prime Minister makes the selection on the advice of the **Clerk of the Privy Council**, who in turn is assisted by a senior appointments office that does much of the leg work (assembling a file on the department's needs and on each of the possible candidates). The **Committee of Senior Officials (COSO)** performs two functions in the process, examining departmental succession plans and conducting performance appraisals. The Prime Minister may consult others about the Clerk's proposal before bringing it to cabinet for decision.

Appointment and dismissal. The statutes establishing departments stipulate that the appointment of DMs is made by the Governor-in-Council (GIC). By convention, the GIC acts on the PM's recommendation. Prime Minister Charles Tupper had a list of 'prerogatives' of the PMO approved by cabinet in 1896; it was subsequently reissued by every Prime Minister from Laurier to King (for the last time by PC 3374, 25 October 1935) (Canada, Privy Council Office, 1987: 9). It is now considered a convention and need not be written down as long as everyone acts in accordance with the custom. The practice of appointment by the GIC on the PM's recommendation entails a rich and complex balance that affects the exercise of power. This is a cabinet appointment, made after the Prime Minister proposes an Order-in-Council, which is not submitted to the full cabinet but does require three other ministerial signatures as well as that of the Prime Minister. Such a procedure means that the person appointed retains the confidence of the government, the cabinet, and the Prime Minister. It is not a ministerial appointment. Therefore, the PM may try to install a particular DM (for example, a seasoned, bilingual, networked official) to assist a particular minister (a newcomer, someone who is unaware of the department's workings, etc.). Only the PM can make the recommendation, which gives him veto power over all such appointments. The power of appointment provided by the Interpretation Act has been understood to include the power of dismissal of DMs: the PM can ask a DM to resign or recommend that cabinet appoint another person to act as DM in the department. On these matters, the Prime Minister is generally advised by the Clerk of the Privy Council. One case of this type was made public by the *Globe and Mail* and is related by Plumptre (1987: 379). The PM's note, an unusual document that may have been requested by the PM's entourage to cover him, stated that the DM in question was 'insensitive to the Minister's role' and had 'lost control of the Department'.

Environment: PM/Minister/ Chief of Staff

The deputy minister inhabits a politically sensitive sphere. Remote from departmental employees and peers, his dealings are with the Prime Minister, ministers, and their **chiefs of staff** (COSs). The chief of staff position is highly contested in Canada. The Mulroney Conservatives experienced numerous conflicts between political appointees and career public servants during their first years of power. When the Liberals returned to power in 1993, they downgraded the chief of staff's role and personnel. The PM recommends the DM's appointment and, accordingly, may at times require the DM's loyalty to counterbalance a minister's tendencies. The PM may occasionally call the DM for direct information on a matter, to express a position on an issue, to send a signal, to discuss a delicate subject, or to request advice on a related matter. However, direct communications between the PMO and a DM is not the rule: a DM would insist on having personal confirmation from the Prime Minister or the minister and will ask to hear directly from him or her, or to be heard directly. Just as it is not usual procedure for the DM to receive a phone call from the PMO, it would be seen as a fatal error (barring exceptional circumstances) for a DM to call the PM directly, without going through the minister (political channels) or the Clerk of the Privy Council (administrative channels). This is hardly surprising, given the various accountability systems in place. The public service is accountable to the minister or Prime Minister for advice provided and for the implementation of political decisions. The chief of staff is accountable to the minister as a partisan political actor whose role is to help him or her to gain and maintain power. The chief of staff should not interfere with the minister/DM relationship. To ensure that the accountability chain is not disrupted, the Gomery Report proposes to 'adopt a code of conduct for political staff, including a provision that bars them from telling bureaucrats what to do' (Gomery Commission, 2006: Recommendation 11).

Relations between deputy ministers and their ministers vary according to the minister's personality and their mutual compatibility. In one cynical description, some ministers reached the top of the mountain the day they were appointed and want only to sit and enjoy the view; others want to roll up their sleeves and get to work on the nitty-gritty details of running a department or hope to leave some monument to the country as their contribution or lasting legacy. Deputy ministers welcome those differing attitudes with varying degrees of enthusiasm. One frustrated minister once commented, 'When you meet the deputy minister for the first time, he is supposed to ask you whether you want to have your main office on Parliament Hill or at the department's HQ. If he insists that you may be better off up on the Hill, near Parliament and colleagues, you may interpret he is afraid of ministerial micromanagement' (Bourgault, 1997c: 13).

Generally, the minister holds a weekly morning meeting with the COS and DM; depending on ministers' preferences, other people, such as the assistant deputy minister (ADM) and senior officials, may also be asked to attend. In addition to this briefing/debriefing, the DM meets with the minister as needed. When there are hot political issues to be dealt with, when pieces of legislation are before the House, when budgets or other strategic documents are in preparation (e.g., an appearance before a House committee), meetings with the minister are more frequent and may be held on a daily basis. Relations may also include a daily review of the minister's briefing book for Question Period when the House is sitting.

Legal Duties and Power

Most statutes establishing departments (with the exception of some regulatory departments such as Revenue, Consumer Affairs, Justice, and Immigration) do not stipulate any specific powers to be exercised by the DM. On the contrary, only general powers are dealt with, and they are assigned only to the minister. When the DM's powers are mentioned, it is stated that the DM shall take 'general advice' from the minister in these matters (Canada, Privy Council Office, 1987: 17).

DMs may exercise power through the minister's authority, subject to 'certain exceptions and constraints' (ibid., 1) as established by the Interpretation Act and convention: 'Words directing or empowering a Minister of the Crown to do an act or a thing, or otherwise applying to him by his name of office, include... his or her deputy.' This provision is followed by an exception for any regulation within the meaning of the Regulations Act (ibid., 24). Moreover, once a minister had taken action on a matter, the DM's hands are tied 'because the Interpretation Act recognizes a deputy as subordinate to his minister'.

As the department's deputy head, the DM is responsible for the management of all of the department's human and financial resources. Those responsibilities were recently expanded as a result of new empowerment approaches adopted by central agencies such as Treasury Board and the Public Service Commission. Briefly put, DMs are now entrusted with full responsibility for all decisions as long as they follow the principles and guidelines established by the central agencies. The new Canada Customs and Revenue Agency may be the most advanced example of this trend. Some powers are delegated to the DM by the central agencies, others by the minister, while in this most recent example the enabling legislation provides the DM with direct powers. Delegated authority can be subdelegated and the DM delegates signing authority to the ADM and the director general (the individual directly beneath the ADM in rank). The DM's role is then to monitor the system, issuing clear guidelines, fine-tuning them, and following up on their application.

In late 2004, the President of the Treasury Board, Reg Alcock, announced new measures in response to the 'sponsorship scandal'. To prevent fraud, the Treasury Board put forth a set of rules framing, among other objectives, the public administration's process pursuit of the enhancement of its transparency. This came as a major setback for the New Public Management's mode of management, such as the Stewardship initiative.

In 2006, the DM's environment was affected by the Federal Accountability Act, enacted on 12 December 2006: the position of **Parliamentary Budget Officer** was created and its holder must be an officer of the Library of Parliament (section 116). As a consequence, the parliamentary committees are gaining slightly more resources to prepare for a DM's appearances before them. The act also creates a **Public Servants Disclosure Protection Tribunal** to protect victims of reprisal and to order disciplinary actions against the perpetrators of such acts (section 201). Public servants now benefit from a structure promoting disclosure of dubious acts, even those committed by a DM. Interestingly, the spectrum of action of this tribunal is quite vast, since not only criminal acts can be brought to its attention. Finally, the DMs are named **Accounting Officers** for their departments and they are responsible for internal auditing. Each DM must establish an audit committee for their department (section 259). A review is necessary every five years to evaluate the relevance and effectiveness of each program (section 260).

The Deputy Minister's Role in the Political System: Service without Servility

The deputy minister is a public servant subject to the Public Service Employment Act and is therefore a non-partisan official. The DM's functions and duties differ from those of staff in the minister's office. The DM is a public employee with special status in terms of recruitment, appointment, and length of tenure. As a public employee (a function formerly defined as 'serving the Crown'), the DM has a duty to the state. The DM performs that duty by loyally and competently serving the government of the day (Kernaghan and Siegel, 1991: 296–7). This means keeping the minister's and cabinet's trust in the DM's professional competency and ethics, and at the same time, as a non-partisan public employee, limiting his or her obedience and acting according to the law. The DM gives advice, protects the minister and the government, acts competently, but will not take a stand to defend or promote a government policy or decision. Neither will the DM agree to do the minister a favour in violation of the law.

Incorporating Cabinet Priorities into Departmental Priorities

The deputy minister is expected to know the priorities, sensitivities, and promises of the government of the day and to incorporate these proactively into the department's agenda, where possible (Osbaldeston, 1989: 20). This means developing or modifying policies, programs, and legislation, preparing budget appropriations, and factoring cabinet priorities into discussions with the provinces, with pressure groups, and in international relations. It is the DM's job to make sure that everyone in the department is reading from the same page and that practical steps are taken to achieve the government's objectives.

Serving the Minister

Deputy ministers answer to their minister, not to cabinet. Some DMs do feel that, ultimately, they must heed cabinet, but, as one deputy said, 'In the last analysis, it is the PM who holds me accountable. In a more indirect way, it is the Minister' (ibid., 18). All DMs recognize direct obligations to the minister as the department head and the department's representative on cabinet (in what Osbaldeston terms a 'highly interactive process') (ibid., 23). Serving the minister essentially means preparing ministerial decisions, since most decisions concerning the administration of the department and the implementation of vertical (or sectoral) legislation (e.g., agricultural policies, health policies) are formally made by the minister with little time, knowledge, or information. Serving the minister also means providing the minister with knowledge, information, advice, orientations, opinions, corporate memory, and other decision support materials. Once the minister has established an approach towards a category of decisions, the authority to make decisions of that type can be delegated to save time for the minister.

In practical terms, there is a weekly morning meeting with the minister and, often, political aides. Meetings may also be held during the week, depending on the legislative agenda, political events (such as crisis), and the minister's involvement in departmental matters. During some periods of the year, the minister and the DM may meet more often in connection with events such as the Throne Speech, the Budget, reports to Parliament, and preparations for the annual executive retreat (strategic planning process) (ibid., 34–5). On a daily basis, the DM is expected to help prepare answers to questions in the House, to gather raw material for speeches, and to reply to technical ministerial correspondence, either under the DM's own name or by preparing drafts for signature by the minister.

The Gomery Report challenges this accepted definition of the relationship between the minister and the DM. It proposes that the DM have the final say in most disagreements with the minister on matters relevant to his or her own accountability. To overrule the position of the DM, the minister would have to invoke an official procedure where he or she would write a letter transmitted to central bodies (Gomery Commission, 2006: Recommendation 5). On the other hand, many 'are opposed to increase the power of unelected officials at the expense of Ministers. The result would be confusion as to who was accountable to Parliament for what' (Ardell et al., 2006). Moreover, they maintain that there is no need to create the proposed procedure to prevent ministers from making decisions contrary to the public's interest. When a DM isn't able to convince the minister not to proceed with an improper decision, he will inform the Clerk of the Privy Council of the situation, who will then bring the matter to the attention of the PM. The final decision will then be made by the PM and the minister, and both will be accountable to the Parliament for the outcome. Ultimately, they may be subject to the sanction of the electorate (Ardell et al., 2006).

Obligation to Answer

In accordance with a recommendation of the 1985 McGrath report on House of Commons reform, which aimed to revitalize the work of Parliament, standing committees of Parliament were given authority to call anyone (including DMs) to answer questions. They already had such authority when dealing with areas in which powers are assigned directly to deputy heads, such as financial and human resources matters. That authority has now been widened. McGrath's recommendation expanded committee powers; the government had to issue guidelines in order to balance the House's right to know and monitor with the House's right to see its Acts implemented effectively. Those guidelines were issued after some difficult official appearances before committees.

The government approved a six-page PCO document, revised in April 2000, that sets out a number of principles regarding the responsibilities of public servants when they appear before parliamentary committees, including the following:

1. The House and Senate, and their committees, have the power to call whomever they see fit, even against the wishes of a minister.
2. Generally, ministers determine which officials will speak on their behalf. It is for ministers to decide which questions they will answer and which questions can be answered by officials.
3. Witnesses testifying before parliamentary committees are expected to answer all questions. However, public servants have a legal responsibility to hold in confidence the information that comes into their possession in the course of their duties. They appear before committees to provide information that ministers could not be expected to provide personally.
4. Public servants have an obligation to behave in a manner that allows ministers to maintain full confidence in their loyalty.
5. When appearing before a committee, public servants must not undermine the principle of ministerial responsibility. They are not directly accountable to Parliament for their actions or for the policies and programs of the government. Matters of policy and political controversy have been reserved for ministers.
6. Public servants have a duty to convey information truthfully to their ministers and, on the minister's behalf, to convey truthfully information which they may properly convey to Parliament.
7. Officials who are asked to be sworn might wish to observe that they are appearing on behalf of their minister to convey factual information and to seek the understanding of the committee for the need to avoid questions that could put them in a position that would conflict with their duty to their minister and their oath of office.
8. Officials have a fundamental duty to advise their ministers frankly on any matters relevant to their departmental and policy responsibilities. Only ministers can properly decide when and to what degree a confidential matter should be disclosed.
9. Testimony under oath could force an official to assume a power of decision in these respects that he or she cannot properly exercise. Committees recognize that the provision of information to committees, beyond that normally accessible to the public, must be a matter of ministerial decision.
10. Officials may give explanations of complex policy matters but they do not defend policy or engage in debate as to policy alternatives.

These principles have generally proven to be workable. There have, however, been some exceptions, such as an early case in which the Opposition tried to embarrass the government by attacking a decision by the Deputy Minister of Immigration and overtly politicized the matter. In the famous Al-Mashat affair, senior officials, a minister's assistant, and the Clerk of the Privy Council passed the blame to each other (see Sutherland, 1991). Conservative ministers were generally highly satisfied with the conduct of their deputy ministers before committees (Bourgault, 1997c: 23).

Role within the Department

DMs perform many roles in the department, many of them on behalf of other authorities. For central agencies, they administer resources; for the minister, they implement the organic statutes and vertical laws for which that the minister is responsible and oversee policy-making in those fields; for cabinet, they align the department's priorities with those of the government; on their own authority, they provide the systems, information, and leadership needed to carry out those tasks or, in Mintzberg's terms, they implement the 'jobframe' through information, people, and action (Mintzberg and Bourgault, 2000). Finally, they contribute personally or by means of the department's resources to assisting the minister in his or her duties.

Administering Departmental Resources

On the minister's behalf, the DM administers the departmental resources provided by the budget. On his or her own authority, the DM makes or authorizes decisions on resource allocation. That authority formerly resided more with the central agencies and ministers; the reform of public management has empowered DMs and their subdelegates (directorates and ADMs). A 1993 study showed that the DMs were allocating 19 per cent of their time to immediate subordinates, more than to ministers, pressure groups, and peers; they were allocating 15 per cent of their time to human resources management, more than to policy-making, program implementation, political relations, and public relations (Bourgault, 1997a: 21). Moreover, the number of Assistant Deputy Ministers (and even associate ADMs!) continues to grow. Although their supervision could be time-consuming for the DMs, it is said to be a long-term investment for the public administration, which will benefit from a pool of high-quality administrators to ensure the succession of the actual DMs.

Implementing Vertical Acts

In addition to the Act establishing the department, there can be anywhere from 10 to 100 Acts that apply to any given sphere. Usually, one minister will be responsible for applying each Act; in rare cases, the responsibility may be shared between more than one minister. A DM must see to applying the Acts for which the department is responsible, in accordance with social needs, or to coordinating implementation with governmental and non-governmental agencies.

Implementing vertical Acts entails drafting rules and regulations, monitoring their application, issuing notices, enforcing the rules, fine-tuning policies, developing programs, making rulings and decisions, and taking action. For this purpose, the minister, the DM, and departmental staff consult within and without the government apparatus, provide opinions, sit on committees and working groups, ask for research materials and information for purposes of analysis, etc.

The departments have headquarters and regional offices to implement policies and programs, central capabilities to monitor policy implementation, and central services to communicate and work with headquarters and provincial counterparts. The DM is responsible for ensuring that the entire apparatus functions smoothly. In the late 1980s there were nearly 40 departments. The last reorganization, in 1993, cut the number of departments from 29 to 23 larger organizations, each responsible for more vertical Acts, more programs and regulations, larger budgets, a larger workforce, and more facilities. These responsibilities consume most of the DM's time.

Policy-Making

Policy-making has always been seen as a key role of the deputy minister: since it is of strategic importance, we expect the department's most prominent manager to be deeply involved in the process. In the past, DMs would spend a larger part of their careers in a given department and became specialists on policy matters. Their position in the organization gives them an overview of developments and makes them the last filter before anything reaches the minister's desk, or in some cases goes to the central agencies. They are at the centre of information processes within the department and between the department and other organizations. This is why Osbaldeston (1989: 17–18) stresses the policy-advisory role and why Swift (1993: 9) considers the advisory role to be so important. Indeed, a DM who is doing his or her job provides official and unofficial advice to many people: the minister, central agency officials, national organizations, etc. In a 1993 study, this writer found that DMs spend 25 per cent of their time on long-term matters and 5 per cent on evaluation, two functions that fall within the general category of policy-making (Bourgault, 1997a: 21).

Role within Peer Group

What Is the Peer Group?

Peer groups have been influential since the beginning of the century. Later, DMs began meeting for a couple of days every year at a retreat 50 kilometres outside Ottawa. In 1940, Clifford Clark, who has been described as 'the one who shaped the mandarinate' (Granatstein, 1982: 14–15), officially founded the Five Lakes Fishing Club 30 miles from Ottawa in Gatineau County. The informal get-together helped build relations between the vertical, insular, command-style departments. Until 1939, the measure of cohesion that did exist had been created by the PM more than by the Privy Council Office.

The peer group consists of the DMs in all departments and in the PCO. It has varied with the number of departments and the number of special advisers with DM rank in the PCO. More recently, the definition has been broadened to include associate deputy ministers. In all, the group comprises from 35 to 50 people. It is a legacy of the pre-Thatcherian British system, in which Whitehall created a pool of corporate wisdom, the group of permanent secretaries. In Canada, the functional peer group began to emerge in the early 1970s with the need for cohesion and for interdepartmental coordination. The reorganization of the PCO in the late 1960s (Hay, 1982: 15) contributed to the normalization of the peer group, but the main reason for the peer group was the enthusiasm of the Clerk of the Privy Council, Gordon Robertson, for horizontal features. The two main changes in this connection were the creation of ministerial committees, with their mirror committees of deputy ministers, and the initiation of peer group appraisal of deputy ministers around 1967 (Bourgault et al., 1993).

The functioning of the peer group goes further than horizontal management. Its corporate culture implies a holistic and long-term integration effort under the formal authority and coordination of the Privy Council. Under this influence, it is expected that the interests of the government prevail over each ministry's own interests. Its members are to have a shared vision and their actions are coordinated by a corporate plan supported by diverse managerial tools such as the evaluation by peers. The corporate culture is omnipresent, influencing the criteria for selection of the DMs, their formation, and the support available to them, as well as encouraging the DMs to socialize together. It is so pervasive that authors such as Savoie characterize it as 'Court Management' (Savoie, 1999). The leadership of the Clerk of the Privy Council is essential to the functioning of the peer group. As the leader of the DMs' community, he or she creates a common perspective, animates the group, steers their orientation, offers personal support, protects the integrity of the management systems, and ensures their periodic revision (Bourgault, 2007b).

Professional Body

In Canada, unlike France, deputy ministers do not belong to a *grand corps* such as the Inspection générale des Finances, the Ingénieurs des mines, the Préfectoral, or the Conseillers d'État, the Cour des Comptes, to name just a few of the 10 bodies to which the *directeurs de cabinet*, *directeurs généraux*, and *secrétaires généraux* of the ministries (each of whom has a portion of the role of a DM in Canada) generally belong (Aberbach et al., 1981: 39); in France there is no single bureaucratic head, since the coordination and direction are done through a political aide (*directeur de cabinet*) who is generally on leave from his/her administrative assignment; this person is in charge of all the ministerial cabinet, which includes the political cabinet (headed by a *Chef de cabinet*) and technical and policy assistants; the cabinet coordinates the work of central directors and regional directors, all of whom are subjected to discretionary nominations and, nevertheless, mostly come from within the administration. And unlike their US equivalents, the positions at the senior or deputy minister level in Canada are permanent: they have a reasonable expectation of continuity if they do their jobs properly and behave appropriately. So there is a functional grouping of these strategic officials who are with the government for an extended period.

The DM category as such is an administrative classification for officials who occupy the position of administrative department head. On the career path, it comes after the EX category, which consists primarily of assistant deputy ministers and directors. Formally, it is not a professional body one enters at a low level and that then defines the course of one's career. Informally, though, the DM category has taken on some of the characteristics of a professional body over the years: these people have a say in selection, in management of the DM group, in individual appraisal, in the development of corporate culture, in operations, and in policies.

Functional Cohesion: Selection, Coordination, Appraisal

The peer group's routine has changed over the past 20 years. At present, the DM breakfast occurs every Wednesday morning from 8:00 to 9:00 a.m. It features the Clerk of the Privy Council and deals with operational issues as well as a debriefing of Tuesday's cabinet meeting. During the 1990s, there was also a weekly DM luncheon. This was a rather social event lasting from noon until two in the afternoon and also involved associate DMs, agency chiefs, and administrative tribunal heads, and was devoted to networking and learning through lectures and discussions. The Coordinating Committee of Deputy Ministers (CCDM) meets for lunch every other Wednesday; it discusses, at alternating meetings, public policy issues and management agenda issues; the meeting is attended by two different sets of DMs. The Treasury Board Secretary Advisory Committee (TBSAC), made up of some 10–12 DMs, will meet on a monthly basis to make advance comments on the projects contemplated by Treasury Board officers. The Committee of Senior Officials (COSO) meets every three weeks on average, depending on the role the Clerk of the Privy Council wants it to play: it may play a major role, giving advice on matters related to DM staffing policies, identifying 'up-and-comers' who are ready for a DM appointment, overseeing the performance appraisal system for DMs, reviewing the information on each prospective appointee, and advising the Clerk (see Bourgault, 2007b). It has also been used to monitor performance and organizational changes within departments.

The peer group also attends to longer-term issues. In 1974, it began holding annual retreats of approximately four days; some years later, these were replaced by three annual two-day seminars to identify issues and form working groups (in the fall), receive and discuss interim reports (winter), and approve final reports (June). Between those meetings, the seven or eight groups of deputy ministers, assisted by other officials, meet, conduct research, and hold discussions on the matters assigned to them, which include policy issues and organizational and administrative concerns. There may also be ad hoc or technical short-term groups created by a DM to address a specific issue, and other advisory groups created by DMs to provide advice (Bourgault, 1997a). DMs are expected to attend those meetings in person; firm believers in horizontal management, they now devote about a third of their time on government-wide corporate matters.

Of the countries we have studied, Canada has one of the most developed forms of corporate management at the top. It is time-consuming and was perceived by the first Conservative governments as a techno-bureaucratic threat (Bourgault and Nugent, 1995). Yet, it serves a self-monitoring function and also has the advantage of facilitating interdepartmental coordination and dialogue at the senior level.

Profile of Deputy Ministers

The profile of deputy ministers was studied by Porter (1965) in the late 1950s, Pond and Chartrand (1969) in the late 1960s, and Campbell and Szablowski (1979) in the 1970s. All of these studies looked at various categories of senior executives. Olsen (1980) deals with assistant deputy ministers. Osbaldeston (1989) lists arrivals and departures. Bourgault (2004) traces the professional, political, and socio-economic profile of DMs from 1867 to 2003. Swift (1993) looks at the professional profile of deputy ministers and associate deputy ministers in the 1990s. Zussman and Varette (1996) compare senior executives in the public and private sectors. We will focus on the studies by Bourgault, Swift, and Zussman and Varette because they are based on homogeneous samples of DMs.

The 2008 federal cohort consists of 33 DMs. Their average age is 54, and 42 per cent of them are women. Ten were born in Ontario, ten come from Quebec, and eight are from Western Canada. Two were born in Atlantic Canada and three are immigrants. Sixty per cent speak English as their first language, 31 per cent French, and 9 per cent were raised in another language. Three DMs of the 13 respondents had a parent working in public administration.

As for their education, 12 per cent have completed a PhD, 64 per cent a master's degree, and 21 per cent a bachelor degree. One DM has not specified any degree. Moreover, almost half of them have a multidisciplinary background (14 out of 33). Fifty-two per cent have a background in humanities (political sciences, history, sociology, and geography) and 67 per cent studied management or economics. Specialization is marginal, with 24 per cent of the DMs having studied law and 6 per cent having studied pure sciences.

Most of the DMs attended Ontario universities (67 per cent). Thirty-nine per cent of the DMs studied at Quebec universities—27 per cent at francophone institutions and 18 per cent at anglophone universities—21 per cent studied in Western Canada, and 6 per cent in Atlantic Canada. Twenty-four per cent attended university outside of Canada.

The DMs (as of 30 April 2008) have held their positions for an average of two and a half years. More precisely, 15.2 per cent of the DMs have been in the position for less than one year, 30.3 per cent between one and two years, 24.2 per cent between two and three years, 18.2 per cent between three and five years, 9.1 per cent between five and seven years, and 3 per cent for more than seven years.

Moreover, 39 per cent of the DMs had previously occupied the same position in one or more other ministries, for an average of five years. This means that 21 of the DMs had no previous experience at this level. But all of them had at least some experience as an associate or assistant DM. When they were appointed to their current positions, one DM had previously occupied a DM position for less than one year, two between one and two years, two for between two and three years, four between three and seven years, and four for more than seven years. The DM with the longest previous DM experience had previously worked ten and a half years as a DM.

Politicization

Politicization is ever a controversial issue. Some argue that governments are entitled to appoint whomever they wish and may legitimately choose people whose loyalty and political views they trust; others argue, out of principle or out of envy, that politicization kills morale, creates cliques, and leads to the appointment of people who are unable to think independently and whose competence will always be considered suspect (Bourgault and Dion, 1989c: 109). While Canada has a rocky history in this regard (Simpson, 1988: 378), it has come to consider non-politicization of the public service as a constitutional convention (Canada, Supreme Court, 1991). However, some observers, such as Aucoin (1995: 118), ask whether low levels of politicization are related to political stability and whether bureaucratic patronage is preferable to political patronage. By design and by nature, the position of DM is politicized to some extent. It is just below the minister and part of its function is to make the minister and cabinet perform well and look good: this is the functional and inescapable sense of politicization, which is totally different from ideological and partisan politicizations. It is a discretionary political appointment made by the Governor-in-Council (GIC). On the other hand, DMs must not cross the line into partisan politics. However, the sponsorship scandal raised questions in 2002 about the nature of politicization of some DMs and senior officials. The nature of the scandal, which involved senior bureaucrats administering contracts designed in the long run to benefit the ruling party, and to promote Canadian unity in violation of election laws, cast doubt on the integrity of those bureaucrats. In his report, Judge Gomery proposes measures to prevent the politicization of the DMs which, despite having triggered controversy, have not yet led to concrete measures (Gomery Commission, 2006). Most critics agree that the solutions proposed to address exceptional circumstances were out of proportion (Ardell et al., 2006).

It is difficult to define objective criteria for determining whether politicization exists. Carrying a party membership card, paying membership dues, making financial contributions, or running as a candidate might be considered clear signs, but there are shrewd citizens who contribute to both main parties or switch parties after seven or 10 years. Less formal indicators might include replacing an effective DM without valid reason, appointing someone from outside, especially a relative (even if he or she has no political involvement), or installing someone with compatible views on policy.

In 1988, after the incoming Mulroney government was accused of politicizing the function, Bourgault and Dion conducted a longitudinal study of deputy ministers (1989b: 124–51). After studying all appointments and departures from 1867 to 1988, we concluded that the number of departures during the 24-month period after an election in which there was a change in ruling party (which ranged from 2.4 per cent in 1911 to 12.5 per cent in 1984) is not significantly greater than after elections in which there was no change in government or during non-election years (an average of 7.4 per cent per year before 1959 and 9.3 per cent since 1959). We also demonstrated that recruitment was almost entirely internal and that when people leave their functions, they generally do so to retire or to occupy another attractive position in the civil service.

Judge Gomery suggests the Clerk of the Privy Council has become politicized over the past 30 years, as power concentrated around the PM. He recommends the split of the Clerk's functions; the Clerk 'should be known as Secretary to the Cabinet and his or her main role should be to represent the public service to the prime minister and the cabinet. The Privy Council Office should be renamed the Cabinet Secretariat. The Secretary of the Treasury Board should assume the title and function of head of the public service' (Gomery Commission, 2006: Recommendation 13). Many disapproved of this recommendation, being of the opinion that the role of this important actor should not be undermined (Ardell et al., 2006). We concur neither with the Judge's observation nor the recommendation; at this level the frontier separating politics and bureaucracy does not exist. DMs are employees of the state loyally serving the government of the day within the limits of the law.

Coping with Transitions

Transitions occur when there is a change in the head of government. They are more significant when there is a change in the governing party after a general election, given the time it takes to build trust and the adversarial tone of election campaigns. Transitions bring three types of changes: in politico-administrative structures (such as committees and departments), in agenda (shifting priorities), and in personnel (new ministers, new political aides, and some new senior officials). Transitions are always a key test of politicization: the more highly politicized a civil service is, the more likely it is to be shaken up and for senior officials to be replaced by others of the right stripe who enjoy the confidence of the politicians.

Let us look at what befell deputy ministers in 1984, when the Tories replaced the Liberals in government. The Conservative transition was depicted as having politicized the ranks of DMs. There was a flurry of activity, including some inflammatory statements by the PM and his Conservative entourage, and numerous skirmishes between ministers, DMs, and the ministers' strengthened chiefs of staff (Bourgault and Dion, 1990). But at the end of the day, Mulroney did not fire many more DMs in his first four years in office than Trudeau had in the previous four years (Bourgault and Dion, 1989a). When Trudeau regained office in 1980 he found all of his former deputy ministers except for four, and when Mulroney first took office in 1984, he found 31 DMs appointed by the previous government. After four years, the Liberals had changed 21 of them and the Conservatives 26; the Liberals had transferred six to other DM positions and the Conservatives four; therefore, only five were still serving the Liberals after four years and one was still serving the Tories. The bottom line is that the difference is slight. The Tories might well argue that it was easy for the Liberals to look good, since Clark's previous Tory government was in office for only a few months and did not have time to bring in its own people.

To promote stability and to reduce political appointments, Gomery's report recommends naming DMs and senior public servants for a minimum of three years, with the expectation that most appointments would last at least five years (Gomery Commission, 2006: Recommendation 6). Despite the rigidity of this recommendation, the administrative community seems to support this idea (Ardell et al., 2006). In our view, this is already what is generally understood on the Hill. Since exceptions always have to be permitted, we do not see what this new rule could bring to the process.

Coping with Minority Governments

While a majority government is assured that it will stay in power for a predictable time, a minority government does not have the same control over its lifespan, the procedures of the House of Commons, and the parliamentary committees. The committees may be excessively zealous in questioning bureaucrats and the ministers. A minority government also fears the possibility of a non-confidence vote, which would precipitate an election. Any government would prefer elections to be held when they have a good chance of re-election. All these factors affect the government's expectations of the DMs' performance.

It would be expected that DMs would have a greater influence on their ministers in a minority government because of the ministers' obvious vulnerability. But interviews conducted in 2007 (Bourgault, 2007c) revealed an unexpected relationship. Minority governments avoid controversial policy issues, pay much attention to administrative details, and may exert more control on management and communications. In turn, senior officials may self-censure to avoid controversy and spend more time dealing with crises, and are expected to accommodate short-term solutions that the administration considers less than ideal, but which are necessary political compromises. The minister would expect his DM to offer realistic propositions which can be implemented quickly. DMs are also expected to be very careful in conducting the government's business, as any mistake could bring about the fall of the government.

Minister's Satisfaction

The discretionary nature of the appointment of DMs and their serving 'at pleasure' fuel an ongoing discussion about the merit system in the public service. The Gomery report stimulates debate by proposing that government 'adopt an open and competitive process for the selection of DMs... where applicants are vetted by a committee of bureaucrats, politicians and outside experts' (Gomery Commission, 2006: Recommendation 12). Judge Gomery agrees that the actual appointment process is an invitation to systemic politicization of the public service, while others claim that Canada is still the country in which politics and administration are most sharply separated, and that the appointment system is designed to provide elected officials with compatible senior bureaucrats capable of helping them implement the program they promised the House. Some critics of the Gomery propositions believe that the Prime Minister needs to ensure that his or her agenda will be implemented in administrative terms and that appointing the DMs is essential to do so (Brown, 2006). Our findings demonstrate that the ministers were not more satisfied with DMs they appointed themselves than with those they kept from preceding governments (Bourgault, 1997c). In the same vein, the tenth recommendation of the Commission suggests removing 'the provisions that enable political staff who have worked for a minister for three years to be appointed to a public service position without competition' and the eighteenth proposes to 'end political involvement in the selection of CEOs and directors of Crown corporations'. These recommendations have triggered less controversy, even if a Globe and Mail journalist remarks 'two of Ottawa's very best deputy ministers today were once Conservative staffers' (Simpson, 2006). The reality is that far more than two fit this description, and that they served as DMs for the other party in power!

Are the politicians really pleased with their DMs? Does it make a difference whether they chose the DMs? With what are they most satisfied and dissatisfied? A 1995 study of former Conservative ministers surveyed half of the 200 or so minister/DM pairings under the Conservative governments of the 1984–93 period. Twenty-one former ministers were interviewed (Bourgault, 1997c: 19). It was found that 81 per cent of ministers were satisfied or very satisfied with their DMs, comparable to the rate found in 1986 in Quebec among former PQ ministers (Bourgault and Dion, 1989a). Most of the dissatisfaction reported by Conservative ministers was caused by two people closely identified with the Liberals and by two others brought in from outside by the Conservatives themselves. In fact, the overall satisfaction rate was the same for DMs they themselves had chosen as for those inherited from the Liberals.

The Conservative ministers were particularly satisfied with the DMs' loyalty, competence, political judgment, willingness to work, discretion, respect for ministerial authority, and performance before House committees, all but the last of which are traditional values of the Canadian public service. They were less satisfied with the DMs' influence in the bureaucracy (29 per cent), management skills (19 per cent), policy-making capacities (19 per cent), ideological compatibility (19 per cent), decision-making abilities (18 per cent), program evaluation skills (18 per cent), and ability to persuade clients and pressure groups (18 per cent). We were expecting the ideological gap; indeed, we thought it might be wider. The dissatisfaction with management, policy-making, and program evaluation skills says a good deal about the disillusionment outsiders may experience after entering government. It may also be consistent with the observations Zussman and Varette (1996) made about the specific career path of DMs; it does not appear that great importance is attached to practical operational experience. What is more surprising is the perceived lack of ability to persuade colleagues, which is the greatest source of dissatisfaction by far. It may be due to normal ministerial impatience with implementing their agenda and removing obstacles, or perhaps to the force of peer power in Ottawa, where an individual DM has to cope with the horizontal system.

Multiple Accountability

The accountability system for deputy ministers has been described as multiple, complex, and at times contradictory. The accountability of the DMs depends on the legal obligations, the powers and the mandates received from the PM, the minister, the Clerk of the Privy Council, central bodies, Parliament, and certain of its agents. A single action can imply different accountabilities on various aspects and contradictions are possible.

Canadian government requires a DM's loyalty to the government's agenda and to the PM as the leader of the government. Moreover, a DM is appointed by cabinet only after being recommended by the PM, so the PM is ultimately the one to whom the DM owes his or her job. The DM is then accountable to the PM for supporting his or her minister and for the application of programs and mandates given by the PM or the cabinet (Bourgault 2006).

According to legislation, the DM is required to assist and serve the minister by taking charge of the daily management of the ministry. Because of the appointment process, the DM may also owe a debt of loyalty to his or her minister (Bourgault, 2006).

The DM operates under the coordinating umbrella of the Clerk of the Privy Council, who was named 'Head of the Public Service' (including DMs) in 1993. Regarded as the 'senior Deputy Minister of the Public Service' (Murray, quoted in Bourgault, 2007a), the Clerk assumes the orientation and coordination of the DM's community at the administrative and social level; he or she supervises the coordination of actions, develops long-term vision, ensures adherence to the governmental agenda, watches performance, promotes collaboration between DMs and organizes social events for DMs (Bourgault, 2007a). The Clerk processes all the preparations for the submission of candidates for DM appointments to the PM and acts as the Prime Minister's deputy minister, which gives him or her some authority over the other deputy ministers. These considerations, taken together, make the DM accountable to some extent to the Clerk. The DM is accountable to the Clerk for his or her ministry's performance and the DM's own performance, for translating the priorities of the Clerk (and thus the priorities of the PM and government) into the activities of the ministry, and for following any particular instructions given by the Clerk (Bourgault, 2006).

The DM is also accountable to the central bodies, which transmit the directives of the cabinet and the ministerial committees. Since these bodies have delegated powers to the DM, such as human resources, finance, and delivering public goods, he or she is accountable for them (Bourgault, 2006).

Some Acts also create specific areas of accountability for DMs; for example, DMs report to Treasury Board on resource management, to the Public Service Commission on staffing processes, to House standing committees when called to testify. Moreover, the DM is answerable to Parliament and its committees for the work of his or her ministry (Bourgault, 2006). Finally, in real life, they also report to the DM community as a whole, since their performance appraisal is processed through COSO, and since they must answer questions from their colleagues at the numerous weekly DM community meetings.

The challenge for the DM is therefore act so as to satisfy the objectives and norms of all these other actors and to be accountable to each of them (Bourgault, 2006)—and still perform coherent and meaningful action.

The multiplicity of DM accountability requirements makes the issue quite complex. 'They are marching to several drums', Langford (1984) comments, and asks whether they are not creating their own beat to the cacophony of sounds. Plumptre, citing the Lambert Commission, observes that 'Some deputies maintain that they are, in effect, accountable only to themselves, and claim to measure their performance against their own standards of excellence' (Plumptre, 1987: 374).

To clarify the situation, we should consider the different meanings of the term 'accountability'. Accountability means 'to account for'. The question then is: account for what, to whom, on what subjects, in how much detail, and with what responsibility for outcomes? British writers have divided the concept into three components: responsibility, reportability, and answerability. DMs are not politically responsible; that responsibility belongs to the minister, who can be asked to resign by a political body. DMs do bear administrative responsibility for their decisions and actions to the minister, the Clerk, and the central agencies administering particular Acts. They have been known to request transfers when things go badly. DMs are responsible for their own personal conduct to the government and the DM community. DMs are also required to report, which means providing requested information. They report to the minister on all issues the minister may have to deal with, to the House on semi-annual departmental reports and on any matter the House requests, to the Auditor General on any matter subject to his jurisdiction; and to the DM community on matters that have been delegated to it. In addition, DMs are answerable to House committees, which means they have to provide factual information without taking a stand or defending or promoting any political position or governmental policy. They must supply facts and figures and explain why a particular course of action was chosen.

Administrative accountability can be exercised through performance appraisals and sanctioned through bonuses, promotions, and constructive reassignments (Bourgault, 1990: 24–5). Canada was the first country to introduce performance appraisals for its most senior personnel (Bourgault et al., 1993). Most developed countries now have systems of this type for their top civil servants (Bourgault, 1997b). The Canadian process is distinctive in that it is collegial, inclusive, participatory, and, above all, creates incentives and a culture to support collaboration. A DM may write a short report on his or her achievements over the year in terms of his or her mandate, as agreed with the Clerk. A visiting committee formed by COSO will meet with the minister and the DM and report to COSO's evaluation committee, which also receives reports on the person from the central agencies. The committee reports to the Clerk, who makes recommendations to the Prime Minister. The PM makes the final decision on the appraisal. The Clerk will then meet with the DM and brief him or her on the results.

Conclusions and Prospects

The nature of the DM's job has been affected by recent developments such as new approaches to answerability, state–citizenry relations, fiscal responsibility, public management, the challenges of new technologies and globalization, and the DM's evolving role, which is changing from manager to 'empowerer'.

Under the new systems of answerability, DMs are required to appear before standing committees on behalf of ministers and answer questions without crossing the fine line and engaging in political debate, and they must present reports on goals, outcomes, and resource use.

New conceptions of state–citizenry relations are affecting departmental operations as a whole: policy-making and service delivery processes are shifting from command-style models to more participative models; more information is being released, making relations with the media, pressure groups, and the provinces trickier for senior officials. DMs must communicate with more people and organizations than ever before, all of whom are claiming the right to be heard: citizens no longer see themselves as subjects of the state; rather, they consider the state to be their servant.

Fiscal constraint has meant budget and program cuts, workforce reductions, and loss of capacity and expertise, making policy decisions more difficult and forcing DMs to deal with external, less predictable resources.

New approaches to public management have ushered in extensive use of contracting as outsourcing and partnering increase. As a result, clearly defined inputs, deliverables, and expected outcomes must be formulated. They have also caused problems with grant management and prompted criticism in cases where resources for the proper control of the use of grants were lacking, even as departments were being asked to deliver more swiftly, more smoothly, and on a more receiver-friendly basis. In this regard, the organization is learning and DMs have to answer complex questions, keep sight of overall objectives, and take corrective action when necessary. (A recent example of the latter is the action plan Minister Jane Stewart brought before the House in response to the Auditor General's report on Human Resources Development Canada in the spring of 2000.)

Globalization is making the DM's job more demanding. DMs no longer control the flow of information; the pressure groups they deal with are able to bypass policy rules through information technology (the free movement of capital is one example); their counterparts are able rapidly to develop joint negotiating positions. As a result, DMs must be on their toes and attentive to their own organization's capacities.

Because of all these demands deputy ministers may find themselves overwhelmed and must rely heavily on their staff. They must impart a vision to them, and that vision must evolve with changing challenges. They must make things happen through people they have enabled and whom they trust. Building that type of relationship with their assistants and subordinates is one of the most critical parts of their new role.

Important Terms and Concepts

Accounting Officer
chief of staff
Committee of Senior Officials (COSO)
deputy minister (DM)
discretionary appointment
Parliamentary Budget Officer
Public Servants Disclosure Protection Tribunal
selection

Study Questions

1. How are deputy ministers designated, selected, appointed, and dismissed?
2. What is the nature of the politically sensitive world that DMs inhabit, and how do they manage to survive within it? What are the relative chances of politicization?
3. What duties does the DM owe to the political realm?
4. What is the DM's peer group, and what is their relative importance in his or her professional life?
5. What did Gomery, its critics, and those promoting the Federal Accountability Act have to say about the role of DMs, and what do you think Bourgault's take on all these is?
6. What does Bourgault mean when he says that 'The accountability system for deputy ministers has been described as multiple, complex, and at times contradictory'?

Useful Websites

Current deputy ministers, Government of Canada:

www2.parl.gc.ca/parlinfo/Compilations/Addresses/DeputyMinister.aspx

Alex Smith. 2008. *The Accountability of Accounting Officers before Parliamentary Committees.* Ottawa: Library of Parliament.

www2.parl.gc.ca/Content/LOP/ResearchPublications/prb0818-e.htm

Jacques Bourgault delivers the 2007 Galimberti Lecture at IPAC: 'The Changing Role of the Deputy Minister in Canadian Governments'.

www.ipac.ca/documents/2007Galimeberti%20LectureEnglish-FINAL.pdf

References

Aberbach, J., R. Putnam, and B. Rockman. 1981. *Bureaucrats and Politicians in Western Democracies.* Cambridge, Mass.: Harvard University Press.

Ardell, Bill, et al. 2006. 'Letter to the Prime Minister on the Federal Sponsorship Scandal', IPAC.

Aucoin, P. 1995. 'Politicians, Public Servants, and Public Management: Getting Government Right', in B. Guy Peters and Donald J. Savoie, eds, *Governance in a Changing Environment.* Montreal and Kingston: CCMD/McGill-Queen's University Press, 113–37.

Bourgault, J. 1990. 'Rules and Practices of Dismissal in the Canadian Higher Civil Service', in A.W. Neilson, ed., *Getting the Pink Slip.* Toronto: IPAC, 18–44.

———. 1997a. 'De Kafka au Net: la lutte de tous les instants pour le contrôle de l'agenda chez les sous-ministres canadiens', *Gestion, revue internationale de gestion* 22, 2: 18–26.

———. 1997b. 'La gestion de la performance dans la haute fonction publique: quelques cas issus du modèle de Whitehall', in M.M. Guay, ed., *Performance et secteur public, réalités, enjeux et paradoxes.* Montreal: PUQ, 193–213.

———. 1997c. *The Satisfaction of Ministers with the Performance of their Deputy Ministers during the Mulroney Governments: 1984–1993.* Ottawa: Canadian Centre for Management Development, Research Paper No. 22.

———. 2004. *Le profil des sous-ministres du gouvernement du Canada.* Ottawa, École de la fonction publique du Canada.

———. 2006. 'Le rôle du sous-ministre du Gouvernement du Canada: sa responsabilité et sa reddition de comptes', in Canada, *Commission d'enquête sur le programme de commandites et les activités publicitaires. Rétablir l'imputabilité. Études.* Volume 1, Le Parlement, les ministres et les sous-ministres. Ottawa, la Commission, 283–329.

———. 2007a. 'Les facteurs contributifs au leadership du greffier dans la fonction publique du Canada', *Administration publique du Canada Canadian Public Administration* 50 (hiver): 541–71.

———. 2007b. 'La gestion corporative au sommet des gouvernements: la pratique canadienne', *Revue internationale des sciences administratives* 73 (juin): 283–300.

———. 2007c. 'Inaugural Galimberti Memorial Lecture: The Changing Role of the Deputy Minister in Canadian Governments'. IPAC Annual Conference, Winnipeg.

———, and S. Dion. 1989a. 'Brian Mulroney a-t-il politisé les sous-ministres?', *Canadian Public Administration* 32, 1: 63–84.

———, and ———. 1989b. 'Governments Come and Go, But What of Senior Civil Servants? Canadian Deputy Ministers and Transitions in Power (1867–1987)', *Governance* 2, 3: 124–51.

———, and ———. 1989c. 'Les gouvernements anti-bureaucratiques face à la haute fonction publique: une comparaison Québec-Ottawa', *Politiques et management public* 7, 2: 97–118.

———, and ———. 1990. 'Managing Conflicts in a Context of Government Change: Lessons from the Federal Government of Canada, 1984–1988', *International Journal for Conflict Management* 1, 4: 375–96.

———, and ———. 1991. *The Changing Profile of Federal Deputy Ministers: 1867–1988.* Ottawa: Canadian Centre for Management Development.

———, ———, and M. Lemay. 1993. 'Performance Appraisals of Top Civil Servants: Creating a Corporate Culture', *Public Administration Review* 53, 1: 73–80.

———, and P. Nugent. 1995. 'Les transitions de gouvernement et la théorie des conflits: le cas de la transition de 1984 au gouvernement du Canada', *Revue Canadienne de Sciences Administratives* 12, 1: 15–26.

Brown, Jim. 2006. 'Gomery Reform Proposals Spark Backlash among Political, Business Elite', Canadian Press Newswire, 6 Mar 2006.

Burns, R.M. 1961. 'The Role of the Deputy Minister', *Canadian Public Administration* 4: 357–62.

Campbell, E.C., and G.J. Szlablowski. 1979. *The Superbureaucrats.* Toronto: Macmillan.

Canada. 1985. *Report of the Special Committee on Reform of the House of Commons* (James A. McGrath, chair). Ottawa: House of Commons.

Canada, Privy Council Office. 1987. *The Office of Deputy Minister*, rev. edn. Ottawa.

Canada, Royal Commission on Financial Management and Accountability (Lambert Commission). 1979. *Final Report.* Ottawa.

Canada, Royal Commission of Inquiry into the Sponsorship Program and Advertising Activities (Gomery Commission). 2005. *Who Is Responsible?* Phase 1 Report. Ottawa.

———. 2006. *Restoring Accountability.* Phase 2 Report. Ottawa.

Canada, Supreme Court. 1991. *Osborne v. Canada* 2 S.C.R. 69.

Des Roches, J.M. 1962. 'The Evolution of the Organization of the Federal Government of Canada', *Canadian Public Administration* 5: 411–23.

Granatstein, J. 1982. *The Ottawa Men.* Toronto: Oxford University Press.

Greene, Ian. 1990. 'Conflict of Interest and the Canadian Constitution: An Analysis of Conflict of Interest for Canadian Cabinet Ministers', *Canadian Journal of Political Science* 23, 2: 233–56.

Hay, M.A. 1982. 'Understanding the PCO: The Ultimate Facilitator', *Optimum* 13, 1: 5–21.

Heintzman, R. 1997. 'Introduction', in J. Bourgault et al., *Public Administration and Public Management: Canadian Experiences.* Quebec City: Publications du Québec, 1–13.

Hodgetts, J.E. 1973. *The Canadian Public Service.* Toronto: University of Toronto Press.

Kernaghan, K., and D. Siegel. 1991. *Public Administration in Canada.* Scarborough, Ont.: Nelson.

Langford, J. 1984. 'Responsibility in the Senior Public Service: Marching to Several Drummers', *Canadian Public Administration* 27, 4: 513–21.

Mintzberg, H., and J. Bourgault. 2000. *Managing Publicly.* Toronto: IPAC.

Olsen, D. 1980. *The State Elite in Canadian Society.* Toronto: McClelland & Stewart.

Osbaldeston, G. 1989. *Keeping Deputy Ministers Accountable.* Scarborough, Ont.: McGraw-Hill Ryerson.

———. 1992. *Organizing to Govern.* Toronto: McGraw-Hill Ryerson.

Plasse, M. 1992. 'Les chefs de cabinets ministériels du gouvernement fédéral canadien: rôle et relation avec la haute fonction publique', *Canadian Public Administration* 30, 3: 317–38.

Plumptre, T. 1987. 'New Perspectives on the Role of the Deputy Minister', *Canadian Public Administration* 30, 3: 376–98.

Pond, K.L., and P.J. Chartrand. 1969. 'Cheminement des carrières de direction dans la fonction publique au Canada', *Relations industrielles* 4, 2: 318–29.

Porter, J. 1965. *The Vertical Mosaic.* Toronto: University of Toronto Press.

Savoie, D. 1999. *Governing from the Centre.* Toronto: University of Toronto Press.

Simpson, J. 1988. *Spoils of Power.* Toronto: Collins.

———. 2006. 'The Gomery Reforms Should First Do No Harm', *The Globe and Mail*, 28 Feb., A1.

Sutherland, S. 1991. 'The Al Mashat Affair: Administrative Accountability in Parliamentary Institutions', *Canadian Public Administration* 34, 4: 573–603.

Swift, F. 1993. *Strategic Management in the Public Service: The Changing Role of the Deputy Minister.* Ottawa: Canadian Centre for Management Development.

Zussman, D., and S. Varette. 1996. 'Today's Leaders: Career Trends of Canada's Private and Public Sector Executives'. Ottawa: Public Management Research Centre and University of Ottawa.

29 Information, Technology, and Canadian Public Administration

David C.G. Brown

University students today have grown up with the Internet and cellular telephones and take them as much for granted as their parents took land-line telephones. And yet even they are aware that the technology is constantly changing and successive waves of new applications are creating new forms of social interaction, economic activity, and ways of doing things (Negroponte, 1995; Tapscott and Caston, 1993). If technology is having this kind of open-ended impact on daily living, its effects on public administration are at least as profound and unpredictable (Snellen and van de Donk, 1998).

Information and technology have been an integral part of public administration from the earliest forms of empire and social governance. Kings had scribes to record their laws and lesser decisions and to make them known, in order to give them a chance of being obeyed. Information was needed about who the subjects were, where they lived, and what they did. Records were needed to keep track of taxes collected and how they were spent, as well as to memorialize the acts of the kings for posterity. These records helped to define the society to itself and to others and to lay the foundations of the modern state. Over time, the nature of the state has been directly tied to the technology for keeping and transmitting records—an administration based on paper records could be larger and more sophisticated than one where the writing medium was stone tablets (Innis, 1950).

This dynamic relationship between information, its technological medium, and governance continues to be a characteristic of public administration in Canada and every other country in the world (Fountain, 2001a). Yet, it is an aspect of public administration that tends to receive less academic attention than the other foundations of public administration, the management of financial and human resources (although for recent Canadian book-length treatments of this and related topics, see Barney, 2005; Borins et al., 2007; Oliver and Sanders, 2004; and Roy, 2006). This chapter is a modest addition to that literature.

In any discussion, it is important to define the terms used. There are two that are particularly important for the purposes of this chapter and two others that are lurking in the background. The first is **information**. The Canadian Oxford Dictionary defines information as 'something told' or knowledge. Information theorists refine this to describe a hierarchy—inspired perhaps by atomic theory—of data, information, and knowledge, each level having a 'value added' building on the ones below it. Some add a fourth level—wisdom—as a reminder that judgment is increasingly a factor in how information is used. In any case, these are all terms to describe content or, in Marshall McLuhan's characterization, the message (McLuhan, 1964).

The second term is technology, which is both the medium and, as political philosophers have observed (Ellul, 1964), the society-shaping dynamic. Our Canadian Oxford Dictionary definition is 'the study or use of the mechanical arts or applied sciences'. This is a very broad definition that attempts to capture the fact that technology takes many forms and is as old as society. It hints at links to engineering, but at its root is based on the Greek word for 'art'. This multi-disciplinary tension between art and science is still very much part of the story.

Our contemporary interest in information and technology comes from the world that has been shaped by the introduction of the Internet and the convergence between several strands of technology—telecommunications, computing and broadcasting—that it represents (Rowland, 2006). In North America we tend to refer to these technological forces as '**information technology**' (**IT**), even though the term '**information and communications technologies**' (**ICTs**) is more accurate and more widely used in the rest of the world. So when the terms 'IT' or 'technology' are used in this chapter they should be understood as encompassing the range of technologies that have been the dominant influences since the mid-1990s. Similarly, the term 'information management' (IM) refers to the various methodologies that have emerged for organizing and using information, especially in the environment created by IT. IT and IM are as inextricably linked as yin and yang, but they do represent distinct starting points in the art and science of public administration.

This chapter explores five elements of the story of information and technology in Canadian public administration. It starts by looking at the promise of IT and the discipline that it has spawned: e-government. The harnessing of information and technology has been a critical underpinning of New Public Management thinking, and a second part of the discussion is to look at the catalytic effects of a central tenet of NPM, a focus on the citizen. The third section considers—briefly, as it is a topic in itself—politics and policy-making in the electronic environment; in effect what is happening at the front end of public administration. The heart of the chapter is the fourth section, which looks at the new spheres and methods of public administration created by IT and IM, and the chapter concludes with a look at their relationship to public sector reform.

If there is an underlying message in this discussion it is that we are in a world where everything is new but nothing is new. As Gow and Hodgetts have observed, 'The public service is part of the development of society. . . . it reflects the society in which it operates, while acting on that same society, shaping it' (Gow and Hodgetts, 2003: 195). We live in a society that more than ever is shaped by information and technology and the implications for public administration are enormous.

The Promise of Information Technology

There is a certain inherent optimism in the application of information technology to public administration, sometimes to the point of wishful thinking. Almost by definition, the potential exceeds the reality and certainly the supply exceeds the demand. It is also an inherently risky field, as invariably the technologies—and thinking about how they can be used—will be different at the beginning of an IT-enabled project or activity than at its end. An important part of this administrative world, therefore, is managing risks and expectations, not to mention costs.

This is not to underestimate the very real and important changes that have been made in public administration in a relatively short time or the speed with which change continues to happen. Indeed, government is faced with a dilemma, because it needs to adjust to externally driven technological forces, which influence every corner of Canadian society, while playing a constructive role in helping Canadians adjust to those forces. As discussed later in this chapter, one result is a very different relationship with the private sector than occurs in other areas of public administration. The tapestry is even richer, when it is considered that technology is both a focus of public policy (a major new industry) and an enabler, an asset to be managed as well as a resource to use in support of other activities, creating a new management discipline that maintains an uneasy balance between medium and content.

These competing elements have given rise to a great deal of thought and discussion within government, but it is fair to say that just as much of the technology has been externally generated, so too have many (if not most) of the ideas on how it should be used. These can be loosely categorized under the heading of *e-commerce*, which has in turn generated the emerging discipline of *e-government*. These rapidly evolving disciplines shape much of the day-to-day application of information and technology in Canadian public administration.

E-Commerce and E-Government

The starting point is electronic commerce. ('**E-commerce**' is a shorthand that allows speakers at conferences to play with e-variants such as 'enabled' or 'enhanced'.) The term has been in use since the early 1980s and tends to focus on online sales and other transactions between businesses and their clients as well as their suppliers. The early foundation was electronic data interchange (EDI), which permitted the sharing of digital information over telephone lines as well as the electronic transfer of funds. The financial industries were leaders in this field and developed applications such as telephone banking and automatic teller machines (ATMs), which combined greater customer control over their finances with cost and efficiency savings for the banks (generated at least in part by the banks transferring basic clerical functions to the customer). These technologies are by now well established, and the ATM and its online offspring in many ways are the 'gold standard' when government provides electronic services to citizens, even though they may not always be as straightforward as managing your own bank or credit card account.

The introduction of the Internet, with its 'graphic user interface', took e-commerce to another level, as its gurus like to say. In fairly short order, the entire range of transactions involving goods and services was available online, using **electronic service delivery (ESD)** tools and methodologies. These were backed up by bringing into the electronic environment the relationships that companies have with their suppliers (e-procurement and supply chain management) as well as internally. The process facilitated the growth and integration of global corporations but also allowed for a wide range of employment relationships, including a growth in tele-working and self-employment.

The driving focus, however, was client-relationship management (CRM), supported by computer-enabled consolidation of data about all aspects of the organization's relationship with the customer. At the 'business' end, this led to consolidation of all the ways ('channels') in which businesses dealt with their clients—by telephone, mail, fax, kiosk, and in person, as well as online—while behind the scenes came the creation of 'data warehouses' and 'data mining' to consolidate and exploit the information that was collected. This in turn gave rise to a new set of day-to-day headaches and challenges, including meeting requirements for security against hackers and other potential forms of tampering, protection of personal information, and identity management in order to maintain the integrity and confidentiality of the increasingly precious database.

Government was not immune to these developments. From the outset, the private sector encouraged government to adopt the new methodologies, both in order to modernize public administration—a long-standing private sector preoccupation—and to establish the public sector as a client for IT goods and services, given that governments are among the largest institutions in the country. While initially not linked to New Public Management, the use of IT rapidly became an integral part of efforts to reinvent and re-engineer government (Andersen, 1999). Perhaps most importantly, vocal segments of the public began asking government to deal with them in the same way that banks, booksellers, and other successful online service providers did. The clincher was the prospect of major savings, even 'doing more with less', through investments in IT when governments faced a major fiscal crunch just at the time that the Internet was coming into the mainstream.

The result has been the emergence of a discipline of e-government, the public sector companion to e-commerce. While definitions of e-government vary, its starting point is the application of technology in the areas of the public sector analogous to where it is in use in the private sector. This began with government financial transactions but has included the full adoption of electronic service delivery, client relationship management, and data management methodologies. All governments in Canada have become fully automated environments in their internal communications and information management, closely resembling in that respect large Canadian corporations and universities. This has included moving aggressively towards primarily online environments in the provision of services to government (as opposed to the public) and in buying goods and services for government from the private sector (e-procurement).

Consideration of e-government of course has to take account of the differences between government and the private sector and therefore how far the e-commerce model can be applied. A broad view is that IT shapes—and will be increasingly dominant—in all of the state's relationships (Brown, 2005). These are most notably how the state interacts with society and the economy, with the citizen and governance institutions, with the international environment, and within itself. The first of these is the focus of public policy, the second raises issues that are addressed under the heading of e-democracy, the third is the stuff of globalization and international relations, while the fourth can be seen as the domain of public administration. The loop is closed, however, as public administration encompasses public sector institutions and processes that are set up to deal with the three other sets of relationships. It is safe to say that no area is untouched by technology and increasingly technology provides the substance as well as the medium.

An Evolving Public Sector Environment

The management and use of information technology has long been a feature of Canadian government. The Constitution Act, 1867 assigns the federal government responsibility for the postal service as well as for railways and telegraph lines that cross provincial boundaries. This has provided the basis for later court rulings assigning Ottawa jurisdiction over telephones, radio, television, and the Internet. At the same time, provinces have developed their own roles in several of these areas that touch on their interests and responsibilities, notably the establishment of provincially owned telephone companies in Western Canada and provincial educational radio and television initiatives.

This evolution was paralleled by the establishment, in the federal government, of departments and regulatory agencies, notably the establishment of a Department of Communications in 1969 that by 1980 had assumed responsibility for both the hardware and the software aspects of telecommunications, broadcasting, and related technologies, thus anticipating their later convergence. The first Canadian regulatory body, the Board of Railway Commissioners, was given authority over telegraphs and the newly regulated telephone industry when it was established in 1908, a mandate that through several evolutions became a central concern of the current Canadian Radio-Television and Telecommunications Commission (CRTC).

These developments were paralleled in the operations of the federal government. It adopted the telephone in the first part of the twentieth century, along with the rest of society, and was also an early user of electronic data processing (computers) after World War II. Based on the advice of the Glassco commission, two common service agencies were established in the 1960s, the Government Telecommunications Agency in the Department of Communications, which supported the federal government's need to operate across the country, and the Computer Services Agency (CSA) in the Department of Supply and Services. In its earliest form, the CSA provided mainframe computing services to government, although individual departments with large-scale requirements, notably Revenue Canada and National Defence, developed their own computing capacity.

In the 1970s and 1980s, science and technology became an increasingly important part of industrial policy and progressively more integrated with the federal department concerned with that area of public policy. By the early 1990s, the growing role of the telecommunications industry and the convergence of computing—a largely unregulated industry—with telecommunications, an area with a long history of government involvement, created a tension between the industry and the communications departments.

The tension came to a head in June 1993 with the reorganization of the machinery of government carried out by Prime Minister Kim Campbell when she formed her cabinet. Every new Prime Minister needs to think about how they wish to organize their ministry and the relationships among government departments. Based on briefings from the Privy Council Office, Campbell made an ambitious series of changes, creating several new departments in areas of public policy where government was expected to play a strong role in the future. Three of these were Industry ('a modern industry department that was attuned to the information revolution and the knowledge economy'), including the hardware side of the old Department of Communications; Human Resources Development; and Canadian Heritage, bringing together federal programs relating to Canadian culture and identity (Mitchell, 2002: 3). The latter included the software side of Communications, including cultural development in a digital environment. Apart from some adjustment in the human resources development portfolio, these changes have remained in place through three subsequent governments of both major political stripes.

The public policy–oriented organizational changes were matched in the Campbell reorganization by changes in central and common service agency responsibilities within government. Drawing on private sector organizational models, a Chief Information Officer (CIO) was appointed within the Treasury Board Secretariat to oversee the use of IT and IM in public administration. In due course this brought together efforts to manage the government's expanding investment in IT, to adopt IT in areas of public administration such as financial and human resources management, and to use technology to improve government services to the public. These were largely policy and horizontal coordination roles in support of Treasury Board ministers. The development and management of new IT-based services to government was assigned to the Government Telecommunications and Informatics Services (GTIS), which combined the previous telecommunications and computer services agencies in a new Department of Public Works and Government Services Canada (PWGSC). Although GTIS has since been recast as the Information Technology Services Branch (ITSB), the basic elements of these common service arrangements also continue to be in place.

The government's recent institutional stability can be explained by policy initiatives that were taken in the aftermath of the 1993 reorganization and that, in retrospect, seem to have captured successfully the sea change that was happening in the larger economy with the introduction of the Internet and its offspring. Two were of particular importance. The first was the appointment by Prime Minister Jean Chrétien, shortly after coming into office in late 1993, of an Information Highway Advisory Council (IHAC). The IHAC was made up of knowledgeable individuals drawn from the IT industry and a wide range of civil society organizations. The several hundred recommendations in its two reports, in 1995 and 1997, set a broad policy framework based on four objectives of government policy: a consumer-driven policy environment conducive to innovation; Canadian content online to strengthen Canadian culture; access by all to the information highway; and better, more affordable government services, with government serving as a model user of the information and a catalyst for the move to the information society more generally (IHAC, 1995, 1997).

The IHAC reports led to a range of initiatives under the theme of Connecting Canadians to develop electronic infrastructure, digitize cultural holdings, and promote access to the Internet. The latter included programs such as SchoolNet, which succeeded in linking every school in Canada to the Internet, and similar initiatives with respect to Canadian libraries, remote communities, and First Nations bands. Government departments also began to establish a presence on the World Wide Web, and the federal government's Internet portal, the **Canada Site** (*www.canada.gc.ca*), was established in 1995.

Two other developments played an important part in shaping the federal government's use of technology during this period. The first was the advent of the year 2000, also known as Y2K, and the apprehended 'millennium bug'. In the early history of computing, memory space for data input was at a premium and the practice developed of using only the last two digits when recording the year in a date. While this posed no problems in the middle of the twentieth century, the realization grew as the end of the century drew near that computers with two-digit dates would consider the transition from 1999 to 2000 to be a move back in time rather than forward, with unknown but potentially disastrous consequences. Companies and governments around the world therefore made a major investment, ostensibly to fix the date problem, but in practice to upgrade their computing environments. In the event, there were few problems—whether because the issue had been dealt with or because it was not as serious as originally thought—but it did provide the occasion for a quantum leap forward in the adoption of information technology by government.

In the wake of the Y2K preparations, the federal government established Government On-Line (GOL), an aggressive effort to place government services to the public on the Internet. Originally launched in 1999, and re-launched with the new millennium on 1 January 2001, GOL continued until 31 March 2006, bridging the Chrétien and Martin governments and the beginning of the Harper government. Led by the Treasury Board Secretariat CIO, GOL's most visible accomplishment was to place the 130 most commonly used government services online. These included both transactional and information services and involved all the major departments and agencies of government.

A centrepiece of the GOL initiative was the organization of these services into 31 electronic 'clusters' which provided a World Wide Web–based electronic single window to the range of government services of interest to groups in society, defined by subject, audience, or life-event (e.g., health, Aboriginals, or exporting abroad). The clusters were in turn organized into three portals ('gateways') for individual Canadians, Canadian businesses, and the international environment, which became a defining element of the Canada site home page (Brown, 2007). In many areas, provincial and municipal governments provide services to the same groups as the federal sites, and this gave rise to considerable inter-jurisdictional collaboration in the gateways and clusters aspects of GOL. The success of this strategy played no small part in Canada being awarded top ranking by the consulting firm Accenture for five years in a row, 2001–5, in its annual international survey of electronic government services to the public (Accenture, 2005).

GOL had two other strands. One was to upgrade the government's electronic infrastructure, and in particular its ability to protect online transactions from interference and compromise. This led to a major investment in a 'secure channel', using public key infrastructure methodologies. After an extended effort, the results received mixed reviews, and it is unclear whether the secure channel will in fact provide the intended level of protection or even be widely used (Roy, 2006). The other strand of GOL was an effort to establish IT and IM as a focus of public administration and to update the related Treasury Board policies. All of these efforts were coordinated by a committee of deputy ministers, mandated by the Cabinet Secretary and supported by a tapestry of more junior-level committees (Brown, 2001). For the period that it was in place, GOL was treated as one of the two main initiatives to reform the federal public sector, complementing efforts to modernize public service human resources management.

All provincial and territorial governments took their own steps to integrate new technologies into their administrative and public policy environments. Several held their own versions of the IHAC process and all appointed their own Chief Information Officers, who faced the Y2K millennium bug and most of the other management challenges that confronted their federal counterpart (Borins, 2007b). Many consolidated their common technology services to government into a single operating environment, some going as far as contracting the work out to the private sector. In addition, all introduced their own Internet sites and took steps to place services online, usually linked to the establishment of a provincial government service-to-the-public agency. As discussed in the next section, this led to collaboration among jurisdictions at an unprecedented level.

The Citizen as Catalyst

The emphasis in e-commerce on **client-centred service** resonated well in the public sector, with its traditional ethos of public service. It also built on a history of government initiatives to improve service to the public, which included the language of service provisions of the Official Languages Act, 1969, the Access to Information Act, 1983, and the Public Service 2000 task force on service to the public in 1989–90. All of these emphasized the importance of government meeting members of the public on the public's terms rather than the government's terms.

The *Blueprint for the Renewal of Government Services*, issued in 1994 as one of the first initiatives of the new Treasury Board CIO, built on this foundation. Its emphasis on the citizen as the organizing focus for applying IT and promotion of 'single-window' approaches paved the way for GOL and two companion Treasury Board–sponsored programs, the Service Improvement Initiative (SII) and Service Canada. Service Canada in particular was inspired by the creation in several provincial governments of agencies to consolidate the delivery of services to the public on behalf of the entire government, a pathfinder being Service New Brunswick. All provinces and territories have adopted some form of this model, but it was only in 2003 that the federal government followed suit and redefined Service Canada as an operational agency.

An early question for GOL and the SII was whether to aim to shift all government service delivery to the electronic channel. It soon became apparent that this was unrealistic, however. One important reason was that a significant proportion of Canadians do not have access to the Internet or their access is constrained by limitations in local electronic infrastructure or their own computing equipment. This was one of the major concerns of the IHAC, which devoted considerable attention to the issue of Internet access, giving rise to the Connecting Canadians initiatives described earlier. A second reason was that most Canadians in fact prefer to have some kind of personal contact when dealing with government—when offered a choice of service channels, telephone is almost invariably ranked first, with in-person contact close behind. Electronic access is most widely seen as an important part of a 'suite' of service channels (Flumian et al., 2007; Kernaghan, 2005). **Service Canada** and its service-to-business counterpart, **Canada Business**, are therefore organized on a 'multi-channel' basis, combining telephone call centres, storefront operations, and mail access. These are complemented by interactive websites, with all channels backed up by a common information database. A similar pattern has been followed with the consolidation of municipal services to the public; these, however, are based on the introduction of a single easily accessible non-emergency telephone number: 311 (Bontis, 2007a).

These developments have helped nudge government towards a new organizational model integrating government into a single 'enterprise' (Kernaghan, 2007a). This model has three components (Borins, 2007a). The first is the single window to the public, which delivers services on behalf of a number of government departments and agencies. This is sometimes referred to as the 'front room'. In the 'middle room' are 'joined-up' departments that continue to have program development and implementation responsibilities, along the lines of the traditional departmental model, but that work in a networked policy environment. The 'back room'—in effect PWGSC's IT Services branch—provides common services to the enterprise, using an integrated technology infrastructure and a common set of technology applications (see also Box 29.1).

Box 29.1 Service Nova Scotia—A GST Technology Back-Story

When the federal Goods and Service Tax was introduced, Revenue Canada created a telephone banking facility for businesses to remit the GST they collected. This was expanded to permit businesses to remit Canada Pension Plan and Employment Insurance premiums on behalf of their staff. In Nova Scotia the provincial government decided to contract with Revenue Canada (now the Canada Revenue Agency) to collect their provincial sales tax, which was then combined with the GST to create a streamlined Harmonized Sales Tax (HST). Later, provincial worker's compensation premiums were added to the tax collection single window, further reducing a business's tax remittance costs.

Revenue Canada already collected provincial personal and corporate income tax, and there was very little left for the provincial tax commission to do. It did, however, have a well-established computing environment. So the tax commission moved out of the tax collection business. It amalgamated with the Registry of Motor Vehicles, Vital Statistics, and the Registry of Joint Stock Companies and, later, with parts of the Department of Housing and Municipal Relations, including the Registry of Deeds and Property Assessment. Together, they form the knowledge backbone of Service Nova Scotia, the agency that delivers provincial and municipal services across the province.

While this model is in practice only partially implemented, it does represent a more holistic approach to organizational responsibilities than was the case during the heyday of New Public Management, with its emphasis on managerial autonomy and empowerment. At the same time, it raises questions about how far the analogy of citizen as client can be taken (Fountain, 2001b). One view is that it works best where the services are optional and desired by the citizen, as opposed to services that are more regulatory in nature, where traditional organizational models may be preferable (Brown, 2007).

Politics and Policy-Making in the Electronic Environment

Public administration takes place in a political environment. Ministers are first and foremost politicians, who have been tested in both the electoral and the parliamentary arenas. Daily they are on duty with the media. They are members of the governing party and they are supported by political advisors. In the Canadian version of the Westminster system, they are the linchpins in the **accountability** chain between the public service, Parliament, and the public. They preside over the policy development process, including when their departments consult the public in the context of policy development or implementation.

IT is having a major—although not uniform—impact on all of these aspects of the Canadian political environment (Alexander and Pal, 1998). It some ways, the political environment has been slower than the public service to make full use of IT, and in certain areas the political world is likely to lag permanently behind. In others, any gap has disappeared, although some commentators argue that broader changes are required in our system of governance before the full potential of technology is realized (Barney, 2005). There is little doubt, however, that the experience and attitudes of politicians with respect to technology have an important influence on the environment in which IT and IM issues are addressed in public administration (Malloy, 2003).

To begin with, IT is not inherently a vote-getter. Politicians want to be seen to be addressing the important issues of the day, and these include ensuring that Canada is equipped to meet the challenges of the knowledge society and economy. This is a high-level objective, however, and usually does not translate into political debate. Politicians do want to support the telecommunications and IT industries and to be sure that governments are using technology to improve service delivery. They are wary, however, of the costs of technology and the risks of cost overruns, which can be dramatic in the case of large technology projects, and which have attracted close scrutiny from the Auditor General (Auditor General, 2005, 2006). They are also sensitive to media stories about security breaches of technology systems and databases and in particular to perceptions of abuse of the personal information of citizens and taxpayers.

As decision-makers, ministers face a major challenge when it comes to technology-linked issues. Very few politicians have a background in computer science or one of the other disciplines involved in technology or information management, but they are often asked to take decisions with a significant technical dimension. As a result, they are more than usually dependent on briefings from their officials, and by the same token they are more open to lobbying by the technology industry. The stakes are even higher when it is considered that the IT industry is one of the few in Canada where government purchasing has a major impact on the industry—public administration decisions are also industrial policy decisions.

This being said, all of Canada's political parties are active users of IT, and it has become an integral part of election campaigns, in particular in communications with party members and the media (Cross, 1998). All candidates now have websites and many use blogs and other techniques to good effect (Kernaghan, 2007b). In the two provincial elections in 2007, YouTube postings of gaffes by opponents became an important part of the campaign (Borins, 2007c). On the other hand, Canada has been very slow to move to electronic voting, perhaps because our first-past-the-post system is comparatively simple and does not involve a major counting effort.

Once elected, a growing number of MPs have personal websites, although the parliamentary system imposes some inherent limitations on how autonomous they can be in presenting their views (Kernaghan, 2007c). The Parliament Buildings are as thoroughly wired as any government office building, and MPs have their share of laptops and wireless communications devices. The House of Commons and Senate have been cautious about technology, however, and IT is not used in conducting parliamentary business, beyond recording for Hansard and broadcast, and some experiments in conducting committee hearings.

Public consultations are an important part of the public policy-making process, and both ministers and public servants are involved. The Internet offers considerable potential as a medium for public consultations, and the federal government has established a central website—www.consultingcanadians.gc.ca—to provide information about all such consultations. The site has been particularly important in the regulatory process and other consultations on specialized topics (Borins and Brown, 2007a). At the same time there has been concern about how representative the views provided on the Internet are of the larger population. It is likely that consultation exercises will increasingly follow the multi-channel path of government service delivery, but there is also evidence that 'virtual' policy communities can in fact be as representative as their in-person counterparts (McNutt, 2006).

An underlying political concern about both e-consultations and electronic service delivery, however, is that their very success in linking public servants and members of the public risks cutting out the middle man or woman—the politician. Known in academic discussions as '**disintermediation**', the extent of this phenomenon has not been systematically studied, but its prospect makes politicians more cautious in how they approach technology.

New Spheres and Methods of Public Administration

The advent of networked information and communications technologies has given new prominence to some very old disciplines of public administration. IT and IM are taking their place as one of the foundations of modern public administration, alongside financial and human resources management. There are new institutions, combining traditional and new models. Information and technology have assumed greater importance as assets of government, and the challenges of managing them are creating a renewed public administration discipline, one that is defined by its interdisciplinary nature. Managing information and technology also calls for skills and working relationships—within and outside government—that have not had much prominence in the past. In turn, there are implications for traditional accountability models—the links between public administration and the world of Parliament and politics.

The Institutional Response to Information and Technology

Beginning with the 1993 Campbell reorganization—although building on earlier roots—a technology-related institutional environment has emerged in the federal government, with comparable, albeit less elaborate, arrangements in provincial governments. The Chief Information Officer (CIO) is one of the senior officials of the Treasury Board Secretariat and provides central agency leadership to a wide network of IT- and IM-related agencies and government-wide 'communities of practice' that are defined by Treasury Board policies. Every department and agency has its own CIO, usually a member of the senior management team and often involved in internal initiatives to renew services to the public and departmental administration.

The emphasis on service delivery has also produced new institutions. Service Canada's role has already been discussed. Organizationally it has varied in its relatively brief existence between being a separate department and a significant unit within the Department of Human Resources and Social Development (HRSDC); in either case it seeks to be the single-window for delivering government services to individual Canadians. Canada Business, a unit in the Department of Industry, plays a similar role with respect to Canadian business, especially the medium and small business sectors which have been given new prominence in the information economy. The Department of Foreign Affairs and International Trade (DFAIT) maintains **Canada International**, an Internet portal for Canadians travelling abroad and foreign residents wishing to know more about Canada. This complements DFAIT's traditional role of maintaining Canadian diplomatic posts abroad on behalf of the entire government.

In the enterprise model, service to the public is paralleled by service to government. The Department of Public Works and Government Services (PWGSC), and the Government Telecommunications and Informatics Services (GTIS) within it, were set up in 1993 on the **common service agency model** that has prevailed since the 1960s, providing centralized services to government departments where it was considered to be desirable for policy or cost reasons. For a number of reasons—not least the difficulty in predicting where technology is going and therefore the risks involved in putting all its IT resources into one basket—the development of IT services and applications in government has evolved on a more collaborative basis, with the emphasis on sharing services among departments and best practices rather than one-size-fits-all approaches. A related issue is 'make or buy'—whether government should develop its own IT capacity or contract out. Driven by these issues, GTIS has undergone its own organizational evolution, becoming the IT Services Branch (ITSB) of PWGSC and spawning a new shared services **special operating agency**.

Other areas of government have also responded to the information age. Three in particular should be noted. The Department of Industry, with responsibilities ranging from supporting scientific research to promoting the IT industry, incorporating new businesses, protecting intellectual property, and regulating the radio spectrum (more important than ever in the wireless environment), has since the IHAC report sought to promote the use of technology in support of innovation and competitiveness in the Canadian economy. The Department of Canadian Heritage is concerned with cultural industries and the use of technology in daily life. One of its agencies, Library and Archives Canada, is leading efforts to digitize cultural and other information holdings, both within government and in the country as a whole. HRSDC is concerned with the employment effects of the knowledge economy, including the new literacy—the essential skills—required to live and work in that economy (Wallace et al., 2005).

IT and Information as Assets of Government

Much of public administration theory and practice is about managing people and money as the primary assets of government. In recent years, the government's information holdings and the technology that houses them have joined the list of key public resources (Lenihan et al., 2002). Even so, the situation is still evolving and even somewhat problematic. Although no one would deny the critical importance of the IT infrastructure, traditional accounting carries it on the government's books as a depreciating asset. Program budgeting, with its emphasis on results, treats technology as a means or input, so it is difficult even to track how much is spent on IT in single year—estimate in 2003–4 placed total annual technology-related spending at just under $5 billion, roughly 10 per cent of total spending on government operations. Almost two-thirds of that amount was on the purchase of IT goods and services from the private sector (Brown, 2007: 63). The Public Accounts assign the government's massive inventory of paper files and other information holdings no value at all! This raises the question of how something that is not valued can be properly managed.

Nevertheless, a considerable effort goes into planning, buying, and running the government's technology and telecommunications infrastructure. PWGSC's ITSB provides the essential 'backbone' and runs a number of mainframe-based computing services for other branches of PWGSC and departments that do not operate their own computing environments. Both ITSB and departments have made extensive investments in moving paper-based activities into an electronic environment. These large projects have not always been successful—indeed, by some measures, most of them have problems to at least some degree (Auditor General, 2006). One aspect of this track record is that government in Canada generally operates on a larger scale than business, and major government computing projects are generally larger and more complex than those in the private sector. In any case, it can be argued that such events are becoming less common as the pathfinder projects are completed and connected and major databases move to second and later generations.

IM as a Discipline of Public Administration

The management of the government's information holdings represents its own challenge. Traditionally, information was kept on paper records in physical files and filing cabinets. When the **Access to Information Act** was passed in 1983 it required government institutions to be able to locate and produce any record under their control within 30 days in response to a request from the public. In order to meet this test, Treasury Board policies were introduced that direct departments to manage their records on a life-cycle basis, from creation or acquisition through initial and secondary use to longer-term disposal or retention. Library and Archives Canada is the ultimate resting place of records that are meant to last. The Access to Information policy established procedures for the public to request records, working with Info Source (www.infosource.gc.ca), a public database of what those records are and where they can be found.

This framework remains in place, but it has become considerably more difficult to administer with the transition to electronic information. Personal computers and databases have greatly expanded the volume of information holdings and the range of ways in which they are held, much of it outside of centrally administered registry systems—even increasingly sophisticated electronic ones. Multiple versions, both paper and electronic, are common and it is often very difficult to know which one should be used. Email has become ubiquitous in a relatively short space of time, and many records are obscured from view as email attachments. These challenges are compounded by new generations of hardware and software, which make it difficult to retrieve electronic files that are more than a few years old. At the same time, court interpretations have made it clear that any retrievable record in any form—including, for example, call logs on government cell phones—is subject to the Access to Information Act.

These are not the only issues addressed by Treasury Board information management policies. The Access to Information Act makes a distinction between records—which are considered internal to a government institution—and published material, including books, press releases, and public websites, which are considered to be in the public domain. The Government Communications policy promotes information dissemination and articulates the government's duty to inform citizens so they may exercise their rights and responsibilities; from that starting point it establishes procedures for government publishing and media relations. More controversial areas of the policy concern advertising, public opinion research, and sponsorship. The federal identity program sets standards for government signage and visual identity in order to facilitate public access and accountability.

Other Treasury Board policies are more oriented towards information protection. The **Privacy Act** and related policies give Canadians the right to see government files about themselves and establish limits on the extent to which they can be seen by others. It also limits the government's ability to take personal information that was collected for one purpose and use it for another. These restrictions, which are based on international standards, have assumed even greater prominence as networked databases create the potential to link previously unconnected information to build profiles of individuals and groups in society. Such information is valuable both to government and to commercial interests, and there is growing pressure to make government data publicly available. Another set of policies deals with government security, the protection of information and other government assets against perceived threats. Varying levels of assessed threats lead to corresponding levels of security classification and protection, adding to the complexity of information management.

The People Effect—New Skills

Few, if any, areas of public service work have been untouched by the introduction of technology and the move to knowledge-based government. All public service desktops are connected to internal electronic networks and through them to the Internet. Their users must handle email and manage their own electronic information. Many public servants are able to take advantage of information and communications technologies to establish more flexible work arrangements; many also see them as a kind of virtual prison, blurring the traditional boundaries between work and personal life.

In addition to these environmental effects, a good deal of the substance of public service work is shaped by information and technology. In addition to the Treasury Board and departmental CIOs, every department has a substantial number of staff whose jobs are defined by Treasury Board information and technology policies or by the management of technology infrastructure and applications. In addition, other administrative disciplines, notably financial management (comptrollership) and human resources management are heavily influenced by technology in how they do their work. Policy and program work relating to the IT industry or the knowledge economy and society also require technical knowledge, and the government has substantial numbers of computer scientists, engineers, librarians, archivists, and other specialists to carry out this work.

One result of this changing skills profile within government is a requirement for interdisciplinary work teams and for public servants of different academic backgrounds to learn how to work together. Engineers and political scientists may not have spent much time with each other as students, but they have to work together in the public service! At the same time, the move towards knowledge work in government places a greater premium on information-finding and information-organizing skills as opposed to the application of specialized knowledge (Bontis, 2007b). The open-ended and costly nature of technology, combined with the considerable reliance on private sector contractors, has brought to the fore skills in areas such as risk management and contract management. All of these demands have also called for new forms of digital leadership (Borins and Brown, 2007b). However, the ability to analyze, synthesize, and advise is as important in public service work as ever.

New Working Relationships

Another skill that is called for in IM- and IT-influenced public administration is relationship management. The networked environment is credited with eliminating time and space and with crossing boundaries. In practice public servants are connected with wide-ranging communities, both within and beyond the traditional departmental structure (e.g., see Box 29.2).

Within government, the growth of service-to-the-public agencies has the effect of separating policy-making from program delivery, often into different ministerial portfolios. This creates practical as well as theoretical issues about accountability and program effectiveness. A similar observation can be made about the consolidation of technology and other administrative services to government in shared or common service agencies, especially when they are in turn contracted out. A related development is the impact of citizen-centred service on Canadian federalism, which goes well beyond the collaboration noted in the discussion of the GOL gateways and clusters (Ambrose et al., 2006).

More than in any other sphere of public administration, the management of information and technology has also created a close working relationship with the private sector (Dutil et al., 2005). This takes several forms. To begin with, the private sector is the source of most technology hardware and software and many of the applications used in government. Government sales are important to vendors and it is also important for government to keep abreast of the technology that is available or in prospect, and its cost (Brown and Kourakos, 2005). Tendering procedures involve one kind of relationship, contract administration another. The private sector also provides consultants to advise on planning, purchasing, using, and servicing IT goods and services.

In many, if not most, of these relationships, government acts as its own technology manager—government managers or project offices supervise the development of new IT-based systems and run the technology-enabled services. The private-sector vendors and consultants are 'on tap, not on top'. A different dynamic comes into play when project management functions are also assumed, under contract, by the private sector. In such public–private partnerships, public services are

Box 29.2 The Technology-Enabled Face of Federalism

As governments appointed CIOs in the 1990s, they began to meet periodically to discuss common problems and concerns, including dealing with a common vendor community and linking governments on the Internet. The Public Sector CIO Council was formed, made up of the 14 federal, provincial, and territorial CIOs plus two representatives of municipal technology organizations and co-chaired by the federal CIO and a provincial counterpart. In a parallel development, the government service delivery agencies formed the Public Service Delivery Council. The two Councils in turn have sponsored a not-for-profit organization, the Institute for Citizen-Centred Service, which conducts research on their behalf. Every year the two councils meet with senior private sector representatives at the Lac Carling conference, which is co-sponsored with the Institute of Public Administration of Canada and *ITWorld Canada*, a technology industry journal.

being provided to the public or to government, but by the private sector, either jointly with government or on its behalf. This puts a premium on governance arrangements for such projects and on balancing the incentives, risks, accountabilities, and liabilities for both sides of the partnership. Two important constraints are that even large private sector firms do not have as deep pockets as government, and government remains ultimately responsible for the decision to invoke this model and for its results.

An added dimension to the private sector relationship is the diversity within the private sector itself. Governments in Canada and around the world deal with a relatively small number of multinational technology and consulting firms, who have broad experience and resources and are skilled at managing large projects. They also tend to offer similar products and services from one jurisdiction to another, with the result that there is considerable similarity in how governments use IT and IM. Their size and importance in developing and providing IT goods and services present governments with a major challenge (Dunleavy et al., 2004). Beyond this multinational tier of vendors there is a wide range of firms, with large Canadian-based companies that themselves have international operations at one end, through medium- and small-sized firms, many with only a handful of employees, down to a large number of individual consultants at the other end. Governments deal with the full spectrum, sometimes working with firms or individuals on a long-term basis that comes close to a traditional public service employment relationship.

Information Technology and Accountability

The extensive use of technology in government raises many questions about accountability, the spinal cord of public administration. Traditional accountability models are under pressure for many reasons, not just from the effects of IT (Aucoin and Jarvis, 2005). One context for such questioning is organizations such as Service Canada, which provide services to the public on behalf of other government programs. This is a departure from the traditional departmental model, in which a minister is accountable for both policy development and its delivery. It remains to be seen how willing ministers and Parliament will be, in practice, in accepting a division of responsibility between these two areas.

A similar issue arises when a minister and department are no longer fully in control of the computing environment supporting the department. A third concern is the increasingly 'real-time' nature of accountability—with current communications technologies, ministers become instantly accountable for the actions and statements of their officials, anytime and anywhere these may occur. Without effective internal communications between ministers and their officials, this continuous accountability loop creates risks for both ministers and their officials.

Some Conclusions: Information, Technology, and Public Sector Reform

In justifying new technology projects, the terms most commonly used by their advocates are 'transformation' and 'innovation'. These evoke the promise of information technology and of knowledge-based government and in many ways reflect a new reality. Governments in the early 1990s did not plan the introduction of a networked working environment featuring single-window electronic service delivery and backed by massive databases. They recognized that new technologies and associated management techniques offered considerable potential to improve, even reform, public services as well as to save money. But few would have been able to foretell the extent to which public administration would change, while in other respects retaining many of its traditional features.

It is a nice question whether change invariably represents reform. Many individual changes undoubtedly represent improvements, and

Government On-Line can credibly claim to have been a reform initiative, significantly changing the face of government service delivery. The modern public service builds on a legacy of past reforms, and the challenge is to continue that process.

This challenge can be illustrated in six issues that arise from the nature of information and technology in the public administration context. The first is the inherent obsolescence of technology—new products and applications are always becoming available along with new ways of using them, generating new social and economic responses as well (Tapscott and Williams, 2006). Governments have some limited ability to influence these developments, but they need to become informed and skilled users if they wish to influence, and not just be shaped by, events. Second, they face a particular problem in addressing the fragmented situation of information management in the knowledge-based institution—this is the area that government managers are most concerned about (Brown, 2007).

Closely related to the information management challenge is the institutional immaturity of information and technology management (McDonald, 2002), especially compared with financial and human resources management. The statutory framework is limited and there is limited integration among the various administrative disciplines that have been discussed in this chapter—many would not even recognize themselves as being in the same script, never mind on the same page!

A fourth challenge is the one articulated by the Information Highway Advisory Council, of maintaining a link between technology strategies and developments for the public sector and those directed at society at large. Government is the largest user of the information highway; it also needs to be a model user.

A particular dilemma relates to public communications. Technology has greatly expanded the nature and availability of communications channels and has added immediacy to the relationship between public administration and the public. Communications have become part of the currency of contemporary politics, with the paradoxical effect of isolating the communications function as a discipline within public administration.

This points to the final challenge. Much of the leadership in moving into the world of information- and technology-based public administration has been provided by the public service itself, with only a limited decision-making role taken by ministers. This situation cannot last, however. As politicians become more aware of and experienced with the tools of information and communications technologies, the question will be what conclusions they form about the technology agenda and how they will express their political will as a result—whether to encourage technology's further development in public administration or to try to control its use and limit its impact.

Important Terms and Concepts

Access to Information Act
accountability
Canada Business
Canada International
Canada Site
Chief Information Officer (CIO)
client-centred service
common service agency model
disintermediation
e-commerce
e-government
electronic service delivery (ESD)
information
information management (IM)
information technology
Privacy Act
Service Canada
special operating agency

Study Questions

1. Canada's federal government was recognized as the top performer in the delivery of e-government from 2000–5. What steps helped it to achieve such a distinction?
2. What is the relationship between information technology and the New Public Management (IT and NPM)?
3. What new spheres and methods of public administration have been created by information technology and information management (IT and IM)?
4. What issues arise from the nature of information and technology in the public administration context, according to Brown?
5. It seems that there are many avenues opened by ICTs: e-government, e-commerce, e-consultation, e-service, e-filing, and so forth. What is your view of how advanced each is in relation to the others, and how of each can be improved?

Useful Websites

Government of Canada site:

www.canada.gc.ca

Canada Business:

www.canadabusiness.ca/eng/

Canada International:

www.canadainternational.gc.ca/ci-ci/splash.aspx

Central federal public consultations site:

www.consultingcanadians.gc.ca

A public database of what federal government records the public may access and where they can be found:

www.infosource.gc.ca

Office of the Auditor General of Canada. Reports on Information Management in the federal government and in specific departments:

www.oag-bvg.gc.ca/internet/English/parl_lpt_e_1727.html

Brown, David. 2001. *The Governance of Government On-Line*, Report to the Treasury Board Secretariat Chief Information Officer. Public Policy Forum, March.

www.ppforum.ca/fr/search/results/taxonomy:92

The last Accenture Report to rank Canada first in e-government (2005):

www.accenture.com/Countries/Canada/Services/By_Subject/Customer_Relationship_Management/R_and_I/LeadershipNewExperiences.htm

References

Accenture. 2005. *Leadership in Customer Service: New Expectations, New Service.*

Alexander, Cynthia J., and Leslie A. Pal. 1998. *Digital Democracy: Policy and Politics in the Wired World.* Don Mills: Oxford University Press.

Ambrose, Rona, Don Lenihan, and John Milloy. 2006. *Managing the Federation: a Citizen-Centred Approach.* Ottawa: Crossing Boundaries.

Andersen, Kim Viborg. 1999. 'Reengineering Public Sector Organizations Using Information Technology', in Richard Heeks, ed., *Reinventing Government in the Information Age: International Practice in IT-Enabled Public Sector Reform.* London: Routledge.

Aucoin, Peter, and Michael D. Jarvis. 2005. *Modernizing Government Accountability: A Framework for Reform.* Ottawa: Canada School of Public Service.

Barney, Darrin. 2005. *Communication Technology.* Vancouver: University of British Columbia Press.

Bontis, Nick. 2007a. 'Citizen Relationship Management in Canadian Cities: Starting to Dial 311', in Borins et al. (2007: 137–54).

———. 2007b. 'Mining the Nation's Intellectual Capital: Knowledge Management in Government', in Borins et al. (2007: 155–82).

Borins, Sandford. 2007a. 'Conceptual Framework', in Borins et al. (2007: 14–36).

———. 2007b. 'What Keeps a CIO Awake at Night? Evidence from the Ontario Government', in Borins et al. (2007: 69–101).

———. 2007c. 'Attack narratives, strategic decisions and the YouTube effect', InterGovWorld blogs, 11 October. Available at: www.intergovworld.com/Blogs/Pages/blogentry.aspx?EntryID=309.

———, and David Brown. 2007a. 'E-Consultation: Technology at the Interface between Civil Society and Government', in Borins et al. (2007: 253–76).

———, and ———. 2007b. 'Digital Leadership: The Human Face of IT', in Borins et al. (2007: 277–301).

———, Kenneth Kernaghan, David Brown, Perri 6, and Fred Thompson. 2007. *Digital State at the Leading Edge*. Toronto: University of Toronto Press.

Braibant, Guy, ed. 1977. *Informatics and Administration*. Brussels: International Institute of Administrative Sciences.

Brown, David. 2001. *The Governance of Government On-Line*, Report to the Treasury Board Secretariat Chief Information Officer. Public Policy Forum, March. Available at: www.ppforum.ca/fr/search/results/taxonomy:92.

———. 2005. 'Electronic Government and Public Administration', *International Review of Administrative Sciences* 71 (2): 241–54.

———. 2007. 'Government On-Line', in Borins et al. (2007: 37–68).

———, and George Kourakos. 2005. *Vendor Engagement Strategy Consultation*, Report prepared on behalf of Public Works and Government Services Canada, April. Available at: www.ppforum.ca/common/assets/publications/en/vendor_engagment_report.pdf.

Canada, Auditor General of Canada (Auditor General). 2005. 'Information Technology Security', Chapter 1 in *February 2005 Status Report of the Auditor General of Canada to the House of Commons*. Ottawa: Public Works and Government Services Canada.

———. 2006. 'Large Information Technology Projects', Chapter 3 in *Report of the Auditor General of Canada to the House of Commons*. Ottawa: Public Works and Government Services Canada.

Canada, Information Highway Advisory Council (IHAC). 1995. *Connection, Community, Content: The Challenge of the Information Highway*. Ottawa: Minister of Supply and Services.

———. 1997. *Preparing Canada for a Digital World*. Ottawa: Industry Canada.

Cross, William. 1998. 'Teledemocracy: Canadian Political Parties Listening to Their Constituents', in Alexander and Pal (1998: 132–48).

Dunleavy, Patrick, Helen Margetts, Simon Bastow, and Jane Tinkler. 2004. 'Government IT Performance and the Power of the IT Industry: A Cross-National Analysis', Paper presented at the American Political Science Association annual conference.

Dutil, Patrick, John Langford, and Jeffrey Roy. 2005. *E-Government and Service Transformation Relationships between Government and Industry: Developing Best Practices. New Directions* Series. Toronto: Institute of Public Administration of Canada.

Ellul, Jacques. 1964. *The Technology Society*. New York: Vintage Books.

Flumian, Maryantonnett, Amanda Coe, and Kenneth Kernaghan. 2007. 'Transforming Service to Canadian: The Service Canada Model', *International Review of Administrative Sciences* 73, 4: 557–68.

Fountain, Jane E. 2001a. *Building the Virtual State: Information Technology and Institutional Change*. Washington, DC: Brookings Institute Press.

———. 2001b. 'Paradoxes of Public Sector Consumer Service', *Governance* 14, 1 (January): 55–73.

Gow, J.I., and J.E. Hodgetts. 2003. 'Where Are We Coming From? Are There any Useful Lessons from Our Administrative History?' *Canadian Public Administration* 46, 2 (Summer): 178–201.

Innis, Harold A. 1950. *Empire and Communications*. Toronto: Oxford University Press.

Kernaghan, Kenneth. 2005. 'Moving Toward the Virtual State: Integrating Services and Service Channels for Citizen-Centred Service Delivery', *International Review of Administrative Sciences* 71, 1: 119–31.

———. 2007a. 'Beyond Bubble Gum and Goodwill: Integrating Service Delivery', in Borins et al. (2007: 102–36).

———. 2007b. 'Moving Beyond Politics as Usual? Online Campaigning', in Borins et al. (2007: 183–223).

———. 2007c. 'Making Political Connections: IT and Political Life', in Borins et al. (2007: 224–52).

———, and Justin Gunraj. 2004. 'Integrating Information Technology into Public Administration: Conceptual and Practical Considerations', in *Canadian Public Administration* 47, 4: 525–46.

Lenihan, Don, Tony Valeri, and David Hume. 2002. *Information as a Public Resource: Leading Canadians in the Information Age*. Ottawa: Centre for Collaborative Government.

McDonald, John. 2002. *The Financial Capability Model and the Records Management Function: An Assessment*. Ottawa: Public Policy Forum.

McLuhan, Marshall. 1964. *Understanding Media: the Extensions of Man*. New York: Signet Books.

McNutt, Kathleen. 2006. 'Research Note: Do Virtual Policy Networks Matter? Tracing Network Structure Online', in *Canadian Journal of Political Science* 39, 2 (June): 391–405.

Malloy, Jonathan. 2003. 'To Better Serve Canadians: How Technology Is Changing the Relationship between Members of Parliament and Public Servants', *New Directions* 9. Toronto: Institute of Public Administration of Canada.

Mitchell, James R. 2002. 'Changing the Machinery of Government', Ideas at Sussex Circle. Available at: www.sussexcircle.com/e/ideas_e.htm.

Negroponte, Nicholas. 1995. *Being Digital*. New York: Vintage Books.

Oliver, E. Lynn, and Larry Sanders, eds. 2004. *E-Government Reconsidered: Renewal of Governance for the Knowledge Age*. Regina: Canadian Plains Research Centre.

Rowland, Wade. 2006. *Spirit of the Web: The Age of Information from Telegraph to Internet*. Toronto: Thomas Allen.

Roy, Jeffrey. 2006. *E-Government in Canada: Transformation for the Digital Age*. Ottawa: University of Ottawa Press.

Snellen, I.Th.M., and W.B.H.J. van de Donk. 1998. *Public Administration in an Information Age: A Handbook*. Amsterdam: IOS Press.

Tapscott, Don, and Art Caston. 1993. *Paradigm Shift: The New Promise of Information Technology*. New York: McGraw-Hill.

———, and Anthony D. Williams. 2006. *Wikinomics: How Mass Collaboration Changes Everything*. New York and Toronto: Portfolio.

Wallace, Theresa, Nicole Murphy, Geneviève Lépine, and David Brown, eds. 2005. *Exploring New Directions in Essential Skills*. Ottawa: Public Policy Forum.

Glossary

ability to pay A criterion increasingly used in arbitration settlements wherein the ramifications of settlements on the financial health of the employer are considered. It is sometimes distinguished from 'pattern settlements', in which an agreement in one occupational group gets applied across the board. (Chapter 10)

Aboriginal According to section 35(2) of the Constitution Act, 1982: '"Aboriginal peoples of Canada" includes the Indian, Inuit, and Métis peoples of Canada'. (Chapters 19, 20, 21)

Access to Information Act An act passed in 1983 that gives the public the right to access government records and states that government agencies must provide the requested records within a reasonable amount of time (30 days). The Act does not apply to records that contain personal information about individual citizens, and sensitive information relating to certain matters of national security may also be exempt. (Chapter 29)

accountability Generally, the assignment of responsibilities, with clear expectations or standards, by a person or body in authority to a specific person or body, who is obligated to answer for performance or non-performance. (Chapters 2, 4, 5, 6, 17, 19, 29)

accounting officers Established by the Federal Accountability Act, this position is given to the deputy minister or head of an agency. The officer is accountable for aspects of the organization and use of departmental resources, but holds less responsibility than similar officers in the UK. (Chapters 4, 26, 28)

administratively formed organization A type of Government organization that is not legally constituted or established, but administratively formed; generally, it is a section, branch, or portion of a ministerial department or Crown agency. (Chapter 3)

adversary system The dominant legal paradigm in the English legal system, now spread worldwide. It assumes that the parties—and hence lawyers—control the process and that the judge (and jury, if necessary) assesses arguments presented rather than being directly involved in the argumentation of the case. (Chapter 7)

advocacy Public support for laws or policies; non-profit organizations often advocate (lobby) for policies for the good of particular groups and/or society as a whole. (Chapter 17)

affirmative action The US term for what Canadians call employment equity. (Chapter 9)

agencies Generally, any non-departmental form in government that is freed from the normal day-to-day operational controls by central government, but for which government may set broad policy directions. (Chapter 14)

agenda-setting The first stage in the policy process; in this stage, a problem is identified by policy actors and a variety of solutions are put forward. (Chapter 22)

Agreement on Internal Trade (AIT) An informal code of conduct that includes rules concerning mobility, procurement, and other trade matters, along with a dispute settlement mechanism negotiated by the federal and provincial governments in 1995, after they had failed to find ways to reduce internal trade barriers and secure the economic union by constitutional reform. (Chapter 23)

alternative dispute resolution (ADR) Patterns of dispute resolution other than the right to strike, namely, the limited right to strike, binding arbitration, arbitration at the request of either party, and the choice of procedure. The choice of ADR mechanism depends on the effects of political pressures, interest groups, special events, and inertia. (Chapters 7, 10, 11)

alternative service delivery Creative public sector restructuring in which government shares governance functions with individuals, community groups, and other entities in order to develop a more cost-effective delivery, improve effectiveness and delivery, and/or promote managerial decision-making closer to the point of delivery. (Chapter 14)

Annual Premiers Conference (APC) A form of first ministers' conference, bringing together the 10 premiers and the leaders of the three territories, that slowly became a regular part of the intergovernmental scene. In 2003, it was reconstituted as the Council of the Federation. (Chapter 23)

answerability The duty to inform and provide explanations to Parliament; usually distinguished from accountability and responsibility. (Chapter 4)

appropriation In government finance, the approval by a legislative body of an organization's budget, and permission to spend amounts in the budget. (Chapter 27)

Auditor General Act, 1976 An act that gave the Officer of the Auditor General increased power over the management of public money and called for accountability in the form of performance audits of bodies and programs that receive public funding. (Chapter 26)

Auditor General of Canada An officer of Parliament often described as the principal 'financial watchdog' in the legislative branch. The Office of the Auditor General is responsible for ensuring the legality and accuracy of expenditures by practising comprehensive/value-for-money auditing; the Auditor General's reports are read by parliamentarians and pundits alike and often set the agenda for public sector reform. (Chapters 4, 6, 26)

audits Control tools used by agencies to assess (usually financial) performance and compliance with agency objectives and methods. (Chapter 27)

'back-loaded' compensation See **deferred (or back-loaded) compensation**.

base wages Typically, the lowest wage rate in a collective agreement. The *effective wage* includes adjustments for the cost-of-living. (Chapter 11)

'big government' An era in the evolution of the federal government in Canada, from 1946 until about 1973, characterized by growing confidence among policy-makers about the capacity of government to remedy the defects of an unregulated capitalist economy and the elaboration of programs to manage social and economic activity and redistribute wealth. Some consider it the most important invention of the twentieth century. (Chapter 12)

Bill C-31 A 1985 bill, later an act, that amended the Indian Act in order to deal with perceived inequities and anomalies. The Act reinstated the status of Registered Indian to individuals who had lost this status through marriage and to their children. It also gave individual bands the ability to apply their own rules of governance within their communities. (Chapters 19, 20, 21)

binding arbitration A method of dispute resolution in the public sector used when the right to strike is not a viable option. An impartial third-party professional determines awards based on such criteria as comparability (the dominant criterion), the employers' ability to pay, and the cost of living. (Chapters 10, 11)

binding wage arbitration See **binding arbitration**.

bounded rationality A limited rationality, arising from information costs and uncertainty. (Chapter 22)

budget In government finance, a key document of an organization's planning process that allocates financial resources in order to achieve policy agendas. Budgets establish internal financial controls and effective cash management. (Chapters 26, 27)

budget base Expenditures that continue from year to year (as distinguished from discretionary spending). (Chapter 26)

budget increments Expenditures or expenditure proposals beyond the budget base. (Chapter 26)

budget office On paper, the budget office is divided between the Department of Finance (responsible for managing the overall federal fiscal policy) and the Treasury Board Secretariat (responsible for the operating budgets of programs and the general management of government). In actuality, the divisions of responsibility are much more complex. (Chapter 26)

budget roles The jobs of spenders, guardians, priority setters, and financial watchdogs. (Chapter 26)

budget shift point A move away from the normal incremental fashion of budgeting; the point when expenditures for a particular department or program area increase quickly and significantly beyond the normal incremental and regular adjustment. (Chapter 26)

budgetary base See **budget base**.

budgetary process The process of deciding on financial priorities, determining sources of funding, and implementing and monitoring budget spending. Individuals with distinct budget roles (spenders, guardians, priority setters, and financial watchdogs) are involved at different stages. (Chapter 26)

bureaucratic engagement model A model that aims to enhance citizen empowerment and representation in government that gained popularity in the late 1980s and 1990s. In this model, individuals are encouraged to participate in government processes and public officials are encouraged to form meaningful relationships with citizens. (Chapter 15)

bureaucratic independence The idea that the public service is an organ of government. This is a reinterpretation of the traditional approach, which holds that the public service is simply the operational arm of the government and, as such, no public servant can make a decision or take any action not authorized by a statute or government directive. Bureaucratic independence recognizes that, while public servants owe a duty of loyalty to the government of the day, certain circumstances may arise that permit them to exercise independence from that government in order to protect the neutrality of the public service and the rule of law. (Chapters 6, 21)

bureaucratic neutrality See **political neutrality**.

C-31 Indians Individuals qualifying for Registered Indian status as a result of Bill C-31. (Chapter 19)

cabinet committees clusters of cabinet ministers, usually grouped on the basis of shared functional responsibilities or, as is the case with committees such as the Treasury Board, brought together to provide coordination of government activities. (Chapter 5)

cabinet formation The process of establishing a responsible government in office, guided by conventions of the Constitution. (Chapter 5)

Canada Business An Internet portal for Canadian business, especially those in the medium and small business sectors. It provides information on topics such as starting a business, government grants, taxes, import and export, hiring practices, and general management operations. It is administered by the Department of Industry. (Chapter 29)

Canada International An Internet portal for Canadians travelling abroad and foreign residents wishing to know more about Canada. (Chapter 29)

Canada Site The federal government's Internet portal, established in 1995. It provides a vast array of information on government-related programs and services, with links to many government departments. (Chapter 29)

Canadian Charter of Rights and Freedoms Set out in the Constitution Act, 1982, the Charter is designed to regulate the policies and actions of governmental organizations (rather than of individuals, to avoid infringing on individual rights); the Charter covers a wide range of issues that include rights of assembly and association, democratic rights, mobility rights, and minority-language rights. (Chapter 9)

Canadian Human Rights Commission Administering under the Canadian Human Rights Act, the Commission ensures compliance with the Employment Equity Act, acts dedicated to achieving non-discrimination in employment and provision of federal services, and assists with equal employment opportunities for designated groups by federally regulated employers. (Chapter 6)

capital budget A type of budget that contains the plans and resource allocations for capital acquisitions to support an organization's programs. They address yearly expenditures for multi-year plans. (Chapter 27)

case management Pre-planning for complex cases, in the form of directions hearings and/or case conferences. (Chapter 7)

caseflow management An organizational principle under which the court is responsible for the continuation of a case from the time it is initiated. Guidelines generally include a schedule for all stages of the case, a way of monitoring the schedule, and procedures to prevent unnecessary delays (for example, fast tracking, case management, and mediation). (Chapter 7)

cash budget Essentially, a simplified version of an operating budget that contains only planned cash receipts and disbursements or expenditures. (Chapter 27)

catch-up The pattern wherein unusually high settlements in the public sector have historically followed periods of higher settlements in the private sector; these periods of high settlements in the public sector tend to be followed by periods in which the private sector again has higher settlements. (Chapter 11)

central agency A public service-wide facilitative and coordination body, directly responsible to the prime minister or premier, established to promote shared knowledge, collegial decision-making, or the setting of government-wide priorities. (Chapters 2, 5)

central executive The collective political and non-political elements of the executive who are engaged in generating and coordinating central policy. (Chapter 5)

chief administrative officer (CAO) The typical form (and title) of appointed administrative managers in Canadian cities. Their main duty is to facilitate relations and communicate information between staff and council. As with all municipal staff in Canada, they report to all councillors collectively.

chief of staff A senior official in a minister's office who is accountable to the minister as a partisan political actor and whose role is to help the minister gain and maintain power. (Chapter 28)

choice of procedure A form of dispute resolution, mostly used at the federal level, where the union is allowed to choose in advance of negotiation either the strike or arbitration route. (Chapter 10)

citizen engagement model A model that aims to substantively involve citizens in administrative processes and everyday governance. In its most extreme form, the model calls for a complete restructuring of government wherein individual citizens hold a status within government similar to that of political officials. (Chapter 15)

citizenship Membership in a political community and participation in its affairs. In the first half of the twentieth century, such participation referred to equal political and civil rights; in the second half, it also implied equal entitlement to basic social and economic rights. (Chapter 17)

city manager An individual appointed (rather than publicly elected) to professionally manage a city. The role is primarily administrative and often involves policy implementation. Compared to chief administrative officers, city managers generally have greater independent authority. (Chapter 25)

civil society The network of voluntary organizations that stands between the state and families/individuals. (Chapter 25)

classical model of federalism An approach to Canadian federalism in which the powers of federal and provincial governments are more evenly balanced, and in which provinces are fully autonomous within their designated areas of jurisdiction. See also **collaborative federalism**. (Chapter 23)

client-centred service An approach to service provision that focuses on the individual needs of clients. In government, it means that the government meets members of the public on their own terms (rather than the government's terms). (Chapter 29)

clusters of power in the executive Departments or institutions in the federal government with similar functions and influence (see also **Finance cluster**, **Foreign Affairs cluster**, **Justice cluster**, **prime ministerial cluster**). (Chapter 2)

code of conduct (statement of values) A set of principles meant to guide and support public servants in all professional activities, and to instill public confidence in government and government organizations. In general, codes of conduct help to preserve and promote values-based behaviour. (Chapter 16)

collaborative arrangements Partnerships in which contributions, objectives, decision-making, and benefits are shared among the involved parties. (Chapter 14)

collaborative federalism In Canada, the most recent iteration of the intergovernmental relationship between provinces/territories and federal government, in which both parties are seen as equals in relation to governance. (Chapter 23)

collaborative leadership Leadership that is committed to the public good, with a focus on communication and relationship building, reliance on public and corporate values (rather than strict rules), and sharing responsibility and accountability across government and private sector partners. (Chapter 13)

collective ministerial responsibility See **collective responsibility**.

collective responsibility Responsibilities held by the cabinet as a whole—to the monarch, to itself, and to the House. Responsibility to the House requires that ministers, in their capacity as members of the cabinet, are collectively responsible for the policies and management of the government as a whole. If the government (the cabinet) loses a vote of confidence in the legislature, it is required to resign. (Chapters 5, 6, 16)

colonial model of federalism In Canada, the centralized federal model created in 1867. It set the provincial–federal government relations in parallel with the previous colony–Britain relationship. In this model, the federal government had power over all major public responsibilities and decisions. (Chapter 23)

Commission of Inquiry into the Sponsorship Program and Advertising Activities (Gomery Commission) Appointed by the Liberal government in February 2004, in response to the 'sponsorship scandal'. The Commission found evidence of mismanagement, and urged clarification of government accountability. Its recommendations included founding an 'accounting officer' regime, creating a Public Service Charter, providing an open and competitive procedure for the selection of deputy ministers and limiting their terms to no less than three years, increasing the resources of the Public Accounts Committee and encouraging members to stay within the Committee for the duration of the Parliament, and CEOs of Crown corporations be appointed on merit and, if necessary, dismissed by the board of directors of that corporation. The Commission's reports led to the formation of the Federal Accountability Act. (Chapter 4)

Committee of Senior Officials (COSO) An advisory to the Clerk of the Privy Council charged with giving advice on matters related to deputy ministers' staffing policies, identifying candidates for DM appointment, overseeing the performance appraisal system for DMs, and reviewing the information on each prospective appointee. (Chapter 28)

common service agency model A model of centralized service provision in which one agency oversees a number of services that are of benefit to many other agencies. In government, this centralization of services is often based on policy or economic factors. (Chapter 29)

common service departments Departments that provide goods and services to other branches of the public sector; most prominent today is the Department of Public Works and Government. (Chapter 2)

compensating wages Non-wage benefits (e.g., safety, job security, good pensions, fringe benefits) paid for additional aspects of employment in the public sector. Such benefits generally make public sector jobs desirable, but some the benefits may dissipate over time, depending on economic and policy circumstances. (Chapter 11)

competing narratives (for public service reform) Different stories or ideas about what should be done about the public service; these narratives, designed to engage followers looking for credible and coherent political strategies, are constructed by political and organizational leaders with varying motives. (Chapter 1)

competitive federalism In Canada, an era of federalism characterized by increased intergovernmental conflict, in which provinces sought autonomy and the federal government resisted these efforts. (Chapter 23)

competitiveness In the late twentieth century, with the emergence of the information economy, the national project emphasized competition in terms of lowering trade barriers, promoting overseas trade, and improving the capacity of workers and firms to be innovative and adapt to the global marketplace. (Chapter 12)

Comptroller General of Canada Chief financial officer within the Treasury Board. Responsibilities include strengthening financial management and accounting policy, financial systems management, internal audits, and community-building across the Government. (Chapter 4)

consensus government In Nunavut and the Northwest Territories, the form of government in place, with structures deriving from traditional Aboriginal culture. In this arrangement, there is no party system and no official opposition; each candidate for office runs as an independent. The legislative assembly chooses the Premier and members of the executive council by secret ballot, but ministerial assignments are made by the Commissioner in Executive Council, who acts upon the advice of the Premier. It is thus possible to be a member of the executive council, in effect cabinet, but not a minister. Executive domination is limited, since the legislature is an active elective chamber and the cabinet is in a minority, necessitating constant compromise. The dynamics are somewhat like those in coalition governments, but with Aboriginal consensus traditions added. (Chapter 20)

constitutional conventions Binding rules of the Constitution that are not set down in writing and which cannot be enforced by the courts. These conventions fill in the gaps in the formal Constitution in order to make it workable. Generally, they define the powers and obligations of government. (Chapters 16, 21)

constitutional federalism In Canada, a period of attempts (most active between 1968 and 1992) to solve problems in federalism by amending key parts of the Constitution. (Chapter 23)

constitutional reform industry A catch-all phrase to describe the main lines of consensus among decentralist forces in Canada from 1968 to 1992. Supporters were interested in strengthening provincial/territorial–federal relationships and argued that the federal spending power should be constitutionally controlled. (Chapter 24)

contract funding (program-based funding) The primary method of financing of non-governmental entities and third-sector organizations through short-term, highly defined contracts with the state. (Chapter 17)

contract or agreement Generally, a means of forming a governmental organization; members of the organization must adhere to the duties set out in the contract or agreement. (Chapter 3)

Contribution Agreements Contractual financial agreements, many still in effect today, established to connect the federal government with individual First Nations bureaucracies after the Department of Citizenship and Immigration devolved its program responsibilities to First Nations governments beginning in the 1950s. (Chapter 19)

conventional bureaucracy Traditional bureaucratic forms in which citizens perceive bureaucrats as insufficiently accountable for their actions and in which public participation in the administrative process is minimal, resulting in feelings of powerlessness. (Chapter 15)

co-operative federalism In Canada, a period of relative intergovernmental harmony (inspired by the common goal of building a welfare state) in which the federal government took the lead, but worked closely with provincial/territorial governments. (Chapter 23)

Crown agency An agency that is assigned powers and duties of its own to be exercised by and in the name of the agency. (Chapter 3)

Crown corporation Crown agencies that have corporate status, generally established in order to provide for independence from external control over financial matters, personnel, and day-to-day activities. Crown corporations include parent Crown corporations, as defined in the Financial Administration Act, along with their wholly owned subsidiaries. (Chapter 3)

cybernetics A mid-twentieth-century theory of the policy sciences, related to systems theory, cybernetics states that an organization—like an organism—monitors, anticipates, and adapts to change in its environment. The most influential cybernetics theorist in the social sciences was Karl Deutsch, who considered not power but information to be central to political analysis and perceived the political system as a network of information channels. Other theorists have stressed cognition and learning within systems. (Chapter 8)

decision-making The third stage in the policy process; in this stage, governments select a particular course of action or non-action. (Chapter 22)

deferred (or back-loaded) compensation Compensation awarded by current governments in which the obligation falls on future generations of taxpayers and politicians; generally used by governments to avoid accountability for their actions. (Chapter 11)

deficit versus debt Deficit is the excess of expenditures over revenues; debt is the accumulated result of deficits, borrowing (loans), and liabilities. (Chapter 26)

delegated powers Governance authority delegated from the Crown. In relation to Aboriginal governance, it is an alternative to the broad, inherited, inherent right of self-government. (Chapter 19)

deliberative democracy An approach to enhancing citizen empowerment in which individuals act in partnership with government representatives to determine what is in the public's best interest. The goal is to create a truly public sphere of political decision-making. (Chapter 15)

democratic administration A form of governance based on citizen empowerment. It began as a form of participatory government (and was originally the intellectual endpoint preferred by both the New Left and the New Right) but has shifted in focus toward greater accountability and transparency in governance. In the twenty-first century, democratic administration is increasingly concerned with the ways that new technologies and globalization can provide opportunities (and challenges) for citizen engagement. (Chapter 15)

democratic deficit A condition in which democratic governments do not adhere to the rules of democracy; often, this deficit results from the practise of closed-door bargaining between governmental elites. (Chapter 23)

democratic values These values include rule of law, accountability, loyalty, and impartiality. (Chapter 16)

department Generally, the term refers to ministerial departments. A ministerial department has no legal powers and duties of its own; powers and duties are assigned to the department's minister, and the department's role is to support its minister. (Chapter 3)

Department of Finance The central department with near-exclusive responsibility for determining federal fiscal aggregates and for maintaining overall fiscal discipline. (Chapter 26)

departmental corporation A type of organization defined in section 2 of the Financial Administration Act as a corporation. By virtue of section 3(1)(a.1) of the Act, such a corporation is required to be 'established by an Act of Parliament' and to perform 'administrative, research, supervisory, advisory, or regulatory functions of a governmental nature'. (Chapter 3)

departmentalized cabinet The form of cabinet that was common at both the federal and provincial levels between 1920 and 1960, coinciding with the rise of the modern administrative state. It featured government departments at the centre of government decision-making and relied on the input of departmental experts. The prime minister (or premier) was dominant, but ministers were relatively autonomous in producing policy, and there was very little government-wide planning. (Chapters 5, 24)

deputy ministers (DMs) Civil servants closest to the political level, DMs are just below ministers in the organizational hierarchy. Their role is to assist and advise the minster. The DM belongs to a category of what are called 'discretionary appointments'—appointments at will by the Governor-in-Council who, by convention, acts on the recommendation of the prime minister. This category also includes ambassadors, CEOs of Crown Corporations, and members of federal agencies, boards, and commissions. However, DMs (and ambassadors) are appointed for an undetermined period, whereas the others are appointed for a set period of time. (Chapters 4, 28)

designated groups The four groups (Aboriginal people, persons with a disability, visible minorities, and women) for which employers must identify and remove barriers to employment under the requirements of the federal Employment Equity Act of 1995. (Chapters 9, 10)

devolution A form of alternative service delivery in which government transfers the responsibility for delivering service to other levels of government and/or profit or non-profit organizations that receive transfer payments to deliver the service. (Chapter 14)

digital governance The use of information technology to 1) design and deliver services within government, 2) to provide the general public with more information and scrutiny and therefore more opportunities to exact accountability from government, and 3) to allow government to manage the technological, content, and regulatory aspects of the 'information highway'. (Chapter 13)

direct delivery A form of alternative service delivery in which government delivers services directly through its ministries, focusing on results, cost recovery, getting the best value for the tax dollar, and customer service. (Chapter 14)

direct expenditures In government budgets, transfers of funds and payments, listed on the expenditure budget of the federal and provincial governments, as compared to **tax expenditures**. (Chapter 26)

direct management approach In relation to the governance of First Nations reserves, a control-oriented approach to governance that was practised by the federal government between the 1950s and the 1980s. In this model, elected First Nations leaders were responsible for band affairs and relationships with the federal (and provincial) government(s). (Chapter 19)

direct taxation A tax levied on an individual (or body) that must be paid by that individual and not passed on to a third party. (Chapter 25)

disentanglement Separating and defining the distinct roles of two levels of government (usually applied to provincial/territorial–local/municipal relationships). (Chapter 25)

disintermediation Cutting out the middle man or woman (e.g., in government–public relations, the politician); a criticism sometimes made of e-consultations and electronic service delivery. (Chapter 29)

dispute resolution Various methods used to end disagreements between employers and employees (and their representatives) when collective bargaining is not successful. (Chapter 10)

duty of loyalty The convention that public servants owe their political master (ultimately, the Crown) full, impartial advice on policy when it is necessary, and they must not publicly criticize the Crown or otherwise contribute to embarrassing either government or its representatives. (Chapter 21)

duty to accommodate A requirement under human rights legislation wherein an employer must make a reasonable effort to accommodate the needs of an employee. (Chapter 9)

ecological perspectives Views (of classes of organizations) that use concepts from biology and ecology—including natural selection, models of environmental change, and how specific organizational forms evolve with other forms—to examine the state of natural species. In political science, these perspectives can help to ascertain how public service institutions have been evolving and what has been selected in and out. (Chapter 8)

e-commerce Trade in which products and services are bought and sold via electronic networks. (Chapter 29)

economic liberalization Government's efforts to reduce barriers to international trade and market relations, often in the form of limiting or eliminating import tariffs. In North America, such efforts have led to the North American Free Trade Agreement. (Chapter 12)

e-government The use of new technologies, particularly information technology, to facilitate government operations. E-government operations include electronic service delivery, financial transactions, government–client relationship management, and data management. (Chapter 29)

electronic commerce See **e-commerce**.

electronic service delivery (ESD) The use of computer networks to provide public services to households and industry. (Chapter 29)

employment equity Legislation that requires an employer to ensure that its workforce is inclusive and representative of the four designated groups in Canada. (Chapters 9, 10, 18)

entitlement programs Programs that ensure the rights of citizens, as granted by government through legislation, for which government is financially obligated (e.g., social assistance programs). (Chapter 27)

essential services Services that are most necessary to the functioning of society and for which there are not viable private sector alternatives (e.g., police services, firefighting); they are usually distinguished from less essential services (e.g., municipal services, teaching). There is a slight tendency across Canadian jurisdictions to restrict the right to strike in the 'most essential' services and to allow it in the 'less essential' services. (Chapter 10)

ethical values These values include integrity, honesty, and fairness. (Chapter 16)

executive federalism In Canada, the combination of federalism and Westminster-style cabinet government, which concentrates power in the executive. It is defined by close intergovernmental relationships among first ministers, ministers, and senior bureaucrats, with political parties and legislatures playing only a minor role. (Chapter 23)

fair wage Wages determined more by political constraints than by profit constraints, often implemented in the public sector. Initiatives such as public sector pay equity and employment equity are forms of a 'fair wage'. (Chapter 11)

Federal Accountability Act Passed in December 2006 in response to the 'sponsorship scandal' and citizens' concerns over the government's ability to manage public services. The Act seeks to improve accountability across the federal government, at the levels of Parliament, departments, and agencies. So far, the Act has introduced a new Public Sector Integrity Commissioner, a Parliamentary Budget Officer, a Public Appointments Commission, an independent Commissioner of Lobbying, and a Conflict of Interest Code. It has also expanded the reach of the Access to Information Act, strengthened internal auditing regimes, and introduced the 'accounting officer' model to federal public administration. (Chapters 2, 3, 4, 5, 6, 13, 19, 26)

federal foundations Independent autonomous organizations designed to promote science, education, technology, and research. These foundations were first proposed in 1997 to address the challenges facing knowledge growth, and they can be established by legislation or as not-for-profit corporations under the Canada Corporations Act or similar legislation. (Chapter 14)

federalism The division of powers between a national (federal) government and regional (provincial, territorial, or state) governments. (Chapter 23)

Federalism of Openness See **Open Federalism**.

feminist analysis of the state Generally, analysis based on the desire for gender equality and/or feminist representation in state institutions. In its most extreme form, this analysis calls for a complete transformation of the traditionally patriarchal nature of the state. (Chapter 15)

feminist movement In relation to modern public administration, a movement that argues for a greater representation of women in the public realm and seeks a re-conceptualization of the public–private dichotomy. (Chapter 18)

final-offer arbitration A situation in dispute resolution in which the arbitrator must choose either the employer's offer or the union's offer; the arbitrator cannot choose a compromise between the two. (Chapter 10)

Finance cluster A group of federal institutions in which the Minister of Finance exercises not so much influence as co-operative networking. This cluster includes the Governor of the Bank of Canada, the Office of the Superintendent of Financial Institutions, and the Treasury Board Secretariat. (Chapter 2)

Financial Administration Act The major financial statute pertaining to federal public administration, the Act outlines requirements for dealing with revenues and expenditures, establishes various forms of public organization and their relative independence, and establishes the Finance Department and the Treasury Board and Treasury Board Secretariat. (Chapters 3, 4, 13)

financial watchdogs Bodies that control public spending after the fact by monitoring, warning, and advising. The main financial watchdog of the federal government is the Office of the Auditor General, but others (with more restricted roles) are the Parliamentary Budget Officer, accounting officers and the chief audit executive in each department, independent procurement officers, and the Public Sector Integrity Commissioner. The watchdogs control public spending after the fact and by warning and advising. (Chapter 26)

First Nations Governance Act A bill that was part of the suite of Indian Act reform legislation (four bills) introduced between 2001 and 2005. It sought to give bands more autonomy in responding effectively to their own needs in terms of leadership selection, self-governance and administration, and financial management. It also included the highly controversial stipulation that the Minister of Indian Affairs could step in and create regulations in cases when a band did not adequately create its own regulations. (Chapter 19)

Foreign Affairs cluster A group of federal institutions that represents Canada on the global front. This cluster includes the Department of Foreign Affairs, the Department of International Trade, the Minister of Finance, and the Department of Justice. (Chapter 2)

formal organization/informal organization Formal organizations are characterized as having bureaucratic form and its underpinnings (such as goals, hierarchy, offices, and legal authority). Informal organizations are concerned with informal and human dimensions, and they involve various leadership styles. The informal is seen as the complement to the formal. (Chapter 8)

frameworks See **spending power frameworks**.

franchising/licensing A form of alternative service delivery in which the government confers to a private firm the right or privilege to sell a product or service, according to prescribed terms and conditions, that unlicensed firms are not allowed to sell. (Chapter 14)

functions of the legislature The contributions to and the effect upon the political system made by Parliament. Some functions are formally recognized or explicit, whereas others are implicit. The functions include policy-making functions, representational functions, and maintenance functions. (Chapter 6)

garbage-can model A model in which public policy-making is viewed as an inherently irrational process in which decision-makers randomly associate problems with solutions. Actors choose problems from the 'garbage', then search for a solution. Solutions are then formed independent from problem-analysis, often by individuals who were not involved in identifying the problem, and solutions are often influenced by personal interests and biases. (Chapter 22)

Gathering Strength A white paper, or plan, released in 1998 by Indian and Northern Affairs Canada in response to the 1996 *Report of the Royal Commission on Aboriginal Peoples*. It supported self-governance for First Nations communities and proposed government departmental commitments for future

First Nations–government relations, particularly in the area of social and economic issues within First Nations communities. (Chapter 19)

gender equality The balance in rights and responsibilities between men and women. (Chapter 18)

general framework (of public administration) A model of the Canadian public service as an institution. A comprehensive version would include the entire system of Canadian public administration. (Chapter 1)

generations X and Y *Generation X* is a term coined by Douglas Coupland, who used the letter *x* to signify the generation's random and contradictory ways. It does not denote a firm demographic, but has been used by various observers to signify the post-boomer generation, or the generation born between 1965 and 1980. Generation Y, also referred to as the Millennials, was the generation after Generation X. Both are typified as posing a problem for public and private employers in that they are likely to expect higher salaries and fuller compensation packages, but without a willingness to work longer hours, compared to individuals from previous generations. (Chapter 13)

globalization An economic, political, social, cultural, and psychological phenomenon that links the local and the global, thus reducing the autonomy of individual nation-states, to a degree unparalleled in history. (Chapter 13)

governance regime In Canada, the regime is a mixture of institutions and power relations that typically concentrates power in the hands of a majority government led by the prime minister. Such a regime can greatly influence the public service on its own, although it often faces resistance from other levels of government, the Opposition, and the media. (Chapter 1)

government machinery/machinery of government The networks that exist within public administration systems and government in general. (Chapter 18)

government power and influence (over public service) In Canada, the cabinet and its members can influence eight areas of the government's relationship with public service: mandate and policy priorities; decision-making processes; appointments of deputy ministers; policy advice from the public service; oversight of departments', agencies', and deputy ministers' performance; public service structure and processes; interest and capabilities of ministerial offices; and the degree of autonomy of Parliament. (Chapter 1)

Great Depression The period of economic crisis from 1929 to 1939, caused by a confluence of many factors. The economic collapse was unparalleled in its severity, and unemployment in Canada increased from 3 per cent in 1929 to 23 per cent in 1933. Governments differed in their policy responses, with Canada taking a less interventionist approach than the US. (Chapter 12)

guardians In relation to finance in Canada, the Department of Finance and the Treasury Board Secretariat. (Chapter 26)

hard budget constraints In the context of globalized markets, constraints on government taxation and expenditure decisions rooted in international capital markets and bond ratings. (Chapter 11)

high-performance workforce A workforce with specialized skills needed for the new information economy. (Chapter 11)

human capital variables Variables such as education and experience that in part determine wages. (Chapter 11)

human rights The right of individuals and groups to not be adversely affected by discrimination based on characteristics such as age, gender, race, or religion. (Chapter 9)

incremental model A model in which policy-making is viewed as a practical exercise concerned with solving problems through trial-and-error processes (often based only on familiar alternatives) rather than through the comprehensive evaluation of all solutions. (Chapter 22)

independent advisor An individual outside the public service who is appointed by the prime minister and/or the cabinet to offer independent advice. (Chapter 2)

independent procurement auditor Introduced in the 2006 Federal Accountability Plan, an auditor charged with reviewing procurement practices across government on an ongoing basis to ensure fairness and transparency and with making recommendations for improvement. (Chapter 26)

Index of Representativeness (IR) A measure of representation relative to labour market availability. IR is calculated numerically through a formula; a value of 100 or above indicates that representation exists. (Chapter 9)

Indian A person registered, or entitled to be registered, in accordance with the Indian Act. One of three Aboriginal groups recognized as in the Constitution Act, 1982, Indians are often differentiated according to three categories: status Indians, non-status Indians, and treaty Indians. (Chapter 19)

Indian Act reform suite Four interrelated pieces of legislation first introduced in the 2001 Speech from the Throne when the federal government committed to 'strengthening its relationship with Aboriginal People': The Specific Claims Legislation Act (Bill C-6), the Land Management Act (Bill C-49), the First Nations Governance Act (Bill C-61, later reintroduced as Bill C-7), and the First Nations Fiscal and Statistical Management Act (Bill C-19). These bills were designed to replace parts of the Indian Act, as an alternative to reforming the entire Act. (Chapter 19)

Indian Register A list compiled by the federal government listing those Indians legally entitled to access federal programming and funding for status Indians. (Chapter 19)

indigenous approaches to public administration In Nunavut, the ways in which the territorial government incorporates Inuit values, culture, and language into its design, operation, and policy initiatives. (Chapter 20)

individual ministerial responsibility See **ministerial responsibility**.

informal organization See formal **organization/informal organization**.

information A hierarchy of data (knowledge) in which each level builds on the one(s) below it. (Chapter 29)

information and communications technologies (ICTs) See **information technology**.

information technology (IT) Computer-mediated technologies that facilitate the gathering, storage, processing, analysis, and transmission of information. (Chapter 29)

inherent right of self-government A broad, inherited right not subject to diminution by the Crown, analogous to 'natural law' in the Western liberal tradition; usually distinguished from the weaker alternative, governance through delegated powers. (Chapter 19)

Inherent Right of Self-Government Policy A policy, introduced in 1995, intended to facilitate negotiations for self-government between individual First Nations communities and the government. It was created to address government obligations under the 1993 report *Creating Opportunity* (the so-called Red Book), and it recognized First Nations' inherent right of self-government (under section 35 of the Canadian Constitution Act, 1982) in matters related to traditional and cultural affairs. (Chapter 19)

inside initiation An agenda-setting style whereby influential groups with special access to decision-makers initiate a policy, presenting both a problem and a solution. Often, these groups want to avoid public discussion and criticism, and the public is not involved in the process. (Chapter 22)

institutionalization of bureaucratic independence Official recognition of, along with efforts to strengthen the institutions that contribute to, bureaucratic independence. (Chapter 21)

institutionalization of the women's movement The fact that women's programs and structures are now viewed as part of legitimate state structures (rather than merely transitory). (Chapter 18)

institutionalized See **institutionalization of the women's movement**.

institutionalized cabinet The form of cabinet that tended to predominate after 1960; it featured formal cabinet structures, established central agencies, and implemented new budgeting and management techniques that emphasized shared knowledge, collegial decision-making, and the formation of government-wide priorities. (Chapters 5, 24)

institutionalized environments A comparative perspective that explores how classes of organizations align with and distance themselves from broader regimes in their environments. (Chapter 8)

institutions of the judicial branch Institutions that exist to support the judiciary administratively while protecting judicial independence, or to supplement the work of the judiciary. (Chapter 2)

institutions of the legislative branch Institutions attached to each house of Parliament; they provide department-like support to the elected representatives. They primarily consist of legal advisors and committee staffs, but also include management experts and financial managers. The Library of Parliament, which serves both houses, is also considered part of this public service. (Chapter 2)

integrated governance A model of governance that involves a multi-level (horizontal or collaborative) government; this has become the dominant model in the new century. Some examples include earlier waves of reform (e.g., shared services, co-provision of services, internal single-window delivery, multi-level governance outsourcing). (Chapter 1)

integrated justice A concept based on the notion of seamless automated (electronic) processes with a single point of entry for data in criminal and civil cases. (Chapter 7)

intergenerational burden Burdens that are shifted to future generations of taxpayers; examples include excessive wage settlements in the public sector, forms of deferred compensation, and the burden associated with health-care expenditures for an aging population. (Chapter 11)

intersectionality Relating to the intersections, or analogous concerns, of gender with other markers of equity (e.g., visible minority status, Aboriginal status, disability). (Chapter 18)

Inuit-oriented public government The system of government in place at the territorial level in Nunavut, where over 85 per cent of the citizens are Inuit, in which focus is on full representation of Aboriginal citizens and on embedding Inuit culture and language in government operations. (Chapter 20)

Inuit Qaujimajatuqangit (IQ) Traditional Inuit knowledge (literally, 'that which is long known by Inuit') meant to provide responsive, accountable government by incorporating traditional Inuit practices and values into government policy and operations. (Chapter 20)

judicial administration A field of study barely a century old concerned with the organization, management, and operation of courts and court systems. (Chapter 7)

judicial administrative independence (administrative independence) Freedom of functioning of courts administration that reflects the unique role of the courts within a traditional cabinet system. One manifestation would be to shift parts of the court administrative staff to a separate judicial administration budget controlled by the judges. (Chapter 7)

judicial impartiality The stipulation that a judge is bound to decide only on the relevant law and facts presented in court. (Chapter 7)

judicial independence The ability of the individual judge to perform his or her adjudicative function, whether in court or in chambers, free from external interference. (Chapter 7)

Justice cluster A group of federal institutions that share, with the Department of Justice, a desire to safeguard the rule of law; it therefore exhibits a unique independence from politics within government. It includes the Minister of Justice and the Director of Public Prosecutions. (Chapter 2)

Keynesian consensus The post-war agreement within many Western nations, including Canada, to support the system of economics proposed by John Maynard Keynes. Keynes had argued that governments should be involved in promoting the economy by creating public policies aimed at increasing aggregate consumer demand in times of economic downturn, in an effort to stimulate the economy. (Chapter 24)

Keynesian welfare state A public-policy organization, developed out of Keynesian economics, that embraces the goal of full employment and a comprehensive social safety net for those unable to achieve self-sufficiency in the market economy. (Chapters 15, 17)

legislative auditors Individuals appointed by legislature to conduct independent audits of government processes and agencies. These auditors report directly to the legislature and are often the only official channel through which legislatures are regularly informed of government's stewardship of public funds. (Chapter 27)

lesson-drawing Policy-makers drawing lessons from past uses of policy instruments. (Chapter 22)

levels of expenditure The range of government budget coverage: strategic (highest level), departmental (mid-level), and unit (lowest level). (Chapter 27)

line departments Departments that administer substantive sectors of public affairs (rather than managing the process of governance itself). (Chapter 2)

line item (budgeting) A type of budget that focuses on the inputs (or costs of operating) of government expenditure, as opposed to the purposes (outputs) for which money is spent. Introduced in 1937 to allow for standard objects of expenditure (supplies, contracts, programs, staff, activities, etc.), the format is still used today, along with other forms of budgeting, such as program budgeting and performance budgeting. It was initially developed to heighten accountability and control, but it lacks an emphasis on public disclosure and comprehensibility. (Chapter 26)

local government A broad term that encompasses both municipalities and special-purpose bodies. (Chapter 25)

Magistrate's Court The court at the lowest level of the judicial hierarchy for much of Canadian history until the middle of the twentieth century; also referred to as 'inferior courts'. Magistrates were usually non-lawyers, serving on a part-time basis at the pleasure of the government. (Chapter 7)

mainstreaming (of gender) The integration of gender into mainstream programs that were not originally established with gender questions first and foremost. The goal is to increase the visibility of gender issues in day-to-day operations. (Chapter 18)

managing diversity An approach to administration that emphasizes recognizing, encouraging, and valuing diversity. (Chapter 18)

marketization The application of market criteria to allocate public resources and also to measure the efficiency of public service producers and suppliers. The goal is reduced cost and increased quality of service resulting from competition between potential producers. (Chapter 17)

mediation The use of professional mediators (or negotiators) not immediately associated with disputing parties to assist in coming to a resolution. In civil society, it is exemplified in such measures as family counselling and workplace committees. (Chapters 7, 17)

merit Worth, or deserving of reward. In employment, it refers to hiring the individual who best meets job requirements. This principle has driven hiring processes in the federal government since 1918, and it has been supplemented in the late twentieth century by considerations of representativeness as a subset of merit. (Chapter 16)

merit system The systems set up by federal and provincial governments to promote merit and combat patronage in government institutions. (Chapter 16)

ministerial responsibility The expression of accountability in the political realm. Until the latter part of the twentieth century, a minister was responsible (culpable) for *every* action that took place in his or her department. The modern realist version of the doctrine recognizes a distinction between official acts of which the minister can reasonably be expected to be aware, and those that the minister could not have known about. The minister may be held culpable for failing to take appropriate corrective action in the event he or she learns of an illegal or inappropriate act. A minister may be asked to resign in certain cases: misleading Parliament, authorizing unreasonable use of executive power, or engaging in immoral conduct unbecoming to a minister of the Crown. (Chapters 4, 6, 16)

ministers Members of cabinet, usually given the direction of a governmental department; neither ministers nor the cabinet are not mentioned in the Constitution, but exist by virtue of convention and, in the case of ministers, statute. (Chapter 4)

mixed social economy model A model, prevalent in the Keynesian welfare state, for social service provision in which services are delivered through a combination of state and privately run and privately administered programs. (Chapter 17)

mobilization An agenda-setting style whereby decision-makers try to move an issue from a formal, or governmental, agenda to a public agenda. Government then tries to enlist support for the issue among the general public. (Chapter 22)

model employer An ideal employer; a quality that is expected from governments because, while they are a major employer, they also have the power to set collective bargaining rules. (Chapter 10)

morphology The theory that an organization evolves like an organism, going through natural stages of growth and maturity, aligning itself with new environments, and even *altering* external environments. (Chapter 8)

municipality A body, governed by elected officials, that is responsible for various government functions and activities at the local level. (Chapter 25)

neo-liberalism An ideological approach to governing and public administration that supports freedom of the market and of the individual. Developed in response to a perceived 'government failure', neo-liberalism encourages a reduced role of the state in economic and social domains, deregulation of labour and financial markets, and the elimination of trade barriers. (Chapter 17)

New Left A socio-political movement, beginning in the 1960s and 1970s, that pursued the empowerment of citizens through increased participation in government policies and programs within the established bureaucracy. Its goal was to redress the social and economic inequalities produced by the market. (Chapter 15)

New Public Management (NPM) A diverse group of ideas and initiatives, originating in the late 1980s and early 1990s, that were inspired by private sector values; these ideas were increasingly popular in governments who sought to lower costs, provide better service, contain deficits, and incorporate new technologies. These precepts were embedded in earlier post-war reports and reforms but were not as influential or integrated as in the newer NPM literature. (Chapters 1, 15, 17, 19)

New Right A right-wing vision of social and economic life, influential in the 1970s through 1990s, that supports minimal state influence on social and economic life, encouraging the state to facilitate rather than regulate the market. In this vision, citizen empowerment can be achieved through increased competition, choice, and freedom of contract between users of public goods and services and the government. (Chapter 15)

'New Social Order' The name given in 1945 to the increased federal role in society and economy. The concept was heavily influenced by British intellectuals such as Keynes, who argued that governments could have avoided the worst effects of the Depression by taking steps (in the form of direct government expenditures, social programs) to promote public demand for goods and services. The shift to the new order was not immediate, but over the next quarter century it was reflected in programs such as the Family Allowance program, Unemployment Insurance, and government-based pension plans, all of which dramatically increased the amount of money the federal government paid directly to citizens. (Chapter 12)

new values These values include service, innovation, quality, and teamwork. Most of the new values fall into the category of professional values. (Chapter 16)

non-competitive factors Factors (e.g., political constraints, the voting power of public servants) that affect public sector wages. Generally, market forces dictate a floor but not a ceiling to public sector wages; as such, non-competitive factors tend to allow public sector wages to rise above (but rarely below) wages paid for comparable positions in the private sector. (Chapter 11)

non-status Indian An Indian not registered as an Indian under the Indian Act and therefore not entitled to the same rights and benefits available to status Indians. Non-status Indians consider themselves Indians or members of a First Nation, but are not legally recognized as Indians because they are unable to prove their status, they have lost their status rights, or they have experienced discriminatory practices. (Chapter 19)

Office of the Auditor General See **Auditor General of Canada**.

Office of the Information Commissioner An office of Parliament that deals with complaints from those alleging denial of rights under the Access to Information Act; officers use statutory investigative and mediation powers, in the fashion of an ombudsman. (Chapter 6)

Office of the Privacy Commissioner An office of Parliament that investigates complaints, conducting audits and pursuing court action, under the Privacy Act and the Personal Information Protection and Electronic Documents Act (PIPEDA). (Chapter 6)

Officers of Parliament Neutral officials independent from the executive government who perform tasks essential to the operation of Parliament, or in the public interest. They report directly to Parliament and not to the executive, and both houses are involved in some fashion in their appointment. In recent years, their numbers and independence has increased. Currently, the Officers of Parliament are the Auditor General (established in 1868), the Chief Electoral Officer (1920), the Official Languages Commissioner (1970), the Privacy Commissioner (1983), the Access to Information Commissioner (1983), the Conflict of Interest and Ethics Commissioner (2007), the Public Sector Integrity Commissioner (2007), and the Commissioner of Lobbying (2008). Officers of the Legislature are the provincial counterparts. (Chapter 6)

Open Federalism (Federalism of Openness) In Canada, the new Conservative Party's approach to federalism and in particular the federal spending power, which emphasizes accountability and an increased voice for provinces/territories in federal decision-making that affects their jurisdictions. This structure was first discussed at the Conservative Party's founding conference in 2005, and it was most clearly enunciated in the 2007 federal budget. (Chapter 24)

organizational differentiation and integration A concept first presented by Lawrence and Lorsch in 1967 to describe the attributes of organizations that successfully adapt to changes in their environments. Differentiation is the segmentation of the organization into distinct subsystems performing a section of the organization's task, and integration is achieving unity of effort among these units. (Chapter 8)

organizational systematics An approach, using concepts from biology, that seeks to identify different species (or organizations) according to reproductive integrity and to inform assessments and debates about the evolving structure and development over a typical life of a species member as well as the evolutionary trajectory of a species as a whole. (Chapter 8)

outside initiation An agenda-setting style whereby a group outside the government articulates a grievance and tries to gain support from other groups in the population in order to create pressure on decision-makers to force the issue onto the formal agenda. The public is often involved in the process. (Chapter 22)

Parliament The federal legislative power 'consisting of the Queen, an Upper House styled the Senate, and the House of Commons' (section 17 of the Constitution Act, 1867). (Chapter 6)

Parliamentary Budget Officer An officer who provides independent analysis of Parliamentary financial and economy-related matters; they often provide financial estimates for proposed actions. (Chapters 6, 26, 28)

partisan political activity Activities held by, or on behalf of, registered political parties. (Chapter 16)

partnerships A formal arrangement in which government agrees to provide services in partnership with other parties where each contributes resources and shares risks and rewards. (Chapter 14)

patronage The practice of appointing and promoting public servants on the basis of partisan political considerations rather than of merit. By the early 1960s such appointments had been largely eliminated from the federal government, but a few, some say functionally useful, patronage appointments remain (e.g., ministerial staff and governor-in-council appointments, although these are outside the merit-based public service). (Chapter 16)

pattern bargaining The tendency to have key settlements emulated across similar groups in the public sector, usually driven by considerations of comparability. Today, considerations of local conditions and the employers' ability to pay have become more prominent than pattern bargaining in dispute settlement. (Chapter 10)

pay equity The comparable worth guideline, embedded in legislation, that requires equal pay for predominately female jobs of equal value to predominately male jobs; equivalent to the US term 'comparable worth'. (Chapter 9)

payments to individuals and institutions Payments made by the federal government to individuals and institutions (usually in the form of grants) in areas related to matters of provincial jurisdiction. (Chapter 24)

Penner Report The report of the Special Parliamentary Committee on Indian Self-Government, established in 1982 and chaired by MP Keith Penner to examine the federal government's overall relationships with Indian people. The report recommended delegated powers of self-government for First Nations communities in respect to certain administrative areas (e.g., education, child care, membership); it also recommended that the federal approval should be required in decisions involving broader areas (e.g., resource use). (Chapter 19)

people values Primarily, values that involve caring and compassion for others on an individual level. (Chapter 16)

performance audits Economic efficiency audits that review the operations of an organization. (Chapter 26)

performance measurement and reporting An aspect of public sector reform that is meant to assist Parliament in its scrutiny function and lead to a sustained focus on substantive policy outcomes. Annually, hundreds of reports on plans and performance are tabled in Parliament, placing a strain on Members' ability to absorb and make practical use of all the information. (Chapter 6)

policy communities A meso- (middle-) level field of study that bridges the gap between the study of policy-making at the macro (societal) level and at the micro level (where there is a restricted number of participants). The study holds that active and potential policy actors share a common focus or outlook or ideational framework. Its focus is broader and more inclusive than that of policy networks; some even see networks as a distinct, more cohesive part or subset of policy communities. (Chapter 8)

policy community A type of policy subsystem, generally composed of a relatively large set of actors (including government policy-makers, representatives of non-governmental organizations, members of the media, academics, and members of the general public) with some knowledge of the policy issue in question. (Chapter 22)

policy cycle The stages in policy development, also called policy stages, or the stagist approach. A policy cycle generally involves agenda-setting, policy formulation, decision-making, policy implementation, and policy evaluation. (Chapter 22)

policy evaluation The fifth stage in the policy process; in this stage, both state and societal actors monitoring the results of policies, often leading to the reconceptualization of policy problems and solutions. (Chapter 22)

policy formulation The second stage in the policy process; in this stage, policy options are developed within government, and infeasible options are excluded. (Chapter 22)

policy implementation The fourth stage in the policy process; in this stage, government put decisions into effect. (Chapter 22)

policy learning The notion that policy actors can learn from the formal and informal evaluation of policies in which they are engaged; this learning often leads actors to modify their positions on issues of policy. (Chapter 22)

policy network A type of policy subsystem, generally composed of fewer actors than in a policy community. Actors are involved with formal government institutions, and they must be knowledgeable about policy areas. Generally, members of the network have established familiar patterns for interaction within the group. (Chapter 22)

policy networks A meso-level field of study that deals with participants (sometimes referred to as 'subgovernments') in a particular area of policy, or of the state apparatus. Most analysts hold that policy networks involve regular, long-term participants in a policy-formulation process that spans government and civil society. The networks may be highly or weakly integrated (stable and interdependent or loosely structured with a multiplicity of relations with other groups), but all are composed of actors, both state and societal, who seek to further their own interests. (Chapter 8)

policy process Variously interpreted, but usually described as the notion of the policy process as an ongoing cycle in which policies are adapted into new forms. (Chapter 22)

policy style The methods government uses to create and implement policies. These methods can vary widely between governments, over time, and between states. (Chapter 22)

policy subsystem A group of policy actors involved in policy formulation; the relevant policy actors are restricted to those who not only have an opinion on a subject but also have some level of knowledge of the subject area. (Chapter 22)

political neutrality The convention that prohibits public servants from engaging in activities that impair or seem to impair their impartiality or the impartiality of the public service as a whole (e.g., partisan political activities). In Canada, the courts have noted that restricting political activities of all public servants is contrary to the *Canadian Charter of Rights and Freedoms*. Consequently, the Public Service Employment Act permits political activities by public servants, as long as their involvement does not affect their impartiality. (Chapters 16, 21)

political rights for public servants In Canada, the rights to vote in elections, to contribute to political parties, to canvass on behalf of a political party or political cause, to express political opinions, and to be nominated for and run for public office. (Chapter 16)

politics–administration dichotomy Originally developed to oppose the spoils system and to promote a more professional business-like public service, this idea holds that administrative areas of government have more in common with business practices (technical implementation) than with political activities (the development of laws, policies, and public values). (Chapters 15, 16)

post-bureaucratic organization model The model based on citizen needs, participatory decision-making, collective action, innovation, and results-based accountability, opposed to the policy culture based on organizational needs, control and command, and procedural accountability. The model is characterized by decentralization of leadership, independent employees, emphasis on innovation, and increased efficiency. (Chapter 13)

Prime Minister's Office A partisan-oriented central agency whose authority derives from the prerogatives of the prime minister. Staffed by officials sympathetic to the party in power, the Office engages in political intelligence-gathering; organizes the prime minister's media relations, correspondence, and timetable; and acts as the liaison between party, government, and Parliament. (Chapter 26)

prime ministerial cluster A group of federal institutions whose lead figure is the head of government; at its highest level are the vital interests of the state and the legitimate exercise of political power. (Chapter 2)

priority setters In relation to finance in Canada, the Prime Minister's Office and the Privy Council Office. (Chapter 26)

Privacy Act, The An act passed in 1983 that gives citizens the right to see government documents that contain information about themselves and restricts access to documents that contain other people's personal information. The act also restricts government agencies from collecting personal information that is not essential to their operations, limits the ability of agencies to share personal information about citizens, and forces agencies to disclose to citizens the reason for collecting personal information. (Chapter 29)

privatization The selling of government-owned enterprises, assets, or controlling interests to the private sector. There have been waves of privatization at various periods in Canadian history, for example the post-World War II divesting of Crown corporations. (Chapters 10, 12, 14, 17)

Privy Council Office A non-partisan central agency that serves as the secretariat for cabinet and its committees, and for coordinating policy development for the Government of Canada. It is also responsible for monitoring government priorities and for liaising between cabinet and department and agencies. It is led by the Clerk of the Privy Council, who is also designated as Secretary of Cabinet and Head of the Public Service. (Chapters 4, 5, 26)

procedural instruments Policy instruments associated with the information and decision-making processes rather than the substance of policy. They support government aims and initiatives by managing state–societal interactions. They indirectly influence the number or nature of actors in the policy subsystems that policy-makers face. Such procedural instruments as government–NGO partnerships, public advisory commissions, roundtables, and information dissemination provide government with means to steer policy processes in its preferred directions by manipulating policy actors and their interrelationships. (Chapter 22)

professional values These values include efficiency, effectiveness, quality, service, innovation, teamwork, and accountability. (Chapter 16)

program budget A type of budget that examines services and programs or program elements (outputs); it also outlines the ways in which the money was spent. This format helps to highlight cross-governmental priorities and complementary and competing expenditures, but can lack adequate information about inputs. (Chapter 26)

Provincial Courts What Magistrate's Courts were transformed into, beginning in Quebec and Ontario in the 1960s, over the next two decades in every province. Their work today is primarily in criminal matters, particularly over young offenders, but some have been given expanded jurisdiction in civil matters and in family law. (Chapter 7)

provincial legislatures The provincial analogue of the federal Parliament, consisting of the legislative assembly and the Queen. Provincial legislatures usually demonstrate more limited staff resources, shorter legislative sessions, less active committee systems, and more executive (cabinet) domination. (Chapter 6)

Public Accounts Committee (PAC) A committee of the federal House of Commons (there are also counterparts in provincial legislatures). It oversees the expenditures of government, complementing the work of standing committees of the House, which provide more specific, departmental oversight. It is also the mechanism through which the Auditor General of Canada reports to Parliament. (Chapters 4, 27)

public comment In general, evaluations (particularly of a political nature), positive or negative, made in public. In Canada, public servants have been traditionally prohibited from engaging in public comment on government policies, parties, or personalities, aside from discussions of a technical or scientific nature or to explain already-established governmental procedures and policies. Nevertheless, as with political activity, the trend is in the direction of extending the permissible rights of public servants to engage in public comment. (Chapter 16)

Public Servant Disclosure Protection Act Also known as the 'whistleblower act', this accountability act provides protection for public servants who disclose wrongdoing within government. The Act requires public servants to follow established procedures in order to secure the handling of sensitive information. In order to obtain protection, whistleblowers must make their disclosure to the Commissioner, must disclose no more information than reasonably necessary, and must not violate confidences of cabinet. (Chapter 21)

Public Servants Disclosure Protection Tribunal A board, established by the Federal Accountability Act, that is charged with protecting public servants who disclose government wrongdoings by ordering disciplinary actions against the party or parties responsible for any unfair suffering the public servant has faced as a result of his or her disclosure. (Chapter 28)

public service A multi-faceted universe of organizations that can be formed to accomplish almost any purpose or objective the government wishes to achieve, subject always to the constitutional limitations imposed by the Constitution Act, 1867 and to the Charter of Rights and Freedoms. (Chapters 3, 6, 20, 21)

public service anonymity The requirement of public servants to provide confidential advice to ministers and to avoid the public spotlight and public attention. (Chapter 16)

public service ethics Commonly held value standards that public servants are expected to operate under. In general, ethics refers to questions of right and wrong (e.g., questions of integrity). (Chapter 16)

Public Service Modernization Act An act of public sector reform in which the federal government and the deputy minister of an organization are held most accountable for actions, while the central agencies act to provide services and oversee the functioning of organizations. (Chapter 14)

Public Service Rearrangement and Transfer of Duties Act An act that provides for the rearrangement of certain departments. It authorizes the Governor-in-Council to reassign or amalgamate departments or departmental branches under another minister, but it does not permit an increase in the number of departments. It is frequently used and permits quick reorganizations of the federal bureaucracy. (Chapter 2)

public service values These values involve enduring social, cultural, and ideological beliefs that influence the choices of public servants. (Chapter 16)

punctuated equilibrium A theory that posits a stable pattern of policy-making punctuated by periods of instability and abrupt change in the agenda-setting stage of the policy process. Normally, there is agreement on problem definition and agenda placement resulting from a dominant policy subsystem (or policy monopoly) that is in control and provides stability. Instability arises with the emergence of new issues and new institutions that come about to deal with these issues; the new institutions in turn upset the previous policy monopoly. Instability opens up the policy agenda for debate, and agenda access, promoted especially by the media, often features criticism of the previously dominant institutions. The new institutions in turn lead to more stability. (Chapter 8)

purchase of service A form of alternative service delivery in which government purchases services through a contract with a private firm, but government retains accountability for the service. (Chapter 14)

queues or shortages The demand or absence of demand for public sector jobs. (Chapter 11)

rational model A model in which policy-making is viewed as a systematic method in which policy-makers establish a goal, explore alternative strategies for achieving the goal, predict the consequences and likelihood of each alternative, and then choose the option with the most benefits and the least risks. (Chapter 22)

regional districts (British Columbia) A system of municipal governance established in British Columbia in the 1960s, designed to bring services to areas that previously had no official municipal government. (Chapter 25)

registered See **registered Indian**.

registered Indian An individual who is legally entitled to access federal programming and funding for status Indian people and who is attached to, or is a member of, a band recognized by federal government. The names of registered Indians appear on the Indian Register. (Chapter 19)

***Report of the Royal Commission on Aboriginal Peoples* (RCAP Report)** The 1996 report of the Royal Commission on Aboriginal Peoples (the Dussault–Erasmus Commission), which supported First Nations self-government within the context of the Canadian Constitution. It called for new relationships with government (including an Aboriginal Parliament and the abolition of DIAND), self-determination through self-government, economic self-sufficiency, and personal and collective healing. Sensitive to the differing needs of the various Aboriginal, it advocated three different models for self-government: the 'national model' (for groups with defined memberships), 'public government' (in regions where Aboriginals form the majority of the population), and 'community of interest government' (an administrative arrangement to serve urban Indians from diverse backgrounds). In this arrangement, First Nations governments would negotiate with provincial governments on a government-to-government basis and with the federal government on a nation-to-nation basis. (Chapter 19)

representation In Canadian employment equity policy, representation signifies the degree to which an organization's workforce reflects each of the four designated groups in the available labour supply. (Chapter 9)

representative public service Public service that is representative in two ways: 1) public servants advocate for (represent) the interests of individuals within the community and 2) the body of public servants reflects (is representative of) the makeup of the community in terms of personal backgrounds (culture, language, sex, socio-economic status, education, race, etc.). (Chapter 20)

responsibility A convention of the Constitution by which ministers are answerable before Parliament for the administration of their particular department and/or portfolio. (Chapter 2)

restorative justice A replacement, popularized by Australian criminologist John Braithwaite, for the system of criminal justice in which all disputes would require a restoration of the balance of relationships within a community, and thus the participation of members of the community in individual cases. (Chapter 7)

retrenchment The drive to restrain expenditures. It has taken different forms in Canada, but the most effective way of achieving this aim has been the reduction of transfers to people and to provinces. (Chapter 12)

revolving funds Funds that are theoretically self-financing and generally permitted to retain all or part of their revenue. (Chapter 27)

role See **budget roles**.

roles of Parliament in relation to the public service In relation to the public service, Parliament plays the following roles: legitimizer, policy-maker, creator, financier, and scutinizer. (Chapter 6)

rolling budget A budget, usually created in smaller organizations, in which expenditures are directly linked to revenues and other available funds. It allows the organization to make continual adjustments to its programs depending on its revenues. (Chapter 27)

royal or Crown prerogative The residual authority, often arbitrary, that is left in the hands of the Crown; it has the power, infrequently used, to create public organizations such as departments. It is the source of authority for the Privy Council Office in Canada, and the rare method of creating royal commissions (the Inquiries Act is the more usual method). (Chapter 3)

rule of law The condition in which all individuals are equally subject to the law and not by arbitrary or discretionary decisions made by government. (Chapter 21)

'sacrality' of the state (or 'sacralized state') A dominant image in popular thought, promoted by the Canadian state in the nineteenth century, and reflected in the symbols and rituals (flags, anthems) designed to promote patriotic love. (Chapter 12)

satisfycing A less-than-optimal criterion for choice that decision-makers use in conditions of bounded rationality (when they do not have full information about all alternatives and all consequences). Decision-makers do not opt for the best solution, but for the most satisfactory one, based on the information they have. (Chapter 22)

scientific management A term usually associated with the work of F.W. Taylor. Essentially, it is the process of taking the knowledge monopoly about task performance from the worker and transferring it to management, who systematize it and train workers according to increasingly more refined methods. (Chapter 8)

self-standing statutes Statutes by which departments are established; they name a department specifically and outline its leadership, management, and responsibilities. (Chapter 2)

separation-of-powers theory The theory that the legislative arm of government makes the laws, the executive arm implements and administers those laws, and the judicial arm adjudicates cases based on those laws. (Chapter 3)

Service Canada An alternative service delivery arrangement in which a wide range of government programs and services from across federal departments and other levels of government are integrated to provide citizens with easy-to-access, personalized service. Individual departments concentrate on developing outcomes-focused policies and programs, while Service Canada concentrates on improving the delivery of programs and services. (Chapters 14, 29)

services Tangible and intangible assistance provided to citizens; some service activities involve partnership between non-profit organizations and the state, while others are independent actions. (Chapter 17)

shared-cost programs In general, a mutually beneficial program in which the cost is shared between two or more affected parties. In Canada, such programs between provinces/territories and the federal government have often led to controversy over the federal spending power, as they often involve great sums of money being paid to the provincial/territorial governments, but they have also resulted in many beneficial social programs. Initially, provinces/territories were required to adhere to strict conditions attached to the funding, but many of these conditions were eliminated when the federal government began to favour block grants and tax transfers to fund social programs. (Chapter 24)

shift point See **budget shift point**.

short-run demand changes Demand changes for public sector workers emanating from proximate factors such as the changing demographics of the population. (Chapter 11)

single-tier systems Systems of local governance in which there is only one level of municipal administration. (Chapter 25)

social capital The recognized value of social networks in coordinating for the benefit of individuals, organizations, and society as a whole. (Chapter 17)

social cohesion A sense of inclusiveness in a given society; the shared impression that all are involved in a common enterprise, share common values, face common challenges, and care enough about each other to accept reduction in the disparities of wealth and income. (Chapter 17)

social contracts In Canada, one measure (among many) employed in the 1980s and early 1990s that effectively controlled public sector wages. In the so-called social contracts, employees were given mandatory unpaid leave days as part of the freezes. (Chapter 10)

social learning In relation to public policy, a form of learning in which ideas and events in the larger policy community penetrate into policy evaluations. (Chapter 22)

Social Union Framework Agreement (SUFA) An agreement in the collaborative federalism mode, signed in 1999, between the federal government and the provinces and territories. It addressed social policy concerns, providing guidelines to guarantee an 'adequate' level of social support for all citizens, and to ensure citizens' mobility rights across Canada. (Chapters 23, 24)

soft budget constraints In the context of globalized markets, constraints on government taxation and expenditure decisions rooted in political processes. (Chapter 11)

Special Operating Agencies (SOAs) Autonomous service units, at both the federal and the provincial levels, that operate under the Financial Administration Act. A type of alternate service delivery mechanism roughly modelled after the Thatcher–Major era 'executive agencies', they are meant to operate in a more independent, business-like manner, involving negotiated agreements between the sponsoring departments and the Treasury Board. In 2010, the federal government had 16 SOAs, most established in the 1990s. (Chapters 6, 14, 29)

special-purpose body (SPB) A body, functioning at the local level, that is usually only responsible for one function (or a set of closely related functions). These bodies are usually very efficient, but can raise issues of accountability, as their managers are sometimes appointed rather than elected. (Chapter 25)

spenders Advocates of increased expenditures, most often departments and agencies. (Chapter 26)

spending power frameworks A series of issues and considerations that could feature in any broad attempt to reform the federal spending power. For example, what would the threshold of provincial consent be for introduction of new spending power programs? And how strictly would provinces have to follow set guidelines in order to qualify for federal compensation? (Chapter 24)

spending power of Parliament The power of Parliament to make payments to people, institutions, or governments in relation to areas in which it (Parliament) does not necessarily have the power to legislate. (Chapter 24)

spending power tests A series of broad conditions that critics of the federal spending power advanced as matters to be met in any reform of the spending power. For example, national objectives should be determined by a co-operative approach rather than a unilateral federal definition, and the federal principle (the principle of non-subordination of one level of government to another in areas of its own jurisdiction) should be followed. (Chapter 24)

Standing Committee on Public Accounts The analogue of the Public Accounts Committee in the UK. (Chapter 4)

status Indian In legal terms, an individual who is legally recognized as Indian under the Indian Act. (Chapter 19)

statute An act of Parliament, commonly used to create a new government entity. A statute may provide for the structure, composition, mandate and/or management of the new body. (Chapter 3)

structural-functional tradition The theory that there are certain functions, or activities, that must be performed for a society or political system in order to survive; these functions are performed by specialized structures in society, although the structures are not always apparent. Some theorists have emphasized the importance of the internal life of organizations—how they struggle with tensions between rational or public goals, informal goals of system maintenance, and interactions with external environments. (Chapter 8)

subordinate legislation (or delegated legislation) A subordinate, or secondary, law-making power delegated to the executive by an act of Parliament (in the form of orders-in-council or regulations made by a minister or agency); authority for creating the legislation comes from a primary, enabling piece of legislation passed by Parliament. Examples of bodies established by subordinate legislation include commissions of inquiry, advisory committees, and review panels. (Chapter 3)

substantive instruments Policy instruments that directly provide goods and services to members of the public or governments. (Chapter 22)

substantive statutes Statutes that create departments in order to achieve a substantive public policy objective; the policy itself, rather than the creation of the department, is the object of the legislation. For example, the Financial Administration Act is concerned with financial management of departments and agencies, but it creates the Department of Finance and the Treasury Board Secretariat. (Chapter 2)

superior and inferior courts Constitutionally, superior courts have what is legally termed 'inherent jurisdiction' (general jurisdiction) in the provinces derived from their link to superior courts in England and their constitutional entrenchment in section 96 of the Constitution Act, 1867. Thus, superior courts have inherent authority to enforce their own orders (e.g., through use of the contempt power). Provincial (inferior) Courts are courts of 'limited jurisdiction'; their jurisdiction is limited to powers conferred by statute. (Chapter 7)

supplementary budgets or estimates Mid-course adjustments needed during the lifespan of a budget. (Chapter 27)

systemic discrimination A policy, procedure, or system that has a valid purpose but also an unintended adverse impact on one or more groups protected by human rights legislation. Remedies are typically varied, as there is often more than one way to change the system while ensuring that the intended purpose is preserved. (Chapter 9)

systemic remedy See **systemic discrimination**.

systems theory A theory of interconnectedness between organizational structures and environments, based on concepts from biology, that was popular in political science and organizational theory in the 1950s and 1960s. One of its most prominent proponents in political science was David Easton, who examined how political systems manage to persist (survive and adapt) through time in the face of the stresses that face them. He found that they do so by converting inputs (demands and supports) into outputs (decisions) and by monitoring and reacting to the environment of the political system. (Chapter 8)

tax expenditures In government budgets, tax measures such as exemptions, deductions, rebates, deferrals, and credits that are used to advance a wide range of economic, social, and other public policy objectives. Because they are buried in legislation and in legal language, tax expenditures amount to a 'hidden area' of budgeting, but in dollar terms they nearly equal the entire direct expenditure budget. (Chapters 26, 27)

territorial consolidation An imperative that dominated the first quarter of twentieth-century Canada and put an imprint on federal public administration. By 1900, Canada had not yet established control of the land over which it claimed sovereignty, and the government deemed it necessary to prioritize the expansion of rail and water transportation, along with immigration services, in order to unify the country. (Chapter 12)

tests See **spending power tests**.

third sector (non-profit sector) The sector between the state and market realms where not-for-profit organizations operate. The primary objective of third-sector organizations is not the redistribution of profit, but the pursuance of the public good. (Chapter 17)

third way A political ideology developed as a balance between the left and the right. It accepts the neo-liberal idea of the problem of 'government failure', and hence the need to be more reliant on market mechanisms to increase society's wealth and provide services. But it also acknowledges 'market failure' and the consequent need for the state and civil society to correct resulting deficiencies. (Chapter 17)

total compensation All wage- and non-wage-related benefits of public sector employment. (Chapter 11)

traditional cabinet The form of cabinet that predominated in the days before the rise of the modern administrative state; ministers' jobs were to articulate and aggregate matters of local and regional political concern. (Chapters 5, 24)

traditional model (of public service) The model of public service values and conventions, based in the 1928 adoption of the merit principle, that dominated the Canadian public service for the early to mid-twentieth century. The merit and recruitment systems allow employees to have full careers in the public service. Elements of the traditional model are still in place, but they are contested, and they have been supplemented by other values from the 1960s and 1970s. (Chapter 1)

traditional values These values include accountability, efficiency, effectiveness, integrity, neutrality, responsiveness, and representativeness. (Chapter 16)

transaction–cost economics A theory pioneered by economist Oliver Williamson in the 1970s and 1980s about how firms grow by substituting internal markets for arrangements with external firms. Firms can lower the transaction costs (of information seeking, transportation, negotiations, contracts, etc.) and uncertainty (of dealing with an outside organization), heighten control, and monitor opportunism by incorporating outside firms within them. Thus, a market relationship is replaced by a hierarchical command relationship. (Chapter 8)

Treasury Board of Canada A cabinet committee of the Queen's Privy Council for Canada presided over by the President of the Privy Council and composed of at least four other ministers; it may act for the Privy Council on all matters relating to general administrative policy, the organization of the federal public administration, financial management, the review of expenditure plans; human resources management, and internal audits. It is served by its own central department, the Treasury Board Secretariat. (Chapter 4)

Treasury Board Secretariat A central department charged with improving cross-governmental management performance, examining departmental spending plans, and acting as the principal employer for the core public administration. It is led by the President of the Treasury Board, whose authority derives from statute. (Chapter 26)

two-tier systems Systems of local governance in which both an upper tier (with broader regional interests, such as a county or a municipality) and a lower tier (e.g., a city or a town) are involved in local public administration. (Chapter 25)

unconditional grants (including equalization) Grants made by the federal government that (apart from statutory subsidies and grants-in-lieu, which are also unconditional but insignificant as a percentage of transfers of this kind) play an important role in the support of provincial/territorial revenues. The most important are 'equalization grants', which are designed to compensate for the low per-capita tax yield in the less-endowed provinces/territories so that all Canadians have access to an average standard of services. (Chapter 24)

unified criminal court A reform, proposed in the 1980s, to the current criminal court division in which only superior courts could hold jury trials and Provincial Court judges could not preside at murder trials; it was designed as a way to erase the difference in status between the two levels. (Chapter 7)

unified family court Specialized family courts with unified jurisdiction now operating in seven provinces of Canada; this organization was designed to overcome the historical division between superior courts and Provincial Courts regarding litigation on family issues. (Chapter 7)

unity of service model A model that empowers a specified agency to enter into and implement agreements with other federal departments and agencies, as well as with Aboriginal governments, to carry out an activity or administer a program, with provinces or public bodies performing a governmental function to carry out an activity. Often the body created will appear to be a national institution, rather than a federal or provincial one—for example, the Canada Revenue Agency (CRA). (Chapter 2)

upper-tier The upper tier in a two-tier local government, with broader interests than those of the lower (geographically smaller) tier. (Chapter 25)

urban asymmetry The condition wherein the federal government makes decisions and builds relationships based on the unique needs of large urban areas and agglomerations, resulting in unequal (unparallel) treatment of different urban areas across the country. (Chapter 24)

wage controls In Canada, legislated controls over federal and provincial public sector wages, common in the 1970s and early 1980s. (Chapter 10)

wage equations Equations that illustrate the sensitivity of public- and private-wage changes to economic conditions such as the business cycle; they can be used to determine whether there is a spillover effect across the sectors. (Chapter 11)

Wagner model A framework for labour relations and collective bargaining originating in the US and imported into Canada, where it gained prominence in the 1940s. First designed for the private sector, and then largely transplanted into the public sector, the model addressed union certification, bargaining over collective agreements, strikes and lockouts, grievance procedures, renegotiation of agreements upon their expiration, and lists of prohibited unfair labour practices. (Chapter 10)

well-performing institution (of public service) An institution that recognizes the importance of strong leadership, core values, adaptability, coordination between component parts, and recruitment as necessary for maintaining organizational competence. (Chapter 1)

White Paper of 1969 A plan that proposed a new philosophy of integration in which all legal distinctions between recognized Indians and other Canadians would be removed. It recommended ending the reserve system, transferring Indian lands to Indian people, repealing the Indian Act, and phasing out DIAND programs. The plan faced opposition and was soon quietly withdrawn. (Chapter 19)

'whole of government' mandates Mandates that involve or encompass various aspects of government operations and organizations. (Chapter 27)

workplace equity Employment standards governed by laws, programs, and concerns related to the fair treatment of employees and the elimination of discrimination in the workplace. (Chapter 9)

Index

C